Cases and Materials on Labor Law:

Process and Policy

Editorial Advisory Board

Little, Brown and Company
Law Book Division

Cases and Materials on Labor Law:

Process and Policy

Second Edition

Douglas L. Leslie
Charles O. Gregory Professor of Law
University of Virginia

LITTLE, BROWN AND COMPANY   Boston and Toronto

Library of Congress Catalog Card No. 84-82266
ISBN 0-316-52161-2

Second edition

HAL

Published simultaneously in Canada
by Little, Brown & Company (Canada) Limited

Printed in the United States of America

To
Sharon Lynn, Doug,
and Jeff

Summary of Contents

Contents

Preface to the Second Edition

The first edition of the casebook has been very successful in the classroom. Its basic design is unchanged in this edition.

This edition introduces economic theory into the materials. Workers, unions, and managers operate in the marketplace, and I believe that analyses of labor law issues will pay increasingly closer attention to microeconomics. The economic materials in the casebook are presented so as to be accessible to students; they raise issues that are unresolved and quite challenging.

An important economic perspective is presented in an essay discussing alternative models of what unions do. The Notes often draw on this essay. Second, the consequences of rule/standard choices by the Labor Board and the courts is a recurring and explicit theme. Third, there is attention to transaction costs and to the role of legal rules as contractual gap-fillers in a bargain context. I believe that these new approaches do not interfere with, but rather enrich, traditional analyses of labor law issues. Without doubt, they offer new ways of looking at the subject.

I have deleted the materials on equal employment opportunity law. A survey of teachers who have adopted the casebook discloses that there is not enough time in the basic labor law course to cover this material.

My special thanks go to my research assistants, Jeffrey Berman and Scott Seeley, who helped me with this second edition, and to my secretary, Linda May.

Douglas Leslie

August 1984

Preface to the First Edition

The conventional wisdom is that a labor survey course should emphasize the employer-employee-union relationship, focusing especially on union representation and collective bargaining. This book adopts that wisdom and therefore makes no substantial departure from the topic coverage found in current labor law casebooks. But even though the scope of the traditional first course in labor law is so limited, I suspect that only a handful of today's teachers of labor law come close to covering all of the doctrine that each of us considers the "bare minimum." The leading casebooks, striving to be exhaustive, have grown in size and complexity, even though the survey course remains what it has been for some time — an introduction to the principal doctrinal developments in the law's treatment of labor issues. Consequently, I set out to see if I could reduce the standard fare to manageable size for a three- or four-hour course without sacrificing coverage of major doctrine or sophisticated analysis.

Because the study of labor law is interesting and very difficult, my working assumption has been that a casebook need make no special effort to make the course challenging. I have attempted to present the subject matter in a fashion that is straightforward and comprehensible to students. The cases are heavily edited; judicial boilerplate and unhelpful (for our purposes) case citations have been excluded. Secondary sources are quoted to facilitate substantive discussion. The notes following the principal cases are intentionally less full of citations than in some other books; they are not written as research aids, but to serve three purposes: to provide information not available in the cases, to preview what is likely to be discussed in class, and to highlight policy and process issues. Asking too many questions is, in my view, as great a disservice as asking none: The student has no idea which issues to key in on, thus impairing classroom discussion; and interstitial, preclass editing of notes (or cases, for that matter) by the teacher is impractical. And, as a research tool, a casebook cannot compete with the labor law looseleaf services without compromising the book's essential purpose.

The emphasis of the book is on policy and process values in labor law. There is no denying that I have my own notions of what should be taken up in class with respect to the principal doctrines and that the notes reflect these notions. I hope that they are congenial to other teachers, and to the students. I believe that I have done what I hoped to, but, as with all books, the final judgment rests with the reader.

Footnotes in the opinions retain their original numbering. My footnotes are indicated by bracketed numbers. Citations are deleted from the opinions without showing ellipses.

Douglas Leslie

July 1978

Acknowledgments

I wish to express my appreciation to the following authors, periodicals, and publishers (as well as those acknowledged in the text) for their permission to reproduce material from their publications:

Atleson, A Union Member's Right of Free Speech and Assembly, 51 Minnesota Law Review 406 (1966). Copyright © 1966 by the University of Minnesota. Reprinted by permission.

Bok and Dunlop, Labor and the American Community (1970). Copyright © 1970 by the Rockefeller Brothers Fund. Reprinted by permission of Simon & Schuster, a division of Gulf & Western.

Burton and Krider, The Role and Consequences of Public Employee Strikes, 79 Yale Law Journal 418 (1970). Copyright © 1970 by The Yale Law Journal Company. Reprinted by permission of The Yale Law Journal Company and Fred B. Rothman & Company.

Cox, Labor Decisions of the Supreme Court at the October Term, 1957, 44 Virginia Law Review 1083 (1958). Copyright © 1958 by the Virginia Law Review. Reprinted by permission of the Virginia Law Review and Fred B. Rothman & Company.

———, Labor Law Preemption Revisited, 85 Harvard Law Review 1352 (1972). Copyright © 1972 by The Harvard Law Review Association. Reprinted by permission.

Cox and Dunlop, Regulation of Collective Bargaining by the National Labor Relations Board, 63 Harvard Law Review 403 (1950). Copyright © 1950 by The Harvard Law Review Association. Reprinted by permission.

Erlich and Posner, An Economic Analysis of Legal Rulemaking, 3 Journal of Legal Studies 257 (1974). Copyright © 1974 by the Journal of Legal Studies. Reprinted by permission.

Getman and Goldberg, The Myth of Labor Board Expertise, 39 University of Chicago Law Review 681 (1972). Copyright © 1972 by The University of Chicago. Reprinted by permission.

Hays, The Future of Labor Arbitration, 74 Yale Law Journal 1034 (1965). Copyright © 1965 by The Yale Law Journal Company. Reprinted by permission of The Yale Law Journal Company and Fred B. Rothman & Company.

Leslie, Right to Control: A Study in Secondary Boycotts and Labor Antitrust, 89 Harvard Law Review 913 (1976). Copyright © 1976 by The Harvard Law Review Association. Reprinted by permission.

Leslie, Labor Bargaining Units, 70 Va. L. Rev. 353 (1984). Copyright © 1984 by The Virginia Law Review Association. Reprinted by permission.

Note, Election Remedies under the Labor-Management Reporting and Disclosure Act, 78 Harvard Law Review 1617 (1965). Copyright © 1965 by The Harvard Law Review Association. Reprinted by permission.

Note, Labor Injunctions and Judge-Made Labor Law: The Contemporary Role of Norris-LaGuardia, 70 Yale Law Journal 71 (1960). Copyright © 1960 by The Yale Law Journal. Reprinted by permission of The Yale Law Journal and Fred B. Rothman & Company.

Note, New Standards for Domination and Support under Section 8(a)(2), 82 Yale Law Journal 71 (1973). Copyright © 1973 by The Yale Law Journal. Reprinted by permission of The Yale Law Journal and Fred B. Rothman & Company.

Reuther, The Brothers Reuther 143 (1976). Copyright © 1976 by Victor G. Reuther. Reprinted by permission of the Houghton Mifflin Company.

Reynolds, Labor Economics and Labor Relations 567 (6th ed. 1974). Copyright © 1974 by Lloyd G. Reynolds. Reprinted by permission of Prentice-Hall, Inc., Englewood Cliffs, New Jersey.

Sigal, Freedom of Speech and Union Discipline: The "Right" of Defamation and Disloyalty, from Proceedings of New York University Seventeenth Annual Conference on Labor 369 (1965). Copyright © 1965 by The Bureau of National Affairs, Washington, D.C. Reprinted by permission.

Weber, Stability and Change in the Structure of Collective Bargaining, from Ulman, ed., Challenges to Collective Bargaining 13 (1967). Copyright © 1967 by The American Assembly, Columbia University. Reprinted by permission of Prentice-Hall, Inc., Englewood Cliffs, New Jersey.

Wellington and Winter, The Limits of Collective Bargaining in Public Employment, 78 Yale Law Journal 1107 (1969). Copyright © 1969 by The Yale Law Journal Company. Reprinted by permission of The Yale Law Journal Company and Fred B. Rothman & Company.

———, More on Strikes by Public Employees, 79 Yale Law Journal 441 (1970). Copyright © 1970 by The Yale Law Journal Company. Reprinted by permission of The Yale Law Journal Company and Fred B. Rothman & Company.

Cases and Materials on Labor Law:

Process and Policy

1

INTRODUCTION

A. HISTORY OF THE U.S. LABOR MOVEMENT AND ITS REGULATION BY LAW

1. A Short History of the Labor Movement and the Development of the Modern Statutory Framework

The earliest workers in America were black slaves or indentured servants. An increase in business activity, however, meant that more as well as different kinds of workers were needed. One reason the number of free workers, or apprentices, grew was that they could be hired and fired on demand. In the skilled trades the relationship between the masters and the apprentices was often a close personal one — apprentices were themselves planning to become master craftsmen after their training was complete.

This similarity did not prevent the apprentices from identifying some goals common to themselves. By the early 1800s labor organizations comprised of skilled workers began to form in the cities. It is not surprising that the skilled craftsmen organized first. They had the education necessary to form and run unions that unskilled workers lacked, and they also had a commitment to their trade because of the time they had invested in apprenticeships. The first strike in America is said to have been called by the Philadelphia printers in 1796.

Early unions were unstable and were often formed to promote a particular issue of interest to the craftsmen. The lack of a formal organization and continuing issues meant that members often drifted away. Also, these early unions met with hostility from employers and the courts. In the famous *Philadelphia Cordwainer's Case* of 1806,[1] the court found that a strike by shoemakers for higher piece rates was a common-law criminal conspiracy. In the next several years strikers were subjected to criminal convictions in other eastern states. Only in 1842, in Commonwealth v. Hunt,[2] a Massachusetts case, was there a departure from

[1] Commonwealth v. Pullis, Philadelphia Mayor's Court (1806), 3 Commons & Gilmore, A Documentary History of American Industrial Society 59 (1910).

[2] 45 Mass. (4 Met.) 111 (1842).

the holdings that a strike was an unlawful conspiracy. That case upheld the right of a union to refuse to work for employers who hired nonunion workers at less than union scale. The lawfulness of concerted action depended, in the court's view, on the union's purpose and the means used to accomplish that purpose.

Early unions were substantially affected by adverse economic conditions. Business depressions reduced their membership and permitted employers to refuse to pay union scale and to fire union members. But unions continued modestly to expand. In the 1820s, unionization spread to hatters, tailors, weavers, and carpenters. Until the 1820s each local craft union operated independently of other unions. In 1827, a group of local unions in Philadelphia formed the first federation of unions organized without regard to craft, the Mechanics Union of Trade Associations. A few such organizations of unions encompassing a variety of crafts within a particular city exist today. These organizations cannot function as agents for collective bargaining, but they can offer sympathetic strike support and be a unified voice in the political process.

City-wide federations also formed in several other cities in the early 1800s, and in 1834 the federations of a number of eastern cities formed the National Trades Union, the first national labor organization. The central issue was the establishment of a ten-hour workday, achieved in 1840 when President Van Buren signed an executive order establishing a ten-hour day for federal employees without any pay loss. But the National Trade Union itself fell victim to a severe depression that began in 1837.

Labor unions in the 1840s were run by intellectuals who had never worked at a manual trade. Their energy often went into forming producers' cooperatives, promoting worker ownership of factories and shops, and seeking land reforms and reorganization of the money system. They were unsuccessful.

In the early 1850s, the first permanent international unions were formed. *International union* is the term for a federation of local unions in the same craft, trade, or industry. Most of these federations have Canadian affiliates, which is why they are called international. International unions were formed in the early 1850s as byproducts of improvements in transportation and communication caused primarily by railroads. Goods produced by low-wage workers in one area could be conveniently shipped by railroad to compete with goods produced in another area. The international union was a tool for dealing with the problems created by this competition. Also, greater numbers of union members were travelling from one city to another looking for work or better wages, and wherever they moved they requested admission to their trades' local union. A major purpose of the new international unions was to work out rules for the transfer of these members.

Union growth was stimulated by a tight labor market during the Civil

War, and in 1866 a new central federation was formed, comprised of local unions in various crafts, central city federations, and international unions. Called the National Labor Union, it lasted only six years. By 1870, the international unions had become unhappy with the National Labor Union's political program, which was directed at social reforms, and many withdrew. The internationals were now becoming the core of the American labor movement. Many kept their membership secret to avoid reprisals.

In addition to the Civil War labor shortage, wartime profits and technological advancement stimulated an increase in capital and a growth of industrialization. As new factories grew in size and employed larger percentages of the nation's work force, the resulting depersonalization of the workplace further eroded personal relationships between managers and workers. Size plus an increased dependence of city workers on factory wages was seen to undermine completely the bargaining power of individual workers with their employers.

While the depression of the 1870s hurt the unions, an economic upturn after 1877 renewed their strength. The Knights of Labor, founded in 1869 as a secret society, came into the open and grew rapidly in the early 1880s. The Knights did not restrict membership to skilled craftsmen; they admitted unskilled workers and some self-employed businessmen, although lawyers and liquor dealers were ineligible. While some locals of the Knights were essentially unions of craftsmen, most locals cut across occupational lines. The Knights were very centralized and, at least in theory, emphasized political action rather than negotiations with employers over wages and working conditions. But while the Knights opposed strikes in principle, they won a spectacular victory in 1885 when the Wabash Railroad, controlled by the entrepreneur Jay Gould, settled a strike by agreeing to end discrimination against members of the Knights. The union's membership soared and reached a peak of 700,000 in 1886.

In late 1886, the Knights of Labor lost several important strikes. In early May, in the aftermath of a strike for an eight-hour day, a further strike in Chicago was called when the employer insisted on retaining strikebreakers. Violence occurred on the picket line and several strikers were killed.

A mass meeting was called by anarchist leaders to protest the deaths of the strikers. When police attempted to break up the meeting, a bomb exploded, killing a policeman and injuring several others. Although neither the Knights of Labor nor craft unions were involved in the Haymarket Riot, as the bombing was called, public opinion turned violently against unions and employer resistance increased. The inexperience of the Knights' leadership and the diversity of its membership left it much less able to withstand adverse public opinion than were the more traditional craft unions. By the early 1890s the Knights had disappeared. Their demise marked an important shift away from political unionism (legislation and producer cooperation) to the business unionism of collective bargaining.

In 1881, the Federation of Organized Trades and Labor Unions was founded. It was reorganized in 1886 as the American Federation of Labor (AFL). Its leading figure was Samuel Gompers of the Cigarmakers Union. An immigrant, Gompers ran this national federation of international unions for every year except one until his death in 1925. The principles of the AFL included (1) every international union was to have complete autonomy in its internal affairs; (2) political support was to cross party lines so that labor could support its friends and punish its enemies regardless of party label; (3) every international was to have exclusive jurisdiction over the workers involved in its craft or trade, and there was to be no organizing in the jurisdiction of another international; (4) the AFL's efforts were to be concentrated on bettering wages, hours, and working conditions through its constituent unions and not through legislative action. The commitment to business unionism was to last until the 1930s. All important international unions, with the exception of certain railroad unions, joined the AFL.

In 1890, the United Mine Workers Union was formed as the first successful "industrial union," a union that sought to organize all wage earners in an industry without regard to skill, craft, or occupation. Late in the decade, the United Mine Workers successfully established themselves in the northern bituminous coal fields from Pennsylvania to Illinois and secured collective bargaining agreements from mine operators.

Other attempts to form industrial unions were not as successful, however. In 1892, the Carnegie Steel Company brought in 300 armed Pinkerton agents to its mill at Homestead, Pennsylvania, which was being struck by members of the Amalgamated Association of Iron, Steel and Tin Workers. Gun battles led to several arrests and the state militia intervened. The union was eventually defeated and thereafter was unable to gain any prominence in the steel industry.

In 1894, another major defeat for an industrial union took place, this time in Chicago in a strike against the Pullman Company. Pullman car shop workers struck the Pullman Company to force restoration of a wage cut. Eugene Debs, the leader of the American Railway Union, an industrial union of railway workers, called out his members in support of the car shop workers and struck the railroad. At the request of the United States Attorney in Chicago, a federal district court issued a broad order against Debs, other union officials, and all other persons conspiring with them, enjoining them from inducing railway workers to refuse to work. Debs disobeyed the injunction and spent six months in jail on a contempt citation. Federal troops were used at the order of President Cleveland to enforce the injunction and the strike collapsed. The union was unable to survive this defeat, and craft unions later became the dominant unions in the railway industry.

The late 1890s saw union membership increasing rapidly, from about 450,000 to nearly 2 million by 1904. In 1905, the AFL's position of leadership was challenged by the Industrial Workers of the World (IWW). The IWW was formed to challenge the philosophy of business unionism that had been followed by the AFL and to present a more radical alternative for workers. The IWW stressed the need to abolish America's wage system and to replace government with worker organizations. It opposed the United States' entry into World War I and it did not survive into the 1920s.

Prior to World War I, the unions' efforts at organizing and achieving collective bargaining agreements had faced active employer resistance, violence on both sides, widespread use of judicial injunctions, and the use of troops. In the celebrated *Danbury Hatters Case,* Loewe v. Lawlor, 208 U.S. 274 (1908), the Supreme Court held that the union's instigation of a boycott of retail stores that sold hats produced by a struck manufacturer violated the Sherman Act and made the union liable for trebled antitrust damages. There were some legislative developments favorable to organized labor and the workers in this period but the overall results were mixed at best, primarily because of disappointments in the courts.

The Department of Labor was created, and in 1914 Congress passed the Clayton Act, which declared that unions were not to be deemed conspiracies in restraint of trade under the federal antitrust laws. Gompers hailed the Clayton Act as labor's Magna Carta, a description that proved to be too optimistic when the Supreme Court gave a highly restrictive reading to the labor provisions of the Act.[3] At the same time, some states were passing protective legislation dealing with minimum wages, child labor, and similar matters. Employers commonly used "yellow dog" contracts, whereby workers on being hired agreed that they would not join a union during the term of employment. These agreements were enforced by courts against unions on the theory that organizing efforts were acts inducing breaches of contract. The Supreme Court approved this interpretation[4] and found laws prohibiting yellow dog contracts unconstitutional.[5]

A tight labor market in World War I helped union growth. Industrial unions in the clothing industry took permanent hold, but a major organizing effort in steel failed in 1919 when a strike of over 300,000 workers was broken. Union expansion was halted by the recession of 1921.

An upswing in the economy from 1923 to 1929 would have been

[3] See, e.g., Duplex Printing Press Co. v. Deering, 254 U.S. 443 (1921).

[4] Hitchman Coal & Coke Co. v. Mitchell, 245 U.S. 229 (1917).

[5] See Adair v. United States, 208 U.S. 161 (1908); Coppage v. Kansas, 236 U.S. 1 (1915).

expected to stimulate union growth, but instead union membership decreased from about 5 million in 1920 to about $3\frac{1}{2}$ million in 1929. Employers in many manufacturing industries continued to resist union organizing efforts and began to couple their active resistance with a new kind of attention to employee welfare and employee relations. Special personnel staffs began to adopt policies of profit sharing, insurance plans, company housing, and other sorts of benefits. Often these changes were accompanied by the formation of company unions — unions dominated by the employers. A bright spot for the unions was the passage in 1926 of the Railway Labor Act, which was jointly drafted by unions and management to guarantee workers in the railway industry the right to bargain collectively. It established federal machinery for resolving labor disputes on the railroads.

The depression beginning in 1929 was initially a severe blow to unions. Membership dropped significantly and wage cuts were accepted. Union membership was actually lower than the unions reported because they carried members on their rolls even though they were no longer working and could not pay dues. As the depression continued, however, a substantial change occurred in the public attitude toward unions, which in turn produced new legislation favorable to unions and their organizing efforts. The Norris-LaGuardia Act of 1932 was the first of these new laws.

WINTER, LABOR INJUNCTIONS AND JUDGE-MADE LABOR LAW: THE CONTEMPORARY ROLE OF NORRIS-LaGUARDIA

70 Yale L.J. 70, 71-76 (1960)

Prior to 1932, federal courts had jurisdiction, mainly in diversity and Sherman Act cases, over a broad range of union activities. Acting without legislative guides, federal judges were inclined to decide labor controversies according to their own predominantly conservative social and political views, and rendered decisions which were generally hostile to the union's use of economic power. Under the prima facie tort doctrine, an intentional injury inflicted through the use of economic pressure was unlawful unless a court found it justified by the self-interest of the defendant union. Moreover, even if the objectives were found to be legitimate, economic pressure could be exerted only through means receiving judicial approbation. The imprecise terms of the Sherman Act furnished another vehicle for restraining union activity, since "restraint of trade" could be found in almost any effective use of economic pressure. Both the tort and Sherman Act doctrines were used to prohibit activities such as secondary boycotts, recognition strikes, make-work practices, and picketing. Attempts to organize nonunion employees were brought within the tort of interference with beneficial contractual relations by judicial protection of the "yellow dog" contract — the employee's promise not to join a union, extracted as a condition of employment. Thus, through this often amorphous body of law, the courts themselves undertook to define the "area of allowable economic conflict."

The foundation of this judicial regulation was the labor injunction. Damage suits had proved unsatisfactory to employers seeking relief against illegal union activities. Unions were often judgment-proof; there were procedural difficulties in suing labor organizations as entities; juries were available to the defendant unions; and such actions rarely provided relief until long after the dispute was over. The injunction, however, did not suffer from these handicaps and provided relatively swift and comprehensive relief. A temporary restraining order against the union could be obtained within a matter of hours. Because decrees often enjoined a broad class of persons and a wide range of activities, including even peaceful persuasion and leaving the job, these prohibitory clauses served as a vehicle for detailed judicial policing of labor disputes. Moreover, violators of the order might be subject to criminal and civil contempt proceedings held without a jury and before the same judge who had issued the original decree.

The initial stages of the injunctive process were particularly subject to procedural inadequacies and substantive error. Since to be effective the temporary injunction had to be issued swiftly, the trial judge's decision was made hastily in an atmosphere often highly-charged with emotion. The amorphous character of the substantive law also contributed to the possibility of error, as did the inadequacy of evidence before the judge. To achieve speed, temporary restraining orders were issued ex parte upon the filing of standardized formbook complaints, and, at the preliminary hearing, temporary injunctions were often issued solely on the basis of slanted, vague affidavits, whose allegations were safe from cross-examination. Errors made in the early stages of the proceedings could, in theory, be corrected by the subsequent full dress trial necessary to the issuance of a permanent injunction, or on appeal. In practice, however, such corrective action would be ineffective, for such proceedings ordinarily came too late to repair the damage to the union. Rather than maintaining the status quo, the temporary injunction usually effected a final settlement of the dispute, for even a brief interruption of the strike could break union morale and hold the union's economic power in check while the employer was free to retaliate. The finality of this remedy was demonstrated by the relative infrequency with which employers sought permanent injunctions.

The Norris-LaGuardia Act can be viewed as a three-pronged attack on judge-made labor law and its administration. First, the act rejected the injunction as a remedy in labor disputes. Second, it declared that federal courts were not the proper agency of the government to formulate substantive labor policy. Third, it repudiated the federal common law of labor relations and established a policy of governmental neutrality in labor disputes as a means of aiding the growth of organized labor. Although the act's policy of governmental neutrality has given way to pervasive federal regulation, its remedial proscriptions and strictures on the role of the judiciary remain fundamental to the scheme of federal labor law.

The view that injunctions per se are an inappropriate remedy in labor disputes is reflected in the broad and unequivocal prohibitions imposed by the act. Federal courts are denied all power to issue both temporary and permanent injunctions in nonviolent labor disputes. In addition to this general statement, section 4 of the act explicitly immunizes specific activities such as refusal to work, picketing, and payment of strike benefits. No distinction is drawn between "lawful" and "unlawful" nonviolent activities; the act renders federal judges powerless even to enjoin action prohibited by substantive law. Moreover, in the limited area where injunctions are permitted in order to prevent violence, the act prescribes detailed procedures which the court must follow. Under section 7, no temporary or permanent injunction may be issued unless supported by oral testimony subject to cross-examination. Furthermore, ex parte orders are available only if necessary to prevent injury to property and lapse after five days. In addition, section 11 grants a jury trial to persons charged with contempt for violations of orders issued under the act.

Withdrawal of the injunctive power not only abolished the use of a particular remedy — it also put federal courts out of the business of making labor policy. Shorn of their only meaningful enforcement powers, federal courts were no longer looked to by litigants as an effective check upon economic coercion. The legislative history of Norris-LaGuardia indicates that the Congress intended this result, believing that institutionally courts were ill-suited to make policy in labor matters. Excessive intervention in labor strife had tarnished the prestige of the federal courts. Entanglement in a struggle between opposing economic classes had destroyed the aura of impartiality essential to a rule of law and had made judges and judicial decisions in this area the center of political debate. This loss of prestige, moreover, was the unavoidable result of judicial interference in labor disputes, for such intervention leads to the assumption of partisan positions. While courts making law in areas such as tort or contract may draw upon generally accepted values, there are few such shared principles in the field of labor relations. Every decision tended to be a political statement, favoring one camp or the other. By immobilizing the judiciary, the act attempted to remove courts from this political stage, leaving the controversial task of formulating labor policy to a more appropriate political institution — the Congress itself.

Interpretation of Norris-LaGuardia as a broad prohibition on judicial formulation of labor policy finds support in specific provisions of the statute. The act outlaws both permanent and temporary injunctions, although the permanent injunction suffered from none of the procedural flaws which marred the temporary decree. And section 13, defining the term "labor dispute" in exceedingly broad terms, radically changed the role of the courts in analyzing labor cases. While older theories, such as the prima facie tort doctrine, had required courts to determine the extent to which a union's self-interest justified coercive action, judicial inquiry under Norris-LaGuardia is limited to the narrow question of whether the union has such an interest in the dispute. Moreover, the broad prohibitions of the act, encompassing almost all labor-management controversies and ignoring all distinctions between lawful and unlawful peaceful activity, indicate congressional fear of judicially created exceptions and a desire to limit judicial discretion in applying the act.[6]

With the election of Franklin D. Roosevelt in 1932, a period of legislative advances began for organized labor and the institution of collective bargaining. The National Industrial Recovery Act (NIRA), passed in 1933, included a section guaranteeing the right of employees "to organize and bargain collectively through representatives of their own choosing, and . . . free from the interference, restraint, or coercion of employers of labor. . . ." The NIRA was invalidated by the Supreme Court in 1935,[7] but Congress responded almost immediately by passing the Wagner Act (the National Labor Relations Act, or NLRA).[8]

Section 7 was the heart of the NLRA. As originally enacted, it read: "Employees shall have the right to self-organization, to form, join or assist labor organizations, to bargain collectively through representatives of their own choosing, and to engage in concerted activities for the purpose of collective bargaining or other mutual aid or protection."

Section 8 implements §7 by listing specific employer unfair labor practices. Section 8(a)(1)[9] is broadest in scope, prohibiting employer interference with the rights guaranteed by §7. Section 8(a)(2) is designed to outlaw employer-formed "company unions." Section 8(a)(3) forbids discrimination on account of union activity in hiring and firing, and §8(a)(4) forbids such discrimination on account of employees testifying or giving charges before the agency charged with implementing the statute. Section 8(a)(5) requires employers to bargain collectively with the duly established representatives of their employees. (See §8(a) in the

[6] The Norris-LaGuardia Act still restricts the power of federal courts to issue injunctions in labor disputes although later statutes give the courts power to issue injunctions at the request of the National Labor Relations Board and at the request of a private party in certain matters relating to the enforcement of collective bargaining agreements. These matters will be taken up in the following chapters.

[7] Schechter Poultry Co. v. United States, 295 U.S. 495 (1935).

[8] The National Labor Relations Act as it appears in the Statutory Supplement incorporates later amendments.

[9] Originally §8(1).

Statutory Appendix, but ignore for now the "provisos" of §§8(a)(2) and 8(a)(3).)

Section 9 of the Wagner Act established the procedures, primarily the secret ballot election in an "appropriate bargaining unit," by which employees can choose whether they want a particular union to represent them.

To administer and interpret both the unfair labor practice and representation provisions of the Act, Congress established an administrative agency, the National Labor Relations Board (NLRB). With respect to unfair labor practices, the NLRB was originally designed to serve both as prosecutor and judge by issuing complaints of violation, having them prosecuted by its staff, and then ruling on their merits. Judicial review by an appropriate federal court of appeals was stipulated by §10 of the Act. The Wagner Act contained no provisions restricting union power.

Under conditions created by the National Industrial Recovery Act and the Wagner Act, union membership more than doubled between 1933 and 1937. The growth was accompanied, however, by conflict within the union movement and by disputes with major employers. Workers in the rubber and automobile industries organized and applied for membership in the AFL, but they wanted to form industrial, not craft, unions in their industry; and the existing international craft unions demanded that the charters of the applicants exclude jurisdiction over workers in occupations claimed by the crafts. This was clearly unacceptable to the new internationals and to certain older AFL industrial internationals such as the United Mine Workers, the Amalgamated Clothing Workers, and the International Ladies' Garment Workers. The issue could not be compromised at the 1935 AFL convention and the vote of the craft international unions prevailed. The industrial unions, led by the United Mine Workers' John L. Lewis, formed a Committee for Industrial Organization, initially intended to work within the AFL. The AFL branded it a "dual organization" and ordered it to disband. After their refusal, the Committee's member internationals were expelled. In 1938, the group changed its name to the Congress of Industrial Organizations (CIO) and functioned as a separate federation of international unions until 1955.

When employers in the automobile and rubber industries refused to recognize the new international unions, the unions seized the factories and declared sit-down strikes. Perhaps the most celebrated of these was the successful sit-down strike at the Flint Works of the General Motors Company in Michigan, which is described at pages 13-28, infra.

The CIO at this time was seeking to organize the basic steel industry on an industrial union basis. The Steel Workers' Organizing Committee, later to become the United Steelworkers of America, was voluntarily recognized in 1937 by United States Steel, but other steel companies refused recognition. This led to strikes marked by violence. On May 30,

1937, ten strikers were killed by police at Republic Steel's South Chicago plant, an incident called the "Memorial Day Massacre." The union lost the strike.

Meanwhile, competition from the CIO was spurring the AFL to increase organizing efforts, and the sharp line between craft and industrial unions began to fade. For example, the AFL's Amalgamated Meat Cutters and Butcher Workmen (retail food) and the International Association of Machinists became industrial unions while maintaining their AFL affiliations.

World War II, like World War I, created a tight labor market and was a period of growth for the unions. In return for no-strike pledges from the unions, President Roosevelt promised to maintain the protections provided by the Wagner Act and the Fair Labor Standards Act, which included premium pay for overtime. The federal government created a War Labor Board, which assisted the unions in winning recognition from employers and in establishing stable collective bargaining relationships. In 1941, for example, the Board ordered the steel companies resisting labor organizing in 1937 to recognize the union.

But as union membership grew from less than 4 million to more than 14 million between 1935 and 1947, the resulting economic power of unions became a cause of worry. During the war, the United Mine Workers engaged in two unpopular, and unlawful, strikes. The end of the war and wartime strike restrictions signaled strikes in many critical industries, causing substantial public inconvenience. One result was the passage in 1947, over President Truman's veto, of the Taft-Hartley Act (the Labor Management Relations Act).

The Taft-Hartley Act amended §8 of the NLRA by adding §8(b)'s prohibition of certain union "bad practices." Forbidden (that is, termed unfair labor practices) were secondary boycotts, jurisdictional strikes over work assignments, and strikes to force an employer to discharge an employee on account of his or her union affiliation, or lack of it. The Office of the General Counsel of the NLRB was established to separate the Board's unfair labor practice prosecutorial and adjudicatory functions. In addition to prosecutorial discretion over unfair labor practice complaints, the General Counsel was given the power and responsibility to seek federal court injunctions against unfair labor practices, especially those committed by unions.

Certain changes were made in the representation provisions of the NLRA, with §7 guaranteeing employees the right to refrain from union activity. Section 301 of the Taft-Hartley Act made collective bargaining agreements enforceable in federal district court and rendered unions capable of suing or being sued in district courts. Section 303 provided private parties injured by a union's secondary boycott with a civil damage remedy. An important effect of the prohibition of various union activities was to oust (preempt) the states' power to regulate those activities. Taft-Hartley represented a shift from the outright promotion of unionization to a more neutral government posture, while it continued the right of employees to be free from employer coercion.

World War II and its aftermath caused ideological conflict in CIO unions. Many of these unions, including the United Mine Workers, had used members of the Communist Party as organizers before the war. John L. Lewis, for one, considered the strongly motivated Communists to be essential to his early organizing efforts. But in the 1940s this dependence caused bitter factional disputes; in some unions the Communists took control, whereas in others (for example, the United Auto Workers) the non-Communists took complete control. The beginning of the Cold War found some union leaders working for the ouster of Communist influence in American unions, and in 1948 several international unions were charged with Communist domination and expelled from the CIO. This attack, and the withdrawal of the United Mine Workers from the CIO in 1940 as a result of a political squabble between John L. Lewis and CIO leaders, left the CIO considerably smaller than the AFL.

The death or retirement of those who had been the leaders of their respective federations during the bitterest days of the rivalry as well as the growing similarity of the two federations made merger a possibility. Additional impetus for reunification was provided by the negotiation of a no-raiding agreement that was subsequently ratified by most of the international unions in the AFL and CIO. Under this agreement, each union agreed not to interfere with existing collective bargaining relationships established by any other signatory union but was free to seek representation rights for any employees who had not been organized. In 1955, the two federations reunited as the American Federation of Labor and the Congress of Industrial Organizations (AFL-CIO).

In the 1950s, congressional hearings uncovered financial abuses in several international unions. The Ethical Practices Committee of the AFL-CIO investigated several internationals and some, most notably the International Brotherhood of Teamsters, were expelled from the federation. This self-policing did not satisfy Congress, however, and in 1959 the Landrum-Griffin Act was enacted.

The principal provisions of the Landrum-Griffin Act (the Labor-Management Reporting and Disclosure Act) are aimed at the regulation of internal union affairs and, more specifically, at the securing of a greater measure of internal union democracy. The Act contains a bill of rights for union members, requires certain union financial disclosures, regulates the use of "trusteeships" over local unions, prescribes procedures for the election of union officers, and provides remedies for financial abuses by union officers. Management interests saw the proposed act as an appropriate opportunity to amend the NLRA in matters affecting union economic power. They secured the passage of amendments broadening the coverage of the secondary boycott provisions of the NLRA and restricting the right of unions to picket in order to obtain representation rights.

The 1960s marked collective bargaining successes and organizational failures by the labor movement. The organizational spirit that had marked the unions in many periods during the first half century was now seen in civil rights groups and the antipoverty and anti-Vietnam War movements. The decade saw a broad range of social legislation, marked by the Civil Rights Act of 1964 as the most notable legislative achievement. Walter Reuther, president of the United Auto Workers, thought the AFL-CIO was stagnating and directed a campaign of criticism against it. This action culminated in the United Auto Workers' disaffiliation from AFL-CIO in 1968. In the meantime, the Teamsters continued to grow and became the largest of the nation's international unions.

In the early 1970s came the institution of wage and price controls, a development vigorously resisted by the majority of the labor unions. In the area of organizational effort, greatest attention was focused on public employees and their increasing militancy and willingness to organize. Nonetheless, in 1977 the raw numbers of unionized employees showed a decline. In 1977 and 1978 the union movement worked for reform of the labor statutes to provide more effective remedies against employers willing to resist union organizing and bargaining efforts by violating the present statutes. The efforts failed.

2. A Case Study in Labor History

Overviews of labor history necessarily lack the flavor of the events. The following account of the United Auto Workers' (UAW) successful attempt to secure bargaining rights for employees of the General Motors Corporation was written by Victor Reuther, a central participant in the struggle. Victor's brother Walter Reuther headed the UAW until his death in an airplane crash in 1970. The account may not be balanced, but its glimpse into labor history is revealing.

V. REUTHER, THE BROTHERS REUTHER
143-170 (1976)

Sit-Down in Flint

Flint was a GM town down to the bone. Eighty percent of Flint families were dependent for their living on Buick, Fisher Body, Chevrolet, or AC Spark Plug. The rest of the working families were on relief. The people were gaunt and seedy-looking; years of unemployment had left hollows in their faces and fear in their eyes. Their housing was more miserable than that in any other highly developed industrial town in the country. In a sense, Flint was a segment of the deep South transported north, for General Motors had primarily employed white Southern workers, who were lured up during the twenties by the growing automobile industry. A large number of them went south again in 1929; the rest suffered the Depression out — on the welfare lines. . . .

When Roy [Reuther, brother of Victor and Walter Reuther,] got there that fall [1934], he began with great patience to meet with auto workers in small groups, often in their homes. He taught such basic subjects as parliamentary procedure, public speaking, labor economics, history of the labor movement. But, as Roy suspected and the La Follette Committee discovered later, at least 25 percent of those in attendance at these . . . classes were Pinkerton men paid by General Motors, and all too often Roy's students found discharge slips in their time-card racks. The company managed in this way to snuff out any hope of rebuilding a strong union. . . .

Sporadic strikes began to break out in some isolated departments of the various GM plants, each followed by the discharge of the workers involved. One worker was discharged simply for wearing his union button. Roy asked for an appointment with Harry Coen, later to become GM vice-president.

"How come," asked Roy, "if you're a Mason, or K of C, or a member of the Elks, it's okay to wear a button, but if you wear a union button you get fired?"

"You're damn right," Coen replied. "Now what are you going to do about it?"

Roy did nothing that day, but made up for lost time later. . . .

With a mere one thousand of the forty-seven thousand GM workers in Flint signed up so far, only the naïve would assume that there was a calculated strategy to strike General Motors at that time. As a matter of fact, there had been talk among CIO officials that, because Chrysler was more unionized and did not seem to be as fierce an antagonist as General Motors, it might be wise to take on Chrysler first. But despite the collective wisdom of the leadership, Fred Pieper, close friend and ally of Homer Martin, called a strike in GM's Fisher Body plant in Atlanta. This precipitate action was taken without consultation with the officers of the international union, though Martin must have been in on it, since he sent telegrams alerting all GM locals across the country. . . .

[T]he die was cast and, prepared or not, the UAW had to summon all its resources to try to bring General Motors to terms. Hence the Fisher Body works in Cleveland was struck under the leadership of Paul Miley, and the word was sent to [Robert] Travis and Roy to get ready for strike action at Fisher Body One in Flint.

The GM management anticipated this possibility and made an attempt to move strategic dies out of the plant, so that the pressing and forming of auto parts might be shifted to factories not likely to be struck. This gambit by GM was what determined the Union's move. In both Fisher One and Two, a sit-down strike was called on December 30 [1936]. . . .

It was obvious that the very nature of the sit-down strike would provide a controversial element. Was it legal? The courts had not officially ruled on the matter. The sit-down had been successful in the Akron rubber strike and the recent skirmish at Kelsey Hayes Wheel. The corporations were, of course, concerned about protecting their capital, invested in tools, equipment, and raw materials, and could invoke the laws that safeguard property rights. Yet to the workers it seemed natural to protest, by means of this essentially peaceful technique, the years of exploitation they had suffered. Their jobs were *their* investments, and they were protecting them. They were no more concerned about the corporation's property rights than was the corporation about the workers' legal rights to unionize, as established by Congress in 1933. I should venture to guess that those who doubted the morality of the sit-down in 1937 were fewer than the doubters among the population in 1775, when American independence was won by challenging the tyrannical laws and regulations of the British Crown.

The first court injunction against the sit-down was issued on January 2 by Circuit Judge Edward D. Black. He ordered the strikers to evacuate the plants, and Sheriff Wolcott deputized 100 auxiliary police — most of them "loyal employees" of GM. When the Sheriff appeared at the gates of Fisher One, where some 500 workers were sitting in, and read aloud the injunction terms, he was literally laughed out of the place, and retreated with boos and catcalls ringing in his ears. Meanwhile, Lee Pressman, general counsel for the national CIO, had been tipped off by an alert newspaperman that he might find it useful to look into Judge Black's GM stock holdings. To Pressman's amazement and glee he learned that the judge owned some 3365 shares, valued then at about $219,000. This fact hit like a delayed bomb in Flint, Detroit, and Washington. Black was asked to disqualify himself, and it was even suggested that he be impeached. GM's image suffered, and the UAW gained support in the community. . . .

I have often been asked whether the idea of the sit-down strike was something brought in surreptitiously from Europe, by hired agents. I find that most unlikely. To my recollection, no one in Flint or Detroit or Akron was even vaguely aware that sit-in strikes had recently occurred in France. In Flint the concept gained support after the success of that first quickie stoppage in Fisher One, when the discharged welders were reinstated. During every short-term strike before that one, the workers had been promised concessions, only to find, when they returned to the plant a few days later, that everything was just as before, and as likely as not the ringleaders of such a strike would be discharged. Such betrayals had made the sit-down strike the only recourse.

Another reason for the workers to remain in the plant instead of marching in picket lines was that they might be free from intimidation by plant police, city police, vigilante groups, and other powers of authority that were always on the side of the corporation. Inside the plant, they gained a sense of security from the very walls and the familiar machines among which they had spent most of their lives.

In 1936-37, only a small minority of workers dared to identify openly with the UAW. The sit-in technique, by allowing a small, highly organized group of laboring men to occupy key areas of a corporation's production process, gave workers control of a situation that affected them. Does this mean that sit-in strikes were immoral because they permitted a minority to force its will on a lethargic and fearful majority? No, I think the facts prove otherwise. Once the fear was calmed, the mass of workers in auto plants made incontrovertibly clear that they wanted a union to represent them — an industrial union to embrace all grades of employees. Furthermore, with all the money that was poured into it, the company's return-to-work movement was not able to persuade the majority outside the plant to act against the minority inside. There was obviously a conviction that the minority was acting in behalf of all. . . .

Inside Fisher One and Fisher Two, the strikers showed their capacity for organization and self-control. A security committee was responsible for protecting the equipment and for blocking the doors against police, company men, or vigilantes. It also guarded against fire hazards; smoking was permitted only in specified sections. A health committee watched over the condition of the men and called a doctor when necessary, and another group provided entertainment. . . .

To get the food in was easy enough at Fisher One, where the strikers were on the ground floor. But at Fisher Two, the downstairs was patrolled regularly by company police, so most of the time the only way we could talk to those inside was to climb a tall ladder that was placed against the front windows. (Twice a day the guard opened the front door downstairs and allowed meals to be brought in.) . . .

Fisher One had a stronger group than Fisher Two because of its long history of unionizing efforts. . . . When GM made its first overt effort to oust the strikers it chose Fisher Two, the easier prey. The attempt took place on the afternoon of January 11. The first indication of impending trouble was the arrival of a contingent of twenty-two plant protection guards, augmenting the force of only eight policemen usually on duty outside the plant. Then all heat in the building was shut off. Up to this time the company had refrained from using this tactic because of pleas from the state authorities and threats by the sit-downers to build wood fires, if necessary, to keep warm. But when GM decided to force a showdown, it did not consult state officials, and relied on the compliant Flint police force.

I was at strike headquarters with Roy and Bob Travis when word of this development came, and we rallied as many volunteers as we could and shifted most of our pickets from Fisher One to Fisher Two. We next heard that police were gathering in some force not too far from Fisher Two. I had been using an improvised sound car, an old Chevrolet with speakers fastened to the roof, for my daily rounds at the two plants, giving news, playing music, talking to the pickets during their long vigil. My voice as well as the music penetrated to the strikers inside. That afternoon I took a circuitous route to avoid the police just beyond the railroad tracks on Chevrolet Avenue and reached Fisher Two's gate on that avenue by back alleys. Bill Carney was with me. We found a silent and grim picket line, slightly larger than before. There were now about 140 on the line, and the atmosphere was both ugly and solemn. [Victor Reuther helped arrange for the strikers to receive food.]

I had just returned to the sound car when I heard shouts: "The police! My God, the police!" Then I saw out of the corner of my eye the first burst of teargas shells from beyond the railroad tracks, in between Chevrolet Four and Five. From where I was parked, in the center of Chevrolet Avenue, I could see the police coming across the tracks and down the avenue. Over the bridge came a group of squad cars whose human occupants holding short, stubby muzzled guns, looked very strange in their gas masks. Then I saw more police on foot, shielding themselves behind the slowly advancing cars. As they got closer, they began lobbing tear-gas shells that had points hard and sharp enough to break through reinforced glass. They were aiming them at the second-floor windows of Fisher Two and into the midst of the pickets. And as they forced their way through, they hurled additional shells at the ground-floor windows, breaking several panes of glass, apparently unaware that all the strikers were upstairs.

We were not unprepared. The second-floor doors were barred with weighted steel dollies, and fire hoses were connected for any emergency. On the roof, at strategic points facing Chevrolet Avenue, the strikers had placed huge piles of pound-and-a-half hinges, and had stretched inner tube rubber between the big steel bars that were part of the roof's structure to use as giant slingshots. As soon as the police began using tear gas and breaking windows, I shouted to the men inside to defend themselves with everything they had. The response was immediate. Every tear-gas missile fired in their direction was followed by a barrage of heavy hinges that struck cars and some of the officers.

The weather was on our side: it was only about sixteen degrees above and no day to be doused with cold water, so when the strikers brought the fire hoses into full play against the police below and the 150 pickets pushed with all their might, the police were driven back across the bridge to regroup and plan new tactics.

The pickets used this interlude to carry away those whose scalps had been cut open by police clubs or who had been directly hit by the tear-gas bombs. Unionists ready to assist the strikers crowded into the opposite end of Chevrolet Avenue. On the roof many more strikers from the second floor had come up to man the hoses and the slingshots. The remaining pickets began to gather up any objects that might be used as weapons — pop bottles, rocks, or hinges shot down during the first attack.

I continued to speak over the microphone, calling on the men and women both inside and out to stand firm and not permit GM to drive them into submission by the unwarranted use of police power. The onlookers had grown into a crowd of thousands. I reminded the strikers and all who could hear me that the UAW had tried to settle the matter over the conference table but had been turned away, that the promises of General Motors had never been kept, and that it was GM's choice to settle by means of force but that we were determined to defend our rights at any cost. I called upon those who stood looking on to come in and help the pickets. A great shout went up every time a group broke away from the sidelines and took up positions in front of the plant alongside the pickets.

Soon the police had regrouped and were marching in a solid phalanx toward us. They seemed intent on knocking out the sound truck. Thank God they hadn't yet brought in the long-range tear-gas missiles; most of their shots fell short but some bombs slithered along the pavement and came to rest immediately under the car. The fumes came seeping through the floorboards and mingled with the acid of the battery that ran the loudspeaker. Because of the possibility of a direct hit, I had to keep my head down close to that battery as I spoke into the microphone, so I soaked my handkerchief in some coffee I had in a thermos and held it to my nose, trying to breathe and keep talking. One observer later wrote: "From the sound car emanated one steady unswerving note. It dominated everything. Reuther's voice was like an inexhaustible furious flood pouring courage into the men."

The second police attack was directed more against those of us outside than at the sit-downers, but the heroic defenders on the roof did a spectacular job of pelting the attackers with hinges from their big slingshots, and kept pouring water down to freeze on the police uniforms, until the police were forced to retreat once again. As they went, they resorted to the vicious revenge I had dreaded: they began to use their firearms, and shot directly into the ranks of our pickets. That night thirteen union men were seriously wounded. . . .

The third attack came. This time they did bring long-range tear-gas missiles, and though the shells were fired from the other side of our barricades, they landed again and again in the midst of the pickets. At one point, with pickets choking and vomiting and staggering away, briefly, to get a whiff of fresh air, suddenly, as if it had been authorized from above, a gust of wind swept down, blowing the tear gas back into the faces of the police. . . .

I am convinced that the police lost not only that night's battle but the whole Flint war by providing us with the finest audience we had ever had. The drama the bystanders witnessed put our point across more cogently than any words could have done, and served to nudge thousands of Flint workers off dead center and into an open commitment to the UAW.

It was beyond midnight when the shelling stopped, and though we spent the rest of the night anticipating another barrage, the police had, we later learned, run out of ammunition. They had appealed to the Detroit police for more, but Detroit must have said, "No, we need ours down here." Thus ended the Battle of the Running Bulls. In the morning Chevrolet Avenue indeed looked like a battlefield of the industrial age — smashed and overturned vehicles, broken windowpanes, shattered bottles, stones, hinges, splintered picket signs, used tear-gas canisters, and everywhere the ice formed by the water that had served so effectively as a defensive weapon. . . .

There must have been considerable bitterness among the General Motors executives, who had been frustrated in their move to use the courts against us, and now in their attempt to oust us with tear gas and bullets. They had not, however, exhausted their arsenal. For some time they had been secretly encouraging and arming a vigilante organization known as the Flint Alliance. This group was to be used to propagandize a back-to-work movement in the city. It was also the tool GM used when it wanted some CIO or UAW organizer brutally beaten up.

We discovered that we too had a strong extra resource: Governor Frank Murphy,[10] a man of principle and sensibility, who had been elected the previous fall. I did not know him personally in 1937, though later in life we became very good friends. He was a true humanitarian: seldom have I met a man who anguished more over the prospect of violence perpetrated against a fellow human being. To be confronted with such a militant situation in Flint so soon after his inauguration created for him a personal dilemma. He was in Lansing, Michigan's capital, when the attack on the Fisher Two sit-downers began, and was kept informed by telephone by both John M. Barringer, Flint's City Manager, and by representatives of the UAW and the CIO. The conflicting reports convinced him that he urgently needed to have an independent view of the events. . . .

[10] Frank Murphy later became a Justice of the United States Supreme Court.

It was Governor Murphy's delicate job to defuse a threatening situation in a neutral fashion, partisan neither to the corporation nor to the UAW. His first act was to mobilize two regiments of the National Guard: "Whatever else may happen, there is going to be law and order in Michigan. The public interest and public safety are paramount. The public authority in Michigan is stronger than either of the parties in the present controversy." . . .

With the National Guard on the scene, the workers lost a good deal of their apprehension and union membership soared. The soldiers appeared in full battle regalia and set up field kitchens, and drab Flint took on the look of an occupied city, but the tension was reduced. I recall that there was considerable camaraderie between our strikers and pickets and the troops stationed near the gate. . . .

On January 14, Governor Murphy brought together in his office in Lansing three men from each side: Knudsen, Smith, and Brown from GM; and Homer Martin, Mortimer, and John Brophy of the CIO. As chief executive, Murphy was sensitive to his responsibility to uphold due process, and since the strikers were "in unlawful possession" of GM property, he was most anxious to get the plant evacuated. But not at the cost of violence. He steadfastly refused to use the troops to force that evacuation. Instead, he worked untiringly to negotiate a compromise. His aim was to get a clear commitment from General Motors that it would negotiate with the UAW on a settlement involving not only the Flint plants but GM plants all over the country, and would cover a seniority system and a structure of representation for the union as well as wages. There was an immediate issue to be settled, too, and this seemed to be the stumbling block for both sides: General Motors was to deliver a signed promise that it would not move the strategic tools and dies from Fisher Two to "safer" plants once the men had evacuated. We in the UAW had a deep suspicion that the company planned to do just that the moment we left. GM refused to sign the promise.

After days of interminable consultations with both sides, early in the morning of January 15 the Governor, haggard and exhausted, announced an agreement, in the form of a letter signed by Knudsen, Smith, and Brown, addressed not to the UAW but to himself. It stated that the UAW had agreed that the strikers would leave the plant premises in Flint, Detroit, and Anderson, Indiana, "as soon as practicable," and that GM would meet with UAW representatives to bargain on the basis of our proposal of January 4. It was indicated in the letter that there would be no discrimination against any worker because of union affiliation and that GM would not remove any equipment from any of the struck plants while negotiations were taking place.

There was one other important clause: General Motors would not try to resume operations in the struck plants during the negotiations, which they would pursue steadily, unless those negotiations took more than fifteen days, in which case the corporation would be free to start up the plants again.

The Flint strikers were not enthusiastic about the terms of the settlement. They wanted a signed agreement that included more concessions before they evacuated the plant where they had endured the sit-down and where pickets had been brutalized. But Mortimer, Travis, Roy, Addes, and Hall reassured them it was a real turnabout on the part of the corporation — in fact, a victory for the union — and that GM could not afford to welch on the terms because the public would then turn against the corporation and more workers would join the union.

In Detroit, Walter met with the Cadillac and Fleetwood strikers and secured their acceptance of the agreement. They marched out of the plant and on that very same day, January 16, received telegrams from General Motors asking them to report for work on January 18, in direct contradiction to the terms of the letter. . . .

The balance of power still lay with the Flint strike. GM had, for some weeks, been promoting an antiunion back-to-work movement of "loyal" employees through the Flint Alliance, headed by George Boysen, former Buick paymaster and former Mayor of the city. An elaborate PR campaign had been mounted to appeal to business and religious groups in the community to support the nonunion workers, who, it was charged, would suffer from more days of idleness. The reactionary group branded the UAW leaders Communists and outside agitators. Its following among the workers came mostly from the less unionized Buick and AC Spark Plug plants.

We had been aware of the threat of the Flint Alliance and had sent trusted UAW men to observe it from within. One of these, Kempton Williams, tipped us off to the plan to arm a large number of foremen and guards to march on Pengelly Hall, our strike headquarters, and drive all union organizers out of town. This was not as serious and alarming, however, as the telegram exchange between Knudsen and Boysen. The latter wired Knudsen, soon after the January 15 letter agreement with Governor Murphy, that the UAW spoke only for a minority of the workers and that the Flint Alliance wanted no settlement with that Union that would imperil the rights of the majority. Knudsen replied that "General Motors will never tolerate domination of its employees by a minority group." This exchange would not in itself have surprised us, but when Knudsen made the fatal blunder of agreeing by telegram to meet formally with members of the Flint Alliance to discuss collective bargaining, we realized that a double-cross was in the offing. . . .

[I]t was too late by now to resurrect the Murphy formula for conciliation. The lines had hardened once more; the atmosphere was tense and grim and remained so in spite of the personal intervention of President Roosevelt in private conversations with Lewis of the [CIO] and Sloan [of GM]. The settlement had been aborted by GM's patent lack of sincerity.

In the midst of this stand-off, GM made an effort to resume production in the Chevrolet units, which, like Buick, had closed down for lack of parts. They scheduled an opening for January 22, and Boysen of the Flint Alliance moved into action, announcing a big rally at which all Flint GM workers could express themselves on the subject of "forceful action" to re-establish their employment rights. This was obviously an open appeal to eject the strikers by force.

Governor Murphy was alerted to the possibility of more and bloody violence, and he called a meeting of the strike leaders along with Boysen, the Sheriff, and the Chief of Police, to discuss the rally. . . .

The exchanges between Boysen and our union leaders were heated. Fortunately, the city officials made it clear to Boysen that they would not tolerate any behavior at the rally that would incite the audience to commit violence. At the actual rally, there were some angry remarks about the CIO, Lewis, and "outside agitators," but Boysen himself kept the commitment he had made to Murphy and cautioned the audience against any destructive actions. The rally, attended largely by about eight thousand Buick and AC Spark Plug workers, whose plants had not been called out on strike, reflected strong back-to-work sentiment. There is no question in my mind that had we been tricked into evacuating the struck plants most GM workers would have gone back to work under prestrike terms with few or no reforms, the UAW would have been broken, and Flint families would have continued to live in poverty and hopelessness.

Knudsen's letter to Governor Murphy promising a settlement became a thoroughly dead letter on January 28, when GM went back to the strategy of using the courts, and sought a new injunction, from a different judge, to evacuate the plants. Vigilante activity increased: organizers Ditzel, Federoff, and Mayo were attacked and badly beaten. Henry Kraus reports in his book, The Many and the Few, that City Manager Barringer, perhaps the most bitterly antiunion official in Flint, plotted the murders of Roy, Bob Travis, and Kraus himself. During my last days in the city, Roy and I slept with a volunteer bodyguard on a mattress on the floor beside us and another guard outside the door. Roy was dragged from the sound truck one day in front of Chevrolet Nine by a bunch of vigilantes, including GM foremen, who smashed the sound equipment and roughed up Roy and the men who were with him. This incident was a measure of the growing terror; it also confirmed our suspicion that the company was going to try to single me out as the major culprit when the court battle was joined. According to them, I was responsible for the Battle of the Running Bulls and they probably thought I was in the sound truck when they attacked it. . . .

The UAW realized that unless the stalemate in Flint were resolved immediately the union would probably not survive. Inspired by desperation, Roy and Bob Travis devised one of the most daring and spectacular bits of strike strategy in the history of the labor movement.

Chevrolet was the biggest moneymaker within General Motors. Only one plant made Chevrolet engines for all the assembly plants around the country: Chevrolet Four. It had not been involved in the strike action, had small union affiliation, and by late January could have been quickly swung back into operation with the help of the Flint Alliance and its back-to-work propaganda. Unless the corporation's nerve could be pinched at this sensitive point, GM would win by waiting it out, and the strike would have been in vain. Roy, Travis, and a few trusted UAW staff members, therefore, plotted a plan of action used in many a military campaign: a feint, by which the enemy, distracted from the main thrust of troops by a minor deployment of forces, is taken off-guard.

Chevrolet Four was very well defended by the company because it was both important and vulnerable. Extra guards, whose motivation had been buttressed by long riot sticks and a pay increase, were installed in the plant. The building was somewhat removed from the main road, and it would have been foolhardy of the UAW to try to arrange a strike in that isolated, heavily armed fortress. It was decided to call an official strike at Chevrolet Nine instead, and let the plans leak out beforehand so that the guards, the riot sticks, and the tear-gas guns would be shifted from Four to Nine. If the ruse worked, then a strike could be brought off in the all-important Number Four.

The plan was cleared with CIO officials in Detroit, who were doubtful of its success but recognized that it just might be a great coup. Only four of five men in Flint besides Travis and Roy knew the real plot. The small, heroic group of union men in Chevrolet Nine, who were to become the sacrificial lambs, were not let in on the secret for fear of an inadvertent leak. They were merely asked, in a series of meetings, if they were willing to call a strike, and with considerable trepidation they agreed.

Walter's job was to bring several carloads of loyal unionists from Detroit's West Side to be on hand for the action, set for February 1. The day arrived. Precisely at three-thirty that afternoon, at the moment between shifts, the leading unionists in Chevrolet Nine threw the switches, downed their tools, and proclaimed a strike. Simultaneously, Roy and Travis brought a large group from a meeting in Pengelly Hall to demonstrate in front of the plant. They had earlier spread the word among the strikers in Fisher One that there would be action in Chevrolet Nine, sure that this decoy plan would reach the corporation through the omnipresent stool pigeons, which indeed proved to be the case. GM *had* been alerted, and when the open call came for a meeting in the union hall on the afternoon of February 1, the company quickly drew all its surplus security forces out of the engine-making plant, Chevrolet Four, and concentrated them inside Nine. When the strike was called, the union men in Nine were completely outnumbered. They defended themselves valiantly, but they were badly mauled, and should be honored in the annals of the labor movement for their sacrifice.

Outside, meanwhile, one sound truck manned by Roy and Powers Hapgood led a big line of demonstrators noisily from Pengelly Hall to Chevrolet Nine, while another sound truck, operated by Merlin Bishop, quietly led a second group to the general vicinity of Number Four. When the demonstrators outside Nine heard the tear-gas shells exploding inside and saw some windows being broken to let in fresh air, they used their picket signs to break more windows and reduce the fumes that were swirling around the uneven conflict.

Now that the General Motors defense was completely engaged in Nine, a signal was given by Roy to Ed Kronk, a stalwart six-foot press operator from Detroit, to pull an American flag out of his shirt. This was the signal for the fifty Detroiters who had come with him to proceed to the Chevrolet Four entrance, where they were joined by Walter, coming from the opposite direction with an equal number of men. They all entered the plant at once and gave the sign to those union members who had been in on the secret plan to throw the switches and declare a strike. Walter recalled later their frenzied effort to block and secure the exit doors with heavy equipment, after letting out all those who wanted no part of a sit-down strike.

The most vital sector of the General Motors empire was thus put under seige. The strikers in Chevrolet Nine gave up around four o'clock and came out, their heads bloody, but bowed only until they heard what had happened in Number Four and realized that they had played the bravest part in the whole affair. Then they became jubilant and, in spite of their wounds and before they would go for medical care, insisted on joining the Number Four picket line and marching around a few times, singing. They bore no grudge, knowing that they could never have put up as convincing a fight as they had if they had known the plan beforehand.

Once again the corporation officials responded by turning off the heat, but when they were told the strikers would make wood fires to keep warm, they turned it on again. This time, however, they were determined to let no food in. The timing had been too close for the organizers to lay in provisions, and there was no access from the street. The idea of dropping food on the roof was frustrated when the pilot was stopped by the city authorities with the threat of being grounded.

Governor Murphy was again hard at work, meeting with National Guard and police and city officials. By 6:30 P.M. the Chief of Police and the Mayor were appealing to him to use the troops. He chose a different course: he had the troop commanders seal off an area of approximately eight acres, taking in Chevrolet Nine and Four, as well as Fisher Body

Two and Chevrolet Two, across from each other on the avenue. Soldiers with fixed bayonets patrolled; the pickets who had been marching and singing outside Chevy Four . . . were dispersed or taken into custody if they resisted; and the sound car driven by Merlin Bishop was impounded. The troops were under strict orders to make no attempt to evict any of the sit-down strikers in the three plants.

Food was thus definitely cut off from all those inside. Governor Murphy's justification was that he had heard reports that individuals who were not Chevrolet workers were participating in the Chevy Four Strike and he did not propose to let food through to outsiders. Delicate discussions then got underway between the Governor and our leaders. The latter suggested that a National Guard delegation go in with them to check the badges of the sit-downers and ask those who were not legitimate to leave. The Guard refused to participate. Travis, Roy, and Henry Kraus went into the plant and found that Powers Hapgood and Walter were the only two who did not belong, the rest having already departed. Walter and Hapgood came out. Somewhat later the Guard made its own independent inspection and reported to the Governor that all the men inside were bona fide Chevrolet workers. The Governor then lifted the ban and allowed food to be taken in.

On that same historic day, Judge Gadola of Flint handed down what was perhaps one of the most sweeping injunctions ever issued during a labor battle. The public might have accepted it if it had not included a denial of basic rights. The judge declared that even peaceful picketing was now illegal in the State of Michigan, and then set a deadline of two days. If the strikers were not out by then, the union would be liable for a $15 million fine. When Sheriff Wolcott appeared at the struck plants to read the text of this injunction, there was no laughter, no cat calling — merely a grim silence. It was clear that the workers were as determined as ever to hold out against all legal and physical odds. They and all the UAW leaders in Flint feared that Governor Murphy would not be able to resist the pressure to use the troops to force evacuation, and that there would be a terrible and bloody confrontation. An urgent call went out to union members in other cities. They came in by hundreds and thousands from Toledo and from Detroit, from Pontiac and Saginaw and Bay City and Lansing, until, by the next morning, a gigantic crowd was milling around the gates of Fisher One.

The Fisher One sit-down strikers sent Governor Murphy an urgent telegram, warning him of a "bloody massacre" that would be "on his head." The Fisher Two men, the heroes of the Battle of the Running Bulls, appealed even more effectively to the Governor's compassionate nature and deep moral sense. I suspect that their message was written in collaboration with someone on the CIO staff. It read:

"Governor, we have decided to stay in the plant. We have no illusions about the sacrifices which this decision will entail. We fully expect that if a violent effort is made to oust us, many of us will be killed, and we take this means of making it known to our wives, to our children, to the people of the State of Michigan and the country that if this result follows from the attempt to eject us, you are the one who must be held responsible for our deaths."

The injunction had set the deadline for 3:00 P.M. on February 3. It was a bitter afternoon, with temperatures near zero, but thousands of sympathizers and union workers participated in the huge demonstration in front of Fisher One. Everyone was waiting for the dénouement. The hour for the enforcement of the injunction came — and went. The National Guard did not appear.

The celebration that followed did not please the local police officials. It seemed as if almost all of Flint was supporting the strike. The City Manager was especially irritated and began that day, allegedly in collusion with the Flint Alliance, to deputize citizens, many of whom were probably vigilantes. If the Governor wouldn't act, they would take care of the evacuation themselves!

Again more meetings and consultations among the Governor, National Guard, and members of the UAW. The latter promised that if the vigilantes were demobilized they, in turn, would see to it that there were no more large demonstrations at the factory gates and that the large picket signs, which looked like weapons, would be banned. They also promised to give notice to the police if they planned any kind of rally or parade. By this time both sides were sincerely anxious to avoid any further violence, and that night a peace settlement between the union and the Flint authorities was reached and announced to the sit-downers and to the crowd of union pickets and sympathizers still congregated in Pengelly Hall.

What most Flint citizens didn't know was that, on the same February 3, negotiations between the UAW and General Motors resumed in Detroit, under the auspices of Governor Murphy and the able federal conciliator, James Dewey. That was why the Governor could spare himself the painful move of using the troops to evict the strikers. John L. Lewis had also come from Washington for the talks. . . .

Frances Perkins, Secretary of Labor, had prevailed on President Roosevelt to make personal phone calls to Knudsen and Lewis to encourage compromise on the main issue that blocked any settlement: the union's demand for sole representation and bargaining rights in the plants that had been struck. . . .

The talks dragged on, and the Governor found it harder and harder to avoid his obligation to enforce the injunction and send the troops in to evacuate the plants. But he was backed in his determination to avoid violence by reassurances from President Roosevelt and by his own convictions. By February 9, when it looked as if he could hold off no longer,

Lewis drafted a telegram right at the conference table and read it aloud to the Governor:

"I do not doubt your ability to call out your soldiers and shoot the members of our union out of those plants, but let me say that when you issue that order I shall leave this conference and I shall enter one of those plants with my own people . . . and the militia will have the pleasure of shooting me out of the plants with them."

According to reliable observers, the Governor went white, grabbed the draft from Lewis's hand, and fled the room. The order to send in the troops was never given, and on February 11 at 2:40 A.M. a completely exhausted but elated Governor announced that an agreement had been reached. The whole country heaved a sigh of relief.

Murphy was praised in the months and years that followed, but he was also cruelly condemned for his failure to enforce the injunction. There is no doubt in my mind that he chose the wiser course: he laid the foundation once and for all for a relationship between labor and management based on well-defined rules rather than on the sheer exertion of money power and military force. It is a temptation for statesmen who have soldiers at their beck and call to use them freely. To practice restraint and suffer the criticism of those who have no real desire for peace — this requires heroism and sacrifice. History has already commemorated Frank Murphy for his unique contribution to social justice in America. He was a man who had the guts to stand firm in support of his convictions.

The peace terms so long awaited hardly took up the space of one typewritten page, but in those few important words the world's largest corporation agreed to recognize the fledgling United Auto Workers as the collective bargaining agent for all employees who were members of that union. Bargaining, based on the union's January 4 demands, was to begin on February 16. It was promised that there would be no discrimination, interference, restraint, or coercion in any GM plant because of union membership or organizing activities. In return, the union promised to terminate the strikes as quickly as possible and get the facilities back into operation. The UAW also agreed that during collective bargaining negotiations it would not engage in strike action or interfere in any way with production. There would be, from then on, an established grievance procedure for the settlement of disputes, and all possibilities offered by the procedure would have to be exhausted before a strike was called.

As part of this package, GM agreed to withdraw the injunctions it had obtained from courts in Flint and Cleveland and to cancel any contempt proceedings or fines. The UAW did not get exclusive bargaining rights for all employees, union or nonunion, but the corporation agreed that, for a period of six months after resumption of work, it would not "bargain or enter agreements with any other union or representative employees of plants on strike." This, in effect, meant six months of exclusive bargaining rights for the UAW in seventeen plants, and this period was considered sufficient for the union to demonstrate, through general Labor Board elections or other appropriate ways, that it did in fact represent a majority of GM workers. . . .

AUTO WORKERS' 25th CONSTITUTIONAL CONVENTION

Labor Relations Reporter (Bureau of National Affairs), Vol. 95, No. 5 (May 23, 1977).

Whatever problems the auto workers face in the next few years, it appears many of them will be external — caused by the energy shortage and its attendant threats to their livelihood — and not generated by internal conflict.

In his keynote address to the union's 25th constitutional convention, retiring president Leonard Woodcock said he is satisfied the union is in "great shape . . . just as good a union as it ever was" and fully capable of carrying on that way.

Having reached UAW's mandatory retirement age of 65, Woodcock has stepped down from the union presidency — a job he has held for seven years — as of May 19.

The gathering of some 2,812 delegates from about 980 locals in the U.S. and Canada opened on May 15 with a healthy list of matters to be considered, among them, the Administration's energy proposals, possible reaffiliation with the AFL-CIO, proposed amendment of the UAW constitution to permit future elections of officers by membership referendum, and the dissatisfactions of groups within the union such as skilled trades and white collar workers.

Woodcock devoted a major portion of his farewell address to the convention to the union's vehement opposition to the Administration's proposals for penalties on "gas-guzzler" automobiles and rebates for fuel efficient ones. The proposal is "not simply wrong because it would affect the automobile industry," Woodcock said, "but because it is an absolutely unnecessary and unwise policy if enacted into law."

In UAW's view, the "mandatory miles per gallon" law, which becomes effective this fall, will be sufficient to force conservation of gasoline. The law requires that the fleet average of each auto company reach 27.5 miles per gallon by 1985 — what Woodcock termed a "100 percent improvement in efficiency in a decade." Manufacturers who fail to meet the miles per gallon averages (interim limits are set for years before 1985) must pay fines of $50 for each mile per gallon by which the fleet average is missed. Woodcock emphasized that the fine is not tax deductible.

His criticisms of the energy proposal completed, Woodcock added that UAW's disagreements in this area do "not mean we are dissatisfied or disillusioned." The union certainly supports, for example, Administration proposals to restructure the social security system, which Woodcock called "a responsible demonstration of concern for the security of this country's workers and their families."

Turning to a matter of internal union affairs, Woodcock took note of the existence of at least nine resolutions submitted to the convention's constitution committee calling for election of international officers by membership referendum instead of by the convention delegates. The resolutions could not affect the choice of Woodcock's successor, Douglas A. Fraser, at this convention, but they could affect future elections.

Woodcock commented that "there are many who sincerely and honestly believe that a referendum system is a more democratic way because it involves everybody" but "I deeply believe ours is a much more democratic system." The UAW president added:

"Now, why do I say it's more democratic? When you have a referendum vote, the people are relatively passive; they are reacting simply to the candidates who are floating around the country and going on television and asking for their support. They are not necessarily involved. The possibility of outside interference is substantially greater in a referendum system, which is fought through the press and through the TV, and which takes for the candidates great sums of money which is constantly subject to litigation."

Woodcock observed that it has been charged that UAW Vice President Fraser's status as the "only one major candidate" for the UAW presidency indicates "that the UAW system is a machine system" and "fixed." But he declared that "there are others who have an absolute right to challenge for that office." Some of them said they would like the job of UAW president, Woodcock said, but they also concluded that "it's more important that we keep this union together and strong in what are going to be even more difficult days ahead."

At its opening session on May 15, the convention was addressed by Coretta Scott King, after the delegates approved a donation of $600,000 over the next two years to the Martin Luther King, Jr. Center for Social Change in Atlanta. The money, to be taken from interest and earnings income of the union strike fund, will go toward the center's construction fund at the rate of $25,000 per month, beginning in June 1977.

Woodcock noted that UAW is well recovered from the financial difficulties it met as a result of the 1970 General Motors strike. As of December 31, 1976, the strike fund stood at $146,399,782, an increase of more than $9 million over 1975. The general operating fund stood at $29,166,685, an increase of more than $7 million over 1975.

The union spent $2,826,975 on organizing in 1976, and of this amount, $244,969 was spent on organizing technical, office and professional workers. UAW participated in 300 representation elections during the year, winning 171 in units with 17,700 potential members and losing 129 elections. Since the union's last convention in 1974, UAW said it has organized 65,404 new workers.

UAW assistance to other unions during 1976 included contributions of $423,372 to United Farm Workers organizing activities, $50,000 to the Rubber Workers' industry-wide strike, and $2,000 to the International Metal Workers Foundation to assist strikers at Massey-Ferguson Company in Barcelona, Spain.

The union's average dues-paying membership stood at 1,358,354 during 1976, compared to 1,356,670 for 1975 — an increase of 1,684. The average monthly dues at the end of 1976 (calculated at the rate of two hours' pay) were $12.81, compared with $12.17 at the end of 1975.

[Among other items, the account closes with a description of an address delivered to the convention by President Carter.]

B. THE MODERN UNION AND ITS ECONOMIC IMPACT

D. BOK AND J. DUNLOP, A PROFILE OF THE LABOR MOVEMENT: ITS MEMBERSHIP AND LEADERSHIP

Labor and the American Community 43-57 (1970)

In 1966, 18.3 million men and women in the United States were paying dues to labor unions.[1] By 1968, the figure is estimated to have exceeded 19 million. The number of employees subject to collective-bargaining agreements is still larger by three quarters of a million, since not all employees covered by collective-bargaining agreements are required to be union members. The past five years have been a period of marked expansion in the total number of union members, reversing a decline which set in with the recession of 1958. Nevertheless, the labor force has grown so rapidly that union membership in 1968, as a percentage of employment in nonagricultural enterprises, was little more than 28 percent compared to the level of 33-34 percent achieved in the middle 1950's. [Figures 1 and 2 present in chart form the data on union

1. This Bureau of Labor Statistics figure excludes approximately 1.4 million members of national and international unions with headquarters in the United States who were in Canada and other areas outside the United States. This figure also excludes many members, who may number over 900,000, exempt from dues payments in whole or in part as provided in union constitutions, by virtue of being unemployed, on strike, retired, apprentices prior to being eligible to membership, or in military service.

FIGURE [1]
Membership of National Unions, 1930-78[11]

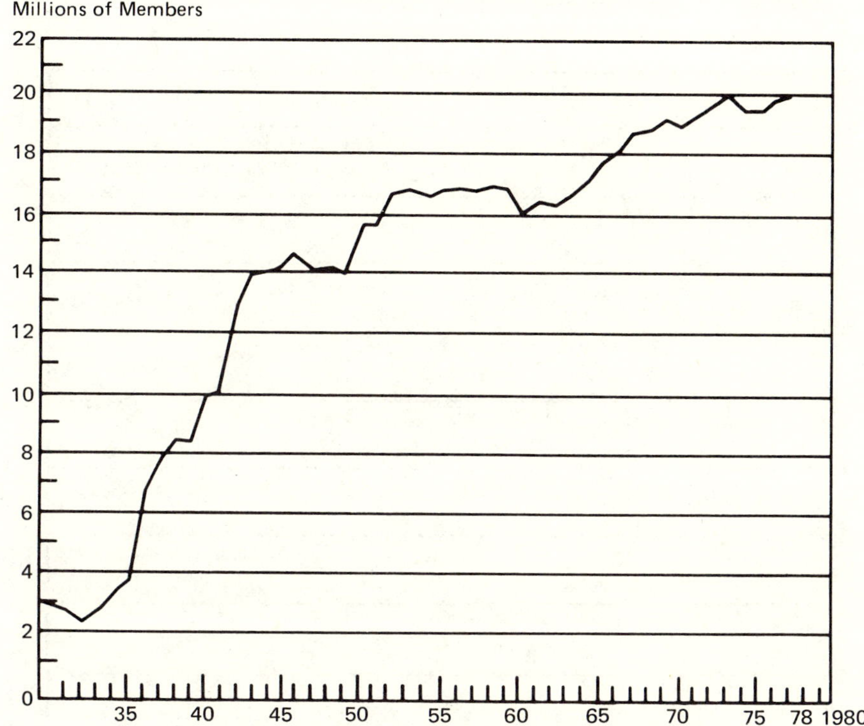

Source: Directory of National Unions and Employee Associations, 1979, U.S. Department of Labor, Bureau of Labor Statistics, Bulletin 2079, Sept. 1980.

[11] Excludes Canadian membership but includes members in other areas outside the United States. Members of AFL-CIO directly affiliated local unions are also included. Members of single-firm and local unaffiliated unions are excluded. For the years 1948-52, midpoints of membership estimates, which were expressed as ranges, were used.

FIGURE [2]
Union Membership As a Percent of Total Labor Force and of Employees in Nonagricultural Establishments, 1930–78[12]

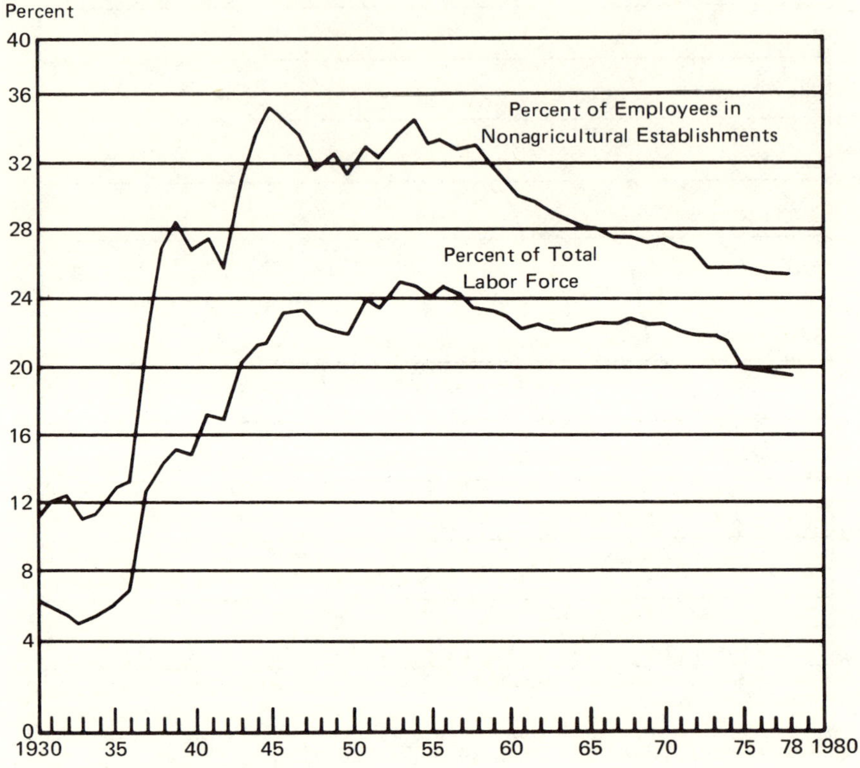

Source: Directory of National Unions and Employee Associations, 1979, U.S. Department of Labor, Bureau of Labor Statistics, Bulletin 2079, Sept. 1980.

[12] See footnote [11], Figure [1].

membership, and union membership as a percentage of nonagricultural employees, for the years 1930-1978.]

Union members are organized into more than 70,000 local unions, which are in turn affiliated with 190 national or international unions (except for fewer than a thousand locals, with an aggregate of little more than a half million members, that are directly affiliated with the AFL-CIO or in single-firm and local unaffiliated unions). Two-thirds of these national unions with more than three-quarters of the membership are affiliated with the AFL-CIO, even after the disaffiliation of Walter Reuther and the Auto Workers in 1968.

The Union Member

Union members do not represent a mirror image of the entire adult population, or even the work force, of this country. Instead they are rather heavily concentrated in certain income ranges, educational levels, industries, occupations and regions.

INCOME

Unionists fall mainly in the middle-income group, with relatively few members numbered among the very rich or the very poor. In 1965, 69.1 percent of union heads of households had incomes ranging from $5,000 to $10,000. Among households headed by nonmembers, only 43.4 percent fell within this income range. Conversely, only 3.9 percent of union household heads received less than $3,000 during the same year, while 14.2 percent earned more than $10,000. For nonunion households, the corresponding figures were substantially larger; 14.3 percent fell below $3,000, while 21.6 percent earned over $10,000.

EDUCATION

Much the same pattern carries over to the area of education. In 1965, 44 percent of all union heads of households had an education that extended through all or part of high school (but not beyond). Only 32 percent of nonunion household heads fell within these categories. At the upper end of the scale, however, the figures were sharply reversed. Only 1.4 percent of all union family heads had received a college diploma and .4 percent had received an advanced degree. Among family heads who were not members of unions, over eight times as many (11.4 percent) had graduated from college, while almost twenty times as many (7.8 percent) had obtained an advanced degree.

SEX

It is well known that women workers are underrepresented in labor unions. Among employees outside the agricultural sector, only one woman in seven belongs to a union, while one man in every three is a member. To some extent, the difference is explained by the heavy employment of women in clerical and sales occupations and in service industries, where unions have traditionally made little headway. But other causes are probably more important. Women can be among the most loyal, determined union members when their sense of injustice is aroused. In general, however, women outside the professions appear not to place the importance that men do on matters connected with employment; they frequently do not conceive of themselves as remaining in a job for a working lifetime. Thus, even in operative and semiskilled occupations, which are quite highly organized, women seem to be less inclined to join unions than men.

INDUSTRY AND OCCUPATION

Union members are distributed most unevenly among different industries, as the following table reveals:

Industry	*Percentage organized*
Transportation, communications, public utilities	74.7%
Construction	70.9
Manufacturing	50.0
Mining	47.2
Government	14.1
Services	10.5
Trade	9.3
Finance, real estate	2.0
Agriculture	.8

These differences are the result of many factors. The variations in the occupational mix of different industries are significant, for unions seem to have much greater appeal in some occupational groups than others. The prevalence of women in certain occupations helps to explain the low rate of unionization in the trade and service sectors. With a few notable exceptions, white-collar workers have traditionally been cool to unions, especially professional and technical employees. On the other hand, blue-collar employees in the skilled and semiskilled categories seem to be the most promising target for unionization. Unskilled laborers tend to fall between these poles. They are usually more susceptible than white-collar workers, but they are also more apt to be foreign-born, easily replaceable, quickly intimidated by hostile employers, subject to considerable turnover and thus often frustrating to union organizers seeking to attract continuing affiliation. These differences reveal themselves dramatically in figures comparing the rates of unionization among occupations.

Occupations	*Percentage organized*
Operatives (semiskilled)	63%
Craftsmen and foremen	50
Laborers (excluding agriculture)	38
Clerical	26
Service	20
Sales Managers Professional and technical	5-10

GEOGRAPHY

Union membership is not distributed throughout the United States in proportion to population or employment. In general terms, the extent of union organization — measured as a fraction of nonagricultural employment — is greatest in the east-northcentral and eastern industrial states and on the West Coast. The extent of organization is least in the South, the Southwest and the Middle West plain states. There are, of course, important variations within these groupings. For example, there appears to be some tendency for employees in metropolitan areas to be slightly more highly organized than employees in smaller communities.

The five states with the largest employment — New York, California, Pennsylvania, Illinois, and Ohio — contain 48 percent of the union members while they employ 38 percent of the nonagricultural work force. These five states have 8.7 million union members.

Many more characteristics of union members could be cited. For example, it is interesting to note that the union movement includes about the same proportion of nonwhites as in the nonagricultural work force and that unions contain a disproportionate number of war veterans and Catholics. But even more important than these demographic factors are the attitudes of union employees on social, political and economic questions. For, in the last analysis, these sentiments will probably have the most direct effects upon the course of union behavior.

As suggested in the first chapter, the opinions of union members are particularly striking in their lack of any special class bias. This remarkable state of affairs has been commented upon by a number of European critics.

"In the experience of the European, industrial strife was a conflict between two classes, almost two distinct orders of mankind, separated from each other by a wide and impossible gulf of habits, attitudes and material conditions. The European was fascinated (in the United States) by the general air of prosperity, the free-and-easy relations between persons on different social levels, the lack of social distinctions, class hostilities, class jealousies, class political issues." [Smuts, European Perception of American Workers 2 (1955)]

Today, the same pattern still reveals itself in opinion surveys on a wide variety of questions. Whether the issue is Vietnam, admission of Red China to the U.N., civil-rights legislation, aid to education, the poverty program, a labor party, or government ownership of essential industries, the opinions of union members come within a very few percentage points of those held by the public at large. The same is true of questions touching on attitudes toward society and government. Union members are no more likely than the general public is to feel, in the language of the interview question, that "the people running the country don't really care what happens to people like yourself." Nor are they more likely to feel that what they think "doesn't count very much" or to fear that they "don't have as good a chance to get ahead as most people." And they are as overwhelmingly disposed as the rest of society is to reject the notion that "nobody understands our problems" or they are "left out of the things going on around us."

It is well to compare these findings with the standard theories that popular writers have expressed about the political sentiments of union members. One view, less prevalent now than two decades ago, maintains that union members are, more than the rest of the population, willing to support sweeping social and economic programs. Another theory has flowered more recently in the wake of repeated claims of "white backlash" in heavily blue-collar areas. According to this opinion, union members were more "progressive" in earlier decades but have become strongly conservative as their wages and conditions have risen to more comfortable middle-class levels.

Neither of these theories is well supported by the facts. According to recent opinion surveys, union members as a group do not exhibit any special desire for drastic social and economic change. They reject, by about the same margin as the general public, such current proposals as a negative income tax and a multibillion-dollar program for the cities. And they are much more anxious that the government finance the war in Vietnam and combat crime in the streets than that it maintain welfare programs and campaign against poverty. Nevertheless, union members are not more conservative about these matters than the rest of the population. If anything, they tend to stand two or three percentage points to the liberal side on matters of race, the United Nations, the poverty program, and most other public issues. These tendencies also seem to be remarkably durable. There has been no apparent shift to the right over the past two or three decades. On racial matters, for example, the attitudes of union members have grown steadily *more* tolerant, not less (along with those of most other segments of the society).

Various forces have contributed to this peculiar lack of class sentiment among union members (and other manual workers). One important factor was the extreme heterogeneity of the American labor force in the formative years of industrialization. During this period, a network of language, racial and religious barriers was thrown up by repeated waves of immigration. Particular ethnic groups gained control over different jobs, while recent immigrants and Negro laborers were excluded from the better jobs and later used as strikebreakers by employers. These experiences produced cleavages that kept the labor movement from achieving the degree of unity reached in Great Britain and Scandinavia.

Labor organizations in America also grew up in a society that stressed the ideals of classlessness, individual initiative, and abundant opportunity, a society in which workers enjoyed the right of suffrage and the opportunity for a free public education. In this atmosphere, employees were less inclined than workers in Europe to submerge their sense of individuality and identify with a working class. Many of them, moreover, were constantly presented with opportunities to leave the ranks of labor for management jobs or opportunities in the West. In contrast to Europe, real wages were high and rose rapidly, and the spread between skilled and unskilled wage rates was especially large. As a result, class solidarity was slow to develop and potential leadership was constantly siphoned off into other pursuits.

In Europe, on the other hand, labor movements arose against the backdrop of a feudal tradition that denied workers access to economic opportunity or political power. Under these conditions, European workers were driven together to make common cause to advance their interests. In the political sphere, for example, workers often had to struggle for a decade or more into the twentieth century to achieve such elementary rights as public education and, more important, universal male suffrage. As public issues, these questions were important enough to arouse the working classes for a sustained political effort. In contrast to the experience of America, where such rights were granted much earlier, in Europe ". . . the arising awareness of the working classes expressed above all an experience of *political alienation* — that is, a sense of not having a recognized position in the civic community or of not having a civic community in which to participate."

The sense of working-class solidarity, of separateness from the rest of society, still remains strong in countries like France and Italy. Elsewhere in Europe, notably in Scandinavia, manual workers seem gradually to have been integrated more closely into the entire population. Yet, traditions of working-class sentiment have left their mark upon the shape of the labor movement throughout the entire continent.

The Unions

The American union movement has certain characteristics that give it a special flavor and set it somewhat apart from most of its counterparts abroad.

SIZE

Despite all of the concern expressed over labor's power, union membership in America is a smaller proportion of the work force than in any of the other major industrial democracies.[2] While this fact is arresting in itself, its significance grows even larger when one realizes that higher levels of unionization have been achieved throughout Western Europe without benefit of the union shop, without elaborate safeguards to protect the workers' right to organize, and without expensive campaigns or professional staffs to organize nonunion employers.

The low levels of unionization in America can be explained largely by two factors. One important factor is a widespread opposition of employers — an attitude no longer prevalent in Europe save in Italy and France. Although American labor leaders often exaggerate the significance of this opposition, its importance can be seen in the ease with

2. Union Membership as Percentage of Nonagricultural Employed Labor Force

	Union membership (thousands)	*Total number employed (thousands)*	*Percentage of organization*
Austria	1,540	2,247	68.5%
Sweden	2,165	3,302	65.6
Belgium	1,700	3,407	49.9
Italy	6,320	14,242	44.4
Australia	1,475	3,448	42.8
England	8,757	22,621	38.7
Netherlands	1,430	3,978	35.9
Germany	7,996	23,733	33.7
France	3,071	10,243	29.0
United States	17,299	60,770	28.5

(Australian data are for 1963; data relating to other countries for 1965.)

Statistical comparisons of union membership among countries should be used with considerable caution, since the meaning of membership varies greatly. In the United States membership is measured by dues payments, but in Europe not only are dues levels much lower, but membership is not reported according to regular dues payments. In addition, it should be emphasized that the political and economic power of the union movement does not bear any simple relation to the proportion of the labor force that is organized; such power depends on several other factors such as the financial strength of the unions, the nature of the party system, etcetera.

which unions can usually organize blue-collar workers once management has been persuaded to remain neutral. Employer opposition, however, does not wholly explain the stunted growth of the American labor movement. Unionization is proportionately much greater in Italy than in the United States despite widespread hostility from employers, and this has been true even though Italian unions have had to cope with severe internal divisions, less impressive achievements at the bargaining table, and an almost total lack of formal organizing efforts. In other countries, moreover, employers were often openly hostile toward unions in the early stages of organization, but their policies eventually changed because they could not overcome the determination of the unions.

A second factor has been the lack of solidarity among workers in the United States. Perhaps opportunities for advancement and geographic movement were greater in this country, thus strengthening the hold on individualism; perhaps employees were influenced by higher wages and rising living standards derived from a chronic scarcity of labor and rapidly increasing productivity. Whatever the explanation, the small size of the United States union movement must probably be attributed in part to the lack of a strongly felt need on the part of many employees to band together for mutual protection. In Europe, on the other hand, feelings of worker solidarity were much stronger. They were typically buttressed by a network of mutually reinforcing institutions based on working-class support — political parties, cooperatives, youth groups, educational programs, and even banks, newspapers and other commercial undertakings. In short, though there is evidence in several countries that class lines may be weakening, the European labor leader has been able to capitalize on a cultural milieu in which union membership has been the natural response of the working man.

UNIONS AND POLITICS

The lack of a distinctive ideology among the working people of this country has also had a marked influence on the political activity of American unions. The labor movement in the United States is unique in failing to produce a political party based explicitly on working-class support. Nor have American unions followed the example of many European countries by splitting into rival organizations based upon party lines. In France and in Italy, there are three large national organizations of workers representing Communist, Socialist, and Christian Democratic ideologies. In Belgium, Socialist and Christian Democrat federations coexist. In the Netherlands separate Catholic, Protestant, and Socialist labor organizations have been established. Cleavages have also developed in the United States, most notably during the thirties, when John L. Lewis and the Congress of Industrial Organizations defied the American Federation of Labor. But characteristically this division took place over pragmatic questions of tactics and jurisdiction in organizing the mass-production industries and not because of any deep-seated differences in religion or political philosophy. In keeping with the nature of the conflict, the differences between the AFL and CIO were submerged twenty years later in the formation of the AFL-CIO.

STRONG LOCAL UNIONS

Unions in this country were generally forced to achieve recognition and establish bargaining relationships on a plant-by-plant basis rather than by agreement with a strong national or regional association of employers. This process encouraged the growth of active local unions in the plant, with important functions to perform. In some industries, of course, control over collective bargaining has gravitated to the national or regional level. But even in these sectors, local unions still retain considerable influence over the administration of the contract and over political and community activities.

The importance of local unions is reflected in the financial holdings of labor organizations in the United States. At the end of 1966, all union bodies had combined assets of $1,839,000,000, and the combined assets of local unions and intermediate bodies[3] exceeded those of the international unions. In the same year, local unions had receipts of $1,256,000,000; intermediate bodies net receipts of $14,000,000 and international unions net receipts of $560,000,000.

This pattern is not encountered abroad. Viable plant locals do exist in Scandinavia, but even there the grievance process is less developed than in this country, and local bodies have little or no control over political matters, organizing other plants, community activities, and similar matters that occupy the attention of many local unions in this country. In Britain and Australia, plant organizations may have a strong influence over local disputes and working conditions, but these bodies often behave quite independently of the national unions, to the frequent embarrassment of their parent organizations. On the continent of Europe, the contrast is even more marked. Local unions rarely exist at all and union representatives in the plant share whatever power they have over grievances and local problems with other institutions, such as the elected workers' councils, over which they have little direct control.

A LOOSE FEDERATION

At higher levels in the union structure, the labor movement in America has remained markedly decentralized in the sense that the central federation has had relatively little authority over its member unions. In

3. Locals of the same international union in a metropolitan area or state often form a district council or state council for purposes of bargaining or organizing. Such bodies typically maintain their own financial status. Intermediate bodies may also be composed of a number of locals in the same industry from different international unions.

part, this is the result of the lack of a class sentiment strong enough to transcend the attachments of workers to their own separate crafts and occupations. In part, the absence of a strong federation reflected the predominance in our labor movement of bargaining rather than political action, for which a powerful central body would have been more necessary to enable the movement to act in unison in election campaigns and lobbying efforts. In any event, the AFL was founded with the explicit understanding that the affiliated unions would retain their autonomy. Throughout its history, the federation had to rely, with mixed success, on persuasion and conciliation instead of exercising formal powers or sanctions. Even today the situation is not much changed. The AFL-CIO has acquired some power to investigate and suspend affiliates for corruption or Communist influence, but it has little or no authority over the bargaining and strike policies of its members, nor is it able to control their membership requirements or political activities.

There are other countries, notably Britain and Australia, where the central federation is also rather weak. But the situation is more often to the contrary. For example, the major Swedish federation negotiates directly with the central employers' organization to establish broad wage guidelines that are binding on its constituent unions. Member unions must also gain the consent of the federation before initiating a strike involving more than 3 percent of their membership and must agree to include various rules in their constitutions safeguarding the rights of individuals with respect to membership, discipline, transfers, and the like. Even in matters involving local grievances and discharges of workers, the federation has ultimate power to enter into binding settlements. In other European countries, the degree of power actually exercised by the central organizations is harder to assess, but certainly the Belgian and Dutch federations are highly centralized, and it is generally assumed that the dominant Communist federations in France and Italy have extensive control over the policies of their member unions.

The Near Unions

It has been assumed that everyone understands what a union is in this country. But any careful newspaper reader will agree that the definition of "union" has become decidedly vague in recent years. A decade ago, the National Education Association, an organization of a million schoolteachers and administrators, prided itself on its status as a thoroughly professional association. Today, the teachers affiliated with N.E.A. have embraced the idea of negotiation with school boards and have resorted to strikes and other collective sanctions to achieve their proposals. Professional associations of nurses have come to engage in mass resignations and other forms of economic pressure to achieve collective agreements. In professional athletics, football, basketball, and baseball associations have all sprung up seeking negotiations and uttering ominous threats of stopping play. Police officers' associations in a few localities have invented the "blue plague," an exotic illness known only to uniformed patrolmen in search of improved benefits. And in Southern California an erstwhile man of the cloth has even tried to organize Catholic priests. The near unions tend to have supervisory employees as members; their members are more independent, have higher incomes, and are more responsive to professional concerns than are members of conventional unions. It is unclear whether these organizations are in transition toward more conventional unions or constitute a more permanent form of employee organization.

Although the total size of the near unions is uncertain, their combined membership is certainly greater than two million persons. With the addition of the near unions, the composition of membership in all employee organizations is less heavily concentrated than in the AFL-CIO alone among income and occupational groups. It is also more diverse in its goals, its strategies and its political outlook.

The Union Leader

In contrast to the labor movements in other countries, unions in the United States boast a much higher number of full-time officials.[4] To some extent, this tendency may reflect a distinctive American attitude toward administration, for business enterprises, universities, and various other private organizations also seem to have particularly large staffs in this country. But the root of the matter, once again, lies in the decentralized pattern of union organization and labor relations in the United States. For the most part, collective bargaining has not consisted of negotiations with huge industrywide employer associations. The predominant tendency has been to conduct separate negotiations with individual plants and companies. As a result, there are a vast number of contracts to be negotiated. Because it is so decentralized, bargaining can also grapple with the particular working conditions of the individual plant to a degree not duplicated abroad. And once the agreement is signed, the local union is the natural agency for taking up the countless individual complaints and questions that arise concerning the application and ad-

4. Ratio of officers to members

United States	1:300
Denmark	1:775
Australia	1:900
Sweden	1:1700
Great Britain	1:2000
Norway	1:2200

— Seymour M. Lipset, "Trade Unions and Social Structure: II," Industrial Relations, February 1962, p. 93.

ministration of the contract. To perform all this work, a host of union officials is required.

Almost all labor leaders have come up from the ranks of the members working in the plants and crafts that the unions represent. Unlike the situation in several other countries, especially in the underdeveloped world, very few of these leaders have backgrounds as lawyers, politicians, editors, professors or intellectuals. Nor are their fathers predominantly found outside the ranks of labor. In a 1967 survey of union presidents, secretary-treasurers, and vice-presidents, 37 percent were found to have fathers who were skilled workers; 17 percent were the sons of semiskilled and unskilled employees; 7 percent were the children of foremen. No more than 11 percent of the fathers owned a business and only 4 percent were executives.

At first glance, these figures seem surprising. In a mobile society without marked class divisions, one might have expected that union leaders would be drawn to a larger extent from different areas of society. But other forces have tugged more strongly in the opposite direction. Intellectuals and professionals are most often drawn to a labor movement as a vehicle for their own political advancement or a force for promoting certain political and social ideals. The American labor movement has been rather unattractive for these purposes, for it has never been profoundly ideological, nor has it provided a particularly easy entry to a political career. Instead, the work of the unions has centered upon the bargaining process and, especially at the lowest levels of the union hierarchy, upon the day-to-day business of administering the working conditions in the shop and factory. These issues require an intimate knowledge of the workplace naturally acquired by union members who have worked in the trade. To the intellectual or the professional man, however, these matters are not only unfamiliar; they are also of precious little interest.

Emerging as he does from the rank and file, the union leader naturally tends to reflect many of the characteristics of his membership. For example, 83 percent of union presidents and secretary-treasurers are said to be Democrats, just as almost all unions have a majority of Democrats among their members. As for education, approximately half of all union leaders in the 1967 survey have no more than a high-school education; while 21 percent have completed college, 25 percent never graduated from high school. The proportion of college graduates among union leaders is appreciably higher than among union members, but it lags well behind the level achieved by businessmen, government officials, and other key groups within the society.

The average age of the national officer of a union is fifty-three — about the same for business executives at the vice-president and president level. According to the 1967 survey, the "typical" national officer is likely to have begun to work at roughly eighteen years of age. But he will probably not have become a union member until his early twenties and will not have joined his present union until three or four years later. Six or seven years after that he will have reached his first elective position in his union local. From local office, he will probably have taken an appointive staff position and then will have become a national officer at approximately age forty-five.

As one might expect, there are marked variations among officials and among unions. For example, union leaders tend to have higher levels of education if they belong to small unions or unions in the transportation, service, or government sectors. In most cases, these differences stem from variations in the type and background of the members in the various unions. Small elite crafts tend to be led by better-educated men. The Airline Pilots or Actors Equity will obviously produce a different kind of leader from that of the Mine Workers or the Laborers.

At one time, much was made of the differences between the leaders of CIO and AFL unions. According to the sociologist C. Wright Mills, "The AFL and CIO are not two differently shaped vessels filled with similar types of leaders. The split between them runs deep: It divides different types of men. They differ in their personal characteristics, in the union experience they have had, and in their social and political outlook." When Mills was writing, the CIO was little more than a decade old. Its young unions were filled with young leaders. Their education was frequently superior to that of the AFL leaders. To Mills, therefore, the AFL seemed largely a gerontocracy — ". . . at its top are older men who are relatively poorly educated and who have authority over much younger men who are relatively better educated."

In the intervening years, these differences have all but disappeared. According to the 1967 survey, the average age of CIO leaders is fifty-three; for AFL leaders, fifty-six. The percentage of CIO leaders who have completed college is twelve; of AFL leaders, twenty-two. In sum, the divergent statistics that Mills developed were largely the accidents of history. They reflected the youth of the CIO and disappeared as soon as these unions increased in age. And as they disappeared, many of the differences in social and political outlook tended to diminish as well.

THE ECONOMICS OF LABOR UNIONS[1]

Economists have models of what unions do, but there is disagreement about what model best describes the "business" of unions. For many years the price theory model of unions has dominated the literature, and by this theory's lights unions (wage monopolists) misallocate society's resources.

1. Portions of this appear in Leslie, Labor Bargaining Units, 70 Va. L. Rev. 353 (1984).

The price theory model posits that wages (salaries and fringe benefits) are set in competitive labor markets, in which supply curves — determined by the number of workers willing to work at particular wage rates — and demand curves — determined by marginal revenue products of workers — intersect to produce a "going wage" that is presented to individual firms. This model treats unions as cartels of workers who seek to raise wages above these competitive levels.

When unions are successful, the costs are borne by consumers in higher prices for goods and services, by nonunion workers who receive wage rates below those that would be set by a competitive labor market, and by workers who lose jobs when firms reduce employment as a result of union wage gains. Only in a labor market subject to imperfections could a union raise wages without causing reduced employment, and even in such a market unions may not be content to push wages only up to the competitive level. When unions are unsuccessful, the costs of organizing the cartel and attempting to raise wages are deadweight social losses. The first section of this discussion develops this model in some detail.

The relational contract model is a partial alternative to the price theory model. Proponents of the relational contract model argue that the price theory model does not adequately explain observed features of many actual labor markets. Wage differentials in local labor markets may be common, wages are downwardly rigid in time of unemployment, firms observe relative wages across employee groups, and unions are stable over the long run notwithstanding competitive product markets. The relational contract model predicts how wages and employment levels would be determined in firms in which important employee skills are learned on the job from other employees, are specific to the firm, and where monitoring of employee cooperativeness by managers is costly.

The role of unions in a relational contract model is unclear. A union might reduce the costs of contracting, thereby improving the welfare of both the firm and its employees, while not imposing costs on consumers or on nonunion workers; or, a union might extract monopoly rents with the effects described in the price theory model. The contention is that actual labor markets can be placed along a spectrum in which price theory model markets occupy one end of the spectrum, relational contracts occupy the other end, and most markets are at neither extreme.

The collective goods model is not a model of labor markets, but is an elaboration of the role of unions in both the price theory and relational contract models. Development of this model begins with the argument that by collectivizing employee "voice" within a particular firm, a union could persuade managers to alter employee compensation packages and other employment terms in ways improving the welfare of a majority of the employees without the use of union monopoly power. The model predicts that voice would be underutilized in the absence of collectivization. The argument is then made that whether it be by voice, purchase or monopoly power, most of the benefits secured for employees by unions are collective goods — goods that employees in a particular group will consume even if they pay no share of the costs of producing the goods, and that will be underproduced absent unionization. The collective goods model is contrasted to the price theory model, which assumes that increased wages are the *only* collective goods produced by unions and that unions therefore rely solely on monopoly power to redistribute wealth from consumers and nonunion workers to union members.

Within the context of the collective goods model the incentives of managers and the costs to the firm of monitoring managerial behavior help explain why managers might oppose union production of many collective goods even though the firm itself would not be harmed, and might be made more profitable, by their production.

Last, we will explore the goals of unions and the related questions of how union members communicate their preferences to union officers and how they monitor officers' performance.

Price Theory and the Wage-Employment Tradeoff

According to the price theory model, unions are in the business of raising wages by monopolizing the labor supply. An example illustrates the model. Suppose a retail store selling widgets is owned and managed by a single owner, *A*. Working alone, owner *A* produces a net revenue of $100 per week.[13] Owner *A* discovers that if he hires a clerk to assist him, he can handle more customers, sell more widgets, and thereby increase his revenue to $150 per week. So long as he pays the clerk less than $50 per week,[14] owner *A* improves his financial position by hiring the clerk.

Owner *A* then determines that adding a second clerk will increase the net revenue of the store to $175. The $25 incremental contribution to the store's revenue occasioned by the addition of the second clerk is called the clerk's marginal revenue product.[15] The $25 incremental contribution to revenue does not necessarily mean that the second clerk himself sells enough widgets to produce the $25 increase in revenue. Part of the increase may come from increased sales by the first clerk made possible by the presence of the second clerk (e.g., the second clerk stocks shelves, freeing the first clerk to attend to more customers).

[13] This example is adapted from A. Kuhn, Labor: Institutions and Economics 280 (1967).

[14] At precisely $50 per week the owner will be indifferent to whether he hires the clerk, but I shall ignore that in order to keep the numbers simpler. This point is applicable to later wage examples as well.

[15] The marginal revenue product is calculated by multiplying the increases in physical product or services sold (or manufactured) by the firm on account of hiring the new employee times the product price. If the firm sells more of its product only by reducing price, the employee's marginal revenue product is found by multiplying the marginal physical product by the marginal revenue. This takes into account the fact that the increase in sales is accompanied by a lower price for the product.

If there is only one clerk available for hire in town, his wage cannot be predicted but a bargaining range can be described. His maximum wage is $50 (his marginal revenue product), which is his worth to the store. His minimum wage is set by the wage that he can secure in another job, or by the wage below which he would prefer to be unemployed. The wage that the clerk can command becomes more definite as we introduce wage competition among clerks into the example.

Assume that the first clerk has negotiated a wage of $50 when a second clerk, identical in every relevant respect to the first clerk, accepts a job with the store at $25 per week. The first clerk can no longer command $50 in wages, for if he persists in demanding $50 the owner would be better off financially by discharging him. A discharge saves the owner $50 in wage payment but costs the owner only $25 in net revenue, a net gain of $25. Neither clerk can expect to bargain for more than $25 in wages. Whether they intend to or not, the clerks are competing with one another. This example illustrates the principle that the maximum wage of identical co-workers is the marginal revenue product of the last worker.

The results change if the clerks act in concert and offer their services to owner *A* only as a package. The maximum wage of each clerk now rises above $25. With no clerks, net revenue to the store is $100; with two clerks, net revenue is $175. So long as the total wage bill is no more than $75, the owner is better off hiring the two-clerk package than he is operating the store alone. If the clerks divide the pay equally,[16] they can command a maximum wage of $37.50 each. The clerks must stick together, however, because they can earn $37.50 only if neither is persuaded to accept $25 from the employer, and only if no other clerks at $25 are available.

Similar results are obtained when a competing widget store and management innovation are added to the example. Assume the town has two stores (store *A* and store *B*) that can use clerks and that they are presented with the same marginal productivity schedules: An owner alone yields net revenue of $100, an owner and one clerk yields net revenue of $150, an owner and two clerks yields net revenue of $175, and a third clerk adds no additional revenue. If the number of available clerks is four and they do not act in concert, each store should have two clerks at $25 each. Now the owner of store *A* discovers a new technique that enables his clerks to handle widgets and customers more effectively. The marginal revenue product of each clerk increases by $50 and a third and fourth clerk now add revenue. The owner of store *A* computes the following schedule:

[16] The clerks would not have to divide the wage bill equally. If the division is unequal, however, the less fortunate clerk may be inclined to drop out of the agreement. Splitting the gains tends to be a natural, but not a required, solution for the clerks. At any wage above $25 a clerk is better off cooperating than he is competing.

	Net revenue	Maximum wage of additional clerk
owner alone	$100	—
one clerk	200	$100
two clerks	275	75
three clerks	325	50
four clerks	350	25
five clerks	350	0

The owner of store *A* would like to have four clerks at $25 each but he can get them only by attracting them from store *B* (which has not yet discovered the new technique). The owner of store *A* would be willing to pay up to $100 for the first clerk, $75 for the second clerk, and $50 for the third clerk. Two clerks are already at store *A*, where they are now worth more than before, and a third can be enticed away from store *B* by a higher wage than he is currently earning. We would thus predict that store *A* will have three clerks at a maximum wage of $50 each and that store *B* will have one clerk at a maximum wage of $50.

Suppose that the four clerks agree among themselves to offer their services to store *A* only as a package. If there were only three clerks and they acted in concert, the owner of store *A* would be faced with a choice of working alone with a net revenue of $100 or of employing three clerks with a net revenue of $325. The owner of store *A* will be financially better off hiring the three-clerk package so long as total wages do not exceed $225. If the three clerks divide the wages equally, they can seek a maximum wage of $75 each. But three clerks acting in concert will have problems with the fourth clerk. Unless he is bribed, or otherwise prevented from bidding, he will undercut the cooperating clerks by offering the owner of store *A* the option of using one clerk and obtaining a new revenue of $200. If this clerk is hired, the three-clerk package will increase net revenue from $200 to $350, yielding each of the three clerks a maximum wage of only $50.

One possibility is that each of the three cooperating clerks will pay the fourth clerk $6.25 to stay at store *B* (with a wage of, say, $50). All four clerks would then earn $68.75. This is a higher wage than any of the clerks could earn absent cooperation. It may be difficult, however, to devise a convenient mechanism for making the weekly payments that persuade the fourth clerk not to bid. One way of making the payment is to present the owner of store *A* with the alternative of taking four clerks at $62.50 each or of getting no clerks at all. If this strategy is successful,[17] it leaves store *B* without a clerk. Cooperation among the clerks will

[17] The $62.50 wage is the maximum the clerks could hope for from store *A*. The owner will try to buy their services for less. Note that there is a $25 deadweight social loss in this example.

be successful only if there are no other clerks available to the owner of store *A* at less than \$68.75 — unavailable either because they do not exist[18] or because by force or persuasion the four clerks prevent them from bidding.[19] Unionization provides a mechanism for effectuating cooperation among the clerks. Cooperation among workers does not guarantee that workers can extract wages equal to their maximum value to the firm, however. The owners of stores *A* and *B* may be aware that the next job opportunities for the cooperating clerks pay less than the wages that are being demanded from the stores. Cooperation has only increased the bargaining range.

The example has assumed a very limited supply of clerks. I now change that assumption and consider a firm that is presented with a supply of applicants at the "going rate" that, given the size of the firm, easily satisfies normal hiring requirements. Assume that a manufacturer of widgets installs his machines and after running tests generates the following data:[20]

Number of workers per hour	*Total product output (widgets) per worker*	*Average hourly output per worker per hour*	*Marginal product*
0	0	0	—
1	5	5.0	5
2	12	6.0	7
3	20	6.7	8
4	28	7.0	8
5	34	6.8	6
6	39	6.5	5
7	42	6.0	3
8	44	5.5	2
9	45	5.0	1
10	45	4.5	0
11	44	4.0	−1
12	42	3.5	−2

[18] Over the short run only four clerks may have the skills necessary to do the job; or perhaps others who possess needed skills refuse for personal reasons to move to this town even for a wage increase. Still, this is a strong assumption.

[19] Assume that store *B* copies the new technique for handling widgets and customers so that its productivity schedule now matches that of store *A*. Absent cooperation among the clerks, the owner of store *B* will have one clerk at a maximum wage of \$50 before the owner introduces the new technique. After the owner introduces the technique, the first clerk will be worth a maximum of \$100 to him and a second clerk will be worth \$75. The owner of store *B* will employ two workers by paying a maximum of \$75 to each. By cooperating with each other the four clerks could say to each store, "Take two clerks at \$87.50 (\$175/2) or get none." The maximum wage is now \$87.50.

[20] The figures are taken from A. Rees, The Economics of Work and Pay 58 (2d ed. 1979). The example assumes increasing marginal revenue product.

If the firm employs six workers, it produces 39 widgets and the average number of widgets produced per worker is 6.5. A move from six to seven employees produces more widgets (42) but the average per employee drops (to 6.0). The marginal product figure of 3 describes the change in product output accomplished by the move from six to seven employees. How many employees will the firm hire? It depends on the employees' wage rate and on the net revenue each widget brings to the firm. If the wage rate were zero, the firm would use nine or ten workers. More than ten results in a reduction of total output, suggesting that workers are getting in one another's way, making production more difficult. Assume that each widget produced yields $1 net revenue to the firm. If the wage rate is $5.50 per hour, the firm will employ five workers. Hiring a sixth would cost the firm $5.50 in wages but would bring the firm only $5 in increased revenue. Similarly, at a $3 per hour wage rate the firm will hire six or seven but not an eighth. When the firm is faced with a wage rate increase, other things remaining the same, it will seek to reduce its level of employment.

Assume that the going rate for workers is $3 per hour. An applicant who demands $8 per hour will be turned down in favor of a $3 applicant. Similarly, a current employee who refuses to continue to work unless his or her wage is increased from $3 to $8 will be discharged to make room for a $3 applicant. Workers currently employed by this firm can gain a wage increase by acting in concert only if they can bar competition from applicants. If there are not enough applicants over the short run to replace the employees who are acting in concert, the employees can bar the applicants' entry by agreeing to continue to work for the firm only on the condition that the firm employ no worker at a wage less than that demanded by the employees.

Unions take this approach when they strike to establish a wage rate. Replacements may be found for some of the strikers, but the firm may not be able to hire enough replacements to operate. The union may also be able to persuade potential replacements that it would be immoral to take the job of a striking employee. The union may also bar replacements by coercing the firm through consumer boycotts and the like. The struck firm is not required to capitulate to the union's demands. Strikers suffer wage losses during the work stoppage and the firm may hope to outwait the employees. The standoff may become a game of "chicken."

There are several reasons why the tradeoff between wage rates and employment levels may not be widely perceived. First, an apparent wage increase imposed by union action may not be a real increase at all; it may only reflect monetary inflation and may possibly be matched by a rise in the selling price of widgets. Second, in some situations had the union not pushed up wages, the firm would have increased employment (because of increased consumer demand for the product, for example). In such a case the new wage rate might reduce or offset entirely an employment level increase and thus not be as noticeable as would a reduction in the number of employees currently employed.

Third, over the short run the firm may be unable to reduce its number of employees because a minimum number is required to operate equipment currently on hand. Finally, the effect of a wage increase on employment, while direct, may be disguised. A firm increases the price of its product because its wages have gone up; it discovers later that sales have fallen off. The decline in sales causes the firm to reduce output and to lay off employees (e.g., the third shift). The firm and the union may attribute the sales downturn to a fall in consumer demand, not appreciating that it is the direct result of the wage increase. This explanation (fallen demand) may be especially plausible when a union forces a wage increase upon all firms producing a particular product (an "industry-wide" wage increase).

Another consequence of an increase in the wage bill caused by cooperative employee (union) activity is that managers have an incentive to substitute machinery for employees. Most firms are able to vary the amount of machinery used in production, although over the short run it is likely that some level of capital is frozen in existing plants and equipment and that only labor inputs are variable.[21] Suppose, for example, a firm finds that to produce a given quantity of product it has the choice of the following combinations of machine hours and employee hours:

1. Machine hours renting at $50,000 per week plus five employees hours at $3 per hour;
2. Machine hours renting at $800 per week plus 60 employee hours at $3 per hour;
3. Machine hours renting at $60 per week plus 7,000 employee hours at $3 per hour.

In this extreme example it is clear that the firm would choose the second option. The point is that at each level of output one combination of machine hours and employee hours is cheapest.

If the costs of renting machines remain constant when a union imposes a wage bill increase on the firm, managers will seek to substitute machine hours for employee hours. The same tendency to substitute machine hours for employee hours occurs without a wage bill increase if currently available machines become cheaper, machines are improved so as to produce more output per dollar invested, or a new machine becomes available that produces output cheaper than employees can at their wage rate. Employees have a direct stake in the potential substitution of machinery for workers.

[21] See A. Cartter & F. Marshall, Labor Economics: Wages, Employment, and Trade Unionism 274-275 (1967).

Some unions seek to reduce or eliminate competition between employees and any factor of production (machinery, prefabricated parts, etc.) that will substitute for employees the union represents. There are many examples of union resistance to innovations such as the automatic packager for the assembly line, the spray gun for paint, and the factory-prefabricated boiler (reducing the number of construction site pipefitters). Employees of a subcontractor present a problem for a union similar to that of machines, for those employees may be nearly a perfect substitute for the firm's employees, and at less cost. Even other groups of the firm's own employees may be competing factors of production.

The "Victims" of Union Monopolization

The discussion has focused on the tradeoff between wages and employment levels and on the substitutability of labor and capital in a single firm. I now extend the price theory model to examine the effects of unionization when numerous firms compete to satisfy consumer demand for a good or service.

We have assumed that one firm among many competing for employee services can find as many workers as it needs at the going wage. But for an industry as a whole this assumption often is unrealistic because of size, especially if workers with special skills are required. As wages go up, more workers will find employment in the industry attractive; as wages fall relative to jobs in other industries, workers will leave the industry. When a union forces up wages more workers will wish to work in the industry; but as we have seen, a rise in wages will cause firms to reduce employment. Workers who would have been happy to accept jobs in the industry at the preunion wage will find fewer jobs available. Thus union wage gains come at the expense of workers who otherwise would be hired. Because it is rare that machines substitute perfectly for employees by producing the same marginal product as employees at the same (preunion) hourly cost, union wage gains also result in lower output and higher prices to consumers, especially if the wage gain is industrywide.

The amount by which a wage increase reduces industry employment depends on the slope of the demand curve for labor and on the price elasticity of the industry's product or service. If the industry's required number of employees varies over a small range regardless of output (e.g., it requires 50 employees to operate a plant, and only 52 to run one at full capacity), then a wage increase will have little effect on employment. The amount by which the industry will reduce output when the cost of production increases also depends on the responsiveness of consumers to a price increase. If consumers are very responsive to a price increase it means that many potential purchasers will reduce or eliminate purchases if the price goes up. A limiting case is when everyone who is inclined at all to buy will do so at x price, but at a price of $x + 1$ no one will buy (as when there is a very close alternative product or service). Another limiting case is when those consumers who want the product at all will buy it at almost any price (a life-saving medicine). The more price-responsive consumers are, the more a wage (or other cost increase) will tend to reduce industry output and employment.

Now consider an industry where a union has organized half of the competing firms. In the absence of the union, a going wage would be established by the interplay of the industry's need for labor and the workers' willingness to accept jobs at particular wages. Let us assume that no firm is large enough to affect this wage rate on its own and that any wage differences between firms reflect only locational dissimilarities (e.g., lower housing prices in a given area). A wage increase imposed by a union on the unionized half of the industry will reduce employment there, for reasons already discussed. Potential employees now unable to find employment in the unionized segment of the industry (and probably others laid off from that segment) will compete for jobs elsewhere, and many of them can be expected to apply for positions in the unorganized segment of the industry. This increased supply of labor tends to drive down wages in the unorganized sector. When this happens, union wage gains can be said to be at the expense of nonunion employees. Moreover, assuming that before unionization both sectors of the industry were operating at the least costly combination of employees and other factors of production, thereby producing output at the lowest cost, neither the organized nor the unorganized sector will operate at that least costly combination after the union imposes its wage rate on half the industry. The industry's total output is reduced and prices to the consumer increase.

Unions have incentives to organize along product lines, on an "industrywide" basis. Over both the long and the short run, the threat to unionized firms from the industry's nonunion firms can be substantial. Assuming that purchasers are unwilling to pay more for a product or service because it is produced by union labor, a union-imposed wage bill driving up production costs yields the unionized firm fewer profits than it would have earned absent the union's intervention. This may reduce the firm's return on invested capital below what it could earn in other industries or in other investments.

In the short run, the firm's assets (location, equipment, expertise) may not be easily transferred and the firm has an incentive to resist unionization and, once unionized, to return to a nonunion status. At the same time that investment capital is moving out of unionized firms, profits in the nonunion sector of the industry are enhanced by a rise in the price of the product and by a decrease in the cost of labor. Because this gives the nonunion sector a greater than average return to investment capital, it will tempt more capital into the industry, driving down the price of the product and making the position of the unionized sector even more untenable. Therefore, a union's interest in organizing an entire industry goes beyond its interest, if any, in increasing its membership.

The union's interest in preventing new nonunion firms from entering a unionized industry is equally acute, and for the same reasons. A non-union entrant with lower labor costs made possible by a nonunion wage rate can price its product below the price established by its unionized competitors and, unless its size makes it relatively insignificant, threaten union gains in unionized firms.

The model is not shown to be defective, its proponents argue, by the presence of union and nonunion firms apparently competing in the same product or service line. Competition between firms may be limited geographically by specialized resources so that competition in the product market is regional or local. Nonunion firms may incur significant costs in preventing unionization of their employees. For example, a nonunion firm may maintain the same wage and benefit scale as its unionized competitors to forestall unionization. Finally, firms in apparent competition may be producing goods or services of unequal quality and purchasers may differentiate. A building constructed by union labor may have a higher quality of workmanship than one constructed by nonunion labor.

Unionized workers are threatened by competition from nonunion firms that have any cost advantages over unionized firms. More enlightened management techniques, inventiveness, and specialized location are examples of efficiencies by which a nonunion firm may endanger a unionized firm and its employees. Whenever unionized firms are threatened, the union predictably will try to organize the nonunion firm, to pressure the nonunion firm to match the union's wage package with the union firms, or to force the nonunion firms out of business. The first alternative protects the union's wage bill and increases its membership. The second ensures that any competitive advantage that the nonunion firm has does not come from a lower wage rate, but it does not protect the unionized firm from other competitive disadvantages. The third alternative completely protects the unionized firms and it also permits the union to concentrate on fewer firms when negotiating and administering bargaining agreements. The unionized firms themselves are benefitted by each of these union responses. Union tools for these purposes include organizing drives, picketing, and employee and consumer boycotts.

Imperfect Labor Markets and Bilateral Monopolies

In a perfectly competitive labor market an individual firm has no power over the wages it pays its employees. If the firm offers less than the going rate, it gets no applicants and current employees quit for higher paying positions with other firms. Because a firm has as many applicants as it needs at the going rate, it is not advantaged by offering a higher wage.

For there to be a perfectly competitive labor market, several conditions must be met.[22] Workers must have knowledge of job opportunities, including vacancies, wages, and other terms of employment (such as the attitudes of frontline supervisors) at other firms in the relevant market; and workers must be rational in the sense of responding to differences in wage and nonwage conditions. Workers must be mobile. Workers cannot act in concert. Firms must attempt to maximize profits, and each firm must represent a sufficiently small share of the market so that its wage and employment levels will not affect the market as a whole. Finally, firms must act individually, not by common agreement, in setting wages and employment levels.

Many labor markets fail to satisfy these conditions in one or more respects. Workers are often ignorant of precise wage rates and working conditions available elsewhere; indeed, workers are sometimes unaware of wage rates within their own firm.[23] Workers may not be willing to risk the uncertainties of a change in employers to capture a small wage or other gain. For a variety of personal reasons, workers may be reluctant to relocate geographically to change employers.[24] Some firms have tacit agreements not to "raid" other firms' employees. Typical practices in many firms impose costs on employees who would change jobs; they include hiring only at bottom-level jobs, discriminating against mobile workers (e.g., refusals to hire the "man without a family"), and maintaining employment benefits (pensions, vacations, job and shift bidding) based on length of service with the employer.

A firm operating in an imperfect labor market has a degree of monopsony power. The typically discussed example of monopsony power is a firm of great size in a small locality. Unlike a firm facing a perfectly competitive labor market, which attracts no applicants at less than the going wage rate, a firm with monopsony power finds that its supply of applicants varies with the wage rate it offers. Recall that a firm in a competitive labor market will continue to add workers until the marginal product of the next worker to be hired is less than his or her

[22] Ibid. at 201.

[23] Professors are commonly ignorant of their colleagues' salaries and this information is often inaccessible. One study found that, like professors, plantation workers in Louisiana were unaware of one another's wages. See Piore, Wage Determination in Low-Wage Labor Markets and the Role of Minimum Wage Legislation, in Unemployment and Inflation 197, 204 (M. Piore, ed., 1979).

[24] On the length of time that American workers ordinarily spend in a single job, see Hall, The Importance of Lifetime Jobs in the U.S. Economy, 72 Am. Econ. Rev. 716 (1982) ("The typical worker today is holding a job which has lasted or will last about eight years. Over a quarter of all workers are holding jobs that will last twenty years or more. Sixty percent hold jobs which will last five years or more.")

wage. The fact that a firm has monopsony power does not change the marginal contribution to the firm's revenue of each additional employee, but the computation of when to stop hiring is more complex.

Assume that to attract the first 100 workers a firm must pay $3 per hour. To attract another 50 workers the firm must pay $4 per hour. If it were no more complex than that, the firm would pay each new group of workers a higher wage until the wage rate required to attract an additional worker was greater than the worker's contribution to revenue. However, it may be impractical for the firm because of administrative costs or potential employee dissatisfaction to maintain more than one wage rate for employees who are, by hypothesis, identical in every respect but their willingness to work at a particular wage. In the likely event that the firm decides to pay these identical employees the same wage, each employee group hired at a higher wage pulls up the wages of existing employees.

At some point the firm is faced with a situation where it could hire the next group of employees at a wage equal to or below the value of their marginal revenue product, but it will not do so because of the effect of the hiring on other employees' wages. Thus in our example, assume the marginal revenue product of the group of 50 applicants is $4 per hour per worker. The "cost" of hiring these workers is $6 per hour because existing workers at $3 per hour must also be raised to $4. The firm will continue to employ 100 workers at $3 per hour.

A union (or a government-mandated wage such as that required by the minimum wage law) that forces a firm with monopsony power to raise wages can increase both wages and employment. For example, if a union in the example were to force a wage rate on the firm of $4 for all present and future employees, that "cost" of hiring the additional 50 employees would be only their actual wage of $4 per hour and the firm would profitably hire them.[25]

Some argue that most labor markets are marked by imperfections that create monopsony power.[26] In many labor markets some employers attract employees at less than a competitively determined going rate. But it is not necessary that all workers in a labor market be mobile and aware of alternative job openings, wage rates, and working conditions for the market to be competitive. So long as a sufficient number of workers respond knowledgeably to differing terms and conditions of employment, firms will have to observe competitive conditions, and ignorant and immobile workers will share the benefits.[27] Whether most

[25] When a union raises wages to competitive levels in a firm that has monopsony power in the labor market, the price of the firm's product will not rise if the firm has been operating in a competitive product market, unless all firms in that product market had monopsony power, which the union has corrected.

[26] Cartter & Marshall, supra n.[21]; C. Mulvey, The Economic Analysis of Trade Unions 52 (1978).

[27] See Schwartz & Wilde, Intervening in Markets on the Basis of Imperfect Information, 127 U. Pa. L. Rev. 630 (1979).

markets are reasonably competitive is both an empirical question and a value judgment as to what is reasonable.

When a firm having monopsony power in the labor market is unionized, a bilateral monopoly is created. The firm's monopsony power tends to keep down the wage rate and employment levels, while the union's monopoly power over the labor supply tends to drive wages and, in this instance, employment levels up. The outcome is indeterminate. The resulting wage rates and employment levels may be closer to those of a competitive labor market than if the firm were not unionized. However, the union could easily under- or over-correct the firm's monopsony power. The union's goal is not to duplicate the result of a competitive labor market.

Criticisms of the Price Theory Model

In the price theory model, wages and employment levels in a firm are determined by marginal revenue products and competitive wage rates. There are two ways that the firm might discover this wage rate and set its employment level.[28] Wages might be set and employees selected by periodic purchases on a spot market. A current employee would have his wage determined by market rates, which would be subject to upward and downward fluctuation as industry supply and demand for labor changed. New employees would be hired on the open market at market rates. Current employees could bid on jobs at the firm that commanded higher wages (promotions), but they would have no advantage over applicants from outside the firm unless they had knowledge or skills specific to this firm that would be useful in the new position. In that case the firm would be willing to pay somewhat more for their services because of reduced training costs. If an employee learned skills or acquired knowledge in a current job that would entail costly training were he or she replaced with a market applicant, the employee could seek a wage premium equal to the costs of training the replacement — although such a request would not necessarily be successful because, as skills specific to the firm, the employee's assets would be of no use to any other firm.[29]

Second, the firm could set wages and other employment conditions through long-term contingency contracts. It is important to the firm's production that employees be induced to acquire skills specific to the firm; but once those skills are acquired, the employee can demand a premium wage. A bilateral monopoly is thus created that results in costly negotiations. The firm would prefer to have applicants compete for

[28] Much of the discussion criticizing the price theory model is suggested by P. Doeringer & M. Piore, Internal Labor Markets and Manpower Analysis (1971), and Ross, Orbits of Coercive Comparison, reprinted in M. Piore, ed., Unemployment and Inflation 94 (1979).

[29] See G. Becker, Investment in Human Capital: A Theoretical Analysis, 70 J. Pol. Econ. 10-25 (Supp. 1962).

long-term employment contracts that would guarantee the applicant that efforts to acquire new skills would be paid for, but in which the applicant would contract to work at a nonpremium wage once the skills were acquired.

The applicant and the firm might, in principle, contract for a period of years (perhaps until the worker's retirement age), the contract providing for the vast array of future events that could affect the employment relationship and setting a schedule of long-term wages tied to market rates. The contract would be complex because the employee would be committing for a long period of time and the conditions of his or her commitment (e.g., specification of required tasks and the orders he or she would be required to take) would have to be specified. Nonetheless, a competitive labor market would set the terms of the contract.

In a spot market method for determining wages, the going rate is observed by all employers and equally qualified workers. Wage rates are equalized in local labor markets and, if corrected for differences in living environments, would be equalized across labor markets as well. If consumer demand for goods and services expands, wages rise; if consumer demand contracts, the spot market reacts to the contraction over time, wages fall and full employment continues. If wages in a local labor market are perceived not to be equalized, several explanations are consistent with the model. The wage differences may reflect differences in job content and skills required. There may be differences in the makeup of the wage package across various employers, some having higher weekly wages, other contributing more heavily to worker pensions or offering a more luxurious working environment. Finally, some markets may be subject to short-term imperfections that cause some workers to be paid more or less than the competitively determined rate.

Critics find this model incomplete in several respects. Wage differentials in local markets are often found and are not adequately explained. If nonequalization of local wage rates is routinely to be explained by differences in skill and job content, then the price theory model does not yield a testable result. The same criticism applies to the assumption that nonequalization signals market imperfections. Lester Thurow points out, "An observer of the economic game should be extremely reluctant to label anything that has existed for long periods of time a 'market imperfection.' If the phenomenon has survived, the chances are high that it is an integral part of the game and not a market imperfection."[30] The contention that wage differences can be explained by differences in the makeup of wage packages seems not to be true. Many firms that offer high wages also pay high fringe benefits.[31] The most important

[30] L. Thurow, Generating Equality 55 (1975).

[31] Many union policies that persist seem inconsistent with the price theory model. Why, if unions and managers are rational maximizers, are there strikes over wage offers that differ from a union's wage demand by only a few cents — far less than the predicted cost of the strike to either the union or the firm? Why do unions seek to equalize wages

criticism of the price theory model is its inability to explain wage rigidity in times of unemployment. Wage reductions caused by increases in the supply of workers during periods of declining demand should solve unemployment. All agree that this does not happen and that the labor market regularly experiences downward wage rigidity. Unions cannot be responsible for downward wage rigidity for too small a percentage of the workforce is unionized, and nonunion sectors also experience unemployment and rigidity.

Finally, the existence of unions may be difficult for the price theory model to explain. Given the prediction that a competitive product market will over the long run drive out firms with high input costs, an economy in which over 20 percent of the firms are unionized and in which unions drive wages above competitive levels will be stable only if unions systematically organize entire product markets and raise barriers to entry, if absent unionization unionized firms would be able to earn supracompetitive profits in labor markets marked by substantial imperfections, if unions have no actual as opposed to apparent effects, or if all nonunion firms match union gains in order to prevent unionization.[32]

The Relational Contract Model

The key premise of the relational contract model[33] of labor markets is that many job skills are learned on the job and are specific to the firm. Employees work in teams and tasks are complex.[34] Skills acquisition is

---

across an industry ("take the wages out of competition")? A rational monopolist would seek to drive each firm's wages to the limit of the firm's ability to pay. Why do unions and employers engage in multiemployer bargaining? Since multiemployer bargaining is by law voluntary on both sides, the employer should refuse if it enhances the power of the union and the union should refuse if it diminishes its power. See the discussion at 568, infra.

[32] See Freeman & Medoff, The Impact of Collective Bargaining: Illusion or Reality? in U.S. Industrial Relations 1950–1980: A Critical Assessment 47 (1982).

[33] An efficiency analysis of internal labor markets, upon which the relational contract model is based, is found in Williamson, Wachter, & Harris, Understanding the Employment Relationship: The Analysis of Idiosyncratic Exchange, 6 Bell J. Econ. 250 (1975); and Williamson, Efficient Labor Organization, Center for the Study of Organizational Innovation (Univ. of Pa. Discussion Paper 123, Feb. 1982). Because the text attempts to synthesize the views of these authors, it may not precisely correspond to their individual views.

[34] Williamson, Wachter & Harris, supra n.[33], list a variety of sources of firm-specific tasks:

> [T]ask idiosyncrasies can arise in at least four ways: (1) equipment idiosyncrasies, due to incompletely standardized, albeit common equipment, the unique characteristics of which become known through experience; (2) process idiosyncrasies, which are fashioned or "adopted" by the worker and his associates in specific operating contexts; (3) informal team accommodations, attributable to mutual adaptation among parties engaged in recurrent contact but which are upset, to the possible detriment of group performance, when the membership is altered; (4) communication idiosyncrasies with respect to information channels and codes that are of value only within the firm.

an ongoing process as the workforce adapts to exogenous changes — in product demand, new technology, and the like. Where tasks are complex, learning by doing is efficient.

The spot market contracting of the price theory model is inadequate when specific skills predominate at a firm. An employee has a powerful incentive not to train newcomers because once a newcomer has acquired specific skills he or she may underbid the current employee in case of a layoff or a promotional opportunity. Forcing a current employee to cooperate in imparting specific skills requires managers to monitor cooperativeness, which is excessively expensive when production is a team effort among employees and lack of cooperation may be subtle.[35]

The goals of a firm's employment system in such a model are to reduce bargaining costs, to rationalize the internal wage structure in terms of objective task considerations, to encourage complete employee cooperation (willingness to train), and to encourage the acquisition of specific skills while minimizing the risks of exploitation.[36] Both the firm and its employees need a mechanism for guaranteeing that employees will cooperate in acquiring firm-specific skills and training other employees, while ensuring that neither the firm nor the employees will be the victim of the other's opportunism. One ideal mechanism would be a contract between an employee and the firm establishing in advance long-term wages and conditions, thereby avoiding later bilateral monopoly bargaining with employees holding those skills. The contract would have to be very complex because it would need to provide for a host of contingencies, such as the nature of managerial orders the employees would be bound to obey, the conditions of discharge and layoff, and standards of promotions and demotions, all under conditions of considerable uncertainty.

Such a complete, contingent contract exists only in theory because the firm and the worker would have to anticipate, bargain out, and reduce to writing a vast array of potential future events and conditions to solve ex ante the bilateral monopoly problem caused by firm-specific skills. The inability to foresee all the contingencies and the costs of bargaining them out in advance and reducing them to writing prevents the actual execution of such individual labor contracts. Even were it possible to anticipate and provide for all future employer and employee claims, the contract would be too complex for an individual employee to understand.

When a formal, complete, contingent contract is impossible, a firm may still obtain efficiency gains by acting in accordance with an implicit relational. In this way, firms avoid strategic behavior by employees by removing wage competition from the job. Wage rates attach to particular

[35] See Alchian & Demsetz, Production, Information Costs, and Economic Organization, 62 Am. Econ. Rev. 777 (1972).

[36] Williamson et al, supra n.[34] at 270.

jobs, and jobs, not workers, carry marginal products. Hiring occurs only at the entry level, and applicants for entry-level positions compete according to their predicted training costs, measured by the background characteristics deemed relevant by the firm. Seniority ladders control promotion, with the limitation that an employee may be punished if the firm discovers poor work habits. Wage differentials are fixed in order to facilitate willingness to give and receive on-the-job training. At least in the short run, the firm will not change wages in response to changes in the supply and demand for labor (thus explaining downward wage rigidity). In times of reduced employment, laid-off employees are not permitted to bid back against current employees at a lower wage. When demand for labor is high or supply low, the employer deescalates the required hiring characteristics; when demand is low or supply high, he or she escalates them.

The relational contract model maintains that workers care about relative wages and working conditions — traditional relationships between and across job classifications. Real world observations underscore the importance of relative wages.[37] The model need not explain why workers value the continuance of relative differentials, although some plausible explanations come to mind. Perhaps workers consider adherence to relative wages "fair" or "just." Bounded rationality may provide a more precise explanation.

How does an employee determine whether he or she is being treated fairly? Surveying the labor market to determine the going rate by analyzing wage and benefit packages, assessing the impact of managerial practices on the plant lifestyles, and making the appropriate discounts for, say, locational differences is impractical. So is computing one's marginal revenue product. Moreover, the employee's marginal productivity as the market sees it is less than the employee's marginal productivity to this firm, because of firm-specific skills. How does an employee compute this firm-specific marginal productivity? The best measure of whether one is being paid fairly may be relative wages within the firm (which is easier to ascertain than is internal marginal productivity) developed over a period of time, and the employer's continued adherence to traditional work rules. In any event, employees are concerned with relative wages and will enforce this concern with a lack of cooperativeness if they become too unhappy.

Managers have incentives to adhere to relative wages and traditional work rules. If wages are too low, employee morale and productivity may be affected; if wages are too high, the firm is competitively disadvantaged in the product market. In either event, a manager's job may be at

[37] There is considerable impressionistic evidence that workers are concerned with relative wages. See Seidman, Bargaining Structure: Some Problems of Complexity and Dislocation, 4 Lab. L.J. 340, 342 (1973).

risk if he or she misses the optimal wage by much. The manager, like the employee, is subject to bounded rationality. The costs of measuring internal productivities are high. Employees are responsive to traditional differentials and a risk-averse manager will respect those differentials. Perhaps a wage rate that turns out to be higher than the firm would have to have paid will not redound so severely to the manager's detriment if it was dictated by historical differentials.

The effects of unionization in a relational contract model are uncertain.[38] A union could serve as a mechanism for formalizing the implicit relational contract. The union would spread the costs of this formalization and enforcement across all of its members. The union could serve as a collector of information about future contingencies and could act as a continuing monitor of managerial good faith and adherence to worker expectations. Thus the union would reduce the problem of employee-bounded rationality through the negotiation and enforcement of collective bargaining agreements, and workers could be assured that traditional wage differentials and customary work rules were maintained or, to the extent that changes in customary differentials and rules would increase the profitability of the firm, that proposed changes by managers were rational from the point of view of the workers. Unions could assist managers in monitoring worker cooperativeness through informal worker social channels. On the other hand, unions can raise barriers to altering customary rules even when the rules interfere substantially with production efficiency.

Because of competitive forces in both the labor and product markets, as well as the lack of firm-specific skills in some industries, some labor markets will more closely resemble the price theory model than the relational contract model. Market forces often dictate wages for entry-level jobs. Moreover, in some industries, especially those marked by low-skilled jobs, a loose attachment to the labor market by workers, and labor intensive firms, wage competition and the lack of customary work rules may predominate.[39] Turnover may be so rapid that social norms do not form. Union sanctions against these firms may be impracticable because jobs do not require on-the-job training, substitute workers are readily available with little or no training costs, and employees in low-skill jobs are easily monitored.

The price theory and relational contract models lie on a spectrum. There are firms at each end of the spectrum, but the majority of firms fall between the two extremes. The goods that unions produce lie along

[38] See P. Doeringer & M. Piore, supra n.[28], at 35-36.

[39] The construction crafts may be an example of a labor market well described by the price theory model. Construction jobs are of relatively short duration. Skills are carried from job to job, and workers do not necessarily continue with the same firm. Thus very few skills are specific to the firm. Frequent wage bidding in times of labor demand fluctuations and union wage monopolizers mark this industry.

a similar spectrum. Where skills are not firm-specific and a firm acts in accordance with the price theory model, a union may be principally concerned with raising wages through monopoly power. Where firm-specific skills predominate, a union may focus on rationalizing an implicit relational contract. Yet one should not assume that either of these descriptions is always accurate. When a firm finds itself in a market that fits the price theory model, a union may attempt to force the managers to adhere to worker desires for relative wages and working conditions. So too, in a market that fits the relational contract model, a union could content itself with raising the levels of relative wages. What a union does may change over time. I suspect that many employees unionize because they feel they are being unfairly treated in matters such as promotions or discipline. Once these problems are corrected, the union looks to wage bargaining to maintain its existence.

The Collective Goods Model

The collective goods model is not a model of labor markets, as are the price theory and relational contract models, but is an elaboration of the role of unions within labor markets. The precise relationship between the collective goods model and the labor market models will be explored as the collective goods model is developed. I introduce the model by first discussing the concept of "collective voice."

In the price theory model of labor markets, in the absence of union constraints a firm determines its wage package (hourly rates, pension contributions, vacations, holidays, etc.) and other employment conditions affecting employees by reacting to the exit and entry of workers. If the firm pays too little, retains oppressive foremen, or offers the "wrong" mix of hourly wages, pension contributions, and the like, employee quit rates (exits) and employment applications (entries) inform the managers of their error.[40]

It is probable, however, that the bulk of a firm's employees will not quit even though they prefer a different mix of, say, hourly wages and pension contributions. Length of service with the firm may have given these employees specific skills not valuable to another firm. Other firms may be willing to hire new employees only in entry-level jobs. Given the many variables that have an impact on an employee in a particular firm, searching for a new employer that offers a preferred mix and that has no other disadvantages may be very costly. But not all the employees will feel constrained to stay with the firm; some will exit in order to find the preferred mix of wages and pension contributions. The exit of these "marginal" employees signals to the firm that something is amiss in the

[40] The exit/voice terminology is developed in A. Hirschman's classic book, Exit, Voice and Loyality (1970).

employment package. Applicants for employment are also marginal employees in this sense, because the inability to attract sufficient applicants to cover normal attrition is a similar signal.

The characteristics of marginal workers may differ significantly from the characteristics of inframarginal employees.[41] Inframarginal employees are those less likely to exit because the costs to them are greater. Marginal employees are usually younger than inframarginal employees, have fewer relocation costs, and are less likely to have skills specific to the firm. To the extent that firms are not constrained to follow customary work rules and observe relative wages, they will tend to tailor their employment packages with the marginal worker in mind because an unhappy inframarginal worker is less likely to signal dissatisfaction by exiting. However, when an unhappy inframarginal employee does exit, the firm can incur a great expense. Training a replacement worker is generally necessary, and these replacement costs are directly proportional to the firm-specific knowledge or skills of the exiting employee. Especially if firm-specific skills are prevalent in the labor market, as the relational contract model suggests, firms should consider exits by inframarginal employees to be a serious matter.

The alternative to exit as a device for signaling dissatisfactions (preferences) is voice. To exercise voice is to complain. An employee can tell the firm's personnel manager that he or she dislikes the current mix of wages and pension contributions. He or she can complain that the lighting over the assembly line is inadequate (workers go home with headaches), or that the food in the firm cafeteria is too salty. Voice is likely to be underused at the workplace. In many instances the improvement desired by a single complaining employee will benefit other workers. These kinds of benefits are "collective goods"; if they are provided to any one person in a group, the benefits cannot feasibly be withheld from others in the group.[42] The discharge of a repressive foreman at the complaint of one worker benefits every other worker victimized by the foreman.

There are several reasons why a good produced by a union may be a collective good. In some instances it may be physically impossible to prevent any worker in the group from consuming the good. Improved factory lighting and air purification systems are examples. Some goods may be nonexcludable for psychological reasons; for instance, if employees would become embittered and uncooperative if they are treated

[41] See Freeman, Individual Mobility and Collective Voice in the Labor Market, 66 Am. Econ. Rev. 361 (1976); and Freeman & Medoff, The Two Faces of Unionism, 57 Pub. Interest 69 (1979).

[42] There are more restrictive definitions of a collective good, but I do not deal with them here. See, e.g., Poulson, Is Collective Bargaining a Collective Good?, 4 J. Lab. Research 349 (1983). For example, if literal nonexcludability is required, it is hard to imagine a good that qualifies.

differently from other employees and do not agree with the rationale for the different treatment, the firm may provide them a good even though it could be physically withheld. A firm may also extend a good to all employees in a group because it is too costly to administer a scheme of different treatment. For example, a union might negotiate a disciplinary procedure covering only its members that requires record-keeping procedures by the managers; the managers might extend the procedure to all employees because it is too costly to keep track of which employees are covered and which are not.

Nonexcludability might be imposed by law, as when a statute forbids a firm from treating unionized employees differently from nonunion employees. Nonexcludability can also be forced on a firm by a union as a part of the union's demands, presumably because of notions of solidarity or fear that excluded workers will undercut the cartel. Finally, there are economies of scale in the production of some goods so that while they are excludable goods, their extension to all employees in the group carries very little cost.

A cost/benefit analysis suggests when a utility-maximizing worker will exercise voice to obtain a collective good.[43] The worker will calculate his or her perceived value of the good times the difference between the probability that effort will secure the good and the likelihood that some other employee will successfully obtain the collective good for the group. This discounted value of the good will be compared to the costs to the worker of exercising voice. Only an altruistic worker will exercise voice if the costs exceed the benefits.

Thus the benefits of a collective good are enjoyed by the entire group, while the costs (absent collectivization) are borne by a single worker. The total value of the good is the sum of the value to each worker who consumes the good. Although the total value may far exceed the cost, the good may not be produced. It is in this sense that (costly) voice is underused when a collective good is sought.

In the workplace the subjective estimate of the costs of securing collective goods by exercising voice may be considerable. Managers may not like workers who complain and they may feel threatened by the complaints. If the complaint is costly to correct, and especially if it explicitly or implicitly criticizes the manager or threatens his or her discretionary authority,[44] the worker may be considered a troublemaker not worth having. If the repressive foreman is not fired or controlled by other managers, the complaining worker is likely to be very uncomfortable.

In this analysis of collective voice, the first thing that unionization of employees and collective bargaining may do is change the mixture of

[43] The classic statement is M. Olson, The Logic of Collective Action (1971). See also T. Schelling, Micromotives and Macrobehavior 83–133 (1978).

[44] The reaction of managers is more fully discussed below.

wages and other benefits (the employment package) and promote voice over exit as a signaling device. A union is a democratically run collective of workers. As such, its "demands" should tend to reflect the average preferences of the entire work force rather than the preferences of marginal workers. If the average preference is for more health insurance in lieu of a portion of salary, unionization makes increased health coverage more likely even though marginal employees prefer wages.[45] The shift from a marginal calculus to an average calculus is not necessarily efficiency-enhancing or normatively preferable, but it may be both. Professor Richard Freeman presents the following example:

> Consider, for example, a situation in which management can choose one of two modes of organizing work, which, exclusive of their impact on workers, have equal profitability. Method *A* greatly reduces the well-being of immobile senior workers, while method *B* has no effect on them but displeases the mobile young slightly. In a market where information is conveyed by quits, the behavior of the young would lead management to choose method *A*, despite the loss of consumer "surplus" to other personnel. In a market with collective bargaining, the union might arbitrage the difference in preference, so that the firm will pick *B*, with a negotiated redistribution giving the young some compensatory benefit and the old a less onerous loss than under *A*. This scenario can be expanded, to take account of different frequencies of quitting under *A* and *B* with similar results. The greater the difference between the losses under the two modes, the greater is the possibility that a superior bargain could be struck through the voice mechanism. I do not claim that the union will, in fact, arbitrage worker preferences correctly for the behavior of the union will depend on its internal organization, organizational goals, and political power of the various groups which are neglected. The possibility is, however, there.[46]

A union could spread the costs of exercising voice over its entire membership. When an individual employee initiates a complaint, the union can spread the costs by processing the complaint on the employee's behalf, by keeping secret the identity of the complainer, and by securing from the firm guarantees against reprisals.[47] (Why in the absence of a union managers themselves might not voluntarily adopt similar protections for employees exercising voice is explored below.)

[45] The preferences of marginal employees cannot be ignored completely, lest the firm find itself with no applicants. This would be in neither the firm's nor the union's best interest. Even when the employment package reflects the preferences of the average employee, the opportunity to exercise voice can make the firm a good long-term prospect for the marginal employee.

[46] Freeman, supra n.[42], at 366.

[47] Voice may be a consumption good for many employees; that is, participation in industrial decision making may have value apart from the instrumental role of voice. The protections brought by unionization make this use of voice possible.

The role of unions in the collective goods model is not limited, however, to optimizing voice, and I now develop a broader model, the collective goods model, which incorporates the analysis of voice. Unionization can facilitate the production of collective goods when voice is not a determinative factor. For example, a worker in a nonunion firm could in theory negotiate an individual employment contract guaranteeing that the firm will discharge him or her only if there is just cause for doing so and that an arbitrator will decide whether a discharge was in fact for just cause. Provisions such as these are rarely found in individual employment contracts, but they typically appear in union collective bargaining agreements. The collective goods model offers explanations for this apparent discrepancy.

First, it is plausible that the young, mobile marginal employee does not value highly a "just cause" guarantee enforced by grievance arbitration and that a firm responding only to exits will not offer these terms of employment. The inframarginal employee, who is less mobile, may be reluctant to request the terms for fear that the managers will interpret the request as signaling the employee's negative evaluation of his or her past or future job performance. A second, independent explanation is that the value to an individual worker of a just cause provision may be low if it can be enforced only by costly court litigation. The risk of discharge for any particular worker may be small. Moreover, the cost to the firm of maintaining a grievance arbitration system (the alternative to court litigation), which involves educating supervisors and record keeping, for one or a few employees may be so high that no single worker or even a small group could "purchase" grievance arbitration by working for the firm at a reduced wage rate.

The employee collective, the union, could purchase this benefit. It can pool the discharge risks of all the workers and collect payments (in the form of reduced wages or other foregone benefits) from the entire workforce. Managers should agree to a just cause clause and grievance arbitration if the purchase price, the reduction in total wage bill, exceeds the costs of implementing and maintaining this term of employment. Thus unions might successfully bargain for these terms even in the absence of monopoly power pressure, such as strikes or picketing, and in a situation where voice alone will not secure the terms.

In a collective goods model unions exist chiefly to secure collective goods for their members. A collective good can be secured in four ways. First, the union can secure a good by collective voice: telling managers what otherwise managers would not know or would learn only at the cost of expensive quits. The union might secure the discharge of a repressive foreman in this fashion. Second, the union might purchase a collective good by agreeing to trade off another benefit of lesser value (e.g., forgo a wage increase). Third, a union might purchase a collective good by providing a participatory substitute for jobsite uncooperativeness of unhappy employees. Unions might initiate or regularize a relational contract and thereby facilitate on-the-job training. If employees who are participating in jobsite decisions are happier and therefore more productive, the firm should be willing to pay for the increased productivity by providing collective goods. Fourth, and perhaps most typical, a union can secure collective goods by exercising monopoly power (strikes, picketing, boycotts, and the like).

Some collective goods for employees may be societal "bads." A taste for racial discrimination may lead a union to secure racially discriminatory hiring rules from the firm. These rules are collective goods from the standpoint of every member with a taste for discrimination, even though others would condemn the rules on moral and other grounds. Some would argue, applying the teachings of the price theory model, that a union strike for a higher wage is a societal "bad" because the union members' gain will be at the expense of consumers and nonunion workers.

Union-imposed wage gains are a collective good for all union members and they may be a collective good for nonmember employees as well if the firm finds it too costly, because of administrative difficulties or worker dissatisfaction, to deny the increase to nonunion workers. Thus a strike for higher wages is an instance of the production of a particular collective good (a higher wage) through union monopoly power. Further elaboration of the relationship between the collective goods model and the price theory model must await an examination of the reaction of managers to a union's production of collective goods.

Managerial Slack

We now consider the reactions of the managers of firms to union attempts to produce collective goods. In order to explain why market forces might not produce certain collective goods for employees without union intervention, I build on the writings of academics that discuss the theory of the firm to suggest reasons why some managers would oppose union production of collective goods.

Assume that there are workplace collective goods that have value to employees in excess of their production costs, so that the firm could do better by offering the collective goods in lieu of a portion of wages. Assume further that managers are slacking[48] by failing to make the collective goods available. A competitive product market might punish a firm whose managers were failing to reduce costs. Moreover, a competitive labor market for managers would eliminate slack if applicants for managerial positions (including those positions available by promotion) could underbid slackers by contracting not to slack. Recent works on the

[48] The term *slack* is suggested in A. Hirschman, supra n.[41].

theory of the firm, however, have argued that the existence of managerial slack is plausible.[49] Professors Frank Easterbrook and Daniel Fischel summarize this literature:

> Corporate managers (which include both officers and members of the board), like all other people, work harder if they can enjoy all of the benefits of their efforts. In a corporation, however, much of the benefit of each manager's performance inures to someone else, whether it be shareholders, bondholders, or other managers. The investors must be given a substantial share of the gains to induce them to put up their money. Because no single manager receives the full benefit of his work, he may find that, at the margin, developing new ventures and supervising old ones takes too much effort to be worthwhile; each manager may reason that someone else is apt to do the work if he does not or to take the rewards even if he does well. No manager will be completely vigilant. So some managers will find it advantageous to shirk responsibilities, consume corporate perquisites, or otherwise take more than the corporation promised to give them.[50]

The problem of slack is not limited to the corporate form of ownership. It applies whenever ownership and management are separate. To reduce slack, owners must monitor managers, managers must bond their own performance, or some combination of both. Especially where ownership is spread over a large number of individuals, owners will underinvest in monitoring. Locating managerial slack requires careful study of the firm, but the benefits of reducing managerial slack do not go in their entirety to the owner who has invested in locating and reducing the slack. Instead, they accrue to all owners. Often a single owner cannot eliminate the slack (discharge the managers, restructure the production processes) without the participation of other owners. Coordinating this participation is costly, and some owners may be unwilling to pay their share of the costs for familiar free rider reasons.

Monitoring devices are available, but at the point where the marginal costs and marginal benefits of monitoring coincide, additional monitoring devices will either be too difficult to implement or their usefulness too circumscribed. High salaries and pensions may reduce managerial slack by giving added bite to the threat of being fired.[51] These monitoring devices presuppose that monitors can distinguish good managerial performances from bad ones, but monitors will find such a task

[49] See Jensen & Meckling, Theory of the Firm: Managerial Behavior, Agency Costs and Ownership Structure, 3 J. Fin. Econ. 305 (1976). See also Alchian & Demseth, Production, Information Costs, and Economic Organization, 62 Am. Econ. Rev. 777 (1972).

[50] Easterbrook & Fischel, The Proper Role of a Target's Management in Responding to a Tender Offer, 94 Harv. L. Rev. 1161, 1170 (1980) [footnotes omitted].

[51] Increasing a manager's equity in the firm may also induce more attentive management. See Alchian & Demseth, supra n.[49], at 782; Jensen & Meckling, supra n.[49], at 313-316.

difficult because it requires them to disaggregate the collective actions of teams of managers and to assign to each manager his or her marginal contribution. Nor can owners expect managers to monitor one another without shirking. As Easterbrook and Fischel note, "Even the most dedicated manager will find it difficult to fire or discipline an old friend when the benefits of ruthlessness will accrue to distant and unknown shareholders."[52] Hirschman[53] and Leibenstein[54] suggest that substantial product market competition can impose stress on managers and diminish slack, but both imply that a sufficiently competitive product market is the exception rather than the rule.

Managers could earn additional money compensation if they chose to relinquish power by adopting monitoring or bonding devices. If cost-effective monitoring and bonding devices do not exist, managerial power is a form of slack. Because it is available to the manager, the firm will charge him or her for it in the form of reduced salary whether it is exercised or not. Even if the manager prefers additional salary to managerial power, inadequacy of monitoring and bonding devices makes substituting money for power too costly. Where cost-effective monitoring or bonding devices are available but are not used, power is a consumption good. Presumably this is always so in a firm managed by its owner.

When unions regularize matters such as discharges by demanding just cause clauses and grievance arbitration, the fact of management resistance does not necessarily mean that unions are impairing the efficiency of the firm. The gain to employees may not be at the firm's expense. The same may be true of employee attempts via the union to participate in production line decisions. Suggestions benefiting the firm will not necessarily be welcomed by managers who see the suggested changes as diminishing their jobsite discretion while giving benefits only to the firm's owners. This analysis may explain, in part, the large sums of money spent by some managers resisting unionization.[55]

The question remains whether managers and owners for whom power is a consumption good will leave a firm in which the union has reduced managerial power by securing collective goods for the workers. Some of these managers will have knowledge and skills specific to the firm that cannot be used elsewhere. Those whose skills are fully marketable have the choice of leaving the firm and joining another in which managerial power is still available as a consumption good, or of staying with the firm at an increased salary. A union in this situation is a moni-

[52] Easterbrook & Fishel, supra n.[50] at 1173.

[53] A. Hirschman, supra n.[40].

[54] Leibenstein, Allocative Efficiency vs. X-Efficiency, Am. Econ. Rev. 392 (1966); Microeconomics and X-Efficiency Theory: If There Is No Crisis, There Ought to Be, Pub. Interest 97 (special ed., 1980).

[55] Compare the large sums of corporate money spent on preventing takeover bids and on "golden parachutes."

toring device forced on unwilling managers. Where managerial power has been the product of slack, because monitoring and bonding were too costly, a union also a monitoring device. Managers need no longer be automatically charged for exercising managerial power and their salaries should increase. Again, those managers who prefer managerial power to increased salary will leave the firm if their skills are fully marketable.

Owner-managers, for whom managerial power is a consumption good, may find it costly, especially over the short run, to withdraw their capital when managerial power is diminished by the firm's unionization. Owners who would sell a firm rather than own a firm that has "gone union" may be selling because they perceive that union monopoly wages will reduce the firm's profitability below the level that an owner could earn elsewhere, or they may be selling because for them power is an important consumption good that they predict will be unavailable after unionization.

Moreover, in the collective goods model, unionization forces managers to develop and use new skills as the firm reacts to increased employee voice and to new ways of dealing with employment relations (e.g., collective bargaining and grievance arbitration). Incumbent managers who do not have those skills and are not optimistic about their ability to acquire them can be expected to spend the firm's money resisting unionization, as would managers who value power and find moving to a nonunion firm to be costly.[56] Unions will find that these managers oppose union-organizing efforts and union attempts to bargain for collective goods once the firm is unionized. It can be predicted that unions will find it difficult in such firms to produce collective goods by purchase or by collective voice, and that threats of strikes or other exercises of monopoly power will be necessary.

[56] It is not necessary to this analysis that managers be aware that they are spending the firm's funds to protect their personal discretion. The theory of cognitive dissonance explains how managers could persuade themselves that they oppose unionization because unions are bad for the firm. The theory is summarized in E. Aronson, The Social Animal 39-100 (3d ed. 1980).

> [C]ognitive dissonance is a state of tension that occurs whenever an individual simultaneously holds two cognitions (ideas, attitudes, beliefs, opinions) that are psychologically inconsistent. . . . Because the occurrence of cognitive dissonance is unpleasant, people are motivated to reduce it. . . . [H]ow do we reduce cognitive dissonance? By changing one or both cognitions in a way so as to render them more compatible (more consonant) with each other, or by adding new cognitions that help bridge the gap between the original cognitions.

In this context the cognition "I am a good manager who does not spend the resources of the firm on my own well-being" is dissonant with the cognition "Spending the firm's money to oppose unions is good for me but not for the firm." The dissonance disappears if "Unions are (very) bad for the firm and (great) efforts should be made by the firm to oppose unionization" replaces the second cognition.

The Effects of Unionization on Productivity

In the price theory model of unionization, unions reduce the productivity of firms. They do this by altering optimal capital-labor ratios, distorting labor markets to the disadvantage of nonunion and unemployed workers, establishing wasteful "work rules" (e.g., restrictions on prefabricated goods, manning requirements), and engaging in costly strikes. Unions in a relational contract model may reduce employee dissatisfaction and thereby promote cooperative training, and they may make it easier for managers to alter traditional, but costly, work rules; but they may instead create inflationary pressures by altering relative wage differentials in such a way that other unions or employee groups are disposed to play catch-up or leap-frog.

In the collective goods model, the effects of unions on productivity also are uncertain. Unions may enhance productivity by reducing employee quits, improving employee morale, motivation and cooperativeness, and pressuring managers so as to reduce slack. Unions may secure collective goods, via monopoly power threats, at the expense of managers rather than the firm. But collective goods may also be secured at the expense of consumers and employment levels.

Productivity effects, even if they were unambiguously negative, would not necessarily call for a condemnation of unionization. The unions' role in promoting collective voice and the production of other collective goods would persuade some of us of the value of unionization to society. Nevertheless, productivity studies undoubtedly are important to normative statements about unions. They also would provide data that would help to evaluate the alternative models of what unions do.

It is difficult to devise empirical studies that reliably assess the effects of unionization on the productivity of a firm. A wage rate imposed by monopoly power that is higher than the market rate would induce the firm, if it could, to substitute more highly skilled employees for less skilled employees.[57] Thus output-per-worker figures comparing union and nonunion workers might show a productivity advantage that would disappear if corrected for this "price effect."[58] Substitution of capital for workers by the firm would show the same effect.

[57] See Brown & Medoff, Trade Unions in the Production Process, 86 J. Pol. Econ. 355, 356 (1978); J. Lewis, Unionism and Relative Wages in the United States: An Empirical Inquiry 45-46 (1963).

[58] For example, one study found that in a comparison of efficiency and costs in the construction industry in two Michigan cities, one heavily unionized and the other not, unions appeared to have had a favorable effect on firm efficiency. The author noted, however, that he was unable to test for the possibility that "the greater efficiency in the union area was due to the rejection of poor workers who could not be paid the high wage rate, [so that] the effect of the union has been merely to redistribute the workers geographically, and the union cannot be credited with improving the general level of efficiency." Mandelstamm, The Effects of Unions on Efficiency in the Residential Construction Industry: A Case Study, 18 Indus. & Lab. Rel. Rev. 503, 521 (1965).

Employee exits are costly to firms when employees have job skills and knowledge specific to the firm, so a collective voice effect of unionization that reduced quits would have a positive productivity effect. However, a union that used monopoly power to produce a higher wage would also reduce quits — high wages and other employment benefits induce workers to stay with the firm. In this situation, productivity gains from reduced exits are more than offset by the union's monopoly extraction (or else the firm would have raised wages without the union's intervention), and the net effect on productivity is negative.[59]

Unless technology is the same in union and nonunion firms, comparing output per worker between these firms is difficult.[60] Also, unless output can be measured in physical terms, the effects of union wages on prices cloud the comparison. Notwithstanding these measurement difficulties, an important recent study was able to find that in one industry unionization had a positive effect on productivity.[61] The study examined six plants in the cement industry that changed from nonunion to union status. The production of cement occurs in highly regional markets. Cement is a homogeneous product, produced to widely accepted specifications. There is little difference in quality between plants, and technology in plants of the same age is relatively standard. These characteristics permitted a careful measure of worker productivity measured by output before and after unionization. The study found that unionization has a positive effect on productivity of about 6 to 8 percent, occurring over a narrow range. Correcting for the possibility that high union wages caused firms to substitute highly skilled for lower skilled workers reduced the differential by only about 1 percent.

Interview data[62] revealed changes in plant practices following unionization. Before unionization, the plants had not strictly adhered to a promotion-from-within practice. In-plant employee mobility depended on decisions of departmental foremen, and hiring from the outside above entry-level jobs was not uncommon. Personalities played a role in promotions, as did favoritism by foremen. Under the union's regime, seniority was the dominant factor in promotions. Formal plantwide job posting and bidding were established by the bargaining agreements.

[59] Professor Freeman's study, using survey data, "has documented the existence of a significant inverse relation between trade unionism and various measures of exit behavior, which exists separate from the effect of unions on wages and the selectivity of innately more stable workers by unions." Freeman, The Exit-Voice Tradeoff in the Labor Market; Unionism, Job Tenure, Quits, and Separations, 94 Q.J. Econ. 643, 666 (1980).

[60] See Brown & Medoff, supra n.[57]. This article found apparent productivity gains associated with unionization that did not seem to be explained by an hypothesis that unions organize the most productive industries or that unions organize the most productive firms within industries.

[61] Clark, The Impact of Unionization on Productivity, 33 Ind. & Lab. Rel. Rev. 451 (1980); see also Clark, Unionization and Productivity: Micro-Econometric Evidence, 95 Q.J. Econ. 613 (1980).

[62] This included examination of the collective bargaining agreements.

Thus the study indicates a shift towards a relational contract as the result of unionization. It is plausible that the shift to a seniority criterion increased the willingness of employees to cooperate with one another and share firm-specific knowledge and that productivity increased accordingly.

The nonunion plants had no formalized system for worker complaints and complaints were seldom made, possibly out of fear of management retaliations. After unionization, the plants had formal grievance systems ending in third-party arbitration. Thus employee voice was increased.

Exit behavior proved difficult to measure but the author concludes that reduced exits did not seem to be an important factor in the productivity increase. This may have been because jobs in the industry tended to be high paying even before unionization. Unionization, according to the study, had a minor upward effect on wage compensation.

The study could neither prove nor disprove an effect of unionization on employee morale. The inconclusiveness appears to result from shortcomings inherent in questionnaires and interviews when the issue is highly impressionistic.

Unionization had a significant impact on management practices. Formalized grievance procedures and a seniority system were instituted. In five of the six plants studied, plant managers had been replaced. In some instances, supervisors were replaced; in other instances, they were retained but retrained. The author argues that "[g]iven the substantial change in the nature of industrial relations, the identification of the old manager with the nonunion regime, and the likelihood that the previous management was involved in attempts to block unionization, the change in plant management is not surprising."[63] In addition to changes in managerial personnel, the study observed important changes in management practices:

> [T]he interviews uncovered changes in management methods in all plants. The magnitude of the change varied from situation to situation, with a more professional, business like approach to labor relations by front-line supervisors the most common adjustment. In four of the six plants we found attempts to increase work effort and work group efficiency primarily through introduction of formal methods of organizational control. The adjustments in formal control procedures took several forms. In essence, however, they amounted to a system of production goals or targets accompanied by procedures for the review and monitoring of performance. The evaluation often occurred in newly introduced staff meetings, which were used for communication, training, and assessment of conditions and progress. Substantial changes in formal procedures were not introduced in all plants. Yet, even where formal procedures were changed only moderately,

[63] Clark, The Impact of Unionization on Productivity, supra n.[61], at 467.

> the interviews suggest that management monitored work performance and manning more closely. . . .
>
> The existence of a pattern of management adjustment across plants organized at different points in time suggests that the observed changes are not due solely to general technical change. While technical change may be at work in the processes we observed, it seems clear from the interviews that unionization had a significant independent effect. Our tentative conclusion, therefore, is that an independent improvement in plant management is one of the key adjustments to unionization. These results may be interpreted as evidence of a modern union "shock effect."[64]

The results may also be interpreted as evidence that managers take extra compensation in the form of discretion (power) and that by controlling this discretion unions produce gains for employees and efficiency gains for the firm. Replacement of plant managers and replacement and retraining of supervisors provide a powerful explanation of why firms, controlled by managers and inadequately monitored by shareholders, would spend considerable money resisting unionization.

The positive effects of unionization on productivity found by this study cannot be generalized to other industries.[65] Several factors bear on union productivity effects. If unionization is followed by stubborn management resistance to collective bargaining, costs are expended, workers are frustrated and noncooperative, and strikes often follow. Moreover, some unions may only be interested in securing wage gains by monopoly power.

Two effects associated with unions — strikes and make-work practices — tend to be overemphasized as evidence of the negative impact of unions on productivity. In the past 20 years, no more than one half of 1 percent of total workdays were lost as the result of strikes in any one year. The yearly average of lost workdays in this period was two-tenths of 1 percent.[66] Although a strike is surely serious business to a struck firm and its employees, the productivity losses to society on account of strikes is not substantial.

The direct impact of strikes can be measured, but that is not true of union make-work practices. Examples of make-work practices are the requirement that more workers be employed than are necessary to do a particular job, restrictions on the types of tools which may be used by workers, prohibitions of prefabricated materials, and unbending insis-

[64] Ibid.

[65] See Pencavel, The Distributional and Efficiency Effects of Trade Unions in Britain, 15 Brit. J. Ind. Rel. 137 (1977); Stone, The Origins of Job Structures in the Steel Industry, in R. Edwards, M. Reich & D. Gordon, Labor Market Segmentation 27-84 (1975).

[66] A Difference of Opinion, Fortune Magazine, Dec. 1, 1980, at 150.

tence on union jurisdictional lines.[67] Determining the impact of make-work rules requires extensive survey data and involves difficult questions of whether a particular rule is a make-work rule or not.

For instance, some local unions of the Painters Union have established a rule that no brush more than four and one half inches wide may be used to apply oil paint. On its face this appears to be a make-work rule designed to extend the time required to complete a job. Two studies[68] have shown, however, that in practice the rule is not restrictive because employers reported that they would not have used wider brushes in any event. Oil paint imposes a heavy drag that tires the hands and wrists, and it requires a "wet edge" that is hard to maintain with a wide brush.

The studies also found restrictive work rules that in practice were not enforced. Without doubt, there are make-work rules that unions do enforce and that have a negative impact on productivity. Individual firms are restrained by such rules but it remains to be shown that the rules have a significant national impact. It may be that union make-work practices are possible only over a narrow range of conditions. One study found that "[a] larger proportion of the industries in which make-work practices are found are local and the product is perishable; if it is not produced today, it will not be produced at all. Examples are the entertainment industries, the waterfront, building construction, railroad service, and bus and street car service."[69]

The Union-Member Relationship

A union's choice of which collective goods to seek depends on the membership's preferences and on how the union as an institution responds to those preferences. In standard economic models of firms, owners maximize profits. No similar unitary goal can be posited for unions because of the tradeoff between wage increases and employment levels. Some commentators, working within the price theory model, have suggested that unions seek to maximize the "wage bill" accruing to its members — the hours of employment times hourly earnings. But there is no intuitive reason why this should be so. A union might weigh hours of employment three times as highly as it values hourly wages.[70] Another suggestion is that unions most value maximizing the wage rate.

[67] For example, the Carpenters Union might follow a rule that only a member of the Union can hammer a nail on jobsite, and that no member of the Union will do work that is not carpentry work (e.g., no member will sweep up the jobsite).

[68] W. Haber & H. Levinson, Labor Relations and Productivity in the Building Trades 164-165 (1956); Mandelstamm, supra n. [58], at 511.

[69] S. Slichter, J. Healy & E. Livernash, The Impact of Collective Bargaining on Management 336 (1960).

[70] See D. Mitchell, Unions, Wages, and Inflation 65 (1980) (citing relevant literature). See also A. Cartter & F. Marshall, Labor Economics; Wages, Employment, and Trade Unionism 276-288 (1967).

The United Mine Workers seem to have adopted this policy from about 1930 to 1950, notwithstanding the substantial reduction in employment that resulted.[71] A third possibility is that union goals change as the demand for labor change. When demand for labor is rising a union might value jobs for laid-off members more highly than increased wages; when the demand for labor is falling, the same union might protect its current wage rate and accept layoffs. No generalization can be made that holds true for all unions.

In a relational contract model, a union's first goal might be the maintenance of its wage rate and customary rules relative to other groups. If the union is composed of groups of employees with wage expectations relative to one another, union officers seeking to stay in office might emphasize the continuation of current differentials.

In the collective goods model, unions maximize the production of collective goods in the workplace. They do this by expending resources up to the point where the costs of producing more collective goods are equal to the value of the goods times the probability that they can be attained. To the extent that the collective good being sought is a monopoly wage, the collective good model does not solve the problem of squaring union goals with the wage-employment tradeoff. But the model has the advantage of incorporating the fact that unions secure many goods other than wages, that some of these goods can be secured by means other than monopoly power, and that certain collective goods secured through monopoly power — those coming at the expense of managers rather than the firm — may not cause reduced employment.

Unions produce collective goods under conditions of uncertainty; for example, they may not know ex ante whether a strike or continued collective bargaining will produce an increase in collective goods. Thus even if all union members shared the same preferences — if they each assigned the same value to particular collective goods — the union's calculation of optimal expenditures would be difficult, and mistakes common. But union members differ in the focus and intensity of their preferences. I next discuss how union members signal preferences, and how they monitor the behavior of union officers.

Union members can signal satisfactions and dissatisfactions to union officers by either voice or exit. Members use voice when they complain, compliment, cajole, or criticize. Voting for or against a candidate for union office is a form of voice. Exits serve as an inadequate signal of preferences in the union context because no individual worker alone can choose whether to purchase unionization.[72] A worker must change employers in order to exercise a personal choice for or against

[71] Ibid. at 280.

[72] The choice must be made by a majority of employees in an appropriate bargaining unit (see Chapter 2).

unionization. Exercising voice by removing a union officer from his or her office may also be underutilized. A coalition of dissatisfied members must be formed to mount the campaign to unseat the incumbent. This action entails startup costs, which may be considerable, especially if the incumbent is thought to have the power and the inclination to retaliate against political opponents. Also, for reasons discussed below, members will tend not to invest in information gathering and other forms of monitoring that would cause changes in union leadership policies.

Because exit is costly, voice is a particularly critical force for change in unions. Change within unions has the same characteristics as change in the workplace: Most changes benefit groups of workers and are collective goods. If members shared both the costs and benefits of producing these collective goods, they would invest up to the point where the marginal (incremental) cost of producing a collective good (for example, the fidelity of a union officer to the union's constitution) just equalled the marginal values of the good.[73] When costs and benefits are not equally shared among all members, many otherwise beneficial collective goods will not be sought. Self-interested individuals will not act to achieve group interests. The individual will calculate the costs of his or her efforts to produce the collective good and compare those costs with the perceived value of the good, discounted by the probability that these efforts will be successful and discounted again by the probability that some other, similarly situated member will act to secure the good.[74] Especially if the union is large, the probability that one person's efforts will secure the good may be negligible. Thus, absent some special benefit, purely self-interested individuals will not contribute to the production of collective goods by paying union dues, giving time and effort to union activities, or informing themselves about workplace or internal union issues, even though they would benefit from these collective goods and they hope others will provide the goods.

Clearly some workers do contribute money, time, and effort to unions. The analysis suggests, however, that because unions are large groups producing collective goods at the workplace and within the union, contributions will be suboptimal.[75] There are several reasons why unions do not falter. Some workers have a sense of loyalty and moral obligation toward their fellows and believe that fair play requires one to pay one's share. A collective bargaining agreement may compel dues contributions. Indeed, the foregoing analysis is the principal argu-

[73] The following discussion draws on M. Olson, The Logic of Collective Action (1971).

[74] Only the latter discount is properly called the free rider problem. Even were the member certain that no one else would act, he or she still might not find it rational to act.

[75] It is suboptimal in the sense that the total contribution will be less than it would be if the costs and benefits were shared equally.

ment for allowing unions to coerce dues contributions. Social pressure from one's fellows may compel contribution toward workplace collective goods, as may the more formal pressure of a picket line. In addition to workplace collective goods that cannot be withheld from a noncontributing worker, there may be goods that the union can withhold. In earlier times, the social and recreational opportunities provided by unions were important to many members, but that is probably not typically true today. Some workers may contribute to the union because they believe that union officers will adequately represent them on workplace issues only if they contribute.

Like the managers of firms, union officers have opportunities for slack. Monitoring of officers is a collective good, and the full benefits of monitoring do not go to the monitor. There may be social sanctions that pressure an individual member to contribute his or her share toward the monitoring of union officers, but in unions that principal monitors are office seekers.[76] They get an individual benefit from their monitoring efforts: the opportunity to replace the incumbent. But especially in a large union, the support of many other members may be necessary in order to have a realistic chance of replacing an incumbent, and there is no straightforward mechanism for purchasing that support. This support (which at least requires information gathering) may not be readily forthcoming because of the calculus of individual contribution to collective goods and the feeling by individuals that their single vote, or other contribution, is not likely to be determinative.

This analysis suggests why some union officers, especially at the national level, may be able to dominate union policy with little fear of loss of office or other reprisals. Yet because union officers must stand for reelection periodically, fear of election defeat sets limits to the power of union officers, much as the product market and the market for managers sets limits on the power of firm managers. The analysis also suggests that officers of small unions would be subject to ouster more often than would officers of large unions, a conclusion supported by impressionistic evidence.[77] Finally, officers or staff members responsible to a small group of workers, such as a job steward, should be more responsive to constituents.

The analysis also shows why it is incorrect to assume that union officers and contract negotiators will necessarily show fidelity to average membership preferences. As is true with any process of group decision making where preferences are nonidentical, coalitions may form within unions, and decisional processes are difficult to predict.

[76] Compare the role of corporate takeovers as a monitoring device.
[77] See D. Bok & J. Dunlop, Labor and the American Community 73 (1970).

C. THE AGENCY: THE STRUCTURE OF THE NATIONAL LABOR RELATIONS BOARD

The principal components of the administrative agency known as the National Labor Relations Board are five Board members, a General Counsel, regional directors, and administrative law judges (for many years called *trial examiners*).

The five Board members are housed in Washington, D.C. They are appointed by the President, with the advice and consent of the Senate, and serve five-year, staggered terms. One board member is designated chairman. On cases of particular importance, all five Board members sit.[78] Routine cases are assigned to a panel of three members.

The General Counsel is also appointed by the President with the advice and consent of the Senate. The General Counsel is responsible for investigating and prosecuting unfair labor practice charges, and for representing the agency in the courts. Most of the unfair labor practice case work is done in the field, in regional offices. Each of the regional offices — there are over 30 — is headed by a regional director appointed by and responsible to the General Counsel.

The regional directors have also been delegated considerable authority to act for the Board in representation cases, cases involving a decision of whether or not to designate a particular union as the exclusive bargaining representative for a group of employees. The details of that delegation are considered in Chapter 2, Section A.

While the Board has jurisdiction over all enterprises whose activities "affect" interstate commerce, the Board has refused to assert jurisdiction over employers not meeting a minimum-volume-of-business test.[79] Thus, of over $3\frac{1}{2}$ million establishments in the retail and service industries, only about 22 percent are large enough to be covered by present Board jurisdictional standards. As an example, for nonretail businesses the minimum business volume that must be involved before the Board will assert jurisdiction is an annual inflow or outflow, direct or indirect, of at least $50,000 across state lines.[80] Other dollar standards are applicable

[78] In a typical year only 5 to 10 percent of the Board's decisions are signed by four or five Board members.

[79] In §14(c) of the Landrum-Griffin Act of 1959, Congress prohibited the Board from declining jurisdiction over labor disputes involving firms that met the Board's jurisdictional criteria on August 1, 1959. Because the Board cannot raise its jurisdictional amounts, inflation increases the Board's jurisdiction. See Meltzer, Inflation and the NLRB, Reg. Mag., Sept.-Oct. 1980, at 43.

[80] *Direct outflow* is defined as goods shipped or services furnished by the employer outside the state. *Indirect outflow* is defined as the sale of goods or services to users meeting any of the Board's jurisdictional standards, excepting the indirect outflow or indirect inflow standard. *Direct inflow* is defined as goods or services furnished the employer directly from outside the state. *Indirect inflow* is defined as goods that originated outside the state, but which the employer purchased from a seller or supplier within the state.

to particular types of enterprises, such as newspapers and local public utilities. No attempt will be made in these materials to survey the variety of Board jurisdictional standards. In the 1959 Act, Congress added §14(c)(1) to the NLRA, which has the effect of prohibiting the Board from declining to assert jurisdiction over any labor dispute over which it would have asserted jurisdiction under the standards prevailing on August 1, 1959. Thus the Board can expand, but no longer contract, its jurisdiction. Where a case falls outside of the Board's jurisdictional standards, the states are permitted to act.

Neither the Board nor the General Counsel initiates cases. Each case must be initiated by a private party. In fiscal year 1983, 48,740 cases were so initiated.[81] Unfair labor practice charges accounted for 39,874 and petitions for employee representation elections numbered 8,089. The Board members issued decisions in 2,606 cases in fiscal 1983. Two points should be appreciated from the latter figure. First, even though the Board decides many cases in three-member panels, 2,606 decisions for five decision makers is a heavy adjudicatory caseload. At the least, this means the Board members must rely heavily on their staff in routine cases. Second, the percentage of cases reaching the Board members shows that the bulk of the agency's activity takes place in the regional offices. To the extent that regional offices are regularly engaged in disposing of cases according to clearly expressed NLRB decisional guidelines, the low percentage reaching the Board may be neither surprising nor disturbing. However, the fact that the Board members' caseload is already heavy enough to preclude significant expansion may cause Board decisions in substantive matters to be designed to reduce caseload rather than promote the policies of the Act, and it may also cause regional directors to refuse to prosecute meritorious cases.

We can look at how the process operates, as well as gain an insight into the relationships of the various NLRB functionaries, by examining how unfair labor practices cases are handled.[82] An unfair labor practice case is initiated when a private party files a "charge" that an unfair labor practice has been committed. The form for such a charge is reproduced in the Statutory Appendix. The regional office is responsible for investigating the charge, although in practice some regional offices clogged with cases may do no more than demand that the charging party produce sufficient evidence to establish a meritorious case. The regional director decides whether to issue a "complaint" in the case, and only if a complaint is issued will the case be heard by the Board.

[81] These figures are obtained from the 46th Annual Report of the National Labor Relations Board (1982), the 1983 Operations Report of the General Counsel, and the Chairman's Task Force on the National Labor Relations Board.

[82] For a more detailed description of unfair labor practice procedures and suggested improvements, see Nolan & Lehr, Improving NLRB Unfair Labor Practice Procedures, 57 Tex. L. Rev. 47 (1978).

Among the factors influencing the choice of whether to issue a complaint are the strength of the evidence, the seriousness of the activity under attack, the caseload of the regional office, and the clarity of Board precedent on the substantive issues raised. If the regional director refuses to issue a complaint, an internal appeal can be taken to a branch of the General Counsel's office in Washington, which affirms well over 90 percent of the refusals, but no appeal can be taken to the Board members or to the courts. The General Counsel's discretion is unreviewable. Before dismissing a charge, i.e., refusing to issue a complaint, regional offices apprise the charging party and afford an opportunity for the charge to be withdrawn. Of the unfair labor practice charges filed in 1983 (39,874), 65.8 percent were either dismissed or were withdrawn before a complaint was issued.

If the regional director issues an unfair labor practice complaint, an attorney from the regional office will prosecute the case. Most complaints (93.6 percent in 1983) are settled by a regional office prior to a hearing. While information is often exchanged during settlement discussions, the Board does not permit prehearing discovery in unfair labor practice cases. The Supreme Court ruled in NLRB v. Robbins Tire & Rubber Co., 437 U.S. 214 (1978), that witnesses' statements in pending unfair labor practice proceedings are exempt from Freedom of Information Act disclosure at least until completion of the hearing. If a hearing is necessary, the charging party may intervene and present evidence, but the General Counsel, by a regional staff attorney, is in control of the case.

Unfair labor practice cases are tried before administrative law judges (ALJs). ALJs are appointed and paid by the Civil Service Commission. They are housed in Washington or San Francisco and travel throughout the country to take evidence in unfair labor practice cases. After taking evidence and receiving briefs, an ALJ issues a recommended decision and order. The decisions routinely recite the evidence in great detail, make credibility resolutions when necessary, and discuss applicable Board precedent. The recommended order will either suggest an appropriate remedy or that the complaint be dismissed.

If no party — respondent, General Counsel, or charging party — files exceptions to the ALJ's recommended decision and order, it will automatically become final. If exceptions are filed, the case file is transferred to the Board's Washington office, and briefs are filed. Oral argument is very rare. The Board will issue a written decision and order. Thus the Board hears no evidence, sees no witnesses; in that sense, it is an appellate tribunal. The Board members' procedures for processing unfair labor practice cases after the ALJ's recommended decision are as follows:[83]

[83] Dawidoff v. Minneapolis Building Trades Council, 430 F. Supp. 322, 324 (D. Minn. 1977) (affidavit of NLRB executive secretary).

(a) The ALJ decision is formally issued by the Executive Secretary and is served on the parties with an order transferring the proceedings to the Board and with an excerpt from the Board's Rules and Regulations regarding appeal to the Board. The rules provide 23 days for the filing of exceptions and supporting briefs. Within 13 days from the last day on which exceptions may be filed, a party opposing the exceptions may file either an answering brief to the exceptions or cross-exceptions and supporting briefs. Within 13 days from the last date on which cross-exceptions may be filed, a brief in opposition to cross-exceptions may be filed. In other words, a maximum time of 49 days, excluding any extensions of time, is provided. However, in any case the parties may expedite the process by filing exceptions and responses within a shorter period of time. Moreover, if no timely exceptions are filed, the Board promptly enters an order adopting the ALJ decision.

(b) Within 10 days after the filing of the initial exceptions with the Board, the case is assigned to one of five Board Members and thereby to the panel which he or she leads. Cases in which Section 10(1) injunctive relief is pending are specially identified as priority cases in which expedited action is required.

(c) Within 49 hours after the Board Member receives a case, it is assigned to a staff attorney for research and analysis.

(d) Depending upon its complexity, difficulty, or priority nature, in from one to three weeks, the usual case is presented to a sub-panel composed of an experienced counsel representing each of the Board Members on the panel, which reaches a tentative decision as to the disposition of the case.

(e) The proposed decision is then drafted by the attorney pursuant to instructions of the sub-panel and reviewed by the supervisory personnel. Again depending on the character of the case, up to three weeks are allowed for drafting and revising the tentative decision.

(f) When the proposed draft decision comports with the tentative decision reached by the sub-panel and has the approval of the originating Board Member, it is circulated among the other two participating panel Members for approval and to the non-participating Members for clearance. Up to two weeks are allowed for this process, again depending on the character of the case.

(g) However, any case may be referred for full Board review by the sub-panel, by any participating panel Member or by any non-participating Member who does not believe the decision as drafted comports with existing Board precedent or policy. If this occurs the time needed for review and decision is obviously extended.

(h) When final agreement has been reached on the decision and order, the case must still be finally edited before it may be reproduced for publication. Approximately one week is needed for these final mechanical procedures before the decision may be issued to the parties.[84]

[84] In some cases, the Board will adopt entirely or substantially the ALJ's recommended decision and order with little or no discussion of its own; this is called *short-forming.*

A Board order is not self-enforcing; that is, the Board has no coercive power to compel adherence to its order. Section 10(e) of the NLRB provides that the Board may petition a specified U.S. Court of Appeals (always including the District of Columbia Court of Appeals) for the enforcement of a Board order. Section 10(f) provides that "[a]ny person aggrieved by a final order of the Board granting or denying in whole or in part the relief sought" may petition a specified Court of Appeals (again including the D.C. Circuit) for review of the order. Both sections provide that "[t]he findings of the Board with respect to questions of fact if supported by substantial evidence on the record considered as a whole shall be conclusive." The Board was affirmed in whole or in part by a Court of Appeals in 81.6 percent of 1983's 338 appellate rulings on Board decisions. Failure to comply with Court of Appeals' enforcement risks a contempt citation. The final review possibility is a writ of certiorari from the U.S. Supreme Court.

Delay is a major problem in the prosecution of unfair labor practice cases. In fiscal 1983, the median time for the disposal of unfair labor practices in the investigative stage was 45 days. Median time from the close of an unfair labor practice hearing to receipt of the ALJ's decision was 139 days. After an ALJ's decision was issued, it took, on the average, 120 days to a Board decision.

2

PROCEDURES FOR THE SELECTION OF A BARGAINING REPRESENTATIVE

A. INTRODUCTION

PRESSURES IN TODAY'S WORKPLACE, OVERSIGHT HEARINGS BEFORE THE SUBCOMMITTEE ON LABOR-MANAGEMENT RELATIONS OF THE COMMITTEE ON EDUCATION AND LABOR

House of Representatives, 96th Cong., 1st Sess., Oct. 16–18, 1979

Statement of Robert A. Georgine, President of the Building and Construction Trades Department of the AFL–CIO

My name is Robert A. Georgine and I am appearing here on behalf of the Building and Construction Trades Department of the AFL–CIO which is composed of 17 affiliated unions and represents approximately 4 million of this nation's construction workers. I would like to begin by commending this Subcommittee for conducting these hearings. The increase in the number of labor relations consultants and the growth of union-busting during the 1970s, is a subject which is of crucial concern to American workers but it is a subject which has received little attention from the government or from the press. I appreciate the opportunity you are providing to expose this threat to American working men and women.

I submit to you that there is a new form of terrorism now running rampant through the factories, offices and job sites of America. It does not involve masked gunmen. There is no skyjacking. There are no tales of bloody violence. It is not part of an extremist cause in a far away land. But what we are seeing today is, in fact, the new psychological terrorists of American industry. Drawn from the ranks of lawyers, labor relations specialists and psychologists, their weapons are emotional intimidation and the subversion of the law. Whenever and wherever working people seek to organize, this guerilla army dressed in three piece suits stands ready to resist. . . .

Here is how they operate. First they seek a psychological profile of the work force. Private files are opened. Supervisors are thoroughly interrogated on the union sympathies of each and every employee. Every worker is required to complete a so-called "attitude survey" to measure what some have termed "employee loyalty."

Secondly, consultants work with supervisors to enlist them as foot-soldiers in the anti-union campaign. In some cases these well-groomed young men use smiles and compliments to win over the company's supervisors. If this fails, direct threats of dismissal are made to supervisors who lack the protection of the Taft-Hartley Act.

After weeks of labor relations education, supervisors are given specific instructions for dealing with individual workers. While the consultants stand behind the scenes, often without anyone knowing they exist, the supervisors carry out the anti-union game plan. Countless cases abound of harassment, interrogation, rumor mongering, discharge, selective promotions and special appeals to personal situations. The consultants also prepare letters and speeches to be delivered by the supervisory staff aimed at the areas of greatest worker vulnerability as devined by their psychological spade-work.

Simultaneously, a series of legal maneuvers are utilized. Unfair labor practices are committed and dilatory motions are filed to delay the NLRB election. While ultimately the company may be found guilty by the NLRB, the benefits of delay outweigh the costs. To many workers the company seems above the law. They watch as the company unilaterally fires, coerces and delays. Remedies will take months and years if they are to occur at all. The consultants have no desire to pursue a rational dialogue. Their appeal is aimed at the basic fears of worker isolation, powerlessness and insecurity. In the end, this "formula" has proven highly successful. One major consulting firm, Modern Management Methods, has had a 98% victory percentage in NLRB elections.

Individual workers who have faced this type of campaign can express far more eloquently than I just what it is like to face an "industrial terrorist." For my part, I would like to give you an overview of this problem. First you must understand that this scene is recurring in hundreds of workplaces across the country at this very moment. It is part of a larger pattern of a growing corporate assault on the trade union movement. History has taught the labor movement that there will always be union-busters. But today supposedly "enlightened" business leaders are encouraging and hiring these anti-union forces and seem willing to risk years of successful cooperation and mutual support between labor and management. . . .

So let me turn now to examining the nature of union-busting in 1979.

The fact is that today the phenomena of union-busting is very different from 1959. Unfair labor practices of all kinds have skyrocketed. Our records show that out of 6,000 organizing campaigns of 10 or more workers, two-thirds involve some form of outside anti-union expertise. By some estimates there are more than 1,000 firms directly and indirectly involved in union-busting activities with more than 1,500 individual practitioners engaged in the full-time activity of preventing unionization efforts. Union-busting is now a major American industry with annual sales well over $½ billion.

These firms and consultants have almost all emerged within the last ten years. The conclusions must be drawn that there is a direct link between the professionalization of union-busting and the skyrocketing abuse of the law. In fact, many consultants openly claim credit for the meteoric rise in decertification and deauthorization elections.

Union-busting is no longer as blatant as the blunt-end of a billyclub. It is a sophisticated science spanning the fields of psychology, law, and personnel administration. The practice of union-busting, like any of these component professions, involves the dissemination of expertise for practical application. We have identified five principal delivery systems by which this union-busting technology is disseminated from the expert into the midst of the workplace. They are: (1) The seminar lecturer who gives companies a two or three day crash course in the art of anti-unionism. (2) The consulting firm composed of psychologists and industrial relations experts. (3) The anti-union law firm which handles the legal strategies of union-busting, including delays, discharges, bargaining to impasse and decertifications. (4) The industrial psychologist who develops and administers the surveys and psychological testing of anti-unionism. (5) The trade association which combines all of these functions and specifically tailors them to the labor relations of an industry.

You must also realize that there are three principal kinds of union-busting. First, there is what is politely called preventive labor relations. Here an internal company program is established to extinguish union aspirations. Potential union-sympathizers are denied jobs. Psychological profiles of employees are developed without the workers' knowledge. Consistent anti-union pressure is applied by the employer, and an emergency legal strategy of delay and dismissal is developed just in case the situation gets out of hand.

The second category of union-busting techniques occur during the ongoing organizing drive. I have already described how one such drive is conducted. Yet businesses have turned to a variety of consultants, lawyers, psychologists and trade associations for guidance in their day-to-day effort to defeat a union organizing campaign.

Finally, there are the "de-unionizing" efforts. While the employer's involvement is strictly regulated in these areas, consultants nevertheless coach firms in how to initiate such proceedings. Over the last ten years largely through the coaching of these consultants the number of decertification elections has increased threefold.

Now let me turn to the five ways in which these types of union-busting techniques are actually "delivered" to employers.

1. SEMINARS

Of all the union-busting delivery systems, none is more blatant than the anti-union seminar. Packaging their wares in slick glossy brochures, mailing them to hundreds of thousands of businesses each year, a handful of so-called educational companies are making big profits off employers who want to bust unions. I have brought with me today a few sample advertisements for these seminars which I would like to enter into the record.

As you can see, the firms go by names like Advanced Management Research; Executive Enterprises, Inc.; Professional Seminar Association; Federal Publications; and West Coast Industrial Relations Association, Inc. Their seminars bear the names "De-Unionizing"; "The Process of Decertification," "How to Maintain Non-Union Status"; "Avoiding Unions"; "Preserving Non-Union Status" and "Making Unions Unnecessary."

I also want you to know that seminars are also offered by trade associations including the American Hospital Association, the Associated Builders and Contractors, and the National Association of Manufacturers. Here you will find courses with similar names being offered to members of these associations.

Yet whether these seminars are given by private companies or by trade associations, they generally follow a similar pattern. They are intensive one to 3-day courses on some aspect of union-busting. Their cost is usually between $300 and $500 and the seminar leaders are almost always drawn from the ranks of active anti-union specialists. Attendance ranges between 35 and 100 executives netting more than $20,000 for a few days work with some minimal overhead expenses.

In many cases, academic institutions including many which receive federal support lend their names to these seminars. They provide no faculty but merely add a touch of legitimacy. Often these courses provide participants with state continuing education credits. Recently Utah's Governor Matheson attacked the notion of an anti-union seminar industry and specifically criticized academic institutions for lending these firms the credibility which they would not otherwise possess.

There is no way to determine the precise number of seminars given each year but a conservative estimate based on existing information would have to place that number at well over two hundred. Thus more than 10,000 business executives pay more than $450 each year to get a crash course on how to beat the union. That's a $4.5 million industry right there.

These seminars fill an important need within the union-busting world. For consultants they provide an easy and even profitable means of meeting potential clients. For large businesses, they represent a relatively cheap means of sampling a consultant's skill before retaining him. While seminar prices are high, the going rate for anti-union services is between $75 and $100 per consultant hour. In addition, the seminars are an excellent way for personnel directors to brush up on the latest tricks of the trade. For small businesses unable to afford a consultant at all, these lectures can provide a basic orientation on how to avoid, beat or "dump" a union.

If this Subcommittee could observe one of these seminars as they are actually conducted you would see just how cynically union-busters view their profession. From the word go, their singular goal is the manipulation of workers' attitudes rather than any rational dialogue about the benefits or costs of unionization. The consultant and his audience always have their eye on the bottom line result of defeating the union. In some cases this means high pressure and "questionable" labor practices. For example, Herbert G. Melnick of Modern Management ("MMM") counsels his audience to keep unfair labor charges "in perspective." Two well-known anti-union attorneys, Alfred T. DeMaris and Francis Coleman, openly advise people on operating in the gray area of the law. Others may take a more "enlightened" approach urging employers to disguise the actual power relations at the workplace with cosmetic changes in salary structure, job classifications and working atmosphere.

I would now like to take you through a seminar. It is a composite seminar derived from several reports we have received on actual seminars. Much of the language is actual quotes from the seminar instructors or from the manuals which are distributed to seminar participants:

You are a businessman from Anywhere, USA and receive a brochure in the mail entitled "Unions: How to Avoid Them, Beat Them and Decertify Them." It takes place over three days at a large hotel in a major American city. Maybe you are facing a union drive; maybe you want to avoid unions or perhaps you wish to rid yourself of an existing union.

On the evening before the first day, you meet the two seminar leaders. They are each experts in their respective fields. The first, an industrial psychologist, is somewhat disarming, sporting a beard, open shirt and rolled-up shirt sleeves. You soon realize that his relaxed jovial manner is a vital tool of his trade which he has practiced for more than two decades with major Fortune "500" companies including IBM, Shell, Dupont and Texas Instruments. The second is a New York lawyer dressed in a custom-made shirt and conservative business suit. He has a direct and business like manner which also comes from years of combating union organizing and assisting management decertification efforts.

The first day is reserved for the psychologist who speaks on how to "Make Unions Unnecessary." He starts off the morning by stating:

"Gentlemen, we are here today because many of you already have a union problem. For some of you an organizing drive is now underway. For others, the union is already a reality and deunionization is desirable. And for a few, who believe that an ounce of prevention is worth a pound of cure, you are here to insure that you never must face a union across a bargaining table.

"All my years in this business have shown me that any management that gets a union deserves it — and they get the kind they deserve. No labor union has ever captured a group of employees without the full cooperation and encouragement of managers who create the need for unionization. Management language does not even have a positive word for operating non-union. The positive approach is: Make Unions Unnecessary.

"In fact, there are really only two approaches to unions, which I call the cactus and the plum. The plum is an easy target for a union since it is not even concerned with unionization. The cactus is tough and prickly — creating an environment clearly opposed to unions."

That first day you learn how to plant the cactus early. For starters the psychologist recommends screening workers in the interview process to weed out union sympathizers. Of course, since direct questions as to union sympathies are illegal he recommends:

"Find out if they are involved in liberal causes; tenant organizations, consumer rights organizations or other activities which would reveal a pro-union tendency. Never hire workers with union backgrounds if you can help it.

"The law says you can't interrogate employees but you can very strongly state your philosophy and tell them what's going on in the plant . . . check into the employee's background. Do the spade work involved with checking referrals. This will tell you whether or not the employee is going to be 'open minded.' "

Finally, the psychologist urges you to pay close attention to the sex and race of your workforce.

"Given a choice between a man and a woman for the same job, always choose a woman, because they are usually the secondary bread winner and because they are 'scared to death' of strikes and violence. Obviously it's absolutely legal to scare the beejesus out of your female employees with threats of strikes, violence and picket lines, and I suggest to you that this is a very good way to scare the hell out of them.

"When you're dealing with minorities, look at it from the perspective of the average black. He sees that the only way that the blacks have gotten any place in this country in the last 20 years is collective action, getting together and raising hell. And there is a fair amount of evidence to support this. So, it is my very strong finding that blacks tend to be more prone to unionization than whites. Now you have EEOC these days and you have to follow the EEOC laws and have whatever the percentage of blacks you are supposed to have. There is no reason for you to be heroes about this and interested in abstract justice or upraising the downtrodden, so don't be heroes about the whole goddam thing and fill up the work force with blacks. If you can keep them at a minimum you're better off.

"I feel the same way about Indians that I do about blacks . . . stay the hell away from Puerto Ricans. Mexicans are O.K. if they feel that their first-line supervisor is their friend and if he speaks Spanish. Cubans are great. They [Cubans, Mexicans and Puerto Ricans] are all Hispanic surnames, so you can stick with one and still keep your EEOC limits."

You soon learn that screening is just a small part of keeping the union out. Once hired, the worker must be initiated into a company with a non-union message. The psychologist teaches:

"Tell them the company operates without unions, and has for a long time. The union didn't get you your job, the union can't keep you your job. Now we are not saying that unions are good or bad, what we are saying is that we don't feel there is a need for them here, and no one has evidently ever felt the need for them because we don't have any.

"But it will take real time and effort . . . to cultivate the non-union spirit of cooperation. Create long-term education programs in industrial relations. An employer is certainly free to educate employees on a number of current topics. You can hold an industrial relations course to include how unions organize . . . and how, when a union comes in, you will lose your ability to deal directly with management. Regularly communicate with employees about the nature of your business, tell them how many union shops are leaving your area and the advantage of being non-union in your area. Tell them that one of a union's greatest strengths is job security but real job security comes from working with a successful firm."

You are soon given a checklist of cosmetic items which must be changed to foster the non-union environment. They are each items which have no real bearing on wages or working conditions. The psychologist warns:

"Never create the impression that we in the ivory tower with the glass and carpet up front saying that you in the factory, in the back without any air-conditioning in the dark don't need a union.

"Don't drive to work in a fancy car.

"Don't call people workers or even employees and don't call bosses, bosses. Everyone should be considered part of the same firm. For instance at IBM everyone is an IBMer.

"Give people titles they respect like technician or engineer.

"Create numerous salary and job levels so that advancement comes early and often for everyone.

"Always stress their career at the firm. Emphasize that unions will hurt career advancement by emphasizing seniority.

"Always respond to employee inquiries. From the highest possible level of the company."

At this point the psychologist pauses, looks at his watch and announces the lunch break. Proceeding to lunch, everyone is furiously discussing what has been said, comparing their situation to the psychologist's recommendations. Over lunch the psychologist drifts from table to table handing out business cards and setting up meetings for people from the same area or industry.

After lunch participants are introduced to the importance of "attitude and value surveys" which the psychologist calls the early warning system for unionization. You receive a sheet with nearly one hundred multiple choice questions which have been used countless times and which he claims have been translated into a dozen languages. The surveys are filled out at work and submitted anonymously. The psychologist explains:

"Anytime you get a bad score on anything having to do with supervisors or work pressure or competence of the management, you are going to have an organizing drive."

For more than an hour, you discuss various strategies and tactics for polling employee attitudes through these value surveys. You learn that years of recycling and standardization have given these tests a rather high degree of correlation with immediate worker attitudes. The audience seems genuinely excited with the prospect of gauging the success of their antiunion campaigns on a regular basis.

The last topic of the day focuses on recruiting first line supervisors into the non-union effort. The psychologist warns that the chief executive officer, whom he calls "Big Daddy," should never directly deal with workers on the unionization issue. Instead, the immediate boss — the first line supervisor — should do the "dirty" anti-union work. The psychologist counsels:

"There are a lot of tribalistic people in low-skill level jobs. The boss is very important to them. A good boss keeps them in the know and talks to each directly.

"Know what's doing, how it's doing and what's with them. Big Daddy is not management, he is a myth. Management is the first line supervisor."

The psychologist goes on to tell you how to motivate supervisors, stressing the danger unions would represent to their authority. He offers a sample speech.

"Tell them if a union comes into the plant, who do you think is going to be affected most. It isn't the president, or the vice-presidents of the company. It's you, Mr. and Mrs. Supervisor. You're the ones who are going to be up against the union every day. You're going to have to deal with the shop steward, with the grievances, with the complaints, with the slowdowns, with the harassment, you're the ones who are going to be dealing with the union on the front line. Let me tell you from experience, it's the supervisors in the company who bear the brunt of the problems and confrontations that come with unionism — and it's the supervisors who have the biggest stake in keeping their company non-union.

"For example, when a discharge is made by a supervisor, the issue will be grieved and an arbitrator will finally decide whether or not the employee should remain in the plant. In more than 80 percent of the recorded cases involving discharge, arbitrators have modified the discipline imposed by the company — and in a great many of these cases, the employee has been reinstated with back pay because the arbitrator's opinion about the reasons for the discharge differed from the supervisor's opinion. And how does that make you look? Once you have 'discharged' someone and two months later he returns to the department after the union has won its case, and he has been reinstated by the arbitrator your control over that particular employee is probably lost forever, and your authority over those whom you supervise is certainly weakened. In fact, you look like a real paper tiger in your own department." . . .

In the second day of a typical anti-union seminar both the psychologist and the lawyer are present. They tell you that in an organizing drive you should adhere to the basic non-union philosophy discussed previously while paying greater attention to the legality of your actions. And in case you misunderstand the lawyer cautions:

"Keep unfair labor practices in perspective. The worst that can happen will be the rescheduling of an election or an order to bargain. The only one who can force you to sign a contract is the union and the only real power they have is a strike."

So you quickly realize that the lawyer's real purpose is not only to teach you the limits of the law but to teach you how to strategically violate it. He teaches:

"Many actions fall into the gray area of the law and some of them the very darkest part of the gray.

"Remember if you commit an unfair labor practice the union could have the election set aside. However, if an election is scheduled and it doesn't look good for the company, pull out all the stops, take the risk."

To solidify your new found understanding of the law they proceed to lay out several illegal tactics which you can almost always get away with. As the lawyer reminds you, "you can cover your tracks . . . if you know ahead of time what you are doing you can avoid charges of [unfair labor practices]." For example, he tells you: "If management keeps careful records of absences and reprimands, it can usually make dismissal of a prounion worker look legitimate."

On spying and surveillance he says: "I know the union meeting's going to be held at the Holiday Inn. I park my car in the lot and watch everybody who comes into the parking lot. That is an act of surveillance. I may not do this. Now, if I just happen to be coming to the Holiday Inn to attend another function and I happen to see certain people go in — I have every right to do that."

But of all the quasi-legal tactics the lawyer offers, delaying the election is singled out in importance.

"Delay is crucial to your strategy . . . Delay in setting up a first conference. . . . Dig up issues on appropriate unit, supervisors, confidential employees, part-time workers. . . . Don't consent [to an election] until all issues are resolved. . . . Then delay hearings. . . . Delay briefs with excuses.

"Stall and delay wherever possible. When 30 percent of the employees have signed cards the union can file for an election. Can you stack the election? Yes — hire new people. Time is on the side of the employer."

With the legal ground rules of counterorganizing established the seminar leaders move on to the next topic — how to plan and conduct the campaign. They give you a sample calendar which outlines steps to be taken against the union including delay tactics such as questioning the bargaining unit size and filing objections to the election if the union should win. Essentially, the campaign involves letters and speeches to workers pitched at certain sensitive issues. These include strikes, alleged union violence, the company's economic position, the viability of nonunion firms in the same industry, the company's right to replace strikers, and the company's alleged right not to agree to union demands.

The lawyer tells you:

"Tell employees that, in your opinion, a union authorization card is just about as secret and confidential as a four party county telephone.

"Tell employees the union can't guarantee them anything. The union can't guarantee that in a contract they will have the same benefits they now have. No union and no law require your company to agree to anything it doesn't want to agree to.

"Tell employees if anyone causes you any trouble at your work or puts you under any pressure to join a union, please let me know and I will undertake to take every legal step to see that it is stopped.

"Tell employees if the union calls you out on an economic strike, the Company has the right to stop paying your insurance premiums."

Letters can be written to convey the same message. In fact, you receive a union-free communications package filled with pre-packaged letters to be sent out during a campaign.

Finally, you receive the following pre-packaged letter accusing the union of producing pre-packaged literature.

"It is always a laugh to read these union propaganda notes. They appear as if they are written by poor, browbeaten and overworked peons, whereas they probably are stereotyped, often-used letters in which only the names are changed, but the aim is the same — to create a breakdown in normally-good employee/employer relations within whatever company that is 'picked-to-parasite.'"

Yet the heart of the anti-union campaign like the non-union prevention program is the supervisor. Since there is little time once the campaign begins, you are advised to start early to slowly educate supervisors. The lawyer reminds you:

"The National Labor Relations Act has defined the term 'employee' to exclude any individual employed as a supervisor. Therefore, it is clear that a supervisor does not enjoy the same legal protections as does a regular employee. Here are the rules:

"1. A supervisor can be required AT THE PRICE OF HIS JOB not to engage in union activities.

"2. He can be required, AT THE PRICE OF HIS JOB, not to become a union member.

"3. A supervisor can be required, AT THE PRICE OF HIS JOB, to engage in lawful anti-union activity."

Once the supervisor is recruited you are advised to use his or her services on a daily basis.

"Do not send letters and notices by U.S. mail . . . have them personally hand carried by the supervisor to employees on work time at their work station."

The supervisors, you learn, should be forced to follow the letters with conversations with their subordinates. The object: On a daily basis workers should hear new arguments against the union. The supervisor then should report back to the campaign coordinator on an almost daily basis. This permits an on-going refinement of strategy and allows management to repeat those themes which have the greatest effect. . . .

Finally, I want to make this point. Anti-union consultants and seminar leaders don't stop here. If the workers overcome these obstacles, as they have in many places, they urge participants not to bargain with the union. "Bargain to the point of boredom," as one consultant puts it and then go right for a decertification effort.

On the third day of the seminar, the audience is much smaller in size. Many of the participants who face organizing drives have already left to begin their campaign. But those who remain want to learn about "de-unionizing," a process which cannot legally be instigated by the employer.

The meeting is held under tight security. No press is allowed. Company names are not used. Tape recorders are expressly prohibited.

Now, it is the psychologist who is absent. Only the lawyer remains. He begins.

"Gentlemen, good morning.

"My partner and I gave you the full scope of services. During the last two days we have given you an idea of how to keep the union out should they come knocking. Today we will be talking about what to do if your initial strategy fails and they should get in. This seminar is entitled 'The Process of Decertification.'"

He continues with a brief summary of recent trends.

"In 1963, when I worked for the NLRB, we got a decertification petition in our office. No one had ever heard of it. Last year there were 600 decertifications and this year there will be more than 1,000. What's happening? I don't know, but my job is to help the process of decertification along.

"Of course in practice it's difficult to turn around employees who have been in a union for a long time. But, it can be done. Careful preparation is needed of at least six to nine months."

As he continues, he hands out a brochure on strike insurance which he suggests may come in handy if you plan to bargain to impasse. In addition, he urges:

"Line up other employers who can handle your work and take care of your customers during the strike. Train supervisors way in advance to do the work of the bargaining unit. Find alternate means of transportation and extra security to ensure that everything goes smoothly.

"Once the groundwork is laid, notify the union that you will put into effect your last offer. Don't give a better wage package, give the same. At that point the union will take their people out on strike. It puts the ball back in the union camp. It's put up or shut up for them at that point. The strike situation represents fertile grounds for decertification. If there are 75 people in and 75 people still out and you have hired 75 replacements [. . .] you can count on the scabs to vote with you. You will probably win the decertification effort.

"You learn that bargaining to impasse is only one weapon in the decertification army.

"Refusal to bargain can be effective, but it is the Russian Roulette approach to de-unionizing. While refusal to bargain immediately puts the union on the defensive, the employer will most likely be found guilty of an unfair labor practice. Nevertheless, it is short and sweet, if you do it yourself the burden is on the union."

And the lawyer teaches you "gimmicks" on how to covertly encourage decertification petitions. He says:

"Of course, the all important question, whether for deauthorization or decertification campaigns, is how to encourage employees to begin the process. There is a gimmick. If the employee asks questions about decertification, it opens up a whole range of information you can supply. If you want an employee to ask you about the information, you can get that question out of him one way or another.

"There isn't a company in this room that can't get an informational request out of an employee. Sometimes, however, you have to create the proper atmosphere. Perhaps there are disgruntled employees or employees who have vocalized disdain for having to join the union in non-right to work states. Perhaps there are employees in right-to-work states who have refused to join the union. Go out and engage them in conversation. Ask them how the union is going. How they like it. How the contract is, etc. Train supervisors to generate such inquiries to provide information. If anyone knows the mood of employees, it is the supervisor.

"Once someone asks for information, you have virtual carte blanche to give them any form of information you please. You couch your opinions in the cloak of information. Tell employees, I have just spoken to my attorney, he has informed me that I cannot urge you to decertify the union, however, even if I wish you to do this, I could not inform you of that and if I wished you not to do it, I could not do that. However, I can tell you what your rights are to decertify the union. I can tell you what the law is. I can tell you why other unions have decertified.

"Example: an employer left decertification pamphlets in the ladies room . . . Three days later, a woman came and said, I noticed pamphlets about decertification in the ladies lounge, can you explain to me what it's all about. The employer asked, 'You mean what decertification is about?' She said, 'Yes,' and bingo, he had the whole 'carte blanche' wide open to him. That is a good example for you to follow."

You soon learn of several ways to carefully assist the decertification committee. The lawyer advises:

"You may want to get your decertification committee a list of names and addresses as soon as possible. Now, should you supply that list to them directly, that could be considered an unfair labor practice. However, the trick here is to wait to distribute the excelsior list the same way as you would wait before an election; however, the show of interest list of which the decertification committee will get a copy and the union will not get a copy due to the confidentiality clause in decertification, can be drawn up differently than it is for an RC election. Give an alphabetical list of names and addresses with home phones on it to the NLRB. Quite naively, give them all that information. That list will then be turned over to the decertification committee and can be very useful indeed. Or, mail that list anonymously to the decertification committee. It is basically a good thing for them to have.

"That various right-to-work committees around the country will be very helpful in counseling employees on how to decertify the union."

The lawyer then provides you with a list of about forty right-to-work committees. . . .

2. LAW FIRMS

The vehicle for the delivery of anti-union expertise is through lawyers and law firms.

While management law firms are nothing new, there is now a breed of management lawyers whose activities are at least questionable from the point of view of professional ethics if not the law as well. One such law firm is Jackson, Lewis, Schnitzler & Kruppman in New York City. Not only does this firm advise individual employers involved in union organizing drives, but an incorporated arm of the law firm also publishes a monthly report called "Preventive Labor Relations." The January, 1978 edition of "Preventive Labor Relations" contains such articles as "Restriction on Solicitation and Distribution," and "The Propriety of Discerning a Job Applicant's Union Sentiments." Subscribers to this report also receive a special offer for an anti-union campaign kit at bulk rates. The kits include preprinted election material, anti-union posters, vote "No" buttons, and other anti-union campaign gimmicks, such as a sample collective bargaining agreement containing nothing but blank pages. . . .

Maybe the Ethics Committees of state and local Bar Associations need to reread the sections on proper attorney conduct. The canons of conduct for lawyers provide "the office of an attorney does not permit, much less does it demand of him for any client, violation of law. . . ." Lawyers pledge that "I will not counsel or maintain any suit or proceeding which shall appear to me to be unjust."

Can the Bar Associations square these canons with advice to stall and delay, with advice to conduct preventive hiring of "psychologically profiled" employees; with advice to thwart elections through new hires; with advice to bargain to an impasse as the central strategy for destroying a union? . . .

3. INDUSTRIAL PSYCHOLOGISTS

The third vehicle through which anti-union expertise is traveling to employers is through industrial psychologists. The science of industrial psychology lies at the very heart of modern union-busting. Its basic objectives are to understand the emotional substratum of the workplace and to harness that understanding in the interest of profits. For the unscrupulous businessman it holds out the promise of a workforce silently manipulated into non-union status.

Since the early fifties, industrial psychologists have performed hundreds of tests to correlate worker attitudes (as measured by personality tests and attitude surveys) with their tendencies to join unions. A recent article by Chester A. Schresheim of the Kent State Graduate School of Business illustrates how this area of expertise can be used to thwart union organizing drives. Professor Schresheim held out the hope that his survey could become an employer early warning system periodically administered to nip union organizing in the bud. He said: ". . . [M]anagement should be concerned about employee sentiments well before a union enters the picture, since pro-union attitudes and job dissatisfaction probably take months (perhaps years) to develop . . . it seems important to stress that to avoid unionization organizations must seek to satisfy employee needs before they even begin to consider seeking union representation, particularly those dealing with economic job satisfaction factors."

The second study was performed by W. Clay Hammer of Duke University and Frank J. Smith of the Sears Roebuck Co. They sampled 87,740 workers. Their test seeks to determine union voting patterns strictly on the basis of attitude survey questions which never refer to unions or labor organizations. These psychologists wrote: "The present study takes advantage of a rare opportunity to examine the attitudes toward work of employees in 250 naturally occurring settings prior to any history of unionization activity. Subsequently, unionization attempts were made in 125 of these settings. A predictive model of unionization activity based on the attitudes of these employees toward work was derived and cross-validated to test our prediction."

Sparing the committee the statistical details, the authors found that such surveys could independently predict the intentions of workers to organize.

Another practitioner of psychological forecasting is Dr. Charles L. Hughes of the Center for Values Research in Dallas. Dr. Hughes also claims to be hard at work correlating worker attitude surveys with the probabilities of union organizing. The attached exhibits contain material from his book "Value Systems Analysis: Theory and Management Applications." As mentioned earlier, Dr. Hughes recommends the use of his attitude analysis as both a "preventive" labor relations technique and to aid in counter-organizing efforts.

An example of the use of these theories is Emery Air Freight which put its warehouse workers on a planned "reinforcement schedule."

The following is a description of Emery's secret antiunion strategy: "Each manager receives two elaborate programmed instruction workbooks prepared in-house and geared to the specific work situation at Emery. One deals with recognition and rewards, the other with feedback. Under recognition and rewards, the workbook enumerates no less than 150 kinds, ranging from a smile and a nod of encouragement, the 'Let my buy you a coffee,' to detailed praise for a job well done.

"In bestowing praise and recognition, Emery follows Skinner pretty closely. There is the same emphasis on reinforcing specific behavior; the same insistence that the behavior be reinforced as soon as possible after it has taken place; the same assertion that you reinforce frequently in the beginning to shape the desired behavior, but that as time goes on, maintaining the desired behavior requires progressively less frequent and unpredictable reinforcement. . . .

"At the gumdrop state, Feeney urges supervisors to supply praise and recognition at least twice a week during the early weeks or months of behavior shaping. It's impractical to require them to provide [enforcement] more frequently — they are too busy, they would forget, etc. Once the desired behavior has been established, managers have more discretion — the key point being the unpredictability of the reinforcement, not the frequency . . . But keep the employee guessing as to when or whether he's going to be praised or recognized." (Organizational Dynamics, 1973).

When questioned about the propriety of this system, an Emery official responded:

"Actually, the charge that you're manipulating people when you use positive reinforcement — I prefer myself to say that you're shaping their behavior — is a hollow one to start with. People in business manipulate their employees all the time — otherwise they would go bankrupt. The only questions are, how effective are you as a manipulator and what ends do you further with your manipulation?" (Ibid).

There are many further examples where psychological principles are being used to predict and alter the behavior of working people often without their knowledge. Whether the object is to prevent unions, counterorganize or merely bolster profit margins there can be no excuse for such hidden manipulations.

Of all the union-busting tactics we are experiencing today, none is more harmful to our American system of collective bargaining. The Wagner Act and all subsequent labor law clearly defends the democratic principle of trade unionism. The use of industrial psychology clearly threatens this principle by aiming management's campaign at unconscious emotions and attitudes. How can free elections occur when one side runs away from rational discourse and chooses to pitch its argument at proven vulnerabilities and fears? . . .

4. CONSULTING FIRMS

The fourth vehicle of antiunionism is the consulting firm itself. Today, the anti-union consultant remains the principle vehicle of union-busting in America. More than 1,000 of these so-called "labor management consultants" now make their presence felt in hundreds of NLRB elections every year.

There are the individuals who do the employer's dirty work. The consultant sets up shop in the company's personnel office or in a hotel near the workplace. Quietly, behind the scenes, the consultant directs the daily action of front-line supervisors. He prepares campaign literature, writes captive audience speeches and in some cases directly seeks to persuade workers to vote against the union. In every case the consultant creates insecurities and confusion. Workers are frightened, supervisors pressured and even top management cannot escape the daily rigors of fighting the union tooth and nail. The only differences among consultants are ones of subtlety and sophistication.

Some are as clumsy as a billy club with tactics that do not extend beyond firing union sympathizers, delaying elections and threatening employees. They work for small fly-by-night operations that gain new clients by waiting at the local NLRB office for representation petitions to be filed.

But for every such industrial ambulance-chaser there are a dozen consultants who hold advanced degrees in labor relations, or Ph.D's in psychology, or law degrees. They work for high budget operations with offices scattered across the country. Clients come almost solely through referrals from lawyers and trade associations. The price is often a hefty $100 per hour plus expenses. With upwards of 50 full-time consultants, some firms are grossing nearly $150,000 per week. . . .

Yet to really understand the impact of such a firm for workers at the workplace, you must study their conduct during a campaign. To give you this perspective I want to briefly discuss another consulting firm, Modern Management Methods, otherwise known as "MMM."

In 1971 former employees of John Sheridan and Associates founded Melnick, Milkus and McKeown, later renamed Modern Management Methods. MMM is located in Deerfield, Illinois, but with branch offices across the country it has been active in almost every state. Its clients are drawn from industries which employ high numbers of female employees, including hospitals, insurance companies, universities, banks and retail stores. The insurance client list includes Equitable, Aetna, Allstate, CNA, Prudential, Travelers and Massachusetts Mutual. Employing more than 50 full-time professionals the firm is active in more than 100 representation elections a year. Raymond F. Mickus, Executive Vice President of MMM, claims to have been personally involved in more than 1,000 union elections in his career. Yet despite such impressive training and experience the firm rarely leaves anything to chance, often assigning as many as seven full-time consultants to an organizing drive. According to the Wall Street Journal such measures pay off yielding the firm a 98-percent victory record. In fact, MMM reportedly offers prospective clients a fee reduction in the event their tactics are unsuccessful. They have been known to tell supervisors, "We never lose."

Like other consulting firms, MMM sends top officers on the lecture circuit in an effort to drum up business. Raymond Mickus is currently appearing at seminars sponsored by Professional Seminar Associates called "Avoiding Unions." The brochure for this seminar is in the exhibits. You will note that the seminar is a highly detailed outline of an anti-union strategy which includes everything from a laundry list of tactics to a discussion on "avoiding the feeling of personal guilt."

Yet the stock in trade of MMM's work is the day-to-day practice of counter-organizing. For example, following an election at St. Elizabeth's Hospital in Massachusetts, the NLRB issued 38 unfair labor practices complaints against the hospital including charges of threats, intimidation, interrogation, surveillance, suspension and discharges for union activity. The organizer in this campaign reported that by the last week of the campaign "the tension was so thick you could cut it with a knife." Many supervisors stayed at home altogether while others found themselves suffering from chronic headaches or repeatedly breaking down in tears after being interrogated by MMM. Workers were in turn grilled by their terrified supervisors. In some cases three-hour long meetings took place between six supervisors and one worker after which the worker broke down in tears and left for the day. In other cases, dismissals or job changes severely disrupted people's lives. High pitched emotional appeals were made to worker loyalty. All the time, the day-to-day work of a hospital went by the wayside. Patient care became secondary in the effort to derail organizing efforts.

We have seen dozens of MMM campaigns over the last few years. In every case, this insidious pattern of psychological terrorism has been repeated. This may sound extreme but let me take you step-by-step through a typical MMM campaign. I think it will show you just how this atmosphere is created and why it has a 98 percent success record behind it.

A petition requesting a union election is filed by 65 percent of all workers at State Hospital. That day this hospital administration calls the State Hospital Association and speaks with the labor director. He is told about a Chicago consulting firm, Modern Management Methods, which while high in price almost never loses. That same week the firm is retained under the following conditions: The firm is given full authority over hospital administration in conducting the campaign. An isolated room with two beds will be put aside for the consultants so that they can spend several days living in the hospital to observe all three shifts of workers. Four consultants will be employed during the life of the campaign at the rates of $60, $75, $85 and $100 dollars per hour. All expenses including hotel room and board at the city's most expensive hotel will be paid by the hospital.

After several weeks two developments begin to unfold. First every worker receives a job evaluation survey which they are told will be used to redesign job classifications. Simultaneously, supervisors are called to attend one-on-one meetings with the consultants to discuss the union attitudes of the workers in their shop.

As it turns out the surveys they use were first distributed by the

Association of Industrial Management (AAIM) in the fifties. The present test was designed to be graded on an eleven point scale measuring job attitudes and responsibilities. It was published with other AAIM material designed to maintain non-union status.

The initial one-on-one meetings cover every supervisor in the hospital and last for several hours. Such meetings are an MMM trademark. After several minutes, supervisors are told that the administration has hired a consulting firm to teach them about labor law since the hospital is in the business of health care and does not understand very much about unions. The consultant then asks questions of the supervisor, her family, her friends and finally her work. Eventually, the consultant goes down a list of workers in her department asking about their job, performance and probable attitude towards the union. As she responds the consultant takes copious notes. Once this process is completed the supervisor is invited to a group meeting with other supervisors to discuss principles of labor law.

Over the course of the next two weeks every supervisor goes through such a one-on-one meeting. After that, labor education meetings with supervisors are held every week. The consultants continue their friendly overtures to supervisors and they gradually become publicly anti-union in conversations with supervisors. On a few occasions supervisors are given literature to hand out to workers and are asked to discuss the union with each of them. The supervisors are then asked to report back one-on-one with a consultant about what was said.

Simultaneously, the hospital has filed objections to the union's proposed unit and appeals every decision until the case goes to the NLRB in Washington. The election is delayed for months. During that time supervisors continue to work with the consultants handing out literature and reporting on what is said. All the time most workers do not know MMM has been hired.

When the election date is finally announced the consultants pick up the pace of the campaign. Meetings with supervisors are held more frequently. They are asked to report on union activities of workers, to interrogate them about their views and push hard for an anti-union answer. Some are even asked to start rumors about the union while still others are required to reassign union leaders to isolated work areas.

Several supervisors object, protesting that the consultant's request will destroy long standing friendships with their subordinates. In response they are threatened with dismissal if their unit is not clearly anti-union by election time. All the time many workers still do not know that a consulting firm is operating.

In the last two weeks company literature and rumors start personally attacking workers. Several firings and job reassignments have taken place. In addition, more company literature is going home. Every worker personally meets directly with a management representative, in some cases two to six representatives, in closed door meetings of up to three hours.

Before the election, the desired effect has been achieved. An atmosphere of tension exists which is associated not with the consultants, who in many cases still clandestinely operate, but with the union. The final result is a management victory. Even after charges are brought and a new election is scheduled, the atmosphere at the workplace has been so poisoned that the union may well lose the second election.

5. TRADE ASSOCIATIONS

The fifth delivery system for antiunion expertise is through the trade associations. Today, the art of union-busting is moving to a higher and more sophisticated plan in the growth of the antiunion trade association. Over the last ten years the chief executive officers in several sectors of the economy have chosen to pool information and resources in an effort to de-unionize their industries. They have hired consultants and lawyers to analyze the unique properties of their specific industries. Then based on their reports, principal firms have achieved consensus on appropriate action. Today in the printing industry we are witnessing the handiwork of the Master Printers Association which spearheaded the elimination of unionized printers across the country.

In the construction industry, we have witnessed a conscious effort to build a major nonunion trade association — the Associated Builders and Contractors. We have seen the major construction users divert their jobs from union to nonunion contractors. We have also watched them encourage union contractors to establish nonunion subsidiaries, an operation known as double breasting.

One of the best examples of anti-unionism by a trade association is the Master Printers of America ("MPA"). At the end of World War II the MPA was an inconsequential trade association. Today it represents two-thirds of the industry. This shift has been accomplished by assisting the deunionization of unionized printers through many methods including specialized "de-unionizing" seminars for their members. For example, on December 1, 1977, the MPA held a decertification seminar at the Chicago Ramada-O'Hare Motel. Sixty printing industry executives from around the country came to learn how to rid themselves of unions. The seminar was led by John Doesburg, General Counsel of the MPA and Francis Coleman, then Assistant General Counsel who has since replaced the retired Doesburg. Both men are retained by the MPA and available to printing industry executives who face union organizing efforts or who seek to rid themselves of an existing union. On this day, they were proselytizing for the MPA's open shop philosophy explaining to executives that it is possible to rid themselves of their union.

The seminar leaders suggested that six to nine months of planning would be required to schedule the movement of machinery and work to other locations. Participants learned that the Master Printers' strike insurance program could be used to weather a strike. They were told to find other nonunion printers to handle their work while the strike was underway. It was also recommended that they withdraw from any multiemployer bargaining group. Finally, they counseled the establishment of "lines of communications" with anti-union employees.

Once these preparations were complete the employers were told to "bargain to impasse" and force the union out on strike. At this point the decertification effort may be initiated by either the anti-union employees or during the strike itself. The seminar leaders then recommended a series of psychological tactics to break the strike including moving finished work out in the full view of the strikers to lower morale and reminding workers that once the contract expires replacements can vote in the decertification election.

Francis Coleman, now General Counsel of the MPA, also suggests a somewhat more subtle approach to deunionizing which can be used beyond the printing industry. He outlines the process of establishing satellite operations or what is more commonly called double-breasted operations. Here he outlines a simple set of steps to establish the legal requirements for independent ownership. At that point a firm can simply transfer operations to its nonunion satellite permitting the union operation to slowly wither away.

Needless to say working through the MPA, printers can tap the union-busting advice of experts such as Coleman and Doesburg. To help this process along the MPA has developed an antiunion kit called the "Stay Free" package. It is a four-inch thick box containing preliminary materials for union-busting efforts, including strike insurance offers, pre-written campaign literature and speeches, listings of upcoming decertification and labor relations seminars, a pamphlet to be given to workers to encourage anti-union activities and awards including the freedom fighter award which is given to workers who do the most to preserve freedom from unions. The criteria include leading decertification drives, deauthorization efforts or massive resignations from the union. . . .

B. THE EXCLUSIVITY PRINCIPLE

Before exploring problems raised when unions attempt to secure bargaining rights, we will examine the stakes for which this game is played — the principle of exclusivity.[1]

[1] See Schatzki, Majority Rule, Exclusive Representation and the Interests of Individual Workers: Should Exclusivity be Abolished?, 123 U. Pa. L. Rev. 897 (1975); Weyand, Majority Rule in Collective Bargaining, 45 Colum. L. Rev. 556 (1945). For a comparative law discussion, see Bok, Reflections on the Distinctive Character of American Labor Laws, 84 Harv. L. Rev. 1394 (1971).

In the spring of 1937 the Supreme Court sustained the constitutionality of both the Railway Labor Act (regulating labor relations in the railway industry) and the National Labor Relations Act. One challenge to the Acts' constitutionality argued that Congress intended to make unlawful employers' bargaining with individual employees, or minority groups, on the employees' own behalf once a union was designated as their bargaining representative. The legislative history tended to show that Congress had precisely that effect in mind, and Supreme Court precedent suggested it was unconstitutional. The constitutionality of the Railway Labor Act was upheld in Virginian Ry. v. System Fedn., 300 U.S. 515 (1937), in which the Court disposed of the argument as follows:

> [The Railway Labor Act] imposes the affirmative duty to treat only with the true representative [of the employees], and hence the negative duty to treat with no other. We think, as the Government concedes in its brief, that the injunction against [the railroad's] entering into any contract concerning rules, rates of pay and working conditions, except with [the respondent union] is designed only to prevent collective bargaining with anyone purporting to represent employees, other than [the respondent union], who has been ascertained to be their true representative. When read in its context it must be taken to prohibit the negotiation of labor contracts, generally applicable to employees in the mechanical department, with any representative other than respondent, but not precluding such individual contracts as [the railroad] may elect to make directly with individual employees.[2]

Two weeks later, in NLRB v. Jones & Laughlin Steel Corp., 301 U.S. 1 (1937), the Court quoted from this passage in making the same construction of the representation provision (§9) of the National Labor Relations Act.

J. I. CASE CO. v. NLRB

321 U.S. 332 (1944)

Jackson, J. . . .

The petitioner, J. I. Case Company, at its Rock Island, Illinois, plant, from 1937 offered each employee an individual contract of employment. The contracts were uniform and for a term of one year. The Company agreed to furnish employment as steadily as conditions permitted, to pay a specified rate, which the Company might redetermine if the job changed, and to maintain certain hospital facilities. The employee agreed to accept the provisions, to serve faithfully and honestly for the term, to comply with factory rules, and that defective work

[2] 300 U.S. at 548-549.

should not be paid for. About 75 percent of the employees accepted and worked under these agreements.

. . . [T]he execution of the contracts was not a condition of employment, nor was the status of individual employees affected by reason of signing or failing to sign the contracts. It is not found or contended that the agreements were coerced, obtained by any unfair labor practice, or that they were not valid under the circumstances in which they were made.

While the individual contracts executed August 1, 1941 were in effect, a C.I.O. union petitioned the [National Labor Relations] Board for certification as the exclusive bargaining representative of the production and maintenance employees. On December 17, 1941 a hearing was held, at which the Company urged the individual contracts as a bar to representation proceedings. The Board, however, directed an election, which was won by the union. The union was thereupon certified as the exclusive bargaining representative of the employees in question in respect to wages, hours, and other conditions of employment.

The union then asked the Company to bargain. It refused, declaring that it could not deal with the union in any manner affecting rights and obligations under the individual contracts while they remained in effect. It offered to negotiate on matters which did not affect rights under the individual contracts, and said that upon the expiration of the contracts it would bargain as to all matters. Twice the Company sent circulars to its employees asserting the validity of the individual contracts and stating the position that it took before the Board in reference to them.

The Board held that the Company had refused to bargain collectively, in violation of [§8(a)(5)] of the National Labor Relations Act; and that the contracts had been utilized, by means of the circulars, to impede employees in the exercise of rights guaranteed by §7 of the Act, with the result that the Company had engaged in unfair labor practices within the meaning of [§8(a)(1)] of the Act. It ordered the Company to cease and desist from giving effect to the contracts, from extending them or entering into new ones, from refusing to bargain and from interfering with the employees; and it required the Company to give notice accordingly and to bargain upon request. . . .

Contract in labor law is a term the implications of which must be determined from the connection in which it appears. Collective bargaining between employer and the representatives of a unit, usually a union, results in an accord as to terms which will govern hiring and work and pay in that unit. The result is not, however, a contract of employment except in rare cases; no one has a job by reason of it and no obligation to any individual ordinarily comes into existence from it alone. The negotiations between union and management result in what often has been called a trade agreement, rather than in a contract of employment. Without pushing the analogy too far, the agreement may be likened to the tariffs established by a carrier, to standard provisions prescribed by supervising authorities for insurance policies, or to utility schedules of rates and rules for service, which do not of themselves establish any relationships but which do govern the terms of the shipper or insurer or customer relationship whenever and with whomever it may be established. Indeed, in some European countries, contrary to American practice, the terms of a collectively negotiated trade agreement are submitted to a government department and if approved become a governmental regulation ruling employment in the unit.

After the collective trade agreement is made, the individuals who shall benefit by it are identified by individual hirings. The employer, except as restricted by the collective agreement itself and except that he must engage in no unfair labor practice or discrimination, is free to select those he will employ or discharge. But the terms of the employment already have been traded out. There is little left to individual agreement except the act of hiring. This hiring may be by writing or by word of mouth or may be implied from conduct. In the sense of contracts of hiring, individual contracts between the employer and employee are not forbidden, but indeed are necessitated by the collective bargaining procedure.

But, however engaged, an employee becomes entitled by virtue of the Labor Relations Act somewhat as a third party beneficiary to all benefits of the collective trade agreement, even if on his own he would yield to less favorable terms. The individual hiring contract is subsidiary to the terms of the trade agreement and may not waive any of its benefits, any more than a shipper can contract away the benefit of filed tariffs, the insurer the benefit of standard provisions, or the utility customer the benefit of legally established rates.

Concurrent existence of these two types of agreement raises problems as to which the National Labor Relations Act makes no express provision. We have, however, held that individual contracts obtained as the result of an unfair labor practice may not be the basis of advantage to the violator of the Act nor of disadvantage to employees. National Licorice Co. v. National Labor Relations Board, 309 U.S. 350. But it is urged that where, as here, the contracts were not unfairly or unlawfully obtained, the court indicated a contrary rule in National Labor Relations Board v. Jones & Laughlin Steel Corp., 301 U.S. 1, 44, 45, and Virginian Ry. Co. v. System Federation, 300 U.S. 515. Without reviewing those cases in detail, it may be said that their decisions called for nothing and their opinions contain nothing which may be properly read to rule the case before us. The court in those cases recognized the existence of some scope for individual contracts, but it did not undertake to define it or to consider the relations between lawful individual and collective agreements, which is the problem now before us.

Care has been taken in the opinions of the Court to reserve a field for the individual contract, even in industries covered by the National Labor Relations Act, not merely as an act or evidence of hiring, but also in the sense of a completely individually bargained contract setting out terms of employment, because there are circumstances in which it may legally be used, in fact, in which there is no alternative. Without limiting the possibilities, instances such as the following will occur: Men may continue work after a collective agreement expires and, despite negotiation in good faith, the negotiation may be deadlocked or delayed; in the interim express or implied individual agreements may be held to govern. The conditions for collective bargaining may not exist; thus a majority of the employees may refuse to join a union or to agree upon or designate bargaining representatives, or the majority may not be demonstrable by the means prescribed by the statute, or a previously existent majority may have been lost without unlawful interference by the employer and no new majority have been formed. As the employer in these circumstances may be under no legal obligation to bargain collectively, he may be free to enter into individual contracts.

Individual contracts, no matter what the circumstances that justify their execution or what their terms, may not be availed of to defeat or delay the procedures prescribed by the National Labor Relations Act looking to collective bargaining, nor to exclude the contracting employee from a duly ascertained bargaining unit; nor may they be used to forestall bargaining or to limit or condition the terms of the collective agreement. "The Board asserts a public right vested in it as a public body, charged in the public interest with the duty of preventing unfair labor practices." National Licorice Co. v. National Labor Relations Board, 309 U.S. 350, 364. Wherever private contracts conflict with its functions, they obviously must yield or the Act would be reduced to a futility.

It is equally clear since the collective trade agreement is to serve the purpose contemplated by the Act, the individual contract cannot be effective as a waiver of any benefit to which the employee otherwise would be entitled under the trade agreement. The very purpose of providing by statute for the collective agreement is to supersede the terms of separate agreements of employees with terms which reflect the strength and bargaining power and serve the welfare of the group. Its benefits and advantages are open to every employee of the represented unit, whatever the type or terms of his pre-existing contract of employment.

But it is urged that some employees may lose by the collective agreement, that an individual workman may sometimes have, or be capable of getting, better terms than those obtainable by the group and that his freedom of contract must be respected on that account. We are not called upon to say that under no circumstances can an individual enforce an agreement more advantageous than a collective agreement, but we find the mere possibility that such agreements might be made no ground for holding generally that individual contracts may survive or surmount collective ones. The practice and philosophy of collective bargaining looks with suspicion on such individual advantages. Of course, where there is great variation in circumstances of employment or capacity of employees, it is possible for the collective bargain to prescribe only minimum rates or maximum hours or expressly to leave certain areas open to individual bargaining. But except as so provided, advantages to individuals may prove as disruptive of industrial peace as disadvantages. They are a fruitful way of interfering with organization and choice of representatives; increased compensation, if individually deserved, is often earned at the cost of breaking down some other standard thought to be for the welfare of the group, and always creates the suspicion of being paid at the long-range expense of the group as a whole. Such discriminations not infrequently amount to unfair labor practices. The workman is free, if he values his own bargaining position more than that of the group, to vote against representation; but the majority rules, and if it collectivizes the employment bargain, individual advantages or favors will generally in practice go in as a contribution to the collective result. We cannot except individual contracts generally from the operation of collective ones because some may be more individually advantageous. Individual contracts cannot subtract from collective ones, and whether under some circumstances they might add to them in matters covered by the collective bargain, we leave to be determined by appropriate forums under the laws of contracts applicable, and to the Labor Board if they constitute unfair labor practices.

It also is urged that such individual contracts may embody matters that are not necessarily included within the statutory scope of collective bargaining, such as stock purchase, group insurance, hospitalization, or medical attention. We know of nothing to prevent the employee's, because he is an employee, making any contract provided it is not inconsistent with a collective agreement or does not amount to or result from or is not part of an unfair labor practice. But in so doing the employer may not incidentally exact or obtain any diminution of his own obligation or any increase of those of employees in the matters covered by collective agreement. Hence we find that the contentions of the Company that the individual contracts precluded a choice of representatives and warranted refusal to bargain during their duration were properly overruled. It follows that representation to the employees by circular letter that they had such legal effect was improper and could properly be prohibited by the Board. . . .

Affirmed.[3]

[3] Roberts, J., dissented.

Notes

1. John Elway is a very highly paid professional football player. A union is the exclusive representative for all the players in the league. Suppose the union decides that it is unfair for backfield stars like Elway to earn hundreds of thousands of dollars per year while linemen earn far less. Better, the union decides, that all players who make a league team should be paid the same — say, $75,000 per year. The union announces to the players that it shall seek such a compensation scheme during the next round of negotiations. Does an upset Elway have to go along with this plan? What are the alternative positions the owners could take?

What are the normative implications of the union's choice? Is the union's proposal understandable in a price theory model of labor markets? Would it also fit within the relational contract or collective goods model?

2. Suppose the union representing the company's employees is disappointed with economic concessions offered by the employer in collective bargaining. It calls the employees out on strike. The company president seeks out striking employees on the picket line, and wherever else he runs into them, and urges them to return to work at existing wage rates while he continues to bargain with the union.

Should the company be found to have violated the Act by bypassing the union? Samuel Bingham's Son Mfg. Co., 80 N.L.R.B. 1612 (1948), suggests the Board would find a violation.

EMPORIUM CAPWELL CO. v. WESTERN ADDITION COMMUNITY ORGANIZATION[4]

420 U.S. 50 (1975)

MARSHALL, J.

This litigation presents the question whether, in light of the national policy against racial discrimination in employment, the National Labor Relations Act protects concerted activity by a group of minority employees to bargain with their employer over issues of employment discrimination. The National Labor Relations Board held that the employees could not circumvent their elected representative to engage in such bargaining. The Court of Appeals for the District of Columbia Circuit reversed and remanded, holding that in certain circumstances the activity would be protected. We now reverse.

[4] See Cantor, Dissident Worker Action, After *The Emporium,* 20 Rutgers L. Rev. 35 (1975).

I

The Emporium Capwell Co. (Company) operates a department store in San Francisco. At all times relevant to this litigation it was a party to the collective-bargaining agreement negotiated by the San Francisco Retailer's Council, of which it was a member, and the Department Store Employees Union (Union) which represented all stock and marketing area employees of the Company. The agreement, in which the Union was recognized as the sole collective-bargaining agency for all covered employees, prohibited employment discrimination by reason of race, color, creed, national origin, age, or sex, as well as union activity. It had a no-strike or lockout clause, and it established grievance and arbitration machinery for processing any claimed violation of the contract, including a violation of the antidiscrimination clause.

On April 3, 1968, a group of Company employees covered by the agreement met with the secretary-treasurer of the Union, Walter Johnson, to present a list of grievances including a claim that the Company was discriminating on the basis of race in making assignments and promotions. The Union official agreed to take certain of the grievances and to investigate the charge of racial discrimination. He appointed an investigating committee and prepared a report on the employees' grievances, which he submitted to the Retailers Council and which the Council in turn referred to the Company. The report described "the possibility of racial discrimination" as perhaps the most important issue raised by the employees and termed the situation at the Company as potentially explosive if corrective action were not taken. It offered as an example of the problem the Company's failure to promote a Negro stock employee regarded by other employees as an outstanding candidate but a victim of racial discrimination.

Shortly after receiving the report, the Company's labor relations director met with Union representatives and agreed to "look into the matter" of discrimination and see what needed to be done. Apparently unsatisfied with these representations, the Union held a meeting in September attended by Union officials, Company employees, and representatives of the California Fair Employment Practices Committee (FEPC) and the local antipoverty agency. The secretary-treasurer of the Union announced that the Union had concluded that the Company was discriminating, and that it would process every such grievance through to arbitration if necessary. Testimony about the Company's practices was taken and transcribed by a court reporter, and the next day the Union notified the Company of its formal charge and demanded that the joint union-management Adjustment Board be convened "to hear the entire case."

At the September meeting some of the Company's employees had expressed their view that the contract procedures were inadequate to handle a systemic grievance of this sort; they suggested that the Union instead begin picketing the store in protest. Johnson explained that the collective agreement bound the Union to its processes and expressed his view that successful grievants would be helping not only themselves but all others who might be the victims of invidious discrimination as well. The FEPC and antipoverty agency representatives offered the same advice. Nonetheless, when the Adjustment Board meeting convened on October 16, James Joseph Hollins, Tom Hawkins, and two other employees whose testimony the Union had intended to elicit refused to participate in the grievance procedure. Instead, Hollins read a statement objecting to reliance on correction of individual inequities as an approach to the problem of discrimination at the store and demanding that the president of the Company meet with the four protestants to work out a broader agreement for dealing with the issue as they saw it. The four employees then walked out of the hearing.

Hollins attempted to discuss the question of racial discrimination with the Company president shortly after the incidents of October 16. The president refused to be drawn into such a discussion but suggested to Hollins that he see the personnel director about the matter. Hollins, who had spoken to the personnel director before, made no effort to do so again. Rather, he and Hawkins and several other dissident employees held a press conference on October 22 at which they denounced the store's employment policy as racist, reiterated their desire to deal directly with "the top management" of the Company over minority employment conditions, and announced their intention to picket and institute a boycott of the store. On Saturday, November 2, Hollins, Hawkins, and at least two other employees picketed the store throughout the day and distributed at the entrance handbills urging consumers not to patronize the store.[2] Johnson encountered the picketing employ-

2. The full text of the handbill read:

*** * BEWARE * * * * BEWARE * * * * BEWARE * ***
EMPORIUM SHOPPERS
"Boycott Is On" "Boycott Is On" "Boycott Is On"

For years at The Emporium black, brown, yellow and red people have worked at the lowest jobs, at the lowest levels. Time and time again we have seen intelligent, hard working brothers and sisters denied promotions and respect.

The Emporium is a 20th Century colonial plantation. The brothers and sisters are being treated the same way as our brothers are being treated in the slave mines of Africa.

Whenever the racist pig at The Emporium injures or harms a black sister or brother, they injure and insult all black people. THE EMPORIUM MUST PAY FOR THESE INSULTS. Therefore, we encourage all of our people to take their money out of this racist store, until black people have full employment and are promoted justly throughout The Emporium.

We welcome the support of our brothers and sisters from the churches, unions, sororities, fraternities, social clubs, Afro-American Institute, Black Panther Party, W.A.C.O. and the Poor Peoples Institute.

ees, again urged them to rely on the grievance process, and warned that they might be fired for their activities. The pickets, however, were not dissuaded, and they continued to press their demand to deal directly with the Company president.

On November 7, Hollins and Hawkins were given written warnings that a repetition of the picketing or public statements about the Company could lead to their discharge. When the conduct was repeated the following Saturday, the two employees were fired.

Western Addition Community Organization (hereinafter respondent), a local civil rights association of which Hollins and Hawkins were members, filed a charge against the Company with the National Labor Relations Board. The Board's General Counsel subsequently issued a complaint alleging that in discharging the two the Company had violated §8(a)(1) of the National Labor Relations Act. After a hearing, the NLRB Trial Examiner found that the discharged employees had believed in good faith that the Company was discriminating against minority employees, and that they had resorted to concerted activity on the basis of that belief. He concluded, however, that their activity was not protected by §7 of the Act and that their discharges did not, therefore, violate §8(a)(1).

The Board, after oral argument, adopted the findings and conclusions of its Trial Examiner and dismissed the complaint. Among the findings adopted by the Board was that the discharged employees' course of conduct "was no mere presentation of a grievance but nothing short of a demand that the [Company] bargain with the picketing employees for the entire group of minority employees."

The Board concluded that protection of such an attempt to bargain would undermine the statutory system of bargaining through an exclusive, elected representative, impede elected unions' efforts at bettering the working conditions of minority employees, "and place on the Employer an unreasonable burden of attempting to placate self-designated representatives of minority groups while abiding by the terms of a valid bargaining agreement and attempting in good faith to meet whatever demands the bargaining representative put forth under that agreement."[6]

6. The Board considered but stopped short of resolving the question of whether the employees' invective and call for a boycott of the Company bespoke so malicious an attempt to harm their employer as to deprive them of the protection of the Act. The Board decision is therefore grounded squarely on the view that a minority group member may not bypass the Union and bargain directly over matters affecting minority employees, and not at all on the tactics used in this particular attempt to obtain such bargaining.

Member Jenkins dissented on the ground that the employees' activity was protected by §7 because it concerned the terms and conditions of their employment. Member Brown agreed but expressly relied upon his view that the facts revealed no attempt to bargain "but simply to urge [the Company] to take action to correct conditions of racial discrimination which the employees reasonably believed existed at the Emporium." 192 N.L.R.B., at 179.

On respondent's petition for review the Court of Appeals reversed and remanded. The court was of the view that concerted activity directed against racial discrimination enjoys a "unique status" by virtue of the national labor policy against discrimination, as expressed in both the NLRA and in Title VII of the Civil Rights Act of 1964, 42 U.S.C. §2000e et seq., and that the Board had not adequately taken account of the necessity to accommodate the exclusive bargaining principle of the NLRA to the national policy of protecting action taken in opposition to discrimination from employer retaliation. The court recognized that protection of the minority-group concerted activity involved in this case would interfere to some extent with the orderly collective-bargaining process, but it considered the disruptive effect on that process to be outweighed where protection of minority activity is necessary to full and immediate realization of the policy against discrimination. In formulating a standard for distinguishing between protected and unprotected activity, the majority held that the "Board should inquire, in cases such as this, whether the union was actually remedying the discrimination to the *fullest extent possible, by the most expedient and efficacious means.* Where union's efforts fall short of this high standard, the minority group's concerted activities cannot lose its section 7 protection." Accordingly, the court remanded the case for the Board to make this determination and, if it found in favor of the employees, to consider whether their particular tactics were so disloyal to their employer as to deprive them of §7 protection under our decision in NLRB v. Electrical Workers, 346 U.S. 464 (1953).

II

Before turning to the central questions of labor policy raised by these cases, it is important to have firmly in mind the character of the underlying conduct to which we apply them. As stated, the Trial Examiner and the Board found that the employees were discharged for attempting to bargain with the company over the terms and conditions of employment as they affected racial minorities. Although the Court of Appeals expressly declined to set aside this finding, respondent has devoted considerable effort to attacking it in this Court, on the theory that the employees were attempting only to present a grievance to their employer within the meaning of the first proviso to §9(a).[12] We see no

12. That proviso states: "That any individual employee or a group of employees shall have the right at any time to present grievances to their employer and to have such grievances adjusted, without the intervention of the bargaining representative, as long as the adjustment is not inconsistent with the terms of a collective-bargaining contract or agreement then in effect. . . ."

Respondent clearly misapprehends the nature of the "right" conferred by this section. The intendment of the proviso is to permit employees to present grievances and to authorize the employer to entertain them without opening itself to liability for dealing directly

occasion to disturb the finding of the Board. Universal Camera Corp. v. NLRB, 340 U.S. 474, 491 (1951). The issue, then, is whether such attempts to engage in separate bargaining are protected by §7 of the Act or proscribed by §9(a).

A

Section 7 affirmatively guarantees employees the most basic rights of industrial self-determination, "the right to self-organization, to form, join, or assist labor organizations, to bargain collectively through representatives of their own choosing, and to engage in other concerted activities for the purpose of collective bargaining or other mutual aid or protection," as well as the right to refrain from these activities. These are, for the most part, collective rights, rights to act in concert with one's fellow employees; they are protected not for their own sake but as an instrument of the national labor policy of minimizing industrial strife "by encouraging the practice and procedure of collective bargaining." 29 U.S.C. §151.

Central to the policy of fostering collective bargaining, where the employees elect that course, is the principle of majority rule. See NLRB v. Jones & Laughlin Steel Corp., 301 U.S. 1 (1937). If the majority of a unit chooses union representation, the NLRA permits it to bargain with its employer to make union membership a condition of employment, thereby imposing its choice upon the minority. 29 U.S.C. §§157, 158(a)(3). In establishing a regime of majority rule, Congress sought to secure to all members of the unit the benefits of their collective strength and bargaining power, in full awareness that the superior strength of some individuals or groups might be subordinated to the interest of the majority. As a result, "[t]he complete satisfaction of all who are represented is hardly to be expected." Ford Motor Co. v. Huffman, 345 U.S. 330, 338 (1953).

In vesting the representatives of the majority with this broad power Congress did not, of course, authorize a tyranny of the majority over minority interests. First, it confined the exercise of these powers to the context of a "unit appropriate for the purposes of collective bargaining,"

---

with employees in derogation of the duty to bargain only with the exclusive bargaining representative, a violation of §8(a)(5). H. R. Rep. No. 245, 80th Cong., 1st Sess., 7 (1947); H. R. Conf. Rep. No. 510, 80th Cong., 1st Sess. (House managers' statement), 46 (1947). The Act nowhere protects this "right" by making it an unfair labor practice for an employer to refuse to entertain such a presentation, nor can it be read to authorize resort to economic coercion. This matter is fully explicated in Black-Clawson Co. v. Machinists, 313 F.2d 179 (C.A.2, 1962). See also Republic Steel v. Maddox, 379 U.S. 650 (1965). If the employees' activity in the present litigation is to be deemed protected, therefore, it must be so by reason of the reading given to the main part of §9(a), in light of Title VII and the national policy against employment discrimination, and not by burdening the proviso to that section with a load it was not meant to carry.

i.e., a group of employees with a sufficient commonality of circumstances to ensure against the submergence of a minority with distinctively different interests in the terms and conditions of their employment. Second, it undertook in the 1959 Landrum-Griffin amendments to assure that minority voices are heard as they are in the functioning of a democratic institution. Third, we have held, by the very nature of the exclusive bargaining representative's status as representative of *all* unit employees, Congress implicitly imposed upon it a duty fairly and in good faith to represent the interests of minorities within the unit. Vaca v. Sipes, [386 U.S. 171 (1967)]; Wallace Corp. v. NLRB, 323 U.S. 248 (1944); cf. Steele v. Louisville & N.R. Co., 323 U.S. 192 (1944). And the Board has taken the position that a union's refusal to process grievances against racial discrimination, in violation of that duty, is an unfair labor practice. Hughes Tool Co., 147 N.L.R.B. 1573 (1964); see Miranda Fuel Co., 140 N.L.R.B. 181 (1962), enforcement denied, 362 F.2d 172 (C.A.2 1963). Indeed, the Board has ordered a union implicated by a collective-bargaining agreement in discrimination with an employer to propose specific contractual provisions to prohibit racial discrimination. See Local Union No. 12, United Rubber Workers of America v. NLRB, 368 F.2d 12 (C.A.5 1966) (enforcement granted).

B

Against this background of long and consistent adherence to the principle of exclusive representation tempered by safeguards for the protection of minority interests, respondent urges this Court to fashion a limited exception to that principle: employees who seek to bargain separately with their employer as to the elimination of racially discriminatory employment practices peculiarly affecting them, should be free from the constraints of the exclusivity principle of §9(a). Essentially because established procedures under Title VII or, as in this case, a grievance machinery, are too time consuming, the national labor policy against discrimination requires this exception, respondent argues, and its adoption would not unduly compromise the legitimate interests of either unions or employers.

Plainly, national labor policy embodies the principles of nondiscrimination as a matter of highest priority, and it is a commonplace that we must construe the NLRA in light of the broad national labor policy of which it is a part. These general principles do not aid respondent, however, as it is far from clear that separate bargaining is necessary to help eliminate discrimination. Indeed, as the facts of this litigation demonstrate, the proposed remedy might have just the opposite effect. The collective-bargaining agreement involved here prohibited without qualification all manner of invidious discrimination and made any claimed violation a grievable issue. The grievance procedure is directed precisely at determining whether discrimination has occurred. That orderly determination, if affirmative, could lead to an arbitral award enforceable in court. Nor is there any reason to believe that the processing of grievances is inherently limited to the correction of individual cases of discrimination. Quite apart from the essentially contractual question of whether the Union could grieve against a "pattern or practice" it deems inconsistent with the nondiscrimination clause of the contract, one would hardly expect an employer to continue in effect an employment practice that routinely results in adverse arbitral decisions.

The decision by a handful of employees to bypass the grievance procedure in favor of attempting to bargain with their employer, by contrast, may or may not be predicated upon the actual existence of discrimination. An employer confronted with bargaining demands from each of several minority groups would not necessarily, or even probably, be able to agree to remedial steps satisfactory to all at once. Competing claims on the employer's ability to accommodate each group's demands, e.g., for reassignments and promotions to a limited number of positions, could only set one group against the other even if it is not the employer's intention to divide and overcome them. Having divided themselves, the minority employees will not be in position to advance their cause unless it be by recourse seriatim to economic coercion, which can only have the effect of further dividing them along racial or other lines. Nor is the situation materially different where, as apparently happened here, self-designated representatives purport to speak for all groups that might consider themselves to be victims of discrimination. Even if in actual bargaining the various groups did not perceive their interests as divergent and further subdivide themselves, the employer would be bound to bargain with them in a field largely pre-empted by the current collective-bargaining agreement with the elected bargaining representative. In this instance we do not know precisely what form the demands advanced by Hollins, Hawkins, et al. would take, but the nature of the grievance that motivated them indicates that the demands would have included the transfer of some minority employees to sales areas in which higher commissions were paid. Yet the collective-bargaining agreement provided that no employee would be transferred from a higher-paying to a lower-paying classification except by consent or in the course of a layoff or reduction in force. The potential for conflict between the minority and other employees in this situation is manifest. With each group able to enforce its conflicting demands—the incumbent employees by resort to contractual processes and the minority employees by economic coercion — the probability of strife and deadlock is high; the likelihood of making headway against discriminatory practices would be minimal.

What has been said here in evaluating respondent's claim that the policy against discrimination requires §7 protection for concerted efforts at minority bargaining has obvious implications for the related claim that legitimate employer and union interests would not be unduly compromised thereby. The court below minimized the impact on the Union in this case by noting that it was not working at cross-purposes with the dissidents, and that indeed it could not do so consistent with its duty of fair representation and perhaps its obligations under Title VII. As to the Company, its obligations under Title VII are cited for the proposition that it could have no legitimate objection to bargaining with the dissidents in order to achieve full compliance with that law.

This argument confuses the employees' substantive right to be free of racial discrimination with the procedures available under the NLRA for securing these rights. Whether they are thought to be dependent upon Title VII or have an independent source in the NLRA, they cannot be pursued at the expense of the orderly collective-bargaining process contemplated by the NLRA. The elimination of discrimination and its vestiges is an appropriate subject of bargaining, and an employer may have no objection to incorporating into a collective agreement the substance of his obligation not to discriminate in personnel decisions; the Company here has done as much, making any claimed dereliction a matter subject to the grievance-arbitration machinery as well as to the processes of Title VII. But that does not mean that an employer may not have strong and legitimate objections to bargaining on several fronts over the implementation of the right to be free of discrimination for some of the reasons set forth above. Similarly, while a union cannot lawfully bargain for the establishment or continuation of discriminatory practices, see Steele v. Louisville & N.R. Co., 323 U.S. 192 (1944); 43 U.S.C. §2000e-2(c)(3), it has a legitimate interest in presenting a united front on this as on other issues and in not seeing its strength dissipated and its stature denigrated by subgroups within the unit separately pursuing what they see as separate interests. When union and employer are not responsive to their legal obligations, the bargain they have struck must yield *pro tanto* to the law, whether by means of conciliation through the offices of the EEOC, or by means of federal-court enforcement at the instance of either that agency or the party claiming to be aggrieved.

Accordingly, we think neither aspect of respondent's contention in support of the right to short-circuit orderly, established processes for eliminating discrimination in employment is well-founded. The policy of industrial self-determination as expressed in §7 does not require fragmentation of the bargaining unit along racial or other lines in order to consist with the national labor policy against discrimination. And in the face of such fragmentation, whatever its effect on discriminatory practices, the bargaining process that the principle of exclusive representation is meant to lubricate could not endure unhampered. . . .

Reversed.[5]

[5] Douglas, J., dissented.

Notes

1. What other result might the Court have reached in the principal case?

2. *Problem.* Smith, a production employee, was docked eight hours' pay after being accused by a supervisor of sleeping on the job. Smith denies any such wrongdoing and the union believes him. The union agreed that it will file a grievance on Smith's behalf pursuant to its collective bargaining agreement and will carry it to arbitration if necessary. Smith, still very angry, stood in the company parking lot with a picket sign for three hours protesting the injustice of the company's action. He was promptly fired. Has the company violated §8(a)(1)? Is *Emporium Capwell* distinguishable? See Colonial Stores, 248 N.L.R.B. 142 (1980).

3. As Justice Marshall notes, in addition to its exclusive power to represent, a union has the duty to represent employees fairly. We shall explore the contours of that duty in Chapter 6.

4. *Union security clauses.* The Court states in *Emporium Capwell* that "[i]f the majority of a unit chooses union representation, the NLRA permits them to bargain with their employer to make union membership a condition of employment. . . ." The statement is misleading and, because the issue of compelled union membership is often relevant in these materials, it is useful to have an early overview of union security devices.[6]

A "union security clause" is a provision in a collective bargaining agreement that describes the obligation of the employees to support the union. Historically, there have been several varieties of these clauses.

a. *Agency shop.* A clause of this sort requires every company employee to pay to the union an amount equal to the union's customary initiation fee and monthly dues. It does not require any employee to become a formal member of the union, to take any oath of obligation, or to observe the internal rules and regulations of the union.

b. *Union shop.* A union shop clause requires an employee to become a member of the union in order to retain his or her job. No one needs to be a member of the union in order to be hired, and every person hired has a prescribed period of time to become a member.

c. *Closed shop.* Under this provision of a bargaining agreement, the employer agrees to hire only union members and to discharge any employee who drops his or her membership status.

The federal regulating legislation is found in §§8(a)(3) and 8(b)(2) of the NLRA. While many collective bargaining agreements have union shop provisions, they are unenforceable as written. Only the agency shop is permitted to operate, although many employees are unaware of

[6] We will examine them in greater detail in Chapter 5.

this. Thus, an employee can be required by a bargaining agreement to pay customary dues and an initiation fee on pain of discharge — but no one can be required to become a "member" to any greater extent than this financial obligation. Section 14(b) of the NLRA permits the states to pass "right to work" legislation, which prohibits employers and unions from exacting even the financial obligations of the agency shop.

C. NATIONAL LABOR RELATIONS BOARD ELECTIONS

Before we look at the variety of problems that may beset unions and employers when a union seeks to become the exclusive bargaining representative for a group of employees, it is useful to have an overview of the process.

1. The Role of the Regional Directors

In 1959, one of the Landrum-Griffin amendments to the NLRA gave the Board the power to delegate the bulk of its decisional powers in representation election cases to the Board's regional directors. The Board made the delegation in 1961. Regional directors are now empowered to decide with respect to election petitions whether a question concerning representation exists, the appropriateness of proposed bargaining units, the validity of challenged ballots, and the accuracy and strength of election objections. The Board itself only hears these matters on a discretionary, case-by-case basis. Thus a regional director's election decision will be final and binding unless review by the Board is sought and obtained on one of the following grounds.[7]

1. That a substantial question of law or policy is raised because of (a) the absence of, or (b) a departure from, officially reported Board precedent.
2. That the regional director's decision on a substantial factual issue is clearly erroneous on the record and such error prejudicially affects the rights of a party.
3. That the conduct of the hearing or any ruling made in connection with the proceeding has resulted in prejudicial error.

[7] The Board has ruled that if a regional director has ordered an election and the Board has granted a request to review, the election should be conducted without delay but the ballots will be impounded pending the Board's decision. Otherwise, the union might be disadvantaged by waning employee support during the delay. 29 C.F.R. §102.67(b) (1983).

4. That there are compelling reasons for reconsideration of an important Board rule or policy.

This delegation reduced the median days required to process representation cases, from the filing of petition to the issuance of decision, from 89 in 1961 to 41 in 1981.

2. Election Petitions

A union ordinarily engages in a campaign for the allegiance of a company's employees prior to invoking NLRB election procedures. Such a campaign may be suggested, and even conducted, by the employees themselves; or it may be initiated by the union without any prior expression of interest by employees. In either event, unions usually consider it very important to gain the support of a majority of employees before approaching the NLRB. Organizational campaigns include the solicitation of company employees by other employees and by outside union organizers. This solicitation may take place at the employer's premises, in the employees' homes, or through the mails. The distribution of handbills and other literature is a major organizing device of many unions. Solicitation of support may be overt or covert depending upon the perceived opposition of the managers.

Petitions for representation elections can be filed by unions and employers.[8] A blank petition is reproduced in the Statutory Appendix. The Board will not conduct an election at a union's request unless the union's petition is supported by a substantial number of employees, which under current Board rules means at least 30 percent of the employees in the unit designated by the petition. Such support is usually shown by signed and dated authorization cards. When a union submits a 30 percent showing of interest, a regional director administratively investigates the authenticity of the cards. The employer is not permitted to see the cards nor to challenge the results of this administrative investigation.[9]

Managers can file an election petition if one or more unions have made a claim on the firm for exclusive recognition.[10] A petition is not warranted merely because a labor organization is campaigning among the employees (lest the employer be able to thwart organizing by forcing a premature election), but the managers can file if there is a claim by the

[8] Employees can also file, but they do so rarely.

[9] Sheffield Corp., 108 N.L.R.B. 349 (1954).

[10] Amperex Electronics Corp., 109 N.L.R.B. 353 (1954); Coca Cola Bottling Div., Walla Walla, Wash., 80 N.L.R.B. 1063 (1948).

union that it represents a majority of the employees, or that it desires the employer to bargain.

Once a petition has been filed by either the union or the employer, the regional director will investigate whether the Board asserts jurisdiction over an employer of this sort and whether there are any bars to the election. If the regional director is preliminarily satisfied that there are no obstacles to holding an election, he or she will attempt to secure the agreement of both the union and the employer to the holding of a consent election. An agreement for a consent election includes a time and place for the ballotting, a designation of the appropriate unit, and determinations of the voting eligibility of particular employees. If the regional director cannot secure an agreement for a consent election, he or she will order a hearing to be conducted by an employee of the regional office. At the hearing, interested parties will litigate all issues relating to the appropriateness of holding the election and the identification of which employees are eligible to vote. The hearing is labeled nonadversarial and so rules of evidence are relaxed and the hearing officer makes no credibility resolutions. In practice, however, the hearings are often highly adversarial.

3. Bars to Holding an Election

NATIONAL LABOR RELATIONS BOARD, 39TH ANNUAL REPORT

54-55 (1974)

In certain circumstances the Board, in the interest of promoting the stability of labor relations, will find that circumstances appropriately preclude the raising of a question concerning representation.

One such circumstance occurs under the Board's contract-bar rules. Under these rules, a present election among employees currently covered by a valid collective-bargaining agreement may, with certain exceptions, be barred by an outstanding contract. Generally, these rules require that, to operate as a bar, the contract must be in writing; properly executed, and binding on the parties; it must be of definite duration and in effect for no more than 3 years; and it must also contain substantive terms and conditions of employment which in turn must be consistent with the policies of the Act. Established Board policy requires that to serve as a bar to an election a contract must be signed by all parties before the rival petition is filed.

The period during the contract term when a petition may be timely filed is ordinarily calculated from the expiration date of the agreement. A petition is timely when filed not more than 90 or less than 60 days before the terminal date of an outstanding contract.[11] Thus, a petition which is filed during the last 60 days of a valid contract will be considered untimely and will be dismissed. During this 60-day insulated period, the parties to the existing contract are free to execute a new or amended agreement without the intrusion of a rival petition, but if no agreement is reached or if the agreement which is reached does not constitute a bar itself then a petition filed after the expiration of the old valid contract will be timely and entertained. In addition, the Board's contract-bar rules do not permit the parties to an existing collective-bargaining relationship to avoid this filing period by executing an amendment or new contract term which prematurely extends the date of expiration of that contract. In the event of such premature extension, the new contract ordinarily will not bar an election.

In American Seating Co., 106 N.L.R.B. 250 (1953), the issue was whether a newly certified union was bound to a collective bargaining agreement that had been negotiated by a predecessor union and which was of too long a duration to operate as an election bar. The Board held the bargaining agreement was not binding.

> The purpose of the Board's rule holding a contract of unreasonable duration not a bar to a new determination of representatives is the democratic one of insuring to employees the right at reasonable intervals of reappraising and changing, if they so desire, their union representation. Bargaining representatives are thereby kept responsive to the needs and desires of their constituents; and employees dissatisfied with their representatives know that they will have the opportunity of changing them by peaceful means at an election conducted by an impartial government agency. Strikes for a change of representatives are thereby reduced and the effects of employee dissatisfaction with their representatives are mitigated. But, if a newly chosen representative is to be hobbled [by being bound to the agreement], a great part of the benefit to be derived from the no-bar rule will be dissipated. There is little point in selecting a new bargaining representative which is unable to negotiate new terms and conditions of employment for an extended period of time.

The incumbent union probably is bound to its bargaining agreement, and so a rival union may gain a tactical advantage by saying that existing terms of the agreement will serve as a floor if the rival union is voted in, and that the only hope for better terms is to replace the incumbent union. The practical effect of the Board's contract bar rules and *American Seating* doctrine has been the establishment of a period of maximum duration — 3 years — for collective bargaining agreements.

[11] The open period in the health care industry is 90 to 120 days prior to the termination of an outstanding contract. Trinity Lutheran Hosp., 218 N.L.R.B. 199 (1975).

The Board treats a bargaining agreement as a bar even though it contains an unlawful provision; however, if it contains a union security clause that is unlawful on its face or that has been found to be unlawful in an unfair labor practice proceeding, the bargaining agreement will no longer serve as a bar. It may be that a racially discriminatory collective bargaining agreement also will not serve as a bar.[12]

Another bar to an election is found in §9(c)(3) of the NLRA: "No election shall be directed in any bargaining unit or any subdivision within which, in the preceding 12-month period, a valid election shall have been held." This means that an election within the past year in a bargaining unit will preclude another election in that unit or a smaller unit; it will not, however, preclude an election in a larger unit, even though the larger unit includes employees who have voted within the past year.[13] In addition, the Board has declared that an election petition is barred if it is filed within 12 months of the actual certification of a union. This is important when a period of time has passed between the election itself and the final ruling on election objections. If the employer should refuse to bargain following a Board certification, thus forcing the representation issue to a court of appeals, the 12-month period will begin only when the employer actually starts bargaining.[14]

4. The Bargaining Unit[15]

Employee elections conducted by the Board are the most important mechanism for a union to secure representation rights for a group of employees. Section 9 of the National Labor Relations Act directs the Board to conduct elections in appropriate bargaining units upon the request of a union. The Board looks at many facts to decide if a proposed unit is appropriate. When a union wins an election, however, the Act does not require managers and unions to confine their collective bargaining to the unit in which the election was conducted. A negotiating unit may evolve that is larger or smaller than the election unit. And unions are not limited to negotiating for goods that have an impact only on the employees within the unit. A bargaining agreement often affects employees outside the unit.

Managers of a firm may voluntarily recognize a union as the representative of all or some of the firm's employees, but the more typical route is through an employee election in "an appropriate bargaining

[12] Cf. Pioneer Bus Co., 140 N.L.R.B. 54 (1962).
[13] Robertson Bros. Dept. Store, 95 N.L.R.B. 271 (1951).
[14] Lamar Hotel, 137 N.L.R.B. 1271 (1962).
[15] See Leslie, Labor Bargaining Units, 70 Va. L. Rev. 353 (1984).

unit." The statute directs the Board to determine whether a unit proposed by a union is appropriate, but beyond that it provides little detailed guidance. According to the Board's opinions there are a few applicable presumptions, but there are no hard-and-fast rules respecting unit appropriateness. Instead, the Board determines unit appropriateness on a case-by-case basis. Courts of Appeals review Board unit determinations, but they owe the Board considerable deference. Some courts have complained that when the Board recites numerous factors without assigning relative weights, it obscures actual rationales; and it has been argued that the Board's purpose is to evade meaningful judicial review.

Two stated principles underlie Board unit determinations. First, the Board is not to search for the most appropriate unit, but is only to decide if a proposed unit is an appropriate unit. Second, the Board will find a proposed unit appropriate only if the employees in the unit share "a community of interest." The meaning of this term is not self-evident, and the consequences (presumably bad) of approving a unit in which the employees do not share a community of interest is not specified. The principle does mean, however, that the union's choice will not necessarily be determinative. It seems also to suggest that the Board will focus on employee interests rather than interests of the union or the firm's managers in its determination. Still, it is not a very helpful standard against which to measure the relevance of particular facts or for determining their relative weight.

Although there is no general standard of unit appropriateness, commentators who have researched the case law have compiled a list of factors considered by the Board. A composite list includes:

1. Similarity of pay and method of computing pay (e.g., weekly salary, hourly, piece-work).
2. Similarity of benefits (e.g., common pension plan, vacation schedule).
3. Similarity of hours of work.
4. Similarity of kind of work performed.
5. Similarity of qualifications, skills, and training.
6. Physical proximity and frequency of contact and transfers.
7. Functional integration of the firm.
8. The firm's supervisory structure (common supervision) and organizational structure, especially as it relates to setting and applying labor relations policies.
9. Bargaining history.
10. Employee desires.
11. Extent of union organization within the firm.

The Board decides unit issues after a union proposes a unit by filing an election petition. Opposition to the unit comes, if at all, from the firm's managers. It is useful to consider the incentives of unions and managers in unit disputes and to speculate whether they correspond to any plausible societal objectives.

Commentators believe that in general a union will propose the largest unit in which it expects to win a representation election, although there has been no empirical verification and little discussion of why this should be so. Perhaps it is obvious why a union would want to sweep in as many employees as possible, but the reasons are worth exploring. First, a large membership may enhance the self-esteem of union leaders. Second, dues contributions of new members may exceed the costs of representing them, reducing costs to incumbent union members. Third, if the union is able to pressure its members to strike by legal or social sanctions, when it could not if they were excluded from the bargaining unit, increased membership may enhance the union's monopoly power. For example, if a supermarket can operate with supervisors when the produce and dairy clerks strike, but cannot operate when the meat department clerks strike, the union has little or no monopoly power representing only produce and dairy clerks. It increases its power representing (unwilling) meat department clerks only if those clerks can be pressured to strike by legal or social mechanisms or persuaded by solidarity arguments.

The union should tend not to seek a broad unit if the costs of representing new members exceed the contributions they make toward the well-being of existing members. If the union "owns" jobs because it is able to limit entry, it will predictably ration future memberships. This seems typical of craft unions in the construction industry, which in fact do little organizing of unrepresented employees.

A plausible surmise is that managers want to minimize the union's power and the costs of collective bargaining, and that they take bargaining unit positions accordingly. On this view, keeping the union out of the firm is the preferred outcome if it can be accomplished at reasonable cost. For managers the best Board ruling usually is one that designates as the only appropriate unit one that is too large for a union to organize.

BIRDSALL, INC.

268 N.L.R.B. No. 16 (1983)

On 20 August 1982 the Regional Director for Region 12 issued a Decision and Direction of Election in the above-entitled proceeding, in which he directed an election to be held in a unit of the Employer's regular full-time and part-time warehouse employees, including receiving and handling (outbound) and receiving and handling (inbound) (BI Consolidated), laborers, checkers, operator/checkers, operators, lead loaders, documentation clerks/forwarders, receiving clerks, special handling clerks, and overage/shortage/damage clerks employed at its 821 Avenue E and 1489 West Eighth Street, Riviera Beach, Florida, facilities. Thereafter, in accordance with §102.67 of the National Labor Relations Board Rules and Regulations, Series 8, as amended, the Employer filed a timely request for review of the Regional Director's decision, contending that a unit of all the Employer's employees is the only appropriate unit.

The National Labor Relations Board, by telegraphic order dated 20 September 1982, granted the Employer's request for review.[2] Thereafter, the Employer filed a supplement to its request for review, and the Petitioner filed a brief in opposition to the Employer's request for review.

The National Labor Relations Board has delegated its authority in this proceeding to a three-member panel.

The Board has considered the entire record in this case and hereby makes the following findings:

The Employer, a Florida corporation within its principal office and place of business at Riviera Beach, in Palm Beach County, Florida, is engaged in the transportation of freight. The Petitioner seeks to represent the unit found appropriate by the Regional Director. There is no evidence of any history of collective bargaining with respect to the Employer's employees.

In addition to the employee classifications included in the unit found appropriate by the Regional Director, the Employer seeks to include the following employees in a "wall-to-wall" unit: jockey drivers, stevedoring employees, Shop I employees, Shop II employees, equipment control employees, container repair employees, marine employees, maintenance employees, and traffic, insurance, and data processing employees.

The unit the Regional Director found appropriate numbers approximately 32 employees, and the all-employee unit the Employer seeks numbers approximately 177 employees.

For the reasons set out below, and based on the record as a whole, we find merit in the Employer's contention that the unit in which the Regional Director has directed an election is not appropriate. Contrary to the Employer, however, who, as noted above, seeks a unit of all its employees, we shall exclude traffic, insurance, data processing, administration, and other office clerical employees from the unit found appropriate herein.[4]

1. The Employer's Facilities

The Employer's facilities are located at four different sites, three of

2. We take administrative notice of the fact that an election was conducted on 17 September 1982, and that the ballots have been impounded pending our Decision on Review.

4. The unit in which we shall direct an election numbers approximately 134 employees.

which are within some proximity to one another. The 821 Avenue E Street facility, also known as the Terminal, houses the Employer's receiving and handling (outbound) operations. It sits on 10 acres of land bounded by Avenue E on the east and by Eighth Street on its north side, and includes the following functions and facilities: yard, rail dock, rail warehouse, LTL[5] warehouse, TL[6] dock, Shop II, and reefer control. One mile west of the 821 Avenue E facility is the 15-acre site at which the Employer's receiving and handling (inbound) operation is located. This facility, also known as BI Consolidated, is located at 1489 Eighth Street, and shall be referred to hereinafter as receiving and handling (inbound).

One block east of the 821 Avenue E Terminal is the port area, an 11-acre site, on which the Employer's marine, container repair, equipment control, and stevedoring operations are located. Finally, the Employer's Shop I facility is located approximately 5 miles south of the Employer's receiving and handling (inbound) facility. The evidence shows that the Employer's operations have expanded gradually over the years, and that the separation between the various sites is the result of what has been a piecemeal expansion process, and does not reflect any particular operational or functional segmentation.

2. The Employer's Operations

The Employer is involved in the transshipment and transportation of freight. Thus, in addition to transporting goods to their final destination via its own ships, the Employer acts as a transfer point for freight which is moved from one conveyance to another.

There are several areas of the Employer's facilities that receive and handle freight. In the Terminal area, freight is received at the LTL warehouse, the TL dock, rail dock, and yard. These areas are collectively referred to as receiving and handling (outbound). Freight is also received at receiving and handling (inbound), and, in the port area, freight is received at stevedoring and equipment control. When a consignment of freight arrives, it is generally processed in the following manner: The freight is checked by a receiving clerk who verifies the paperwork traveling with that particular consignment and prepares a checker's tally, or interchange, which reflects the amount of freight coming in, as well as its condition. The freight is then unloaded by a checker or operator/checker, who "cubes" the consignment, thereby determining the volume or weight which is used as the basis for freight charges. There may be

5. "LTL" refers to "less-than-trailer load" and designates those shipments of freight which are not sufficient to fill an entire trailer (container).

6. "TL" refers to "trailer load," and designates a shipment of freight which fills an entire trailer (container).

further contact between the receiving clerk and the checker or operator/checker if there is a question relating to the validity of the paperwork, or if some of the freight is missing. The operator/checker then passes the paperwork to a documentation clerk, also referred to as a documentation forwarder, who matches the paperwork received from the checker with the shipper's paperwork, and enters a complete inventory of that consignment into the computer. The documentation clerk thereafter completes the preparatory stages for assigning a rate, or cost, for the shipping. During this process, if the documentation clerk discovers any discrepancy between what the shipper says his "cubes" are and the Employer's measurements, the documentation clerk will ask the checkers to recube the consignment, and will oversee the recubing process. The above-described operation applies to both TL and LTL shipments.

With respect to TL shipments, a jockey driver will bring a trailer, into which the TL load is placed; the jockey driver thereafter brings the loaded trailer to the appropriate area for shipping. The documentation clerk then sends the paperwork to the office, from which it is sent to the correct ship. Inasmuch as the TL shipment will fill an entire container, such shipment can be loaded directly onto a trailer (container) as it is received, thus obviating the need for warehousing.

If the consignment is less-than-trailer-load (LTL), it is necessary to gather together more than one shipment to fill a container (trailer). In this situation, when sufficient freight has been received, the documentation clerks will determine, based on weight and cube, which consignments will be assigned to a common container, and will then notify the checker or operator/checker, who will retrieve the particular consignments and load the freight into a waiting trailer. The jockey driver has responsibility for bringing up empty containers and removing loaded ones from the area. The checker and operator/checker will have prepared a trailer manifest, which is then brought to the documentation clerk, who compiles all the paperwork and sends it to the main office to eventually be placed on the ship.

The jockey drivers are primarily responsible for moving both empty and loaded containers from one area to another, and from one facility to another, as well as for washing containers. In addition, a jockey driver will assist in loading containers on an as-needed basis. There are employees at the port facility who perform jockey driver work, but are classified as equipment operators because they operate both jockey trucks and forklifts. The evidence also shows that the Employer abandoned its "pool" arrangement and now assigns its jockey drivers to receiving and handling (inbound and outbound), and reefer control, although it does move jockey drivers to different areas and jobs on an as-needed basis.

Also located at the LTL warehouse are the overage/shortage/damage clerk and the special handling clerk. The overage/shortage/damage clerk, who also serves as hazardous materials clerk, is in constant contact with the other receiving and handling (outbound) employees, advising them concerning the shipping of certain hazardous materials and checking on discrepancies and damage of consignments of freight. The special handling clerk is a contact person for the Employer's large customers who need special service. Thus, the special handling clerk maintains five or six accounts and personally follows the freight through the Employer's transshipment process. Receiving and handling (outbound) also employs a lead loader and two laborers, who generally work throughout the area and are involved, like the other classifications, in maintaining the flow of freight.

In addition to receiving and handling (outbound), the Terminal area at 821 Avenue E houses reefer control and Shop II. Reefer control is responsible for moving and maintaining the Employer's refrigeration containers and equipment, and employs two employees, a jockey driver and a washer/operator. Shop II is responsible for the repair of containers, forklifts, trucks, and chassis. Shop II is in constant contact with receiving and handling. Thus operator/checkers will carry equipment to the shop to have it repaired, and the Shop II employees will often go onsite to repair equipment. On these onsite occasions, the employee in that particular area whose equipment is down will often assist the shop employee in making repairs. Such assistance is mandatory with respect to the larger equipment. Several Shop II employees are located in the stevedoring area at the Employer's port facility, and while they administratively report to the Shop II superintendent, they are directed on a day-to-day basis by the stevedoring foreman.

Like receiving and handling, the Employer's stevedoring section receives and handles freight and employs operator/checkers and operators who utilize forklifts. The stevedoring employees also load and unload the Employer's ships and receive incoming containers. On many occasions receiving and handling employees will be sent to stevedoring if help is needed unloading ships.

Equipment control is located at the Employer's port facility, and its primary function is keeping track of the Employer's equipment. This function often requires that these employees travel to the other operational areas to complete the tracing, locating, and moving of equipment. Equipment control is the check-in point for outside deliveries of cargo to the port. The equipment control employees thus perform a receiving and handling function, and several of these employees operate forklifts.

The container repair section, which is also located in the port area and shares space with the marine employees, performs maintenance work on the Employer's containers. Although container repair shares tools and facilities with the marine section, the container repair employees report to stevedoring. These employees, who often utilize forklifts, also spend time in stevedoring and equipment control, repairing containers onsite.

The marine employees are responsible for the maintenance of the Employer's ships while in port. Like Shops I and II, the marine section primarily utilizes mechanics and welders, and the maintenance and repair work performed by marine section employees parallels that done by the shop employees.

Shop I employees repair containers and container chassis. The Shop I employees often perform onsite repairs on heavy equipment and thus spend time in Shop II, equipment control, receiving and handling, and stevedoring.

The Employer also employs maintenance employees who care for the buildings and grounds, and who also use forklifts in performing their duties.

The Employer's 821 Avenue E facility houses its traffic, data processing, insurance, and administrative sections. The traffic section is responsible for booking cargo, sales, marketing, assignment of freight to a particular ship, rating of freight, and making sure that the paperwork follows the appropriate consignment of freight onto the ship. The data processing section oversees the Employer's computer operations. The insurance section is responsible for insuring cargo, vessels, vehicles, and other equipment. The Employer's administrative section includes its personnel office, as well as its management personnel and attendant office clerical staff. There is little or no interchange or contact between these groups of employees and the Employer's other employees. Between March 1980 and July 1982, the hearing date, two traffic employees received permanent transfers to receiving and handling (outbound), and one data processing employee permanently transferred to equipment control. There were no temporary interchanges involving any of the above groups, nor is there any evidence of their utilization on an as-needed basis.

The Employer's operations manager, Alan Campbell, reports directly to the Employer's president, Birdsall. Campbell's peers, who also report directly to Birdsall, are as follows: Rick Murrell, sales and marketing manager, with authority over the traffic section; James McIntire, insurance; Bill Whitesill, personnel director; B.D. Sory, Shop I superintendent; Tony Sanchez, Shop II superintendent; Ernie Phillips, marine superintendent; and John Spillane, treasurer, who has authority over data processing. Campbell, as operations manager, oversees the remainder of the Employer's operations. Some of these managers look to Campbell for administrative guidance. The evidence also shows that Hud Warren, assistant operations manager, assists Campbell in the areas of stevedoring, equipment control, and container repair. Jim Soles has similar responsibility with respect to receiving and handling (outbound). With respect to line supervision, four foremen rotate jobs on a 3- to 6-month basis in receiving and handling (outbound). At receiving and handling (inbound), a foreman reports to a supervisor who, in turn, reports to Campbell; the foremen in stevedoring, equipment control, and container repair report to Hud Warren. There is also a foreman in the Employer's marine section.

The Employer maintains a system of wage levels that are applied companywide, and its fringe benefits are the same for all hourly employees. When an individual is hired, he or she receives training for the particular job to be performed. The new employee also goes through an orientation process so as to develop a familiarity with all areas of the Employer's operation, the duration of the orientation depending on the position for which the employee was hired.[7] Consistent with this employerwide orientation process, there is a policy of allowing employees to bid on available jobs on a companywide basis, so that job advancement is not restricted to the section in which the employee is hired, or to which he or she is currently assigned.

During the period between March 1980 and July 1982, 32 employees were permanently transferred from one section to another; only 7 of these transfers involved data processing and traffic employees, operational divisions which we shall exclude from the unit found appropriate. The remaining 25 permanent transfers involved operational divisions which shall be included in the appropriate unit. The Employer also utilizes two methods of temporary transfers. The first type, and the one most frequently resorted to, occurs when employees are used on an as-needed basis, as, for instance, when a large consignment of freight needs to be quickly unloaded or processed. In such instances, employees from many operational areas are mobilized on an *ad hoc* basis to satisfy a short-term need.

During the busy season, September through February, receiving and handling (outbound) employees work in stevedoring on a frequent basis helping to load and unload vessels. Throughout the year, employees are regularly shifted to various operational divisions, depending on the

7. Alan Campbell, the Employer's operations manager, testified concerning the orientation process:

> [I]t's impossible for any one employee, assigned to work in any one area, to go in and effectively do his job without knowing what's taking place at all of the other areas.
>
> So when a new employee is hired . . . he will physically work in various areas and become familiar with them, and then finally end up locating and doing his permanent work in a specific area.

Campbell testified further concerning the need for the orientation process:

> [T]he skills that most people need . . . are not skills that are isolated into any one area.
>
> [I]f you are an operator, your skills in operating . . . transcend being able to drive a forklift.
>
> You would have to go and learn about what operating that piece of equipment means in all areas because you could just as easily be called on to go operate that piece of equipment in any area.

amount of freight passing through a particular area. Likewise, it is not unusual for a stevedoring employee, for example, having been sent to receiving and handling to pick up a container to be brought to the port area, and finding that the loading has not yet been completed, to assist in the loading process in order to expedite getting the container to the ship. The other type of temporary transfer, or area interchange, occurs when an employee is needed in a particular job on a 1- to 3-week basis. The record reflects that, between March 1980 and July 1982, 21 such area interchanges took place.

3. The Regional Director's Determination

Citing *A. Harris & Co.,* 116 N.L.R.B. 1628 (1956), the Regional Director found the "warehouse employees for both receiving and handling (outbound) and (inbound) . . . [to have] a community of interest separate and apart from the employees of the other sections."[10] The Regional Director stated that "[u]nlike other employee groups, these employees are engaged almost exclusively in traditional warehousing duties." The Regional Director, in making the unit determination, also relied on his findings that the receiving and handling (inbound) and (outbound) employees are geographically separated from other employees; that they are subject to separate supervision; that transfers of the receiving and handling employees to other employee groups are not significant; that on-the-job contact among the groups of employees does not establish regular and substantial integration or interaction sufficient to preclude a separate unit; that employees in many sections have mechanical or craft skills not possessed by the receiving and handling employees; and that stevedoring and equipment control operators are paid at a higher rate than receiving and handling operators.

Analysis and Conclusions

Based upon a consideration of all the facts, and contrary to the Regional Director, we find a unit limited to the Employer's receiving and handling (inbound) and (outbound) employees to be inappropriate.

Before engaging in a factual analysis, we think it instructive to restate the concept underlying the congressional mandate, set forth in §9(b) of the Act, that we determine "the unit appropriate for the purposes of collective bargaining." In Kalamazoo Paper Box Corporation, 136 N.L.R.B. 134, 137 (1962), the Board stated:

10. The Regional Director specifically excluded jockey drivers from the unit, citing H. P. Wasson & Company, 153 N.L.R.B. 1499, 1501 (1965), and Cal-Maine Farms, Inc., 249 N.L.R.B. 944 (1980). The Regional Director also directed that the reefer control washer/operator vote subject to challenge, concluding that he was unable to determine if the latter classification shares a community of interest with the included classifications.

> In determining the appropriate unit, the Board delineates the grouping of employees within which freedom of choice may be given collective expression. At the same time it creates the context within which the process of collective bargaining must function. Because the scope of the unit is basic to and permeates the whole of the collective-bargaining relationship, each unit determination, in order to further effective expression of the statutory purposes, must have a direct relevancy to the circumstances within which collective bargaining is to take place. For, if the unit determination fails to relate to the factual situation with which the parties must deal, efficient and stable collective bargaining is undermined rather than fostered.

Thus, in determining the unit appropriate for collective bargaining herein, a consideration of the various employee classifications or functions is incomplete without an analysis of how they interact within the Employer's operational scheme so as to carry out its business purpose.

As a first step, and central to our analysis, we note that the Employer herein is engaged in the transportation and transshipment of consignments of freight, and its operations are therefore geared toward the movement and temporary storage of those consignments. Simply put, and as is clear from the above recitation of facts, the Employer's operation is highly integrated and adaptive, and, contrary to the Regional Director, cannot be artificially characterized as, or divided into, warehousing and nonwarehousing functions. The Regional Director's reliance on A. Harris & Co., as well as more recent cases involving combined retail and warehouse establishments, is, therefore, misplaced.

Indeed, the factual reality of the Employer's operation compels a determination that a broader unit is appropriate. Thus, although the Employer's business is carried on at four facilities,[14] it operates with a high degree of functional integration, including substantial interchangeability and contact among employees. As described above, the Employer's business purpose and operations require that employees be frequently shifted from one area to another on an *ad hoc* basis, and the promptness of the response to the Employer's quickly varying requirements is essential if the freight is to be moved in an expeditious and orderly fashion. Thus, while the Employer utilizes a more administratively formal system of temporary inter-area 1- to-3-week transfers whereby employees fill in for vacationing or ill coworkers, it is the "as-needed" flexibility of the work force which is far more operationally crucial, and gives the Employer's business its distinctive character.

14. We note that the Employer's physical layout was not preplanned, nor does it reflect any particular operational organization which might require separate facilities. To the contrary, the record reflects that, as the Employer's business grew, it attempted to acquire property as near its existing facilities as possible. In addition, the Board has held that a difference in the situs of employment does not necessarily require separate bargaining units, particularly where there is evidence of a community of interest among the employer's employees. See, e.g., Peerless Products Company, 114 N.L.R.B. 1586 (1955).

In the same vein and with respect to job bidding, all jobs are posted on an employerwide basis, and all employees are permitted to bid on any job, regardless of their current assignment. It also should be noted that the Employer's orientation procedure familiarizes new employees with all aspects of the Employer's operation. Finally, as is fully described above, movement of freight from one operational area to another results in much contact among employees in different departments. It is thus clear that the Employer's operation requires and promotes a substantial degree of employee contact and functional integration.

Likewise, the Employer maintains uniform working conditions for all its employees. The Employer has a single personnel office located in the administration area at 821 Avenue E, and its personnel policies, practices, wage scale, and fringe benefits are applied to all hourly employees. Given all these factors supporting a finding that the employees in the broader unit share a community of interest, the fact that various departments are separately supervised does not require a different result. The Pierce-Williams Company, 76 N.L.R.B. 1002 (1948).

Based on all of the above, and the record as a whole, we shall, contrary to the Regional Director, include the employees in the following additional operational divisions in the unit found appropriate herein: stevedoring, equipment control, container repair, Shop I, Shop II, marine, maintenance, and reefer control. We shall also include jockey drivers, but, in accordance with the Employer's operational scheme, they shall be included as part of the respective operational divisions to which they are assigned.

Like receiving and handling (inbound and outbound), stevedoring and equipment control utilize forklifts and receive and handle freight. Thus, stevedoring loads and unloads cargo from the Employer's vessels, and its employees frequently receive assistance from receiving and handling, and other employees, on an as-needed basis. Equipment control, in addition to tracing the Employer's equipment, also serves as the check-in point for cargo deliveries at the port area. With respect to its tracing function, the equipment control employees have frequent contact with other employees, including receiving and handling. Thus, the equipment control employees must locate, inventory, and move equipment, including forklifts and containers, and during this process, travel to, and interact with, the Employer's other operational divisions. In addition, the stevedoring and equipment control employees share the same working conditions as all other employees included in the broader unit.

The Employer's maintenance functions are performed by container repair, Shop I, Shop II, marine and maintenance. Thus, container repair (which uses forklifts), Shop I, and Shop II are involved in repairing and maintaining the Employer's containers. Shops I and II also repair the Employer's moving equipment, such as trucks, forklifts, and chassis; employees at both shops frequently make onsite repairs at other operational areas, including receiving and handling, and are assisted by the employees in those areas. In addition, several Shop II employees are located at stevedoring, and while they administratively report to the Shop II superintendent, they are directed, on a day-to-day basis, by the stevedoring foreman. Marine, which shares space and tools with container repair, performs repair and maintenance work on the Employer's vessels. The marine employees board the ships with the stevedoring employees and perform their duties while the ships are being loaded and unloaded. The Employer's maintenance section, which like other operational divisions utilizes forklifts, is responsible for the care and upkeep of the Employer's buildings and grounds. The container repair, Shops I and II, marine, and maintenance employees share the same working conditions as employees included in the broader unit. Finally, these employees serve a function analogous to maintenance employees in a production and maintenance unit. Thus, insofar as these employees maintain and repair the equipment and facilities which are directly involved in the moving of freight, they form an integral part of the Employer's operations, and we include them in the unit we find appropriate.

Contrary to the Regional Director, and based on the record evidence, we shall also include jockey drivers, and the washer/operator to reefer control, in the unit found appropriate herein. As noted above, jockey drivers do not constitute a separate operational department, but are assigned, on an individual basis, to receiving and handling (inbound and outbound) and reefer control, respectively, and, in the course of performing their duties, have contact with employees in most of the Employer's operational departments. In addition, the jockey drivers share the same working conditions as all other employees included in the broader unit. With respect to the reefer control washer/operator, the record clearly reflects that the reefer control department employs one jockey driver and one washer/operator. The evidence further shows that these employees specialize in refrigerated equipment: its movement and placement, and maintaining the cleanliness of the equipment. As such, the washer/operator performs duties similar to operators in other operational divisions. Finally, the washer/operator shares the same working conditions as all other employees included in the broader unit.

We also find, based on the record evidence, that the Employer's employees in the traffic, data processing, insurance, and administration departments do not share a community of interest with the other employees. As discussed above, while these employees are located at the 821 Avenue E facility, they are primarily concerned with paperwork, recordkeeping, administration, and with respect to traffic, the sales and marketing requirements of the Employer's business. Unlike, for example, the checkers or documentation clerks, the traffic, data processing, insurance, and administrative employees do not physically follow the freight, nor are they located in the areas where freight is handled. Further, they have little or no contact, or interchange, with the included employees, and their skills — typing, filing, computer, and administrative — are more accurately described as office clerical. We therefore find them to be office clerical employees, and we shall exclude them from the unit we find appropriate. See, e.g., Victory Grocery Company, a Division of E. J. Keefe Company, 129 N.L.R.B. 1415, 1417 (1961).

Based upon a consideration of all of the evidence, we conclude that the facts of this case do not support a finding that a separate warehouse unit is appropriate. We therefore find the broader unit, described below, is appropriate.

In view of the foregoing, and as the Petitioner has not indicated that it will not proceed to an election in the broader unit found appropriate, we order that the election conducted 17 September 1982 be vacated and direct an election in the unit we find appropriate, as described below:[15]

> All full-time and regular part-time employees of the Employer in the following operational divisions: receiving and handling (outbound), receiving and handling (inbound), stevedoring, equipment control, reefer control, container repair, Shop I, Shop II, marine, and maintenance at its Riviera Beach, Florida, facilities, excluding all traffic employees, data processing employees, insurance employees, administrative office employees, office clerical employees, guards, and supervisors as defined in the Act.

MALLINCKRODT CHEMICAL WORKS
162 N.L.R.B. 387 (1966)

[Petitioner union, the International Brotherhood of Electrical Workers, filed a representation petition seeking to represent the employer's instrument mechanics. These mechanics had for many years been represented by the Atomic Workers' Union as a part of a bargaining unit of production and maintenance workers. The question before the Board was whether to "sever" the mechanics from the existing unit, and if the petitioner won the election, to permit them to be represented separately.]

The Employer's Operations

The Employer is engaged . . . in the purification of uranium ore and the manufacture of uranium metal under a cost plus fixed fee contract

15. As the unit we find appropriate is larger than that requested, the Petitioner is accorded a period of 10 days in which to submit the requisite showing of interest to support an election. In the event the Petitioner does not wish to proceed to an election, it may withdraw its petition without prejudice by notice to the Regional Director within 7 days from the date of this Decision on Review, Order, and Direction of Election.

with the Atomic Energy Commission. It is the single facility contracting with AEC whose production process fully embraces the step-by-step extraction of uranium from its adulterated ores and converting it into a finished product in the form of solid metals, ultimately to be used by AEC and the Department of Defense.

The Employer's uranium division occupies a 200-acre tract consisting of between 40 and 50 buildings, staffed by about 560 employees. Of these, fully half are guards, supervisors, professional, technical, and clerical employees. The remaining production and maintenance unit is comprised of 130 production operators and approximately 150 maintenance employees of which 12 are instrument mechanics, the classification which Petitioner seeks to sever. At the remand hearing, the Employer established that its production process is highly complex and that its capital equipment required an expenditure upward of $25 million. In a great part of the Employer's operation, which is continuous, the product progresses through a closed-pipe system. Most waste and scrap materials are recirculated through the system, ultimately to be consumed in the fabrication of uranium in designated shapes. No other end product is produced, and no intermediate products are stored or merchandised. Yet, it is possible to, and the plant does, shut down on weekends and holidays. When the process is recommenced after a planned shutdown, there is some loss in product integrity until such time as the proper balance is achieved among the several systems. An unplanned shutdown necessitated by an operational failure could result in several days' production loss. Not surprisingly, many of the processes involve the handling of highly volatile, explosive, and inflammable materials, at which times special precautions must be taken. . . .

Coordination of the Instrument Mechanics in the Production Process

It is the principal function of the instrument mechanic to make adjustments and alterations on improperly operating instruments so that the production process may continue unimpeded. Close to three-fourths of the repairs performed by the instrument mechanics occur at the place of the breakdown, that is, on the production line. While the job requirements of operator and instrument mechanic are clearly defined and do not overlap, the operator is required to work with and does assist the mechanic in order to permit a speedy repair and the continuation of production. It is also necessary that the activities between the two be coordinated so that the operator may read the panel and relay the reading to the instrument mechanic. The operator also manually operates the instrument in order to see that it is functioning properly. We conclude from the foregoing that the instrument mechanic's role in the Employer's production process is uniquely and integrally a part upon which the production flow is dependent.

Instrument Mechanics as Craftsmen

The instrument shop is set apart physically from other departments at Weldon Spring. In charge of the 12 instrument mechanics is a foreman who reports directly to the superintendent of the instrument department. The superintendent in turn is responsible to the department manager. The instrument mechanic is identified by the blue hat which he must wear. . . .

It is clear that the instrument mechanics are skilled workmen who work under separate supervision, and we find that the instrument mechanics constitute an identifiable group of skilled employees similar to groups we have previously found to be journeymen or craft instrument mechanics. . . .

Reconsideration of the *American Potash* Doctrine

Petitioner, relying on its showing that the instrument mechanics are craftsmen and on its claim that it qualifies as a traditional representative of such craftsmen, contends it has met the requirements set forth in the *American Potash* decision[4] for obtaining a craft severance election. On the other hand, the Employer, though not receding from its contention that the instrument mechanics are not true craftsmen and that the Petitioner is not, in any event, the traditional representative of such mechanics, argues that the *American Potash* decision improperly makes the question of severance turn solely on affirmative findings with respect to the above issues, ignoring many other relevant and weighty considerations. In this latter respect, the Employer places particular emphasis on the fact that the *American Potash* decision precludes, for all practical purposes, consideration of the duration and character of the representation which craft employees have received while being represented in a more inclusive unit, and completely rules out any consideration of the effect that integration of the functions of the craft employees involved in the proceeding with the overall production processes of the employer may have on the Board's unit determination. With respect to both points, the Employer urges that to the extent the *American Potash* decision forbids realistic consideration of bargaining history and integration of the craft employees' functions in the production process unless the case involves one of the so-called *National Tube* industries, it is plainly discriminatory in application and requires reversal.

We believe there is much force to the Employer's arguments and contentions, and we have undertaken in this and other cases a review of our present policies regarding severance elections.

At the outset, it is appropriate to set forth the nature of the issue confronting the Board in making unit determinations in severance cases.

4. A ıerican Potash & Chemical Corporation, 107 N.L.R.B. 1418.

Underlying such determinations is the need to balance the interest of the employer and the total employee complement in maintaining the industrial stability and resulting benefits of an historical plantwide bargaining unit as against the interest of a portion of such complement in having an opportunity to break away from the historical unit by a vote for separate representation. The Board does not exercise its judgment lightly in these difficult areas. Each such case involves a resolution of "what would best serve the working man in his effort to bargain collectively with his employer, and what would best serve the interest of the country as a whole." It is within the context of this declared legislative purpose that Congress has delegated to the Board the obligation to determine appropriate bargaining units. We do not believe that the Board can properly, or perhaps even lawfully, discharge its statutory duties by delegating the performance of so important a function to a segment of the affected employee body. . . .

The cohesiveness and special interest of a craft or departmental group seeking severance may indicate the appropriateness of a bargaining unit limited to that group. However, the interests of all employees in continuing to bargain together in order to maintain their collective strength, as well as the public interest and the interests of the employer and the plant union in maintaining overall plant stability in labor relations and uninterrupted operation of integrated industrial or commercial facilities, may favor adherence to the established patterns of bargaining.

The problem of striking a balance has been the subject of Board and congressional concern since the early days in the administration of the Wagner Act. In the *American Can* decision,[7] the Board refused to allow craft severance in the face of a bargaining history on a broader basis. The so-called *American Can* doctrine was not, however, rigidly applied to rule out all opportunities for craft severance. Nevertheless, when Congress amended the Wagner Act in 1947 by enactment of the Taft-Hartley Act, it added a proviso to §9(b), stating in pertinent part: "The Board shall . . . not . . . (2) decide that any craft unit is inappropriate on . . . the ground that a different unit has been established by a prior Board determination, unless a majority of the employees in the proposed craft unit vote against separate representation."

Though the legislative history indicates that this proviso grew out of congressional concern that the *American Can* doctrine unduly restricted the rights of craft employees to seek separate representation, it is equally clear that Congress did not intend to take away the Board's discretionary authority to find craft units to be inappropriate for collective-bargaining purposes if a review of *all* the facts, both *pro* and *con* severance, led to

7. American Can Company, 13 N.L.R.B. 1252. See also Pressed Steel Car Company, Inc., 69 N.L.R.B. 629.

such result. Thus, as stated in Senate Report No. 105 on S. 1126, submitted by Senator Taft:

> Since the decision in the *American Can* case (13 N.L.R.B. 1252), where the Board refused to permit craft unions to be 'carved out' from a broader beginning unit already established, the Board, except under unusual circumstances, has virtually compelled skilled artisans to remain part of a comprehensive plant unit. The committee regards the application of this doctrine as inequitable. *Our bill still leaves to the Board discretion to review all the facts in determining the appropriate unit,* but it may not decide that any craft unit is inappropriate on the ground that a different unit has been established by a prior Board determination. [Emphasis supplied.] . . .

Shortly after the enactment of §9(b)(2), the Board, in the *National Tube* case [76 N.L.R.B. 1199], dismissed a craft severance petition filed on behalf of a group of bricklayer craftsmen who were employed in the basic steel industry. After an exhaustive analysis of the section and its legislative history, the Board concluded that:

> (1) the only restriction imposed by §9(b)(2) is that a prior Board determination cannot be the basis for denying separate representation to a craft group; (2) under the language of the statute there is nothing to bar the Board from considering either a prior determination or the bargaining history of a particular employer as a factor, even if not controlling, in determining the appropriateness of a proposed craft unit; (3) there is nothing in either statute or legislative history to preclude the Board from considering or giving such weight as it deems necessary to the factors of bargaining history in an industry, the basic nature of the duties performed by the craft employees in relation to those of the production employees, the integration of craft functions with the overall production processes of the employer, and many other circumstances upon which the Board has customarily based its determination as to the appropriateness or inappropriateness of a proposed unit.

The bricklayer unit was there found to be inappropriate because of the existence of such a pattern and history of bargaining in the basic steel industry and because the functions of the craft bricklayers were intimately connected with the basic steel production process which was highly integrated in nature. In subsequent cases, the same grounds were relied upon for denying the formation of craft units in the wet milling, basic aluminum, and lumbering industries.

In the *American Potash* decision, the Board, in effect, reversed the *National Tube* decision as to both the proper construction of §9(b)(2) and the propriety of denying craft severance on the basis of integrated production processes in an industry where the prevailing pattern of bargaining is industrial in character. . . .

It is apparent that the decision in *American Potash* was predicated in substantial part on the view that §9(b)(2) virtually forecloses discretion and compels the Board to grant craft severance. This view represented an almost diametrically opposite construction of the statute from that adopted by the Board in *National Tube.* On the basis of what has already been indicated herein respecting the legislative history of the section, we believe the revised construction of the statute adopted in *American Potash* was erroneous. . . .

[W]e now consider whether the tests laid down in the *American Potash* case nevertheless permit a satisfactory resolution of the issues posed in severance cases. We find that they do not. *American Potash* established two basic tests: (1) the employees involved must constitute a true craft or departmental group, and (2) the union seeking to carve out a craft or departmental unit must be one which has traditionally devoted itself to the special problems of the group involved. These tests do serve to identify and define those employee groups which normally have the necessary cohesiveness and special interests to distinguish them from the generality of production and maintenance employees, and place in the scales of judgment the interests of the craft employees. However, they do not consider the interests of the other employees and thus do not permit a weighing of the craft group against the competing interests favoring continuance of the established relationship. Thus, by confining consideration solely to the interests favoring severance, the *American Potash* tests preclude the Board from discharging its statutory responsibility to make its unit determinations on the basis of all relevant factors, including those factors which weigh against severance. In short, application of these mechanistic tests leads always to the conclusion that the interests of craft employees always prevail. It does this, moreover, without affording a voice in the decision to the other employees, whose unity of association is broken and whose collective strength is weakened by the success of the craft or departmental group in pressing its own special interests.

Furthermore, the *American Potash* decision makes arbitrary distinctions between industries by forbidding the application of the *National Tube* doctrine to other industries whose operations are as highly integrated, and whose plantwide bargaining patterns are as well established, as is the case in the so-called *National Tube* industries. In fact, the *American Potash* decision is inherently inconsistent in asserting that ". . . it is not the province of this Board to dictate the course and pattern of labor organization in our vast industrial complex," while, at the same time, establishing rules which have that very effect. Thus, *American Potash* clearly "dictate[s] the course and pattern of labor organization" by establishing rigid qualifications for unions seeking craft units and by automatically precluding severance of all such units in *National Tube* industries.

It is patent, from the foregoing, that the *American Potash* tests do not effectuate the policies of the Act. We shall, therefore, no longer allow our inquiry to be limited by them. Rather, we shall, as the Board did prior to *American Potash*, broaden our inquiry to permit evaluation of all considerations relevant to an informed decision in this area. The following areas of inquiry are illustrative of those we deem relevant:

1. Whether or not the proposed unit consists of a distinct and homogeneous group of skilled journeymen craftsmen performing the functions of their craft on a nonrepetitive basis, or of employees constituting a functionally distinct department, working in trades or occupations for which a tradition of separate representation exists.
2. The history of collective bargaining of the employees sought and at the plant involved, and at other plants of the employer, with emphasis on whether the existing patterns of bargaining are productive of stability in labor relations, and whether such stability will be unduly disrupted by the destruction of the existing patterns of representation.
3. The extent to which the employees in the proposed unit have established and maintained their separate identity during the period of inclusion in a broader unit, and the extent of their participation or lack of participation in the establishment and maintenance of the existing pattern of representation and the prior opportunities, if any, afforded them to obtain separate representation.
4. The history and pattern of collective bargaining in the industry involved.
5. The degree of integration of the employer's production processes, including the extent to which the continued normal operation of the production processes is dependent upon the performance of the assigned functions of the employees in the proposed unit.
6. The qualifications of the union seeking to "carve out" a separate unit, including that union's experience in representing employees like those involved in the severance action.[15]

In view of the nature of the issue posed by a petition for severance, the foregoing should not be taken as a hard and fast definition or an inclusive or exclusive listing of the various considerations involved in making unit determinations in this area. No doubt other factors worthy

15. With respect to this factor, we shall no longer require, as a sine qua non for severance, that the petitioning union qualify as a "traditional representative" in the *American Potash* sense. The fact that a union may or may not have devoted itself to representing the special interests of a particular craft or traditional department group of employees is a factor which will be considered in making our unit determinations in this area.

of consideration will appear in the course of litigation.[16] We emphasize the foregoing to demonstrate our intention to free ourselves from the restrictive effect of rigid and inflexible rules in making our unit determinations. Our determinations will be made only after a weighing of all relevant factors on a case-by-case basis, and we will apply the same principles and standards to all industries.[17]

Turning to the facts of this case, we conclude that it will not effectuate the policies of the Act to permit the disruption of the production and maintenance unit by permitting Petitioner to "carve out" a unit of instrument mechanics. Our conclusion is predicated on the following considerations.

The Employer is engaged in the production of uranium metal. It is the only enterprise in the country which is engaged in all phases of such production. All of its finished product is sold to the Atomic Energy Commission. Continued stability in labor relations at such facilities is vital to our national defense.

The Employer produces uranium metal by means of a highly integrated continuous flow production system which the record herein shows is beyond doubt as highly integrated as are the production processes of the basic steel, basic aluminum, wet milling, and lumbering industries. The process itself is largely dependent upon the proper functioning of a wide variety of instrument controls which channel the raw materials through the closed-pipe system and regulate the speed of flow of the materials as well as the temperatures within different parts of the system. These controls are an integral part of the production system. The instrument mechanics' work on such controls is therefore intimately related to the production process itself. Indeed, in performing such work, they must do so in tandem with the operators of the controls to insure that the system continues to function while new controls are installed, and existing controls are calibrated, maintained, and repaired.

The instrument mechanics have been represented as part of a production and maintenance unit for the last 25 years. The record does not

16. We are in a period of industrial progress and change which so profoundly affect the product, process, operational technology, and organization of industry that a concomitant upheaval is reflected in the types and standards of skills, the working arrangements, job requirements, and community of interests of employees. Through modern technological development, a merging and overlapping of old crafts is taking place and new crafts are emerging. Highly skilled workers are, in some situations, required to devote those skills wholly to the production process itself, so that old departmental lines no longer reflect a homogeneous grouping of employees.

17. To the extent that *American Potash* forecloses inquiry into all relevant factors, and to the extent that it limits consideration of the factors of industry bargaining history and integration operations to cases arising in the so-called National Tube Industries, it is overruled. To the extent that the decisions in *National Tube Company,* supra, *Permauente Metals Co.,* supra, *Corn Products Refining Company,* supra, *Weyerhaeuser Timber Company,* supra, and decisions relying thereon, may be read as automatically foreclosing craft or departmental severance or the initial formation of such units in unorganized plants in the industries involved, they are hereby overruled.

demonstrate that their interests have been neglected by their bargaining representative. In fact, the record shows that their pay rates are comparable to those received by the skilled electricians who are currently represented by the Petitioner, and that such rates are among the highest in the plant. The instrument mechanics have their own seniority system for purposes of transfer, layoff, and recall. Viewing this long lack of concern for maintaining and preserving a separate group identity for bargaining purposes, together with the fact that Petitioner has not traditionally represented the instrument mechanic craft, we find that the interests served by maintenance of stability in the existing bargaining unit of approximately 280 production and maintenance employees outweigh the interests served by affording the 12 instrument mechanics an opportunity to change their mode of representation.

We conclude that the foregoing circumstances present a compelling argument in support of the continued appropriateness of the existing production and maintenance unit for purposes of collective bargaining, and against the appropriateness of a separate unit of instrument mechanics. In reaching this conclusion, we have not overlooked the fact that the instrument mechanics do not constitute an identifiable group of skilled journeymen mechanics, similar to groups the Board heretofore has found entitled to severance from an overall unit. However, it appears that the separate community of interests which these employees enjoy by reason of their skills and training has been largely submerged in the broader community of interests which they share with other employees by reason of long and uninterrupted association in the existing bargaining unit, the high degree of integration of the employer's production processes, and the intimate connection of the work of these employees with the actual uranium metal-making process itself. We find, accordingly, that the unit sought by the Petitioner is inappropriate for the purposes of collective bargaining. We shall, therefore, dismiss the petition.[16]

Notes

1. Consider whether the three models in Chapter 1's discussion of the economics of labor unions offer descriptive or normative criteria for Labor Board bargaining unit policy.

In the price theory model of labor markets, unions are labor monopolists that seek to raise the wages of their members through strikes and other cartel activities. Is there a place for a normative theory of bargaining units in a price theory model? Isn't the optimal amount of union monopoly power over wages in a competitive labor market zero?

[16] Member Fanning dissented.

Given certain distributional goals, one could construct a rationale within the price theory model for promoting unionization and enhancing union monopoly power over wages. The point would be to maximize monopoly gains so as to redistribute as many gains as possible to union members. Then one must ask, why limit unions to appropriate units at all? Absent miscalculations by a union, its power will be maximized by permitting it to select its own unit. One goal might be to encourage unions to spread the monopoly gains across the firm's work force. If bargaining goals are formulated by majority vote of the union's members, or some similar but less formal participatory process, the larger the unit, presumably the more the gains will be spread.

There is another reason why a single bargaining unit might be preferred to two or more smaller units. If two groups of employees each have the power to close down the firm by striking, and they are in separate bargaining units, they will need to coordinate their bargaining demands. Absent coordination, there is a danger that both groups will attempt to extract the entire monopoly gain from the firm. To avoid a situation where the combined wage demands of the two groups exceed the firm's ability to pay, the groups must coordinate not only strike strategy but wage demands. It may be that this "demand coordination" is easier when the two groups are in a single bargaining unit. If a single union represents the two groups, demand coordination occurs within the union; and for the purpose of deciding goals and strategies, the two bargaining units are functionally a single negotiating unit. The interesting question is whether demand coordination within a single union is likely to be less costly or less subject to misunderstandings and stalemates than is a similar coordination attempt between two unions.

Now consider bargaining unit policy in a relational contract model. The statutory bargaining unit presumption favoring unionization promotes explicit relational contracting, which has the potential to reduce friction by substituting a single bilateral monopoly for many bilateral monopolies and to encourage employee cooperativeness in acquiring and transmitting firm-specific skills. The presumption does not discriminate, however, between firms on the basis of whether firm-specific skills predominate. The presumption favoring unionization also does not carry with it a rationale for denying a union its proposed unit. One argument for denying a proposed unit is that there may be economies of scale in relational contracting. If a bargaining unit covers only a few employees, they may be unwilling to bear the contracting costs of collecting adequate information and negotiating a comprehensive agreement. A presumption favoring a single-location unit might be seen as an effort to alleviate this problem. If employees favor a unit smaller than location-wide, it may mean that they are willing to bear these contracting costs or it may mean that their purpose in unionizing is wage monopolization.

In a relational contracts model, firm-specific skills predominate, and wage differentials and customary rules will tend to stabilize over time. The work force tends to coalesce into "relative groups," employees with common wage rates and working conditions. Employees in a relative group will be conscious of sharing a special identity of interests, among which are common expectations of how managers will treat them vis-a-vis other relative groups. The approval of a single-location unit, or the insistence by the Board on such a unit, will put relative groups together in a single unit. It is unclear how this will affect the ability of managers to secure consent to changes in established wage differentials and customary work rules. The problem resembles the need for demand coordination in a price theory model. Relative groups will tend to resolve their conflicts within the union rather than in a series of separate negotiations with managers. It is unclear, however, whether this will lead to more or less resistance to change.

Finally, does the collective goods model suggest a bargaining unit policy? An instructive, but imperfect, analogy is to a city producing public goods for its citizens. There might be various notions of what constitutes optimal production of public goods by the government, depending on one's normative perspective. By optimal production, I mean that which duplicates the result that would occur if purely voluntary cooperation were costless, preferences were honestly revealed, and contributions to costs (taxes) were made according to benefits received.

If the government's coercive power does not reach all those who benefit from a public good's production, or if it reaches and taxes some who do not benefit, the optimal level of production will not be reached. Failure to sweep in all the beneficiaries results in underproduction, and it allows some people to enjoy the benefits of the public good for free. When the government taxes nonbeneficiaries, public goods are overproduced and beneficiaries do not shoulder the full costs.

A single government often produces many different public goods, and who benefits from their production varies with the characteristics of the good. Because governments have start-up and other administrative costs, it is usually too costly to have a separate government for each public good.

In this theory, there are advantages in having three groups be coextensive: those who decide which public good will be produced and at what level, those who will benefit from the public good, and those who will pay the direct and indirect (i.e., those who prefer that the good not be produced) costs of producing the good. I call this "coextensive grouping." Coextensive grouping minimizes positive and negative externalities and improves the chances that the collective good will neither be overproduced nor underproduced. It also minimizes the probability that production of the good will result in an unintended wealth redistribution. Coextensive grouping is the ideal for optimal production, but the costs of separate governments for each public good and the costs of setting individualized taxes for everyone receiving a benefit or suffering a detriment, no matter how small, are likely to be too high. Citizens might agree to a taxing and decision scheme spread across time and across groups if they thought that they would be extrabenefitted by the production of some goods and less benefitted by the production of others, that these effects would fall randomly, and that overall there would be an excess of benefits over costs to them.

Unions differ from cities in several relevant respects, a couple of which will be mentioned here. First, the statute does not permit separate bargaining units for separate collective goods. Second, a strike may impose costs on employees who will not benefit from it even if it is successful, but unlike the taxation of nonbeneficiaries by a city, the strike costs imposed on nonbeneficiaries does not give the union increased resources with which to secure a greater level of benefits. Third, very little is known about how a union decides which collective goods to seek, and at what level. Given these distinguishing characteristics, is the notion of coextensive grouping helpful in thinking about labor bargaining units?

2. By a memorandum of June 24, 1968, the Executive Secretary of the Board advised the regional offices:

> Since the Board's decision in *Mallinckrodt Chemical Works* which substantially changed the *American Potash* doctrine, the Board has issued a number of decisions strictly applying the standards established in *Mallinckrodt.* The thrust of all these cases indicates that the Board will not sever from an existing production and maintenance or other overall unit any craft, department, or other subdivision of such unit except under very strong factual circumstances.

In the same memorandum the regional offices were advised that most severance petitions could be dismissed without a hearing. Sharp, Craft Certification: New Expansion of an Old Concept, 33 Ohio St. L.J. 102, 105 n.16 (1972).

This is not the only doctrine with respect to which the Board recites a litany of factors and then reaches the same result in virtually all cases — here, denying craft severance. Lawyers have not been successful in attacking the practice. In any given case there is enough evidence favoring the Board's conclusion to sustain it in the court of appeals. The courts have not been receptive to the argument that an examination of all the cases in a particular area shows a result-oriented decision process that is an abuse of the Board's discretion.

3. *Globe elections.* One union may seek an election in an overall production and maintenance unit at the same time that a craft union seeks an election among only the craftsmen. If the factors are evenly balanced on the issue of which is the more appropriate unit, the Board theoretically may hold a "Globe" election, the name coming from Globe Machine

& Stamping Co., 3 N.L.R.B. 294 (1937). A separate vote is held among the craft employees. If a majority of them vote for the craft union, they will be separately represented. If they vote against the craft union, their votes will be pooled with the employees voting in the overall unit. Thus the craftsmen can opt for separate representation but cannot opt out entirely. The matter is of only academic interest because in recent years the Board has been unwilling to find the other factors evenly balanced.[17]

4. *Exclusions and interventions.* The hearing that establishes the bargaining unit should also dispose of the matters of employee exclusions from the unit and of rival union intervention. Section 2(3) directs the Board to exclude certain groups of employees: for example, supervisors and independent contractors.[18] Whether a given employee is a supervisor may be a contested issue. If a unit consists of production but not maintenance employees, the parties may contest whether a particular employee should be deemed to be production or maintenance. The parties' positions on issues of unit inclusion often depend on their prediction of how the contested employees will vote.

A rival union can secure a place on the election ballot by showing support from just a single employee. If the rival union seeks full intervention,[19] it must have a 10 percent showing of interest. This will enable the rival to block a consent election and to participate fully in the representation hearing. However, if the rival seeks a unit substantially different from that described in the petition, it must produce a 30 percent showing of interest from the unit it seeks.

5. Bargaining Unit Implications of Multiemployer Bargaining

When two or more employers in the same industry have been organized, they may find advantages in joining together to bargain as a multiemployer group. Some legal and economic implications of multiemployer bargaining will be considered in Chapter 4 when we take up the nature of the duty to bargain. What should be noted here are the implications of multiemployer bargaining for the procedures by which unions gain and lose representative status.

Multiemployer bargaining is consensual. Neither an employer nor a

[17] Section 9(b) requires Globe elections for all professional employees, but they also have the choice to remain unrepresented; that is, they may opt out of the large unit without choosing another union.

[18] Sections 9(b)(1) and (3) require that special treatment be given to professional employees and guards.

[19] "Full intervention" means that the rival union can block a consent election and force a hearing. If there is to be a hearing in any event, a rival union may participate without a 10 percent showing.

union may insist that the other commence or continue multiemployer bargaining. If a union seeks a bargaining unit consisting of more than one employer and the employers have no history of unionization on a multiemployer basis, the unit will be held inappropriate absent the consent of the employers. But consider the case in which a union has achieved representative status with respect to a single employer who thereafter bargains (with the union's consent) on a multiemployer basis. If a rival union petitions to displace the incumbent, a startling development occurs. If the employer continues in the multiemployer group, the Board is quite likely to rule that the unit has metamorphosed into a multiemployer unit and that the rival union may only petition for all the employees encompassed by the multiemployer group.[20]

Yet if the employer makes a timely withdrawal from multiemployer bargaining, the rival union's petition will be entertained. This rule seems startling because it gives the employer power to assist or thwart the rival union by defining the unit, and it is arguably inconsistent with §8(a)(2). It also stymies employees who wish to replace their current union with, say, a more militant union. Perhaps "industrial stability" is worth this cost.

6. Balloting and Postelection Procedures

If the unit petitioned for is found appropriate and there are no bars to holding an election, an employee of the regional office will conduct a secret ballot election among the employees. Polling places and times will be designated. The ballots will list the name of the union seeking representation and also a "no union" choice.[21] If the right of a particular employee to vote is disputed, his or her ballot may be challenged and set aside. When the voting is completed the ballots are counted. If the margin is great enough that challenged ballots cannot affect the outcome, they will be discarded; otherwise the regional director will have to decide their validity. For a union to win the election, it must receive the votes of half of those voting (not those eligible to vote) plus one. If more

[20] Similarly, where units at separate locations of a single employer have been individually unionized but have a history of bargaining together, the unit will be treated by the Board as employer-wide. If the employees at one location vote for the union, and thereafter bargain along with similarly unionized employees from other locations to a common bargaining agreement, the newly represented employees may find themselves trapped. The unit may be transformed into a multilocation unit. The union can now be ousted only by a majority vote of the employees at all locations. For example, in Westinghouse Electric Corp., 618 F.2d 107 (4th Cir.), cert. denied, 449 U.S. 975 (1980), a 45-employee unit previously certified by the Board was held to be merged into a 20,000-employee, 42-location, multiplant unit. Therefore, a decertification petition for the 45-employee unit was dismissed.

[21] If two unions seek representation in the same unit, a "neither" choice will be on the ballot.

than one union is on the ballot and no category (a union or the "neither" choice) can garner a majority, §9(c)(3) directs a run-off of the top two vote-getting categories.

Should any party object to the manner in which the election was held or to conduct that may have affected the result of the election, it has five days from the tally of ballots to file objections with the regional director. The regional director may or may not hold a hearing on these objections, but in either event, the regional director will render a decision that is only subject to discretionary Board review.

Section 10(f) of the NLRA permits a "person aggrieved by a final order of the Board" to petition for review of the order in a court of appeals. Both the finding of an unfair labor practice and the dismissal of an unfair labor practice complaint[22] qualify as final orders, but neither the certification of a union nor a refusal to certify constitutes a final order.[23] Where the Board certifies a union and the employer objects to the certification (on the grounds of pre-election misconduct, or bargaining unit inappropriateness, for example), the employer may refuse to bargain with the union. A §8(a)(5) complaint alleging an unlawful refusal to bargain will issue against the employer and the Board will issue a summary judgment[24] and a bargaining order.

If the employer refuses to comply with the order and forces the case to the court of appeals, the employer will defend by raising the representation issues. On questions deemed particularly subject to Board expertise, such as bargaining unit appropriateness, the courts often defer substantially to the Board. On questions of pre-election misconduct, the courts are more likely to take a careful look. But in any event, the employer has a day in court on the representation issues. If an employer challenges a union's election victory and persists through the court of appeals, a two-year delay in bargaining is routine. Attorneys for unions denied certification have yet to find a route to the court of appeals.[25]

Where pre-election conduct is alleged to be an unfair labor practice and to warrant setting aside an election victory, if the regional director decides to go to complaint on the unfair labor practice charge, the unfair practice complaint and the election objection will be consolidated before an administrative law judge. On review of the ALJ's recommended decision, the Board will decide both whether an unfair labor practice has been committed and whether the election should be set aside. The unfair labor practice order is appealable to a court of appeals, but the representation issue is not.[26] Thus, even if the court reverses the Board

[22] Recall that there is no court review of an unfair labor practice *charge*.

[23] AFL v. NLRB, 308 U.S. 401 (1940).

[24] The Board will not relitigate the representation issues even though the regional director alone ruled on the issues and the Board refused discretionary review.

[25] But see p. 316, infra.

[26] NLRB v. Monroe Tube Co., 545 F.2d 1320 (2d Cir. 1976).

on the unfair labor practice issue involving the same facts and consolidated in the same proceeding, it will not interfere with the representation issue of whether to order a rerun election.

In Leedom v. Kyne, 358 U.S. 184 (1958), the Supreme Court permitted district court review of a representation issue. The Board had held appropriate a bargaining unit consisting of both professional and nonprofessional employees. The professional employees sued in district court to set aside the certification of the union for that unit. The Supreme Court upheld the district court's jurisdiction:

> This suit is not one to "review," in the sense of that term as used in the Act, a decision of the Board made within its jurisdiction. Rather, it is one to strike down an order of the Board made in excess of its delegated powers and contrary to a specific prohibition in the Act. Section 9(b)(1) [prohibiting such a mixed unit] is clear and mandatory.

Kyne has been narrowly applied and employers have seldom been successful in sustaining district court jurisdiction. In Boire v. Greyhound Corp., 376 U.S. 473 (1964), the Supreme Court denied the jurisdiction of the district court to hear a challenge to a Board finding in a representation case that two companies were joint employers:

> The *Kyne* exception is a narrow one, not to be extended to permit plenary District Court review of Board orders in certification proceedings whenever it can be said that an erroneous assessment of the particular facts before the Board has led it to a conclusion which does not comport with the law.

D. THE PROTECTION OF PROPERTY[27]

NLRB v. BABCOCK & WILCOX CO.
351 U.S. 105 (1956)

REED, J.

In each of these cases the employer refused to permit distribution of union literature by nonemployee union organizers on company-owned parking lots. The National Labor Relations Board, in separate and unrelated proceedings, found in each case that it was unreasonably difficult

[27] On campaign tactics generally, see Bok, The Regulation of Campaign Tactics, in Representation Elections under the National Labor Relations Act, 78 Harv. L. Rev. 38 (1964); Getman, Goldberg & Herman, Union Representation Elections: Law and Reality (1976); Symposium, Four Perspectives on Union Representation Elections, 28 Stan. L. Rev. 1163 (1976); Weiler, Promises to Keep: Securing Workers' Rights of Self-Organization under the NLRA, 96 Harv. L. Rev. 1769 (1983); Williams, Janus & Huhn, NLRB Regulation of Election Conduct (1974).

for the union organizer to reach the employees of company property and held that, in refusing the unions access to parking lots, the employers had unreasonably impeded their employees' right to self-organization in violation of §8(a)(1) of the National Labor Relations Act.

The plant involved in National Labor Relations Board v. Babcock & Wilcox Co., is a company engaged in the manufacture of tubular products such as boilers and accessories, located on a 100-acre tract about one mile from a community of 21,000 people. Approximately 40 percent of the 500 employees live in that town and the remainder live within a 30-mile radius. More than 90 percent of them drive to work in private automobiles and park on a company lot that adjoins the fenced-in plant area. The parking lot is reached only by a driveway 100 yards long which is entirely on company property excepting for a public right-of-way that extends 31 feet from the [middle] of the highway to the plant's property. Thus, the only public place in the immediate vicinity of the plant area at which leaflets can be effectively distributed to employees is that place where this driveway crosses the public right-of-way. Because of the traffic conditions at that place the Board found it practically impossible for union organizers to distribute leaflets safely to employees in [motor cars] as they enter or leave the lot. The Board noted that the company's policy on such distribution had not discriminated against labor organizations and that other means of communications, such as the mail and telephones, as well as the homes of the workers, were open to the union.[1] The employer justified its refusal to allow distribution of literature on company property on the ground that it had maintained a consistent policy of refusing access to all kinds of pamphleteering and that such distribution of leaflets would litter its property.

The Board found that the parking lot and the walkway from it to the gatehouse, where employees punched in for work, were the only "safe and practicable" places for distribution of union literature. The Board viewed the place of work as so much more effective a place for communication of information that it held the employer guilty of an unfair labor practice for refusing limited access to company property to union organizers. It therefore ordered the employer to rescind its no-distribution order for the parking lot and walkway, subject to reasonable and nondiscriminating regulations "in the interest of plant efficiency and discipline,

1. "Other union contacts with employees: In addition to distributing literature to some of the employees, as shown above, during the period of concern herein the Union has had other contacts with some of the employees. It has communicated with over 100 employees of Respondent on 3 different occasions by sending literature to them through the mails. Union representatives have communicated with many of Respondent's employees by talking with them on the streets of Paris, by driving to their homes and talking with them there, and by talking with them over the telephone. All of these contacts have been for the purpose of soliciting the adherence and membership of the employees in the Union." 109 N.L.R.B., at 492-493.

but not as to deny access to union representatives for the purpose of effecting such distribution." 109 N.L.R.B., at 486.

The Board petitioned the Court of Appeals for the Fifth Circuit for enforcement. That court refused enforcement on the ground the statute did not authorize the Board to impose a servitude on the employer's property where no employee was involved. [The facts of the other two cases are omitted.]

In each of these cases the Board found that the employer violated §8(a)(1) of the National Labor Relations Act, making it an unfair labor practice for an employer to interfere with employees in the exercise of rights guaranteed in §7 of that Act. . . .

These holdings were placed on the Labor Board's determination of LeTourneau Company of Georgia, 54 N.L.R.B. 1253. In the *LeTourneau* case the Board balanced the conflicting interests of employees to receive information on self-organization on the company's property from fellow employees during nonworking time, with the employer's right to control the use of his property and found the former more essential in the circumstances of that case. Recognizing that the employer could restrict employees' union activities when necessary to maintain plant discipline or production, the Board said: "Upon all the above considerations, we are convinced, and find, that the respondent, in applying its 'no-distributing' rule to the distribution of union literature by its employees on its parking lots has placed an unreasonable impediment on the freedom of communication essential to the exercise of its employees' right to self-organization," Le Tourneau Company of Georgia, 54 N.L.R.B. at page 1262. This Court affirmed the Board. Republic Aviation Corp. v. National Labor Relations Board, 324 U.S. 793, 801. . . .

The Board has applied its reasoning in the *LeTourneau* case without distinction to situations where the distribution was made, as here, by nonemployees. In these present cases the Board has set out the facts that support its conclusions as to the necessity for allowing nonemployee union organizers to distribute union literature on the company's property. In essence they are that nonemployee union representatives, if barred, would have to use personal contacts on streets or at home, telephones, letters or advertised meetings to get in touch with the employees. The force of this position in respect to employees isolated from normal contacts has been recognized by this Court and by others. We recognize, too, that the Board has the responsibility of "'applying the Act's general prohibitory language in the light of the infinite combinations of events which might be charged as violative of its terms.'" National Labor Relations Board v. Stowe Spinning Co., 336 U.S. 226, 231.

We are slow to overturn an administrative decision. It is our judgment, however, that an employer may validly post his property against nonemployee distribution of union literature if reasonable efforts by the union through other available channels of communication will enable it to reach the employees with its message and if the employer's notice or order does not discriminate against the union by allowing other distribution. In these circumstances the employer may not be compelled to allow distribution even under such reasonable regulations as the orders in these cases permit.

This is not a problem of always open or always closed doors for union organization on company property. Organization rights are granted to workers by the same authority, the National Government, that preserves property rights. Accommodation between the two must be obtained with as little destruction of one as is consistent with the maintenance of the other. The employer may not affirmatively interfere with organization; the union may not always insist that the employer aid organization. But when the inaccessibility of employees makes ineffective the reasonable attempts by nonemployees to communicate with them through the usual channels, the right to exclude from property has been required to yield to the extent needed to permit communication of information on the right to organize.

The determination of the proper adjustments rests with the Board. Its rulings, when reached on findings of fact supported by substantial evidence on the record as a whole, should be sustained by the courts unless its conclusions rest on erroneous legal foundations. Here the Board failed to make a distinction between rules of law applicable to employees and those applicable to nonemployees.

The distinction is one of substance. No restriction may be placed on the employees' right to discuss self-organization among themselves, unless the employer can demonstrate that a restriction is necessary to maintain production or discipline. Republic Aviation Corp. v. National Labor Relations Board, 324 U.S. 793, 803. But no such obligation is owed nonemployee organizers. Their access to company property is governed by a different consideration. The right of self-organization depends in some measure on the ability of employees to learn the advantages of self-organization from others. Consequently, if the location of a plant and the living quarters of the employees place the employees beyond the reach of reasonable union efforts to communicate with them, the employer must allow the union to approach his employees on his property. No such conditions are shown in these records.

The plants are close to small well-settled communities where a large percentage of the employees live. The usual methods of imparting information are available. See, e.g., note 1, supra. The various instruments of publicity are at hand. Though the quarters of the employees are scattered they are in reasonable reach. The Act requires only that the employer refrain from interference, discrimination, restraint or coercion in the employees' exercise of their own rights. It does not require that the employer permit the use of its facilities for organization when other means are readily available.

Labor Board v. Babcock & Wilcox Co., is affirmed.[28]

Notes

1. How would *Babcock* be applied to a lumber camp organizing drive in a remote forest? Would the union have an easier time organizing a factory beside a busy freeway in Chicago? In Monogram Models, 192 N.L.R.B. 705 (1971), the Board in a divided opinion refused to adopt a "big city rule" for a plant located in a metropolitan area. The majority ruled against a right of access for union organizers: "The test established [in *Babcock*] was not one of relative convenience, but rather whether the location of the plant and the living quarters of the employees place the employees beyond the reach of reasonable union efforts to communicate with them." A dissenting Board member argued that the majority's result

> requires a union to make extraordinary efforts without regard to the economic impracticability or tactical disadvantages that, in the union's view, may be inherent in certain methods of communication. [This] requirement . . . . is contrary to the mandate of [*Babcock*]. . . .

Does the result in *Monogram* turn on a matter of statutory interpretation?

2. It would be reasonable after reading *Babcock* to conclude that in access cases the Board will look carefully to determine whether reasonable efforts will enable a union to reach employees with its message. In fact, you would be quite justified in advising your union or management clients in all cases that the union will not be granted access. The only cases in which the Board has granted access are ones where employees lived on the employer's property. In all cases but one,[29] the courts of appeals have refused to enforce Board access orders in *Babcock*-type cases. The Supreme Court is aware of this. It wrote in a preemption case "[t]hat the burden imposed on the Union [by *Babcock*] is a heavy one is evidenced by the fact that the balance struck by the Board and the courts under the *Babcock* accommodation principle has rarely been struck in favor of trespassory organizational activity."[30] Does this change your view of the *Babcock* decision?

[28] Harlan, J., took no part in the decision.

[29] That case is NLRB v. S & H Grossinger's, 372 F.2d 26 (2d Cir. 1967), involving employees living on the premises of a resort. The Second Circuit has since indicated an unwillingness even to follow that case. NLRB v. New Pines, 468 F.2d 427 (2d Cir. 1972).

[30] Sears, Roebuck & Co. v. San Diego Dist. Council of Carpenters, 436 U.S. 180, 205 (1978).

There is a slightly better chance that an outside union will be granted access to a firm's property if the access is sought as a remedy for the firm's unfair labor practices, which have impeded the union's ability to organize employees. See Note, NLRB Orders Granting Unions Access to Company Property, 68 Cornell L. Rev. 895 (1983).

3. The Court in *Babcock* draws a critical distinction between the rights of employees and nonemployees. One consideration supporting such a distinction is the language of §§7 and 8(a)(1), which protect only the rights of "employees." Thus in those cases in which it is an unfair labor practice to deny nonemployee organizers access to company property, the interference is with the employees' right to hear, not the organizers' right to speak. A second consideration is the employer's interest in securing his or her property from strangers. Would an employee have the right to stay on company premises after the end of his or her shift to distribute union literature?[31]

In the next case the pickets are not seeking to organize the employer but to exert pressure for economic benefits. The case is presented here because its constitutional analysis also applies to organizational appeals. You should pay close attention to the discussions of whether the *statutory* rights should strike a different balance depending on whether the picketing is organizational or economic. Note that the case does not deal with the issue of whether state law should be preempted; we shall take up that issue in a later chapter.

HUDGENS v. NLRB
424 U.S. 507 (1976)

STEWART, J.

A group of labor union members who engaged in peaceful primary picketing within the confines of a privately owned shopping center were threatened by an agent of the owner with arrest for criminal trespass if they did not depart. The question presented is whether this threat violated the National Labor Relations Act. The National Labor Relations Board concluded that it did, 205 N.L.R.B. 628, and the Court of Appeals for the Fifth Circuit agreed. 501 F.2d 161. . . .

The petitioner, Scott Hudgens, is the owner of the North DeKalb Shopping Center, located in suburban Atlanta, Ga. The center consists of a single large building with an enclosed mall. Surrounding the building is a parking area which can accommodate 2,640 automobiles. The

[31] The Board has held "no" with respect to plant interiors and other working areas, "yes" with respect to parking lots., GTE Lenkurt, 204 N.L.R.B. 921 (1973); Tri-County Medical Center, 222 N.L.R.B. 1089 (1973).

shopping center houses 60 retail stores leased to various businesses. One of the lessees is the Butler Shoe Company. Most of the stores, including Butler's, can be entered only from the interior mall.

In January 1971, warehouse employees of the Butler Shoe company went on strike to protest the company's failure to agree to demands made by their union in contract negotiations.[1] The strikers decided to picket not only Butler's warehouse but its nine retail stores in the Atlanta area as well, including the store in North DeKalb Shopping Center. On January 22, 1971, four of the striking warehouse employees entered the center's enclosed mall carrying placards which read, "Butler Shoe Warehouse on Strike, AFL-CIO, Local 315." The general manager of the shopping center informed the employees that they could not picket within the mall or on the parking lot and threatened them with arrest if they did not leave. The employees departed but returned a short time later and began picketing in an area of the mall immediately adjacent to the entrances of the Butler store. After the picketing had continued for approximately 30 minutes, the shopping center manager again informed the picketers that if they did not leave they would be arrested for trespassing. The pickets departed.

The union subsequently filed with the Board an unfair labor practice charge against Hudgens, alleging interference with rights protected by §7 of the Act. Relying on this Court's decision in Amalgamated Food Employees Union Local 590 v. Logan Valley Plaza, Inc., 391 U.S. 308, the Board entered a cease-and-desist order against Hudgens, reasoning that because the warehouse employees enjoyed a First Amendment right to picket on the shopping center property, the owner's threat of arrest violated §8(a)(1) of the Act.[3] Hudgens filed a petition for review in the Court of Appeals for the Fifth Circuit. Soon thereafter this Court decided Lloyd Corp. v. Tanner, 407 U.S. 551, and Central Hardware Co. v. NLRB, 407 U.S. 539, and the Court of Appeals remanded the case to the Board for reconsideration in the light of those two decisions.

The Board, in turn, remanded to an administrative law judge, who made finding of fact, recommendations and conclusions to the effect that Hudgens had committed an unfair labor practice by excluding the pickets. This result was ostensibly reached under the statutory criteria set forth in NLRB v. Babcock & Wilcox Co., 351 U.S. 105, a case which held that union organizers who seek to solicit for union membership may

1. The Butler warehouse was not located within the North DeKalb Shopping Center.

3. Hudgens v. Local 315, Retail, Wholesale and Department Store Union, 192 N.L.R.B. 671 (1971), Section 8(a)(1) makes it an unfair labor practice for "an employer" to "restrain, or coerce employees" in the exercise of their §7 rights. While Hudgens was not the employer of the employees involved in this case, it seems to be undisputed that he was an employer engaged in commerce within the meaning of §§2(6) and (7) of the Act. The Board has held that a statutory "employer" may violate §8(a)(1) with respect to employees other than his own. See Austin Co., 101 N.L.R.B. 1257, 1258-1259. See also §2(13) of the Act.

intrude on an employer's private property if no alternative means exist for communicating with the employees. But the administrative law judge's opinion also relied on this Court's constitutional decision in *Logan Valley* for a "realistic view of the facts." The Board agreed with the findings and recommendation of the administrative law judge, but departed somewhat from his reasoning. It concluded that the picketers were within the scope of Hudgens' invitation to members of the public to do business at the shopping center, and that it was, therefore, immaterial whether or not there existed an alternative means of communicating with the customers and employees of the Butler store.

Hudgens again petitioned for review in the Court of Appeals for the Fifth Circuit, and there the Board changed its tack and urged that the case was controlled not by *Babcock & Wilcox,* but by Republic Aviation Corp. v. NLRB, 324 U.S. 793, a case which held that an employer commits an unfair labor practice if he enforces a no-solicitation rule against employees on his premises who are also union organizers, unless he can prove that the rule is necessitated by special circumstances. The Court of Appeals enforced the Board's cease-and-desist order but on the basis of yet another theory. While acknowledging that the source of the pickets' rights was §7 of the Act, the Court of Appeals held that the competing constitutional and property right considerations discussed in Lloyd Corp v. Tanner, supra, "burde[n] the General Counsel with the duty to prove that other locations less intrusive upon Hudgens' property rights than picketing inside the mall were either unavailable or ineffective," 501 F.2d, at 169, and that the Board's General Counsel had met that burden in this case.

In this Court the petitioner Hudgens continues to urge that *Babcock & Wilcox Co.* is the controlling precedent, and that under the criteria of that case the judgment of the Court of Appeals should be reversed. The respondent union agrees that a statutory standard governs, but insists that, since the §7 activity here was not organizational as in *Babcock* but picketing in support of a lawful economic strike, an appropriate accommodation of the competing interests must lead to an affirmance of the Court of Appeals' judgment. The respondent Board now contends that the conflict between employee picketing rights and employer property rights in a case like this must be measured in accord with the commands of the First Amendment, pursuant to the Board's asserted understanding of Lloyd Corp. v. Tanner, supra, and that the judgment of the Court of Appeals should be affirmed on the basis of that standard. . . .

In the present posture of the case the most basic question is whether the respective rights and liabilities of the parties are to be decided under the criteria of the National Labor Relations Act alone, under a First Amendment standard, or under some combination of the two. It is to that question, accordingly, that we now turn.

It is, of course, a commonplace that the constitutional guarantee of free speech is a guarantee only against abridgment of government, federal or state. Thus, while statutory or common law may in some situations extend protection or provide redress against a private corporation or person who seeks to abridge the free expression of others, no such protection or redress is provided by the Constitution itself.

This elementary proposition is little more than a truism. But even truisms are not always unexceptionably true, and an exception to this one was recognized almost 30 years ago in the case Marsh v. Alabama, 326 U.S. 501. In *Marsh,* a Jehovah's Witness who had distributed literature without a license on a sidewalk in Chickasaw, Ala., was convicted of criminal trespass. Chickasaw was a so-called company town, wholly owned by the Gulf Shipbuilding Corporation. It was described in the Court's opinion as follows:

"Except for [ownership by a private corporation] it has all the characteristics of any American town. The property consists of residential buildings, streets, a system of sewers, a sewage disposal plant and a 'business block' on which business places are situated. A deputy of the Mobile County Sheriff, paid by the company, serves as the town's policeman. Merchants and service establishments have rented the stores and business places on the business block and the United States uses one of the places as a post office from which six carriers deliver mail to the people of Chickasaw and the adjacent area. The town and the surrounding neighborhood, which can not be distinguished from the Gulf property by anyone not familiar with the property lines, are thickly settled, and according to all indications the residents use the business block as their regular shopping center. To do so, they now, as they have for many years, make use of a company-owned paved street and sidewalk located alongside the store fronts in order to enter and leave the stores and the post office. Intersecting company-owned roads at each end of the business block lead into a four-lane public highway which runs parallel to the business block at a distance of thirty feet. There is nothing to stop highway traffic from coming onto the business block and upon arrival a traveler may make free use of the facilities available there. In short the town and its shopping district are accessible to and freely used by the public in general and there is nothing to distinguish them from any other town and shopping center except the fact that the title to the property belongs to a private corporation." 326 U.S., at 502-503.

The Court pointed out that if the "title" to Chickasaw had "belonged not to a private but to a municipal corporation and had appellant been arrested for violating a municipal ordinance rather than a ruling by those appointed by the corporation to manage a company town it would have been clear that appellant's conviction must be reversed." 326 U.S., at 504. Concluding that Gulf's "property interests" should not be allowed to lead to a different result in Chickasaw, which did "not function differently from any other town," 326 U.S., at 506-508, the Court invoked the First and Fourteenth Amendments to reverse the appellant's conviction.

It was the *Marsh* case that in 1968 provided the foundation for the Court's decision in Amalgamated Food Employees Union Local 590 v. Logan Valley Plaza, Inc., 391 U.S. 308. That case involved peaceful picketing within a large shopping center near Altoona, Pa. One of the tenants of the shopping center was a retail store that employed a wholly nonunion staff. Members of a local union picketed the store, carrying signs proclaiming that it was nonunion and that its employees were not receiving union wages or other union benefits. The picketing took place on the shopping center's property in the immediate vicinity of the store. A Pennsylvania court issued an injunction that required all picketing to be confined to public areas outside the shopping center, and the Supreme Court of Pennsylvania affirmed the issuance of this injunction. This Court held that the doctrine of the *Marsh* case required reversal of that judgment.

The Court's opinion pointed out that the First and Fourteenth Amendments would clearly have protected the picketing if it had taken place on a public sidewalk:

> It is clear that if the shopping center premises were not privately owned but instead constituted the business area of a municipality, which they to a large extent resemble, petitioners could not be barred from exercising their First Amendment rights there on the sole ground that title to the property was in the municipality. . . . [S]treets, sidewalks, parks, and other similar public places are so historically associated with the exercise of First Amendment rights that access to them for the purpose of exercising such rights cannot constitutionally be denied broadly and absolutely. 391 U.S., at 315.

The Court's opinion then reviewed the *Marsh* case in detail, emphasized the similarities between the business block in Chickasaw, Ala., and the Logan Valley shopping center and unambiguously concluded: "The shopping center here is clearly the functional equivalent of the business district of Chickasaw involved in *Marsh.*" 391 U.S., at 318.

Upon the basis of that conclusion, the Court held that the First and Fourteenth Amendments required reversal of the judgment of the Pennsylvania Supreme Court. . . .

Four years later the Court had occasion to reconsider the *Logan Valley* doctrine in Lloyd Corp v. Tanner, 407 U.S. 551. That case involved a shopping center covering some 50 acres in downtown Portland, Ore. On a November day in 1968 five young people entered the mall of the shopping center and distributed handbills protesting the then ongoing American military operations in Vietnam. Security guards told them to leave, and they did so "to avoid arrest." 407 U.S., at 556. They subsequently brought suit in a federal district court, seeking declaratory and injunctive relief. The trial court ruled in their favor, holding that the distribution of handbills on the shopping center's property was protected by the First and Fourteenth Amendments. The Court of Appeals for the Ninth Circuit affirmed the judgment, 446 F.2d 545, expressly relying on this Court's *Marsh* and *Logan Valley* decisions. This Court reversed the judgment of the Court of Appeals.

The Court in its *Lloyd* opinion did not say that it was overruling the *Logan Valley* decision. Indeed a substantial portion of the Court's opinion in *Lloyd* was devoted to pointing out the differences between the two cases, noting particularly that, in contrast to the hand-billing in *Lloyd*, the picketing in *Logan Valley* had been specifically directed to a store in the shopping center and the picketers had had no other reasonable opportunity to reach their intended audience. 407 U.S., at 561-567. But the fact is that the reasoning of the Court's opinion in *Lloyd* cannot be squared with the reasoning of the Court's opinion in *Logan Valley*.

It matters not that some members of the Court may continue to believe that the *Logan Valley* case was rightly decided. Our institutional duty is to follow until changed the law as it now is, not as some members of the Court might wish it to be. And in the performance of that duty we make clear now, if it was not clear before, that the rationale of *Logan Valley* did not survive the Court's decision in the *Lloyd* case. Not only did the *Lloyd* opinion incorporate lengthy excerpts from two of the dissenting opinions in *Logan Valley*, the ultimate holding in *Lloyd* amounted to a total rejection of the holding in *Logan Valley*:

> The basic issue in this case is whether respondents, in the exercise of asserted First Amendment rights, may distribute handbills on Lloyd's private property contrary to its wishes and contrary to a policy enforced against *all* handbilling. In addressing this issue, it must be remembered that the First and Fourteenth Amendments safeguard the rights of free speech and assembly by limitations on *state* action, not on action by the owner of private property used nondiscriminatorily for private purposes only. . . . 407 U.S., at 567.
>
> Respondents contend . . . that the property of a large shopping center is "open to the public," serves the same purposes as a "business district" of a municipality, and therefore has been dedicated to certain types of public use. The argument is that such a center has sidewalks, streets, and parking areas which are functionally similar to facilities customarily provided by municipalities. It is then asserted that all members of the public, whether invited as customers or not, have the same right of free speech as they would have on the similar public facilities in the streets of a city or town.
>
> The argument reaches too far. The Constitution by no means requires such an attenuated doctrine of dedication of private property to public use. The closest decision in theory, Marsh v. Alabama, supra, involved the assumption by a private enterprise of all of the attributes of a state-created municipality and the exercise by that enterprise of semi-official municipal

> functions as a delegate of the State. In effect, the owner of the company town was performing the full spectrum of muncipal powers and stood in the shoes of the State. In the instant case there is no comparable assumption or exercise of municipal functions or power. 407 U.S., at 568-569. . . .
>
> We hold that there has been no such dedication of Lloyd's privately owned and operated shopping center to public use as to entitle respondents to exercise therein the asserted First Amendment rights. . . . 407 U.S., at 570.

If a large self-contained shopping center *is* the functional equivalent of a municipality, as *Logan Valley* held, then the First and Fourteenth Amendments would not permit control of speech within such a center to depend upon the speech's content. For while a municipality may constitutionally impose reasonable time, place, and manner regulations on the use of its streets and sidewalks for First Amendment purposes, and may even forbid altogether such use of some of its facilities, what a municipality may *not* do under the First and Fourteenth Amendments is to discriminate in the regulation of expression on the basis of the content of that expression. "[A]bove all else, the First Amendment means that government has no power to restrict expression because of its message, its ideas, its subject matter, or its contents." Police Department of Chicago v. Mosley, 408 U.S. 92, 95. It conversely follows, therefore, that if the respondents in the *Lloyd* case did not have a First Amendment right to enter that shopping center to distribute handbills concerning Vietnam, then the respondents in the present case did not have a First Amendment right to enter this shopping center for the purpose of advertising their strike against the Butler Shoe Company.

We conclude, in short, that under the present state of the law the constitutional guarantee of free expression has no part to play in a case such as this.

From what has been said it follows that the rights and liabilities of the parties in this case are dependent exclusively upon the National Labor Relations Act. Under the Act the task of the Board, subject to review by the courts, is to resolve conflicts between §7 rights and private property rights, "and to seek a proper accommodation between the two." Central Hardware Co. v. NLRB, 407 U.S. 539, 543. What is "a proper accommodation" in any situation may largely depend upon the content and the context of the §7 rights being asserted. The task of the Board and the reviewing courts under the Act, therefore, stands in conspicuous contrast to the duty of a court in applying the standards of the First Amendment, which requires "above all else" that expression must not be restricted by government "because of its message, its ideas, its subject matter, or its content."

In the *Central Hardware* case, and earlier in the case of NLRB v. Babcock & Wilcox Co., the Court considered the nature of the Board's task in this area under the Act. Accommodation between employees' §7 rights and employers' property rights, the Court said in *Babcock & Wilcox,* "must be obtained with as little destruction of one as is consistent with the maintenance of the other." 351 U.S., at 112.

Both *Central Hardware* and *Babcock & Wilcox* involved organizational activity carried on by nonemployees on the employers' property.[10] The context of the §7 activity in the present case was different in several respects which may or may not be relevant in striking the proper balance. First, it involved lawful economic strike activity rather than organizational activity. Second, the §7 activity here was carried on by Butler's employees (albeit not employees of its shopping center store), not by outsiders. See NLRB v. Babcock & Wilcox Co., 351 U.S., at 111-113. Third, the property interests impinged upon in this case were not those of the employer against whom the §7 activity was directed, but of another.

The *Babcock & Wilcox* opinion established the basic objective under the Act: accommodation of §7 rights and private property rights "with as little destruction of one as is consistent with the maintenance of the other." The locus of that accommodation, however, may fall at differing points along the spectrum depending on the nature and strength of the respective §7 rights and private property rights asserted in any given context. In each generic situation, the primary responsibility for making this accommodation must rest with the Board in the first instance. . . .

For the reasons stated in this opinion, the judgment is vacated and the case is remanded to the Court of Appeals with directions to remand to the National Labor Relations Board, so that the case may be there considered under the statutory criteria of the National Labor Relations Act alone.

Vacated and remanded.[32]

MARSHALL, J., with whom BRENNAN, J., joins, dissenting.

[Justice Marshall first argued that the Court should have declined to decide the First Amendment issue because it was not substantially relied upon in the proceedings below, and because of the policy of avoiding constitutional issues when statutory grounds are available.]

On the merits of the purely statutory question that I believe is presented to the Court, I would affirm the judgment of the Court of Appeals. To do so, one need not consider whether consumer picketing by

10. A wholly different balance was struck when the organizational activity was carried on by employees already rightfully on the employer's property, since the employer's management interests rather than his property interests were there involved. Republic Aviation Corp. v. NLRB, 324 U.S. 793. This difference is "one of substance." NLRB v. Babcock & Wilcox., 351 U.S., at 113.

[32] Powell, J., and Burger, C.J., in a separate concurring opinion joined in the opinion of the Court. White, J., concurred in the judgment. Stevens, J., took no part in the decision.

employees is subject to a more permissive test under §7 than the test articulated in *Babcock & Wilcox* for organizational activity by nonemployees. In *Babcock & Wilcox* we stated that an employer "must allow the union to approach his employees on his property"[5] if the employees are "beyond the reach of reasonable efforts to communicate with them," 351 U.S., at 113 — that is, if "other means" of communication are not "readily available." Id., at 114. Thus the general standard that emerges from *Babcock & Wilcox* is the ready availability of reasonably effective alternative means of communication with the intended audience.

In *Babcock & Wilcox* itself, the intended audience was the employees of a particular employer, a limited identifiable group; and it was thought that such an audience could be reached effectively by means other than entrance onto the employer's property — for example, personal contact at the employees' living quarters, which were "in reasonable reach." Id., at 113. In this case, of course, the intended audience was different, and what constitutes reasonably effective alternative means of communication also differs. As the Court of Appeals noted, the intended audience in this case "was only identifiable as part of the citizenry of greater Atlanta until it approached the store, and thus for the picketing to be effective, the location chosen was crucial unless the audience could be known and reached by other means." 501 F.2d at 168. Petitioner contends that the employees could have utilized the newspapers, radio, television, direct mail, handbills, and billboards to reach the citizenry of Atlanta. But none of those means is likely to be as effective as on-location picketing: the initial impact of communication by those means would likely be less dramatic, and the potential for dilution of impact significantly greater. As this Court has observed:

> "Publication in a newspaper, or by distribution of circulars, may convey the same information or make the same charge as do those patrolling a picket line. But the very purpose of a picket line is to exert influences, and it produces consequences, different from other modes of communication. The loyalties and responses evoked and exacted by picket lines are unlike those flowing from appeals by printed word." Hughes v. Superior Court, 339 U.S. 460, 465 (1950).

In addition, all of the alternatives suggested by petitioner are considerably more expensive than on-site picketing. Certainly *Babcock & Wilcox* did not require resort to the mass media,[6] or to more individualized efforts on a scale comparable to that which would be required to reach the intended audience in this case.

Petitioner also contends that the employees could have picketed on

5. It is irrelevant, in my view, that the property in this case was owned by the shopping center owner rather than by the employer. The nature of the property interest is the same in either case.

6. The only alternative means of communication referred to in *Babcock & Wilcox* were "personal contacts on streets or at home, telephones, letters or advertised meetings to get in touch with the employees." 351 U.S., at 111.

the public right-of-way, where vehicles entered the shopping center. Quite apart from considerations of safety, that alternative was clearly inadequate: prospective customers would have had to read the picketers' placards while driving by in their vehicle — a difficult task indeed. Moreover, as both the Board and the Court of Appeals recognized, picketing at an entrance used by customers of all retail establishments in the shopping center, rather than simply customers of the Butler Shoe Company store, may well have invited undesirable secondary effects.

In short, I believe the Court of Appeals was clearly correct in concluding that "alternatives to picketing inside the mall were either unavailable or inadequate." 501 F.2d at 169. Under *Babcock & Wilcox*, then, the picketing in this case was protected by §7. I would affirm the judgment of the Court of Appeals on that basis.

[In part III of his dissenting opinion, Justice Marshall argued for retaining the First Amendment protection announced in *Logan Valley* "when the picketing is related to the function of the shopping center and when there is no other reasonable opportunity to convey the message to the intended audience."]

Notes

1. An aside on Supreme Court decision making. *Logan Valley* is now clearly overruled, but did it get its day in the Supreme Court? Even if the Court has changed its mind on the compatibility of *Logan Valley* and *Lloyd*, is it so clear that *Lloyd* is the correct result as to warrant no discussion?

2. On remand in *Hudgens* the Board held that the picketing was protected and that Scott Hudgens had violated §8(a)(1) by threatening the pickets with arrest for trespassing. The Board first noted that both economic strike activity and organizational activity are protected by §7. According to the Board, the fact that the pickets were employees entitled them to at least as much protection as was afforded the nonemployee organizers in *Babcock*. The case thus turned on how §7 rights and private property rights were to be accommodated.

> One difference between organizational campaigns as opposed to economic strike situations is that in the former the §7 rights being protected are those of the intended audience (the employees sought to be organized), and in the latter the §7 rights are those of the persons attempting to communicate with *their* intended audience, the public as well as the employees. A further distinction between organizational and economic strike activity becomes apparent when the focus shifts to the characteristics of the audience at which the §7 activity in question is directed. In an organizational campaign, the group of employees whose support the union seeks is specific and often is accessible by means of communication other than direct entry of the union organizers onto the employer's prop-

erty, such as meeting employees on the street, home visits, letters, and telephone calls.

Here, the pickets' intended audience comprised two distinct groups: (1) those members of the buying public who might, when seeing Butler's window display inside the Mall, think of doing business with the one employer, and (2) the employees at the Butler store. Although the non-striking employees at the Butler store were obviously a clearly defined group, the potential customers (the more important component of the intended audience) became established as such only when individual shoppers decide to enter the store.

Hudgens contends that *Babcock & Wilcox* should be read to require that, if television, radio, and newspaper advertising is available, the picketers' §7 rights must yield to property rights regardless of the expense involved and regardless of the fact that such forms of communication, in order to reach the intended audience, necessarily must also reach the general populace. As to these contentions, the Administrative Law Judge found, and we agree, that the mass media, appropriately used by the North DeKalb Center and its merchants to attract customers from the Metropolitan Atlanta area, are not "reasonable" means of communication for employee pickets seeking to publicize their labor dispute with a single store in the Mall. Furthermore, Hudgens' suggested approach would undercut Board and Court precedent recognizing and protecting such picketing as the most effective way of reaching those who would enter a struck employer's premises, including situations in which the entrance to the employer's property is on land owned by another. . . .

As to Hudgens' suggestion that the pickets could have used public streets and sidewalks, the Administrative Law Judge pointed out that Butler is only 1 of 60 stores fronting on the same common inside walkways, that the closest public area — i.e., not privately owned — is 500 feet away from the store, and that a message announced orally or by picket sign at such a distance from the focal point would be too greatly diluted to be meaningful. Further, we find merit in the General Counsel's contentions that safety considerations, the likelihood of enmeshing neutral employers, and the fact that many people become members of the pickets' intended audience on impulse all weigh against requiring the pickets to remove to public property, or even to the sidewalks surrounding the Mall. 230 N.L.R.B. 414 (1977).

3. In Seattle–First National Bank v. NLRB, 651 F.2d 1272 (9th Cir. 1980), the union engaged in an economic strike against a restaurant located on the forty-sixth floor of an office building. It picketed on the forty-sixth floor in front of the restaurant's entrance and the owner was held to have violated §8(a)(1) when he threatened to have the pickets arrested. The court relied on *Scott Hudgens,* and especially on its findings that the pickets could not identify potential customers of a particular store within a mall. Furthermore, in *Hudgens* shoppers buying on impulse might not know that they were potential customers of a particular store when they entered the mall; thus the union had the right to enter and picket in front of the target store.

This precedent was thought especially apt because in the instant case many people using the restaurant were workers in the office building and might have forgotten the pickets' message by lunchtime. However, most of the dinnertime customers did not work in the building. The court held that "even if the union can adequately inform most of the restaurant's customers of the existence of the strike without stationing picketers on the forty-sixth floor, the union cannot fully implement its §7 rights without confronting the customers in front of the restaurant." The court also indicated that more limited rights might be granted in the case of organizational picketing.

4. *Problem.* A general contractor in the construction industry requires officials of any union representing jobsite employees to check in at the general contractor's office before conducting business on jobsite, to state the nature of the union official's business with sufficient particularity to satisfy the general contractor that the matter cannot be handled off-premises, and to permit a representative of the contractor to accompany the official while on the jobsite. Is this a §8(a)(1) violation? See Villa Avila, 253 N.L.R.B. 76 (1980).

E. SOLICITATION AND DISTRIBUTION OF LITERATURE

The next case, as well as many others in this chapter, illustrates ground rules that the courts and the NLRB have developed for union organizing drives. Underlying the cases are two subtle lines of inquiry. First, what are the appropriate principles of decision? Need the right to organize actually be interfered with in order for there to be a violation? What sorts of cases require scienter, and when will a legitimate business justification for a discriminatory act save the day for the alleged violator? Second, what are the institutional roles of the NLRB and the courts in resolving these issues? May NLRB expertise be presumed? Does the statute permit needs of administrative and judicial economy to influence doctrinal development?

REPUBLIC AVIATION CORP. v. NLRB
324 U.S. 793 (1945)

REED, J.

In the *Republic Aviation Corporation* case, the employer, a large and rapidly growing military aircraft manufacturer, adopted, well before any union activity at the plant, a general rule against soliciting which read as follows: "Soliciting of any type cannot be permitted in the factory or offices."

The Republic plant was located in a built-up section of Suffolk County, New York. An employee persisted after being warned of the rule in soliciting union membership in the plant by passing out application cards to employees on his own time during lunch periods. The employee was discharged for infraction of the rule and, as the National Labor Relations Board found, without discrimination on the part of the employer toward union activity.

Three other employees were discharged for wearing UAW-CIO union steward buttons in the plant after being requested to remove the insignia. The union was at that time active in seeking to organize the plant. The reason which the employer gave for the request was that as the union was not then the duly designated representative of the employees, the wearing of the steward buttons in the plant indicated an acknowledgment by the management of the authority of the stewards to represent the employees in dealing with the management and might impinge upon the employer's policy of strict neutrality in union matters and might interfere with the existing grievance system of the corporation.

The Board was of the view that wearing union steward buttons by employees did not carry any implication of recognition of that union by the employer where, as here, there was no competing labor organization in the plant. The discharges of the stewards, however, were found not to be motivated by opposition to the particular union or, we deduce, to unionism.

The Board determined that the promulgation and enforcement of the "no solicitation" rule violated §[8(a)(1)] of the National Labor Relations Act as it interfered with, restrained and coerced employees in their rights under §7 and discriminated against the discharged employees under §[8(a)(3)]. It determined also that the discharge of the stewards violated §§[8(a)(1) and 8(a)(3)]. As a consequence of its conclusions as to the solicitation and the wearing of the insignia, the Board entered the usual cease and desist order and directed the reinstatement of the discharged employees with back pay and also the rescission of "the rule against solicitation in so far as it prohibits union activity and solicitation on company property during the employees' own time." 51 N.L.R.B. 1186, 1189. . . . [The Court granted certiorari in *Republic Aviation* and in Le Tourneau Co. v. National Labor Relations Board, which raised the same issue.]

These cases bring here for review the action of the National Labor Relations Board in working out an adjustment between the undisputed right of self-organization assured to employees under the Wagner Act and the equally undisputed right of employers to maintain discipline in their establishments. Like so many others, these rights are not unlimited in the sense that they can be exercised without regard to any duty which the existence of rights in others may place upon employer or employee.

Opportunity to organize and proper discipline are both essential elements in a balanced society.

The Wagner Act did not undertake the impossible task of specifying in precise and unmistakable language each incident which would constitute an unfair labor practice. On the contrary that Act left to the Board the work of applying the Act's general prohibitory language in the light of the infinite combinations of events which might be charged as violative of its terms. Thus a "rigid scheme of remedies" is avoided and administrative flexibility within appropriate statutory limitations obtained to accomplish the dominant purpose of the legislation. So far as we are here concerned, that purpose is the right of employees to organize for mutual aid without employer interference. This is the principle of labor relations which the Board is to foster.

The gravamen of the objection of both *Republic* and *Le Tourneau* to the Board's orders is that they rest on a policy formulated without due administrative procedure. To be more specific it is that the Board cannot substitute its knowledge of industrial relations for substantive evidence. The contention is that there must be evidence before the Board to show that the rules and orders of the employers interfered with and discouraged union organization in the circumstances and situations of each company. Neither in the *Republic* nor the *Le Tourneau* cases can it properly be said that there was evidence or a finding that the plant's physical location made solicitation away from company property ineffective to reach prospective union members. Neither of these is like a mining or lumber camp where the employees pass their rest as well as their work time on the employer's premises, so that union organization must proceed upon the employer's premises or be seriously handicapped. . . .

[The] statutory plan for an adversary proceeding requires that the Board's orders on complaints of unfair labor practices be based upon evidence which is placed before the Board by witnesses who are subject to cross-examination by opposing parties. Such procedure strengthens assurance of fairness by requiring findings on known evidence. Such a requirement does not go beyond the necessity for the production of evidential facts, however, and compel evidence as to the results which may flow from such facts. An administrative agency with power after hearings to determine on the evidence in adversary proceedings whether violations of statutory commands have occurred may infer within the limits of the inquiry from the proven facts such conclusions as reasonably may be based upon the facts proven. One of the purposes which lead to the creation of such boards is to have decisions based upon evidential facts under the particular statute made by experienced officials with an adequate appreciation of the complexities of the subject which is entrusted to their administration.

In the *Republic Aviation* case the evidence showed that the petitioner was in early 1943 a non-urban manufacturing establishment for military production which employed thousands. It was growing rapidly. Trains and automobiles gathered daily many employees for the plant from an area on Long Island, certainly larger than walking distance. The rule against solicitation was introduced in evidence and the circumstances of its violation by the dismissed employee after warning [were] detailed.

As to the employees who were discharged for wearing the buttons of a union steward, the evidence showed in addition the discussion in regard to their right to wear the insignia when the union had not been recognized by the petitioner as the representative of the employees. Petitioner looked upon a steward as a union representative for the adjustment of grievances with the management after employer recognition of the stewards' union. Until such recognition petitioner felt that it would violate its neutrality in labor organization if it permitted the display of a steward button by an employee. From its point of view, such display represented to other employees that the union already was recognized.

No evidence was offered that any unusual conditions existed in labor relations, the plant location or otherwise to support any contention that conditions at this plant differed from those occurring normally at any other large establishment. . . .

These were the facts upon which the Board reached its conclusions as to unfair labor practices. The Intermediate Report in the *Republic Aviation* case, 51 N.L.R.B. at 1195, set out the reason why the rule against solicitation was considered inimical to the right of organization.[6] This was approved by the Board. Id., 1186. The Board's reasons for concluding that the petitioner's insistence that its employees refrain from wearing steward buttons appear at page 1187 of the report.[7] In the *Le Tourneau Company* case the discussion of the reasons underlying the findings was much more extended. 54 N.L.R.B. 1253, 1258 et seq. We insert in the note below a quotation which shows the character of the Board's opinion.[8] Furthermore, in both opinions of the Board full citation of

6. 51 N.L.R.B. 1195: "Thus under the conditions obtaining in January, 1943, the respondent's employees, working long hours in a plant engaged entirely in war production and expanding with extreme rapidity, were entirely deprived of their normal right to 'full freedom of association' in the plant on their own time, the very time and place uniquely appropriate and almost solely available to them therefor. The respondent's rule is therefore in clear derogation of the rights of its employees guaranteed by the Act."

7. We quote an illustrative portion. 51 N.L.R.B. 1187, 1188: "We do not believe that the wearing of a steward button is a representation that the employer either approves or recognizes the union in question as the representative of the employees, especially when, as here, there is no competing labor organization in the plant. Furthermore, there is no evidence in the record herein that the respondent's employees so understood the steward buttons or that the appearance of union stewards in the plant affected the normal operation of the respondent's grievance procedure. On the other hand, the right of employees to wear union insignia at work has long been recognized as a reasonable and legitimate form of union activity, and the respondent's curtailment of that right is clearly violative of the Act."

8. 54 N.L.R.B. at 1259, 1260: "As the Circuit Court of Appeals for the Second Circuit has held, 'It is not every interference with property rights that is within the Fifth Amend-

authorities was given including Matter of Peyton Packing Company, 49 N.L.R.B. 828, 50 N.L.R.B. 355, hereinafter referred to.

The Board has fairly, we think, explicated in these cases the theory which moved it to its conclusions in these cases. The excerpts from its opinions just quoted show this. The reasons why it has decided as it has are sufficiently set forth. We cannot agree, as Republic urges, that in these present cases reviewing courts are left to "sheer acceptance" of the Board's conclusions or that its formulation of policy is "cryptic."

Not only has the Board in these cases sufficiently expressed the theory upon which it concludes that rules against solicitation or prohibitions against the wearing of insignia must fall as interferences with union organization but in so far as rules against solicitation are concerned, it had theretofore succinctly expressed the requirements of proof which it considered appropriate to outweigh or overcome the presumption as to rules against solicitation. In the *Peyton Packing Company* case, 49 N.L.R.B. 828, at 843, hereinbefore referred to, the presumption adopted by the Board is set forth.[10]

Although this definite ruling appeared in the Board's decisions, no motion was made in the court by Republic or Le Tourneau after the Board's decisions for leave to introduce additional evidence to show unusual circumstances involving their plants or for other purposes. Such a motion might have been granted by the Board or court in view of the fact that the Intermediate Report in the *Republic Aviation* case was dated

---

ment and . . . inconvenience or even some dislocation of property rights, may be necessary in order to safeguard the right to collective bargaining.' The Board has frequently applied this principle in decisions involving varying sets of circumstances, where it has held that the employer's right to control his property does not permit him to deny access to his property to persons whose presence is necessary there to enable the employees effectively to exercise their right to self-organization and collective bargaining, and in those decisions which have reached the courts, the Board's position has been sustained. Similarly, the Board has held that, while it was 'within the province of an employer to promulgate and enforce a rule prohibiting union solicitation during working hours,' it was 'not within the province of an employer to promulgate and enforce a rule prohibiting union solicitation by an employee outside of working hours, although on company property,' the latter restriction being deemed an unreasonable impediment to the exercise of the right to self-organization."

10. 49 N.L.R.B. at 843, 844: "The Act, of course, does not prevent an employer from making and enforcing reasonable rules covering the conduct of employees on company time. Working time is for work. It is therefore within the province of an employer to promulgate and enforce a rule prohibiting union solicitation during working hours. Such a rule must be presumed to be valid in the absence of evidence that it was adopted for a discriminatory purpose. It is no less true that time outside working hours, whether before or after work, or during luncheon or rest periods, is an employee's time to use as he wishes without unreasonable restraint, although the employee is on company property. It is therefore not within the province of an employer to promulgate and enforce a rule prohibiting union solicitation by an employee outside of working hours, although on company property. Such a rule must be presumed to be an unreasonable impediment to self-organization and therefore discriminatory in the absence of evidence that special circumstances make the rule necessary in order to maintain production or discipline."

May 21, 1943, and that in *Le Tourneau* November 11, 1943, while the opinion in the *Peyton Packing Company* case was given as late as May 18, 1943. We perceive no error in the Board's adoption of this presumption. The Board had previously considered similar rules in industrial establishments and the definitive form which the *Peyton Packing Company* decision gave to the presumption was the product of the Board's appraisal of normal conditions about industrial establishments. Like a statutory presumption or one established by regulation, the validity, perhaps in a varying degree, depends upon the rationality between what is proved and what is inferred.

In the *Republic Aviation* case, petitioner urges that irrespective of the validity of the rule against solicitation, its application in this instance did not violate §[8(a)(3)], because the rule was not discriminatorily applied against union solicitation but was impartially enforced against all solicitors. It seems clear, however, that if a rule against solicitation is invalid as to union solicitation on the employer's premises during the employee's own time, a discharge because of violation of that rule discriminates within the meaning of §[8(a)(3)] in that it discourages membership in a labor organization.[33]

Notes

1. With respect to its antisolicitation rule, was the company's interference with organizational rights intentional? Did its rule actually impede the union's organizational efforts? Compare the Board's language in Cooper Thermometer Co., 154 N.L.R.B. 502, 503 n.2 (1965): "[I]nterference, restraint and coercion under §8(a)(1) of the Act does not turn on the employer's motive or on whether it succeeded or failed. The test is whether the employer engaged in conduct which, it may reasonably be said, tends to interfere with the free exercise of employee rights under the Act."

The Court has no trouble in *Republic Aviation* finding that the employee discharges violated §8(a)(3). Professor Getman comments: "The Court's analysis is unclear: to the extent the opinion equates discrimination with discouragement it denies any separate meaning to the former. But it is clear that the court used discrimination to signify something other than a distinction between employees. The only way in which it may properly be said that the employer discriminated was in treating employees differently from the way he would have treated them had they not engaged in union solicitation. Discrimination as thus used includes any employer action taken in response to union activity."[34]

[33] Roberts, J., dissented.

[34] Getman, Section 8(a)(3) of the NLRA and the Effort to Insulate Free Employee Choice, 32 U. Chi. L. Rev. 735, 737 (1965).

A literal reading of §§7 and 8(a)(1) would demand that every employer interference with employee organizational rights be deemed an unfair labor practice. *Babcock* and *Republic Aviation* are two of many cases making it clear that the Board and the courts are to consider legitimate employer interests in deciding which employer acts violate the statute. The interplay between §7 interference and employer business interests will be considered in greater detail when we examine the use of economic weapons in Chapter 3.

2. An otherwise valid rule restricting solicitation/distribution is unlawful if promulgated for discriminatory reasons. Should an employer who has never restricted employee solicitation/distribution be permitted to adopt restrictions when a union organizing drive begins? The Board approved such an adoption where the employer was able to show an observable decline in productivity caused by solicitation shortly after the start of a union organizing drive.[35]

EASTEX, INC. v. NLRB
437 U.S. 556 (1978)

POWELL, J. . . .

Petitioner is a company that manufactures paper products in Silsbee, Tex. Since 1954, petitioner's production employees have been represented by Local 801 of the United Paperworkers International Union. . . . Since Texas is a "right-to-work" state by statute, Local 801 is barred from obtaining an agreement with petitioner requiring all production employees to become union members.

In March 1974, officers of Local 801, seeking to strengthen employee support for the union and perhaps recruit new members in anticipation of upcoming contract negotiations with petitioner, decided to distribute a union newsletter to petitioner's production employees. The newsletter was divided into four sections. The first and fourth sections urged employees to support and participate in the union and, more generally, extolled the benefits of union solidarity. The second section encouraged employees to write their legislators to oppose incorporation of the state "right-to-work" statute into a revised state constitution then under consideration, warning that incorporation would "weake[n] Unions and improv[e] the edge business has at the bargaining table." The third section noted that the President recently had vetoed a bill to increase the federal minimum wage from $1.60 to $2.00 per hour, compared this action to the increase of prices and profits in the oil industry under administration policies, and admonished: "As working men and women we must

[35] Bankers Club, 218 N.L.R.B. 22 (1975); North American Rockwell Corp., 195 N.L.R.B. 1046 (1972).

defeat our enemies and elect our friends. If you haven't registered to vote, please do so today." [The company refused to permit union officials or employees to distribute the newsletter in nonworking areas of the plant. The union filed a §8(a)(1) charge.]

At a hearing on the charge, [the company's personnel director] testified that he had no objection to the first and fourth sections of the newsletter. He had denied permission to distribute the newsletter because he "didn't see any way in which [the second and third sections were] related to our association with the Union." The Administrative Law Judge held that although not all of the newsletter had immediate bearing on the relationship between petitioner and Local 801, distribution of all its contents was protected under §7 as concerted activity for the "mutual aid or protection" of employees. Because petitioner had presented no evidence of "special circumstances" to justify a ban on the distribution of protected matter by employees in nonworking areas during nonworking time, the Administrative Law Judge held that petitioner had violated §8(a)(1) and ordered petitioner to cease and desist from the violation. The Board affirmed the Administrative Law Judge's rulings, findings, and conclusions, and adopted his recommended order.

The Court of Appeals enforced the order. 550 F.2d 198 (5th Cir. 1977). It rejected petitioner's argument that the "mutual aid or protection" clause of §7 protects only concerted activity by employees that is directed at conditions that their employer has the authority or power to change or control. Without expressing an opinion as to the full range of §7 rights "when exercised off the employer's property," 550 F.2d, at 202, the court purported to balance those rights against the employer's property rights and concluded that "whatever is reasonably related to the employees' *jobs* or to their status or condition as employees in the plant may be the subject of such handouts as we treat of here, distributed on the plant premises in such a manner as not to interfere with the work. . . ." Id., at 203 (emphasis in original). The court further held that all of the material in the newsletter here met this test. Id., at 204-205.[9]

Because of apparent differences among the Courts of Appeals as to the scope of rights protected by the "mutual aid or protection" clause of §7, see n.17, infra, we granted certiorari.

II

Two distinct questions are presented. The first is whether, apart from the location of the activity, distribution of the newsletter is the kind of

9. The court went on to disapprove the alternative ground for the Board's decision stating that "the presence of some §7 protected material will not rescue that which is significantly not protected." 550 F.2d, at 205. We do not find it necessary to express an opinion as to the correctness of this statement. In an opinion denying rehearing and rehearing en banc, the court reaffirmed that it had balanced the employer's and employees' rights, and it deleted two references in its first opinion to the First Amendment. 556 F.2d 1280 (C.A.5 1977).

concerted activity that is protected from employer interference by §§7 and 8(a)(1) of the National Labor Relations Act. If it is, then the second question is whether the fact that the activity takes place on petitioner's property gives rise to a countervailing interest that outweighs the exercise of §7 rights in that location. See Hudgens v. NLRB, 424 U.S. 507, 521-523 (1976); Central Hardware Co. v. NLRB, 407 U.S. 539, 542-545 (1972); NLRB v. Babcock & Wilcox Co., 351 U.S. 105, 112 (1956); Republic Aviation Corp. v. NLRB, 324 U.S. 793, 797-798 (1945). We address these questions in turn.

A

. . . Petitioner contends that the activity here is not within the "mutual aid or protection" language [of §7] because it does not relate to a "specific dispute" between employees and their own employer "over an issue which the employer has the right or power to affect." . . . In support of its position, petitioner asserts that the term *employees* in §7 refers only to employees of a particular employer, so that only activity by employees on behalf of themselves or other employees of the same employer is protected. Petitioner also argues that the term *collective bargaining* in §7 "indicates a direct bargaining relationship whereas 'other mutual aid or protection' must refer to activities of a similar nature. . . ." Thus, in petitioner's view, under §7 "the employee is only protected for activity within the scope of the employment relationship." Petitioner rejects the idea that §7 might protect any activity that could be characterized as "political," and suggests that the discharge of an employee who engages in any such activity would not violate the Act.

We believe that petitioner misconceives the reach of the "mutual aid or protection" clause. The "employees" who may engage in concerted activities for "mutual aid or protection" are defined by §2(3) of the Act to "include any employee, and shall not be limited to the employees of a particular employer, unless this subchapter explicitly states otherwise. . . ." This definition was intended to protect employees when they engage in otherwise proper concerted activities in support of employees of employers other than their own. In recognition of this intent, the Board and the courts long have held that the "mutual aid or protection" clause encompasses such activity. Petitioner's argument on this point ignores the language of the Act and its settled construction.

We also find no warrant for petitioner's view that employees lose their protection under the "mutual aid or protection" clause when they seek to improve terms and conditions of employment or otherwise improve their lot as employees through channels outside the immediate employee-employer relationship. The 74th Congress knew well enough that labor's cause often is advanced on fronts other than collective bargaining and grievance settlement within the immediate employment context. It recognized this fact by choosing, as the language of §7 makes clear, to protect concerted activities for the somewhat broader purpose of "mutual aid or protection" as well as for the narrower purposes of "self-organization" and "collective bargaining." Thus, it has been held that the "mutual aid or protection" clause protects employees from retaliation by their employers when they seek to improve working conditions through resort to administrative and judicial forums, and that employees' appeals to legislators to protect their interests as employees are within the scope of this clause. To hold that activity of this nature is entirely unprotected — irrespective of location or the means employed — would leave employees open to retaliation for much legitimate activity that could improve their lot as employees. As this could "frustrate the policy of the Act to protect the right of workers to act together to better their working conditions," NLRB v. Washington Aluminum Co., 370 U.S. 9, 14 (1962), we do not think that Congress could have intended the protection of §7 to be as narrow as petitioner insists.[17]

It is true, of course, that some concerted activity bears a less immediate relationship to employees' interests as employees than other such activity. We may assume that at some point the relationship becomes so attenuated that an activity cannot fairly be deemed to come within the "mutual aid or protection" clause. It is neither necessary nor appropriate, however, for us to attempt to delineate precisely the boundaries of the "mutual aid or protection" clause. That task is for the Board to

17. Petitioner relies upon several cases said to construe §7 more narrowly than do we. NLRB v. Leslie Metal Arts Co., 509 F.2d 811 (C.A.6 1975), and Shelly & Anderson Furniture Mfg. Co. v. NLRB, 497 F.2d 1200 (C.A.9 1974), both quote the same treatise for the proposition that to be protected under §7, concerted activity must seek "a specific remedy" for a "work-related complaint or grievance." 509 F.2d, at 813, and 497 F.2d, at 1202-1203, quoting 18B T. Kheel, Labor Law §10.02[3], pp. 10-21 (1973). It was unnecessary in those cases to decide whether the protection of §7 went beyond the treatise's formulation, for the activity in both cases was held to be protected. Moreover, in stating its "rule," the treatise relied upon takes no note of the cases cited in nn. 13, 15, and 16, supra. Cf. R. Gorman, Labor Law 296-302 (1976). The Courts of Appeals for the Sixth and Ninth Circuits themselves have taken a broader view of the "mutual aid or protection" clause than the reference to the treatise in the above-cited cases would seem to suggest. See, e.g., Kellogg Co. v. NLRB, 457 F.2d 519, 522-523 (C.A.6 1972), and cases there cited; Kaiser Engineers v. NLRB, supra, at 1384-1385.

Similarly, although the Court of Appeals for the Fourth Circuit stated in NLRB v. Bretz Fuel Co., 210 F.2d 392 (1954), that "concerted activity is protected only where such activity is intimately connected with the employees' immediate employment," id., at 396, the holding in that case turned more on the fact that the activity there consisted of a wildcat strike in violation of a collective-bargaining agreement than on a narrow view of the "mutual aid or protection" clause. See id., at 397-398.

This leaves only G & W Electric Specialty Co. v. NLRB, 360 F.2d 873 (C.A.7 1966), which refused to enforce a Board order because the concerted activity there — circulation of a petition concerning management of an employee-run credit union — "involved no request for any action upon the part of the Company and did not concern a matter over which the Company had control." Id., at 876, *C & W Electric* cites no authority for its narrowing of §7, and it ignores a substantial weight of authority to the contrary, including the Seventh Circuit's own prior holding in Fort Wayne Corrugated Paper Co. v. NLRB, supra, at 874. See n.13, supra. We therefore do not view any of these cases as persuasive authority for petitioner's position.

perform in the first instance as it considers the wide variety of cases that come before it.[18] Republic Aviation Corp. v. NLRB, 324 U.S., at 798; Phelps Dodge Corp. v. NLRB, 313 U.S. 177, 194 (1941). To decide this case, it is enough to determine whether the Board erred in holding that distribution of the second and third sections of the newsletter is for the purpose of "mutual aid or protection."

The Board determined that distribution of the second section, urging employees to write their legislators to oppose incorporation of the state "right-to-work" statute into a revised state constitution, was protected because union security is "central to the union concept of strength through solidarity" and "a mandatory subject of bargaining in other than right-to-work states." 215 N.L.R.B., at 274. The newsletter warned that incorporation could affect employees adversely "by weakening Unions and improving the edge business has at the bargaining table." The fact that Texas already has a "right-to-work" statute does not render employees' interest in this matter any less strong, for, as the Court of Appeals noted, it is "one thing to face a statutory scheme which is open to legislative modification or repeal" and "quite another thing to face the prospect that such a scheme will be frozen in a concrete constitutional mandate." 550 F.2d, at 205. We cannot say that the Board erred in holding that this section of the newsletter bears such a relation to employees' interests as to come within the guarantee of the "mutual aid or protection" clause. . . .

The Board held that distribution of the third section, criticizing a Presidential veto of an increase in the federal minimum wage and urging employees to register to vote to "defeat our enemies and elect our friends," was protected despite the fact that petitioner's employees were paid more than the vetoed minimum wage. It reasoned that the "minimum wage inevitably influences wage levels derived from collective bargaining, even those far above the minimum," and that "concern by [petitioner's] employees for the plight of other employees might gain support for them at some future time when they might have a dispute

18. See Ford Motor Co., 221 N.L.R.B. 663, 666 (1975), enf'd, 546 F.2d 418 (3d Cir. 1976) (holding distribution on employer's premises of a "purely political tract" unprotected even though "the election of any political candidate may have an ultimate effect on employment conditions"); cf. Ford Motor Co. (Rouge Complex), 233 N.L.R.B. No. 102 (1977), decision of Administrative Law Judge, p. 8 (concession of General Counsel that distributions on employer's premises of literature urging participation in Revolutionary Communist Party celebration, and of Party's newspaper, were unprotected). The Board has not yet made clear whether it considers distributions like those in the above-cited cases to be unprotected altogether, or only on the employer's premises.

In addition, even when concerted activity comes within the scope of the "mutual aid or protection" clause, the forms such activity permissibly may take may well depend on the object of the activity. "The argument that the employer's lack of interest or control affords a legitimate basis for holding that a subject does not come within 'mutual aid or protection' is unconvincing. The argument that economic pressure should be unprotected in such cases is more convincing." Getman, The Protection of Economic Pressure by Section 7 of the National Labor Relations Act, 115 U. Pa. L. Rev. 1195, 1221 (1967).

with their employer." 215 N.L.R.B., at 274 (internal quotation marks omitted). We think that the Board acted within the range of its discretion in so holding. Few topics are of such immediate concern to employees as the level of their wages. The Board was entitled to note the widely recognized impact that a rise in the minimum wage may have on the level of negotiated wages generally, a phenomenon that would not have been lost on petitioner's employees. The union's call, in the circumstances of this case, for these employees to back persons who support an increase in the minimum wage, and to oppose those who oppose it, fairly is characterized as concerted activity for the "mutual aid or protection" of petitioner's employees and of employees generally.

In sum, we hold that distribution of both the second and the third sections of the newsletter is protected under the "mutual aid or protection" clause of §7.[20]

B

The question that remains is whether the Board erred in holding that petitioner's employees may distribute the newsletter in nonworking areas of petitioner's property during nonworking time. Consideration of this issue must begin with the Court's decisions in Republic Aviation Corp. v. NLRB, supra, and NLRB v. Babcock & Wilcox Co., 351 U.S. 105 (1956). In *Republic Aviation* the Court upheld the Board's ruling that an employer may not prohibit its employees from distributing union organizational literature in nonworking areas of its industrial property during nonworking time, absent a showing by the employer that a ban is necessary to maintain plant discipline or production. This ruling obtained even though the employees had not shown that distribution off the employer's property would be ineffective. 324 U.S., at 798-799, 801. In the Court's view, the Board had reached an acceptable "adjustment between the undisputed right of self-organization assured to employees under the Wagner Act and the equally undisputed right of employers to maintain discipline in their establishments." Id., at 797-798.[21]

20. Petitioner argues that the "right to work" and minimum wage issues are "political," and that advancing a union's political views is not protected by §7. As almost every issue can be viewed by some as political, the clear purpose of the "mutual aid or protection" clause would be frustrated if the mere characterization of conduct or speech removed it from the protection of the Act. . . . Moreover, what may be viewed as political in one context can be viewed quite differently in another. There may well be types of conduct or speech that are so purely political or so remotely connected to the concerns of employees as employees as to be beyond the protection of the clause. But this is a determination that should be left for case-by-case consideration. Cf. cases cited in n.18, supra.

21. In *Republic Aviation* the Court also upheld Board rulings that employees may solicit other employees to join a union on the employer's property during nonworking time, and may wear union insignia on the employer's property. The Board since has distinguished between distributions of literature and oral solicitation, holding that the latter but not the former may take place in working areas during nonworking time. Stoddard-Quirk Mfg. Co., 138 N.L.R.B. 615 (1962).

In *Babcock & Wilcox,* on the other hand, nonemployees sought to enter an employer's property to distribute union organizational literature. The Board applied the rule of *Republic Aviation* in this situation, but the Court held that there is a distinction "of substance" between "rules of law applicable to employees and those applicable to nonemployees." 351 U.S., at 113. The difference was that the nonemployees in *Babcock & Wilcox* sought to trespass on the employer's property, whereas the employees in *Republic Aviation* did not. Striking a balance between §7 organizational rights and an employer's right to keep strangers from entering on its property, the Court held that the employer in *Babcock & Wilcox* was entitled to prevent "nonemployee distribution of union literature [on its property] if reasonable efforts by the union through other available channels of communication will enable it to reach the employees with its message. . . ." Id., at 112. The Court recently has emphasized the distinction between the two cases: "A wholly different balance was struck when the organizational activity was carried on by employees already rightfully on the employer's property, since the employer's management interests rather than his property interests were there involved." Hudgens v. NLRB, 424 U.S., at 521-522, n.10; see also Central Hardware Co. v. NLRB, 407 U.S., at 543-545.

It is apparent that the instant case resembles *Republic Aviation* rather closely. Here, as there, employees sought to distribute literature in nonworking areas of their employer's industrial property during nonworking time. Here, as there, the employer has not attempted to show that distribution would interfere with plant discipline or production. And here, as there, distribution of the newsletter clearly would be protected by §7 against employer discipline if it took place off the employer's property. The only possible ground of distinction is that part of the newsletter in this case does not address purely organizational matters, but rather concerns other activity protected by §7. The question, then, is whether this difference required the Board to apply a different rule here than it applied in *Republic Aviation.*

Petitioner contends that the Board must distinguish among distributions of protected matter by employees on an employer's property on the basis of the content of each distribution. Echoing its earlier argument, petitioner urges that the *Republic Aviation* rule should not be applied if a distribution "does not involve a request for any action on the part of the employer, or does not concern a matter over which the employer has any degree of control. . . ." In petitioner's view, distribution of any other matter protected by §7 would be an "unnecessary intrusio[n] on the employer's property rights," in the absence of a showing by employees that no alternative channels of communication with fellow employees are available.

We hold that the Board was not required to adopt this view in the case at hand. In the first place, petitioner's reliance on its property right is largely misplaced. Here, as in *Republic Aviation*, petitioner's employees are "already rightfully on the employer's property," so that in the context of this case it is the "employer's management interests rather than [its] property interests" that primarily are implicated. *Hudgens*, supra, at 521-522, n.10. As already noted, petitioner made no attempt to show that its management interests would be prejudiced in any way by the exercise of §7 rights proposed by its employees here. Even if the mere distribution by employees of material protected by §7 can be said to intrude on petitioner's property rights in any meaningful sense, the degree of intrusion does not vary with the content of the material. Petitioner's only cognizable property right in this respect is in preventing employees from bringing literature onto its property and distributing it there — not in choosing which distributions protected by §7 it wishes to suppress.[22]

On the other side of the balance, it may be argued that the employees' interest in distributing literature that deals with matters affecting them as employees, but not with self-organization or collective bargaining, is so removed from the central concerns of the Act as to justify application of a different rule than in *Republic Aviation*. Although such an argument may have force in some circumstances, see *Hudgens*, supra, at 522, the Board to date generally has chosen not to engage in such refinement of its rules regarding the distribution of literature by employees during nonworking time in nonworking areas of their employers' property. We are not prepared to say in this case that the Board erred in the view it took.

It is apparent that the complexity of the Board's rules and the difficulty of the Board's task might be compounded greatly if it were required to distinguish not only between literature that is within and without the protection of §7, but also among subcategories of literature within that protection. In addition, whatever the strength of the employees' §7 interest in distributing particular literature, the Board is entitled to view the intrusion by employees on the property rights of their employer as quite limited in this context as long as the employer's management interests are adequately protected. The Board also properly may take into account the fact that the plant is a particularly appropriate place for the distribution of §7 material, because it "is the one place where [employees] clearly share common interests and where they tradi-

22. In addition, we doubt whether the test proposed by petitioner for the protection of its property rights can be squared with *Republic Aviation* itself, for the organizational literature in that case did not "involve a request for any action on the part of the employer, or . . . concern a matter over which the employer [had] any degree of control."

To be sure, if the material distributed on the premises of the employer were inflammatory to the point of threatening disorder or other interruption of the normal functioning of the business, the exception noted in *Republic Aviation* with respect to interference with discipline or production would be fully applicable. See Procter & Gamble Mfg. Co., 160 N.L.R.B. 334, 395 (1966).

tionally seek to persuade fellow workers in matters affecting their union organizational life and other matters related to their status as employees." Gale Products, 142 N.L.R.B. 1246, 1249 (1963).

We need not go so far in this case, however, as to hold that the *Republic Aviation* rule properly is applied to every in-plant distribution of literature that falls within the protective ambit of §7. This is a new area for the Board and the courts which has not yet received mature consideration. It may be that the "nature of the problem, as revealed by unfolding variant situations," requires "an evolutionary process for its rational response, not a quick, definitive formula as a comprehensive answer." Electrical Workers v. NLRB, 366 U.S. 667, 674 (1961). For this reason, we confine our holding to the facts of this case.

Petitioner concedes that its employees were entitled to distribute a substantial portion of this newsletter on its property. In addition, as we have held above, the sections to which petitioner objected concern activity which petitioner, in the absence of a countervailing interest of its own, is not entitled to suppress. Yet petitioner made no attempt to show that its management interests would be prejudiced in any manner by distribution of these sections, and in our view any incremental intrusion on petitioner's property rights from their distribution together with the other sections would be minimal. Moreover, it is undisputed that the union undertook the distribution in order to boost its support and improve its bargaining position in upcoming contract negotiations with petitioner. Thus, viewed in context, the distribution was closely tied to vital concerns of the act. In these circumstances, we hold that the Board did not err in applying the *Republic Aviation* rule to the facts of this case. The judgment of the Court of Appeals therefore is affirmed.

WHITE, J., concurring. . . .

I agree that the employees here were engaged in activity protected by §7, at least in the sense that the employer could not discharge employees for propagandizing their fellow workers with materials concerning minimum wages and right-to-work laws, so long as the distribution takes place off the employer's property. I agree further that under current law and the facts and claims in this record, the distributions could take place on the employer's property. Accordingly, the Board was entitled to have its order enforced and I join the judgment and opinion of the Court.

In doing so, I should say that it is not easy to explain why an employer need permit his property to be used for distributions about subjects unrelated to his relationship with his employees simply because it is convenient for the latter to use his property in this manner and simply because there is no interference with "management interests." Ownership of property normally confers the right to control the use of that property. Here there was no finding by the Board that the literature sought to be distributed was connected with the bargaining relationship; and I doubt that federal law requires the employer *always* to permit his property to be used for solicitations and distributions having §7 protection, even by and among employees in nonworking areas and during nonworking times. Such distributions might concern goals and ends about which his work force, considered as a whole, as well as the public, may be deeply divided, with which he may have no sympathy whatsoever, or in connection with which he would not care to have it inferred that he supports one side or the other. All of these, if substantiated by the record, would appear to be substantial factors to be weighed in the balance when determining whether the employer has violated the Labor Act's strictures concerning his relationship with his employees.

However this may be, on the record before us, I am content to affirm the judgment of the Court of Appeals.

REHNQUIST, J., with whom BURGER, C.J. joins, dissenting. . . .

The Court today cites no case in which it has ever held that anyone, whether an employee or a nonemployee, has a protected right to engage in anything other than organizational activity on an employer's property. The simple question before us is whether Congress has authorized the Board to displace an employer's right to prevent the distribution on his property of political material concerning matters over which he has no control. In eschewing any analysis of this question, in deference to the supposed expertise of the Board, the Court permits a "'yielding' of property rights" which is certainly not "temporary"; and I cannot conclude that the deprivation of such a right of property can be dismissed as "minimal." It may be that Congress has power under the Commerce Clause to require an employer to open his property to such political advocacy, but, if Congress intended to do so, "such a legislative intention should be found in some definite and unmistakable expression." *Fansteel,* 306 U.S., at 255. Finding no such expression in the Act, I would not permit the Board to balance away petitioner's right to exclude political literature from its property. . . .

Notes

1. In Beth Israel Hospital v. NLRB, 437 U.S. 483 (1978), the Court invalidated a rule promulgated by a hospital barring solicitation and distribution of literature in a hospital cafeteria. A majority of the Justices were unpersuaded that special considerations of patient care rendered *Republic Aviation* rules inapplicable. Of critical importance to the entire Court was the fact that there was no convenient access to employees in other areas of the hospital, and that less than 2 percent of the use of the cafeteria was by patients.

2. *Problem.* After *Eastex,* would a union have a §7 right to distribute, in nonworking areas of a plant, propaganda relating solely to the union's support of candidates seeking election to the Michigan Supreme Court, the United States Senate, and the governorship of the state of Michigan? See Firestone Steel Products Co., 244 N.L.R.B. 148 (1979).

NLRB v. UNITED STEELWORKERS (NUTONE AND AVONDALE MILLS)

357 U.S. 357 (1957)

FRANKFURTER, J.

These two cases, argued in succession, are controlled by the same considerations and will be disposed of in a single opinion. In one case the National Labor Relations Board ruled that it was not an unfair labor practice for an employer to enforce against his employees a no-solicitation rule, in itself concededly valid, while the employer was himself engaged in anti-union solicitation in a context of separate unfair labor practices. This ruling was reversed by a Court of Appeals. In the second case the Board on the basis of similar facts, except that the employer's anti-union solicitation by itself constituted a separate unfair labor practice, found the enforcement of the rule to have been an unfair labor practice, but another Court of Appeals denied enforcement of the Board's order. . . .

No. 81. — In April of 1953 the respondent Steelworkers instituted a campaign to organize the employees of respondent Nutone, Inc., a manufacturer of electrical devices. In the early stages of the campaign, supervisory personnel of the company interrogated employees and solicited reports concerning the organizational activities of other employees. Several employees were discharged; the Board later found that the discharges had been the result of their organizational activities. In June the company began to distribute, through its supervisory personnel, literature that, although not coercive, was clearly anti-union in tenor. In August, while continuing to distribute such material, the company announced its intention of enforcing its rule against employees' posting signs or distributing literature on company property or soliciting or campaigning on company time. The rule, according to these posted announcements, applied to "all employees — whether they are for or against the union." Later the same month a representation election was held, which the Steelworkers lost.

In a proceeding before the Board commenced at the instance of the Steelworkers, the company was charged with a number of violations of the Act alleged to have taken place both before and after the election, including the discriminatory application of the no-solicitation rule. The Board found that the pre-election interrogation and solicitation by supervisory personnel and the discharge of employees were unfair labor practices; it also found that the company had, in violation of the Act, assisted and supported an employee organization formed after the election. However, the Board dismissed the allegation that the company had discriminatorily enforced its no-solicitation rule. The Steelworkers sought review of this dismissal in the United States Court of Appeals for the District of Columbia Circuit, and the Board petitioned for enforcement of its order in the same court. The Court of Appeals concluded that it was an unfair labor practice for the company to prohibit the distribution of organizational literature on company property during nonworking hours while the company was itself distributing anti-union literature; and it directed that the Board's order be modified accordingly and enforced as modified.

No. 289. — In the fall of 1954 the Textile Workers conducted an organizational campaign at several of the plants of respondent Avondale Mills. A number of individual employees were called before supervisory personnel of the company, on the ground that they had been soliciting union membership, and informed that such solicitation was in violation of plant rules and would not be tolerated in the future. The rule had not been promulgated in written form, but there was evidence that it had been previously involved in a nonorganizational context. During this same period, both in these interviews concerning the rule and at the employees' places of work, supervisory personnel interrogated employees concerning their organizational views and activities and solicited employees to withdraw their membership cards from the union. This conduct was in many cases accompanied by threats that the mill would close down or that various employee benefits would be lost if the mill should become organized. Subsequently three employees, each of whom had been informed of the no-solicitation rule, were laid off and eventually discharged for violating the rule.

As a result of charges filed with the Board by the Textile Workers, a complaint was brought against the company alleging that it had committed a number of unfair labor practices, including the discriminatory invocation of the no-solicitation rule and the discharge of employees for its violation. The Board found that the interrogation, solicitation and threatening of employees by the company's supervisory personnel were unfair labor practices. Moreover, it found that resort to the no-solicitation rule and discharge of the three employees for its violation were discriminatory and therefore in violation of the Act; it further held that, even if the rule had not been invoked discriminatorily, the discharge of one of the employees had resulted solely from his organizational activities apart from any violation of the rule and was therefore an unfair labor practice. The Board ordered the cessation of these practices and the reinstatement of the discharged employees. 115 N.L.R.B. 840. Upon the Board's petitioning for enforcement in the Court of Appeals for the Fifth Circuit, the company contested only the portions of the Board's findings and order relating to the rule and the discharges. The court enforced the uncontested portions of the order but, finding insufficient evidence of discrimination in the application of the no-solicitation rule, denied enforcement to the portion of the order relating to the rule and to two of the discharges. As to the third discharge, the court agreed with the Board that is was the result of discrimination unrelated to a violation of the rule, and the court enforced the portion of the Board's order directing the employee's reinstatement. 242 F.2d 669.

Employer rules prohibiting organizational solicitation are not in and of themselves violative of the Act, for they may duly serve production, order and discipline. See Republic Aviation Corp. v. Labor Board, 324 U.S. 793; Labor Board v. Babcock & Wilcox Co., 351 U.S. 105. In neither of the cases before us did the party attacking the enforcement of the no-solicitation rule contest its validity. Nor is the claim made that an employer may not, under proper circumstances, engage in non-coercive anti-union solicitation; indeed, his right to do so is protected by the so-called "employer free speech" provision of §8(c) of the Act. Contrariwise, as both cases before us show, coercive anti-union solicitation and other similar conduct run afoul of the Act and constitute unfair labor practices irrespective of the bearing of such practices on enforcement of a no-solicitation rule. The very narrow and almost abstract question here derives from the claim that, when the employer himself engages in anti-union solicitation that if engaged in by employees would constitute a violation of the rule — particularly when his solicitation is coercive or accompanied by other unfair labor practices — his enforcement of an otherwise valid no-solicitation rule against the employees is itself an unfair labor practice. We are asked to rule that the coincidence of these circumstances necessarily violates the Act, regardless of the way in which the particular controversy arose or whether the employer's conduct to any considerable degree created an imbalance in the opportunities for organizational communication. For us to lay down such a rule of law would show indifference to the responsibilities imposed by the Act primarily on the Board to appraise carefully the interests of both sides of any labor-management controversy in the diverse circumstances of particular cases and in light of the Board's special understanding of these industrial situations.

There is no indication in the record in either of these cases that the employees, or the union on their behalf, requested the employer, himself engaging in anti-union solicitation, to make an exception to the rule for pro-union solicitation. There is evidence in both cases that the employers had in the past made exceptions to their rules for charitable solicitation. Notwithstanding the clear anti-union bias of both employers, it is not for us to conclude as a matter of law — although it might well have been open to the Board to conclude as a matter of industrial experience — that a request for a similar qualification upon the rule for organizational solicitation would have been rejected. Certainly the employer is not obliged voluntarily and without any request to offer the use of his facilities and the time of his employees for pro-union solicitation. He may very well be wary of a charge that he is interfering with, or contributing support to, a labor organization in violation of §8(a)(2) of the Act.

No attempt was made in either of these cases to make a showing that the no-solicitation rules truly diminished the ability of the labor organizations involved to carry their messages to the employees. Just as that is a vital consideration in determining the validity of a no-solicitation rule, see Republic Aviation Corp. v. Labor Board, supra, at 797-798; Labor Board v. Babcock & Wilcox Co., supra, at 112, it is highly relevant in determining whether a valid rule has been fairly applied. Of course the rules had the effect of closing off one channel of communication; but the Taft-Hartley Act does not command that labor organizations as a matter of abstract law, under all circumstances, be protected in the use of every possible means of reaching the minds of individual workers, nor that they are entitled to use a medium of communication simply because the employer is using it.

No such mechanical answers will avail for the solution of this non-mechanical, complex problem in labor-management relations. If, by virtue of the location of the plant and of the facilities and resources available to the union, the opportunities for effectively reaching the employees with a pro-union message, in spite of a no-solicitation rule, are at least as great as the employer's ability to promote the legally authorized expression of his anti-union views, there is no basis for invalidating these "otherwise valid" rules. The Board, in determining whether or not the enforcement of such a rule in the circumstances of an individual case is an unfair labor practice, may find relevant alternative channels available for communications on the right to organize. When this important issue is not even raised before the Board and no evidence bearing on it adduced, the concrete basis for appraising the significance of the employer's conduct is wanting.

We do not at all imply that the enforcement of a valid no-solicitation rule by an employer who is at the same time engaging in anti-union solicitation may not constitute an unfair labor practice. All we hold is that there must be some basis, in the actualities of industrial relations, for such a finding. The records in both cases — the issues raised in the proceedings — are barren of the ingredients for such a finding. Accordingly the judgment in No. 81 is reversed, insofar as it sets aside and requires the Board to modify its order, and the cause is remanded to the Court of Appeals for proceedings not inconsistent with this opinion; in all other respects, it is affirmed. The judgment in No. 289 is affirmed.

It is so ordered.[36]

[36] Black, J., and Douglas, J., dissented. Warren, C.J., dissented in part and concurred in part.

Notes

1. Consider the Board opinions in *Nutone* and *Avondale*. In Nutone, Inc., 112 N.L.R.B. 1153 (1955), the Board held 3-1 that the employer could prohibit employee solicitation even while his or her supervisors were soliciting antiunion support:

> The Trial Examiner . . . predicated a finding of unlawful conduct on his conclusion that the respondent "broke its own rules . . . by campaigning against the Union in the normal arena and the most effective one for reaching employees . . . while simultaneously denying access to it by the union." We are in disagreement with this conclusion. Valid plant rules against solicitation and other forms of union activity do not control an employer's actions. Management prerogative certainly extends far enough so as to permit an employer to make rules that do not bind himself.

Only nine months later, in Avondale Mills, 115 N.L.R.B. 840 (1956), the Board, with two new members, unanimously held that supervisor solicitation was evidence of a discriminatory purpose in the employer's maintenance of an employee no-solicitation rule:

> It is settled law that a rule prohibiting union solicitation during working hours is valid provided it is not promulgated or utilized in order to prevent or impede the organization of its employees. In the present case, such a discriminatory purpose is revealed in the Trial Examiner's factual findings and the evidence in the record. . . . that the respondent was prompted to invoke the no-solicitation rule by a desire to prevent unionization of its employees rather than by consideration of plant production and efficiency, as the Respondent urges, is also indicated by the fact that talking on a variety of subjects was permitted in the plant. This included union discussions in which both employees and supervisors participated. Indeed, supervisors utilized these and other occasions during working hours to make threats of reprisals and to interrogate employees concerning their union membership and sympathies, which conduct the Trial Examiner found violated §8(a)(1) of the Act.[8] Finally, there is no concrete evidence in the record showing the extent, if any, that production was impaired by union solicitation.

Which is the best course for the Supreme Court or a court of appeals on review of *Avondale*: enforce, relying on Board expertise; refuse to enforce, relying on the unexplained inconsistency in the cases; remand to the Board with a demand for a more reasoned analysis; or decide the issue itself?

2. Note the effect of the Court's decision in *Nutone*. The legality of

8. The Board's decision in Nutone, Inc., 112 N.L.R.B. 1153, does not preclude reliance on the antiunion conduct of the Respondent's supervisors as evidence of discriminatory motivation underlying the adoption or revival of the no-union-solicitation rule.

maintaining a facially valid no-solicitation/distribution rule to which supervisors are not bound is determined by considering, on a case-by-case basis, whether the union's ability to carry its message has been "truly diminished." Companies will not be likely to restrict their supervisors' solicitations, for, assuming no election is pending, their legal exposure is very limited. The no-solicitation/distribution rule may not be challenged; or if it is challenged, the company can drop it with no cost, or defend it (while maintaining it) by the expenditure of legal fees — the ultimate risk being a cease and desist order. Liability beyond the company's own attorneys' fees is risked only if an employee is discharged for violating the rule, and such a discharge may be unnecessary.

3. As we shall see, the NLRB only decides contested cases; it does not engage in formal, administrative rule making. Nonetheless, in it decisions the Board has developed precise rules regarding an employer's restrictions on oral solicitation and the distribution of literature. An employer may prohibit his or her workers from oral solicitation only during the workers' "working time."[37] That is, discipline for oral solicitation occurring when the employees involved are not on their working time will result in §§8(a)(1) and (3) violations even though the solicitation occurs on company premises and in working areas.

The employer's permissible restrictions on the distribution of literature are broader. The employer may forbid the distribution of literature by employees in working areas of the establishment during both working and nonworking time.[38] However, an otherwise valid rule may still be held a violation of the Act if it is adopted for a discriminatory purpose or applied in a discriminatory manner.[39] Conversely, even a normally invalid rule will be upheld in the rare case in which an employer can show special circumstances inherent in the nature of the business operation to justify it.[40]

Are rules of general application consistent with *Babcock* and *Nutone*? This issue is illustrated by the NLRB's decision in May Dept. Stores Co., 136 N.L.R.B. 797 (1962). The respondent owned a department store and prohibited union solicitation in the selling areas of the store during the employees' working and nonworking time. The Board in prior cases had developed a special rule for department stores that permitted this broad prohibition as a special exception to the NLRB's general doctrine because union solicitation in the presence of customers might have an adverse effect on the business. In the instant case, while prohibiting union solicitation, the employer made noncoercive, antiunion speeches to massed assemblies of employees on the department store property but denied the union's request for equal time and access to address the same employees.

[37] Essex Intl., 211 N.L.R.B. 749 (1974).
[38] Stoddard-Quirk Mfg. Co., 138 N.L.R.B. 615 (1962).
[39] State Chemical Co., 166 N.L.R.B. 455 (1967).
[40] May Dept. Stores Co., 59 N.L.R.B. 976 (1944).

A majority of the Board held that the cumulative effect of the broad company prohibition and the company's own captive audience speech violated the Act. In response to the company's reliance on *Nutone* and *Babcock*, the majority discussed generally the advantages that companies have in presenting their views of organizing issues on company premises during working time while relegating "the union and its employee supporters to relatively catch-as-catch-can methods of rebuttal. . . ." While the Board spoke in terms of an "imbalance in opportunities for organizational communication," it did not look at the impact of this employer's practices on the ability of this particular union to reach the employees at the May Department Store. A dissenting Board member stated, "I do not think . . . a true diminution can be established merely by showing that as a general proposition department store employees can be more easily reached through the avenues of communication open to their employer than through the avenues open to a union." How would you have decided the case on appeal?[41]

The Board has suffered under the burden of an increasingly heavy case load. Would it be proper for a court to consider the effect of a general rule, such as that announced by the Board in *May*, on administrative costs?

What are the comparative advantages and disadvantages of legal rules that require the accumulation and weighing of many facts versus legal "rules of thumb"? This kind of question recurs throughout the course, in a variety of contexts. It is the subject of the following essay.

EHRLICH AND POSNER, AN ECONOMIC ANALYSIS OF LEGAL RULEMAKING

2 J. Legal Stud. 257 (1974)

This article . . . discusses the degree of precision or specificity with which a legal command is expressed as a determinant of the efficiency of the legal process. . . . We are not concerned here with the question why some activities are regulated and others not.

If we want to prevent driving at excessive speeds, one approach is to post specific speed limits and to declare it unlawful per se to exceed those limits; another is to eschew specific speed limits and simply declare that driving at unreasonable speeds is unlawful. Any choice along the specificity-generality continuum will generate a unique set of costs and benefits. This article discusses the conditions under which greater specificity or greater generality is the efficient choice and makes a preliminary effort to appraise the efficiency of the choices actually made by the legal process.

[41] The Court of Appeals for the Sixth Circuit refused to enforce the Board's order. May Dept. Stores Co. v. NLRB, 316 F.2d 797 (6th Cir. 1963); but see Montgomery Ward & Co. v. NLRB, 339 F.2d 889 (6th Cir. 1965).

I. Preliminary Issues

To facilitate exposition, we will sometimes treat the specificity-generality continuum as if it were a dichotomy between "rules" and "standards." The term "standard" denotes in our usage a general criterion of social choice; efficiency (and its counterparts in legal terminology, such as reasonableness) is an example. A standard indicates the kinds of circumstances that are relevant to a decision on legality and is thus open-ended. That is, it is not a list of all the circumstances that might be relevant but is rather the criterion by which particular circumstances presented in a case are judged to be relevant or not. In an automobile collision case governed by the negligence standard these circumstances would be the speed and weight of the vehicles, their design, the time of day, the layout of the highway, the weather, and any other factors that might affect the question how the sum of the expected accident costs and the accident-avoidance costs could have been minimized.

A rule withdraws from the decision maker's consideration one or more of the circumstances that would be relevant to decision according to a standard. Suppose that if it is proved that the following car in a rear-end collision was driving within 100 feet of the preceding car, the driver of the following car will be liable for the costs of the accident. This is a rule rather than a standard because, were the case to be decided under the general negligence standard, other circumstances besides the distance between the two cars would have to be considered, such as the ability of the driver of the preceding car to avoid stopping short. The simplest kind of rule, then, takes the form: if *X*, then *Y*, where *X* is a single, simple, determinate fact (e.g., the car's speed) and *Y* is a definite, unequivocal legal consequence — a judgment of liability or nonliability — that follows directly from proof of *X* (e.g., driver has violated traffic code). It should be clear, therefore, that we are using the term "rule" in a somewhat special sense; "general rule" would be a contradiction in our usage.

The difference between a rule and a standard is a matter of degree — the degree of precision. The efficiency standard itself could be regarded as a rule of social choice designed to implement a broader standard (the greatest happiness of the greatest number of people), while a rule that required the weighing of many circumstances (unlike our hypothetical rear-end rule, which required the weighing of only one, distance) would be like a standard. Our fundamental concern is with precision of law rather than with choosing between rule and standard as such. . . .

Rule and standard are not merely alternative forms in which to express the commands of the law. Standards are also criteria of rules. If the standard governing automobile accident cases were income equality rather than efficiency, the specific rules of accident law would be different from what they are. But while rules may implement standards, they need not do so, as can be seen by a comparison of rules, such as those of common law fields like torts, that derive (we believe) from coherent and intelligible social policies, with rules, characteristic of much of the economic legislation of modern welfare states, that are the outcome of a power struggle between opposing political factions, such as the rules of taxation. (We do not suggest that all legislative rules are of this character.)

If the social goal is efficiency, a set of particular rules of accident law can be formulated to maximize attainment of the goal; arguably, most of the rules and doctrines of tort law are of this type. One doubts that the rules of tax law (governing rates, deductions, and the like) could be derived in similar fashion. Taxation has goals — to raise revenue, to foster certain notions of distributive justice, and to avoid creating incentives to engage in inefficient activities — but they are often, perhaps typically, in conflict; they do not constitute a single, coherent standard. It does not follow that there are no rules of taxation; there are more rules of taxation than of negligence. But they do not comprise a logical system in the sense that, told "the purpose" of the system and something about the activities taxed, one could deduce the rules — at least it would be much harder to do so than in the case of the tort system. If this analysis is correct, arbitrariness, political favoritism, covert influence, and the like — the very abuses associated with "discretionary justice" — may sometimes be more prevalent in an area, such as taxation, where decision is guided primarily by rules than in one where a less exact standard is operating.

II. The Optimum Precision of Legal Obligation: A Static Approach

We shall consider in this part the benefits and costs associated with different choices along the continuum between the highly specific rule and the highly general standard and discuss the optimum choice — the choice that maximizes the excess of benefits over costs. Our analysis will be rather abstract owing to the problem of measuring the relevant costs and benefits and to the absence of a readily identifiable empirical counterpart to the concept of precision of legal obligation (it is obvious that simply counting the number of rules in an area of law will not yield a reliable measure of it). We emphasize, however, that the *concept* of legal precision is unambiguous — the fewer and simpler the facts to which definite legal consequences attach, the more precise is a legal obligation. And we do not despair of measuring legal precision, especially within (rather than across) fields of law. We do not doubt, for example, that the so-called "per se" rules of antitrust law can be shown to be more precise than the "Rule of Reason" under which some antitrust questions are decided.

Several points should be kept in mind throughout the analysis:

1. Rules are addressed to two audiences: people who might violate (or be accused of violating) the law, and participants in the process of determining whether a violation has occurred (judges, lawyers, etc.). The effects of the choice between rule and standard on the first group we shall call effects on "primary behavior," as contrasted with the effects of the choice on law enforcement and other activities of the legal system.
2. The legislature's choice whether to enact a standard or a set of precise rules is implicitly also a choice between legislative and judicial rulemaking. A general legislative standard creates a demand for specification. This demand is brought to bear on the courts through the litigation process and they respond by creating rules particularizing the legislative standard. Thus an appraisal of the efficiency of a legislative decision to enact a standard requires consideration of the differences in costs and benefits between legislative rules and judge-made rules (precedents).

   Sometimes the demand for specificity is satisfied by private rulemakers rather than by courts. This is especially likely to occur in areas where courts use standards rather than rules. Potential defendants may be unwilling to let their employees make the difficult decisions involved in applying a standard to particular circumstances, so they formulate rules of conduct to guide the employees. We do not discuss these private rules in this article but they are undoubtedly an important feature of legal regulation.
3. The analysis in this part is primarily static. We postpone to Part III a discussion of how the costs and benefits of a rule or standard are affected by changes through time in the relevant social or economic conditions.

A. ELEMENTS OF THE MODEL

1. Benefits of Rules

a. *Primary behavior.* A perfectly detailed and comprehensive set of rules brings society nearer to its desired allocation of resources by discouraging socially undesirable activities and encouraging socially desirable ones. This is because detailing the law efficiently (the importance of this qualification will become clear later) results in an increase in the expected gain from engaging in socially desirable activity relative to that from engaging in undesirable activity.

It does this by increasing the (subjective) probabilities that the undesirable activity is punishable and that the desirable is not. The cost of an activity includes any expected punishment costs. The expected punishment cost of engaging in an activity is the product of (1) the subjective probability of the participant's being apprehended and convicted and (2) the cost to him of the penalty that will be imposed if he is convicted. The probability of apprehension and conviction, in turn, is the product of (1) the probability that the activity in which the person is engaged will be deemed illegal and (2) the probability that, if so, he will be charged and convicted for his participation in it. The more (efficiently) precise and detailed the applicable substantive standard or rule is, the higher is the probability that the activity will be deemed illegal if it is in fact undesirable (the kind of activity the legislature wanted to prevent) and the lower is the probability that the activity will be deemed illegal if it is in fact desirable. Thus the expected punishment cost of undesirable activity is increased and that of desirable activity reduced.

We offer two additional observations about the impact of precision of legal obligation on primary behavior. First, it has an indirect effect on that behavior through its effect on law enforcement activity (public or private), a point developed in the next subsection. Second, efficient *statutory* rules can be expected to have a greater effect on primary behavior than efficient judge-made rules. The statute precedes the precedent. The legislature's choice is between promulgating its own rule and leaving it to the courts to fashion a rule after a case (or series of cases) comes to them — the latter a protracted process. In addition, the statutory rule is likely to have a broader scope than the judge-made rule. Since the parties to a lawsuit, who define the issues in the suit, are generally individuals or individual firms that are not interested in obtaining a broad rule, a court tends to create a rule limited to situations very similar to that of the case at hand. The nature of the legislative process is such that ordinarily only substantial interest groups, rather than single individuals, can invoke it. The result is that most legislative rules control a relatively broad span of activity.

b. *Legal-system behavior.* Here we consider the benefits of greater precision of legal obligation in terms of its effects on behavior within the legal system.

(1) An increase in precision increases the probability of convicting the guilty and of acquitting the innocent ("guilty" here meaning engaged in socially undesirable activities and "innocent" engaged in socially desirable activities). Stated differently, it increases the marginal productivity of expenditures by the law enforcer (public or private) on prosecuting the guilty, reduces the marginal productivity of his expenditures on prosecuting the innocent, reduces the marginal productivity of the guilty defendant's litigation expenditures, and increases the marginal productivity of the innocent defendant's litigation expenditures. The combination of these effects should induce an increase in prosecutorial resources in cases involving guilty defendants, a decrease in defendants' expenditures in those cases, an increase in defense expenditures in cases

where the defendant is in fact innocent, and a decrease in prosecutorial expenditures in those cases. The net result should be a further increase in the probability of convicting the guilty and of acquitting the innocent, resulting in a further increase in the efficiency of primary behavior.

(2) The reduction in the amount of socially undesirable activity brought about both directly and (through the greater efficiency of law enforcement expenditures) indirectly by rule precision should reduce the total number of cases brought and hence the total amount of resources devoted to legal dispute resolution. In addition, fewer cases will be brought that arise out of socially desirable activities. Also, the sum of the parties' expenditures in those cases that are litigated may be lower. This is because a rule withdraws from a lawsuit many of the issues that would have been litigable were the case decided under a standard and it seems likely that there are diminishing — often very rapidly diminishing — returns to proof of a point.

(3) If a legal dispute occurs, the fact that the outcome of the dispute, if it is litigated, will be determined by application of a rule rather than a standard should make it easier for the parties to predict the outcome. According to the economic analysis of the settlement of legal disputes out of court, an increase in the predictability of the outcome of litigation should result in an increase in the settlement rate. Since the costs of litigating are generally higher than the costs of settling a dispute out of court, an increase in the settlement rate (at least within a broad range) should reduce the total costs of legal dispute resolution.

(4) The choice of rule versus standard affects the speed, and hence indirectly the costs and benefits, of legal dispute resolution. Because of the sequential character of a trial, an increase in the number of issues to be litigated will lengthen the trial. Decision by standard therefore increases the interval between an incident giving rise to a legal dispute and final judicial resolution of the dispute. The principal effects, so far as relevant here, are to increase the costs of legal error through the effect of delay in causing evidence to decay and to foster settlements in some classes of cases.

(5) Rules reduce the costs of organizing and communicating information for use in resolving legal disputes. A rule that the driver of the following car is liable in a rear-end collision amounts to saying that since experience has shown that the driver of that car can usually avert the collision at moderate cost, the benefits of determining the question still another time are likely to be less than the costs of doing so. The rule summarizes what has been learned in the prior adjudications.

(6) Decision according to rule facilitates the social control of decision makers. Where the correct outcome of a litigation is highly uncertain due to the number of circumstances that must be weighed and the uncertain weight of each, detection of an incompetent or corrupt outcome is more difficult.

We note in closing that the *net* benefits of legal rules may be smaller in cases where private rules are an alternative. The creation of a legal rule may simply shift the rulemaking function from the private to the public sector.

2. *The Costs of Legal Rules*

Several different sorts of cost are associated with greater precision of legal obligation. Some of these costs arise from the fact that making law more precise often involves making it more detailed in order to minimize the costs of overinclusion and underinclusion, which, as we are about to see, are generated by precise rules.

a. Obtaining and correctly evaluating information concerning the various combinations of events or circumstances under which the general standard that the set of rules is designed to implement should be activated are costly. The cost is presumably greater the more heterogeneous the conduct sought to be regulated (more on heterogeneity below).

b. Formulating a rule, once the appropriate scope of the desired prohibition has been determined, involves a cost. This cost, we conjecture, is greatest when the rule is a statutory rule and the conduct to be regulated is politically controversial. The formulation of a statutory rule requires negotiation among the legislators. This makes legislative production an extremely expensive form of production: the analysis of transaction costs in other contexts suggests that the costs of legislative negotiation are likely to be substantial due to the number of legislators whose agreement must be secured. The costs of negotiation will be even higher when a proposed rule is controversial, that is, costly to a politically effective segment of the community.

Transaction costs tend to increase rapidly with the number of parties whose agreement is necessary for the transaction to occur. This suggests that there are practical limits to increasing the size of a legislature. Hence as the amount and complexity of social activity increase over time, we can expect to find that legislatures, rather than expanding, will delegate more and more of the legislative function to bodies that do not produce rules through negotiation among a large number of people — i.e., to executive and administrative agencies and to courts — as has in fact happened. . . . A related prediction, one also supported by at least casual observation, is that over time judicial interpretation of statutes will become more flexible. As the costs of legislative enactment increase, courts will be more reluctant to apply principles of strict statutory construction, which have the effect of confining to the legislature the task of keeping statutes up to date.

c. Greater specificity of legal obligation generates allocative inefficiency as a result of the necessarily imperfect fit between the coverage of a rule and the conduct sought to be regulated. Our earlier assumption of a perfect fit was unrealistic. The inherent ambiguity of language and the limitations of human foresight and knowledge limit the practical ability of the rulemaker to catalog accurately and exhaustively the circumstances that should activate the general standard. Hence the reduction of a standard to a set of rules must in practice create both overinclusion and underinclusion. Some conduct is prohibited that would be permitted if the standard that the rules are designed to implement were applied directly to it; other conduct is permitted that would be prohibited under a direct application of the standard. Both effects impose social costs similar to those that an indefinite standard imposes since, as we saw earlier, such a standard, *in application,* will both over- and underinclude.

The problem of underinclusion can be solved by backing up the rule with a standard. It can be made unlawful to drive more than 60 miles per hour *or* to drive at any lower speed that is unreasonably fast in the particular circumstances. The result of adding a standard is, however, to sacrifice some benefits from governance by rules.

The problem of overinclusion is frequently dealt with by delegation to enforcement officials of authority to waive application of the rule: the policeman need not give a traffic ticket to the speeding driver who is en route to a hospital in an emergency. In principle one could rewrite the rule to specify all the possible exceptions; but in practice it may be cheaper to allow *ad hoc* exceptions to be made at the enforcement level — as recognized by even the severest critics of official discretion. Again, however, some benefits of governance by rules are sacrificed by recognizing exceptions based on implicit use of an overriding standard.

Our discussion of overinclusion requires two qualifications. First, where the sanction for violation of a legal rule or standard imposes on the violator a cost just equal to the social costs of the violation — simple damages in tort or contract actions approximate such a sanction — socially valuable violations will not be deterred. A rule that makes injurers liable for all of their accidents whether or not they are negligent (strict liability) should not deter them from engaging in behavior that results in nonnegligent (efficient) accidents, since, by definition, their liability will be less than the benefits they obtain from such activity.

Another respect in which our analysis of overinclusion needs to be qualified involves situations where the costs of transactions among the people subject to the rule are low. An example of a rule operating in such a context is the Statute of Frauds, which provides that certain types of contract (e.g., for the sale of land) are unenforceable unless reduced to writing. If the criterion for enforcing contracts for the sale of land were a reasonableness or efficiency standard, many oral land contracts would have to be enforced as expressing the true intentions of the parties. But it does not follow that the Statute of Frauds frustrates many valuable transactions. Since prospective contracting parties can assure enforcement by making a written contract, the major cost associated with the Statue of Frauds, viewed as an overinclusive rule, is not the prevention of valuable transactions but the legal and negotiating expenses necessary to comply with the rule. These expenses are probably modest.

The major benefit is a reduction in the cost of resolving contract disputes. The cost of proving the existence and terms of a contract is reduced; the probability of an erroneous decision is reduced; and the predictability of the outcome of contract litigation is increased.

The problems of overinclusion and underinclusion are more serious the greater the heterogeneity (or ambiguity, or uncertainty) of the conduct intended to be affected. If speeding were a homogeneous phenomenon — as it would be, for example, if driving at a speed of more than 70 miles per hour were always unreasonably fast and driving at a lesser speed never unreasonably fast — it could be effectively proscribed by a uniform speed limit of 70 with no residual prohibition of unreasonably fast driving. But speeding is in fact heterogeneous. It includes some driving at very low speeds and excludes some very fast driving, depending on a multitude of particular circumstances. A single speed limit or even a large number of separate speed limits must exclude a great deal of conduct that is really speeding and include a great deal that is not really speeding.

d. We have assumed up to now that an increase in the specificity of a legal prohibition always increases the certainty of the prohibition. This is incorrect; it may reduce it, thereby imposing the sorts of cost usually associated with standards. Compare the following alternative methods of defining the crime of statutory rape: sexual intercourse with a female under 16; sexual intercourse with a female who the defendant knows or should know is under 16. The first rule is more precise on its face than the second, but more uncertain in its application to primary behavior because it may be hard for potential defendants to determine age accurately. The first rule may induce the defendant (especially if risk averse) to confine his attentions to females obviously much older than 16. Observe, however, that it imparts greater certainty than the second rule to the litigation process since, in a legal proceeding, the female's actual age can be ascertained more readily than the defendant's knowledge. As we saw earlier, greater certainty at the litigation stage indirectly increases the efficiency of primary behavior. So the costs of the first rule may be lower than the costs of the second rule after all.

This example makes clear that precision can be measured only by reference to whom the rule is addressed to. It may be precise to one audience (adjudicators), imprecise to another (potential violators). The example also suggests an additional point about the costs of overinclusion: they may be low if the lawful conduct deterred (here, intercourse with females who look younger than 16 but are not) is not considered socially very valuable.

III. The Dynamics of Legal Rules

Thus far we have largely ignored the costs and benefits associated with the time dimension of legal regulation. Clearly, however, the efficient (or just) solution to a problem may change over time with changes in the economic and technological factors shaping the problem. For example, the development of the air brake, the spark arrester, the electric crossing signal, the steel car, and other railroad safety devices successively altered the relative costs of accident avoidance by railroads and by potential victims of railroad accidents, obsoleting rules of railroad accident law based on the relative costs of avoidance by injurer and by victim as they had existed prior to the development of the safety devices in question. An important cost of legal regulation by means of rules is thus the cost of altering rules to keep pace with economic and technological change.

Obsolescence is not so serious a problem with regulation by standard. Standards are relatively unaffected by changes over time in the circumstances in which they are applied, since a standard does not specify the circumstances relevant to decision or the weight of each circumstance but merely indicates the kinds of circumstance that are relevant. The standard of efficiency, and its legal counterpart in the accident area, due care, directs the decision maker to determine what behavior by the parties would have minimized the sum of the expected accident costs and the accident-avoidance costs. This precept can be obeyed even though the relevant costs, and hence the optimizing course of conduct, change radically over time. One is therefore not surprised that the negligence standard has changed little since it was introduced some 150 years ago, while specific rules of accident law have changed frequently and substantially.

In general, the more detailed a rule is, the more often it will have to be changed. The greater detailedness of a very precise rule is thus also a source of additional costs, the costs of changing rules. These include the costs, discussed earlier, of producing the new rule plus additional costs arising from the fact that change in the law is a source of uncertainty. A transaction may be subject to a precise and definite rule but if there is a possibility that the rights of the parties to the transaction will in fact be determined by application of a different rule those rights are uncertain. Another name for uncertainty in this context is imperfect precision: if a rule can be changed, one can no longer say definitely that if circumstance X is present, legal consequence Y will follow. Thus the greater the amount of detail in a rule, the lower will be the costs of imperfect precision in one respect and the higher they will be in another. . . .

NLRB v. MAGNAVOX CO.
415 U.S. 322 (1974)

Since 1954, the company had maintained a rule prohibiting employees from distributing literature even in nonworking areas during nonworking time, although it did provide bulletin boards for the posting of "noncontroversial" notices. The company's collective bargaining agreement with the union representing its employees authorized the company to issue rules for the "maintenance of orderly conditions on plant property." Nonetheless, the union filed a §8(a)(1) charge challenging the validity of the no-distribution rule. The NLRB had decided in an earlier case[42] that a union would not be permitted to waive the distribution rights of employees whose goal was to supplant the union with another representative, and in the instant case extended its holding to encompass literature supporting the union. The court of appeals denied enforcement, holding the waiver valid as applied to the union and its supporters. The Supreme Court reversed.

The Court acknowledged that a union can waive the employees' right to strike in a lawful collective bargaining agreement,[43] but distinguished the instant case on several grounds. The Court found that the place of work is uniquely appropriate for the dissemination of views concerning the bargaining representative and bargaining issues, and rejected the argument that the use of a bulletin board was a fair substitute. It held that employees supporting the union should have as great a §7 right to distribute literature as those opposed to the union. The Court concluded: "As we noted in *Republic Aviation Corp.,* the Board may well conclude that considerations of production or discipline may make controls necessary. No such evidence existed here and the trial examiner so found. Accordingly, this is not the occasion to balance the availability of alternative channels of communication against a legitimate employer business justification for barring or limiting in-plant communications."

Three dissenting justices would have affirmed the court of appeals. They argued that the Court's ruling will have an unsettling effect on the stability of collective bargaining between employers and unions, and they would invalidate such a waiver only in the exceptional circumstances where it could be shown that union supporters were unable to effectively respond to the propaganda made by opponents in their literature.

Note

The Court did not discuss *Nutone*. Should it have?

NLRB v. WYMAN-GORDON CO.

394 U.S. 759 (1969)

Fortas, J. announced the judgment of the Court and delivered an opinion in which Warren, C.J., Stewart, J., and White, J. join.

[42] Gale Products, 142 N.L.R.B. 1246 (1963).
[43] Mastro Plastics Corp. v. NLRB, 350 U.S. 270 (1956), discussed at p. 344, infra.

On the petition of the International Brotherhood of Boilermakers and pursuant to its powers under §9 of the National Labor Relations Act, the National Labor Relations Board ordered an election among the production and maintenance employees of the respondent company. At the election, the employees were to select one of two labor unions as their exclusive bargaining representative, or to choose not to be represented by a union at all. In connection with the election, the Board ordered the respondent to furnish a list of the names and addresses of its employees who could vote in the election, so that the unions could use the list for election purposes. The respondent refused to comply with the order, and the election was held without the list. Both unions were defeated in the election.

The Board upheld the union's objections to the election because the respondent had not furnished the list, and the Board ordered a new election. The respondent again refused to obey a Board order to supply a list of employees, and the Board issued a subpoena ordering the respondent to provide the list or else produce its personnel and payroll records showing the employees' names and addresses. The Board filed an action in the United States District Court for the District of Massachusetts seeking to have its subpoena enforced or to have a mandatory injunction issued to compel the respondent to comply with its order.

The District Court held the Board's order valid and directed the respondent to comply. 270 F. Supp. 280 (1967). The United States Court of Appeals for the First Circuit reversed. 397 F.2d 394 (1968). The Court of Appeals thought that the order in this case was invalid because it was based on a rule laid down in an earlier decision by the Board, Excelsior Underwear, Inc., 156 N.L.R.B. 1236 (1966), and the *Excelsior* rule had not been promulgated in accordance with the requirements that the Administrative Procedure Act prescribed for rule-making, 5 U.S.C. §553. We granted certiorari to resolve a conflict among the circuits concerning the validity and effect of the *Excelsior* rule.

I

The *Excelsior* case involved union objections to the certification of the results of elections that the unions had lost at two companies. The companies had denied to the unions a list of the names and addresses of employees eligible to vote. In the course of the proceedings, the Board "invited certain interested parties" to file briefs and to participate in oral argument of the issue whether the Board should require the employer to furnish lists of employees. Various employer groups and trade unions did so, as amici curiae. After these proceedings, the Board issued its decision in *Excelsior*. It purported to establish the general rule that such a list must be provided, but it declined to apply its new rule to the companies involved in the *Excelsior* case. Instead, it held that the rule would apply "only in those elections that are directed, or consented to, subsequent to 30 days from the date of [the] Decision." Id., at 1240, n.5.

Specifically, the Board purported to establish "a requirement that will be applied in all election cases. That is, within 7 days after the Regional Director has approved a consent-election agreement entered into by the parties . . . , or after the Regional Director or the Board has directed an election . . . the employer must file with the Regional Director an election eligibility list, containing the names and addresses of all the eligible voters. The Regional Director, in turn, shall make this information available to all parties in the case. Failure to comply with this requirement shall be grounds for setting aside the election whenever proper objections are filed." Id., at 1239-1240.

Section 6 of the National Labor Relations Act empowers the Board "to make . . . , in the manner prescribed by the Administrative Procedure Act, such rules and regulations as may be necessary to carry out the provisions of this Act." The Administrative Procedure Act contains specific provisions governing agency rule-making, which it defines as "an agency statement of general or particular applicability and future effect." 5 U.S.C. §551(4). The Act requires among other things, publication in the Federal Register of notice of proposed rule-making and of hearing; opportunity to be heard; a statement in the rule of its basis and purposes; and publication in the Federal Register of the rule as adopted. The Board asks us to hold that it has direction to promulgate new rules in adjudicatory proceedings, without complying with the requirements of the Administrative Procedure Act.

The rule-making provisions of that Act, which the Board would avoid, were designed to assure fairness and mature consideration of rules of general application. They may not be avoided by the process of making rules in the course of adjudicatory proceedings. There is no warrant in law for the Board to replace the statutory scheme with a rule-making procedure of its own invention. Apart from the fact that the device fashioned by the Board does not comply with statutory command, it obviously falls short of the substance of the requirements of the Administrative Procedure Act. The "rule" created in *Excelsior* was not published in the Federal Register, which is the statutory and accepted means of giving notice of a rule as adopted; only selected organizations were given notice of the "hearing," whereas notice in the Federal Register would have been general in character; under the Administrative Procedure Act, the term or substance of the rule would have to be stated in the notice of hearing, and all interested parties would have an opportunity to participate in the rule-making.

The Solicitor General does not deny that the Board ignored the rule-making provisions of the Administrative Procedure Act.[3] But he appears

3. The Board has never utilized the Act's rule-making procedures. It has been criticized for contravening the Act in this manner. See, e.g., 1 Davis, Administrative Law §6.13

to argue that *Excelsior's* command is a valid substantive regulation, binding upon this respondent as such, because the Board promulgated it in the *Excelsior* proceeding, in which the requirements for valid adjudication had been met. This argument misses the point. There is no question that, in an adjudicatory hearing, the Board could validly decide the issue whether the employer must furnish a list of employees to the union. But that is not what the Board did in *Excelsior*. The Board did not even apply the rule it made to the parties in the adjudicatory proceedings, the only entities that could properly be subject to the order in that case. Instead, the Board purported to make a rule: i.e., to exercise its quasi-legislative power.

Adjudicated cases may and do, of course, serve as vehicles for the formulation of agency policies, which are applied and announced therein. See Friendly, The Federal Administrative Agencies 36-52 (1962).[4] They generally provide a guide to action that the agency may be expected to take in future cases. Subject to the qualified role of *stare decisis* in the administrative process, they may serve as precedents. But this is far from saying, as the Solicitor General suggests, that commands, decisions, or policies announced in the adjudication are "rules" in the sense that they must, without more, be obeyed by the affected public.

In the present case, however, the respondent itself was specifically directed by the Board to submit a list of the names and addresses of its employees for use by the unions in connection with the election. This direction, which was part of the order directing that an election be held, is unquestionably valid. Even though the direction to furnish the list was followed by citation to "Excelsior Underwear, Inc., 156 NLRB No. 111," it is an order in the present case that the respondent was required to obey. Absent this direction by the Board, the respondent was under no compulsion to furnish the list because no statute and no validly adopted rule required it to do so.

Because the Board in an adjudicatory proceeding directed the respondent itself to furnish the list, the decision of the Court of Appeals for the First Circuit must be reversed.

(Supp. 1967); Peck, The Atrophied Rule-Making Powers of the National Labor Relations Board, 70 Yale L.J. 720 (1961).

4. The Solicitor General argues that this Court has previously approved "rules" articulated by the Board in the adjudication of particular cases without questioning the propriety of that procedure. He cites Republic Aviation Corp., v. NLRB, 324 U.S. 793 (1945); NLRB v. A. J. Tower Co., 329 U.S. 324 (1946); NLRB v. Seven-Up Bottling Co., 344 U.S. 244 (1953); and Brooks v. NLRB, 348 U.S. 96 (1954). In none of these cases has this Court ruled upon or sanctioned the exercise of quasi-legislative power — i.e., rule-making — without compliance with §6 of the NLRA and the rule-making provisions of the Administrative Procedure Act.

II

The respondent also argues that it need not obey the Board's order because the requirement of disclosure of employees' names and addresses is substantively invalid. This argument lacks merit. The objections that the respondent raises to the requirement of disclosure were clearly and correctly answered by the Board in its *Excelsior* decision. All of the United States Courts of Appeals that have passed on the question have upheld the substantive validity of the disclosure requirement, and the court below strongly intimated a view that the requirement was substantively a proper one, 397 F.2d, at 396.

We have held in a number of cases that Congress granted the Board a wide discretion to ensure the fair and free choice of bargaining representatives. The disclosure requirement furthers this objective by encouraging an informed employee electorate and by allowing unions the right of access to employees that management already possesses. It is for the Board and not for this Court to weigh against this interest the asserted interest of employees in avoiding the problems that union solicitation may present.

[The Court then ruled that production of the list of names and addresses was within the NLRB's subpoena power.]

The judgment of the Court of Appeals is reversed, and the case is remanded to the District Court with directions to reinstate its judgment.

[Justice Black, joined by Justices Brennan and Marshall, agreed that the Board's order requiring the production of the list was valid, but argued that the Board had the discretion of whether to proceed by adjudication or rule-making in *Excelsior.* Justices Douglas and Harlan dissented in separate opinions arguing the Board's *Excelsior* procedure violated the Administrative Procedure Act and thus invalidated the order to produce the list.]

Notes

1. Why didn't the Court apply *Babcock* and *Nutone* in this case? The following excerpt from the NLRB's brief to the Supreme Court in *Wyman-Gordon* may help explain Part II of the Court's opinion.

> 1. The Company contends (Resp. Br., pp. 12-15) that, under the decisions of this Court in National Labor Relations Board v. Babcock & Wilcox Co., 351 U.S. 105 and National Labor Relations Board v. United Steelworkers (Nutone, Inc.), 357 U.S. 357, the Board's authority to compel disclosure of employees' names and addresses is limited to cases where unions have no

alternative means of communicating with the employees.[33] But both *Babcock* and *Nutone* dealt with the circumstances under which an employer commits an unfair labor practice, in violation of §8 of the Act, by denying his employees access to union communications. As the Board noted in *Excelsior,* the resolution of that issue depends on different considerations than those presented in determining the reasonableness of an employee-list rule for purposes of an election conducted under §9. As the Board further pointed out, "The existence of alternative channels of communication is relevant only when the opportunity to communicate made available by the Board would interfere with a significant employer interest — such as the employer's interest in controlling the use of the property owned by him."

Here, unlike in *Babcock* and *Nutone,* there is no necessity to balance, for "the employer has no significant interest in the secrecy of employee names and addresses." Moreover, the Board expressly stated that it was not, in *Excelsior,* considering or determining the question whether an employer's failure to provide an employee list would constitute an unfair labor practice under §8(a)(1). . . .

2. In NLRB v. Bell Aerospace Co., 416 U.S. 267 (1974), the Court indicated that the Board has far greater discretion as to whether it will engage in rule making or case-by-case adjudication than is suggested by the majority in *Wyman-Gordon.*

Whether or not rule making is required by statute, is it the preferable course for the NLRB? What values are at stake?[44]

F. CAMPAIGN PROPAGANDA

The regulation of employer and union campaign propaganda by the NLRB and the appellate courts has produced watershed cases laying down general principles, followed by vigorous disagreement over their application to particular cases. It is neither possible nor profitable to trace here the detailed course of the various lines of authority in their many applications. General themes, however, are readily apparent. One

33. The board in *Excelsior,* although acknowledging that, in some cases, "a party *might* be able to communicate with a substantial portion of the electorate even without possessing their names and addresses," concluded "that the access of *all* employees to such communications can be insured only if all parties have the names and addresses of all the voters" (A. 18).

[44] See Bernstein, The NLRB's Adjudication-Rule Making Dilemma under the Administrative Procedure Act, 79 Yale L. Rev. 571 (1970); Peck, A Critique of National Labor Relations Board Performance in Policy Formulation: Adjudication and Rule Making, 117 U. Pa. L. Rev. 254 (1968); Shapiro. The Choice of Rule Making or Adjudication in the Development of Administrative Policy, 78 Harv. L. Rev. 921 (1965).

is the indisputable fact that many employees fear the power of the employer over their jobs. Another is the public interest in a fully informed employee electorate. A third is the right of employers to exercise freedom of speech.

It is clear that employer opposition is a major impediment to union organizing. Unions faced with a neutral employer have an easier time organizing employees. After the Wagner Act was passed in 1935, the NLRB took the position that the Act required the employer to stay neutral when employees were faced with the choice of whether to select a collective bargaining agent. Employers were deemed to have no legitimate interest in the issue. The passage of §8(c) in 1947 was intended to reverse this doctrine by ensuring that employers could exercise free speech and voice opposition to unionization.

In 1948, the NLRB held that §8(c) is applicable only in unfair labor practice cases and not in representation cases.[45] The Board developed its "laboratory standards" test for deciding whether union or employer propaganda should overturn a completed election. The theory is that conduct that does not amount to an unfair labor practice may nonetheless show a faulty election environment (one that does not meet laboratory standards of fairness), fatally infecting the election and requiring a re-run.[46] Through the 1950s, the NLRB showed an increased willingness to police the accuracy of campaign propaganda, especially last minute propaganda when there was no chance of rebuttal. Misleading statements, deliberate or not, could overturn an election.

1. Misrepresentation

MIDLAND NATIONAL LIFE INSURANCE CO.

263 N.L.R.B. No. 24, 110 L.R.R.M. 1489 (1982)

[In April of 1978, the union lost a representation election by a vote of 127 to 75. The Board found that the employer had committed unfair labor practices and ordered a second election. This order was enforced

[45] General Shoe Corp., 77 N.L.R.B. 124 (1948). The Board does admit that the First Amendment applies in representation cases. Dal-Tex Optical Co., 137 N.L.R.B. 1782, 1787 n.11 (1962).

[46] On the relationship between conduct amounting to an unfair labor practice and conduct interfering with the election, the Board has stated: "[C]onduct violative of §8(a)(1) is, a fortiori, conduct which interferes with free and untrammeled choice in an election. Dal-Tex Optical Co., 137 N.L.R.B. 1782 (1962). The only recognized exception to this policy is where the violations are such that it is virtually impossible to conclude that they could have affected the results of the election. This determination is based, inter alia, on the number of violations, their severity, the extent of dissemination, the size of the unit and other relevant factors." Super Thrift Markets, 233 N.L.R.B. 409 (1977).

by a court of appeals in the spring of 1980, and the second election was held in the fall of 1980. The vote was a tie, which meant the union lost, but a Board hearing officer found that the employer had engaged in conduct interfering with the election and he recommended that a third election be held.]

I

The facts are not complex. On the afternoon of October 15, 1980, the day before the election, the Employer distributed campaign literature to its employees with their paychecks. One of the distributions was a six-page document which included photographs and text depicting three local employers and their involvements with the Petitioner. The document also contained a reproduction of a portion of the Petitioner's 1979 financial report (hereinafter LMRDA report) submitted to the Department of Labor pursuant to the provisions of the Labor Management Reporting and Disclosure Act of 1959. The Petitioner learned of the document the next morning, 3½ hours before the polls were to open.

The first subject of the document, Meilman Food, Inc., was portrayed in "recent" pictures as a deserted facility, and was described in accompanying text as follows: "They too employed between 200 and 300 employees. This Local 304A struck this plant — violence ensued. *Now all of the workers are gone*! What did the Local 304A do for them? Where is the 304A union job security?" Jack Smith, the Petitioner's business representative, testified that Local 304A, the Petitioner, had been the representative of Meilman's employees, but that neither the Petitioner nor Meilman's employees had been on strike when the plant closed. He added that the employees had been working for at least 1½ years following the strike and prior to the closure of the facility.

The second and third employers pictured and discussed in the document were Luther Manor Nursing Home and Blue Cross/Blue Shield. The text accompanying the pictures of Luther Manor explained that:

> [a]lmost a year ago this same union that tells you they will "make job security" (we believe you are the only ones who can do that) and will get you more pay, told the employees of LUTHER MANOR (again, here in Sioux Falls) . . . the union would get them a contract with job security and more money. Unfortunately Local 304A did not tell the Luther Manor employees what year or century they were talking about. Today the employees have no contract. Most of the union leaders left to work elsewhere. Their job security is the same (depends upon the individual as it always has). There has been no change or increase in wages or hours. The union has sent in three different sets of negotiators. Again, promises and performance are two different things. All wages, fringes, working conditions are remaining the same while negotiations continue.

The text accompanying the pictures of Blue Cross stated that "this same Local union won an election at Blue Cross/Blue Shield after promising less restrictive policies, better pay and more job security. Since the election a good percentage of its former employees are no longer working there. Ask them! The employees have been offered a wage increase — *next year* of 5% . . . ."

Smith testified that the Petitioner took over negotiations at Luther Manor and at Blue Cross on or about July 1, 1980, after the Petitioner had merged with Retail Clerks, Local 1665, and that Retail Clerks, Local 1665, not the Petitioner, had conducted the prior negotiations and won the election at Blue Cross.

Assessing the statements concerning these local employers, the Hearing Officer concluded that, in its description of Meilman Food, the Employer intended to instill in the minds of its employees the false impression that the Petitioner had conducted a strike at Meilman, that violence had ensued, and that, as a direct result of the strike, all of the employees at Meilman were terminated. Evaluating the statements about Luther Manor and Blue Cross, the Hearing Officer found that the Employer had misrepresented the labor organization involved, and had implied that the Petitioner was an ineffectual and inefficient bargaining representative who would cause employees to suffer.

The Employer's distribution also included a portion of the Petitioner's 1979 LMRDA report which listed information concerning the Petitioner's assets, liabilities, and cash receipts and disbursements for the reporting period. Three entries on the reproduced page were underlined: total receipts, reported at $508,946; disbursements "On Behalf of Individual Members," reported at zero; and total disbursements, reported at $492,701. Other entries on the reproduced page showed disbursements of $93,185 to officers, and $22,662 to employees. The accompanying text stated that $141,000 of the Petitioner's funds went to "union officers and officials and those who worked for them," and that "NOTHING — according to the report they filed with the U.S. Government was spent 'on behalf of the individual members.' [sic]"

The Hearing Officer found that the report actually showed that the Petitioner disbursed only $115,847 to its officers and employees, a difference of $25,000, and that the Employer's statement attributed 19 percent more in income to the officials and employees than was actually received. He further found that, while the report showed that no sums had been spent "on behalf of the individual members," the instructions for the LMRDA report required that entry to reflect disbursements for "other than normal operating purposes," and that the Employer failed to include this fact in its distribution.

In accordance with his findings outlined above, the Hearing Officer concluded that the document distributed by the Employer contained numerous misrepresentations of fact of a substantial nature designed to portray the Petitioner as an organization staffed by highly paid officials and employees who were ineffectual as bargaining representatives, and that as a consequence employees would suffer with respect to job security and compensation. The Hearing Officer also determined that the document was distributed on the afternoon before the election, that the Petitioner did not become aware of it until approximately 10 A.M. election day, 2½ hours before the preelection conference and 3½ hours before the polls were to open, and that, owing to the nature of the misrepresentations, the Petitioner did not have sufficient time to respond effectively. Applying the standard found in General Knit of California, Inc.,[8] and Hollywood Ceramics Company, Inc.,[9] the Hearing Officer accordingly recommended that the objection be sustained and that a third election be directed.

We have decided to reject the Hearing Officer's recommendations and to certify the results of the election. We do so because, after painstaking evaluation and careful consideration, we have resolved to return to the sound rule announced in Shopping Kart Food Market, Inc.[10] and to overrule General Knit and Hollywood Ceramics. Before discussing the controlling factors which underlie our decision, we believe it would be instructive to review briefly the Board's past treatment of this troublesome area.

II

During the years under the Wagner Act, the Board made no attempt to regulate campaign propaganda, and concerned itself solely with conduct which might tend to coerce employees in their election choice. As the Board stated in Maywood Hosiery Mills, Inc., 64 N.L.R.B. 146, 150 (1945), "we cannot censor the information, misinformation, argument, gossip, and opinion which accompany all controversies of any importance and which, perceptively or otherwise, condition employees' desires and decisions; nor is it our function to do so." "[E]mployees," as the Board acknowledged even then, "undoubtedly recognized [campaign] propaganda for what it is, and discount it." Corn Products Refining Company, 58 N.L.R.B. 1441, 1442 (1944).

Following the enactment of the Taft-Hartley amendments, the Board continued to disregard issues concerning the truth or falsity of campaign propaganda.[11] N. P. Nelson Iron Works, Inc., 78 N.L.R.B. 1270, 1271 (1948); Carrollton Furniture Manufacturing Company, 75 N.L.R.B.

8. 239 N.L.R.B. 619 (1978).
9. 140 N.L.R.B. 221 (1962).
10. 228 N.L.R.B. 1311 (1977).
11. In considering the Taft-Hartley amendments to the Act, Congress expressed no disapproval of the Board's refusal to regulate such campaign propaganda, and in fact sought to reduce even further the Board's ability to restrict speech by enacting §8(c). See NLRB v. The Golub Corporation, et al., 388 F.2d 921 (2d Cir. 1967).

710, 712 (1948). Again relying on the ability of employees to recognize and assess campaign propaganda for what it is, the Board entrusted these matters to the "good sense" of the voters. Id. In an apparent effort to remove itself further from controversies of this nature, the Board also imposed a duty upon the parties to correct "inaccurate or untruthful statements by any of them." Id.

Even as it was refusing to consider the truth or falsity of campaign propaganda, the Board announced its "laboratory conditions" standard. General Shoe Corporation, 77 N.L.R.B. 124 (1948). Assessing certain conduct it characterized as "calculated to prevent a free and untrammeled choice by the employees," the Board noted that "[a]n election can serve its true purpose only if the surrounding circumstances enable employees to register [such a] choice for or against a bargaining representative." Id. at 126. Recounting that it had in the past set aside elections where the "record reveal[ed] conduct so glaring that it is almost certain to have impaired employees' freedom of choice," the Board found that it "[could] not police the details surrounding every election," and reasserted its belief that "in the absence of excessive acts employees can be taken to have expressed their true convictions in the secrecy of the polling booth." Id. The majority also stated that, contrary to the "apparent" view of the dissenters in the case, the criteria applied to representation proceedings should not be the same as that applied to unfair labor practice proceedings. "In election proceedings, it is the Board's function to provide a laboratory in which an experiment may be conducted, under conditions as nearly ideal as possible, to determine the uninhibited desires of the employees." Id. at 127. However, as was subsequently explained in The Liberal Market, Inc., 108 N.L.R.B. 1481, 1482 (1954), the Board had a realistic recognition that elections did "not occur in a laboratory where controlled or artificial conditions may be established," and that, accordingly, the Board's goal was "to establish ideal conditions insofar as possible," and to assess "the actual facts in the light of realistic standards of human conduct." Id.

Exhibiting the understanding and realism espoused in *Liberal Market,* the Board recognized a limited exception to its general rule barring an examination of the effect of the truth or falsity of campaign propaganda upon the election results. Thus, where it appeared that employees were deceived as to the source of campaign propaganda by trickery or fraud, and that they could therefore neither recognize nor evaluate propaganda for what it was, the Board set aside the election. United Aircraft Corporation, 103 N.L.R.B. 102 (1953). See also The Timken-Detroit Axle Company, 98 N.L.R.B. 790 (1952). In those situations, the Board found that election standards had been "lowered . . . to a level which impaired the free and informed atmosphere requisite to an untrammeled expression of choice by the employees." United Aircraft Corporation, 103 N.L.R.B. at 105.

It was not until 20 years after the Board began establishing standards for elections that it deviated from its practice of refusing to consider the truth or falsity of campaign propaganda. In The Gummed Products Company, 112 N.L.R.B. 1092 (1955), the Board set aside an election where the union deliberately misrepresented wage rates it had negotiated with another employer. Recognizing that it "normally [would] not censor or police preelection propaganda by parties to elections, absent threats or acts of violence," the Board noted that "some limits" had been imposed. Id. at 1093. "Exaggerations, inaccuracies, partial truths, name-calling, and falsehoods, while not condoned, may be excused as legitimate propaganda, provided they are not so misleading as to prevent the exercise of free choice by employees in the election of their bargaining representative. The ultimate consideration is whether the challenged propaganda has lowered the standards of campaigning to the point where it may be said that the uninhibited desires of the employees cannot be determined in an election." Id. at 1093-94.

The Board refined this standard 7 years later in Hollywood Ceramics Company, Inc., 140 N.L.R.B. 221 (1962). Overruling prior cases which indicated that intent to mislead was an element of the standard, the Board stated that "an election should be set aside only where there has been a misrepresentation or other similar campaign trickery, which involves a substantial departure from the truth, at a time which prevents the other party or parties from making an effective reply, so that the misrepresentation, whether deliberate or not, may reasonably be expected to have a significant impact on the election." Id. at 224.

In 1977, after 15 years of experience under this rule, a majority of the Board decided in Shopping Kart Food Market, Inc., 228 N.L.R.B. 1311 (1977), to overrule *Hollywood Ceramics,* and to return to Board practice which had preceded *Gummed Products.* Thus, the Board stated that it would "no longer probe into the truth or falsity of the parties' campaign statements," but would instead recognize and rely on employees "as mature individuals who are capable of recognizing campaign propaganda for what it is and discounting it." Id. at 1311, 1313. Consistent with this view, the majority also held that the Board would intervene "in instances where a party has engaged in such deceptive campaign practices as improperly involving the Board and its processes, or the use of forged documents which render the voters unable to recognize the propaganda for what it is." Id. at 1313.

A scant 20 months later, the Board reversed itself, overruled *Shopping Kart,* and reinstated the *Hollywood Ceramics* standard. General Knit of California, Inc., 239 N.L.R.B. 619 (1978). Finding that the rule propounded in *Shopping Kart* was "inconsistent with [the Board's] responsibility to insure fair elections," the Board stated that "there are certain circumstances where a particular misrepresentation . . . may materially affect an election," and that such an election should be set aside "in order to maintain the integrity of Board elections and thereby protect employee free choice." Id. at 620.

Many lessons and conclusions can be drawn from this summary of the Board's past practice regarding the role of misrepresentations in Board elections and, no doubt, many will be. However, one lesson which cannot be mistaken is that reasonable, informed individuals can differ, and indeed have differed, in their assessment of the effect of misrepresentations on voters and in their views of the Board's proper role in policing such misrepresentations. No one can or does dispute the ultimate purpose of this controversy, that is the necessity of Board procedures which insure the fair and free choice of a bargaining representative. The sole question facing us is how that "fair and free choice" is best assured.

III

We begin with the recognition that Congress has entrusted a wide degree of discretion to the Board to establish the procedures necessary to insure the fair and free choice of bargaining representatives by employees. NLRB v. A. J. Tower Co., 329 U.S. 324, 330 (1946). In carrying out this task, "the Board must act so as to give effect to the principle of majority rule set forth in §9(a)" of the Act. Id. at 331.

Although the Board's exercise of discretion must be consistent with the principle of majority rule, the Supreme Court has held that the Board is not precluded from making "practical adjustments designed to protect the election machinery from the ever-present dangers of abuse and fraud." Id. In making these rules, the Board must weigh and accommodate not only the principle of majority rule, but several other conflicting factors, such as preserving the secrecy of the ballot, insuring the certainty and finality of election results, and minimizing unwarranted and dilatory claims by those opposed to the election results. Id.

Accordingly, a Board rule governing a representation proceeding need not be an "absolute guarantee" that the election will, without exception, reflect the choice of a majority of the voting employees. Rather, the rule simply must be "consistent with" and constitute a "justifiable and reasonable adjustment of the democratic process." Id. at 332, 333.

For numerous reasons, we find that the rule we announce today constitutes just such a "justifiable and reasonable adjustment" of our democratic electoral processes. By returning to the sound principles espoused in *Shopping Kart*, not only do we alleviate the many difficulties attending to the *Hollywood Ceramics* rule, but we also insure the certainty and finality of election results, and minimize unwarranted and dilatory claims attacking those results.

As was discussed earlier, an election would be set aside under *Hollywood Ceramics*:

> . . . only where there has been a misrepresentation or other similar campaign trickery, which involves a substantial departure from the truth, at a time which prevents the other party . . . from making an effective reply, so that the misrepresentation, whether deliberate or not, may reasonably be expected to have a significant impact on the election.[13]

As an initial matter, it is apparent that reasonable, informed individuals can differ on the multitude of subjective issues encompassed in this rule. When does a particular statement involve a "substantial" departure from the "truth"? Under what conditions has there been time for an "effective reply"? May the misrepresentation "reasonably be expected" to have a "significant impact" upon the election? As Professor Derek C. Bok concluded in his classic work on the Board's election procedures, restrictions on the content of campaign propaganda requiring truthful and accurate statements "resist every effort at a clear formulation and tend inexorably to give rise to vague and inconsistent rulings which baffle the parties and provoke litigation."[14]

The Board's experience under the *Hollywood Ceramics* rule bears this out. As was found in *Shopping Kart,* although the adoption of the *Hollywood Ceramics* rule "was premised on assuring employee free choice its administration has in fact tended to impede the attainment of that goal. The ill effects of the rule include extensive analysis of campaign propaganda, restriction of free speech, variance in application as between the Board and the courts, increasing litigation, and a resulting decrease in the finality of election results."[15]

In sharp contrast to the *Hollywood Ceramics* standard, *Shopping Kart* "draws a clear line between what is and what is not objectionable."[16] Thus, "elections will be set aside 'not on the basis of the *substance* of the representation, but the deceptive *manner* in which it was made.' . . . As long as the campaign material is what it purports to be, i.e., mere propaganda of a particular party, the Board would leave the task of evaluating its contents solely to the employees."[17] Where, due to forgery, no voter could recognize the propaganda "for what it is," Board intervention is warranted. Further, unlike *Hollywood Ceramics,* the rule in *Shopping Kart* lends itself to definite results which are both predictable and speedy. The incentive for protracted litigation is greatly reduced,

13. 140 N.L.R.B. at 224.

14. The Regulation of Campaign Tactics in Representation Elections Under the National Labor Relations Act, 78 Harv. L. Rev. 38, 85 (1964).

15. 228 N.L.R.B at 1312. Our dissenting colleagues choose to ignore all of the bases for our determination to overrule *General Knit* except that of administrative convenience. We reject the characterization that our only purpose is to cut down the level of litigation of election objections, though we agree that is one worthy goal served by our decision today.

16. General Knit of California, Inc., 239 N.L.R.B. 619, 629 (1978) (Member Penello dissenting).

17. Id.

as is the possibility of disagreement between the Board and the courts. Because objections alleging false or inaccurate statements can be summarily rejected at the first stage of Board proceedings, the opportunity for delay is almost nonexistent.[18] Finally, the rule in *Shopping Kart* "furthers the goal of consistent and equitable adjudications" by applying uniformly to the objections of both unions and employers.

In addition to finding the *Hollywood Ceramics* rule to be unwieldy and counterproductive, we also consider it to have an unrealistic view of the ability of voters to assess misleading campaign propaganda. As is clear from an examination of our treatment of misrepresentations under the Wagner Act, the Board had long viewed employees as aware that parties to a campaign are seeking to achieve certain results and to promote their own goals. Employees, knowing these interests, could not help but greet the various claims made during a campaign with natural skepticism. The "protectionism" propounded by the *Hollywood Ceramics* rule is simply not warranted. On the contrary, as we found in *Shopping Kart,* "we believe that Board rules in this area must be based on a view of employees as mature individuals who are capable of recognizing campaign propaganda for what it is and discounting it."

This fact is apparently recognized to a certain extent even under *Hollywood Ceramics.* Thus, although the Board determined that a substantial misrepresentation had been made, the election would not be set aside if it also appeared that there had been ample time to respond. This result would obtain no matter how egregious the error or falsity, and regardless of whether in fact a response had been made.

We appreciate that today's decision is likely to cause concern, just as did *General Knit*'s quick retreat from *Shopping Kart* in 1978. Accordingly, we do not take this step lightly. We take it because of our emphatic belief that the rule in *Shopping Kart* is the most appropriate accommodation of all the interests here involved, and should be given a fair chance to succeed. Unlike its predecessor, it is a clear, realistic rule of easy application which lends itself to definite, predictable, and speedy results. It removes impediments to free speech by permitting parties to speak without fear that inadvertent errors will provide the basis for endless delay or overturned elections, and promotes uniformity in national labor law by minimizing the basis for disagreement between the Board and the

18. The figures cited by our dissenting colleagues purporting to compare the "number of elections in which allegations of misleading statements were ruled upon" before and after *Shopping Kart* hardly establish that the policy change we enunciate today will not have the desired effects. That parties continued to file misrepresentation objections in 1978 simply demonstrated their acknowledgment of the reality that *Shopping Kart* could be overturned by a shift of one Board Member. In fact, that is what occurred when former Member Truesdale replaced former Member Walther on the Board. In any event, had our dissenting colleagues been more amenable to giving *Shopping Kart* a reasonable chance to take life, perhaps their point might have some merit.

courts of appeals. Weighing the benefits flowing from reinstatement of the *Shopping Kart* rule against the possibility that some voters may be misled by erroneous campaign propaganda, a result that even *Hollywood Ceramics* permits, we find that the balance unquestionably falls in favor of implementing the standard set forth in *Shopping Kart.*

In reaching this decision, we note that "[a]dministrative flexibility is . . . one of the principal reasons for the establishment of the regulatory agencies [because it] permits valuable experimentation and allows administrative policies to reflect changing policy views." Boyd Leedom, et al. v. International Brotherhood of Electrical Workers, Local Union No. 108, AFL–CIO, 278 F.2d 237, 243 (D.C. Cir. 1960). As is obvious from today's decision, the policy views of the Board have changed. We cannot permit earlier decisions to endure forever if, in our view, their effects are deleterious and hinder the goals of the Act. The nature of administrative decisionmaking relies heavily upon the benefits of the cumulative experience of the decisionmakers. Such experience, in the words of the Supreme Court, "begets understanding and insight by which judgments . . . are validated or qualified or invalidated. The constant process of trial and error, on a wider and fuller scale than a single adversary litigation permits, differentiates perhaps more than anything else the administrative from the judicial process." NLRB v. J. Weingarten, Inc., 420 U.S. 251, 265-266 (1975).

Cumulative experience need not produce the same understanding and insight. Reasonable minds can and indeed have differed over the most appropriate resolution of this issue. That no one can dispute. However, we again express our emphatic belief that on balance the rule in *Shopping Kart* best accommodates and serves the interests of all.

In sum, we rule today that we will no longer probe into the truth or falsity of the parties' campaign statements, and that we will not set elections aside on the basis of misleading campaign statements.[24] We will, however, intervene in cases where a party has used forged documents which render the voters unable to recognize propaganda for what it is.[25] Thus, we will set an election aside not because of the substance of the representation, but because of the deceptive manner in which it was made, a manner which renders employees unable to evaluate the forgery for what it is. As was the case in *Shopping Kart,* we will continue to protect against other campaign conduct, such as threats, promises, or the like, which interferes with employee free choice.

24. In accordance with our usual practice, we shall apply our new policy not only "to the case in which the issue arises," but also "to all pending cases in whatever stage." Deluxe Metal Furniture Company, 121 N.L.R.B. 995, 1006-07 (1958). . . .

25. United Aircraft Corporation, Pratt & Whitney Aircraft Division, 103 N.L.R.B. 102 (1953). See our discussion of this case in part II, supra.

Of course, as stated in *Shopping Kart,* we will also set elections aside when an official Board document has been altered in such a way as to indicate an endorsement by the Board of a party to the election. Allied Electric Products, Inc., 109 N.L.R.B. 1270 (1954).

Accordingly, inasmuch as the Petitioner's objection alleges nothing more than misrepresentations, it is hereby overruled. Because the tally of ballots shows that the Petitioner failed to receive a majority of the valid ballots cast, we shall certify the results.

Members FANNING and JENKINS, dissenting:

For the second time in five years, a bare majority of the Board has abandoned the flexible and balanced *Hollywood Ceramics* standard for determining when election campaign misrepresentations have overstepped the bounds of tolerability and substituted an ultra-permissive standard that places a premium on the well-timed use of deception, trickery, and fraud.[27] In reestablishing the *Shopping Kart* rule, the present majority adds nothing to the debate that has accompanied the seesawing of Board doctrine in this area. Instead, the majority reiterates the familiar theme of the "unrealistic view of the ability of voters to assess misleading campaign propaganda" (which it attributes to *Hollywood Ceramics*) and the promise of elimination of delays caused by the processing of misrepresentation objections.

The considerations that went into *Hollywood Ceramics,* as the brief history set forth by the instant majority shows, represented the accumulated wisdom and experience of several generations of Board Members, from the *General Shoe* case in the 1940's, through *Gummed Products* in 1955 and *Hollywood Ceramics* in 1962. And the stated policies behind *Hollywood Ceramics* belie the majority's claim that it is based on an overprotectionist, condescending view of employees:

> The basic policy underlying this rule, as well as the other rules in this election field, is to assure the employees full and complete freedom of choice in selecting a bargaining representative. The Board seeks to maintain, as closely as possible, laboratory conditions for the exercise of this basic right of the employees. One of the factors which may so disturb these conditions as to interfere with the expression of this free choice is gross misrepresentation about some material issue in the election. It is obvious

27. Arguably, it is the present majority that for the first time establishes such a permissive standard. For then-Chairman Murphy, concurring in *Shopping Kart,* supra, 228 N.L.R.B. at 1314, agreed with the "basic principles" set forth in *Hollywood Ceramics,* but worried that its "ruling has been expanded and misapplied as to have extended far from the original intent of the Board." Then-Chairman Murphy did not abandon analysis of the substance of the misrepresentation, as the present majority does. Rather, she sought to preserve some flexibility by taking the position that an election should be set aside "where a party makes an egregious mistake of fact." Id. at 1314. Moreover, she rejected the suggestion by her colleagues of the *Shopping Kart* majority that her concept of "egregious mistake of fact" was a very narrow one. Id. at 1314 fn. 24 and 1315 fn. 31. And, dissenting in *General Knit of California,* supra, then-Member Murphy, applying her "egregious mistake of fact" standard, characterized the issue presented in that case as "whether an accurate statement which is slightly ambiguous" could be the basis for setting aside the election. 239 N.L.R.B. at 633. Thus, her departure from *Hollywood Ceramics* would appear to have been more rhetorically than empirically radical.

that where employees cast their ballots upon the basis of a material misrepresentation, such vote cannot reflect their uninhibited desires, and they have not exercised the kind of choice envisaged by the Act. . . .

The Board has limited its intervention . . . because an election by secret ballot, conducted under Government auspices, should not be lightly set aside, and because we realize that additional elections upset the plant routine and prevent stable labor-management relations. We are also aware that absolute precision of statement and complete honesty are not always attainable in an election campaign, nor are they expected by the employees. Election campaigns are often hotly contested and feelings frequently run high. At such times a party may, in its zeal, overstate its own virtues and the vices of the other without essentially impairing "laboratory conditions." Accordingly, in reaching its decision in cases where objections to elections have been filed alleging that one party misrepresented certain facts, the Board must balance the right of the employees to an untrammeled choice, and the right of the parties to wage a free and vigorous campaign with all the normal legitimate tools of electioneering.[29]

What the majority does now is to give up, in the interest of possibly reducing litigation, a speculative thing at best, any attempt to balance the rights of the employees and the campaigners.[30] However, their goal, which, as the Board noted in *General Knit,* must never take precedence over preservation of the integrity of the electoral process, seems to have eluded the Board's prior attempt under *Shopping Kart.* For, according to an internal audit conducted for the General Counsel, the number of elections in which allegations of misleading statements were ruled upon increased from 327 in 1976, the year before *Shopping Kart* was decided, to 357 in 1978, the first full year after *Shopping Kart* was in effect, this despite a decrease (from 8,899 to 8,464) in the total number of elections conducted in those respective years.[31]

In return for the illusory benefits of speed and a speculative lightening of its workload, the majority today errs in relinquishing the Board's obligation to put some limits on fraud and deceit as campaign tools. It is apparent that the system contemplated by §9 of the Act for representation elections has survived reasonably well during the decades in which the Board has taken a role in insuring the integrity of its elections. Indeed, the majority does not suggest deregulating the election process other than with respect to misrepresentations. In this connection, we are

29. 140 N.L.R.B. at 223-224.

30. We find incomprehensible the majority's additional suggestion that the *Shopping Kart* rule (presumably as compared with the *Hollywood Ceramics* rule) "'furthers the goal of consistent and equitable adjudications' by applying uniformly to the objections of both unions and employers." To our knowledge, no rule ever contemplated by the Board has treated misrepresentations by unions and employers differently.

31. The number of misrepresentation cases was even higher in 1977, the year in which *Shopping Kart* was decided. However, the total number of elections held in 1977 was substantially higher than in either 1976 or 1978.

especially puzzled by the distinction the majority draws between forgery, which it will regulate, and other kinds of fraud, which it will not. The majority states that forgeries "render the voters unable to recognize the propaganda for what it is." Yet it is precisely the Board's traditional perception that there are some misrepresentations which employees can recognize "for what they are" and others which, in the Board's considered judgment, they cannot, that has made the *Hollywood Ceramics* doctrine so effective. In place of this approach, under which judgments take into account the facts of each case, the majority creates an irrebuttable presumption that employees can recognize all misrepresentations, however opaque and deceptive, except forgeries. Employees' free choice in elections, the only reason we run elections, must necessarily be inhibited, distorted, and frustrated by this new rule. To the majority, this is less important than the freedom to engage in lies, trickery, and fraud. Under the new rule, important election issues will be ignored in favor of irresponsible charges and deceit. Under *Hollywood Ceramics,* the Board did not attempt to sanitize elections completely but only to keep the campaign propaganda within reasonable bounds. Those bounds have now disappeared. Why?

Albeit today's American employees may be better educated, in the formal sense, than those of previous generations, and may be in certain respects more sophisticated, we do not honor them by abandoning them utterly to the mercies of unscrupulous campaigners, including the expert cadre of professional opinion molders who devise campaigns for many of our representation elections. In political campaigns, which are conducted over a much longer period of time and are subject to extensive media scrutiny, the voters have ready access to independent sources of information concerning the issues. In representation campaigns, they do not. Thus, it has been observed that: "Promises are often written on the wind, but statements of fact are the stuff upon which men and women make serious value judgments . . . and rank and file employees must largely depend on the company and the union to provide the data. . . ."[32] As we said in our dissent in *Shopping Kart,* the very high level of participation in Board elections as compared with political elections speaks well for the Board's role in insuring a measuring of responsibility in campaigning.[33] On the other hand, absent some external restraint, the campaigners will have little incentive to refrain from any last-minute deceptions that might work to their short-term advantage.

32. J. I. Case v. NLRB, 555 F.2d 202, 205 (8th Cir. 1977). As the cited case illustrates, the courts, although they have not hesitated to disagree with the Board's application of the *Hollywood Ceramics* standard to particular facts, have accepted its principles readily.

33. Perhaps it is not practicable to regulate political campaign propaganda as the Board traditionally has policed representation campaigns, because elected Government positions must be filled within a very brief period after the election. As noted above, however, our system of majority collective-bargaining representation has not been endangered by *Hollywood Ceramics.*

In sum, we are able to agree with the majority on very little. But one point of agreement is the majority's statement that, "The sole question facing us here is how [the fair and free choice of a bargaining representative] is best assured." For the reasons set forth above, and also for the reasons set forth in *General Knit* and our dissent in *Shopping Kart,* we find it impossible to answer that question by abandoning one of the most effective means the Board has yet devised for assuring that desired result.

Turning to the facts of the instant case, the Employer misrepresented to the employees that a strike called by the Union led directly to the closing of a large local employer and that the Union had bargained extensively with two other local employers without success. These were substantial misrepresentations concerning the central issue in the choice of a bargaining representative — its effectiveness. But the Employer did not limit itself to simple misrepresentations. It stepped beyond that and engaged in an elaborately conceived fraud when it presented and commented upon an excerpt from the Form LM-2 financial report the Union was required to file with the U.S. Department of Labor. Line 71 of the form, showing union disbursements "on behalf of individual members," appears to show that the Union made no such disbursements during the reporting year. The Employer both underlined that item and emphasized it in a separate notation. The Employer contrasted this negative disbursement figure with a figure which overstated by 19 percent the moneys paid to union officers and "those that worked for them." This contrast was designed, of course, to show that the hard-earned money collected from the Union's members benefited only union officials. What the excerpt and the Employer's notations concealed, however, was that the Labor Department's instructions for completing line 71 specifically exclude from disbursements "on behalf of individual members," all normal operating expenses. Thus, while a reader in possession of the instructions might realize that the Union's operating expenses, including salaries for the Union's staff, are incurred with the objective of benefiting all the members, the Employer carefully disguised this fact, egregiously distorted what the Union does with its members' money, and ingeniously made the Union itself appear to be the source of this misinformation. In addition, how many employees are going to read and understand this complicated form?

The Employer's fraudulent misstatement of the contents of this Government document is analogous to the mischaracterization of this Board's documents, and is at least equally objectionable. See Formco, Inc., 233 N.L.R.B. 61 (1977). Here, in sum, we have a fraudulent misrepresentation of a most serious and extreme nature, forming part of a series of material misrepresentations. Such conduct can hardly have failed to affect the election, especially since, with a tally of 107 to 107, the change of a single vote may have changed the outcome.

The majority through this decision is giving our election processes, possibly the most important part of installing a viable collective-bargaining relationship, over to the possible excesses of the participants and eliminating the Board from its statutory oversight responsibilities. Why? Accordingly, we must dissent.

Notes

1. Is the Board majority saying that voters are sophisticated enough to ferret out the actual facts and give the lie to misrepresentations, or that they are sophisticated enough to know that they will be lied to? Do you expect that employers and unions, educated by the Getman, Goldberg and Herman study and the Board's opinion in this case, will cease pouring large sums of money into propaganda campaigns?

2. The Board relied on *Shopping Kart Food Market* to dismiss union election objections in Thomas E. Gates & Sons, 229 N.L.R.B. 705 (1977). Shortly before the election and (according to Chairman Fanning's dissenting opinion) at a time when the union had no opportunity to reply, the employer told the employees by letter that the union's current contract with other employers provided for a base rate of $9.19 per hour with additional fringe benefits amounting to $2.13 per hour for a total of $11.32 per hour. The employer was currently paying $12.38 per hour. In fact, the union's current contract provided for $11.09 per hour with additional fringe benefits of $2.13 per hour, for a total of $13.22 per hour.

If you were an employee, would the employer's letter have influenced your vote? Since the case involved no unfair labor practice, there was no way for the union to take it to a court of appeals.

3. Managers file election objections because they hope to reverse a union's election victory, and even if they are unsuccessful, they may profit from delaying their obligation to bargain. Unions must have different reasons than do managers for filing election objections after an election defeat. If a union's objections are successful, a rerun election will be ordered. The union can have a new election without litigating election objections, however, if it waits a year and files a new petition. In many cases the reason for filing election objections must be their propaganda value. In Dayton Tire & Rubber Co., 242 N.L.R.B. 154 (1979), for example, the Board was still trying to decide whether or not to order a second election almost two years after the union's loss in the first election.

4. *The Getman study.* In 1976, Professors Getman, Goldberg, and Herman challenged the "behavioral assumptions" behind the NLRB's regulation of campaign conduct with a detailed empirical analysis of 31 union representation elections. In light of their findings, the authors recommended substantial deregulation of the representation election process.

The authors argued that they had identified implicit behavioral assumptions in the Board's regulation of election conduct. Those assumptions are (1) that employees' precampaign voting dispositions are not strongly held and are easily changed by the campaign; (2) that employees attend closely to the issues raised in the campaign and make their final decision based on those issues; and (3) that unlawful campaign tactics are likely to have a coercive effect, constraining employee free choice.

To test the validity of the Board's assumptions, and in particular to measure the effect of unlawful campaigning, Getman and his coauthors interviewed employees at different stages of selected election campaigns. They asked how individual employees intended to vote before the campaign began and how they ultimately voted, and also sought to determine which campaign issues employees remembered after the election. In choosing elections to study, the authors applied selection criteria designed to identify hotly contested elections with a high likelihood of vigorous, possibly unlawful campaigning. In 28 of the 31 elections in the final sample, at least one party engaged in substantial campaigning. Unlawful campaigning occurred in 22 of the elections, based either on an official NLRB decision or, where no formal charges were filed, on an informal finding by an NLRB administrative law judge retained by the authors.

Based on the data, the Getman study made three major findings. First, contrary to the Board's alleged assumption that employees' precampaign voting intent is not strongly held, the study found that employee predispositions were closely correlated to actual votes in the election. Using measures of employees' precampaign attitudes toward their jobs and toward unions in general, as well as employees' precampaign voting intent, the authors were able to correctly predict the postcampaign votes of 81 percent of the employees. Precampaign intent was the most powerful predictor of vote: 94 percent of the employees intending to vote for the company, and 82 percent of those intending to vote for the union, ultimately voted in accordance with their intent.

Second, the study found that following the election, employees remembered little about the content of the campaigns of either the union or the employer. Employees recalled 10 percent of the company campaign issues and 7 percent of the union issues, a result described by the authors as contradicting the Board's alleged assumption that employees are closely attentive to the campaign. Not only were employees unable to recall a large proportion of campaign issues, but they were generally unable to remember the details of issues they did recall. For example, only 22 percent of the employees who remembered union campaign statements referring to wages obtained elsewhere by the union could recall the amount of the union's claim within 10 percent.

Another finding related to campaign familiarity was that while both company voters and union voters had similar recall of company campaign issues, union voters had a significantly higher recall of union campaign issues than did company voters. The study associates this phenomenon with a finding that a much greater percentage of employees attend company campaign meetings than union campaign meetings, and that while most of those employees attending union meetings were already union supporters, the opposite was not true of the audience at company meetings.

Third, and most important, the study found that unlawful campaigning has no greater effect on employee voting behavior than lawful campaigning, a result at odds with the Board's implicit assumption that unlawful campaign tactics often coerce union supporters into voting against the union. Using either official NLRB decisions or an informal finding by an administrative law judge, the authors divided the elections studied into (1) those with unlawful campaigning by the company serious enough to warrant a bargaining order; (2) those with unlawful campaigning, but not serious enough for a remedial bargaining order;[47] and (3) those with no unlawful campaigning, or "clean elections."

The authors then classified as potential union voters employees who either were undecided prior to the campaign or had expressed prounion attitudes or voting intent. An analysis of actual votes found that there was no group of potential union voters in which a significantly greater proportion voted against the union in bargaining order elections than in clean elections, or in elections involving less serious unlawful campaigning. While the percentage of undecided employees voting against the union increased from 60 percent in clean elections to 65 percent in unlawful elections, and to 79 percent in bargaining order elections, the increases were not statistically significant.

Asserting that the existing scheme of Board regulation of election campaigns is based on invalid assumptions, the authors present a package of recommendations. They propose (1) completely to deregulate oral and written campaign communications; (2) to permit unions to hold campaign meetings on working time and premises whenever a company has engaged in such activity; and (3) to impose stronger sanctions against managerial retaliation for union activity.

Some academic writers have criticized the Getman study. They raise a number of points, including sample selection, the authors' apparent acceptance of their own "null hypothesis," the study's focus on the average worker rather than the election verdict, and the failure to consider other rationales for NLRB regulation of representation elections.

Getman and his coauthors chose to study elections with a high potential for vigorous, possibly unlawful campaigning. Reviewers have criticized the resulting sample for lacking a control group of elections with a low potential for unlawful campaigning, and hence for failing to provide

[47] We study remedial bargaining orders beginning at p. 253 infra.

data indicating how voters behave in less heated circumstances.[48] In a response to critics,[49] the authors of the Getman study suggest that the control group consists of the 9 of the 31 elections in which the Board would find no unlawful campaigning. But critics point out that the Getman study itself found that employee perceptions of unlawful campaigning are unrelated to Board findings thereof. Therefore, the factors making an unlawful campaign likely may also polarize employee positions and result in hardened predispositions in advance of the campaign, skewing the sample toward elections in which the campaign is less likely to further influence employee opinion.

Professor Paul Weiler levels the following criticisms:

> A closer look at the Getman study . . . reveals two critical flaws in its analysis. The first consists in the study's appraisal of the evidence of the impact of coercive campaigning by employers. The authors actually found that, among the surveyed workers who had indicated before the campaign either that they were undecided or that they favored the union, the percentage of votes against unionization was somewhat higher after an illegal employer campaign than after a clean one. The magnitude of the difference, however, was too small to pass a 99% test of statistical significance. Thus, the authors asserted, one could not conclude with certainty that the observed relation was attributable to anything but chance. This sort of statistical judgment is hardly sufficient for the making of legal policy. It may be legitimate for Getman and his coauthors to conclude that their own data do not demonstrate with certainty that employer coercion affects employee voting, but it is entirely unjustified to infer from that fact alone that the contrary is true. . . .
>
> In any event, that data gathered by Getman and his coauthors have been used by another scholar, William Dickens, to calculate the actual probabilities that the employer campaigns had varying levels of impact. Dickens' best estimate was that, in the average campaign studied, unfair labor practices reduced the number of prounion votes by 4%. The reduction was 15% when the unfair labor practices took the form of specific threats or actions against union supporters. Furthermore, when both legal and illegal practices were taken into account, it was more than 99% certain that the typical employer campaign reduced by at least 5% the probability that the average voter would vote for unionization, and it was more than 90% certain that the campaign reduced that probability by at least 10%.[50]

Criticizing the study's focus on the average voter, Weiler asserts:

[48] Eames, An Analysis of the Union Voting Study from a Trade Unionist's Point of View, 28 Stan. L. Rev. 1181 (1976); Shapiro, Why Do Voters Vote? (Book Review), 86 Yale L.J. 1532 (1977).

[49] Goldberg, Getman & Brett, Union Representation Elections: Law and Reality: The Authors Respond to the Critics, 79 Mich L. Rev. 564 (1981).

[50] Weiler, Promises To Keep: Securing Workers' Rights to Self-Organization under the NLRA, 96 Harv. L. Rev. 1769, 1783-1784 (1983).

> [t]he importance of the campaign lies in its effect on the ultimate election verdict, and a small shift in the number of workers voting for union representation may have a substantial effect on the number of union victories. . . . The number of election results changed by employer coercion . . . depends not only on how many votes are affected in all campaigns combined, but also on how close the elections are and on how the affected voters are distributed among the different employee units. . . .
>
> The elections studied by Getman and his coauthors show how shifts among small numbers of critically located voters can have large effects on the overall success of union organizing efforts. The unions studied won just over one-fourth (eight of thirty-one) of the elections studied. To win a majority of these elections, the union would have had to be successful in eight more campaigns. A shift of only 2% of the total votes cast in the thirty-one elections, if those 2% had been carefully allocated, would have been sufficient to provide eight additional victories.[51]

2. Promises, Predictions, and Threats

NLRB v. GISSEL PACKING CO.
395 U.S. 575 (1969)

[Under this case caption the Court decided four cases dealing with the right of unions to be certified without an election in certain circumstances. We shall consider that portion of the Court's opinion below. What follows is the Court's discussion of the contention of one employer, Sinclair, that the NLRB had improperly sustained election objections against Sinclair and found it to have violated §8(a)(1).]

Warren, C.J. . . .

[Petitioner Sinclair,] a producer of mill rolls, wire, and related products at two plants in Holyoke, Massachusetts, was shut down for some three months in 1952 as the result of a strike over contract negotiations with the American Wire Weavers Protective Association, the representative of petitioner's journeymen and apprentice wire weavers from 1933 to 1952. The Company subsequently reopened without a union contract, and its employees remained unrepresented through 1964, when the Company was acquired by an Ohio corporation, with the Company's former president continuing as head of the Holyoke, Massachusetts, division. In July 1965, the International Brotherhood of Teamsters, Local Union No. 404, began an organizing campaign among petitioner's Holyoke employees and by the end of the summer had obtained authorization cards from 11 of the Company's 14 journeymen wire weavers

[51] Ibid. at 1784-1785.

choosing the Union as their bargaining agent. On September 20, the Union notified petitioner that it represented a majority of its wire weavers, requested that the Company bargain with it, and offered to submit the signed cards to a neutral third party for authentication. After petitioner's president declined the Union's request a week later, claiming, inter alia, that he had a good faith doubt of majority status because of the cards' inherent unreliability, the Union petitioned, on November 8, for an election that was ultimately set for December 9.

When petitioner's president first learned of the Union's drive in July, he talked with all of his employees in an effort to dissuade them from joining a union. He particularly emphasized the results of the long 1952 strike, which he claimed "almost put our company out of business," and expressed worry that the employees were forgetting the "lessons of the past." He emphasized, secondly, that the Company was still on "thin ice" financially, that the Union's "only weapon is to strike," and that a strike "could lead to the closing of the plant," since the parent company had ample manufacturing facilities elsewhere. He noted, thirdly, that because of their age and the limited usefulness of their skills outside their craft, the employees might not be able to find re-employment if they lost their jobs as a result of a strike. Finally, he warned those who did not believe that the plant could go out of business to "look around Holyoke and see a lot of them out of business." The president sent letters to the same effect to the employees in early November, emphasizing that the parent company had no reason to stay in Massachusetts if profits went down.

During the two or three weeks immediately prior to the election on December 9, the president sent the employees a pamphlet captioned: "Do you want another 13-week strike?" stating, inter alia, that: "We have no doubt that the Teamsters Union can again close the Wire Weaving Department and the entire plant by a strike. We have no hopes that the Teamsters Union Bosses will not call a strike. . . . The Teamsters Union is a strike happy outfit." Similar communications followed in late November, including one stressing the Teamsters' "hoodlum control." Two days before the election, the Company sent out another pamphlet that was entitled: "Let's Look at the Record," and that purported to be an obituary of companies in the Holyoke-Springfield, Massachusetts, area that had allegedly gone out of business because of union demands, eliminating some 3,500 jobs; the first page carried a large cartoon showing the preparation of a grave for the Sinclair Company and other headstones containing the names of other plants allegedly victimized by the unions. Finally, on the day before the election, the president made another personal appeal to his employees to reject the Union. He repeated that the Company's financial condition was precarious; that a possible strike would jeopardize the continued operation of the plant;

and that age and lack of education would make re-employment difficult. The Union lost the election 7-6, and then filed both objections to the election and unfair labor practice charges which were consolidated for hearing before the trial examiner.

The Board agreed with the trial examiner that the president's communications with his employees, when considered as a whole, "reasonably tended to convey to the employees the belief or impression that selection of the Union in the forthcoming election could lead [the Company] to close its plant, or to the transfer of the weaving production, with the resultant loss of jobs to the wire weavers." Thus, the Board found that under the "totality of the circumstances" petitioner's activities constituted a violation of §8(a)(1) of the Act. The Board further agreed with the trial examiner that petitioner's activities, because they "also interfered with the exercise of a free and untrammeled choice in the election," and "tended to foreclose the possibility" of holding a fair election, required that the election be set aside. [The First Circuit enforced the Board's order.]

We consider finally petitioner Sinclair's First Amendment challenge to the holding of the Board and the Court of Appeals for the First Circuit. At the outset we note that the question raised here most often arises in the context of a nascent union organizational drive, where employers must be careful in waging their anti-union campaign. As to conduct generally, . . . unfair labor practices, with their varying consequences, create certain hazards for employers when they seek to estimate or resist unionization efforts. But so long as the differences involve conduct easily avoided, such as discharge, surveillance, and coercive interrogation, we do not think that employers can complain that the distinctions are unreasonably difficult to follow. Where an employer's antiunion efforts consist of speech alone, however, the difficulties raised are not so easily resolved. The Board has eliminated some of the problem areas by no longer requiring an employer to show affirmative reasons for insisting on an election and by permitting him to make reasonable inquiries. We do not decide, of course, whether these allowances are mandatory. But we do note that an employer's free speech right to communicate his views to his employees is firmly established and cannot be infringed by a union or the Board. Thus, §8(c) merely implements the First Amendment by requiring that the expression of "any views, argument, or opinion" shall not be "evidence of an unfair labor practice," so long as such expression contains "no threat of reprisal or force or promise of benefit" in violation of §8(a)(1). Section 8(a)(1), in turn, prohibits interference, restraint or coercion of employees in the exercise of their right to self-organization.

Any assessment of the precise scope of employer expression, of course, must be made in the context of its labor relations setting. Thus, an employer's rights cannot outweigh the equal rights of the employees to associate freely, as those rights are embodied in §7 and protected by §8(a)(1) and the proviso to §8(c). And any balancing of those rights must take into account the economic dependence of the employees on their employers, and the necessary tendency of the former, because of that relationship, to pick up intended implications of the latter that might be more readily dismissed by a more disinterested ear. Stating these obvious principles is but another way of recognizing that what is basically at stake is the establishment of a nonpermanent, limited relationship between the employer, his economically dependent employee and his union agent, not the election of legislators or the enactment of legislation whereby that relationship is ultimately defined and where the independent voter may be freer to listen more objectively and employers as a class freer to talk. Cf. New York Times Co. v. Sullivan, 376 U.S. 254 (1964).

Within this framework, we must reject the Company's challenge to the decision below and the findings of the Board on which it was based. The standards used below for evaluating the impact of an employer's statements are not seriously questioned by petitioner and we see no need to tamper with them here. Thus, an employer is free to communicate to his employees any of his general views about unionism or any of his specific views about a particular union, so long as the communications do not contain a "threat of reprisal or force or promise of benefit." He may even make a prediction as to the precise effects he believes unionization will have on his company. In such a case, however, the prediction must be carefully phrased on the basis of objective fact to convey an employer's belief as to demonstrably probable consequences beyond his control or to convey a management decision already arrived at to close the plant in case of unionization. See Textile Workers v. Darlington Mfg. Co., 380 U.S. 263, 274, n. 20 (1965). If there is any implication that an employer may or may not take action solely on his own initiative for reasons unrelated to economic necessities and known only to him, the statement is no longer a reasonable prediction based on available facts but a threat of retaliation based on misrepresentation and coercion, and as such without the protection of the First Amendment. We therefore agree with the court below that "[c]onveyance of the employer's belief, even though sincere, that unionization will or may result in the closing of the plant is not a statement of fact unless, which is most improbable, the eventuality of closing is capable of proof." 397 F.2d 157, 160. As stated elsewhere, an employer is free only to tell "what he reasonably believes will be the likely economic consequences of unionization that are outside his control," and not "threats of economic reprisal to be taken solely on his own volition." NLRB v. River Togs, Inc., 382 F.2d 198, 202 (C.A. 2d Cir. 1967).

Equally valid was the finding by the court and the Board that petitioner's statements and communications were not cast as a prediction of "demonstrable 'economic consequences,' " 397 F.2d, at 160, but rather as a threat of retaliatory action. The Board found that petitioner's speeches, pamphlets, leaflets, and letters conveyed the following message: that the company was in a precarious financial condition; that the "strike-happy" union would in all likelihood have to obtain its potentially unreasonable demands by striking, the probable result of which would be a plant shutdown, as the past history of labor relations in the area indicated; and that the employees in such a case would have great difficulty finding employment elsewhere. In carrying out its duty to focus on the question: "[W]hat did the speaker intend and the listener understand?" (A. Cox, Law and the National Labor Policy 44 (1960)), the Board could reasonably conclude that the intended and understood import of that message was not to predict that unionization would inevitably cause the plant to close but to threaten to throw employees out of work regardless of the economic realities. In this connection, we need go no further than to point out (1) that petitioner had no support for its basic assumption that the union, which had not yet even presented any demands, would have to strike to be heard, and that it admitted at the hearing that it had no basis for attributing other plant closings in the area to unionism; and (2) that the Board has often found that employees, who are particularly sensitive to rumors of plant closings, take such hints as coercive threats rather than honest forecasts.

Petitioner argues that the line between so-called permitted predictions and proscribed threats is too vague to stand up under traditional First Amendment analysis and that the Board's discretion to curtail free speech rights is correspondingly too uncontrolled. It is true that a reviewing court must recognize the Board's competence in the first instance to judge the impact of utterances made in the context of the employer-employee relationship. But an employer, who has control over that relationship and therefore knows it best, cannot be heard to complain that he is without an adequate guide for his behavior. He can easily make his views known without engaging in "brinkmanship" when it becomes all too easy to "overstep and tumble [over] the brink," Wausau Steel Corp. v. NLRB, 377 F.2d 369, 372 (C.A. 7th Cir. 1967). At the least he can avoid coercive speech simply by avoiding conscious overstatements he has reason to believe will mislead his employees. . . .

Notes

1. How would you evaluate the following employer statements?

a. As you all know, we have a good deal of competition from other companies in this city. Yet we have been able to maintain a good share of the work that is available. Why? Well, the answer is simple. We are the only company in the city making our product that has not been organized by this union. As soon as the union gets in, it forces wages up. There is no doubt that if they get in here, they will try to force us to raise our wages. Now you may think that's a good thing, but we don't think so. If the union succeeds, there is every probability that we will not be able to do as much business as we have in the past. You know that our competitors are bigger and have more automated machinery. We have been thinking for a long time that we could reduce our costs by moving this plant to the southern United States or by replacing many employees with automated machinery. If the union is voted in here, we are going to have to consider those possibilities again.

b. The law does not require us to do anything more than sit down with the union in good faith. It does not force us to give you a single benefit. And you can be sure that if the union is voted in here, we will begin bargaining from scratch.

c. Although the NLRB has held that the union is seeking an election in an appropriate bargaining unit, we do not agree and intend to take this issue to the court of appeals. Our attorney informs us that even if the union wins the election, it may take as much as several years before the court of appeals finally decides whether or not the union is your lawful bargaining agent.

2. *Problem.* During a union campaign prior to a representation election the employer distributed a letter to company employees signed by the company president containing the following language:

> The company handouts explain in detail exactly how the Sayre employees have received special treatment from North American Car [Sayre's parent company]. Your wages, fringe benefits and company sponsored activities all exceed those of any BRC [Brotherhood of Railway Carmen] union shop. We want to continue to consider the Sayre employees as a *special* group. If you vote for the union, you'll simply be considered as another BRC union shop and dealt with accordingly. . . .
>
> The Sayre employees and even the unions themselves have indicated that the Sayre shop pays very good wages. We intend to continue increasing wages every year just as we have in the past, and in doing so we will be taking into consideration the increase in cost of living. You have more flexibility without a union contract because your wages are reviewed once each year. The BRC union contracts fix wages for three years at a time, and those contracts do not have an unlimited cost of living provision either.
>
> If you go union, everything is subject to *renegotiation.* This means your fringe benefits, wages and company sponsored activities could possibly change or be reduced. Unions frequently give away benefits in exchange for a closed union shop provision and a check-off clause. . . .

> What about the employees at Roscoe and Staples who have lost thousands of dollars and been permanently replaced because they followed the union's leadership in demanding more than the company could agree to?
>
> I encourage all of you to keep your jobs rather than possibly being permanently replaced in the event of a strike — Keep your individual right to speak for yourself — Keep your standing as the *special North American Car Shop* for wages and fringe benefits are higher than at the other BRC shops.
>
> I am very encouraged about the future of the Sayre shop. There's no reason why it can't continue to be the *special* shop in the North American Car Organization. On the other hand, if you vote union, you'll be dealt with just like any other union shop.
>
> I sincerely believe that the union can't and won't do anything for you — in fact, it could work to your disadvantage.

The union lost the election. Should the election be overturned? See North American Car Corp., 253 N.L.R.B. No. 128 (1980).

3. Would it violate §8(a)(1) for a corporate board of directors to exhibit shortly before a representation election a corporate resolution stating that the company will go out of business if the union is voted in?

3. Questioning, Polling, and Surveillance

Suppose an employer, confronted by a union claim that it represents a majority of his or her employees, asks individual employees whether they do, in fact, wish to have the union represent them. If the questioning contains no hint of retaliation, should it be deemed either an unfair labor practice or conduct that would overturn the employer's later election victory?

ROSSMORE HOUSE
269 N.L.R.B. No. 198, 116 L.R.R.M. 1025 (1984)

[An administrative law] judge found that the Respondent interrogated employee Warren Harvey in violation of §8(a)(1) of the Act. We disagree, and for the reasons set forth below, we overrule existing Board law supporting the judge's conclusions.

The Respondent operates a residential retirement hotel that provides food and lodging to its guests. On 26 or 27 July employee Warren Harvey contacted union representatives and arranged for an employee meeting at his house 31 July. In the meantime Harvey distributed authorization cards to fellow employees. At the suggestion of a union representative, a mailgram was sent to the Respondent following the 31 July meeting; the mailgram stated that Harvey and another employee were forming a union organizing committee with knowledge that their activities were protected under the Act. The mailgram's purpose was to protect the rights of the organizing committee.

When the Respondent's manager, Tvenstrup, received the mailgram on the morning of 1 August he walked into the kitchen with the mailgram and approached Harvey. According to Tvenstrup's testimony, he asked Harvey, "Is this true?" Harvey answered affirmatively, and Tvenstrup said, "Okay, thank you," and started walking away. Harvey said, "I am sorry; it is nothing personal," and Tvenstrup said "Okay," and proceeded to his office. Tvenstrup testified that he had been unaware of any union activity and did not believe the mailgram when he received it.

Harvey testified that Tvenstrup walked into the kitchen waving the mailgram. His version is as follows:

> he said, "What is this about a union?" . . . I told him, "That's right about the union. We're going to have a union because of the lack of benefits, lack of insurance, lack of job security, vacations without pay". . . . After I told him that, he said that Mr. and Mrs. Tsay were not going to like it and that they would fight it, have to fight it to the hilt, and I said, "Well, it's nothing personal. We just want better conditions." And he said, "Well, as manager, I will have to fight it too."

The next incident took place 7 August. According to Harvey's credited testimony, he was leaving the facility after work when the Respondent's owners, the Tsays, approached him. Mr. Tsay stated, "The manager tells me you're trying to get a union in here," and asked why. Harvey replied that it was "because of the low pay, no benefits and lack of job security." Tsay then asked whether the Union charged a fee to join and, when Harvey said yes, Tsay said he would talk to the manager about it.

The judge found the Respondent's statement in both instances to be unlawful interrogations under §8(a)(1) of the Act, eliciting Paceco[5] and Anaconda Co.[6] In Paceco[7] the Board stated:

> [A]n interrogation of an employee's union sympathies or his reasons for supporting a union need not be uttered in the context of threats or promises in order to be coercive. The probing of such views, even addressed to employees who have openly declared their prounion sympathies, reasonably tends to interfere with the free exercise of employee rights under the Act, and, consequently, is coercive.

More recently, in PPG Industries,[8] the Board held that questions

5. 237 N.L.R.B. 399, 99 L.R.R.M. 1544 (1978), vacated in part and remanded in part, 601 F.2d 180. (5th Cir. 1979), supp. dec. 247 N.L.R.B. 1405 (1980).
6. 241 N.L.R.B. 1091.
7. 237 N.L.R.B. 399-400.
8. 251 N.L.R.B. 1146, 105 L.R.R.M. 1434.

concerning union sympathies, even when addressed to open and active union supporters in the absence of threats or promises, are inherently coercive.

Before the line of cases culminating in the PPG decision, the Board had declined to find violations in such circumstances. In B. F. Goodrich Footwear Co.,[10] the Board found no violation when a supervisor asked two employees who were open union partisans how they felt about the union. The Board noted that no other unlawful conduct occurred with respect to either employee and concluded that "the nature of the inquiry, in the total context of all the circumstances here, is [not] sufficient to establish the kind of interference, restraint, or coercion which we have found to constitute a violation of §8(a)(1) in quite different contexts." Similarly, in Stumpf Motor Co.,[11] the Board held that the respondent's asking "a self-proclaimed and known union adherent" what he thought of the union did not violate §8(a)(1), but was merely a conversation opener.

In PPG, however, the Board overruled Stumpf and B. F. Goodrich. The PPG board stated, "The type of questioning at issue conveys an employer's displeasure with employees' union activity and thereby discourages such activity in the future. The coercive impact of these questions is not diminished by the employees' open union support or by the absence of attendant threats."

We will no longer apply the PPG standard. We conclude that PPG improperly established a per se rule that completely disregarded the circumstances surrounding an alleged interrogation and ignored the reality of the workplace. Such a per se approach had been rejected by the Board 30 years ago[13] when it set forth the basic test for evaluating whether interrogations violate the Act: whether under all of the circumstances the interrogation reasonably tends to restrain, coerce, or interfere with rights guaranteed by the Act. Our view is consonant with that expressed by the Seventh Circuit Court of Appeals in Midwest Stock Exchange v. NLRB:[14]

> It is well established that interrogation of employees is not illegal per se. §8(a)(1) of the Act prohibits employers only from activity which in some manner tends to restrain, coerce or interfere with employee rights. To fall within the ambit of §8(a)(1), either the words themselves or the context in which they are used must suggest an element of coercion or interference.

In Graham Architectural Products v. NLRB,[15] the Third Circuit recently adopted the same approach, as follows:

10. 201 N.L.R.B. 353 (1973).
11. 208 N.L.R.B. 431, 432 (1974).
13. Blue Flash Express, 109 N.L.R.B. 591 (1954).
14. 635 F.2d 1255, 1267 (7th Cir. 1980).
15. 697 F.2d 534, 541 (3d Cir. 1983).

> In deciding whether questioning in individual cases amounts to the type of coercive interrogation that 8(a)(1) proscribes, one must remember two general points. Because production supervisors and employees often work closely together, one can expect that during the course of the workday they will discuss a range of subjects of mutual interest, including ongoing unionization efforts. To hold that any instance of casual questioning concerning union sympathies violates the Act ignores the realities of the workplace. Moreover, as the United States Supreme Court recognized in NLRB v. Gissel Packing Co., 395 U.S. 575, 89 S. Ct. 1918, 23 L. Ed. 2d 547, 71 L.R.R.M.2481 (1969), the First Amendment permits employers to communicate with their employees concerning an ongoing union organizing campaign 'so long as the communications do not contain a threat of reprisal or force or promise of benefit.' Id. at 618, 89 S. Ct. at 1942. This right is recognized in §8(c) of the Act. If §8(a)(1) of the Act deprived the employers of any right to ask non-coercive questions of their employees during such a campaign, the Act would directly collide with the Constitution. What the Act proscribes is only those instances of true 'interrogation' which tend to interfere with the employees' right to organize.

After careful consideration, we conclude, in agreement with Member Hunter's dissent in Donnelly Mfg. Co.,[17] that PPG improperly establishes a per se rule that completely disregards the circumstances surrounding an alleged interrogation and ignores the reality of the workplace. Accordingly, we overrule PPG and similar cases to the extent they find that an employer's questioning open and active union supporters about their union sentiments, in the absence of threats or promises, necessarily interferes with, restrains, or coerces employees in violation of §8(a)(1) of the Act.[20]

In this case, Harvey, an active union supporter, openly declared his union ties by means of a mailgram to the Respondent. We find no violation of §8(a)(1) of the Act under either version of the conversation between Tvenstrup and Harvey concerning the contents of the telegram and Tvenstrup's intention to oppose the Union. Nor do we find any violation regarding the second incident when the Respondent's owner asked Harvey why he wanted a union and whether the Union charged a fee. Under the totality of the circumstances, we find the Respondent's

17. 265 N.L.R.B. No. 196, 112 L.R.R.M. 1143 (Dec. 27, 1982).

20. Our dissenting colleague mischaracterizes our holding here by stating that we will not weigh the setting and nature of interrogations involving open and active union supporters. Experience convinces us that there are myriad situations in which interrogations may arise. Out duty is to determine in each case whether, under the dictates of §8(a)(1), such interrogations violate the Act. Some factors which may be considered in analyzing alleged interrogations are: (1) the background; (2) the nature of the information sought; (3) the identity of the questioner; and (4) the place and method of interrogation. See Bourne v. NLRB, 332 F.2d 47 (2d Cir. 1964). These and other relevant factors are not to be mechanically applied in each case. Rather, they represent some areas of inquiry that may be considered in applying the Blue Flash test of whether under all the circumstances the interrogation reasonably tends to restrain, coerce, or interfere with rights guaranteed by the Act.

questioning of Harvey to be noncoercive, and therefore we shall dismiss the complaint in its entirety.

The complaint is dismissed.

ZIMMERMAN, Member, dissenting in part:

I dissent from the overruling of PPG Industries. I reject my colleagues' claim that PPG established a per se rule that disregards the circumstances surrounding an alleged interrogation and ignores the "reality of the workplace." On the contrary, it is my colleagues who have established a per se rule by their decision in this case. They hold that, absent an accompanying threat of reprisal or promise of benefit, the interrogation of an open union adherent will not violate §8(a)(1). Unlike the PPG standard, this new per se rule gives no weight to the setting and nature of the interrogation. It ignores the reality that employers sometimes use subtle coercion during an organizing campaign and fails to recognize that even open union adherents may be intimidated by such coercion. . . .

Notes

1. What effects do you predict the Board's choice of a standard instead of a rule will have in this case?
2. The *Blue Flash* criteria are as follows:

> Absent unusual circumstances, the polling of employees by an employer will be violative of §8(a)(1) of the Act unless the following safeguards are observed: (1) the purpose of the poll is to determine the truth of a union's claim of majority, (2) this purpose is communicated to the employees, (3) assurances against reprisal are given, (4) the employees are polled by secret ballot, and (5) the employer has not engaged in unfair labor practices or otherwise created a coercive atmosphere.

Are these still the Board's criteria? It is difficult to believe that the Board's expertise in this subject has increased unless it can cite data not earlier available. If it has no such data, one must conclude the decision is political. What are the implications of that conclusion? Wouldn't it be more straightforward for a political party that has just taken control of the Board to publish a list of new rules?

4. Third Party Interference

Employer unfair labor practice responsibility for the acts of third parties is governed by §§2(2) and 2(13) of the Act. Supervisors are almost always considered agents of their employer unless their activity is minor and not clothed with apparent authority. The acts of outsiders, such as citizen groups and other involvements by the community, can be laid at the employer's feet only on a finding of agency. But although unfair labor practice liability is limited by agency, agency need not necessarily be shown in order to set aside an election. Thus where acts of the community have created an environment hostile to the union organizing drive, an employer election victory may be set aside by the NLRB. Consistency in the Board's decisions is not always obvious, however. Thus rumors spread by citizen groups, the media, or employees to the effect that the employer might close down or move his or her operation in the case of a union victory may or may not warrant setting aside the election.[52]

G. EMPLOYER ECONOMIC RESISTANCE TO ORGANIZING

1. Retaliation Against Protected Activities[53]

BOB'S CASING CREWS v. NLRB

458 F.2d 1301 (5th Cir. 1972)

GOLDBERG, J.

This is a petition for review of an order of the National Labor Relation Board issued against Bob's Casing Crews, Inc., and a cross-application for enforcement of a Board order. . . .

This case has been decided by the Board and reviewed by this Court once before. In the original proceeding the Board, agreeing with the Trial Examiner, found that one Billy Ray Loper was refused employment by the petitioner because he walked off the job at Red's Casing Crews, Inc. The Board further found that Loper's action in walking off the job at Red's constituted activity protected by §7 of the National Labor Relations Act. Therefore, the Board concluded that the petitioner's refusal to rehire Loper was violative of §8(a)(1) of the Act. On appeal of

[52] Compare Marlowe Mfg. Co., 213 N.L.R.B. 278 (1974) (leaflet threatening plant closure distributed by employees held not grounds for overturning an election) with Richland's, 220 N.L.R.B. 83 (1975) (threat of plant closure unlawful where employer knew state legislator had mailed letters containing the threat to employees; failure of employer to repudiate constituted ratification).

[53] See Christensen & Svanoe, Motive and Intent in the Commission of Unfair Labor Practices: The Supreme Court and the Fictive Formality, 77 Yale L.J. 1269 (1968); Getman, Section 8(a)(3) of the NLRA and the Effort to Insulate Free Employee Choice, 32 U. Chi. L. Rev. 735 (1965); Oberer, The Scienter Factor in Sections 8(a)(1) and (3) of the Labor Act: Of Balancing, Hostile Motives, Dogs and Tails, 52 Cornell L.Q. 491 (1967).

that original order this Court found that "[t]he record does establish that Loper's activity at Red's was a factor in the Company's decision not to reemploy him. However, this factor may have been a legitimate business reason, unless it can be shown that Loper's conduct at Red's was protected 'concerted activity.'" Accordingly, this Court remanded the case for a determination of whether or not Loper's conduct at Red's Casing Crews, Inc. was indeed protected "concerted activity." Bob's Casing Crews, Inc. v. NLRB, 5th Cir. 1970, 429 F.2d 261, 263-264. Pursuant to our direction, a further hearing was held before a trial examiner and the following was established.

In August of 1968 Red's Casing Crews, Inc. was hired by Standard Oil Company of Texas to "lay down" some 10,000 feet of casing at a location approximately 160 miles from Odessa, Texas. Billy Loper was a member of the casing crew which arrived at the job site on August 5. As the crew was preparing for work, a representative of Standard Oil approached Crew Hauler Shelton and requested that the crew, in addition to laying down the 10,000 feet of casing, pick up some 10,000 feet of drill pipe. The entire crew discussed the additional job order and decided that they would perform the initial job but would be too tired to pick up the drill pipe. Accordingly, Shelton agreed to attempt to arrange for a relief crew to pick up the drill pipe. At about noon on the same day, one of Red's field representatives arrived at the job site and began talking with Shelton. Loper approached the two men and told them that the crew wanted relief for the picking up of the drill pipe and that if the crew were not relieved, they would walk off the job. In the early morning hours of August 6 the initial job order was completed; a relief crew arrived to pick up the drill pipe; and the original crew members returned to their homes in Odessa. During the afternoon of August 6, Shelton visited Loper at his home and told him that Red's president and owner had instructed Shelton to fire Loper because he had threatened to walk off the job the night before. On the basis of these facts the trial examiner and the Board concluded that Loper's activities at Red's constituted protected, concerted activity within the meaning of the National Labor Relations Act. Therefore, the Board reaffirmed its original decision and order holding that the petitioner's refusal to hire Loper because he engaged in protected, concerted activity at Red's violated §8(a)(1) of the Act. From this reaffirmance of the Board's order, the petitioner appeals.

The Company first asserts that the findings of the Board are not supported by substantial evidence. Essentially, the petitioner contends that the evidence at the hearings revealed (1) that Loper acted alone and not in concert with any other crew members, (2) that no protest was ever made by Loper to Red's concerning the work at the job site, (3) that Loper never threatened to walk off the job, (4) that Loper was never discharged at Red's, and (5) that Loper lied to the petitioner at the time he sought to be rehired. All of these alleged facts are based on evidence offered by the Company which was discredited by the Trial Examiner and the Board. The findings of the Trial Examiner and the Board, as set forth above, are based principally upon the testimony of Loper. To the extent that the petitioner asserts that the testimonial conflicts between Loper and the Company witnesses should have been resolved differently, we note that it is established law that credibility choices are for the Board. In addition, we cannot conclude that the testimony relied on the Trial Examiner and the Board "carries its own death wound" and that the discredited evidence "carries its own irrefutable truth." Pittsburgh S.S. Co. v NLRB, 1949, 337 U.S. 656, 660, quoting from NLRB v. Robbins Tire & Rubber Co., 5 Cir. 1947, 161 F.2d 798, 800. While the record in this case contains a considerable amount of evidence in support of the Company's asserted facts, it also encompasses admissible evidence validating the findings of both the Trial Examiner and the Board. Therefore, we conclude that the record as a whole evinces substantial evidence in support of the Board's findings.

We next turn to the petitioner's assertion that the activity engaged in by Loper while working for Red's was not protected, concerted activity within the meaning of §7 of the Act. Petitioner does not deny that under §7 employees have the right to protest concertedly to management a particular condition of their employment which they consider objectionable and to strike or threaten to strike in support of their protestations. However, petitioner does contend that §7 encompasses only activity which is in protest of then-existing conditions of employment. Essentially, the Company argues that no matter how nefarious an employer's proposed changes in working conditions might be, employees have no right to concert in order to frustrate that malefaction until they have experienced its malign embraces. We do not think such a "try it — you'll like it" philosophy is embodied in §7 of the Act. This is evidenced principally by those decisions holding that a sympathy strike is protected, concerted activity under §7 of the Act. But independently of any judicial precedent, we are simply unable to convince ourselves that, though an employer's future impositions be ever so ominous and foreseeable, a union's concerting is so frozen to the status quo under §7 that the union possesses absolutely no mobility to object. A union cannot be cast solely as a neanderthal of the past or a lamb of the present. Indeed, if it be given any role, it must be that of a lion seeking havens of betterment in the company's plant. Therefore, we conclude that under §7 employees have the right to ameliorate both present and future working conditions, and that Loper's conduct in the instant case falls within the protective ambit of that provision.

Turning our attention to the petitioner's procedural objections, we first consider the Company's argument that the charge and complaint in this case are barred by §10 of the Act. Section 10(b) provides in part "[t]hat no complaint shall issue based upon any unfair labor practice occurring more than six months prior to the filing of the charge with the Board and the service of a copy thereof upon the person against whom such charge is made. . . ." 29 U.S.C.A. §160(b). The original charge in this case alleged that the petitioner discriminated against Loper by refusing to employ him because of his union membership and his activities in behalf of the union. The complaint, which was filed some two and a half months after the union filed its original charge, asserts that the petitioner refused to rehire Billy Loper on August 7, 1968, because he engaged in concerted activities for the purpose of collective bargaining or mutual aid or protection. The Company contends that the failure of the Board's complaint to list in detail the concerted activities in which Loper engaged is fatal to the Board's order. It is the Company's position that it was not apprised of the details until February 20, 1969, and that this notice constituted an amendment to the complaint which was barred by §10(b) because it was issued more than six months subsequent to the filing of the charge. We first note that the six-months limitation of §10(b), by its own terms, applies to the filing of a charge and not to the issuance of a complaint. Moreover, it is settled law that particularity of pleading is not required of a complaint issued by the Board. Finally, even assuming arguendo that the complaint was not sufficiently detailed to put the petitioner on notice at the original hearing as to the precise facts at issue, the Company is in no position to claim any prejudice by any such omission since it knew of the alleged details concerning Loper's concerted activity at Red's long before they were established at the rehearing.

Having determined that the petitioner's objections to the Board's order are without merit, we conclude that the Board's cross-application to enforce its order should be granted.

Enforced.

Notes

1. If Loper had been fired for trying unsuccessfully to persuade other employees to refuse the drill pipe work, his activity would have been accorded §7 protection. Do you see why?

2. No violation of §8(a)(3) was alleged in *Bob's Casing Crews* because Loper's activity did not involve a union. If it had, the Board would have found both §8(a)(3) and §8(a)(1) violations.

3. Suppose Bob's Casing Crews alleges that Loper had given a negative answer to a job application form's inquiry into whether he had ever been discharged by a previous employer. The company then makes alternative arguments:

a. Loper was refused employment because he falsified his application; and
b. the company has a policy against hiring anyone who has been discharged by a previous employer and the company was unaware of the circumstances of Loper's discharge at Red's Casing Crews.

Should either argument be a defense? In formulating your answer, consider the Supreme Court's decision in NLRB v. Burnup & Sims, 379 U.S. 21 (1964). The employer discharged two employees in the good faith belief that they were planning to dynamite the employer's property to achieve recognition for the union. The Board found that the dynamite threat had not been made, and that the discharges thus violated §§8(a)(1) and (3). The employer's good faith was no defense. The Supreme Court affirmed the finding of a §8(a)(1) violation and found it unnecessary to reach the issue of §8(a)(3) liability.

4. The normal remedy in a case like *Bob's Casing Crews* is a cease and desist order and an order to offer the applicant employment with backpay and interest. From the backpay is deducted monies earned elsewhere by the applicant in the interim period, and a deduction is also made for monies that the applicant failed to earn without excuse. This remedy was approved by the Supreme Court in Phelps Dodge Corp. v. NLRB, 313 U.S. 177 (1941).

The Court rejected two arguments. First, it was contended that the remedial language of §10(c) permitting "affirmative action, including reinstatement of employees with or without backpay" precludes an order to hire an applicant since the applicant is not an "employee" nor is he or she being "reinstated." Second, it was argued that §2(3)'s reference to an employee "who has not obtained any other regular and substantially equivalent employment" shows an intent to deny the hiring remedy where the discriminatee has found equivalent employment.

Query whether these remedies, coming four years after the incident, were satisfactory to Billy Loper or sufficient to deter similar conduct in the future. A cease and desist order plus backpay is also the remedy when an employee is discriminatorily discharged. Some employers when faced with a union organizing drive will determine that the chilling effect on employees of seeing union supporters fired is worth more than the cost of the backpay awards, a remedy usually coming too late by several years to affect the union's campaign.

EDWARD G. BUDD MANUFACTURING CO. v. NLRB

138 F.2d 86 (3d Cir. 1943), cert. denied, 321 U.S. 778 (1943)

BIGGS, J. . . .

The complaint . . . alleges that the petitioner, in September, 1933, created and foisted a labor organization, known as the Budd Employee

Representation Association, upon its employees and thereafter contributed financial support to the Association and dominated its activities. The amended complaint also alleges that in July, 1941, the petitioner discharged an employee, Walter Weigand, because of his activities on behalf of the union. . . .

The petitioner denies these charges as does the Association which was permitted to intervene. After extensive hearings before a trial examiner the Board on June 10, 1942 issued its decision and order, requiring the disestablishment of the Association and the reinstatement of Weigand.

The case of Walter Weigand is extraordinary. If ever a workman deserved summary discharge it was he. He was under the influence of liquor while on duty. He came to work when he chose and he left the plant and his shift as he pleased. In fact, a foreman on one occasion was agreeably surprised to find Weigand at work and commented upon it. Weigand amiably stated that he was enjoying it.[6] He brought a woman (apparently generally known as the "Duchess") to the rear of the plant yard and introduced some of the employees to her. He took another employee to visit her and when this man got too drunk to be able to go home, punched his time-card for him and put him on the table in the representatives' meeting room in the plant in order to sleep off his intoxication. Weigand's immediate superiors demanded again and again that he be discharged, but each time higher officials intervened on Weigand's behalf because as was naively stated he was "a representative." In return for not working at the job for which he was hired, the petitioner gave him full pay and on five separate occasions raised his wages. One of these raises was general; that is to say, Weigand profited by general wage increase throughout the plant, but the other four raises were given Weigand at times when other employees in the plant did not receive wage increases.

The petitioner contends that Weigand was discharged because of cumulative grievances against him. But about the time of the discharge it was suspected by some of the representatives that Weigand had joined the complaining CIO union. One of the representatives taxed him with this fact and Weigand offered to bet a hundred dollars that it could not be proved. On July 22, 1941, Weigand did disclose his union membership to the vice-chairman (Rattigan) of the Association and to another representative (Mullen) and apparently tried to persuade them to support the union. Weigand asserts that the next day he with Rattigan and Mullen, were seen talking to CIO organizer Reichwein on a street corner. The following day, according to Weigand's testimony, Mullen came to Weigand at the plant and stated that Weigand, Rattigan and himself had been seen talking to Reichwein and that he, Mullen, had just had an interview with Personnel Director McIlvain and Plant Manager Mahan.

6. Weigand stated that he was carried on the payroll as a "rigger." He was asked what was a rigger. He replied: "I don't know; I am not a rigger."

According to Weigand, Mullen said to him, "Maybe you didn't get me in a jam." And, "We were seen down there." The following day Weigand was discharged.

[A]n employer may discharge an employee for a good reason, a poor reason or no reason at all so long as the provisions of the National Labor Relations Act are not violated. It is, of course, a violation to discharge an employee because he has engaged in activities on behalf of a union. Conversely an employer may retain an employee for a good reason, a bad reason or no reason at all and the reason is not a concern of the Board. But it is certainly too great a strain on our credulity to assert, as does the petitioner, that Weigand was discharged for an accumulation of offenses. We think that he was discharged because his work on behalf of the CIO had become known to the plant manager. That ended his sinecure at the Budd plant. The Board found that he was discharged because of his activities on behalf of the union. The record shows that the Board's finding was based on sufficient evidence.

The order of the Board will be enforced.

Notes

1. Evaluate the following argument that might have been made on Weigand's behalf to the court of appeals:

> Certainly there is evidence in the record that Weigand had broken some company rules, but that is irrelevant. The purpose of the Act is a public purpose, not concerned with the guilt, innocence or quality of individual employees. The effect of Weigand's discharge on other employees cannot be doubted: it is no longer safe to support the CIO union at Budd Manufacturing. The only way to loose the fear from these employees is to carry out the public policy by reinstating Weigand and making him whole.
>
> Nor does it matter what the subjective motivation of the company may have been. The Act does seek to deter anti-union conduct by punishing employers, but it does much more than that. See NLRB v. Burnup & Sims, 379 U.S. 21 (1964). Weigand's discharge was instantaneous upon the company's learning of his CIO activity — employees could see his discharge as nothing other than a reprisal for his union beliefs. That was a violation of §8(a)(1) notwithstanding what may have been inside the plant manager's head at the time.

How should the company's brief respond? What are the alternatives for the court of appeals? Compare Frosty Morn Meats v. NLRB, 296 F.2d 617, 621 (5th Cir. 1961):

> If in the absence of a discriminating motive the employee would not have been fired, his discharge deprives him of a right he would otherwise have had to continue his job while participating in union activities. Such dis-

charges make other employees apprehensive that if they join a union they endanger their jobs. The inquiry must be made even where the discharged employee had done something that might warrant his discharge, since if it is something that the employer might pass over in another instance the firing of the union employee can be discriminatory. If, however, the misdeeds of the employee are so flagrant that he would almost certainly be fired anyway there is no room for discrimination to play a part. The employee will not have been harmed by the employer's union animus, and neither he nor any others will be discouraged from membership in a union, since all will understand that the employee would have been fired anyway. It must be remembered that the statute prohibits discrimination, and that the focus on dominant motivation is only a test to reveal whether discrimination has occurred. Discrimination consists in treating like cases differently. If an employer fires a union sympathizer or organizer, a finding of discrimination rests on the assumption that in the absence of the union activities he would have treated the employee differently.

When an employee gives his employer as much reason to fire him as Judkins did, by refusing to follow instructions and by giving not only his supervisors but also his fellow employees the impression that he was uncooperative, there is no basis for the conclusion that the employer has treated him differently than he would have treated a non-union employee. As a speculative matter, it may or may not be true that union animus loomed larger in the employer's motivation than Judkin's shortcomings as a worker. But when the evidence of just cause for discharge is as great as it is here, the record as a whole does not support the conclusion that the discharged employee was deprived of any right because of union activities. The power of reinstatement is remedial. It is not punitive. It is not to penalize an employer for anti-unionism by forcing on the pay-roll an employee unfit to stay on the job.

2. If Weigand accepts reinstatement, is his tenure likely to be long and happy? Consider these results from a study in one of the Board's regional offices in the early 1970s.

One major fact emerges from this longitudinal study, and that is the fact that it is the discriminatee who suffers. Of the original 217 ordered reinstatement, a full 129 refused it. Of that group, 114 refused it because of fear of company backlash. . . .

There were originally 88 employees who accepted reinstatement. Of that number, only 72 actually received it. The remainder were placed on preferential hiring lists and not heard from again. This brings attention to the 72 who were reinstated.

By January of 1973, 86.9 percent of those originally reinstated had terminated employment or had been discharged. Two years later, an additional six percent joined them. . . . In summary, of the 72 originally reinstated, 95.8 percent were gone in eight years.[54]

[54] Chaney, The Reinstatement Remedy Revisited, 32 Lab. L.J. 357, 363-364 (1981).

3. *Problem.* Managers fired an employee for going into a supervisor's office without permission and copying down names and addresses for transmission to the union organizers. The Board held the discharge violated §§8(a)(3) and 8(a)(1) because there was no attempt by the employee to conceal what he was doing and the employer had never treated these records as confidential.[55] Right result? Right reasons?

4. Where employees engaged in a union organizing drive commit acts of physical destruction of the employer's property, the Board may refuse to order their reinstatement on the ground that to reinstate would not "effectuate the policies of the Act." An alternative ground is to rely on that portion of §10(c) reading: "No order of the Board shall require the reinstatement of any individual as an employee who has been suspended or discharged, or the payment to him of any back pay, if such individual was suspended or discharged for cause." Should either of these rationales have helped Budd Manufacturing? Should they have helped Bob's Casing Crews?

In Clear Pine Mouldings, 268 N.L.R.B. No. 173, 115 L.R.R.M. 1221 (1984), the question was whether words, unaccompanied by "sticks and stones," would prevent reinstatement. The Board's opinion stated:

> Section 7 of the Act gives employees the right to peacefully strike, picket, and engage in other concerted activities for the purpose of collective bargaining or other mutual aid or protection. Section 7 also grants employees the equivalent right to "refrain from" these activities.
>
> Previously, the Board has held that "not every impropriety committed in the course of a strike deprives an employee of the protective mantle of the Act" and that "minor acts of misconduct must have been in the contemplation of Congress when it provided for the right to strike. . . ."[6] However, the Board has also acknowledged that "serious acts of misconduct which occur in the course of a strike may disqualify a striker from the protection of the Act."[7]
>
> The difficulty lies in deciding whether particular strike misconduct results in the loss of statutory protection the employees otherwise would have. In the past, the Board has held that verbal threats by strikers, "not accompanied by any physical acts or gestures that would provide added emphasis or meaning to [the] words," do not constitute serious strike misconduct warranting an employer's refusal to reinstate the strikers.[8] On the other hand, the Board has held that verbal threats which are accompanied by physical movements or contacts, such as hitting cars, do constitute

[55] Southern & Western Lumber Co., d/b/a/ Gray Flooring, 212 N.L.R.B. 668 (1974).

6. Coronet Casuals, 207 N.L.R.B. 304, 305 (1973).

7. Id. at 304.

8. W. C. McQuaide, Inc. 220 N.L.R.B. 593, 594 (1975), enf. denied in pertinent part, 552 F.2d 519 (3d Cir. 1977). See also A. Duie Pyle, Inc., 263 N.L.R.B. 744 (1982); Georgia Kraft Co., 258 N.L.R.B. 908, 912-913 (1981), enfd. 696 F.2d 931 (11th Cir. 1983), cert. granted 52 U.S.L.W. 3386 (Nov. 14, 1983) (No. 83-103); Arrow Industries, 245 N.L.R.B. 1376 (1979); MP Industries, 227 N.L.R.B. 1709, 1711 (1977).

serious strike misconduct.[9] The Board summarized its standard for finding strike misconduct based on verbal threats in *Coronet Casuals,* where it stated that "absent violence . . . a picket is not disqualified from reinstatement despite . . . making abusive threats against nonstrikers. . . ."[10]

We disagree with this standard because actions such as the making of abusive threats against nonstriking employees equate to "restraint and coercion" prohibited elsewhere in the Act and are not privileged by §8(c) of the Act. Although we agree that the presence of physical gestures accompanying a verbal threat may increase the gravity of verbal conduct, we reject the per se rule that words alone can never warrant a denial of reinstatement in the absence of physical acts. Rather, we agree with the United States Court of Appeals for the First Circuit that "[a] serious threat may draw its credibility from the surrounding circumstances and not from the physical gestures of the speaker."[11] We also agree with the United States Court of Appeals for the Third Circuit that an employer need not "countenance conduct that amounts to intimidation and threats of bodily harm."[12] In *McQuaide,* the Third Circuit applied the following objective test for determining whether verbal threats by strikers directed at fellow employees justify an employer's refusal to reinstate: ' "whether the misconduct is such that, under the circumstances existing, it may reasonably tend to coerce or intimidate employees in the exercise of rights protected under the Act.' "[13] We believe this is the correct standard and we adopt it. . . .

In deciding whether reinstatement should be ordered after an unfair labor practice strike, the Board has in the past balanced the severity of the employer's unfair labor practices that provoked the strike against the gravity of the striker's misconduct.[24] We do not agree with this test. There is nothing in the statute to support the notion that striking employees are free to engage in or escalate violence or misconduct in proportion to their individual estimates of the degree of seriousness of an employer's unfair labor practices. Rather, it is for the Board to fashion remedies and policies which will discourage unfair labor practices and the resort to violence and unlawful coercion by employers and employees alike. In cases of picket

9. Hedstrom Co., 235 N.L.R.B. 1198, 1198-1199 (1978), enfd. 629 F.2d 305 (3d Cir. 1980); Pepsi Cola Bottling Co., 203 N.L.R.B. 183 (1973), enfd. in pertinent part 496 F.2d 226 (4th Cir. 1974); Alabaster Lime Co., 194 N.L.R.B. 1116 (1972).

10. Coronet Casuals, 207 N.L.R.B. at 304-305.

11. Associated Grocers of New England v. NLRB, 562 F.2d 1333, 1336 (1st Cir. 1977), denying enf. in part to 227 N.L.R.B. 1200.

12. NLRB v. W. C. McQuaide, Inc., 552 F.2d 519, 527 (3d Cir. 1977), denying enf. in part to 220 N.L.R.B. 593 (1975). We read the *McQuaide* standard to essentially adopt a "reasonably tends to restrain and coerce" measure for the loss of reinstatement rights.

13. Id. at 528 (quoting Operating Engineers Local 542 v. NLRB, 328 F.2d 850, 852-853 (3d Cir. 1964), cert. denied, 379 U.S. 826).

24. *Coronet Casuals,* 207 N.L.R.B. at 305 fn. 15. See also NLRB v. Thayer Co., 213 F.2d 748 (1st Cir. 1954), cert. denied, 348 U.S. 883 (1955), which holds that, where collective action is precipitated by an employer's unfair labor practice, a finding that the employees' conduct is not protected under §7 does not, ipso facto, preclude the Board from ordering the employer to reinstate the employees if such an order would effectuate the purposes of the Act, and which uses the same balancing test to determine whether reinstatement is warranted.

line and strike misconduct, we will do this by denying reinstatement and backpay to employees who exceed the bounds of peaceful and reasoned conduct. . . .

5. *Problem.* The company discharged an employee because of his union activity. One month after the discharge the employee willfully and unlawfully failed to report earnings to the State Unemployment Benefits Commission for the purpose of obtaining benefits to which he was not entitled. Should this preclude the Board from awarding reinstatement with full backpay? See Alumbaugh Coal Corp. v. NLRB, 635 F.2d 1380 (8th Cir. 1980).

6. In Bill Johnson's Restaurants v. NLRB, 103 S. Ct. 2161 (1983), waitresses filed an unfair labor practice charge against their employer alleging the discriminatory discharge of a fellow worker. They also picketed the restaurant protesting the discharge. The employer filed a state court lawsuit alleging that the waitresses had engaged in mass picketing, harassed customers, blocked entrances, and created a threat to public safety. A libel count alleged that the waitresses had distributed leaflets containing false and outrageous statements about the employer. The suit asked for a temporary restraining order, preliminary and permanent injunctive relief, compensatory damages, and $500,000 in punative damages. One of the waitresses filed an unfair labor practice charge against the restaurant contending that the lawsuit was in retaliation for the waitresses' protected, concerted activities.

An Administrative Law Judge found the restaurant to have committed several unfair labor practices, one of which was the filing of the state civil suit. The ALJ applied a Board rule that it is an unfair labor practice for an employer to institute a civil lawsuit for the purpose of penalizing or discouraging its employees from filing charges with the Board or seeking the Board's processes. On the basis of facts brought out in a four-day hearing, the ALJ found that the allegations in the employer's state court suit were unfounded. The Board adopted the ALJ's report and recommendations. The Board ordered the employer to withdraw its state court suit and to reimburse the legal expenses of the waitresses. A court of appeals affirmed.

The Supreme Court reversed:

> To summarize, we hold that the Board may not halt the prosecution of a state-court lawsuit, regardless of the plaintiff's motive, unless the suit lacks a reasonable basis in fact or law. Retaliatory motive and lack of reasonable basis are both essential prerequisites to the issuance of a cease-and-desist order against a state suit. The Board's reasonable basis inquiry must be structured in a manner that will preserve the state plaintiff's right to have a state court jury or judge resolve genuine material factual or state-law legal disputes pertaining to the lawsuit. Therefore, if the Board is called upon to determine whether a suit is unlawful prior to the time that the

state court renders final judgment, and if the state plaintiff can show that such genuine material factual or legal issues exist, the Board must await the results of the state-court adjudication with respect to the merits of the state suit. If the state proceedings result in a judgment adverse to the plaintiff, the Board may then consider the matter further and, if it is found that the lawsuit was filed with retaliatory intent, the Board may find a violation and order appropriate relief. In short, then, although it is an unfair labor practice to prosecute an unmeritorious lawsuit for a retaliatory purpose, the offense is not enjoinable unless the suit lacks a reasonable basis. . . .[15]

7. Suppose in *Bill Johnson's Restaurants* one or more of the picketing waitresses had been discharged by the employer for participating in the picketing but were later found to have been supervisors at the time of the picketing. Are the supervisors protected? The Board holds not.

Whether and under what circumstances the discharge of a supervisor will violate the Act has been a recurring issue in recent years—an issue which has divided the Board and has produced sometimes confusing and inconsistent decisions. As noted above, the Administrative Law Judge relied on *DRW Corporation,* [248 N.L.R.B. 828.] (1980) where a panel of the Board found that the respondent violated §8(a)(1) by discharging a supervisor as part of "a pattern of conduct aimed at coercing employees in the exercise of their §7 rights." After careful consideration, we conclude that the so-called "integral part" or "pattern of conduct" line of cases, as typified by *DRW Corporation,* supra, and cases cited therein, misreads the intent of Congress when it amended the Act to exclude specifically "any individual employed as a supervisor" from the definition of the term "employee." Accordingly, we have determined to overrule *DRW* and similar cases. Rather than simply overruling *DRW,* however, we deem it advisable to review the development of the law in this area because we wish to empha-

15. On remand, the state court's denial of summary judgment on the libel count should be given careful consideration before a cease-and-desist order is issued, unless petitioner is deemed to have waived this point by failing to bring the state court's ruling to the attention of the ALJ prior to his decision. . . . In the ordinary case, although the Board is not bound in a res judicata sense by such a state-court ruling, we see no reason why the state court's own judgment on the question whether the lawsuit presents triable factual issues should not be entitled to deference. In any event, such a state-court decision should not be disregarded without a cogent explanation for doing so.

Petitioner also argues that weight should be given to the fact that a federal District Court denied the Board's petition for temporary injunctive relief. See ibid. At least in the context of the present case, we disagree, because here the District Court denied relief not because it felt that petitioner's lawsuit raised triable issues, but because it was of the erroneous view that a state suit could never be enjoined unless it sought "an unlawful objective, as, for example, when a union sues to enforce an unlawful contract." App. to Brief for Petitioner C5.

It appears that only the libel count remains pending before the state court. If petitioner's other claims have been finally adjudicated to be lacking in merit, on remand the Board may reinstate its finding that petitioner acted unlawfully by prosecuting these unmeritorious claims if the Board adheres to its previous finding that the suit was filed for a retaliatory purpose.

size that in certain circumstances the discharge of a supervisor may violate §8(a)(1) of the Act.

As noted above, the 1947 amendments to the National Labor Relations Act narrowed the definition of the term "employee" by excluding from §2(3) "any individual employed as a supervisor." As recognized by the U.S. Supreme Court, the practical effect of the amendments was to free "employers to discharge supervisors without violating the Act's restraints against discharges on account of labor union membership." *Beasley* v. *Food Fair of North Carolina,* 416 U.S. 653, 654-655 (1974). Indeed, down through the years the Board has consistently held that a supervisor may be discharged for union activity.

Notwithstanding the general exclusion of supervisors from coverage under the Act, the discharge of a supervisor may violate §8(a)(1) in certain circumstances, none of which are present here. Thus, an employer may not discharge a supervisor for giving testimony adverse to an employer's interest either at an NLRB proceeding or during the processing of an employee's grievance under the collective-bargaining agreement. Similarly, an employer may not discharge a supervisor for refusing to commit unfair labor practices, or because the supervisor fails to prevent unionization. In all these situations, however, the protection afforded supervisors stems not from any statutory protection inuring to them, but rather from the need to vindicate employees' exercise of their §7 rights.

We are in full agreement that the discharge of a supervisor in the circumstances described above violates §8(a)(1) of the Act because such discharge interferes with the exercise of employees' §7 rights. However, the "integral part" or "pattern of conduct" line of cases unduly extends these circumstances. Examination of this line of cases discloses that they differ from the other categories of supervisory discharge cases in several respects. Supervisors in the "integral part" or "pattern of conduct" cases were, themselves, active for the union or participated in the concerted activity. Other than the fact that the supervisors were discharged contemporaneously with rank-and-file employees, it is difficult to distinguish these cases from those in which the Board has found that the discharge of a supervisor does not violate the Act. The "integral part" or "pattern of conduct" line of cases has produced inconsistent decisions which cannot be reconciled with the statute, so that all concerned—employers, unions, and, indeed, supervisors, themselves—have no clear guidelines as to when supervisors may be lawfully discharged.

The confusion in this area, in our judgment, stems from extension of the rationale of the seminal *Pioneer Drilling* case[11] to factual situations in which the only common denominator was a "pattern of pervasive unfair labor practices." In *Pioneer,* it was customary practice in the drilling industry for rank-and-file employees to depend on the continued employment of the drillers who had hired and supervised them. Thus, it was reasonable for the Board to find the discharge of the supervisors to be a mechanism to effectuate the employer's efforts to rid itself of union adherents in gen-

11. Pioneer Drilling Co., Inc., 162 N.L.R.B. 918 (1967), enfd. in pertinent part 391 F.2d 961, 962-963 (10th Cir. 1968).

eral, and to find it necessary to reinstate the driller, along with the employees, as an effective remedy. Examination of the cases after *Pioneer Drilling* . . . shows that the factual situation in *Pioneer Drilling* has been unduly extended to apply the Act's protection to supervisors who merely join with rank-and-file employee protected activity and who are then subjected to the same discharge or other disciplinary treatment unlawfully meted out to those employees. No matter how appealing from an equitable standpoint, the "integral part" or "pattern of conduct" line of cases disregards the fact that *employees,* but not *supervisors,* are protected against discharge for engaging in union or concerted activity. The results must be the same under the Act whether the supervisors engage in union or concerted activity by themselves or along with employees. . . .

[A]lthough we recognize that the discharge of a supervisor for engaging in union or concerted activity almost invariably has a secondary or incidental effect on employees, we believe that, when a supervisor is discharged either because he or she engaged in union or concerted activity or because the discharge is contemporaneous with the unlawful discharge of statutory employees, or both, this incidental or secondary effect on the employees is insufficient to warrant an exception to the general statutory provision excluding supervisors from the protection of the Act. Thus, it is irrelevant that an employer may have hoped, or even expected, that its decision to terminate a supervisor for his union or concerted activity would cause employees to reconsider, and perhaps abandon, their own concerted or union activity. No matter what the employer's subjective hope or expectation, that circumstance cannot change the character of its otherwise lawful conduct.[56]

NLRB v. TRANSPORTATION MANAGEMENT CORP., 103 S. Ct. 2469 (1983): When Santillo, a bus driver, began solicitating on behalf of a union, his supervisor took offense and, after making several antiunion remarks, discharged Santillo. The reasons given for the discharge were that Santillo had left his keys in his bus and had taken unauthorized breaks.

The Board held that the General Counsel had the burden of proving that the discharge was motivated, at least in part, by a desire to discourage union activities, and that the General Counsel had carried that burden. Applying its decision in Wright Line, 251 N.L.R.B. 1083 (1980), enforced, 662 F.2d 899 (1st Cir. 1981), cert. denied, 455 U.S. 989 (1982), the Board ruled that the employer had the burden of proving by a preponderance of the evidence that the worker would have been fired even if he had not been involved with the union. The First Circuit Court of Appeals refused to enforce. It held that the General Counsel should have had the burden of proving that Santillo would not have been fired had it not been for his union activities.

[56] Parker-Robb Chevrolet, 262 N.L.R.B. No. 58, 110 L.R.R.M. 1289 (1982).

The Supreme Court reversed. The Board's rule is reasonable because "[t]he employer is a wrongdoer; he has acted out of a motive that is declared illegitimate by the statute. It is fair that he bear the risk that the influence of legal and illegal motives cannot be separated, because he knowingly created the risk and because the risk was created not by innocent activity but by his own wrongdoing."

2. Offers and Inducements

NLRB v. EXCHANGE PARTS
375 U.S. 405 (1964)

[While a representation election was pending the employer announced the granting of certain economic benefits to employees. The purpose of the grant of benefits was to induce the employees to vote against the union, but the benefits were granted unconditionally and without implication that they would be withdrawn if the union won the election. The NLRB found the grant of benefits violative of §8(a)(1) but the circuit court denied enforcement.]

HARLAN, J. . . .

We think the Court of Appeals was mistaken in concluding that the conferral of employee benefits while a representation election is pending, for the purpose of inducing employees to vote against the union, does not "interfere with" the protected right to organize.

The broad purpose of §8(a)(1) is to establish "the right of employees to organize for mutual aid without employer interference." Republic Aviation Corp. v. NLRB, 324 U.S. 793, 798. We have no doubt that it prohibits not only intrusive threats and promises but also conduct immediately favorable to employees which is undertaken with the express purpose of impinging upon their freedom of choice for or against unionization and is reasonably calculated to have that effect. In Medo Photo Supply Corp. v. NLRB, 321 U.S. 678, 686, this Court said: "The action of employees with respect to the choice of their bargaining agents may be induced by favors bestowed by the employer as well as by his threats or domination." Although in that case there was already a designated bargaining agent and the offer of "favors" was in response to a suggestion of the employees that they would leave the union if favors were bestowed, the principles which dictated the result there are fully applicable here. The danger inherent in well-timed increases in benefits is the suggestion of a fist inside the velvet glove. Employees are not likely to miss the inference that the source of benefits now conferred is also the source from which future benefits must flow and which may dry up if it is not obliged. The danger may be diminished if, as in this case, the benefits are conferred permanently and unconditionally. But the absence of conditions or threats pertaining to the particular benefits conferred would be of controlling significance only if it could be presumed that no question of additional benefits or renegotiation of existing benefits would arise in the future; and, of course, no such presumption is tenable.

It is true, as the court below pointed out, that in most cases of this kind the increase in benefits could be regarded as "one part of an overall program of interference and restraint by the employer," 304 F.2d, at 372, and that in this case the questioned conduct stood in isolation. Other unlawful conduct may often be an indication of the motive behind a grant of benefits while an election is pending, and to that extent it is relevant to the legality of the grant; but when as here the motive is otherwise established, and employer is not free to violate §8(a)(1) by conferring benefits simply because it refrains from other, more obvious violations. We cannot agree with the Court of Appeals that enforcement of the Board's order will have the "ironic" result of "discouraging benefits for labor." 304 F.2d, at 376. The beneficence of an employer is likely to be ephemeral if prompted by a threat of unionization which is subsequently removed. Insulating the right of collective organization from calculated good will of this sort deprives employees of little that has lasting value.

Reversed.

Notes

1. A reduction in benefits to coerce employee votes violates §8(a)(1). There the remedy is a cease and desist order and a retroactive restoration of benefits. In *Exchange Parts,* the Board entered a cease and desist order but stated that it was not to be construed to require that the economic benefits be withdrawn. Thus in the latter case, the employer risks the posting of a notice that an unfair labor practice has been committed and that the union can obtain a rerun election without waiting a year and obtaining a new showing of interest.

Who do you understand is the beneficiary of the Court's ruling—the work force, the union? Do any of the three models of unionization suggest a normative basis for preventing managers from bribing employees not to vote for the union? Would the form of the bribe matter?

2. Unions often file simultaneous election objections and unfair labor practice charges against employers. Where the employer is found to have violated §8(a)(1) or §8(a)(3) the NLRB almost invariably finds the

conduct to warrant setting aside an election vote against the union.[57] Do you understand the Court in *Exchange Parts* to be holding that the employer's motive was an essential element in the §8(a)(1) violation? Should motive be critical if only election objections, and not unfair labor practice charges, were filed?

3. The NLRB has established rules for deciding which sorts of benefits and promises of benefits will overturn an election, and possibly also be §8(a)(1) violations. The only benefits that an employer can bestow before an election must be of a traditional sort, such as merit or percentage wage increases reflecting a start of a fiscal or calendar year, or reflecting an industry-wide wage increase. To the extent that the granting of wage increases is deemed discretionary, the employer must act very cautiously.

But the employer can also run into difficulty if he postpones benefits because of a pending election. Thus, in one case,[58] the employer's letter stated that the employees at his other stores were receiving salary increases, but that he was not permitted by law to grant increases at the store where the election was pending. The NLRB overturned the election vote against the union because the employer had not made it clear that the wage increases granted at other stores would be granted at this store regardless of the results of the election.

Clearly employer offers of benefits contingent on the union losing the election are bad, whether any actual effect on voters is shown or not, but a union's promise to obtain benefits if it wins is not unlawful. The NLRB reasons that the union stands in a different relation to the employees than does the employer.

4. Suppose during a union organizing campaign, the company president approachs a group of workers at the assembly line and says: "I didn't know you people were unhappy—come into my office and tell me your problems and we'll see what we can do."

Any violation of the Act?[59]

5. Suppose for Christmas the employer has always given his employees turkeys. Can he do so again if a union election is pending? Can he give hams this year? Should the NLRB be in the business of regulating this sort of conduct?[60]

[57] See p. 207 n.[46], supra.

[58] Great Atlantic & Pacific Tea Co., 101 N.L.R.B. 1118 (1952). Accord, NLRB v. Otis Hospital, 545 F.2d 252 (1st Cir. 1976); but see Newberry v. NLRB, 442 F.2d 897 (2d Cir. 1971); NLRB v. Big Three Industrial Gas & Equip. Co., 441 F.2d 774 (5th Cir. 1975).

[59] Board case law appears to distinguish between employer solicitation of employee complaints and such solicitations accompanied by an implied promise to remedy them. Only the latter is deemed unlawful. See Cherokee Culvert Co., 262 N.L.R.B. 917 (1982); Montgomery Ward & Co., 225 N.L.R.B. 112 (1976).

[60] The current Board does not think so. See Benchmark Indus., 270 N.L.R.B. No. 8 (1984) (holding it is permissible for an employer to discontinue Christmas hams without bargaining with the union because hams are merely "token items").

6. In NLRB v. Savair Mfg. Co., 414 U.S. 27 (1974), the Court held that the NLRB should have set a union election victory aside where the union had promised that if it won the election, it would waive its initiation fee for all employees signing cards before the election. The Court reasoned that the purchasing of authorization cards in this manner creates an artificial showing of employee support likely to mislead other employees, and that employees who signed might feel morally obligated to vote for the union. It also noted that employees who did not sign the authorization cards might fear the wrath of the union if the union prevailed. The Court indicated, however, that a pre-election offer by the union to waive initiation fees for everyone if the union won the election would not necessarily be objectionable.

3. Union Certification as a Remedy for Employer Misconduct

NLRB v. GISSEL PACKING CO.[61]
395 U.S. 575 (1969)

WARREN, C.J.

These cases involve the extent of an employer's duty under the National Labor Relations Act to recognize a union that bases its claim to representative status solely on the possession of union authorization cards, and the steps an employer may take, particularly with regard to the scope and content of statements he may make, in legitimately resisting card-based recognition. The specific questions facing us here are whether the duty to bargain can arise without a Board election under the Act; whether union authorization cards, if obtained from a majority of employees without misrepresentation or coercion, are reliable enough generally to provide a valid, alternate route to majority status; whether a bargaining order is an appropriate and authorized remedy where an employer rejects a card majority while at the same time committing unfair labor practices that tend to undermine the union's majority and make a fair election an unlikely possibility; and whether certain specific statements made by an employer to his employees constituted such an election-voiding unfair labor practice and thus fell outside the protection of the First Amendment and §8(c) of the Act.[62] For reasons given below, we answer each of these questions in the affirmative. . . .

[61] For a discussion urging a reconsideration of the use of authorization cards to establish an employer's duty to bargain, see Weiler, Promises to Keep: Securing Workers' Right to Self-Organization under the NLRA, 96 Harv. L. Rev. 1769 (1983).

[62] The part of the Court's opinion dealing with the employer speech issue was reproduced at p. 225, supra.

I

In each of the cases from the Fourth Circuit, the course of action followed by the Union and the employer and the Board's response were similar. In each case, the Union waged an organizational campaign, obtained authorization cards from a majority of employees in the appropriate bargaining unit, and then, on the basis of the cards, demanded recognition by the employer. All three employers refused to bargain on the ground that authorization cards were inherently unreliable indicators of employee desires; and they either embarked on, or continued, vigorous antiunion campaigns that gave rise to numerous unfair labor practice charges. In *Gissel,* where the employer's campaign began almost at the outset of the Union's organizational drive, the Union did not seek an election, but instead filed three unfair labor practice charges against the employer, for refusing to bargain in violation of §8(a)(5), for coercion and intimidation of employees in violation of §8(a)(1), and for discharge of Union adherents in violation of §8(a)(3). In *Heck's* an election sought by the Union was never held because of nearly identical unfair labor practice charges later filed by the Union as a result of the employer's antiunion campaign, initiated after the Union's recognition demand. And in *General Steel,* an election petitioned for by the Union and won by the employer was set aside by the Board because of the unfair labor practices committed by the employer in the pre-election period.

In each case, the Board's primary response was an order to bargain directed at the employers, despite the absence of an election in *Gissel* and *Heck's* and the employer's victory in *General Steel.* More specifically, the Board found in each case (1) that the Union had obtained valid authorization cards[4] from a majority of the employees in the bargaining unit and was thus entitled to represent the employees for collective bargaining purposes; and (2) that the employer's refusal to bargain with the Union in violation of §8(a)(5) was motivated, not by a "good faith" doubt of the Union's majority status, but by a desire to gain time to dissipate that status. The Board based its conclusion as to the lack of good faith doubt on the fact that the employers had committed substantial unfair labor practices during their antiunion campaign efforts to resist recognition. Thus, the Board found that all three employers had engaged in

4. The cards used . . . unambiguously authorized the Union to represent the signing employee for collective bargaining purposes; there was no reference to elections. Typical of the cards was the one used in the Charleston campaign in *Heck's,* and it stated in relevant part:

> Desiring to become a member of the above Union of the International Brotherhood of Teamsters, Chauffeurs, Warehousemen and Helpers of America, I hereby make application for admission to membership. I hereby authorize you, your agents or representatives to act for me as collective bargaining agent on all matters pertaining to rates of pay, hours, or any other conditions of employment.

restraint and coercion of employees in violation of §8(a)(1)—in *Gissel,* for coercively interrogating employees about Union activities, threatening them with discharge, and promising them benefits; in *Heck's,* for coercively interrogating employees, threatening reprisals, creating the appearance of surveillance, and offering benefits for opposing the Union; and in *General Steel,* for coercive interrogation and threats of reprisals, including discharge. In addition, the Board found that the employers in *Gissel* and *Heck's* had wrongfully discharged employees for engaging in Union activities in violation of §8(a)(3). And, because the employers had rejected the card-based bargaining demand in bad faith, the Board found that all three had refused to recognize the Unions in violation of §8(a)(5).

Only in *General Steel* was there any objection by an employer to the validity of the cards and the manner in which they had been solicited, and the doubt raised by the evidence was resolved in the following manner. The customary approach of the Board in dealing with allegations of misrepresentation by the Union and misunderstanding by the employees of the purpose for which the cards were being solicited has been set out in Cumberland Shoe Corp., 144 N.L.R.B. 1268 (1963) and reaffirmed in Levi Strauss & Co., 172 N.L.R.B. No. 57 (1968). Under the *Cumberland Shoe* doctrine, if the card itself is unambiguous (i.e., states on its face that the signer authorizes the Union to represent the employee for collective bargaining purposes and not to seek an election), it will be counted unless it is proved that the employee was told that the card was to be used *solely* for the purpose of obtaining an election. In *General Steel,* the trial examiner considered the allegations of misrepresentation at length and, applying the Board's customary analysis, rejected the claims with findings that were adopted by the Board. . . .

Consequently, the Board ordered the companies to cease and desist from their unfair labor practices, to offer reinstatement and back pay to the employees who had been discriminatorily discharged, to bargain with the Unions on request, and to post the appropriate notices.

On appeal, the Court of Appeals for the Fourth Circuit, in per curiam opinions in each of the three cases (398 F.2d 336, 337, 339), sustained the Board's findings as to the §§8(a)(1) and (3) violations, but rejected the Board's findings that the employers' refusal to bargain violated §8(a)(5) and declined to enforce those portions of the Board's orders directing the respondent companies to bargain in good faith. The court . . . held that the 1947 Taft-Hartley amendments to the Act, which permitted the Board to resolve representation disputes by certification under §9(c) only by secret ballot election, withdrew from the Board the authority to order an employer to bargain under §8(a)(5) on the basis of cards, in the absence of NLRB certification, unless the employer knows independently of the cards that there is in fact no representation dispute. The court held that the cards themselves were so inherently unreliable that their use gave an employer virtually an automatic, good faith claim that such a dispute existed, for which a secret election was necessary. Thus, these rulings established that a company could not be ordered to bargain unless (1) there was no question about a union's majority status (either because the employer agreed the cards were valid or had conducted his own poll so indicating), or (2) the employer's §§8(a)(1) and (3) unfair labor practices committed during the representation campaign were so extensive and pervasive that a bargaining order was the only available Board remedy irrespective of a card majority. . . .

II

In urging us to reverse the Fourth Circuit and to affirm the First Circuit, the National Labor Relations Board contends that we should approve its interpretation and administration of the duties and obligations imposed by the Act in authorization card cases. The Board argues (1) that unions have never been limited under §9(c) of either the Wagner Act or the 1947 amendments to certified elections as the sole route to attaining representative status. Unions may, the Board contends, impose a duty to bargain on the employer under §8(a)(5) by reliance on other evidence of majority employee support, such as authorization cards. Contrary to the Fourth Circuit's holding, the Board asserts, the 1947 amendments did not eliminate the alternative routes to majority status. The Board contends (2) that the cards themselves, when solicited in accordance with Board standards which adequately insure against union misrepresentation, are sufficiently reliable indicators of employee desires to support a bargaining order against an employer who refuses to recognize a card majority in violation of §8(a)(5). The Board argues (3) that a bargaining order is the appropriate remedy for the §8(a)(5) violation, where the employer commits other unfair labor practices that tend to undermine union support and render a fair election improbable.

Relying on these three assertions, the Board asks us to approve its current practice, which is briefly as follows. When confronted by a recognition demand based on possession of cards allegedly signed by a majority of his employees, an employer need not grant recognition immediately, but may, unless he has knowledge independently of the cards that the union has a majority, decline the union's request and insist on an election, either by requesting the union to file an election petition or by filing such a petition himself under §9(c)(1)(B). If, however, the employer commits independent and substantial unfair labor practices disruptive of election conditions, the Board may withhold the election or set it aside, and issue instead a bargaining order as a remedy for the various violations. A bargaining order will not issue, of course, if the union obtained the cards through misrepresentation or coercion or if the employer's unfair labor practices are unrelated generally to the representation campaign. Conversely, the employers in these cases urge us to adopt the views of the Fourth Circuit.

There is more at issue in these cases than the dispute outlined above between the Board and the four employers, however, for the Union argues that we should accord a far greater role to cards in the bargaining area than the Board itself seeks in this litigation. In order to understand the differences between the Union and the Board, it is necessary to trace the evolution of the Board's approach to authorization cards from its early practice to the position it takes on oral argument before this Court. Such an analysis requires viewing the Board's treatment of authorization cards in three separate phases: (1) under the *Joy Silk* doctrine, (2) under the rules of the *Aaron Brothers* case, and (3) under the approach announced at oral argument before this Court.

The traditional approach utilized by the Board for many years has been known as the *Joy Silk* doctrine. Joy Silk Mills, Inc., 85 N.L.R.B. 1263 (1949), enforced, 87 U.S. App. D.C. 360, 185 F.2d 732 (1950). Under that rule, an employer could lawfully refuse to bargain with a union claiming representative status through possession of authorization cards if he had a "good faith doubt" as to the union's majority status; instead of bargaining, he could insist that the union seek an election in order to test out his doubts. The Board, then, could find a lack of good faith doubt and enter a bargaining order in one of two ways. It could find (1) that the employer's independent unfair labor practices were evidence of bad faith, showing that the employer was seeking time to dissipate the union's majority. Or the Board could find (2) that the employer had come forward with no reasons for entertaining any doubt and therefore that he must have rejected the bargaining demand in bad faith. An example of the second category was Snow & Sons, 134 N.L.R.B. 709 (1961), enforced, 308 F.2d 687 (C.A. 9th Cir. 1962), where the employer reneged on his agreement to bargain after a third party checked the validity of the card signatures and insisted on an election because he doubted that the employees truly desired representation. The Board entered a bargaining order with very broad language to the effect that an employer could not refuse a bargaining demand and seek an election instead "without a valid ground therefor," 134 N.L.R.B., at 710-711.

The leading case codifying modifications to the *Joy Silk* doctrine was Aaron Brothers, 158 N.L.R.B. 1077 (1966). There the Board made it clear that it had shifted the burden to the General Counsel to show bad faith and that an employer "will not be held to have violated his bargaining obligation . . . simply because he refuses to rely upon cards, rather than an election, as the method for determining the union's majority." 158 N.L.R.B., at 1078. Two significant consequences were emphasized. The Board noted (1) that not every unfair labor practice would automatically result in a finding of bad faith and therefore a bargaining order;

the Board implied that it would find bad faith only if the unfair labor practice was serious enough to have the tendency to dissipate the union's majority. The Board noted (2) that an employer no longer needed to come forward with reasons for rejecting a bargaining demand. The Board pointed out, however, that a bargaining order would issue if it could prove that an employer's "course of conduct" gave indications as to the employer's bad faith. . . .

Although the Board's brief before this Court generally followed the approach as set out in *Aaron Brothers,* supra, the Board announced at oral argument that it had virtually abandoned the *Joy Silk* doctrine altogether. Under the Board's current practice, an employer's good faith doubt is largely irrelevant, and the key to the issuance of a bargaining order is the commission of serious unfair labor practices that interfere with the election processes and tend to preclude the holding of a fair election. Thus, an employer can insist that a union go to an election, regardless of his subjective motivation, so long as he is not guilty of misconduct; he need give no affirmative reasons for rejecting a recognition request, and he can demand an election with a simple "no comment" to the union. The Board pointed out, however, (1) that an employer could not refuse to bargain if he *knew,* through a personal poll for instance, that a majority of his employees supported the union, and (2) that an employer could not refuse recognition initially because of questions as to the appropriateness of the unit and then later claim, as an afterthought, that he doubted the union's strength.

The Union argues here that an employer's right to insist on an election in the absence of unfair labor practices should be more circumscribed, and a union's right to rely on cards correspondingly more expanded, then the Board would have us rule. The union's contention is that an employer, when confronted with a card-based bargaining demand, can insist on an election only by filing the election petition himself immediately under §9(c)(1)(B) and not by insisting that the Union file the election petition, whereby the election can be subjected to considerable delay. If the employer does not himself petition for an election, the Union argues, he must recognize the Union regardless of his good or bad faith and regardless of his other unfair labor practices, and should be ordered to bargain if the cards were in fact validly obtained. And if this Court should continue to utilize the good faith doubt rule, the Union contends that at the least we should put the burden on the employer to make an affirmative showing of his reasons for entertaining such doubt.

Because the employers' refusal to bargain in each of these cases was accompanied by independent unfair labor practices which tend to preclude the holding of a fair election, we need not decide whether a bargaining order is ever appropriate in cases where there is not interference with the election processes. . . .

III

A

The first issue facing us is whether a union can establish a bargaining obligation by means other than a Board election and whether the validity of alternate routes to majority status, such as cards, was affected by the 1947 Taft-Hartley amendments. The most commonly traveled route for a union to obtain recognition as the exclusive bargaining representative of an unorganized group of employees is through the Board's election and certification procedures under §9(c) of the Act; it is also, from the Board's point of view, the preferred route. A union is not limited to a Board election, however, for, in addition to §9, the present Act provides in §8(a)(5) as did the Wagner Act in §8(5), that "[i]t shall be an unfair labor practice for an employer . . . to refuse to bargain collectively with the representatives of his employees, subject to the provisions of section 9(a)." Since §9(a), in both the Wagner Act and the present Act, refers to the representative as the one "designated or selected" by a majority of the employees without specifying precisely how that representative is to be chosen, it was early recognized that an employer had a duty to bargain whenever the union representative presented "convincing evidence of majority support." Almost from the inception of the Act, then, it was recognized that a union did not have to be certified as the winner of a Board election to invoke a bargaining obligation; it could establish majority status by other means under the unfair labor practice provision of §8(a)(5)—by showing convincing support, for instance, by a union-called strike or strike vote, or, as here, by possession of cards signed by a majority of the employees authorizing the union to represent them for collective bargaining purposes.[11]

We have consistently accepted this interpretation of the Wagner Act and the present Act, particularly as to the use of authorization cards. See, e.g., United Mine Workers v. Arkansas Flooring Co., 351 U.S. 62 (1956). . . . [We] find unpersuasive the Fourth Circuit's view that the 1947 Taft-Hartley amendments, enacted some nine years before our decision in *United Mine Workers*, supra, require us to disregard that case. Indeed, the 1947 amendments weaken rather than strengthen the position taken by the employers here and the Fourth Circuit below. An early version of the bill in the House would have amended §8(5) of the Wagner Act to permit the Board to find a refusal-to-bargain violation only where an employer had failed to bargain with a union "currently recognized by the employer or certified as such [through an election]

11. The right of an employer lawfully to refuse to bargain if he had a good faith doubt as to the Union's majority status, even if in fact the Union did represent a majority, was recognized early in the administration of the Act. See NLRB v. Remington Rand, Inc., 94 F.2d 862, 868 (C.A. 2d Cir.), cert. denied, 304 U.S. 576 (1938).

under section 9." Section 8(a)(5) of H.R. 3020, 80th Cong., 1st Sess. (1947). The proposed change, which would have eliminated the use of cards, was rejected in Conference (H.R. Conf. Rep. No. 510, 80th Cong., 1st Sess., 41 (1947)), however, and we cannot make a similar change in the Act simply because, as the employers assert, Congress did not expressly approve the use of cards in rejecting the House amendment. Nor can we accept the Fourth Circuit's conclusion that the change was wrought when Congress amended §9(c) to make election the sole basis for *certification* by eliminating the phrase "any other suitable method to ascertain such representatives," under which the Board had occasionally used cards as a certification basis. A certified union has the benefit of numerous special privileges which are not accorded unions recognized voluntarily or under a bargaining order[14] and which, Congress could determine, should not be dispensed unless a union has survived the crucible of a secret ballot election.

The employers rely finally on the addition to §9(c) of subparagraph (B), which allows an employer to petition for an election whenever "one or more individuals or labor organizations have presented to him a claim[15] to be recognized as the representative defined in section 9(a)." That provision was not added, as the employers assert, to give them an absolute right to an election at any time; rather, it was intended, as the legislative history indicates, to allow them, after being asked to bargain, to test out their doubts as to a union's majority in a secret election which they would then presumably not cause to be set aside by illegal antiunion activity.[16] We agree with the Board's assertion here that there is no

14. E.g., protection against the filing of new election petitions by rival unions or employees seeking decertification for 12 months (§9(c)(3)), protection for a reasonable period, usually one year, against any disruption of the bargaining relationship because of claims that the union no longer represents a majority (see Brooks v. NLRB, 348 U.S. 96 (1954)), protection against recognitional picketing by rival unions (§8(b)(4)), and freedom from the restrictions placed in work assignments disputes by §8(b)(4)(D), and on recognitional and organizational picketing by §8(b)(7).

15. Under the Wagner Act, which did not prescribe who would file election petitions, the Board had ruled that an employer could seek an election only when two unions presented conflicting bargaining requests on the ground that if he were given the same election petition rights as the union, he could interrupt union drives by demanding an election before the union had obtained majority status. The 1947 amendments resolved the difficulty by providing that an employer could seek an election only after he had been requested to bargain.

16. The Senate report stated that the "present Board rules . . . discriminate against employers who have reasonable grounds for believing that labor organizations claiming to represent their employees are really not the choice of the majority." S. Rep. No. 105, 80th Cong., 1st Sess., 10 (1947). Senator Taft stated during the debates:

> Today an employer is faced with this situation. A man comes into his office and says, "I represent your employees. Sign this agreement, or we strike tomorrow." . . . The employer has no way in which to determine whether this man really does represent his employees or does not. The bill gives him the right to go to the Board . . . and say, "I want an election. I want to know who is the bargaining agent for my employees." 93 Cong. Rec. 3838 (1947).

suggestion that Congress intended §9(c)(1)(B) to relieve any employer of his §8(a)(5) bargaining obligation where, without good faith, he engaged in unfair labor practices disruptive of the Board's election machinery. And we agree that the policies reflected in §9(c)(1)(B) fully support the Board's present administration of the Act; for an employer can insist on a secret ballot election, unless, in the words of the Board, he engages "in contemporaneous unfair labor practices likely to destroy the union's majority and seriously impede the election." Brief for the Board, p. 36.

In short, we hold that the 1947 amendments did not restrict an employer's duty to bargain under §8(a)(5) solely to those unions whose representative status is certified after a Board election.

B

We next consider the question whether authorization cards are such inherently unreliable indicators of employee desires that, whatever the validity of other alternative routes to representative status, the cards themselves may never be used to determine a union's majority and to support an order to bargain. In this context, the employers urge us to take the step the 1947 amendments and their legislative history indicate Congress did not take, namely, to rule out completely the use of cards in the bargaining arena. Even if we do not unhesitatingly accept the Fourth Circuit's view in the matter, the employers argue, at the very least we should overrule the *Cumberland Shoe* doctrine and establish stricter controls over the solicitation of the cards by union representatives.[18]

The objections to the use of cards voiced by the employers and the Fourth Circuit boil down to two contentions: (1) that, as contrasted with the election procedure, the cards cannot accurately reflect an employee's wishes, either because an employer has not had a chance to present his views and thus a chance to insure that the employee choice was an informed one, or because the choice was the result of group pressures and not individual decision made in the privacy of a voting booth; and

18. In dealing with the reliability of cards, we should re-emphasize what issues we are not confronting. As pointed out above, we are not here faced with a situation where an employer, with "good" or "bad" subjective motivation, has rejected a card-based bargaining request without good reason and has insisted that the Union go to an election while at the same time refraining from committing unfair labor practices that would tend to disturb the "laboratory conditions" of that election. We thus need not decide whether, absent election interference by an employer's unfair labor practices, he may obtain an election only if he petitions for one himself; whether, if he does not, he must bargain with a card majority if the Union chooses not to seek an election; and whether, in the latter situation, he is bound by the Board's ultimate determination of the card results regardless of his earlier good faith doubts, or whether he can still insist on a Union-sought election if he makes an affirmative showing of his positive reasons for believing there is a representation dispute. In short, a union's right to rely on cards as a freely interchangeable substitute for elections where there has been no election interference is not put in issue here; we need only decide whether the cards are reliable enough to support a bargaining order where a fair election probably could not have been held, or where an election that was held was in fact set aside.

(2) that quite apart from the election comparison, the cards are too often obtained through misrepresentation and coercion which compound the cards' inherent inferiority to the election process. Neither contention is persuasive, and each proves too much. The Board itself has recognized, and continues to do so here, that secret elections are generally the most satisfactory — indeed the preferred — method of ascertaining whether a union has majority support. The acknowledged superiority of the election process, however, does not mean that cards are thereby rendered totally invalid, for where an employer engages in conduct disruptive of the election process, cards may be the most effective — perhaps the only — way of assuring employee choice. As for misrepresentation, in any specific case of alleged irregularity in the solicitation of the cards, the proper course is to apply the Board's customary standards (to be discussed more fully below) and rule that there was no majority if the standards were not satisfied. It does not follow that because there are some instances of irregularity, the cards can never be used; otherwise, an employer could put off his bargaining obligation indefinitely through continuing interference with elections.

That the cards, though admittedly inferior to the election process, can adequately reflect employee sentiment when that process has been impeded, needs no extended discussion, for the employers' contentions cannot withstand close examination. The employers argue that their employees cannot make an informed choice because the card drive will be over before the employer has had a chance to present his side of the unionization issues. Normally, however, the union will inform the employer of its organization drive early in order to subject the employer to the unfair labor practice provisions of the Act; the union must be able to show the employer's awareness of the drive in order to prove that his contemporaneous conduct constituted unfair labor practices on which a bargaining order can be based if the drive is ultimately successful. . . . Further, the employers argue that without a secret ballot an employee may, in a card drive, succumb to group pressures or sign simply to get the union "off his back" and then be unable to change his mind as he would be free to do once inside a voting booth. But the same pressures are likely to be equally present in an election, for election cases arise most often with small bargaining units where virtually every voter's sentiments can be carefully and individually canvassed. And no voter, of course, can change his mind after casting a ballot in an election even though he may think better of his choice shortly thereafter.

The employers' second complaint, that the cards are too often obtained through misrepresentation and coercion, must be rejected also in view of the Board's present rules for controlling card solicitation, which we view as adequate to the task where the cards involved state their purpose clearly and unambiguously on their face. We would be closing our eyes to obvious difficulties, of course, if we did not recognize that there have been abuses, primarily arising out of misrepresentations by union organizers as to whether the effect of signing a card was to designate the union to represent the employee for collective bargaining purposes or merely to authorize it to seek an election to determine that issue. And we would be equally blind if we did not recognize that various courts of appeals and commentators have differed significantly as to the effectiveness of the Board's *Cumberland Shoe* doctrine to cure such abuses. . . .

We need make no decision as to the conflicting approaches used with regard to dual-purpose cards, for in each of the five organization campaigns in the four cases before us the cards used were single-purpose cards, stating clearly and unambiguously on their face that the signer designated the union as his representative. . . .

In resolving the conflict among the circuits in favor of approving the Board's *Cumberland* rule, we think it sufficient to point out that employees should be bound by the clear language of what they sign unless that language is deliberately and clearly canceled by a union adherent with words calculated to direct the signer to disregard and forget the language above his signature. There is nothing inconsistent in handing an employee a card that says the signer authorizes the union to represent him and then telling him that the card will probably be used first to get an election. Elections have been, after all, and will continue to be, held in the vast majority of cases; the union will still have to have the signatures of 30% of the employees when an employer rejects a bargaining demand and insists that the union seek an election. We cannot agree with the employers here that employees as a rule are too unsophisticated to be bound by what they sign unless expressly told that their act of signing represents something else. . . .

We agree, however, with the Board's own warnings in Levi Strauss & Co., 172 N.L.R.B. No. 57, 68 L.R.R.M. 1338, 1341, and n. 7 (1968), that in hearing testimony concerning a card challenge, trial examiners should not neglect their obligation to ensure employee free choice by a too easy mechanical application of the *Cumberland* rule.[27] We also accept

27. In explaining and reaffirming the *Cumberland Shoe* doctrine in the context of unambiguous cards, the Board stated:

> Thus the fact that employees are told in the course of solicitation that an election is contemplated, or that a purpose of the card is to make an election possible, provides in our view insufficient basis in itself for vitiating unambiguously worded authorization cards on the theory of misrepresentation. A different situation is presented, of course, where union organizers solicit cards on the explicit or indirectly expressed representation that they will use such cards only for an election and subsequently seek to use them for a different purpose. . . .

The Board stated further in a footnote:

> The foregoing does not of course imply that a finding of misrepresentation is confined to situations where employees are expressly told in haec verba that the 'sole' or 'only' purpose of the cards is to obtain an election. The Board has never

the observation that employees are more likely than not, many months after a card drive and in response to questions by company counsel, to give testimony damaging to the union, particularly where company officials have previously threatened reprisals for union activity in violation of §8(a)(1). We therefore reject any rule that requires a probe of an employee's subjective motivations as involving an endless and unreliable inquiry. We reiterate that nothing we say here indicates our approval of the *Cumberland Shoe* rule when applied to ambiguous, dual-purpose cards.

The employers argue as a final reason for rejecting the use of the cards that they are faced with a Hobson's choice under current Board rules and will almost inevitably come out the loser. They contend that if they do not make an immediate, personal investigation into possible solicitation irregularities to determine whether in fact the union represents an uncoerced majority, they will have unlawfully refused to bargain for failure to have a good faith doubt of the union's majority; and if they do make such an investigation, their efforts at polling and interrogation will constitute an unfair labor practice in violation of §8(a)(1) and they will again be ordered to bargain. As we have pointed out, however, an employer is not obligated to accept a card check as proof of majority status, under the Board's current practice, and he is not required to justify his insistence on an election by making his own investigation of employee sentiment and showing affirmative reasons for doubting the majority status. See Aaron Brothers, 158 N.L.R.B. 1077, 1078. If he does make an investigation, the Board's recent cases indicate that reasonable polling in this regard will not always be termed violative of §8(a)(1) if conducted in accordance with the requirements set out in Struksnes Construction Co., 165 N.L.R.B. No. 102 (1967). And even if an employer's limited interrogation is found violative of the Act, it might not be serious enough to call for a bargaining order. As noted above, the Board has emphasized that not "any employer conduct found violative of Section 8(a)(1) of the Act, regardless of its nature or gravity, will necessarily support a refusal-to-bargain finding," *Aaron Brothers,* supra, at 1079.

C

Remaining before us is the propriety of a bargaining order as a remedy for a §8(a)(5) refusal to bargain where an employer has committed

---

suggested such a mechanistic application of the foregoing principles, as some have contended. The Board looks to substance rather than to form. It is not the use or nonuse of certain key or 'magic' words that is controlling, but whether or not the totality of circumstances surrounding the card solicitation is such, as to add up to an assurance to the card signer that his card will be used for no purpose other than to help get an election. 172 N.L.R.B. No. 57, 68 L.R.R.M. 1338, 1341-1342, and n. 7.

independent unfair labor practices which have made the holding of a fair election unlikely or which have in fact undermined a union's majority and caused an election to be set aside. We have long held that the Board is not limited to a cease-and-desist order in such cases, but has the authority to issue a bargaining order without first requiring the union to show that it has been able to maintain its majority status. And we have held that the Board has the same authority even where it is clear that the union, which once had possession of cards from a majority of the employees, represents only a minority when the bargaining order is entered. We see no reason now to withdraw this authority from the Board. If the Board could enter only a cease-and-desist order and direct an election or a rerun, it would in effect be rewarding the employer and allowing him "to profit from [his] own wrongful refusal to bargain," Franks Bros. [v. NLRB, 321 U.S. 702, 704 (1944)], while at the same time severely curtailing the employees' right freely to determine whether they desire a representative. The employer could continue to delay or disrupt the election processes and put off indefinitely his obligation to bargain;[30] and any election held under these circumstances would not be likely to demonstrate the employees' true, undistorted desires.[31]

The employers argue that the Board has ample remedies, over and above the cease-and-desist order, to control employer misconduct. The Board can, they assert, direct the companies to mail notices to employees, to read notices to employees during plant time and to give the union access to employees during working time at the plant, or it can seek a court injunctive order under §10(j) as a last resort. In view of the Board's power, they conclude, the bargaining order is an unnecessarily harsh remedy that needlessly prejudices employees' §7 rights solely for the

30. The Board indicates here that its records show that in the period between January and June 1968, the median time between the filing of an unfair labor practice charge and a Board decision in a contested case was 388 days. But the employer can do more than just put off his bargaining obligation by seeking to slow down the Board's administrative processes. He can also affect the outcome of a rerun election by delaying tactics, for figures show that the longer the time between a tainted election and a rerun, the less are the union's chances of reversing the outcome of the first election. See n. 31, infra.

31. A study of 20,153 elections held between 1960 and 1962 shows that in the 267 cases where rerun elections were held over 30% were won by the party who caused the election to be set aside. See Pollitt, NLRB Re-Run Elections: A Study, 41 N.C.L. Rev. 209, 212 (1963). The study shows further that certain unfair labor practices are more effective to destroy election conditions for a longer period of time than others. For instance, in cases involving threats to close or transfer plant operations, the union won the rerun only 29% of the time, while threats to eliminate benefits or refuse to deal with the union if elected seemed less irremediable with the union winning the rerun 75% of the time. Id., at 215-216. Finally, time appears to be a factor. The figures suggest that if a rerun is held too soon after the election before the effects of the unfair labor practices have worn off, or too long after the election when interest in the union may have waned, the chances for a changed result occurring are not as good as they are if the rerun is held sometime in between those periods. Thus, the study showed that if the rerun is held within 30 days of the election or over nine months after, the chances that a different result will occur are only one in five; when the rerun is held within 30-60 days after the election, the chances for a changed result are two in five. Id., at 221.

purpose of punishing or restraining an employer. Such an argument ignores that a bargaining order is designed as much to remedy past election damage[32] as it is to deter future misconduct. If an employer has succeeded in undermining a union's strength and destroying the laboratory conditions necessary for a fair election, he may see no need to violate a cease-and-desist order by further unlawful activity. The damage will have been done, and perhaps the only fair way to effectuate employee rights is to re-establish the conditions as they existed before the employer's unlawful campaign. There is, after all, nothing permanent in a bargaining order, and if, after the effects of the employer's acts have worn off, the employees clearly desire to disavow the union, they can do so by filing a representation petition. . . .

Before considering whether the bargaining orders were appropriately entered in these cases, we should summarize the factors that go into such a determination. While refusing to validate the general use of a bargaining order in reliance on cards, the Fourth Circuit nevertheless left open the possibility of imposing a bargaining order, without need of inquiry into majority status on the basis of cards or otherwise, in "exceptional" cases marked by "outrageous" and "pervasive" unfair labor practices. Such an order would be an appropriate remedy for those practices, the court noted, if they are of "such a nature that their coercive effects cannot be eliminated by the application of traditional remedies, with the result that a fair and reliable election cannot be had." NLRB v. Logan Packing Co., 386 F.2d 562, 570 (C. A. 4th Cir. 1967); see also NLRB v. Heck's, Inc., 398 F.2d 337, 338. The Board itself, we should add, has long had a similar policy of issuing a bargaining order, in the absence of a §8(a)(5) violation or even a bargaining demand, when that was the only available, effective remedy for substantial unfair labor practices.

The only effect of our holding here is to approve the Board's use of the bargaining order in less extraordinary cases marked by less pervasive practices which nonetheless still have the tendency to undermine majority strength and impede the election processes. The Board's authority to issue such an order on a lesser showing of employer misconduct is appropriate, we should reemphasize, where there is also a showing that at one point the union had a majority; in such a case, of course, effectuating ascertainable employee free choice becomes as important a goal as deterring employer misbehavior. In fashioning a remedy in the exercise

32. The employers argue that the Fourth Circuit correctly observed that, "in the great majority of cases, a cease and desist order with the posting of appropriate notices will eliminate any undue influences upon employees voting in the security of anonymity." NLRB v. Logan Packing Co., 386 F.2d, at 570. It is for the Board and not the courts, however, to make that determination, based on its expert estimate as to the effects on the election process of unfair labor practices of varying intensity. In fashioning its remedies under the broad provisions of §10(c) of the Act, the Board draws on a fund of knowledge and expertise of its own, and its choice of remedy must therefore be given special respect by reviewing courts. . . .

of its discretion, then, the Board can properly take into consideration the extensiveness of an employer's unfair practice in terms of their past effect on election conditions and the likelihood of their recurrence in the future. If the Board finds that the possibility of erasing the effects of past practices and of ensuring a fair election (or a fair rerun) by the use of traditional remedies, though present, is slight and that employee sentiment once expressed through cards would, on balance, be better protected by a bargaining order, then such an order should issue (see n. 32, supra).

We emphasize that under the Board's remedial power there is still a third category of minor or less extensive unfair labor practices, which, because of their minimal impact on the election machinery, will not sustain a bargaining order. There is, the Board says, no per se rule that the commission of any unfair practice will automatically result in a §8(a)(5) violation and the issuance of an order to bargain. See *Aaron Brothers,* supra.

With these considerations in mind, we turn to an examination of the orders in these cases. In *Sinclair,* the Board made a finding, left undisturbed by the First Circuit, that the employer's threats of reprisal were so coercive that, even in the absence of a §8(a)(5) violation, a bargaining order would have been necessary to repair the unlawful effect of those threats.[34] The Board therefore did not have to make the determination called for in the intermediate situation above that the risks that a fair rerun election might not be possible were too great to disregard the desires of the employees already expressed through the cards. The employer argues, however, that its communications to its employees were protected by the First Amendment and §8(c) of the Act (29 U.S.C. §158(c)), whatever the effect of those communications on the union's majority or the Board's ability to ensure a fair election; it is to that contention that we shall direct our final attention in the next section.

In the three cases from the Fourth Circuit, on the other hand, the Board did not make a similar finding that a bargaining order would have been necessary in the absence of an unlawful refusal to bargain. Nor did it make a finding that, even though traditional remedies might be able to ensure a fair election, there was insufficient indication that an election (or a rerun in *General Steel*) would definitely be a more reliable test of the employees' desires than the card count taken before the unfair labor practices occurred. The employees argue that such findings would not be warranted, and the court below ruled in *General Steel* that available remedies short of a bargaining order could guarantee a fair election. 398 F.2d 339, 340, n. 3. We think it possible that the requisite findings

34. Under the doctrine of Bernel Foam Prod. Co., 146 N.L.R.B. 1277 (1964), there is nothing inconsistent in the Union's filing an election petition and thereby agreeing that a question of representation exists, and then filing a refusal-to-bargain charge after the election is lost because of the employer's unfair labor practices.

were implicit in the Board's decisions below to issue bargaining orders (and to set aside the election in *General Steel*); and we think it clearly inappropriate for the court below to make any contrary finding on its own (see n. 32, supra). Because the Board's current practice at the time required it to phrase its findings in terms of an employer's good or bad faith doubts, however, the precise analysis the Board now puts forth was not employed below, and we therefore remand these cases for proper findings. . . .

Notes

1. Should the Court have been so sanguine at the Board changing its rationale between the filing of the brief and oral argument (p. 258, supra)? One interpretation is that the Board's practice was so poorly articulated that its brief writers could not discern it; another is that the Board decided late in the game that its current position was not wholly defensible.

2. In Linden Lumber Div. v. NLRB, 419 U.S. 817 (1974), the Court decided the question reserved in footnote 18 of *Gissel.* A 5-4 majority held that the Board does not abuse its discretion by refusing to issue a bargaining order against an employer who, without committing unfair labor practices that impair the election process, refuses to recognize the union on the basis of cards and/or recognitional picketing, and also refuses to file an election petition. Not only are authorization cards often deemed suspect, in the Court's view, but not even a majority of employees on the picket line necessarily establishes the union's representative majority. "Fear may indeed prevent some [employees] from crossing a picket line; or sympathy for strikers, not the desire to have the particular union in the saddle, may influence others." The Court therefore approved the Board's abandonment of a good faith test for employer refusals to bargain in this context.

The Court also rejected the contention that the failure of the employer to file a representation petition demonstrates the lack of a good faith doubt of the union's majority status. The Court hypothesized a controversy between an employer and a union over the appropriateness of proposed bargaining units. The employer should have the right to challenge the union's requested unit; but if the employer files a petition for the bargaining unit he or she deems appropriate, the petition will be dismissed unless it coincides with the unit sought by the union. Forcing the employer to file is thus no guarantee against delay. The Court ruled that where a union is refused recognition, the union has the burden of taking the next step and filing an election petition unless the employer is engaged in unfair labor practices warranting a *Gissel* remedy.

3. At what point in time should it be determined whether the em-

ployer's misconduct is of a sort that a fair and reliable election cannot be had? Possibilities are the time of the misconduct, the time the Board enters the remedial order for the unfair labor practices, or even at the time that a court of appeals is called on to enforce the Board's order. In one case where the Board had not adequately set out its reasons for imposing a *Gissel* bargaining order, the court of appeals held that such an order could be justified only on the basis of facts existing at the time the case was remanded to the Board. NLRB v. Armcor Indus., 588 F.2d 821 (3d Cir. 1978). See Note, 'After All, Tomorrow is Another Day': Should Subsequent Events Affect the Validity of Bargaining Orders? 31 Stan. L. Rev. 506 (1979).

4. Is a bargaining order in a *Gissel*-type case justified because it is the only effective remedy for certain §§8(a)(1) and 8(a)(3) violations, or because the employer has been found to violate §8(a)(5) by coupling his or her refusal to bargain with antiunion misconduct? This might make a practical difference if after the election the employer reduces wages (or other economic benefits) for purely economic reasons but without bargaining with the union. As we shall study later, a unilateral change in economic benefits without bargaining with a lawfully designated union violates §8(a)(5). The union is likely to demand a backpay remedy for the economic reductions. In Steel-Fab, 212 N.L.R.B. 363 (1974), the Board, by a 3-2 majority, found a §8(a)(1) violation after employer election misconduct but expressly refused to find a §8(a)(5) violation. Thus, unilateral changes made before the §8(a)(1) bargaining order violated the Act only if motivated by antiunion animus. This refusal to make *Gissel* bargaining orders retroactive was reversed in Trading Port, 219 N.L.R.B. 298 (1975), where the Board grounded its order on §8(a)(5).

5. The Board has split along political lines on the question of whether it can and should issue a bargaining order on account of employer electioneering unfair labor practices, in the absence of a union showing that at one time it had majority employee support. In United Dairy Farmers Coop. Assn., 242 N.L.R.B. 1026 (1979), one Board member argued that the Board lacks authority to issue such a bargaining order. Two other members concluded that the Board may have such authority, but they declined to exercise this discretionary power. In their view, it is less destructive of the purposes of the Act to order a second election than to risk imposing a bargaining order when the employees do not support the union. Two dissenting members concluded that the Board does have the authority and would have issued the order in this case.

Then in Conair Corp., 261 N.L.R.B. 1189 (1982), the Board issued a bargaining order even though the union could not show it had ever attained majority status.

In the most recent installment, the Board has held it lacks the authority. See Gourmet Foods, 270 N.L.R.B. No. 113 (1984).

6. How should the Board go about deciding whether conduct is "out-

rageous" and "pervasive," or "less pervasive" but still with a "tendency to undermine majority strength and impede the election processes"? What evidence should it seek to determine if a fair election is possible notwithstanding employer misconduct? Several courts of appeals have demanded that the Board give specific reasons why a fair rerun election is impossible.[63]

In this connection, consider the following.

GETMAN AND GOLDBERG, THE MYTH OF LABOR BOARD EXPERTISE

39 U. Chi. L. Rev. 681-684 (1974)

One of the central assumptions underlying the administration of the National Labor Relations Act is that the National Labor Relations Board has special expertise to determine the impact of employer conduct on the exercise of employee rights guaranteed by the Act. The Board is presumed able to determine, for example, whether discriminatory employer conduct is "inherently destructive" of the right to strike or has only a "comparatively slight" effect on that right. Similarly, the Supreme Court has assumed that the Board can take into account "imponderable subtleties" in weighing the effect of employer speech on employee exercise of the right of self-organization and that the Board knows whether an employer ban on union solicitation on company premises will prevent effective organization. Most recently, in NLRB v. Gissel Packing Co., the Court affirmed the Board's ability, on the basis of its "expert estimate as to the effects on the election process of unfair labor practices of varying intensity," to order an employer to bargain with a union that has not been chosen by a majority of his employees.

The assumption that the Board has the ability to assess the actual impact of employer — or union — conduct is a fiction. Although it has been administering the National Labor Relations Act for over thirty-five years, the Board has never engaged in an effort to determine empirically whether a particular type of conduct has a coercive impact. The Board has not required, or even permitted, the introduction of evidence as to whether particular conduct had a harmful impact on employees. As the Board has stated: "In evaluating the interference resulting from specific conduct, the Board does not attempt to assess its actual effect on employees, but rather concerns itself with whether it is reasonable to conclude that the conduct tended to prevent the free formation and expression of the employees' choice." Thus, the elaborate structure of Board rules concerning the circumstances under which it will find a tendency to coerce employee choice is not grounded in any respect on factual data. It

[63] See, e.g., NLRB v. Pilgrim Foods, 591 F.2d 110 (1st Cir. 1978).

rests, rather, on guesses or assumptions. There is, moreover, nothing in the collective activities or experience of the Board that insures the accuracy of the assumptions upon which these rules are based. As pointed out in a recent article:

> The Board's staff consists mostly of lawyers and a few researchers who are primarily concerned with the statistics of the Board's own operations and with legal case analysis. . . .
>
> What the Board lacks notably is (1) specific information about labor-management practices and employee attitudes and reactions that may be pertinent to its work, and (2) any systematic means of monitoring the impact of Board and Court NLRB doctrine upon industrial practice. . . . Thus, the Board's decision-making fails to provide a bridge between Board members, and the real world of labor relations.[8]

One wonders why the courts have accepted the myth that the Board possesses expertise to determine the impact of employer or union conduct on employee free choice. Court opinions, which abound with references to the Board's expertise, rarely discuss the question of how the Board acquired its special competence. In part, the courts appear simply to have assumed that because the Board constantly rationalizes its rules in terms of the policies, language, and legislative history of the NLRA, it has thereby acquired an understanding of the practical implications of its decisions. But the process of elaborating and harmonizing rules of decision cannot lead to the development of expertise as long as the assumptions upon which the rules rest remain untested.

The courts' uncritical acceptance of the myth of the Board's expertise may also be due in part to its usefulness in allocating institutional responsibility. The myth helps to justify a fairly limited scope of review. Since the courts possess no greater knowledge of the impact of employer and union conduct on employees than does the Board, it is sensible of the courts to permit the Board to make and apply the basic rules with little interference. The Board is in a better position to establish a coherent pattern of regulation, serving the significant interest of treating like cases alike. From this point of view, the Board's practice of finding unfair labor practices on the basis of specific rules deduced from assumptions about impact on employees has much to commend it. It has helped to direct the attention of the Board and the reviewing courts to the question whether the decision in a particular case is consistent with the general holding of similar cases — and away from the question whether employee free choice was interfered with, a question that neither the Board nor the courts are capable of answering.

8. Bernstein, The N.L.R.B's Adjudication-Rule Making Dilemma under the Administrative Procedure Act, 79 Yale L.J. 571, 577-578 (1970).

4. Avoidance by Domination or Assistance

NOTE, NEW STANDARDS FOR DOMINATION AND SUPPORT UNDER §8(a)(2)

82 Yale L.J. 510, 511-516 (1973)

Section 8(a)(2) of the National Labor Relations Act, which makes it unlawful[2] for an employer to interfere with, dominate, or support any labor organization,[4] has been vigorously enforced to maintain a strict dichotomy between labor and management. . . .

I. Traditional Standards under §8(a)(2)

A. THE PER SE RULE

Although never made explicit, the traditional standard in §8(a)(2) cases is essentially a per se rule. Any employer support of a labor organization is illegal beyond a certain critical level, regardless of the character of the challenged organization, the intent of the employer, or the will of the employees.[11] Under this per se rule, virtually the only question ever

2. A cease and desist order is used in case of a relatively minor violation, and requires an end to employer interference with the labor organization. In more serious cases of support under §8(a)(2), the order may require temporary suspension of recognition as the collective bargaining agent, if such recognition has been given. In cases of complete domination, the employer is required to disestablish the organization, and is forever barred from recognizing it as the collective bargaining representative. The Board has broad discretion concerning the nature of its remedies. NLRA §10(a), (c).

4. The NLRA defines a labor organization as follows: "The term 'labor organization' means any organization of any kind, or any agency or employee representation committee or plan, in which employees participate and which exists for the purpose, in whole or in part, of dealing with employers concerning grievances, labor disputes, wages, rates of pay, hours of employment, or conditions of work." NLRA §2(5).

This definition was intentionally made broad enough to include not only normal unions, but also employees' committees and employers' representation plans. However, purely social organizations are exempt. Hudson Dispatch, 68 N.L.R.B. 115, 124 (1946). Employer contentions that a challenged organization does not fall within the statutory definition, and for that reason does not constitute a violation, have nearly always failed. Subsequent amendments of the Act have not altered this definitional breadth. Therefore, for the purposes of §8(a)(2), a labor organization need not meet the internal requirements of the Labor Management Reporting and Disclosure Act of 1939 (Landrum-Griffin Act), or even have a formal structure at all. Nonetheless, attempting to defend §8(a)(2) complaints on the ground that the challenged organization does not constitute a labor organization has been one of the most enduring (and bootless) employer approaches to this section.

11. The fact that employees express a desire to be represented by a labor organization has been said not to be determinative of, or even relevant to, the question of whether that organization has in fact been dominated and assisted by the employer. NLRB v. Newport News Shipbldg. & Dry Dock Co., 308 U.S. 241 (1939); NLRB v. Brown Paper Mill Co., 108 F.2d 867 (5th Cir. 1940), cert. denied, 310 U.S. 651 (1940).

litigated is whether the challenged actions are sufficient to constitute the illegal quantum of support.

In practice, this rigid rule has meant that an employer may be found in violation if he assists in or defrays the costs of elections for a labor organization; helps in or is present at the drawing of its charter; arranges for its attorney; supplies a place or refreshments for its meeting; furnishes any direct financial support, no matter how meager; provides indirect financial aid, as, for example, from vending machines or the plant store; allows the organization to use his safe, mimeograph machine, or telephone; or provides secretarial services. In short, an employer must leave a union or other labor organization scrupulously alone, or the Board, usually upon the complaint of an outside union or a dissident employee, will force him to do so.[25]

Once sufficient employer assistance is shown, no defense is available. Thus, in NLRB v. Newport News Shipbuilding & Drydock Co.,[26] the Supreme Court affirmed the disestablishment of an employer-assisted labor organization under §8(a)(2), in explicit disregard of "uncontradicted" findings that the company had "good motives" in assisting the organization, that the organization operated "to the apparent satisfaction of employees," that the company practiced no discrimination or coercion of any kind, that the employees were free to join other labor organizations, and that the organization had solved labor disputes and promoted industrial tranquillity.

While §8(a)(2) actions frequently arise because of the indiscretions of otherwise independent local unions, the clearest case of the per se rule in action is the Board's unforgiving hostility to in-plant, employer-sponsored, non-union "employees' committees."[29] Whether termed "shop committees," "grievance councils," or "employees' representation plans," virtually all such organizations are illegal under the traditional doc-

25. It is an over-simplification to assert that the examples enumerated in the text outline the parameters of §8(a)(2). In fact, the parameters are unknown, because the Board declines to make clear the precise type or amount of assistance needed to trigger a violation. Rather, the Board maintains that it does not view individual actions, but instead considers the "totality" of a situation. 2 NLRB Ann. Rep. 95 (1937). It is therefore extremely difficult to find the precise basis for the Board's holding in any case or to extract from the Board's description of the "totality" those separate actions which of themselves, will or will not support a §8(a)(2) violation. For this reason, the Board's totality approach has been criticized as "indiscriminate lumping." The Board's decisions can in fact be quite unpredictable. Thus, no single instance of assistance such as enumerated is technically a violation; rather, it is evidence of a violation. The Board's long record with §8(a)(2) cases, however, indicates a low level of tolerance for such assistance.

26. 308 U.S. 241, 251 (1939).

29. Generally, an employees' committee is an independent labor organization, unaffiliated with a national union and considerably less formal than even an independent local. Typically, it has a vague structure and purpose, frequently has no dues, by-laws, or constitution, and deals with management on such varied topics as terms and conditions of employment, grievances, safety, recreation, or any other matter. Its distinguishing feature is that the degree of management participation is considerably greater than in more formal unions.

trine.[30] Thus, violations have been found not only where the employer actually formed the committee, but also where he caused it to be formed or where the organization never developed the characteristics of an independent entity, such as a constitution, by-laws, dues, meetings, or collective aggreements. It has been held a violation of §8(a)(2) to suggest the formation of an employees' committee, to be its sustaining force, or to deal with one on an interim basis. In general, the enduring and singleminded goal of the Board and the courts has been to force the employer to "refrain from any action which will place him on both sides of the bargaining table."

B. THE ADVERSARY MODEL OF LABOR RELATIONS

During the 1930's there was undoubtedly a need for such an uncompromising rule. In 1935, the year in which the NLRA was enacted, employer-dominated labor organizations such as the "Employee Representation Plans" fostered by the defunct National Industrial Recovery Act accounted for over 2,500,000 workers. These organizations were, for the most part, patent creatures of management, mere charades of representation which hampered outside organizing, and organized labor fought bitterly to have such "company unions" outlawed forever. The argument that "collective bargaining becomes a mockery when the spokesman of the employees is the marionette of the employer" was persuasive to the Congress, and the Board was consequently given broad power under §8(a)(2) to combat employer interference. So armed, the Board and the courts began a vigorous enforcement effort, and the strict per se approach developed quickly.

Only in light of labor's struggle against the early company unions is the per se rule intelligible. Standing alone, it is not entirely logical; outright employer assistance by itself need be neither detrimental nor improper. In fact, when a labor organization is gratuitously given an office or a typist, that would appear to be a benefit. The per se prohibition on such assistance is understandable only when coupled with the presumption that employer assistance to labor organizations is necessarily subversive to the interests of the employees.

Since many would agree — the unions most vigorously — that the NLRA represented the triumph of one ideology over another, it is not surprising that there is an entire series of such presumptions implicit in the Act. Some of these presumptions, which together may be called the

30. At first, the NLRB's hostility to this type of organization was institutionalized. It differentiated between unaffiliated independent locals affiliated with national unions by completely disestablishing the former and just temporarily withholding recognition from the latter, in cases of employer assistance. In response to protests that independents could be just as effective as affiliated unions, and ought to be treated equally, Congress included in the Taft-Hartley Act a specific directive that independents were to be treated equally. 29 U.S.C. §160(c) (1970). The Board has followed this directive.

"adversary model" of labor relations, include: There exists an inherent conflict of interest between employers and employees; this conflict leads to hostility; employers wish to subvert the interests of their employees; no informed employee would align himself with his employer; any organization of employees in which management plays a part is thus necessarily a fraud and contrary to the employees' best interests.

II. The Need for New Standards

A. THE DECLINE OF THE COMPANY UNION

Today, however, the more blatant forms of company unionism have largely disappeared.[44] While employer attempts to manipulate through assistance continue to pose some problems, the concept of independently organized labor has achieved general acceptance. Cases involving §8(a)(2) are increasingly less common,[46] and ideological discussion of the subject has virtually ceased. As early as 1953, a former Board chairman declared the company union problem to be "almost dead." The issue, in short, has given way to more pressing controversies.

Simultaneously, other developments have rendered the existence of company unions less threatening. Section 8(a)(2) was not only a protective device for individual workers, but also a means for promoting the growth of organized labor. Yet as organized labor has achieved maturity, public policy efforts have turned from nurturing unions to limiting and regulating them. The early threat, actual or perceived, of management's co-optation of the labor movement is no longer a problem.

On this ground alone, it can be argued that it is now inappropriate to follow the stringent per se rule. If the justification for outlawing even non-detrimental assistance lay in the overall threat of massive company co-optation, then, to the extent that company unionism no longer poses such a threat, the law should fashion more subtle standards to differentiate truly detrimental cases of employer assistance from non-detrimental ones. The per se rule, a meat cleaver once appropriate for hacking through the mass of company unions, needs to be replaced with a scalpel for excising occasional malignancies.

44. Most contemporary §8(a(2) complaints have nothing to do with classic "company unionism." Rather, they are essentially disputes between regular unions over which shall be the certified collective bargaining agent. Thus, current cases typically involve situations in which an employer recognizes a minority union or helps one union gain favor over another with his employees, or continues to check off dues after a union security agreement has expired.

46. In 1938, §8(a)(2) charges constituted 19.5% of all unfair labor practice complaints. Between 1941 and 1949, they constituted 9.8%, and between 1961 and 1969, 6.3%. By 1970, the figure has dropped to 4.5%. 1-35 NLRB Ann. Rep. (1936-70) (percentages derived from yearly statistics).

Note

Problem. The employer, Sparks Nugget, established an "employees' council" for use by employees unable to resolve disputes with their supervisors. Under company rules, each employee department votes annually for an employee representative on the council. When it meets to resolve grievances, the council is composed of the employer's director of employee relations, who sits as chairman, an employee member elected from the grievant's department, and a third member selected by the first two from the management of a department other than that of the grievant. The council receives testimony and exhibits from the grievant and the grievant's supervisor. The council then makes a decision that is binding on all involved. Has the employer violated §8(a)(2) by establishing the council? See Sparks Nugget, 230 N.L.R.B. 275 (1977).

INTERNATIONAL LADIES' GARMENT WORKERS' UNION [BERNHARD-ALTMANN CORP.] v. NLRB

366 U.S. 731 (1961)

Clark, J.

We are asked to decide in this case whether it was an unfair labor practice for both an employer and a union to enter into an agreement under which the employer recognized the union as exclusive bargaining representative of certain of his employees, although in fact only a minority of those employees had authorized the union to represent their interests. The Board found that by extending such recognition, even though done in the good-faith belief that the union had the consent of a majority of employees in the appropriate bargaining unit, the employer interfered with the organizational rights of his employees in violation of §8(a)(1) of the National Labor Relations Act and that such recognition also constituted unlawful support to a labor organization in violation of §8(a)(2). In addition, the Board found that the union violated §8(b)(1)(A) by its acceptance of exclusive bargaining authority at a time when in fact it did not have the support of a majority of the employees, and this in spite of its bona fide belief that it did. Accordingly, the Board ordered the unfair labor practices discontinued and directed the holding of a representation election. . . .

We agree with the Board and the Court of Appeals that such extension and acceptance of recognition constitute unfair labor practices, and that the remedy provided was appropriate.

In October 1956 the petitioner union initiated an organizational campaign at Bernhard-Altmann Texas Corporation's knitwear manufacturing plant in San Antonio, Texas. No other labor organization was similarly engaged at that time. During the course of that campaign, on July 29, 1957, certain of the company's Topping Department employees went on strike in protest against a wage reduction. That dispute was in no way related to the union campaign, however, and the organizational efforts were continued during the strike. Some of the striking employees had signed authorization cards solicited by the union during its drive, and, while the strike was in progress, the union entered upon a course of negotiations with the employer. As a result of those negotiations, held in New York City where the home offices of both were located, on August 30, 1957, the employer and union signed a "memorandum of understanding." In that memorandum the company recognized the union as exclusive bargaining representative of "all production and shipping employees." The union representative asserted that the union's comparison of the employee authorization cards in its possession with the number of eligible employee representatives of the company furnished it indicated that the union had in fact secured such cards from a majority of employees in the unit. Neither employer nor union made any effort at that time to check the cards in the union's possession against the employee roll, or otherwise, to ascertain with any degree of certainty that the union's assertion, later found by the Board to be erroneous, was founded on fact rather than upon good-faith assumption. The agreement, containing no union security provisions, called for the ending of the strike and for certain improved wages and conditions of employment. It also provided that a "formal agreement containing these terms" would "be promptly drafted . . . and signed by both parties within the next two weeks."

Thereafter, on October 10, 1957, a formal collective bargaining agreement, embodying the terms of the August 30 memorandum, was signed by the parties. The bargaining unit description set out in the formal contract, although more specific, conformed to that contained in the prior memorandum. It is not disputed that as of execution of the formal contract the union in fact represented a clear majority of employees in the appropriate unit. In upholding the complaints filed against the employer and union by the General Counsel, the Board decided that the employer's good-faith belief that the union in fact represented a majority of employees in the unit on the critical date of the memorandum of understanding was not a defense, "particularly where, as here, the Company made no effort to check the authorization cards against its payroll records." 122 N.L.R.B. 1289, 1292. Noting that the union was "actively seeking recognition at the time such recognition was granted," and that "the Union was [not] the passive recipient of an unsolicited gift bestowed by the Company," the Board found that the union's execution of the August 30 agreement was a "direct deprivation" of the nonconsenting majority employees' organizational and bargaining rights.

Accordingly, the Board ordered the employer to withhold all recognition from the union and to cease giving effect to agreements entered into with the union;[7] the union was ordered to cease acting as bargaining representative of any of the employees until such time as a Board-conducted election demonstrated its majority status, and to refrain from seeking to enforce the agreements previously entered.

At the outset, we reject as without relevance to our decision the fact that, as of the execution date of the formal agreement on October 10, petitioner represented a majority of the employees. As the Court of Appeals indicated, the recognition of the minority union on August 30, 1957, was "a *fait accompli* depriving the majority of the employees of their guaranteed right to choose their own representative." 280 F.2d at page 621. It is, therefore, of no consequence that petitioner may have acquired by October 10 the necessary majority if, during the interim, it was acting unlawfully. Indeed, such acquisition of majority status itself might indicate that the recognition secured by the August 30 agreement afforded petitioner a deceptive cloak of authority with which to persuasively elicit additional employee support.

Nor does this case directly involve a strike. The strike which occurred was in protest against a wage reduction and had nothing to do with petitioner's quest for recognition. Likewise, no question of picketing is presented. Lastly, the violation which the Board found was the grant by the employer of exclusive representation status to a minority union, as distinguished from an employer's bargaining with a minority union for its members only. Therefore, the exclusive representation provision is the vice in the agreement, and discussion of "collective bargaining," as distinguished from "exclusive recognition," is pointless. Moreover, the insistence that we hold the agreement valid and enforceable as to those employees who consented to it must be rejected. On the facts shown, the agreement must fail in its entirety. It was obtained under the erroneous claim of majority representation. Perhaps the employer would not have entered into it if he had known the facts. Quite apart from other conceivable situations, the unlawful genesis of this agreement precludes its partial validity. In their selection of a bargaining representative, §9(a) of the Wagner Act guarantees employees freedom of choice and majority rule. J. I. Case Co. v. National Labor Relations Board, 321 U.S. 332, 339. . . .

Bernhard-Altmann granted exclusive bargaining status to an agency selected by a minority of its employees, thereby impressing that agent upon the nonconsenting majority. There could be no clearer abridgment of §7 of the Act, assuring employees the right "to bargain collectively through representatives of their own choosing" or "to refrain from"

7. However, the terms and conditions of employment fixed by the agreement were not required to be varied or abandoned. We take it that the Board's order restraining the union and employer from dealing will, in any event, terminate after the election is held.

such activity. It follows, without need of further demonstration, that the employer activity found present here violated §8(a)(1) of the Act which prohibits employer interference with, and restraint of, employee exercise of §7 rights. Section 8(a)(2) of the Act makes it an unfair labor practice for an employer to "contribute . . . support" to a labor organization. The law has long been settled that a grant of exclusive recognition to a minority union constitutes unlawful support in violation of that section, because the union so favored is given "a marked advantage over any other in securing the adherence of employees," National Labor Relations Board v. Pennsylvania Greyhound Lines, 303 U.S. 261, 267. In the Taft-Hartley Law, Congress added §8(b)(1)(A) to the Wagner Act, prohibiting, as the Court of Appeals held, "unions from invading the rights of employees under §7 in a fashion comparable to the activities of employers prohibited under §8(a)(1)." 280 F.2d at page 620. It was the intent of Congress to impose upon unions the same restrictions which the Wagner Act imposed on employers with respect to violations of employee rights.

The petitioner, while taking no issue with the fact of its minority status on the critical date, maintains that both Bernhard-Altmann's and its own good-faith beliefs in petitioner's majority status are a complete defense. To countenance such an excuse would place in permissibly careless employer and union hands the power to completely frustrate employee realization of the premise of the Act — that its prohibitions will go far to assure freedom of choice and majority rule in employee selection of representatives. We find nothing in the statutory language prescribing *scienter* as an element of the unfair labor practices here involved. The act made unlawful by §8(a)(2) is employer support of a minority union. Here that support is an accomplished fact. More need not be shown, for, even if mistakenly, the employees' rights have been invaded. It follows that prohibited conduct cannot be excused by a showing of good faith.

This conclusion, while giving the employee only the protection assured him by the Act, places no particular hardship on the employer or the union. It merely requires that recognition be withheld until the Board-conducted election results in majority selection of a representative. The Board's order here, as we might infer from the employer's failure to resist its enforcement, would apparently result in similarly slight hardship upon it. We do not share petitioner's apprehension that holding such conduct unlawful will somehow induce a breakdown, or seriously impede the progress of collective bargaining. If an employer takes reasonable steps to verify union claims, themselves advanced only after careful estimate — precisely what Bernhard-Altmann and petitioner failed to do here — he can readily ascertain their validity and obviate a Board election. We fail to see any onerous burden involved in requiring responsible negotiators to be careful, by cross-checking, for example, well-analyzed employer records with union listings or authorization cards. Individual and collective employee rights may not be trampled upon merely because it is inconvenient to avoid doing so. Moreover, no penalty is attached to the violation. Assuming that an employer in good faith accepts or rejects a union claim of majority status, the validity of his decision may be tested in an unfair labor practice proceeding. If he is found to have erred in extending or withholding recognition, he is subject only to a remedial order requiring him to conform his conduct to the norms set out in the Act, as was the case here. No further penalty results. We believe the Board's remedial order is the proper one in such cases.

Affirmed.

Douglas, J., with whom Black, J., concurs, dissenting in part.

I agree that, under the statutory scheme, a minority union does not have the standing to bargain for all employees. That principle of representative government extends only to the majority. But where there is no majority union, I see no reason why the minority union should be disabled from bargaining for the minority of the members who have joined it. Yet the order of the Board, now approved, enjoins petitioner union from acting as the exclusive bargaining representative "of any of the employees," and it enjoins the employer from recognizing the union as the representative of "any of its employees." . . .

I think the Court is correct insofar as it sets aside the exclusive recognition clause in the contract. I think it is incorrect in setting aside the entire contract. First, that agreement secured valuable benefits for the union's members regarding wages and hours, work standards and distribution, discharge and discipline, holidays, vacations, health and welfare fund, and other matters. Since there was no duly selected representative for all the employees authorized in accordance with the Act, it certainly was the right of the employee union members to designate the union or any other appropriate person to make this contract they desired. To hold the contract void as to the union's voluntary members seems to me to go beyond the competency of the Board under the Act and to be unsupported by any principle of contract law. Certainly there is no principle of justice or fairness with which I am familiar that requires these employees to be stripped of the benefits they acquired by the good-faith bargaining of their designated agent. Such a deprivation gives no protection to the majority who were not members of the union and arbitrarily takes from the union members their contract rights.

Second, the result of today's decision is to enjoin the employer from dealing with the union as the representative of its own members in any manner, whether in relation to greivances or otherwise, until it is certified as a majority union. A case for complete disestablishment of the union cannot be sustained under our decisions.

Notes

1. Suppose that in *Budd Manufacturing* Weigand was carried on the company payroll but spent all his time transacting union business. Section 8(a)(2) violation?

2. The dissent in *Bernhard-Altmann* suggests that a members-only collective bargaining agreement with a minority union is legal. There are two contrary arguments. Since under §8(a)(3) an employer cannot differentiate between employees on account of their union status, a wage increase secured by the union for its members would have to be paid to nonmembers as well. Thus the "minority" union would be setting terms for all employees, and that smacks of exclusivity. Second, if for some reason §8(a)(3) is deemed inapplicable, a wage rate secured for only union members would surely attract nonmembers to the union ranks, seemingly violating §8(a)(2).

3. Should it violate §8(a)(2) for an employer and a union to enter into a collective bargaining agreement that will not go into effect unless and until the union secures a majority of employees? Does the existence of such an agreement interfere with or facilitate a free and knowledgeable choice by employees as to whether they desire union representation?

4. How long is an agreement of the *Bernhard-Altmann* sort subject to challenge: Is "assistance" a continuing violation of the Act? Section 10(b) of the Act establishes a six-month statute of limitations for the filing of unfair labor practice charges. At one time the Board's theory was that such an agreement gave rise to a continuing violation; that is, each time the agreement was applied or enforced, it constituted a new violation. The Supreme Court reversed the Board in Local Lodge 1424, Machinists v. NLRB, 362 U.S. 418 (1960). The Court stated:

> It is doubtless true that §10(b) does not prevent all use of evidence relating to events transpiring more than six months before the filing and service of an unfair labor practice charge. However, in applying rules of evidence as to the admissibility of past events, due regard for the purposes of §10(b) requires that two different kinds of situations be distinguished. The first is one where occurrences within the six-month limitations period in and of themselves may constitute, as a substantive matter, unfair labor practices. There, earlier events may be utilized to shed light on the true character of matters occurring within the limitations period; and for that purpose §10(b) ordinarily does not bar such evidentiary use of anterior events.
>
> The second situation is that where conduct occurring within the limitations period can be charged to be an unfair labor practice only through reliance on an earlier unfair labor practice. There the use of the earlier unfair labor practice is not merely "evidentiary," since it does not simply lay bare a putative current unfair labor practice. Rather, it serves to cloak with illegality that which was otherwise lawful. And where a complaint based upon that earlier event is time-barred, to permit the event itself to

be so used in effect results in reviving a legally defunct unfair labor practice.

How would a charge that a union is under the domination of an employer fare under this test? Could Bob's Casing Crews have refused to hire Billy Loper if his application was acted upon more than six months after his discharge from Red's Casing Crews?

5. Suppose an employer has had bargaining agreements with an incumbent union for many years. This year the agreement has expired and negotiations are under way when a rival union notifies the employer that it claims to represent a majority of the employer's employees and has filed a representation petition with the Board. May the employer continue to bargain with the incumbent union? For many years the Board held that continued negotiations constitute a §8(a)(2) violation if the rival has raised "a real question of representation."[64] This was called the Board's *Midwest Piping* doctrine.[65]

The doctrine was overruled in RCA Del Caribe, 262 N.L.R.B. 963 (1982). Under the new rule an employer may negotiate and execute a bargaining agreement with the incumbent union; indeed, the employer violates §8(a)(5) if he or she withdraws from bargaining solely because of the filing of the petition. The Board's majority stated that if the incumbent prevails in the representation election, any contract executed between it and the employer will be binding, but if the challenging union wins the election, the contract between the employer and the incumbent is void.

5. Going Out of Business and Runaway Shops

In the next case we consider whether an employer can close down with impunity rather than deal with the union. The case also includes an important discussion of the relationship between §§8(a)(1) and (3).

TEXTILE WORKERS UNION v. DARLINGTON MANUFACTURING CO.

380 U.S. 263 (1965)

Harlan, J.

We here review judgments of the Court of Appeals setting aside and refusing to enforce an order of the National Labor Relations Board which found respondent Darlington guilty of an unfair labor practice by

[64] Shea Chemical Corp., 121 N.L.R.B. 1027 (1958).
[65] From Midwest Piping & Supply Co., 63 N.L.R.B. 1060 (1945).

reason of having permanently closed its plant following petitioner union's election as the bargaining representative of Darlington's employees.

Darlington Manufacturing Company was a South Carolina corporation operating one textile mill. A majority of Darlington's stock was held by Deering Milliken, a New York "selling house" marketing textiles produced by others. Deering Milliken in turn was controlled by Roger Milliken, president of Darlington, and by other members of the Milliken family. The National Labor Relations Board found that the Milliken family, through Deering Milliken, operated 17 textile manufacturers, including Darlington, whose products manufactured in 27 different mills, were marketed through Deering Milliken.

In March 1956 petitioner Textile Workers Union initiated an organizational campaign at Darlington which the company resisted vigorously in various ways, including threats to close the mill if the union won a representation election. On September 6, 1956, the union won an election by a narrow margin. When Roger Milliken was advised of the union victory, he decided to call a meeting of the Darlington board of directors to consider closing the mill. Mr Milliken testified before the Labor Board:

> I felt that as a result of the campaign that had been conducted and the promises and statements made in these letters that had been distributed [favoring unionization], that if before we had had some hope, possible hope of achieving competitive [costs] . . . by taking advantage of new machinery that was being put in, that this hope had diminished as a result of the election because a majority of the employees had voted in favor of the union. . . . (R. 457).

The board of directors met on September 12 and voted to liquidate the corporation, action which was approved by the stockholders on October 17. The plant ceased operations entirely in November, and all plant machinery and equipment were sold piecemeal at auction in December.

The union filed charges with the Labor Board claiming that Darlington had violated §§8(a)(1) and (3) of the National Labor Relations Act by closing its plant, and §8(a)(5) by refusing to bargain with the union after the election. The Board, by a divided vote, found that Darlington had been closed because of the antiunion animus of Roger Milliken, and held that to be a violation of §8(a)(3). The Board also found Darlington to be part of a single integrated employer group controlled by the Milliken family through Deering Milliken; therefore Deering Milliken could be held liable for the unfair labor practices of Darlington. Alternatively, since Darlington was a part of the Deering Milliken enterprise, Deering Milliken had violated the Act by closing part of its business for a discriminatory purpose. The Board ordered back pay for all Darlington employees until they obtained substantially equivalent work or were put on preferential hiring lists at the other Deering Milliken mills. Respondent Deering Milliken was ordered to bargain with the union in regard to details of compliance with the Board order. 139 N.L.R.B. 241. . . . The Court of Appeals held that even accepting arguendo the Board's determination that Deering Milliken had the status of a single employer, a company has the absolute right to close out a part or all of its business regardless of antiunion motives. The court therefore did not review the Board's finding that Deering Milliken was a single integrated employer. We granted certiorari. . . .

We hold that so far as the Labor Relations Act is concerned, an employer has the absolute right to terminate his entire business for any reason he pleases, but disagree with the Court of Appeals that such right includes the ability to close part of a business no matter what the reason. We conclude that the cause must be remanded to the Board for further proceedings.

Preliminarily it should be observed that both petitioners argue that the Darlington closing violated §8(a)(1) as well as §8(a)(3) of the Act. We think, however, that the Board was correct in treating the closing only under §8(a)(3). Section 8(a)(1) provides that it is an unfair labor practice for an employer "to interfere with, restrain, or coerce employees in the exercise of" §7 rights. Naturally, certain business decisions will, to some degree, interfere with concerted activities by employees. But it is only when the interference with §7 rights outweighs the business justification for the employer's action that §8(a)(1) is violated. See, e.g., National Labor Relations Board v. United Steelworkers, 357 U.S. 357; Republic Aviation Corp. v. National Labor Relations Board, 324 U.S. 793. A violation of §8(a)(1) alone therefore presupposes an act which is unlawful even absent a discriminatory motive. Whatever may be the limits of §8(a)(1), some employer decisions are so peculiarly matters of management prerogative that they would never constitute violations of §8(a)(1), whether or not they involved sound business judgment, unless they also violated §8(a)(3). Thus it is not questioned in this case that an employer has the right to terminate his business, whatever the impact of such action on concerted activities, if the decision to close is motivated by other than discriminatory reasons.[10] But such action, if discriminatorily

10. It is also clear that the ambiguous act of closing a plant following the election of a union is not, absent an inquiry into the employer's motive, inherently discriminatory. We are thus not confronted with a situation where the employer "must be held to intend the very consequences which foreseeably and inescapably flow from his actions. . . ." (NLRB v. Erie Resistor Corp., 373 U.S. 221, 228), in which the Board could find a violation of §8(a)(3) without an examination into motive. See Radio Officers v. NLRB, 347 U.S. 17, 42-43; Local 357, International Brotherhood of Teamsters, etc. v. NLRB, 365, U.S. 667, 674-676.

motivated, is encompassed within the literal language of §8(a)(3). We therefore deal with the Darlington closing under that section.

I

We consider first the argument, advanced by the petitioner union but not by the Board, and rejected by the Court of Appeals, that an employer may not go completely out of business without running afoul of the Labor Relations Act if such action is prompted by a desire to avoid unionization.[11] Given the Board's findings on the issue of motive, acceptance of his contention would carry the day for the Board's conclusion that the closing of this plant was an unfair labor practice, even on the assumption that Darlington is to be regarded as an independent unrelated employer. A proposition that a single businessman cannot choose to go out of business if he wants to would represent such a startling innovation that it should not be entertained without the clearest manifestation of legislative intent or unequivocal judicial precedent so construing the Labor Relations Act. We find neither.

So far as legislative manifestation is concerned, it is sufficient to say that there is not the slightest indication in the history of the Wagner Act or of the Taft-Hartley Act that Congress envisaged any such result under either statute.

As for judicial precedent, the Board recognized that "[t]here is no decided case directly dispositive of Darlington's claim that it had an absolute right to close its mill, irrespective of motive." 139 N.L.R.B., at 250. . . .

The AFL-CIO suggests in its amicus brief that Darlington's action was similar to a discriminatory lockout, which is prohibited "'because designed to frustrate organizational efforts, to destroy or undermine bargaining representation, or to evade the duty to bargain.'" One of the purposes of the Labor Relations Act is to prohibit the discriminatory use of economic weapons in an effort to obtain future benefits. The discriminatory lockout designed to destroy a union, like a "runaway shop," is a lever which has been used to discourage collective employee activities in the future. But a complete liquidation of a business yields no such future benefit for the employer, if the termination is bona fide.[14] It may be motivated more by spite against the union than by business reasons, but it is not the type of discrimination which is prohibited by the Act. The

11. The Board predicates its argument on the finding that Deering Milliken was an integrated enterprise, and does not consider it necessary to argue that an employer may not go completely out of business for antiunion reasons. Brief for National Labor Relations Board, p. 3, n. 2.

14. The Darlington property and equipment could not be sold as a unit, and were eventually auctioned off piecemeal. We therefore are not confronted with a sale of a going concern, which might present different considerations under §§8(a)(3) and (5).

personal satisfaction that such an employer may derive from standing on his beliefs and the mere possibility that other employers will follow his example are surely too remote to be considered dangers at which the labor statutes were aimed.[15] Although employees may be prohibited from engaging in a strike under certain conditions, no one would consider it a violation of the Act for the same employees to quite their employment en masse, even if motivated by a desire to ruin the employer. The very permanence of such action would negate any future economic benefit to the employees. The employer's right to go out of business is no different.

We are not presented here with the case of a "runaway shop,"[16] whereby Darlington would transfer its work to another plant or open a new plant in another locality to replace its closed plant. Nor are we concerned with a shutdown where the employees, by renouncing the union, could cause the plant to reopen. Such cases would involve discriminatory employer action for the purpose of obtaining some benefit in the future from the employees in the future. We hold here only that when an employer closes his entire business, even if the liquidation is motivated by vindictiveness toward the union, such action is not an unfair labor practice.[20]

II

While we thus agree with the Court of Appeals that viewing Darlington as an independent employer the liquidation of its business was not an unfair labor practice, we cannot accept the lower court's view that the same conclusion necessarily follows if Darlington is regarded as an integral part of the Deering Milliken enterprise.

15. Cf. NLRA §8(c). Different considerations would arise were it made to appear that the closing employer was acting pursuant to some arrangement or understanding with other employers to discourage employee organizational activities in their businesses.

16. E.g., NLRB v. Preston Feed Corp., 4 Cir., 309 F.2d 346; NLRB v. Wallick, 3 Cir., 198 F.2d 477. An analogous problem is presented where a department is closed for antiunion reasons but the work is continued by independent contractors.

20. Nothing we have said in this opinion would justify an employer's interfering with employee organizational activities by threatening to close his plant, as distinguished from announcing a decision to close already reached by the board of directors or other management authority empowered to make such a decision. We recognize that this safeguard does not wholly remove the possibility that our holding may result in some deterrent effect on organizational activities independent of that arising from the closing itself. An employer may be encouraged to make a definitive decision to close on the theory that its mere announcement before a representation election will discourage the employees from voting for the union, and thus his decision may not have to be implemented. Such a possibility is not likely to occur, however, except in a marginal business; a solidly successful employer is not apt to hazard the possibility that the employees will call his bluff by voting to organize. We see no practical way of eliminating this possible consequence of our holding short of allowing the Board to order an employer who chooses so to gamble with his employees not to carry out his announced intention to close. We do not consider the matter of sufficient significance in the overall labor-management relations picture to require or justify a decision different from the one we have made.

The closing of an entire business, even though discriminatory, ends the employer-employee relationship; the force of such a closing is entirely spent as to that business when termination of the enterprise takes place. On the other hand, a discriminatory partial closing may have repercussions on what remains of the business, affording employer leverage for discouraging the free exercise of §7 rights among remaining employees of much the same kind as that found to exist in the "runaway shop" and "temporary closing" cases. Moreover, a possible remedy open to the Board in such a case, like the remedies available in the "runaway shop" and "temporary closing" cases, is to order reinstatement of the discharged employees in the other parts of the business. No such remedy is available when an entire business has been terminated. By analogy to those cases involving a continuing enterprise we are constrained to hold, in disagreement with the Court of Appeals, that a partial closing is an unfair labor practice under §8(a)(3) if motivated by a purpose to chill unionism in any of the remaining plants of the single employer and if the employer may reasonably have foreseen that such closing would likely have that effect.

While we have spoken in terms of a "partial closing" in the context of the Board's finding that Darlington was part of a larger single enterprise controlled by the Milliken family, we do not mean to suggest that an organizational integration of plants or corporations is a necessary prerequisite to the establishment of such a violation of §8(a)(3). If the persons exercising control over a plant that is being closed for antiunion reasons (1) have an interest in another business, whether or not affiliated with or engaged in the same line of commercial activity as the closed plant, of sufficient substantiality to give promise of their reaping a benefit from the discouragement of unionization in that business; (2) act to close their plant with the purpose of producing such a result; and (3) occupy a relationship to the other business which makes it realistically foreseeable that its employees will fear that such business will also be closed down if they persist in organizational activities, we think that an unfair labor practice has been made out.

Although the Board's single employer finding necessarily embraced findings as to Roger Milliken and the Milliken family which, if sustained by the Court of Appeals, would satisfy the elements of "interest" and "relationship" with respect to other parts of the Deering Milliken enterprise, that and the other Board findings fall short of establishing the factors of "purpose" and "effect" which are vital requisites of the general principles that govern a case of this kind.

Thus, the Board's findings as to the purpose and foreseeable effect of the Darlington closing pertained *only* to its impact on the Darlington employees. No findings were made as to the purpose and effect of the closing with respect to the employees in the other plants comprising the Deering Milliken group. It does not suffice to establish the unfair labor practice charged here to argue that the Darlington closing necessarily had an adverse impact upon unionization in such other plants. We have heretofore observed that employer action which has a foreseeable consequence of discouraging concerted activities generally does not amount to a violation of §8(a)(3) in the absence of a showing of motivation which is aimed at achieving the prohibited effect. See Local 357 International Brotherhood of Teamsters v. National Labor Relations Board, 365 U.S. 667, and the concurring opinion therein, at 677.

In an area which trenches so closely upon otherwise legitimate employer prerogatives, we consider the absence of Board findings on this score a fatal defect in its decision. The Court of Appeals for its part did not deal with the question of purpose and effect at all, since it concluded that an employer's right to close down his entire business because of distaste for unionism, also embraced a partial closing so motivated.

Apart from this, the Board's holding should not be accepted or rejected without court review of its single employer finding, judged, however, in accordance with the general principles set forth above. Review of that finding, which the lower court found unnecessary on its view of the cause, now becomes necessary in light of our holding in this part of our opinion, and is a task that devolves upon the Court of Appeals in the first instance. In these circumstances, we think the proper disposition of this cause is to require that it be remanded to the Board so as to afford the Board the opportunity to make further findings on the issue of purpose and effect. This is particularly appropriate here since the cases involve issues of first impression. If such findings are made, the cases will then be in a posture for further review by the Court of Appeals on all issues. Accordingly, without intimating any view as to how any of these matters should eventuate, we vacate the judgments of the Court of Appeals and remand the cases to that court with instructions to remand them to the Board for further proceedings consistent with this opinion. It is so ordered.

Judgments of Court of Appeals vacated and cases remanded with instructions.[66]

Notes

1. Shouldn't Justice Harlan have stated the issue in this way: "We do not doubt that an employer has the absolute right to terminate his entire business for any reason he pleases, but the issue is whether the statute commands that as a cost of his decision he respond in damages and make the employees whole for their discriminatory treatment"?

2. Would the following paragraph be appropriate for the Court's opinion?

[66] Goldberg, J., and Stewart, J., took no part in the decision.

> Section 8(a)(3) requires "discrimination . . . to encourage or discourage membership in any labor organization." Where an employer is going out of business entirely, and thus will no longer have any employees, it is highly likely that his purpose is to discourage unionization. An exception would be shown only by proof that he intended to discourage unionism at other businesses owned by him or others. Our decision in Republic Aviation v. NLRB, 324 U.S. 793 (1945) commands no different result. There an employee was discharged for violating a no-solicitation rule held to be so overinclusive as to interfere with §7 rights. The proscribed discouragement was not the effect on the discharged employee, but the effect on other employees who would fear similar treatment. And while we could presume the unlawful intent and effect in *Republic,* no such presumption is warranted in the instant case for the reasons outlined above.

3. Even when the employer is privileged to discontinue operations, he may be obligated to bargain with an incumbent union over the effects of the closing. The Board's remedy for a failure to bargain is as follows. The employer has to bargain with the union about the effects of the discontinuance of operation and to pay employees amounts, at the rate of their normal wages when last in the company's employ, from five days after the date of the NLRB decision until the occurrance of the earliest of the following conditions: (1) the date the company bargains to agreement with the union on those subjects pertaining to the effects; (2) a bona fide impasse in bargaining occurs; (3) the union fails to request bargaining within five days of the Board's decision, or to commence negotiations within five days of the company's notice of its desire to bargain with the union; or (4) the subsequent failure of the union to bargain in good faith. The upper limit on the sum paid to any employees is the amount each would have earned as wages from the time the company discontinued its operation to the time each secured equivalent employment elsewhere, or the date on which the company has offered to bargain, whichever occurs first. But in no event shall the sum be less than such employees would have earned for a two-week period at the last rate of their normal wages when last in the company's employ. National Car Rental, 252 N.L.R.B. No. 27 (1980). What is this remedy trying to accomplish?

4. Re footnote 16 of *Darlington,* why is the subcontracting of a department more analogous to a runaway shop than to a *Darlington* close-down? Would the result in the subcontracting case depend on whether it had a tendency to — or was intended to — chill unionism in other parts of the plant? The employer may try to justify the subcontracting on the ground that in light of the wages he or she is likely to have to pay to the unionized department, subcontracting is more economical.

5. On remand in *Darlington* the Board found (1) that the persons controlling Darlington had sufficient interest in and relationship with Deering Milliken and other affiliated corporations to establish a single

enterprise, and (2) that the purpose and effect of Darlington's closing was to chill unionism in other mills of the Deering Milliken group. Consequently, the Board ordered Darlington and Deering Milliken to pay back wages until the employees obtained substantially equivalent employment or were put on a preferential hiring list at other Deering Milliken mills. 165 N.L.R.B. 1074 (1967), enforcement granted, 397 F.2d 760 (4th Cir. 1968), cert. denied, 393 U.S. 1023 (1969).

In 1974, after locating and interviewing the 553 former Darlington employees who were potential claimants, the NLRB regional office issued backpay specifications. Deering Milliken's disagreement with the specifications led to a backpay compliance proceeding before an Administrative Law Judge, who held hearings, received briefs, and heard oral arguments. In late 1980, the General Counsel proposed a compromise $5 million backpay settlement, which was accepted by Deering Milliken and by a vote of the former employees (or their survivors) — 24 years after the Darlington mill was closed.

6. *Runaway shops*. From A.B.A., Section of Labor Relations Law, The Developing Law 122 (C. Morris, ed., 1971).

> The problem of the "runaway shop" has confronted the Board in a number of cases. If the employer's purpose in moving his business is to discourage union membership or collective bargaining, he violates §8(a)(3). The Board's remedy is to order reinstatement to jobs with back pay and moving expenses (or reimbursement for increased costs in traveling to and from the new work location). The difficult cases are those in which an employer is proved to have been anti-union in feeling but nevertheless had good economic reason for moving his business. If the preponderant motive for moving is economic necessity, anti-union animus does not make the move an unfair labor practice.

This is an accurate statement of the case law, but does that case law make any sense? Consider the following employer statements:

> I oppose unions as a matter of principle. I am moving my plant to South Carolina so I won't have to deal with them.
>
> I oppose unions as a matter of principle. I am moving my plant to South Carolina because wage rates are lower there and I can be more competitive.

Different result?

Consider also the Board's decision in Co-Ed Garment Co., 231 N.L.R.B. 848 (1977), where the Board found that the employer ("Respondent") did not violate §8(a)(3) when he moved his operations from Festus, Missouri to Greenwood, Mississippi:

> The Respondent had voluntarily bargained with the Union for nearly 20 years. By early 1976, it had suffered substantial financial losses for at least

two years, and its liabilities exceeded its assets. The Respondent unsuccessfully sought an understanding with the union so that it could continue operations, and also sought higher piece rates from the Girl Scouts, its principal customer, in excess of the 3-percent increase offered, but was turned down. Rather than suggesting a discriminatory motive, the record indicates that the Respondent sought to continue its operation in Festus and that its relocation was for legitimate reasons unconnected to any intention to discourage or chill union activity.

If the employer faced with majority employee support for the union has fled to Florida for discriminatory (as opposed to economic) reasons, should the Board order the employer to bargain with the union in Florida? Judge (now Chief Justice) Burger said no in Local 57, ILGWU v. NLRB, 374 F.2d 295 (D.C. Cir. 1967), cert. denied, 387 U.S. 942 (1967):

> In our view the Board should not seek to "discipline" the Employer at the expense of the new Florida employees. Such a remedy is, on face, arbitrary; the Board ought not to rob Peter to punish Paul.

Judge McGowan, dissenting on this point, argued: "Weighing the efficacy of alternative approaches, and drawing upon past experience to guide the choice between them, are inherent in the Board's remedial powers."

6. Double-Breasted Employers[67]

SOUTH PRAIRIE CONSTRUCTION CO. v. OPERATING ENGINEERS, LOCAL 627

425 U.S. 800 (1976)

Per Curiam.

Respondent Union filed a complaint in 1972 with the National Labor Relations Board alleging that South Prairie Construction Co. (South Prairie) and Peter Kiewit Sons' Co. (Kiewit) had violated §§8(a)(5) and (1) by their continuing refusal to apply to South Prairie's employees the collective-bargaining agreement in effect between the Union and Kiewit. The Union first asserted that since South Prairie and Kiewit are wholly owned subsidiaries of Peter Kiewit Sons', Inc. (PKS), and engage in highway construction in Oklahoma, they constituted a single "employer" within the Act for purposes of applying the Union-Kiewit agreement. That being the case, the Union contended, South Prairie was obligated

[67] See Bornstein, The Emerging Law of the "Double Breasted" Operation in the Construction Industry, 28 Lab. L.J. 77 (1977).

to recognize the Union as the representative of a bargaining unit drawn to include South Prairie's employees.[1] Disagreeing with the Administrative Law Judge on the first part of the Union's claim, the Board concluded that South Prairie and Kiewit were in fact separate employers, and dismissed the complaint.

On the Union's petition for review, the Court of Appeals for the District of Columbia Circuit canvassed the facts of record. It discussed, inter alia, the manner in which Kiewit, South Prairie, and PKS functioned as entities; PKS' decision to activate South Prairie, its nonunion subsidiary, in a State where historically Kiewit had been the only union highway contractor among the latter's Oklahoma competitors; and the two firms' competitive bidding patterns on Oklahoma highway jobs after South Prairie was activated in 1972 to do business there.

Stating that it was applying the criteria recognized by this Court in Radio Union v. Broadcast Service, 380 U.S. 255 (1965),[3] the Court of Appeals disagreed with the Board and decided that on the facts presented Kiewit and South Prairie were a single "employer." It reasoned that in addition to the 'presence of a very substantial qualitative degree of centralized control of labor relations," the facts "evidence a substantial qualitative degree of interrelation of operations and common management — one that we are satisfied would not be found in the arm's length relationship existing among unintegrated companies." 171 U.S. App. D.C. 102, 108, 109, 518 F.2d 1040, 1046, 1047 (1975). The Board's finding to the contrary was, therefore, in the view of the Court of Appeals "not warranted by the record." Id., at 109, 518 F.2d, at 1047.

Having set aside this portion of the Board's determination, however, the Court of Appeals went on to reach and decide the second question presented by the Union's complaint which had not been passed upon by the Board. The court decided that the employees of Kiewit and South Prairie constituted the appropriate unit under §9 of the Act for purposes of collective bargaining. On the basis of this conclusion, it decided that these firms had committed an unfair labor practice by refusing "to recognize Local 627 as the bargaining representative of South Prairie's employees or to extend the terms of the Union's agreement with Kiewit to South Prairie's employees." Id., at 112, 518 F.2d, at 1050. The case was remanded to the Board for "issuance and enforcement of an appropriate order against . . . Kiewit and South Prairie." Ibid.

1. . . . On the facts of this case, the Union first had to establish that Kiewit and South Prairie were a single "employer." If it succeeded, the existence of a violation under §8(a)(5) would then turn on whether under §9 the "employer unit" was the "appropriate" one for collective-bargaining purposes.

3. "[I]n determining the relevant employer, the Board considers several nominally separate business entities to be a single employer where they comprise an integrated enterprise, N.L.R.B. Twenty-first Ann. Rep. 14-15 (1956). The controlling criteria, set out and elaborated in Board decisions, are interrelation of operations, common management, centralized control of labor relations and common ownership." 380 U.S., at 256.

Petitioners South Prairie and the Board in their petitions here contest the action of the Court of Appeals in setting aside the Board's determination on the "employer" question. But their principal contention is that the Court of Appeals invaded the statutory province of the Board when it proceeded to decide the §9 "unit" question in the first instance, instead of remanding the case to the Board so that it could make the initial determination. While we refrain from disturbing the holding of the Court of Appeals that Kiewit and South Prairie are an "employer," see NLRB v. Pittsburgh S. S. Co., 340 U.S. 498 (1951),[5] we agree with petitioners' principal contention.

The Court of Appeals was evidently of the view that since the Board dismissed the complaint it had necessarily decided that the employees of Kiewit and South Prairie would not constitute an appropriate bargaining unit under §9. But while the Board's opinion referred to its cases in this area and included a finding that "the employees of each constitute a separate bargaining unit," 206 N.L.R.B. 562, 563 (1973), its brief discussion was set in the context of what it obviously considered was the dispositive issue, namely, whether the two firms were separate employers. We think a fair reading of its decision discloses that it did not address the "unit" question on the basis of any assumption, arguendo, that it might have been wrong on the threshold "employer" issue.[6]

Section 9(b) of the Act directs the Board to "decide in each case whether, in order to assure to employees the fullest freedom in exercising the rights guaranteed by this Act, the unit appropriate for the purposes of collective bargaining shall be the employer unit, craft unit, plant unit, or subdivision thereof. . . ."

The Board's cases hold that especially in the construction industry a determination that two affiliated firms constitute a single employer "does not necessarily establish that an employerwide unit is appropriate, as the factors which are relevant in identifying the breadth of an employer's operation are not conclusively determinative of the scope of an appropriate unit." Central New Mexico Chapter, National Electrical Contractors Assn., Inc., 152 N.L.R.B. 1604, 1608 (1965).

The Court of Appeals reasoned that the Board's principal case on the "unit" question, *Central New Mexico Chapter,* supra, was distinguishable because there the two affiliated construction firms engaged in different

5. "Were we called upon to pass on the Board's conclusions in the first instance or to make an independent review of the review by the Court of Appeals, we might well support the Board's conclusion and reject that of the court below. But Congress has charged the Courts of Appeals and not this Court with the normal and primary responsibility for granting or denying enforcement of Labor Board orders." 340 U.S. 498, 502.

6. The Administrative Law Judge's decision in favor of the Union included a conclusion that the pertinent employees of Kiewit and South Prairie constituted an appropriate unit under §9(b). But that conclusion was, of course, preceded by the determination that the two firms were a single employer. In disagreeing on the "employer" issue, the Board was not compelled to reach the §9(b) question in order to dismiss the complaint.

types of contracting. It thought that this fact was critical to the Board's conclusion in that case that the employees did not have the same "community of interest" for purposes of identifying an appropriate bargaining unit. Whether or not the Court of Appeals was correct in this reasoning, we think that for it to take upon itself the initial determination of this issue was "incompatible with the orderly function of the process of judicial review." NLRB v. Metropolitan Ins. Co., 380 U.S. 438, 444 (1965). Since the selection of an appropriate bargaining unit lies largely within the discretion of the Board, whose decision, "if not final, is rarely to be disturbed," Packard Motor Co. v. NLRB, 330 U.S. 485, 491 (1947), we think the function of the Court of Appeals ended when the board's error on the "employer" issue was "laid bare." FPC v. Idaho Power Co., 344 U.S. 17, 20 (1952).

As this Court stated in NLRB v. Food Store Employees, 417 U.S. 1, 9 (1974): "It is a guiding principle of administrative law, long recognized by this Court, that 'an administrative determination in which is imbedded a legal question open to judicial review does not impliedly foreclose the administrative agency, after its error has been corrected, from enforcing the legislative policy committed to its charge.' FCC v. Pottsville Broadcasting Co., 309 134, 145 (1940)."

In foreclosing the Board from the opportunity to determine the appropriate bargaining unit under §9, the Court of Appeals did not give "due observance [to] the distribution of authority made by Congress as between its power to regulate commerce and the reviewing power which it has conferred upon the courts under Article III of the Constitution." FCC v. Pottsville Broadcasting Co., 309 U.S. 134, 141 (1940).

The petitions for certiorari are accordingly granted, and that part of the judgment of the Court of Appeals which set aside the determination of the Board on the question of whether Kiewit and South Prairie were a single employer is affirmed. That part of the judgment which held that the two firms' employees constituted the appropriate bargaining unit for purposes of the Act, and which directed the Board to issue an enforcement order, is vacated, and the case is remanded to the Court of Appeals for proceedings consistent with this opinion.

Note

The facts of *South Prairie* are typical of the construction industry in some parts of the country. Some general contractors will let construction subcontracts out only to unionized subcontractors (often called *specialty contractors*; these subcontractors usually limit their work to a particular trade, such as sheet metal work, electrical work, or pipefitting). When there is competition between union and nonunion general contractors, a unionized specialty contractor may see a lot of work going to nonunion companies and decide to play both sides of the fence.

The unionized contractor may form a separate corporation to do nonunion work. Either new equipment is purchased or else existing equipment is transferred from the unionized operation. A long-time supervisory employee is put "in charge" of the new business. Often both corporations lack any regular complement of employees. When a subcontract comes up for bids from a unionized general contractor, the unionized specialty subcontractor will bid and, if successful, will call the union hall for employees. If the general contractor permits open bidding (that is, it accepts bids from nonunion specialty contractors), the nonunion corporation will bid and, if successful, will hire its employees for this job from the area's nonunion workers.

As the *South Prairie* opinion indicates, there are two strands of doctrine that permit this "double-breasted" employer to maintain two operations. First, the Board is likely to find that the two corporations are separate employers by applying the criteria set out in footnote 3 of the Court's opinion. Second, even assuming the corporations are a single employer, a bargaining unit encompassing both may not be "appropriate" in the Board's view.[68]

Should the Board strike down the double-breasted employer arrangement? If so, under what section of the Act? Consider whether the double-breasted employer scheme constitutes unlawful discrimination, or whether it merely reflects the economics of the marketplace.

H. ORGANIZATIONAL PICKETING

1. Constitutional Protection of Picketing

The following case deals with whether the Constitution affords protection for organizational[69] picketing against state and — by necessary implication — federal interference. It outlines the twisting history of the Supreme Court's treatment of the issue. The case does not consider whether federal law regulating organizational picketing preempts the state from acting; that issue will be taken up in Chapter 7.

[68] The Board so ruled on remand in *South Prairie*.

[69] There have been attempts to distinguish organizational from recognitional picketing — the former being appeals to employees to cast their lot with the union, the latter being pressure on an employer to recognize the union as his or her employees' representative notwithstanding the employees' wishes. Unions seldom made such a distinction and picket lines usually had both effects, rendering the distinction more academic than actual. The federal statutory treatment, §8(b)(7), expressly encompasses both.

TEAMSTERS LOCAL 695 v. VOGT
354 U.S. 284 (1957)

Frankfurter, J.

This is one more in the long series of cases in which this Court has been required to consider the limits imposed by the Fourteenth Amendment on the power of a Statute to enjoin picketing. . . . Respondent owns and operates a gravel pit in Oconomowoc, Wisconsin, where it employs 15 to 20 men. Petitioner unions sought unsuccessfully to induce some of respondent's employees to join the unions and commenced to picket the entrance to respondent's place of business with signs reading, "The men on this job are not 100% affiliated with the A.F.L." "In consequence," drivers of several trucking companies refused to deliver and haul goods to and from respondent's plant, causing substantial damage to respondent. Respondent thereupon sought an injunction to restrain the picketing.

The trial court did not make the finding, requested by respondent, "That the picketing of plaintiff's premises has been engaged in for the purpose of coercing, intimidating and inducing the employer to force, compel, or induce its employees to become members of defendant labor organizations, and for the purpose of injuring the plaintiff in its business because of its refusal to in any way interfere with the rights of its employees to join or not to join a labor organization." It nevertheless held that by virtue of Wis. Stat. §103.535, prohibiting picketing in the absence of a "labor dispute," the petitioners must be enjoined from maintaining any pickets near respondent's place of business, from displaying at any place near respondent's place of business signs indicating that there was a labor dispute between respondent and its employees or between respondent and any of the petitioners, and from inducing others to decline to transport goods to and from respondent's business establishment.

On appeal, the Wisconsin Supreme Court at first reversed, relying largely on A. F. of L. v. Swing, 312 U.S. 321, to hold §103.535 unconstitutional, on the ground that picketing could not constitutionally be enjoined merely because of the absence of a "labor dispute." 270 Wis. 315, 71 N.W.2d 359.

Upon reargument, however, the court withdraw its original opinion. Although the trial court had refused to make the finding requested by respondent, the Supreme Court, noting that the facts as to which the request was made were undisputed, drew the inference from the undisputed facts and itself made the finding. It canvassed the whole circumstances surrounding the picketing and held that "One would be credulous, indeed, to believe under the circumstances that the union had no thought of coercing the employer to interfere with its employees in their right to join or refuse to join the defendant union." Such picketing, the court held, was for "an unlawful purpose," since Wis. Stat. §111.06(2)(b) made it an unfair labor practice for an employee individually or in concert with others to "coerce, intimidate or induce any employer to interfere with any of his employees in the enjoyment of their legal rights . . . or to engage in any practice with regard to his employees which would constitute an unfair labor practice if undertaken by him on his own initiative." Relying on Building Service Employees v. Gazzam, 339 U.S. 532, and Pappas v. Stacey, 151 Me. 36, 116 A.2d 497, the Wisconsin Supreme Court therefore affirmed the granting of the injunction on this different ground. 270 Wis. 321a, 74 N.W.2d 749. [The Court granted certiorari.]

It is not too surprising that the response of States — legislative and judicial — to use of the injunction in labor controversies should have given rise to a series of adjudications in this Court relating to the limitations on state action contained in the provisions of the Due Process Clause of the Fourteenth Amendment. It is also not too surprising that examination of these adjudications should disclose an evolving, not a static, course of decision.

The series begins with Truax v. Corrigan, 257 U.S. 312, in which a closely divided Court found it to be violative of the Equal Protection Clause — not of the Due Process Clause — for a State to deny use of the injunction in the special class of cases arising out of labor conflicts. The considerations that underlay that case soon had to yield, through legislation and later through litigation, to the persuasiveness of undermining facts. Thus, to remedy the abusive use of the injunction in the federal courts (see Frankfurter and Greene, The Labor Injunction), the Norris-LaGuardia Act, 47 Stat. 70, 29 U.S.C. §101, withdraw, subject to qualifications, jurisdiction from the federal courts to issue injunctions in labor disputes to prohibit certain acts. Its example was widely followed by state enactments.

Apart from remedying the abuses of the injunction in this general type of litigation, legislatures and courts began to find in one of the aims of picketing an aspect of communication. This view came to the fore in Senn v. Tile Layers Union, 301 U.S. 468, where the Court held that the Fourteenth Amendment did not prohibit Wisconsin from authorizing peaceful stranger picketing by a union that was attempting to unionize a shop and to induce an employer to refrain from working in his business as a laborer.

Although the Court had been closely divided in the *Senn* case, three years later, in passing on a restrictive instead of a permissive state statute, the Court made sweeping pronouncements about the right to picket in holding unconstitutional a statute that had been applied to ban all picketing, with "no exceptions based upon either the number of persons engaged in the proscribed activity, the peaceful character of their demeanor, the nature of their dispute with an employer, or the restrained character and the accurateness of the terminology used in notifying the public of the facts of the dispute." Thornhill v. Alabama, 310 U.S. 88, 99. As the statute dealt at large with all picketing, so the Court broadly assimilated peaceful picketing in general to freedom of speech, and as such protected against abridgment by the Fourteenth Amendment.

These principles were applied by the Court in A. F. of L. v. Swing, 312 U.S. 321, to hold unconstitutional an injunction against peaceful picketing, based on a State's common-law policy against picketing when there was no immediate dispute between employer and employee. On the same day, however, the Court upheld a generalized injunction against picketing where there had been violence because "it could justifiably be concluded that the momentum of fear generated by past violence would survive even though future picketing might be wholly peaceful." Milk Wagon Drivers Union v. Meadowmoor Dairies, 312 U.S. 287, 294.

Soon, however, the Court came to realize that the broad pronouncements, but not the specific holding, of *Thornhill* had to yield "to the impact of facts unforeseen," or at least not sufficiently appreciated. Cases reached the Court in which a State had designed a remedy to meet a specific situation or to accomplish a particular social policy. These cases made manifest that picketing, even though "peaceful," involved more than just communication of ideas and could not be immune from all state regulation. "Picketing by an organized group is more than free speech, since it involves patrol of a particular locality and since the very presence of a picket line may induce action of one kind or another, quite irrespective of the nature of the ideas which are being disseminated." Bakery Drivers Local v. Wohl, 315 U.S. 769, 776 (concurring opinion); see Carpenters Union v. Ritter's Cafe, 315 U.S. 722, 725-728.

These latter two cases required the Court to review a choice made by two States between the competing interests of unions, employers, their employees, and the public at large. In the *Ritter's Cafe* case, Texas had enjoined as a violation of its antitrust law picketing of a restaurant by unions to bring pressure on its owner with respect to the use of nonunion labor by a contractor of the restaurant owner in the construction of a building having nothing to do with the restaurant. The Court held that Texas could, consistent with the Fourteenth Amendment, insulate from the dispute a neutral establishment that industrially had no connection with it. This type of picketing certainly involved little, if any, "communication."

In Bakery Drivers Local v. Wohl, 315 U.S. 769, in a very narrowly restricted decision, the Court held that because of the impossibility of otherwise publicizing a legitimate grievance and because of the slight effect on "strangers" to the dispute, a State could not constitutionally prohibit a union from picketing bakeries in its efforts to have independent peddlers, buying from bakers and selling to small stores, conform to certain union requests. Although the Court in *Ritter's Cafe* and *Wohl* did not question the holding of *Thornhill,* the strong reliance on the particular facts in each case demonstrated a growing awareness that these cases involved not so much questions of free speech as review of the balance struck by a State between picketing that involved more than "publicity" and competing interests of state policy. . . .

The implied reassessments of the broad language of the *Thornhill* case were finally generalized in a series of cases sustaining injunctions against peaceful picketing, even when arising in the course of a labor controversy, when such picketing was counter to valid state policy in a domain open to state regulation. The decisive reconsideration came in Giboney v. Empire Storage & Ice Co., 336 U.S. 490. A union, seeking to organize peddlers, picketed a wholesale dealer to induce it to refrain from selling to nonunion peddlers. The state courts, finding that such an agreement would constitute a conspiracy in restraint of trade in violation of the state antitrust laws, enjoined the picketing. This Court affirmed unanimously:

"It is contended that the injunction against picketing adjacent to Empire's place of business is an unconstitutional abridgment of free speech because the picketers were attempting peacefully to publicize truthful facts about a labor dispute. . . . . But the record here does not permit this publicizing to be treated in isolation. For according to the pleadings, the evidence, the findings, and the argument of the appellants, the sole immediate object of the publicizing adjacent to the premises of Empire, as well as the other activities of the appellants and their allies, was to compel Empire to agree to stop selling ice to nonunion peddlers. Thus all of appellants' activities . . . constituted a single and integrated course of conduct, which was in violation of Missouri's valid law. In this situation, the injunction did no more than enjoin an offense against Missouri law, a felony." Id., at 497-498.

The Court therefore concluded that it was "clear that appellants were doing more than exercising a right of free speech or press. . . . They were exercising their economic power together with that of their allies to compel Empire to abide by union rather than by state regulation of trade." Id., at 503.

The following Term, the Court decided a group of cases applying and elaborating on the theory of *Giboney*. In Hughes v. Superior Court, 339 U.S. 460, the Court held that the Fourteenth Amendment did not bar use of the injunction to prohibit picketing of a place of business solely to secure compliance with a demand that its employees be hired in percentage to the racial origin of its customers. "We cannot construe the Due Process Clause as precluding California from securing respect for its policy against involuntary employment on racial lines by prohibiting systematic picketing that would subvert such policy." Id., at 466. The Court also found it immaterial that the state policy had been expressed by the judiciary rather than by the legislature.

On the same day, the Court decided Teamsters Union v. Hanke, 339 U.S. 470, holding that a State was not restrained by the Fourteenth Amendment from enjoining picketing of a business, conducted by the owner himself without employees, in order to secure compliance with a demand to become a union shop. Although there was no one opinion for the Court, its decision was another instance of the affirmance of an injunction against picketing because directed against a valid public policy of the State.

A third case, Building Service Employees v. Gazzam, 339 U.S. 532, was decided the same day. Following an unsuccessful attempt at unionization of a small hotel and refusal by the owner to sign a contract with the union as bargaining agent, the union began to picket the hotel with signs stating that the owner was unfair to organized labor. The State, finding that the object of the picketing was in violation of its statutory policy against employer coercion of employees' choice of bargaining representative, enjoined picketing for such purpose. This Court affirmed, rejecting the argument that "the *Swing* case, supra, is controlling. . . . In that case this Court struck down the State's restraint of picketing based solely on the absence of an employer-employee relationship. An adequate basis for the instant decree is the unlawful objective of the picketing, namely, coercion by the employer of the employees' selection of a bargaining representative. Peaceful picketing for any lawful purpose is not prohibited by the decree under review." Id., at 539.

A similar problem was involved in Plumbers Union v. Graham, 345 U.S. 192, where a state court had enjoined, as a violation of its "Right to Work" law, picketing that advertised that nonunion men were being employed on a building job. This Court found that there was evidence in the record supporting a conclusion that a substantial purpose of the picketing was to put pressure on the general contractor to eliminate nonunion men from the job and, on the reasoning of the cases that we have just discussed, held that the injunction was not in conflict with the Fourteenth Amendment.

This series of cases, then, established a broad field in which a State, in enforcing some public policy, whether of its criminal or its civil law, and whether announced by its legislature or its courts, could constitutionally enjoin peaceful picketing aimed at preventing effectuation of that policy.

In the light of this background, the Maine Supreme Judicial Court in 1955 decided, on an agreed statement of facts, the case of Pappas v. Stacey, 151 Me. 36, 116 A.2d 497. From the statement, it appeared that three union employees went on strike and picketed a restaurant peacefully "for the sole purpose of seeking to organize other employees of the Plaintiff, ultimately to have the Plaintiff enter into collective bargaining and negotiations with the Union. . . ." Maine had a statute providing that workers should have full liberty of self-organization, free from restraint by employers or other persons. The Maine Supreme Judicial Court drew the inference from the agreed statement of facts that "there is a steady and exacting pressure upon the employer to interfere with the free choice of the employees in the matter of organization. To say that the picketing is not designed to bring about such action is to forget an obvious purpose of picketing — to cause economic loss to the business during noncompliance by the employees with the request of the union." 151 Me., at 42, 116 A.2d, at 500. It therefore enjoined the picketing, and an appeal was taken to this Court.

The whole series of cases discussed above allowing, as they did, wide discretion to a State in the formulation of domestic policy, and not involving a curtailment of free speech in its obvious and accepted scope, led this Court, without the need for further argument, to grant appellee's motion to dismiss the appeal in that it no longer presented a substantial federal question. 350 U.S. 870.

The *Stacey* case is this case. As in *Stacey,* the present case was tried without oral testimony. As in *Stacey,* the highest state court draw the inference from the facts that the picketing was to coerce the employer to put pressure on his employees to join the union, in violation of the declared policy of the State. (For a declaration of similar congressional policy, see §8 of the National Labor Relations Act.) The cases discussed above all hold that, consistent with the Fourteenth Amendment, a State may enjoin such conduct.

Of course, the mere fact that there is "picketing" does not automatically justify its restraint without an investigation into its conduct and purposes. State courts, no more than state legislatures, can enact blanket prohibitions against picketing. Thornhill v. Alabama and A. F. of L. v. Swing, supra. The series of cases following *Thornhill* and *Swing* demonstrate that the policy of Wisconsin enforced by the prohibition of this picketing is a valid one. In this case, the circumstances set forth in the opinion of the Wisconsin Supreme Court afford a rational basis for the inference it drew concerning the purpose of the picketing. No question was raised here concerning the breadth of the injunction, but of course its terms must be read in the light of the opinion of the Wisconsin Supreme Court, which justified it on the ground that the picketing was for the purpose of coercing the employer to coerce his employees. "If astuteness may discover argumentative excess in the scope of the [injunction] beyond what we constitutionally justify by this opinion, it will be open to petitioners to raise the matter, which they have not raised here, when the [case] on remand [reaches] the [Wisconsin] court." Teamsters Union v. Hanke, 339 U.S., at 480-481.

Therefore, having deemed it appropriate to elaborate on the issues in the case, we affirm.

Affirmed.[70]

Douglas, J., with whom Warren, C. J., and Black, J., concur, dissenting.

The Court has now come full circle. In Thornhill v. Alabama, 310 U.S. 88, 102, we struck down a state ban on picketing on the ground that "the dissemination of information concerning the facts of a labor dispute must be regarded as within that area of free discussion that is guaranteed by the Constitution." Less than one year later, we held that the First

[70] Whittaker, J., took no part in the decision.

Amendment protected organizational picketing on a factual record which cannot be distinguished from the one now before us. A. F. of L. v. Swing, 312 U.S. 321. Of course, we have always recognized that picketing has aspects which make it more than speech. Bakery Drivers Local v. Wohl, 315 U.S. 769, 776-777 (concurring opinion). That difference underlies our decision in Giboney v. Empire Storage & Ice Co., 336 U.S. 490. There, picketing was an essential part of "a single and integrated course of conduct, which was in violation of Missouri's valid law." Id., at 498. And see Labor Board v. Virginia Power Co., 314 U.S. 469, 477-478. We emphasized that "there was clear danger, imminent and immediate, that unless restrained, appellants would succeed in making [the state] policy a dead letter. . . . " 336 U.S., at 503. Speech there was enjoined because it was an inseparable part of conduct which the State constitutionally could and did regulate.

But where, as here, there is no rioting, no mass picketing, no violence, no disorder, no fisticuffs, no coercion — indeed nothing but speech — the principles announced in *Thornhill* and *Swing* should give the advocacy of one side of a dispute First Amendment protection.

The retreat began when, in Teamsters Union v. Hanke, 339 U.S. 470, four members of the Court announced that all picketing could be prohibited if a state court decided that that picketing violated the State's public policy. The retreat became a rout in Plumbers Union v. Graham, 345 U.S. 192. It was only the "purpose" of the picketing which was relevant. The state court's characterization of the picketers' "purpose" had been made well-nigh conclusive. Considerations of the proximity of picketing to conduct which the State could control or prevent were abandoned, and no longer was it necessary for the state court's decree to be narrowly drawn to proscribe a specific evil. Id., at 201-205 (dissenting opinion).

Today, the Court signs the formal surrender. State courts and state legislatures cannot fashion blanket prohibitions on all picketing. But, for practical purposes, the situation now is as it was when Senn v. Tile Layers Union, 301 U.S. 468, was decided. State courts and state legislatures are free to decide whether to permit or suppress any particular picket line for any reason other than a blanket policy against all picketing. I would adhere to the principle announced in *Thornhill.* I would adhere to the result reached in *Swing.* I would return to the test enunciated in *Giboney* — that this form of expression can be regulated or prohibited only to the extent that it forms an essential part of a course of conduct which the State can regulate or prohibit. I would reverse the judgment below.

Note

"Give me liberty or give me death." Is that an example of free speech? Suppose it were said by an official of the Pipefitters' Union on a construction jobsite and, as a result, 60 pipefitters walk off the job? How would the dissent in *Vogt* treat such a case?

We return to issues of constitutional protection of picketing in Chapter 3, in connection with secondary boycotts.

2. In Defense of Minority Picketing

Is there anything to be said for allowing organizational picketing? Certainly it can be argued that coercion is the very essence of such picketing: the attempt to bludgeon an employer and/or his or her employees to accept an unwanted union. The NLRB took precisely this position in 1957 when it held that picketing by a minority union (one not in fact representing a majority of the employer's employees) interfered with employees' §7 rights and thus violated §8(b)(1)(A). The Supreme Court reversed in NLRB v. Drivers Local 639 [Curtis Bros.], 362 U.S. 274 (1960). The Court held "that §8(b)(1)(A) is a grant of power to the Board limited to authority to proceed against union tactics involving violence, intimidation, and reprisal or threats thereof — conduct involving more that the general pressures upon persons employed by the affected employers implicit in economic strikes." The Court was not unmindful that a contrary decision would have largely mooted the detailed provisions of §8(b)(7), passed between the time of the Board's decision and the case reaching the Supreme Court.

But *Curtis Bros.* does not treat the fundamental inquiry: Shouldn't Congress outlaw minority picketing? Organizational picketing may be directed in part at the product market consumer, but the principal effect of many such picket lines (and the intended effect of the majority) is to persuade unionized employees of other employers to "honor" (refuse to cross) the line, thus preventing the employer sought to be organized from obtaining raw materials or delivering the finished product or service. It is to the advantage of these "honoring" employees to respect the picket line if they can expect reciprocity should their roles be reversed. Do any of the three models of unionization suggest a normative ground for permitting organizational picketing?

3. Section 8(b)(7): An Overview[71]

The next case begins with a treatise-style overview of §8(b)(7). It is helpful to read §8(b)(7) and §10(l) (authorizing district court injunctions) in the Statutory Appendix before carefully working your way through the Board's discussion. On the substantive issue involved in the

[71] See Dunau, Some Aspects of the Current Interpretation of Section 8(b)(7), 52 Geo. L.J. 220 (1964); Meltzer, Organizational Picketing and the NLRB: Five on a Seesaw, 30 U. Chi. L. Rev. 78 (1962).

case — whether §8(b)(7) prevents organizational picketing by a union that enjoyed the support of the majority of employees, which it then lost because of employer unfair labor practices — the Board's opinion is meant for future cases. The dispute between these parties has long since passed and no civil damage liability attaches to a violation of §8(b)(7).

HOD CARRIERS LOCAL 840 (BLINNE CONSTRUCTION CO.)

135 N.L.R.B. 1153 (1962)

[In 1961, the Board found that the respondent union in this case had violated §8(b)(7)(C). Subsequently, President Kennedy made new appointments to the Board and a motion for reconsideration was granted.]

Before proceeding to determine the application of §8(b)(7)(C) to the facts of the instant case, it is essential to note the interplay of the several subsections of §8(b)(7), of which subparagraph (C) is only a constituent part.

The section as a whole, as is apparent from its opening phrases, prescribes limitation only on picketing for an object of "recognition" or "bargaining" (both of which terms will hereinafter be subsumed under the single term "recognition") or for an object of organization. Picketing for other objects is not proscribed by this section. Moreover, not all picketing for recognition or organization is proscribed. A "currently certified" union may picket for recognition or organization of employees for whom it is certified. And even a union which is not certified is barred from recognition or organization picketing only in three general areas. The first area, defined in subparagraph (A) of §8(b)(7), relates to situations where another union has been lawfully recognized and a question concerning representation cannot appropriately be raised.[5] The second area, defined in subparagraph (B), relates to situations where, within the preceding 12 months, a "valid election" has been held.

The intent of subparagraphs (A) and (B) is fairly clear. Congress concluded that where a union has been lawfully recognized and a question concerning representation cannot appropriately be raised, or where the employees within the preceding 12 months have made known their views concerning representation, both the employer and employees are entitled to immunity from recognition or organization picketing for prescribed periods.

5. It will be noted, of course, that subparagraph (A) represents a substantial enlargement upon the prohibition already embodied in §8(b)(4)(C) of the Taft-Hartley Act, which merely insulates certified unions from proscribed "raiding" by rival labor organizations. Subparagraph (A) affords protection to lawfully recognized unions which do not have certified status and also incorporates, in effect, the Board's contract-bar rules relating to the existence of a question concerning representation.

Congress did not stop there, however. Deeply concerned with other abuses, most particularly "blackmail" picketing, Congress concluded that it would be salutary to impose even further limitations on picketing for recognition or organization. Accordingly, subparagraph (C) provides that even where such picketing is not barred by the provisions of (A) or (B) so that picketing for recognition or organization would otherwise be permissible, such picketing is limited to a reasonable period not to exceed 30 days unless a representation petition is filed prior to the expiration of that period.[7] Absent the filing of such a timely petition, continuation of the picketing beyond the reasonable period becomes an unfair labor practice. On the other hand, the filing of a timely petition stays the limitation and picketing may continue pending the processing of the petition. Even here, however, Congress by the addition of the first proviso to subparagraph (C) made it possible to foreshorten the period of permissible picketing by directing the holding of an expedited election pursuant to the representation petition.

The expedited election procedure is applicable, of course, only in a §8(b)(7)(C) proceeding, i.e., where an 8(b)(7)(C) unfair labor practice charge has been filed. Congress rejected efforts to amend the provisions of §9(c) of the Act so as to dispense generally with preelection hearings. Thus, in the absence of an 8(b)(7)(C) unfair labor practice charge, a union will not be enabled to obtain an expedited election by the mere device of engaging in recognition or organization picketing and filing a representation petition.[10] And on the other hand, a picketing union which files a representation petition pursuant to the mandate of §8(b)(7)(C) and to avoid its sanctions will not be propelled into an expedited election, which it may not desire, merely because it has filed such a petition. In both the above situations, the normal representation procedures are applicable; the showing of a substantial interest will be required, and the preelection hearing directed in §9(c)(1) will be held. . . .

Subparagraphs (B) and (C) serve different purposes. But it is especially significant to note their interrelationship. Congress was particularly concerned, even where picketing for recognition or organization was otherwise permissible, that the question concerning representation which gave rise to the picketing be resolved as quickly as possible. It was for this reason that is provided for the filing of a petition pursuant to which the Board could direct an expedited election in which the employees could freely indicate their desires as to representation. If, in the free exercise of their choice, they designate the picketing union as their bar-

7. Section 9(c) of the Act permits such a petition to be filed "by an employee or group of employees or any individual or labor organization acting in their behalf" or "by an employer."

10. [T]he Board has ruled . . . that a charge filed by a picketing union or a person "fronting" for it may not be utilized to invoke an expedited election.

gaining representative, that union will be certified and it will by the express terms of §8(b)(7) be exonerated from the strictures of that section. If, conversely, the employees reject the picketing union, that union will be barred from picketing for 12 months thereafter under the provisions of subparagraph (B).

The scheme which Congress thus devised represents what that legislative body deemed a practical accommodation between the right of a union to engage in legitimate picketing for recognition or organization and abuse of that right. One caveat must be noted in that regard. The congressional scheme is, perforce, based on the premise that the election to be conducted under the first proviso to subparagraph (C) represents the free and uncoerced choice of the employee electorate. Absent such a free and uncoerced choice, the underlying question concerning representation is not resolved and, more particularly, subparagraph (B) which turns on the holding of a "valid election" does not become operative.

There remains to be considered only the second proviso to subparagraph (C). In sum, that proviso removes the time limitation imposed upon, and preserves the legality of, recognition or organization picketing falling within the ambit of subparagraph (C), where that picketing merely advises the public that an employer does not employ members of, or have a contract with, a union unless an effect of such picketing is to halt pickups or deliveries, or the performance of services. Needless to add, picketing which meets the requirements of the proviso also renders the expedited election procedure inapplicable.

Except for the final clause in §8(b)(7) which provides that nothing in that section shall be construed to permit any act otherwise proscribed under §8(b) of the Act, the foregoing sums up the limitations imposed upon recognition or organization picketing by the Landrum-Griffin amendments. However, at the risk of laboring the obvious, it is important to note that structurally, as well as grammatically, subparagraphs (A), (B), and (C) are subordinate to and controlled by the opening phrases of §8(b)(7). In other words, the thrust of all the §8(b)(7) provisions is only upon picketing for an object of recognition or organization, and not upon picketing for other objects. Similarly, both structurally and grammatically, the two provisos in subparagraph (C) appertain only to the situation defined in the principal clause of that subparagraph.

Having outlined, in concededly broad strokes, the statutory framework of §8(b)(7) and particularly subparagraph (C) thereof, we may appropriately turn to a consideration of the instant case which presents issues going to the heart of that legislation.

The relevant facts may be briefly stated. On February 2, 1960, all three common laborers employed by Blinne at the Fort Leonard Wood jobsite signed cards designating the Union to represent them for purposes of collective bargaining. The next day the Union demanded that Blinne recognize the Union as the bargaining agent for the three laborers. Blinne not only refused recognition but told the Union it would transfer one of the laborers, Wann, in order to destroy the Union's majority. Blinne carried out this threat and transferred Wann 5 days later, on February 8. Following this refusal to recognize the Union and the transfer of Wann the Union started picketing at Fort Wood. The picketing, which began on February 8, immediately following the transfer of Wann, had three announced objectives: (1) recognition of the Union; (2) payment of the Davis-Bacon scale of wages; and (3) protest against Blinne's unfair labor practices in refusing to recognize the Union and in threatening to transfer and transferring Wann.

The picketing continued, with interruptions due to bad weather, until at least March 11, 1960, a period of more than 30 days from the date the picketing commenced.[15] The picketing was peaceful, only one picket was on duty, and the picket sign he carried read "C. A. Blinne Construction Company, unfair." The three laborers on the job (one was the replacement for Wann) struck when the picketing started.

The Union, of course, was not the certified bargaining representative of the employees. Moreover, no representation petition was filed during the more than 30 days in which picketing was taking place. On March 1, however, about 3 weeks after the picketing commenced and well within the statutory 30-day period, the Union filed unfair labor practice charges against Blinne, alleging violations of §§8(a)(1), (2), (3), and (5). On March 22, the Regional Director dismissed the §§8(a)(2) and (5) charges, whereupon the Union forthwith filed a representation petition under §9(c) of the Act.[16] Subsequently on April 20, the Regional Director approved a unilateral settlement agreement with Blinne with respect to the §§8(a)(1) and (3) charges which had not been dismissed. In the settlement agreement, Blinne neither admitted nor denied that it had committed unfair labor practices.[17]

General Counsel argues that a violation of §8(b)(7)(C) has occurred within the literal terms of that provision because (1) the Union's picketing was concededly for an object of obtaining recognition; (2) the Union was not currently certified as the representative of the employees involved; and (3) not petition for representation was filed within 30 days of the commencement of the picketing. Inasmuch as the Union made no contention that its recognition picketing was "informational" within the

15. Subsequently, on April 5, 1960, Judge Moore in the United States District Court for the Eastern District of Missouri, upon application of the Regional Director of the Board, entered a temporary injunction restraining further picketing.

16. As already noted, this was more than 30 days after the picketing commenced.

17. Although the transcript in these proceedings for obvious reasons makes no reference to the disposition of the representation petition filed by the Union on March 22, it is a matter of public record and known to the parties that the petition was dismissed on April 26, 1960, for the reason that "the unit sought appears to be inappropriate and is also expected to go out of existence within about four months."

meaning of the second proviso to subparagraph (C) or that it otherwise comported with the strictures of that proviso, General Counsel contends that a finding of unfair labor practice is required.

Respondent Union, for its part, points to the manifest inequity of such a finding and argues that Congress could not have intended so incongruous a result. In essence, its position is that it was entitled to recognition because it represented all the employees in the appropriate unit, that Blinne by a series of unfair labor practices deprived the Union and the employees it sought to represent of fundamental rights guaranteed by the Act, and that the impact of a finding adverse to the Union would be to punish the innocent and reward the wrongdoer. More specifically, Respondent argues that §8(b)(7)(C) was not intended to apply to picketing by a majority union and that, in any event, Blinne's unfair labor practices exonerated it from the statutory requirement of filing a timely representation petition.

The Trial Examiner found on the basis of the evidence in the record that the Union represented all the employees in what he "assumed" in the absence of adequate evidence to be an appropriate unit. He found further that Blinne "not only rejected the principle of collective bargaining but was willing to and did engage in further unfair labor practices to insure that his obligations under the statute would not be met." Notwithstanding that, in this frame of reference, "the equities . . . so obviously rest with the picketing union," the Trial Examiner "reluctantly" concluded that §8(b)(7) deprived employees of rights considered fundamental under other provisions of the Act. Accordingly, he found that Respondent Union had violated §8(b)(7)(C) of the Act and entered a cease-and-desist order framed in the language of that provision. . . .

As already noted, Respondent advances two major contentions. The first is that §8(b)(7)(C) does not apply to picketing by a majority union in an appropriate unit; the second is that employer unfair labor practices are a defense to a charge of an 8(b)(7) violation. We deal with the contentions in that order.

A. The Contention That §8(b)(7)(C) Does Not Proscribe Picketing for Recognition or Organization by a Majority Union

Respondent, urging the self-evident proposition that a statute should be read as a whole, argues that §8(b)(7)(C) was not designed to prohibit picketing for recognition by a union enjoying majority status in an appropriate unit. Such picketing is for a lawful purpose inasmuch as §§8(a)(5) and 9(a) of the Act specifically impose upon an employer the duty to recognize and bargain with a union which enjoys that status. Accordingly, Respondent contends, absent express language requiring such a result, §8(b)(7)(C) should not be read in derogation of the duty so imposed.

There is grave doubt that the argument here made is apposite in this case.[18] But, assuming its relevance, we find it to be without merit. To be sure, the legislative history is replete with references that Congress in framing the 1959 amendments was primarily concerned with "blackmail" picketing where the picketing union represented none or few of the employees whose allegiance it sought. Legislative references susceptible to an interpretation that Congress was concerned with the evils of majority picketing are sparse. Yet it cannot be gainsaid that §8(b)(7) by its explicit language exempts only "currently certified unions" from its proscriptions. Cautious as we should be to avoid a mechanical reading of statutory terms in involved legislative enactments, it is difficult to avoid giving the quoted words, essentially words of art, their natural construction. Moreover, such a construction is consonant with the underlying statutory scheme which is to resolve disputed issues of majority status, whenever possible, by the machinery of a Board election. Absent unfair labor practices or preelection misconduct warranting the setting aside of the election, majority unions will presumably not be prejudiced by such resolution. On the other hand, the admitted difficulties of determining majority status without such an election are obviated by this construction.

Congress was presumably aware of these considerations. In any event, there would seem to be here no valid considerations requiring that Congress be assumed to have intended a broader exemption that the one it actually afforded.

B. The Contention That Employer Unfair Labor Practices Are a Defense to a Charge of a §8(b)(7)(C) Violation

We turn now to the second issue, namely, whether employer unfair labor practices are a defense to an §8(b)(7)(C) violation. As set forth in the original Decision and Order, the Union argues that Blinne was engaged in unfair labor practices within the meaning of §§8(a)(1) and (3) of the Act; that it filed appropriate unfair labor practice charges against Blinne within a reasonable period of time after the commencement of the picketing; that it filed a representation petition as soon as the §§8(a)(2) and (5) allegations of the charges were dismissed; that the §§8(a)(1) and (3) allegations were in effect sustained and a settlement agreement was subsequently entered into with the approval of the Board; and that, therefore, this sequence of events should satisfy the requirements of §8(b)(7)(C).

18. The argument here is based, as it must be, on the premise that Respondent not only represented a majority of the employees but that this majority status was in an appropriate unit. The latter proposition is by no means established. The Trial Examiner "assumed" the existence of an appropriate unit for purposes of his analysis. The dismissal of the 8(a)(5) charge and, particularly, the subsequent dismissal of the representation petition and the reason given therefor tend to invalidate his assumption.

The majority of the Board in the original Decision and Order rejected this argument. Pointing out that the representation petition was concededly filed more than 30 days after the commencement of the picketing, the majority concluded that the clear terms of §8(b)(7)(C) had been violated.

The majority also addressed itself specifically to the Union's contention that §8(b)(7)(C) could not have been intended by Congress to apply where an employer unfair labor practice had occurred. Its opinion alludes to the fact that the then Senator, now President, Kennedy had proposed statutory language to the effect that any employer unfair labor practice would be a defense to a charge of an §8(b)(7) violation both with respect to an application to the courts for a temporary restraining order and with respect to the unfair labor practice proceeding itself. The majority noted that the Congress did not adopt this proposal but instead limited itself merely to the insertion of a proviso in §10(1) prohibiting the application for a restraining order under §8(b)(7)(C) if there was reason to believe that a §8(a)(2) violation existed. Accordingly, the majority concluded that Congress had specifically rejected the very contention which Respondent urged.

The dissenting member in the original Decision and Order took sharp issue with the majority. In his view, the majority failed to "look to the provisions of the whole law and its object and policy." Conceding that §8(b)(7)(C) in terms outlawed recognition picketing for more than 30 days unless a representation petition was filed, he emphasized that the cited section also provided for an expedited election if such a petition was filed. The purpose of the election is to obtain a free and uncoerced expression of the employees' desires as to their representation. Where unfair labor practices have taken place, however, such a free and uncoerced expression is precluded and the filing of a representation petition would be a futility. Indeed, consistent Board practice, presumably known to Congress, is to stay representation proceedings and elections thereunder until the effect of existing unremedied unfair labor practices is dissipated. Accordingly, the dissenting member concluded that the failure of a picketing union to file a timely petition in the face of employer unfair labor practices should not be made the basis for a finding of a violation under §8(b)(7)(C) of the Act.

The dissenting opinion likewise did not find the majority's reliance upon the proviso to §10(1) persuasive. On the basis of the relevant legislative history, the dissent concluded that this proviso was intended merely to implement §8(b)(7)(A) of the Act, that is, to insure that a union which was the beneficiary of a "sweetheart agreement" with an employer could not derive the benefit of injunctive relief that would otherwise be accorded by virtue of the provisions of subparagraph (A).

In retrospect, both the majority and dissenting opinions are not without logic or respectable foundation. Certainly, the narrow proviso embodied in §10(1), and the failure to embrace a proposal that would exempt recognition and organization picketing from the §8(b)(7)(C) bar where employer unfair labor practices had been committed, suggest that Congress was reluctant to grant such an exemption. Conversely, as the dissenting opinion argues, to hold that employer unfair labor practices sufficient to affect the results of an election are irrelevant in an §8(b)(7)(C) context seems incongruous and inconsistent with the overall scheme of the Act.

Fortified by the advantages of hindsight and added deliberation as to the ramifications of the majority and minority opinions, we are now of the view that neither opinion affords a complete answer to the question here presented. It seems fair to say that Congress was unwilling to write an exemption into §8(b)(7)(C) dispensing with the necessity for filing a representation petition wherever employer unfair labor practices were alleged. . . . On the other hand, it strains credulity to believe that Congress proposed to make the rights of union and employees turn upon the results of an election which, because of the existence of unremedied unfair labor practices, is unlikely to reflect the true wishes of the employees. . . .

The facts of the instant case may be utilized to demonstrate the practical operation of the legislative scheme. Here the union had filed unfair labor practice charges alleging violations by the employer of §§8(a)(1), (2), (3), and (5) of the Act. General Counsel found the allegations of §8(a)(2) and (5) violations groundless. Hence had these allegations stood alone and had a timely petition been on file, an election could have been directed forthwith and the underlying question concerning representation out of which the picketing arose could have been resolved pursuant to the statutory scheme. The failure to file a timely petition frustrated that scheme.[24]

24. We would, however, have had a much different case here if the §8(a)(5) charge had been found meritorious so as to warrant issuance of a complaint. A representation petition assumes an unresolved question concerning representation. A §8(a)(5) charge, on the other had, presupposes that no such question exists and that the employer is wrongfully refusing to recognize or bargain with a statutory bargaining representative. Because of this basic inconsistency, the Board has over the years uniformly refused to entertain representation petitions where a meritorious charge of refusal to bargain has been filed and, indeed, has dismissed any representation petition which may already have been on file. The same considerations apply where a meritorious §8(a)(5) charge is filed in a §8(b)(7)(C) context. Congressional acquiescence in the Board's long-standing practice prior to the enactment of §8(b)(7)(C) imports, in our view, congressional approval of a continuation of that practice thereafter. Cf. Gullett Gin Co. v. NLRB, 340 U.S. 361, 366. Accordingly, where a meritorious 8(a)(5) charge was filed in an 8(b)(7)(C) situation, the Board dismissed the representation petition. See Robert P. Scott, Inc. v. Rothman, 46 L.R.R.M. 2793 (D.C.D.C.); Colony Materials, Inc. v. Rothman, 46 L.R.R.M. 2794 (D.C.D.C.). So here, if a meritorious §8(a)(5) charge had been filed, a petition for representation would not have been required.

But this situation, as we have already demonstrated, is not presented in the instant case and is footnoted here only to mark the boundaries of our holding in the situation which is presented. It is regrettable, therefore, that in respect to the only substantive matter discussed in their separate opinion our respected colleagues, Members Rodgers and Leedom, have focused their attention upon this fringe issue. Nevertheless, they do not persuade us even in this regard. We assert, to be sure, that the filing of a representation petition will not

On the other hand, the §§8(a)(1) and (3) charges were found meritorious. Under these circumstances, and again consistent with uniform practice, no election would have been directed notwithstanding the currency of a timely petition; the petition would be held in abeyance pending a satisfactory resolution of the unfair labor practice charges.[25] The aggrieved union's right to picket would not be abated in the interim and the sole prejudice to the employer would be the delay engendered by its own unfair labor practices.[26] The absence of a timely petition, however, precludes disposition of the underlying question concerning representation which thus remains unresolved even after the §§8(a)(1) and (3) charges are satisfactorily disposed of. Accordingly, to condone the refusal to file a timely petition in such situations would be to condone the flouting of a legislative judgment. Moreover, and most important, to impose a lesser requirement would fly in the face of the public interest which promoted that judgment.

Conclusion

Because we read §8(b)(7)(C) as requiring in the instant case the filing of a timely petition and because such a petition was admittedly not filed until more than 30 days after the commencement of the picketing, we find that Respondent violated §8(b)(7)(C) of the Act. As previously noted, it is undisputed that "an object" of the picketing was for recognition. It affords Respondent no comfort that its picketing was also in protest against the discriminatory transfer of an employee and against payment of wages at a rate lower than that prescribed by law. Had Respondent confined its picketing to these objectives rather than, as it did, include a demand for recognition, we believe none of the provisions of §8(b)(7) would be applicable.[29] Under the circumstances here, however, §8(b)(7)(C) is applicable.

---

be required of a union when it has filed a meritorious §8(a)(5) charge, but will be required where it has filed other §8(a) charges. The point of the distinction — a point which our colleagues inexplicably ignore — is simply this: a meritorious §8(a)(5) case moots the question concerning representation which the petition is designed to resolve; other 8(a) charges merely delay the time when that unresolved question can be submitting to a free election by the employees. Indeed, our colleagues concede . . . that a §8(a)(5) charge, found meritorious after investigation, dictates a dismissal of a pending representation petition, and, hence, on their own analysis, to require the union to file a petition in such circumstances is to require the union to perform a futile act.

25. The Board's practice of declining to entertain, or dismissing, representation petitions does not apply to situations involving unlawful interference or unlawful discrimination. The inconsistency latent in the refusal-to-bargain situation is not present in the latter situations and uniform practice has been merely to hold such petitions in abeyance.

26. To be sure, we would not permit a union to benefit by itself committing unfair labor practices to delay the holding of an election and thereby stay the sanctions of §8(b)(7).

29. As noted at the outset, §8(b)(7) is directed only at recognition and organization picketing and not at picketing for other objects including so-called protest picketing

Accordingly, having concluded as in the original decision herein that a violation of §8(b)(7)(C) has occurred, albeit for differing reasons, we reaffirm the Order entered therein.[72]

Notes

1. Section 8(b)(7) prohibits only picketing and threats to picket. It does not prohibit strikes or forms of publicity other than picketing. Occasionally a case will raise the issue of whether the union's activity is picketing. The Board has held, for example, that when union protesters put their signs in a snow bank next to the employer's premises and watched from the warmth of their cars, emerging to answer questions about the signs and speak to delivery drivers, they engaged in picketing.[73] The board has reasoned that some sort of confrontation between the union protesters and the targets of their appeal is necessary to constitute picketing. Thus the posting of a sign on a pole with the union picketers watching from a nearby house may or may not be picketing,

---

against unfair labor practices. There is ample legislative history to substantiate the proposition that Congress did not intend to outlaw picketing against unfair labor practices as such. See, for example, 105 Daily Cong. Rec. 5756, 5766, 15121, 15907, 16400, 16541; 2 Legis. Hist. 1361, 1384, 1429, 1714. Absent other evidence (such as is present in this case) of an organizational, recognition, or bargaining objective it is clear that Congress did not consider picketing against unfair labor practices as such to be also for proscribed objectives and, hence, outlawed. Parenthetically, it follows that a cease-and-desist order issued against picketing in violation of §8(b)(7) will enjoin only picketing for recognition, bargaining, or organization and will not be a bar to protest picketing against unfair labor practices.

We are aware that this analysis runs counter to what the majority of the Board had held in Lewis Food Company, 115 N.L.R.B. 890, namely, that a strike to compel reinstatement of a discharged employee was necessarily a strike to force or require the employer "to recognize and bargain" with the union as to such matter. Implicit in that holding was the broader proposition that any strike or picketing in support of a demand which could be made through the process of collective bargaining was a strike or picketing for recognition or bargaining. Included in this category, presumably, would be picketing against substandard wages or working conditions in a competing plant, or a strike in support of an economic demand at a bargaining table where neither recognition nor willingness to bargain are really in issue but ony the reluctance of the employer to grant the particular economic demand. Cf. *Cartage,* a companion case to the instant case and cited in footnote 3, which presents a closely related issue but in which a majority of the Board (Chairman McCulloch and Member Brown dissenting) voted to deny reconsideration. We might well concede that in the long view all union activity, including strikes and picketing, has the ultimate economic objective of organization and bargaining. But we deal here not with abstract economic ideology. Congress itself has drawn a sharp distinction between recognition and organization picketing and other forms of picketing, thereby recognizing, as we recognize, that a real distinction does exist. The *Lewis Food* issue and its ramifications are not crucial in this case. Moreover, the *Lewis Food* case itself has now been reversed in any event. Local 259, International Union United Automobile, etc. (Fanelli Ford Sales, Inc.), 133 N.L.R.B. 1468; see also Miratti's Inc., 132 N.L.R.B. 699.

[72] Members Rogers and Leedom dissented and Member Fanning concurred in part and dissented in part.

[73] See Teamsters Union 182 (Woodward Motors), 135 N.L.R.B. 851 (1962), enforced, 314 F.2d 53 (2d Cir. 1963).

depending on why the organizers are present. If by staying nearby they intend to have the same effect as they would if they stood with the sign, then they are picketing; but if their presence is only a necessary precaution to safeguard the sign, they are not picketing.[74] The Board has applied the following test:

The important feature of picketing appears to be the posting by a labor organization or by strikers of individuals at the approach to a place of business to accomplish a purpose which advances the cause of the union, such as keeping employees away from work or keeping customers from the employer's business.[75]

This test permits the Board to find picketing in the congregation of a group of union men for the purposes of protesting outside an employer's place of business even though the men carry no identifying signs.

The difficulty with the test is that it tends to obliterate a distinction between picketing and handbilling. In the *Stoltze* case the distribution of handbills was held to constitute picketing when it continued after unlawful placard picketing had stopped. But as we shall examine in greater detail when we study secondary boycotts, the distinction between picketing and handbilling is considered crucial for some purposes under the Act. Some would deem it improper for the Board to merge concepts of picketing and handbilling for §8(b)(7) purposes while drawing a significant distinction between the two in interpreting other provisions of §8(b).

2. The remedy for a §8(b)(7) violation is a §10(1) injunction (sought in federal district court by a regional director upon the filing of a charge deemed meritorious) and a cease and desist order (entered by the Board at the end of the unfair labor practice proceedings). The Act provides no damage remedy for a §8(b)(7) violation. However, employees picketing in violation of §8(b)(7) lose their §7 protection and can be discharged by their employer.[76] *Striking* for recognition does not occasion the loss of §7 protection.[77] Do you see why?

3. The period of 30 days described in §8(b)(7)(C) is a *maximum*. Factors that will shorten the period are violence and intimidation by the union, and severe economic damage to the employer.

4. Lest it escaped your notice in *Blinne* (see, e.g., n.10), there will be an expedited election pursuant to §8(b)(7)(C) only if the *employer* files the §8(b)(7) charge.

5. Suppose the union has engaged in organizational picketing, files a petition, and loses the election. The employer then discharges two em-

[74] See NLRB v. United Furniture Workers, 337 F.2d 936 (2d Cir. 1964).

[75] Lumber & Sawmill Workers Local 2797 (Stoltze Land & Lumber Co.), 156 N.L.R.B. 388, 394 (1965); also see Teamsters Local 688 (Levitz Furniture Co.), 205 N.L.R.B. 1131 (1973).

[76] Claremont Polychemical Corp., 196 N.L.R.B. 613 (1972).

[77] Ibid.

ployees who were active in the campaign. The picketing continues but now the signs protest the discriminatory discharges. Section 8(b)(7)(B) violation? See *Blinne,* n.29. Would it matter if the General Counsel refuses to go to complaint? Or if the General Counsel settles the case for reinstatement without back pay?

6. To better understand how §8(b)(7) works and the strategies involved, consider the following hypothetical case. The employer operates a factory that has four departments: shipping, production, maintenance, and sanitation. On June 1, the union begins picketing for recognition as the representative of the shipping department's employees. The employer's position (and the union knows it) is that the shipping department is an inappropriate bargaining unit; that is, only a unit of employees of all four departments would constitute an appropriate group for a Board election, in the employer's view.

The union's first option is to continue picketing without filing an election petition in the hope that the employer will succumb and recognize the union as the representative for the shipping unit. The employer has two responses. First, he or she can wait until picketing has continued for 30 days and then file a §8(b)(7)(C) charge. A §10(1) injunction will then issue and, unless the union files an election petition, that will be the end of the representation matter. Even if the union files a petition (remember, 30 days of picketing have passed), an injunction against the picketing will issue, and the employer can demand a full hearing on the appropriateness of the unit.

The unit question may be difficult, or the employer may engage in stalling tactics and the election will be delayed. And if the employer prevails on the unit issue, the union's petition will be dismissed. The employer's second option is to file a §8(b)(7)(C) charge within the first 30 days of picketing. The regional director will hold the charge in abeyance until either 30 days have passed (or a shorter period, if it constitutes a "reasonable period of time"), or until an election petition is filed. If the union files a petition, or if the employer himself files such a petition (and this is likely if the picketing is having a detrimental effect on the employer's business), an expedited election will be ordered and the §8(b)(7)(C) charge will be dismissed.

The union may decide to file an election petition during the first 30 days of picketing. In that event, the employer has two choices. He or she can tolerate the picketing while the normal pre-election Board procedures are exhausted, or else file a §8(b)(7)(C) charge. The effect of the charge will be the ordering of an expedited election, and the charge will be dismissed as that order is entered.

Thus for an expedited election, there must be recognitional picketing, an election petition, and a §8(b)(7)(C) charge filed by the employer. An expedited election means that there is not likely to be a pre-election hearing on the appropriateness of proposed bargaining units; and even if there is a hearing, it will be of an abbreviated sort, with no briefs filed.[78] The regional director will designate and election to be held *in the smallest appropriate unit that includes all the picketing employees.* The union will argue that the shipping department is an appropriate unit and should be so designated. The employer will argue for the designation of a plant-wide unit including all four departments — for in his or her view that is the smallest "appropriate" unit that includes the shipping department employees. If the union wins the election, it can continue picketing without fear of being enjoined. But if the union loses the election (and it is likely to if the plant-wide unit is designated), then the employer will file a §8(b)(7)(B) charge and the union's further recognitional picketing will be enjoined.

7. We saw in the Notes following the *Gissel* case (p. 269, supra) that when the Board entered a *Gissel*-type bargaining order, it at one time refused to find a §8(a)(5) violation (grounding the bargaining order instead on §§8(a)(1) and (3) violations). Thus a union, faced with pervasive employer unfair labor practices and concluding that a representation election would be fruitless, would only file §§8(a)(1) and (3) charges because the General Counsel would refuse to go to complaint on any accompanying §8(a)(5) charge. Presumably, then, recognitional picketing by the union would have violated §8(b)(7) on authority of *Blinne.* The Board's change in policy respecting the entry of §8(a)(5) bargaining orders should now preclude a finding that continued recognitional picketing violates §8(b)(7).

8. Should a union be able to obtain review of an adverse Board unit determination through the use of §8(b)(7)? Suppose the union engages in recognitional picketing and the employer files an election petition for a unit unacceptable to the union. If the regional director orders an election in the unit requested by the employer and the union loses the election but continues picketing, can the union litigate the adverse unit determination in the court of appeals on the ground that no §8(b)(7)(B) "valid election" precludes its picketing?[79]

NLRB v. IRON WORKERS LOCAL 103, 434 U.S. 335 (1978): Section 8(f) of the National Labor Relations Act permits construction industry firms and unions to enter into "prehire agreements." The firm agrees to recognize the union as the bargaining representative of its employees and to observe specified wages, hours, and working conditions, even though the union has not attained majority status. The firm is likely to

[78] Also, the union will not be required to demonstrate a showing of interest and the employer will not be required to produce an *Excelsior* list of employee names and addresses. The Board will not engage in pre-election review of the regional director's bargaining unit determinations and the like.

[79] One case supports such a contention. American Bread Co. v. NLRB, 411 F.2d 147 (6th Cir. 1969). Also see NLRB v. Teamsters Local 182, 314 F.2d 53 (2d Cir. 1963).

have no employees when it signs the agreement. This permits the firm to bid on "union only" construction jobs, and to have access to the union hiring hall.

In this case a construction industry local union signed a prehire agreement with the Higdon Construction Company. At about the same time, the Higdon Contracting Company was formed for the express purpose of doing construction work with nonunion labor. The union picketed a jobsite at which the Higdon Contracting Company was working, protesting that the prehire agreement had been violated. The Board found that the two Higdon companies were a single employer, but it also held that picketing to enforce a prehire agreement when the union had never attained majority status and when no election petition had been filed within a reasonable time violated §8(b)(7)(C). A court of appeals reversed, reasoning that the validity of a §8(f) prehire agreement carried with it the right to picket to enforce the agreement.

The Supreme Court reversed the court of appeals and held that the Board's rule was a reasonable construction of the statute. The effect of a prehire agreement is only to shield the signatory union and the firm against unfair labor practice liability, it does not shield the union from liability for recognitional picketing when the union pickets to enforce the agreement nor does it give rise to a duty to bargain by the firm. Three Justices dissented.

Note

In Dee Cee Floor Covering, Inc., 232 N.L.R.B. 421 (1977), union members had performed work under collective bargaining agreements between the union and Dee Cee. When that firm went out of business and was replaced by Dagin-Akrab Floor Coverings (a successor or an alter ego) the union signed a new agreement, identical to the contract with Dee Cee. A few months later, Dagin-Akrab was awarded a contract at Fort Riley, Kansas, which it planned to perform nonunion. Terms different than those set out in the bargaining agreement were unilaterally set by the company and the union filed a §8(a)(5) charge. The Board rejected the union's argument that, because it had represented a majority of Dee Cee's employees on prior sites, failure to follow the agreement violated the Act: "[T]he union must demonstrate its majority at each new jobsite in order to invoke the provisions of Section 8(a)(5). . . ." This result is criticized as being inconsistent with sound policy and Board precedent in Barr and Jacobson, The Enforceability of Construction Industry Prehire Agreements after *Higdon,* 3 Indus. Rel. L.J. 517 (1979).

The Board's General Counsel has taken the position that *Dee Cee* is applicable to representation relationships in the construction industry established through §8(f) procedures but not to those established through §9(a) procedures. If a union has established majority status under §9(a), the union becomes the representative at all sites "present and prospective without the need to reprove majority at each future site." Office of the General Counsel Memorandum 79-32, Guidelines for Handling Section 8(f) Cases (1979).

4. Section 8(b)(7): Publicity Picketing

In the next case the union pickets the employer hoping to secure recognition, but the picketing is directed at consumers and halts no deliveries. The employer argues that the recognitional intent brings the picketing within §8(b)(7), and the union relies on the publicity proviso of §8(b)(7)(C).

SMITLEY d/b/a CROWN CAFETERIA v. NLRB

327 F.2d 351 (9th Cir. 1964)

DUNIWAY, J. . . .

The findings of the Board as to the facts are not attacked. It found, in substance, that the unions picketed the cafeteria for more than thirty days before filing a representation petition under §9(c) of the Act, that an object of the picketing was to secure recognition, that the purpose of the picketing was truthfully to advise the public that petitioners employed non-union employees or had no contract with the unions, and that the picketing did not have the effect of inducing any stoppage of deliveries or services to the cafeteria by employees of any other employer. The matter was twice heard by the Board, which first concluded, by a majority of 3 to 2, that the picketing did violate the statute in question (130 N.L.R.B. 570), and then held, following a change in its membership, and by a majority of 3 to 2, that the picketing did not violate the statute (135 N.L.R.B. 1183). We conclude that the views of the Board, as stated after its second consideration of the matter, are correct, and that the statute has not been violated.

The Board states its interpretation of the section, including the proviso quoted above, as follows:

"Congress framed a general rule covering all organizational or recognitional picketing carried on for more than 30 days without the filing of a representation petition. Then, Congress excepted from that rule picketing which, although it had an organizational or recognitional objective, was addressed primarily to the public, was truthful in nature, and did not interfere to any significant extent with deliveries or the rendition of services by the employees of any other employer."

We think that this is the correct interpretation. It will be noted that subdivision (7) of subsection (b), section 8, quoted above, starts with the general prohibition of picketing "where an object thereof is forcing or requiring an employer to recognize or bargain with a labor organization" (This is often called recognitional picketing) ". . . or forcing or requiring the employees of an employer to accept or select such labor organization. . . ." (This is often called organizational picketing), ". . . unless such labor organization is currently certified as the representative of such employees: . . ." This is followed by three subparagraphs, (A) (B) and (C). Each begins with the same word, "where." (A) deals with the situation "where" the employer has lawfully recognized another labor organization and a question of representation cannot be raised under §9(c). (B) refers to the situation "where," within the preceding 12 months, a valid election under §9(c) has been conducted. (C), with which we are concerned, refers to a situation "where" there has been no petition for an election under §9(c) filed within a reasonable period of time, not to exceed thirty days, from the commencement of the picketing. Thus, §8(b)(7) does not purport to prohibit all picketing having the named "object" of recognitional or organizational picketing. It limits the prohibition of such picketing to three specific situations.

There are no exceptions or provisos in subparagraphs (A) and (B), which describe two of those situations. There are, however, two provisos in subparagraph (C). The first sets up a special procedure for an expedited election under §9(c). The second is the one with which we are concerned. It is an exception to the prohibition of "such picketing," i.e., recognitional or organizational picketing, being a proviso to a prohibition of such picketing "where" certain conditions exist. It can only mean, indeed, it says, that "such picketing," which otherwise falls within subparagraph (C), is not prohibited if it falls within the terms of the proviso. That proviso says that subparagraph (C) is not to be construed to prohibit "any picketing" for "the purpose" of truthfully advising the public (including consumers) that an employer does not employ members of, or have a contract with, a labor organization. To this exception there is an exception, stated in the last "unless" clause, namely, that "such picketing," i.e., picketing where "an object" is recognitional or organizational, but which has "the" excepting "purpose," would still be illegal if an effect were to induce any individual employee of other persons not to pick up, deliver, or transport any goods, or not to perform any services. Admittedly, the picketing here does not fall within the "unless" clause in the second proviso to subparagraph (C). It does, however, fall within the proviso, since it does have "the purpose" that brings it within the proviso. It also has "an object" that brings it within the first sentence of subsection (b) and the first clause of subdivision (7), and within the circumstances stated in the opening clause of subparagraph (C). If it did not have "an object" bringing it within subdivision (7), it would not be prohibited at all. Moreover, if it did have that "object," it still would not be prohibited at all, unless it occurred in circumstances described in subparagraph (A), (B) or (C). Here, neither (A) or (B) applies; (C) does. But, unlike (A) or (B), it has an excepting proviso. Unless that proviso refers to picketing having as "an object" either recognition or organization, it can have no meaning, for it would not be an exception or proviso to anything. It would be referring to conduct not prohibited in §8(b) at all.

Petitioners urge that if the picketing has as "an object" of recognition or organization, then it is still illegal, even though it has "the purpose" of truthfully advising the public, etc., within the meaning of the second proviso to subparagraph (C). It seems to us, as it did to the Board, that to so construe the statute would make the proviso meaningless. The hard realities of union-employer relations are such that it is difficult, indeed almost impossible, for us to conceive of picketing falling within the terms of the proviso that did not also have as "an object" obtaining a contract with the employer. This is normally the ultimate objective of any union in relation to an employer who has employees whose jobs fall within the categories of employment that are within the jurisdiction of the union, which is admittedly the situation here.

We note that the Court of Appeals for the Second Circuit has reached a similar conclusion. In NLRB v. Local 3, International Bhd. of Electrical Workers, 2 Cir., 1963, 317 F.2d 193, that court considered the section at some length, and said:

> It seems, however, much more realistic to suppose that Congress framed a general rule covering the field of recognitional and organizational picketing, conducted under alternate sets of circumstances described in subparagraphs (A), (B), and (C), and then excepted from the operation of the rule, as it applied to the circumstances set forth in subparagraph (C), a comparatively innocuous species of picketing having the immediate purpose of informing or advising the public, even though its ultimate object was success in recognition and organization. . . .
>
> One of the principal difficulties in construing and applying subparagraph (C) is that §8(b)(7) contains the partially synonymous words, 'object' and 'purpose,' used in two distinct contexts but to which much of the same evidence is relevant. These are: 'where an object thereof is forcing or requiring an employer to recognize or bargain . . .' and 'for the purpose of truthfully advising the public. . . .' It does not necessarily follow that, where an object of the picketing is forcing or requiring an employer to recognize or bargain, the purpose of the picketing, in the context of the second proviso, is not truthfully to advise the public, etc. The union may legitimately have a long range or strategic objective of getting the employer to bargain with or recognize the union and still the picketing may be permissive. This proviso gives the union freedom to appeal to the unorganized public for spontaneous popular pressure upon an employer; it is intended, however, to exclude the invocation of pressure by organized labor groups or members of unions, as such.

> The permissible picketing is, therefore, that which through the dissemination of certain allowed representations, is designed to influence members of the unorganized public, as individuals, because the impact upon the employer by way of such individuals is weaker, more indirect and less coercive.

We agree.

Both sides have reviewed legislative history. We think this unnecessary, because we think that the meaning of the statute is clear. We also find the history inconclusive, but it seems to us to point somewhat more strongly toward the view that we here adopt than to the contrary view. Petitioners rely on language used by Senator Kennedy, who was one of the sponsors of the bill in the Senate and one of the Senate Conferees, in which he referred to the second proviso as permitting "purely informational" picketing. Counsel for petitioners frankly conceded, however, at oral argument, that most of the legislative history is against the view that he urged, and we agree. A discussion of legislative history appears in the dissent to the Board's first opinion, (130 N.L.R.B. 576-77) and we therefore do not repeat it here. We think that even Senator Kennedy's comment, upon which petitioners most heavily rely, taken in context, was not intended to have the limiting effect which petitioners would give it. Senator Kennedy was more concerned, on the one hand, with the economic pressure involved in recognitional and organizational picketing, and on the other hand, with the right of labor truthfully to advise the public that the employer was non-union, or that the employer did not have a contract with the union, than he was with whether or not, in addition to having an informational purpose described in the proviso, there was also a recognitional or organizational object. See 105 Cong. Rec. 17898 (1959). See also Cox, The Landrum-Griffin Amendments to the National Labor Relations Act, 44 Minn. L. Rev. 258, 267. Mr. Cox, now the Solicitor General, was then Senator Kennedy's chief advisor on the bill.

We think that, in substance, the effect of the second proviso to subparagraph (C) is to allow recognitional or organizational picketing to continue if it meets two important restrictions: (1) it must be addressed to the public and be truthful and (2) it must not induce other unions to stop deliveries or services. The picketing here meet those criteria.

The petition is denied.

Notes

1. What do you understand to have been the employer's theory in *Crown Cafeteria?* On its theory when would the proviso protect union

picketing? How does the court's decision accord with the three models of unionization?

2. If the signs are couched in the language of the proviso to §8(b)(7)(C), should it matter that the union pickets both consumer and employee entrances?

3. Would the following sign fall within the proviso: "Notice to Members of Organized Labor and Their Friends — This Establishment Is Non-Union — Please Do Not Patronize"?[80]

4. One stopped delivery will not necessarily take the union's picketing out of the proviso. The Board has held that the interruptions or stoppages must have "disrupted, interfered with, or curtailed the employer's business."[81]

5. Area Standards Picketing[82]

HOUSTON BUILDING AND
CONSTRUCTION TRADES COUNCIL
(CLAUDE EVERETT CONSTRUCTION CO.)
136 N.L.R.B. 321 (1962)

. . . The facts as found by the Trial Examiner are not in dispute. The Respondent, a council of local unions in the building and construction industry in the Houston, Texas, area, inquired on March 8, 1961, about the wage rates of Claude Everett Construction Company, a general construction contractor in that area. The Respondent's representative was told by Wilson, the Company's construction superintendent, that it operated an "open shop," and that its wages rates were lower than those negotiated in the area by the local unions which were members of the Respondent. On March 10, 1961, the Respondent wrote to the Company protesting its "substandard" wages and threatening to picket its construction site on March 13, unless "prevailing" rates were paid. When this letter had not been answered by March 16, the Respondent began picketing the Company's jobsite with a sign which read as follows:

> Houston Building and Construction Trades Council, AFL-CIO protests substandard wages and conditions being paid on this job by Claude Everett Company. Houston Building and Construction Trade Council does not intend by this picket line to induce or encourage the employees of any other employer to engage in a strike or a concerted refusal to work.

Such picketing continued for more than 30 days without the filing of a petition under §9(c) of the Act. The Respondent has never been certi-

[80] It was the sign in *Crown Cafeteria.*

[81] Retail Clerks Local 324 (Barker Bros.), 138 N.L.R.B. 478 (1962), enforced, 328 F.2d 431 (9th Cir. 1964).

[82] See Rosen, Area Standards Picketing, 23 Lab. L.J. 67 (1972); Comment, 1968 Duke L.J. 767.

fied as the representative of the Company's employees. The parties stipulated at the hearing that the picketing interfered with deliveries and services by inducing individuals employed by suppliers, service companies, and common carriers not to make pickups or deliveries or to perform services for the Company.

The Trial Examiner found that the Respondent picketed the Company to require it to conform its wage rates to those paid by employers having union contracts. Relying on the original Board decision in the *Calumet Contractors* case,[2] he concluded that such picketing violated §8(b)(7)(C) of the Act. Subsequent to the issuance of his Intermediate Report, however, the Board, having reconsidered the *Calumet Contractors* case,[3] found the picketing there involved not unlawful, and stated that:

> . . . Respondent's admitted objective to require the Association . . . to conform standards of employment to those prevailing in the area, is not tantamount to, nor does it have an objective of, recognition or bargaining. A union may legitimately be concerned that a particular employer is undermining area standards of employment by maintaining lower standards. It may be willing to forgo recognition and bargaining provided subnormal working conditions are eliminated from area considerations.

While the *Calumet Contractors* case arose under §8(b)(4)(C) of the Act, which prohibits only recognitional picketing, whereas the instant case arose under §8(b)(7)(C), which proscribes both recognitional and organizational picketing, the language of both subsections is similar, and the rationale in that case is equally applicable herein. The Respondent in the present case did not, in its conversation with the Company, its letter to the Company, or its picket sign, claim to represent the Company's employees, request recognition by the Company, or solicit employees of the Company to become members of any of the locals which are members of the Respondent. Moreover, the undisputed testimony of Executive Secretary Graham reveals that the Respondent Union has on numerous occasions in the past made similar protests against substandard wages paid by other employers without ever requesting recognition as the bargaining representative of their employees. Thus, it is clear, from the entire record, that the objective of the Respondent's picketing was to induce the Company to raise its wage rates to the union scale prevailing in the area. We cannot, as do our dissenting colleagues, equate this attempt to maintain area wage standards with conduct "forcing or requiring an employer to recognize or bargain with a labor organization as the representative of his employees, or forcing or requiring the employ-

2. International Hod Carriers, Building and Common Laborers' Union of America, Local No. 41, AFL-CIO (Calumet Contractors Association), 130 N.L.R.B. 78.

3. International Hod Carriers, Building and Common Laborers' Union of America, Local No. 41, AFL-CIO (Calumet Contractors Association), 133 N.L.R.B. 512 (Members Rodgers and Leedom dissenting).

ees . . . to accept or select such labor organization as their collective bargaining representative," the conduct proscribed by §8(b)(7).

Nor do we agree with our dissenting colleagues that the fact that the picketing interfered with deliveries and services in itself constitutes a violation of §8(b)(7)(C). To determine the effect of §8(b)(7)(C), we must look at the section in its entirety, in accord with the long-established principle of statutory construction that a legislative enactment is to be read in its entirety, not in bits and pieces. It is clear that this section, read as a whole, declares picketing by an uncertified union unlawful if it has a recognitional or organizational objective and if a petition has not been filed within a reasonable time, and that the interruption-of-deliveries clause does not enter into the picture unless the picketing can first be shown to have such a prohibited objective. . . .

Our dissenting colleagues interpret the second proviso of subparagraph (C) as though it creates a completely independent unfair labor practice, without reference to the fact that it is a subsidiary clause in a section which initially prohibits picketing with a recognitional or organizational objective. Such a reading would remove the proviso from its statutory setting, an interpretive result we feel constrained to avoid.

Accordingly, on the basis of the facts in the present case and of "the thrust of all the §8(b)(7) provisions," we find that the Respondent's picketing did not have a recognitional or organizational objective, and, therefore, that it did not violate the Act even though the picketing interfered with deliveries and services. Accordingly, we shall dismiss the complaint.

Members Rodgers and Leedom, dissenting. . . .

We take exception to our colleagues' holding that picketing an employer in order to compel it to change wages and conditions of employment of its employees does not have as an objective recognition or organization. Their holding does not withstand scrutiny in the light of industrial realities.

As to whether there was a recognitional objective in the present case, it is undenied that the Respondent Union was demanding a change in the Company's wage rates to conform to standards in the area. The alternative open to the Company was either to suffer a picket line or to comply with the Respondent Union's demand. Our colleagues, however, choose to view the problem unrealistically. For, they fail to take into consideration either the extent to which the standards of the Respondent Union are applicable to the Company's operations, the complications attendant upon changing a wage pattern, or the many factors that determine the pattern. Otherwise, they would readily concede that any effort on the part of the Company to adjust the Respondent's wage demand to its circumstances would have necessitated negotiations; that such negotiations would constitute bargaining with the Respondent Union as though it were the representative of the Company's employees;

and that such recognition and bargaining would manifestly be the result of the Respondent forcing or requiring the Company by a picket line, to ". . . recognize or bargain with a labor organization as the representative of [its] employees . . ." in violation of §8(b)(7).

Nor can we lose sight of the organizational objective implicit in Respondent's picketing. We note further that the picket sign, after protesting the Company's "substandard wages and conditions," expressly disclaimed any intent of the Respondent that "the employees of any other employer" should engage in a work stoppage. The sign was silent as to the Respondent's intent with regard to the Company's employees. By dint of this omission, Respondent's real purpose is emphasized. For the Union was thereby calling upon the Company's employees to join with it in getting the Company to change its existing wage rates — clearly organizational and recognitional objectives.

Nor can the Respondent Union take refuge in the proviso to §8(b)(7)(C) to protect its recognitional or organizational picketing. In this regard, it is obvious that the picketing did not conform to the language of the proviso and the Respondent Union makes no claim to the contrary.

Moreover, we would find that the Respondent, in effect, admitted a violation of §8(b)(7)(C) when it stipulated that its picketing interrupted the Company's deliveries and services. In our separate opinion upon reconsideration of the *Stork Restaurant*[10] case, we pointed out why it is consistent with the statute to hold that so-called informational picketing violates the Act when it interrupts deliveries or services. Accordingly, even assuming that we have here informational picketing within the intendment of the proviso, there was a violation of §8(b)(7)(C) because of the admitted interruption in the Company's deliveries and services.

Notes

1. The disagreement between the majority and the dissent is obvious, but is the ground for decision as obvious? Does the case turn on a technical statutory interpretation, the intent of the union officials planning the picket line, the practical effect on the employer, a choice of economic models, or some other standard?

2. Two arguments for deeming all area standards picketing to have a recognitional purpose are: (a) since the "area standards" are meant to be union standards, and the union sets them, this is a form of recognition," and (b) since there are advantages to an employer being unionized (in the construction industry, for example, some general contractors will subcontract only to unionized subcontractors), an employer pressured to

10. Chefs, Cooks, Pastry Cooks and Assistants, Local 89, etc. (Stork Restaurant, Inc.), 135 N.L.R.B. 1173 (Members Rogers and Leedom dissenting).

pay union wages will have a natural tendency to sign a union bargaining agreement.

3. In addition to wage rates, fringe benefits — such as pension and health and welfare contributions, travel pay, overtime and show-up time guarantees, holiday pay and the like — constitute significant parts of a union's economic package. How many of these can the union seek by area standards picketing? Surely it cannot seek the union's standard area collective bargaining agreement, presumably with the recognition clause and union-run grievance and arbitration clauses stricken, for that would be deemed recognitional. Yet striking out other clauses is likely to put the unionized employers at a competitive disadvantage. That is a dilemma of area standards picketing.

4. The Board will look at several factors to see if picketing defended as area standards actually has a recognitional purpose. These include:

a. the timing of the announcement of objective (i.e., an earlier demand for recognition hurts the union);
b. the nature of the contacts with the employer and the employees;
c. whether the employer is in fact substandard and the union knows it; and
d. correct language on the signs.

This is not a balancing test; any slip by the union is likely to be fatal.

Suppose that at the same time the union is engaged in area standards picketing at the employer's place of business, it places an advertisement in the paper informing the public that the employer does not employ the union's members. Is the picketing lawful? See IBEW, Local 453 (Southern Sun Elec. Corp.), 252 N.L.R.B. 719 (1980).

5. A union tells its lawyer that it seeks to organize an employer, but has little support from the employees and fears picketing will be enjoined by the Board. Is it ethical for the lawyer to advise the union how to set up an area standards picket?

I. LOSS OF REPRESENTATIVE STATUS[83]

BROOKS v. NLRB
348 U.S. 96 (1954)

FRANKFURTER, J.

The National Labor Relations Board conducted a representation election in petitioner's Chrysler-Plymouth agency on April 12, 1951. District

[83] See Ray, Withdrawal of Recognition from an Incumbent Union under the National Labor Relations Act: An Appraisal, 28 Vill. L. Rev. 868 (1983).

Lodge No. 727, International Association of Machinists, won by a vote of eight to five, and the Labor Board certified it as the exclusive bargaining representative on April 20. A week after the election and the day before the certification, petitioner received a handwritten letter signed by 9 of the 13 employees in the bargaining unit stating: "We, the undersigned majority of the employees . . . are not in favor of being represented by Union Local No. 727 as a bargaining agent."

Relying on this letter . . . . , petitioner refused to bargain with the union. The Labor Board found that petitioner had thereby committed an unfair labor practice in violation of §§8(a)(1) and 8(a)(5) of the amended National Labor Relations Act. . . .

The issue before us is the duty of an employer toward a duly certified bargaining agent if, shortly after the election which resulted in the certification, the union has lost, without the employer's fault, a majority of the employees from its membership.

Under the original Wagner Act, the Labor Board was given the power to certify a union as the exclusive representative of the employees in a bargaining unit when it had determined by election or "any other suitable method," that the union commanded majority support. §9(c). In exercising this authority the Board evolved a number of working rules, of which the following are relevant to our purpose:

(a) A certification, if based on a Board-conducted election, must be honored for a "reasonable" period, ordinarily "one year," in the absence of "unusual circumstances."

(b) "Unusual circumstances" were found in at least three situations: (1) the certified union dissolved or became defunct; (2) as a result of a schism, substantially all the members and officers of the certified union transferred their affiliation to a new local or international; (3) the size of the bargaining unit fluctuated radically within a short time.

(c) Loss of majority support after the "reasonable" period could be questioned in two ways: (1) employer's refusal to bargain, or (2) petition by a rival union for a new election.

(d) If the initial election resulted in a majority for "no union," the election — unlike a certification — did not bar a second election within a year.

The Board uniformly found an unfair labor practice where, during the so-called "certification year," an employer refused to bargain on the ground that the certified union no longer possessed a majority. While the courts in the main enforced the Board's decisions, they did not commit themselves to one year as the determinate content of reasonableness. The Board and the courts proceeded along this line of reasoning:

(a) In the political and business spheres, the choice of the voters in an election binds them for a fixed time. This promotes a sense of responsibility in the electorate and needed coherence in administration. These considerations are equally relevant to healthy labor relations.

(b) Since an election is a solemn and costly occasion, conducted under safeguards to voluntary choice, revocation of authority should occur by a procedure no less solemn than that of the initial designation. A petition or a public meeting — in which those voting for and against unionism are disclosed to management, and in which the influences of mass psychology are present — is not comparable to the privacy and independence of the voting booth.

(c) A union should be given ample time for carrying out its mandate on behalf of its members, and should not be under exigent pressure to produce hothouse results or be turned out.

(d) It is scarcely conducive to bargaining in good faith for an employer to know that, if he dillydallies or subtly undermines, union strength may erode and thereby relieve him of his statutory duties at any time, while if he works conscientiously toward agreement, the rank and file may, at the last moment, repudiate their agent.

(e) In situations, not wholly rare, where unions are competing, raiding and strife will be minimized if elections are not at the hazard of informal and short-term recall.

Certain aspects of the Labor Board's representation procedures came under scrutiny in the Congress that enacted the Taft-Hartley Act in 1947. Congress was mindful that, once employees had chosen a union, they could not vote to revoke its authority and refrain from union activities, while if they voted against having a union in the first place, the union could begin at once to agitate for a new election. The National Labor Relations Act was amended to provide that (a) employees could petition the Board for a decertification election, at which they would have an opportunity to choose no longer to be represented by a union [§9(c)(1)(A)(ii)]; (b) an employer, if in doubt as to the majority claimed by a union without formal election or beset by the conflicting claims of rival unions, could likewise petition the Board for an election [§9(c)(1)(B)]; (c) after a valid certification or decertification election had been conducted, the Board could not hold a second election in the same bargaining unit until a year had elapsed [§9(c)(3)]; (d) Board certification could only be granted as the result of an election [§9(c)(1)], though an employer would presumably still be under a duty to bargain with an uncertified union that had a clear majority.

The Board continued to apply its "one-year certification" rule after the Taft-Hartley Act came into force, except that even "unusual circumstances" no longer left the Board free to order an election where one had taken place within the preceding 12 months. Conflicting views became manifest in the Courts of Appeals when the Board sought to enforce orders based on refusal to bargain in violation of its rule. Some Circuits sanctioned the Board's position. The Court of Appeals for the Sixth Circuit denied enforcement. The Court of Appeals for the Third Circuit held that a "reasonable" period depended on the facts of the particular case. . . .

Petitioner contends that whenever an employer is presented with evidence that his employees have deserted their certified union, he may forthwith refuse to bargain. In effect, he seeks to vindicate the rights of his employees to select their bargaining representative. If the employees are dissatisfied with their chosen union, they may submit their own grievance to the Board. If an employer has doubts about his duty to continue bargaining, it is his responsibility to petition the Board for relief, while continuing to bargain in good faith at least until the Board has given some indication that his claim has merit. Although the Board may, if the facts warrant, revoke a certification or agree not to pursue a charge of an unfair labor practice, these are matters for the Board; they do not justify employer self-help or judicial intervention. The underlying purpose of this statute is industrial peace. To allow employers to rely on employee's right in refusing to bargain with the formally designated union is not conducive to that end, it is inimical to it. Congress has devised a formal mode for selection and rejection of bargaining agents and has fixed the spacing of elections, with a view of furthering industrial stability and with due regard to administrative prudence.

We find wanting the arguments against these controlling considerations. In placing a nonconsenting minority under the bargaining responsibility of an agency selected by a majority of the workers, Congress has discarded common-law doctrines of agency. It is contended that since a bargaining agency may be ascertained by methods less formal than a supervised election, informal repudiation should also be sanctioned where decertification by another election is precluded. This is to make situations that are different appear the same. Finally, it is not within the power of this court to require the Board, as is suggested, to relieve a small employer, like the one involved in this case, of the duty that may be exacted from an enterprise with many employees.

To be sure, what we have said has special pertinence only to the period during which a second election is impossible. But the Board's view that the one-year period should run from the date of certification rather than the date of election seems within the allowable area of the Board's discretion in carrying out congressional policy. Otherwise, encouragement would be given to management or a rival union to delay certification by spurious objections to the conduct of an election and thereby diminish the duration of the duty to bargain. Furthermore, the Board has ruled that one year after certification the employer can ask for an election or, if he has fair doubts about the union's continuing majority, he may refuse to bargain further with it. This, too, is a matter appropriately determined by the Board's administrative authority. . . .

Affirmed.

Notes

1. Where the employer recognizes the union without an election, there is no certification. The Board will preclude a petition in that circumstance only "for a reasonable period," often less than a year.[84]

2. Section 9(c)(1) of the NLRA permits an employee, group of employees, or an individual or union acting on their behalf to file a petition for a decertification election. For there to be such an election, a union must be currently certified or recognized by the employer and the petitioner must produce a showing that 30 percent or more of the current employees support decertification. Partial decertifications are not permitted; the election will be held in the incumbent union's bargaining unit. An employer is not permitted to file a decertification petition and commits a §8(a)(1) violation if he or she instigates or assists a decertification petition.

3. The employer who doubts the current majority status of an incumbent union is not without recourse, however. Section 9(c)(1)(B) permits an employer to file an election petition when presented with a claim for recognition. This includes a claim for continued recognition by an incumbent union. Fearing that an unrestricted right to demand an election would force incumbent unions to elections at the end of every bargaining agreement, disrupting the bargaining process, the Board held in U.S. Gypsum Co., 157 N.L.R.B. 652 (1966).

> [I]n petitioning the Board for an election to question the continued majority of a previously certified incumbent union, an employer, in addition to showing the union's claim for continued recognition, must demonstrate by objective considerations that it has some reasonable grounds for believing that the union has lost its majority status since its certification.

Absent such a showing, the employer's petition will be dismissed. The regional director will determine the adequacy of the showing and it will not be litigable by the union.

The employer's other option upon doubting the incumbent union's current majority is to refuse to bargain with the union. Whether the employer commits a §8(a)(5) violation by such a refusal produced disagreement among the Board members in Stoner Rubber Co., 123 N.L.R.B. 1440 (1959). There the employer had both refused to bargain with the union and instituted unilateral economic changes. Two Board members reasoned that after the certification year expired the union enjoyed only a presumption of continued majority status. The burden of

[84] In Brennan's Cadillac, 231 N.L.R.B. 225 (1977), for example, the employer voluntarily recognized the union, negotiations broke down, and some employees withdrew from the union. The Board held, 3-2, that the employer could refuse further recognition of the union even though only five months had elapsed.

proof is initially on the employer to "produce sufficient evidence to cast serious doubt on the union's continued majority status." If the employer carried his or her burden, it is then up to the General Counsel to prove that as of the refusal to bargain date the union in fact represented a majority of the employees.

Another Board member would not find employer unilateral action to constitute a violation so long as he or she demonstrates a good faith doubt of the union's majority status. The final two Board members would permit an employer to withdraw recognition if he or she entertains a good faith doubt of the union's majority status, but they would find a violation when unilateral action is taken before the union has "an opportunity to protect its established position and reaffirm its statutory entitlement to recognition." Such unilateral action would itself tend to undercut the union's majority status.

It is now clear that in the refusal to bargain case, as in the §9(c)(1)(B) case, the employer's good faith doubt must be based on objective considerations.[85] Also, an employer will not be permitted to rely on a loss of majority caused by his or her own unfair labor practices. To establish a "good faith doubt based on objective considerations" employers have sometimes relied upon declines in union dues-payers, high employee turnover, polls of the employees, rumors of employee dissatisfaction, sudden changes in union bargaining posture, and failure of the union to communicate with the employer over a period of time. They have not always been successful.

There appears to be disagreement among the circuits[86] on whether the employer's refusal to bargain should be found to have violated §8(a)(5) when the employer establishes a good faith doubt of the union's majority status but the General Counsel proves the union, in fact, enjoyed a majority. The Board's present view is that if the employer established a reasonably based doubt, the union's actual majority status is irrelevant.[87]

Since the Board, with Supreme Court approval in *Gissel,* no longer inquires into an employer's good faith when the employer refuses to recognize a nonincumbent union, should the rules respecting withdrawal of recognition or election petitions to challenge an incumbent's majority status be changed to reflect this new policy, or are these fundamentally different situations?

4. *Problem.* The Office Employees Union had exclusive bargaining rights for the 60 employees at Westwood Import Company's facility in

[85] Terrell Machine Co., 173 N.L.R.B. 1480 (1969). The same presumption is accorded when a union has been recognized voluntarily and a "reasonable period" has passed.

[86] Compare NLRB v. Dayton Motels, Inc., 474 F.2d 328 (6th Cir. 1973) with Automated Business Systems v. NLRB, 497 F.2d 262 (6th Cir. 1974).

[87] Arkay Packaging Corp., 227 N.L.R.B. 397 (1976), petition for review denied, 575 F.2d 1045 (2d Cir. 1978).

San Francisco. Westwood then moved its facility to Hayward, California for economic reasons. Hayward is about 35 miles from San Francisco. Operations and equipment are substantially the same at the new location as they were at the old location. Twenty-four employees from the San Francisco location transferred to the Haywood location, where they now constitute 40 percent of Westwood's work force. Westwood has refused to recognize the union at the Hayward facility, claiming a good faith doubt as to the union's majority status. Has Westwood violated §8(a)(5)? Would it matter whether a collective bargaining agreement was in effect at the San Francisco location at the time that Westwood moved to Hayward? See Westwood Import Co., 251 N.L.R.B. No. 162 (1980).

5. We shall see later in Chapter 3 (p. 373, infra) that employees who strike for economic benefits may be permanently replaced by their employer with new employees. If a substantial number of striker replacements are hired, the employer may claim the union no longer enjoys majority support and either petition for a new election or refuse to bargain with the union. Without more facts, this is not likely in the Board's view to justify a refusal to bargain because of the Board's principle that replacements for economic strikers are presumed to support the union in the same ratio as those whom they have replaced.[88] The courts of appeals have not always accepted this presumption.[89]

Assuming, though, that the employer has a reasonably held doubt, §9(c)(3) of the NLRA provides that economic strikers are entitled to vote in an election if it is conducted within 12 months of the commencement of the strike. The replacements will also vote. Similarly, within that 12-month period, any attempt to show a reasonably placed doubt of majority status must take the strikers into account.[90]

If the employer has precipitated the strike by committing unfair labor practices, the strikers will be permitted to vote in any election without regard to the 12-month limitation and their replacements will not be eligible to vote.[91]

6. Another circumstance in which the union may lose its representative status is when the employer changes ownership and the doctrine of "successorship" is applied. We shall examine that doctrine after we explore the role of grievance arbitration in the administration of collective bargaining agreements.[92]

[88] See Windham Community Memorial Hosp. 230 N.L.R.B. 1070 (1977).

[89] See, e.g., National Car Rental Sys. v. NLRB, 594 F.2d 1203 (8th Cir. 1979).

[90] Pioneer Flour Mills v. NLRB, 427 F.2d 983 (5th Cir. 1970).

[91] Tampa Sand & Material Co., 137 N.L.R.B. 1549 (1962).

[92] See pp. 693-728, infra.

3

ECONOMIC PRESSURE FOR BENEFITS

A. EMPLOYER WEAPONS, OFFENSIVE AND DEFENSIVE

In the context of treating employer pressure for economic benefits, we examine further here the concept of "protected concerted activity." A variety of issues are raised. First, what sorts of employee activity are deemed protected? In some instances protection will be deemed to have been waived (recall NLRB v. Magnavox Co., p. 200, supra); in other instances employee actions will be seen as so indefensible that even though they were undertaken for mutual aid and protection, the activities will be found undeserving of protected status. In both of the above types of situations, an employer is free to use his or her full economic power against the employees.

Second, if an activity is protected, what countermeasures is an employer nonetheless privileged to take? While §7 was enacted to prohibit employers from punishing employees for engaging in economic pressure to secure benefits, it is clear that an employer may put the employees and their union to a test of economic power, and that in so doing the employer may defend his or her own economic interest. The cases in this section disclose that sometimes a business justification for an employer countermeasure will prevent unfair labor practice liability, and other times it will not. The elusive issue of employer intent is raised in many of the cases.

1. Discharge and Replacement of Employees[1]

NLRB v. LOCAL 1229, IBEW
[JEFFERSON STANDARD BROADCASTING CO.]
346 U.S. 464 (1953)

BURTON, J.

The issue before us is whether the discharge of certain employees by their employer constituted an unfair labor practice, within the meaning of §§8(a)(1) and 7 of the Taft-Hartley Act, justifying their reinstatement by the National Labor Relations Board. For the reason that their discharge was "for cause" within the meaning of §10(c) of that Act, we sustain the Board in not requiring their reinstatement.

In 1949, the Jefferson Standard Broadcasting Company (here called the company) was a North Carolina corporation engaged in interstate commerce. Under a license from the Federal Communications Commission, it operated, at Charlotte, North Carolina, a 50,000-watt radio station, with call letters WBT. It broadcast 10 to 12 hours daily by radio and television. The television service, which it started July 14, 1949, representing an investment of about $500,000, was the only such service in the area. Less than 50 percent of the station's programs originated in Charlotte. The others were piped in over leased wires, generally from New York, California or Illinois from several different networks. Its annual gross revenue from broadcasting operations exceeded $100,000 but its television enterprise caused it a monthly loss of about $10,000 during the first four months of that operation, including the period here involved. Its rates for television advertising were geared to the number of receiving sets in the area. Local dealers had large inventories of such sets ready to meet anticipated demands.

The company employed 22 technicians. In December 1948, negotiations to settle the terms of their employment after January 31, 1949, were begun between representatives of the company and of the respondent Local Union No. 1229, International Brotherhood of Electrical Workers, American Federation of Labor (here called the union). The negotiations reached an impasse in January 1949, and the existing contract of employment expired January 31. The technicians, nevertheless, continued to work for the company and their collective-bargaining negotiations were resumed in July, only to break down again July 8. The main point of disagreement arose from the union's demand for the renewal of a provision that all discharges from employment be subject to arbitration and the company's counterproposal that such arbitration be limited to the facts material to each discharge, leaving it to the company to determine whether those facts gave adequate cause for discharge.

July 9, 1949, the union began daily peaceful picketing of the company's station. Placards and handbills on the picket line charged the company with unfairness to its technicians and emphasized the company's

[1] See Getman, The Protection of Economic Pressure by Section 7 of the National Labor Relations Act, 115 U. Pa. L. Rev. 1195 (1967); Schatzki, Some Observations and Suggestions Concerning a Misnomer — "Protected Concerted Activities," 47 Tex. L. Rev. 378 (1969).

refusal to renew the provision for arbitration of discharges. The placards and handbills named the union as the representative of the WBT technicians. The employees did not strike. They confined their respective tours of picketing to their off-duty hours and continued to draw full pay. There was no violence or threat of violence and no one has taken exception to any of the above conduct.

But on August 24, 1949, a new procedure made its appearance. Without warning, several of its technicians launched a vitriolic attack on the quality of the company's television broadcasts. Five thousand handbills were printed over the designation "WBT TECHNICIANS." These were distributed on the picket line, on the public square two or three blocks from the company's premises, in barber shops, restaurants and busses. Some were mailed to local businessmen. The handbills made no reference to the union, to a labor controversy or to collective bargaining. They read:

> IS CHARLOTTE A SECOND-CLASS CITY?
>
> You might think so from the kind of Television programs being presented by the Jefferson Standard Broadcasting Co. over WBTV. Have you seen one of their television programs lately? Did you know that all the programs presented over WBTV are on film and may be from one day to five years old. There are no local programs presented by WBTV. You cannot receive the local baseball games, football games or other local events because WBTV does not have the proper equipment to make these pickups. Cities like New York, Boston, Philadelphia, Washington receive such programs nightly. Why doesn't the Jefferson Standard Broadcasting Company purchase the needed equipment to bring you the same type of programs enjoyed by other leading American cities? Could it be that they consider Charlotte a second-class community and only entitled to the pictures now being presented to them?
>
> WBT TECHNICIANS

This attack continued until September 3, 1949, when the company discharged ten of its technicians, whom it charged with sponsoring or distributing these handbills. The company's letter discharging them tells its side of the story.[4]

September 4, the union's picketing resumed its original tenor and, September 13, the union filed with the Board a charge that the com-

4. Dear Mr. . . . ,

When you and some of our other technicians commenced early in July to picket against this Company, we felt that your action was very ill-considered. We were paying you a salary of . . . per week, to say nothing of other benefits which you receive as an employee of our Company, such as time-and-a-half pay for all work

pany, by discharging the above-mentioned ten technicians, had engaged in an unfair labor practice. . . .

The Board found that one of the discharged men had neither sponsored nor distributed the "Second-Class City" handbill and ordered his reinstatement with back pay. It then found that the other nine had sponsored or distributed the handbill and held that the company, by discharging them for such conduct, had not engaged in an unfair labor practice. The Board, accordingly, did not order their reinstatement. One member dissented. . . . [T]he union petitioned the Court of Appeals for the District of Columbia Circuit for a review of the Board's order and for such a modification of it as would reinstate all ten of the discharged technicians with back pay. That court remanded the cause to the Board for further consideration and for a finding as to the "unlawfulness" of the conduct of the employees which had led to their discharge. 202 F.2d 186.[7] . . .

In its essence, the issue is simple. It is whether these employees, whose

---

beyond eight hours in any one day, three weeks vacation each year with full pay, unlimited sick leave with full pay, liberal life insurance and hospitalization, for you and your family, and retirement and pension benefits unexcelled anywhere. Yet when we were unable to agree upon the terms of a contract with your Union, you began to denounce us publicly as "unfair."

And ever since early July while you have been walking up and down the street with placards and literature attacking us, you have continued to hold your job and receive your pay and all the other benefits referred to above.

Even when you began to put out propaganda which contained many untruths about our Company and great deal of personal abuse and slander, we still continued to treat you exactly as before. For it has been our understanding that under our labor laws, you have a very great latitude in trying to make the public believe that your employer is unfair to you.

Now, however, you have turned from trying to persuade the public that we are unfair to you and are trying to persuade the public that we give inferior service to them. While we are struggling to expand into and develop a new field, and incidentally losing large sums of money in the process, you are busy trying to turn customers and the public against us in every possible way, even handing out leaflets on the public streets advertising that our operations are "second-class," and endeavoring in various ways to hamper and totally destroy our business. Certainly we are not required by law or common sense to keep you in our employment and pay you a substantial salary while you thus do your best to tear down and bankrupt our business.

You are hereby discharged from our employment. Although there is nothing requiring us to do so, and the circumstances certainly do not call for our doing so, we are enclosing a check payable to your order for two weeks' advance or severance pay.

Very truly yours,
Jefferson Standard Broadcasting Company
By: CHARLES H. CRUTCHFIELD
Vice President

7. The Court of Appeals said:

Protection under §7 of the Act . . . is withdrawn only from those concerted activities which contravene either (a) specific provisions or basic policies of the Act

contracts of employment had expired, were discharged "for cause." They were discharged solely because, at a critical time in the initiation of the company's television service, they sponsored or distributed 5,000 handbills making a sharp, public, disparaging attack upon the quality of the company's product and its business policies, in a manner reasonably calculated to harm the company's reputation and reduce its income. The attack was made by them expressly as "WBT TECHNICIANS." It continued ten days without indication of abatement. The Board found that —

"It [the handbill] occasioned widespread comment in the community, and caused Respondent to apprehend a loss of advertising revenue due to dissatisfaction with its television broadcasting service.

"In short, the employees in this case deliberately undertook to alienate their employer's customers by impugning the technical quality of his product. As the Trial Examiner found, they did not misrepresent, at least wilfully, the facts they cited to support their disparaging report. And their ultimate purpose — to extract a concession from the employer with respect to the terms of their employment — was lawful. That purpose, however, was undisclosed; the employees purported to speak as experts, in the interest of consumers and the public at large. They did not indicate that they sought to secure any benefit for themselves, *as employees,* by casting discredit upon their employer." 94 N.L.R.B., at 1511.

The company's letter shows that it interpreted the handbill as a demonstration of such detrimental disloyalty as to provide "cause" for its refusal to continue in its employ the perpetrators of the attack. We agree.

Section 10(c) of the Taft-Hartley Act expressly provides that "No order of the Board shall require the reinstatement of any individual as an employee who has been suspended or discharged, or the payment to him of any back pay, if such individual was suspended or discharged for cause." There is no more elemental cause for discharge of an employee than disloyalty to his employer. It is equally elemental that the Taft-Hartley Act seeks to strengthen, rather than to weaken, that cooperation, continuity of service and cordial contractual relation between employer and employee that is born of loyalty to their common enterprise.

Congress, while safeguarding, in §7, the right of employees to engage

---

or of related federal statutes, or (b) specific rules of other federal or local law that is not incompatible with the Board's governing statute. . . .

We think the Board failed to make the finding essential to its conclusion that the concerted activity was unprotected. Sound practice in judicial review of administrative orders precludes this court from determining "unlawfulness" without a prior consideration and finding by the Board. 91 U.S. App. D.C., at 335, 336, 202 F.2d, at 188, 189.

in "concerted activities for the purpose of collective bargaining or other mutual aid or protection," did not weaken the underlying contractual bonds and loyalties of employer and employee. The conference report that led to the enactment of the law said:

> [T]he courts have firmly established the rule that under the existing provisions of section 7 of the National Labor Relations Act, employees are not given any right to engage in unlawful or other improper conduct. . . .
>
> . . . Furthermore, in section 10(c) of the amended act, as proposed in the conference agreement, it is specifically provided that no order of the Board shall require the reinstatement of any individual or the payment to him of any back pay if such individual was suspended or discharged for cause, and this, of course, applies with equal force whether or not the acts constituting the cause for discharge were committed in connection with a concerted activity. H.R. Rep. No. 510, 80th Cong., 1st Sess. 38-39. . . .

Many cases reaching their final disposition in the Courts of Appeals furnish examples emphasizing the importance of enforcing industrial plant discipline and of maintaining loyalty as well as the rights of concerted activities. The courts have refused to reinstate employees discharged for "cause" consisting of insubordination, disobedience or disloyalty. In such cases, it often has been necessary to identify individual employees, somewhat comparable to the nine discharged in this case, and to recognize that their discharges were for causes which were separable from the concerted activities of others whose acts might come within the protection of §7. It has been equally important to identify employees, comparable to the tenth man in the instant case, who participated in simultaneous concerted activities for the purpose of collective bargaining or other mutual aid or protection but who refrained from joining the others in separable acts of insubordination, disobedience or disloyalty. In the latter instances, this sometimes led to a further inquiry to determine whether their concerted activities were carried on in such a manner as to come within the protection of §7.

The cases illustrate the responsibility that falls upon the Board to find the facts material to such decisions. The legal principle that insubordination, disobedience or disloyalty is adequate cause for discharge is plain enough. The difficulty arises in determining whether, in fact, the discharges are made because of such a separable cause or because of some other concerted activities engaged in for the purpose of collective bargaining or other mutual aid or protection which may not be adequate cause for discharge.

In the instant case the Board found that the company's discharge of the nine offenders resulted from their sponsoring and distributing the "Second-Class City" handbills of August 24 — September 3, issued in their name as the "WBT TECHNICIANS." Assuming that there had been no pending labor controversy, the conduct of the "WBT TECHNI-

CIANS" from August 24 through September 3 unquestionably would have provided adequate cause for their disciplinary discharge within the meaning of §10(c). Their attack related itself to no labor practice of the company. It made no reference to wages, hours or working conditions. The policies attacked were those of finance and public relations for which management, not technicians, must be responsible. The attack asked for no public sympathy or support. It was a continuing attack, initiated while off duty, upon the very interests which the attackers were being paid to conserve and develop. Nothing could be further from the purpose of the Act than to require an employer to finance such activities. Nothing would contribute less to the Act's declared purpose of promoting industrial peace and stability.

The fortuity of the coexistence of a labor dispute affords these technicians no substantial defense. While they were also union men and leaders in the labor controversy, they took pains to separate those categories. In contrast to their claims on the picket line as to the labor controversy, their handbill of August 24 omitted all reference to it. The handbill diverted attention from the labor controversy. It attacked public policies of the company which had no discernible relation to that controversy. The only connection between the handbill and the labor controversy was an ultimate and undisclosed purpose or motive on the part of some of the sponsors that, by the hoped-for financial pressure, the attack might extract from the company some future concession. A disclosure of that motive might have lost more public support for the employees than it would have gained, for it would have given the handbill more the character of coercion than of collective bargaining. Referring to the attack, the Board said "In our judgment, these tactics, in the circumstances of this case, were hardly less 'indefensible' than acts of physical sabotage." 94 N.L.R.B., at 1511. In any event, the findings of the Board effectively separate the attack from the labor controversy and treat it solely as one made by the company's technical experts upon the quality of the company's product. As such, it was as adequate a cause for the discharge of its sponsors as if the labor controversy had not been pending. The technicians, themselves, so handled their attack as thus to bring their discharge under §10(c).

The Board stated "We . . . do not decide whether the disparagement of product involved here would have justified the employer in discharging the employees responsible for it, had it been uttered in the context of a conventional appeal for support of the union in the labor dispute." Id., at 1512, n. 18. This underscored the Board's factual conclusion that the attack of August 24 was not part of an appeal for support in the pending dispute. It was a concerted separable attack purporting to be made in the interest of the public rather than in that of the employees.

We find no occasion to remand this cause to the Board for further specificity of findings. Even if the attack were to be treated, as the Board has not treated it, as a concerted activity wholly or partly within the scope of those mentioned in §7, the means used by the technicians in conducting the attack have deprived the attackers of the protection of that section, when read in the light and context of the purpose of the Act.[13]

Accordingly, the order of the Court of Appeals remanding the cause to the National Labor Relations Board is set aside, and the cause is remanded to the Court of Appeals with instructions to dismiss respondent's petition to modify the order of the Board.

FRANKFURTER, J., whom BLACK, J., and DOUGLAS, J., join, dissenting. . . .

On this central issue — whether the Court of Appeals rightly or wrongly found that the Board applied an improper criterion — this Court is silent. It does not support the Board in using "indefensible" as the legal litmus nor does it reject the Court of Appeals' rejection of that test. This Court presumably does not disagree with the assumption of the Court of Appeals that conduct may be "indefensible" in the colloquial meaning of that loose adjective, and yet be within the protection of §7.

Instead, the Court, relying on §10(c) which permits discharges "for cause," points to the "disloyalty" of the employees and finds sufficient "cause" regardless of whether the handbill was a "concerted activity" within §7. Section 10(c) does not speak of discharge "for disloyalty." If Congress had so written that section, it would have overturned much of the law that had been developed by the Board and the courts in the twelve years preceding the Taft-Hartley Act. The legislative history makes clear that Congress had no such purpose but was rather expressing approval of the construction of "concerted activities" adopted by the Board and the courts. Many of the legally recognized tactics and weapons of labor would readily be condemned for "disloyalty" were they employed between man and man in friendly personal relations. In this connection it is significant that the ground now taken by the Court,

13. See Labor Board v. Rockaway News Co., 345 U.S. 71 (discharge, for violation of an obligation to make deliveries, even though crossing a picket line, sustained); Auto Workers v. Wisconsin Board, 336 U.S. 245, 255-263 (arbitrary unannounced interruptions of work, not protected by §7); Southern S.S. Co. v. Labor Board, 316 U.S. 31 (discharge of seamen, for disobedience on shipboard while away from home port, sustained); Allen-Bradley Local v. Wisconsin Board, 315 U.S. 740 (mass picketing, unprotected); Hotel Employees' Local v. Wisconsin Board, 315 U.S. 437 (violence, while picketing, unprotected); Labor Board v. Sands Manufacturing Co., 306 U.S. 332 (discharge, for repudiation of employee's agreement, sustained); Labor Board v. Fansteel Corp., 306 U.S. 240 (discharge for tortious conduct, violence or sit-down strike, sustained); and see Associated Press v. Labor Board, 301 U.S. 103, 132; Labor Board v. Jones & Laughlin, 301 U.S. 1, 45-46. See also, Cox, The Right to Engage in Concerted Activities, 26 Ind. L.J. 319 (1951); Recent Cases, 66 Harv. L. Rev. 1321 (1953).

insofar as it is derived from the provision of §10(c) relating to discharge "for cause," was not invoked by the Board in justification of its order.

To suggest that all actions which in the absence of a labor controversy might be "cause" — or, to use the words commonly found in labor agreements, "just cause" — for discharge should be unprotected, even when such actions were undertaken as "concerted activities, for the purpose of collective bargaining," is to misconstrue legislation designed to put labor on a fair footing with management. Furthermore, it would disregard the rough and tumble of strikes, in the course of which loose and even reckless language is properly discounted.

"Concerted activities" by employees and dismissal "for cause" by employers are not dissociated legal criteria under the Act. They are like the two halves of a pair of shears. Of course, as the Conference Report on the Taft-Hartley Act said, men on strike may be guilty of conduct "in connection with a concerted activity" which properly constitutes "cause" for dismissal and bars reinstatement. But §10(c) does not obviate the necessity for a determination whether the distribution of the handbill here was a legitimate tool in a labor dispute or was so "improper," as the Conference Report put it, as to be denied the protection of §7 and to constitute a discharge "for cause." It is for the Board, in the first instance, to make these evaluations, and a court of appeals does not travel beyond its proper bounds in asking the Board for greater explicitness in light of the correct legal standards for judgment.

The Board and the courts of appeals will hardly find guidance for future cases from this Court's reversal of the Court of Appeals, beyond that which the specific facts of this case may afford. More than that, to float such imprecise notions as "discipline" and "loyalty" in the context of labor controversies, as the basis of the right to discharge, is to open the door wide to individual judgment by Board members and judges. One may anticipate that the Court's opinion will needlessly stimulate litigation.

Section 7 of course only protects "concerted activities" in the course of promoting legitimate interests of labor. But to treat the offensive handbills here as though they were circulated by the technicians as interloping outsiders to the sustained dispute between them and their employer is a very unreal way of looking at the circumstances of a labor controversy. Certainly there is nothing in the language of the Act or in the legislative history to indicate that only conventional placards and handbills, headed by a trite phrase such as "UNFAIR TO LABOR," are protected. In any event, on a remand the Board could properly be asked to leave no doubt whether the technicians, in distributing the handbills, were, so far as the public could tell, on a frolic of their own or whether this tactic, however unorthodox, was no more unlawful than other union behavior previously found to be entitled to protection.

It follows that the Court of Appeals should not be reversed.

Notes

1. In NLRB v. Washington Aluminum Co., 370 U.S. 9 (1962), seven employees left work without permission to protest the cold temperature in their shop. They had not made a specific demand on their employer. The firm discharged them. The Court held that the employer's interest in keeping the employees on the job (presumably a company "rule") was outweighed by the interference with §7 rights, and that the activity was protected:

> Section 10(c) of the Act does authorize an employer to discharge employees for "cause" and our cases have long recognized this right on the part of an employer. But this, of course, cannot mean that an employer is at liberty to punish a man by discharging him for engaging in concerted activities which §7 of the Act protects. And the plant rule in question here purports to permit the company to do just that for it would prohibit even the most plainly protected kinds of concerted work stoppages until and unless the permission of the company's foreman was obtained.
>
> It is of course true that §7 does not protect all concerted activities, but that aspect of the section is not involved in this case. The activities engaged in here do not fall within the normal categories of unprotected concerted activities such as those that are unlawful, violent or in breach of contract. Nor can they be brought under this Court's more recent pronouncement which denied the protection of §7 to activities characterized as "indefensible" because they were found to show a disloyalty to the workers' employer which this Court deemed unnecessary to carry on the workers' legitimate concerted activities. The activities of these seven employees cannot be classified as "indefensible" by any recognized standard of conduct.

2. Striking paint company employees distributed handbills captioned "Beware Paint Substitute." The handbills warned that because of the strike, the paint was "not being made by the well-trained employees who have always made the paint you have always bought" (it was being produced by supervisors). Such paint might, they said, peel and crack. The handbill concluded, "You will be informed when you can again buy B.P.S. paint which is made by the regular employees." The Board held this was not protected activity. Neither the reference to the strike nor the truthfulness of the handbill was deemed to distinguish the case from *Jefferson Standard.* Patterson Sargent Co., 115 N.L.R.B. 1627 (1956). Should the court of appeals reverse?

3. A strike timed to endanger physical equipment in a plant has been held to be unprotected, NLRB v. Marshall Car Wheel & Foundry Co., 218 F.2d 409 (5th Cir. 1955); but a strike does not lose its protection merely because it is intentionally called to maximize its economic effect by interfering with an employer's peak business activity.

4. In Dobbs Houses v. NLRB, 325 F.2d 531 (5th Cir. 1963), a restau-

rant supervisor, popular with the employees, was discharged. A large group of employees walked off the job in protest and 16 were discharged. The Board held the walkoff was protected activity and argued to the court that "employees may not be discharged for making known their ideas on managerial supervision, where that supervision is so directly related to their own employment that their actions can properly be denoted as activities for their mutual aid and protection."

Two precedents confronted the court. In NLRB v. Phoenix Mutual Life Ins. Co., 167 F.2d 983 (7th Cir. 1948), cert. denied, 335 U.S. 845, the Seventh Circuit held that two insurance salesmen engaged in protected activity when they partially drafted a letter to central management recommending that their assistant cashier be promoted to a vacant cashier's job. The actions were protected because the cashier's position "bore a reasonable relation to conditions of [the salesmen's] employment." And in NLRB v. Guernsey-Muskingun Elec. Co-op., 285 F.2d 8 (6th Cir. 1960), the Sixth Circuit found the activity of three employees to be protected when they complained at different times about the capability of a foreman. Nonetheless, the *Dobbs* court denied enforcement with the following argument:

> A test which must be met to determine the protected character of the employees' activity is that the means be reasonably related to the ends sought to be achieved. The cases where the courts have found that employees' protest activity against a change in supervisory personnel was unprotected have all involved strikes. While the fact of a strike may not of itself be decisive, such conduct must be contrasted with the incomplete letter in *Phoenix* and the several complaints in *Guernsey*. At any rate it is our conclusion that the course taken by the waitresses here, walking out at the height of the dinner hour and staying out for the entire night, was an unreasonable way to make known their concern to the employer over their mistaken belief that Cooper had been discharged. The Board urges that a strike is not rendered unprotected because of "the availability to the employees of other concerted activities short of striking . . . [or] the reasonableness or wisdom of their selection of a particular course of action." In support of this position the Board cites NLRB v. Washington Aluminum Co., 370 U.S. 9 and NLRB v. Mackay Radio & Television Co., 304 U.S. 333. We do not disagree with the proposition of law stated, but it is premature. The reasonableness of a course of action must be determined initially to ascertain whether in fact it is protected. The cause of the employees' grievance must be considered in determining the reasonableness of their course of conduct undertaken in protest. We have not here reached the stage of *Washington Aluminum*. There the men were working under intolerably cold conditions. Without a union or grievance procedure, concerted activity to protest took the form of a walkout. The conditions there were within the proper realm of employee interest, and the walkout, while extreme under the circumstances, was reasonably related to the complaint. Under the law as we find it, a mass departure by waitresses during the

> dinner hour is not a reasonable method of protest against the firing of a supervisor who enjoys their esteem. Order vacated and enforcement denied.

Is this a correct reading of *Jefferson Standard* and *Washington Aluminum*?

5. In addition to the activities listed in note 13 of *Jefferson Standard,* strikes to force an employer to commit an unfair labor practice (e.g., recognize a minority union) and to grant a wage increase rendered unlawful by federal statute have been declared unprotected. The Board and the courts have also held unprotected intermittent, unannounced ("quickie") strikes, sitdown strikes, slowdowns, and refusals to perform selected pieces of work.

With respect to the last category, consider NLRB v. Montgomery Ward & Co., 157 F.2d 486 (8th Cir. 1946). Employees at one of the employer's plants refused to process orders from another plant where a strike was in progress. The employer discharged them. Their refusal was held unprotected.

> It was implied in the contract of hiring that these employees would do the work assigned to them in a careful and workmanlike manner; that they would comply with all reasonable orders and conduct themselves so as not to work injury to the employer's business; that they would serve faithfully and be regardful of the interests of the employer during the term of their service, and carefully discharge their duties to the extent reasonably required. . . . Any employee may, of course, be lawfully discharged from disobedience of the employer's directions in breach of his contract. . . . While these employees had the undoubted right to go on a strike and quit their employment, they could not continue to work and remain at their positions, accept the wages paid them and at the same time select what part of their allotted tasks they cared to perform of their own volition, or refuse openly or secretly to the employer's damage, to do other work. 157 F.2d at 496.

Reconsider *Bob's Casing Crews,* p. 236, supra. Doesn't this argument suggest that if Billy Loper and the crew walk off the job rather than pick up the pipe, they are protected; but if they refuse to pick up the pipe while remaining available for other work, they may be discharged? Is this distinction reasonable? What would be the status of a concerted refusal to work overtime?

6. It is a general rule that employees have no §7 protection when they strike in breach of a no-strike clause in a collective bargaining agreement, but an important exception was grafted onto the rule in Mastro Plastics Corp. v. NLRB, 350 U.S. 270 (1956). A rival union was seeking to oust the incumbent union at the employer's plant. The employer, opposing the rival union but fearing the incumbent union was not strong enough to withstand the challenge, gave unlawful assistance to

yet a third union. An employee supporter of the incumbent union was fired for his activities attempting to overcome the effects of the employer's unlawful assistance. The employer's activities and the discharge of the employee precipitated a plantwide strike that was in apparent breach of an unqualified no-strike clause in the collective bargaining agreement between the employer and the incumbent union. When the strikers made an unconditional offer to return to work, the employer refused and declared them discharged. The Supreme Court affirmed the Board's reinstatement order.

The Court first made it clear that when a strike is in protest of an employer's unfair labor practices, "the striking employees do not lose their status and are entitled to reinstatement with back pay, even if replacements for them have been made." The Court then "assume[d] that the employees, by explicit contractual provision, could have waived their right to strike against such unfair labor practices" and stated the issue to be whether the agreement's no-strike clause constituted such a waiver:

> Petitioners argue that the words "any strike" leave no room for interpretation and necessarily include all strikes, even those against unlawful practices destructive of the foundation on which collective bargaining must rest. We disagree. We believe that the contract, taken as a whole, deals solely with the economic relationship between the employers and their employees. It is a typical collective-bargaining contract dealing with terms of employment and the normal operations of the plant. It is for one year and assumes the existence of a lawfully designated bargaining representative. Its strike and lockout clauses are natural adjuncts of an operating policy aimed at avoiding interruptions of production prompted by efforts to change existing economic relationships. The main function of arbitration under the contract is to provide a mechanism for avoiding similar stoppages due to disputes over the meaning and application of the various contractual provisions.
>
> To adopt petitioners' all-inclusive interpretation of the clause is quite a different matter. That interpretation would eliminate, for the whole year, the employees' right to strike, even if petitioners, by coercion, ousted the employers' lawful bargaining representative and, by threats of discharge, caused the employees to sign membership cards in a new union. Whatever may be said of the legality of such a waiver when explicitly stated, there is no adequate basis for implying its existence without a more compelling expression of it than appears in §5 of this contract. . . .

The Court therefore held the strike to be protected activity.

Mastro Plastics raises difficult issues. Does the case stand for the proposition that absent explicit language, a no-strike clause should be interpreted to exclude every unfair labor practice strike, or are the only strikes deemed excluded from such a clause those protesting employer unfair labor practices that are destructive of the union's representational status? In Arlan's Department Stores, 133 N.L.R.B. 802 (1961), the Board held that only strikes "against serious unfair labor practices [are] immune from general no strike clauses." The Board later defined "serious" as "destructive of the foundation on which collective bargaining must rest" (quoting *Mastro Plastics*). Member Fanning, dissenting, argued:

> In my opinion, the clear import of this section of the Court's opinion [in *Mastro Plastics*] is that a general no-strike clause in a collective-bargaining agreement for the term of the agreement bars only the right to strike over the "subject matter of the contract" which deals solely with the economic relationship between the employers and their employees, a so-called "economic" strike, and does not bar a strike to protest unfair labor practices in the absence of an express waiver to that effect *because such a strike is outside the scope of the contract.* The Court did not say that the gravity or degree of the unfair labor practices was the operative factor in removing an unfair labor practice strike from coverage of the contract, but rather that by its very nature such a strike was not covered by a contract dealing solely with the parties' economic relationship. . . . Query, moreover, as to what test my colleagues would apply to determine whether particular unfair labor practices are sufficiently serious to apply *Mastro Plastics*? I believe that all unfair labor practices found by the Board to be violative of the Act are serious, and in the words of the Court "destructive of the foundation on which collective bargaining must rest." In fact, in the instant case the unfair labor practice which caused the strike was a discriminatory discharge of a leader in a rival union movement in violation of §8(a)(3), and such a violation "goes to the very heart of the Act." How then in any event, even applying the majority's theory that *Mastro Plastics* requires "serious" unfair labor practices, can the majority say that the unfair labor practice here was not serious enough to protect the employees' right to strike in protest thereof? And this, of course, is the fallacy of the majority's position, for even a single unfair labor practice by an employer, as here, is destructive of the rights guaranteed to employees under §7. Nor can the majority validly contend that the instant case is any different in principle from *Mastro Plastics* because the employer's unfair labor practices here were designed to destroy a rival union movement, whereas in that case the employer sought to encourage a rival union — in either case, the employees are deprived of their §7 right to freely select their bargaining representative. In fact, it might well be argued that where, as Member Leedom and I find here, both the employer and the incumbent union commit unfair labor practices to prevent a change of bargaining representative, there is an even more serious interference with the employees' freedom of selection than in the *Mastro Plastics* situation where only the employer commits unfair labor practices to replace the incumbent.

Would a court or an arbitrator in a damage action brought against the striking union be free to construe a broad no-strike clause as encompassing unfair labor practice strikes?

NLRB v. J. WEINGARTEN, INC.

420 U.S. 251 (1975)

BRENNAN, J. . . .

[Leura Collins worked at a retail food-service facility at one of the company's stores. An undercover security guard, hired to prevent shoplifting and employee dishonesty, observed Collins at work for two days because of a report that Collins was taking money from a cash register. The guard reported to the store manager that he could find nothing wrong, but at the same time a fellow employee of Collins reported that Collins had just made a purchase without paying the full price. When Collins was summoned for questioning, she asked the store manager several times to call the union steward or other union representative to the interview. These requests were denied. Collins' explanation of the purchase was checked and verified.

When Collins was told that the matter was closed, she burst into tears and informed the store manager and guard that the only thing she had ever gotten from the store without paying for it was her free lunch; further interrogation ensued because the store manager understood that company policy did not permit free lunches at this facility. Collins again asked for a union representative to be present and was again refused. When a call to company headquarters disclosed uncertainty over whether free lunches were permitted at this facility, the interrogation ended.

Collins told the union of the incident and an unfair labor practice charge was filed. The Board held that the company violated §8(a)(1) by denying an employee's request to have a union representative present at an investigatory interview that the employee reasonably believed might result in discipline. The Fifth Circuit denied enforcement.]

II

The Board's construction that §7 creates a statutory right in an employee to refuse to submit without union representation to an interview which he reasonably fears may result in his discipline was announced in its decision and order of January 28, 1972, in Quality Mfg. Co., 195 N.L.R.B. 197, considered in Garment Workers v. Quality Mfg. Co., 420 U.S. 276. In its opinions in that case and in Mobil Oil Corp., 196 N.L.R.B. 1052, decided May 12, 1972, three months later, the Board shaped the contours and limits of the statutory right.

First, the right inheres in §7's guarantee of the right of employees to act in concert for mutual aid and protection. In *Mobil Oil,* the Board stated:

> An employee's right to union representation upon request is based on Section 7 of the Act which guarantees the right of employees to act in

> concert for 'mutual aid and protection.' The denial of this right has a reasonable tendency to interfere with, restrain, and coerce employees in violation of §8(a)(1) of the Act. Thus, it is a serious violation of the employee's individual right to engage in concerted activity by seeking the assistance of his statutory representative if the employer denies the employee's request and compels the employee to appear unassisted at an interview which may put his job security in jeopardy. Such a dilution of the employee's right to act collectively to protect his job interests is, in our view, unwarranted interference with his right to insist on concerted protection, rather than individual self-protection, against possible adverse employer action. Ibid.

Second, the right arises only in situations where the employee requests representation. In other words, the employee may forgo his guaranteed right and, if he prefers, participate in an interview unaccompanied by his union representative.

Third, the employee's right to request representation as a condition of participation in an interview is limited to situations where the employee reasonably believes the investigation will result in disciplinary action.[5] Thus the Board stated in *Quality:*

"We would not apply the rule to such run-of-the-mill shop-floor conversations as, for example, the giving of instructions or training or needed corrections of work techniques. In such cases there cannot normally be any reasonable basis for an employee to fear that any adverse impact may result from the interview, and thus we would then see no reasonable basis for him to seek the assistance of his representative." 195 N.L.R.B., at 199.

Fourth, exercise of the right may not interfere with legitimate employer prerogatives. The employer has no obligation to justify his refusal to allow union representation, and despite refusal, the employer is free to carry on his inquiry without interviewing the employee, and thus leave to the employee the choice between having an interview unaccompanied by his representative, or having no interview and forgoing any benefits that might be derived from one. . . .

Fifth, the employer has no duty to bargain with any union representative who may be permitted to attend the investigatory interview. The Board said in *Mobil,* "we are not giving the Union any particular rights with respect to predisciplinary discussions which it otherwise was not able to secure during collective-bargaining negotiations." 196 N.L.R.B., at 1052 n. 3. The Board thus adhered to its decisions distinguishing

5. . . . The key objective fact in this case is that the only exception to the requirement in the collective-bargaining agreement that the employer give a warning notice prior to discharge is "if the cause of such discharge is dishonesty." Accordingly, had respondent been satisfied, based on its investigatory interview, that Collins was guilty of dishonesty, Collins could have been discharged without further notice. That she might reasonably believe that the interview might result in disciplinary action is thus clear.

between disciplinary and investigatory interviews, imposing a mandatory affirmative obligation to meet with the union representative only in the case of the disciplinary interview. The employer has no duty to bargain with the union representative at an investigatory interview. "The representative is present to assist the employee, and may attempt to clarify the facts or suggest other employees who may have knowledge of them. The employer, however, is free to insist that he is only interested, at that time, in hearing the employee's account of the matter under investigation." Brief for Petitioner 22.

III

The Board's holding is a permissible construction of "concerted activities for . . . mutual aid or protection" by the agency charged by Congress with enforcement of the Act, and should have been sustained.

The action of an employee in seeking to have the assistance of his union representative at a confrontation with his employer clearly falls within the literal wording of §7 that [e]mployees shall have the right . . . to engage in . . . concerted activities for the purpose of . . . mutual aid or protection." Mobil Oil Corp. v. NLRB, 482 F.2d 842, 847 (C.A.7 1973). This is true even though the employee alone may have an immediate stake in the outcome; he seeks "aid or protection" against a perceived threat to his employment security. The union representative whose participation he seeks is, however, safeguarding not only the particular employee's interest, but also the interests of the entire bargaining unit by exercising vigilance to make certain that the employer does not initiate or continue a practice of imposing punishment unjustly. The representative's presence is an assurance to other employees in the bargaining unit that they, too, can obtain his aid and protection if called upon to attend a like interview. Concerted activity for mutual aid or protection is therefore as present here as it was held to be in NLRB v. Peter Cailler Kohler Swiss Chocolates Co., 130 F.2d 503, 505-506 (C.A.2 1942), cited with approval by this Court in Houston Contractors Assn. v. NLRB, 386 U.S. 664, 668-669 (1967):

> "When all the other workmen in a shop make common cause with a fellow workman over his separate grievance, and go out on strike in his support, they engage in a 'concerted activity' for 'mutual aid or protection,' although the aggrieved workman is the only one of them who has any immediate stake in the outcome. The rest know that by their action each of them assures himself, in case his turn ever comes, of the support of the one whom they are all then helping; and the solidarity so established is 'mutual aid' in the most liberal sense, as nobody doubts."

The Board's construction plainly effectuates the most fundamental purposes of the Act. In §1, the Act declares that it is a goal of national labor policy to protect "the exercise by workers of full freedom of association, self-organization, and designation of representatives of their own choosing, for the purpose of . . . mutual aid or protection." To that end the Act is designed to eliminate the "inequality of bargaining power between employees . . . and employers." Ibid. Requiring a lone employee to attend an investigatory interview which he reasonably believes may result in the imposition of discipline perpetuates the inequality the Act was designed to eliminate, and bars recourse to the safeguards the Act provided "to redress the perceived imbalance of economic power between labor and management." American Ship Building Co. v. NLRB, 380 U.S. 300, 316 (1965). Viewed in this light, the Board's recognition that §7 guarantees an employee's right to the presence of a union representative at an investigatory interview in which the risk of discipline reasonably inheres is within the protective ambit of the section " 'read in the light of the mischief to be corrected and the end to be attained.' " NLRB v. Hearst Publications, Inc., 322 U.S. 111, 124 (1944).

The Board's construction also gives recognition to the right when it is most useful to both employee and employer. A single employee confronted by an employer investigating whether certain conduct deserves discipline may be too fearful or inarticulate to relate accurately the incident being investigated, or too ignorant to raise extenuating factors. A knowledgeable union representative could assist the employer by eliciting favorable facts, and save the employer production time by getting to the bottom of the incident occasioning the interview. Certainly his presence need not transform the interview into an adversary contest. Respondent suggests nonetheless that union representation at this stage is unnecessary because a decision as to employee culpability or disciplinary action can be corrected after the decision to impose discipline has become final. In other words, respondent would defer representation until the filing of a formal grievance challenging the employer's determination of guilt after the employee has been discharged or otherwise disciplined. At that point, however, it becomes increasingly difficult for the employee to vindicate himself, and the value of representation is correspondingly diminished. The employer may then be more concerned with justifying his actions that re-examining them. . . .

The judgment is reversed and the case is remanded with direction to enter a judgment enforcing the Board's order.

It is so ordered.[2]

POWELL, J., with whom STEWART, J., joins, dissenting.

Section 7 of the National Labor Relations Act guarantees to employees the right to "engage in . . . concerted activities for the purpose of collective bargaining or other mutual aid or protection." The Court

[2] Burger, C.J., dissented.

today construes that right to include union representation or the presence of another employee[1] at any interview the employee reasonably fears might result in disciplinary action. In my view, such an interview is not *concerted activity* within the intendment of the Act. An employee's right to have a union representative or another employee present at an investigatory interview is a matter that Congress left to the free and flexible exchange of the bargaining process. . . .

Congress' goal in enacting federal labor legislation was to create a framework within which labor and management can establish the mutual rights and obligations that govern the employment relationship. "The theory of the Act is that free opportunity for negotiation with accredited representatives of employees is likely to promote industrial peace and may bring about the adjustments and agreements which the Act in itself does not attempt to compel." NLRB v. Jones & Laughlin Steel Corp., 301 U.S. 1, 45 (1937). The National Labor Relations Act only creates the structure for the parties' exercise of their respective economic strengths; it leaves definition of the precise contours of the employment relationship to the collective-bargaining process. . . . Section 7 protects those rights that are essential to employee self-organization and to the exercise of economic weapons to exact concessions from management and demand a voice in defining the terms of the employment relationship. It does not define those terms itself.

The power to discipline or discharge employees has been recognized uniformly as one of the elemental prerogatives of management. Absent specific limitations imposed by statute or through the process of collective bargaining, management remains free to discharge employees at will. See Steelworkers v. Warrior & Gulf Co., 363 U.S. 574, 583 (1960). An employer's need to consider and undertake disciplinary action will arise in a wide variety of unpredictable situations. The appropriate disciplinary response also will vary significantly, depending on the nature and severity of the employee's conduct. Likewise, the nature and amount of information required for determining the appropriateness of disciplinary action may vary with the severity of the possible sanction and the complexity of the problem. And in some instances, the employer's legitimate need to maintain discipline and security may require an immediate response.

This variety and complexity necessarily call for flexible and creative adjustment. As the Court recognizes, the question of union participation in investigatory interviews is a standard topic of collective bargaining.[8]

1. While the Court speaks only of the right to insist on the presence of a union representative, it must be assumed that the §7 right today recognized, affording employees the right to act "in concert" in employer interviews, also exists in the absence of a recognized union. Cf. NLRB v. Washington Aluminum Co., 370 U.S. 9 (1962).

8. The history of a similar case, Mobil Oil, 196 N.L.R.B. 1052 (1972), enforcement denied, 482 F.2d 842 (C.A.7 1973), illustrates how the Board has substituted its judgment

Many agreements incorporate provisions that grant and define such rights, and arbitration decisions increasingly have begun to recognize them as well. Rather than vindicate the Board's interpretation of §7, however, these developments suggest to me that union representation at investigatory interviews is a matter that Congress left to the bargaining process. Even after affording appropriate deference to the Board's meandering interpretation of the Act, I conclude that the right announced today is not among those that Congress intended to protect in §7. The type of personalized interview with which we are here concerned is simply not "concerted activity" within the meaning of the Act.

Notes

1. In a companion case, International Ladies' Garment Workers v. Quality Mfg. Co., 420 U.S. 276 (1975), the Supreme Court upheld the Board's finding of an unfair labor practice where the union representative, as well as the employee called in for the investigatory interview, was disciplined for insisting that a union representative be present at the interview.

2. In Certified Grocers, 227 N.L.R.B. 1211 (1977), an employee was called to a supervisor's office to receive notice of a two-week layoff for low production. The employee requested to have a union representative present and to see his performance records. Both requests were refused. The Board held, 2-1, that the refusal to permit union representation violated §8(a)(1) and ordered the employer to expunge the layoff notice from the employee's records and give him backpay for the layoff. Is this an unwarranted extension of *Weingarten*? The *Certified Grocers* case was overruled in Baton Rouge Waterworks, 246 N.L.R.B. 995 (1979). The current rule is that an employer can refuse to allow a union representative to be present at a meeting with an employee if the purpose of the meeting is to announce discipline already decided upon. See Houston Coca-Cola, 251 N.L.R.B. 860 (1980).

---

for that of the collective-bargaining process. During negotiations leading to the establishment of a collective-bargaining agreement in that case, the union advanced a demand that existing provisions governing suspension and discharge be amended to provide for company-union discussions prior to disciplinary action. The employer refused to accede to that demand and ultimately prevailed, only to find his efforts at the bargaining table voided by the Board's interpretation of the statute.

Chairman Miller subsequently suggested that the union can waive the employee's §7 right to the presence of a union representative. See Western Electric Co., 198 N.L.R.B. 82 (1972). The Court today provides no indication whether such waivers in the collective-bargaining process are permissible. Cf. NLRB v. Magnavox Co., 415 U.S. 322 (1974).

3. If Ms. Collins had been discharged for dishonesty, what remedy? The Board established its standards in Kraft Foods, 251 N.L.R.B. 598 (1980). The General Council can make a prima facie showing of the appropriateness of a make-whole remedy by proving that the employer conducted an investigatory interview in violation of *Weingarten* rights and that the employee whose rights were violated was later disciplined for conduct that was the subject of the unlawful interview. When this showing is made, the burden shifts to the employer, who must demonstrate that a decision to discipline the employee was not based on information obtained at the unlawful interview. If the employer meets this burden, the Board will issue a cease and desist order that will not provide for reinstatement with back pay. Cf. NLRB v. Transportation Management Corp., at p. 249, supra.

NLRB v. CITY DISPOSAL SYSTEMS

— U.S. —, 104 S. Ct. 1505 (1984)

BRENNAN, J. . . . delivered the opinion of the Court.

James Brown, a truck driver employed by respondent, was discharged when he refused to drive a truck that he honestly and reasonably believed to be unsafe because of faulty brakes. Article XXI of the collective-bargaining agreement between respondent and Local 247 of the International Brotherhood of Teamsters, Chauffeurs, Warehousemen and Helpers of America, which covered Brown, provides:

> [t]he Employer shall not require employees to take out on the streets or highways any vehicle that is not in safe operating condition or equipped with safety appliances prescribed by law. It shall not be a violation of the Agreement where employees refuse to operate such equipment unless such refusal is unjustified.

The question to be decided is whether Brown's honest and reasonable assertion of his right to be free of the obligation to drive unsafe trucks constituted "concerted activit[y]" within the meaning of §7 of the National Labor Relations Act. The National Labor Relations Board (NLRB or Board) held that Brown's refusal was concerted activity within §7, and that his discharge was, therefore, an unfair labor practice under §8(a)(1) of the Act. The Court of Appeals disagreed and declined enforcement. 683 F.2d 1005 (C.A.6 1982). At least three other Courts of Appeals, however, have accepted the Board's interpretation of "concerted activities" as including the assertion by an individual employee of a right grounded in a collective-bargaining agreement. We granted certiorari to resolve the conflict and now reverse.

I

The facts are not in dispute in the current posture of this case. Respondent, City Disposal System, Inc. (City Disposal), hauls garbage for the City of Detroit. Under the collective-bargaining agreement with Local Union No. 247, respondent's truck drivers haul garbage from Detroit to a land fill about 37 miles away. Each driver is assigned to operate a particular truck, which he or she operates each day of work, unless that truck is in disrepair.

James Brown was assigned to truck No. 245. On Saturday, May 12, 1979, Brown observed that a fellow driver had difficulty with the brakes of another truck, truck No. 244. As a result of the brake problem, truck No. 244 nearly collided with Brown's truck. After unloading their garbage at the land fill, Brown and the driver of truck No. 244 brought No. 244 to respondent's truck-repair facility, where they were told that the brakes would be repaired either over the weekend or in the morning of Monday, May 14.

Early in the morning of Monday, May 14, while transporting a load of garbage to the land fill, Brown experienced difficulty with one of the wheels of his own truck — No. 245 — and brought that truck in for repair. At the repair facility, Brown was told that, because of a backlog at the facility, No. 245 could not be repaired that day. Brown reported the situation to his supervisor, Otto Jasmund, who ordered Brown to punch out and go home. Before Brown could leave, however, Jasmund changed his mind and asked Brown to drive truck No. 244 instead. Brown refused, explaining that "there's something wrong with that truck. . . . [S]omething was wrong with the brakes . . . there was a grease seal or something leaking causing it to be affecting the brakes." Brown did not, however, explicitly refer to Article XXI of the collective-bargaining agreement or to the agreement in general. In response to Brown's refusal to drive truck No. 244, Jasmund angrily told Brown to go home. At that point, an argument ensued and Robert Madary, another supervisor, intervened, repeating Jasmund's request that Brown drive truck No. 244. Again, Brown refused, explaining that No. 244 "has got problems and I don't want to drive it." Madary replied that half the trucks had problems and that if respondent tried to fix all of them it would be unable to do business. He went on to tell Brown that "[w]e've got all this garbage out here to haul and you tell me about you don't want to drive." Brown responded, "Bob, what you going to do, put the garbage ahead of the safety of the men?" Finally, Madary went to his office and Brown went home. Later that day, Brown received word that he had been discharged. He immediately returned to work in an attempt to gain reinstatement but was unsuccessful.

On May 15, the day after the discharge, Brown filed a written grievance, pursuant to the collective-bargaining agreement, asserting that truck No. 244 was defective, that it had been improper for him to have been ordered to drive the truck, and that his discharge was therefore also improper. The union, however, found no objective merit in the grievance and declined to process it.

On September 7, 1979, Brown filed an unfair labor practice charge with the NLRB, challenging his discharge. The Administrative Law Judge (ALJ) found that Brown had been discharged for refusing to operate truck No. 244, that Brown's refusal was covered by §7 of the NLRA, and that respondent had therefore committed an unfair labor practice under §8(a)(1) of the Act. The ALJ held that an employee who acts alone in asserting a contractual right can nevertheless be engaged in concerted activity within the meaning of §7:

> [W]hen an employee makes complaints concerning safety matters which are embodied in a contract, he is acting not only in his own interest, but is attempting to enforce such contract provisions in the interest of all the employees covered under the contract. Such activity we have found to be concerted and protected under the Act, and the discharge of an individual for engaging in such activity to be in violation of §8(a)(1) of the Act. 256 N.L.R.B., at 454 (quoting *Roadway Express, Inc.*, 217 N.L.R.B. 278, 279 (1975)).

The NLRB adopted the findings and conclusions of the ALJ and ordered that Brown be reinstated with backpay.

On a petition for enforcement of the Board's order, the Court of Appeals disagreed with the ALJ and the Board. Finding that Brown's refusal to drive truck No. 244 was an action taken solely on his own behalf, the Court of Appeals concluded that the refusal was not a concerted activity within the meaning of §7. This holding followed the court's prior decision in ARO, Inc. v. NLRB, 596 F.2d 713 (C.A.6 1979), in which the Court of Appeals had held:

> For an individual claim or complaint to amount to concerted action under the Act it must not have been made solely on behalf of an individual employee, but it must be made on behalf of other employees or at least be made with the object of inducing or preparing for group action and have some arguable basis in the collective bargaining agreement. Id., at 718.

II

Section 7 of the NLRA provides that "[e]mployees shall have the right to . . . join or assist labor organizations, to bargain collectively through representatives of their own choosing, and to engage in other concerted activities for the purpose of collective bargaining or other mutual aid or protection." 29 U.S.C. §157 (emphasis added). The NLRB's decision in this case applied the Board's longstanding "*Interboro* doctrine," under which an individual's assertion of a right grounded in a collective-bargaining agreement is recognized as "concerted activit[y]" and therefore accorded the protection of §7.[6] See Interboro Contractors, Inc., 157 N.L.R.B. 1295, 1298 (1966), enforced, 388 F.2d 495 (C.A.2 1967); Bunney Bros. Construction Co., 139 N.L.R.B. 1516, 1519 (1962). The Board has relied on two justifications for the doctrine: First, the assertion of a right contained in a collective-bargaining agreement is an extension of the concerted action that produced the agreement, *Bunney Bros. Construction,* supra, at 1519; and second, the assertion of such a right affects the rights of all employees covered by the collective-bargaining agreement. *Interboro Contractors,* supra, at 1298.

We have often reaffirmed that the task of defining the scope of §7 "is for the Board to perform in the first instance as it considers the wide variety of cases that come before it," Eastex, Inc. v. NLRB, 437 U.S. 556, 568 (1978), and, on an issue that implicates its expertise in labor relations, a reasonable construction by the Board is entitled to considerable deference, NLRB v. Iron Workers, 434 U.S. 335, 350 (1978); NLRB v. Hearst Publications, Inc., 322 U.S. 111, 130-131 (1944). The question for decision today is thus narrowed to whether the Board's application of §7 to Brown's refusal to drive truck No. 244 is reasonable.[7] Several reasons persuade us that it is.

A

Neither the Court of Appeals nor respondent appears to question that an employee's invocation of a right derived from a collective-bargaining agreement meets §7's requirement that an employee's action be taken "for purposes of collective bargaining or other mutual aid or protection." As the Board first explained in the *Interboro* case, a single employee's invocation of such rights affects all the employees that are covered by the collective-bargaining agreement. *Interboro Contractors, Inc.,* supra, at 1298. This type of generalized effect, as our cases have demonstrated, is sufficient to bring the actions of an individual em-

6. The NLRB has recently held that, where a group of employees are not unionized and there is no collective-bargaining agreement, an employee's assertion of a right that can only be presumed to be of interest to other employees is not concerted activity. Meyers Industries, 268 N.L.R.B. No. 73 (1984). The Board, however, distinguished that case from the cases involving the *Interboro* doctrine, which is based on the existence of a collective-bargaining agreement. The *Meyers* case is thus of no relevance here.

7. Respondent argues that because "the scope of the 'concerted activities' clause in §7 is essentially a jurisdictional or legal question concerning the coverage of the Act," we need not defer to the expertise of the Board. Brief for Respondent 13. We have never, however, held that such an exception exists to the normal standard of review of Board interpretations of the Act: indeed, we have not hesitated to defer to the Board's interpretation of the Act in the context of issues substantially similar to that presented here. E.g. NLRB v. Weingarten, Inc., 420 U.S. 251, 266-267 (1975) (right under §7 to have union representative present at investigatory interview of employee). See also Bayside Enterprises, Inc. v. NLRB, 429 U.S. 298, 302-303 (1977) (definition of agricultural workers).

ployee within the "mutual aid or protection" standard, regardless of whether the employee has his own interests most immediately in mind. See, e.g., Weingarten v. NLRB, 420 U.S. 251, 260-261 (1974).

The term "concerted activit[y]" is not defined in the Act but it clearly enough embraces the activities of employees who have joined together in order to achieve common goals. See, e.g., Meyers Industries, 268 N.L.R.B. No 73, at 3 (1984). What is not self-evident from the language of the Act, however, and what we must elucidate, is the precise manner in which particular actions of an individual employee must be linked to the actions of fellow employees in order to permit it to be said that the individual is engaged in concerted activity. We now turn to consider the Board's analysis of that question as expressed in the *Interboro* doctrine.

Although one could interpret the phrase, "to engage in concerted activities," to refer to a situation in which two or more employees are working together at the same time and the same place toward a common goal, the language of §7 does not confine itself to such a narrow meaning. In fact, §7 itself defines both joining and assisting labor organizations — activities in which a single employee can engage — as concerted activities.[8] Indeed, even the courts that have rejected the *Interboro* doctrine recognize the possibility that an individual employee may be engaged in concerted activity when he acts alone. They have limited their recognition of this type of concerted activity, however, to two situations: (1) that in which the lone employee intends to induce group activity, and (2) that in which the employee acts as a representative of at least one other employee. See, e.g., Aro, Inc. v. NLRB, 596 F.2d at 713, 717 (C.A.6 1979); NLRB v. Northern Metal Co., 440 F.2d 881, 884 (C.A.3 1971). The disagreement over the *Interboro* doctrine, therefore, merely reflects differing views regarding the nature of the relationship that must exist between the action of the individual employee and the actions of the group in order for §7 to apply. We cannot say that the Board's view of that relationship, as applied in the *Interboro* doctrine, is unreasonable.

The invocation of a right rooted in a collective-bargaining agreement is unquestionably an integral part of the process that gave rise to the agreement. That process — beginning with the organization of a union, continuing into the negotiation of a collective-bargaining agreement, and extending through the enforcement of the agreement — is a single, collective activity. Obviously, an employee could not invoke a right grounded in a collective-bargaining agreement were it not for the prior negotiating activities of his fellow employees. Nor would it make sense for a union to negotiate a collective-bargaining agreement if individual employees could not invoke the rights thereby created against their employer. Moreover, when an employee invokes a right grounded in the

8. Section 7 lists these and other activities initially and concludes the list with the phrase "*other* concerted activities," thereby indicating that the enumerated activities are deemed to be "concerted." See supra, at n. 1.

collective-bargaining agreement, he does not stand alone. Instead, he brings to bear on his employer the power and resolve of all his fellow employees. When, for instance, James Brown refused to drive a truck he believed to be unsafe, he was in effect reminding his employer that he and his fellow employees, at the time their collective-bargaining agreement was signed, had extracted a promise from City Disposal that they would not be asked to drive unsafe trucks. He was also reminding his employer that if it persisted in ordering him to drive an unsafe truck, he could reharness the power of that group to ensure the enforcement of that promise. It was just as though James Brown was reassembling his fellow union members to reenact their decision not to drive unsafe trucks. A lone employee's invocation of a right grounded in his collective-bargaining agreement is, therefore, a concerted activity in a very real sense.

Furthermore, the acts of joining and assisting a labor organization, which §7 explicitly recognizes as concerted, are related to collective action in essentially the same way that the invocation of a collectively bargained right is related to collective action. When an employee joins or assists a labor organization, his actions may be divorced in time, and in location as well, from the actions of fellow employees. Because of the integral relationship among the employees' actions, however, Congress viewed each employee as engaged in concerted activity. The lone employee could not join or assist a labor organization were it not for the related organizing activities of his fellow employees. Conversely, there would be limited utility in forming a labor organization if other employees could not join or assist the organization once it is formed. Thus, the formation of a labor organization is integrally related to the activity of joining or assisting such an organization in the same sense that the negotiation of a collective-bargaining agreement is integrally related to the invocation of a right provided for in the agreement. In each case, neither the individual activity nor the group activity would be complete without the other.[10]

10. Of course, at some point an individual employee's actions may become so remotely related to the activities of fellow employees that it cannot reasonably be said that the employee is engaged in concerted activity. For instance, the Board has held that if an employer were to discharge an employee for purely personal "griping," the employee could not claim the protection of §7. See, e.g., Capital Ornamental Concrete Specialties, Inc., 248 N.L.R.B. 851 (1980).

In addition, although the Board relies entirely on its interpretation of §7 as support for the *Interboro* doctrine, it bears noting that under §8(a)(1), an employer commits an unfair labor practice if he or she "interfere[s] with, [or] restrain[s]" concerted activity. It is possible, therefore, for an employer to commit an unfair labor practice by discharging an employee who is not himself involved in concerted activity, but whose actions are related to other employees' concerted activities in such a manner as to render his discharge an interference or restraint on those activities. In the context of the *Interboro* doctrine, for instance, even if an individual's invocation of rights provided for in a collective-bargaining agreement, for some reason, were not concerted activity, the discharge of that individual would still be an unfair labor practice if the result were to restrain or interfere with the concerted activity of negotiating or enforcing a collective-bargaining agreement.

The *Interboro* doctrine is also entirely consistent with the purposes of the Act, which explicitly include the encouragement of collective bargaining and other "practices fundamental to the friendly adjustment of industrial disputes arising out of differences as to wages, hours, or other working conditions." 29 U.S.C. §151. Although, as we have said, there is nothing in the legislative history of §7 that specifically expresses the understanding of Congress in enacting the "concerted activities" language, the general history of §7 reveals no inconsistency between the *Interboro* doctrine and congressional intent. That history begins in the early days of the labor movement, when employers invoked the common law doctrines of criminal conspiracy and restraint of trade to thwart workers' attempts to unionize. See Automobile Workers, Local 232 v. Wisconsin Employment Relations Board (Briggs & Stratton), 336 U.S. 245, 257-258 (1949). As this Court recognized in NLRB v. Jones & Laughlin Steel Corp., 301 U.S. 1, 33 (1937), a single employee at that time "was helpless in dealing with an employer; . . . he was dependent ordinarily on his daily wage for the maintenance of himself and his family; . . . if the employer refused to pay him the wages that he thought fair, he was nevertheless unable to leave the employ and resist arbitrary and unfair treatment; . . . union was essential to give laborers opportunity to deal on an equality with their employer."

Congress's first attempt to equalize the bargaining power of management and labor, and its first use of the term "concert" in this context, came in 1914 with the enactment of §§6 and 20 of the Clayton Act, which exempted from the antitrust laws certain types of peaceful union activities. 15 U.S.C. §17; 29 U.S.C. §52.[11] There followed, in 1932, the Norris-LaGuardia Act, which declared that "the individual . . . worker shall be free from the interference, restraint, or coercion, of employers . . . in self-organization or in *other concerted activities for the purpose of collective bargaining or other mutual aid or protection*." 29 U.S.C. 102 (emphasis added). This was the source of the language enacted in §7. It was adopted first in §7(a) of the National Industrial Recovery Act and then, in 1935, in §7 of the NLRA. See generally Gorman & Finkin, The Individual and the Requirement of "Concert" under the National Labor Relations Act, 130 U. Pa. L. Rev. 286, 331-346 (1981).

Against this background, it is evident that, in enacting §7 of the NLRA, Congress sought generally to equalize the bargaining power of the employee with that of his employer by allowing employees to band together in confronting an employer regarding the terms and conditions of their employment. There is no indication that Congress intended to limit this protection to situations in which an employee's activity and that of his fellow employees combine with one another in any particular way.

11. In §20 of the Clayton Act, Congress provided that "no . . . injunction shall prohibit any person or persons, whether singly or *in concert*, from . . . ceasing to perform any work [or other specified activities]." 29 U.S.C. §52 (emphasis added).

Nor, more specifically, does it appear that Congress intended to have this general protection withdrawn in situations in which a single employee, acting alone, participates in an integral aspect of a collective process. Instead, what emerges from the general background of §7 — and what is consistent with the Act's statement of purpose — is a congressional intent to create an equality in bargaining power between the employee and the employer throughout the entire process of labor organizing, collective bargaining, and enforcement of collective-bargaining agreements.

The Board's *Interboro* doctrine, based on a recognition that the potential inequality in the relationship between the employee and the employer continues beyond the point at which a collective-bargaining agreement is signed, mitigates that inequality throughout the duration of the employment relationship, and is, therefore, fully consistent with congressional intent. Moreover, by applying §7 to the actions of individual employees invoking their rights under a collective-bargaining agreement, the *Interboro* doctrine preserves the integrity of the entire collective-bargaining process; for by invoking a right grounded in a collective-bargaining agreement, the employee makes that right a reality, and breathes life, not only into the promises contained in the collective-bargaining agreement, but also into the entire process envisioned by Congress as the means by which to achieve industrial peace.

To be sure, the principal tool by which an employee invokes the rights granted him in a collective-bargaining agreement is the processing of a grievance according to whatever procedures his collective-bargaining agreement establishes. No one doubts that the processing of a grievance in such a manner is concerted activity within the meaning of §7. See, e.g., NLRB v. Ford Motor Co., 683 F.2d 156, 159 (C.A.6 1982); Crown Central Petroleum Corp. v. NLRB, 430 F.2d 724, 729 (C.A.5 1970). Indeed, it would make little sense for §7 to cover an employee's conduct while negotiating a collective-bargaining agreement, including a grievance mechanism by which to protect the rights created by the agreement, but not to cover an employee's attempt to utilize that mechanism to enforce the agreement.

In practice, however, there is unlikely to be a bright-line distinction between an incipient grievance, a complaint to an employer, and perhaps even an employee's initial refusal to perform a certain job that he believes he has no duty to perform. It is reasonable to expect that an employee's first response to a situation that he believes violates his collective-bargaining agreement will be a protest to his employer. Whether he files a grievance will depend in part on his employer's reaction and in part upon the nature of the right at issue. In addition, certain rights might not be susceptible of enforcement by the filing of a grievance. In such a case, the collective-bargaining agreement might provide for an alternative method of enforcement, as did the agreement involved in this case, see supra, at 1, or the agreement might be silent on the matter. Thus, for a variety of reasons, an employee's initial statement to an employer to the effect that he believes a collectively bargained right is being violated, or the employee's initial refusal to do that which he believes he is not obligated to do, might serve as both a natural prelude to, and an efficient substitute for, the filing of a formal grievance. As long as the employee's statement or action is based on a reasonable and honest belief that he is being, or has been, asked to perform a task that he is not required to perform under his collective-bargaining agreement, and the statement or action is reasonably directed toward the enforcement of a collectively bargained right, there is no justification for overturning the Board's judgment that the employee is engaged in concerted activity, just as he would have been had he filed a formal grievance.

The fact that an activity is concerted, however, does not necessarily mean that an employee can engage in the activity with impunity. An employee may engage in concerted activity in such an abusive manner that he loses the protection of §7. See, e.g., Crown Central Petroleum Corp. v. NLRB, 430 F.2d 724, 729 (C.A.5 1970); Yellow Freight System, Inc., 247 N.L.R.B. 177, 181 (1980). Cf. Eastex, Inc. v. NLRB, 437 U.S. 556 (1978) (finding concerted activity nonetheless unprotected); NLRB v. Babcock & Wilcox Co., 351 U.S. 105 (1956) (same). Furthermore, if an employer does not wish to tolerate certain methods by which employees invoke their collectively bargained rights, he is free to negotiate a provision in his collective-bargaining agreement that limits the availability of such methods. No-strike provisions, for instance, are a common mechanism by which employers and employees agree that the latter will not invoke their rights by refusing to work. In general, if an employee violates such a provision, his activity is unprotected even though it may be concerted. Mastro Plastics Corp. v. NLRB, 350 U.S. 270 (1956). Whether Brown's action in this case was unprotected, however, is not before us.

B

Respondent argues that the *Interboro* doctrine undermines the arbitration process by providing employees with the possibility of provoking a discharge and then filing an unfair labor practice claim. Brief of Respondent 34-42. This argument, however, misses the mark for several reasons. First, an employee who purposefully follows this route would run the risk that the Board would find his actions concerted but nonetheless unprotected, as discussed above.

Second, the *Interboro* doctrine does not shift dispute resolution from the grievance and arbitration process to NLRB adjudication in any way that is different from the alternative position adopted by the Court of Appeals, and pressed upon us by respondent. As stated above, see supra, at 5, the Court of Appeals would allow a finding of concerted activity if two employees together invoke a collectively bargained right, if a lone employee represents another employee in addition to himself when he invokes the right, or if the lone employee invokes the right in a manner that is intended to induce at least one other employee to join him. In each of these situations, however, the underlying substance of the dispute between the employees and the employer is the same as when a single employee invokes a collectively bargained right by himself. In each case the employees are claiming that their employer violated their collective-bargaining agreement, and if the complaining employee or employees in those situations are discharged, their unfair labor practice action would be identical to an action brought by an employee who has been discharged for invoking a collectively bargained right by himself. Because the employees in each of these situations are equally well positioned to go through the grievance and arbitration process, there is no basis for singling out the *Interboro* doctrine as undermining that process any more than would the approach of respondent and the Courts of Appeals that have rejected the doctrine.

Finally, and most importantly, to the extent that the factual issues raised in an unfair labor practice action have been, or can be, addressed through the grievance process, the Board may defer to that process. See Collyer Insulated Wire, 192 N.L.R.B. 837 (1971); Spielberg Manufacturing Co., 112 N.L.R.B. 1080 (1955). There is no reason, therefore, for the Board's interpretation of "concerted activit[y]" in §7 to be constrained by a concern for maintaining the integrity of the grievance and arbitration process.

III

In this case, the Board found that James Brown's refusal to drive truck No. 244 was based on an honest and reasonable belief that the brakes on the truck were faulty. Brown explained to each of his supervisors his reason for refusing to drive the truck. Although he did not refer to his collective-bargaining agreement in either of these confrontations, the agreement provided not only that "[t]he Employer shall not require employees to take out on the streets or highways any vehicle that is not in safe operating condition," but also that "[i]t shall not be a violation of the Agreement where employees refuse to operate such equipment, unless such refusal is unjustified." See supra, at 1. There is no doubt, therefore, nor could there have been any doubt during Brown's confrontations with his supervisors, that by refusing to drive truck No. 244, Brown was invoking the right granted him in his collective-bargaining agreement to be free of the obligation to drive unsafe trucks. Moreover, there can be no question but that Brown's refusal to drive the truck was reasonably well directed toward the enforcement of that right. Indeed, it would appear that there were no other means available by which Brown could have enforced the right. If he had gone ahead and driven truck No. 244, the issue may have been moot.

Respondent argues that Brown's action was not concerted because he did not explicitly refer to the collective-bargaining agreement as a basis for his refusal to drive the truck. Brief of Respondent 21-22. The Board, however, has never held that an employee must make such an explicit reference for his actions to be covered by the *Interboro* doctrine, and we find that position reasonable. We have often recognized the importance of "the Board's special function of applying the general provisions of the Act to the complexities of industrial life." NLRB v. Erie Resistor Corp., 373 U.S. 221, 236 (1963). As long as the nature of the employee's complaint is reasonably clear to the person to whom it is communicated, and the complaint does, in fact, refer to a reasonably perceived violation of the collective-bargaining agreement, the complaining employee is engaged in the process of enforcing that agreement. In the context of a workplace dispute, where the participants are likely to be unsophisticated in collective-bargaining matters, a requirement that the employee explicitly refer to the collective-bargaining agreement is likely to serve as nothing more than a trap for the unwary.

Respondent further argues that the Board erred in finding Brown's action concerted based only on Brown's reasonable and honest belief that truck No. 244 was unsafe. Brief of Respondent 38. Respondent bases its argument on the language of the collective-bargaining agreement, which provides that an employee may refuse to drive an unsafe truck "unless such refusal is unjustified." In the view of respondent, this language allows a driver to refuse to drive a truck only if the truck is objectively unsafe. Regardless of whether respondent's interpretation of the agreement is correct, a question as to which we express no view, this argument confuses the threshold question whether Brown's conduct was concerted with the ultimate question whether that conduct was protected. The rationale of the *Interboro* doctrine compels the conclusion that an honest and reasonable invocation of a collectively bargained right constitutes concerted activity, regardless of whether the employee turns out to have been correct in his belief that his right was violated. See supra, Part II. No one would suggest, for instance, that the filing of a grievance is concerted only if the grievance turns out to be meritorious. As long as the grievance is based on an honest and reasonable belief that a right had been violated, its filing is a concerted activity because it is an integral part of the process by which the collective-bargaining agreement is enforced. The same is true of other methods by which an employee enforces the agreement. On the other hand, if the collective-bargaining agreement imposes a limitation on the means by which a right may be invoked, the concerted activity would be unprotected if it went beyond that limitation. See supra, at 14.

In this case, because Brown reasonably and honestly invoked his right to avoid driving unsafe trucks, his action was concerted. It may be that the collective-bargaining agreement prohibits an employee from refusing to drive a truck that he reasonably believes to be unsafe, but that is, in fact, perfectly safe. If so, Brown's action was concerted but unprotected. As stated above, however, the only issue before this Court and the only issue passed upon by the Board or the Court of Appeals is whether Brown's action was concerted, not whether it was protected.

IV

The NLRB's *Interboro* doctrine recognizes as concerted activity an individual employee's reasonable and honest invocation of a right provided for in his collective-bargaining agreement. We conclude that the doctrine constitutes a reasonable interpretation of the Act. Accordingly, we accept the Board's conclusion that James Brown was engaged in concerted activity when he refused to drive truck No. 244. We therefore reverse the judgment of the Court of Appeals and remand the case for further proceedings consistent with this opinion, including an inquiry into whether respondent may continue to defend this action on the theory that Brown's refusal to drive truck No. 244 was unprotected, even if concerted.

O'CONNOR, J., with whom BURGER, C. J., POWELL, J., and REHNQUIST, J., join, dissenting.

Under the *Interboro* doctrine, an individual employee is deemed to have engaged in "concerted activity," within the meaning of §7 of the National Labor Relations Act (Act), 29 U.S.C. §157, if the right he reasonably and in good faith asserts is grounded in his employer's collective bargaining agreement.[1] On this view, the reasonable, good faith assertion of a right contained in the collective bargaining agreement is said to be an extension of the concerted action that produced the agreement; alternatively, the reasonable, good faith assertion of the contract right is said to affect the rights of all the other employees in the work force. See ante, at 6. Thus, if the employer "interfere[s] with, restrains, or coerces" the employee in response to the latter's assertion of the alleged contract right, the *Interboro* doctrine enables the employee to file a §8(a)(1) unfair labor practice charge with the National Labor Relations Board (Board). See 29 U.S.C. §158(a)(1). Although the concepts of individual action for personal gain and "concerted activity" are intuitively incompatible,[2] the

1. See Interboro Contractors, Inc., 157 N.L.R.B. 1295, 1298 (1966), enforced, 388 F.2d 495 (CA2 1967); see also Bunney Bros. Construction Co., 139 N.L.R.B. 1516, 1519 (1962).

2. The Court and the Board agree that the Act cannot be read to cover, or to give the Board jurisdiction over, purely personal, though work related, claims of individual employees. See ante, at n. 10; Brief for the National Labor Relations Board 16, and n. 9. They

Court today defers to the Board's judgment that the *Interboro* doctrine is necessary to safeguard the exercise of rights previously won in the collective bargaining process. Since I consider the *Interboro* doctrine to be an exercise in undelegated legislative power by the Board, I respectfully dissent.

In my view, the fact that the right the employee asserts ultimately can be grounded in the collective bargaining agreement is not enough to make the individual's self-interested action concerted. If it could, then *every* contract claim could be the basis for an unfair labor practice complaint. But the law is clear that an employer's alleged violation of a collective agreement cannot, by itself, provide the basis for an unfair labor practice complaint. See NLRB v. C & C Plywood, 385 U.S. 421, 427-428 (1967); Dowd Box Co. v. Courtney, 368 U.S. 502, 509-513 (1962). Congress once considered a proposal that would have given the Board "general jurisdiction over all alleged violations of collective bargaining agreements." NLRB v. C & C Plywood, supra, at 427. But it realized that "[t]o have conferred upon the National Labor Relations Board generalized power to determine the rights of parties under all collective agreements would have been a step toward governmental regulation of the terms of those agreements." Ibid. Thus, Congress expressly decided that, "[o]nce [the] parties have made a collective bargaining contract[,] the enforcement of that contract should be left to the usual processes of the law and not to the . . . Board." H. R. Conf. Rep. No. 510, 80th Cong., 1st Sess., 42 (1946). By basing the determination whether activity is "concerted" on the assertion's ultimate grounding in the collective bargaining agreement,[3] the *Interboro* doctrine's extension of the concerted activity proviso transfers the final authority for interpreting all contracts and for resolving all contract disputes back to the Board. This arrogation of power violates Congress' decision to the contrary.

Of course, the Board has considerable discretion to act on contractual matters which are incident to unfair labor practice proceedings. See NLRB v. C & C Plywood, supra. But the fact that the Board can resolve contractual matters incident to unfair labor practice disputes does not give it authority to make unfair labor practice claims out of the contractual disputes themselves. The statutory authority to interpret *some* con-

---

also agree that the mere fact that an asserted right can be presumed to be of interest to other employees is not a sufficient basis for labeling it "concerted." See ante, at n. 6; Meyers Industries, 268 N.L.R.B. — (1984).

3. The *Interboro* doctrine is especially disturbing in this respect, since it does not require the individual expressly to refer to the contract provision supporting the claim or even to be aware of the existence of the agreement. See ante, at 16-17; accord, App. to Pet. for Cert. 18a-19a. One would think that a rule defining "concerted activity" would require the employee to have some idea that he is engaging in it.

tract provisions is not authority to resolve *all* labor contract disputes.[4] Congress' decision not to give the Board this broad power indicates that it considered the difference between individual and concerted activity to be a meaningful one. Indeed, when viewed in light of the scheme Congress created for enforcing labor contract rights, the *Interboro* doctrine turns out to be nothing less than a Trojan Horse dressed up in legal form.

This Court has previously recognized that the labor laws were designed to encourage employees to act together. See, e.g., NLRB v. Weingarten, Inc., 420 U.S. 251, 260-264 (1975). Even a single employee acting in good faith and asserting a right contained in the collective bargaining agreement may be too fearful, inarticulate, or lacking in skill to relate accurately either the event being investigated or the relevant extenuating factors. Other disinterested employees, especially knowlegeable union stewards, can assist the employee and the employer in eliciting the relevant facts and in preventing misunderstandings and hard feelings. The participation of other employees may save production time, reduce administrative expenses, and avoid unnecessary discharges and disciplinary action. By providing an increased degree of statutory coverage to employees participating in that process, the labor laws encourage and preserve the "practice and procedure of collective bargaining." Emporium Capwell Co. v. Western Addition Community Organization, 420 U.S. 50, 62 (1975). The fact that two employees receive coverage where one acting alone does not is therefore entirely consistent with the labor laws' emphasis on collective action. See NLRB v. Allis-Chalmers Mfg. Co., 388 U.S. 175, 180 (1967); Republic Steel Corp. v. Maddox, 379 U.S. 650, 653 (1965).

The Court and the Board insist that, because the group has previously expressed interest in the right now being asserted, the individual's self-interested expression must be treated as "concerted" to ensure that meaning is given to the contract rights. This argument is mistaken. It confuses the employees' substantive contract entitlements with the process by which those entitlements are to be vindicated. When employees act together in expressing a mutual concern, contractual or otherwise, their action is "concerted" and the statute authorizes them to seek vindication through the Board's administrative processes.[5] In contrast, when

4. The Court rather glibly suggests that, to the extent factual issues raised in an unfair labor practice proceeding have been, or can be, addressed through the grievance process, the Board will defer to that process. See ante, at 15. Yet the Court does not discuss why the Board did not defer to that process in this case, where the union determined that there was no objective basis to the grievance. Id., at 4. Moreover, as I have discussed at some length elsewhere, the Board hardly applies its deferral criteria evenhandedly or consistently. See Schaefer v. NLRB, — U.S. — (1983) (O'CONNOR, J., dissenting). Finally, the question whether deferral will occur or is appropriate is relevant only if the Board has jurisdiction in the first place, and that is precisely the issue the Court must decide today.

5. The Board may, of course, require the employees to first seek satisfaction from contractual arbitration and grievance procedures. See William E. Arnold Co. v. Carpenters

an employee acts alone in expressing a personal concern, contractual or otherwise, his action is not "concerted"; in such cases, the statute instructs him to seek vindication through his union, and where necessary, through the courts. See Republic Steel Corp. v. Maddox, 379 U.S. 650 (1965); Hines v. Anchor Motor Freight, Inc., 424 U.S. 554 (1976). Under either scenario, the integrity of the rights won in the collective bargaining process and the rights of all other employees are preserved. The question is whether these rights will be vindicated by administrative or by private and judicial processes. It is clear that Congress believes "day-to-day adjustments in the contract and working rules, resolutions of new problems not covered by existing agreements, and the *protection of employee rights already secured by contract,*" Conley v. Gibson, 355 U.S. 41, 46 (1957) (emphasis added), are more suitably handled, not by the Board, but by the employees' collective representative and, if necessary, the courts. See supra, at 2-3. The *Interboro* doctrine is therefore against Congress' judgment as to how contract rights are best vindicated.

Finally, the *Interboro* doctrine makes little sense when applied to the facts of this case. There is no evidence that employee James Brown discussed the truck's alleged safety problem with other employees, sought their support in remedying the problem, or requested their or his union's assistance in protesting to his employer. He did not seek to warn others of the problem or even initially to file a grievance through his union. He simply asserted that the truck was not safe enough for *him* to drive. James Brown was not engaging in "concerted activity" in any reasonable sense of the term, and therefore his employer could not have violated §8(a)(1) of the Act when it discharged him. The fact that the right asserted can be found in the collective bargaining agreement may be relevant to whether activity of that type should be "protected," but not to whether it is "concerted." The *Interboro* doctrine is, in my view, unreasonable in concluding otherwise.

I do not mean to imply by this dissent that conduct should not be considered "concerted" because it is engaged in by only a single employee. The crucial issue is, as the Court notes, the precise nature of the relationship that must exist between the action of an individual employee and the actions of the group. See ante, at 7-8. An employee certainly engages in "concerted activity" when he acts with or expressly on behalf of one or more of the other employees. And, as several of the courts of appeals have concluded, the statutory language can even be stretched to cover an individual who takes action with the proven object of inducing, initiating, or preparing for group action. See, e.g., Aro, Inc.

District Council of Jacksonville and Vicinity, 417 U.S. 12 (1974). But that deferral decision can properly be made only *after* an unfair labor practice is properly filed, which requires a determination whether "concerted activity" is involved in the first instance.

v. NLRB, 596 F.2d 713, 717 (C.A.6 1979); NLRB v. Northern Metal Co., 440 F.2d 881, 884 (C.A.3 1971); see also Kohls v. NLRB, 629 F.2d 173, 176-177 (C.A.D.C. 1980). But it stretches the language past its snapping point to cover an employee's action that is taken solely for personal benefit.

Accordingly, I respectfully dissent.

Notes

1. In *Meyers Industries,* cited in note 6 of *City Disposal Systems,* a firm discharged an employee because of his safety complaints and his refusal to drive a truck after reporting its condition to the Tennessee Public Service Commission. The Board found the employee's actions leading to his discharge not to be concerted activity.

> In general, to find an employee's activity to be "concerted," we shall require that it be engaged in with or on the authority of other employees, and not solely by and on behalf of the employee himself. Once the activity is found to be concerted, an §8(a)(1) violation will be found if, in addition, the employer knew of the concerted nature of the employee's activity, the concerted activity was protected by the Act, and the adverse employment action at issue (e.g., discharge) was motivated by the employee's protected concerted activity. . . . It will no longer be sufficient for the General Counsel to set out the subject matter that is of alleged concern to a theoretical group and expect to establish concert of action thereby.

The actions of the employee in the instant case did not meet the standard because he alone refused to drive the truck and trailer (although another employee was making a similar complaint at about the same time), and he alone contacted public authorities. There was no union involved.

In *Meyers,* the Board pulled back from a model of concerted activity that might be thought to have been expansive. In the course of its opinion it reviews many prior cases on the meaning of concerted activity, but it does not discuss any precedent with the question of whether employer intent or knowledge must be shown to make out a §8(a)(1) violation. Is the quoted passage consistent with *Darlington,* supra at p. 282, for example?

2. Does the collective goods model suggest a basis for distinguishing concerted from unconcerted activities? Did James Brown seek a collective good? Did the worker in *Meyers*? Consider that there is a characterization problem here. Refusing to drive an unsafe truck may be an individualized good, whereas "safety" is a collective good. Moreover, a collective good may be secured by a single employee who has no interest in the welfare of others. Do you think §7 should be read to protect every

attempt to produce a collective good, perhaps because otherwise collective goods will be underproduced, or should the *process* of production play a decisive role?

A PRELIMINARY ESSAY ON STATUTORY ENTITLEMENTS

The purpose of this essay is to analyze the functions that statutory entitlements serve in labor-management collective bargaining contexts. For instance, in *Weingarten* the Supreme Court held that unions have the statutory right to have a union representative present when an employee is called into an investigatory (disciplinary) interview by managers. In *City Disposal Systems,* the Court ruled that certain actions by an individual employee are protected by §7 unless waived in a collective bargaining agreement. Had the Court ruled the other way in either of those cases, presumably the unions could have secured identical rights through collective bargaining with employers. And after the Court's decisions in those cases, dissatisfied employers could bargain for a waiver from unions. *Mastro Plastics* is another example, and many more such cases are discussed in later chapters.

One way of beginning to think about these questions is to ask, "If the union didn't buy the right before, why don't they sell it now?" For example, assume that before the Supreme Court's decision in *Weingarten,* unions believed that employees had no right to union representation in an investigatory interview unless they negotiated such a right in their bargaining agreement. Assume further that such terms were seldom negotiated. After the Supreme Court's decision would you expect to find frequent waivers of the right by unions? If not, why not? I begin by making the following assumptions:

1. There are no transactions costs.
2. Entitlements are clear.
3. Parties have perfect information (they know one another's preferences).
4. Contracts are enforceable and statutory entitlements can be waived.

On these assumptions, in a market context, statutory entitlements function as contractual gap-fillers or "off-the-rack" terms. To illustrate, assume two jurisdictions East State and West State, which are identical except for a difference in a particular statutory entitlement. *R* and *U* are private parties who find it beneficial to enter into a binding contract with one another. Call one matter that is bound up in the contract *x,* which might be the time of delivery, a warranty, or a measure of damages in case of a breach. The legal rule in West State is that absent a contract term, *R* gets *x*;[3] the rule in East State is that absent a contract term, *U* gets *x*. We can predict that in West State, if *R* values *x* more highly than *U* does, *R* will purchase it from *U* as part of the contract; but if *U* values it more than *R* does, *x* will remain as the statute places it.

A similar analysis applies in East State: If *U* values *x* more than *R* does, *U* will buy it as part of the contract; but if *R* values it more highly, there will be no transfer. So long as the rule makers allow *x* to be bought and sold (waived), *x* will end up[4] in the hands of the contracting party who values it the more highly. This is true regardless of its initial placement as a statutory entitlement.

The next question is whether the alternative statutory entitlements have distributional effects in this simplified hypothetical. First, consider the situation in which there is a competitive market in the subject matter of the contract. Suppose the state legislature passes a statute saying that every household contracting for the services of a plumber must provide the plumber with free coffee unless the plumber waives this right. The price for plumbing before the coffee law was passed was $17/hour, and plumbers value on-the-job coffee at $2/hour. After the law is passed, we would expect to see two prices for plumbing: $15/hour with coffee and $17 with a waiver of coffee.[5]

An example in a different context illustrates the same point. Suppose the federal government were to promulgate a regulation that all wheat must be delivered by sellers to buyers in burlap bags, as opposed to open boxcars, unless the buyer and seller stipulate to the contrary. Prior to the regulation wheat is selling for $1/bushel, and the cost to the seller to put a bushel of wheat in a burlap bag is $0.07. While there may be a time lag while buyers and sellers adjust to the new regulation, it seems clear that the price of a bushel of wheat after the regulation will be $1.07/bushel in burlap bags, and $1/bushel with a waiver of the regulation. I conclude that, given the assumptions, in a deep market a statutory entitlement has no distributive effects (wealth redistributions).

The union/management collective bargaining context is not a competitive market situation; it is a peculiar kind of bilateral monopoly. In more typical bilateral monopolies, there are no other potential contracting parties on either side of the transaction and both parties stand to gain from the transaction. Consider the effects of a statutory entitlement in the typical bilateral monopoly case. Assume that the two parties to a bilateral monopoly (again, *R* and *U*) decide that each would be better off with a contractual exchange and that the value of the contractual "pie" is

[3] For example, the time of delivery is in *R*'s favor, or there is an implied warranty running in his or her favor, etc.

[4] E.g., the time of delivery will change, or there will be no implied warranty.

[5] The regulation may be so misguided that the only price ordinarily offered is $17/hour with the waiver.

$300. The outcomes for *U* range from a low of $1 to a high of $299. *R* has an identical range.

Suppose the Supreme Court, construing a regulatory statute, declares that unless the contract provides otherwise, *U* has a particular contractual right, *x*. In construing the statute, the Court has not increased the bargaining range for either party even though *x* has a positive value to each side.[6] The Court's rule has no distributive effect; it merely serves as a contractual term for those agreements that do not provide to the contrary. Absent transactions costs, we can also predict that *x* will end up in the hands of the party who values it the most; for no matter who is the better bargainer, once the bargain is struck if *x* is in the hands of the party who values it less, there is mutual gain to be made from selling the right to the other party. The placement of the right by the Court will have neither allocative nor distributive effect.

Now consider the special case of union/management collective bargaining. Collective bargaining can be seen as a zero-sum game in which the managers are forced to give the union items of value because otherwise the union will inflict injury on both the firm and on itself (its members) by striking. Managers can be said to "possess" many assets of value to the union. These include wage increases, seniority promotions, grievance and arbitration procedures, "just cause" disciplinary guarantees, promises of notice before plant relocation or shutdown, and a host of other potential contractual promises. Among the calculations that managers must make before giving the union any of these assets are the likelihood that the union will strike, the duration and seriousness of the strike from the managers' standpoint and from that of the employees, and the effect of particular promises on union demands in future years.

Suppose the Supreme Court, interpreting the labor statutes, rules that if the union and the managers reach an agreement that does not expressly mention seniority promotions, the union gets this asset;[7] and if the parties fail to reach an agreement, the union gets this asset. The union has an "entitlement" to seniority promotions. If seniority promotions have a high enough value to the union, it may be content with that asset and abandon its strike threat. And if the managers show great determination not to yield to any other of the union's demands, settling for seniority promotions in the context of no agreement may again be the union's choice. But seniority promotions may have a value below the union's minimum expectation — that is, the union requires more or else it will strike. Suppose, for instance, that the union puts a money value of $10,000 on seniority promotions. If the union's minimum settlement point without regard for this entitlement would have been $8,000, the

[6] If this is not intuitive, contrast it with a governmental award of $50 to any party successfully reaching a contract.

[7] Thus seniority promotions are an implied term in the agreement.

Court's action will redistribute wealth from managers to the union.[8] If the union's minimum settlement point would instead have been $15,000, the entitlement will have neither allocative nor distributional effects.

In the real world, where assumptions are relaxed, my hunch is that investigation would reveal that there are many instances of statutory entitlements where unions and managers initially assumed that a particular "right" was in the hands of, say, management and few if any bargaining agreements transferred the right to a union; yet after a Court decision declaring the right to belong to the unions, there were few instances of waiver. The question is why such waivers are not common.

One possibility is that the entitlement is trivial. The cost of negotiating to put the right in the hand of the party that values it the most is greater than the value of the right to that party. By cost of negotiating I mean the expense of meeting and exchanging information.[9] Such an entitlement has both allocative and distributional effects. I think it is unlikely that many of the entitlements are trivial in this sense.

A second theory is what I call the batch theory. After a collective bargaining agreement is reached (either finally, or provisional on membership ratification), union negotiators must explain to the membership which assets were secured in collective bargaining and persuade the members that the negotiators did a good job. When the asset "belongs" to the managers (that is, the managers will have the asset unless the union expressly secures it in collective bargaining), negotiators must persuade the members that the union was not powerful enough to get the asset. They can do so by relying on the high value that managers gave to the asset as well as the limits on the union's power. They need not establish the value to management, only that it was "high."

Similar persuasion is necessary when the Court has given the asset to the union but the union's negotiators have bargained it away. The negotiators would say, "We sold the asset back to the employer." A problem may arise in explaining to the members what the negotiators got from the managers in return for the asset. Terms in collective bargaining agreements may be negotiated in "batches." That is, a contract proposal containing many terms is presented and a counterproposal comes back with many terms changed. The differences are dickered over, other proposals are exchanged, and agreement is reached. The point is that the negotiators may be unable to say precisely what they got for a particular asset; that trade-off was submerged in a host of trades. Because the negotiators have given up something of value without being able to identify its quid pro quo, they may be especially vulnerable to critics

[8] The analysis assumes that the managers do not have the ability to injure the union (in the absence of an agreement) and thereby force the union to give back the asset.

[9] Another sense in which negotiating costs can be greater than the entitlement is if negotiations over the issue are likely to lead to a breakdown and a strike, and the costs of the strike are greater than the entitlement.

within the union. To avoid this criticism, negotiators may refuse to bargain away assets granted by statute.

A third theory I call the preference exposure theory. Often a useful strategy in negotiations is to understate or overstate one's true preferences. Suppose that a union assigns a value of ten to an asset, the managers assign it a value of two, and the union owns it unless it bargains it away. We can predict that the managers will not offer enough to buy the asset and that it will remain with the union. The union may discover the value of the asset to the managers, but the managers may not find out the actual value that the union assigns to the asset — only that it is greater than two. Should the Court now assign the asset to the managers, the union will have to purchase it. Since they assign it a considerably higher value than the managers do, the purchase should be made at something between two and ten.

In making the purchase, the union may have to disclose its true preference for the good, although to the extent that it strategically understates its preference, the price may be closer to two than to ten. Suppose that in addition to the first asset (*a*), there is a second good, *b*, and that in purchasing *a* from the managers the union will necessarily reveal some information about its preference for *b*. Now the cost to the union is outside (higher than) the two-to-ten range. The true cost includes the loss of strategic advantage in unwillingly conveying information to the managers about *b*. The price of *a* may now be greater than ten, and the union will not purchase it. This analysis would explain why the union would not sell *a* if it owned it but also would not buy it if it were placed by the Court with the managers.

A fourth theory explains union-manager interaction by the offer/asking price theory. This theory posits that the minimum price at which the union would be willing to sell an item of value that it owns may be higher than the price at which the union would be willing to buy it, and that this effect can be independent of transactions costs and wealth effects. For some, this asserted discrepancy is not intuitively plausible, and its application in a collective bargaining context is unclear.

I am not prepared at this time to draw normative conclusions from this analysis. It seems to me, however, that evaluations of a considerable number of rules in labor law ought to take this line of analysis into account.

NLRB v. MACKAY RADIO & TELEGRAPH CO.
304 U.S. 333 (1938)

[The union called an economic strike against the Mackay Company and the company brought in replacements for the striking employees. Some of the strikers became persuaded that the strike was not going to be successful and asked to return to their jobs. The company informed them that some of the replacements had been promised permanent positions. Eventually the company designated five union leaders as those who were deemed to have been permanently replaced. The Board found a violation on the ground that the company's selection criterion (extent of union activity) was discriminatory and found it unnecessary to decide the general issue of the legality of permanent replacement of strikers. The court of appeals refused to enforce the Board's order that the strikers be reinstated with backpay; the Supreme Court reversed.]

Roberts, J. . . .

The strikers remained employees under §2(3) of the act which provides: "The term 'employee' shall include . . . any individual whose work has ceased as a consequence of, or in connection with, any current labor dispute or because of any unfair labor practice, and who has not obtained any other regular and substantially equivalent employment. . . ." Within this definition the strikers remained employees for the purpose of the act and were protected against the unfair labor practices denounced by it.

It is contended that the Board lacked jurisdiction because respondent was at no time guilty of any unfair labor practice. . . . There is no evidence and no finding that the respondent was guilty of any unfair labor practice in connection with the negotiations. . . . On the contrary, it affirmatively appears that the respondent was negotiating with the authorized representatives of the union. Nor was it an unfair labor practice to replace the striking employees with others in an effort to carry on the business. Although §13 of the act, provides, "Nothing in this Act shall be construed so as to interfere with or impede or diminish in any way the right to strike," it does not follow that an employer, guilty of no act denounced by the statute, has lost the right to protect and continue his business by supplying places left vacant by strikers. And he is not bound to discharge those hired to fill the places of strikers, upon the election of the latter to resume their employment, in order to create places for them. The assurance by respondent to those who accepted employment during the strike that if they so desired their places might be permanent was not an unfair labor practice, nor was it such to reinstate only so many of the strikers as there were vacant places to be filled. But the claim put forward is that the unfair labor practice indulged by the respondent was discrimination in reinstating striking employees by keeping out certain of them for the sole reason that they had been active in the union. As we have said, the strikers retained, under the act, the status of employees. Any such discrimination in putting them back to work is, therefore, prohibited by §8.

The Board's findings as to discrimination are supported by evidence. . . .

The Board found, and we cannot say that its finding is unsupported, that, in taking back six of the eleven men and excluding five who were active union men, the respondent's officials discriminated against the latter on account of their union activities and that the excuse given that they did not apply until after the quota was full was an afterthought and not the true reason for the discrimination against them.

As we have said, the respondent was not bound to displace men hired to take the strikers' places in order to provide positions for them. It might have refused reinstatement on the grounds of skill or ability, but the Board found that it did not do so. It might have resorted to any one of a number of methods of determining which of its striking employees would have to wait because five men had taken permanent positions during the strike, but it is found that the preparation and use of the list, and the action taken by respondent, was with the purpose to discriminate against those most active in the union. There is evidence to support these findings. . . .[10]

NLRB v. ERIE RESISTOR CORP.

373 U.S. 221 (1963)

[When the collective bargaining agreement expired, the union called a strike for new terms. All the unit employees joined the strike. Under intensive competitive pressure and unable to maintain production using nonunit employees, the company, after notifying the strikers, hired replacements and promised them that they would not be laid off or discharged at the end of the strike. The area was suffering from extreme unemployment. Later in the strike, the company notified the union that it was according both the replacements and any strikers who would return to work 20 years' additional seniority that could be used as a credit against future layoffs, but could not be used for other employee benefits based on years of service. The strikers voted to continue the strike, now in protest of the seniority grant as well as for economic benefits. However, many employees returned to work and the union eventually capitulated and called off the strike.

The union contended the seniority grant was an unfair labor practice. The trial examiner found the policy was adopted for legitimate economic reasons and not for illegal or discriminatory purposes. The Board held that specific evidence of subjective intent to discriminate was not a necessary element in finding a violation and that the employer's insistence that its overriding purpose in granting the super-seniority was to keep its plant open was unacceptable since "to excuse such conduct would greatly diminish, if not destroy, the right to strike guaranteed by

[10] Cardozo, J., and Reed, J., took no part in the decision.

the Act, and would run directly counter to the guarantees of §§8(a)(1) and (3) that employees shall not be discriminated against for engaging in protected concerted activities."]

WHITE, J. . . .

The question before us is whether an employer commits an unfair labor practice under §8(a) . . . when he extends a 20-year seniority credit to strike replacements and strikers who leave the strike and return to work. . . . The Court of Appeals rejected as unsupportable the rationale of the Board that a preferential seniority policy is illegal however motivated.

> We are of the opinion that inherent in the right of an employer to replace strikers during a strike is the concomitant right to adopt a preferential seniority policy which will assure the replacements some form of tenure, provided the policy is adopted *solely* to protect and continue the business of the employer. We find nothing in the Act which proscribes such a policy. Whether the policy adopted by the Company in the instant case was illegally motivated we do not decide. The question is one of fact for decision by the Board. 303 F.2d, at 364.

It consequently denied the Board's petition for enforcement and remanded the case for further findings.

We think the Court of Appeals erred in holding that, in the absence of a finding of specific illegal intent, a legitimate business purpose is always a defense to an unfair labor practice charge. Cases in this Court dealing with unfair labor practices have recognized the relevance and importance of showing the employer's intent or motive to discriminate or to interfere with union rights. But specific evidence of such subjective intent is "not an indispensable element of proof of violation." Radio Officers v. Labor Board, 347 U.S. 17, 44. "Some conduct may by its very nature contain the implications of the required intent; the natural foreseeable consequences of certain action may warrant the inference. . . . The existence of discrimination may at times be inferred by the Board, for 'it is permissible to draw on experience in factual inquiries.' " Teamsters Local v. Labor Board, 365 U.S. 667, 675.

Though the interest necessary for an unfair labor practice may be shown in different ways, proving it in one manner may have far different weight and far different consequences than proving it in another. When specific evidence of a subjective intent to discriminate or to encourage or discourage union membership is shown, and found, many otherwise innocent or ambiguous actions which are normally incident to the conduct of a business may, without more, be converted into unfair labor practices. Labor Board v. Jones & Laughlin Steel Corp., 301 U.S. 1, 46 (discharging employees); Associated Press v. Labor Board, 301 U.S. 103, 132 (discharging employees); Phelps Dodge Corp. v. Labor Board, 313 U.S. 177 (hiring employees). Compare Labor Board v.

Brown-Dunkin Co., 287 F.2d 17, with Labor Board v. Houston Chronicle Publishing Co., 211 F.2d 848 (subcontracting union work); and Fiss Corp., 43 N.L.R.B. 125, with Jacob H. Klotz, 13 N.L.R.B. 746 (movement of plant to another town). Such proof itself is normally sufficient to destroy the employer's claim of a legitimate business purpose, if one is made, and provides strong support to a finding that there is interference with union rights or that union membership will be discouraged. Conduct which on its face appears to serve legitimate business ends in these cases is wholly impeached by the showing of an intent to encroach upon protected rights. The employer's claim of legitimacy is totally dispelled.

The outcome may well be the same when intent is founded upon the inherently discriminatory or destructive nature of the conduct itself. The employer in such cases must be held to intend the very consequences which foreseeably and inescapably flow from his actions and if he fails to explain away, to justify or to characterize his actions as something different than they appear on their face, an unfair labor practice charge is made out. But, as often happens, the employer may counter by claiming that his actions were taken in the pursuit of legitimate business ends and that his dominant purpose was not to discriminate or to invade union rights but to accomplish business objectives acceptable under the Act. Nevertheless, his conduct *does* speak for itself — it *is* discriminatory and it *does* discourage union membership and whatever the claimed overriding justification may be, it carries with it unavoidable consequences which the employer not only foresaw but which he must have intended. As is not uncommon in human experience, such situations present a complex of motives and preferring one motive to another is in reality the far more delicate task, reflected in part in decisions of this Court,[7] of weighing the interests of employees in concerted activity against the interest of the employer in operating his business in a particular manner and of balancing in the light of the Act and its policy the intended consequences upon employee rights against the business ends to be served by the employer's conduct.[8] This essentially is the teaching

7. See, e.g., Labor Board v. Mackay Radio & Tel. Co., 304 U.S. 333; Republic Aviation Corp. v. Labor Board, 324 U.S. 793; Labor Board v. Babcock & Wilcox Co., 351 U.S. 105; Labor Board v. Truck Drivers Union, 353 U.S. 87.

8. In a variety of situations, the lower courts have dealt with and rejected the approach urged here that conduct otherwise unlawful is automatically excused upon a showing that it was motivated by business exigencies. Thus, it has been held that an employer cannot justify the discriminatory discharge of union members upon the ground that such conduct is the only way to induce a rival union to remove a picket line and permit the resumption of business, or rearrange the bargaining unit because of an expected adverse effect on production, or defend a refusal to bargain in good faith on the ground that unless the employer's view prevails dire consequences to the business will follow, or refuse exclusive recognition to a union for fear that such recognition will bring reprisals from rival unions, or discriminate in his business operations against employees of rival unions or without union affiliation solely in order to keep peace in the plant and avoid disruption of business. Indeed, many employers doubtless could conscientiously assert that their unfair labor practices were not malicious but were prompted by their best judgment as to the interests of their business. Such good-faith motive itself, however, has not been deemed an absolute defense to an unfair labor practice charge.

of the Court's prior cases dealing with this problem and, in our view, the Board did not depart from it.

The Board made a detailed assessment of super-seniority and, to its experienced eye, such a plan had the following characteristics:

1. Super-seniority affects the tenure of all strikers whereas permanent replacement, proper under *Mackay,* affects only those who are, in actuality, replaced. It is one thing to say that a striker is subject to loss of his job at the strike's end but quite another to hold that in addition to the threat of replacement, all strikers will at best return to their jobs with seniority inferior to that of the replacements and of those who left the strike.
2. A super-seniority award necessarily operates to the detriment of those who participated in the strike as compared to nonstrikers.
3. Super-seniority made available to striking bargaining unit employees as well as to new employees is in effect offering individual benefits to the strikers to induce them to abandon the strike.
4. Extending the benefits of super-seniority to striking bargaining unit employees as well as to new replacements deals a crippling blow to the strike effort. At one stroke, those with low seniority have the opportunity to obtain the job security which ordinarily only long years of service can bring, while conversely, the accumulated seniority of older employees is seriously diluted. This combination of threat and promise could be expected to undermine the strikers' mutual interest and place the entire strike effort in jeopardy. The history of this strike and its virtual collapse following the announcement of the plan emphasize the grave repercussions of super-seniority.
5. Super-seniority renders future bargaining difficult, if not impossible, for the collective bargaining representative. Unlike the replacement granted in *Mackay* which ceases to be an issue once the strike is over, the plan here creates a cleavage in the plant continuing long after the strike is ended. Employees are henceforth divided into two camps: those who stayed with the union and those who returned before the end of the strike and thereby gained extra seniority. This breach is re-emphasized with each subsequent layoff and stands as an ever-present reminder of the dangers connected with striking and with union activities in general.

In the light of this analysis, super-seniority by its very terms operates to discriminate between strikers and non-strikers, both during and after a strike, and its destructive impact upon the strike and union activity cannot be doubted. The origin of the plan, as respondent insists, may have been to keep production going and it may have been necessary to offer super-seniority to attract replacements and induce union members to leave the strike. But if this is true, accomplishment of respondent's business purpose inexorably was contingent upon attracting sufficient replacements and strikers by offering preferential inducements to those who worked as opposed to those who struck. We think the Board was entitled to treat this case as involving conduct which carried its own indicia of intent and which is barred by the Act unless saved from illegality by an overriding business purpose justifying the invasion of union rights. The Board concluded that the business purpose asserted was insufficient to insulate the super-seniority plan from the reach of §8(a)(1) and §8(a)(3), and we turn now to a review of that conclusion.

The Court of Appeals and respondent rely upon *Mackay* as precluding the result reached by the Board but we are not persuaded. Under the decision in that case an employer may operate his plant during a strike and at its conclusion need not discharge those who worked during the strike in order to make way for returning strikers. It may be, as the Court of Appeals said, that "such a replacement policy is obviously discriminatory and may tend to discourage union membership." But *Mackay* did not deal with super-seniority, with its effects upon all strikers, whether replaced or not, or with its powerful impact upon a strike itself. Because the employer's interest must be deemed to outweigh the damage to concerted activities caused by permanently replacing strikers does not mean it also outweighs the far greater encroachment resulting from super-seniority in addition to permanent replacement.

We have no intention of questioning the continuing vitality of the *Mackay* rule, but we are not prepared to extend it to the situation we have here. . . . [I]n view of the deference paid the strike weapon by the federal labor laws and the devastating consequences upon it which the Board found was and would be precipitated by respondent's inherently discriminatory super-seniority plan, we cannot say the Board erred in the balance which it struck here. Although the Board's decisions are by no means immune from attack in the courts as cases in this Court amply illustrate, its findings here are supported by substantial evidence, its explication is not inadequate, irrational or arbitrary, and it did not exceed its powers or venture into an area barred by the statute. "The ultimate problem is the balancing of the conflicting legitimate interests. The function of striking that balance to effectuate national labor policy is often a difficult and delicate responsibility, which the Congress committed primarily to the National Labor Relations Board, subject to limited judicial review." Labor Board v. Truck Drivers Union, 353 U.S. 87, 99. . . .[11]

[11] Harlan, J., concurred.

Notes

1. Evaluate the following as an argument to the Supreme Court:

> We concede that the *Mackay* "rule" approving the permanent replacement of economic strikers has been widely and uncritically applied. But repeated applications do not make it correct. Employees join together and strike for economic benefits; as a result, under *Mackay* not only do they fail to gain benefits, *they lose their jobs*. Nothing could be more discriminatory, no act could be more destructive of the right to organize for a common cause, than the loss of a person's means of livelihood. There is no warrant in the statute for reaching a mystical ad hoc balance between §7 rights and the right of management to have a weapon sufficient to bludgeon organized employees out of existence.
>
> Nor is the *Mackay* decision worthy of stare decisis deference. The rule was dictum and its formulation was without input from the agency charged by Congress with implementing the statute. Second, the opinion fails to mention, if indeed it appreciated at all, that on any principled view of the statute the right to hire permanent replacements should not be a relevant inquiry unless and until the employer can prove convincingly that temporary replacements were unavailable.
>
> Finally, the rule is capricious in operation. When employment is high, replacements are difficult or impossible to find; when community employment is low, the employer will easily replace the strikers. The right to replace may be no right at all in a small rural town in Iowa, but outcome-determinative of a strike in Cleveland. Thus the efficacy of a strike depends on matters of location and the level of employment, matters totally irrelevant to the merits of the dispute. . . .

2. In *Erie Resistor,* what precisely was the relevance of the fact, if it was a fact, that the employer could not secure replacements unless he or she offered them super-seniority?

3. What does it mean to say that a new employee is a "permanent replacement" for a striker? It is highly unlikely that the new employee has an enforceable employment contract that extends over a period of time. And if such an individual employment contract did exist, wouldn't it be subject to attack on *J. I. Case* grounds (supra, at p. 306) and on the ground that it is a grant of super-seniority illegal under *Erie Resistor*? But if there is no enforceable employment contract, the employer can discharge the new employees at his or her pleasure.[12] Thus isn't it at the employer's whim whether to call the new employees "permanent" and visit the discharge penalty upon the strikers?

The following is excerpted from Associated Grocers, 253 N.L.R.B. 31 (1980):

[12] If the employer makes a promise of permanent jobs to replacements that satisfies common law contract rules, federal law will not preempt the enforcement of the contract in state court. See Belknap v. Hale, infra at p. 857.

The facts as found by the Administrative Law Judge do not support his conclusion that as of May 10, 1978, all strike replacements were hired as permanent employees. The more than 1,000 replacements hired during the April 12 to October 4 strike signed a statement acknowledging that their employment was temporary. On May 10 all then current employees received a letter from Respondent's president, Nichols, advising them that they had been hired as permanent employees entitled to company benefits after a 90-day probationary period. Between May 10 and May 18, 237 employees signed an acknowledgment at the bottom of the letter. However, because of a communication failure between Nichols and his personnel managers, replacements hired after May 10 received and signed only the original statement acknowledging temporary status. . . .

Permanent replacement of strikers in order to continue business operations is a legitimate business justification for refusing to reinstate economic strikers upon appropriate application. NLRB v. Mackay Radio & Telegraph Co., 304 U.S. 333 (1939). However, it is an affirmative defense and Respondent has the burden of proof. NLRB v. Fleetwood Trailer Co., Inc., 389 U.S. 375 (1967); W. C. McQuaide, Inc., 237 N.L.R.B. 177 (1978); National Fresh Fruit and Vegetable Company and Quality Banana Co., Inc., 227 N.L.R.B. 2014 (1977), enforcement denied on other grounds 565 F.2d 1331 (5th Cir. 1978). Here, the burden was satisfied only with respect to the 237 employees who signed the May 10 letter acknowledging permanency. Each of those 237 employees and Respondent had a mutual understanding and commitment on the permanent nature of their employment. Conversely, replacements hired after May 10 acknowledge that their employment was temporary and received no assurance that their employment was permanent. The permanency of the post May 10 replacements was established only in the mind of Respondent's president, a showing insufficient to satisfy Respondent's burden. Covington Furniture, 212 N.L.R.B. 214, 219-220 (1974); cf. Superior National Bank and Trust, 246 N.L.R.B. No. 123 (1979).

The Union made appropriate application on behalf of the strikers in its October 4 mailgram to Respondent, unconditionally offering to return to work. Respondent refused to take back all of the strikers immediately since it maintained that all replacements were permanent. Economic strikers must be reinstated upon appropriate application, absent a legitimate business justification which can include permanent replacement. Mackay Radio, 304 U.S. 333. As the Administrative Law Judge found that the strikers had been permanently replaced, he found Respondent's refusal to immediately reinstate strikers justified. However, as set forth above, we do not agree that all strike replacements were permanent. Thus, by refusing to reinstate on and after October 4 those economic strikers who had not been permanently replaced, Respondent violated §§8(a)(3) and (1) of the Act.

Alternatively, can't all replacements be deemed permanent on the ground that to oust them in favor of returning strikers violates §§8(a)(3), (2), and (1)? Would a strike settlement agreement calling for such an ouster be lawful?

4. In NLRB v. International Van Lines, 409 U.S. 48 (1972), the Court adopted the generally viewed meaning of the *Mackay* rule, that an economic striker may not be discharged but may be replaced. Thus a striker's right to his or her job upon an unconditional offer to return to work depends on whether a permanent replacement has actually been secured.[13]

Even if the striker's job has been filled, some employment rights remain. In Laidlaw Corp., 171 N.L.R.B. 1366 (1968), enforced, 414 F.2d 99 (7th Cir. 1969), cert. denied, 397 U.S. 920 (1970), the NLRB held that

> economic strikers who unconditionally apply for reinstatement at a time when their positions are filled by permanent replacements: (1) remain employees; (2) are entitled to full reinstatement upon the departure of replacements unless they have in the meantime acquired regular and substantially equivalent employment, or the employer can sustain his burden of proof that the failure to offer full reinstatement was for legitimate and substantial business reasons.

5. As the Court indicated in *Mastro Plastics*, supra at p. 344, where a strike is in protest of an employer's unfair labor practice, strikers have a right to their jobs upon an unconditional offer to return to work notwithstanding that the employer has called their replacements permanent. Also, a strike that begins as an economic strike may be converted to an unfair labor practice strike if the employer commits unfair labor practices during its duration that prolong the strike.[14] The Board so held in *Erie Resistor*.

Whether the strikers have shifted from an economic motive to one in protest of the employer's misdeeds is a question of fact for the Board — and it is likely that the unfair labor practice will have to be of a serious nature before the Board will find there has been such a conversion. When the union claims that a strike has been precipitated by unfair labor practices, the employer faces a dilemma. The employer has no right to refuse to reinstate unfair labor practice strikers even though they have been replaced, yet a determination of whether the employer has in fact committed an unfair labor practice may take years to resolve. Is it unfair to put an employer in such a position or does it represent a necessary qualification of his or her right to replace? Is the only employer put to the dilemma one who has engaged in unfair labor practice brinksmanship?

[13] In Abilities & Goodwill, 241 N.L.R.B. 27 (1979), enforcement denied, 612 F.2d 6 (1st Cir. 1979), the Board, 3-2, overruled prior doctrine, which held that an unlawfully discharged striker had a right to backpay only from the time that the striker made a request for reinstatement and an unconditional offer to return to work. The employer's backpay obligation now begins at the time of the unlawful discharge.

[14] See Stewart, Conversion of Strikes: Economic to Unfair Labor Practice: I, II, 45 Va. L. Rev. 1322 (1959), 49 Va. L. Rev. 1297 (1963).

6. Whether a strike is deemed economic or in protest of an unfair labor practice may also control the reinstatement rights of strikers who have engaged in misconduct. In NLRB v. Thayer Co., 213 F.2d 748 (1st Cir.), cert. denied, 348 U.S. 883 (1954), the court held that an economic striker discharged for conduct unprotected by §7 could not be reinstated by the Board because the employer had committed no unfair labor practice to which a remedial order could attach. But, if the strike were caused or prolonged by an employer unfair labor practice, the Board could remedy the unfair labor practice with the reinstatement of strikers guilty of (unprotected) misconduct so long as their conduct did not constitute "cause" under §10(c).

According to the First Circuit, the Board should "balance the severity of the employer's unfair labor practice which provoked the industrial disturbance against whatever employee misconduct occurred during the strike." Do you see why the court adopted such a balancing test? What sorts of employee misconduct in your view would always preclude reinstatement?

7. *The status of employees to cross a picket line at another's place of business.* It is a principle of at least part of the trade union movement that a union member does not cross a picket line, whether established by his or her own or another's union. Where a delivery person refuses to cross a picket line at a customer's place of business, can he or she be discharged or replaced? Resolution of this simple question turns out to be very difficult.

An employer, responding to the union's contention that the refusal to cross a picket line is protected by §7, has several arguments:

a. The refusal is not protected §7 activity because (1) it is not concerted, (2) it is a partial work stoppage, (3) it is in breach of a no-strike clause, (4) where the picket line is itself violative of the Act (e.g., a §8(b)(7) violation), the refusal is for an unlawful purpose;
b. Although the refusal may be §7 activity, discharge is permissible because the discharge/replacement distinction is unwarranted in this context; and
c. The refusal itself violates the secondary boycott provisions of the Act, thus permitting discharge.

Even though only one of the employer's employees refuses to cross the picket line at the customer's premises, the Board and courts have had no difficulty deeming it concerted activity. An early rationale was provided by Judge Learned Hand in NLRB v. Peter Cailler Kohler Swiss Chocolates Co., 130 F.2d 503, 505-506 (2d Cir. 1942):

> When all the other workmen in a shop make common cause with a fellow workman over his separate grievance, and go out on strike in his support,

> they engage in a "concerted activity" for "mutual aid or protection," although the aggrieved workman is the only one of them who has any immediate stake in the outcome. The rest know that by their action each one of them assures himself, in case his turn ever comes, of the support of the one whom they are all then helping, and the solidarity so established is "mutual aid" in the most literal sense, as nobody doubts. So too of those engaging in a "sympathetic strike," or secondary boycott; the immediate quarrel does not itself concern them, but by extending the number of those who will make the enemy of one the enemy of all, the power of each is vastly increased. It is one thing how far a community should allow such power to grow; but, whatever may be the proper place to check it, each separate extension is certainly a step in "mutual aid or protection." It is true that in the past courts often fail to recognize the interest which each might have in a solidarity so obtained, but it seems to us that the Act has put an end to this.[15]

Arguments that a refusal to cross a picket line is a partial work stoppage, and thus unprotected, either have not been made to the Board and courts or have been ignored in the opinions. Professor Julius Getman argues that since such refusals to cross involve no serious economic hardship to the employer, they should not fall within the rule that partial strikes are unprotected activity.[16]

To evaluate some of the employer's other arguments we must look to NLRB v. Rockway News Supply Co., 345 U.S. 71 (1953). In that case an employee had been discharged for refusing to cross a picket line although no replacement had been secured when this employee was "fired." The collective bargaining agreement between the employer and the union provided that "[n]o strikes . . . or other cessation of work . . . shall be ordered or sanctioned by any party hereto. . . ." A labor arbitrator in a breach of contract action had ruled that the employer had not breached the bargaining agreement by discharging the employee, perhaps relying on contract negotiations where the union demanded, but failed to secure, a contract clause stating "no man shall be required to cross a picket line."

The Court upheld the discharge against an attack that it was an unfair labor practice, stating "an employee's breach of [a bargaining] agreement may be made grounds for his discharge without violating §7 of the Act." But the Court was not content to rely on this ground of decision; it also rendered its view of the case absent the breach of contract issue:

> The actual controversy here is within a very narrow scope, so narrow that the Board in its opinion said:

[15] Recall the Supreme Court quoted the first half of this paragraph in *Weingarten*, supra at p. 347.

[16] Getman, the Protection of Economic Pressure by §7 of the National Labor Relations Act, 115 U. Pa. L. Rev. 1195, 1226 n. 133 (1967).

> Although Waugh's refusal to cross the picket line was a protected activity, the Respondent, as a normal incident of its right to maintain its operations, could have required Waugh to elect whether to perform all his duties or, as a striker, to vacate his job and make way for his replacement by the Respondent. Instead the Respondent discharged Waugh.

The Court of Appeals said [197 F.2d 114], "we cannot follow the Board's reasoning." Nor can we. The distinction between discharge and replacement in this context seems to us as unrealistic and unfounded in law as the Court of Appeals found it. This application of the distinction is not sanctioned by NLRB v. Mackay Radio & Telegraph Co., 304 U.S. 333, 347. It is not based on any difference in effect upon the employee. And there is no finding that he was not replaced either by a new employee or by transfer of duties to some non-objecting employee, as would appear necessary if the respondent were to maintain the operation. Substantive rights and duties in the field of labor-management do not depend on verbal ritual reminiscent of medieval real property law.

In subsequent cases the Board has held that where the employer can demonstrate that a discharge preserves the efficient operation of the business, neither the terminology of the employment severance (discharge or replacement) nor the chronological order of the severance and the replacement will control. Key factors in determining whether the employer had a legitimate economic justification are whether the refusal to cross had a substantial adverse effect on the business (could another employee have been conveniently assigned to do the work?) and whether the employer in fact hired replacements.[17] In L. G. Everist, 142 N.L.R.B. 193 (1963), the Board held that an employee discharged for refusing to cross a picket line is entitled to reinstatement if he or she unconditionally applies before a replacement is hired. The Eighth Circuit refused to enforce, 334 F.2d 312 (8th Cir. 1964), feeling that the Board's ruling was too reminiscent of the discharge-replacement distinction condemned in *Rockway*.

What is the employer's economic interest in the picket line cases? Your answer may help you decide whether the Board or the Eighth Circuit has the better of the argument in *L. G. Everist,* and also whether it is particularly relevant that the picket line honored might be itself illegal. If you find the legality of the picketing to be relevant, also consider the plight of the delivery person who, confronted with a decision of whether to honor a picket line at a customer's place of business, must decide whether the picketing violates, say, §8(b)(7), and must decide on pain of discharge.

We will examine the secondary boycott aspects of refusal to cross picket lines in a later chapter. Suffice it to say here that the secondary boycott issues confound, not simplify, the matter.

[17] See Overnight Transportation Co., 154 N.L.R.B. 1271 (1965); Redwing Carriers, 137 N.L.R.B. 1545 (1962).

2. Lockouts[18]

The next two cases deal with employer lockouts, but they also are significant for their discussions of the tests for liability under §§8(a)(3) and (1).

NLRB v. BROWN
380 U.S. 278 (1965)

BRENNAN, J.

The respondents, who are members of a multiemployer bargaining group, locked out their employees in response to a whipsaw strike against another member of the group. They and the struck employer continued operations with temporary replacements. The National Labor Relations Board found that the struck employer's use of temporary replacements was lawful but that the respondents had violated §§8(a)(1) and (3) of the National Labor Relations Act by locking out their regular employees and using temporary replacements to carry on business. 137 N.L.R.B. 73. . . .

Five operators of six retail food stores in Carlsbad, New Mexico, make up the employer group. The stores had bargained successfully on a group basis for many years with Local 462 of the Retail Clerks International Association. Negotiations for a new collective-bargaining agreement to replace the expiring one began in January 1960. Agreement was reached by mid-February on all terms except the amount and effective date of a wage increase. Bargaining continued without result, and on March 2 the Local informed the employers that a strike had been authorized. The employers responded that a strike against any member of the employer group would be regarded as a strike against all. On March 16, the union struck Food Jet, Inc., one of the group. The four respondents, operating five stores, immediately locked out all employees represented by the Local, telling them and the Local that they would be recalled to work when the strike against Food Jet ended. The stores, including Food Jet, continued to carry on business by using management personnel, relatives of such personnel, and a few temporary employees; all of the temporary replacements were expressly told that the arrangement would be discontinued when the whipsaw strike ended. Bargaining continued until April 22 when an agreement was reached. The employers immediately released the temporary replacements and restored the strikers and the locked-out employees to their jobs.

[18] See Bernhardt, Lockouts: An Analysis of Board and Court Decisions Since Brown and American Ship, 25 Cornell L. Rev. 221 (1972); Meltzer, The Lockout Cases, 1965 Sup. Ct. Rev. 87; Oberer, Lockouts and the Law: The Importance of American Shipbuilding and Brown Foods, 51 Cornell L.Q. 193 (1966).

The Board and the Court of Appeals agreed that the case was to be decided in light of our decision in the so-called *Buffalo Linen* case, National Labor Relations Board v. Truck Drivers Union, 353 U.S. 87. There we sustained the Board's finding that, in the absence of specific proof of unlawful motivation, the use of a lockout by members of a multiemployer bargaining unit in response to a whipsaw strike did not violate either §8(a)(1) or §8(a)(3). We held that, although the lockout tended to impair the effectiveness of the whipsaw strike, the right to strike "is not so absolute as to deny self-help by employers when legitimate interests of employees and employers collide. . . . The ultimate problem is the balancing of the conflicting legitimate interests." 353 U.S., at 96. We concluded that the Board correctly balanced those interests in upholding the lockout, since it found that the nonstruck employers resorted to the lockout to preserve the multiemployer bargaining unit from the disintegration threatened by the whipsaw strike. But in the present case the Board held, two members dissenting, that the respondents' continued operations with temporary replacements constituted a "critical difference" from *Buffalo Linen* — where all members of the employer group shut down operations — and that in this circumstance it was reasonable to infer that the respondents did not act to protect the multiemployer group, but "for the purpose of inhibiting a lawful strike." 137 N.L.R.B., at 76. Thus the respondents' act was both a coercive practice condemned by §8(a)(1) and discriminatory conduct in violation of §8(a)(3).

The Board's decision does not rest upon independent evidence that the respondents acted either out of hostility toward the Local or in reprisal for the whipsaw strike. It rests upon the Board's appraisal that the respondents' conduct carried its own indicia of unlawful intent, thereby establishing, without more, that the conduct constituted an unfair labor practice. It was disagreement with this appraisal, which we share, that led the Court of Appeals to refuse to enforce the Board's order. It is true that the Board need not inquire into employer motivation to support a finding of an unfair labor practice where the employer conduct is demonstrably destructive of employee rights and is not justified by the service of significant or important business ends. See, e.g., National Labor Relations Board v. Erie Resistor Corp., 373 U.S. 221, National Labor Relations Board v. Burnup & Sims, Inc., 379 U.S. 21.

We agree with the Court of Appeals that, in the setting of this whipsaw strike and Food Jet's continued operations, the respondents' lockout and their continued operations with the use of temporary replacements, viewed separately or as a single act, do not constitute such conduct. We begin with the proposition that the Act does not constitute the Board as an "arbiter of the sort of economic weapons the parties can use in seeking to gain acceptance of their bargaining demands." National Labor Relations Board v. Insurance Agents, 361 U.S. 477, 497. In the absence of proof of unlawful motivation, there are many economic weapons which an employer may use that either interfere in some measure with concerted employee activities, or which are in some degree discriminatory and discourage union membership, and yet the use of such economic weapons does not constitute conduct that is within the prohibition of either §8(a)(1) or §8(a)(3). . . .

In the circumstances of this case, we do not see how the continued operations of respondents and their use of temporary replacements imply hostile motivation any more than the lockout itself; nor do we see how they are inherently more destructive of employee rights. Rather, the compelling inference is that this was all part and parcel of respondents' defensive measure to preserve the multiemployer group in the face of the whipsaw strike. Since Food Jet legitimately continued business operations, it is only reasonable to regard respondents' action as evincing concern that the integrity of the employer group was threatened unless they also managed to stay open for business during the lockout. For with Food Jet open for business and respondents' stores closed, the prospect that the whipsaw strike would succeed in breaking up the employer association was not at all fanciful. The retail food industry is very competitive and repetitive patronage is highly important. Faced with the prospect of a loss of patronage to Food Jet, it is logical that respondents should have been concerned that one or more of their number might bolt the group and come to terms with the Local, thus destroying the common front essential to multiemployer bargaining. The Court of Appeals correctly pictured the respondents' dilemma in saying, "If . . . the struck employer does choose to operate with replacements and the other employers cannot replace after lockout, the economic advantage passes to the struck member, the nonstruck members are deterred in exercising the defensive lockout, and the whipsaw strike . . . enjoys an almost inescapable prospect of success." 319 F.2d at 11. Clearly respondents' continued operations with the use of temporary replacements following the lockout were wholly consistent with a legitimate business purpose.

Nor are we persuaded by the Board's argument that justification for the inference of hostile motivation appears in the respondents' use of temporary employees rather than some of the regular employees. It is not commonsense, we think, to say that the regular employees were "willing to work at the employers' terms." 137 N.L.R.B., at 76. It seems probable that this "willingness" was motivated as much by their understandable desire to further the objective of the whipsaw strike — to break through the employers' united front by forcing Food Jet to accept the Local's terms — as it was by a desire to work for the employers under the existing unacceptable terms. As the Board's dissenting members put it, "These employees are willing to receive wages while their brethren in the rest of the associationwide unit are exerting whipsaw pressure on one employer to gain benefits that will ultimately accrue to all employees in the associationwide unit, including those here locked out." 137 N.L.R.B., at 78. Moreover, the course of action to which the Board would limit the respondents would force them into the position of aiding and abetting the success of the whipsaw strike and consequently would render "largely illusory," 137 N.L.R.B., at 78-79, the right of lockout recognized by *Buffalo Linen;* the right would be meaningless if barred to nonstruck stores that find it necessary to operate because the struck stores does so.

The Board's finding of a §8(a)(1) violation emphasized the impact of respondents' conduct upon the effectiveness of the whipsaw strike. It is no doubt true that the collective strength of the stores to resist that strike is maintained, and even increased, when all stores stay open with temporary replacements. The pressures on the employees are necessarily greater when none of the union employees is working and the stores remain open. But these pressures are no more than the result of the Local's inability to make effective use of the whipsaw tactic. Moreover, these effects are no different from those that result from the legitimate use of any economic weapon by an employer. Continued operations with the use of temporary replacements may result in the failure of the whipsaw strike, but this does not mean that the employers' conduct is demonstrably so destructive of employee rights and so devoid of significant service to any legitimate business end that it cannot be tolerated consistently with the Act. Certainly then, in the absence of evidentiary findings of hostile motive, there is no support for the conclusion that respondents violated §8(a)(1).

Nor does the record show any basis for concluding that respondents violated §8(a)(3). Under that section both discrimination and a resulting discouragement of union membership are necessary, but the added element of unlawful intent is also required. In *Buffalo Linen* itself the employers treated the locked-out employees less favorably because of their union membership, and this may have tended to discourage continued membership, but we rejected the notion that the use of the lockout violated the statute. The discriminatory act is not by itself unlawful unless intended to prejudice the employees' position because of their membership in the union; some element of antiunion animus is necessary. We have determined that the "real motive" of the employer is an alleged §8(a)(3) violation is decisive, if any doubt still persisted, we laid it to rest in Radio Officers' Union v. National Labor Relations Board, [347 U.S. 17] where we reviewed the legislative history of the provision and concluded that Congress clearly intended the employer's purpose in discriminating to be controlling.

We recognize that, analogous to the determination of unfair practices under §8(a)(1), when an employer practice is inherently destructive of employee rights and is not justified by the service of important business ends, no specific evidence of intent to discourage union membership is necessary to establish a violation of §8(a)(3). This principle, we have said, is "but an application of the common-law rule that a man is held to intend the foreseeable consequences of his conduct." Radio Officers' Union v. National Labor Relations Board, supra, at 45. For example, in National Labor Relations Board v. Erie Resistor Corp., supra, we held that an employer's action in awarding superseniority to employees who worked during a strike was discriminatory conduct that carried with it its own indicia of improper intent. The only reasonable inference that could be drawn by the Board from the award of superseniority — balancing the prejudicial effect upon the employees against any asserted business purpose — was that it was directed against the striking employees because of their union membership; conduct so inherently destructive of employee interests could not be saved from illegality by an asserted overriding business purpose pursued in good faith. But where, as here, the tendency to discourage union membership is comparatively slight, and the employers' conduct is reasonably adapted to achieve legitimate business ends or to deal with business exigencies we enter into an area where the improper motivation of the employers must be established by independent evidence. When so established; antiunion motivation will convert an otherwise ordinary business act into an unfair labor practice.

We agree with the Court of Appeals that respondents' conduct here clearly fits into the latter category, where actual subjective intent is determinative, and where the Board must find from evidence independent of the mere conduct involved that the conduct was primarily motivated by an antiunion animus. While the use of temporary nonunion personnel in preference to the locked-out union members is discriminatory, we think that any resulting tendency to discourage union membership is comparatively remote, and that this use of temporary personnel constitutes a measure reasonably adapted to the effectuation of a legitimate business end. Here discontent on the part of the Local's membership in all likelihood is attributable largely to the fact that the membership was locked out as the result of the Local's whipsaw strategem. But the lockout itself is concededly within the rule of *Buffalo Linen.* We think that the added dissatisfaction, with its resultant pressure on membership, attributable to the fact that the nonstruck employers remain in business with temporary replacements is comparatively insubstantial. First, the replacements were expressly used for the duration of the labor dispute only; thus, the displaced employees could not have looked upon the replacements as threatening their jobs. At most the union would be forced to capitulate and return its members to work on terms which, while not as desirable as hoped for, were still better than under the old contract. Second, the membership, through its control of union policy, could end the dispute and terminate the lockout at any time simply by agreeing to the employers' terms and returning to work on a regular basis. Third, in light of the union-shop provision that had been carried forward into the new contract from the old collective-bargaining agreement, it would appear that a union member would have nothing to gain and much to lose, by quitting the union. Under all these circumstances, we cannot say that the employers' conduct had any great tendency to discourage union membership. Not only was the prospect of discouragement of membership comparatively remote, but the respondents' attempt to remain open for business with the help of temporary replacements was a measure reasonably adapted to the achievement of a legitimate end — preserving the integrity of the multiemployer bargaining unit.

When the resulting harm to employee rights is thus comparatively slight, and a substantial and legitimate business end is served, the employers' conduct is prima facie lawful. Under these circumstances the finding of an unfair labor practice under §8(a)(3) requires a showing of improper subjective intent. Here, there is no assertion by either the union or the Board that the respondents were motivated by antiunion animus, nor is there any evidence that this was the case. . . .

In sum, the Court of Appeals was required to conclude that there was not sufficient evidence gathered from the record as a whole to support the Board's finding that respondents' conduct violates §8(a)(3). . . .[6]

Affirmed.

GOLDBERG, J., whom WARREN, C. J., joins, concurring. . . .

. . . There would be grave doubts as to whether the act of locking out employees and hiring permanent replacements is justified by any legitimate interest of the nonstruck employers, for *Buffalo Linen* makes clear that the test in such a situation is not whether parity is achieved between struck and nonstruck employers, but, rather, whether the nonstruck employers' actions are necessary to counteract the whipsaw effects of the strike and to preserve the employer bargaining unit. Since in this case the nonstruck employers did nothing more than hire temporary replacements, an activity necessary to counter whipsawing by the union and to preserve the bargaining unit, I agree that, applying *Buffalo Linen*, the judgment of the Court of Appeals should be affirmed.

WHITE, J., dissenting. . . .

The Court reasons that *Buffalo Linen* gave the nonstruck employer in a multiemployer unit a "right" to lock out whenever a member of the

6. We do not here decide whether the case would be the same had the struck employer exercised its prerogative to hire permanent replacements for the strikers under our rule in National Labor Relations Board v. Mackay Radio & Telegraph Co., 304 U.S. 333, and the non-struck employers had then hired permanent replacements for their locked-out employees.

unit is struck so that a parity of economic advantage or disadvantage between the struck and nonstruck employers can be maintained. In order to maintain parity where the struck employer hires replacements, the nonstruck employers must also be free to hire replacements, lest the right to lock out to protect the unit be illusory. And they need not offer these jobs to the locked-out employees desiring to work, lest the parity between the struck and nonstruck employers be lost and the right to lock out be meaningless. If this reasoning is sound, the nonstruck employers can not only lock out employees who belong to the union because of their union membership but also hire permanent as well as temporary nonunion replacements whenever the struck employer hires such replacements, for parity may well so require. But I cannot accept this reasoning.

One, *Buffalo Linen* established no unqualified "right" of employers in a multi-employer unit to lock out. . . .

Two, the threat to the integrity of the multiemployer unit, the consideration that was decisive in *Buffalo Linen,* is obviously very different where the struck employer continues operations with replacements; it certainly cannot be assumed that the struck employer operating with replacements is at the same disadvantage vis-à-vis the nonstruck employers as the employer in *Buffalo Linen* whose operations were totally shut down by the union. Indeed, there was no showing here that the struck employer was substantially disadvantaged at all, and the Board found that there was "no economic necessity . . . for the other members shutting down." 137 N.L.R.B. 73, at 77. . . .

Three, the disparity between the struck employer who resumes operations and the nonstruck employers who choose to lock out to maintain a unit front is caused by the unilateral action of one of the employer members of the unit and not by the union's whipsawing tactic. The integrity of the multiemployer unit may be important, but surely that consideration cannot justify employer tandem action destructive of concerted activity.

Four, the Court asserts that the right of nonstruck employers to hire temporary replacements, and to refuse to hire union men, is but a concomitant of the right to lock out to preserve the multiemployer group. The santification of the multiemployer unit ignores the fundamental rule that an employer may not displace union members with nonunion members solely on account of union membership, the prototype of discrimination under §8(a)(3), and may not maintain operations and refuse to retain or hire nonstriking union members, notwithstanding that most of the union members and most of the workers at that very plant are on strike. The struck employer need not continue operations, but if he does, he may not give a preference to employees not affiliated with the striking union, any more than he may do so after the strike, for §7 explicitly and unequivocally protects the right of employees to engage and not to engage in a concerted activity and §8(a)(3) clearly prohibits discrimination which discourages union membership. If dismissing and replacing nonstriking union members at a struck plant discourages union membership and interferes with concerted activities, I fail to understand how this same conduct at a nonstruck plant, even if in the name of multiemployer parity and unity, has a different effect on employee rights. . . .

Finally, I cannot agree with the Court's fundamental premise on which its balance of rights is founded: that a lockout followed by the hiring of nonunion men to operate the plant has but a "slight" tendency to discourage union membership, which includes participation in union activities, and to impinge on concerted activity generally. This proposition overturns the Board's longheld views on the effect of lockouts and dismissal of union members. Moreover, it is difficult to fathom the logic or industrial experience which on the one hand dictates that a guarantee to strike replacements that they will not be laid off after a strike is "inherently destructive of employee interests," although based on a legitimate and important business justification, Erie Resistor, 373 U.S. 221, and yet at the same time dictates that the dismissal of and refusal to hire nonstriking union members, who desire to work, because other union members working for a different employer have struck, have but a slight unimportant inhibiting effect on the affiliation with the union and on concerted activities. I think the Board's finding that this activity substantially burdens concerted activities and discourages union membership is far more consistent with *Erie Resistor* and industrial realities. . . .

AMERICAN SHIP BUILDING CO. v. NLRB
380 U.S. 300 (1965)

[The bulk of the American Ship Building Company's ship repair business took place in the winter months when the freezing of the Great Lakes renders shipping impossible. Its limited summer business had to be performed quickly to minimize immobilization of the ships. On August 9, 1961, collective bargaining negotiations between the company and a group of eight unions reached impasse after two months' bargaining. In a decade of collective bargaining agreements, each one had been preceded by a strike. The union proposed a six-month extension of the current agreement and, although the union protested to the contrary, the company feared the union would strike as soon as a ship entered the yard or during the busy winter months. Thus on August 11 the employees received a notice from the company that read: "Because of the labor dispute which has been unresolved since August 1, 1961, you are laid off until further notice." Negotiations resumed shortly after these layoffs and on October 27 a new contract was reached. The employees were recalled on the following day.

An NLRB trial examiner found that the employer was reasonably apprehensive of a strike at some point and was motivated and economically justified in laying off the employees when it did. The Board, 3-2, rejected the conclusion that the employer could reasonably anticipate a strike, found the layoff motivated by a desire to bring economic pressure to secure prompt settlement of the dispute on favorable terms, and held that the layoff violated §§8(a)(3) and (1).]

STEWART, J. . . .

Both the Board and the examiner assumed, within the established pattern of Board analysis, that if the employer had shut down its yard and laid off its workers solely for the purpose of bringing to bear economic pressure to break an impasse and secure more favorable contract terms, an unfair labor practice would be made out. . . . The Board has, however, exempted certain classes of lockouts from proscription. "Accordingly, it has held that lockouts are permissible to safeguard against . . . loss where there is reasonable ground for believing that a strike was threatened or imminent." [Quaker State Oil Refining Corp., 121 N.L.R.B. 334, 337.] Developing this distinction in its rulings, the Board has approved lockouts designed to prevent seizure of a plant by a sit-down strike, to forestall repetitive disruptions of an integrated operation by "quickie" strikes, to avoid spoilage of materials which would result from a sudden work stoppage, and to avert the immobilization of automobiles brought in for repair.

In analyzing the status of the bargaining lockout under §§8(a)(1) and (3) of the National Labor Relations Act, it is important that the practice with which we are here concerned be distinguished from other forms of temporary separation from employment. No one would deny that an employer is free to shut down his enterprise temporarily for reasons of renovation or lack of profitable work unrelated to his collective bargaining situation. Similarly, we put to one side cases where the Board has concluded on the basis of substantial evidence that the employer has used a lockout as a means to injure a labor organization or to evade his duty to bargain collectively. What we are here concerned with is the use of a temporary layoff of employees solely as a means to bring economic pressure to bear in support of the employer's bargaining position, after an impasse has been reached. This is the only issue before us, and all that we decide.[8]

To establish that this practice is a violation of §8(a)(1), it must be shown that the employer has interfered with, restrained, or coerced employees in the exercise of some right protected by §7 of the Act. The

8. Contrary to the views expressed in a concurring opinion filed in this case, we intimate no view whatever as to the consequences which would follow had the employer replaced its employees with permanent replacements or even temporary help. Cf. National Labor Relations Board v. Mackay Radio & Telegraph Co., 304 U.S. 333.

Board's position is premised on the view that the lockout interferes with two of the rights guaranteed by §7: the right to bargain collectively and the right to strike. In the Board's view, the use of the lockout "punishes" employees for the presentation of and adherence to demands made by their bargaining representatives and so coerces them in the exercise of their right to bargain collectively. It is important to note that there is here no allegation that the employer used the lockout in the service of designs inimical to the process of collective bargaining. There was no evidence and no finding that the employer was hostile to its employees' banding together for collective bargaining or that the lockout was designed to discipline them for doing so. It is therefore inaccurate to say that the employer's intention was to destroy or frustrate the process of collective bargaining. What can be said is that it intended to resist the demands made of it in the negotiations and to secure modification of these demands. We cannot see that this intention is in any way inconsistent with the employees' rights to bargain collectively.

Moreover, there is no indication, either as a general matter or in this specific case, that the lockout will necessarily destroy the unions' capacity for effective and responsible representation. The unions here involved have vigorously represented the employees since 1952, and there is nothing to show that their ability to do so has been impaired by the lockout. Nor is the lockout one of those acts which are demonstrably so destructive of collective bargaining that the Board need not inquire into employer motivation, as might be the case, for example, if an employer permanently discharged his unionized staff and replaced them with employees known to be possessed of a violent antiunion animus. Cf. National Labor Relations Board v. Erie Resistor Corp., 373 U.S. 221. The lockout may well dissuade employees from adhering to the position which they initially adopted in the bargaining, but the right to bargain collectively does not entail any "right" to insist on one's position free from economic disadvantage. Proper analysis of the problem demands that the simple intention to support the employer's bargaining position as to compensation and the like be distinguished from a hostility to the process of collective bargaining which could suffice to render a lockout unlawful. See National Labor Relations Board v. Brown, 380 U.S. 278.

The Board has taken the complementary view that the lockout interferes with the right to strike protected under §§7 and 13 of the Act in that it allows the employer to pre-empt the possibility of a strike and thus leave the union with "nothing to strike against." Insofar as this means that once employees are locked out, they are deprived of their right to call a strike against the employer because he is already shut down, the argument is wholly specious, for the work stoppage which would have been the object of the strike has in fact occurred. It is true that recognition of the lockout deprives the union of exclusive control of the timing and duration of work stoppages calculated to influence the result of collective bargaining negotiations, but there is nothing in the statute which would imply that the right to strike "carries with it" the right exclusively to determine the timing and duration of all work stoppages. The right to strike as commonly understood is the right to cease work — nothing more. No doubt a union's bargaining power would be enhanced if it possesed not only the simple right to strike but also the power exclusively to determine when work stoppages should occur, but the Act's provisions are not indefinitely elastic, content-free forms to be shaped in whatever manner the Board might think best conforms to the proper balance of bargaining power.

Thus, we cannot see that the employer's use of a lockout solely in support of a legitimate bargaining position is in any way inconsistent with the right to bargain collectively or with the right to strike. Accordingly, we conclude that on the basis of the findings made by the Board in this case, there has been no violation of §8(a)(1).

Section 8(a)(3) prohibits discrimination in regard to tenure or other conditions of employment to discourage union membership. Under the words of the statute there must be both discrimination and a resulting discouragement of union membership. It has long been established that a finding of violation under this section will normally turn on the employer's motivation. Thus when the employer discharges a union leader who has broken shop rules, the problem posed is to determine whether the employer has acted purely in disinterested defense of shop discipline or has sought to damage employee organization. It is likely that the discharge will naturally tend to discourage union membership in both cases, because of the loss of union leadership and the employees' suspicion of the employer's true intention. But we have consistently construed the section to leave unscathed a wide range of employer actions taken to serve legitimate business interests in some significant fashion, even though the act committed may tend to discourage union membership. See e.g., National Labor Relations Board v. Mackay Radio & Telegraph Co., 304 U.S. 333, 347. Such a construction of §8(a)(3) is essential if due protection is to be accorded the employer's right to manage his enterprise. See Textile Workers' Union v. Darlington Mfg. Co., 880 U.S. 263.

This is not to deny that there are some practices which are inherently so prejudicial to union interests and so devoid of significant economic justification that no specific evidence of intent to discourage union membership or other antiunion animus is required. In some cases, it may be that the employer's conduct carries with it an inference of unlawful intention so compelling that it is justifiable to disbelieve the employer's protestations of innocent purpose. Radio Officers' Union v. National Labor Relations Board, supra, 347 U.S. at 44-45; National Labor Relations Board v. Erie Resistor Corp., supra. Thus where many have broken a shop rule, but only union leaders have been discharged, the Board need not listen too long to the plea that shop discipline was simply being enforced. In other situations, we have described the process as the "far more delicate task . . . of weighing the interests of employees in concerted activity against the interest of the employer in operating his business in a particular manner. . . ." National Labor Relations Board v. Erie Resistor Corp., supra, 373 U.S. at 229.

But this lockout does not fall into that category of cases arising under §8(a)(3) in which the Board may truncate its inquiry into employer motivation. As this case well shows, use of the lockout does not carry with it any necessary implication that the employer acted to discourage union membership or otherwise discriminate against union members as such. The purpose and effect of the lockout were only to bring pressure upon the union to modify its demands. Similarly, it does not appear that the natural tendency of the lockout is severely to discourage union membership while serving no significant employer interest. In fact, it is difficult to understand what tendency to discourage union membership or otherwise discriminate against union members was perceived by the Board. There is no claim that the employer locked out only union members, or locked out any employee simply because he was a union member; nor is it alleged that the employer conditioned rehiring upon resignation from the union. It is true that the employees suffered economic disadvantage because of their union's insistence on demands unacceptable to the employer, but this is also true of many steps which an employer may take during a bargaining conflict, and the existence of an arguable possibility that someone may feel himself discouraged in his union membership or discriminated against by reason of that membership cannot suffice to label them violations of §8(a)(3) absent some unlawful intention. The employer's permanent replacement of strikers, his unilateral imposition of terms, or his simple refusal to make a concession which would terminate a strike — all impose economic disadvantage during a bargaining conflict, but none is necessarily a violation of §8(a)(3).

To find a violation of §8(a)(3), then, the Board must find that the employer acted for a proscribed purpose. Indeed, the Board itself has always recognized that certain "operative" or "economic" purposes would justify a lockout. But the Board has erred in ruling that only these purposes will remove a lockout from the ambit of §8(a)(3), for that section requires an intention to discourage union membership or otherwise discriminate against the union. There was not the slightest evidence and there was no finding that the employer was actuated by a desire to discourage membership in the union as distinguished from a desire to affect the outcome of the particular negotiations in which it was involved. We recognize that the "union membership" which is not to be discouraged refers to more than the payment of dues and that measures taken to discourage participation in protected union activities may be found to come within the proscription. However, there is nothing in the Act which gives employees the right to insist on their contract demands, free from the sort of economic disadvantage which frequently attends bargaining disputes. Therefore, we conclude that where the intention proven is merely to bring about a settlement of a labor dispute on favorable terms, no violation of §8(a)(3) is shown. . . .

The Board has justified its ruling in this case and its general approach to the legality of lockouts on the basis of its special competence to weigh the competing interests of employers and employees and to accommodate these interests according to its expert judgment. "The Board has reasonably concluded that the availability of such a weapon would so substantially tip the scales in the employer's favor as to defeat the Congressional purpose of placing employees on a par with their adversary at the bargaining table." To buttress its decision as to the balance struck in this particular case, the Board points out that the employer has been given other weapons to counterbalance the employees' power of strike. The employer may permanently replace workers who have gone out on strike, or, by stockpiling and subcontracting, maintain his commercial operations while the strikers bear the economic brunt of the work stoppage. Similarly, the employer can institute unilaterally the working conditions which he desires once his contract with the union has expired. Given these economic weapons, it is argued, the employer has been adequately equipped with tools of economic self-help.

There is of course no question that the Board is entitled to the greatest deference in recognition of its special competence in dealing with labor problems. In many areas its evaluation of the competing interests of employer and employee should unquestionably be given conclusive effect in determining the application of §§8(a)(1), (3), and (5). However, we think that the Board construes its functions too expansively when it claims general authority to define national labor policy by balancing the competing interests of labor and management.

While a primary purpose of the National Labor Relations Act was to redress the perceived imbalance of economic power between labor and management, it sought to accomplish that result by conferring certain affirmative rights on employees and by placing certain enumerated restrictions on the activities of employers. The Act prohibited acts which interfered with, restrained, or coerced employees in the exercise of their rights to organize a union, to bargain collectively, and to strike; it proscribed discrimination in regard to tenure and other conditions of employment to discourage membership in any labor organization. The central purpose of these provisions was to protect employee self-organization and the process of collective bargaining from disruptive interferences by employers. Having protected employee organization in countervailance to the employers' bargaining power, and having established a system of collective bargaining whereby the newly coequal adversaries might resolve their disputes, the Act also contemplated resort to economic weapons should more peaceful measures not avail. Sections

8(a)(1) and (3) do not give the Board a general authority to assess the relative economic power of the adversaries in the bargaining process and to deny weapons to one party or the other because of its assessment of that party's bargaining power. National Labor Relations Board v. Brown, 280 U.S. 278. In this case the Board has, in essence, denied the use of the bargaining lockout to the employer because of its conviction that use of this device would give the employer "too much power." In so doing, the Board has stretched §§8(a)(1) and (3) far beyond their functions of protecting the rights of employee organization and collective bargaining. What we have recently said in a closely related context is equally applicable here:

> [W]hen the Board moves in this area . . . it is functioning as an arbiter of the sort of economic weapons the parties can use in seeking to gain acceptance of their bargaining demands. It has sought to introduce some standard of properly 'balanced' bargaining power, or some new distinction of justifiable and unjustifiable, proper and 'abusive' economic weapons into . . . the Act. . . . We have expressed our belief that this amounts to the Board's entrance into the substantive aspects of the bargaining process to an extent Congress has not countenanced. National Labor Relations Board v. Insurance Agents' International Union, 361 U.S. 477.

We are unable to find that any fair construction of the provisions relied on by the Board in this case can support its finding of an unfair labor practice. Indeed, the role assumed by the Board in this area is fundamentally inconsistent with the structure of the Act and the function of the sections relied upon. The deference owed to an expert tribunal cannot be allowed to slip into a judicial inertia which results in the unauthorized assumption by an agency of major policy decisions properly made by Congress. Accordingly, we hold that an employer violates neither §8(a)(1) nor §8(a)(3) when, after a bargaining impasse has been reached, he temporarily shuts down his plant and lays off his employees for the sole purpose of bringing economic pressure to bear in support of his legitimate bargaining position.

Reversed.

WHITE, J., concurring in the result. . . .

In my view the issue posed in this case is whether an employer who in fact anticipates a strike may inform customers of this belief to protect his commercial relationship with customers and to safeguard their property thereby discouraging business, and then lay off employees for whom there is no available work. I, like the trial examiner, think he may, and do not think this conduct can be impeached under §§8(a)(1) and (3) by merely asserting that the employer and his customers were erroneous in believing a strike was imminent. . . . Since I think an employer's decision to lay off employees because of lack of work is not ordinarily barred by the Act, and since neither the Board nor the Court properly can ignore this claim, I would reverse the Board's order, but without reaching out to decide an issue not at all presented by this case.

Since the Court does rule on the status of the bargaining lockout under the National Labor Relations Act, I feel constrained to state my views. This Court has long recognized that the Labor Relations Act "did not undertake the impossible task of specifying in precise and unmistakable language each incident which would constitute an unfair labor practice," but "left to the Board the work of applying the Act's general prohibitory language in the light of the infinite combinations of events which might be charged as violative of its terms." Republic Aviation Corp. v. National Labor Relations Board, 324 U.S. 793, 798. Thus the legal status of the bargaining lockout, as the Court indicated in National Labor Relations Board v. Truck Drivers Union, etc., 353 U.S. 87, 96, is to be determined by "the balancing of the conflicting legitimate interests."

The Board has balanced these interests here — the value of the lockout as an economic weapon against its impact on protected concerted activities, including the right to strike, for which the Act has special solicitude, and has determined that the employer's interest in obtaining a bargaining victory does not outweigh the damaging consequences of the lockout. . . . The Court rejects this reasoning on the ground that the lockout is not conduct "demonstrably so destructive of collective bargaining that the Board need not inquire into employer motivation." Since the employer's true motive is to bring about settlement of the dispute on favorable terms, there can be no substantial discouragement of union membership or interference with concerted activities. And the right to strike is only the right to cease work, which the lockout only encourages rather than displaces.

This tour de force denies the Board's assessment of the impact on employee rights and this truncated definition of the right to strike, nowhere supported in the Act, is unprecedented. Until today the employer's true motive or sole purpose has not always been determinative of the impact on employee rights. Republic Aviation Corp. v. National Labor Relations Board, 324 U.S. 793; Radio Officers' Union v. National Labor Relations Board, 347 U.S. 17; National Labor Relations Board v. Truck Drivers Union, etc., 353 U.S. 87; National Labor Relations Board v. Erie Resistor Corp., 373 U.S. 221; National Labor Relations Board v. Burnup & Sims, Inc., 379 U.S. 21. The importance of the employer's right to hire replacements to continue operations, or of his right to fire employees he has good reason to believe are guilty of gross misconduct was not doubted in *Erie Resistor* and *Burnup & Sims*. Nonetheless the Board was upheld in its determination that the award of super-seniority to strike replacements and discharge of the suspected employee were unfair labor practices. Of course, such conduct is taken in the pursuit of legitimate business ends, but nonetheless the "conduct *does* speak for itself . . . [i]t carries with it unavoidable consequences which the employer not only foresaw but which he must have intended." *Erie Resistor,* 373 U.S., at 228. I would have thought it apparent that loss of jobs for an indefinite period, and the threatened loss of jobs, which the Court's decision assuredly sanctions, cf. Textile Workers' Union v. Darlington Mfg. Co., 380 U.S., at 274, because of the union's negotiating activity, itself protected conduct under §7, hardly encourage affiliation with a union.

If the Court means what it says today, an employer may not only lock out after impasse consistent with §§8(a)(1) and (3), but replace his locked-out employees with temporary help, cf. National Labor Relations Board v. Brown, 380 U.S. 278 or perhaps permanent replacements, and also lock out long before an impasse is reached. . . .

Goldberg, J., with whom Warren, C. J., joins, concurring in the result.

I concur in the Court's conclusion that the employer's lockout in this case was not a violation of either §8(a)(1) or §8(a)(3). I reach this result not for the Court's reasons, but because, from the plain facts revealed by the record, it is crystal clear that the employer's lockout here was justifiable. The very facts recited by the Court in its opinion show that this employer locked out its employees in the face of a threatened strike under circumstances where, had the choice of timing been left solely to the unions, the employer and its customers would have been subject to economic injury over and beyond the loss of business normally incident to a strike upon the termination of the collective bargaining agreement. A lockout under these circumstances has been recognized by the Board itself to be justifiable and not a violation of the labor statutes. . . .

My view of this case would make it unnecessary to deal with the broad question of whether an employer may lock out his employees solely to bring economic pressure to bear in support of his bargaining position. The question of which types of lockout are compatible with the labor statute is a complex one as this decision and the other cases decided today illustrate. . . .

The Court not only overlooks the factual diversity among different types of lockout, but its statement of the rules governing unfair labor practices under §§8(a)(1) and (3) does not give proper recognition to the fact that "[t]he ultimate problem [in this area] is the balancing of the conflicting legitimate interests." National Labor Relations Board v. Truck Drivers Union, etc., 353 U.S. 87, 96.

The Court states that employer conduct, not actually motivated by antiunion bias, does not violate §8(a)(1) or §8(a)(3) unless it is "demonstrably so destructive of collective bargaining," ante, at 962, or "so prejudicial to union interests and so devoid of significant economic justification" that no antiunion animus need be shown. This rule departs substantially from both the letter and the spirit of numerous prior decisions of the Court. See, e.g., National Labor Relations Board v. Truck Drivers Union, etc., supra, 353 U.S., at 96; Republic Aviation Corp. v. National Labor Relations Board, 324 U.S. 793; National Labor Relations Board v. Babcock & Wilcox Co., 351 U.S. 105; National Labor Relations Board v. Burnup & Sims, Inc., 379 U.S. 21.

These decisions demonstrate that the correct test for determining whether §8(a)(1) has been violated in cases not involving an employer antiunion motive is whether the business justification for the employer's action outweighs the interference with §7 rights involved. In Republic Aviation Corp. v. National Labor Relations Board, supra, for example, the Court affirmed a Board holding that a company "no-solicitation" rule was invalid as applied to prevent solicitation of employees on company property during periods when employees were free to do as they pleased, not because such a rule was "demonstrably . . . destructive of collective bargaining," but simply because there was no significant employer justification for the rule and there was a showing of union interest, though far short of a necessity, in its abolition. See also, National Labor Relations Board v. Burnup & Sims, Inc., supra.

A similar test is applicable in §8(a)(3) cases where no antiunion motive is shown. The Court misreads Radio Officers' Union v. National Labor Relations Board, 347 U.S. 17, and National Labor Relations Board v. Erie Resistor Corp., supra, in stating that the test in such cases under §8(a)(3) is whether practices "are inherently so prejudicial to union interests and so devoid of significant economic justification that no specific evidence of intent to discourage union membership or other antiunion animus is required." *Radio Officers* did not restrict the application of §8(a)(3) in cases devoid of antiunion motive to the extreme situations encompassed by the Court's test. Rather, in holding applicable the common-law rule that a man is presumed to intend the foreseeable consequences of his own actions, the Court extended the reach of §8(a)(3) to all cases in which a significant antiunion effect is foreseeable regardless of the employer's motive. In such cases the Court, in *Erie Resistor Corp.*, held that conduct might be determined by the Board to violate §8(a)(3) where the Board's determination resulted from a reasonable "weighing [of] the interests of employees in concerted activity against the interest of the employer in operating his business in a particular manner and . . . [from] balancing in the light of the Act and its policy the intended consequences upon employee rights against the business ends to be served by the employer's conduct." 373 U.S., at 229.

These cases show that the tests as to whether an employer's conduct violates §8(a)(1) or violates §8(a)(3) without a showing of antiunion motive come down to substantially the same thing: whether the legitimate economic interests of the employer justify his interference with the rights of his employees — a test involving "the balancing of the conflicting legitimate interests." National Labor Relations Board v. Truck Drivers Union, etc., supra, 353 U.S., at 96. As the prior decisions of this Court have held, "[t]he function of striking . . . [such a] balance . . . often a difficult and delicate responsibility, . . . Congress committed primarily to the National Labor Relations Board, subject to limited judicial review." Ibid.

This, of course, does not mean that reviewing courts are to abdicate their function of determining whether, giving due deference to the Board, the Board has struck the balance consistently with the language and policy of the Act. See National Labor Relations Board v. Brown, supra; National Labor Relations Board v. Truck Drivers Union, etc., supra. Nor does it mean that reviewing courts are to rubber-stamp decisions of the Board where the application of principles in a particular case is irrational or not supported by substantial evidence on the record as a whole. Applying these principles to the factual situation here presented, I would accept the Board's carefully limited rule, fashioned by the Board after weighing the "conflicting legitimate interests" of employers and union, that a lockout does not violate the Act where used to "safeguard against unusual operational problems or hazards or economic loss where there is reasonable ground for believing that a strike [is] . . . threatened or imminent." Quaker State Oil Refining Corp., [121 N.L.R.B.] at 337. This rule is consistent with the policies of the Act and based upon the actualities of industrial relations. I would, however, reject the determination of the Board refusing to apply this rule to this case, for the undisputed facts revealed by the record bring this case clearly within the rule. . . .

Notes

1. Suppose every three years Ford Motor Company, General Motors Corporation, and Chrysler Corporation bargain separately with the United Auto Workers' Union (UAW). The UAW selects one of the employers as its target company and bargains only with it, holding other negotiations in abeyance. If a strike against the target company is necessary, UAW members at the other companies may contribute money to a strike fund to support the striking workers. The bargaining agreement reached with the target company will not be binding on the other companies, and strikes against them have occasionally been necessary, but the agreement regularly sets a settlement pattern for the other two companies. This year Ford has been selected as the target company; extensive negotiations have taken place but no agreement has yet been reached. There have been no negotiations with General Motors or Chry-

sler, and UAW members at all three companies are working at the rates set by the expired agreements. The UAW now strikes Ford. Can General Motors and Chrysler lawfully lock out?

2. What do you understand to have been the union's argument in *Brown*? Did the union have a viable argument that the employer's action in *Brown* had a greater discriminatory impact on locked-out employees than the lockout in *Buffalo Linen*?

Is an offensive lockout plus permanent replacements any different from outright discharge for organizing? Is a *Buffalo Linen* lockout plus permanent replacements on firmer footing? Suppose the struck employer has hired permanent replacements?

3. Devise an argument that an offensive lockout plus temporary replacements violates §§8(a)(3) and 8(a)(1) under the standards set out in *American Ship* and *Brown*.

Should an employer whose employees have recently unionized be permitted to use an offensive lockout to reach a favorable first contract?

4. Since the Court has retreated from Justice White's argument that the treatment of employer motive under §§8(a)(1) and (3) actually reflects "the far more delicate task . . . of weighing the interests of employees in concerted activity against the interest of the employer in operating his business in a particular manner and of balancing . . . the intended consequences upon employee rights against the business ends to be served by the employer's conduct," conceptualizing the motive issue has proved difficult, especially in the light of the variety of views espoused by the Justices in the lockout cases.

Another decision of importance is NLRB v. Great Dane Trailers, 388 U.S. 26 (1967). The employer was found to have violated §8(a)(3) when he refused to pay striking employees vacation benefits accrued under a terminated collective bargaining agreement while he announced an intention to pay such benefits to striker replacements, returning strikers, and nonstrikers who had been at work on a certain date during the strike. After noting that the treatment of the strikers was "discrimination in its simplest form" and was without doubt capable of discouraging membership in a labor organization by discouraging participation in concerted activities, the Court, per Warren, C. J., turned to the motivation inquiry:

> First, if it can reasonably be concluded that the employer's discriminatory conduct was "inherently destructive" of important employee rights, no proof of an antiunion motivation is needed and the Board can find an unfair labor practice even if the conduct was motivated by business considerations. Second, if the adverse effect of the discriminatory conduct on employee rights is "comparatively slight," an antiunion motivation must be proved to sustain the charge if the employer has come forward with evidence of legitimate and substantial business justifications for the conduct. Thus, in either situation, once it has been proved that the employer en-

> gaged in discriminatory conduct which could have adversely affected employee rights to some extent, the burden is upon the employer to establish that he was motivated by legitimate objectives since proof of motivation is most accessible to him.

Since the employer in the instant case had offered no proof of a legitimate and substantial business justification, the Court sustained the Board's finding of a violation.

Suppose the president of the Great Dane Company had testified that vacation benefits had been denied strikers in order to save money? Does the *Great Dane* test help you devise your argument for the illegality of an offensive lockout coupled with temporary replacements? If the Board had had the foresight to anticipate the *Great Dane* test, would it have avoided the "mistake" it made in *American Ship*?

5. One month after the bargaining agreement expired, the employer gave nonbargaining unit employees a 10 percent wage increase. The employer did not extend this increase to unit employees because their union refused to extend their collective bargaining agreement. After an additional eight months of bargaining, the union proposed that the 10 percent wage increase be extended retroactively to unit employees. The union showed that unit employees were as skilled as nonunit employees, that labor supply and demand factors justified no lower wage, and that the employer had a policy of standardizing employee benefits. The employer refused to make the wage increase retroactive. Although not claiming any "inability to pay," the employer contended that "according retroactivity after nine months of negotiations might prove a future disincentive to the prompt conclusion of a collective bargaining agreement." Sections 8(a)(3) and 8(a)(1) violation? See South Shore Hosp. v. NLRB, 630 F.2d 40 (1st Cir. 1980).

In Interstate Paper Supply Co., 251 N.L.R.B. No. 189 (1980), the Board held that an employer could not declare that while employees were engaged in an economic strike they could not accrue seniority credit. The Board held that, under *Great Dane,* the employer could permanently replace these employees but could not otherwise disadvantage them.

6. One way of looking at the employer intent cases is suggested by Thomas Christensen and Andrea Svanoe, supra p. 236 n. [53], at 1325:

> It is difficult to disagree with Justice White's observation in *Erie Resistor* that, in determining the legality of such conduct, what the Board and the Court are really doing is resolving the tension between the employer's ability to continue his business successfully and the employee's exercise of rights guaranteed under §7. Indeed, in *Buffalo Linen* the nature of the decision to be made — a choice between conflicting interests — was openly acknowledged by the Court, as was the Board's superior ability initially to make that choice. When, however, as in the cases just discussed, this choice

between conflicting interests was converted into an analysis of competing and frequently unprovable motives, the essence of what was to be decided became obscured and the process of adjudication was basically altered. The resulting concealment of the real issues involved may help account for the obvious attraction of the motive concept to a majority of the Court. It is a difficult and delicate matter to state to the Board that the Supreme Court disagrees as to the assessment the agency has made of the value of a lockout or a hiring hall to employers or unions, respectively. It is far easier to assert that the Board has erred as to the legal concept of motive than that the Court takes a different view of the respective importance of the economic interests at stake.

B. UNION WEAPONS: SECONDARY BOYCOTTS

1. Overview

The subject of secondary boycotts is difficult and the statute is seldom clarifying. "Boycott," of course, implies a refusal to deal and "secondary" suggests the presence of an employer other than the one with whom the union has its dispute. From this line of logic comes a celebrated definition of the secondary boycott:

> The gravamen of a secondary boycott is that its sanctions bear, not upon the employer who alone is the party to the dispute, but upon some third party who has no concern in it. Its aim is to compel him to stop business with the employer in the hope that this will induce the employer to give in to his employees' demands. IBEW v. NLRB, 181 F.2d 34, 37 (2d Cir. 1950), per Judge Learned Hand

The secondary boycott has historically been a union tactical weapon in drives to organize employees and to seek economic benefits. Why outlaw the secondary boycott? Consider the following three arguments. First, it is unfair to the primary employer (the one with whom the union has its dispute, either organizational or economic) to permit the union to enlist the aid of a secondary employer in what should be an intrafamily struggle; the enlistment of the secondary distorts the economics of the marketplace. Take as an example the mutually dependent relationships between manufacturer, distributor, and retailer. A union should not, the argument goes, be allowed to choose the most vulnerable of these three enterprises and, by pressuring it to boycott the others, force the others to comply with union demands.

Second, it is unfair to the secondary employer to subject it to union economic coercion merely because the secondary does business with an offending employer over which it has no control. Third, the proliferation of labor disputes injures the public and should thus be minimized; since the secondary boycott makes two (or more) disputes out of one, it should be prohibited.

Counterarguments come less easily to mind, but consider a few of the possible responses. First, fairness is, after all, in the eye (or the pocket) of the beholder. The argument that secondary boycotts distort competitive markets depends on market definition. Where the employers are interdependent, there is no reason to arbitrarily limit the focus of union pressure to a "primary" employer. The real question as to the legitimacy of the secondary boycott is union power, but union power does not turn on the use of a single weapon. The secondary boycott will not make a weak union strong, and its prohibition will not make a strong union weak. Nor are secondary boycotts necessarily more harmful to secondary employers than the effects of primary strikes; a distributor may be devastated by a primary strike that closes down a major manufacturer. There is no reason to single out secondary boycotts for special treatment. As to the third argument, the public impact of a strike depends on the nature of the employer and the duration of the strike, not on whether it is primary or secondary.

Whether the pro or con argument is the stronger, the fact is that Congress set out in 1947 to prohibit the secondary boycott. As Senator Taft stated during the Congressional debates:

> All this provision of the bill does is to reverse the effect of the law as to secondary boycotts. It has been set forth that there are good secondary boycotts and bad secondary boycotts. Our committee heard evidence for weeks and never succeeded in having anyone tell us any difference. . . . So we have so broadened the provision dealing with secondary boycotts as to make them an unfair labor practice. 93 Cong. Rec. 4198 (1947).

The policies remain critical, however, for how can one distinguish primary from secondary activity without knowing what the union is seeking to accomplish? To say that all parties would not agree on whether particular conduct is primary or secondary is to seriously understate the controversy. The materials that follow raise the primary/secondary issue in several contexts.

The relevant statutory sections are §§8(b)(4)(A) and (B), 8(e), 10(l), and 303 of the Labor-Management Relations Act. Briefly stated, §8(b)(4)(B) prohibits a union from engaging in, persuading other employees to engage in, or coercing an employer to engage in a secondary boycott. Section 8(e) declares unlawful a bargaining agreement clause wherein one employer agrees with the union to engage in a secondary boycott of another employer. Section 8(b)(4)(A) prohibits a strike to secure a clause that violates §8(e). Sections 303 and 10(l) are remedial.

Section 10(1) requires regional directors to seek district court injunctions whenever they have reasonable cause to believe §8(b)(4) is being violated. Section 303 permits a private party injured by a violation of §8(b)(4) to recover actual damages in federal district court.

The most complex sections are §§8(b)(4)(A) and (B). You might think of them as follows:

means
objects
exceptions ("*provisos*")

There are two prohibited means, which labor lawyers call *i* and *double-i* conduct. The former prohibits the union from engaging in a full or partial strike or inducing or encouraging other employees to do so; the latter prohibits the union from threatening, coercing, or restraining any person.

The forbidden objects correspond to clauses (A), (B), and (C). Clause (A) has a dual prohibition: The union cannot force an employer to enter into a bargaining agreement clause violative of §8(e), nor can it force an employer or self-employed person to join a union. Clause (B) is the key provision. The forbidden objects are forcing any person "to cease handling products of any other producer" or "to cease doing business with any other person." Clause (C), the forerunner of §8(b)(7)'s recognitional picketing provisions and not really a secondary boycott provision at all, makes it a forbidden object to force an employer to recognize or bargain with a union if another union has been certified (striking against a certification).

There are three provisos, or exceptions, to §8(b)(4): The first affirmatively protects primary strikes and picketing; the second affords union members some protection from §8(b)(4) liability when they honor a picket line at another employer's place of business; and the third covers some appeals to consumers.

Professor David Feller diagrams §8(b)(4) as shown on page 409, infra.[19]

Note that nowhere does §8(b)(4) use the word *secondary,* and *primary* appears only in a proviso. Consider the effect of a literal reading of the statute on the most ordinary sort of strike, one called by a union to force

[19] Carrier Air Conditioning v. NLRB, 547 F.2d 1178, 1189 (2d Cir. 1976).

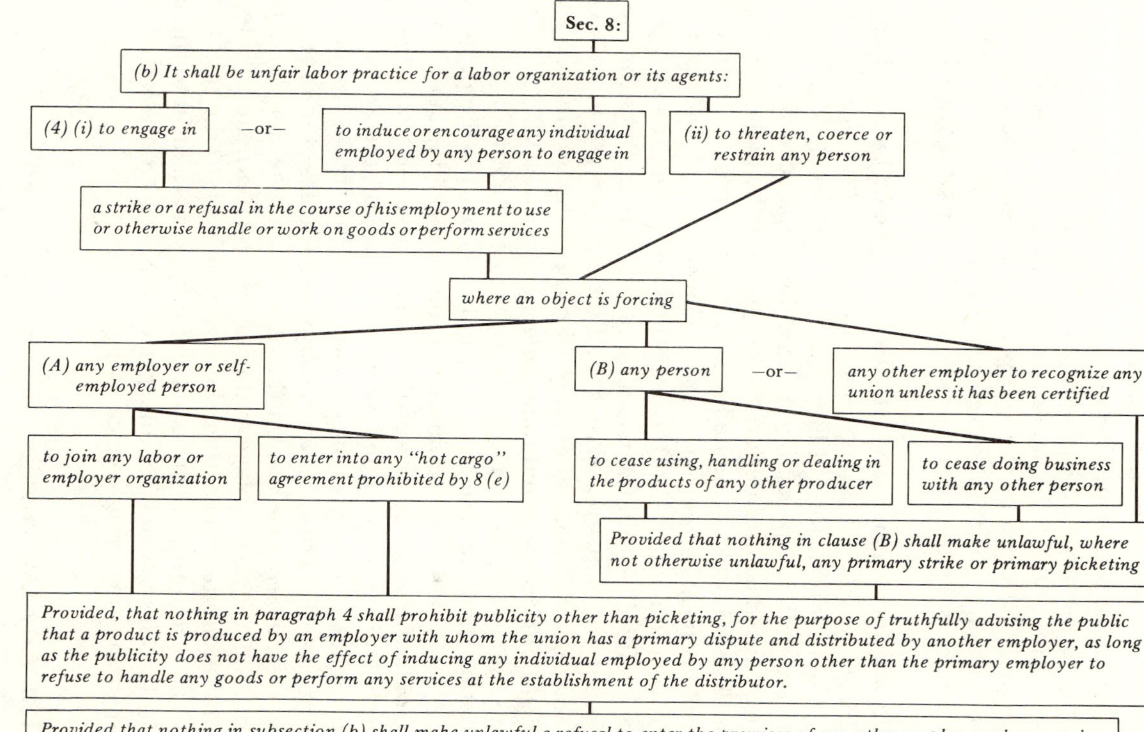
Sec. 8:
(b) It shall be unfair labor practice for a labor organization or its agents:
(4) (i) to engage in
—or—
to induce or encourage any individual employed by any person to engage in
(ii) to threaten, coerce or restrain any person
a strike or a refusal in the course of his employment to use or otherwise handle or work on goods or perform services
where an object is forcing
(A) any employer or self-employed person
(B) any person
—or—
any other employer to recognize any union unless it has been certified
to join any labor or employer organization
to enter into any "hot cargo" agreement prohibited by 8 (e)
to cease using, handling or dealing in the products of any other producer
to cease doing business with any other person
Provided that nothing in clause (B) shall make unlawful, where not otherwise unlawful, any primary strike or primary picketing
Provided, that nothing in paragraph 4 shall prohibit publicity other than picketing, for the purpose of truthfully advising the public that a product is produced by an employer with whom the union has a primary dispute and distributed by another employer, as long as the publicity does not have the effect of inducing any individual employed by any person other than the primary employer to refuse to handle any goods or perform any services at the establishment of the distributor.
Provided that nothing in subsection (b) shall make unlawful a refusal to enter the premises of any other employer where a union which the employer is required to recognize is on strike

an employer whose employees the union represents to raise wages. The union calls out all the employer's rank and file employees and sets up a peaceful picket line around the employer's premises. The union intends, of course, that the employer will not be able to continue operating and will be forced to give in to the union's demands. The union has thus engaged in a strike where an object is forcing a person (its employer) to cease doing business with other persons (its employer's customers and suppliers). Section 8(b)(4)(B), literally read, has been violated although the strike would be saved by the first proviso. Prior to the 1959 amendments there was no "primary strike" proviso and §8(b)(4)(B) read essentially the same as it does now (it was numbered §8(b)(4)(A) prior to 1959).

But this does not mean that all strikes accompanied by picketing were unlawful prior to 1959. The Supreme Court made that clear in 1951 in NLRB v. International Rice Milling Co., 341 U.S. 66 (1951). That case involved recognitional picketing around the employer's place of business, which caused a customer's truck not to cross the picket line to pick up goods. The statute's prohibited means in 1951 spoke of encouraging a "concerted refusal" by employees to perform services, and the Court's very narrow holding was that the inducement of a single truck was not a "concerted refusal" within the meaning of the statute. But near the end of the opinion the Court relied on §13 of the Act to say "[t]hat Congress did not seek, by §8(b)(4), to interfere with the ordinary strike. . . ."

In 1959, Congress reversed the *holding* of *International Rice Milling* by removing the word "concerted" from the definition of prohibited means, but by then the case had come to be known for the proposition that §8(b)(4) does not reach traditional, primary picketing at the employer's place of business. In other words, the statute cannot be read literally.

But if not literally, how? The cases that follow show the Board and the courts struggling to interpret the secondary boycott sections. You should read the cases with a critical eye not only on the "rules of the game" that are being established, but also on the question of whether the decision makers are looking to language and policy to reach principled interpretations of the statute, or whether they are reading into the statute their own notions of the proper limits on union power. Central to the latter inquiry is the question of what interpretation should control: that of the Board or of the reviewing courts.

2. The Ally Doctrine[20]

In the congressional debates of 1947 leading to the passage of §8(b)(4), Senator Taft said that the secondary boycott "provision makes

[20] See Levin, "Wholly Unconcerned": The Scope and Meaning of the Ally Doctrine under §8(b)(4) of the NLRB, 119 U. Pa. L. Rev. 283 (1970).

it unlawful to resort to a secondary boycott to injure the business of a third person who is wholly unconcerned in the disagreement between an employer and his employees." 93 Cong. Rec. 4198 (1947). From this legislative history was born the ally doctrine.

NLRB v. BUSINESS MACHINE & OFFICE APPLIANCE MECHANICS CONFERENCE BOARD, LOCAL 459 [ROYAL TYPEWRITER CO.]

228 F.2d 553 (2d Cir. 1955), cert. denied, 351 U.S. 962 (1956)

LUMBARD, J.

The National Labor Relations Board seeks enforcement of an order directing the Union to cease and desist from certain picketing and to post appropriate notices. . . . On about March 23, 1954, the Union, being unable to reach agreement with Royal on the terms of a contract, called the Royal service personnel out on strike. The service employees customarily repair typewriters either at Royal's branch offices or at its customers' premises. Royal has several arrangements under which it is obligated to render service to its customers. First, Royal's warranty on each new machine obligates it to provide free inspection and repair for one year. Second, for a fixed periodic fee Royal contracts to service machines not under warranty. Finally, Royal is committed to repairing typewriters rented from it or loaned by it to replace machines undergoing repair. Of course, in addition Royal provides repair services on call by non-contract users.

During the strike Royal differentiated between calls from customers to whom it owed a repair obligation and others. Royal's office personnel were instructed to tell the latter to call some independent repair company listed in the telephone directory. Contract customers, however, were advised to select such an independent from the directory, to have the repair made, and to send a receipted invoice to Royal for reimbursement for reasonable repairs within their agreement with Royal. Consequently many of Royal's contract customers had repair services performed by various independent repair companies. In most instances the customer sent Royal the unpaid repair bill and Royal paid the independent company directly. Among the independent companies paid directly by Royal for repairs made for such customers were Typewriter Maintenance and Sales Company and Tytell Typewriter Company. . . .

During May 1954 the Union picketed four independent typewriter repair companies who had been doing work covered by Royal's contracts pursuant to the arrangement described above. The Board found this picketing unlawful with respect to Typewriter Maintenance and Tytell. Typewriter Maintenance was picketed for about three days and Tytell for several hours on one day. In each instance the picketing, which was peaceful and orderly, took place before entrances used in common by employees, deliverymen and the general public. The signs read substantially as follows (with the appropriate repair company name inserted):

Notice To The Public Only
Employees Of Royal Typewriter Co.
On Strike

Tytell Typewriter Company Employees
Are Being Used As Strikebearers

Business Machine & Office Appliance
Mechanics Union, Local 459, IUE-CIO

Both before and after this picketing, which took place in mid-May, Tytell and Typewriter Maintenance did work on Royal accounts and received payment directly from Royal. Royal's records show that Typewriter Maintenance's first voucher was passed for payment by Royal on April 20, 1954 and Tytell's first voucher was passed for payment on May 3, 1954. After these dates each independent serviced various of Royal's customers on numerous occasions and received payment directly from Royal. . . .

On the above facts the Trial Examiner and the Board found that both the customer picketing and the repair company picketing violated §8(b)(4) of the National Labor Relations Act. . . . We are of the opinion that the Board's finding with respect to the repair company picketing cannot be sustained. The independent repair companies were so allied with Royal that the Union's picketing of their premises was not prohibited by §8(b)(4)[(B)].

We approve the "ally" doctrine which had its origin in a well reasoned opinion by Judge Rifkind in the Ebasco case, Douds v. Metropolitan Federation of Architects, Engineers, Chemists & Technicians, Local 231, D.C.S.D.N.Y. 1948, 75 F. Supp. 672, 676. Ebasco, a corporation engaged in the business of providing engineering services, had a close business relationship with Project, a firm providing similar services. Ebasco subcontracted some of its work to Project and when it did so Ebasco supervised the work of Project's employees and paid Project for the time spent by Project's employees on Ebasco's work plus a factor for overhead and profit. When Ebasco's employees went on strike, Ebasco transferred a greater percentage of its work to Project, including some jobs that had already been started by Ebasco's employees. When Project refused to heed the Union's requests to stop doing Ebasco's work, the Union picketed Project and induced some of Project's employees to cease work. On these facts Judge Rifkind found that Project was not "doing business" with Ebasco within the meaning of §8(b)(4)[(B)] and that the Union had therefore not committed an unfair labor practice under that section. He reached this result by looking to the legislative history of the Taft-Hartley Act and to the history of the secondary boycotts which it sought to outlaw. He determined that Project was not a person " 'wholly unconcerned in the disagreement between an employer and his employees' " such as §8(b)(4)[(B)] was designed to protect. This result has been described as a proper interpretation of the Act by its principal sponsor, Senator Taft, 95 Cong. Rec. (1949) 8709, and President Eisenhower in his January 1954 recommendations to Congress for revision of the Act included a suggestion which would make this rule explicit.

Here there was evidence of only one instance where Royal contacted an independent (Manhattan Typewriter Service, not named in the complaint) to see whether it could handle some of Royal's calls. Apart from that incident there is no evidence that Royal made any arrangement with an independent directly. It is obvious, however, that what the independents did would inevitably tend to break the strike. As Judge Rifkind pointed out in the Ebasco case: "The economic effect upon Ebasco's employees was precisely that which would flow from Ebasco's hiring strikebreakers to work on its own premises." And at 95 Cong. Rec. (1949) page 8709 Senator Taft said: "The spirit of the Act is not intended to protect a man who in the last case I mentioned is cooperating with a primary employer and taking his work and doing the work which he is unable to do because of the strike."

President Eisenhower's recommendation referred to above was to make it explicit "that concerted action against (1) an employer who is performing 'farmed-out' work for the account of another employer whose employees are on strike . . . will not be treated as a secondary boycott." Text of President's Message to Congress on Taft-Hartley Amendments, January 11, 1954. . . .

Moreover, there is evidence that the secondary strikes and boycotts sought to be outlawed by §8(b)(4)[(B)] were only those which had been unlawful at common law. 93 Cong. Rec. (1947) 3950, 4323 (Senator Taft). And although secondary boycotts were generally unlawful, it has been held that the common law does not proscribe union activity designed to prevent employers from doing the farmed-out work of a struck employer. Iron Molders Union No. 125 of Milwaukee, Wis. v. Allis-Chalmers Co., 7 Cir., 1908, 166 F. 45, 51. Thus the picketing of the independent typewriter companies was not the kind of secondary activity which §8(b)(4)[(B)] of the Taft-Hartley Act was designed to outlaw. Where an employer is attempting to avoid the economic impact of a strike by securing the services of others to do his work, the striking union obviously has a great interest, and we think a proper interest, in preventing those services from being rendered. This interest is more fundamental than the interest in bringing pressure on customers of the primary employer. Nor are those who render such services completely uninvolved in the primary strike. By doing the work of the primary employer they secure benefits themselves at the same time that they aid the primary employer. The ally employer may easily extricate himself from the dispute and insulate himself from picketing by refusing to do that work. A case may arise where the ally employer is unable to determine that the work he is doing is "farmed-out." We need not decide whether the picketing of such an employer would be lawful, for that is not the situation here. The existence of the strike, the receipt of checks from Royal, and the picketing itself certainly put the independents on notice that some of the work they were doing might be work farmed-out by Royal. Wherever they worked on new Royal machines they were probably aware that such machines were covered by a Royal warranty. But in any event, before working on a Royal machine they could have inquired of the customer whether it was covered by a Royal contract and refused to work on it if it was. There is no indication that they made any effort to avoid doing Royal's work. The Union was justified in picketing them in order to induce them to make such an effort. We therefore hold that an employer is not within the protection of §8(b)(4)[(B)] when he knowingly does work which would otherwise be done by the striking employees of the primary employer and where this work is paid for by the primary employer pursuant to an arrangement devised and originated by him to enable him to meet his contractual obligations. The result must be the same whether or not the primary employer makes any direct arrangement with the employers providing the services. . . .

Enforcement of the Board's order is therefore in all respects denied.[21]

HAND, J. (concurring). . . .

[It] seems to me that both "independents" had so far associated themselves with Royal in the controversy with its employees as to forfeit their privilege as neutrals. After the picketing began both necessarily knew of the strike against Royal; indeed, the Union's representative spoke to each of them. I altogether agree that they were nevertheless entitled to do work for Royal's customers. One does not make oneself a party to the dispute with a primary employer by taking over the business that the strike has prevented him from doing. On the other hand if a secondary employer, knowing of the strike, not only accepts the customer of the primary employer but takes his pay, not from the customer but from the primary employer, I do not see any relevant difference in doing so from accepting a subcontract from the primary employer, which would certainly forfeit the exemption. As I understand §8(b)(4)[(B)], it is meant to protect from industrial pressure employers, who have not made common cause with the primary employer. The theory is that they should be free to carry on their businesses without being subject to sanctions that

[21] Medina, J., concurred.

are reasonable between parties to the dispute. When, however, a secondary employer accepts business for which the primary employer pays him, although it is not an inevitable inference that, but for the strike, the primary employer would have done the business himself, I see no reason why he should not be compelled to prove that the primary employer would not have done it, if he could have. Therefore I think that, even though the Union meant to induce a strike of the "independents' " employees, it was within its rights.

Notes

1. Is Senator Taft's 1947 statement sufficient support for the court's conclusion that the independents have lost their statutory protection? (Note that the court does not credit Senator Taft for the "wholly unconcerned" language.) Both Senator Taft and President Eisenhower were apparently of the view that the ally doctrine deserved a place in the statute, but their comments referred to by the court came several years after §8(b)(4) was passed. Is it proper to grant a statutory exception on the basis of such statements? If in 1949 Senator Taft had said instead, "This *Ebasco* case is without foundation in the statute; we never had such an exception in mind and I oppose it now," would this have demanded a different result in *Royal Typewriter*?

2. Suppose a strike by a laundry workers' union shuts down the largest laundry and dry cleaning establishment in the city. Can the union picket the other laundry and dry cleaning companies in the city on the authority of *Royal Typewriter*?

Can you reconcile the following cases? In each, consider the economic effect on the struck employer.

a. Tugboat employees struck, suspending tugboat operations. Pier operators who normally used the tugboats to dock arriving ships used their own employees to pull ships in by hand with cables. Held, the pier operators were not allies. Longshoremen's Local 333 (New York Shipping Assn.), 107 N.L.R.B. 686 (1954).
b. Striking employees of a barge company were replaced by strikebreakers. When the barge came to the pier for loading, the strikebreakers withdrew, and the barge's customer had its own employees load the barge. Held, the customer was an ally. Master, Mates & Pilots Local 28 (Ingram Barge Co.), 136 N.L.R.B. 1175 (1962), enforced, 321 F.2d 376 (D.C. Cir. 1963).

Do these cases suggest a factor that could be substituted for *Royal Typewriter*'s requirement that there be an arrangement?

3. Existing case law holds that a union can picket an ally asking the

ally's employees to stop all work, not just "struck work."[22] If you were opposing the approval of this rule in a circuit which had never passed on it, how would you respond to the following argument?

> . . . Such a result is demanded by both theory and policy. An ally's protection from secondary boycotts is lost either because it is not "doing business" with the primary or because it is not another "person" under the statute; no theory is available by which it is an ally for part of its work, but not for the remainder. And should the union appeal to the ally's employees to cease doing only the struck work, complying employees would lose their §7 protection by engaging in a partial strike. Finally, limiting the doctrine in such a fashion would permit allies to avoid economic pressure by removing identifying marks from struck work materials and commingling them with primary materials.

4. Suppose the salesmen of an auto dealer are engaged in an economic strike and picketing. Since truck drivers delivering new cars from the factory won't cross the picket lines, the employer directs the cars to be delivered, unloaded, and stored at a secondary site. The salesmen have never participated in the unloading of cars. Can the salesmen picket the secondary site under the ally doctrine?[23]

Suppose Local 7 is picketing a printing plant for recognition and the employer arranges to have all the printing transferred to an independent plant. Is the independent plant an ally? Should it be necessary that some of the first plant's employees join Local 7's picket line?

5. Suppose an employer decides for economic reasons to subcontract part of his or her operations to a secondary employer. If the union representing the employees who will lose their jobs as a result of the subcontract objects and pickets but the employer subcontracts anyway, will the secondary employer be an ally? Contrast the situation where the employees of one department go out on strike. Suffering the economic pressure of the strike and picketing, the employer decides to permanently subcontract out the work of that department. Where can the now laid-off workers picket?

6. Suppose part of the Maytag Company (a washing machine manufacturer) is a small shop making pulley belts of rubber for motors incorporated into Maytag's washing machines. A strike of Maytag's pulley-belt workers causes Maytag to purchase pulley belts from National Supplier, a manufacturer of all sorts of pulley belts. Is National an ally? Two arguments militate against such a finding.[24] First, it would require all suppliers to investigate a customer's labor status before every sale. Second, the primary employees have adequate opportunity to stop deliveries of the product at the primary premises. Are you persuaded?

[22] Shopmen's Local 501, Iron Workers (Oliver Whyte Co.), 120 N.L.R.B. 856 (1958).
[23] See Teamsters Local 868 (Mercer Storage Co.), 156 N.L.R.B. 67 (1965).
[24] See Levin, supra n.20, at 296 and n.49.

7. *The "integrated-enterprise" ally.* Consider a company engaged in the printing and binding of books. The company takes an author's manuscript, sets it in type, and prints it on paper, which it then cuts and binds into a finished book. Such a company might have only one bargaining unit, with all employees represented by the same union, but it is more likely to have several bargaining units — for example, typographers, paper handlers, printing pressmen, bindery workers, and others. But suppose that instead of remaining one company, the owners decide to incorporate two separate operations. Thus all the manufacturing processes except the binding will be done by one corporation, and the binding will be done by the second corporation. Especially if the same individuals own both corporations and control both operations, and if the operations are housed in the same building, the two corporations will be allies (and probably alter egos) and a union in a dispute with the bindery operation will be able to appeal to nonbindery employees without running afoul of §8(b)(4)(B).[25]

The question is why? Assuming it is the common ownership, control and straight-line operation, what happens if one or more of these factors are missing? Apparently common ownership standing alone is not enough and even where the same corporation operates two businesses (a leading case involves a nationwide newspaper chain),[26] the businesses are likely not to be allies if they exercise independent control over their operations. Actual (as opposed to potential) common control of operations, especially labor relations policy, is considered a factor strongly supporting an ally finding — and will probably be enough when combined with common ownership, as will common ownership plus straight-line operations at the same location. The status of permutations is very hard to predict.

A basic point bears emphasis. If a single employer at one location is composed of several bargaining units, all his or her employees are primary. That is, strikers from one bargaining unit can appeal to employees from other bargaining units without running into §8(b)(4) problems.

In the following case the circuit court had held for the union, relying heavily on *Ebasco* and the integrated-enterprise ally doctrine. The union continued this reliance before the Supreme Court.

NLRB v. DENVER BUILDING & CONSTRUCTION TRADES COUNCIL

341 U.S. 675 (1951)

BURTON, J.

The principal question here is whether a labor organization committed an unfair labor practice, within the meaning of §8(b)(4)[(B)] of the

[25] See, e.g., Lithographers Local 235 (Henry Wurst, Inc.), 187 N.L.R.B. 490 (1970).
[26] Los Angeles Newspaper Guild (Hearst Corp.), 185 N.L.R.B. 305 (1970).

National Labor Relations Act by engaging in a strike, an object of which was to force the general contractor on a construction project to terminate its contract with a certain subcontractor on that project. For the reasons hereafter stated, we hold that such an unfair labor practice was committed.

In September, 1947, Doose & Lintner was the general contractor for the construction of a commercial building in Denver, Colorado. It awarded a subcontract for electrical work on the building, in an estimated amount of $2,300, to Gould & Preisner, a firm which for 20 years had employed nonunion workmen on construction work in that city. The latter's employees proved to be the only nonunion workmen on the project. Those of the general contractor and of the other subcontractors were members of unions affiliated with the respondent Denver Building and Construction Trades Council.

In November a representative of one of those unions told Gould that he did not see how the job could progress with Gould's nonunion men on it. Gould insisted that they would complete the electrical work unless bodily put off. The representative replied that the situation would be difficult for both Gould & Preisner and Doose & Lintner.

January 8, 1948, the Council's Board of Business Agents instructed the Council's representative "to place a picket on the job stating that the job was unfair" to it. In keeping with the Council's practice, each affiliate was notified of that decision. That notice was a signal in the nature of an order to the members of the affiliated unions to leave the job and remain away until otherwise ordered. Representatives of the Council and each of the respondent unions visited the project and reminded the contractor that Gould & Preisner employed nonunion workmen and said that union men could not work on the job with nonunion men. They further advised that if Gould & Preisner's men did work on the job, the Council and its affiliates would put a picket on it to notify their members that nonunion men were working on it and that the job was unfair. All parties stood their ground.

January 9, the Council posted a picket at the project carrying a placard stating "This Job Unfair to Denver Building and Construction Trades Council." He was paid by the Council and his picketing continued from January 9 through January 22. During that time the only persons who reported for work were the nonunion electricians of Gould & Preisner. January 22, before Gould & Preisner had completed its subcontract, the general contractor notified it to get off the job so that Doose & Lintner could continue with the project. January 23, the Council removed its picket and shortly thereafter the union employees resumed work on the project. Gould & Preisner protested this treatment but its workmen were denied entrance to the job.

On charges filed by Gould & Preisner, the Regional Director of the National Labor Relations Board issued the complaint in this case against the Council and the respondent unions. It alleged that they had engaged in a strike or had caused strike action to be taken on the project by employees of the general contractor and of other subcontractors, an object of which was to force the general contractor to cease doing business with Gould & Preisner on that project. [The Board found the strike to be secondary, the court of appeals found it primary.]

While §8(b)(4) does not expressly mention "primary" or "secondary" disputes, strikes or boycotts, that section often is referred to in the Act's legislative history as one of the Act's "secondary boycott sections." . . .

We must first determine whether the strike in this case had a proscribed object. The conduct which the Board here condemned is readily distinguishable from that which it declined to condemn in the Rice Milling case, 341 U.S. 665. There the accused union sought merely to obtain its own recognition by the operator of a mill, and the union's pickets near the mill sought to influence two employees of a customer of the mill not to cross the picket line. In that case we supported the Board in its conclusion that such conduct was no more than was traditional and permissible in a primary strike. The union did not engage in a strike against the customer. It did not encourage concerted action by the customer's employees to force the customer to boycott the mill. It did not commit any unfair labor practice proscribed by §8(b)(4).

In the background of the instant case there was a longstanding labor dispute between the Council and Gould & Preisner due to the latter's practice of employing nonunion workmen on construction jobs in Denver. The respondent labor organizations contend that they engaged in a primary dispute with Doose & Lintner alone, and that they sought simply to force Doose & Lintner to make the project an all-union job. If there had been no contract between Doose & Lintner and Gould & Preisner there might be substance in their contention that the dispute involved no boycott. If, for example, Doose & Lintner had been doing all the electrical work on this project through its own nonunion employees, it could have replaced them with union men and thus disposed of the dispute. However, the existence of the Gould & Preisner subcontract presented a materially different situation. The nonunion employees were employees of Gould & Preisner. The only way that respondents could attain their purpose was to force Gould & Preisner itself off the job. This, in turn, could be done only through Doose & Lintner's termination of Gould & Preisner's subcontract. The result is that the Council's strike, in order to attain its ultimate purpose, must have included among its objects that of forcing Doose & Lintner to terminate that subcontract. On that point, the Board adopted the following finding: "That *an* object, if not the only object, of what transpired with respect to . . . Doose & Lintner was to force or require them to cease doing business with Gould & Preisner seems scarcely open to question, in view of all of the facts. And it is clear at least as to Doose & Lintner, that that purpose was achieved." (Emphasis supplied.) 82 N.L.R.B. at 1212.

We accept this crucial finding. It was an object of the strike to force the contractor to terminate Gould & Preisner's subcontract. We hold also that a strike with such an object was an unfair labor practice within the meaning of §8(b)(4)[(B)]. It is not necessary to find that the *sole* object of the strike was that of forcing the contractor to terminate the subcontractor's contract. This is emphasized in the legislative history of the section.

We agree with the Board also in its conclusion that the fact that the contractor and subcontractor were engaged on the same construction project, and that the contractor had some supervision over the subcontractor's work, did not eliminate the status of each as an independent contractor or make the employees of one the employees of the other. The business relationship between independent contractors is too well established in the law to be overridden without clear language doing so. The Board found that the relationship between Doose & Lintner and Gould & Preisner was one of "doing business" and we find no adequate reason for upsetting that conclusion.

Finally, §8(c) safeguarding freedom of speech has no significant application to the picket's placard in this case. Section 8(c) does not apply to a mere signal by a labor organization to its members, or to the members of its affiliates, to engage in an unfair labor practice such as a strike proscribed by §8(b)(4)[(B)]. That the placard was merely such a signal, tantamount to a direction to strike, was found by the Board. ". . . the issues in this case turn upon acts by labor organizations which are tantamount to directions and instructions to their members to engage in strike action. The protection afforded by Section 8(c) of the Act to the expression of 'any views, argument or opinion' does not pertain where, as here, the issues raised under Section 8(b)(4)[(B)] turn on official directions or instructions to a union's own members." 82 N.L.R.B. at 1213. . . . The judgment of the Court of Appeals accordingly is reversed and the case is remanded to it for procedure not inconsistent with this opinion.[27]

Douglas, J., with whom Reed, J., joins, dissenting.

The employment of union and nonunion men on the same job is a basic protest in trade union history. That was the protest here. The union was not out to destroy the contractor because of his antiunion attitude. The union was not pursuing the contractor to other jobs. All the union asked was that union men not be compelled to work alongside nonunion men on the same job. As Judge Rifkind stated in an analogous case, "the union was not extending its activity to a front remote from the immediate dispute but to one intimately and indeed inextricably united to it."[1]

The picketing would undoubtedly have been legal if there had been no subcontractor involved — if the general contractor had put nonunion men on the job. The presence of a subcontractor does not alter one

[27] Jackson, J., dissented.

1. Douds v. Metropolitan Federation, D.C., 73 F. Supp. 672, 677.

whit the realities of the situation; the protest of the union is precisely the same. In each the union was trying to protect the job on which union men were employed. If that is forbidden, the Taft-Hartley Act makes the right to strike, guaranteed by §13, dependent on fortuitous business arrangements that have no significance so far as the evils of the secondary boycott are concerned. I would give scope to both §8(b)(4) and §13 by reading the restrictions of §8(b)(4) to reach the case where an industrial dispute spreads from the job to another front.

Notes

1. The union might have said to the general contractor, "We don't want you to put Gould & Preisner off the job, just persuade it to employ union electricians. We are not going to refer you any workers until you do." The union could then have argued that it had no object of forcing one person to "cease doing business with" another person. Such an argument was rejected in NLRB v. Local 825, Operating Engineers, 400 U.S. 297 (1971), the Court holding that "[t]he clear implication of the demands was that [the general] would be required either to force a change in the [subcontractor's] policy or to terminate [the subcontractor's] contract."

2. Employers on a construction site produce a single product, a building, by the closely coordinated operations of several companies. The departments of a tractor factory could be similarly independently owned, but are not. Is it fair to make decisions on restricting unions based on such accidents of industrial ownership? The answer turns on how one defines "fair," and for that we must look to the policies underlying the secondary boycott prohibitions. At least one arguable policy — striking an acceptable balance of power between union and management — can be gauged only on an industry-by-industry basis. Yet there appears to be no statutory language in §8(b)(4)(B) warranting such an approach. You should consider, nonetheless, whether the Court may have been trying to do that in *Denver Building Trades* when it refused, with little explanation, to apply the integrated-enterprise ally doctrine. To put it another way, in what other industries is "[t]he business relationship between independent contractors . . . too well established in the law to be overridden without clear language doing so"?

3. Appeals to Secondary Employees[28]

Consider a primary strike (e.g., one for higher wages) by a union against a manufacturing company. Why does the union picket? It may

[28] See Goetz, Secondary Boycotts and the LMRA: A Path Through the Swamp, 19 U. Kan. L. Rev. 651 (1971); Lesnick, The Gravamen of the Secondary Boycott, 62 Colum.

be to persuade the primary employees to cease work, or if the primary employees are already off the job but their work is being done by supervisors or replacements, it may be to persuade the latter group to stop work. In either event, the success of the picket line for this purpose is likely to be apparent early in the game; for although those crossing the line today may decide to honor it tomorrow, it is more likely that initial decisions to honor or not will stand. Yet even if the appeal to primary employees is demonstrably unsuccessful, the union may continue picketing in order to appeal to secondary employees, such as those delivering raw materials, picking up finished goods and the like, not to cross the picket line. The efficacy of these appeals may well determine the ultimate success of the strike. The extent to which the law allows or disallows these appeals to secondary employees is thus a major determinant of union power.

In the early cases following the passage of §8(b)(4), the Board adopted a geographical approach to union appeals to secondary employees (employees of a secondary employer). The Board reasoned that Congress had not intended to prohibit primary strikes or primary picket lines. Since, in the Board's view, one object of all primary picketing is to persuade third persons not to do business at the primary employer's premises, this object could not be deemed forbidden lest it have the unintended effect of banning picketing at a primary premises, the most traditional sort of primary picketing. In a series of cases in the early 1950s, the Board held that a union could appeal to secondary employees not to do any work on primary premises. Such appeals might come from pickets, solicitations at the homes of secondary employees, unfair lists, and the like.

The Board also developed geographic rules to govern the legality of picketing when primary employees worked away from the primary employer's premises. Thus when a primary employer's truck made deliveries at secondary premises, the Board held that picketing around the truck was permissible because the union's object of influencing the customer to stop doing business with the primary at the primary's premises was a legitimate object of the picketing. The truck was a roving primary situs and it was appropriate for the pickets to follow that situs so long as the picketing was strictly limited to the area around the truck while it sat at the secondary premises. It was in the context of these rules that the following case was decided.

L. Rev. 1363 (1962); St. Antoine, What Makes Secondary Boycotts Secondary? Southwestern Legal Foundation, Eleventh Annual Institute on Labor Law 5 (1965); Zimmerman, Secondary Picketing and the Reserved Gate: The *General Electric* Doctrine, 47 Va. L. Rev. 1164 (1961).

SAILORS' UNION OF THE PACIFIC & MOORE DRY DOCK CO.

92 N.L.R.B. 547 (1950)

[Samsoc, a Greek-owned shipping corporation, withdrew a contract to transport gypsum from an American ship, whose employees were represented by the Sailor's Union of the Pacific, and gave it to the S.S. Phopho, a Samsoc ship. The Phopho was placed in the Moore Dry Dock shipyard for refitting by Moore Dry Dock employees to permit the ship to carry the gypsum. A crew, none of whom was a Sailors' Union member, was hired and began training on the ship while it was at the shipyard. When the Sailors' Union was denied recognition for Phopho sailors, it sent pickets to the shipyard. It asked to be allowed to picket adjacent to the ship, but was refused. It then picketed the entrance to the shipyard and sent letters to Moore Dry Dock employees explaining the dispute and asking them not to work on the Phopho. Picket signs emphasized that the dispute was with the Phopho's owner. The picketing had no effect on the Phopho's sailors; but the Moore Dry Dock employees ceased work on the Phopho, although they continued to work on other ships.]

Section 8(b)(4)[(B)] is aimed at secondary boycotts and secondary strike activities. It was not intended to proscribe primary action by a union having a legitimate labor dispute with an employer. Picketing at the premises of a primary employer is traditionally recognized as primary action even though it is "necessarily designed to induce and encourage third persons to cease doing business with the picketed employer." . . . Hence, if Samsoc, the owner of the S.S. Phopho, had had a dock of its own in California to which the Phopho had been tied up while undergoing conversion by Moore Dry Dock employees, picketing by the Respondent at the dock site would unquestionably have constituted *primary* action, even though the Respondent might have expected that the picketing would be more effective in persuading Moore employees not to work on the ship than to persuade the seamen aboard the Phopho to quit that vessel. The difficulty in the present case arises therefore, not because of any difference in picketing objectives, but from the fact that the Phopho was not tied up at its own dock, but at that of Moore, while the picketing was going on in front of the Moore premises.

In the usual case, the situs of a labor dispute is the premises of the primary employer. Picketing of the premises is also picketing of the situs. . . . But in some cases the situs of the dispute may not be limited to a fixed location; it may be ambulatory. Thus in the *Shultz*[9] case, a major-

9. [International Brotherhood of Teamsters, etc. (Schultz Refrigerated Service, Inc.), 87 N.L.R.B. 502.]

ity of the Board held that the truck upon which a truck driver worked was the situs of a labor dispute between him and the owner of the truck. Similarly, we hold in the present case that, as the Phopho was the place of employment of the seamen, it was the situs of the dispute between Samsoc and the Respondent over working conditions aboard that vessel.

When the situs is ambulatory, it may come to rest temporarily at the premises of another employer. The perplexing question is: Does the right to picket follow the situs while it is stationed at the premises of a secondary employer, when the only way to picket that *situs* is in front of the secondary employer's premises? Admittedly, no easy answer is possible. Essentially the problem is one of balancing the right of a union to picket at the site of its dispute as against the right of a secondary employer to be free from picketing in a controversy in which it is not directly involved.

When a secondary employer is harboring the situs of a dispute between a union and a primary employer, the right of neither the union to picket nor of the secondary employer to be free from picketing can be absolute. The enmeshing of premises and situs qualifies both rights. In the kind of situation that exists in this case, we believe that picketing of the premises of a secondary employer is primary if it meets the following conditions: (a) The picketing is strictly limited to times when the situs of dispute is located on the secondary employer's premises; (b) at the time of the picketing the primary employer is engaged in its normal business at the situs; (c) the picketing is limited to places reasonably close to the location of the situs; and (d) the picketing discloses clearly that the dispute is with the primary employer. All these conditions were met in the present case.

(a) During the entire period of the picketing the Phopho was tied up at a dock in the Moore shipyard.

(b) Under its contract with Samsoc, Moore agreed to permit the former to put a crew on board the Phopho for training purposes during the last 2 weeks before the vessel's delivery to Samsoc. At the time the picketing started on February 17, 1950, 90 percent of the conversion job had been completed, practically the entire crew had been hired, the ship's oil bunkers had been filled, and other stores were shortly to be put aboard. The various members of the crew commenced work as soon as they reported aboard the Phopho. Those in the deck department did painting and cleaning up; those in the steward's department, cooking and cleaning up; and those in the engine department, oiling and cleaning up. The crew were thus getting the ship ready for sea. They were on board to serve the purposes of Samsoc, the Phopho's owners, and not Moore. The normal business of a ship does not only begin with its departure on a scheduled voyage.

The multitudinous steps of preparation, including hiring and training a crew and putting stores aboard, are as much a part of the normal business of a ship as the voyage itself. We find, therefore, that during the entire period of the picketing, the Phopho was engaged in its normal business.

(c) Before placing its pickets outside the entrance to the Moore shipyard, the Respondent Union asked, but was refused, permission to place its pickets at the dock where the Phopho was tied up. The Respondent therefore posted its pickets at the yard entrance which, as the parties stipulated, was as close to the Phopho as they could get under the circumstances.

(d) Finally, by its picketing and other conduct the Respondent was scrupulously careful to indicate that its dispute was solely with the primary employer, the owners of the Phopho. Thus the signs carried by the pickets said only that the Phopho was unfair to the Respondent. The Phopho and not Moore was declared "hot." Similarly, in asking cooperation of other unions, the Respondent clearly revealed that its dispute was with the Phopho. Finally, Moore's own witnesses admitted that no attempt was made to interfere with other work in progress in the Moore yard.

We believe that our dissenting colleagues' expressions of alarm are based on a misunderstanding of our decision. We are not holding, as the dissenters seem to think, that a union which has a dispute with a shipowner over working conditions of seamen aboard a ship may lawfully picket the premises of an independent shipyard to which the shipowner has delivered his vessel for overhaul and repair. We are only holding that, if a shipyard permits the owner of a vessel to use its dock for the purpose of readying the ship for its regular voyage by hiring and training a crew and putting stores aboard ship, a union representing seamen may then, within the careful limitations laid down in this decision, lawfully picket in front of the shipyard premises to advertise its dispute with the shipowner. . . .

Under the circumstances of this case, we therefore find that the picketing practice followed by the Respondent was primary and not secondary and therefore did not violate §8(b)(4)[(B)] of the Act.[29]

Note

The *Moore Dry Dock* test was designed to permit appeals to secondary employees not to do any work at the primary premises while minimizing the possibility that the appeals would persuade secondary employees to cease doing all work for the secondary employer.

[29] Members Reynolds and Murdock dissented.

About 1954, the Board began a shift from a geographical to a literal approach to the statute. Now the theory was that the statute demanded that union appeals to secondary employees were to be avoided entirely. Rules were established to permit appeals to primary employees while prohibiting appeals to secondary employees except insofar as they were "incidental" (unavoidable?) effects of a primary picket line. If picketing induced secondary employees to stop work for their employer and the object of the picketing was to pressure the secondary employer to cease doing business with the primary, there was a violation. The forbidden object was easily shown, in the Board's view, if a union picketed a primary situs when secondary employees but no primary employees were present.

Where the premises were owned by the primary employer but secondary employees had to work there over an "extended" period of time, the union had to insulate secondary employees from the dispute by following the standards set out in *Moore Dry Dock.* Where primary employees worked at a secondary premises, the union would also have to comply with *Moore Dry Dock* in setting up its picket line. And in the latter situation, the Board ruled that where the union had adequate opportunity to picket at the primary premises, any picketing of the secondary premises would be a violation of §8(b)(4) notwithstanding compliance with *Moore Dry Dock.*

Moore Dry Dock thus remained good Board law, but it had changed from a rule designed to minimize the effect of permissible appeals to secondary employees on their employers to a rule forbidding all appeals to secondary employees. Only if occasional secondary employees approached a primary picket line (established in conformity with *Moore Dry Dock*) and refused to cross, was an appeal to a secondary employee a permissible "incidental" effect of the picket line. This literal approach did not always fare well in the courts of appeal.

In 1961, the Supreme Court influenced the course of the doctrinal development by its decision in *General Electric,* which follows. Before reading that case, it is valuable to have some information on the briefs that were filed. The case involves a primary employer who set out separate gates for the use of secondary employees working at the primary's premises. The International Union of Electrical Workers (petitioning union) argued that an employer may use a separate gate for §8(b)(4) purposes only for employees of a secondary employer who perform no services at all for the primary, since all other appeals are part and parcel of primary picketing.

Amici briefs filed by other unions argued that a picketing union can appeal to all employees so as to shut down all primary and secondary operations at the primary premises. The General Electric company maintained that a direct appeal to any secondary employee violates §8(b)(4). Board counsel contended that the union should not be permitted to appeal to the employees of neutral employers who use the premises "in a substantial and continuous manner as a regular work place," but that appeals to neutrals making only occasional deliveries to General Electric should be permissible. The argued distinction was that appeals to the former group of employees have far greater impact than appeals to the occasional deliveryman.

LOCAL 761, INTERNATIONAL UNION OF ELECTRICAL WORKERS v. NLRB [GENERAL ELECTRIC CO.]

366 U.S. 667 (1961)

Frankfurter, J.

General Electric Corporation operates a plant outside of Louisville, Kentucky, where it manufactures washers, dryers, and other electrical household appliances. The square-shaped, thousand-acre, unfenced plant is known as Appliance Park. A large drainage ditch makes ingress and egress impossible except over five roadways cross culverts, designated as gates.

Since 1954, General Electric sought to confine the employees of independent contractors, described hereafter, who work on the premises of the Park, to the use of Gate 3-A and confine its use to them. The undisputed reason for doing so was to insulate General Electric employees from the frequent labor disputes in which the contractors were involved. Gate 3-A is 550 feet away from the nearest entrance available for General Electric employees, suppliers, and deliverymen. Although anyone can pass the gate without challenge, the roadway leads to a guardhouse where identification must be presented. Vehicle stickers of various shapes and colors enable a guard to check on sight whether a vehicle is authorized to use Gate 3-A. Since January 1958, a prominent sign has been posted at the gate which states: "Gate 3-A For Employees Of Contractors Only — G. E. Employees Use Other Gates." On rare occasions, it appears, a General Electric employee was allowed to pass the guardhouse, but such occurrence was in violation of company instructions. There was no proof of any unauthorized attempts to pass the gate during the strike in question.

The independent contractors are utilized for a great variety of tasks on the Appliance Park premises. Some do construction work on new buildings; some install and repair ventilating and heating equipment; some engage in retooling and rearranging operations necessary to the manufacture of new models; others do "general maintenance work." These services are contracted to outside employers either because the company's employees lack the necessary skill or manpower, or because the work can be done more economically by independent contractors. The latter reason determined the contracting of maintenance work for which the Central Maintenance department of the company bid competitively with the contractors. While some of the work done by these contractors had on occasion been previously performed by Central

Maintenance, the findings do not disclose the number of employees of independent contractors who were performing these routine maintenance services, as compared with those who were doing specialized work of a capital-improvement nature.

The Union, petitioner here, is the certified bargaining representative for the production and maintenance workers who constitute approximately 7,600 of the 10,500 employees of General Electric at Appliance Park. On July 27, 1958, the Union called a strike because of 24 unsettled grievances with the company. Picketing occurred at all the gates, including Gate 3-A, and continued until August 9 when an injunction was issued by a Federal District Court. The signs carried by the pickets at all gates read: "Local 761 On Strike G. E. Unfair." Because of the picketing, almost all of the employees of independent contractors refused to enter the company premises.

Neither the legality of the strike or of the picketing at any of the gates except 3-A nor the peaceful nature of the picketing is in dispute. The sole claim is that the picketing before the gate exclusively used by employees of independent contractors was conduct proscribed by §8(b)(4)[(B)].

The Trial Examiner recommended that the Board dismiss the complaint. He concluded that the limitations on picketing which the Board had prescribed in so-called "common situs" cases were not applicable to the situation before him, in that the picketing at Gate 3-A represented traditional primary action which necessarily had a secondary effect of inconveniencing those who did business with the struck employer. He reasoned that if a primary employer could limit the area of picketing around his own premises by constructing a separate gate for employees of independent contractors, such a device could also be used to isolate employees of his suppliers and customers, and that such action could not relevantly be distinguished from oral appeals made to secondary employees not to cross a picket line where only a single gate existed.

The Board rejected the Trial Examiner's conclusion. It held that, since only the employees of the independent contractors were allowed to use Gate 3-A, the Union's object in picketing there was "to enmesh these employees of the neutral employers in its dispute with the Company," thereby constituting a violation of §8(b)(4)[(B)] because the independent employees were encouraged to engage in a concerted refusal to work "with an object of forcing the independent contractors to cease doing business with the Company."[2] The Court of Appeals for the District of Columbia granted enforcement of the Board's order. . . .

2. Member Fanning concurred in the result, reasoning that the common-situs criteria set out by the Board in Sailors' Union of the Pacific (Moore Dry Dock), 92 N.L.R.B. 547, could be applied to situations where the primary employer owned the premises, and that the requirement that the picketing take place reasonably close to the situs of the labor dispute had therefore been violated by the picketing around Gate 3-A.

I

Section 8(b)(4)[(B)] . . . could not be literally construed; otherwise it would ban most strikes historically considered to be lawful, so-called primary activity. "While §8(b)(4) does not expressly mention 'primary' or 'secondary' disputes, strikes or boycotts, that section often is referred to in the Act's legislative history as one of the Act's 'secondary boycott sections.' " National Labor Relations Board v. Denver Building & Const. Trades Council, 341 U.S. 675, 686. "Congress did not seek by §8(b)(4), to interfere with the ordinary strike. . . ." National Labor Relations Board v. International Rice Milling Co., 341 U.S. 665, 672. The impact of the section was directed toward what is known as the secondary boycott whose "sanctions bear, not upon the employer who alone is a party to the dispute, but upon some third party who has no concern in it." International Brotherhood of Electrical Workers, Local 501 v. National Labor Relations Board, 2 Cir., 181 F.2d 34, 37. Thus the section "left a striking labor organization free to use persuasion, including picketing, not only on the primary employer and his employees but on numerous others. Among these were secondary employers who were customers or suppliers of the primary employer and persons dealing with them . . . and even employees of secondary employers so long as the labor organization did not . . . 'induce or encourage the employees of any employer to engage, in a strike or a concerted refusal in the course of their employment' . . ." National Labor Relations Board v. Local 294, International Brotherhood of Teamsters, 2 Cir., 284 F.2d 887, 889. . . .

Important as is the distinction between legitimate "primary activity" and banned "secondary activity," it does not present a glaringly bright line. The objectives of any picketing include a desire to influence others from withholding from the employer their services or trade. See Sailors' Union of the Pacific (Moore Dry Dock), 92 N.L.R.B. 547. "[I]ntended or not, sought for or not, aimed for or not, employees of neutral employers do take action sympathetic with strikers and do put pressure on their own employers." Seafarers International Union, etc. v. National Labor Relations Board, 105 U.S. App. D.C. 211, 265 F.2d 585, 590. "It is clear that, when a union pickets an employer with whom it has a dispute, it hopes, even if it does not intend, that all persons will honor the picket line, and that hope encompasses the employees of neutral employers who may in the course of their employment (deliverymen and the like) have to enter the premises." Id., at page 591. "Almost all picketing, even at the situs of the primary employer and surely at that of the secondary, hopes to achieve the forbidden objective, whatever other motives there may be and however small the chances of success." Local 294, supra, 284 F.2d at page 890. But picketing which induces secondary employees to respect a picket line is not the equivalent of picketing which has an object of inducing those employees to engage in concerted conduct against their employer in order to force him to refuse to deal with the struck employer. National Labor Relations Board v. International Rice Milling Co., supra.

However difficult the drawing of lines more nice than obvious, the statute compels the task. Accordingly, the Board and the courts have attempted to devise reasonable criteria drawing heavily upon the means to which a union resorts in promoting its cause. Although "[n]o rigid rule which would make . . . [a] few factors conclusive is contained in or deducible from the statute," Sales Drivers, etc. v. National Labor Relations Board, 97 U.S. App. D.C. 173, 229 F.2d 514, 157, "[I]n the absence of admissions by the union of an illegal intent, the nature of acts performed shows the intent." Seafarers International Union, etc., supra, 265 F.2d at page 591.

The nature of the problem, as revealed by unfolding variant situations, inevitably involves an evolutionary process for its rational response, not a quick, definitive formula as a comprehensive answer. And so, it is not surprising that the Board has more or less felt its way during the fourteen years in which it has had to apply §8(b)(4)[(B)], and has modified and reformed its standards on the basis of accumulating experience. . . .

II

The early decisions of the Board following the Taft-Hartley amendments involved activity which took place around the secondary employer's premises. For example, in Wadsworth Building Co., [81 N.L.R.B. 802] the union set up a picket line around the situs of a builder who had contracted to purchase prefabricated houses from the primary employer. The Board found this to be illegal secondary activity. . . . In contrast, when picketing took place around the premises of the primary employer, the Board regarded this as valid primary activity. In Oil Workers International Union (Pure Oil Co.), 84 N.L.R.B. 315, Pure had used Standard's dock and employees for loading its oil onto ships. The companies had contracted that, in case of a strike against Standard, Pure employees would take over the loading of Pure oil. The union struck against Standard and picketed the dock, and Pure employees refused to cross the picket line. The Board held this to be a primary activity, although the union's action induced the Pure employees to engage in a concerted refusal to handle Pure products at the dock. The fact that the picketing was confined to the vicinity of the Standard premises influenced the Board not to find that an object of the activity was to force Pure to cease doing business with Standard, even if such was a secondary effect.

"A strike, by its very nature, inconveniences those who customarily do business with the struck employer. Moreover, any accompanying picketing of the employer's premises is necessarily designed to induce and encourage third persons to cease doing business with the picketed employer. It does not follow, however, that such picketing is therefore proscribed by §8(b)(4)[(B)] of the Act." 84 N.L.R.B., at 318.

In United Electrical Workers (Ryan Construction Corp.), 85 N.L.R.B. 417, Ryan had contracted to perform construction work on a building adjacent to the Bucyrus plant and inside its fence. A separate gate was cut through the fence for Ryan's employees which no employee of Bucyrus ever used. The Board concluded that the union — on strike against Bucyrus — could picket the Ryan gate, even though an object of the picketing was to enlist the aid of Ryan employees, since Congress did not intend to outlaw primary picketing.

"When picketing is wholly at the premises of the employer with whom the union is engaged in a labor dispute, it cannot be called 'secondary' even though, as is virtually always the case, an object of the picketing is to dissuade all persons from entering such premises for business reasons. It makes no difference whether 1 or 100 other employees wish to enter the premises. It follows in this case that the picketing of Bucyrus premises, which was primary because in support of a labor dispute *with Bucyrus,* did not lose its character and become 'secondary' at the co-called Ryan gate because Ryan employees were the only persons regularly entering Bucyrus premises at that gate." 85 N.L.R.B., at 418. See also General Teamsters (Crump, Inc.), 112 N.L.R.B. 311.

Thus, the Board eliminated picketing which took place around the situs of the primary employer — regardless of the special circumstances involved — from being held invalid secondary activity under §8(b)(4)[(B)].

However, the impact of the new situations made the Board conscious of the complexity of the problem by reason of the protean forms in which it appeared. This became clear in the "common situs" cases — situations where two employers were performing separate tasks on common premises.[30] The Moore Dry Dock case, supra, laid out the Board's new standards in this area. There, the union picketed outside an entrance to a dock where a ship, owned by the struck employer, was being

[30] What is a "common situs"? If it means a single premises at which is found both a primary and secondary employee, the term is irrelevant, for every primary premises visited by a secondary employee (e.g., a deliveryman) would be a common situs. Only a secondary situs where no primary employees work would be excluded from the definition; in the instant case, Appliance Park would be a common situs by this use of the term. Alternatively, a common situs could be one on which primary and secondary employees both work but which is owned by a third employer. But the term would then turn on the legal ownership of the property and it is not apparent that this has any relevance to secondary boycott policy (suppose the land on which Appliance Park sat was leased by General Electric?). Consider whether Justice Frankfurter is offering yet another definition here, a definition that may bear a relationship to the test for the legality of appeals to secondary employees set out later in the opinion. The inquiry is important for later the Board will hold that *General Electric* does not apply to "common situs" picketing.

trained and outfitted. Although the premises picketed were those of the secondary employer, they constituted the only place where picketing could take place; furthermore, the objectives of the picketing were no more aimed at the employees of the secondary employer — the dock owner — than they had been in the *Pure Oil* and *Ryan* cases. The Board concluded, however, that when the situs of the primary employer was "ambulatory" there must be a balance between the union's right to picket and the interest of the secondary employer in being free from picketing. It set out four standards for picketing in such situations which would be presumptive of valid primary activity: (1) that the picketing be limited to times when the situs of dispute was located on the secondary premises, (2) that the primary employer be engaged in his normal business at the situs, (3) that the picketing take place reasonably close to the situs, and (4) that the picketing clearly disclose that the dispute was only with the primary employer. These tests were widely accepted by reviewing federal courts. As is too often the way of law or, at least, of adjudications, soon the *Dry Dock* tests were mechanically applied so that a violation of one of the standards was taken to be presumptive of illegal activity. For example, failure of picket signs clearly to designate the employer against whom the strike was directed was held to be violative of §8(b)(4)[(B)].

In Local 55 (PBM), 108 N.L.R.B. 363, the Board for the first time applied the *Dry Dock* test, although the picketing occurred at premises owned by the primary employer. There, an insurance company owned a tract of land that it was developing, and also served as the general contractor. A neutral subcontractor was also doing work at the site. The union, engaged in a strike against the insurance company, picketed the entire premises, characterizing the entire job as unfair, and the employees of the subcontractor walked off. The Court of Appeals for the Tenth Circuit enforced the Board's order which found the picketing to be illegal on the ground that the picket signs did not measure up to the *Dry Dock* standard that they clearly disclose that the picketing was directed against the struck employer only. 218 F.2d 226.[31]

The Board's application of the *Dry Dock* standards to picketing at the premises of the struck employer was made more explicit in Retail Fruit & Vegetable Clerks (Crystal Palace Market), 116 N.L.R.B. 856. The owner of a large common market operated some of the shops within, and leased out others to independent sellers. The union, although given permission to picket the owner's individual stands chose to picket outside the entire market. The Board held that this action was violative of §8(b)(4)[(B)] in that the union did not attempt to minimize the effect of its picketing, as required in a common-situs case, on the operations of the neutral employers utilizing the market. "We believe . . . that the foregoing principles should apply to all common situs picketing, in-

[31] In a future case, see p. 444, infra, the Board will say that the Court here cited the *PBM* case with approval. Do you agree?

cluding cases where, as here, the picketed premises are owned by the primary employer." 116 N.L.R.B., at 859. The *Ryan* case, supra, was overruled to the extent it implied the contrary. The Court of Appeals for the Ninth Circuit, in enforcing the Board's order, specifically approved its disavowance of an ownership test. 249 F.2d 591. The Board made clear that its decision did not affect situations where picketing which had effects on neutral third parties who dealt with the employer occurred at premises occupied solely by him. "In such case, we adhere to the rule established by the Board . . . that more latitude be given to picketing at such separate primary premises than at premises occupied in part (or entirely) by secondary employers." 116 N.L.R.B., at 860, n. 10.

In rejecting the ownership test in situations where two employers were performing work upon a common site, the Board was naturally guided by this Court's opinion in *Rice Milling,* in which we indicated that the location of the picketing at the primary employer's premises was "not necessarily conclusive" of its legality. 341 U.S., at page 671. Where the work done by the secondary employees is unrelated to the normal operations of the primary employer, it is difficult to perceive how the pressure of picketing the entire situs is any less on the neutral employer merely because the picketing takes place at property owned by the struck employer. The application of the *Dry Dock* tests to limit the picketing effects to the employees of the employer against whom the dispute is directed carries out the "dual congressional objectives of preserving the right of labor organizations to bring pressure to bear on offending employers in primary labor disputes and of shielding unoffending employers and others from pressures in controversies not their own." National Labor Relations Board v. Denver Building & Const. Trades Council, supra, 341 U.S. at page 692.[32]

III

From this necessary survey of the course of the Board's treatment of our problem, the precise nature of the issue before us emerges. With due regard to the relation between the Board's function and the scope of judicial review of its rulings, the question is whether the Board may apply the *Dry Dock* criteria so as to make unlawful picketing at a gate utilized exclusively by employees of independent contractors who work on the struck employer's premises. The effect of such a holding would not bar the union from picketing at all gates used by the employees, suppliers, and customers of the struck employer. Of course an employer

[32] This, then, is the Court's test (pickets can appeal to secondary employees doing "related work"; if the work is unrelated, the pickets must attempt to insulate secondary employees by conforming to *Moore Dry Dock*). You should consider whether the court means this test to apply at only the primary site or is it to apply at secondary and "common" sites as well. In other words, is location, as well as related work, a factor?

may not, by removing all his employees from the situs of the strike, bar the union from publicizing its cause, see Local 618, Automotive, Petroleum, etc. v. National Labor Relations Board, 8 Cir., 249 F.2d 332. The basis of the Board's decision in this case would not remotely have that effect, nor any such tendency for the future.

The Union claims that, if the Board's ruling is upheld, employers will be free to erect separate gates for deliveries, customers, and replacement workers which will be immunzied from picketing. This fear is baseless. The key to the problem is found in the type of work that is being performed by those who use the separate gate. It is significant that the Board has since applied its rationale, first stated in the present case, only to situations where the independent workers were performing tasks unconnected to the normal operations of the struck employer — usually construction work on his buildings. In such situations, the indicated limitations on picketing activity respect the balance of competing interests that Congress has required the Board to enforce. On the other hand, if a separate gate were devised for regular plant deliveries, the barring of picketing at that location would make a clear invasion on traditional primary activity of appealing to neutral employees whose tasks aid the employer's everyday operations. The 1959 Amendments to the National Labor Relations Act, which removed the word "concerted" from the boycott provisions, included a proviso that "nothing contained in this clause (B) shall be construed to make unlawful, where not otherwise unlawful, any primary strike or primary picketing." The proviso was directed against the fear that the removal of "concerted" from the statute might be interpreted so that "the picketing at the factory violates section 8(b)(4)[(B)] because the pickets induce the truck drivers employed by the trucker not to perform their usual services where an object is to compel the trucking firm not to do business with the . . . manufacturer during the strike." Analysis of the bill prepared by Senator Kennedy and Representative Thompson, 105 Cong. Rec. 16589.

In a case similar to the one now before us, the Court of Appeals for the Second Circuit sustained the Board in its application of §8(b)(4)[(B)] to a separate-gate situation. "There must be a separate gate marked and set apart from other gates; the work done by the men who use the gate must be unrelated to the normal operations of the employer and the work must be of a kind that would not, if done when the plant were engaged in its regular operations, necessitate curtailing those operations." United Steelworkers of America, AFL-CIO v. National Labor Relations Board, 2 Cir., 289 F.2d 591, 595. These seem to us controlling considerations.

IV

The foregoing course of reasoning would require that the judgment below sustaining the Board's order be affirmed but for one consideration, even though this consideration may turn out not to affect the result. The legal path by which the Board and the Court of Appeals reached their decisions did not take into account that if Gate 3-A was in fact used by employees of independent contractors who performed conventional maintenance work necessary to the normal operations of General Electric, the use of the gate would have been a mingled one outside the bar of §8(b)(4)[(B)]. In short, such mixed use of this portion of the struck employer's premises would not bar picketing rights of the striking employees. While the record shows some such mingled use, it sheds no light on its extent. It may well turn out to be that the instances of these maintenance tasks were so insubstantial as to be treated by the Board as de minimis. We cannot here guess at the quantitative aspect of this problem. It calls for Board determination. For determination of the questions thus raised, the case must be remanded by the Court of Appeals to the Board.

Reversed.[33]

Two major questions are left after *General Electric*: What is "related work," and does the related-work test apply to union appeals to secondary employees away from the primary premises?

Consider first the following attempt to provide a workable and principled standard for deciding whether work is "related."

LESNICK, THE GRAVAMEN OF THE SECONDARY BOYCOTT

62 Colum. L. Rev. 1412-1414 (1962)

[The union's "intent" that is significant for Section 8(b)(4)(B) purposes], in my view, is the intent to subject the secondary to pressure different in kind from that generated against him by a primary strike. I say different "in kind" because, depending on economic relationships, the pressure of a secondary boycott may be no more severe than that felt as a result of a strike against one with whom the secondary does business. Yet a difference in kind there is.

If a company finds that one of its customers or suppliers has been shut by a strike,[240] normal business relations between the two employers automatically cease; employees of the company seeking to enter the struck plant will find it closed, and the strikers will, of course, not be performing whatever work has been necessary to the doing of business with the secondary. The extent of injury to that company will depend on the particular economic relationships. It may or may not feel compelled

[33] Warren, C. J., and Black, J., concurred in the result. Douglas, J., dissented.

240. I am here, of course, using the term "strike" to include picketing which seeks to induce strike action.

to seek to induce the other employer to settle the dispute. In either event, the pressure generated flows entirely from the disruption of the struck employer's business. If, now, the struck employer is continuing to operate, but the employees of the secondary refuse to enter, the effect on the company is no different. In the one case, the gates are physically locked; in the other, though literally open, they are in effect impassable. The legislative policy, for the most part protecting successful strike activity despite the described effect on secondary employers, suggests the inapplicability of a policy designed to protect secondary and not primary employers from identical effects flowing from wholly or partially unsuccessful strike activity.[241]

Suppose, however, that a picket induces one of the company's drivers, not only to turn away from the struck plant, but to refuse to make deliveries to any other company, so long as his employer continues to attempt to deal with the struck company. Such pressure, whatever its strength, is "essentially different" in that it does not grow out of the interference with the primary's business threatened by the strike against it. It seeks to jump that hurdle and conscript the neutral by subjecting it to independent, directly applied loss of service that would not otherwise be suffered even were the struck plant to cease operations entirely. Here, I submit, the protection afforded to secondary employers by §8(b)(4) is called into play, and that afforded the strike by the act is not at stake.

A similar analysis can be made as to secondary site picketing. An employer who processes materials manufactured by another will feel significantly the loss of trade flowing from the shutting down by a strike of the manufacturer's operations. If the strike fails to close the primary's doors, but "roving situs" pickets induce secondary employees to refuse to unload goods delivered by the primary's nonstriking employees, the effect on the secondary is largely the same as if the delivery, by reason of the success of the strike, could not have been attempted. But if the pickets induce secondary employees to quit all work, whether connected with the primary or not, or induce employees of third persons to refuse to enter the secondary premises, pressure wholly apart from that which could attend the disruption of the primary's business is felt.

In considering the applicability of this analysis to secondary site activities, however, complicating considerations arise. When no primary employees are present at the secondary site, the act plainly condemns inducement of secondary employees to refuse to work on materials coming there from the primary, even though the inducement be only "partial," that is, limited to those materials. Yet it is clear that the strike, if successful in closing down the primary employer's business, would de-

241. See Local 1976, United Bhd. of Carpenters v. NLRB, 357 U.S. 93, 99 (1958). By "successful" strike, I refer, of course, to one that succeeds in closing the primary's plant, not one that wins its bargaining objectives.

prive the secondary of the opportunity to work on such "hot goods." The suggested rationale, then, can not encompass all secondary employee refusals to work that are no broader than those which would "automatically" be occasioned by the disruption of the primary's operation through a wholly successful strike. Only the effect of loss of the primary's *employees* may be considered. The crucial question, thus modified, is: does the picketing union intend to subject the secondary employer to a loss of the services of his employees broader in impact than would be directly caused by the unavailability, as a result of the complete success of the strike, of the services of the primary employees? If so, the picketing is secondary; otherwise, it is primary.

Professor Lesnick argued that under this formulation almost every secondary employee working at the primary's premises will be engaged in related work. The test is, in his view, equally applicable to picketing at a secondary site, but in the typical case most secondary employees would be engaged in unrelated work and thus *Moore Dry Dock* standards would apply.

UNITED STEELWORKERS OF AMERICA v. NLRB [CARRIER CORP.], 376 U.S. 492 (1964): The union's dispute was with the Carrier Corporation. Along the south boundary of Carrier's property was a 35-foot railroad right-of-way used for deliveries to Carrier and to three other companies in the area. The railroad spur ran across a public road that bounded Carrier's property on the west, and through a gate in a continuous chain-link fence that enclosed both the property of Carrier and the railroad right-of-way. The gate was accessible only to railroad employees. The union picketed at this gate and was charged with secondary picketing when its members appealed to railroad employees who were making pickups and deliveries at Carrier.

The Board held the picketing was primary and was legalized by the primary picketing proviso to §8(b)(4)(B). The Board relied on the *General Electric* case and the fact that the work of the railroad employees was in connection with the normal operations of the struck employer. A court of appeals reversed, holding that *General Electric* was inapposite because the picketing occurred on the premises of a secondary employer.

The Supreme Court agreed with the Board and reversed the court of appeals. According to the Court, "[t]he location of the picketing is an important but not decisive factor. . . . The railroad gate adjoined company property and was in fact the railroad entrance gate to the Carrier plant. For the purposes of §8(b)(4) picketing at a situs so proximate and related to the employer's day-to-day operations is no more illegal than if it had occurred at a gate owned by Carrier." The Court then held that the fact that some of the picketing was violent had no bearing on whether it was a secondary boycott proscribed by the statute.

Notes

1. Does the *General Electric* test bear a similarity to the struck work-ally doctrine in that both "struck work" and "related work" assist the primary employer in outlasting the strike?

In Local 32B-32J, Service Employees International Union (Dalton School), 248 N.L.R.B. No. 133 (1980), the union was on strike against the company that supplied janitorial and maintenance services to a school. School employees performed cleaning work during the strike. The Board held that *General Electric* did not permit the union to picket the school because the struck work neither benefited the primary employer economically nor permitted him to escape the impact of the strike.

2. Partially disagreeing with the Lesnick formulation, Professor (then practitioner) St. Antoine asked, "is the legality of appeals to deliverymen not to supply newspapers to struck newsstands going to turn on whether the papers customarily are handed across the counter to the dealer or tossed to the curb beside the stand?"[34]

The distinction between the primary's product and the services of primary employees is crucial to Lesnick's formulation, and even if that formulation proves unpersuasive, the distinction must play some role in the related-work test, for it is clearly unlawful to "follow the product" in these circumstances. Compare the case of an independent contractor performing routine maintenance service on General Electric's assembly lines (and presume the work can be done whether or not the lines are running) with the independent retailer of General Electric products who deals exclusively in these products. The work of neither the maintenance contractor nor the retailer depends on the immediate availability of the primary (General Electric) employees, but if the primary strike were completely successful the work of both would cease. Yet it seems clear that direct appeals to the maintenance employees would be lawful whereas appeals to the retailer's employees would violate §8(b)(4)B).

How are we to distinguish the two, save on a geographical basis? And for that matter, how do we classify receiving dock employees of the independent retailer who unload the General Electric delivery truck while the driver is across the street drinking coffee? If you take the position that the dock workers are doing related work, what about other employees who stock the retailer's shelves?

Reconsider the facts of *Moore Dry Dock.* Were the shipyard's employees doing related work?

3. Assume a case where the *Moore Dry Dock* standards are applicable but one of the criteria is not met. Should a district court judge enjoin the

[34] St. Antoine, What Makes Secondary Boycotts Secondary? Southwestern Legal Foundation, Eleventh Annual Institute on Labor Law 5, 32 (1965).

picketing pending the outcome of the §8(b)(4)(B) charge before the Board, or should the judge only enjoin further picketing that fails to conform with the criteria?

4. The Board's pre-*General Electric* rule[35] that the existence of primary premises where the union could adequately publicize its dispute will usually invalidate picketing at secondary premises was partially reversed in IBEW, Local 861 (Plauche Electric), 135 N.L.R.B. 250 (1962). The significance of the primary's separate place of business is no longer in the nature of a per se rule, but remains one factor to be considered in a case-by-case determination.

BUILDING & CONSTRUCTION TRADES COUNCIL OF NEW ORLEANS (MARKWELL & HARTZ, INC.)

155 N.L.R.B. 319 (1965)

. . . [W]e are asked to decide whether a union, in furtherance of a primary dispute with a general contractor [M & H] in the construction industry, may lawfully engage in jobsite picketing at gates reserved and set apart from exclusive use of neutral subcontractors. . . . Respondent asserts that, as the work of the subcontractors purportedly related to the normal operations of M & H, the Supreme Court's decisions in Local 761, International Union of Electrical, Radio and Machine Workers, AFL-CIO (General Electric Co.) v. NLRB and United Steelworkers of America, AFL-CIO (Carrier Corp.) v. NLRB, compel dismissal of the complaint herein. We do not agree with the Respondent's position. . . .

Without passing upon whether the subcontractor gates involved herein were established and maintained in accordance with the *General Electric* requirements, we are of the opinion that the principles expressed in that case are inapposite in determining whether a union may lawfully extend its dispute with a general contractor on a construction site by picketing gates reserved for exclusive use of subcontractors also engaged on that project. Rather, we believe that this issue must be resolved in the light of the *Moore Dry Dock* standards, traditionally applied by the Board in determining whether picketing at a common situs is protected primary activity.

Unlike *General Electric* and *Carrier Corp.,* both of which involved picketing *at the premises of a struck manufacturer,* the picketing in the instant case occurred at a construction project on which M & H, the primary employer, was but one of several employers operating on premises owned and operated by a third party, the Jefferson Parish Water Works. Picketing of neutral and primary contractors under such conditions has been traditionally viewed as presenting a "common situs" problem.

[35] Brewery & Beverage Drivers Local 67 (Washington Coca-Cola Bottling Works), 107 N.L.R.B. 299 (1953), enforced, 220 F.2d 380 (D.C. Cir. 1955).

Over the years, the distinction between common situs picketing and that which occurs at premises occupied solely by the struck employer has been a guiding consideration in Board efforts to strike a balance between the competing interests underlying the boycott provisions of the Act. Mindful of the fact that "Congress did not seek, by §8(b)(4), to interfere with the ordinary strike," the Board has given wide latitude to picketing and related conduct confined to the sole premises of the primary employer. On the other hand, in the interest of shielding "unoffending employers" from disputes not their own, the Board has taken a more restrictive review of common situs picketing, requiring that it be conducted so as "to minimize its impact on neutral employees insofar as this can be done without substantial impairment of the effectiveness of the picketing in reaching the primary employees."

In accordance with the foregoing, the Board, in determining whether a labor organization, when picketing a common situs, has taken all reasonable precaution to prevent enmeshment of neutrals, traditionally applies the limtiations set forth in the *Moore Dry Dock* case. In our opinion, application of these standards to all common situs situations, including those, which like the instant case, involve picketing of gates reserved exclusively for neutral contractors on a construction project, serves the "dual congressional objectives" underlying the boycott provisions of the Act.

The instant facts, when considered in the light of the legislative history and decisional precedent, do not warrant a departure from our long-established policy with respect to common situs picketing. Quite to the contrary, our continued adherence to the *Moore Dry Dock* standards in such cases comports with the clear expression of Congress, in enacting the "primary strike and picketing" proviso, that said proviso ". . . does not eliminate, restrict, or modify the limitations on picketing at the site of a primary dispute that are in existing law."[14] Nor do the Supreme Court's decisions in *General Electric* and *Carrier* detract from our conclusions in this regard; for, the mere fact that picketing of a neutral gate *at premises of a struck employer,* may in proper circumstances be lawful primary action, does not require a like finding when a labor organization

14. As indicated by the following statement on the part of the House conferees, the enactment of specific language protecting primary activity was accompanied by express preservation of the *Denver Building Trades* and *Moore Dry Dock* cases:

> . . . the amendment adopted by the committee of conference contains a provision "that nothing contained in clause (B) of this paragraph (4) shall be construed to make unlawful, where not otherwise unlawful, any primary strike or primary picketing." The purpose of this provision is to make it clear that the changes in §8(b)(4) do not overrule or qualify the present rules of law permitting picketing at the site of a primary labor dispute. This provision does not eliminate, restrict, or modify the limitations on picketing at the site of a primary labor dispute that are in existing law. See, for example, NLRB v. Denver Building and Construction Trades Council, et al. (341 U.S. 675 (1951); . . . Moore Drydock Co. (81 N.L.R.B. 1108) [sic]; . . . 1 Leg. Hist. 942 (1959)).

applies *direct* pressure upon secondary employers engaged on a common situs. That the Supreme Court had no intention of overriding this historic distinction is evidenced by its express approval of the *Moore Dry Dock* standards,[16] and its observation that the *General Electric* case did not present a common situs situation to which the *Moore Dry Dock* standards should apply.[17] It is plain, therefore, that the Court did not seek to interfere with the Board's traditional approach to common situs problems; rather, the Court's decisions in *General Electric* and *Carrier Corp.*, merely represent an implementation of the concomitant policy that lenient treatment be given to strike action taking place at the separate premises of a struck employer. . . .

The dissent does not persuade us otherwise. The dissent's analysis, although well-stated and on first reading not unreasonable as an application of *General Electric* standards in a construction industry setting, nevertheless runs counter to firmly established principles governing common situs picketing in that industry. Simply because the work of the neutral subcontractors in one sense is "related to M & H's normal operations," our dissenting colleagues would exonerate the pickets' appeals to the secondary employees to honor the picket line aimed at M & H. And notwithstanding their suggestion (in footnote 35) that they would apply the "related work" standard only where the dispute is with a general contractor, the plain logic of their position is equally applicable where the primary dispute is with a building construction *sub*contractor whose employees are working closely with employees of other subcontractors or those of the general contractors. Given the close relation — which is not only characteristic of but almost inevitable at many stages of a building construction project — of the work duties of the various other employees with those of the primary subcontractor, the principle of the dissent would also permit picket line appeals to the employees of the neutral general contractor and other subcontractors whatever the situation as to common or separate gates.

But it was precisely this claim, that the *close* working relations of various building construction contractors on a common situs involved them in a common undertaking which destroyed the neutrality and thus the immunity of secondary employers and employees to picket line appeals, that the Supreme Court rejected in *Denver Building Trades.* And there is not the slightest intimation by the Court in *General Electric* or *Carrier* that it was reversing or revising the rule in *Denver*. Although our dissenting colleagues disclaim such a purpose, by applying the "close relation to normal operations" test of *General Electric,* the theory of the dissent, if logically extended, is one that would in effect reverse *Denver* not only where the overarching general contractor on the building site is

16. Local 761, IUE (General Electric Co.), v. NLRB, supra, 679.

17. Steelworkers (Carrier Corp.) v. NLRB, supra, 497.

the primary employer, but also, where the intertwined work of a construction *sub*contractor is the primary target.

We are not constrained, without much plainer indications from the Court of an intention to effect such a reversal, to apply principles laid down by the Court in an entirely different set of circumstances to a situation in which the prior Board and court interpretations of the statutory protection established for neutrals are clear and have been long understood by the parties to labor-management relations and by the Congress.[23]

For the reasons stated, we conclude that Respondent violated §§8(b)(4)(i) and (ii)(B) of the Act by inducing employees of [the subcontractors] to engage in work stoppages, and by restraining and coercing said Employers, for an object of forcing or requiring them to cease doing business with M & H. . . .

[In a lengthy dissenting opinion, Members Fanning and Jenkins argued that the related-work test should be applied in the instant case. In footnote 35 they attempted to distinguish the case where the union's dispute was with a construction subcontractor:]

35. [W]e do not imply that simply because a union has a dispute with one subcontractor on a construction project, appeals to employees of other subcontractors using different gates constitute primary appeals within the meaning of the *General Electric* decision. In such situations, the work of the employees of the neutral general contractor and subcontractors, though obviously bearing a close relationship to the work of the primary employees, is nevertheless not work which the primary subcontractor has obligated himself to perform or which lies within his power to control or to assign to whomsoever he sees fit. It is therefore not "related to the normal operations of the [primary] employer" nor does it "otherwise contribut[e] to the operations which the strike is endeavoring to halt" within the meaning of the *General Electric* and *Carrier* decisions. In similar fashion, we would not, in the direct converse of the *General Electric* case where the primary dispute is with a General Electric subcontractor, apply the *General Electric* principles to preclude General Electric from setting up separate gates for its own employees and those of subcontractors not involved in the dispute for the purpose of confining the picketing to those gates used by the employees of the struck primary subcontractor and his suppliers.

[The dissenting opinion then considered the related-work issue:]

In applying the *General Electric* standards to the instant case, we find that the work of [the subcontractors] was related to the normal operations of M & H, the general contractor. In this connection it is relevant

23. See, for example, the recurrent hearings and committee reports on consideration of "situs picketing" legislation.

that employees of the named subcontractors were scheduled to work during the picketing period together with the employees of M & H in completing the filtration plant expansion job.[38] In addition, during this period, M & H's project engineer and superintendent were to work with the subcontractors to insure that M & H's commitment to the owner was performed in compliance with project specifications. We find that M & H's portion of the work on this job was part of its normal operations, as was completing of the entire project, and that the work of the subcontractors was related to both M & H's work on the job and its responsibility to complete the project itself, and hence related to M & H's normal operations. We, accordingly, hold that the work of the subcontractors failed to meet the "unrelated work" condition and, on this basis, we find that Respondent had the right to appeal to the employees of the subcontractors to honor its picket line around M & H's operations. . . .

Notes

1. The Fifth Circuit enforced (2-1) the Board's order in Markwell & Hartz v. NLRB, 387 F.2d 79 (5th Cir. 1967), cert. denied, 391 U.S. 914 (1968). One judge ruled that the related-work test of *General Electric* applied and that *Denver Building Trades* "authoritatively" held that the work of a construction general contractor and subcontractor were unrelated. A concurring judge found the work to be related but held that since the picketing was at a common situs, "where two or more employers are performing separate tasks on common premises," *Moore Dry Dock* criteria applied. A dissenting judge would apply the related-work test whether the union's dispute was with the construction general contractor or subcontractor and would have remanded to the Board for a finding of whether there was related work in this case.[36]

2. Consider the Board's opinion in *Markwell & Hartz* at notes 14, 16, and 17:

a. With respect to the opinion at note 14, are we to consider the "preservation" of these cases by the conferees as tantamount to legislation? If so, isn't the *General Electric* decision itself patently erroneous since it substantially modifies the use to which *Moore Dry Dock* can be put? The list of cases that the House conferees have been deemed by the Board to have "preserved" was edited by the Board. The original list included *Washington Coca-Cola,*

38. M & H undertook to perform about 80% of the project with its own employees, while subcontracting the balance. It also appears that M & H in certain instances could not work until completion of a subcontractor's phase of the job, while in others subcontractors would have to hold up while M & H was performing.

[36] The Board remains split over the *Markwell & Hartz* issue. See Sacramento Council of Carpenters (Malek Construction Co.), 244 N.L.R.B. 890 (1979).

which the Board overruled three years before its decision in *Markwell & Hartz.* See p. 439, supra.

b. The opinion at note 16 describes *General Electric* as expressly approving the *Moore Dry Dock* standards. When the Court describes the development of a doctrine should it be taken to have approved all of the doctrine's constituent parts?

c. A careful reading of the *Carrier* opinion would reveal precious little support for the Board's text at note 17 in *Markwell & Hartz.*

3. What is a common situs? In Carpenters, Local 470 (Mueller-Anderson), 224 N.L.R.B. 315 (1976), enforced, 564 F.2d 1360 (9th Cir. 1977), the Board again split 3-2 on the application of *General Electric* to construction industry picketing. The majority held that *Moore Dry Dock,* not *General Electric,* applied where the union's dispute was with a general contractor engaged in building an apartment complex on land that it owned:

> [We] attach no legal significance to the fact that the general contractor was engaged in erecting an apartment complex on land which it owned. In *General Electric,* the Supreme Court traced the evolution of the *Moore Dry Dock* doctrine. It discussed and cited with approval Local Union No. 55, and Carpenters' District Council of Denver (Professional and Business Men's Life Insurance Company), 108 N.L.R.B. 363 (1954), enfd. 218 F.2d 226 (C.A. 10), which is on all fours with the present case. In that case an insurance company, acting as general contractor, was building a housing project on land which it owned: A neutral subcontractor was also working at the site. The respondent union was engaged in a dispute with the insurance company and picketed the entire site. The Board and the court found that the picketing was unlawful because it did not conform with the *Moore Dry Dock* standards. The Supreme Court in this same case discussed and cited with approval Retail Fruit & Vegetable Clerks Union, Local 1017 (Retail Grocers Association of San Francisco), 116 N.L.R.B. 856 (1956), enfd. 249 F.2d 591 (C.A. 9, 1957), where the Board again applied the *Moore Dry Dock* principles to a common situs situation even though the premises were owned by the primary employer. The Board stated (116 N.L.R.B. at 859):
>
>> We can see no logical reason why the legality of such picketing should depend on title to property. The impact on neutral employees of picketing which deviates from the standards outlined above is the same whether the common premises are owned by their own employer or by the primary employer.
>
> More recently the Board made the same point in General Teamsters, Warehouse and Dairy Employees Union Local No. 126 (Ready Mixed Concrete, Inc.), 200 N.L.R.B. 253 (1972) (Members Fanning and Jenkins dissenting), where the Board stated (fn. 5):
>
>> Although *Moore Dry Dock* involved picketing at the common situs of a secondary employer, its rule has been extended by the Board to picketing at the situs of a primary employer where a secondary or neutral employer is engaged. . . . [Citations omitted.]

> In *Markwell and Hartz,* the Board affirmed, with court approval, that the legality of picketing at a common situs in the construction industry, including picketing of gates reserved exclusively for neutral contractors at the project, is to be determined under the *Moore Dry Dock* standards rather than by the special guidelines laid down by the Supreme Court in *General Electric.*
>
> As pointed out above, under *Moore Dry Dock* standards it is immaterial that the picketing occurred at a construction site owned by the primary employer or that the general contractor was engaged in erecting a building on its behalf. The decision in this case therefore involves an application of *Markwell and Hartz* in light of precedents relating to *Moore Dry Dock.* It does not involve in the words of the dissent "a sweeping extension of the *Markwell and Hartz* case."
>
> Since Respondent's picketing on and after April 9, 1975, did not comport with *Moore Dry Dock,* we find on the basis of the entire record that an object of the picketing was to force or require secondary employers to cease doing business with Anderson and that the picketing was therefore violative of §§8(b)(4)(i) and (ii)(B) of the Act.

On the basis of this decision, should the related-work doctrine or the *Moore Dry Dock* criteria apply to the facts of *General Electric*?

4. In 1975, the unions, after repeated efforts, were able to secure congressional passage of the common situs picketing bill. The purpose was to overrule *Denver Building Trades* and render construction contractors and subcontractors allies. Section 8(b)(4) was to be amended by adding the following proviso:

> Provided further, That nothing contained in clause (B) of this paragraph (4) shall be construed to prohibit any strike or refusal to perform services or any inducement of any individual employed by any employer primarily engaged in the construction industry on the site to strike or refuse to perform services at the site of the construction, alteration, painting, or repair of a building, structure, or other work and directed at any of several employers who are in the construction industry and are jointly engaged as joint venturers or in the relationship of contractors and subcontractors in such constructions, alteration, painting, or repair at such site. . . .

President Ford vetoed the bill and Congress failed to override.

Problem

Now try your hand at the following problem. You will need to read the next section before answering several of the questions.

Associated Wholesalers (AW) is a wholesaler of groceries to retail supermarkets. Its employees are presently engaged in an economic strike. The striking employees are warehousemen and truck drivers who deliver merchandise to the stores. Consider the following:

1. AW supervisors deliver groceries to Kroger (a retail grocery). Can the union pickets follow?
2. AW subcontracts its delivery services to Independent Truckers Co. (IT). Can the pickets follow IT trucks to Kroger's? Can the union picket the IT home office asking IT drivers to stop all work? Can the AW pickets follow IT's delivery of drugs from a drug wholesaler to its customer? Would any of the answers be different if Kroger had hired IT to pick up groceries at AW?
3. Suppose Kroger employees come to the warehouse to pick up groceries. Can the AW employees picketing at the warehouse appeal to Kroger employees not to cross the picket line? Can the pickets follow the Kroger trucks back to Kroger and ask Kroger employees there not to unload?
4. Can the president of the union go to the manager of Kroger and ask her not to purchase merchandise from AW while the union is on strike?
5. a. Can the union picket Kroger with a sign reading:

   > Local One on strike against Associated Wholesalers. Please do not purchase groceries distributed by Associated Wholesalers. The union has no dispute with Kroger.

   b. If Kroger purchases all its canned vegetables from AW, could the union picket Kroger asking consumers not to purchase canned vegetables if an effect of the picket line is that Kroger's checkout personnel won't cross it?
   c. What handbilling, if any, could the union engage in if Kroger purchases only its canned vegetables from AW? Could the union president tell the Kroger manager, "Quit buying from AW or the union will go on television and radio calling for a complete consumer boycott of Kroger"?
6. Suppose Bayless (another retail grocery) does no business with AW but the union discovers that Sam Bayless owns 72 percent of the stock of Bayless (and is also chairman of the board) and also owns 67 percent of the stock of Associated Wholesalers. Can the union picket Bayless on an integrated enterprise theory?

4. Appeals to Consumers[37]

NLRB v. SERVETTE, 377 U.S. 46 (1964): Servette was a wholesale distributor of specialty merchandise to retail supermarkets. As part of their strategy in a dispute with Servette, union representatives asked

[37] See Engel, Secondary Consumer Picketing, Following the Struck Product, 52 Va. L. Rev. 189 (1966); Lewis, Consumer Picketing and the Court — The Questionable Yield of Tree Fruits, 49 Minn. L. Rev. 479 (1965).

supermarket managers to discontinue stocking merchandise supplied by Servette. The representatives warned the managers that if they failed to comply, the union would handbill the market asking consumers not to purchase named items distributed by Servette. Servette argued that the appeal to the managers was encompassed by both (i) and (ii) of §8(b)(4); that the managers were "individuals" induced to refuse to handle commodities as described by (i); and that the handbilling warning was threatening and coercive under (ii). Servette contended that the handbilling would not be protected by the publicity proviso because no products were "produced" by Servette.

The Supreme Court found no violation. Agreeing that the managers were "individuals" encompassed by (i), the Court nonetheless found the appeal lawful:

> In the instant case . . . the Local, in asking the managers not to handle Servette items, was not attempting to induce or encourage them to cease performing their managerial duties in order to force their employers to cease doing business with Servette. Rather the managers were asked to make a managerial decision which the Board found was within their authority to make. Such an appeal would not have been a violation of §8(b)(4)(A) before 1959, and we think the legislative history of the 1959 amendments makes it clear that the amendments were not meant to render such an appeal an unfair labor practice.

The 1959 amendment adding (i), according to the Court, was intended to reverse *International Rice Milling*'s requirement that inducements be of "concerted" activity, and to prohibit inducements of persons not included in the NLRA's definition of *employee* (e.g., agricultural laborers, supervisors, railway employees). The congressional intent was, therefore, to prohibit appeals to management discretion only when the appeal constituted (ii) threats or coercion.

The Court then held that a threat to engage in handbilling that is itself protected by the publicity proviso was not prohibited by §8(b)(4)(B). The Court found the purpose of the proviso to be broad enough to include goods distributed by an employer with whom the union had a dispute.

EDWARD J. DeBARTOLO CORP. v. NLRB, — U.S. — , 103 S. Ct. 2926 (1983): The union had a labor dispute with High, a general building contractor. High was building a department store for Wilson in a shopping center in Florida. Wilson had a standard lease agreement with DeBartolo, the owner and operator of the shopping center, as did most of the other 85 tenants of the center. The union distributed handbills at all four entrances to the shopping center while the Wilson store was under construction. The handbills stated that the contractors building Wilson's store were paying substandard wages and asked consumers not to patronize any of the stores in the mall until DeBartolo promised that all construction at the mall would be done by contractors paying fair wages and benefits.

The Board did not decide whether the handbilling was a form of "coercion" or "restraint" within §8(b)(4) because it found that the handbilling was exempted by the "publicity proviso" to that section. The Board reasoned that Wilson and all the other tenants of the shopping center would derive a substantial benefit from the product that High was producing, Wilson's new store. DeBartolo and all the tenants were said to be in a "symbiotic" relationship. A court of appeals enforced.

The Supreme Court reversed. The Court assumed that High was a "producer" within the meaning of the proviso, and it was willing to assume further that Wilson was a "distributor" of High's product, but it refused to find that the other tenants were distributors of High's product. The "symbiotic" relationship analysis was rejected because it "would almost strip the distribution requirement of its limiting effect. It diverts the inquiry away from the relationship between the primary and secondary employers and toward the relationship between two secondary employers. It then tests that relationship by a standard so generous that it will be satisfied by virtually any secondary employer that a union might want consumers to boycott." The Court then refused to consider a constitutional challenge to the statutory prohibition because the Board had not yet decided whether the handbilling was a form of "restraint" or "coercion." The case was remanded to the Board for that purpose.

Note

It is common for large department stores at shopping centers to pay rent at a rate substantially below the rate charged to smaller stores, and sometimes a large store will be charged no rent at all. The large store acts as a magnet. It draws shoppers who then patronize the smaller stores almost incidentally.

Had the members of the Supreme Court liked the Board's result in this case, we probably would have found in the Court's opinion references to the Board's expertise and comments about the Board's role as the primary interpreter of the statute. Not liking the result in this case, the Court doesn't include such language.[38]

[38] One wonders if word processors have assisted the Court in this respect. Stock paragraphs extolling deference and the agency's expertise could be loaded into one of the function keys on a word processor. When a Justice doesn't like the Board's result, the Justice (or the Justice's clerk) doesn't hit the key.

NLRB v. FRUIT & VEGETABLE PACKERS & WAREHOUSEMEN, LOCAL 760 [TREE FRUITS]
377 U.S. 58 (1964)

BRENNAN, J. . . .

The question in this case is whether the respondent unions violated [§8(b)(4)(ii)(B)] when they limited their secondary picketing of retail stores to an appeal to the customers of the stores not to buy the products of certain firms against which one of the respondents was on strike.

Respondent Local 760 called a strike against fruit packers and warehousemen doing business in Yakima, Washington. The struck firms sold Washington State apples to the Safeway chain of retail stores in and about Seattle, Washington. Local 760 . . . instituted a consumer boycott against the apples in support of the strike. They placed pickets who walked back and forth before the customers' entrances of 46 Safeway stores in Seattle. The pickets — two at each of 45 stores and three at the 46th store — wore placards and distributed handbills which appealed to Safeway customers, and to the public generally, to refrain from buying Washington State apples, which were only one of numerous food products sold in the stores.[3]

3. The placard worn by each picket stated: "To the Consumer: Non-Union Washington State apples are being sold at this store. Please do not purchase such apples. Thank you. Teamsters Local 760, Yakima, Washington."

A typical handbill read:

DON'T BUY
WASHINGTON STATE
APPLES
The 1960 CROP OF WASHINGTON STATE APPLES IS BEING
PACKED BY NON-UNION FIRMS

Included in this non-union operation are twenty-six firms in the Yakima Valley with which there is a labor dispute. These firms are charged with being

UNFAIR

by their employees who, with their union, are on strike and have been *replaced by* non-union strikebreaking workers employed under substandard wage scales and working conditions.

In justice to these striking union workers who are attempting to protect their living standards and their right to engage in good-faith collective bargaining, we request that you

DON'T BUY
WASHINGTON STATE
APPLES

TEAMSTERS UNION LOCAL 769
YAKIMA, WASHINGTON

This is not a strike against any store or market.

(P.S. — **PACIFIC FRUIT & PRODUCE CO.** is the only firm packing Washington State Apples under a union contract.)

Before the pickets appeared at any store, a letter was delivered to the store manager informing him that the picketing was only an appeal to his customers not to buy Washington State apples, and that the pickets were being expressly instructed "to patrol peacefully in front of the consumer entrances of the store, to stay away from the delivery entrances and not to interfere with the work of your employees, or with deliveries to or pickups from your store." A copy of written instructions to the pickets — which included the explicit statement that "you are also forbidden to request that the customers not patronize the store" — was enclosed with the letter.

Since it was desired to assure Safeway employees that they were not to cease work, and to avoid any interference with pickups or deliveries, the pickets appeared after the stores opened for business and departed before the stores closed. At all times during the picketing, the store employees continued to work, and no deliveries or pickups were obstructed. Washington State apples were handled in normal course by both Safeway employees and the employees of other employers involved. Ingress and egress by customers and others was not interfered with in any manner.

[The Board held the picketing violated §8(b)(4)[5] and was not saved by the last proviso to that section. The D.C. Court of Appeals] rejected the Board's construction and held that the statutory requirement of a showing that respondents' conduct would "threaten, coerce, or restrain" Safeway could only be satisfied by affirmative proof that a substantial economic impact on Safeway had occurred, or was likely to occur as a result of the conduct. Under the remand the Board was left "free to reopen the record to receive evidence upon the issue whether Safeway was in fact threatened, coerced, or restrained." . . .

The Board's reading of the statute — that the legislative history and the phrase "other than picketing" in the proviso reveal a congressional purpose to outlaw all picketing directed at customers at a secondary site — necessarily rested on the finding that Congress determined that such picketing always threatens, coerces or restrains the secondary employer. We therefore have a special responsibility to examine the legislative history for confirmation that Congress made that determination. Throughout the history of federal regulation of labor relations, Congress has consistently refused to prohibit peaceful picketing except where it is used as a means to achieve specific ends which experience has shown are undesirable. "In the sensitive area of peaceful picketing Con-

5. The complaint charged violations of both subsections (i) and (ii) of §8(b)(4). The Board held, however, that as the evidence indicated "that Respondents' picketing was directed at consumers only, and was not intended to 'induce or encourage' employees of Safeway or of its suppliers to engage in any kind of action, we find that by such picketing Respondents did not violate §8(b)(4)(i)(B) of the Act." 132 N.L.R.B. at 1177. See also National Labor Relations Board v. Servette, Inc., 377 U.S. 46.

gress has dealt explicitly with isolated evils which experience has established flow from such picketing." National Labor Relations Board v. Drivers etc. Local Union, 362 U.S. 274. We havc recognized this congressional practice and have not ascribed to Congress a purpose to outlaw peaceful picketing unless "there is the clearest indication in the legislative history," ibid., that Congress intended to do so as regards the particular ends of the picketing under review. Both the congressional policy and our adherence to this principle of interpretation reflect concern that a broad ban against peaceful picketing might collide with the guarantees of the First Amendment.

We have examined the legislative history of the amendments to §8(b)(4), and conclude that it does not reflect with the requisite clarity a congressional plan to proscribe all peaceful consumer picketing at secondary sites, and, particularly, any concern with peaceful picketing when it is limited, as here, to persuading Safeway customers not to buy Washington State apples when they traded in the Safeway stores. All that the legislative history shows in the way of an "isolated evil" believed to require proscription of peaceful consumer picketing at secondary sites was its use to persuade the customers of the secondary employer to cease trading with him in order to force him to cease dealing with, or to put pressure upon, the primary employer. This narrow focus reflects the difference between such conduct and peaceful picketing at the secondary site directed only at the struck product. In the latter case, the union's appeal to the public is confined to its dispute with the primary employer, since the public is not asked to withhold its patronage from the secondary employer, but only to boycott the primary employer's goods. On the other hand, a union appeal to the public at the secondary site not to trade at all with the secondary employer goes beyond the goods of the primary employer, and seeks the public's assistance in forcing the secondary employer to cooperate with the union in its primary dispute.[7] This is not to say that this distinction was expressly alluded to in the debates. It is to say, however, that the consumer picketing carried on in this case is not attended by the abuses at which the statute was directed.

The story of the 1959 amendments, which we have detailed at greater length in our opinion filed today in National Labor Relations Board v. Servette, Inc., 377 U.S. 46, begins with the original §8(b)(4) of the National Labor Relations Act. Its prohibition, in pertinent part, was confined to the inducing or encouraging of "the employees of any employer

7. The distinction between picketing a secondary employer merely to "follow the struck goods," and picketing designed to result in a generalized loss of patronage, was well established in the state cases by 1940. The distinction was sometimes justified on the ground that the secondary employer, who was presumed to receive a competitive benefit from the primary employer's nonunion, and hence lower, wage scales, was in "unity of interest" with the primary employer and sometimes on the ground that picketing restricted to the primary employer's product is "a primary boycott against the merchandise."

to engage in, a strike or a concerted refusal . . . to . . . handle . . . any goods . . ." of a primary employer. This proved to be inept language. Three major loopholes were revealed. Since only inducement of "employees" was proscribed, direct inducement of a supervisor or the secondary employer by threats of labor trouble was not prohibited. Since only a "strike or a concerted refusal" was prohibited, pressure upon a single employee was not forbidden. Finally, railroads, airlines and municipalities were not "employers" under the Act and therefore inducement or encouragement of their employees was not unlawful.

When major labor relations legislation was being considered in 1958 the closing of these loopholes was important to the House and to some members of the Senate. But the prevailing Senate sentiment favored new legislation primarily concerned with the redress of other abuses, and neither the Kennedy-Ives bill, which failed of passage in the House in the Eighty-fifth Congress, nor the Kennedy-Ervin bill, adopted by the Senate in the Eighty-sixth Congress, included any revision of §8(b)(4). Proposed amendments of §8(b)(4) offered by several Senators to fill the three loopholes were rejected. The Administration introduced such a bill, and it was supported by Senators Dirksen and Goldwater. Senator Goldwater, an insistent proponent of stiff boycott curbs, also proposed his own amendments. We think it is especially significant that neither Senator, nor the Secretary of Labor in testifying in support of the Administration's bill, referred to consumer picketing as making the amendments necessary.[10] Senator McClellan, who also offered a bill to curb boycotts, mentioned consumer picketing but only such as was "pressure in the form of dissuading customers *from dealing with* secondary employers." (Emphasis supplied.) It was the opponents of the amendments who, in expressing fear of their sweep, suggested that they might proscribe consumer picketing. Senator Humphrey first sounded the warning early in April. Many months later, when the Conference bill was before the Senate, Senator Morse, a conferee, would not support the Conference bill on the express ground that it prohibited consumer picketing. But we have often cautioned against the danger, when interpret-

10. It is true that Senator Goldwater referred to consumer picketing when the Conference bill was before the Senate. His full statement reads as follows: "the House bill . . . closed up every loophole in the boycott section of the law including the use of a secondary consumer picket line, an example of which the President gave on his nationwide TV program on August 6. . . ." 105 Cong. Rec. 17904, II Leg. Hist. 1437. The example given by the President was this: "The employees [of a furniture manufacturer] vote against joining a particular union. Instead of picketing the furniture plant itself, unscrupulous organizing officials . . . picket the stores which sell the furniture. . . . How can anyone justify this kind of pressure against stores which are not involved in any dispute? . . . This kind of section is designed to make the stores bring pressure on the furniture plant and its employees. . . ." 105 Cong. Rec. 19954, II Leg. Hist. 1842. Senator Goldwater's own definition of what he meant by a secondary consumer boycott is even more clearly narrow in scope: "A secondary consumer, or customer, boycott involves the refusal of consumers or customers to buy the products or services of one employer in order to force him to stop doing business with another employer." 105 Cong. Rec. 17074, II Leg. Hist. 1386.

ing a statute, of reliance upon the views of its legislative opponents. In their zeal to defeat a bill, they understandably tend to overstate its reach. "The fears and doubts of the opposition are no authoritative guide to the construction of legislation. It is the sponsors that we look to when the meaning of the statutory words is in doubt." Schwegmann Bros. v. Calvert Distillers Corp., 341 U.S. 384, 394-395. The silence of the sponsors of amendments is pregnant with significance since they must have been aware that consumer picketing as such had been held to be outside the reach of §8(b)(4). We are faithful to our practice of respecting the congressional policy of legislating only against clearly identified abuses of peaceful picketing when we conclude that the Senate neither specified the kind of picketing here involved as an abuse, nor indicated any intention of banning all consumer picketing.

The House history is similarly beclouded, but what appears confirms our conclusion. From the outset the House legislation included provisions concerning secondary boycotts. The Landrum-Griffin bill, which was ultimately passed by the House, embodied the Eisenhower Administration's proposals as to secondary boycotts. The initial statement of Congressman Griffin in introducing the bill which bears his name, contains no reference to consumer picketing in the list of abuses which he thought required the secondary boycott amendments. Later in the House debates he did discuss consumer picketing, but only in the context of its abuse when directed against shutting off the patronage of a secondary employer.

In the debates before passage of the House bill he stated that the amendments applied to consumer picketing of customer entrances to retail stores selling goods manufactured by a concern under strike, if the picketing were designed to "coerce or to restrain the employer of [the] second establishment, to get him not to do business with the manufacturer . . . ," and further that, "of course, this bill and any other bill is limited by the constitutional right of free speech. If the purpose of the picketing is to *coerce the retailer not to do business* with the manufacturer" — then such a boycott could be stopped. (Italics supplied.)

. . . When Congress meant to bar picketing per se, it made its meaning clear; for example, §8(b)(7) makes it an unfair labor practice, "to picket or cause to be picketed any employer. . . ." In contrast, the prohibition of §8(b)(4) is keyed to the coercive nature of the conduct, whether it be picketing or otherwise.

Senator Kennedy presided over the Conference Committee. He and Congressman Thompson prepared a joint analysis of the Senate and House bills. This analysis pointed up the First Amendment implications of the broad language in the House revisions of §8(b)(4) stating,

"The prohibition [of the House bill] reaches not only picketing but leaflets, radio broadcasts and newspaper advertisements, thereby interfering with freedom of speech. . . .

". . . [O]ne of the apparent purposes of the amendment is to prevent unions from appealing to the general public as consumers for assistance in a labor dispute. This is a basic infringement upon freedom of expression."

This analysis was the first step in the development of the publicity proviso, but nothing in the legislative history of the proviso alters our conclusion that Congress did not clearly express an intention that amended §8(b)(4) should prohibit all consumer picketing. Because of the sweeping language of the House bill, and its implications for freedom of speech, the Senate conferees refused to accede to the House proposal without safeguards for the right of unions to appeal to the public, even by some conduct which might be "coercive." The result was the addition of the proviso. But it does not follow from the fact that some coercive conduct was protected by the proviso, that the exception "other than picketing" indicates that Congress had determined that all consumer picketing was coercive.

No Conference Report was before the Senate when it passed the compromise bill, and it had the benefit only of Senator Kennedy's statement of the purpose of the proviso. He said that the proviso preserved

> the right to appeal to consumers by methods other than picketing asking them to refrain from buying goods made by nonunion labor *and* to refrain from trading with a retailer who sells such goods. . . . We were not able to persuade the House conferees to permit picketing in front of that secondary shop, but were able to persuade them to agree that the unions shall be free to conduct informational activity short of picketing. In other words, the union can hand out handbills at the shop . . . and can carry on all publicity short of having ambulatory picketing. . . . (Italics supplied.)

This explanation does not compel the conclusion that the Conference Agreement contemplated prohibiting any consumer picketing at a secondary site beyond that which urges the public, in Senator Kennedy's words, to "refrain from trading with a retailer who sells such goods." To read into the Conference Agreement, on the basis of a single statement, an intention to prohibit all consumer picketing at a secondary site would depart from our practice of respecting the congressional policy not to prohibit peaceful picketing except to curb "isolated evils" spelled out by the Congress itself.

Peaceful consumer picketing to shut off all trade with the secondary employer unless he aids the union in its dispute with the primary employer, is poles apart from such picketing which only persuades his customers not to buy the struck product. The proviso indicates no more than that the Senate conferees' constitutional doubts led Congress to authorize publicity other than picketing which persuades the customers of a secondary employer to stop all trading with him, but not such publicity which has the effect of cutting off his deliveries or inducing his employees to cease work. On the other hand, picketing which persuades the customers of a secondary employer to stop all trading with him was also to be barred.

In sum, the legislative history does not support the Board's finding that Congress meant to prohibit all consumer picketing at a secondary site, having determined that such picketing necessarily threatened, coerced or restrained the secondary employer. Rather, the history shows that Congress was following its usual practice of legislating against peaceful picketing only to curb "isolated evils."

This distinction is opposed as "unrealistic" because, it is urged, all picketing automatically provokes the public to stay away from the picketed establishment. The public will, it is said, neither read the signs and handbills, nor note the explicit injunction that "This is not a strike against any store or market." Be that as it may, our holding today simply takes note of the fact that Congress has never adopted a broad condemnation of peaceful picketing, such as that urged upon us by petitioners, and an intention to do so is not revealed with that "clearest indication in the legislative history," which we require.

We come then to the question whether the picketing in this case, confined as it was to persuading customers to cease buying the product of the primary employer, falls within the area of secondary consumer picketing which Congress did clearly indicate its intention to prohibit under §8(b)(4)(ii). We hold that it did not fall within that area, and therefore did not "threaten, coerce, or restrain" Safeway. While any diminution in Safeway's purchases of apples due to a drop in consumer demand might be said to be a result which causes respondents' picketing to fall literally within the statutory prohibition, "it is a familiar rule that a thing may be within the letter of the statute and yet not within the statute, because not within its spirit nor within the intention of its makers." Holy Trinity Church v. United States, 143 U.S. 457, 459.

When consumer picketing is employed only to persuade customers not to buy the struck product, the union's appeal is closely confined to the primary dispute. The site of the appeal is expanded to include the premises of the secondary employer, but if the appeal succeeds, the secondary employer's purchases from the struck firms are decreased only because the public has diminished its purchases of the struck product. On the other hand, when consumer picketing is employed to persuade customers not to trade at all with the secondary employer, the latter stops buying the struck product, not because of a falling demand, but in response to pressure designed to inflict injury on his business generally. In such case, the union does more than merely follow the struck product; it creates a separate dispute with the secondary employer.[20]

We disagree therefore with the Court of Appeals that the test of "to threaten, coerce, or restrain" for the purposes of this case is whether Safeway suffered or was likely to suffer economic loss. A violation of §8(b)(4)(ii)(B) would not be established, merely because respondents' picketing was effective to reduce Safeway's sales of Washington State apples, even if this led or might lead Safeway to drop the item as a poor seller.

The judgment of the Court of Appeals is vacated and the case is remanded with direction to enter judgment setting aside the Board's order. It is so ordered.[39]

Harlan, J., whom Stewart, J., joins, dissenting. . . .

Nothing in the statute lends support to the fine distinction which the Court draws between general and limited product picketing. The enactment speaks pervasively of threatening, coercing, or restraining any person; the proviso differentiates only between modes of expression, not between types of secondary consumer picketing. For me, the Court's argument to the contrary is very unconvincing.

The difference to which the Court points between a secondary employer merely lowering his purchases of the struck product to the degree of decreased consumer demand and such an employer ceasing to purchase one product because of consumer refusal to buy any products, is surely too refined in the context of reality. It can hardly be supposed that in all, or even most, instances the result of the type of picketing involved here will be simply that suggested by the Court. Because of the very nature of picketing there may be numbers of persons who will refuse to buy at all from a picketed store, either out of economic or social conviction or because they prefer to shop where they need not brave a picket line. Moreover, the public can hardly be expected always to know or ascertain the precise scope of a particular picketing operation. Thus in cases like this, the effect on the secondary employer may not always be limited to a decrease in his sales of the struck product. And even when that is the effect, the employer may, rather than simply reducing purchases from the primary employer, deem it more expedient to turn to another producer whose product is approved by the union.

The distinction drawn by the majority becomes even more tenuous if

20. For example: If a public appeal directed only at a product results in a decline of 25% in the secondary employer's sales of that product, the corresponding reduction of his purchases of the product is due to his inability to sell any more. But if the appeal is broadened to ask that the public cease all patronage, and if there is a 25% response, the secondary employer faces this decision: whether to discontinue handling the primary product entirely, even though he might otherwise have continued to sell it at the 75% level, in order to prevent the loss of sales of other products.

[39] Douglas, J., took no part in the decision.

a picketed retailer depends largely or entirely on sales of the struck product. If, for example, an independent gas station owner sells gasoline purchased from a struck gasoline company, one would not suppose he would feel less threatened, coerced, or restrained by picket signs which said "Do not buy X gasoline" than by signs which said "Do not patronize this gas station." To be sure Safeway is a multiple article seller, but it cannot well be gainsaid that the rule laid down by the Court would be unworkable if its applicability turned on a calculation of the relation between total income of the secondary employer and income from the struck product. . . .

In the light of the foregoing [legislative history], I see no escape from the conclusion that §8(b)(4)(ii)(B) does prohibit *all* consumer picketing. There are, of course, numerous times in the debates of both houses in which consumer picketing is referred to generally or the reference is made with an example of an appeal to consumers not to purchase at all from the secondary employer. But it is remarkable that every time the possibility of picketing of the sort involved in this case was considered, it was assumed to be prohibited by the House bill. Admittedly, in the House, appeals to refrain from purchase of the struck product were discussed only by opponents of the House bill; however, only one of two inferences can be drawn from the silence of the bill's supporters. Either the distinction drawn by this Court was not considered of sufficient significance to require comment, or the proponents recognized a difference between the two types of consumer picketing but assumed that the bill encompassed both. Under either supposition, the conclusion reached by the Court in regard to the picketing involved here is untenable.

Under my view of the statute the constitutional issue is therefore reached. Since the Court does not discuss it, I am content simply to state in summary form my reasons for believing that the prohibitions of §8(b)(4)(i)(B), as applied here, do not run afoul of constitutional limitations. This Court has long recognized that picketing is "inseparably something more [than] and different" from simple communication. Hughes v. Superior Court, 339 U.S. 460, 464; see, e.g., Building Service Employees v. Gazzam, 339 U.S. 532, 537; Bakery Drivers v. Wohl, 315 U.S. 769, 776; (concurring opinion of Douglas, J.). Congress has given careful and continued consideration to the problems of labor-management relations, and its attempts to effect an accommodation between the right of unions to publicize their position and the social desirability of limiting a form of communication likely to have effects caused by something apart from the message communicated, are entitled to great deference. The decision of Congress to prohibit secondary consumer picketing during labor disputes is, I believe, not inconsistent with the protections of the First Amendment, particularly when, as here, other methods of communication are left open.

Contrary to my Brother Black, I think the fact that Congress in prohibiting secondary consumer picketing has acted with a discriminating eye is the very thing that renders this provision invulnerable to constitutional attack. That Congress has permitted other picketing which is likely to have effects beyond those resulting from the "communicative" aspect of picketing does not, of course, in any way lend itself to the conclusion that Congress here has aimed to "prevent dissemination of information about the facts of a labor dispute." Even on the highly dubious assumption that the "non-speech" aspect of picketing is always the same whatever the particular context, the social consequences of the "noncommunicative" aspect of picketing may certainly be thought desirable in the case of "primary" picketing and undesirable in the case of "secondary" picketing, a judgment Congress has indeed made in prohibiting secondary but not primary picketing.

I would enforce the Board's order.

[Justice BLACK, concurring, found Congress to have intended to preclude the union's picketing and believed the prohibition to violate the First Amendment.]

Note

Do you find the following persuasive?

> *Tree Fruits* upsets the delicate balance Congress legislated in §8(b)(4)(B). Certainly we can be sympathetic to a union appeal to the public not to purchase the products of an employer who flouts the employee-freedom provisions of the NLRA or runs a sweatshop, but we can just as easily condemn the consumer boycott engaged in by an unscrupulous union embittered at losing a representation election. The fact is that Congress drew the balance on different grounds than the justness of the union's appeal.
>
> Everyone schooled in industrial relations knows that the effect of many, if not most, picket lines is to serve as a signal to other union employees to stop work — a signal to the employees of the employer selling the "hot" goods and its suppliers and deliverymen. It was precisely for this reason that Congress outlawed secondary consumer picketing. Why permit such picketing, reasoned Congress, when if the purpose is actually to appeal to consumers, handbilling and radio and television appeals will do just as well? So Congress outlawed secondary consumer picketing and went even further: It prohibited handbilling if its effect was to serve as a signal.
>
> The *Tree Fruits* Court turned this balance on its head. Not only is secondary consumer picketing lawful — a misreading of the statute's plain meaning — but the logic of the opinion is inescapable: If the retailer deals solely in the product of the offending employer, the union can picket for a total boycott; and, even more significantly, since product picketing is

deemed not to fall within §8(b)(4) at all, the fact that the picket line does serve as a signal to employees is irrelevant. The Court relied on unpersuasive legislative history to distort an unambiguous statute — the case should be overruled at the first opportunity.

NLRB v. RETAIL STORE EMPLOYEES LOCAL 100 [SAFECO], 444 U.S. 1011 (1980): The Safeco Title Insurance Company maintained close business relationships with five local title insurance companies. Over 90 percent of the gross incomes of the local title companies derived from the sale of Safeco insurance policies. Safeco had substantial stock holdings in each of the five companies but did not exercise control over their daily operations. Unable to reach a collective bargaining agreement with Safeco, the union picketed the five local title insurance companies publicizing its dispute with Safeco.

The Supreme Court, per Justice Powell, held the union had violated §8(b)(4)(ii)(B). *Tree Fruits* was distinguished:

> The product picketed in *Tree Fruits* was but one item among the many that made up the retailer's trade. If the appeal against such a product succeeds, the Court observed, it simply induces the neutral retailer to reduce his orders for the product or "to drop the item as a poor seller." The decline in sales attributable to consumer rejection of the struck product puts pressure upon the primary employer, and the marginal injury to the neutral retailer is purely incidental to the product boycott. The neutral therefore has little reason to become involved in the labor dispute. In this case, on the other hand, the title companies sell only the primary employer's product and perform the services associated with it. Secondary picketing against consumption of the primary product leaves responsive consumers no realistic option other than to boycott the title companies altogether. If the appeal succeeds, each company "stops buying the struck product, not because of a falling demand, but in response to pressure designed to inflict injury on [its] business generally." Thus, "the union does more than merely follow the struck product; it creates a separate dispute with the secondary employer." . . . Product picketing that reasonably can be expected to threaten neutral parties with ruin or substantial loss simply does not square with the language or the purpose of §8(b)(4)(ii)(B). Since successful picketing would put the title companies to a choice between their survival and the severance of their ties with Safeco, the picketing plainly violates the statutory ban. . . .

In a footnote to this passage, the opinion states:

> If secondary picketing were directed against a product representing a major portion of a neutral's business, but significantly less than that represented by a single dominant product, neither *Tree Fruits* nor today's decision necessarily would control. The critical question would be whether, by encouraging consumers to reject the struck product, the secondary appeal is reasonably likely to threaten the neutral party with ruin or substantial loss. Resolution of the question in each case will be entrusted to the Board.

The constitutional issue proved to be quite easy for Justice Powell. Describing the union's picketing as an attempt to coerce a neutral party to join the fray and therefore to be an "unlawful objective," the Justice concluded that the statutory prohibition "imposes no impermissible restrictions upon constitutionally protected speech." Other Justices took issue with Justice Powell's easy disposition of the constitutional issue. Writing separately on this point, Justice Blackmun "concurr[ed] in the result . . . only because I am reluctant to hold unconstitutional Congress' delicate balance between union freedom of expression and the ability of neutral employers, employees, and consumers to remain free from coerced participation in industrial strife.

Justice Stevens also declined to join Justice Powell's opinion on the constitutional question. Justice Stevens wrote, "I agree with the Court that this content-based restriction is permissible, but not simply because it is in furtherance of objectives deemed unlawful by Congress. That a statute proscribes the otherwise lawful expression of views in a particular manner and at a particular location cannot in itself totally justify the restriction. Otherwise the First Amendment would place no limit on Congress' power." Contrasting the picketing in this case to handbilling carrying the same message, Justice Stevens rested his result on the following reasoning:

> The statutory ban in this case affects only that aspect of the union's efforts to communicate its views that calls for an automatic response to a signal, rather than a reasoned response to an idea. And the restriction on picketing is limited in geographical scope to sites of neutrals in the labor dispute. Because I believe that such restrictions on conduct are sufficiently justified by the purpose to avoid embroiling neutrals in a third party's labor dispute, I agree that the statute is consistent with the First Amendment.

Justice Brennan, writing for himself and for Justices White and Marshall, dissented from the Court's disposition of the statutory issue.

> The *Tree Fruits* test reflects the distinction between economic damage sustained by the secondary firm solely by virtue of its dependence upon the primary employer's goods, and injuries inflicted upon interests of the secondary firm that are unrelated to the primary dispute — injuries that are calculated to influence the secondary retailer's conduct with respect to the primary dispute. . . . Appeals to boycott nonprimary goods sold by a secondary retailer place more at stake for the retailer than the risk it has assumed by handling the primary employer's product. Four considerations indicate that this broader pressure is highly undesirable from the standpoint of labor policy. First, nonprimary product boycotts distort the strength of consumer response to the primary dispute; the secondary retailer's decision to continue purchasing the primary employer's line becomes a function of consumer reaction to the primary conflict *amplified* by the impact of the boycott upon nonprimary goods. . . . Second, although

> it seems proper to compel the producer or retailer of an individual primary product to internalize the costs of labor conflict engendered in the course of the item's production, a nonprimary product boycott may unfairly impose multiple costs upon the secondary retailer who does not wish to terminate his relationship with the primary employer. Third, nonprimary product boycotts attack interests of the secondary firm that are not derivative of the interests of the primary enterprise; because the retailer thereby becomes an independent disputant, the primary labor controversy may be aggravated and complicated. Finally, by affecting the sales of nonprimary goods handled by the secondary firm, the disruptive effect of the primary dispute is felt even by those businesses that manufacture and sell nonprimary products to the secondary retailer.

Note

The union was carrying its message to consumers in this case. No consumer who honored the union's request to stop patronizing the title companies committed a violation of law, civil or criminal. Thus it could not be argued that the union was engaged in a call for an unlawful conspiracy, or the like. Moreover, the content of the union's message was lawful, because the union could have communicated it with impunity had they done it by handbilling, or through newspaper and television advertisements. Finally, there is adequate Supreme Court precedent for the proposition that peaceful picketing, standing alone, is entitled to constitutional protection. In light of this, is Justice Powell's treatment of the constitutional issue persuasive? What of the concurring opinions?

In NAACP v. Claiborne Hardware Co., 458 U.S. 886 (1982), the Supreme Court reversed, on constitutional grounds, a state prohibition of a call for a consumer boycott of white merchants in Claiborne County, Mississippi. The boycotters demanded that county government officials desegregate schools, improve black residential neighborhoods, hire blacks for positions on the police force, and take other similar steps. The boycott was intended to pressure white merchants into pressuring elected officials to take these steps. After finding that the call for a boycott enjoyed constitutional protection, the Court had the following to say about the labor cases:

> The presence of protected activity, however, does not end the relevant constitutional inquiry. Governmental regulation that has an incidental effect on First Amendment freedoms may be justified in certain narrowly defined instances. A nonviolent and totally voluntary boycott may have a disruptive effect on local economic conditions. This Court has recognized the strong governmental interest in certain forms of economic regulation, even though such regulation may have an incidental effect on rights of speech and association. See Giboney v. Empire Storage, 336 U.S. 490; NLRB v. Retail Store Employees Union, 447 U.S. 607. The right of busi-

ness entities to "associate" to suppress competition may be curtailed. National Soc. of Professional Engineers v. United States, 435 U.S. 679. Unfair trade practices may be restricted. Secondary boycotts and picketing by labor unions may be prohibited, as part of Congress' striking of the delicate balance between union freedom of expression and the ability of neutral employers, employees, and consumers to remain free from coerced participation in industrial strife. NLRB v. Retail Store Employees Union, supra, at 617-618. See International Longshoremen's Assoc. v. Allied International, 456 U.S. 212.

In the cited case, *International Longshoremen's Assoc.,* ILA members, acting at the order of their union's president, refused to handle cargo arriving from or destined for the Soviet Union. They were protesting the Soviet actions in Afghanistan. The Court held that the union was violating the statutory prohibition against secondary boycotts. The Court reasoned:

> [It is not] a defense to the application of §8(b)(4) that the reason for the ILA boycott was not a labor dispute but a political dispute with a foreign nation. §8(b)(4) contains no such limitation. . . .
>
> We would create a large and undefinable exception to the statute if we accepted the argument that "political" boycotts are exempt from the secondary boycott provision. The distinction between labor and political objectives would be difficult to draw in many cases. In the absence of any limiting language in the statute or legislative history, we find no reason to conclude that Congress intended such a potentially expansive exception to a statutory provision purposefully drafted in broadest terms. . . .
>
> Application of §8(b)(4) to the ILA's activity in this case will not infringe upon the First Amendment rights of the ILA and its members. We have consistently rejected the claim that secondary picketing by labor unions in violation of §8(b)(4) is protected activity under the First Amendment. . . . It would seem even clearer that conduct designed not to communicate but to coerce merits still less consideration under the First Amendment. 456 U.S. 212, 224-226 (1982).

5. "Hot Cargo" Agreements[40]

UNITED BROTHERHOOD OF CARPENTERS & JOINERS, LOCAL 1976 v. NLRB [SAND DOOR], 357 U.S. 93 (1958): The Court decided three cases under this caption. In the first, the Carpenters Union negotiated a collective bargaining agreement clause with a general construction contractor providing that "workmen shall not be required to handle non-union material." When nonunion doors were

[40] See Lesnick, Job Security and Secondary Boycotts: The Reach of NLRA §§8(b)(4) and 8(e), 113 U. Pa. L. Rev. 1000 (1965); Comment, 71 Yale L.J. 158 (1961); Note, 57 Va. L. Rev. 1280 (1971).

brought onto the job site, the carpenters refused to install them, relying on the clause. The other two cases grew out of a dispute between the Machinists Union and a manufacturing company. The Teamsters Union ordered its members working for common carriers not to handle freight produced by the manufacturing company. The Teamsters relied on a provision in their bargaining agreement with the carriers providing that "members of the Union shall not be allowed to handle or haul freight to or from an unfair company, provided, this is not a violation of the Labor Management Relations Act of 1947. . . ."

The Court first noted that nothing in the statute prohibited an employer from voluntarily boycotting another employer, nor did it prohibit a union from persuading an employer to do so unless the union used prohibited means of persuasion (including a strike or a concerted refusal to handle).

The union argued that a strike (or concerted refusal to handle) to enforce a bargaining agreement clause voluntarily entered into did not violate §8(b)(4)(A).[41] If the employer has entered into a contract with such a clause it is no longer a disinterested party to the dispute. The Court disagreed, holding that §8(b)(4)(A) contemplated that a secondary employer would have at the time the question arises a choice, free from union pressure, of whether or not to boycott. Thus, the contract clause was not a defense to a strike for a secondary boycott.

The Court went on to say that while neither the execution nor the voluntary observance of a hot cargo clause (the common term for these clauses) violated §8(b)(4)(A), the Board was permitted to presume conclusively that an employer's observance was nonvoluntary where the union had ordered its members not to handle the hot goods. But, the Court noted, it "does not necessarily follow from the fact that the unions cannot invoke the contractual provision in the manner in which they sought to do so in the present cases that it may not, in some totally different context not now before the Court, still have legal radiations affecting the relations between the parties."

Note

In the 1959 amendments Congress enacted §8(e) and new §8(b)(4)(A), substantially altering the law of hot cargo clauses. The suspicion was that few, if any, employers ever signed hot cargo agreements on a truly voluntary basis. An employer having signed such a clause — realizing that the alternative was a strike "for higher wages," etc. — was free (under *Sand Door*) to renege on the clause, but only if he or she were willing to endure the union's wrath at the next round of negotiations.

[41] §8(b)(4)(A) was amended and renumbered §8(b)(4)(B) in 1959.

Language in *Sand Door* was read to mean that such clauses might be peacefully enforced by a court or arbitrator. The Senate thus voted to outlaw hot cargo agreements in the trucking industry, where their use was common and effective. The House broadened the prohibition to include all industries covered by the NLRA on the rationale that what was bad for one industry was bad for another, although the House did not have evidence of the extent to which such clauses existed in other industries or the uses to which they were put.

The broadened version was enacted but exceptions were carved for the construction and the apparel and clothing industries. Unions in the clothing and apparel industry are permitted by a proviso to §8(e) to strike for and enter into hot cargo agreements without violating §§8(e) or 8(b)(4)(A), and to strike to enforce them without violating §8(b)(4)B). Historically, manufacturers in this industry were typified by their low capitalization and ability to subcontract almost instantaneously to highly mobile employers working in shifting, hard-to-discover locations. Only if unions were allowed to secure and enforce hot cargo agreements with manufacturers and jobbers could conditions in the industry be improved. These unions successfully made their case to Congress in 1959.

The construction industry exemption is narrow in scope, relating only to "contracting or subcontracting of work to be done at the site of the construction." In National Woodwork Mfrs. Assn. v. NLRB, 386 U.S. 612 (1967), the Court held that the exemption offers no protection to a clause that covers work to be performed at a factory and brought to the job site. A strike to obtain a hot cargo clause permitted by the construction industry exemption was held by a line of Board cases to violate §8(b)(4)(A), but the Board met resistance from the courts of appeals, and in Building & Construction Trades Council (Centlivre Village Apartments), 148 N.L.R.B. 854 (1964), relented, holding such strikes were lawful. Unlike its treatment of the clothing industry, §8(e) does not remove the construction industry from the constraints of §8(b)(4). Thus the Board, with court approval, has held that strikes to enforce such clauses violate §8(b)(4)(B)[42] although peaceful enforcement of the clauses through arbitration or court action is lawful.[43]

The rationale for the construction industry exemption and a major limitation on its operation were set out by the Supreme Court in Connell Constr. Co. v. Plumbers Local 100, 421 U.S. 616 (1975). The union sought to organize construction subcontractors by picketing a construction general contractor for an agreement that it would subcontract job-

[42] Operating Engineers Local 825 (Nichols Elec. Co.), 140 N.L.R.B. 458, enforced, 326 F.2d 213 (3d Cir. 1964); Bay Counties District Council of Carpenters (Jones & Jones, Inc.), 154 N.L.R.B. 1598, enforced, 382 F.2d 593 (9th Cir. 1967), cert. denied, 398 U.S. 1037 (1968).

[43] California Dump Truck Owners Assn., 227 N.L.R.B. 269 (1976) (enforcement of contract clause through grievance arbitration is not §8(b)(4) threat or coercion regardless of clause's lawfulness under §8(e)); Hughes Markets, 218 N.L.R.B. 680 (1975) (resort to court).

site work only to companies having a bargaining agreement with the union. Defending itself from an allegation that it was violating the antitrust laws, the union argued that the clause and the strike fell within §8(e)'s construction industry exemption. The Court found that Congress' intent in enacting the exemption was to allow unions to protect their members from having to work alongside of nonunion workmen (and the resultant strife) on construction job sites. But the union in the instant case represented none of the general contractor's employees and the scope of the agreement was not limited to job sites where the union's members would necessarily be working, nor would the clause prevent the use of other nonunion subcontractors. Unwilling to assume Congress intended to legitimatize this sort of "top-down" organizing by enacting §8(e), the Court held that the construction industry exemption "extends only to agreements in the context of collective-bargaining relationships and . . . possibly to common-situs relationships on particular job sites as well."

In Woelke & Romero Framing, v. NLRB, 456 U.S. 645 (1982), the Court retreated from the dictum in the *Connell* opinion. It upheld a Board ruling that it was lawful for a union in the construction industry that has a bargaining relationship with a construction firm to secure a clause from the firm limiting job site subcontracting to unionized firms even though the clause is not limited to particular job sites.

The District of Columbia Circuit Court of Appeals has held that a prehire contract under §8(f) of the Act qualifies as a collective bargaining relationship for *Connell* purposes, thus bringing a subcontracting clause in a prehire agreement within the proviso to §8(e). Donald Schriver v. NLRB, 635 F.2d 859 (D.C. Cir. 1980).

Read the next case with the following problem in mind. Your union client is presently negotiating a new collective bargaining agreement with a manufacturing company. The union wants to insert clauses in the agreement affording its members their maximum protection, consistent with the labor statutes, in the following areas: freedom to honor picket lines at the employer's premises and while making deliveries, without fear of being discharged or replaced; freedom to refuse to work on raw materials that are subject to a labor dispute at the supplier's, without incurring disciplinary measures; and a restriction on the employer's right to subcontract work without the union's prior consent.

TRUCK DRIVERS, LOCAL 413 v. NLRB

334 F.2d 539 (D.C. Cir.), cert. denied, 379 U.S. 916 (1964)

WRIGHT, J.

[The Board found the disputed clauses void under §8(e).]

A preliminary issue is whether it is the *object,* the *effect,* or the express or implied *terms* of the challenged clauses which are relevant to the §8(e) charge. The unions suggest an object test, by parity of reasoning with §8(b)(4)(B)'s secondary boycott provisions. The Trial Examiner, in one of these companion cases considered the effect of the clauses to be relevant to their validity under §8(e), and took extensive evidence of their effect. The Board, however, at the instance of its General Counsel, held that the implementation of a contract was not relevant to its validity under §8(e), that extrinsic evidence of object alone was not determinative, and that the contract must be tested by its terms, express or implied. We agree.

The Picket Line Clause

A key provision in the union contracts protects the right of individual employees to refuse to cross picket lines by immunizing them against employer discipline. This picket line clause is broadly worded to achieve maximum application permitted by the law. The Board held that under §8(e) of the Act the clause may validly apply only to certain types of picket lines; the union apparently would apply it to all.

The clause provides:

> It shall not be a violation of this Agreement and it shall not be cause for discharge or disciplinary action in the event an employee refuses to enter upon any property involved in a labor dispute or refuses to go through or work behind any picket line, including the picket line of Unions party to this Agreement and including picket lines at the Employer's place or places of business.

The Board concedes that the contract clause may permissibly operate to protect refusals to cross a picket line where the line is in connection with a *primary* dispute at the *contracting* employer's *own premises.* This seems clearly correct. Employees who refuse to cross such a line are entitled to the same protection as strikers under §§7 and 13 of the Act. The refusal to cross being a protected activity, the union and the employer may provide by contract that such refusal shall not be grounds for discharge. See National Labor Relations Board v. Rockaway News Co., 345 U.S. 71, 80 (1953).

A different result must be reached where the picket line at the contracting employer's own premises is itself in promotion of a *secondary* strike or boycott. Refusal to cross that line would itself be secondary activity. To the extent that the clause would protect such refusal to cross, it would then be authorizing a secondary strike, and would pro tanto be void under §8(e) of the Act. There is no merit to the unions' suggestion that this clause is outside the reach of §8(e) because it protects *individual* refusals, not *union*-induced refusals. We read our own cases as having rejected this argument.

The Board also held that the clause may validly protect refusals to cross a picket line at the premises of *another* employer if that picket line meets the conditions expressed in the proviso[44] to §8(b)(4) of the Act. Clearly this is the law.

The remaining question concerns refusals to cross a picket line at *another* employer's premises where that line does *not* meet the conditions of the §8(b)(4) proviso.[45] The unions maintain that refusal to cross any lawful primary picket line is primary activity under the Act and that protection thereof in the bargaining agreement falls outside the ambit of §8(e). The Board held that refusal to cross a non-proviso picket line constitutes secondary activity, and that contractual protection of such activity violates §8(e).

[The court examined the legislative history of the 1959 amendments and was persuaded that Congress did not intend §8(e) to prohibit agreements sanctioning refusals to cross primary picket lines.] It would seem that even without this legislative history, a similar conclusion would be demanded by the case law. It has been clear since *Rockaway News* that whenever refusal to cross a picket line is a protected activity, unions and employers may sign contracts providing that the refusal shall not be ground for discharge. In *Rockaway News* the activity in question was within the §8(b)(4) proviso, but the Court did not limit the principle there announced to proviso activity. The Board itself recently held in the *Redwing*[11] and *Everist*[12] cases that refusal to cross a primary picket line was indeed a protected activity, without even considering whether the picket lines met the terms of the §8(b)(4) proviso. And, in *Redwing,* we affirmed the Board's holding "that the employees had in fact engaged in *protected* concerted activity when they refused to cross the picket line," also without regard to whether the proviso was satisfied. Sub nom. Teamsters, Chauffeurs & Helpers Local U. No. 79 v. N.L.R.B., 117 U.S. App. D.C. 84, 325 F.2d 1011, 1012 (1963). In fact, we are aware of no case which limits protection of refusal to cross a primary picket line to §8(b)(4) proviso situations.

Similar conclusions are suggested by National Labor Relations Board v. International Rice Milling Co., [341 U.S. 665 (1951)], and Electrical Workers Local 761 v. National Labor Relations Board, 366 U.S. 667 (1961). Since "appealing to neutral employees whose tasks aid the employer's everyday operations" is a "traditional primary activity," id. at 681 of 366 U.S., primary picketing retains its primary characteristic even

[44] The proviso reads: "That nothing contained in this subsection (b) shall be construed to make unlawful a refusal by any person to enter upon the premises of any employer (other than his own employer), if the employees of such employer are engaged in a strike ratified or approved by a representative of such employees whom such employer is required to recognize under this Act. . . ."

[45] E.g., an organizational picket line at another employer's premises.

11. Redwing Carriers, Inc., et al., 137 N.L.R.B. 3545 (1962).

12. L. G. Everist, Inc., et al., 142 N.L.R.B. No. 20 (1963).

though it induces deliverymen to refuse to cross the line. Thus it seems clear that refusal to cross a lawful primary picket line, absent demonstrated secondary intent, is itself primary, and as such falls outside the Act's proscriptions against secondary activity. Since §8(e) is limited to secondary activity, a provision in the bargaining agreement immunizing the exercise of this protected right against employer discipline does not violate it. See National Labor Relations Board v. Rockaway News Co., supra.

The Struck Goods Clause

A second section of the collective bargaining agreement which is in dispute concerns Struck Goods. It reads: . . .

> [(a)] It shall not be a violation of this Agreement and it shall not be a cause for discharge or disciplinary action if any employee refuses to perform any service which, but for the existence of a controversy between a labor union and any other person (whether party to this Agreement or not), would be performed by the employees of such person.
>
> [(b)] Likewise, it shall not be a violation of the Agreement and it shall not be a cause for discharge or disciplinary action if any employee refuses to handle any goods or equipment transported, interchanged, handled or used by any carrier or other person, whether a party to this Agreement or not, at any of whose terminals or places of business there is a controversy between such carrier, or person, or its employees on the one hand and a labor union on the other hand; and such rights may be exercised where such goods or equipment are being transported, handled or used by the originating, interchanging or succeeding carriers or persons, whether parties to this agreement or not. . . .

In considering clause (a) of this section, the Board acknowledged that it may lawfully apply where the relationship between the contracting employer and the employer with a labor dispute is so close as to render them "allies."

[The Court then described the ally doctrine as developed in *Ebasco* and *Royal Typewriter*.]

The Trial Examiner found clause (a) to be limited in scope to the "ally" doctrine, and therefore valid. But the Board read the clause as impermissibly broad, in that under it employees of the contracting employer might refuse to perform services which met the *first* test of [*Royal Typewriter*] ("otherwise done by the striking employees"), even if the *second* test of that rule were not met ("pursuant to an arrangement").

We agree with the Board that to the extent clause (a) protects refusals to work beyond the scope of the ally doctrine, it authorizes a secondary boycott, and so is pro tanto void under §8(e) of the Act. We refrain from defining the exact limits of the ally doctrine, however, and do not decide whether the [*Royal Typewriter*] tests are adequate for all variations in factual situations. Such spelling out is best left for the elucidating process of gradual inclusion and exclusion provided by specific cases.

Clause (b) of the Struck Goods section, set out above, seems to be a typical hot cargo clause, prohibited by §8(e) of the Act. The unions contend, however, that this clause — like others in the contract — is immune from §8(e)'s prohibition because it protects the freedom of decision of the individual laborer, rather than creates a power of decision in the union itself. Since few workers will exercise their rights under these clauses, the unions argue, there will be no substantial interference with the business of the employer, particularly in view of the provisions of clause (c). The short answer to this contention is that it has already been rejected by this court. [Citing cases] Moreover, the legislative history of the 1959 amendments equates these "employee-rights" clauses with other hot cargo clauses. . . .

We must conclude, therefore, as did the Board, that this clause (b) is void under §8(e) of the Act and that clause (c) does not save it.

The Subcontracting Clause

The third major challenged provision of the collective bargaining agreements here concerns Subcontracting:

"The Employer agrees to refrain from using the services of any person who does not observe the wages, hours and conditions of employment established by labor unions having jurisdiction over the type of services performed."[13]

The Board found this clause was secondary, and therefore void under §8(e) of the Act. It reasoned:

"Like the typical hot cargo clause itself, a subcontractor clause is secondary where it limits, *not the fact of subcontracting* — either prohibiting it outright or conditioning it upon, e.g., current full employment in the unit — but the *persons with whom* the signatory employer may subcontract. . . ."

This Board position groups together, as secondary, contract clauses which impose boycotts on subcontractors not signatory to union agreements, and those which merely require subcontractors to meet the equivalent of union standards in order to protect the work standards of the employees of the contracting employer. But the distinction between these two types of clauses is vital. Union-signatory subcontracting clauses are secondary, and therefore within the scope of §8(e), while union-standards subcontracting clauses are primary as to the contracting employer.

This clause would be a union-signatory clause if it required subcon-

13. Since this clause is entitled "Subcontracting," we assume — in the absence of any indication to the contrary — that its scope is limited to the contracting out of work which otherwise would be performed by members of the bargaining unit.

tractors to have collective bargaining agreements with petitioner unions or their affiliates, or with unions generally. We interpret it, however, as merely requiring that subcontractors observe the equivalent of union wages, hours, and the like.[14] Since we find that this clause only requires union standards, and not union recognition, we . . . rule it primary, and thus outside §8(e)'s prohibitions. . . .

There remains the question of the appropriate relief. As to some sections of the contract, we have found the clauses to have a valid scope of operation under the law, but to be prohibited by law from operating outside that scope. Though the Board's decree is ambiguous, a section of its opinion suggests that in such a situation of partially-valid clauses, the entire clauses as written should be struck down. If this is the Board's view, we do not agree.

Ordinarily, the rubric of not rewriting the contract for the parties does bear some relation to labor contracts. Every collective bargaining agreement is the resultant of opposing forces, representing their relative strengths and positions. To limit clauses won by one side, while leaving in effect the remainder of the contract, would upset the balance struck at the bargaining table. Indeed, these considerations would suggest that, not just the challenged clauses, but the entire labor contract should be voided as a whole, if one part must be struck down.

But these considerations do not govern in situations such as here. This is not a case where the unions, by sacrificing other dearly desired privileges, have won from employers acceptance of clauses in the contract, clearly intended to confer union rights, but later found to violate the Act. Rather the clauses here seem purposefully to be drawn in broad terms to achieve maximum application permitted by the new amendments to the Act. Both unions and employers must have anticipated that these amendments would not permit the clauses to be given the most expansive reading the bare words allowed. A more narrow reading, or even a partial excision, must have been within the contemplation of the experienced counsel who purposefully cast the clauses in such general terms. . . .

We therefore conclude that a decree should be drafted condemning the challenged contract clauses only to the extent found unlawful by this court.

Enforced in part and set aside in part.

Notes

1. Is footnote 14 consistent with the first paragraph of the court's opinion? So long as the union enforces the clause peacefully, i.e., with-

14. The Board's processes are adequate, we take it, to insure that substantial compliance with union standards or the equivalent will suffice under such a clause, and that the union will not be allowed to use it as a device to limit subcontracting to union firms.

out using a strike or other prohibited means, what jurisdiction would the Board have?

2. If a union in a breach of contract action against an employer asks a court to enforce a broad no-subcontracting clause, should the court examine the clause for §8(e) validity? What should the court do if the clause is valid on its face but is sought to be enforced in circumstances rendering it secondary? Conversely, suppose the clause as written is overbroad (and thus violative of §8(e)), but enforcement is sought in a situation in which its operation is clearly primary?

3. If the Board or a court is to rewrite an overbroad clause, won't maximum protection be secured for the union's members by drafting an unlawful clause?

6. Identifying the Primary (Work Preservation)

NATIONAL WOODWORK MANUFACTURERS ASSN. v. NLRB

386 U.S. 612 (1967)

Brennan, J. . . .

Frouge Corporation, a Bridgeport, Connecticut, concern, was the general contractor on a housing project in Philadelphia. Frouge had a collective bargaining agreement with the Carpenters' International Union under which Frouge agreed to be bound by the rules and regulations agreed upon by local unions with contractors in areas in which Frouge had jobs. Frouge was therefore subject to the provisions of a collective bargaining agreement between the Union and an organization of Philadelphia contractors, the General Building Association, Inc. A sentence in a provision of that agreement entitled Rule 17 provides that ". . . No member of this District Council will handle . . . any doors . . . which have been fitted prior to being furnished on the job. . . ." Frouge's Philadelphia project called for 3,600 doors. Customarily, before the doors could be hung on such projects, "blank" or "blind" doors would be mortised for the knob, routed for the hinges, and beveled to make them fit between jambs. These are tasks traditionally performed in the Philadelphia area by the carpenters employed on the jobsite. However, precut and prefitted doors ready to hang may be purchased from door manufacturers. Although Frouge's contract and job specifications did not call for premachined doors, and "blank" or "blind" doors could have been ordered, Frouge contracted for the purchase of premachined doors from a Pennsylvania door manufacturer which is a member of the National Woodwork Manufacturers Association. The Union ordered its carpenter members not to hang the doors when they arrived at the jobsite. Frouge thereupon withdrew the prefabricated doors and substituted "blank" doors which were fitted and cut by its carpenters on the jobsite.

The National Woodwork Manufacturers Association and another filed charges with the National Labor Relations Board against the Union alleging that by including the "will not handle" sentence of Rule 17 in the collective bargaining agreement the Union committed the unfair labor practice under §8(e) of entering into an "agreement . . . whereby [the] employer . . . agrees to cease or refrain from handling . . . any of the products of any other employer . . ." and alleging further that in enforcing the sentence against Frouge, the Union committed the unfair labor practice under §8(b)(4)(B) of "forcing or requiring any person to cease using . . . the products of any other . . . manufacturer. . . ." The National Labor Relations Board dismissed the charges, 149 N.L.R.B. 646. The Board adopted the findings of the Trial Examiner that the "will not handle" sentence in Rule 17 was language used by the parties to protect and preserve cutting out and fitting as unit work to be performed by the jobsite carpenters. The Board also adopted the holding of the Trial Examiner that both the sentence of Rule 17 itself and its maintenance against Frouge were therefore "primary" activity outside the prohibitions of §§8(e) and 8(b)(4)(B). [The Seventh Circuit found a §8(e) violation but no §8(b)(4)(B) violation.]

I

Even on the doubtful premise that the words of §8(e) unambiguously embrace the sentence of Rule 17, this does not end inquiry into Congress' purpose in enacting the section. It is a "familiar rule, that a thing may be within the letter of the statute and yet not within the statute, because not within its spirit nor within the intention of its makers." Holy Trinity Church v. United States, 143 U.S. 457, 459. . . .

Strongly held opposing views have invariably marked controversy over labor's use of the boycott to further its aims by involving an employer in disputes not his own. But congressional action to deal with such conduct has stopped short of proscribing identical activity having the object of pressuring the employer for agreements regulating relations between him and his own employees. That Congress meant §§8(e) and 8(b)(4)(B) to prohibit only "secondary" objectives clearly appears from an examination of the history of congressional action on the subject; we may, by such an examination, "reconstitute the gamut of values current at the time when the words were uttered."

[The Court reviewed the history of statutory and judicial treatment of the secondary boycott. The Court examined Allen Bradley Co. v. Local 3, I.B.E.W., 325 U.S. 797, (1945), a celebrated anti-trust case involving an extensive network of product boycotts designed to monopolize the work of electrical contracting and manufacturing for the unionized employees of New York City employers. The case played a heavy role in the 1947 debates leading up to §8(b)(4)'s passage. The Court proceeded to distinguish *Allen Bradley* from the instant case.]

[T]he boycott in *Allen Bradley* was carried on, not as a shield to preserve the jobs of Local 3 members, traditionally a primary labor activity, but as a sword, to reach out and monopolize all the manufacturing job tasks for Local 3 members. It is arguable that Congress may have viewed the use of the boycott as a sword as different from labor's traditional concerns with wages, hours, and working conditions. But the boycott in the present cases was not used as a sword; it was a shield carried solely to preserve the members' jobs. We therefore have no occasion today to decide the questions which might arise where the workers carry on a boycott to reach out to monopolize jobs or acquire new job tasks when their own jobs are not threatened by the boycotted product.[19] . . .

In effect Congress, in enacting §8(b)(4)(A) of the Act . . . barred as a secondary boycott union activity directed against a neutral employer, including the immediate employer when in fact the activity directed against him was carried on for its effect elsewhere.

Indeed, Congress in rewriting §8(b)(4)(A) as §8(b)(4)(B) took pains to confirm the limited application of the section to such "secondary" conduct. The word "concerted" in former §8(b)(4) was deleted to reach secondary conduct directed to only one individual. This was in response to the Court's holding in National Labor Relations Board v. International Rice Milling Co., 341 U.S. 665, that "concerted" required proof of inducement of two or more employees. But to make clear that the deletion was not to be read as supporting a construction of the statute as prohibiting the incidental effects of traditional primary activity, Congress added the proviso that nothing in the amended section "shall be construed to make unlawful, where not otherwise unlawful, any primary strike or primary picketing." Many statements and examples proffered in the 1959 debates confirm this congressional acceptance of the distinction between primary and secondary activity.

II

The Landrum-Griffin Act amendments in 1959 were adopted only to close various loopholes in the application of §8(b)(4)(A) which had been exposed in Board and court decisions.

Section 8(e) simply closed still another loophole. In Local 1976, United Brotherhood of Carpenters, etc., v. National Labor Relations

19. We likewise do not have before us in these cases, and express no view upon, the antitrust limitations, if any, upon union-employer work-preservations or work-extension agreements.

Board (Sand Door), 357 U.S. 93, the Court held that it was no defense to an unfair labor practice charge under §8(b)(4)(A) that the struck employer had agreed, in a contract with the union, not to handle nonunion material. However, the Court emphasized that the mere execution of such a contract provision (known as a "hot cargo" clause because of its prevalence in Teamsters Union contracts), or its voluntary observance by the employer, was not unlawful under §8(b)(4)(A). Section 8(e) was designed to plug this gap in the legislation by making the "hot cargo" clause itself unlawful. The *Sand Door* decision was believed by Congress not only to create the possibility of damage actions against employers for breaches of "hot cargo" clauses, but also to create a situation in which such clauses might be employed to exert subtle pressures upon employers to engage in "voluntary" boycotts. Hearings in late 1958 before the Senate Select Committee explored seven cases of "hot cargo" clauses in Teamsters Union contracts, the use of which the Committee found conscripted neutral employers in Teamsters organizational campaigns.

This loophole-closing measure likewise did not expand the type of conduct which §8(b)(4)(A) condemned. Although the language of §8(e) is sweeping, it closely tracks that of §8(b)(4)(A), and just as the latter and its successor §8(b)(4)(B) did not reach employees' activity to pressure their employer to preserve for themselves work traditionally done by them, §8(e) does not prohibit agreements made and maintained for that purpose. [The Court found support for its conclusion in the 1959 legislative history of §8(e).]

The only mention of a broader reach for §8(e) appears in isolated statements by opponents of that provision, expressing fears that work preservation agreements would be banned. These statements have scant probative value against the backdrop of the strong evidence to the contrary. Too, "we have often cautioned against the danger, when interpreting a statute, of reliance upon the views of its legislative opponents. In their zeal to defeat a bill, they understandably tend to overstate its reach." National Labor Relations Board v. Fruit & Vegetable Packers, etc., 377 U.S. 58, 66. "It is the sponsors that we look to when the meaning of the statutory words is in doubt." Schwegmann Bros. v. Calvert Distillers Corp., 341 U.S. 384, 394-395.

In addition to all else, "[t]he silence of the sponsors of [the] amendments is pregnant with significance . . ." National Labor Relations Board v. Fruit & Vegetable Packers, etc., supra, 377 U.S. at 66. Before we may say that Congress meant to strike from workers' hands the economic weapons traditionally used against their employers' efforts to abolish their jobs, that meaning should plainly appear. "[I]n this era of automation and onrushing technological change, no problems in the domestic economy are of greater concern than those involving job security and employment stability. Because of the potentially cruel impact upon the lives and fortunes of the working men and women of the

Nation, these problems have understandably engaged the solicitous attention of government, of responsible private business, and particularly of organized labor." Fibreboard Paper Prods. Corp. v. National Labor Relations Board, 379 U.S. 203, 225 (concurring opinion of Stewart, J.). We would expect that legislation curtailing the ability of management and labor voluntarily to negotiate for solutions to these significant and difficult problems would be preceded by extensive congressional study and debate, and consideration of voluminous economic, scientific, and statistical data. The silence regarding such matters in the Eighty-sixth Congress is itself evidence that Congress, in enacting §8(e), had no thought of prohibiting agreements directed to work preservation. . . .

Moreover, our decision in *Fibreboard Paper Prods. Corp.*, supra, implicitly recognizes the legitimacy of work preservation clauses like that involved here. Indeed, in the circumstances presented in *Fibreboard*, we held that bargaining on the subject was made mandatory by §8(a)(5) of the Act, concerning as it does "terms and conditions of employment," §8(d). *Fibreboard* involved an alleged refusal to bargain with respect to the contracting-out of plant maintenance work previously performed by employees in the bargaining unit. The Court recognized that the "termination of employment which . . . necessarily results from the contracting out of work performed by members of the established bargaining unit," supra, at 210, is "a problem of vital concern to labor and management. . . ." supra, at 211. . . . It would therefore be incongruous to interpret §8(e) to invalidate clauses over which the parties may be mandated to bargain and which have been successfully incorporated through collective bargaining in many of this Nation's major labor agreements. . . .

The Woodwork Manufacturers Association and amici who support its position advance several reasons, grounded in economic and technological factors, why "will not handle" clauses should be invalid in all circumstances. Those arguments are addressed to the wrong branch of government. . . .

III

The determination whether the "will not handle" sentence of Rule 17 and its enforcement violated §8(e) and §8(b)(4)(B) cannot be made without an inquiry into whether, under all the surrounding circumstances,[38] the Union's objective was preservation of work for Frouge's employees, or whether the agreements and boycott were tactically calculated to satisfy union objectives elsewhere. Were the latter the case, Frouge, the

38. As a general proposition, such circumstances might include the remoteness of the threat of displacement by the banned product or services, the history of the labor relations between the union and the employers who would be boycotted, and the economic personality of the industry. See Comment, 62 Mich. L. Rev. 1176, 1185 et seq. (1964).

boycotting employer, would be a neutral bystander, and the agreement or boycott would, within the intent of Congress, become secondary. There need not be an actual dispute with the boycotted employer, here the door manufacturer, for the activity to fall within this category, so long as the tactical object of the agreement and its maintenance is that employer, or benefits to other than the boycotting employees or other employees of the primary employer thus making the agreement or boycott secondary in its aim. The touchstone is whether the agreement or its maintenance is addressed to the labor relations of the contracting employer vis-à-vis his own employees. This will not always be a simple test to apply. But "[h]owever difficult the drawing of lines more nice than obvious, the statute compels the task." Local 761, Inter. Union of Electrical, etc., Workers v. National Labor Relations Board, 366 U.S. 667, 674.

That the "will not handle" provision was not an unfair labor practice in these cases is clear. The finding of the Trial Examiner, adopted by the Board, was that the objective of the sentence was preservation of work traditionally performed by the jobsite carpenters. This finding is supported by substantial evidence, and therefore the Union's making of the "will not handle" agreement was not a violation of §8(e).

Similarly, the Union's maintenance of the provision was not a violation of §8(b)(4)(B). The Union refused to hang prefabricated doors whether or not they bore a union label, and even refused to install prefabricated doors manufactured off the jobsite by members of the Union. This and other substantial evidence supported the finding that the conduct of the Union on the Frouge jobsite related solely to preservation of the traditional tasks of the jobsite carpenters. . . .

Memorandum of HARLAN, J.

In joining the Court's opinion, I am constrained to add these few words by way of underscoring the salient factors which, in my judgment, make for the decision that has been reached in these difficult cases.

1. The facts as found by the Board and the Court of Appeals show that the contractual restrictive-product rule in question, and the boycott in support of its enforcement, had as their sole objective the protection of union members from a diminution of work flowing from changes in technology. Union members traditionally had performed the task of fitting doors on the jobsite, and there is no evidence of any motive for this contract provision and its companion boycott other than the preservation of that work. This, then, is not a case of a union seeking to restrict by contract or boycott an employer with respect to the products he uses, for the purpose of acquiring for its members work that had not previously been theirs.

2. The only question thus to be decided, and which is decided, is whether Congress meant, in enacting §§8(b)(4)(B) and 8(e) of the National Labor Relations Act, to prevent this kind of labor-management arrangement designed to forestall possible adverse effects upon workers arising from changing technology.
3. Because of the possibly profound impacts that the answer to this question may have upon labor-management relations and upon other aspects of the economy, both sides of today's division in the Court agree that we must be especially careful to eschew a resolution of the issue according to our own economic ideas and to find one in what Congress has done. It is further agreed that in pursuing the search for the true intent of Congress we should not stop with the language of the statute itself, but must look beneath its surface to the legislative history.
4. It is recognized by court and counsel on both sides that the legislative history of §8(b)(4)(B), with which §8(e), it is agreed, is to be taken pari passu, contains only the most tangential references to problems connected with changing technology. Also, a circumspect reading of the legislative record evincing Congress' belief that the statutory provisions in question prohibited agreements and conduct of the kind involved in Allen Bradley Co. v. Local Union No. 3, etc., 325 U.S. 797, will not support a confident assertion that Congress also had in mind the sort of union-management activity before us here. And although it is arguable that Congress, in the temper of the times, would have readily accepted a proposal to outlaw work-preservation agreements and boycotts, even, as here, in their most limited sense, such a surmise can hardly serve as a basis for the construction of an existing statute.
5. We are thus left with a legislative history which, on the precise point at issue, is essentially negative, which shows with fair conclusiveness only that Congress was not squarely faced with the problem these cases present. In view of Congress' deep commitment to the resolution of matters of vital importance to management and labor through the collective bargaining process, and its recognition of the boycott as a legitimate weapon in that process, it would be unfortunate were this Court to attribute to Congress, on the basis of such an opaque legislative record, a purpose to outlaw the kind of collective bargaining and conduct involved in these cases. Especially at a time when Congress is continuing to explore methods for meeting the economic problems increasingly arising in this technological age from scientific advances, this Court should not take such a step until Congress has made unmistakably clear that it wishes wholly to exclude collective bargaining as one avenue of approach to solutions in this elusive aspect of our economy.

STEWART, J., whom BLACK, J., DOUGLAS, J., and CLARK, J., join, dissenting. . . .

The Court undertakes a protracted review of legislative and decisional history in an effort to show that the clear word of the statute should be disregarded in these cases. But the fact is that the relevant history fully confirms that Congress meant what it said, and I therefore dissent.

The Court concludes that the Union's conduct in these cases falls outside the ambit of §8(b)(4) because it had an ultimate purpose that the Court characterizes as "primary" in nature — the preservation of work for union members. But §8(b)(4) is not limited to boycotts that have as their only purpose the forcing of any person to cease using the products of another; it is sufficient if that result is "an object" of the boycott. Legitimate union objectives may not be accomplished through means proscribed by the statute. See National Labor Relations Board v. Denver Bldg. & Const. Trades Council, 341 U.S. 675, 688-689. Without question, preventing Frouge from using prefitted doors was "an object" of the Union's conduct here.

It is, of course, true that courts have distinguished "primary" and "secondary" activities, and have found the former permitted despite the literal applicability of the statutory language. But the Court errs in concluding that the product boycott conducted by the Union in these cases was protected primary activity. As the Court points out, a typical form of secondary boycott is the visitation of sanctions on Employer A, with whom the union has no dispute, in order to force him to cease doing business with Employer B, with whom the union does have a dispute. But this is not the only form of secondary boycott that §8(b)(4) was intended to reach. The Court overlooks the fact that a product boycott for work preservation purposes has consistently been regarded by the courts, and by the Congress that passed the Taft-Hartley Act, as a proscribed "secondary boycott."

[The dissent argued that in passing §8(b)(4) Congress intended to outlaw product boycotts as typified by those in *Allen Bradley*.]

The Court seeks to avoid the thrust of this legislative history stemming from *Allen Bradley* by suggesting that in the present cases, the product boycott was used to preserve work opportunities traditionally performed by the Union, whereas in *Allen Bradley* the boycott was originally designed to create new job opportunities. But it is misleading to state that the union in *Allen Bradley* used the product boycott as a "sword." The record in that case establishes that the boycott was undertaken for the defensive purpose of restoring job opportunities lost in the depression. Moreover, the Court is unable to cite anything in *Allen Bradley*, or in the Taft-Hartley Act and its legislative history, to support a distinction in the applicability of §8(b)(4) based on the origin of the job opportunities sought to be preserved by a product boycott. The Court creates its sword and shield distinction out of thin air; nothing could more clearly indicate that the Court is simply substituting its own concepts of desirable labor policy for the scheme enacted by Congress. . . .

Finally, the Court's reliance on Fibreboard Paper Prods. Corp. v. National Labor Relations Board, 379 U.S. 203, is wholly misplaced. That case involved an employer's use of workers hired by an independent contractor to perform in its own plant maintenance work formerly done by its own employees. This reassignment of work was held by the Court to be a mandatory subject of collective bargaining. The circumscribed nature of the decision is established by the Court's careful observation that "The Company's decision to contract out the maintenance work did not alter the Company's basic operation. The maintenance work still had to be performed in the plant . . . the Company merely replaced existing employees with those of an independent contractor to do the same work under similar conditions of employment. Therefore, to require the employer to bargain about the matter would not significantly abridge his freedom to manage the business." 379 U.S., at 213.

An employer's decision as to the products he wishes to buy presents entirely different issues. That decision has traditionally been regarded as one within management's discretion, and *Fibreboard* does not indicate that it is a mandatory subject of collective bargaining, much less a permissible basis for a product boycott made illegal by federal labor laws. . . .

NLRB v. ENTERPRISE ASSN. OF PIPEFITTERS[46]

429 U.S. 507 (1977)

[The Pipefitters Union signed a bargaining agreement with a construction subcontractor (Hudik) which provided that pipe threading and cutting would be performed on job site by the subcontractor's unionized employees. Hudik then bid successfully on a subcontract put out by a general contractor (Austin), which provided that Hudik would install factory (Slant/Fin) prefabricated climate control units. When the units arrived on the job, Hudik's union employees refused to install them. The Board held that the clause was valid since its purpose was to preserve work traditionally done by Hudik's pipefitters but that the refusal to handle the prefabricated units violated §8(b)(4)(B) because control over whether factory units would be installed was vested in Austin, not Hudik. Since the object of the pressure against Hudik (the refusal to handle) was to affect the policies of another employer (Austin), there was a prohibited secondary boycott.]

WHITE, J. . . .

[46] See Leslie, Right to Control: A Study in Secondary Boycotts and Labor Antitrust, 89 Harv. L. Rev. 904 (1976).

II

In setting aside the Board's order, the Court of Appeals disagreed with the Board on both legal and factual grounds. We deal first with the Court of Appeals' proposition that "an employer who is struck by his own employees for the purpose of requiring him to do what he has lawfully contracted to do to benefit those employees can [n]ever be considered a neutral bystander in a dispute not his own." 521 F.2d, at 903 (footnote omitted). Under this view, a strike or refusal to handle undertaken to enforce such a contract would not itself warrant an inference that the union sought to satisfy secondary, rather than primary, objectives, whatever the impact on the immediate employer or on other employers might be. Thus, where a union seeks to enforce a work-preservation agreement by a strike or work stoppage, the existence of the agreement would always provide an adequate defense to a §8(b)(4) unfair labor practice charge. This approach is untenable under the Act and our cases construing it. [The Court relied on the holding of Local 1976, United Brotherhood of Carpenters v. NLRB (Sand Door) — that an employer's promise in a bargaining agreement was no defense to a §8(b)(4)(B) charge — as a complete response to the court of appeals' reasoning. Neither the enactment of §8(e) nor the decision in *National Woodwork* overruled this aspect of *Sand Door*.]

There is thus no doubt that the collective-bargaining provision that pipes be cut by hand on the job and that the work be conducted by units of two is not itself a sufficient answer to a §8(b)(4)(B) charge. The substantial question before us is whether, with or without the collective-bargaining contract, the union's conduct at the time it occurred was proscribed secondary activity within the meaning of the section. If it was, the collective-bargaining provision does not save it. If it was not, the reason is that §8(b)(4)(B) did not reach it, not that it was immunized by the contract. Thus, regardless of whether an agreement is valid under §8(e), it may not be enforced by means that would violate §8(b)(4).[8]

III

The Court of Appeals was also of the view that the Board's "control" test, under which the union commits an unfair labor practice under §8(b)(4)(B) when it coerces an employer in order to obtain work that the

8. The validity of the will-not-handle provision in this case was not challenged by the charging party, and the Board referred to it as a valid provision. Because the scope of the prohibitions in §§8(b)(4)(B) and 8(e) are essentially identical, except where the proscriptions in §8(e) are limited by the provisos in that section, the Court of Appeals regarded as anomalous that a valid provision in a collective-bargaining contract could not be enforced through economic pressure exerted by the union. This conclusion ignores the substance of our decision in *Sand Door*. Even though a work-preservation provision may be valid in its intendment and valid in its application in other contexts, efforts to apply the provision so as to influence some other than the immediate employer are prohibited by §8(b)(4)(B). . . .

employer has no power to assign, is invalid as a matter of law because it fails to comply with the *National Woodwork* standard that the union's conduct be judged in light of all the relevant circumstances. Again, we think the Court of Appeals was in error. . . .

Nor is it the case that the Board, in applying its control standard, failed to consider all of the relevant circumstances. Surely the fact that the Board distinguishes between two otherwise identical cases because in the one the employer has control of the work and in the other he has no power over it does not indicate that the Board has ignored any material circumstance. The contrary might more rationally be inferred. Of course, the Board may assign to the presence or absence of control much more weight than would the Court of Appeals, but this far from demonstrates a departure from the totality-of-the-circumstances test recognized in *National Woodwork.*

[The Court described the Board's long adherence to the right to control doctrine.]

IV

Wholly apart from its determination that the union's conduct was justified as a measure to enforce its collective-bargaining contract and that the Board applied an incorrect standard for determining liability, the Court of Appeals held that since there was "no substantial evidence . . . in this record that the union's purpose was also 'to satisfy union objectives elsewhere,' the Board's decision holding the union guilty of §8(b)(4)(B) violation may not stand." 521 F.2d, at 904. We disagree.

That there existed inducement and coercion within the meaning of §8(b)(4) is not disputed. The issue is whether "an object" of the inducement and the coercion was to cause the cease-doing-business consequences prohibited by §8(b)(4), the resolution of which in turn depends on whether the product boycott was "addressed to the labor relations of [Hudik] . . . vis-à-vis his own employees," *National Woodwork,* 386 U.S., at 645, or whether the union's conduct was "tactically calculated to satisfy [its] objectives elsewhere," id., at 644.[16]

16. The dissenters now assert a different definition of what constitutes prohibited secondary activity:

> "If the purpose of a contract provision, or of economic pressure on an employer is to secure benefits for that employer's own employees, it is primary; if the object is to affect the policies of some other employer toward his employees, the contract or its enforcement is secondary." *National Woodwork* did not, however, adopt this standard for applying the proscriptions of §8(b)(4)(B). The distinction between primary and secondary activity does not always turn on which group of employees the union seeks to benefit. There are circumstances under which the union's conduct is secondary when one of its purposes is to influence directly the conduct of an employer other than the struck employer. In these situations, a union's efforts to influence the conduct of the nonstruck employer are not rendered primary simply because it seeks to benefit the employees of the struck employer. *National Woodwork* itself

There is ample support in the record for the Board's resolution of this question. The union sought to enforce its contract with Hudik by a jobsite product boycott by which the steamfitters asserted their rights to the cutting and threading work on the Norwegian Home project. It is uncontrovertible that the work at this site could not be secured by pressure on Hudik alone and that the union's objectives could not be obtained without exerting pressure on Austin as well. That the union may also have been seeking to enforce its contract and to convince Hudik that it should bid on no more jobs where prepiped units were specified does not alter the fact that the union refused to install the Slant/Fin units and asserted that the piping work on the Norwegian Home job belonged to its members.[17] It was not error for the Board to conclude that the

---

embraced the view that the union's conduct would be secondary if its tactical object was to influence another employer:

"There need not be an actual dispute with the boycotted employer, here the door manufacturer, for the activity to fall within this category, so long as the tactical object of the agreement and its maintenance is that employer, or benefits to other than the boycotting employees or other employees of the primary employer thus making the agreement or boycott secondary in its aim." 386 U.S., at 645.

Under the standard announced, we found no unfair labor practice in *National Woodwork*. Frouge, the struck employer, was faced with the choice of either giving the cutting and fitting work to its own employees or giving it to the door manufacturer. Cf. Fibreboard Corp. v. NLRB, 379 U.S. 203 (1964). The Court sustained the Board's finding that the union's sole object was to influence Frouge to give the work to its own employees. The union thus had no object of influencing the door manufacturer, even though any influence that the union had on Frouge would have had incidental effect on persons with whom Frouge had commercial dealings. Cf. NLRB v. Operating Engineers, 400 U.S. 297, 304 (1971) ("Some disruption of business relationships is the necessary consequence of the purest form of primary activity").

The *National Woodwork* opinion also noted that the Court then had no occasion "to decide the questions which might arise where the workers carry on a boycott to reach out to monopolize jobs or acquire new job tasks." 386 U.S., at 630-631. That reservation was apparently meaningless, for under the theory of the dissent, seemingly derived from *National Woodwork* itself, striking workers may legally demand that their employer cease doing business with another company even if the union's object is to obtain new work so long as that work is for the benefit of the striking employees. If, for example, Hudik had in the past used prepiped units without opposition from the union, and the union had demanded that Hudik not fulfill its contract with Austin on the Norwegian Home job — all for the benefit of Hudik employees — it would appear that the dissenters' approach would exonerate the union. Respondents take the same view. Tr. of Oral Arg. 22. We disagree, for the union's object would necessarily be to force Hudik to cease doing business with Austin, not to preserve, but to aggrandize, its own position and that of its members. Such activity is squarely within the statute.

Here, of course, the union sought to acquire work that it never had and that its employer had no power to give it, namely, the piping work on units specified by any contractor or developer who prefers and uses prepiped units. By seeking the work at the Norwegian Home, the union's tactical objects necessarily included influencing Austin; this conduct falls squarely within the statement of *National Woodwork* that a union's activity is secondary if its tactical object is to influence the boycotted employer.

17. "It is not necessary to find that the sole object of the strike" was secondary so long as one of the union's objectives was to influence another employer by inducing the struck employer to cease doing business with that other employer. See NLRB v. Denver Bldg. Council, 341 U.S. 675, 689 (1951).

union's objectives were not confined to the employment relationship with Hudik but included the object of influencing Austin in a manner prohibited by §8(b)(4)(B).

The Court of Appeals was of the view that other inferences from the facts were possible. The court, for example, could "clearly see that it was possible for Hudik-Ross to settle the labor dispute which it had created. The record is void of any suggestion that Hudik-Ross attempted to negotiate a compromise with the union under which the union would have agreed to install the climate control units in exchange for extra pay or other special benefits." 172 U.S. App. D.C., at 239, 521 F.2d, at 899. How this observation impugns the Board's finding with respect to the union's object is not clear. The union simply refused to handle the Slant/Fin units and asserted that under the contract the cutting and threading work belonged to them. The common-sense inference from these facts is that the product boycott was in part aimed at securing the cutting and threading work at the Norwegian Home job, which could only be obtained by exerting pressure on Austin . . .

The judgment of the Court of Appeals is reversed.

Brennan, J., with whom Stewart, J., and Marshall, J., join, dissenting.

I dissent. Today's holding that union members exert secondary pressure in violation of §8(b)(4)(B) of the National Labor Relations Act by striking their own employer to protest his conceded violation of a lawful work-preservation provision in the parties' collective-bargaining agreement is patently precluded by National Woodwork Mfrs. Assn. v. NLRB, 386 U.S. 612 (1967). . . .

Two principles follow from [*National Woodwork*]. First, §§8(b)(4)(B) and 8(e) prohibit only conduct which is secondary, as that term has generally been understood in American labor law. If the purpose of a contract provision, or of economic pressure on an employer, is to secure benefits for that employer's own employees, it is primary; if the object is to affect the policies of some other employer toward his employees, the contract or its enforcement is secondary. Second, work preservation is necessarily a primary goal. Pressure undertaken in order to preserve work traditionally performed by unit members aims at benefits for those members, and centers on a conflict between the employees and their employer, which, although it has secondary effects on other employers, as does the use of almost any economic weapon in a labor dispute, can only be regarded as primary. Thus, if a contract clause is intended to preserve work, its objective, and the objective of pressure to enforce it, is primary, and therefore legitimate. Only if examination of "all the surrounding circumstances" indicated that the purpose of the clause is not work preservation, but rather "to satisfy union objectives elsewhere," would the provision violate §8(e) and its enforcement by economic pressure violate §8(b)(4)(B). . . .

It defies reality to deny that the union's principal dispute was with Hudik, the immediate employer of its members. It was Hudik which had acceded to the union's demand for the work-preservation clause particularly desired by its employees for their own protection. And it was Hudik which breached that clause. Nothing whatever in the record even remotely suggests that the union had any quarrel with Slant/Fin or Austin. Those companies were simply the vehicles used by Hudik to effect the breach which created the primary dispute between it and its own employees and their union. Nor is there the slightest basis for a suggestion that the true purpose of the work-preservation clause or the pressure applied to enforce it was to benefit employees "other than the boycotting employees or other employees of [Hudik]." Id., at 645.

The Court maintains that the collective-bargaining agreement between Enterprise and Hudik is irrelevant to the determination of whether the union exerted primary or secondary pressure, relying on Carpenters v. NLRB, 357 U.S. 93 (1958) (Sand Door). With all respect, this totally misapprehends the relevance of the agreement to the issue before us, and misapplies *Sand Door*. . . .

Sand Door holds that pressure to enforce a *secondary* boycott clause remains secondary, despite the then legality of the clause itself; it is not authority that union pressure to enforce a concededly *primary* work-preservation clause (which, since the enactment of §8(e), is legal only because it is primary), is anything but primary pressure. The union here does not argue, as in *Sand Door,* that pressure otherwise secondary is magically transformed into primary pressure by an employer's prior agreement to support a secondary boycott. Rather, §§8(b)(4) and 8(e) are "to be taken pari passu," *National Woodwork,* supra, at 649 (Harlan, J., concurring), so that pressure to enforce an employer to honor a clause of a collective-bargaining agreement admittedly primary, because intended to preserve work traditionally performed by unit members, is also primary. In short, the agreement in this case, as the Board found, was for a primary purpose; pressure brought to compel Hudik to agree to it would have been primary; and pressure brought to enforce it when Hudik breached it, whether by ordering prefabricated units himself, as in *National Woodwork,* or by entering a contract that required it to breach it, was no less primary. . . . [47]

Notes

1. In a companion case to *National Woodwork,* the Court held that there was no §8(b)(4)(B) violation where employees represented by one local refused to handle goods in order to preserve traditional work for

[47] Stewart, J., also dissented separately.

other employees of the same employer represented by a sister local.[48] The fact that all the workers were employed by the primary employer rendered the work preservation attempt primary.

The Board and the Second Circuit have held that a union may not preserve work for "members generally" without running afoul of §§8(b)(4) and 8(e). The context was a bargaining agreement clause with a shipowner whereby the owner agreed not to sell the ship to a buyer who would not recognize the union as the representative of its sailors. Since there was no guarantee that the individual sailors manning the ship at that time would continue if it were sold in conformity with the agreement, the clause was deemed the equivalent of a union signatory clause and unlawful.[49]

Is this reasoning inconsistent with *National Woodwork*? As a construction industry case, it is highly likely that the contractors got their carpenters through the union hiring hall and that no particular carpenters were continuously employed.

2. Does the rationale of *National Woodwork* protect a union's attempt to acquire work for the employees it represents but which they have not previously done? In Meat Drivers Local 710 v. NLRB, 335 F.2d 709 (D.C. Cir. 1964), the court held that a union could seek to "recapture" work it had lost some time before; so long as the work fell within the bargaining unit and was "fairly claimable," efforts to secure it were primary. Other court and Board cases have given the doctrine a narrower construction. The *National Woodwork* "sword and shield" analogy is colorful, but what has it to do with the theory on which the case is based or with any policy conceivably underlying the secondary boycott prohibitions?

Does footnote 16 of *Enterprise Assn.* now preclude the "fairly claimable" argument? Isn't the final paragraph of that footnote inconsistent with the Board's finding, apparently approved by the Court, that the clause at issue constituted a valid work preservation attempt?

If a union has monopoly power in the labor market with respect to a certain job task, why would it seek to use this power to acquire other job tasks? Shouldn't the union be satisfied with extracting its maximum monopoly rents with respect to the work that it has? The same question applies to jurisdictional disputes between unions.

3. In *Enterprise Assn.*, what is the majority's test for determining whether an employer is a primary or a secondary? The dissent's? Which has the more persuasive argument on the relevance of *Sand Door*?

Would the majority permit the union to picket Austin? If not, doesn't this mean that there is no primary employer in this situation? If you conclude that the union can picket Austin, aren't you forced also to

[48] Houston Insulation Contractors Assn. v. NLRB, 386 U.S. 664 (1967).
[49] NLRB v. National Maritime Union, 486 F.2d 907 (2d Cir. 1972).

conclude that a union can picket a customer (or potential customer) of its employer to force the customer to swing business the employer's way, thus providing work for the union's members?

Enterprise Assn. may moot the work preservation defense in the construction industry. For example, in the next National Woodwork case the owner's architect should specify prefabricated doors.

NLRB v. INTERNATIONAL LONGSHOREMEN'S ASSN., 440 U.S. 1042 (1980): Prior to World War II the bulk of cargo for shipping by ocean vessels in and out of the Port of New York was loaded and unloaded by members of the International Longshoremen's Union (ILA) on a piece-by-piece basis. After the war, containerized cargo became increasingly popular. The method uses reusable metal containers, which are as large as 8 × 8 × 40 feet. Containers can be moved on and off vessels unopened, and special vessels are constructed to facilitate containerized cargo. A container can be attached to the tractor of a truck and transported to and from the pier like a conventional trailor.

Use of containers substantially reduced shipping costs. It also reduced the work for ILA members, as did the shipping companies' practice of making their containers available to shippers and consolidators for loading and unloading away from the pier. In 1958 the ILA protested the use of large containers. For ten years a controversy between the ILA and the New York Shipping Association over the use of the container was largely unresolved. During some periods loaded containers were handled by the ILA; at other times, the union insisted on reloading containers at the pier. After a 57-day strike in 1969, the ILA and the Shipping Association signed a bargaining agreement providing that containers (1) owned or leased by a Shipping Association member, (2) coming from or going to an employer who would load or unload the containers but was not the beneficial owner of the cargo, or (3) which were coming or going to a point within 50 miles of the Port of New York, would be loaded and unloaded at the dock by ILA members. The agreement stipulated liquidated damages for a violation.

The bargaining agreement was challenged by consolidators located within 50 miles of the port who used non-ILA labor and who were denied containers by members of the shipping association and by truckers who delivered cargo to those consolidators. The Board found the agreement violated §8(e) of the Act. It reasoned that the agreement sought to acquire for ILA members work that had historically been performed not by longshoremen but by employees of the consolidators and truckers.

The Supreme Court reversed the Board, holding that the Board's description of the work in controversy as "the off-pier stuffing and stripping of containers" was "incorrect as a matter of law." The Board "must focus on the work of the bargaining unit employees, not on the work of other employees who may be doing the same or similar work. . . ." The Court noted that if the Board's reasoning was persuasive it followed that *National Woodwork* was incorrectly decided because the Carpenters in that case would have been seeking to acquire work, the factory prefabrication of doors away from the construction site. But the Court drew back from deciding that the ILA in this case was preserving traditional work.

> [T]he Board's determination that the work of longshoremen has historically been the loading and unloading of ships should be only the beginning of analysis. The next step is to look at how the contracting parties sought to preserve that work, to the extent possible, in the face of a massive technological change that largely eliminated the need for cargo handling at intermediate stages of the intermodal transportation of goods, and to evaluate the relationship between traditional longshore work and the work which the Rules attempt to assign to ILA members.

The case was remanded to the Board for that determination.

Four Justices dissented, in an opinion authored by Chief Justice Burger. Agreeing that the case turned on the definition of the work in controversy, he argued that there were alternative perspectives of the work — the perspective of the ILA members and the perspective of the consolidators and truckers.

> A door may be a door in the carpenter's world, and a pipe may be a pipe to the plumber, but a "container" can be seen as sometimes like the hold of a ship, sometimes like the trailer of a truck — and sometimes an independent component.

Notes

1. Footnote 8 of *Enterprise Assn.* indicates that the validity of the work preservation clause itself was not challenged although the Board referred to it as "a valid work preservation clause . . . for the purpose of preserving work they had traditionally performed." However, in earlier right to control cases, complaints charging §8(e) violations were filed but were dismissed by the Board without discussion, although the Board found that refusals to handle violated §8(b)(4)(B). In the *ILA* case, the Board found violations of both sections. These cases suggest there is a problem inherent in the relationship between §§8(b)(4)(B) and 8(e).

The Court in *National Woodwork* told us that a contract clause is to be scrutinized for §8(e) validity at the time the clause is entered into. But if the agreement is valid as written (e.g., *Enterprise Assn.* and *National Woodwork*), is the employer without a remedy when the clause is peacefully enforced in secondary circumstances? Such would have been the case in *Enterprise Assn.* if the union had handled the offending prefabricated units but sued Hudik for breach of contract damages, and in *National Woodwork* if the Carpenters Union had enforced in court a "no prefabricated doors" clause when it was trying to organize the factory. Isn't this the same result that would have been reached after *Sand Door* was decided, and which Congress tried to change by passing §8(e)? Consider the following suggestion:[50]

> There are two ways to attack the problem. One is to consider seeking damages to be "coercion" within the meaning of §8(b)(4)(B); the other is to determine the validity under §8(e) of the underlying obligation in light of the contract's actual construction and administration.
>
> The first approach tends to strain the statutory language. It is clear that a damage suit designed to enforce a "hot cargo" clause permitted under the construction industry proviso to §8(e) does not violate §8(b)(4)(B), even though striking or picketing would. This result suggests that peaceful enforcement does not amount to "coercion" within the meaning of §8(b)(4)(B). Although arguably "coercion" should be defined in the light of §8(e) to include damage actions only if the underlying obligation would violate that section, such a reading makes the word "coercion" troublingly equivocal.
>
> The difficulty with the alternative approach, testing the underlying contract, as administered, against §8(e), is that the statute prohibits "entering into" hot cargo agreements, suggesting that such agreements must be evaluated on their face. The policy underlying this position is to avoid striking down an otherwise valid clause, like a work preservation guarantee, merely because the union has attempted to enforce it in circumstances in which a secondary objective exists. But if a collective bargaining provision is not invalid when so applied, and the union's efforts to obtain damages for breach of the agreement is not "coercion" under §8(b)(4)(B), there will be a dangerous gap in the congressional policy against secondary boycotts. A possible way to plug this loophole is to evaluate agreements not only on their face but as applied; a contract valid on its face but not as applied could be preserved for all other applications.

2. *Problem.* The employees of the Kroger Grocery Company are represented by Local 123, Retail Clerks Union. Kroger is now bargaining for a new collective bargaining agreement. Located in the southeast corner of the Kroger store is the potato chip department. In this area are sold various brands and varieties of prepackaged goods. The union has demanded a bargaining agreement clause reading: "All shelves in the potato chip department shall be stocked by Kroger employees." A Kroger manager reports that included in the potato chip department are:

[50] Leslie, supra n. [46], at 913-914.

a. Kroger brand potato chips, which have always been stocked by Kroger clerks;
b. Treato-Lay Corn Chips, an established product heretofore stocked by employees of the Treato-Lay Company; and
c. Nibbles, a new product made of soybeans shaped as potato chips, which is scheduled to arrive at Kroger in several months.

Is the union's demand lawful?

3. *Problem.* A clause in the bargaining agreement of the Charatan Pipe Company's bargaining agreement, now two years old, with the Pipe Carver's Union reads: "Charatan will not subcontract any bargaining unit work during the term of this agreement without the union's consent." The union recently filed a damage suit alleging that Charatan breached its agreement by subcontracting to the Preben Holm Company the carving of certain prime, straight-grain pipes. Charatan's answer to the complaint admits subcontracting without the union's consent, but alleges further that the union has given its consent to several previous subcontracts. In every instance in which the union has given its consent, Charatan alleges, the subcontractors' employees were represented by the Pipe Carver's Union. Preben Holm, however, is nonunion.

The union moves to strike the defense and for summary judgment on the contract liability issue. What result?

4. *Problem.* Smedlach, Inc. has decided to purchase several ocean vessels and to carry containerized cargo out of the Port of New York. It realizes that to be successful in that port it must sign a bargaining agreement with the International Longshoremen's Association (ILA). It would prefer to have its containers stuffed and stripped by independent consolidators because it understands that consolidator employees are paid less than ILA members. Smedlach wants to know if it can somehow avoid the ramifications of the majority opinion in *NLRB v. International Longshoremen's Assn.* Smedlach says it has four options in organizing its business:

a. Containers can be owned by Smedlach and provided to the consolidators;
b. Containers can be owned by Smedlach and leased to the consolidators;
c. Smedlach and the consolidators can sign a contract obligating Smedlach to accept containers owned by Smedlach and stuffed by the consolidators;
d. Containers can be owned by the consolidators.

Advise Smedlach.

7. Jurisdictional Disputes Between Unions[51]

NLRB v. RADIO & TELEVISION BROADCAST ENGINEERS, LOCAL 1212 [CBS]

364 U.S. 573 (1961)

Black, J.

This case, in which the Court of Appeals refused to enforce a cease-and-desist order of the National Labor Relations Board, grew out of a "jurisdictional dispute" over work assignments between the respondent union, composed of television "technicians," and another union, composed of "stage employees." Both of these unions had collective bargaining agreements in force with the Columbia Broadcasting System and the respondent union was the certified bargaining agent for its members, but neither the certification nor the agreements clearly apportioned between the employees represented by the two unions the work of providing electric lighting for television shows. This led to constant disputes, extending over a number of years, as to the proper assignment of this work, disputes that were particularly acrimonious with reference to "remote lighting," that is, lighting for telecasts away from the home studio. Each union repeatedly urged Columbia to amend its bargaining agreement so as specifically to allocate remote lighting to its members rather than to members of the other union. But, as the Board found, Columbia refused to make such an agreement with either union because "the rival locals had failed to agree on the resolution of this jurisdictional dispute over remote lighting." Thus feeling itself caught "between the devil and the deep blue," Columbia chose to divide the disputed work between the two unions according to criteria improvised apparently for the sole purpose of maintaining peace between the two. But, in trying to satisfy both of the unions, Columbia has apparently not succeeded in satisfying either. During recent years, it has been forced to contend with work stoppages by each of the two unions when a particular assignment was made in favor of the other.

The precise occasion for the present controversy was the decision of Columbia to assign the lighting work for a major telecast from the Waldorf-Astoria Hotel in New York City to the stage employees. When the technicians' protest of this assignment proved unavailing, they refused to operate the cameras for the program and thus forced its cancellation. This caused Columbia to file the unfair labor practice charge which started these proceedings, claiming a violation of §8(b)(4)(D) of the National Labor Relations Act. That section clearly

[51] See Leslie, The Role of the NLRB and the Courts in Resolving Union Jurisdictional Disputes, 75 Colum. L. Rev. 1470 (1975); Player, Work Assignment Disputes under §10(k): Putting the Substantive Cart before the Procedural Horse, 52 Tex. L. Rev. 417 (1974).

makes it an unfair labor practice for a labor union to induce a strike or a concerted refusal to work in order to compel an employer to assign particular work to employees represented by it rather than to employees represented by another union, unless the employer's assignment is in violation of "an order or certification of the Board determining the bargaining representative for employees performing such work. . . ." Obviously, if §8(b)(4)(D) stood alone, what this union did in the absence of a Board order or certification entitling its members to be assigned to these particular jobs would be enough to support a finding of an unfair labor practice in a normal proceeding under §10(c) of the Act. But when Congress created this new type of unfair labor practice by enacting §8(b)(4)(D) as part of the Taft-Hartley Act in 1947, it also added §10(k) to the Act. Section 10(k) quite plainly emphasizes the belief of Congress that it is more important to industrial peace that jurisdictional disputes be settled permanently than it is that unfair labor practice sanctions for jurisdictional strikes be imposed upon unions. Accordingly, §10(k) offers strong inducements to quarrelling unions to settle their differences by directing dismissal of unfair labor practice charges upon voluntary adjustment of jurisdictional disputes. And even where no voluntary adjustment is made, "the Board is empowered and directed," by §10(k), "to hear and determine the dispute out of which such unfair labor practice shall have arisen," and upon compliance by the disputants with the Board's decision the unfair labor practice charges must be dismissed.

In this case respondent failed to reach a voluntary agreement with the stage employees union so the Board held the §10(k) hearing as required to "determine the dispute." The result of this hearing was a decision that the respondent union was not entitled to have the work assigned to its members because it had no right to it under either an outstanding Board order or certification, as provided in §8(b)(4)(D), or a collective bargaining agreement. The Board refused to consider other criteria, such as the employer's prior practices and the custom of the industry, and also refused to make an affirmative award of the work between the employees represented by the two competing unions. The respondent union refused to comply with this decision, contending that the Board's conception of its duty to "determine the dispute" was too narrow in that this duty is not at all limited, as the Board would have it, to strictly legal considerations growing out of prior Board orders, certifications or collective bargaining agreements. It urged, instead, that the Board's duty was to make a final determination, binding on both unions, as to which of the two unions' members were entitled to do the remote lighting work, basing its determination on factors deemed important in arbitration proceedings, such as the nature of the work, the practices and customs of this and other companies and of these and other unions, and upon other factors deemed relevant by the Board in the light of its experience in the field of labor relations. On the basis of its decision in the §10(k) proceeding and the union's challenge to the validity of that decision, the Board issued an order under §10(c) directing the union to cease and desist from striking to compel Columbia to assign remote lighting work to its members. The Court of Appeals for the Second Circuit refused to enforce the cease-and-desist order, accepting the respondent's contention that the Board had failed to make the kind of determination that §10(k) requires. . . .

We agree . . . that §10(k) requires the Board to decide jurisdictional disputes on their merits and conclude that in this case that requirement means that the Board should affirmatively have decided whether the technicians or the stage employees were entitled to the disputed work. The language of §10(k), supplementing §8(b)(4)(D) as it does, sets up a method adopted by Congress to try to get jurisdictional disputes settled. The words "hear and determine the dispute" convey not only the idea of hearing but also the idea of deciding a controversy. And the clause "the dispute out of which such unfair labor practice shall have arisen" can have no other meaning except a jurisdictional dispute under §8(b)(4)(D) which is a dispute between two or more groups of employees over which is entitled to do certain work for an employer. To determine or settle the dispute as between them would normally require a decision that one or the other is entitled to do the work in dispute.[52] Any decision short of that would obviously not be conducive to quieting a quarrel between two groups which, here as in most instances, is of so little interest to the employer that he seems perfectly willing to assign work to either if the other will just let him alone. This language also indicates a congressional purpose to have the Board do something more than merely look at prior Board orders and certifications or a collective bargaining contract to determine whether one or the other union has a clearly defined statutory or contractual right to have the employees it represents perform certain work tasks. For, in the vast majority of cases, such a narrow determination would leave the broader problem of work assignments in the hands of the employer, exactly where it was before the enactment of §10(k) — with the same old basic jurisdictional dispute likely continuing to vex him, and the rival unions, short of striking, would still be free to adopt other forms of pressure upon the employer. The §10(k) hearing would therefore accomplish little but a restoration of the pre-existing situation, a situation already found intolerable by Congress and by all parties concerned. If this newly granted Board power to hear and determine jurisdictional disputes had meant no more than that, Congress certainly would have achieved very little to solve the knotty problem of wasteful work stoppages due to such disputes.

[The Court reviewed the legislative history of §10(k).] The Board

[52] If the striking union wins the §10(k) award it does *not* mean that the work goes to its members. It only means that the union can continue to strike free from the restraints of §8(b)(4)(D). The employer is still free to refuse the union's demand for the work.

contends, however, that this interpretation of §10(k) should be rejected, despite the language and history of that section. In support of this contention, it first points out that §10(k) sets forth no standards to guide it in determining jurisdictional disputes on their merits. From this fact, the Board argues that §8(b)(4)(D) makes the employer's assignment decisive unless he is at the time acting in violation of a Board order or certification and that the proper interpretation of §10(k) must take account of this right of the employer. It is true, of course, that employers normally select and assign their own individual employees according to their best judgment. But here, as in most situations where jurisdictional strikes occur, the employer has contracted with two unions, both of which represent employees capable of doing the particular tasks involved. The result is that the employer has been placed in a situation where he finds it impossible to secure the benefits of stability from either of these contracts, not because he refuses to satisfy the unions, but because the situation is such that he cannot satisfy them. Thus, it is the employer here, probably more than anyone else, who has been and will be damaged by a failure of the Board to make the binding decision that the employer has not been able to make. We therefore are not impressed by the Board's solicitude for the employer's right to do that which he has not been, and most likely will not be, able to do. It is true that this forces the Board to exercise under §10(k) powers which are broad and lacking in rigid standards to govern their application. But administrative agencies are frequently given rather loosely defined powers to cope with problems as difficult as those posed by jurisdictional disputes and strikes. It might have been better, as some persuasively argued in Congress, to intrust this matter to arbitrators. But Congress, after discussion and consideration, decided to intrust this decision to the Board. It has had long experience in hearing and disposing of similar labor problems. With this experience and a knowledge of the standards generally used by arbitrators, unions, employers, joint boards and others in wrestling with this problem, we are confident that the Board need not disclaim the power given it for lack of standards. Experience and common sense will supply the grounds for the performance of this job which Congress has assigned the Board. . . .

The Board's next contention is that respondent's interpretation of §10(k) should be rejected because it is inconsistent with other provisions of the Taft-Hartley Act. The first such inconsistency urged is with §§8(a)(3) and 8(b)(2) of the Act on the ground that the determination of jurisdictional disputes on their merits by the Board might somehow enable unions to compel employers to discriminate in regard to employment in order to encourage union membership. . . . [We] feel entirely confident that the Board, with its many years of experience in guarding against and redressing violations of §§8(a)(3) and 8(b)(2), will devise means of discharging its duties under §10(k) in a manner entirely harmonious with those sections. A second inconsistency is urged with §303 of the Taft-Hartley Act, which authorizes suits for damages suffered because of jurisdictional strikes. The argument here is that since §303 does not permit a union to establish, as a defense to an action for damages under that section, that it is entitled to the work struck for on the basis of such factors as practice or custom, a similar result is required here in order to preserve "the substantive symmetry" between §303 on the one hand and §§8(b)(4)(D) and 10(k) on the other. This argument ignores the fact that this Court has recognized the separate and distinct nature of these two approaches to the problem of handling jurisdictional strikes. Since we do not require a "substantive symmetry" between the two, we need not and do not decide what effect a decision of the Board under §10(k) might have on actions under §303. . . .

We conclude therefore that the Board's interpretation of its duty under §10(k) is wrong and that under that section it is the Board's responsibility and duty to decide which of two or more employee groups claiming the right to perform certain work tasks is right and then specifically to award such tasks in accordance with its decision. Having failed to meet that responsibility in this case, the Board could not properly proceed under §10(c) to adjudicate the unfair labor practice charge. The Court of Appeals was therefore correct in refusing to enforce the order which resulted from that proceeding.

Affirmed.

INTERNATIONAL LONGSHOREMEN'S & WAREHOUSEMEN'S UNION, LOCAL 50 (BRADY-HAMILTON STEVEDORE CO.)

244 N.L.R.B. 275 (1979)

Second Supplemental Decision and Order

The background to this proceeding . . . is as follows. In a proceeding under §10(k) of the National Labor Relations Act . . . the Board awarded to employees represented by the Charging Party (herein called Engineers) work involving the operation of "barge-mounted floating whirly-type cranes," which lift logs from the water for loading on ships at the companies' Astoria, Oregon, operations.[2] The Respondent's refusal to comply with that award gave rise to the present unfair labor practice proceeding in which the Board in its original Decision[3] found that the Respondent engaged in conduct proscribed by §8(b)(4)(i) and (ii)(D) of the Act. In reaching its result, the Board, in effect, confirmed the decision it had reached in the §10(k) proceeding that engineers, and not longshoremen, were entitled to operate the barge-mounted floating

2. 181 N.L.R.B. 315 (1970).
3. 193 N.L.R.B. 266 (1971).

whirley-type cranes. In so concluding the Board held that the factors of skill, efficiency, safety, past practice, and acquiescence favored assignment to engineers. It further concluded that the Respondent's certification and its contract with the Pacific Maritime Association did not cover the disputed work. It gave no weight to the Employers' assignment of the work.

In the subsequent enforcement proceeding, the court[4] agreed with the Board that at the time of the work stoppage giving rise to the dispute the engineers were more skilled, more efficient, and safer crane operators and that past practice and acquiescence favored employees represented by the Engineers. However, the court concluded that the Respondent's agreement did assign the disputed work to longshoremen and that the Employers did prefer that the work be so assigned. The court further concluded that under its policy the Board gives controlling weight to the factors of contract coverage and employer preference and stated in effect that absent "convincing reasoning by the Board to the contrary" it would find the assignment to the engineers arbitrary and capricious. It then remanded the case to the Board for further proceedings consistent with its opinion.

Thus, on remand the Board was faced with the court's findings and conclusions that, as the Board had found, skill, efficiency, safety, past practice, and acquiescence favored assignment to engineers but that contract coverage and employer preference favored assignment to the longshoremen. However, after considering the matter in the light of the court's remand, the Board concluded in its Supplemental Decision and Order that "in the circumstances of this case" it could not attach controlling weight to the factors of contract coverage or assignment of the work and that employer preference "at best equally favors assignment to both longshoremen and operating engineers."[5] It thus reaffirmed its previous conclusion that Respondent had violated the Act as alleged.

The Board has, sua sponte, decided to reconsider the Supplemental Decision and Order and for reasons set forth below rescinds that decision and order and dismisses the complaint in this preceeding. . . .

We accept, as we must, that the court's opinion establishes the law of this case, as we recognized in our Supplemental Decision. Nevertheless, in that Decision we, in effect, redetermined the question of contract coverage, concluded that its extension to cover the work here in dispute was basically nothing more than an ad hoc, ex post facto rationalization of the Respondent's claim for such work and thus, as noted above, this factor was entitled to little weight with respect to the assignment of the disputed work involved in this proceeding. Also, with respect to the Employers' preference we have reexamined the whole question and con-

4. NLRB v. International Longshoremen's & Warehousemen's Union, Local No. 50, 504 F.2d 1209 (9th Cir. 1974).

5. 223 N.L.R.B. at 1039.

cluded that assignment of the work to longshoremen was compelled by the Respondent's coercive tactics, that it thus did not represent a free choice by the Employers, and, consequently, that the Employers' preference favored neither party.

Upon our reconsideration of these matters, we have concluded that the court did not remand this case for the Board to reconsider the issues of contract coverage and employer preference for purposes of the assignment of the disputed work. Rather, the court established as the law of this proceeding that the Respondent's contract with the Pacific Maritime Association without qualification assigned the disputed work to longshoremen and that the Employers preferred that longshoremen perform the work. Consequently, our task under the remand was and is to determine if those factors supporting an award to engineers override the contract coverage and employer preference supporting an award to longshoremen. We hold that they do not.

As the court emphasized, we have consistently placed great weight on the factors of contract coverage and employer preference in making work assignment awards. Here, we awarded the work to the engineers on lesser factors primarily because of our earlier holding rejecting the claim that the Respondent's contract covered the disputed work and finding no unequivocal indication of employer preference for employees represented by Respondent to perform such work. It now having been determined that the contract covers the work, it follows from the provisions of that agreement that the Employers are obligated to train longshoremen to perform the work properly and safely. Thus, the contract anticipated the problem of the lack of longshore expertise and provided a corrective for it. In these circumstances, the weight to be accorded skill, efficiency, and safety in supporting an award to the engineers is greatly diminished. In any event, we now find that, in view of the contract coverage and employer preference, the operation of the floating whirly cranes at Astoria should have been awarded to longshoremen. Consequently, the Respondent, by striking to secure assignment of that work to the employees it represents, did not violate §§8(b)(4)(i) and (ii)(D). We shall, therefore, rescind our Supplemental Decision and Order and dismiss the complaint.

Notes

Consider the following problem.[53] A local of the Carpenters' Union and Metro Construction, a general contractor in the construction industry, enter into a collective bargaining agreement that provides that car-

[53] Parts of the discussion are taken from Leslie, supra n. [46].

penters shall perform the task of attaching metal duct work to wooden ceiling beams on Metro's construction projects. Metro normally retains carpentry work and some other minor work on its projects and subcontracts the rest of it to other employers. While the bargaining agreement is still in effect, Metro subcontracts out the duct installation on a major construction project to Suburban Sheet Metal Company, whose employees are represented by the Sheet Metal Workers' Union. The Carpenters' Union strikes Metro over its breach of contract. Metro files a §8(b)(4)(D) charge.

1. The Carpenters' Union claims it is striking to preserve work traditionally done by its members. Should that be a defense to a jurisdictional dispute charge? In Local 8, ILWU (Waterway Terminals Co.), 185 N.L.R.B. 186 (1970), enforcement denied, 467 F.2d 1011 (9th Cir. 1972), Waterway terminated a subcontract and assigned the previously subcontracted work to its own employees. The union representing the subcontractor's employees picketed Waterway, and Waterway filed a jurisdictional dispute charge. The Board held that this was not a jurisdictional dispute between Waterway's and the subcontractor's employees, but was rather a protest of the loss of work by the subcontractor's employees.

The Board distinguished an earlier precedent by contrasting the situation at issue, in which a union seeks reinstatement of particular discharged employees, from one in which the union seeks the return of work for members to be dispatched from the hiring hall. The Board made it clear that the controlling issue was the union's intent in picketing. Since the union's sole consideration was its demand for restoration of the "job rights of terminated employees," the strike was not to be considered a jurisdictional dispute even though the Board conceded that another union was actively competing for the work. On appeal, the Ninth Circuit reversed, holding that a jurisdictional dispute was present.

2. Should the Carpenters' Union want this dispute to proceed to a §10(k) hearing? The decision of the Ninth Circuit in *Brady-Hamilton* is remarkable for its candor, but probably not for its approach. From 1961 through the end of 1970 the Board affirmed the employer's preference for which union should be awarded the work in 95.1 percent of all §10(k) cases; and 96.5 percent of the awards involving the construction industry confirmed the employer's preference.

The factors the Board purports to consider are the skills of the respective employee groups, company and industry practice, agreements between the unions involved, bargaining agreement guarantees, awards of arbitrators, the employer's preference, and the effect of the award on the employer's efficiency. The coincidence of employer preference and §10(k) award can be explained on the ground that an employer operating in its own economic self-interest will consider the same factors as does the Board, or on the ground that the number of jurisdictional strikes will be reduced if the union to which the employer is disinclined is precluded from striking. Is the latter ground consistent with *CBS*?

Should Metro or Suburban Sheet Metal be considered the "assigning employer" for §10(k) purposes? Consider how the factors will stack up on each alternative. The Board will deem Suburban the assigning employer.

3. The AFL-CIO has had from time to time a private arbitration panel to resolve jurisdictional disputes between affiliated unions. It has been inoperative since 1981. If the Carpenters' Union and the Sheet Metal Workers' Union (but not the employers) take this dispute to an AFL-CIO panel, or similar private panel, for an award of the work to one union or the other, should this be deemed a "voluntary adjustment" under §10(k)? The Supreme Court held no in NLRB v. Plasterers Local 79, 404 U.S. 116 (1971). The employer is deemed one of the "parties to the dispute" under §10(k) and his or her stipulation to the settlement mechanism is a prerequisite for Board deferral.

Employers in most jurisdictional disputes have two interests. First, they wish to remove themselves from the dilemma of being caught between two warring factions, each of whom will strike if the work goes to the other (CBS's "the devil and the deep blue"). Second, they want the work assignment to go according to their preference. Did Congress intend to protect both interests in passing §§8(b)(4)(D) and 10(k)? Should this have been relevant in *Plasterers Local 79*?

4. Suppose instead of, or in addition to, striking, the Carpenters' Union sued Metro for breach of contract damages. The Board has held that if the union seeks damages but refrains from striking there has been no prohibited conduct.[54] The Ninth Circuit has disagreed in the context of a §8(b)(4)(B) violation.[55]

Where the union not receiving the employer's assignment brings a contract damage action, the union receiving it may threaten to strike if the work is taken from its members. This response will draw both unions into a §10(k) hearing (at least the Board so rules), where the Board is very likely to affirm the employer's preference. Is the losing union's breach of contract claim now precluded? In Carey v. Westinghouse Electric Corp., 375 U.S. 261 (1964), the union and the employer had agreed that all breach of contract disputes would be submitted to a private arbitrator (a common practice). The Supreme Court held that the agreement to arbitrate should be enforced even though the breach of contract issue raised by the union arguably involved a jurisdictional or represen-

[54] Local 49, Sheet Metal Workers (Los Alamos Constructors), 206 N.L.R.B. 473 (1973); but see International Longshoremen's Assn. (Consolidated Express), 221 N.L.R.B. 956 (1975) (liquidated damages).

[55] Associated General Contractors of California v. NLRB, 514 F.2d 433 (9th Cir. 1975).

tational dispute with another union subject to NLRB procedures. In stating its reasons, the Court said:

> Should the Board disagree with the arbiter, by ruling, for example, that the employees involved in the controversy are members of one bargaining unit or another, the Board's ruling would, of course, take precedence; and if the employer's action had been in accord with that ruling, it would not be liable for damages. . . .

Lower courts have construed *Carey* to require that a collective bargaining agreement arbitration award cannot be enforced where the Board has ruled contrary to the arbitration award in a §10(k) hearing. Is this required by *Carey*? Is it sound policy?

5. If the Carpenters' Union had struck in order to obtain the bargaining agreement clause guaranteeing it the ductwork, would that have been a §8(b)(4)(D) violation? If you are inclined to think it was, what sort of §10(k) hearing could the Board hold if the Carpenters' Union struck a multiemployer bargaining association of general contractors for a clause guaranteeing the Carpenters all the work spelled out in the Carpenters' constitution (perhaps running several pages) — the agreement to cover all job sites in southern California for the next three years and to include a liquidated damage clause?

6. Local 107, Highway Truck Drivers (Safeway Stores), 134 N.L.R.B. 1320 (1964), the Board held that if one of the unions to a jurisdictional dispute effectively renounces the work, §§10(k) and 8(b)(4)(D) proceedings are aborted because, the Board reasoned, after the disclaimer the only dispute is between the employer and the claiming union.

Exceptions have subsequently all but swallowed up the rule. Where the union disclaims but its employee-members perform the work at the employer's request (perhaps as they are required to do by a collective bargaining agreement), the Board will entertain §8(b)(4)(D) charges and proceed to a §10(k) hearing.[56]

In Local 1291, ILA (Pocahontis Steamship Co.) 152 N.L.R.B. 676 (1965), enforced, 368 F.2d 107 (3d Cir. 1966), cert. denied, 386 U.S. 1033 (1967), the Longshoremen's Union claimed that their members should be given the work of going on board a Pocahontis ship and operating an electrical switch to open and close hatches. Ship employees, represented by the National Maritime Union, at all times advised the Board that their members made no claim whatsoever to this particular work and would refuse to do it. The Board found the disclaimer not

[56] But see Teamsters Local 85 (United California Express & Storage Co.), 236 N.L.R.B. 157 (1978), where the Board held, 3-2, that a union's disclaimer was not invalidated when its members continued to claim the work. Prior cases were distinguished on the ground that union officers had condoned or given affirmative support to the members' claims even while officially disclaiming the work on the union's behalf.

controlling on the ground that the seamen represented by the Maritime Union were compensated on a monthly salary basis and would therefore suffer no hardship by giving up the work. Although the employees in fact refused to do the work when ordered by their employer, the Board ruled that "they cannot lawfully refuse because to do so would involve a breach of their collective-bargaining contract and possible infringement of applicable maritime law."

Was this a jurisdictional dispute? Would the case apply to a jurisdictional dispute on a construction job site?

7. The typical §10(k) award reads: "We determine the dispute before us by awarding the work in dispute to those employees represented by [Local 1], but not to that union or its members."

Does that solve the §§8(a)(3) and 8(b)(2) preferential hiring problems? Suppose there are competing demands but no strike or strike threat. Would an employer violate §8(a)(3) by taking disputed work away from one employee group and giving it to another?[57]

8. Damages for §8(b)(4) Violations

Section 303 provides a civil damage remedy in federal district court for violations of §8(b)(4). Either a primary or a secondary employer may sue. Neither punitive damages nor an injunction is permissible in a §303 suit. State remedies for secondary boycotts are preempted by §303 although state causes of action for violence remain and a federal court may take pendent jurisdiction over such a claim.[58]

Section 303 suits and §8(b)(4) Board proceedings have been deemed independent. A §303 suit may be brought before, during, or after Board unfair labor practice proceedings. In companion cases in 1952, the Sixth Circuit affirmed a Board ruling that a union had not violated §8(b)(4) and at the same time affirmed a damage award against the union pursuant to §303.[59] But where the Board rules on the §8(b)(4) complaint before a §303 judgment is entered, the majority of recent cases have held the Board decision is res judicata in the §303 action. If the union loses before the Board, it has had a chance to fully litigate the merits; but if the union wins before the Board, has the employer had a full opportunity to litigate?

Suppose the union in a dispute with employer *A* pickets employer *B*

[57] See Brady-Hamilton Stevedore Co., 198 N.L.R.B. 147 (1972) (held, 3-2, no violation where strike threat), petition for review denied, 504 F.2d 1222 (9th Cir. 1974); contra, Teamsters Local 484 (Oroweat Baking Co.), 214 N.L.R.B. 941 (1974).

[58] Teamsters Local 20 v. Morton, 377 U.S. 252 (1964).

[59] United Brick & Clay Workers v. Deena Artware, 198 F.2d 637 (6th Cir. 1952); NLRB v. Deena Artware, 198 F.2d 645 (6th Cir. 1952), cert. denied, 345 U.S. 906 (1953).

claiming *B* is an ally. The General Counsel issues a §8(b)(4)(B) complaint and secures a §10(l) injunction, which halts all picketing. Subsequently the economic dispute between the union and the employer *A* is permanently settled. Should the Board now decide the merits of the §8(b)(4)(B) complaint and enter a cease and desist order, or should it dismiss the complaint as moot?

4

NEGOTIATION OF COLLECTIVE BARGAINING AGREEMENTS

A. BARGAINING IN GOOD FAITH[1]

Sections 8(a)(5), 8(b)(3), and 8(d) set out the duty to bargain in good faith that is imposed on both employers and unions. The several themes that run through this chapter all fall under the general inquiry: How are the Board and the courts to judge negotiations for the presence or absence of good faith? Mindreading isn't possible; thus the Board is forced to look at the procedures of bargaining, the content of economic positions (as evidenced by proposals), or both.

Militating against any inquiry into bargaining content is the value placed on freedom to contract. One purpose of the national labor laws is to create a framework within which employers and unions can freely hammer out bargaining agreements, the terms to be premised on the sincere wish to reach an agreement and determined by the persuasiveness and relative economic power of the employer and the union. Consider four of the responses that might be made by an employer faced with a union's demand to bargain: The employer flatly refuses to meet with the union; the employer meets, listens to union proposals, and rejects them without making any counterproposals; the employer meets, listens, and demands an agreement giving the employer unfettered management discretion over all matters; and the employer meets, listens, and offers unreasonable substantive proposals.

Presumably everyone would agree that the first option violates the duty to bargain. But consider: If the employer has sufficient relative economic power to adopt this tactic even though the employees have collectivized, is not its use appropriate in a framework emphasizing gov-

[1] See Cox, The Duty to Bargain in Good Faith, 71 Harv. L. Rev. 1401 (1958); Gross, Cullen & Hanslowe, Good Faith in Labor Negotiations: Tests and Remedies, 53 Cornell L. Rev. 1009 (1968); Smith, Evolution of the "Duty to Bargain" Concept in American Law, 39 Mich. L. Rev. 1065 (1941).

ernment nonintervention in substantive bargaining? The countervailing argument is that the employer should not be permitted to exercise his or her economic power to this end because of the end's inconsistency with the premise of a sincere attempt to reach a bargaining agreement.

Does this premise also outlaw the other three employer responses? The question becomes particularly knotty when you consider the issue of the reasonableness of positions. Is an offer far below the expectation of the union, or of the employees, to be deemed unreasonable? Or is it the expectation of the Board that counts? The reasonableness of an employer's proposals should, in the employer's view, depend on the economic context: the ability of the union to call the employees out on strike, the ease of securing replacements, the propensity of secondary employees to honor a picket line, the employer's position in the product market, and so on. But, the union argues, the employer's relative economic strength does not permit it to refuse to bargain. Where is government intervention to yield to freedom to exercise economic power? And throughout that inquiry, the critical corollary: What remedy for a refusal to bargain?

NLRB v. AMERICAN NATIONAL INSURANCE CO., 343 U.S. 395 (1952): The newly certified Office Employees Union, seeking its first collective bargaining agreement with the employer, submitted a proposed contract covering such issues as wages, hours, and promotions and including a clause establishing a grievance procedure that culminated in grievance arbitration during the life of the contract. While the employer agreed to a few of the union's terms, the bulk of the union's demands were met with a counterproposal for the following clause:

> The right to select and hire, to promote to a better position, to discharge, demote or discipline for cause, and to maintain discipline and efficiency of employees and to determine the schedules of work is recognized by both union and company as the proper responsibility and prerogative of management to be held and exercised by the company, and while it is agreed that an employee feeling himself to have been aggrieved by any decision of the company in respect to such matters, or the union in his behalf, shall have the right to have such decision reviewed by top management officials of the company under the grievance machinery hereinafter set forth, it is further agreed that the final decision of the company made by such top management officials shall not be further reviewable by arbitration.

The Board found that the employer's insistence on such a clause was a per se violation of §8(a)(5).

In the Supreme Court, the Board conceded that a "management functions" clause was not necessarily an unlawful contract term and, in various forms, was a common industrial practice. Nor was the employer's refusal of the union's arbitration demand a violation. The Board argued that the challenged clause covered "conditions of employment," which are appropriate bargaining subjects under §§8(d) and 9(a), and that to fulfill its bargaining obligation the employer must, at a minimum, agree to include in a contract fixed standards for work schedules and other terms and conditions of employment. Since the challenged clause provided no fixed standards but accorded complete flexibility to management, it could be requested but not insisted upon.

The Supreme Court, per Vinson, C. J., rejected the Board's argument and its result. First emphasizing that the Act is designed to promote collective bargaining without regulating the content of agreements or even compelling agreement itself, the Court stated that

> the Act does not encourage a party to engage in fruitless marathon discussions at the expense of frank statement and support of his position. And it is equally clear that the Board may not, either directly or indirectly, compel concessions or otherwise sit in judgment upon the substantive terms of collective bargaining agreements.

It followed that the Board's finding of a per se violation had to be rejected:

> Any fears the Board may entertain that use of management functions clauses will lead to evasion of an employer's duty to bargain collectively as to "rates of pay, wages, hours and conditions of employment" do not justify condemning all bargaining for management functions clauses covering any "condition of employment" as per se violations of the Act. The duty to bargain collectively is to be enforced by application of the good faith bargaining standards of §8(d) to the facts of each case rather than by prohibiting all employers in every industry from bargaining for management functions clauses altogether.

Notes

1. Evaluate the following employer statements to the union:

a. "We won't bargain with you."
b. "Our bargaining demand is that we retain the absolute right to set wages and manage the business and we want a bargaining agreement clause to that effect."

Isn't the Supreme Court telling the Board that the first statement is a violation but the second is not? Consider the following commentary:[2]

[2] Cox & Dunlop, Regulation of Collective Bargaining by the National Labor Relations Board, 63 Harv. L. Rev. 389, 403-405, 421-422 (1950).

A priori the bare words of §8(a)(5) are open to two conflicting interpretations, which may be stated somewhat argumentatively as follows: *First.* Section 8(a)(5) makes it an unfair labor practice "to refuse to bargain collectively" with the representative designated by a majority of the employees. Section 9(a) plainly declares that the representative's authority extends to "rates of pay, wages, hours of employment, or other conditions of employment." Therefore, the employer must bargain with respect to each such subject and . . . a refusal to discuss a subject covered by the quoted phrase is an unfair labor practice. Nor can this duty be satisfied by going through the forms of bargaining; the employer must have an open mind and sincere desire to reach an agreement. But although an employer must discuss every subject embraced within §9(a), he complies with the duty to bargain if he negotiates in good faith any question as to whether a specific term or condition of employment (1) should be established by the collective agreement; or (2) should be fixed periodically by joint management-union determination within the framework of the contract; or (3) should be left to management's discretion or individual bargaining without the intervention of the bargaining agent.

Second. Under §§8(a)(5) and 9(a) an employer must bargain collectively with respect to each subject embraced within the quoted phrase. The essential policy of the statute is that industrial peace can be achieved by taking from management exclusive control over wages, hours, and the other aspects of the employment relationship defined by §9(a). For that reason the Supreme Court and courts of appeals have repeatedly held that §8(a)(5) makes unilateral action by an employer an unfair labor practice. The employer who insists upon unilateral control of any "condition of employment" is therefore guilty of an unfair labor practice even though he backs his position by argument and negotiates in good faith.

The choice between these interpretations will determine how the line is to be drawn between the area of exclusive management functions on the one side and the sphere of joint management-union responsibility on the other. Similar questions will have to be decided in drawing a line between the sphere of joint responsibility and the union's internal affairs. Under the first interpretation the lines would be drawn by managements and unions in the course of their annual contract negotiations and, if they could not agree, by recourse to economic weapons. Under the second interpretation the line would be drawn by the NLRB and the courts. Since pensions and merit increases are held to be covered by §9(a), management could not bargain for exclusive responsibility without running afoul of §8(a)(5); decisions with respect to them would have to be joint decisions. Similarly the Board and courts would decide as issues of statutory construction whether letting subcontracts and scheduling shifts are management's functions or problems requiring joint determination. We believe not only that the former method of allocating responsibility is the wiser alternative but also that it rests on the sounder interpretation of the NLRA. . . .

[E]ven if we may assume that it is an unfair labor practice for an employer to insist even in good faith upon retaining the power to take unilateral action with respect to all proper subjects of collective bargaining, non constat that it is an unfair labor practice to take that position in good faith with respect to some proper subjects of collective bargaining. The latter proposition is not the logical corollary of the former. The two have different significance in the evolution of collective bargaining relations and different practical consequences. Furthermore there is no employee participation when workers are forced to strike in order to induce the employer to surrender control over even one term of employment. But employees whose representatives negotiate the familiar collective bargaining agreements containing a management clause not only share in fixing the terms and conditions of their employment taken as a whole but participate, as shown above, in the disposition of matters authority over which is reserved to management. . . . [S]ince employers who genuinely accept the principles of collective bargaining do not refuse to make any commitment to the union, a company's insistence upon retaining freedom to change every term or condition of employment is convincing evidence that any negotiations were a sham because the company's mind was sealed "against even the thought of entering into an agreement with the union." Possibly the inference of bad faith can be drawn from an employer's insistence upon retaining freedom to make unilateral changes in the basic wage scale even though he offers to agree on other items. Minimum wage rates are so widely regarded as matters for joint determination that in the absence of extraordinary circumstances one would suspect that the employer who sought to make them his prerogative was endeavoring to avoid contracting with the union. Common knowledge and experience do not furnish the necessary basis for such an inference, however, in the case of the employer who, while he treats wages, hours, and many other terms of employment as matters for joint determination in a collective bargaining agreement, seeks also to have responsibility for particular items such as merit increases and subcontracting allocated to management.

2. One court's interpretation of *American National:*

It is true, as stated in NLRB v. American National Ins. Co., that the Board may not "sit in judgement upon the substantive terms of collective bargaining agreements." But at the same time is seems clear that if the Board is not to be blinded by empty talk and by the mere surface motions of collective bargaining, it must take some cognizance of the reasonableness of the positions taken by an employer in the course of bargaining negotiations.

Thus if an employer can find nothing whatever to agree to in an ordinary current-day contract submitted to him, or in some of the union's related minor requests, and if the employer makes not a single serious proposal meeting the union at least part way, then certainly the Board must be able to conclude that this is at least some evidence of bad faith, that is, of a desire not to reach an agreement with the union. In other words, while the Board cannot force an employer to make a 'concession' on any specific issue or to adopt any particular position, the employer is obliged to make *some* reasonable effort in *some* direction to compose his differences with the union, if §8(a)(5) is to be read as imposing any substantial obligation at all. NLRB v. Reed & Prince Mfg. Co., 205 F.2d 131, 134-135 (1st Cir. 1953).

3. *Problem.* The employer proposes a 50¢ per hour across the board wage increase and other minor benefit improvements to a newly certified union. The union refuses the offer and recommends a strike to the employees. The employees vote not to strike. The union requests another session with the employer "for further bargaining"; and when the parties meet, the employer announces that he is reducing his offer to a 20¢ per hour increase. Section 8(a)(5) violation? If so, what remedy?

NLRB v. INSURANCE AGENTS' INTERNATIONAL UNION, 361 U.S. 477 (1960). In an attempt to bring economic pressure against an insurance company, the union, representing district agents, announced a "Work Without a Contract" program. Member agents refused for a time to solicit new business, refused to follow reporting procedures, arrived late at work, refused to attend business conferences and picketed various company offices. The Board found that while the union had a sincere desire to reach an agreement, its tactics constituted a violation of §8(b)(3).

The Supreme Court, per Brennan, J., disagreed.

> [We] think the Board's approach involves an intrusion into the substantive aspects of the bargaining process—again, unless there is some specific warrant for its condemnation of the precise tactics involved here. The scope of §8(b)(3) and the limitations on Board power which were the design of §8(d) are exceeded, we hold, by inferring a lack of good faith not from any deficiencies of the union's performance at the bargaining table by reason of its attempted use of economic pressure, but solely and simply because tactics designed to exert economic pressure were employed during the course of the good-faith negotiations. Thus the Board in the guise of determining good or bad faith in negotiations could regulate what economic weapons a party might summon to its aid. And if the Board could regulate the choice of economic weapons that may be used as part of collective bargaining, it would be in a position to exercise considerable influence upon the substantive terms on which the parties contract. As the parties' own devices became more limited, the Government might have to enter even more directly into the negotiation of collective agreements. Our labor policy is not presently erected on a foundation of government control of the results of negotiations. Nor does it contain a charter for the National Labor Relations Board to act at large in equalizing disparities of bargaining power between employer and union.

Agreeing arguendo that the agents were engaged in unprotected activity, thus permitting them to be discharged by the employer, the Court found that to be irrelevant to the issue of good faith bargaining.

NLRB v. TRUITT MANUFACTURING CO.
351 U.S. 149 (1956)

BLACK, J. . . .

The question presented by this case is whether the National Labor Relations Board may find that an employer has not bargained in good faith where the employer claims it cannot afford to pay higher wages but refuses requests to produce information substantiating its claim.

The dispute here arose when a union representing certain of respondent's employees asked for a wage increase of 10 cents per hour. The company answered that it could not afford to pay such an increase, it was undercapitalized, had never paid dividends, and that an increase of more than 2½ cents per hour would put it out of business. The union asked the company to produce some evidence substantiating these statements, requesting permission to have a certified public accountant examine the company's books, financial data, etc. This request being denied, the union asked that the company submit "full and complete information with respect to its financial standing and profits," insisting that such information was pertinent and essential for the employees to determine whether or not they should continue to press their demand for a wage increase. A union official testified before the trial examiner that "[W]e were wanting anything relating to the Company's position, any records or what have you, books, accounting sheets, cost expenditures, what not, anything to back the Company's position that they were unable to give any more money." The company refused all the requests, relying solely on the statement that "the information . . . is not pertinent to this discussion and the company declines to give you such information; you have no legal right to such."

[The Board found a §8(a)(5) violation and ordered the information supplied.] The company raised no objection to the Board's order on the ground that the scope of information required was too broad or that disclosure would put an undue burden on the company. Its major argument throughout has been that the information requested was irrelevant to the bargaining process and related to matters exclusively within the province of management. Thus we lay to one side the suggestion by the company here that the Board's order might be unduly burdensome or injurious to its business. In any event, the Board has therefore taken the position in cases such as this that "It is sufficient if the information is made available in a manner not so burdensome or time-consuming as to impede the process of bargaining." And in this case the Board has held substantiation of the company's position requires no more than "reasonable proof."

We think that in determining whether the obligation of good-faith bargaining has been met the Board has a right to consider an employer's refusal to give information about its financial status. While Congress did not compel agreement between employers and bargaining representatives, it did require collective bargaining in the hope that agreements would result. Section 204(a)(1) of the Act admonishes both employers and employees to "exert every reasonable effort to make and maintain agreements concerning rates of pay, hours, and working conditions. . . ." In their effort to reach an agreement here both the union and the company treated the company's ability to pay increased wages as highly relevant. The ability of an employer to increase wages without injury to his business is a commonly considered factor in wage negotiations. Claims for increased wages have sometimes been abandoned because of an employer's unsatisfactory business condition; employees have even voted to accept wage decreases because of such conditions.

Good-faith bargaining necessarily requires that claims made by either bargainer should be honest claims. This is true about an asserted inability to pay an increase in wages. If such an argument is important enough to present in the give and take of bargaining, it is important enough to require some sort of proof of its accuracy. And it would certainly not be farfetched for a trier of fact to reach the conclusion that bargaining lacks good faith when an employer mechanically repeats a claim of inability to pay without making the slightest effort to substantiate the claim. . . . We agree with the Board that a refusal to attempt to substantiate a claim of inability to pay increased wages may support a finding of a failure to bargain in good faith.

The Board concluded that under the facts and circumstances of this case the respondent was guilty of an unfair labor practice in failing to bargain in good faith. We see no reason to disturb the findings of the Board. We do not hold, however, that in every case in which economic inability is raised as an argument against increased wages it automatically follows that the employees are entitled to substantiating evidence. Each case must turn upon its particular facts. The inquiry must always be whether or not under the circumstances of the particular case the statutory obligation to bargain in good faith has been met.

Notes

1. Did the Truitt Co. lack a sincere desire to reach an agreement? If that inquiry is irrelevant, are *Truitt* and *Insurance Agents'* consistent?

2. Is the Court suggesting that the refusal of the Truitt Co. to substantiate a plea of economic inability was merely one factor supporting an overall finding of subjective bad faith? What other evidence in the case supports such a finding? If you discover none, what does it mean to say that "[e]ach case must turn upon its particular facts"?

3. Why should an employer plea of inability to pay be a prerequisite to a disclosure duty? Might not the union need this information to formulate bargaining demands independent of such a plea? The union might ask, for example, for figures disclosing the labor component of production costs. The Board has held that employers have a duty to disclose wage data during negotiations, and must disclose information necessary for the union to administer a bargaining agreement.[3] On the other hand, the Supreme Court has held that a firm's interest in preserving the secrecy of psychological test scores is sufficient to deny a union's disclosure request, and to deny a similar request for individual test scores absent the employee's consent.[4]

Is the role of a legally imposed duty to disclose information different in a relational contracts model from its role in a collective goods model? Has it any role in a price theory model?

4. Does the employer have a reciprocal right to information? For example, can an employer insist on being told what economic demands the union has made on the employer's competitors, or the terms of the union's other bargaining agreements? What sorts of union statements, if any, would trigger a disclosure duty?

NLRB v. KATZ
369 U.S. 736 (1962)

Brennan, J.

Is it a violation of the duty "to bargain collectively" imposed by §8(a)(5) of the National Labor Relations Act for an employer, without first consulting a union with which it is carrying on bona fide contract negotiations, to institute changes regarding matters which are subjects of mandatory bargaining under §8(d) and which are in fact under discussion? The National Labor Relations Board answered the question affirmatively in this case, in a decision which expressly disclaimed any finding that the totality of the respondents' conduct manifested bad faith in the pending negotiations. A divided panel of the Court of Appeals for the Second Circuit denied enforcement of the Board's cease-and-desist order, finding in our decision in National Labor Relations Board v. Insurance Agents' Union, 361 U.S. 477, a broad rule that the statutory duty to bargain cannot be held to be violated, when bargaining is in fact being carried on, without a finding of the respondent's subjective bad faith in negotiating.

[The employer unilaterally granted merit increases, a system of automatic wage increases and a new sick-leave policy although those subjects

[3] See NLRB v. Acme Industrial Co., 385 U.S. 432 (1967).
[4] Detroit Edison Co. v. NLRB, 440 U.S. 301 (1979).

were under discussion in negotiations and no bargaining impasse had been reached.]

The duty "to bargain collectively" enjoined by §8(a)(5) is defined by §8(d) as the duty to "meet . . . and confer in good faith with respect to wages, hours, and other terms and conditions of employment." Clearly, the duty thus defined may be violated without a general failure of subjective good faith; for there is no occasion to consider the issue of good faith if a party has refused even to negotiate *in fact* — "to meet . . . and confer" — about any of the mandatory subjects. A refusal to negotiate *in fact* as to any subject which is within §8(d), and about which the union seeks to negotiate, violates §8(a)(5) though the employer has every desire to reach agreement with the union upon an over-all collective agreement and earnestly and in all good faith bargains to that end. We hold that an employer's unilateral change in conditions of employment under negotiation is similarly a violation of §8(a)(5), for it is a circumvention of the duty to negotiate which frustrates the objectives of §8(a)(5) much as does a flat refusal.[11]

The unilateral actions of the respondent illustrate the policy and practical considerations which support our conclusion. We consider first the matter of sick leave. A sick-leave plan had been in effect since May 1956, under which employees were allowed ten paid sick-leave days annually and could accumulate half the unused days, or up to five days each year. Changes in the plan were sought and proposals and counterproposals had come up at three bargaining conferences. In March 1957, the company, without first notifying or consulting the union, announced changes in the plan, which reduced from ten to five the number of paid sick-leave days per year, but allowed accumulation of twice the unused days, thus increasing to ten the number of days which might be carried over. This action plainly frustrated the statutory objective of establishing working conditions through bargaining. Some employees might view the change to be a diminution of benefits. Others, more interested in accumulating sick-leave days, might regard the change as an improvement. If one view or the other clearly prevailed among the employees, the unilateral action might well mean that the employer had either uselessly dissipated trading material or aggravated the sick-leave issue. On the other hand, if the employees were more evenly divided on the merits of the company's changes, the union negotiators, beset by conflicting factions, might be led to adopt a protective vagueness on the issue of sick leave, which also would inhibit the useful discussion contemplated by Congress in imposing the specific obligation to bargain collectively.

Other considerations appear from consideration of the respondents'

11. Compare NLRB v. Crompton-Highland Mills, 337 U.S. 217. . . . Crompton-Highland Mills sustained the Board's conclusion that the employer's unilateral grant of a wage increase substantially greater than any it had offered to the union during negotiations which had ended in impasse clearly manifested bad faith and violated the employer's duty to bargain.

unilateral action in increasing wages. At the April 4, 1957, meeting the employers offered, and the union rejected, a three-year contract with an immediate across-the-board increase of $7.50 per week, to be followed at the end of the first year and again at the end of the second by further increases of $5 for employees earning less than $90 at those times. Shortly thereafter, without having advised or consulted with the union, the company announced a new system of automatic wage increases whereby there would be an increase of $5 every three months up to $74.99 per week; an increase of $5 every six months between $75 and $90 per week; and a merit review every six months for employees earning over $90 per week. It is clear at a glance that the automatic wage increase system which was instituted unilaterally was considerably more generous than that which had shortly theretofore been offered to and rejected by the union. Such action conclusively manifested bad faith in the negotiations, NLRB v. Crompton-Highland Mills, 337 U.S. 217, and so would have violated §8(a)(5) even on the Court of Appeals' interpretation, though no additional evidence of bad faith appeared. An employer is not required to lead with his best offer; he is free to bargain. But even after an impasse is reached he has no license to grant wage increases greater than any he has ever offered the union at the bargaining table, for such action is necessarily inconsistent with a sincere desire to conclude an agreement with the union.[12]

The respondents' third unilateral action related to merit increases, which are also a subject of mandatory bargaining. The matter of merit increases had been raised at three of the conferences during 1956 but no final understanding had been reached. In January 1957, the company, without notice to the union, granted merit increases to 20 employees out of the approximately 50 in the unit, the increases ranging between $2 and $10. This action too must be viewed as tantamount to an outright refusal to negotiate on that subject, and therefore as a violation of §8(a)(5), unless the fact that the January raises were in line with the company's long-standing practice of granting quarterly or semiannual merit reviews — in effect, were a mere continuation of the status quo — differentiates them from the wage increases and the changes in the sick-leave plan. We do not think it does. Whatever might be the case as to so-called "merit raises" which are in fact simply automatic increases to which the employer has already committed himself, the raises here in question were in no sense automatic, but were informed by a large measure of discretion. There simply is no way in such case for a union to know whether or not there has been a substantial departure from past practice, and therefore the union may properly insist that the company negotiate as to the procedures and criteria for determining such increases.

12. Of course, there is no resemblance between this situation and one wherein an employer, after notice and consultation, "unilaterally" institutes a wage increase identical with one which the union has rejected as too low.

It is apparent from what we have said why we see nothing in *Insurance Agents'* contrary to the Board's decision. The union in that case had not in any way whatever foreclosed discussion of any issue, by unilateral actions or otherwise. The conduct complained of consisted of partial-strike tactics designed to put pressure on the employer to come to terms with the union negotiators. We held that Congress had not, in §8(b)(3), the counterpart of §8(a)(5), empowered the Board to pass judgment on the legitimacy of any particular economic weapon used in support of genuine negotiations. But the Board *is* authorized to order the cessation of behavior which is in effect a refusal to negotiate, or which directly obstructs or inhibits the actual process of discussion, or which reflects a cast of mind against reaching agreement. Unilateral action by an employer without prior discussion with the union does amount to a refusal to negotiate about the affected conditions of employment under negotiation, and must of necessity obstruct bargaining, contrary to the congressional policy. It will often disclose an unwillingness to agree with the union. It will rarely be justified by any reason of substance. It follows that the Board may hold such unilateral action to be an unfair labor practice in violation of §8(a)(5), without also finding the employer guilty of over-all subjective bad faith. While we do not foreclose the possibility that there might be circumstances which the Board could or should accept as excusing or justifying unilateral action, no such case is presented here. . . .

Reversed and remanded.[5]

Notes

1. A toy store negotiating with its clerks in early November fears a strike near Christmas will severely damage its business. The union is currently demanding a $2 per hour increase, and the store has offered a 50¢ per hour increase. The store now announces a 50¢ per hour pay cut, effective immediately. Lawful (*Insurance Agents'* and *American Ship Building*) or unlawful (*Katz*)?

Suppose, on the same facts, the store has been struck three weeks before Christmas. The store offers replacements $1 per hour more than the current rate (and 50¢ per hour more than its offer to the union). Violation?

2. The Board regularly holds that a unilateral decrease in economic benefits by an employer prior to a bargaining impasse is unlawful. Consider the following by a commentator arguing that where an employer unilaterally decreases employment benefits such as wages or holiday pay, *American Ship Building* forecloses the Board from finding a violation:

[5] Frankfurter, J., and White, J., took no part in the decision.

> Let us now assume that the employer intends, or hopes, the unilateral decrease to be permanent. First, despite the employer's intention, it is difficult to imagine, as a general matter, the unilateral decrease accomplishing a split between the union and the employees. This is true because neither the union nor the employees welcome the decrease, and they will fight to have it rescinded and to have the loss restored. Therefore, if the union and employees are strong enough, the decrease will be temporary only. On the other hand, if the employer can make the decrease "stick," why should he have to wait until there is an impasse in bargaining? Second, the change cannot possibly discourage discussion of the issue at the bargaining table, nor will it wean the employees from the union. After all, it was the desire to have better conditions of employment that motivated the employees to designate the union in the first place, and if conditions get worse, the general assumption must be that the need for a union is greater; also, the effect of the decrease will be to force the employees more closely together, perhaps into united outrage, in response to the employer's conduct. None of the underlying reasoning that justifies finding a violation where there is a unilateral increase is applicable where the unilateral action is a decrease in employment benefits. The employees will hardly become satisfied with the change or desire it permanently. The union will not feel inhibited in demanding a repeal. There will be no appreciable effect on the bargaining since, presumably, the employer had already proposed, or was about to propose, or could propose, the change and, accordingly, the matter was an item for negotiations in any event.[6]

Convinced?

3. Once the bargaining agreement between the employer and the union has expired, the employer is contractually free to change wages, hours, and working conditions. This freedom is substantially qualified by §8(a)(5) and the holding in *Katz.* Conceivably, every term of an expired bargaining agreement covering a mandatory subject to bargaining might be immune from unilateral change. However, employers have been permitted to unilaterally discontinue union shop and checkoff provisions, but not super-seniority for union officials or the grievance procedure.[7]

[6] Schatzki, The Employer's Unilateral Act— A Per Se Violation — Sometimes, 44 Tex. L. Rev. 470, 502-503 (1966).

[7] See NLRB v. Cone Mills Corp., 373 F.2d 595, 597 (4th Cir. 1967); Marine & Shipbuilding Workers v. NLRB, 320 F.2d 615 (3d Cir. 1963). In Hilton-Davis Chem. Co., 185 N.L.R.B. 241 (1970), the employer was permitted to unilaterally suspend arbitration procedure after contract termination. The *Hilton-Davis* case was apparently overruled in American Sink Top & Cabinet Co., 242 N.L.R.B. 408 (1979). The Board relied on the Supreme Court's decision in Nolde Bros. v. Local Bakery Workers Local 358, 430 U.S. 243 (1977), at p. 712, infra, to hold the employer violated §8(a)(5) when he unilaterally terminated an expired bargaining agreement's arbitration clause by refusing to arbitrate the grievance of an employee discharged after the agreement expired. Can you devise a principle for determining to which provisions of an expired bargaining agreement the *Katz* duty to bargain should attach?

NLRB v. GENERAL ELECTRIC CO.

418 F.2d 736 (2d Cir. 1959), cert. denied, 397 U.S. 965 (1970)

KAUFMAN, J. . . .

General Electric, a New York Corporation, is the largest and perhaps best known manufacturer of electrical equipment, appliances, and the like. Its products — manufactured in all the 50 states — range from refrigerators to atomic energy plants, from submarines to light bulbs. In 1960, it employed about 250,000 men and women; of these only 120,000 were unionized. The IUE is an international union, affiliated with the AFL-CIO, and had a total membership of about 300,000. In 1960 it represented some 70,000 of the 120,000 unionized GE employees, formally grouped in more than 105 bargaining units, and was far and away the largest single union with whom GE dealt. The next largest, the United Electrical Workers (UE), represented only 10,000 members, and the remaining 50,000 unionized employees were split among some 100-odd other unions or bargaining agents who dealt independently with GE. A high proportion of GE employees are supervisory or managerial personnel, who are available to the company in the event of a strike.

The present action has its roots deep in the history of prior negotiations and bargaining relationships. Before 1950, the major union was the UE. In 1946, negotiations reached an impasse and resulted in a serious and crippling strike. GE eventually capitulated, and agreed to a settlement that it later characterized as a "debacle," and beyond the company's ability to meet.

GE's response came in the form of a new approach to employee relations, urged by one of its vice presidents, Lemuel R. Boulware. Although GE generally objects to use of the term, describing it as a "hostile label," the tactic of "Boulwareism" associated with his name soon became the hallmark of the company's entire attitude towards its employees.

In many respects, GE's negotiating policy after the 1946 strike followed a predictable course. The Company had been concerned over the antipathy many of the employees displayed during the strike. It decided that it was no longer enough to act in a manner that it thought becoming for a "good" employer; it had to insure that the employees recognized and appreciated the Company's efforts in their behalf. The problem was perceived as a failure to apply GE's highly successful consumer product merchandising techniques to the employment relations field.

The new plan was threefold. GE began by soliciting comments from its local management personnel on the desires of the work force, and the type and level of benefits that they expected. These were then translated into specific proposals, and their cost and effectiveness researched, in order to formulate a "product" that would be attractive to the employees, and within the Company's means. The last step was the most important, most innovative, and most often criticized. GE took its "product" —

now a series of fully-formed bargaining proposals — and "sold" it to its employees and the general public. Through a veritable avalanche of publicity, reaching awesome proportions prior to and during negotiations, GE sought to tell its side of the issues to its employees. It described its proposals as a "fair, firm offer," characteristic of its desire to "do right voluntarily," without the need for any union pressure or strike. In negotiations, GE announced that it would have nothing to do with the "blood-and-threat-and-thunder" approach, in which each side presented patently unreasonable demands, and finally chose a middle ground that both knew would be the probable outcome even before the beginning of the bargaining. The Company believed that such tactics diminished the company's credibility in the eyes of its employees, and at the same time appeared to give the union credit for wringing from the Company what it had been willing to offer all along. Henceforth GE would hold nothing back when it made its offer to the Union; it would take all the facts into consideration, and make that offer it thought right under all the circumstances. Though willing to accept Union suggestions based on facts the Company might have overlooked, once the basic outlines of the proposal had been set, the mere fact that the Union disagreed would be no ground for change. When GE said firm, it meant firm, and it denounced the traditional give and take of the so-called auction bargaining as "flea bitten eastern type of cunning and dishonest but pointless haggling."

To bring its position home to its employees, GE utilized a vast network of plant newspapers, bulletins, letters, television and radio announcements, and personal contacts through management personnel.

Side by side with its policies of "doing right voluntarily" through a "firm, fair offer," GE also pursued a policy of guaranteeing uniformity among unions, and between union and non-union employees. Thus all unions received substantially the same offer, and unrepresented employees were assured that they would gain nothing through representation that they would not have had in any case. Prior to 1960, GE held up its proposed benefits for unrepresented employees until the unions agreed, or until the old contract with the Union expired.

[The Board found General Electric to have violated §8(a)(5) by engaging in Boulwareism during its 1960 negotiations.]

The Company and the dissenting opinion seem to take the novel position that the holding in *Insurance Agents'* — that the Board might not forbid a partial strike during bargaining — ousts the Board's control over bargaining tactics. But in NLRB v. Katz, 369 U.S. 736 (1962), the Court held that at least one tactic — instituting unilateral changes during bargaining — was forbidden, for it put a bargainable topic outside the reach of the bargaining process. GE has done no less; it has, if anything, done more. By its communications and bargaining strategy it in effect painted itself into a corner on *all* bargainable matters.

In order to avoid any misunderstanding of our holding, some additional discussion is in order. We do not today hold that an employer may not communicate with his employees during negotiations. Nor are we deciding that the "best offer first" bargaining technique is forbidden. Moreover, we do not require an employer to engage in "auction bargaining," or, as the dissent seems to suggest, compel him to make concessions, "minor" or otherwise.

Our dissenting brother's peroration conjures up the dark spectre that we have taken a "portentous step" which "'contains seeds of danger for unions'" as well as employers. This picturesque characterization is unfortunate for it is a scare-phrase which tends to distract from the facts in this case. It paints over with a broad stroke the care we have taken to spell out the bounds of our opinion. We hold that an employer may not so combine "take-it-or-leave-it" bargaining methods with a widely publicized stance of unbending firmness that he is himself unable to alter a position once taken. It is this specific conduct that GE must avoid in order to comply with the Board's order, and not a carbon copy of every underlying event relied upon by the Board to support its findings. Such conduct, we find, constitutes a refusal to bargain "in fact." NLRB v. Katz, 369 U.S. 736, 743 (1962). It also constitutes, as the facts of this action demonstrate, an absence of subjective good faith, for it implies that the Company can deliberately bargain and communicate as though the Union did not exist, in clear derogation of the Union's status as exclusive representative of its members under §9(a). . . .

The petition for review is denied, and the petition for enforcement of the Board's order is granted.

Waterman, C.J. (concurring).

I fully concur with my brother Kaufman. Without differing from the majority opinion in any way and without reiterating its arguments, I would challenge my brother Friendly's dissenting assertion that the standard set forth by Judge Kaufman for determining overall bad faith is vague or difficult to apply. A company may make a firm, fair offer to the union and may stand by that offer, but the company should not be permitted to advertise to its employees that it believes in the firmness of its offers for the sake of firmness.

We recognize that a company is entitled to insist on the terms of its original offer if it believes that the union can be made to accept that offer. That GE refused to yield to union demands without giving reasons based upon cost, maintained a "stiff and unbending" posture, used a unilateral letter of intent when final agreement was reached, failed to make significant concessions, and publicized its offer without waiting for union suggestions do not indicate anything except that GE made and stood by what it conceived to be a fair, firm offer.

What makes these practices unfair is GE's "widely publicized stance of unbending firmness," that is, GE's communications to its employees that firmness was one of the company's independent policies. Two distinct evils derive from such publicity. First, publicity regarding firmness tends to make the company seal itself into its original position in such a way that, even if it wished to change that position at a later date, its pride and reputation for truthfulness are so at stake that it cannot do so. Second, publicity regarding firmness fixes in the minds of employees the idea that the company has set itself up as their representative and therefore that the union is superfluous. Doubtless these evils exist to some extent whenever a company makes, and stands by, a firm fair offer even when there is no company publicity of the kind here involved. However, it seems clear that publicity tends to amplify these undesirable tendencies to the point that, in a case such as this one, the amplification can well be construed to have been activated by a company motive not to bargain in good faith.

On the other side of the ledger there is very little positive good which can derive from company publicity which indicates that a company believes in firmness for firmness' sake. The free speech benefits of publicity in labor negotiations lie in the fact that informed employees will better know whether to vote for or against a strike and how to evaluate the union's performance on their behalf. These benefits can all be reaped by a company which advertises the terms of an offer and its belief that these terms are fair, without also stating that as a matter of policy it can never be persuaded to change the advertised terms. Such advertisement could only tend to convince employees that because firmness is a company policy it is also a company policy to ignore the union. A company, of course, can advertise its belief that its offer is fair, and that, at the particular time, it sees no reason to change its offer even to forestall a strike. This kind of statement is different from advertising that it is company policy never to change any offer in response to union pressure.

This view does not differ from that of the NLRB, nor does it indicate that the Board reached the right result for the wrong reasons. The trial examiner, whose opinion the Board adopted, specifically condemned GE's declarations that "a union could obtain no added benefits that it would not otherwise grant." 150 N.L.R.B. at 279. Because of this dominant wrong, we agree with the trial examiner that other aspects of the communications program also evidenced bad faith on the facts of this case although not as a matter of law. 150 N.L.R.B. at 274. It does no violence to the doctrine of SEC v. Chenery Corp., 318 U.S. 80, 95 (1943) to point out which of those factors correctly relied upon by an agency in the case at hand will also be instrumental in determining decisions in the future.

[Judge Friendly, dissenting, would have upheld General Electric's publicity as §8(c) free speech, and its "fair, firm offer" posture as protected by §8(d)'s ban on requiring concessions.]

Notes

1. Do you agree with the following?

> The Board and the court saw G.E.'s tactic as a bypass of the bargaining representative to deal directly with employees. G.E. views bargaining more realistically as a battle over the allegiance of employees with the weapons being honesty and persuasiveness. The decision to outlaw Boulwareism shows the Board and the court to be intractably wedded to the traditional form of closed-door jawboning bargaining and adamantly opposed to innovation.

2. Suppose a construction industry union presents its standard area collective bargaining agreement to a new employer in the locality. The employer asks "to talk about it." The union business agent responds, "We can talk all you want but you should know two things. The picket signs are in my car, and we are not about to let you undercut the union employees in this city by signing a better bargaining agreement than your competitors have." Refusal to bargain? Remedy? In *General Electric*, it was a cease and desist order.

B. SUBJECTS OF BARGAINING

NLRB v. WOOSTER DIVISION OF BORG-WARNER CORP.
356 U.S. 342 (1958)

BURTON, J.

In these cases an employer insisted that its collective-bargaining contract with certain of its employees include: (1) a "ballot" clause calling for a prestrike secret vote of those employees (union and nonunion) as to the employer's last offer, and (2) a "recognition" clause which excluded, as a party to the contract, the International Union which had been certified by the National Labor Relations Board as the employees' exclusive bargaining agent, and substituted for it the agent's uncertified local affiliate. The Board held that the employer's insistence upon either of such clauses amounted to a refusal to bargain, in violation of §8(a)(5) of the National Labor Relations Act, as amended. The issue turns on whether either of these clauses comes within the scope of mandatory collective bargaining as defined in §8(d) of the Act. For the reasons hereafter stated, we agree with the Board that neither clause comes within that definition. Therefore, we sustain the Board's order directing the employer to cease insisting upon either clause as a condition precedent to accepting any collective-bargaining contract.

Read together, [§§8(a)(5) and 8(d)] establish the obligation of the employer and the representative of its employees to bargain with each other in good faith with respect to "wages, hours, and other terms and conditions of employment. . . ." The duty is limited to those subjects, and within that area neither party is legally obligated to yield. National Labor Relations Board v. American Insurance Co., 343 U.S. 395. As to other matters, however, each party is free to bargain or not to bargain and to agree or not to agree.

The company's good faith has met the requirements of the statute as to the subjects of mandatory bargaining. But that good faith does not license the employer to refuse to enter into agreements on the ground that they do not include some proposal which is not a mandatory subject of bargaining. We agree with the Board that such conduct is, in substance, a refusal to bargain about the subjects that are within the scope of mandatory bargaining. This does not mean that bargaining is to be confined to the statutory subjects. Each of the two controversial clauses is lawful in itself. Each would be enforceable if agreed to by the unions. But it does not follow that, because the company may propose these clauses, it can lawfully insist upon them as a condition to any agreement.

Since it is lawful to insist upon matters within the scope of mandatory bargaining and unlawful to insist upon matters without, the issue here is whether either the "ballot" or the "recognition" clause is a subject within the phrase "wages, hours, and other terms and conditions of employment" which defines mandatory bargaining. The "ballot" clause is not within that definition. It relates only to the procedure to be followed by the employees among themselves before their representative may call a strike or refuse a final offer. It settles no term or condition of employment—it merely calls for an advisory vote of the employees. It is not a partial "no-strike" clause. A "no-strike" clause prohibits the employees from striking during the life of the contract. It regulates the relations between the employer and the employees.

The "ballot" clause, on the other hand, deals only with relations between the employees and their unions. It substantially modifies the collective-bargaining system provided for in the statute by weakening the independence of the "representative" chosen by the employees. It enables the employer, in effect, to deal with its employees rather than with their statutory representative. The "recognition" clause likewise does not come within the definition of mandatory bargaining. The statute requires the company to bargain with the certified representative of its employees. It is an evasion of that duty to insist that the certified agent not be a party to the collective-bargaining contract. The Act does not prohibit the voluntary addition of a party, but that does not authorize the employer to exclude the certified representative from the contract.[8]

[8] Frankfurter, J., concurred in part and dissented in part.

Harlan, J., whom Clark, J., and Whittaker, J., join, concurring in part and dissenting in part. . . .

Over twenty years ago this Court said in its first decision under the Wagner Act: "The theory of the act is that *free opportunity for negotiation* with accredited representatives of employees is likely to promote industrial peace and may bring about the adjustments and agreements which the act in itself does not attempt to compel." National Labor Relations Board v. Jones & Laughlin Steel Corp., 301 U.S. 1. (Italics added.) Today's decision proceeds on assumptions which I deem incompatible with this basic philosophy of the original labor Act, which has retained its vitality under the amendments effected by the Taft-Hartley Act. I fear that the decision may open the door to an intrusion by the Board into the substantive aspects of the bargaining process which goes beyond anything contemplated by the National Labor Relations Act or suggested in this Court's prior decisions under it. . . .

Notes

1. If the AFL-CIO had been inclined to file an amicus brief in *Borg-Warner,* which side should it have supported?

2. Suppose five different unions represent bargaining units at the employer's printing plant and bargain separately. Would the employer violate §8(a)(5) by insisting to impasse on a June 1, 1987, expiration date for each bargaining agreement? He or she might prefer, for example, a single strike by all employees to five separate strikes.

3. *Problem.* In recent years many unionized manufacturing concerns with operations in northern states have opened plants in sunbelt states, sometimes in communities that are very resistant to union organizing efforts. Unions have an easier time of organizing the new plants if the employer does not disseminate antiunion propaganda but adopts a neutral posture. In negotiating collective bargaining agreements at northern plants, some unions have sought contractual commitments that the employer will maintain neutrality in union organizing compaigns at other locations. Is this a mandatory subject of bargaining? Would such a commitment violate §8(a)(2)? See Lone Star Steel Co. v. NLRB, 639 F.2d 545 (10th Cir. 1980).

4. Is a clause requiring the union to institute internal union disciplinary proceedings against members engaging in unauthorized (wildcat) strikes in breach of contract a mandatory subject of bargaining?

5. Are you persuaded that *Borg-Warner* is sound policy? One might argue that it makes agreement easier to reach by removing noncentral issues from bargaining and that it narrows the range of detrimental economic impact that flows from negotiations where either the employer or the union has overwhelming economic power.

On the other hand, the doctrine tends to drive issues underground at the expense of forthright discussion — a union whose proposal has been rejected as a nonmandatory subject may thereafter take an intractable position on mandatory issues. Employers with sufficient economic power to resist a particular union demand may instead label it nonmandatory and thus needlessly invite Board litigation. And is not the doctrine particularly mischievous because of the difficulty in determining whether a subject is mandatory or not?

Consider another objection:

> The administrative and judicial processes are ill-suited to drawing a line between proper subjects for collective bargaining and management functions. The NLRB is staffed chiefly by lawyers who lack practical experience in industrial management and collective bargaining, and judges are not familiar with the problems. The adversary character of NLRB proceedings focuses attention upon what the immediate parties did or said at the expense of information bearing upon the underlying questions of policy. Casting in terms of statutory interpretation such issues as whether subcontracting and plant location are proper for collective bargaining gives undue prominence to legal techniques at the expense of policy considerations. If the government is to answer the question, its decision ought not to be controlled by the phrase "wages, hours and other terms and conditions of employment," by refined implications found in other sections of the statute, by legislative history, or by related statutory or judicial precedents.
>
> The demarcation lines between the sphere of joint responsibility and the respective prerogatives of management and union should be drawn at different points in different industries. An appropriate subject for collective bargaining in one industry may be highly inappropriate in another. The determination depends upon the industry's customs and history, the previous employer-employee relationships, technological problems and demands, and other factors. A government determination, especially one cast as an interpretation of a statutory phrase, subjects everyone to the same rule. Shift schedules, subcontracting, and the volume of production become either subjects upon which the employer is required to bargain at the request of the union in every industry or else no union can press a demand upon the issue to the point of an impasse.
>
> A line drawn by statutory interpretation is unduly rigid because of its permanence as well as its uniformity. Once made decisions can be altered only by revision of the statute. The history of collective bargaining since the Wagner Act reveals significant changes in the subject matter of negotiations. Indeed any definition of their appropriate scope written in 1937 would look foolish today. Collective bargaining is too dynamic for us to decide today what should be required or permissible subjects of collective bargaining tomorrow.
>
> The character of contract negotiations is radically changed as soon as one party is put under a court decree, violation of which will be punishable as contempt. The necessity for phrasing one's bargaining position with

scrupulous exactness, the use of threats of contempt as negotiating counters, the delays of running to court to obtain a ruling, all should be avoided if alternatives are available. In the end both parties suffer.[9]

FIBREBOARD PAPER PRODUCTS CORP. v. NLRB[10]

379 U.S. 203 (1964)

WARREN, C. J.

This case involves the obligation of an employer and the representative of his employees under §§8(a)(5), 8(d) and 9(a) of the National Labor Relations Act to "confer in good faith with respect to wages, hours, and other terms and conditions of employment." The primary issue is whether the "contracting out" of work being performed by employees in the bargaining unit is a statutory subject of collective bargaining under those sections.

Petitioner, Fibreboard Paper Products Corporation (the Company), has a manufacturing plant in Emeryville, California. . . . Local 1304, United Steelworkers of America, AFL-CIO (the Union) has been the exclusive bargaining representative for a unit of the Company's maintenance employees. . . .

The Company, concerned with the high cost of its maintenance operation, had undertaken a study of the possibility of effecting cost savings by engaging an independent contractor to do the maintenance work. At the July 27 meeting, the Company informed the Union that it had determined that substantial savings could be effected by contracting out the work upon expiration of its collective bargaining agreements with the various labor organizations representing its maintenance employees. The Company delivered to the Union representatives a letter which stated in pertinent part:

> For some time we have been seriously considering the question of letting out our Emeryville maintenance work to an independent contractor, and have now reached a definite decision to do so effective August 1, 1959.
>
> In these circumstances, we are sure you will realize that negotiation of a new contract would be pointless. However, if you have any questions, we will be glad to discuss them with you.

After some discussion of the Company's right to enter a contract with a third party to do the work then being performed by employees in the bargaining unit, the meeting concluded with the understanding that the parties would meet again on July 30.

[9] Cox, Labor Law Decisions of the Supreme Court at the October Term, 44 Va. L. Rev. 1057, 1083-1084 (1958).

[10] See Rabin, *Fibreboard* and the Termination of Bargaining Unit Work: The Search for Standards in Defining the Scope of the Duty to Bargain, 71 Colum. L. Rev. 803 (1971); Rabin, The Decline and Fall of *Fibreboard,* N.Y.U. Twenty-Fourth Annual Conference on Labor Law 237 (1972).

By July 30, the Company had [retained] Fluor Maintenance, Inc., to do the maintenance work. Fluor had assured the Company that maintenance cost could be curtailed by reducing the work force, decreasing fringe benefits and overtime payments, and by preplanning and scheduling the services to be performed. . . .

At the July 30 meeting, the Company's representative, in explaining the decision to contract out the maintenance work, remarked that during bargaining negotiations in previous years the Company had endeavored to point out through the use of charts and statistical information "just how expensive and costly our maintenance work was and how it was creating quite a terrific burden upon the Emeryville plant." He further stated that unions representing other Company employees "had joined hands with management in an effort to bring about an economical and efficient operation," but "we had not been able to attain that in our discussions with this particular Local." The Company also distributed a letter stating that "since we will have no employees in the bargaining unit covered by our present Agreement, negotiation of a new or renewed Agreement would appear to us to be pointless." On July 31, the employment of the maintenance employees represented by the Union was terminated and Fluor employees took over. That evening the Union established a picket line at the Company's plant.

The Union filed unfair labor practice charges against the Company, alleging violations of §§8(a)(1), 8(a)(3) and 8(a)(5). [The Board initially dismissed the complaint but then granted a motion to reconsider and found a §8(a)(5) violation.] Because of the limited grant of certiorari, we are concerned here only with whether the subject upon which the employer allegedly refused to bargain — contracting out of plant maintenance work previously performed by employees in the bargaining unit, which the employees were capable of continuing to perform — is covered by the phrase "terms and conditions of employment" within the meaning of §8(d).

The subject matter of the present dispute is well within the literal meaning of the phrase "terms and conditions of employment." A stipulation with respect to the contracting out of work performed by members of the bargaining unit might appropriately be called a "condition of employment." The words even more plainly cover termination of employment which, as the facts of this case indicate, necessarily results from the contracting out of work performed by members of the established bargaining unit.

The inclusion of "contracting out" within the statutory scope of collective bargaining also seems well designed to effectuate the purposes of the National Labor Relations Act. One of the primary purposes of the Act is to promote the peaceful settlement of industrial disputes by subjecting labor-management controversies to the mediatory influence of negotiation. The Act was framed with an awareness that refusals to confer and negotiate had been one of the most prolific causes of industrial strife.

To hold, as the Board has done, that contracting out is a mandatory subject of collective bargaining would promote the fundamental purpose of the Act by bringing a problem of vital concern to labor and management within the framework established by Congress as most conducive to industrial peace.

The conclusion that "contracting out" is a statutory subject of collective bargaining is further reinforced by industrial practices in this country. While not determinative, it is appropriate to look to industrial bargaining practices in appraising the propriety of including a particular subject within the scope of mandatory bargaining. Industrial experience is not only reflective of the interests of labor and management in the subject matter but is also indicative of the amenability of such subjects to the collective bargaining process. Experience illustrates that contracting out in one form or another has been brought, widely and successfully, within the collective bargaining framework. Provisions relating to contracting out exist in numerous collective bargaining agreements,[7] and "[c]ontracting out work is the basis of many grievances; and that type of claim is grist in the mills of the arbitrators." United Steelworkers of America, etc. v. Warrior & Gulf Nav. Co., 363 U.S. 574, 584.

The situation here is not unlike that presented in Local 24, of Intern. Broth. of Teamsters, etc. v. Oliver, 358 U.S. 283, where we held that conditions imposed upon contracting out work to prevent possible curtailment of jobs and the undermining of conditions of employment for members of the bargaining unit constituted a statutory subject of collective bargaining. The issue in that case was whether state antitrust laws could be applied to a provision of a collective bargaining agreement which fixed the minimum rental to be paid by the employer motor carrier who leased vehicles to be driven by their owners rather than the carrier's employees. We held that the agreement was upon a subject matter as to which federal law directed the parties to bargain and hence that state antitrust laws could not be applied to prevent the effectuation of the agreement. We pointed out that the agreement was a "direct frontal attack upon a problem thought to threaten the maintenance of the basic wage structure established by the collective bargaining contract. The inadequacy of a rental which means that the owner makes up his excess costs from his driver's wages not only clearly bears a close relation to labor's efforts to improve working conditions but is in fact of vital concern to the carrier's employed drivers; an inadequate rental might

7. A Department of Labor study analyzed 1,687 collective bargaining agreements, which applied to approximately 7,500,000 workers (about one-half of the estimated work force covered by collective bargaining agreements). Among the agreements studied, approximately one-fourth (378) contained some form of a limitation on subcontracting.

mean the progressive curtailment of jobs through withdrawal of more and more carrier-owned vehicles from service." Id., at 294.

Thus, we concluded that such a matter is a subject of mandatory bargaining under §8(d). The only difference between that case and the one at hand is that the work of the employees in the bargaining unit was let out piecemeal in *Oliver,* whereas here the work of the entire unit has been contracted out. . . .

The facts of the present case illustrate the propriety of submitting the dispute to collective negotiation. The Company's decision to contract out the maintenance work did not alter the Company's basic operation. The maintenance work still had to be performed in the plant. No capital investment was contemplated; the Company merely replaced existing employees with those of an independent contractor to do the same work under similar conditions of employment. Therefore, to require the employer to bargain about the matter would not significantly abridge his freedom to manage the business.[11]

The Company was concerned with the high cost of its maintenance operation. It was induced to contract out the work by assurances from independent contractors that economies could be derived by reducing the work force, decreasing fringe benefits, and eliminating overtime payments. These have long been regarded as matters peculiarly suitable for resolution within the collective bargaining framework, and industrial experience demonstrates that collective negotiation has been highly successful in achieving peaceful accommodation of the conflicting interests. Yet, it is contended that when an employer can effect cost savings in these respects by contracting the work out, there is no need to attempt to achieve similar economies through negotiation with existing employees or to provide them with an opportunity to negotiate a mutually acceptable alternative. The short answer is that, although it is not possible to say whether a satisfactory solution could be reached, national labor policy is founded upon the congressional determination that the chances are good enough to warrant subjecting such issues to the process of collective negotiation. . . .

We are thus not expanding the scope of mandatory bargaining to hold, as we do now, that the type of "contracting out" involved in this case — the replacement of employees in the existing bargaining unit with those of an independent contractor to do the same work under similar conditions of employment — is a statutory subject of collective bargaining under §8(d). Our decision need not and does not encompass other forms of "contracting out" or "subcontracting" which arise daily in our complex economy.[8]

[11] Recall that *Darlington* was decided a year later.

8. As the Solicitor General points out, the terms "contracting out" and "subcontracting" have no precise meaning. They are used to describe a variety of business arrangements altogether different from that involved in this case.

The only question remaining is whether, upon a finding that the Company had refused to bargain about a matter which is a statutory subject of collective bargaining, the Board was empowered to order the resumption of maintenance operations and reinstatement with back pay. We believe that it was so empowered. . . . There has been no showing that the Board's order restoring the status quo ante to insure meaningful bargaining is not well designed to promote the policies of the Act. Nor is there evidence which would justify disturbing the Board's conclusion that the order would not impose an undue or unfair burden on the Company. . . .

The judgment of the Court of Appeals is affirmed.[12]

Stewart, J., with whom Douglas, J., and Harlan, J., join, concurring. . . .

While employment security has properly been recognized in various circumstances as a condition of employment, it surely does not follow that every decision which may affect job security is a subject of compulsory collective bargaining. Many decisions made by management affect the job security of employees. Decisions concerning the volume and kind of advertising expenditures, product design, the manner of financing, and sales, all may bear upon the security of the workers' jobs. Yet it is hardly conceivable that such decisions so involve "conditions of employment" that they must be negotiated with the employees' bargaining representative.

In many of these areas the impact of a particular management decision upon job security may be extremely indirect and uncertain, and this alone may be sufficient reason to conclude that such decisions are not "with respect to . . . conditions of employment." Yet there are other areas where decisions by management may quite clearly imperil job security, or indeed terminate employment entirely. An enterprise may decide to invest in labor-saving machinery. Another may resolve to liquidate its assets and go out of business. Nothing the Court holds today should be understood as imposing a duty to bargain collectively regarding such managerial decisions, which lie at the core of entrepreneurial control. Decisions concerning the commitment of investment capital and the basic scope of the enterprise are not in themselves primarily about conditions of employment, though the effect of the decision may be necessarily to terminate employment. If, as I think clear, the purpose of §8(d) is to describe a limited area subject to the duty of collective bargaining, those management decisions which are fundamental to the basic direction of a corporate enterprise or which impinge only indirectly upon employment security should be excluded from that area. . . .

[12] Goldberg, J., took no part in the decision.

Notes

1. Was the majority opinion attempting to limit its decision to the facts of this case? Which facts made the case especially appealing for imposing a duty to bargain?

2. The following illustrates the Board's approach after *Fibreboard.*

> We believe, however [that the imposition of a duty to bargain is] controlled by the rationale the courts have generally adopted in closely related cases, that decisions such as this, in which a significant investment or withdrawal of capital will affect the scope and ultimate direction of an enterprise, are matters essentially financial and managerial in nature. They thus lie at the very core of entrepreneurial control and are not the types of subjects which Congress intended to encompass within "rates of pay, wages, hours of employment, or other conditions of employment." Such managerial decisions ofttimes require secrecy as well as the freedom to act quickly and decisively. They also involve subject areas as to which the determinative financial and operational considerations are likely to be unfamiliar to the employees and their representatives.

General Motors Corp., 191 N.L.R.B. 951, 952 (1971), aff'd sub nom. UAW Local 864 v. NLRB, 470 F.2d 422 (D.C. Cir. 1972).

3. In Ford Motor Co. v. NLRB, 441 U.S. 488 (1979), the Court upheld a Board holding that prices for in-plant cafeteria and vending machine food and beverages are mandatory subjects of bargaining. The Court emphasized that the Board's conclusion should be accepted unless it was "an unreasonable or unprincipled construction of the statute."

Several factors supported the Board's decision, according to the Court. It was reasonable for the Board to conclude that the availability and price of in-plant food were matters of deep concern to workers. The price of food was not thought to be among those "managerial decisions, which lie at the core of enterpreneurial control" (quoting Justice Stewart's concurrence in *Fibreboard*). Because employees care about the matter, national labor policy is advanced by channelling disputes over food prices into collective bargaining rather than leaving such disputes to fester until strikes or other disruptions occur. Finally, many collective bargaining agreements contain provisions with respect to in-plant food practices, lending the support of industrial practice to the Board's conclusion.

The Court rejected Ford's argument that the subject of food prices is too trivial to warrant classification as a mandatory bargaining subject, and that prices are not mandatory subjects because they do not "vitally affect" terms and conditions of employment.

4. *Problem.* The Maytag Company, a manufacturer of washing machines, has a department that makes pulley belts to be incorporated into the machines. It recently decided to discontinue making pulley belts and

to purchase them from National Supplier. It announced to the Pulley-Belt Workers Union, representing only this bargaining unit, that the department has been terminated and the pulley-belt workers laid off. Has Maytag violated §8(a)(5)? What are the practical effects of such a holding? Did Maytag and the union have anything to talk about? One effect of finding that the decision to terminate was a mandatory subject is that the union may picket the Maytag plant. The union is prohibited from picketing if the decision is nonmandatory.

5. Does *Fibreboard* provide employers and unions with practical standards to determine if a bargaining subject is mandatory or nonmandatory? For example, the Board has held that interest arbitration clauses (those providing that if the parties are unable to reach agreement on new contract terms, an arbitrator shall be selected to determine the new contract) do not constitute mandatory subjects of bargaining.[13]

Various Board members have suggested three reasons for finding the clause nonmandatory: It falls without the statutory language describing mandatory subjects; it would interfere with the statutory right to use economic force in collective bargaining; and it is capable of self-perpetuation since the arbitrator might include another such clause in the designated agreement. Are you persuaded by these reasons?

Another interesting issue is what the Board should do, if anything, where the parties have agreed to interest arbitration and one party raises a nonmandatory subject of bargaining and attempts to submit it to the arbitrator. The Board recently held that a union violates §8(b)(3) by insisting on sending a nonmandatory subject to interest arbitration. Sheet Metal Workers Local 38 (Elmsford Sheet Metal Works), 231 N.L.R.B. 699, enforced, 575 F.2d 394 (2d Cir. 1978).

NLRB v. FIRST NATIONAL MAINTENANCE CORP.

452 U.S. 666 (1981)

BLACKMUN, J. . . .

Must an employer, under its duty to bargain in good faith "with respect to wages, hours, and other terms and conditions of employment," §§8(d) and 8(a)(5) of the National Labor Relations Act, negotiate with the certified representative of its employees over its decision to close a part of its business? In this case, the National Labor Relations Board (the Board) imposed such a duty on petitioner with respect to its decision to terminate a contract with a customer, and the United States Court of Appeals, although differing over the appropriate rationale, enforced its order.

[13] Columbus Printing Pressmen & Assistants Union No. 252, 219 N.L.R.B. 268 (1975).

I

Petitioner, First National Maintenance Corporation (FNM), is a New York corporation engaged in the business of providing housekeeping, cleaning, maintenance, and related services for commercial customers in the New York City area. It supplies each of its customers, at the customer's premises, contracted-for labor force and supervision in return for reimbursement of its labor costs (gross salaries, FICA and FUTA taxes, and insurance) and payment of a set fee. It contracts for and hires personnel separately for each customer, and it does not transfer employees between locations.

During the Spring of 1977, petitioner was performing maintenance work for the Greenpark Care Center, a nursing home in Brooklyn. Its written agreement dated April 28, 1976, with Greenpark specified that Greenpark "shall furnish all tools, equipment [sic], materials, and supplies," and would pay petitioner weekly "the sum of five hundred dollars plus the gross weekly payroll and fringe benefits." Its weekly fee, however, had been reduced to $250 effective November 1, 1976. The contract prohibited Greenpark from hiring any of petitioner's employees during the term of the contract and for 90 days thereafter. Petitioner employed approximately 35 workers in its Greenpark operation.

Petitioner's business relationship with Greenpark, seemingly, was not very remunerative or smooth. In March 1977, Greenpark gave petitioner the 30 days' written notice of cancellation specified by the contract, because of "lack of efficiency." This cancellation did not become effective, for FNB's work continued after the expiration of that 30-day period. Petitioner, however, became aware that it was losing money at Greenpark. On June 30, by telephone, it asked that its weekly fee be restored at the $500 figure and, on July 6, it informed Greenpark in writing that it would discontinue its operations there on August 1 unless the increase were granted. By telegram on July 25, petitioner gave final notice of termination.

While FNM was experiencing these difficulties, District 1199, National Union of Hospital and Health Care Employees, Retail, Wholesale and Department Store Union, AFL-CIO (the union), was conducting an organization campaign among petitioner's Greenpark employees. On March 31, 1977, at a Board-conducted election, a majority of the employees selected the union as their bargaining agent. On July 12, the union's vice president, Edward Wecker, wrote petitioner, notifying it of the certification and of the union's right to bargain, and stating: "We look forward to meeting with you or your representative for that purpose. Please advise when it will be convenient." Petitioner neither responded nor sought to consult with the union.

On July 28, petitioner notified its Greenpark employees that they would be discharged 3 days later. Wecker immediately telephoned petitioner's secretary-treasurer, Leonard Marsh, to request a delay for the purpose of bargaining. Marsh refused the offer to bargain and told Wecker that the termination of the Greenpark operation was purely a matter of money, and final, and that the 30-days' notice provision of the Greenpark contract made staying on beyond August 1 prohibitively expensive. Wecker discussed the matter with Greenpark's management that same day, but was unable to obtain a waiver of the notice provision. Greenpark also was unwilling itself to hire the FNM employees because of the contract's 90-day limitation on hiring. With nothing but perfunctory further discussion, petitioner on July 31 discontinued its Greenpark operation and discharged the employees.

The union filed an unfair labor practice charge against petitioner, alleging violations of the Act's §§8(a)(1) and (5). After a hearing held upon the Regional Director's complaint, the administrative law judge made findings in the union's favor. Relying on Ozark Trailers, Inc., 161 N.L.R.B. 561 (1966), he ruled that petitioner had failed to satisfy its duty to bargain concerning both the decision to terminate the Greenpark contract and the effect of that change upon the unit employees.[4] The judge reasoned:

> That the discharge of a man is a change in his conditions of employment hardly needs comment. In these obvious facts, the law is clear. When an employer's work complement is represented by a union and he wishes to alter the hiring arrangements, be his reason lack of money or a mere desire to become richer, the law is no less clear that he must first talk to the union about it. . . . If Wecker had been given an opportunity to talk, something might have been worked out to transfer these people to other parts of [petitioner's] business. . . . Entirely apart from whether open discussion between the parties — with the Union speaking on behalf of the employees as was its right — might have persuaded [petitioner] to find a way of continuing this part of its operations, there was always the possibility that Marsh might have persuaded Greenpark to use these same employees to continue doing its maintenance work, either as direct employees or as later hires by a replacement contractor. [242 N.L.R.B. 462, 465 (1979).[5]]

4. The administrative law judge rejected petitioner's contention that it had satisfied, by that single phone call to Wecker, its duty to bargain about the termination.

5. The judge further found that petitioner's "regular and usual" method of operation involved "taking on, finishing, or discontinuing this or that particular job," 242 N.L.R.B., at 466, and that "[t]here was no capital involved when it decided to terminate the Greenpark job. The closing of this one spot in no sense altered the nature of its business, nor did it substantially affect its total size." Ibid. The administrative law judge therefore found inapplicable the Board's ruling in Brockway Motor Trucks, Division of Mack Trucks, Inc., 230 N.L.R.B. 1002, 1003 (1977), enf. denied, 582 F.2d 720 (C.A.3 1978), that an employer's decision to close part of its business is not a mandatory subject of bargaining if it involves such a "'significant investment or withdrawal of capital' as to 'affect the scope and ultimate direction of the enterprise,'" quoting from General Motors Corp., GMC Truck & Coach Div., 191 N.L.R.B. 951, 952 (1971).

The administrative law judge recommended an order requiring petitioner to bargain in good faith with the union about its decision to terminate its Greenpark service operation and its consequent discharge of the employees, as well as the effects of the termination. He recommended, also, that petitioner be ordered to pay the discharged employees backpay from the date of discharge until the parties bargained to agreement, or the bargaining reached impasse, or the union failed timely to request bargaining, or the union failed to bargain in good faith.

The National Labor Relations Board adopted the administrative law judge's findings without further analysis, and additionally required petitioner, if it agreed to resume its Greenpark operations, to offer the terminated employees reinstatement to their former jobs or substantial equivalents; conversely, if agreement was not reached, petitioner was ordered to offer the employees equivalent positions, to be made available by discharge of subsequently-hired employees, if necessary, at its other operations.

The United States Court of Appeals for the Second Circuit, with one judge dissenting in part, enforced the Board's order, although it adopted an analysis different from that espoused by the Board. 627 F.2d 596 (1980).[6] The Court of Appeals reasoned that no per se rule could be formulated to govern an employer's decision to close part of its business. Rather, the court said, §8(d) creates a *presumption* in favor of mandatory bargaining over such a decision, a presumption that is rebuttable "by showing that the purposes of the statute would not be furthered by imposition of a duty to bargain," for example, by demonstrating that "bargaining over the decision would be futile," or that the decision was due to "emergency financial circumstances," or that the "custom of the industry, shown by the absence of such an obligation from typical collective bargaining agreements, is not to bargain over such decisions."

The Court of Appeal's decision in this case appears to be at odds with decisions of other Courts of Appeals,[7] some of which decline to require

6. Because the court adopted different grounds for enforcement of the Board's order, it was error to enforce without a remand to the Board for further examination of the evidence and proper factfinding. NLRB v. Pipefitters, 429 U.S. 507, 522, n.9 (1977); SEC v. Chenery Corp., 318 U.S. 80, 95 (1943).

7. The Court of Appeals in this case, for example, agreed, 627 F.2d at 601, with the Third Circuit in Brockway Motor Trucks, Etc. v. NLRB, 582 F.2d 720 (1978), that a presumption in favor of bargaining was to be established, but it analyzed differently how that presumption would be rebutted. The Third Circuit had decided that the competing interests of the employer and the employees, under the particular circumstances, must be weighed, and it had remanded the case before it to the Board for factfinding into the circumstances behind the partial closing. See also Equitable Gas Co. v. NLRB, 637 F.2d 980 (C.A.3 1981) (subcontracting); ABC Trans-National Transport, Inc. v. NLRB, 642 F.2d 675 (C.A.3 1981) (partial closing); NLRB v. Royal Plating & Polishing Co., 350 F.2d 191 (C.A.3 1965) (partial closing). Several courts have agreed with the Second Circuit. See, e.g., Davis v. NLRB, 617 F.2d 1264 (C.A.7 1980) (change of full-service restaurant to self-service cafeteria); NLRB v. Production Molded Plastics, Inc., 604 F.2d 451 (C.A.6 1979) (plant closing).

bargaining over any management decision involving "a major commitment of capital investment" or a "basic operational change" in the scope or direction of an enterprise,[8] and some of which indicate that bargaining is not mandated unless a violation of §8(b)(3) (a partial closing motivated by antiunion animus) is involved.[9] The Court of Appeals for the Fifth Circuit has imposed a duty to bargain over partial closing decisions. See NLRB v. Winn-Dixie Stores, Inc., 361 F.2d 512, cert. denied, 385 U.S. 935 (1966). The Board itself has not been fully consistent in its rulings applicable to this type of management decision.[10]

Because of the importance of the issue and the continuing disagreement between and among the Board and the Courts of Appeals, we granted certiorari.

II

A fundamental aim of the National Labor Relations Act is the establishment and maintenance of industrial peace to preserve the flow of interstate commerce. NLRB v. Jones & Laughlin Steel Corp., 301 U.S. 1 (1937). Central to achievement of this purpose is the promotion of collective bargaining as a method of defusing and channeling conflict between labor and management.[11] Section 1 of the Act. Congress ensured that collective bargaining would go forward by creating the National

8. See, e.g., NLRB v. International Harvester Co., 618 F.2d 85 (C.A.9 1980); NLRB v. Adams Dairy, Inc., 350 F.2d 108 (C.A.8 1965), cert. denied, 382 U.S. 1011 (1966); NLRB v. Transmarine Navigation Corp., 380 F.2d 933 (C.A.10 1967); Royal Typewriter Co. v. NLRB, 533 F.2d 1030 (C.A.8 1976); NLRB v. Rapid Bindery, Inc., 293 F.2d 170 (C.A.2 1961); NLRB v. Thompson Transport Co., 406 F.2d 698 (C.A.10 1969).

9. See, e.g., Morrison Cafeterias Consolidated, Inc. v. NLRB, 431 F.2d 254 (C.A.8 1970); NLRB v. Drapery Mfg. Co., 425 F.2d 1026 (C.A.8 1970); NLRB v. William J. Burns International Detective Agency, Inc., 346 F.2d 897 (C.A.8 1965).

10. Compare National Car Rental System, Inc., 252 N.L.R.B. No. 27, p. 15 (1980) (employer's decision to terminate car leasing operations at one location not a mandatory subject because "'essentially financial and managerial in nature,' involving a 'significant investment or withdrawal of capital, affecting the scope and ultimate direction of an enterprise,'" quoting from General Motors Corp., GMC Truck & Coach Div., 191 N.L.R.B., at 952), and Summit Tooling Co., 195 N.L.R.B. 479, 480 (1972) (decision to close a subsidiary not a mandatory subject because "its practical effect was to take the Respondent out of the business of manufacturing tool and tooling products"), with Ozark Trailers, Inc., 161 N.L.R.B. 561, 567, 568 (1966) (employer's decision to shut down one of multiple plants was a mandatory subject because it was "a decision directly affecting terms and conditions of employment" and "interests of employees are of sufficient importance that their representatives ought to be consulted in matters affecting them"). See also Kingwood Mining Co., 210 N.L.R.B. 844 (1974), aff'd, sub nom. United Mine Workers v. NLRB, 169 U.S. App. D.C. 301, 551 F.2d 1018 (1975).

11. "Experience has abundantly demonstrated that the recognition of the right of employees to self-organization and to have representatives of their own choosing for the purpose of collective bargaining is often an essential condition of industrial peace. Refusal to confer and negotiate has been one of the most prolific causes of strife. This is such an outstanding fact in the history of labor disturbances that it is a proper subject of judicial notice and requires no citation of instances." NLRB v. Jones & Laughlin Steel Corp., 301 U.S., at 42 (upholding the constitutionality of the Act).

Labor Relations Board and giving it the power to condemn as unfair labor practices certain conduct by unions and employers that it deemed deleterious to the process, including the refusal "to bargain collectively." §§3 and 8.

Although parties are free to bargain about any legal subject, Congress has limited the mandate or duty to bargain to matters of "wages, hours, and other terms and conditions of employment." A unilateral change as to a subject within this category violates the statutory duty to bargain and is subject to the Board's remedial order. NLRB v. Katz, 369 U.S. 736 (1962). Conversely, both employer and union may bargain to impasse over these matters and use the economic weapons at their disposal to attempt to secure their respective aims. NLRB v. American National Ins. Co., 343 U.S. 395 (1952).[13] Congress deliberately left the words "wages, hours, and other terms and conditions of employment" without further definition, for it did not intend to deprive the Board of the power further to define those terms in light of specific industrial practices.[14]

Nonetheless, in establishing what issues must be submitted to the process of bargaining, Congress had no expectation that the elected union representative would become an equal partner in the running of the business enterprise in which the union's members are employed. Despite the deliberate openendedness of the statutory language, there is an undeniable limit to the subjects about which bargaining must take place: "Section 8(a) of the Act, of course, does not immutably fix a list of subjects for mandatory bargaining. . . . But it does establish a limita-

13. A matter that is not a mandatory subject of bargaining, unless it is illegal, may be raised at the bargaining table to be discussed in good faith, and the parties may incorporate it into an enforceable collective-bargaining agreement. Labor and management may not, however, insist on it to the point of impasse. NLRB v. Borg-Warner Corp., 356 U.S. 342 (1958).

14. In enacting the Labor Management Relations Act, 1947, Congress rejected a proposal in the House to limit the subjects of bargaining to "(i) [w]age rates, hours of employment, and work requirements; (ii) procedures and practices relating to discharge, suspension, lay-off, recall, seniority, and discipline, or to promotion, demotion, transfer and assignment within the bargaining unit; (iii) conditions, procedures, and practices governing safety, sanitation, and protection of health at the place of employment; (iv) vacations and leaves of absence; and (v) administrative and procedural provisions relating to the foregoing subjects." H.R. 3020 §2(11), 80th Cong., 1st Sess. (1947). The adoption, instead, of the general phrase now part of §8(d) was clearly meant to preserve future interpretation by the Board. See H.R. Rep. No. 245, 80th Cong., 1st Sess., 71 (1947) (minority report) ("The appropriate scope of collective bargaining cannot be determined by a formula; it will inevitably depend upon the traditions of an industry, the social and political climate at any given time, the needs of employers and employees, and many related factors. What are proper subject matters for collective bargaining should be left in the first instance to employers and trade-unions, and in the second place, to any administrative agency skilled in the field and competent to devote the necessary time to a study of industrial practices and traditions in each industry or area of the country, subject to review by the courts. It cannot and should not be strait-jacketed by legislative enactment."); H.R. Conf. Rep. No. 510, 80th Cong., 1st Sess., 34-35 (1947). Specific references in the legislative history to plant closings, however, are inconclusive. See 79 Cong. Rec. 7673, 9682 (1935) (comments of Sen. Walsh and Rep. Griswold).

tion against which proposed topics must be measured. In general terms, the limitation includes only issues that settle an aspect of the relationship between the employer and the employees." Chemical & Alkali Workers v. Pittsburgh Plate Glass Co., 404 U.S. 157, 178 (1971). See also Ford Motor Co. v. NLRB, 441 U.S. 488 (1979); Fibreboard Paper Products Corp. v. NLRB, 379 U.S. 203 (1964); Teamsters v. Oliver, 358 U.S. 283 (1959).

Some management decisions, such as choice of advertising and promotion, product type and design, and financing arrangements, have only an indirect and attenuated impact on the employment relationship. See *Fibreboard,* 379 U.S., at 223 (Stewart, J., concurring). Other management decisions, such as the order of succession of layoffs and recalls, production quotas, and work rules, are almost exclusively "an aspect of the relationship" between employer and employee. *Chemical Workers,* 404 U.S., at 178. The present case concerns a third type of management decision, one that had a direct impact on employment, since jobs were inexorably eliminated by the termination, but had as its focus only the economic profitability of the contract with Greenpark, a concern under these facts wholly apart from the employment relationship. This decision, involving a change in the scope and direction of the enterprise, is akin to the decision whether to be in business at all, "not in [itself] primarily about conditions of employment, though the effect of the decision may be necessarily to terminate employment." *Fibreboard,* 379 U.S., at 223 (Stewart, J., concurring). Cf. Textile Workers v. Darlington Co., 380 U.S. 263, 268 (1965) ("an employer has the absolute right to terminate his entire business for any reason he pleases"). At the same time, this decision touches on a matter of central and pressing concern to the union and its member employees: the possibility of continued employment and the retention of the employees' very jobs. See Brockway Motor Trucks, Etc. v. NLRB, 582 F.2d 720, 735-736 (C.A.3 1978); Ozark Trailers, Inc., 161 N.L.R.B. 561, 566-568 (1966).

Petitioner contends it had no duty to bargain about its decision to terminate its operations at Greenpark. This contention requires that we determine whether the decision itself should be considered part of petitioner's retained freedom to manage its affairs unrelated to employment.[15] The aim of labeling a matter a mandatory subject of bargaining, rather than simply permitting, but not requiring, bargaining, is to "promote the fundamental purpose of the Act by bringing a problem of vital concern to labor and management within the framework established by Congress as most conducive to industrial peace," *Fibreboard,* 379 U.S., at 211. The concept of mandatory bargaining is premised on the belief that

15. There is no doubt that petitioner was under a duty to bargain about the results or effects of its decision to stop the work at Greenpark, or that it violated that duty. Petitioner consented to enforcement of the Board's order concerning bargaining over the effects of the closing and has reached agreement with the union on severance pay.

collective discussions backed by the parties' economic weapons will result in decisions that are better for both management and labor and for society as a whole. *Ford Motor Co.,* 441 U.S., at 500-501; *Borg-Warner,* 356 U.S., at 350 (condemning employer's proposal of "ballot" clause as weakening the collective-bargaining process). This will be true, however, only if the subject proposed for discussion is amendable to resolution through the bargaining process. Management must be free from the constraints of the bargaining process[17] to the extent essential for the running of a profitable business. It also must have some degree of certainty beforehand as to when it may proceed to reach decisions without fear of later evaluations labeling its conduct an unfair labor practice. Congress did not explicitly state what issues of mutual concern to union and management it intended to exclude from mandatory bargaining.[18] Nonetheless, in view of an employer's need for unencumbered decision-making, bargaining over management decisions that have a substantial impact on the continued availability of employment should be required only if the benefit, for labor-management relations and the collective bargaining process, outweighs the burden placed on the conduct of the business.

The Court in *Fibreboard* implicitly engaged in this analysis with regard to decision to subcontract for maintenance work previously done by unit employees. Holding the employer's decision a subject of mandatory bargaining, the Court relied not only on the "literal meaning" of the statutory words, but also reasoned:

> The Company's decision to contract out the maintenance work did not alter the Company's basic operation. The maintenance work still had to be performed in the plant. No capital investment was contemplated; the Company merely replaced existing employees with those of an independent contractor to do the same work under similar conditions of employment. Therefore, to require the employer to bargain about the matter would not significantly abridge his freedom to manage the business. [379 U.S., at 213.]

17. The employer has no obligation to abandon its intentions or to agree with union proposals. On proper subjects, it must meet with the union, provide information necessary to the union's understanding of the problem, and in good faith consider any proposals the union advances. In concluding to reject a union's position as to a mandatory subject, however, it must face the union's possible use of strike power. See generally Fleming, The Obligation to Bargain in Good Faith, 47 Va. L. Rev. 988 (1961).

18. The subjects over which mandatory bargaining has been required have changed over time. Employers and unions have been required to bargain over such diverse topics as profit-sharing plans, Winn-Dixie Stores, Inc. v. NLRB, 567 F.2d 1343 (C.A.5), cert. denied, 439 U.S. 985 (1978); layoffs and recalls, see Awrey Bakeries, Inc. v. NLRB, 548 F.2d 138 (C.A.6 1976); contractual clauses concerning race discrimination, see Wichita Eagle & Beacon Publishing Co., 222 N.L.R.B. 742 (1976); and "most favored nation" clauses, Dolly Madison Industries, Inc., 182 N.L.R.B. 1037 (1970). See also *Borg-Warner,* 356 U.S., at 353 (Harlan, J., concurring in part and dissenting in part).

The Court also emphasized that a desire to reduce labor costs, which is considered a matter "peculiarly suitable for resolution within the collective bargaining framework," id., at 214, was at the base of the employer's decision to subcontract:

> It was induced to contract out the work by assurances from independent contractors that economies could be derived by reducing the work force, decreasing fringe benefits, and eliminating overtime payments. These have long been regarded as matters peculiarly suitable for resolution within the collective bargaining framework, and industrial experience demonstrates that collective negotiation has been highly successful in achieving peaceful accommodation of the conflicting interests. [Id., at 213-214.]

The prevalence of bargaining over "contracting out" as a matter of industrial practice generally was taken as further proof of the "amenability of such subjects to the collective bargaining process." Id., at 211.

With this approach in mind, we turn to the specific issue at hand: an economically-motivated decision to shut down part of a business.

III

A

Both union and management regard control of the decision to shut down an operation with the utmost seriousness. As has been noted, however, the Act is not intended to serve either party's individual interest, but to foster in a neutral manner a system in which the conflict between these interests may be resolved. It seems particularly important, therefore, to consider whether requiring bargaining over this sort of decision will advance the neutral purposes of the Act.

A union's interest in participating in the decision to close a particular facility or part of an employer's operations springs from its legitimate concern over job security. The Court has observed: "The words of [§8(d)] . . . plainly cover termination of employment which . . . necessarily results" from closing an operation. *Fibreboard,* 379 U.S., at 210. The union's practical purpose in participating, however, will be largely uniform: it will seek to delay or halt the closing. No doubt it will be impelled, in seeking these ends, to offer concessions, information, and alternatives that might be helpful to management or forestall or prevent the termination of jobs.[19] It is unlikely, however, that requiring bargain-

19. We are aware of past instances where unions have aided employers in saving failing businesses by lending technical assistance, reducing wages and benefits or increasing production, and even loaning part of earned wages to forestall closures. See S. Slichter, J. Healy & E. Livernash, The Impact of Collective Bargaining on Management 845-851 (1960); C. Golden & H. Rutenberg, The Dynamics of Industrial Democracy 263-291 (1942). See also United Steel Workers, Etc. v. U.S. Steel Corp., 492 F. Supp. 1 (N.D. Ohio), aff'd in part and vacated in part, 631 F.2d 1264 (C.A.6 1980) (union sought to purchase

ing over the decision itself, as well as its effect, will augment this flow of information and suggestions. There is no dispute that the union must be given a significant opportunity to bargain about these matters of job security as part of the "effects" bargaining mandated by §8(a)(5). See, e.g., NLRB v. Royal Plating & Polishing Co., 350 F.2d 191, 196 (C.A.3 1965); NLRB v. Adams Dairy, Inc., 350 F.2d 108 (C.A.8 1965), cert. denied, 382 U.S. 1011 (1966). And, under §8(a)(5), bargaining over the effects of a decision must be conducted in a meaningful manner and at a meaningful time, and the Board may impose sanctions to insure its adequacy. A union, by pursuing such bargaining rights, may achieve valuable concessions from an employer engaged in a partial closing. It also may secure in contract negotiations provisions implementing rights to notice, information, and fair bargaining. See BNA, Basic Patterns in Union Contracts 62-64 (9th ed., 1979).

Moreover, the union's legitimate interest in fair dealing is protected by §8(a)(3), which prohibits partial closings motivated by anti-union animus, when done to gain an unfair advantage. Textile Workers v. Darlington Co., 380 U.S. 263 (1965). Under §8(a)(3) the Board may inquire into the motivations behind a partial closing. An employer may not simply shut down part of its business and mask its desire to weaken and circumvent the union by labeling its decision "purely economic."

Thus, although the union has a natural concern that a partial closing decision not be hastily or unnecessarily entered into, it has some control over the effects of the decision and indirectly may ensure that the decision itself is deliberately considered. It also has direct protection against a partial closing decision that is motivated by an intent to harm a union.

Management's interest in whether it should discuss a decision of this kind is much more complex and varies with the particular circumstances. If labor costs are an important factor in a failing operation and the decision to close, management will have an incentive to confer voluntarily with the union to seek concessions that may make continuing the business profitable. Cf. U.S. News & World Report, Feb. 9, 1981, p. 74; BNA, Labor Relations Yearbook — 1979, p. 5 (UAW agreement with Chrysler Corp. to make concessions on wages and fringe benefits). At other times, management may have great need for speed, flexibility, and secrecy in meeting business opportunities and exigencies.[20] It may face

---

failing plant); 104 Lab. Rel. Rep. 239 (1980) (employee ownership plan instituted to save company); id., at 267-268 (union accepted pay cuts to reduce plant's financial problems). These have come about without the intervention of the Board enforcing a statutory requirement to bargain.

20. See International Assn. of Machinists & Aerospace Workers v. Northeast Airlines, Inc., 473 F.2d 549, 556-557 (C.A.1), cert. denied, 409 U.S. 845 (1972); Raskin Packing Co., 246 N.L.R.B. No. 15 (1979); M & M Transportation Co., 239 N.L.R.B. 73 (1978); Goetz, The Duty to Bargain about Changes in Operations, 1964 Duke L.J. 1, 9-10. Cf. Detroit Edison Co. v. NLRB, 440 U.S. 301, 316 (1979) (noting the "danger of inadvertent leaks" in giving union confidential information).

significant tax or securities consequences that hinge on confidentiality, the timing of a plant closing, or a reorganization of the corporate structure. The publicity incident to the normal process of bargaining may injure the possibility of a successful transition or increase the economic damage to the business. The employer also may have no feasible alternative to the closing, and even good-faith bargaining over it may be both futile and cause the employer additional loss.

There is an important difference, also, between permitted bargaining and mandated bargaining. Labeling this type of decision mandatory could afford a union a powerful tool for achieving delay, a power that might be used to thwart management's intentions in a manner unrelated to any feasible solution the union might propose. See Comment, "Partial Terminations" — A Choice Between Bargaining Equality and Economic Efficiency, 14 U.C.L.A.L. Rev. 1089, 1103-1105 (1967). In addition, many of the cases before the Board have involved, as this one did, not simply a refusal to bargain over the decision, but a refusal to bargain at all, often coupled with other unfair labor practices. In these cases, the employer's action gave the Board reason to order remedial relief apart from access to the decisionmaking process. It is not clear that a union would be equally dissatisfied if an employer performed all its bargaining obligations apart from the additional remedy sought here.

While evidence of current labor practice is only an indication of what is feasible through collective bargaining, and not a binding guide, see *Chemical Workers,* 404 U.S., at 176, that evidence supports the apparent imbalance weighing against mandatory bargaining. We note that provisions giving unions a right to participate in the decisionmaking process concerning alteration of the scope of an enterprise appear to be relatively rare. Provisions concerning notice and "effects" bargaining are more prevalent. See II BNA, Collective Bargaining Negotiations and Contracts §65:201-233 (1981); U.S. Dept. of Labor, Bureau of Labor Statistics, Bull. 2065. Characteristics of Major Collective Bargaining Agreements, January 1, 1978, pp. 96, 100, 101, 102-103 (charting provisions giving interplant transfer and relocation allowances; advance notice of layoffs, shutdowns, and technological changes; and wage-employment guarantees; no separate tables on decision-bargaining, presumably due to rarity). See also U.S. Dept. of Labor, Bull. No. 1425-10, Major Collective Bargaining Agreements, Plant Movement, Transfer, and Relocation Allowances (July 1969).

Further, the presumption analysis adopted by the Court of Appeals seems ill suited to advance harmonious relations between employer and employee. An employer would have difficulty determining beforehand whether it was faced with a situation requiring bargaining or one that involved economic necessity sufficiently compelling to obviate the duty to bargain. If it should decide to risk not bargaining, it might be faced ultimately with harsh remedies forcing it to pay large amounts of backpay to employees who likely would have been discharged regardless of bargaining, or even to consider reopening a failing operation. See, e.g., Electrical Products Div. of Midland-Ross Corp., 239 N.L.R.B. 323 (1978), enf'd, 617 F.2d 977 (C.A.3 1980), cert. denied, 452 U.S. 685 (1981). Cf. Lever Brothers Co. v. International Chemical Workers Union, 554 F.2d 115 (C.A.4 1976) (enjoining plant closure and transfer to permit negotiations). Also, labor costs may not be a crucial circumstance in a particular economically-based partial termination. See, e.g., NLRB v. International Harvester Co., 618 F.2d 85 (C.A.9 1980) (change in marketing structure); NLRB v. Thompson Transport Co., 406 F.2d 698 (C.A. 10 1969) (loss of major customer). And in those cases, the Board's traditional remedies may well be futile. See ABC Trans-National Transport, Inc. v. NLRB, 642 F.2d 675 (C.A. 3 1981) (although employer violated its "duty" to bargain about freight terminal closing, court refused to enforce order to bargain). If the employer intended to try to fulfill a court's direction to bargain, it would have difficulty determining exactly at what stage of its deliberations the duty to bargain would arise and what amount of bargaining would suffice before it could implement its decision. Compare Burns Ford, Inc., 182 N.L.R.B. 753 (1970) (one week's notice of layoffs sufficient), and Hartmann Luggage Co., 145 N.L.R.B. 1572 (1964) (entering into executory subcontracting agreement before notifying union not a violation since contract not yet final), with Royal Plating & Polishing Co., 148 N.L.R.B. 545, 555 (1964), enf. denied, 350 F.2d 191 (C.A.3 1965) (two weeks' notice before final closing of plant inadequate). If an employer engaged in some discussion, but did not yield to the union's demands, the Board might conclude that the employer had engaged in "surface bargaining," a violation of its good faith. See NLRB v. Reed & Prince Mfg. Co., 205 F.2d 131 (C.A.1), cert. denied, 346 U.S. 887 (1953). A union, too, would have difficulty determining the limits of its prerogatives, whether and when it could use its economic powers to try to alter an employer's decision, or whether, in doing so, it would trigger sanctions from the Board. See, e.g., International Offset Corp., 210 N.L.R.B. 854 (1974) (union's failure to realize that shutdown was imminent, in view of successive advertisements, sales of equipment, and layoffs, held a waiver of right to bargain); Shell Oil Co., 149 N.L.R.B. 305 (1965) (union waived its right to bargain by failing to request meetings when employer announced intent to transfer a few days before implementation).

We conclude that the harm likely to be done to an employer's need to operate freely in deciding whether to shut down part of its business purely for economic reasons outweighs the incremental benefit that might be gained through the union's participation in making the decision[22] and we hold that the decision itself is *not* part of §8(d)'s "terms and

22. In this opinion we of course intimate no view as to other types of management decisions, such as plant relocations, sales, other kinds of subcontracting, automation, etc., which are to be considered on their particular facts. See, e.g., International Ladies' Garment Workers Union v. NLRB, 150 U.S. App. D.C. 71, 463 F.2d 907 (1972) (plant reloca-

conditions," see n.12, supra, over which Congress has mandated bargaining.[23]

B

In order to illustrate the limits of our holding, we turn again to the specific facts of this case. First, we note that when petitioner decided to terminate its Greenpark contract, it had no intention to replace the discharged employees or to move that operation elsewhere. Petitioner's sole purpose was to reduce its economic loss, and the union made no claim of anti-union animus. In addition, petitioner's dispute with Greenpark was solely over the size of the management fee Greenpark was willing to pay. The union had no control or authority over that fee. The most that the union could have offered would have been advice and concessions that Greenpark, the third party upon whom rested the success or failure of the contract, had no duty even to consider. These facts

---

tion predominantly due to labor costs); Weltronic Co. v. NLRB, 419 F.2d 1120 (C.A.6 1969), cert. denied, 398 U.S. 938 (1970) (decision to move plant three miles); Dan Dee West Virginia Corp., 180 N.L.R.B. 534 (1970) (decision to change method of distribution, under which employee-drivers became independent contractors); Young Motor Truck Service, Inc., 156 N.L.R.B. 661 (1966) (decision to sell major portion of business). See also Schwarz, Plant Relocation or Partial Termination — The Duty to Decision-Bargain, 39 Ford. L. Rev. 8-1, 100-102 (1970).

23. Despite the contentions of amicus AFL-CIO our decision in Order of Railroad Telegraphers v. Chicago & N.W.R. Co., 362 U.S. 330 (1960), does not require that we find bargaining over this partial closing decision mandatory. In that case, a union certified as bargaining agent for certain railroad employees requested that the railroad bargain over its decision to close down certain stations thereby eliminating a number of jobs. When the union threatened to strike over the railroad's refusal to bargain on this issue, the railroad sought an injunction in federal court. Construing the scope of bargaining required by §2, First, of the Railway Labor Act, 45 U.S.C. §152, the Court held that the union's effort to negotiate was not "an unlawful bargaining demand," 362 U.S., at 341, and that the District Court was precluded from enjoining the threatened strike by §4 of the Norris-LaGuardia Act, 29 U.S.C. §104, which deprives federal courts of "jurisdiction to issue any restraining order or temporary or permanent injunction in any case involving or growing out of any labor dispute to prohibit any person or persons participating or interested in such dispute . . . from . . . [c]easing or refusing to perform any work. . . . " Although the Court in part relied on an expansive interpretation of §2, First, which requires railroads to "exert every reasonable effort to make and maintain agreements concerning rates of pay, rules, and working conditions," and §13(c) of the Norris-LaGuardia Act, 29 U.S.C. §113(c), defining "labor dispute" as "any controversy concerning terms or conditions of employment," its decision also rested on the particular aims of the Railway Labor Act and national transportation policy. See 362 U.S., at 336-338. The mandatory scope of bargaining under the Railway Labor Act and the extent of the prohibition against injunctive relief contained in Norris-LaGuardia are not coextensive with the National Labor Relations Act and the Board's jurisdiction over unfair labor practices. See Chicago & N.W.R. Co. v. Transportation Union, 402 U.S. 570, 579, n.11 (1971) ("parallels between the duty to bargain in good faith and the duty to exert every reasonable effort, like all parallels between the NLRA and the Railway Labor Act, should be drawn with the utmost care and with full awareness of the differences between the statutory schemes"). Cf. Boys Market, Inc. v. Retail Clerks, 398 U.S. 235 (1970); Buffalo Forge Co. v. United Steelworkers of America, 428 U.S. 397 (1976).

in particular distinguish this case from the subcontracting issue presented in *Fibreboard.* Further, the union was not selected as the bargaining representative or certified until well after petitioner's economic difficulties at Greenpark had begun. We thus are not faced with an employer's abrogation of ongoing negotiations or an existing bargaining agreement. Finally, while petitioner's business enterprise did not involve the investment of large amounts of capital in single locations, we do not believe that the absence of "significant investment or withdrawal of capital," General Motors Corp., GMC Truck & Coach Div., 191 N.L.R.B., at 952, is crucial. The decision to halt work at this specific location represented a significant change in petitioner's operations, a change not unlike opening a new line of business or going out of business entirely.

The judgement of the Court of Appeals, accordingly, is reversed and the case is remanded to that court for further proceedings consistent with this opinion.

It is so ordered.

Brennan, J., with whom Marshall, J., joins, dissenting.

. . . As this Court has noted, the words "terms and conditions of employment" plainly cover termination of employment resulting from a management decision to close an operation. Fibreboard Paper Products Corp. v. NLRB, 379 U.S. 203, 210 (1964). As the Court today admits, the decision to close an operation "touches on a matter of central and pressing concern to the union and its member employees." Moreover, as the Court today further concedes, Congress deliberately left the words "terms and conditions to employment" indefinite, so that the NLRB would be able to give content to those terms in light of changing industrial conditions. In the exercise of its congressionally-delegated authority and accumulated expertise, the Board has determined that an employer's decision to close part of its operations affects the "terms and conditions of employment" within the meaning of the Act, and is thus a mandatory subject for collective bargaining. Ozark Trailers, Inc., 161 N.L.R.B. 561 (1966). Nonetheless, the Court today declines to defer to the Board's decision on this sensitive question of industrial relations, and on the basis of pure speculation reverses the judgment of the Board and of the Court of Appeals. I respectfully dissent.

Court bases its decision on a balancing test. It states that "bargaining over management decisions that have a substantial impact on the continued availability of employment should be required only if the benefit, for labor-management relations and the collective-bargaining process, outweighs the burden placed on the conduct of the business." I cannot agree with this test, because it takes into account only the interests of *management;* it fails to consider the legitimate employment interests of the workers and their Union. Cf. Brockway Motor Trucks v. NLRB, 582 F.2d 720, 734-740 (C.A.3 1978) (balancing of interests of workers in retaining their jobs against interests of employers in maintaining unhindered control over corporate direction). This one-sided approach hardly serves "to foster in a neutral manner" a system for resolution of these serious, two-sided controversies.

Even if the Court's statement of the test were accurate, I could not join in its application, which is based solely on speculation. Apparently, the Court concludes that the benefit to labor-management relations and the collective-bargaining process from negotiation over partial closings is minimal, but it provides no evidence to that effect. The Court acknowledges that the Union might be able to offer concessions, information, and alternatives that might obviate or forestall the closing, but it then asserts that "[i]t is unlikely, however, that requiring bargaining over the decision . . . will augment this flow of information and suggestions." Recent experience, however, suggests the contrary. Most conspicuous, perhaps, were the negotiations between Chrysler Corporation and the United Auto Workers, which led to significant adjustments in compensation and benefits, contributing to Chrysler's ability to remain afloat. See Wall St. Journal, Oct. 26, 1979, at 3, col. 1. Even where labor costs are not the direct cause of a company's financial difficulties, employee concessions can often enable the company to continue in operation — if the employees have the opportunity to offer such concessions.*

The Court further presumes that management's need for "speed, flexibility, and secrecy" in making partial closing decisions would be frustrated by a requirement to bargain. In some cases the Court might be correct. In others, however, the decision will be made openly and deliberately, and considerations of "speed, flexibility, and secrecy" will be inapposite. Indeed, in view of management's admitted duty to bargain over the effects of a closing, it is difficult to understand why additional bargaining over the closing itself would necessarily unduly delay or publicize the decision.

I am not in a position to judge whether mandatory bargaining over partial closings *in all cases* is consistent with our national labor policy, and neither is the Court. The primary responsibility to determine the scope of the statutory duty to bargain has been entrusted to the NLRB, which should not be reversed by the courts merely because they might prefer another view of the statute. Ford Motor Co. v. NLRB, 441 U.S. 488, 495-497 (1979); see NLRB v. Erie Resistor Corp., 373 U.S. 221, 236 (1963). I therefore agree with the Court of Appeals that employers presumptively

* Indeed, in this case, the Court of Appeals found: "On the record, . . . there is sufficient reason to believe that, given the opportunity, the union might have made concessions, by accepting reduction in wages or benefits (take-backs) or a reduction in the work force, which would in part or in whole have enabled Greenpark to give FNM an increased management fee. At least, if FNM had bargained over its decision to close, that possibility would have been tested, and management would still have been free to close the Greenpark operation if bargaining did not produce a solution." 627 F.2d 596, 602 (C.A.2 1980).

have a duty to bargain over a decision to close an operation, and that this presumption can be rebutted by a showing that bargaining would be futile, that the closing was due to emergency financial circumstances, or that, for some other reason, bargaining would not further the purposes of the National Labor Relations Act. 627 F.2d 596, 601 (C.A.2 1980). I believe that this approach is amply supported by recent decisions of the Board. E.g., Brooks-Scanlon, Inc., 246 N.L.R.B. No. 76, 102 L.R.R.M. 1606 (1979); Raskin Packing Co, 246 N.L.R.B. No. 15, 102 L.R.R.M. 1489 (1979); M. & M. Transportation Co., 239 N.L.R.B. 73 (1978). With respect to the individual facts of this case, however, I would vacate the judgment of the Court of Appeals, and remand to the Board for further examination of the evidence. See SEC v. Chenery Corp., 318 U.S. 80, 94-95 (1943).

Note

Reconsider the essay on statutory gap-fillers, supra at p. 369. How does that discussion bear on this case?

OTIS ELEVATOR CO.

269 N.L.R.B. No. 162, 115 L.R.R.M. 1281 (1984)

On 25 March 1981 the National Labor Relations Board issued a Decision and Order in this proceeding, finding that the Respondent had engaged in unfair labor practices in violation of §§8(a)(5) and (1) of the National Labor Relations Act, as amended. The Board held that the Respondent had violated the Act by: (1) refusing to bargain with the Union over its decision to transfer and consolidate certain unit work from its Mahwah, New Jersey, facility to other facilities in East Hartford, Connecticut; (2) refusing to provide the Union with information relevant to the Respondent's decision; and (3) refusing to bargain with the Union over the effects of the Respondent's decision.

The Union and the Respondent filed petitions for review of the Board's Decision and Order with the United States Court of Appeals for the District of Columbia Circuit, and the Board filed a cross-application for enforcement of its Order. On 12 August 1981 the court granted the Board's motion to remand this case to the Board for reconsideration in light of the Supreme Court's decision in First National Maintenance v. NLRB, 452 U.S. 666 (1981).

On 11 September 1981 the Board informed the parties that it intended to reconsider this case and invited them to submit statements of position. All parties filed statements of position.

I

The Board has reconsidered its Decision and Order in this case in light of the Supreme Court's opinion in *First National Maintenance.* We conclude that Respondent was free to decide to discontinue its research and development activities in Mahwah, New Jersey, and to consolidate them with its operation in East Hartford, Connecticut, unrestrained by §§8(a)(5) and 8(d) of the Act. Acknowledging that its decision touched on a matter of central concern to the Union and to the employees it represented, we nevertheless find under the guidance of *First National Maintenance* that the decision turned not upon labor costs, but instead turned upon a change in the nature and direction of a significant facet of its business. Thus it constituted a managerial decision of the sort which is at the core of entrepreneurial control outside the limited scope of §8(d).

Our understanding of the Court's construction of §8(d) is best explicated by Mr. Justice Stewart's concurring opinion in Fibreboard Corp. v. NLRB, 379 U.S. 203, 217 (1964), explicitly relied on by the Court in *First National Maintenance*:

> If, as I think clear, the purpose of §8(d) is to describe a limited area subject to the duty of collective bargaining, those management decisions which are fundamental to the basic direction of a corporate enterprise or which impinge only indirectly upon employment security should be excluded from the area. 379 U.S. at 223.

II

United Technologies acquired Otis Elevator Company in 1975. A review was then made of Otis' engineering organization and the state of Otis' technological development. Based on that review, a formal evaluation of Otis' operations was undertaken by Booz-Allen & Hamilton and by the President of Otis, Robert Cole. In addition, Otis' vice-president, Dr. William M. Foley, independently studied the Company's existing technology. All three studies showed that Otis' technology was outdated, having resulted in product designs that were too expensive and not competitive. Otis' share of the world elevator market was steadily declining, and the Company was selling its products at less than cost in order to remain in the market. Otis' engineering activity was scattered throughout North America, and work performed in one location was being duplicated elsewhere. In particular, the Respondent did research and development work in Parsippany, New Jersey, and did similar work at its outdated and inadequate engineering center in Mahwah, New Jersey. By contrast, United Technologies had a major research and development center in East Hartford, Connecticut, employing approximately 1,000 employees, some of whom were working on elevator-related research projects for Otis.

Based upon its review of Otis' problems, the Respondent decided to terminate Otis research and development operations in Parsippany and Mahwah and to consolidate them at its facility in East Hartford, Connecticut. The Respondent's management believed that consolidation of research and development functions in close proximity to United Technologies would strengthen the overall engineering effort and enable Otis to redesign its product to reduce its production costs. In July 1977, Otis closed its Parsippany facility, transferred its research and development operations to East Hartford, and relocated there approximately 30 Parsippany employees. In the fall of 1977, Vice President Foley recommended a merger of the Mahwah product improvement effort (part of the Otis engineering division) with the overlapping Otis research and development function now located in East Hartford. In October 1977 President Cole approved Dr. Foley's recommendation to transfer the Mahwah production improvement group to East Hartford.

As part of the research and development consolidation. Otis began construction of a research center, including an elevator test tower, adjacent to Otis' North American Operations headquarters in East Hartford, with which it would share computer facilities. The new research center represented a capital investment of between two and three-one-half million dollars.

On 2 December 1977 Dr. Foley informed the Mahwah employees of Otis' plans: by July 1979 there would be a research and development center in East Hartford housing research, development, product engineering, product improvement, testing, and cost reduction operations. The Mahwah facility would continue to house contract engineering, final drafting, data handling, data release, and worldwide data distribution. As part of its plan, Otis transferred 17 unit employees from Mahwah to East Hartford.

We conclude that the Respondent's decision to discontinue its research and development functions in Mahwah, New Jersey and to transfer those functions to its facility in East Hartford, Connecticut, was not subject to mandatory bargaining. . . .

In this case the Respondent decided to discontinue its research and development operations in Parsippany and in Mahwah, New Jersey and to consolidate them in East Hartford, Connecticut, to improve its research and development and hopefully the marketability of its product. Good or bad, this type of decision is beyond the reach of §8(d). The Respondent made its decision because of its opinion that its technology was dated, its product was not competitive, its Mahwah research and development operation duplicated other operations, and because a newer and larger research and development center was available in East Hartford.[3] These facts establish that the Respondent's decision did not

3. In any particular case, although perhaps not here, either the soundness of the judgment or the value of these concerns might be debatable. We see no value in such a debate. Whatever the merits of the decision, so long as it does not turn upon labor costs, §8(d) of the Act does not apply.

turn upon labor costs[4] even though that factor may have been one of the circumstances which stimulated the evaluation process which generated the decision. Despite the *evident effect* on employees, the critical factor to a determination whether the decision is subject to mandatory bargaining is the essence of the decision itself, i.e., whether it turns upon a change in the nature or direction of the business, or turns upon labor costs; *not* its effect on employees nor a union's ability to offer alternatives. The decision at issue here clearly turned upon a fundamental change in the nature and direction of the business, and thus was not amenable to bargaining.

We see no need to reexamine the full scope of the Court's analysis in *First National Maintenance.* The Court discussed at length the Board's extant decisions and the opinions of the Courts of Appeals in this difficult area. For all the reasons given by the Court, we find that the Respondent's decision here turned upon a fundamental change in the nature and direction of the business, and for that reason is excluded from the limited area of bargaining described by §8(d).

III

The Board, before the Supreme Court decided *First National Maintenance,* had applied its approach to plant closure to other managerial decisions which affected both the direction of the business and employees. The Court's opinion rejected that approach. The Court's view that predictability in this area is necessary for both labor and management leads us to elaborate on our present view of §8(d) as it impacts upon management decisions, other than partial closings, to change the nature of the enterprise.

In footnote 22 of its opinion the Supreme Court excluded from its ruling questions whether other types of management decisions, such as plant relocations, sales, various kinds of subcontracting, automation, etc., are excluded from mandatory bargaining. In view of the Court's rejection of the Board's approach we have decided to follow the Court's lead and to rely on the analysis of Justice Stewart's opinion in *Fibreboard* . . . .

Thus, for the reasons the Court gave in *First National Maintenance* (inter alia, management's need for predictability, flexibility, speed, secrecy, and to operate profitably), we hold that excluded from §8(d) of the Act are decisions which affect the scope, direction, or nature of the business.[5] For example, we are aware that in the past the Board's deci-

4. We note there is no allegation present that the Respondent acted for antiunion reasons, or from a desire to modify or lower labor costs . . . .

5. Such decisions include, inter alia, decisions to sell a business or a part thereof, to dispose of its assets, to restructure or to consolidate operations, to subcontract, to invest in labor-saving machinery, to change the methods of finance or of sales, advertising, product

sions reflected an almost reflexive response to "subcontracting" decisions as requiring bargaining. We emphasize, again, that the appellation of the decision is not important. Fibreboard "subcontracting" must be bargained not because the decision turns upon the label, but because in fact the decision turns upon a reduction of labor costs. In *First National Maintenance* the Court explained that its holding in *Fibreboard* derived from the fact that the employer's decision to subcontract did not turn upon a change in the basic operation, but rather turned upon a reduction of labor costs.

In contrast, if Adams Dairy, 137 N.L.R.B. 815 (1962), enf. denied in relevant part 350 F.2d 108 (8th Cir. 1965), cert. denied 382 U.S. 1011 (1966), were before us today, we would hold that decision to "subcontract" is *not* subject to §8(d), because the employer's decision there to discontinue its own distribution operation and to contract out that function turned upon a fundamental change in the scope and direction of the enterprise. The employer retained no control over the equipment or the employees in the subcontractors' distribution system. Further, no alter ego or other sham devices were employed to disguise a unilateral reduction in labor costs in an operation over which the employer maintained surreptitious control. As the Court of Appeals said: "[T]here is a change in basic operating procedure in that the dairy liquidated that part of its business handling distribution of milk product. . . ." 350 F.2d at 111. Included within §8(d), however, in accordance with the teachings of *Fibreboard*, are all decisions which turn upon a reduction of labor costs. This is true whether the decision may be characterized as subcontracting, reorganization, consolidation, or relocation, if the decision in fact turns on direct modification of labor costs and not on a change in the basic direction or nature of the enterprise. We note in this regard our recent decision in Milwaukee Spring II, 268 N.L.R.B. No. 87 (Jan. 23, 1984). In *Milwaukee Spring II* the parties stipulated that the employer's decision to relocate work from its unionized plant to a nonunion plant turned upon a reduction of its labor costs, and that the decision thus was a mandatory subject of bargaining. Had the parties not stipulated, we would have so held. Indeed, in *Milwaukee Spring II*, the Respondent recognized the decision as such, and did in fact bargain in good faith to impasse with the Union concerning wages.

We also recognize that these decisions do not fit neatly into categories.

---

design, and all other decisions akin to the foregoing. See generally Machinists v. Northeast Airlines, 473 F.2d 549 (1st Cir. 1972), cert. denied 409 U.S. 845 (1972), arising under the Federal Aviation Act of 1958, Sec. 408, 49 U.S.C.A. Sec. 1378, and Railway Labor Act, Sec. 2, subd. 1, 45 U.S.C.A. Sec. 152, subd. 1, where the court held that Northeast Airlines had no duty to bargain over its decision to merge into Delta Air Lines. The court held that *Fibreboard* did not guarantee union participation in a decision to merge. "[M]erger negotiations require a secrecy, flexibility and quickness antithetical to collective bargaining." 473 F.2d at 557 cited with approval in First National Maintenance, 452 U.S. at 683 fn. 20.

Such decisions often involve elements of one or more types of decisions, such as the termination, relocation, and consolidation of the research and development operations in this case. As we noted before, it is also evident that labor costs often are among the considerations which cause management to decide to alter the scope or direction of its business. The Court in *First National Maintenance* stated with respect to partial closings that: "If labor costs are an important factor in a failing operation and the decision to close, management will have an incentive to confer voluntarily with the Union to seek concessions that may make continuing the business profitable." 452 U.S. at 682. The Court nevertheless found that this factor was insufficient to put the decision within §8(d), despite its acknowledgement that in the past unions had aided employers by various devices to save faltering businesses. The Court reasoned that if labor costs were a factor, that element of the decision could be adequately dealt with in effects bargaining. We discern no substantial reason why this analysis is not equally applicable to other decisions which turn upon a significant change in the nature or direction of a business. . . .[14]

Notes

1. From *Guidelines of NLRB General Counsel under First National Maintenance*, Daily Labor Reporter, April 15, 1982:

> [T]he Court expressly limited its holding in *First National Maintenance* to economically motivated decisions to go partially out of business. The Court stated that it "intimate[d] no view as to other types of management decisions, such as plant relocations, sales, subcontracting, automation, etc. . . ."
>
> Some of these decisions are clearly different in kind from a decision to close a portion of a business. Thus, for example, decisions to relocate a plant, to subcontract unit work, to eliminate unit jobs through automation, or to consolidate operations are not "akin to [a] decision whether to be in business at all." That is, the employer does not plan to withdraw from business activity, either wholly or partially. Instead, the employer intends to remain in the same business, albeit elsewhere (relocation), or at one location rather than several (consolidation).
>
> Since these decisions are different in kind from a decision to go completely out of business, the region will be required to investigate and analyze each case in light of the *First National Maintenance* balancing test. Thus, the Region must investigate the question of whether, and to what

[14] Member Dennis concurred separately. Member Zimmerman dissented on another issue.

> extent, a particular decision in a given case involves factors which would make bargaining burdensome. On the other side of the scale, the Region must investigate the question of whether a bargaining requirement could be beneficial for labor-management relations and the collective-bargaining process. In this regard, the Region should focus on whether the employer's decision was based on labor costs or other factors that would be amenable to resolution through the collective bargaining process.
>
> If the factors which indicate that the decision is amenable to the process of collective bargaining clearly outweigh the factors which indicate that bargaining would be "burdensome" to the decision-making employer, the Region should issue complaint. . . . If the balance tips clearly the other way, the Region should dismiss. . . . If the balance does not tip clearly either way, the case should be submitted to [the General Counsel's Advice Branch in Washington].
>
> [I]f the case involves an employer's decision to go wholly out of business for economic reasons, . . . the case should ordinarily be dismissed. . . . The same conclusion would obtain in a case involving an economically-motivated decision to terminate a distinct line of business. . . .
>
> Similarly, if the case involves an economically-motivated decision to go partially out of business, the Region should ordinarily dismiss. . . .
>
> A decision to sell a business, . . . and to no longer remain in the business, would appear akin to the type of decision to which *First National Maintenance* is applicable. Thus, such a decision is essentially a decision not to be in business at all. . . .
>
> Accordingly, the Region should ordinarily dismiss such charges. . . .

2. *Problems.* a. The Marriot Corporation operates a commissary that prepares and distributes food products to restaurants in several states. One of the commissary's departments processed shrimp. Because of a rise in the price of raw shrimp and certain processing problems, Marriot contracted with Fishking, a seafood processing company, to supply Marriot with processed shrimp. Marriot then laid off 12 department employees and discontinued its shrimp-processing operation. Its shrimp-processing equipment was sold to Fishking and other related equipment was returned to its lessor. Freezer and hydraulic equipment used in the shrimp-processing operation was diverted to other uses, as was the plant area formerly devoted to shrimp processing.

Marriot did not notify the union representing its shrimp-processing employees nor bargain with the union over its decision. Has Marriot violated §8(a)(5)? Do you need more facts? See Marriot Corp., 264 N.L.R.B. 1369 (1982).

b. Are work preservation clauses, such as the one involved in *National Woodwork*, now nonmandatory subjects of bargaining? After they read *Otis Elevator*, how would you expect managers to characterize their opposition to particular work preservation clauses?

C. MULTIEMPLOYER AND MULTIUNION BARGAINING

CHARLES D. BONANNO, INC. v. NLRB
454 U.S. 404 (1982)

WHITE, J.

The issue here is whether a bargaining impasse justifies an employer's unilateral withdrawal from a multiemployer bargaining unit. The National Labor Relations Board (Board) concluded that an employer attempting such a withdrawal commits an unfair labor practice in violation of §§8(a)(5) and 8(a)(1) of the National Labor Relations Act (Act) by refusing to execute the collective-bargaining agreement later executed by the union and the multiemployer association. The Court of Appeals for the First Circuit enforced the Board's order. Both the Board and the Court of Appeals recognized that several other Courts of Appeals had previously rejected the Board's position on this issue. We granted certiorari to resolve the conflict among the Circuits on this important question of federal labor law. We affirm the judgment of the Court of Appeals.

I

The factual findings of the Administrative Law Judge were affirmed by the Board and are undisputed. Petitioner, Charles D. Bonanno Linen Service, Inc. (Bonanno), is a Massachusetts corporation engaged in laundering, renting, and distributing linens and uniforms. Teamsters Local No. 25 (Union) represents its drivers and helpers as well as those of other linen supply companies in the area. For several years, Bonanno has been a member of the New England Linen Supply Association (Association), a group of 10 employers formed to negotiate with the Union as a multiemployer unit and a signatory of the contracts negotiated between the Union and the Association. On February 19, 1975, Bonanno authorized the Association's negotiating committee to represent it in the anticipated negotiations for a new contract. Bonanno's president became a member of the committee.

The Union and the Association held 10 bargaining sessions during March and April. On April 30, the negotiators agreed upon a proposed contract, but four days later the Union members rejected it. By May 15, according to the stipulations of the parties, the Union and the Association had reached an impasse over the method of compensation: the Union demanded that the drivers be paid on commission, while the Association insisted on continuing payment at an hourly rate.

Several subsequent meetings failed to break the impasse. On June 23, the Union initiated a selective strike against Bonanno. In response, most Association members locked out their drivers. Despite sporadic meetings, the stalemate continued throughout the summer. During this period two of the employers met secretly with the Union, presumably in an effort to reach a separate settlement. These meetings, however, never reached the level of negotiations.

Bonanno hired permanent replacements for all of its striking drivers. On November 21, it notified the Association by letter that it was "withdrawing from the Association with specific respect to negotiations at this time because of an ongoing impasse with Teamsters Local 25." Bonanno mailed a copy of its revocation letter to the Union and read the letter over the phone to a Union representative.

Soon after Bonanno's putative withdrawal, the Association ended the lockout. It told the Union that it wished to continue multiemployer negotiations. Several negotiating sessions took place between December and April, without Bonanno participating. In the middle of April, the Union abandoned its demand for payment on commission and accepted the Association's offer of a revised hourly wage rate. With this development, the parties quickly agreed on a new contract, dated April 23, 1976, and given retroactive effect to April 18, 1975.

Meanwhile, on April 9, 1976, the Union had filed the present action, alleging that Bonanno's purported withdrawal from the bargaining unit constituted an unfair labor practice. In a letter dated April 29, the Union informed Bonanno that because the Union had never consented to the withdrawal, it considered Bonanno to be bound by the settlement just reached. In a reply letter, Bonanno denied that it was bound by the contract.

An Administrative Law Judge concluded, after a hearing, that no unusual circumstances excused Bonanno's withdrawal from the multiemployer bargaining unit. The Board affirmed, ordering Bonanno to sign and implement the contract retroactively. In a supplemental decision, the Board explained the basis of its decision that Bonanno's attempt to withdraw from the multiemployer was untimely and ineffective. The Court of Appeals enforced the Board's order.

II

The standard for judicial review of the Board's decision in this case was established by NLRB v. Truck Drivers, 353 U.S. 87 (1957) (Buffalo Linen). There, the Union struck a single employer during negotiations with a multiemployer bargaining association. The other employers responded with a lockout. Negotiations continued, and an agreement was reached. The Union, claiming that the lockout violated its rights under §§7 and 8 of the Act, then filed charges with the Board. The Board rejected the claim, but the Court of Appeals held that the lockout was an unfair practice.

This Court in turn reversed. That the Act did not expressly authorize or deal with multiemployer units or with lockouts in that context was recognized. Nonetheless, multiemployer bargaining had "long antedated the Wagner Act" and had become more common as employers, in the course of complying with their duty to bargain under the Act, "sought through group bargaining to match increased union strength." 353 U.S., at 94-95 (footnote omitted). Furthermore, at the time of the debates on the Taft-Hartley amendments, Congress had rejected a proposal to limit or outlaw multiemployer bargaining. The debates and their results offered "cogent evidence that in many industries multiemployer bargaining basis was a vital factor in the effectuation of the national policy of promoting labor peace through strengthened collective bargaining." Id., at 95.[3] Congress' refusal to intervene indicated that it intended to leave to the Board's specialized judgment the resolution of conflicts between union and employer rights that were bound to arise in multiemployer bargaining. In such situations, the Court said:

> The ultimate problem is the balancing of the conflicting legitimate interests. The function of striking that balance to effectuate national labor policy is often a difficult and delicate responsibility, which the Congress committed primarily to the National Labor Relations Board, subject to limited judicial review. Id., at 96.

Thus, the Court of Appeals' rejection of the Board's justification of the lockout as an acceptable effort to maintain the integrity of the multiemployer unit and its refusal to accept the lockout as a legitimate response to the whipsaw strike had too narrowly confined the exercise of the Board's discretion. Id., at 97.

Multiemployer bargaining has continued to be the preferred bargaining mechanism in many industries,[4] and as *Buffalo Linen* predicted, it has

3. As the Court of Appeals explained in this case:

> Multiemployer bargaining offers advantages to both management and labor. It enables smaller employers to bargain "on an equal basis with a large union" and avoid "the competitive disadvantages resulting from non-uniform contractual terms." NLRB v. Truck Drivers Local 449, 353 U.S. 87, 96 . . . (1957). At the same time, it facilitates the development of industry-wide, worker benefit programs that employers otherwise might be unable to provide. More generally, multiemployer bargaining encourages both sides to adopt a flexible attitude during negotiations; as the Board explains, employers can make concessions "without fear that other employers will refuse to make similar concessions to achieve a competitive advantage," and a union can act similarly "without fear that the employees will be dissatisfied at not receiving the same benefits which the union might win from other employers." Brief, at 10. Finally, by permitting the union and employers to concentrate their bargaining resources on the negotiation of a single contract, multiemployer bargaining enhances the efficiency and effectiveness of the collective bargaining process and thereby reduces industrial strife. 630 F.2d, at 28.

4. A recent survey of major collective-bargaining agreements (those covering 1,000 or more employees) found that of 1,536 major agreements, 648 (42%) were multiemployer agreements and that 3,238,400 employees were covered by these agreements. U.S. Bureau of Labor Statistics, Dept. of Labor, Bull. No. 2065, Characteristics of Major Collective Bargaining Agreements — January 1, 1978, p. 12, table 1.8 (1980).

raised a variety of problems requiring resolution. One critical question concerns the rights of the union and the employers to terminate the multiemployer bargaining arrangement. Until 1958, the Board permitted both employers and the union to abandon the unit even in the midst of bargaining. But in Retail Associates, 120 N.L.R.B. 388 (1958), the Board announced guidelines for withdrawal from multiemployer units. These rules, which reflect an increasing emphasis on the stability of multiemployer units, permit any party to withdraw prior to the date set for negotiation of a new contract or the date on which negotiations actually begin, provided that adequate notice is given. Once negotiations for a new contract have commenced, however, withdrawal is permitted only if there is "mutual consent" or "unusual circumstances" exist. Id., at 395.

The Board's approach in *Retail Associates* has been accepted in the courts, as have its decisions that unusual circumstances will be found where an employer is subject to extreme financial pressures or where a bargaining unit has become substantially fragmented. But as yet there is no consensus as to whether an impasse in bargaining in a multiemployer unit is an unusual circumstance justifying unilateral withdrawal by the Union or by an employer. After equivocating for a time, the Board squarely held that an impasse is not such an unusual circumstance. Hi-Way Billboards, Inc., 206 N.L.R.B. 22 (1973). The Court of Appeals for the Fifth Circuit refused enforcement of that decision, 500 F.2d 181 (1974), although it has since modified its views and now supports the Board. Similar decisions by the Board were also overturned by the Courts of Appeals in three other Circuits. NLRB v. Beck Engraving Co., 522 F.2d 475 (C.A.3 1975); NLRB v. Independent Assn. of Steel Fabricators, 582 F.2d 135 (C.A.2 1978); H. & D., Inc. v. NLRB, 105 L.R.R.M. 3070 (C.A.9 1980), cert. pending, No. 80-1498. After again considering the question in this case, the Board issued its decision reaffirming its position that an impasse is not an unusual circumstance justifying withdrawal. Its decision was sustained and enforced by the Court of Appeals for the First Circuit.

III

We agree with the Board and with the Court of Appeals. The Board has recognized the voluntary nature of multiemployer bargaining. It neither forces employers into multiemployer units nor erects barriers to withdrawal prior to bargaining. At the same time, it has sought to further the utility of multiemployer bargaining as an instrument of labor peace by limiting the circumstances under which any party may unilaterally withdraw during negotiations. Thus, it has reiterated the view expressed in *Hi-Way Billboards* that an impasse is not sufficiently destructive of group bargaining to justify unilateral withdrawal. As a recurring feature in the bargaining process, impasse is only a temporary deadlock or hiatus in negotiations "which in almost all cases is eventually broken, through either a change of mind or the application of economic force." Charles D. Bonanno Linen Service, Inc., 243 N.L.R.B. 1093, 1093-1094 (1979). Furthermore, an impasse may be "brought about intentionally by one or both parties as a device to further, rather than destroy, the bargaining process." Id., at 1094. Hence, "there is little warrant for regarding an impasse as a rupture of the bargaining relation which leaves the parties free to go their own ways." Ibid. As the Board sees it, permitting withdrawal at impasse would as a practical matter undermine the utility of multiemployer bargaining.[8]

Of course, the ground rules for multiemployer bargaining have not come into being overnight. They have evolved and are still evolving, as the Board, employing its expertise in the light of experience, has sought to balance the "conflicting legitimate interests" in pursuit of the "national policy of promoting labor peace through strengthened collective bargaining." Buffalo Linen, 353 U.S., at 95, 96. The Board might have struck a different balance from the one it has, and it may be that some or all of us would prefer that it had done so. But assessing the significance of impasse and the dynamics of collective bargaining is precisely the kind of judgment that *Buffalo Linen* ruled should be left to the Board. We cannot say that the Board's current resolution of the issue is arbitrary or contrary to law.

If the Board's refusal to accept an impasse, standing alone, as an unusual circumstance warranting withdrawal were the only issue in this case, we would affirm without more. But several Courts of Appeals have rejected *Hi-Way Billboards* on the grounds that impasse may precipitate a strike against one or all members of the unit and that upon impasse the Board permits the union to execute interim agreements with individual employers. These Courts of Appeals consider the possibility of such events as sufficient grounds for any employer in the unit to withdraw.

In *Beck Engraving Co.*, for example, the Court of Appeals for the Third Circuit held that an impasse followed by a selective strike justified unilateral withdrawal from the bargaining unit. Because at that juncture labor relations law, as interpreted by the Board, would permit the union to execute an interim agreement with the struck employer, the Court of Appeals concluded that the union and the employer entering into such an agreement would be given unfair advantage against other employers if the latter were not permitted to withdraw from the unit. The Court of

8. The Board explains that if withdrawal were permitted at impasse, the parties would bargain under the threat of withdrawal by any party who was not completely satisfied with the results of the negotiations. That is, parties could precipitate an impasse in order to escape any agreement less favorable than the one expected. In addition, it is precisely at and during impasse, when bargaining is temporarily replaced by economic warfare, that the need for a stable, predictable bargaining unit becomes acute in order that the parties can weigh the costs and possible benefits of their conduct. Brief for Respondent NLRB 24-25.

Appeals thought the employer's right to withdraw and the union's privilege of executing interim contracts should mature simultaneously. It concluded that the Board's approach too drastically upset the bargaining equilibrium to be justified in the name of maintaining the stability of the bargaining unit.

The Board's reasons for adhering to its *Hi-Way Billboards* position are telling. They are surely adequate to survive judicial review. First, it is said that strikes and interim agreements often occur in the course of negotiations prior to impasse and that neither tactic is necessarily associated with impasse. Second, it is "vital" to understand that the Board distinguishes "between interim agreements which contemplate adherence to a final unitwide contract and are thus not antithetical to group bargaining and individual agreements which are clearly inconsistent with, and destructive of, group bargaining." 243 N.L.R.B., at 1096. In Sangamo Construction Co., 188 N.L.R.B. 159 (1971), and Plumbers and Steamfitters Union No. 323 (P.H.C. Mechanical Contractors), 191 N.L.R.B. 592 (1971), the agreements arrived at with the struck employers were only temporary: both the union and the employer executing the interim agreement were bound by any settlement resulting from multiemployer bargaining. "[I]n both cases, since the early signers maintained a vested interest in the outcome of final union-association negotiations, the multiemployer unit was neither fragmented nor significantly weakened," 243 N.L.R.B., at 1096, and unilateral withdrawal was not justified.

On the other hand, where the union, not content with interim agreements that expire with the execution of a unitwide contract, executes separate agreements that will survive unit negotiations, the union has so "effectively fragmented and destroyed the integrity of the bargaining unit," ibid., as to create an "unusual circumstance" under *Retail Associates* rules. Cf. Typographic Service Co., 238 N.L.R.B. 1565 (1978). Furthermore, the Board has held that the execution of separate agreements that would permit either the union or the employer to escape the binding effect of an agreement resulting from group bargaining is a refusal to bargain and an unfair labor practice on the part of both the union and any employer executing such an agreement. Teamsters Union Local No. 378 (Olympia Automobile Dealers Assn.), 243 N.L.R.B. 1086 (1979). The remaining members of the unit thus can insist that parties remain subject to unit negotiations in accordance with their original understanding.

The Board therefore emphatically rejects the proposition that the negotiation of truly interim, temporary agreements, as distinguished from separate, final contracts, is "inconsistent with the concept of multiemployer bargaining units," 243 N.L.R.B., at 1096. Although interim agreements establish terms and conditions of employment for one or more employer members of the unit pending the outcome of renewed group bargaining, all employers, including those executing interim agreements, have an "equivalent stake" in the final outcome because the "resulting group agreement would then apply to all employers, including each signer of an interim agreement." Ibid. Such interim arrangements "preclude a finding that the early signers had withdrawn from the unit." Ibid. Although the Board concedes that interim agreements exert economic pressure on struck employers, this fact should no more warrant withdrawal than the refusal of one employer to join with others in a lockout.[9] In any event, the Board's view is that interim agreements, on balance, tend to deter rather than promote unit fragmentation since they preserve a continuing mutual interest by all employer members in a final associationwide contract.

The Board also rests on this Court's admonition that the Board should balance "conflicting legitimate interests" rather than economic weapons and bargaining strength. Its conclusion is that the interest in unit stability, recognized as a major consideration by both *Buffalo Linen* and NLRB v. Brown, 380 U.S. 278 (1965), adequately justifies enforcement of the obligation to bargain despite the execution of a temporary agreement.

Of course, no interim or separate agreements were executed in this case. But neither did the impasse initiate any right to execute an agreement inconsistent with the duty to abide by the results of group bargaining. Some Courts of Appeals, taking a different view of the interests involved, question the legitimacy of enforcing the duty to bargain where impasse has occurred and interim agreements have been or may be executed. We think the Board has confined itself within the zone of discretion entrusted to it by Congress. The balance it has struck is not inconsistent with the terms or purposes of the Act, and its decision should therefore be enforced.

IV

The Chief Justice, in dissent, is quite right that this case turns in major part on the extent to which the courts should defer to the Board's judg-

9. The Board adopts the language of the First Circuit below: "the uneven application of economic pressure per se is not inconsistent with multiemployer bargaining." 630 F.2d, at 33. In addition it points out that the employer also has additional weapons at its disposal for exerting economic pressure. It can engage in a lockout, make unilateral changes in working conditions if they are consistent with the offers the union has rejected, hire replacements to counter the loss of striking employees, and try to blunt the effectiveness of an anticipated strike by stockpiling inventories, readjusting contract schedules, or transferring work from one plant to another. The Board further notes that interim agreements do not always have the effect the Union desires. The signing of an interim agreement may not weaken the association's determination to resist the union's demands, see Plumbers & Steamfitters Union No. 323 (P.H.C. Mechanical Contractors), 191 N.L.R.B. 592 (1971), and the eventual contract settlement may have terms more favorable to the employers than the interim agreements, requiring the union to give up its temporary gains, see Associated Shower Door Co., 205 N.L.R.B. 677 (1973), enf'd on other grounds, 512 F.2d 230 (C.A.9), cert. denied, 423 U.S. 893 (1975). Brief for Respondent NLRB 33, nn. 48 and 49.

ment with respect to the critical factors involved. He is also correct in restating the Court's admonition in *Brown*, supra, at 291, that "[r]eviewing courts are not obliged to stand aside and rubber-stamp their affirmance of administrative decisions that they deem inconsistent with a statutory mandate or that frustrate the congressional policy underlying a statute." But the Chief Justice does not suggest that the Board seeks here to promote illegitimate ends. Both he and the Board strive to further labor peace through effective collective bargaining. Hence, if the Board's assessment of the impact of impasse and interim agreements on those goals is accepted, it is plain that its decision in this case is consistent with its mandate and promotes the underlying congressional purpose.

The Chief Justice, candidly accepting that the issue is one of balancing the legitimate interests involved, nonetheless disputes the Board's judgment regarding the underlying factors with respect to what would best serve the statutory goals. He rejects the Board's assessment of the significance of impasse and interim agreements in the multiemployer bargaining context and substitutes his own views. For example, he finds that the impasse in this case "was no 'temporary deadlock or hiatus in negotiations' as the Board claims; this was instead a complete breakdown in negotiations coupled with a prolonged strike and lock-out."[10] He also states, contrary to the Board's judgment, that when the parties have remained at impasse for a long period, "withdrawal of one or a few employers may facilitate rather than frustrate bargaining." Thus, the Chief Justice avers, it would be "more consistent with [the goals of industrial peace] to permit withdrawal and allow negotiation of separate agreements than to force the parties into escalated economic warfare."

The Chief Justice may be quite right. There is obviously room for differing judgments, however, as the conflicting judgments of the Courts of Appeals and the strong views of the Board on the issues now before us make clear. But the dissenting Justices would have us substitute our judgment for those of the Board with respect to the issues that Congress intended the Board should resolve. This we are unwilling to do. If the courts are to monitor so closely the agency's assessment of the kind of factors involved in this case, the role of the judiciary in administering regulatory statutes will be enormously expanded and its work will become more complex and time-consuming. We doubt that this is what Congress intended in subjecting the Board to judicial review. Indeed, we so held in *Buffalo Linen*.

We agree that the National Labor Relations Act does not constitute the Board as an "arbiter of the sort of economic weapons the parties can use in seeking to gain acceptance of their bargaining demands," NLRB v. Insurance Agents, 361 U.S. 477, 497 (1960), or give "the Board a

10. The dissent here ignores *Buffalo Linen*'s recognition of whipsawing as a legitimate weapon of economic persuasion in the course of collective bargaining. See Buffalo Linen, 353 U.S., at 90, n. 7.

general authority to assess the relative economic power of the adversaries in the bargaining process and to deny weapons to one party or the other because of its assessment of that party's bargaining power," American Ship Building Co. v. NLRB, 380 U.S. 300, 317 (1965). But the Board has refused to enter that proscribed area, despite the urging of several Courts of Appeals. Instead, it looked at its statutory mandate and duty — to promote labor peace through strengthened collective bargaining — in developing its rule.

In *Brown* itself the Court disagreed with the Board and held that no unfair labor practice occurred when members of a multiemployer unit hired temporary replacements following a lockout. Maintaining the stability of the multiemployer unit was the key to that decision: the Court reasoned that without temporary replacements "the prospect that the whipsaw strike would succeed in breaking up the employer association was not at all fanciful." Brown, 380 U.S., at 284. In contrast to its action in *Brown*, the Board in this case has developed a rule which, although it may deny an employer a particular economic weapon, does so in the interest of the proper and pre-eminent goal, maintaining the stability of the multiemployer unit. Because the Board has carefully considered the effect of its rule on that goal, we should defer to its judgment.

Affirmed.

Stevens, J., concurring.

The Court's holding today does not impair an employer's freedom to structure the manner in which it will conduct collective bargaining. Its opinion, which I join, recognizes the voluntary nature of multiemployer bargaining, and notes that the Board "neither forces employers into multiemployer units nor erects barriers to withdrawal prior to bargaining."

The mere fact that an employer bargains in conjunction with other employers does not necessarily mean that it must sign any contract that is negotiated by the group. The Board requires that, to be bound by the terms of group negotiation, the members of an employer association must "have indicated from the outset an unequivocal intention to be bound in collective bargaining by group rather than individual action," and the union representing their employees must "[have] been notified of the formation of the group and the delegation of bargaining authority to it, and [have] assented and entered upon negotiations with the group's representative." Weyerhaeuser Co., 166 N.L.R.B. 299, 299 (1967), enf'd, 130 U.S. App. D.C. 176, 398 F.2d 770 (1968). This test is well established in the Courts of Appeals. Absent such an unequivocal commitment to be bound by group action, an employer is free to withdraw from group negotiation at any time, or simply to reject the terms of the final group contract. See *Komatz Construction,* supra; Ruan Transport Corp., 234 N.L.R.B. 241 (1978). In the instant case, petitioner has never questioned the unequivocal character of its commitment to participate in and to be bound by the results of group negotiation.

The Court's holding does not preclude an employer from explicitly conditioning its participation in group bargaining on any special terms of its own design. Presumably, an employer could refuse to participate in multiemployer bargaining unless the union accepted the employer's right to withdraw from the bargaining unit should an impasse develop. The union or the other members of the bargaining unit of course may reject such a condition; in such a case, however, the employer simply would be forced to choose between agreeing to be bound by the terms of group negotiation without a right of withdrawal at impasse, or forgoing the advantages of multiemployer bargaining and bargaining on its own.

BURGER, C.J., with whom REHNQUIST, J., joins, dissenting.

The Court today affirms the National Labor Relations Board's finding that withdrawal of an employer from a multiemployer bargaining unit, after a long drawn-out and unproductive bargaining impasse, constitutes an unfair labor practice by the employer in violation of §§8(a)(1) and (5) of the National Labor Relations Act. In addition, the Court indicates that withdrawal is not permissible even after the union has negotiated separate agreements with other members of the bargaining unit.[1] The Court bases its holding in large part on deference to the views of the Board. Although judicial review of the Board's balancing of conflicting interests is limited, "the balance struck by the Board is [not] immune from judicial examination and reversal in proper cases." NLRB v. Brown, 380 U.S. 278, 290-291 (1965). When the Board's decisions create an artificial and unwarranted imbalance of economic weapons, the courts are not bound to show abject deference to the Board's views. Today the Court perpetuates an unsupportable imbalance and in so doing damages the very multiemployer bargaining mechanism it seeks to protect — a mechanism of great value to both unions and employers.[2]

1. "Whipsawing" describes any one of several tactics by which a union creates a situation in which some but not all employers in a multiemployer group are closed or hampered by a strike or lockout. A union may call a strike against one or a few of the employers or, in the fact of a lockout, it may negotiate a separate agreement with one or a few employers. Some of the employers are thus unable to conduct business as usual while others are fully operational. The theory behind whipsawing is that the impaired employers, seeing their competitors enjoying a market advantage and fearing that those competitors will increase their market share at the expense of the impaired employer, will be under irresistible pressure to yield to the union's demands.

2. The multiemployer mode of bargaining, traditionally seen as a defensive reaction by small employers, has become perhaps as important for unions as for employers. As counsel for the union in this case stated during oral argument, the limited funds and personnel of unions often make it very difficult for a union to negotiate separate agreements with each employer in industries where employer units are small.

I

The Court holds that the occurrence of an impasse, without more, does not *automatically* trigger a right of an employer to withdraw from a multiemployer bargaining unit. If the Court went no further, my objections would be minimal. In this case, however, there was much more than a mere impasse. At the time of the petitioner's withdrawal from the bargaining unit, the negotiations had been stalemated for more than six months, a selective strike and unitwide lockout had kept employees away from their jobs for five months, and there were no signs that the parties would return to the bargaining table. This was no "temporary deadlock or hiatus in negotiations" as the Board claims; this was instead a complete breakdown in negotiations coupled with a prolonged strike and lockout.[3] Nevertheless, the Court holds employers in the multiemployer group could not withdraw.

The Court then goes on, stating that even when the union negotiates separate "interim" agreements with individual employers the remaining employers cannot withdraw from the bargaining group. Thus, with all of the members of a multiemployer group closed down or crippled by a strike or a lockout, the union is permitted to "divide and conquer" by coming to terms with some of the employers, allowing them to resume operations with a full staff. With one or more competitors fully back in business, the ability of the remaining employers to resist the union demands becomes greatly — and unfairly — diminished. Unable to withdraw, the remaining employers have no defense; they are forced either to submit to the union's demands or to allow fellow members of the group to profit from the strike or lockout. The effect of today's decision is "to deny self-help by employers when legitimate interests of employees and employers collide." NLRB v. Truck Drivers, 353 U.S. 87, 96 (1957) (Buffalo Linen).

The Board has purported to follow an evenhanded approach to multiemployer bargaining. The Evening News Assn., 154 N.L.R.B. 1494 (1965), enf'd sub nom. Detroit Newspaper Publishers Assn. v. NLRB, 372 F.2d 569 (C.A.6 1967). By allowing the union to negotiate interim agreements in order to whipsaw the employer group and yet denying the employers the necessary defense of withdrawal, the Board is hardly living up to its asserted — and mandated — commitment to evenhandedness.

II

Maintenance of industrial peace requires balancing the interests of labor with those of management; the Court holds that the "difficult

3. As the Board conceded during oral argument, its rule, now endorsed by this Court, prohibits withdrawal even if an impasse and a strike or lockout lasts as long as two years.

responsibility" of striking this balance lies with the Board subject only to "limited judicial review." But judicial review, although limited, is not absent:

> [T]he phrase "limited judicial review" [does] not mean that the balance struck by the Board is immune from judicial examination and reversal in proper cases. . . . [W]here, as here, the review is not of a question of fact, but of a judgment as to the proper balance to be struck between conflicting interests, "[t]he deference owed to an expert tribunal cannot be allowed to slip into a judicial inertia which results in the unauthorized assumption by an agency of major policy decisions properly made by Congress." NLRB v. Brown, supra, at 290-292, quoting American Ship Building Co. v. NLRB, 380 U.S. 300, 318 (1965).

The Court's deferral to the Board's conclusion that its rules advance the national labor policy by enhancing stability and promoting collective bargaining represents just the kind of uncritical judicial rubberstamping we have often condemned. NLRB v. Brown, supra, at 291.

Contrary to the Board's conclusory statements, accepted by the Court, employers who execute interim agreements do not have an equivalent stake in promptly securing a reasonable final agreement. Such employers are able to operate fully while their competitors are hampered by a strike or defensive lockout; employers covered by interim agreements have a natural economic interest in prolonging the deadlock, thereby increasing their competitive advantage over the employers who remain in the multiemployer group.

The Court also accepts the Board's naked assertion that "interim agreements . . . deter rather than promote unit fragmentation." It is difficult to imagine an event more likely to fragment a multiemployer group than a union's successful whipsawing. Certainly employers will be reluctant to continue their association with other employers who are now encouraged by the Board — and by this Court — selfishly to permit themselves to be used to force the group to yield to the union demands.[4]

Even without the negotiation of interim agreements, when the parties have remained at impasse for a lengthy period, withdrawal of one or a

4. The Court places great reliance on the notion that the union is only allowed to negotiate interim agreements with individual employers and that negotiation of permanent separate agreements not tied to the final association agreement would permit the remaining employers to withdraw from the unit. This reliance may be misplaced. In Tobey Fine Papers of Kansas City, 245 N.L.R.B. 1393 (1979), enf'd, 659 F.2d 841, 107 L.R.R.M. 2221 (C.A.8 1981), the Board did not permit an employer to withdraw from a multiemployer group even though 2 of the 14 members (representing 42% of the group's employees) had withdrawn with union consent and negotiated separate, permanent agreements. The Board held that "it does not follow ipso facto that execution of individual separate final contracts with [withdrawn] Association members either proves an intention to destroy, or necessarily causes the fragmentation of, a multiemployer unit." 245 N.L.R.B., at 1395.

few employers may facilitate rather than frustrate bargaining. The present case is illustrative. Bargaining between the Teamsters and the association was at a stalemate when Bonanno Linen decided to withdraw. That withdrawal did not cause the immediate "disintegration" of the bargaining unit, but instead provided the impetus for the union and the remaining employers ultimately to return to the bargaining table and reach agreement. Thus, Bonanno Linen's withdrawal can be seen as fostering the group collective-bargaining process rather than hindering it. In any event, an employer's withdrawal from the multiemployer group is no more disruptive of the bargaining process than a union's decision to use "divide and conquer" tactics.

Industrial peace, it must be remembered, is the primary objective of the federal labor laws; multiemployer bargaining is simply one of many tools used to try to achieve that goal for the benefit of both sides. When a union and a group of employers have reached an impasse and further negotiations would appear to be an exercise in futility, it is more consistent with that goal to permit withdrawal and allow negotiation of separate agreements than to force the parties into escalated economic warfare. Because of differing concerns, it is likely that employers will be able to negotiate agreements individually even though efforts to reach a group agreement failed. By instead forcing the parties to use their economic weapons, the Board's rule runs counter to the congressional goal of industrial peace.

III

In addition to arguing that its rule barring withdrawal upon impasse enhances the stability of multiemployer groups and promotes collective bargaining, the Board contends that an impasse is neither sufficiently unusual nor adequately determinable to support withdrawal. "Impasse" is a term of art in labor law; the presence of an impasse triggers other important consequences. At impasse, for example, either party may decline to negotiate further. See, e.g., NLRB v. Webb Furniture Corp., 366 F.2d 314, 315 (C.A.4 1966). In addition, at impasse an employer may unilaterally make changes in terms and conditions of employment provided that the changes are consistent with the proposals it made at the bargaining table.

Because unions and employers have important rights which arise upon impasse, the Board and the courts have acquired considerable experience in determining whether an impasse exists. See, e.g., NLRB v. Tex-Tan, Inc., supra; Taft Broadcasting Co., supra. It makes little sense to say, as the Board does here, that on the one hand an impasse is too common and indeterminable to permit withdrawal from a multiemployer bargaining unit while on the other hand maintaining that an impasse is sufficiently momentous and ascertainable to allow employers to stop bargaining and make unilateral changes. Moreover, if the Board, after nearly 40 years of dealing with the concept, finds impasse too ill-defined to permit withdrawal, it is high time that the Board exercise its presumed expertise and establish more definite guidelines to identify impasse. Unions and employers are entitled to that guidance.

The Court also accepts the Board's contention that "impasse may be 'brought about intentionally by one of the parties,'" and asserts that "permitting withdrawal at impasse would as a practical matter undermine the utility of multiemployer bargaining." The Court explains that permitting withdrawal upon impasse would allow employers to "precipitate an impasse in order to escape any agreement less favorable than the one expected." This argument ignores a basic element of impasse: impasse is reached only when a stalemate — a breakdown in bargaining — occurs after good-faith negotiations. NLRB v. Crompton-Highland Mills, Inc., 337 U.S. 217 (1949); Cone Mills Corp. v. NLRB, 413 F.2d 445, 450 (C.A.4 1969). Intentionally refusing to agree in order to create an impasse and thus facilitate withdrawal — or trigger any of the other rights available upon impasse — is hardly good-faith bargaining. The Board has ample means to deal with feigned bargaining.

IV

I would have little difficulty with a rule that a brief cessation of bargaining, without more, does not trigger a right to withdraw from a multiemployer bargaining unit. But the Board has gone much further. No impasse, we are told, no matter how long it lasts or how far apart the parties remain, permits withdrawal. Employers may not withdraw even after the union has negotiated separate agreements with some of the employers in order to force the others in the group into compliance. Absent a more reasonable alternative than that offered by the Board, I would adopt the rule of the Second, Third, and Ninth Circuits and permit withdrawal upon impasse.

O'CONNOR, J., with whom POWELL, J., joins, dissenting.

I join the Chief Justice in the introductory comments and Part I of his dissent. However, I write separately because I believe labor peace would be advanced by avoiding the absolute positions adopted both by the majority and by the dissent of the Chief Justice. Because I am convinced that the Board should examine the circumstances surrounding and following an impasse to determine whether an unusual circumstance sufficient to justify withdrawal has occurred, and because I cannot accept the Court's conclusory statements concerning the effects of all interim agreements, I respectfully dissent.

I

The Court agrees with the Board that an impasse is not an unusual circumstance "sufficiently destructive of group bargaining to justify unilateral withdrawal." The Board adopted that position after identifying an impasse as (1) simply a "temporary deadlock or hiatus in negotiations" (2) which may be brought about intentionally by one of the parties and (3) which in almost all cases is "eventually broken, either through a change of mind or the application of economic force." Charles D. Bonanno Linen Service, Inc., 243 N.L.R.B. 1093, 1093-1094 (1979). There are, of course, impasses that fit this description. Others do not. Unfortunately, having developed its premise, the Board has chosen to ignore the reasons which justified it and now "reasons" that an impasse, regardless of duration, does not justify employer withdrawal. The problem with the Board's approach is that it reasons by definition. That is, while an impasse may be a temporary deadlock, a deadlock cannot be made temporary simply by calling it an impasse. Thus, while the rule may be efficient, it does not contribute to principled decisionmaking. This case provides an excellent example of the result which obtains when the Board applies a general rule without analysis of the particular factual situation.

More than a temporary lull in negotiations developed here. When Bonanno withdrew from the bargaining unit in November, the parties had been deadlocked for more than six months. Nevertheless, although the Board defines an impasse as a "temporary" deadlock, it inexplicably views the passage of time as irrelevant to the question of whether something more than a "hiatus" in negotiations was involved.

Closely related to the Board's view of an impasse as temporary is its view that an impasse is not an unusual circumstance because it is broken in almost all cases either through a change of mind or by the application of economic forces. However, in this case the Board did not determine whether, when Bonanno withdrew, the parties were likely to have broken the impasse. The union and association had unsuccessfully utilized the most common economic weapons: the union had called a selective strike; association members had locked out their drivers; and Bonanno had hired replacement drivers. The Board made no finding that the arsenal of this union or these employers contained additional economic weapons which, if used, might have ended the impasse.

Moreover, neither the Board nor any party to the negotiations suggested that Bonanno precipitated the May 15 impasse as a means to excuse its withdrawal from the association. The Board's third identifying feature of an impasse is thus also missing from this situation.

The impasse which all parties agree existed on May 15 may fit the Board's definition of impasse; the situation which existed on November 21 does not. The point is not that this Court should substitute its judgment as to the "significance of impasse and the dynamics of collective bargaining" for that of the Board. The point is that the Board should be required to analyze, not simply label, a deadlock in negotiations. If the Board had utilized its expertise to examine the facts of this case, it well might have found a complete breakdown in negotiations, not a temporary impasse. When such a complete breakdown occurs, I would afford an employer a right to withdraw.

II

Neither can I agree with the Court's conclusion that employers who execute interim agreements invariably maintain an equivalent stake in securing a final agreement and that interim agreements always deter fragmentation of the employer unit. That conclusion, like the "impasse rule" adopted today, sweeps too broadly. The conclusion is least likely to be accurate when applied to a highly competitive industry which relies upon skilled workers and counts heavily upon repetitive patronage. If one member of a struck employer association in such an industry reaches an interim agreement, he will gain a competitive advantage sufficient to produce a natural and powerful interest in prolonging the deadlock. In fact, the Board has found that an employer with such an advantage is less likely to push for prompt settlement of the labor dispute. See, e.g., Connell Typesetting Co., 212 N.L.R.B. 918 (1974). Moreover, as we recognized in NLRB v. Brown, 380 U.S. 278 (1965), the notion that allowing a practice which unfairly advantages one employer would "succeed in breaking up the employer association was not at all fanciful." Id., at 284. Likewise, when an interim agreement affords one employer a competitive advantage, the notion that allowing the agreement will promote fragmentation of the bargaining unit is not at all fanciful.

Other factors could also affect the impact of an interim agreement. For instance, an agreement between a union and the employer of 40 percent of a work force could shatter a bargaining unit. Such an agreement with an employer of two percent of the work force might have little effect. No magic inheres in the word "interim," as none inheres in "impasse." Identification of an agreement as "interim" rather than "final" is the beginning, not the end, of the required analysis of the agreement's effect on the bargaining unit. Yet, today the Court gives blanket approval of any interim agreement.[3] Here too, I would require the Board to apply its expertise to determine the effect of such an agreement in a

3. By adopting a per se rule that interim agreements never fragment the bargaining unit, the Court takes a position more extreme than that urged by the Board. At least until today, the Board has allowed employer withdrawal when interim agreements resulted in unit fragmentation. Approval of a rule so favorable to one party in negotiations is hardly the way to encourage multiemployer bargaining or industrial peace.

particular instance rather than approve the Board's practice of decision by label. If an agreement, interim or final, operates to fragment a bargaining unit, I would allow withdrawal by an employer.

III

The goal of multiemployer bargaining is to promote "labor peace through strengthened collective bargaining." NLRB v. Truck Drivers, 353 U.S. 87, 95 (1957). Neither a complete breakdown in negotiations nor a fragmented bargaining unit furthers that goal. Because today's decision allows both, I dissent.

NOTE, AN ESSAY ON MULTIEMPLOYER BARGAINING[15]

The legal rules covering multiemployer bargaining are relatively straightforward. Suppose that there are six separately owned firms in a local industry, and that a single union represents all the employees at each firm. If the union and the managers of the firms consent, the firms may negotiate as a single entity with the union. This multiemployer bargaining has several effects. A firm that consents to multiemployer bargaining may not withdraw from the unit during negotiations without the consent of the union[16] and is bound to honor the agreement. A union may not coerce a firm to enter into multiemployer bargaining; it must respect a firm's decision to go it alone. (If the union represents only a particular group of employees at each of the firms, the same rules apply, but the multiemployer agreement will only cover those employees.)

If separate unions represent the clerks at each firm, multiemployer negotiations are still possible if the firms and the unions consent, but no union may be coerced into the negotiations. A union that engages in multiemployer bargaining has a powerful advantage over rival unions that would displace it as the bargaining representative because the Board rules that while a multiemployer negotiating unit is intact, it is the only appropriate bargaining (election) unit. In the example above, a rival union's petition for an election in a single firm will be dismissed so long as the incumbent union and the firm are engaged in multiemployer negotiations or are parties to a multiemployer agreement. The rival union can only obtain an election that covers all the clerks in the multiemployer unit.

[15] The essay is excerpted from Leslie, Labor Bargaining Units, 790 Va. L. Rev. 353 (1984).

[16] Some courts have held that withdrawal also requires the consent of the other employers.

Because multiemployer bargaining requires the consent of both union and managers, it is something of a puzzle why it is so common. If it enhances the power of either side, the other should not consent to it. Perhaps firms join multiemployer bargaining groups to control the product market. When managers meet for the ostensible purpose of formulating responses to union demands, they have the opportunity to discuss product prices, output, and technological competition, and so to coordinate cartel behavior in the product market. The union receives a share of the monopoly rents for agreeing to this form of bargaining.[17] Firms must cast their agreement in terms of product price or output, because common agreement on wage matters alone leaves the firms in competition with respect to other factors of production and yields no supracompetitive profits. If this view of multiemployer bargaining is correct, there should be considerable evidence of employer cartel behavior as firms and unions seek to police output and pricing agreements. The absence of such evidence suggests that the theory probably does not explain most multiemployer bargaining.

An alternative theory of multiemployer bargaining does not depend on product market control to explain managerial incentives. In a perfectly competitive, price theory labor market, the manager of a firm has no discretion over wages and other compensation terms. When a union secures bargaining rights at the firm and demands a monopoly wage, however, the manager now has some discretion. He or she can resist the union's demands to a greater or to a lesser degree, while managers in competing firms make similar choices. Assume that his or her goal is to minimize the sum of wage rents and strike costs imposed by the union. The manager can do better or worse than competitors, which will be reflected in his or her wages and job security. Risk-averse managers, or those who believe themselves to be underskilled in this role, might agree to multiemployer bargaining just to avoid this competition. Multiemployer bargaining assures managers that they and their competitors will pay the same wage rates. A manager might agree even though the multiemployer rate is higher than the union's average gain would be absent multiemployer bargaining. A union is compensated by this wage premium.[18]

[17] Otherwise, the union's best course is to seek to exercise its full monopoly power vis-a-vis individual firms.

[18] The analysis is altered only slightly if the labor market was imperfect prior to unionization of the firms. In an imperfect labor market, managers have some control over the wage rate. If managers have perfect information, the optimal wage/employment level (from the firm's point of view) will be set with no risk to the individual manager; but with imperfect information, a manager will be uncertain as to the optimal wage. Presumably some managers will be better at this than others. In an imperfect market with imperfect information, unionization replaces one form of uncertainty with another. Multiemployer bargaining removes the uncertainty of how a manager will perform in setting compensation rates.

According to this theory, unions earn a wage premium in multiemployer bargaining, which is negotiated by risk-averse managers.[19] The resulting upward pressure on product prices lessens product demand; and although no single firm bears the entire loss in demand, this loss is "seen" by the multiemployer association. The association will have an incentive to keep down the union's wage premium.

It is important to the firms in the multiemployer group that firms outside the group be charged the same wage premium. It is no surprise, then, to find a union that has negotiated a wage rate in multiemployer negotiations insisting on that same wage rate from any firm in the same product market that bargains on an individual basis. Moreover, a union that has negotiated a multiemployer wage is usually better able to persuade the employees of a firm not bound by the negotiations of the unfairness of accepting a lesser rate from their employer. Employees who would not have struck over a matter of a few pennies had they been negotiating in isolation will now strike rather than accept less than the multiemployer rate. The union's credibility in the single-employer negotiations is enhanced.[20]

The viability of a wage premium in multiemployer negotiations depends on there being barriers to entry in the appropriate product market. Unionized firms cannot pay wage premiums indefinitely while competing in every other respect with firms not subject to the premium. The wage premium theory of multiemployer bargaining predicts that multiemployer bargaining would be more prevalent in concentrated industries.

In a relational contract model, unions seek to drive up wages through the use of monopoly power, but they also facilitate comprehensive relational contracting. It is possible that the pervasiveness of multiemployer bargaining shows that wage monopolization is more important than relational contracting. It seems unlikely that a network of relative wages and other working conditions often extends across firms or that a good secured by a union at one firm will involve externalities at another. So, one might conclude, a multiemployer agreement is unlikely to be a comprehensive relational contract. The counterargument notes that multiemployer bargaining agreements ordinarily contain a host of terms in addition to wage terms. This may suggest that multiemployer bargaining, like single-firm bargaining, promotes relational contracting, but that

[19] Risk-neutral managers are better off by staying out of multiemployer bargaining and avoiding the wage premium — as should managers who are especially skilled at wage setting. The union has a strong incentive to force these managers to adopt the wage rate negotiated by the multiemployer group. Although the Labor Board insists that the union refrain from pressuring a firm to join multiemployer bargaining, the statute does not prevent the union from seeking the same wage from a firm in the industry that has not agreed to multiemployer bargaining. See United Mine Workers v. Pennington, 381 U.S. 657, 663-664 (1965), at p. 630, infra.

[20] Getting more is probably equally difficult.

the resultant rationalized network of relative wage and other terms will not be tied to individualized history at particular firms.[21]

The relationship of multiemployer bargaining to the collective goods model is also instructive. Assume that for wage premium reasons firms and a union chose multiemployer bargaining. The union can forgo other collective goods, negotiate those goods into the multiemployer agreement, or tailor the goods to the needs of employees at each firm in separate negotiations. Which alternative a union chooses presumably depends on a comparison of transactions costs. When all issues are resolved in multiemployer bargaining, the employees of a single firm lose flexibility in their choice between alternative bundles of collective goods. Still, it may be more costly to bargain on wages alone in the multiemployer negotiations and to leave the negotiation of other collective goods to separate negotiations with a particular firm.[22]

To the extent the union must exercise or threaten to exercise monopoly power to secure these collective goods, it must find a way to allocate some of its power to the wage premium issue and the remainder to the individualized collective goods issues. But monopoly power in the form of strikes and other disruptions is not finely divisible. Managers will be reluctant to agree to a wage premium in multiemployer bargaining if the union retains its power to again exercise its monopoly power in single-firm negotiations for tailored collective goods, and the union has no mechanism for guaranteeing that it will exercise its power in the appropriate moderation in those later negotiations. Transaction costs may be minimized by handling all the issues in multiemployer negotiations and forgoing flexibility.

None of the models of the business of labor unions suggests a very persuasive, benign rationale for multiemployer bargaining. Either it is a mask for employer cartel behavior, or, more probably, a means by which managers slack at the price of a wage premium paid by the firm to its unionized workers.

Multiunion bargaining is considerably rarer than multiemployer bargaining but, as the following case shows, is not unprecedented.

GENERAL ELECTRIC CO. v. NLRB

412 F.2d 512 (2d Cir. 1969)

Feinberg, J. . . .

General Electric is a New York corporation which manufactures and sells electrical equipment and related products, including many for the

[21] The historical pattern of relationships at a particular firm is thus supplanted by the terms of the multiemployer agreement, terms applicable to all firms in the multiemployer group. An alternative, but less likely, possibility is that the multiemployer agreement contains the important monopoly wage terms but that equally important nonwage terms rationalizing a particular firm's internal labor market have been negotiated outside the multiemployer agreement.

[22] Another round of meetings is costly, but this is probably a minor consideration.

national defense and atomic energy programs. It employs about 290,000 people in over 60 plants and 400 other installations, such as service shops and warehouses. It operates in all of the 50 states. About half of its employees are represented by more than 80 unions in about 150 bargaining units. Approximately 80,000 employees in some 90 of these units are represented by the IUE [International Union of Electrical, Radio and Machine Workers]. . . .

For some time, the IUE and other unions representing the Company's employees had been concerned over the results of their separate efforts to bargain with General Electric. According to the unions, the Company had successfully followed a practice of divide and conquer in the past by making a separate "fair, firm offer" almost simultaneously to each union and then whipsawing one against the other. In any event, dissatisfied with the results of their prior separate efforts, the unions in 1965 formed a Committee on Collective Bargaining (CCB), consisting eventually of the IUE and seven other international unions whose locals also had agreements with General Electric. The avowed purposes of the members of the CCB were to coordinate bargaining in 1966 with General Electric and its chief competitor, Westinghouse Electric Corporation, to formulate national goals, and otherwise to support one another.

[The company refused to meet with the CCB even though it was told that the seven non-IUE members were nonvoting and were present to aid the IUE and not to represent their own members. The Board found the company's refusal to violate §§8(a)(5) and (1) and ordered General Electric to bargain with the negotiating committee of the IUE in the future.]

The basic question before us is whether a union's inclusion of members of other unions on its bargaining committee justifies an employer's refusal to bargain. . . . In general, either side can choose as it sees fit and neither can control the other's selection, a proposition confirmed in a number of opinions, some of fairly ancient vintage. For example, the following asserted objections to bargaining representatives have all been rejected as defenses to charges of refusal to bargain: that a local union president could not act for the international union in grievance handling; that an AFL "general organizer," not a member or officer of the union, could not bargain for the latter; that employees could not be represented by a local union, a majority of whose members were employed by a rival industry and which the employees were not eligible to join; and that an international union representative could not negotiate for a local.

There have been exceptions to the general rule that neither side can choose its bargaining representatives freely, but they have been rare and confined to situations so infected with ill-will, usually personal, or conflict of interest as to make good-faith bargaining impractical. Thus, the freedom to select representatives is not absolute, but that does not detract from its significance. Rather the narrowness and infrequency of approved exceptions to the general rule emphasizes its importance. Thus, in arguing that employees may not select members of other unions as "representatives of their own choosing" on a negotiating committee, the Company clearly undertakes a considerable burden, characterized in an analogous situation as the showing of a "clear and present" danger to the collective bargaining process. . . .

The Board held that a mixed-union negotiating committee is not per se improper and that absent a showing of "substantial evidence of ulterior motive or bad faith" an employer commits an unfair labor practice unless it bargains with such a group. The Company and amicus attack the Board rule on a number of grounds. They claim that the rule will inevitably allow the injection of conflicting interests and "outside and extraneous influences" into the bargaining process, will make the always difficult task of determining the motives of the other side an impossibility, is an improper effort by the Board to adjust economic power, and finally is unworkable because an employer confronted with bad faith or ulterior motives can only break off negotiations with the mixed group and file unfair labor practices charges with the Board, an option disruptive of collective bargaining at best and in actuality no remedy at all.

The claim that outside influences and alleged conflicts require an outright ban on mixed-union committees is not weighty in view of the cases discussed above. Equally unpersuasive is the assertion that the Board made an improper effort to adjust economic power. The Board gave no such rationale for its decision. Of course, it would be nonsense to pretend that IUE's purpose was not to increase its bargaining strength, but that goal is a normal one for unions or employers. That Board application of an old policy to a new situation may have such an effect does not vitiate a rule if it is otherwise justified. The possibility that there will be improper attempts to ignore unit boundaries is, of course, real. The Company argues that different unions certified for separate units may not force an employer to bargain with them jointly as to all units on any subject, despite the implications of United States Pipe & Foundry Co. v. NLRB, 298 F.2d 873 (5th Cir.), cert. denied, 370 U.S. 919 (1962), which approved an arrangement whereby three unions conditioned their agreements in separate but substantially simultaneous negotiations upon a joint demand for common contract expiration dates. The Board did not come to grips with this problem, and we similarly do not now consider the extent to which the law permits cooperation in bargaining among unions or employers. . . .

The point is that the chance that negotiators may improperly press impermissible subjects is inherent in the bargaining process, and therefore must be taken. As to the increased difficulty in determining motives of the other side, we agree that this may occur. However, although evidence that bargaining for other employees is being attempted may be difficult to obtain, the Board is certainly capable of making such a determination when a case comes before it. Indeed, the dangers foreseen could exist even if there were no members of other unions on a committee if, for example, the unions were to meet together immediately before and after each bargaining session. Surely an employer would not be justified because of that fact alone in refusing to meet even though evidence of an attempt by the unions to merge bargaining units or to obtain a common bargaining agreement would, if anything, be more difficult to produce. We agree that a mixed-union committee could make it easier to press such plans illegally, although not by that much, in view of modern communication techniques. Nevertheless, cooperation between unions is not improper up to a point and it is for the Board in the first instance to determine whether the line has been crossed. In view of the overall policy of encouraging free selection of representatives, we agree with the Board's rejection of a per se rule which bans mixed-union committees.

Thus, we have decided that it was improper for the Company to refuse to bargain in August 1966 on the ground that members of other unions were on the IUE committee. However, we must still deal with the Company's claim that in any event it could refuse to meet with the IUE committee because the CCB was attempting to use it to impose joint bargaining upon the Company and because the IUE was "locked-in" to an agreement whereby it would not accept any offer made by the Company until the other unions did.

The Board rejected these contentions without deciding whether either factor would have justified a refusal to meet. Instead, the Board held that the Company had the duty once the IUE had retreated from its advocacy of joint bargaining, to put the negotiators to the test. [The court agreed with the Board.]

Notes

1. When unions representing separate bargaining units demand of an employer that their bargaining agreements have common expiration dates, or that a settlement with any union is conditional on the employer reaching a satisfactory settlement with the other unions, the unions' usual goal is increasing their economic power. Where no one union can successfully shut down the employer by a strike, the strategy may have its intended effect. Also, where the effectiveness of a single union's strike depends on whether the other unions will honor its picket line, the strategy may relieve tensions between unions over the issue of whether picket lines will be honored.

An employer who resists these union demands, or attacks them before the Board as a union refusal to bargain, presumably does so in order to prevent the unions from augmenting their economic power. The employer's contention is likely to be that the unions are attempting to alter the established bargaining units.

2. What advantages are there to multiunion bargaining from an employer's perspective? In the construction industry, for example, local unions have occasionally engaged in "leap-frogging" ("if the Sheet Metal Workers got a 75¢ per hour increase, we Pipefitters are worth $1.25 per hour more"). Is multiunion bargaining a solution? Why would the unions agree? Could a workable statutory requirement to this effect be drafted?

D. BARGAINING DURING THE TERM OF AN EXISTING AGREEMENT

The fact that an employer and a union have signed a collective bargaining agreement does not necessarily end the matter of a duty to bargain. First, the collective bargaining agreement will not explicitly cover every matter that might arise between the parties during its term. The *Jacobs* case, which follows, considers whether there should be a duty to bargain over subjects of concern to one or both of the parties, but which are not covered by the agreement and may or may not have been discussed in negotiations.

Second, we saw in *Katz*, supra, that an employer's unilateral change of a term or condition of employment during negotiations is likely to violate §8(a)(5). Should a similar unilateral change during the term of an agreement and with respect to a matter covered by the agreement also be deemed a §8(a)(5) violation? The *Pittsburgh Plate Glass* case treats this issue. Cutting across both areas is the question of the proper interplay between a §8(a)(5) Board action and a breach of contract action, cognizable by the courts. *C & C Plywood* and *Collyer Insulated Wire* go to the question of whether the Board can and should adjudicate under §8(a)(5) matters that are redressable in breach of contract actions or that raise issues of contract interpretation.

1. Subjects Not Covered by the Agreement[23]

JACOBS MANUFACTURING CO.
94 N.L.R.B. 1214 (1951)

. . . In July 1948, the Respondent and the Union executed a 2-year bargaining contract which, by its terms, could be reopened 1 year after

[23] See Cox & Dunlop, The Duty to Bargain Collectively during the Term of an Existing Agreement, 63 Harv. L. Rev. 1097 (1950); Findling & Colby, Regulation of Collective Bargaining by the National Labor Relations Board — Another View, 51 Colum. L. Rev. 170 (1951).

its execution date for discussion of "wage rates."[1] In July 1949 the Union invoked the reopening clause of the 1948 contract, and thereafter gave the Respondent written notice of its "wage demands." In addition to a request for a wage increase, these demands included a request that the Respondent undertake the entire cost of an existing group insurance program, and another request for the establishment of a pension plan for the Respondent's employees. When the parties met thereafter to consider the Union's demands, the Respondent refused to discuss the Union's pension and insurance requests on the ground that they were not appropriate items of discussion under the reopening clause of the 1948 contract.

The group insurance program to which the Union alluded in its demands was established by the Respondent before 1948. It was underwritten by an insurance company, and provided life, accident, health, surgical, and hospital protection. All the Respondent's employees were eligible to participate in the program, and the employees shared its costs with the Respondent. When the 1948 contract was being negotiated, the Respondent and the Union had discussed changes in this *insurance program*, and had agreed to increase certain of the benefits as well as the costs. However, neither the changes thereby effected, nor the insurance program itself, was mentioned in the 1948 contract.

As indicated by the Union's request, there was no pension plan for the Respondent's employees in existence in 1949. The subject of *pensions*, moreover, had not been discussed during the 1948 negotiations; and, like insurance, that subject is not mentioned in the 1948 contract.

a. For the reasons stated below, Chairman Herzog and Members Houston and Styles agree with the Trial Examiner's conclusion that the Respondent violated §8(a)(5) of the Act by refusing to discuss the matter of *pensions* with the Union. . . .

We are satisfied that the 1948 contract did not in itself impose on the Respondent any obligation to discuss pensions or insurance. The reopening clause of that contract refers to *wage rates*, and thus its intention appears to have been narrowly limited to matters directly related to the amount and manner of compensation for work. For that reason, a requirement to discuss pensions or insurance cannot be predicated on the language of the contract.

On the other hand, a majority of the Board believes that, regardless of the character of the reopening clause, the Act itself imposed upon the Respondent the duty to discuss *pensions* with the Union during the period in question.

It is now established as a principle of law that the matter of pensions is

1. Article XIX, section 5, of the 1948 contract stated: "After the expiration of one year from the date hereof either party may request a meeting after fifteen days' written notice, the purpose of which shall be to discuss wage rates of employees covered by this agreement. . . ."

a subject which falls within the area where the statute requires bargaining. And, as noted above, the 1948 contract between the Respondent and the Union was silent with respect to the subject of pensions; indeed, the matter had never been raised or discussed by the parties. The issue raised, therefore, is whether the Respondent was absolved of the obligation to discuss pensions because of the limitation contained in §8(d) of the amended Act dealing with the duty to discuss or agree to the modification of an existing bargaining contract. The pertinent portion of §8(d) of the Act provides:

> [T]he duties so imposed shall not be construed as requiring either party to discuss or agree to any modification of the terms and conditions contained in a contract for a fixed period, if such modification is to become effective before such terms and conditions can be reopened under the provisions of the contract.

. . . The crucial point at issue here, as in the earlier cases, is the construction to be given the phase "terms and conditions *contained in* a contract." (Emphasis supplied.) The Board, in the *Tide Water* case [85 N.L.R.B. 1096], concluded that the pertinent portion of §8(d)

> *refers to terms and conditions which have been integrated and embodied into a writing.* Conversely it does not have reference to matters relating to "wages, hours and other terms and conditions of employment," which have not been reduced to writing. As to the written terms of the contract either party may refuse to bargain further about them, under the limitations set forth in the paragraph, without committing an unfair labor practice. With respect to unwritten terms dealing with "wages, hours and other terms and conditions of employment," the obligation remains on both parties to bargain continuously.

Thus, as already construed by this Board in the *Tide Water* case, §8(d) does not itself license a party to a bargaining contract to refuse, during the life of the contract, to discuss a bargainable subject unless it has been made a part of the agreement itself. Applied here, therefore, the *Tide Water* construction of §8(d) means that the Respondent was obligated to discuss the Union's pension demand.

Members Houston and Styles have carefully reexamined the Board's construction of §8(d) in the *Tide Water* case, and are persuaded that the view the Board adopted in the *Tide Water* case best effectuates the declared policy of the Act. Chairman Herzog, while joining in the result with respect to the obligation to bargain here concerning pensions — never previously discussed by the parties — joins in the rationale herein *only* to the extent that it is consistent with his views separately recited below, concerning the insurance program.

By making mandatory the discussion of bargainable subjects not already covered by a contract, the parties to the contract are encouraged to arrive at joint decisions with respect to bargainable matters, that, at least to the party requesting discussion, appear at the time to be of some importance. The Act's policy of "encouraging the practice and procedure of collective bargaining" is consequently furthered. A different construction of §8(d) in the circumstances — one that would permit a party to a bargaining contract to avoid discussion when it was sought on subject matters not contained in the contract — would serve, at its best, only to dissipate whatever the good will that had been engendered by the previous bargaining negotiations that led to the execution of a bargaining contract; at its worst, it could bring about the industrial strife and the production interruptions that the policy of the Act also seeks to avert.

The significance of this point cannot be overemphasized. It goes to the heart of our disagreement with our dissenting colleague, Member Reynolds. His dissent stresses the need for "contract stability," and asserts that the furtherance of sound collective bargaining requires that the collective bargaining agreement be viewed as fixing, for the term of the contract, all aspects of the employer-employee relationship, and as absolving either party of the obligation to discuss, during that term, even those matters which had never been raised, or discussed in the past. We could hardly take issue with the virtue of "contract stability," at least in the abstract, and we would certainly agree that everyone is better off when, in negotiating an agreement, the parties have been able to foresee what all the future problems may be, to discuss those problems, and either to embody a resolution of them in the contract, or to provide that they may not be raised again during the contract. But we are here concerned with the kind of case in which, for one reason or another, this has *not* been done, and the question is what best effectuates the policies of the Act in *such* a case. . . .

The construction of §8(d) adopted by the Board in the *Tide Water* case serves also to simplify, and thus to speed, the bargaining process. It eliminates the pressure upon the parties at the time when a contract is being negotiated to raise those subjects that may not then be of controlling importance, but which might in the future assume a more significant status. It also assures to both unions and employers that, if future conditions require some agreement as to matters about which the parties have not sought, or have not been able to obtain agreement, then some discussion of those matters will be forthcoming when necessary.

We cannot believe that Congress was unaware of the foregoing considerations when it amended the Act by inserting §8(d), or that it sought, by the provision in question, to freeze the bargaining relationship by eliminating any mandatory discussion that might lead to the addition of new subject matter to an existing contract. What §8(d) does do is to reject the pronouncements contained in some pre-1947 Board and court decisions — sometimes dicta, sometimes necessary to the holding — to the effect that the duty to bargain continues even as to those matters upon which the parties have reached agreement and which are set forth in the terms of a written contract. But we believe it does no more. Those bargainable issues which have never been discussed by the parties, and which are in no way treated in the contract, remain matters which both the union and the employer are obliged to discuss at any time.

In so holding, we emphasize that under this rule, no less than in any other circumstance, the duty to bargain implies only an obligation to *discuss* the matter in question in good faith with a sincere purpose of reaching some agreement. It does not require that either side agree, or make concessions. And if the parties originally desire to avoid later discussion with respect to matters not specifically covered in the terms of an executed contract, they need only so specify in the terms of the contract itself. Nothing in our construction of §8(d) precludes such an agreement, entered into in good faith, from foreclosing future discussion of matters not contained in the agreement.[13]

b. Chairman Herzog, for reasons set forth in his separate opinion, believes that — unlike the pensions issue — the Respondent was under no obligation to bargain concerning the *group insurance program.*

However, Members Houston and Styles — a minority of the Board on this issue — are of the further opinion that the considerations discussed above leading to the conclusion that the Respondent was obligated to discuss the matter of pensions, also impel the conclusion that the Respondent was obligated to discuss the Union's group insurance demand. . . .

Members Houston and Styles believe, moreover, that the view adopted by Chairman Herzog on the insurance issue is subject to the same basic criticism as is the view of Member Reynolds — it exalts "contract stability" over industrial peace; it eliminates mandatory collective bargaining on subjects about which one of the parties *now* wants discussion, and concerning which it may well be willing to take economic action if discussion is denied, solely because the matter has once been discussed in a manner which may warrant an inference that the failure to mention

13. For an example of a contract in which such a provision was incorporated, see the contract between United Automobile Workers of America and General Motors Corporation, set forth in Labor Relations Manual (BNA), Vol. 26, p. 63, 91, which states:

> (154) The parties acknowledge that during the negotiations which resulted in this agreement, each had the unlimited right and opportunity to make demands and proposals with respect to any subject or matter not removed by law from the area of collective bargaining, and that the understandings and agreements arrived at by the parties after the exercise of that right and opportunity are set forth in this agreement. Therefore, the Corporation and the Union, for the life of this agreement, each voluntarily and unqualifiedly waives the right, and each agrees that the other shall not be obligated, to bargain collectively with respect to any subject or matter not specifically referred to or covered in this agreement, even though such subjects or matter may not have been within the knowledge or contemplation of either or both of the parties at the time that they negotiated or signed this agreement.

that subject in the contract was part of the bargain. Members Houston and Styles are constrained to reject the view of Chairman Herzog for the further reason that it would establish a rule which is administratively unworkable, and would inject dangerous uncertainty into the process of collective bargaining. Apart from the extremely difficult problems of proof — illustrated in this very case — which would constantly confront the Board in cases of this type, the parties to collective bargaining negotiations would always be faced with this question after a subject has been *discussed* — "Have we really *negotiated*, or are we under an obligation to discuss the subject further if asked to?" To this query the rule of the *Tide Water* case gives a clear and concise answer: "You are obligated to discuss any bargainable subject upon request unless you have reduced your agreement on that subject to writing or unless you have agreed in writing not to bargain about it during the term of the contract." Members Houston and Styles would apply that rule without deviation. . . .

Chairman HERZOG, concurring in part:

I believe that this Respondent was *not* under a duty to discuss the Union's *group insurance* demand. The individual views which lead me, by a different road, to the result reached on this issue by Members Reynolds and Murdock, are as follows:

Unlike the issue of pensions, concerning which the contract is silent and the parties did not negotiate at all in 1948, the subject of group insurance was fully discussed while the Respondent and the Union were negotiating the agreement. True, that agreement is silent on the subject, so it cannot literally be said that there is a term "contained in" the 1948 contract relating to the group insurance program. The fact remains that during the negotiations which preceded its execution, the issue was consciously explored. The record reveals that the Union expressly requested that the preexisting program be changed so that the Respondent would assume its entire cost, the very proposal that was again made as part of the 1949 midterm demand which gave rise to this case. The Respondent rejected the basic proposal on this first occasion, but agreement was then reached — although outside the written contract — to increase certain benefits under the group insurance program.

In my opinion, it is only reasonable to assume that rejection of the Union's basic proposal, coupled in this particular instance with enhancement of the substantive benefits, constituted a part of the contemporaneous "bargain" which the parties made when they negotiated the entire 1948 contract. In the face of this record as to what the parties discussed and did, I believe that it would be an abuse of this Board's mandate to throw the weight of Government sanction behind the Union's attempt to disturb, in midterm, a bargain sealed when the original agreement was reached.

To hold otherwise would encourage a labor organization — or, in a §8(b)(3) case, an employer — to come back, time without number, during the term of a contract, to demand resumed discussion of issues which, although perhaps not always incorporated in the written agreement, the other party had every good reason to believe were put at rest for a definite period. I do not think that the doctrine of the *Tide Water* case was ever intended to go so far as to extend to facts like these, or that it should be so extended. Without regard to the niceties of construing the words of §8(d) of the amended Act, I am satisfied that it would be both inequitable and unwise to impose a statutory obligation to bargain in situations of this sort. That would serve only to stimulate uncertainty and evasion of commitments at a time when stability should be the order of the day.

Member REYNOLDS, concurring separately and dissenting in part. . . .

[It] is my opinion that §8(d) imposes no obligation on either party to a contract to bargain on any matter during the term of the contract except as the express provisions of the contract may demand. This is a result reasonably compatible with the particular §8(d) language involved, as well as with §8(d) as a whole. Moreover, not only does the result accord stability and dignity to collective bargaining agreements, but it also gives substance to the practice and procedure of collective bargaining.

It is well established that the function of collective bargaining agreements is to contribute stability, so essential to sound industrial relations. Contractually stabilized industrial relations enable employers, because of fixed labor costs, to engage in sound long-range production planning, and employees, because of fixed wage, seniority, promotion, and grievance provisions, to anticipate secure employment tenure. Hence, when an employer and a labor organization have through the processes of collective bargaining negotiated an agreement containing the terms and conditions of employment for a definite period of time, their total rights and obligations emanating from the employer-employee relationship should remain fixed for that time. Stabilized therefore are the rights and obligations of the parties with respect to all bargainable subjects whether the subjects are or are not specifically set forth in the contract. To hold otherwise and prescribe bargaining on unmentioned subjects would result in continued alteration of the total rights and obligations under the contract, thus rendering meaningless the concept of contract stability. . . . Many items are not mentioned in a collective bargaining agreement either because of concessions at the bargaining table or because one of the parties may have considered it propitious to forego raising one subject in the hope of securing a more advantageous deal on another. Subjects traded off or foregone should, under these circumstances, be as irrevocably settled as those specifically covered and settled by the agreement. To require bargaining on such subjects during midterm debases initial contract negotiations. . . .[24]

Notes

1. In NLRB v. Jacobs Mfg. Co., 196 F.2d 680 (2d Cir. 1952), the court agreed that the employer was subject to a duty to bargain over the pensions since the subject was neither discussed in negotiations nor embodied in the agreement. The court did not decide whether discussion of a subject during negotiations relieved the employer of his or her duty to bargain over a union request for a contractual provision covering the subject.

2. A union engaged in midterm bargaining may bc prohibited by the agreement's no-strike clause from striking in support of its bargaining position. Consider also the restrictions of §8(d) on the union's right to strike. That section provides for a mandatory 60-day cooling-off period with notice to appropriate mediation agencies at the end of a bargaining agreement's term before the union can strike. The sanction for a strike within the insulated period is that striking employees lose their protected status and may be discharged. In NLRB v. Lion Oil Co., 352 U.S. 282 (1957), the Court held that where there is a formal contract reopener on one or more terms, the union may strike (assuming proper notice and the passage of 60 days) without running afoul of §8(d) even though the contract as a whole has not expired. There is no definitive authority on whether a similar rule would apply in the absence of a reopener but on a matter subject to midterm bargaining under the *Jacobs* decision.

3. Wouldn't an employer be wise to always insist on the precise clause set out in footnote 13 of *Jacobs*, called a "zipper clause"? Since *Jacobs*, the Board has held that a zipper clause will constitute an effective waiver of the right to bargain only if the clause expressly waives the right to negotiate over the particular subject in "clear and unmistakable" language.

As to waiver by bargaining history, the Board has held that such a waiver occurs only if a subject has been "fully discussed" or "consciously explored" and the union has "consciouslv yielded" or "clearly and unmistakably waived its interest in the matter."[25] In Stuart Radiator Core Mfg. Co., 173 N.L.R.B. 125 (1968), the employer insisted on a broad zipper clause, a broad management rights clause, and a limited arbitration clause; the Board found a §8(a)(5) violation.

[24] Member Murdock also dissented.

[25] See The Bunker Hill Co., 208 N.L.R.B. 27 (1973), modified, 210 N.L.R.B. 343 (1974); Proctor Mfg. Corp., 131 N.L.R.B. 1166 (1961).

2. Unilteral Changes during the Term of an Agreement

ALLIED CHEMICAL & ALKALI WORKERS LOCAL 1 v. PITTSBURGH PLATE GLASS CO.

404 U.S. 157 (1971)

BRENNAN, J.

Under the National Labor Relations Act, mandatory subjects of collective bargaining include pension and insurance benefits for active employees, and an employer's mid-term unilateral modification of such benefits constitutes an unfair labor practice. This cause presents the question whether a mid-term unilateral modification that concerns, not the benefits of active employees, but the benefits of already retired employees also constitutes an unfair labor practice. . . .

Since 1949, Local 1, Allied Chemical and Alkali Workers of America, has been the exclusive bargaining representative for the employees "working" on hourly rates of pay at the Barberton, Ohio, facilities of respondent Pittsburgh Plate Glass Co. In 1950, the Union and the Company negotiated an employee group health insurance plan, in which, it was orally agreed, retired employees could participate by contributing the required premiums, to be deducted from their pension benefits. This program continued unchanged until 1962, except for an improvement unilaterally instituted by the Company in 1954 and another improvement negotiated in 1959.

In 1962 the Company agreed to contribute two dollars per month toward the cost of insurance premiums of employees who retired in the future and elected to participate in the medical plan. The parties also agreed at this time to make 65 the mandatory retirement age. In 1964 insurance benefits were again negotiated, and the Company agreed to increase its monthly contribution from two to four dollars, applicable to employees retiring after that date and also to pensioners who had retired since the effective date of the 1962 contract. It was agreed, however, that the Company might discontinue paying the two-dollar increase if Congress enacted a national health program.

In November 1965, Medicare, a national health program, was enacted. The 1964 contract was still in effect, and the Union sought midterm bargaining to renegotiate insurance benefits for retired employees. The Company responded in March 1966 that, in its view, Medicare rendered the health insurance program useless because of a non-duplication-of-benefits provision in the Company's insurance policy, and stated, without negotiating any change, that it was planning to (a) reclaim the additional two-dollar monthly contribution as of the effective date of Medicare; (b) cancel the program for retirees; and (c) substitute the payment of the three-dollar monthly subscription fee for supplemental Medicare coverage for each retired employee.

The Union acknowledged that the Company had the contractual right to reduce its monthly contribution, but challenged its proposal unilaterally to substitute supplemental Medicare coverage for the negotiated health plan. The Company, as it had done during the 1959 negotiations without pressing the point, disputed the Union's right to bargain in behalf of retired employees, but advised the Union that upon further consideration it had decided not to terminate the health plan for pensioners. The Company stated instead that it would write each retired employee, offering to pay the supplemental Medicare premium if the employee would withdraw from the negotiated plan. Despite the Union's objections the Company did circulate its proposal to the retired employees, and 15 of 190 retirees elected to accept it. The Union thereupon filed unfair labor practice charges. . . . [The] Company was ordered to cease and desist from refusing to bargain collectively about retirement benefits and from making unilateral adjustments in health insurance plans for retired employees without first negotiating in good faith with the Union. The Company was also required to rescind, at the Union's request, any adjustment it had unilaterally instituted and to mail and post appropriate notices.

[The Court held that pensioners "are not 'employees' within the meaning of the collective-bargaining obligations of the Act," nor are they includable in the union's bargaining unit.]

Even if pensioners are not bargaining unit "employees," are their benefits, nonetheless, a mandatory subject of collective bargaining as "terms and conditions of employment" of the active employees who remain in the unit? The Board held, alternatively, that they are, on the ground that they "vitally" affect the "terms and conditions of employment" of active employees principally by influencing the value of both their current and future benefits. . . .

Section 8(d) of the Act, of course, does not immutably fix a list of subjects for mandatory bargaining. But it does establish a limitation against which proposed topics must be measured. In general terms, the limitation includes only issues that settle an aspect of the relationship between the employer and employees. See, e.g., NLRB v. Wooster Division of Borg-Warner Corp., 356 U.S. 342 (1958). Although normally matters involving individuals outside the employment relationship do not fall within that category, they are not wholly excluded. In Teamsters v. Oliver, 358 U.S. 283 (1959), for example, an agreement had been negotiated in the trucking industry, establishing a minimum rental that carriers would pay to truck owners who drove their own vehicles in the carriers' service in place of the latter's employees. Without determining whether the owner-drivers were themselves "employees," we held that the minimum rental was a mandatory subject of bargaining, and hence immune from state antitrust laws, because the term "was integral to the establishment of a stable wage structure for clearly covered employee-drivers." Similarly, in Fibreboard Paper Products Corp. v. NLRB, 379 U.S., at 215, we held that "the type of 'contracting out' involved in this case — the replacement of employees in the existing bargaining unit with those of an independent contractor to do the same work under similar conditions of employment — is a statutory subject of collective bargaining. . . ." As we said there, "the work of the employees in the bargaining unit was let out piecemeal in *Oliver*, whereas here the work of the entire unit has been contracted out."

The Board urges that *Oliver* and *Fibreboard* provide the principle governing this cause. The Company, on the other hand, would distinguish those decisions on the ground that the unions there sought to protect employees from outside threats, not to represent the interests of third parties. We agree with the Board that the principle of *Oliver* and *Fibreboard* is relevant here; in each case the question is not whether the third-party concern is antagonistic to or compatible with the interests of bargaining-unit employees, but whether it vitally affects the "terms and conditions" of their employment.[19] But we disagree with the Board's assessment of the significance of a change in retirees' benefits to the "terms and conditions of employment" of active employees.

The benefits that active workers may reap by including retired employees under the same health insurance contract are speculative and insubstantial at best. As the Board itself acknowledges in its brief, the relationship between the inclusion of retirees and the overall insurance rate is uncertain. Adding individuals increases the group experience and thereby generally tends to lower the rate, but including pensioners, who are likely to have higher medical expenses, may more than offset that effect. In any event, the impact one way or the other on the "terms and conditions of employment" of active employees is hardly comparable to the loss of jobs threatened in *Oliver* and *Fibreboard*. . . .

The mitigation of future uncertainty and the facilitation of agreement on active employees' retirement plans, that the Board said would follow from the union's representation of pensioners, are equally problematical. Under the Board's theory, active employees undertake to represent pensioners in order to protect their own retirement benefits, just as if they were bargaining for, say, a cost-of-living escalation clause. But there is a crucial difference. Having once found it advantageous to bar-

19. This is not to say that application of *Oliver* and *Fibreboard* turns only on the impact of the third-party matter on employee interests. Other considerations, such as the effect on the employer's freedom to conduct his business, may be equally important. See Fibreboard Paper Products Corp. v. National Labor Relations Board, supra, at 217. (Stewart, J., concurring.) But we have no occasion in this case to consider what, if any, those considerations may be.

gain for improvements in pensioners' benefits, active workers are not forever thereafter bound to that view or obligated to negotiate in behalf of retirees again.[20] To the contrary, they are free to decide, for example, that current income is preferable to greater certainty in their own retirement benefits or, indeed, to their retirement benefits altogether. By advancing pensioners' interests now, active employees, therefore, have no assurance that they will be the beneficiaries of similar representation when they retire. The insurance against future contingencies that they may buy in negotiating benefits for retirees is thus a hazardous and, therefore, improbable investment, far different from a cost-of-living escalation clause that they could contractually enforce in court. See n. 20, supra. We find, accordingly, that the effect that the Board asserts bargaining in behalf of pensioners would have on the negotiation of active employees' retirement plans is too speculative a foundation on which to base an obligation to bargain. . . .

The question remains whether the Company committed an unfair labor practice by offering retirees an exchange for their withdrawal from the already negotiated health insurance plan. . . . The Board's trial examiner ruled that the Company's action is offering retirees a change in their health plan did not amount to a "modification" of the collective-bargaining agreement in violation of §8(d), since the pensioners had merely been given an additional option that they were free to accept or decline as they saw fit. The Board rejected that conclusion on the ground that there were several possible ways of adjusting the negotiated plan to the Medicare provisions and the Company "modified" the contract by unilaterally choosing one of them. The Company now urges, in effect, that we adopt the views of the trial examiner. We need not resolve, however, whether there was a "modification" within the meaning of §8(d), because we hold that even if there was, a "modification" is a prohibited unfair labor practice only when it changes a term that is a mandatory rather than a permissive subject of bargaining.

Paragraph (4) of §8(d), of course, requires that a party proposing a modification continue "in full force and effect . . . all the terms and conditions of the existing contract" until its expiration. Viewed in isolation from the rest of the provision, that language would preclude any distinction between contract obligations that are "terms and conditions of employment" and those that are not. But in construing §8(d), "'we must not be guided by a single sentence or member of a sentence, but

20. Since retirees are not members of the bargaining unit, the bargaining agent is under no statutory duty to represent them in negotiations with the employer. This does not mean that when a union bargains for retirees — which nothing in this opinion precludes if the employer agrees — the retirees are without protection. Under established contract principles, vested retirement rights may not be altered without the pensioner's consent. The retiree, moreover, would have a federal remedy under §301 of the Labor Management Relations Act for breach of contract if his benefits were unilaterally changed.

look to the provisions of the whole law, and to its object and policy.'" Mastro Plastics Corp. v. National Labor Relations Board, 350 U.S. 270, 285 (1956). Seen in that light, §8(d) embraces only mandatory topics of bargaining. The provision begins by defining "to bargain collectively" as meeting and conferring "with respect to wages, hours, and other terms and conditions of employment." It then goes on to state that "the duty to bargain collectively shall also mean" that mid-term unilateral modifications and terminations are prohibited. Although this part of the section is introduced by a "proviso" clause, it quite plainly is to be construed *in pari materia* with the preceding definition. Accordingly, just as §8(d) defines the obligation to bargain to be with respect to mandatory terms alone, so it prescribes the duty to maintain only mandatory terms without unilateral modification for the duration of the collective-bargaining agreement. . . .

The structure and language of §8(d) point to a more specialized purpose than merely promoting general contract compliance. The conditions for a modification or termination set out in paragraphs (1) through (4) plainly are designed to regulate modifications and terminations so as to facilitate agreement in place of economic warfare. . . .

If that is correct, the distinction that we draw between mandatory and permissive terms of bargaining fits the statutory purpose. By once bargaining and agreeing on a permissive subject, the parties, naturally, do not make the subject a mandatory topic of future bargaining. When a proposed modification is to a permissive term, therefore, the purpose of facilitating accord on the proposal is not at all in point, since the parties are not required under the statute to bargain with respect to it. The irrelevance of the purpose is demonstrated by the irrelevance of the procedures themselves of §8(d). Paragraph (2), for example, requires an offer "to meet and confer with the other party for the purpose of negotiating a new contract or a contract containing the proposed modifications." But such an offer is meaningless if a party is statutorily free to refuse to negotiate on the proposed change to the permissive term. The notification to mediation and conciliation services referred to in paragraph (3) would be equally meaningless, if required at all. We think it would be no less beside the point to read paragraph (4) of §8(d) as requiring continued adherence to permissive as well as mandatory terms. The remedy for a unilateral mid-term modification to a permissive term lies in an action for breach of contract, not in an unfair-labor-practice proceeding.

As a unilateral mid-term modification of a permissive term such as retirees' benefits does not, therefore, violate §8(d), the judgment of the Court of Appeals is

Affirmed.[26]

[26] Douglas, J., dissented.

Notes

1. The Milwaukee Spring Company has a unionized facility in Milwaukee, Wisconsin, and a nonunion facility in McHenry, Illinois. During the term of a collective bargaining agreement at the Milwaukee facility, the firm asked the union to forgo a wage increase stipulated in the agreement and to make other contractual concessions. The firm proposed moving its Milwaukee operations to McHenry. When the union refused to make the requested concessions, the firm began to move the facility. This resulted in layoffs in Milwaukee. The firm concedes that it is relocating solely to save labor costs. While it has the "ability" to pay the contractually stipulated wage, it can earn a greater return on investment capital by moving. The firm has bargained with the union about the move but has not gotten the union's consent to it. The firm is ready to bargain over the effects of the move. The union's contract does not expressly forbid the relocation. Has the firm had an unlawful midterm modification? See Milwaukee Spring Div. of Illinois Coil Spring Co., 265 N.L.R.B. 206 (1982).[27]

2. Should the restrictive concept of "mandatory subject of bargaining" control the extent of the employer's duty to refrain from midterm modifications without bargaining in good faith to impasse? If the union has a breach of contract remedy in the courts, why should the Board become involved in midterm *modification* issues at all? Is the simple answer that §8(d) requires it to? Could the Board refuse?

3. Board Treatment of Breach of Contract Issues

NLRB v. C & C PLYWOOD CORP.
385 U.S. 421 (1967)

STEWART, J. . . .

In August 1962, the Plywood, Lumber, and Saw Mill Workers Local No. 2405 was certified as the bargaining representative of the respondent's production and maintenance employees. The agreement which resulted from collective bargaining contained the following provision:

Article XVII
WAGES

A. A classified wage scale has been agreed upon by the Employer and Union, and has been signed by the parties and thereby made a part of the written agreement. The Employer reserves the right to pay a premium rate over and above the contractual classified wage rate to reward any

[27] Recall that this case is discussed in *Otis Elevator*, supra.

> particular employee for some special fitness, skill, aptitude or the like. The payment of such a premium rate shall not be considered a permanent increase in the rate of that position and may, at sole option of the Employer, be reduced to the contractual rate. . . .

The agreement also stipulated that wages should be "closed" during the period it was effective and that neither party should be obligated to bargain collectively with respect to any matter not specifically referred to in the contract. Grievance machinery was established, but no ultimate arbitration of grievances or other disputes was provided.

Less than three weeks after this agreement was signed, the respondent posted a notice that all members of the "glue spreader" crews would be paid $2.50 per hour if their crews met specified biweekly (and later weekly) production standards, although under the "classified wage scale" referred to in the above quoted Art. XVII of the agreement, the members of these crews were to be paid hourly wages ranging from $2.15 to $2.29, depending upon their function within the crew. When the union learned of this premium pay plan through one of its members, it immediately asked for a conference with the respondent. During the meetings between the parties which followed this request, the employer indicated a willingness to discuss the terms of the plan, but refused to rescind it pending those discussions.

It was this refusal which prompted the union to charge the respondent with an unfair labor practice in violation of §§8(a)(5) and (1). . . . [The] Board ruled the union had not ceded power to the employer unilaterally to change the wage system as it had. For while the agreement specified different hourly pay for different members of the glue spreader crews and allowed for merit increases for "particular employee[s]," the employer had placed all the members of these crews on the same wage scale and had made it a function of the production output of the crew as a whole.

In refusing to enforce the Board's order, the Court of Appeals did not decide that the premium pay provision of the labor agreement had been misinterpreted by the Board. Instead, it held the Board did not have jurisdiction to find the respondent had violated §8(a) of the Labor Act, because the "existence . . . of an unfair labor practice [did] not turn entirely upon the provisions of the Act, but arguably upon a good-faith dispute as to the correct meaning of the provisions of the collective-bargaining agreement. . . ." 351 F.2d, at 228.

The respondent does not question the proposition that an employer may not unilaterally institute merit increases during the term of a collective agreement unless some provision of the contract authorizes him to do so. The argument is, rather, that since the contract contained a provision which *might* have allowed the respondent to institute the wage plan in question, the Board was powerless to determine whether that provision *did* authorize the respondent's action, because the question was one for a state or federal court under §301 of the Act.

In evaluating this contention, it is important first to point out that the collective bargaining agreement contained no arbitration clause. The contract did provide grievance procedures, but the end result of those procedures, if differences between the parties remained unresolved, was economic warfare, not "the therapy of arbitration." Carey v. Westinghouse Electric Corp., 375 U.S. 261, 272. . . .

The respondent's argument rests primarily upon the legislative history of the 1947 amendments to the National Labor Relations Act. It is said that the rejection by Congress of a bill which would have given the Board unfair labor practice jurisdiction over all branches of collective bargaining agreements shows that the Board is without power to decide any case involving the interpretation of a labor contract. . . . But in this case the Board has not construed a labor agreement to determine the extent of the contractual rights which were given the union by the employer. It has not imposed its own view of what the terms and conditions of the labor agreement should be. It has done no more than merely enforce a statutory right which Congress considered necessary to allow labor and management to get on with the process of reaching fair terms and conditions of employment — "to provide a means by which agreement may be reached." The Board's interpretation went only so far as was necessary to determine that the union did not agree to give up these statutory safeguards. Thus, the Board, in necessarily construing a labor agreement to decide this unfair labor practice case, has not exceeded the jurisdiction laid out for it by Congress. . . .

If the Board in a case like this had no jurisdiction to consider a collective agreement prior to an authoritative construction by the courts, labor organizations would face inordinate delays in obtaining vindication of their statutory rights. Where, as here, the parties have not provided for arbitration, the union would have to institute a court action to determine the applicability of the premium pay provision of the collective bargaining agreement.[15] If it succeeded in court, the union would then have to go back to the Labor Board to begin an unfair labor practice proceeding. It is not unlikely that this would add years to the already lengthy period required to gain relief from the Board. Congress cannot

15. The precise nature of the union's case in court is not readily apparent. If damages for breach of contract were sought, the union would have difficulty in establishing the amount of injury caused by respondent's action. For the real injury in this case is to the union's status as bargaining representative, and it would be difficult to translate such damage into dollars and cents. If an injunction were sought to vindicate the union's contractual rights, the problem of the applicability of the Norris-LaGuardia Act would have to be faced. A federal injunction issuing from a court with §301 jurisdiction might be barred by §7 of that Act. Thus, it may be that the only remedy in court which would be available to the union would be a suit for a declaratory judgment, assuming such a suit in these circumstances would be maintainable under state or federal law.

have intended to place such obstacles in the way of the Board's effective enforcement of statutory duties. For in the labor field, as in few others, time is crucially important in obtaining relief.

The legislative history of the Labor Act, the precedents interpreting it, and the interest of its efficient administration thus all lead to the conclusion that the Board had jurisdiction to deal with the unfair labor practice charge in this case. We hold that the Court of Appeals was in error in deciding to the contrary. . . .

Reversed and remanded.

Notes

1. In a companion case, NLRB v. Acme Industrial Co., 385 U.S. 432 (1967), the union demanded that the company furnish it with information regarding the removal of certain machinery from the plant. The union suspected either the subcontracting of work (barred by the bargaining agreement) or the transfer of work to another location (giving employees transfer rights under the agreement). The union filed grievances alleging bargaining agreement violations, and the company refused the request for information.

The Supreme Court sustained a Board finding that the refusal to provide the information violated §8(a)(5), rejecting the company's argument that it was for the arbitrator in the first instance to decide the relevancy of the requested information. The Court reasoned that the Board was not making a binding construction of the contract nor was it deciding the merits of the union's breach of contract claims. Rather, the Board was aiding the arbitration process by mandating the transfer of information that would enable the union to better "sift out unmeritorious claims."

2. In NLRB v. Huttig Sash & Door Co., 377 F.2d 964 (8th Cir. 1967), the court held that the Board could act in a *C & C Plywood* situation even though the bargaining agreement contained an arbitration clause.

For more than 20 years the Board has, in cases deemed appropriate, voluntarily deferred to existing arbitration awards when the awards effectively disposed of unfair labor practice issues. This deferral policy is popularly known as the *Spielberg* doctrine.[28] As originally applied, the deferral requirements were the disposal of the unfair labor practice issue by an arbitration decision already rendered, a procedurally fair arbitration proceeding that bound all parties, and a decision by the arbitrator that was "not clearly repugnant to the purposes and policies of the Act." Later in the doctrine's development, the Board held that it would not defer unless the arbitrator had considered the precise issue

[28] From Spielberg Mfg. Co., 112 N.L.R.B. 1080 (1955), its case of origin.

that would be before the Board,[29] although the Board may have later pulled back from this requirement.[30]

In Olin Corp., 268 N.L.R.B. No. 86, 115 L.R.R.M. 1056 (1984), the Board set out the following *Spielberg* standards:

> We would find that an arbitrator has adequately considered the unfair labor practice issue if (1) the contractual issue is factually parallel to the unfair labor practice issue, and (2) the arbitrator was presented generally with the facts relevant to resolving the unfair labor practice. . . . And, with regard to the inquiry into the "clearly repugnant" standards, we would not require an arbitrator's award to be totally consistent with Board precedent. Unless the award is palpably wrong, i.e., unless the arbitrator's decision is not susceptible to an interpretation consistent with the Act, we will defer.

The Board has held that it will not defer to an arbitration award involving the rights of an individual employee unless his or her rights were adequately represented in the arbitration proceeding.[31]

COLLYER INSULATED WIRE[32]

192 N.L.R.B. 837 (1971)

[During the term of a bargaining agreement the employer unilaterally increased the wage rates for two employee groups and directed that the hourly removal and cleaning of a large worm gear be done by a single maintenance machinist rather than two, as was the current practice. The employer contended that these actions were sanctioned by the bargaining agreement as interpreted in the light of past practice. The bargaining agreement granted the employer the power to review wage rates and differentials and permitted "adjustments in individual rates from time to time to remove inequalities or for other proper reasons." It prohibited changes in the existing general pay scale. The bargaining agreement contained an arbitration clause but the union had not invoked it, choosing instead to file a §8(a)(5) refusal to bargain charge.]

We find merit in Respondent's exceptions that because this dispute in its entirety arises from the contract between the parties, and from the

[29] See, e.g., Monsanto Chemical Co., 130 N.L.R.B. 1097 (1961).

[30] See Electronic Reproduction Service Corp., 213 N.L.R.B. 110 (1974). In Pioneer Finishing Corp., 247 N.L.R.B. 1299 (1980), enforced, 667 F.2d 199 (1st Cir. 1981), the Board held that it would not defer to completed arbitration because the arbitrator did not "adequately address" the unfair labor practice issues.

[31] See Jacobs Transfer, 201 N.L.R.B. 210 (1973).

[32] See Isaacson & Zifchak, Agency Deferral to Private Arbitration of Employment Disputes, 73 Colum. L. Rev. 1383 (1973); Schatzki, NLRB Resolution of Contract Disputes under §8(a)(5), 50 Tex. L. Rev. 225 (1972); Zimmer, Wired for Collyer: Rationalizing NLRB and Arbitration Jurisdiction, 48 Ind. L.J. 141 (1973); Getman, Collyer Insulated Wire: A Case of Misplaced Modesty, 49 Ind. L.J. 57 (1973).

parties' relationship under the contract, it ought to be resolved in the manner which that contract prescribes. We conclude that the Board is vested with authority to withhold its processes in this case, and that the contract here made available a quick and fair means for the resolution of this dispute including, if appropriate, a fully effective remedy for any breach of contract which occurred. We conclude, in sum, that our obligation to advance the purposes of the Act is best discharged by the dismissal of this complaint.

In our view, disputes such as these can better be resolved by arbitrators with special skill and experience in deciding matters arising under established bargaining relationships than by the application by this Board of a particular provision of our statute. . . .

The question whether the Board should withhold its process arises, of course, only when a set of facts may present not only an alleged violation of the Act but also an alleged breach of the collective-bargaining agreement subject to arbitration. Thus, this case like each such case compels an accommodation between, on the one hand, the statutory policy favoring the fullest use of collective bargaining and the arbitral process and, on the other, the statutory policy reflected by Congress' grant to the Board of exclusive jurisdiction to prevent unfair labor practices.

[The opinion then partially traces the development of the *Spielberg* doctrine.]

The circumstances of this case weigh heavily in favor of deferral. [T]his dispute arises within the confines of a long and productive collective-bargaining relationship. The parties before us have, for 35 years, mutually and voluntarily resolved the conflicts which inhere in collective bargaining. [N]o claim is made of enmity by Respondent to employees' exercise of protected rights. Respondent here has credibly asserted its willingness to resort to arbitration under a clause providing for arbitration in a very broad range of disputes and unquestionably broad enough to embrace this dispute.

Finally, the dispute is one eminently well suited to resolution by arbitration. The contract and its meaning in present circumstances lie at the center of this dispute. In contrast, the Act and its policies become involved only if it is determined that the agreement between the parties, examined in the light of its negotiating history and the practices of the parties thereunder, did not sanction Respondent's right to make the disputed changes, subject to review if sought by the Union, under the contractually prescribed procedure. That threshold determination is clearly within the expertise of a mutually agreed-upon arbitrator. In this regard we note especially that here, the dispute between these parties is the very stuff of labor contract arbitration. The competence of a mutually selected arbitrator to decide the issue and fashion an appropriate remedy, if needed, can no longer be gainsaid. . . . It is true, manifestly, that we cannot judge the regularity or statutory acceptability of the result in an arbitration proceeding which has not occurred. However, we are unwilling to adopt the presumption that such a proceeding will be invalid under *Spielberg* and to exercise our decisional authority at this juncture on the basis of a mere possibility that such a proceeding might be unacceptable under *Spielberg* standards. That risk is far better accommodated, we believe, by the result reached here of retaining jurisdiction against an event which years of experience with labor arbitration have now made clear is a remote hazard. . . .

When the parties have contractually committed themselves to mutually agreeable procedures for resolving their disputes during the period of the contract, we are of the view that those procedures should be afforded full opportunity to function. The long and successful functioning of grievance and arbitration procedures suggests to us that in the overwhelming majority of cases, the utilization of such means will resolve the underlying dispute and make it unnecessary for either party to follow the more formal, and sometimes lengthy, combination of administrative and judicial litigation provided for under our statute. At the same time, by our reservation of jurisdiction, infra, we guarantee that there will be no sacrifice of statutory rights if the parties' own processes fail to function in a manner consistent with the dictates of our law. This approach, we believe, effectuates the salutary policy announced in *Spielberg,* which the dissenting opinion correctly summarizes as one of not requiring the "serious machinery of the Board where the record indicates that the parties are in the process of resolving their dispute in a manner sufficient to effectuate the policies of the Act." . . .

Member FANNING, dissenting. . . .

The time limits for the resolution of grievances with respect to these unilateral changes have passed and, so far as the collective-bargaining agreement is concerned, those putative grievances must be deemed to be settled.

Clearly then the effect of the majority's decision is a direction to the parties to arbitrate a grievance which is no longer contractually arbitrable. The complaint is dismissed, but jurisdiction is retained, presumably to give the Union an opportunity to file a grievance under a time-expired contractual provision, with the implicit threat to the Respondent that the Board will assert jurisdiction, upon a proper motion, if Respondent is unwilling now to submit to arbitration. The majority's insistence that the parties' statutory rights cannot be adjudicated in this case except through the authority of an arbitrator verges on the practice of compulsory arbitration. . . .

I find it impossible to accept the majority's assertion that an arbitrator rather than the Board, with the help of its staff and Trial Examiner, has more expertise and is more competent to judge such a dispute in a manner to effectuate the policies of the Act. The law is perfectly clear that an employer's unilateral action in granting nonautomatic wage increases without prior discussion or bargaining with the Union is violative of §8(a)(5) of the Act. Such conduct, the Supreme Court has held, "must of necessity obstruct bargaining, contrary to the Congressional policy." NLRB v. Katz, 369 U.S. 736, 747. . . .

The effect of the majority's decision in the instant case is clearly a reversal of the established *Spielberg* line of cases. In the future applicable standards for review of arbitration awards will not be followed. Neither the existence of an actual award, the fairness of the arbitrator's opinion or its impingement upon the policies of the Act will be considered by the Board in dismissing complaints of this nature. Under the majority's accommodation theory even consideration of the nature and scope of the alleged unfair labor practices will not receive the Board's attention. The impact of the majority's decision may be said to go beyond compulsory arbitration. For it means that in the future the Board will not concern itself with the *fact* or the *regularity* of the arbitral process, but will strip the parties of statutory rights merely on the *availability* of such a procedure.

The majority does not frame the primary issue in this case in terms calculated to resolve a particular dispute in a particular case. Rather, a new standard for the nonassertion of jurisdiction is announced, embracing a whole class of employers who have entered into contracts with unions containing a grievance-arbitration clause. In the future, complaints based upon such disputes, without regard to the seriousness of the alleged unfair labor practices, may not be litigated before this Board. . . .

Assuming arguendo the power of the Board to refuse to entertain charges in cases of this type, the policy of embarking upon such a program is open to serious question. Arbitrators are employed to interpret and apply a specific collective-bargaining agreement. Generally, they are loath to intrude into the area of public rights or national labor policy. These questions historically have been the prime concern of the Board, which was established by Congress exclusively for this purpose. Understandably, an arbitrator, paid jointly by a union and an employer to adjudicate their private rights and obligations, may be unwilling to suggest that one of them is in violation of the National Labor Relations Act and to direct a remedy appropriate to such a finding. The function of good arbitration involves not only the resolution of a particular dispute, but the fostering of a harmonious relationship between the parties to collective bargaining. To endow the arbitrator's award in all cases involving contract interpretation with the imprimatur of Board approval is, in my opinion, a disservice to the arbitrator, the parties before him, and the effectuation of a sound national labor policy.[33]

[33] Member Brown concurred and Member Jenkins dissented.

Notes

1. Suppose the employer has given employees turkeys each Christmas throughout the company's history. Last year the employer was organized by the union and signed a collective bargaining agreement. The employer's Christmas practice was mentioned neither in negotiations nor in the agreement. The next Christmas produced no turkeys. If the matter is brought to an arbitrator under the bargaining agreement, how should the arbitrator rule? How should the Board decide it in a §8(a)(5) charge (assuming no deferral)? Is prearbitration deferral appropriate? On essentially these facts, the Board (3-2) deferred to arbitration in Radioear Corp., 199 N.L.R.B. 1161 (1972). The bargaining agreement contained a broad zipper clause and no "maintenance of benefits" clause.

2. Is the *Collyer* majority correct in asserting arbitrators have the greater expertise in these cases? In fact finding? With respect to the employment history and practices of a particular employer? While some bargaining agreements designate a permanent arbitrator to decide all disputes, most agreements call for arbitrators to be selected on a case-by-case basis; the arbitrator in a given case is likely to have had no prior experience with the employer and union in question.

3. Is *Collyer* a way to reduce the Board's caseload? If so, would that be a proper ground for decision? It would seem that such an effect depends on the General Counsel's refusal to go to complaint in *Collyer* cases. The same reasoning is applicable in *Spielberg* cases; yet before the new standards,[34] the Board would explore the arbitrator's treatment with care.[35]

4. In National Radio Co., 198 N.L.R.B. 527 (1972), the employer was charged with violating §8(a)(5) by unilaterally imposing a condition that union representatives record and report their movements in the plant while processing grievances on compensated time, and with violating §8(a)(3) by discharging an employee for refusing to comply with the reporting requirement. The General Counsel claimed the discharge had been motivated by antiunion animus. In a 3-2 decision the Board announced the application of *Collyer* to §8(a)(3) cases.

Thereafter, an arbitrator found that the discharge was neither antiunion motivated nor a contract violation. Even if the employer's reporting requirement violated the contract, in the arbitrator's view, it was the duty of the employee to comply with the rule and challenge it through the grievance process. The arbitrator did not rule on the question of whether the reporting clause's unilateral adoption violated §8(a)(5). The grievant returned to the Board, which again declined (3-2) to consider the merits. 205 N.L.R.B. 1179 (1973).

[34] See p. 592, supra.
[35] See G & H Products, 261 N.L.R.B. 298 (1982).

Rejecting the contention that since the §8(a)(5) allegation had not been decided by the arbitrator the Board must hear the case, the Board stated:

> [A]s the arbitrator noted, the Charging Party initially did not ask him to resolve the issue of the propriety of the manner in which the rule had been promulgated in the arbitration and subsequently did not avail itself of the unopposed opportunity to expand the scope of the arbitration procedure to include that issue. Finally, at no time prior to the issuance of the award did the Board receive a timely motion from the Charging Party that any issue as to the propriety of the rule or the nature of its promulgation had not been resolved by amicable settlement in the grievance procedure or had not been submitted to arbitration.

205 N.L.R.B. at 1180.

What jurisdiction did the arbitrator have to consider the §8(a)(5) issue? If the reporting rule was unilaterally promulgated in violation of §8(a)(5), wouldn't its enforcement violate §§8(a)(3) and (1) on the authority of *Republic Aviation,* supra at p. 170? If so, or if you find *Republic Aviation* not dispositive of the issue, isn't it clear that only the Board has either the authority or the expertise to adjudicate the matter?

Following a change in Board personnel, *National Radio* was overruled in General American Transportation Corp., 228 N.L.R.B. 808 (1977). Two Board members continued to adhere to *Collyer* in its broadest applications. Members Fanning and Jenkins contended that the Board lacks the statutory power to Collyerize cases. Member Murphy was the swing vote. Her decision to defer depended on the nature of the unfair labor practice alleged:

> In cases alleging violations of §§8(a)(5) and 8(b)(3), based upon conduct assertedly in derogation of the contract, the principal issue is whether the complained-of conduct is permitted by the parties' contract. Such issues are eminently suited to the arbitral process and resolution of the contract issue by an unfair labor practice issue. On the other hand, in cases alleging violations of §§8(a)(1), 8(a)(3), 8(b)(1)(A), and 8(b)(2), although arguably also involving a contract violation, the determinative issue is not whether the conduct is permitted by the contract, but whether the conduct was unlawfully motivated or whether it otherwise interfered with, restrained, or coerced employees in the exercise of the rights guaranteed them by §7 of the Act. In these situations, an arbitrator's resolution of the contract issue will not dispose of the unfair labor practice allegation. Nor is the arbitration process suited for resolving employee complaints of discrimination under §7. . . .

Member Murphy also stated that where an unfair labor practice complaint alleges both a §8(a)(5) violation (where she would defer) and a violation where she would not defer, she would not "fragmentize" the case by deferring on any of the charges.[36]

ALEXANDER v. GARDNER-DENVER CO.
415 U.S. 35 (1974)

[Employee Alexander, a black, filed a grievance under a collective bargaining agreement alleging that he had been discharged by his employer without proper cause. In upholding the discharge, an arbitrator made no reference to Alexander's contention that his discharge was the result of racial discrimination. After being notified by the EEOC of his right to sue, Alexander filed a Title VII action against the company. The district court held that Alexander, having voluntarily pursued his grievance to final arbitration under the collective bargaining agreement, was bound by the arbitrator's award and precluded from bringing a Title VII suit. The Tenth Circuit affirmed.]

Powell, J. . . .

III

Title VII does not speak expressly to the relationship between federal courts and the grievance-arbitration machinery of collective bargaining agreements. It does, however, vest federal courts with plenary powers to enforce the statutory requirements; and it specifies with precision the jurisdictional prerequisites that an individual must satisfy before he is entitled to institute a lawsuit. In the present case, these prerequisites were met when petitioner (1) filed timely a charge of employment discrimination with the Commission, and (2) received and acted upon the Commission's statutory notice of the right to sue. . . . There is no suggestion in the statutory scheme that a prior arbitral decision either forecloses an individual's right to sue or divests federal courts of jurisdiction.

In addition, legislative enactments in this area have long evinced a general intent to accord parallel or overlapping remedies against discrimination. In the Civil Rights Act of 1964 Congress indicated that it considered the policy against discrimination to be of the "highest priority." Newman v. Piggie Park Enterprises, [390 U.S.] at 402. Consistent with this view, Title VII provides for consideration of employment-discrimination claims in several forums. See 42 U.S.C. §2000e-5(b) (1970 ed., Supp. II) (EEOC); 42 U.S.C. §2000e-5(c) (1970 ed., Supp. II) (state and local agencies); 42 U.S.C. § 2000e-5(f) (1970 ed., Supp. II) (federal courts). And, in general, submission of a claim to one forum does not

[36] See Texaco, 233 N.L.R.B. 375 (1977).

preclude a later submission to another. See 42 U.S.C. §§2000e-5(b) and (f) (1970 ed., Supp. II); McDonnell Douglas Corp. v. Green, [411 U.S. 792]. Moreover, the legislative history of Title VII manifests a congressional intent to allow an individual to pursue independently his rights under both Title VII and other applicable state and federal statutes. The clear inference is that Title VII was designed to supplement, rather than supplant, existing laws and institutions relating to employment discrimination. In sum, Title VII's purpose and procedures strongly suggest that an individual does not forfeit his private cause of action if he first pursues his grievance to final arbitration under the nondiscrimination clause of a collective bargaining agreement.

In reaching the opposite conclusion, the District Court relied in part on the doctrine of election of remedies.[10] That doctrine, which refers to situations where an individual pursues remedies that are legally or factually inconsistent, has no application in the present context. In submitting his grievance to arbitration, an employee seeks to vindicate his contractual right under a collective bargaining agreement. By contrast, in filing a lawsuit under Title VII, an employee asserts independent statutory rights accorded by Congress. The distinctly separate nature of these contractual and statutory rights is not vitiated merely because both were violated as a result of the same factual occurrence. And certainly no inconsistency results from permitting both rights to be enforced in their respectively appropriate forums. The resulting scheme is somewhat analogous to the procedure under the National Labor Relations Act, as amended, where disputed transactions may implicate both contractual and statutory rights. Where the statutory right underlying a particular claim may not be abridged by contractual agreement, the Court has recognized that consideration of the claim by the arbitrator as a contractual dispute under the collective bargaining agreement does not preclude subsequent consideration of the claim by the National Labor Relations Board as an unfair labor practice charge or as a petition for clarification of the union's representation certificate under the Act. Carey v. Westinghouse Corp., 375 U.S. 261 (1964). Cf. Smith v. Evening News Assn., 371 U.S. 195 (1962). There, as here, the relationship between the forums is complementary since consideration of the claim by both forums may promote the policies underlying each. Thus, the ra-

10. The District Court adopted the reasoning of the Sixth Circuit in Dewey v. Reynolds Metals Co., 429 F.2d 324, 332 (1970), affirmed by an equally divided Court, 402 U.S. 689 (1971), which was apparently based in part on the doctrine of election of remedies. The Sixth Circuit, however, later described *Dewey* as resting instead on the doctrine of equitable estoppel and on "themes of res judicata and collateral estoppel." Newman v. Avco Corp., 451 F.2d 743, 746 n. 1 (C.A.6 1971). Whatever doctrinal label is used, the essence of these holdings remains the same. The policy reasons for rejecting the doctrines of election of remedies and waiver in the context of Title VII are equally applicable to the doctrines of res judicata and collateral estoppel.

tionale behind the election-of-remedies doctrine cannot support the decision below.[14]

We are also unable to accept the proposition that petitioner waived his cause of action under Title VII. . . . [W]e think it clear that there can be no prospective waiver of an employee's rights under Title VII. It is true, of course, that a union may waive certain statutory rights related to collective activity, such as the right to strike. These rights are conferred on employees collectively to foster the processes of bargaining and properly may be exercised or relinquished by the union as collective bargaining agent to obtain economic benefits for unit members. Title VII, on the other hand, stands on plainly different ground; it concerns not majoritarian processes, but an individual's right to equal employment opportunities. Title VII's strictures are absolute and represent a congressional command that each employee be free from discriminatory practices. Of necessity, the rights conferred can form no part of the collective bargaining process since waiver of these rights would defeat the paramount congressional purpose behind Title VII. In these circumstances, an employee's rights under Title VII are not susceptible for prospective waiver. . . .

The actual submission of petitioner's grievance to arbitration in the present case does not alter the situation. Although presumably an employee may waive his cause of action under Title VII as part of a voluntary settlement, mere resort to the arbitral forum to enforce contractual rights constitutes no such waiver. Since an employee's rights under Title VII may not be waived prospectively, existing contractual rights and remedies against discrimination must result from other concessions already made by the union as part of the economic bargain struck with the employer. It is settled law that no additional concession may be exacted from any employee as the price for enforcing those rights. J. I. Case Co. v. NLRB, 321 U.S. 332, 338-339 (1944).

Moreover, a contractual right to submit a claim to arbitration is not displaced simply because Congress also has provided a statutory right against discrimination. Both rights have legally independent origins and are equally available to the aggrieved employee. This point becomes apparent through consideration of the role of the arbitrator in the system of industrial self-government. As the proctor of the bargain, the arbitrator's task is to effectuate the intent of the parties. His source of authority is the collective bargaining agreement, and he must interpret and apply that agreement in accordance with the "industrial common law

14. Nor can it be maintained that election of remedies is required by the possibility of unjust enrichment through duplicative recoveries. Where, as here, the employer has prevailed at arbitration, there, of course, can be no duplicative recovery. But even in cases where the employee has first prevailed, judicial relief can be structured to avoid such windfall gains. . . . Furthermore, if the relief obtained by the employee at arbitration were fully equivalent to that obtainable under Title VII, there would be no further relief for the court to grant and hence no need for the employee to institute suit.

of the shop" and the various needs and desires of the parties. The arbitrator, however, has no general authority to invoke public laws that conflict with the bargain between the parties:

"[A]n arbitrator is confined to interpretation and application of the collective bargaining agreement; . . . He may of course look for guidance from many sources, yet his award is legitimate only so long as it draws its essence from the collective bargaining agreement. When the arbitrator's words manifest an infidelity to this obligation, courts have no choice but to refuse enforcement of the award." United Steelworkers of America v. Enterprise Wheel & Car Corp., 363 U.S. 593, 597 (1960). If an arbitral decision is based "solely upon the arbitrator's view of the requirements of enacted legislation," rather than on interpretation of the collective bargaining agreement, the arbitrator has "exceeded the scope of the submission," and the award will not be enforced. Ibid. Thus the arbitrator has authority to resolve only questions of contractual rights, and this authority remains regardless of whether certain contractual rights are similar to, or duplicative of, the substantive rights secured by Title VII.

IV

The District Court and the Court of Appeals reasoned that to permit an employee to have his claim considered in both the arbitral and judicial forums would be unfair since this would mean that the employer, but not the employee, was bound by the arbitral award. In the District Court's words, it could not "accept a philosophy which gives the employee two strings to his bow when the employer has only one." . . . This argument mistakes the effect of Title VII. Under the *Steelworkers* trilogy, an arbitral decision is final and binding on the employer and employee, and judicial review is limited as to both. But in instituting an action under Title VII, the employee is not seeking review of the arbitrator's decision. Rather, he is asserting a statutory right independent of the arbitration process. An employer does not have "two strings to his bow" with respect to an arbitral decision for the simple reason that Title VII does not provide employers with a cause of action against employees. An employer cannot be the victim of discriminatory employment practices. . . .

The District Court and the Court of Appeals also thought that to permit a later resort to the judicial forum would undermine substantially the employer's incentive to arbitrate and would "sound the death knell for arbitration clauses in labor contracts." . . . Again, we disagree. The primary incentive for an employer to enter into an arbitration agreement is the union's reciprocal promise not to strike. . . . It is not unreasonable to assume that most employers will regard the benefits derived from a no-strike pledge as outweighing whatever costs may result from according employees an arbitral remedy against discrimination in addition to their judicial remedy under Title VII. Indeed, the severe consequences of a strike may make an arbitration clause almost essential from both the employees' and the employer's perspective. Moreover, the grievance-arbitration machinery of the collective bargaining agreement remains a relatively inexpensive and expeditious means for resolving a wide range of disputes, including claims of discriminatory employment practices. Where the collective bargaining agreement contains a nondiscrimination clause similar to Title VII, and where arbitral procedures are fair and regular, arbitration may well produce a settlement satisfactory to both employer and employee. An employer thus has an incentive to make available the conciliatory and therapeutic processes of arbitration which may satisfy an employee's perceived need to resort to the judicial forum, thus saving the employer the expense and aggravation associated with a lawsuit. For similar reasons, the employee also has a strong incentive to arbitrate grievances, and arbitration may often eliminate those misunderstandings or discriminatory practices that might otherwise precipitate resort to the judicial forum.

V

Respondent contends that even if a preclusion rule is not adopted, federal courts should defer to arbitral decisions on discrimination claims where: (i) the claim was before the arbitrator; (ii) the collective bargaining agreement prohibited the form of discrimination charged in the suit under Title VII; and (iii) the arbitrator has authority to rule on the claim and to fashion a remedy.[17] Under respondent's proposed rule, a court would grant summary judgment and dismiss the employee's action if the above conditions were met. The rule's obvious consequence in the present case would be to deprive the petitioner of his statutory right to attempt to establish his claim in a federal court.

At the outset, it is apparent that a deferral rule would be subject to many of the objections applicable to a preclusion rule. The purpose and procedures of Title VII indicate that Congress intended federal courts to exercise final responsibility for enforcement of Title VII; deferral to arbitral decisions would be inconsistent with that goal. Furthermore, we have long recognized that "the choice of forums inevitably affects the scope of the substantive right to be vindicated." U.S. Bulk Carriers v. Arguelles, 400 U.S. 351, 359-360 (1971) (Harlan, J., concurring). Respondent's deferral rule is necessarily premised on the assumption that arbitral processes are commensurate with judicial processes and that

17. Respondent's proposed rule is analogous to the NLRB's policy of deferring to arbitral decisions on statutory issues in certain cases. See Spielberg Mfg. Co., 112 N.L.R.B. 1080, 1082 (1955).

Congress impliedly intended federal courts to defer to arbitral decisions on Title VII issues. We deem this supposition unlikely.

Arbitral procedures, while well suited to the resolution of contractual disputes, make arbitration a comparatively inappropriate forum for the final resolution of rights created by Title VII. This conclusion rests first on the special role of the arbitrator, whose task is to effectuate the intent of the parties rather than the requirements of enacted legislation. Where the collective bargaining agreement conflicts with Title VII, the arbitration must follow the agreement. To be sure, the tension between contractual and statutory objectives may be mitigated where a collective bargaining agreement contains provisions facially similar to those of Title VII. But other facts may still render arbitral processes comparatively inferior to judicial processes in the protection of Title VII rights. Among these is the fact that the specialized competence of arbitrators pertains primarily to the law of the shop, not the law of the land. United Steelworkers of America v. Warrior & Gulf Navigation Co., 363 U.S. 574, 581-583 (1960). Parties usually choose an arbitrator because they trust his knowledge and judgment concerning the demands and norms of industrial relations. On the other hand, the resolution of statutory or constitutional issues is a primary responsibility of courts, and judicial construction has proved especially necessary with respect to Title VII, whose broad language frequently can be given meaning only by reference to public law concepts.

Moreover, the factfinding process in arbitration usually is not equivalent to judicial factfinding. The record of the arbitration proceedings is not as complete; the usual rules of evidence do not apply; and rights and procedures common to civil trials, such as discovery, compulsory process, cross-examination, and testimony under oath, are often severely limited or unavailable. . . . And as this Court has recognized, "[a]rbitrators have no obligation to the court to give their reasons for an award." United Steelworkers of America v. Enterprise Wheel & Car Corp., 363 U.S., at 598. Indeed, it is the informality of arbitral procedure that enables it to function as an efficient, inexpensive, and expeditious means for dispute resolution. This same characteristic, however, makes arbitration a less appropriate forum for final resolution of Title VII issues than the federal courts.

It is evident that respondent's proposed rule would not allay these concerns. Nor are we convinced that the solution lies in applying a more demanding deferral standard, such as that adopted by the Fifth Circuit in Rios v. Reynolds Metals Co., 467 F.2d 54 (1972).[20] As respondent

20. In *Rios*, the court set forth the following deferral standard:

First, there may be no deference to the decision of the arbitrator unless the contractual right coincides with rights under Title VII. Second, it must be plain that the arbitrator's decision is in no way violative of the private rights guaranteed by Title VII, nor of the public policy which inheres in Title VII. In addition, before defer-

points out, a standard that adequately insured effectuation of Title VII rights in the arbitral forum would tend to make arbitration a procedurally complex, expensive, and time-consuming process. And judicial enforcement of such a standard would almost require courts to make de novo determinations of the employees' claims. It is uncertain whether any minimal savings in judicial time and expense would justify the risk to vindication of Title VII rights.

A deferral rule also might adversely affect the arbitration system as well as the enforcement scheme of Title VII. Fearing that the arbitral forum cannot adequately protect their rights under Title VII, some employees may elect to bypass arbitration and institute a lawsuit. The possibility of voluntary compliance or settlement of Title VII claims would thus be reduced, and the result could well be more litigation, not less.

We think, therefore, that the federal policy favoring arbitration of labor disputes and the federal policy against discriminatory employment practices can best be accommodated by permitting an employee to pursue fully both his remedy under the grievance-arbitration clause of a collective bargaining agreement and his cause of action under Title VII. The federal court should consider the employee's claim de novo. The arbitral decision may be admitted as evidence and accorded such weight as the court deems appropriate.[21]

The judgment of the Court of Appeals is reversed.

Note

Does *Gardner-Denver* deliver a fatal blow to the Board's *Collyer* doctrine?

---

ring, the district court must be satisfied that (1) the factual issues before it are identical to those decided by the arbitrator; (2) the arbitrator had power under the collective agreement to decide the ultimate issue of discrimination; (3) the evidence presented at the arbitral hearing dealt adequately with all factual issues; (4) the arbitrator actually decided the factual issues presented to the court; (5) the arbitration proceeding was fair and regular and free of procedural infirmities. The burden of proof in establishing these conditions of limitation will be upon the respondent as distinguished from the claimant. 467 F.2d, at 58.

21. We adopt no standards as to the weight to be accorded an arbitral decision, since this must be determined in the court's discretion with regard to the facts and circumstances of each case. Relevant factors include the existence of provisions in the collective bargaining agreement that conform substantially with Title VII, the degree of procedural fairness in the arbitral forum, adequacy of the record with respect to the issue of discrimination, and the special competence of particular arbitrators. Where an arbitral determination gives full consideration to an employee's Title VII rights, a court may properly accord it great weight. This is especially true where the issue is solely one of fact, specifically addressed by the parties and decided by the arbitrator on the basis of an adequate record. But courts should ever be mindful that Congress, in enacting Title VII, thought it necessary to provide a judicial forum for the ultimate resolution of discriminatory employment claims. It is the duty of courts to assure the full availability of this forum.

E. BARGAINING REMEDIES[37]

H. K. PORTER CO. v. NLRB
397 U.S. 99 (1970)

BLACK, J.

After an election respondent United Steelworkers Union was, on October 5, 1961, certified by the National Labor Relations Board as the bargaining agent for certain employees at the Danville, Virginia, plant of the petitioner, H. K. Porter Co. Thereafter negotiations commenced for a collective bargaining agreement. Since that time the controversy has seesawed between the Board, the Court of Appeals for the District of Columbia Circuit, and this Court. This delay of over eight years is not because the case is exceedingly complex, but appears to have occurred chiefly because of the skill of the company's negotiators in taking advantage of every opportunity for delay in an act more noticeable for its generality than for its precise prescriptions. The entire lengthy dispute mainly revolves around the union's desire to have the company agree to "check off" the dues owed to the union by its members, that is, to deduct those dues periodically from the company's wage payments to the employees. The record shows, as the Board found, that the company's objection to a checkoff was not due to any general principle or policy against making deductions from employees' wages. The company does deduct charges for things like insurance, taxes, and contributions to charities, and at some other plants it has a checkoff arrangement for union dues. The evidence shows, and the court below found, that the company's objection was not because of inconvenience, but solely on the ground that the company was "not going to aid and comfort the union." Efforts by the union to obtain some kind of compromise on the checkoff request were all met with the same staccato response to the effect that the collection of union dues was the "union's business" and the company was not going to provide any assistance. Based on this and other evidence the Board found, and the Court of Appeals approved the finding, that the refusal of the company to bargain about the checkoff was not made in good faith, but was done solely to frustrate the making of any collective bargaining agreement. In May 1966, the Court of Appeals upheld the Board's order requiring the company to cease and desist from refusing to bargain in good faith and directing it to engage in further collective bargaining, if requested by the union to do so, over the checkoff.

In the course of that opinion, the Court of Appeals intimated that the Board conceivably might have required petitioner to agree to a checkoff provision as a remedy for the prior bad-faith bargaining, although the

[37] See McDowell & Huhn, NLRB Remedies for Unfair Labor Practices (1976); St. Antoine, A Touchstone for Labor Board Remedies, 14 Wayne L. Rev. 1039 (1968).

order enforced at that time did not contain any such provision. 363 F.2d, at 275-276, n. 16. In the ensuing negotiations the company offered to discuss alternative arrangements for collecting the union's dues, but the union insisted that the company was required to agree to the checkoff proposal without modification. [Acting on a motion to clarify its opinion, the court of appeals remanded the case to the Board. The Board ordered the company to agree to the checkoff provision.] We granted certiorari to consider whether the Board in these circumstances has the power to remedy the unfair labor practice by requiring the company to agree to check off the dues of the workers. For reasons to be stated we hold that while the Board does have power under the Labor Management Relations Act, to require employers and employees to negotiate, it is without power to compel a company or a union to agree to any substantive contractual provision of a collective bargaining agreement. . . .

The object of this Act was not to allow governmental regulation of the terms and conditions of employment, but rather to ensure that employers and their employees could work together to establish mutually satisfactory conditions. The basic theme of the Act was that through collective bargaining the passions, arguments, and struggles of prior years would be channeled into constructive, open discussions leading, hopefully, to mutual agreement. But it was recognized from the beginning that agreement might in some cases be impossible, and it was never intended that the Government would in such cases step in, become a party to the negotiations and impose its own views of a desirable settlement. This fundamental limitation was made abundantly clear in the legislative reports accompanying the 1935 Act.

[The Court then discussed the legislative history leading to the passage of §8(d).] The parties to the instant case are agreed that this is the first time in the 35-year history of the Act that the Board has ordered either an employer or a union to agree to a substantive term of a collective bargaining agreement.

Recognizing the fundamental principle "that the National Labor Relations Act is grounded on the premise of freedom of contract," 389 F.2d, at 300, the Court of Appeals in this case concluded that nevertheless in the circumstances presented here the Board could properly compel the employer to agree to a proposed checkoff clause. The Board had found that the refusal was based on a desire to frustrate agreement and not on any legitimate business reason. On the basis of that finding the Court of Appeals approved the further finding that the employer had not bargained in good faith, and the validity of that finding is not now before us. Where the record thus revealed repeated refusals by the employer to bargain in good faith on this issue, the Court of Appeals concluded that ordering agreement to the checkoff clause "may be the only means of assuring the Board, and the court, that [the employer] no longer harbors an illegal intent." 389 F.2d, at 299.

In reaching this conclusion the Court of Appeals held that §8(d) did not forbid the Board from compelling agreement. That court felt that "[s]ection 8(d) defines collective bargaining and relates to a determination of *whether* a . . . violation has occurred and not to the *scope* of the remedy which may be necessary to cure violations which have already occurred." 389 F.2d, at 299. We may agree with the Court of Appeals that as a matter of strict, literal interpretation of that section it refers only to deciding when a violation has occurred, but we do not agree that that observation justifies the conclusion that the remedial powers of the Board are not also limited by the same considerations that led Congress to enact §8(d). It is implicit in the entire structure of the Act that the Board acts to oversee and referee the process of collective bargaining, leaving the results of the contest to the bargaining strengths of the parties. It would be anomalous indeed to hold that while §8(d) prohibits the Board from relying on a refusal to agree as the sole evidence of bad faith bargaining, the Act permits the Board to compel agreement in that same dispute. The Board's remedial powers under §10 of the Act are broad, but they are limited to carrying out the policies of the Act itself. One of these fundamental policies is freedom of contract. While the parties' freedom of contract is not absolute under the Act, allowing the Board to compel agreement when the parties themselves are unable to do so would violate the fundamental premise on which the Act is based — private bargaining under governmental supervision of the procedure alone, without any official compulsion over the actual terms of the contract.

In reaching its decision the Court of Appeals relied extensively on the equally important policy of the Act that workers' rights to collective bargaining are to be secured. In this case the Court apparently felt that the employer was trying effectively to destroy the union by refusing to agree to what the union may have considered its most important demand. Perhaps the court, fearing that the parties might resort to economic combat, was also trying to maintain the industrial peace which the Act is designed to further. But the Act as presently drawn does not contemplate that unions will always be secure and able to achieve agreement even when their economic position is weak, nor that strikes and lockouts will never result from a bargaining to impasse. It cannot be said that the Act forbids an employer or a union to rely ultimately on its economic strength to try to secure what it cannot obtain through bargaining. It may well be true, as the Court of Appeals felt, that the present remedial powers of the Board are insufficiently broad to cope with important labor problems. But it is the job of Congress, not the Board or the courts, to decide when and if it is necessary to allow governmental review of proposals for collective bargaining agreements and compulsory submission to one side's demands. The present Act does not envision such a process.

The judgment is reversed and the case is remanded to the Court of Appeals for further action consistent with this opinion.

Reversed and remanded.[38]

HARLAN, J., concurring.

I join in the Court's opinion on the understanding that nothing said therein is meant to disturb or question the primary determination made by the Board and sustained by the Court of Appeals, that petitioner did not bargain in "good faith," and thus may be subjected to a bargaining order enforceable by a citation for contempt if the Board deems such a proceeding appropriate.

Notes

1. Doesn't Justice Black at the end of the opinion find himself in disagreement with the Board's finding of a refusal to bargain? Would the case have been better decided squarely on that ground?

2. Presumably in the next case of this sort the Board is to enter an order that the employer "cease and desist from refusing to bargain in good faith with the union." If the company persists in its refusal to grant the checkoff, shouldn't the Board have its bargaining order enforced in a court of appeals and then apply for a contempt sanction? What would the company have to do to avoid the contempt sanction?

3. Where an employer and a union have agreed in fact to bargaining agreement terms but one of the parties repudiates and refuses to sign, there is ample authority upholding the Board's power to order the document signed and the agreement honored. Then in NLRB v. Strong, 393 U.S. 357 (1969), an employer made an untimely withdrawal from a multiemployer bargaining association and refused to honor the agreement subsequently reached between the association and the union. The Board ordered the employer to sign the contract and pay retroactively the fringe benefits called for in the agreement. The court upheld the Board's authority against the employer's challenge that the Board was improperly inserting itself into contract enforcement. No §8(d) challenge to the Board's order was discussed. Should it have been?

EX-CELL-O CORP.

185 N.L.R.B. 107 (1970)

[The United Auto Workers Union (UAW) won a representation election among Ex-Cell-O's employees. The company filed election objec-

[38] Douglas, J., and Stewart, J., dissented. White, J., and Marshall, J., took no part in the decision.

tions charging UAW campaign misrepresentations but the Board refused to sustain them. The company refused to bargain, relying on the asserted invalidity of the election. The General Counsel filed a §§8(a)(5) and (1) complaint. The UAW requested that in addition to the standard order to bargain, the Board should issue a "make-whole" order requiring the company to compensate employees for monies lost on account of the refusal to bargain.]

It is not disputed that Respondent refused to bargain with the Union, and we hereby affirm the Trial Examiner's conclusion that Respondent thereby violated §§8(a)(1) and (5) of the Act. The compensatory remedy which he recommends, however, raises important issues concerning the Board's powers and duties to fashion appropriate remedies in its efforts to effectuate the policies of the National Labor Relations Act.

It is argued that such a remedy exceeds the Board's general statutory powers. In addition, it is contended that it cannot be granted because the amount of employee loss, if any, is so speculative that an order to make employees whole would amount to the imposition of a penalty. And the position is advanced that the adoption of this remedy would amount to the writing of a contract for the parties, which is prohibited by §8(d).

We have given most serious consideration to the Trial Examiner's recommended financial reparations Order, and are in complete agreement with his finding that current remedies of the Board designed to cure violations of §8(a)(5) are inadequate. A mere affirmative order that an employer bargain upon request does not eradicate the effects of an unlawful delay of 2 or more years in the fulfillment of a statutory bargaining obligation. It does not put the employees in the position of bargaining strength they would have enjoyed if their employer had immediately recognized and bargained with their chosen representative. It does not dissolve the inevitable employee frustration or protect the Union from the loss of employee support attributable to such delay. The inadequacy of the remedy is all the more egregious where, as in the recent NLRB v. Tiidee Products, Inc.,[6] case, the court found that the employer had raised "frivolous" issues in order to postpone or avoid its lawful obligation to bargain. We have weighed these considerations most carefully. For the reasons stated below, however, we have reluctantly concluded that we cannot approve the Trial Examiner's Recommended Order that Respondent compensate its employees for monetary losses incurred as a consequence of Respondent's determination to refuse to bargain until it had tested in court the validity of the Board's certification.

Section 10(c) of the Act is not so broad as to permit the punishment of a particular respondent or a class of respondents. Nor is the statutory

6. 426 F.2d 1243 (D.C. Cir. 1970).

direction to the Board so compelling that the Board is without discretion in exercising the full sweep of all its power, for it would defeat the purposes of the Act if the Board imposed an otherwise proper remedy that resulted in irreparable harm to a particular respondent and hampered rather than promoted meaningful collective bargaining. Moreover, as the Supreme Court recently emphasized, the Board's grant of power does not extend to compelling agreement. (H. K. Porter Co., Inc., v. NLRB.) It is with respect to these three limitations upon the Board's power to remedy a violation of §8(a)(5) that we examine the UAW's requested remedy in this case.

The Trial Examiner concluded that the proposed remedy was not punitive, that it merely made the employees partially whole for losses occasioned by the Respondent's refusal to bargain, and was much less harsh than a backpay order for discharged employees, which might require the Respondent to pay wages to these employees as well as their replacements. Viewed solely in the context of an assumption of employee monetary losses resulting directly from the Respondent's violation of §8(a)(5), as finally determined in court, the Trial Examiner's conclusion appears reasonable. There are, however, other factors in this case which provide counterweights to that rationale. In the first place, there is no contention that this Respondent acted in a manner flagrantly in defiance of the statutory policy. On the contrary, the record indicates that this Respondent responsibly fulfills its legally established collective-bargaining obligations. It is clear that Respondent merely sought judicial affirmance of the Board's decision that the election of October 22, 1964, should not be set aside on the Respondent's objections. In the past, whenever an employer has sought court intervention in a representation proceeding the Board has argued forcefully that court intervention would be premature, that the employer had an unquestioned right under the statute to seek court review of any Board order before its bargaining obligation became final. Should this procedural right in §8(a)(5) cases be tempered by a large monetary liability in the event the employer's position in the representation case is ultimately found to be without merit? Of course, an employer or a union which engages in conduct later found in violation of the Act, does so at the peril of ultimate conviction and responsibility for a make-whole remedy. But the validity of a particular Board election tried in an unfair labor practice case is not, in our opinion, an issue on the same plane as the discharge of employees for union activity or other conduct in flagrant disregard of employee rights. There are wrongdoers and wrongdoers. Where the wrong in refusing to bargain is, at most, a debatable question, though ultimately found a wrong, the imposition of a large financial obligation on such a respondent may come close to a form of punishment for having elected to pursue a representation beyond the Board and to the courts. The desirability of a compensatory remedy in a case remarkably similar to the instant case was recently considered by the Court of Appeals for the District of Columbia in United Steelworkers [Quality Rubber Manufacturing Company, Inc.] v. NLRB, 430 F.2d 519. There the court, distinguishing *Tiidee Products* supra, indicated that the Board was warranted in refusing to grant such a remedy in an §8(a)(5) case where the employer "desired only to obtain an authoritative determination of the validity of the Board's decision." It is not clear whether the court was of the opinion that the requested remedy was within the Board's discretion or whether it would have struck down such a remedy as punitive in view of the technical nature of the respondent's unfair labor practice. In any event, we find ourselves in disagreement with the Trial Examiner's view that a compensatory remedy as applied to the Respondent in the instant case is not punitive "in any sense of the word."

In *Tiidee Products* the court . . . was of the opinion that the remedy was proper where the employer had engaged in a "manifestly unjustifiable refusal to bargain" and where its position was "palpably without merit." As in *Quality Rubber,* the court in *Tiidee Products* distinguished those cases in which the employer's failure to bargain rested on a "debatable question." With due respect for the opinion of the Court of Appeals for the District of Columbia, we cannot agree that the application of a compensatory remedy in §8(a)(5) cases can be fashioned on the subjective determination that the position of one respondent is "debatable" while that of another is "frivolous." [The opinion then describes the *H. K. Porter* case.]

It is argued that the instant case is distinguishable from *H. K. Porter* in that here the requested remedy merely would require an employer to compensate employees for losses they incurred as a consequence of their employer's *failure to agree* to a contract he *would* have agreed to *if* he had bargained in good faith. In our view, the distinction is more illusory than real. The remedy in *H. K. Porter* operates prospectively to bind an employer to a specific contractual term. The remedy in the instant case operates retroactively to impose financial liability upon an employer flowing from a *presumed* contractual agreement. The Board infers that the latter contract, though it never existed and does not and need not exist, was *denied* existence by the employer because of his refusal to bargain. In either case the employer has not agreed to the contractual provision for which he must accept full responsibility *as though he had agreed to it.* Our colleagues contend that a compensatory remedy is not the "writing of a contract" because it does not "specify new or continuing terms of employment and does not prohibit changes in existing terms and conditions." But there is no basis for such a remedy unless the Board finds, as a matter of fact, that a contract would have resulted from bargaining. The fact that the contract, so to speak, is "written in the air" does not diminish its financial impact upon the recalcitrant employer who, willy-nilly, is forced to accede to terms never mutually established by the parties. Despite the admonition of the Supreme Court that §8(d) was intended to mean what it says, i.e., that the obligation to bargain "does not compel either party to agree to a proposal or require the making of a concession," one of the parties under this remedy is forced by the Government to submit to the other side's demands. It does not help to argue that the remedy could not be applied unless there was substantial evidence that the employer would have yielded to these demands during bargaining negotiations. Who is to say in a specific case how much an employer is prepared to give and how much a union is willing to take? Who is to say that a favorable contract would, in any event, result from the negotiations? And it is only the employer of such good will as to whom the Board might conclude that he, at least, would have given his employees a fair increase, who can be made subject to a financial reparations order; should such an employer be singled out for the imposition of such an order? To answer these questions the Board would be required to engage in the most general, if not entirely speculative, inferences to reach the conclusion that employees were deprived of specific benefits as a consequence of their employer's refusal to bargain.

Much as we appreciate the need for more adequate remedies in §8(a)(5) cases, we believe that, as the law now stands, the proposed remedy is a matter for Congress, not the Board. In our opinion, however, substantial relief may be obtained immediately through procedural reform, giving the highest possible priority to §8(a)(5) cases combined with full resort to the injunctive relief provisions of §§10(j) and (e) of the Act. . . .

[Members McCulloch and Brown argued for the "make-whole" remedy. First finding that §10(c)'s authorization of "affirmative action" orders is broad enough to support a "make-whole" remedy, they then relied on the fact that employees denied the opportunity to bargain for a considerable time because of the employer's refusal suffer actual economic loss. Further, the refusal to bargain may last for years while the case moves through Board hearings to a court of appeals, and the union is quite likely to lose substantial employee support. Thus with only the outlay of attorney fees, the recalcitrant employer can avoid the cost of a bargaining agreement for as much as several years and be met at the end by a weakened union unable to bargain effectively. They argued that a make-whole remedy in this situation was compensatory and barred neither as a penalty nor by §8(d). The speculativeness of such an order could be avoided by looking at bargaining agreements at other plants of this employer, at the settlement patterns of other unionized employers in the same geographic area and industry, or at national averages. The employer would be permitted to adduce evidence showing that a contract probably would not have been reached, or that no compensation increase would have resulted from any contract that might have been signed.]

Notes

1. The Board's holding in *Ex-Cell-O* was sustained by the District of Columbia Circuit, 449 F.2d 1058 (D.C. Cir. 1971), on the ground that the company's objections to the certification were "fairly debatable" rather than "frivolous" or in "bad faith." This distinction was initially formulated by the court in IUE v. NLRB [Tiidee Products], 426 F.2d 1243 (D.C. Cir. 1970), cert. denied, 400 U.S. 950 (1970), where the employer's election objections were found to be "patently frivolous." *H. K. Porter* did not, in the court's view, bar a make-whole remedy because the remedy would compensate for past wrongs rather than dictate future terms and would be based on a Board assessment of the contract the parties would have actually agreed upon had bargaining taken place.

On remand of Tiidee Products, 194 N.L.R.B. 1234 (1972), a unanimous Board refused to issue a make-whole award even though the employer's attack on the certification was frivolous. The Board found that it was impossible to construct what agreement would have been reached (as opposed to "should" have been reached — deemed foreclosed by §8(d)) had the employer bargained in good faith.

The Board agreed, however, that a special remedy was warranted for such a violation. It ordered the employer to reimburse the NLRB and the union their litigation expenses, to provide the union reasonable access to company bulletin boards, to mail a signed copy of the Board's order to each employee, and to make available to the union for one year the names and addresses of all employees currently employed. The Board rejected the union's request for organizational expenses and for lost dues and initiation fees. The District of Columbia Circuit, 502 F.2d 349 (D.C. Cir. 1974), upheld the refusal to grant the make-whole remedy, yielding to the Board's exercise of discretion.

2. Is a §10(j) injunction an adequate alternative remedy in refusal to bargain cases? In fiscal 1981, the Board filed only 41 requests for §10(j) injunctions against employers. Also, note that a §10(j) injunction will be sought after the union is certified but before the Board issues a decision in the §8(a)(5) complaint. Suppose the employer has committed outrageous unfair labor practices and the union has lost the election. The general counsel files a complaint seeking a bargaining order. Would a §10(j) injunction be appropriate? What would be the status of a collective bargaining agreement reached in these cases if the Board ruled for the employer in the unfair labor practice proceeding?

3. Aren't there cases where a Board "penalty" will "effectuate the policies of the Act"? The magnitude of a remedy is a very important determinant of its deterrent effect. To call a particular remedy a "penalty," and thus lay it aside, merely blinks the issue.

The labor movement has attempted legislative reform without success. In 1978 unions lobbied for NLRA amendments that would give a make-whole remedy in certain refusal to bargain cases, disbar from government contracts employers who refuse to bargain, and award double backpay to discriminatorily discharged employees. Mild as these reforms seem, they failed to pass.

5

LIMITATIONS ON THE CONTENT OF COLLECTIVE BARGAINING AGREEMENTS

A. ANTITRUST LIMITATIONS ON DEMANDS AND AGREEMENTS[1]

The goal of unions that is of the greatest interest as a matter of antitrust regulation is the one described by the price theory model: to push wages and working conditions above competitive levels by unionizing (cartelizing) workers. The antitrust laws, on the other hand, seek to increase consumer welfare by promoting efficiency. Ordinarily, this involves protecting competitive markets against artificial restraints. Throughout this century courts, and occasionally the Congress, have grappled with finding labor's place in the thicket of antitrust regulation.

The Sherman Act was passed in 1890 to curtail business monopolies and trade restraints, but in the years immediately following its enactment lower federal courts applied it more often to union than to employer business activity. The first of these cases to reach the Supreme Court was Loewe v. Lawlor (Danbury Hatters),[2] involving a union-instigated nationwide boycott of nonunion hats. In the Supreme Court the unions failed to mount a substantial attack on the Sherman Act's applicability to union activities, and a unanimous Court held labor was not exempt. The thrust of court regulation in these early years was not directed against instances of union monopoly power (e.g., industrywide unions) but against certain union practices. While the primary strike was deemed only an indirect restraint on competition and ordinarily lawful,

[1] See Leslie, Principles of Labor Antitrust, 66 Va. L. Rev. 1183 (1980); Meltzer, Labor Unions, Collective Bargaining and the Antitrust Laws, 32 U. Chi. L. Rev. 659, 676 (1965); Winter, Collective Bargaining and Competition: The Application of Antitrust Standards to Union Activities, 73 Yale L.J. 14, 49-50 (1963).

[2] 208 U.S. 274 (1908).

primary and secondary consumer boycotts and secondary employee boycotts were struck down.

In 1914, Congress passed the Clayton Act. Section 6 provides that the "labor of a human being is not a commodity or article of commerce" and that the antitrust laws are not to be construed to forbid the existence of unions or to restrain them "from lawfully carrying out the legitimate objects thereof." Section 20 bars the issuance of injunctions in cases arising out of disputes "between employers and employees" concerning "terms and conditions of employment." It also sets out certain union activities (e.g., quitting work) that are not to be considered violations of any federal law. But the sections are partially obscured by the use of qualifiers such as "lawful" and "unlawful."

Whatever hopes unions had for Clayton Act immunity were dashed by Duplex Printing Press Co. v. Deering,[3] a Supreme Court case involving a secondary boycott. The Court held that §6 did not confer antitrust immunity "where . . . [unions] depart from . . . normal and legitimate objects. . . ." Since §20 by its terms applied to "a case between an employer and employees, or between employers and employees," the Court construed it to protect only workers in a proximate relation to the dispute — the employees of the primary employer.

A curious turn was taken in two Supreme Court opinions involving the same facts, a violent union shutdown of the Coronado Coal Company's mine following a lockout and attempted nonunion operation by the employer. In *Coronado I,*[4] the Court said the evidence tended to show "a local motive" of the union, a reaction to the lockout. If this were so, there was no antitrust violation. Evidence at a second trial showed that the union viewed Coronado's coal production as a serious threat to union wages at other companies and therefore to union organizing efforts. This was enough to make out a violation in *Coronado II.*[5] A strike with a "local motive" was "ordinarily an indirect or remote obstruction to . . . commerce," but where "the intent . . . is shown to be to restrain or control the supply entering and moving in interstate commerce, or the price of it in interstate markets, [the] action is a direct violation of the Anti-Trust Act. . . ." No strike was needed to activate this intent-oriented test.

In United States v. Brims,[6] unionized carpentry manufacturers felt the competitive pinch of nonunion manufacturers paying lower wages. The union obtained the agreement of area building contractors that union carpenters were not required to work on nonunion millwork. *Coronado II* and the secondary strike decisions were the precedent for a Supreme Court finding of illegality.

[3] 254 U.S. 443 (1921).
[4] United Mine Workers v. Coronado Coal Co., 259 U.S. 344 (1922).
[5] Coronado Coal Co. v. UMW, 268 U.S. 295 (1925).
[6] 272 U.S. 549 (1926).

The *Coronado* cases illustrated the shortcomings of two tests for union antitrust liability: proof of a direct effect on the product market test and of subjective intent. If a direct effect on the product market will support union antitrust liability, many ordinary strikes, such as those for higher wages, will be illegal. A successful strike always has a direct effect on the product market, as the union uses its control of the supply of workers to block production.[7] The success of the strike will depend on whether production can be blocked until the union's demands are met.

The *Coronado* cases attempt to limit the scope of the product market test by making antitrust liability turn on whether the union's subjective intent was to extend its organization (lawful) or to attack product market competitors of unionized firms (unlawful). There are two difficulties with this distinction. First, although an increase in membership may be an end in itself for the union, the price theory model shows that organizing efforts may also be motivated by a desire to protect current members from the increased resistance that unionized employers put up when their competitive position is threatened by nonunion firms. These motives may exist concurrently. Rigorous use of the subjective intent test might limit each union to organizing the employees of a single firm. Second, under a subjective intent test liability will tend to turn on whether the union's lawyers have carefully advised union officers what to say.

In the *Coronado* period and after, some courts used the antitrust laws to regulate labor. The principal regulatory device was the labor injunction. The next development was legislative. The Norris-LaGuardia Act of 1932 drastically limited the federal courts' injunctive power in labor disputes. It was passed not only because the injunction had been discredited by overuse, but also because of a belief that the antitrust laws were a poor vehicle for the formulation of national labor policy and that federal courts were poor formulators. In 1935 the passage of the Wagner Act signaled a greater willingness by Congress to assume its proper role of policy maker and further showed that that policy was to be, at least initially, the fostering of union organization and collective bargaining. But the Supreme Court's attitude was not preordained, and the new enactments failed to mention the Sherman Act.

APEX HOSIERY CO. v. LEADER
310 U.S. 469 (1940)

STONE, J.

Petitioner, a Pennsylvania corporation, is engaged in the manufacture, at its factory in Philadelphia, of hosiery, a substantial part of which

[7] In a perfectly competitive product market the loss of the struck firm's output will not affect the market price of the product.

is shipped in interstate commerce. It brought the present suit in the federal district court for Eastern Pennsylvania against respondent Federation, a labor organization, and its officers, to recover treble the amount of damage inflicted on it by respondents in conducting a strike at petitioner's factory alleged to be a conspiracy in violation of the Sherman Anti-Trust Act, §1. The trial to a jury resulted in a verdict for petitioner in the sum of $237,310, respondents saving by proper motions and exceptions the question whether the evidence was sufficient to establish a violation of the Sherman Act. The trial judge trebled the verdict to $711,932.55. . . . The Court of Appeals for the Third Circuit reversed. . . .

The facts are undisputed. There was evidence from which the jury could have found as follows. Petitioner employs at its Philadelphia factory about twenty-five hundred persons in the manufacture of hosiery, and manufactures annually merchandise of the value of about $5,000,000. Its principal raw materials are silk and cotton, which are shipped to it from points outside the state. It ships interstate more than 80 percent of its finished product, and in the last eight months of 1937 it shipped in all 274,791 dozen pairs of stockings. In April, 1937, petitioner was operating a non-union shop. A demand of the respondent Federation at that time for a closed shop agreement came to nothing. On May 4, 1937, when only eight of petitioner's employees were members of the Federation, it ordered a strike. Shortly after midday on May 6, 1937, when petitioner's factory was shut down, members of the union, employed by other factories in Philadelphia who had stopped work, gathered at petitioner's plant. Respondent Leader, president of the Federation, then made a further demand for a closed shop agreement. When this was refused Leader declared a "sit down strike." Immediately, acts of violence against petitioner's plant and the employees in charge of it were committed by the assembled mob. It forcibly seized the plant, whereupon, under union leadership, its members were organized to maintain themselves as sit-down strikers in possession of the plant, and it remained in possession until June 23, 1937, when the strikers were forcibly ejected pursuant to an injunction ordered by the Court of Appeals for the Third Circuit.

The locks on all gates and entrances of petitioner's plant were changed; only strikers were given keys. No others were allowed to leave or enter the plant without permission of the strikers. During the period of their occupancy, the union supplied them with food, blankets, cots, medical care, and paid them strike benefits. While occupying the factory, the strikers willfully wrecked machinery of great value, and did extensive damage to other property and equipment of the company. All manufacturing operations by petitioner ceased on May 6th. As the result of the destruction of the company's machinery and plant, it did not resume even partial manufacturing operations until August 19, 1937. The record discloses a lawless invasion of petitioner's plant and destruction of its property by force and violence of the most brutal and wanton character, under leadership and direction of respondents, and without interference by the local authorities.

For more than three months, by reason of respondents' acts, manufacture was suspended at petitioner's plant and the flow of petitioner's product into interstate commerce was stopped. When the plant was seized, there were on hand 130,000 dozen pairs of finished hosiery, of a value of about $800,000, ready for shipment on unfilled orders, 80 percent of which were to be shipped to points outside the state. Shipment was prevented by the occupation of the factory by the strikers. Three times in the course of the strike respondents refused requests made by petitioner to be allowed to remove the merchandise for the purpose of shipment in filling the orders. . . .

It is not denied, and we assume for present purposes, that respondents by substituting the primitive method of trial by combat, for the ordinary processes of justice and more civilized means of deciding an industrial dispute, violated the civil and penal laws of Pennsylvania which authorize the recovery of full compensation and impose criminal penalties for the wrongs done. But in this suit, in which no diversity of citizenship of the parties is alleged or shown, the federal courts are without authority to enforce state laws. Their only jurisdiction is to vindicate such federal right as Congress has conferred on petitioner by the Sherman Act and violence, as will appear hereafter, however reprehensible, does not give the federal courts jurisdiction. . . .

[T]he jury's verdict must be taken as a finding supported by evidence that respondents intended to prevent petitioner's shipments in interstate commerce in the sense that respondents must be taken to have intended the natural and probable consequences of their acts. . . . Concededly the purpose of the strikers and their principal objective were to compel petitioner to yield to their demands for a union shop, but it is a matter of common knowledge and experience that the stoppage of a large manufacturing plant, which the strikers did intend, whose product is distributed generally to consumers throughout the country, would prevent its shipments in interstate commerce. . . .

But the Sherman Act admittedly does not condemn all combinations and conspiracies which interrupt interstate transportation. In In re Debs, 158 U.S. 564, 600, this Court declined to consider whether the stoppage of trains on an interstate railroad resulting from a strike, was a violation of the Sherman Act — a question which it has not since been called on to decide. It is not seriously contended here that a conspiracy to derail and rob an interstate train, even though it were laden with 100,000 dozen pairs of stockings, necessarily would involve a violation of the Sherman Act. This Court has never applied the Act to laborers or to others as a means of policing interstate transportation, and so the question to which we must address ourselves is whether a conspiracy of strikers in a labor dispute to stop the operation of the employer's factory in order to enforce their demands against the employer is the kind of restraint of trade or commerce at which the Act is aimed, even though a natural and probable consequence of their acts and the only effect on trade or commerce was to prevent substantial shipments interstate by the employer.

A point strongly urged in behalf of respondents in brief and argument before us is that Congress intended to exclude labor organizations and their activities wholly from the operation of the Sherman Act. To this the short answer must be made that for the thirty-two years which have elapsed since the decision of Loewe v. Lawlor, 208 U.S. 274, this Court, in its efforts to determine the true meaning and application of the Sherman Act has repeatedly held that the words of the act, "Every contract, combination . . . or conspiracy in restraint of trade or commerce," do embrace to some extent and in some circumstances labor unions and their activities; and that during that period Congress, although often asked to do so, has passed no act purporting to exclude labor unions wholly from the operation of the Act. On the contrary Congress has repeatedly enacted laws restricting or purporting to curtail the application of the Act to labor organizations and their activities, thus recognizing that to some extent not defined they remain subject to it. . . .

While we must regard the question whether labor unions are to some extent and in some circumstances subject to the Act as settled in the affirmative, it is equally plain that this Court has never thought the Act to apply to all labor union activities affecting interstate commerce. The prohibitions of the Sherman Act were not stated in terms of precision or of crystal clarity and the Act itself did not define them. In consequence of the vagueness of its language, perhaps not uncalculated, the courts have been left to give content to the statute, and in the performance of that function it is appropriate that courts should interpret its word in the light of its legislative history and of the particular evils at which the legislation was aimed. . . .

The critical words which circumscribe the judicial performance of this function so far as the present case is concerned are "Every . . . combination . . . or conspiracy in restraint of trade or commerce." Since in the present case, as we have seen, the natural and predictable consequence of the strike was the restraint of interstate transportation the precise question which we are called upon to decide is whether that restraint resulting from the strike maintained to enforce union demands by compelling a shutdown of petitioner's factory is the kind of "restraint of trade or commerce" which the Act condemns.

In considering whether union activities like the present may fairly be deemed to be embraced within this phrase, three circumstances relating to the history and application of the Act which are of striking significance must first be taken into account. The legislative history of the Sherman Act as well as the decisions of this Court interpreting it, show that it was not aimed at policing interstate transportation or movement of goods and property.

. . . It was another and quite a different evil at which the Sherman Act was aimed. It was enacted in the era of "trusts" and of "combinations" of businesses and of capital organized and directed to control of the market by suppression of competition in the marketing of goods and services, the monopolistic tendency of which had become a matter of public concern. The end sought was the prevention of restraints to free competition in business and commercial transactions which tended to restrict production, raise prices or otherwise control the market to the detriment of purchasers or consumers of goods and services, all of which had come to be regarded as a special form of public injury. . . .

A second significant circumstance is that this Court has never applied the Sherman Act in any case, whether or not involving labor organizations or activities, unless the Court was of opinion that there was some form of restraint upon commercial competition in the marketing of goods or services and finally this Court has refused to apply the Sherman Act in cases like the present in which local strikes conducted by illegal means in a production industry prevented interstate shipment of substantial amounts of the product but in which it was not shown that the restrictions on shipments had operated to restrain commercial competition in some substantial way.

The common law doctrines relating to contracts and combinations in restraint of trade were well understood long before the enactment of the Sherman law. They were contracts for the restriction or suppression of competition in the market, agreements to fix prices, divide marketing territories, apportion customers, restrict production and the like practices, which tend to raise prices or otherwise take from buyers or consumers the advantages which accrue to them from free competition in the market. Such contracts were deemed illegal and were unenforcible at common law. But the resulting restraints of trade were not penalized and gave rise to no actionable wrong. Certain classes of restraints were not outlawed when deemed reasonable, usually because they served to preserve or protect legitimate interests, previously existing, of one or more parties to the contract.

In seeking more effective protection of the public from the growing evils of restraints on the competitive system effected by the concentrated commercial power of "trusts" and "combinations" at the close of the nineteenth century, the legislators found ready at their hand the common law concept of illegal restraints of trade or commerce. In enacting the Sherman law they took over that concept by condemning such restraints wherever they occur in or affect commerce between the states.

They extended the condemnation of the statute to restraints effected by any combination in the form of trust or otherwise, or conspiracy, as well as by contract or agreement, having those effects on the competitive system and on purchasers and consumers of goods or services which were characteristic of restraints deemed illegal at common law, and they gave both private and public remedies for the injuries flowing from such restraints.

That such is the scope and effect of the Sherman Act was first judicially recognized and expounded in the classic opinion in United States v. Addyston Pipe & Steel Co., 85 F. 271, affirmed, 175 U.S. 211, written by Judge, later Chief Justice, Taft, and concurred in by Justice Harlan and Judge, later Justice, Lurton, of this Court. This Court has since repeatedly recognized that the restraints at which the Sherman law is aimed, and which are described by its terms, are only those which are comparable to restraints deemed illegal at common law, although accomplished by means other than contract and which, for constitutional reasons, are confined to transactions in or which affect interstate commerce.

In Standard Oil Co. v. United States, 221 U.S. 1, 54, 55, 58, decided in 1911, this Court, speaking through Chief Justice White, pointed out that the restraint of trade contemplated by §1 of the Act took its origin from the common law, and that the Sherman Act was adapted to the prevention, in modern conditions, of conduct or dealing effecting the wrong, at which the common law doctrine was aimed. This, it was said, is "the dread of enhancement of prices and of other wrongs which it was thought would flow from the undue limitation on competitive conditions caused by contracts or other acts of individuals or corporations, . . ." The Court declared that "the statute was drawn in the light of the existing practical conception of the law of restraint of trade," and drew the conclusion that the restraints which were condemned by the statute are those which, following the common law analogy, are "unreasonable or undue." This view was followed and more explicitly stated in United States v. American Tobacco Co., 221 U.S. 106, 179, where it was said:

> . . . it was held in the *Standard Oil* case that as the words "restraint of trade" at common law and in the law of this country at the time of the adoption of the Anti-Trust Act only embraced acts or contracts or agreements or combinations which operated to the prejudice of the public interests by unduly restricting competition or unduly obstructing the due course of trade or which, either because of their inherent nature or effect or because of the evident purpose of the acts, etc., injuriously restrained trade, that the words as used in the statute were designed to have and did have but a like significance.

In thus grounding the "rule of reason" upon the analogy of the common law doctrines applicable to illegal restraints of trade the Court gave a content and meaning to the statute in harmony with its history and plainly indicated by its legislative purpose. Labor cases apart, which will presently be discussed, this Court has not departed from the conception of the Sherman Act as affording a remedy, public and private, for the public wrongs which flow from restraints of trade in the common law sense of restriction or suppression of commercial competition. In the cases considered by this Court since the *Standard Oil* case in 1911 some form of restraint of commercial competition has been the *sine qua non* to the condemnation of contracts, combinations or conspiracies under the Sherman Act, and in general restraints upon competition have been condemned only when their purpose or effect was to raise or fix the market price. It is in this sense that it is said that the restraints, actual or intended, prohibited by the Sherman Act are only those which are so substantial as to affect market prices. Restraints on competition or on the course of trade in the merchandising of articles moving in interstate commerce is not enough, unless the restraint is shown to have or is intended to have an effect upon prices in the market or otherwise to deprive purchasers or consumers of the advantages which they derive from free competition.

The question remains whether the effect of the combination or conspiracy among respondents was a restraint of trade within the meaning of the Sherman Act. This is not a case of a labor organization being used by combinations of those engaged in an industry as the means or instrument for suppressing competition or fixing prices. See United States v. Brims, 272 U.S. 549; Local 167 v. United States, 291 U.S. 293. Here it is plain that the combination or conspiracy did not have as its purpose restraint upon competition in the market for petitioner's product. Its object was to compel petitioner to accede to the union demands and an effect of it, in consequence of the strikers' tortious acts, was the prevention of the removal of petitioner's product for interstate shipment. So far as appears the delay of these shipments was not intended to have and had no effect on prices of hosiery in the market, and so was in that respect no more a restraint forbidden by the Sherman Act than the restriction upon competition and the course of trade held lawful in Appalachian Coals v. United States, supra, because notwithstanding its effect upon the marketing of the coal it nevertheless was not intended to and did not affect market price.

A combination of employees necessarily restrains competition among themselves in the sale of their services to the employer; yet such a combination was not considered an illegal restraint of trade at common law when the Sherman Act was adopted, either because it was not thought to be unreasonable or because it was not deemed a "restraint of trade." Since the enactment of the declaration in §6 of the Clayton Act that "the labor of a human being is not a commodity or article of commerce . . . nor shall such [labor] organizations, or the members thereof, be held or construed to be illegal combinations or conspiracies in the restraint of trade under the antitrust laws," it would seem plain that restraints on the sale of the employee's services to the employer, however much they curtail the competition among employees, are not in themselves combinations or conspiracies in restraint of trade or commerce under the Sherman Act.

Strikes or agreements not to work, entered into by laborers to compel employers to yield to their demands, may restrict to some extent the power of employers who are parties to the dispute to compete in the market with those not subject to such demands. But under the doctrine applied to non-labor cases, the mere fact of such restrictions on competition does not in itself bring the parties to the agreement within the condemnation of the Sherman Act. Appalachian Coals v. United States, supra. Furthermore, successful union activity, as for example consummation of a wage agreement with employers, may have some influence on price competition by eliminating that part of such competition which is based on differences in labor standards. Since, in order to render a labor combination effective it must eliminate the competition from nonunion made goods, see American Steel Foundries v. Tri-City Central Trades Council, 257 U.S. 184, 209, an elimination of price competition based on differences in labor standards is the objective of any national labor organization. But this effect on competition has not been considered to be the kind of curtailment of price competition prohibited by the Sherman Act.[24] And in any case, the restraint here is, as we have seen, of a different kind and has not been shown to have any actual or intended effect on price or price competition. [The opinion then discussed its prior decisions in this area.]

24. Federal legislation aimed at protecting and favoring labor organizations and eliminating the competition of employers and employees based on labor conditions regarded as substandard, through the establishment of industry-wide standards both by collective bargaining and by legislation setting up minimum wage and hour standards, supports the conclusion that Congress does not regard the effects upon competition from such combinations and standards as against public policy or condemned by the Sherman Act.

The Norris-LaGuardia Act, 47 Stat. 70, 29 U.S.C. §§101-115, limiting the use of injunctions in labor disputes, is predicated on the policy that "under prevailing economic conditions," it is necessary that the worker "have full freedom of association . . . to negotiate the terms and conditions of his employment." The Railway Labor Act of 1934, 48 Stat. 1185, 45 U.S.C. §§151-164, provided for independence of railroad employees in the matter of self-organization. The National Labor Relations Act, 49 Stat. 449, 29 U.S.C. §§151-166, was passed to protect the workers in the "exercise of full freedom of association, self-organization, and designation of representatives of their own choosing for the purpose of negotiating the terms and conditions of their employment . . ." and expressly protects the right of self-organization, recognizes the strike as a proper union weapon and permits closed-shop contracts.

The Public Contracts Act, 49 Stat. 2036, 41 U.S.C. §§35-48, was aimed at preventing price competition in government bidding based on wage cutting and authorizes the establishment of minimum wage standards. The Fair Labor Standards Act of 1938, 52 Stat. 1060, 29 U.S.C. §§201-219, likewise seeks to eliminate competition which thrived upon low wages and substandard working conditions.

This series of acts clearly recognizes that combinations of workers eliminating competition among themselves and restricting competition among their employers based on wage cutting are not contrary to the public policy.

These cases show that activities of labor organizations not immunized by the Clayton Act are not necessarily violations of the Sherman Act. Underlying and implicit in all of them is recognition that the Sherman Act was not enacted to police interstate transportation, or to afford a remedy for wrongs, which are actionable under state law, and result from combinations and conspiracies which fall short, both in their purpose and effect, of any form of market control of a commodity, such as to "monopolize the supply, control its price, or discriminate between its would-be purchasers." These elements of restraint of trade, found to be present in the *Second Coronado* case and alone to distinguish it from the *First Coronado* case and the *Leather Workers* case, are wholly lacking here. We do not hold that conspiracies to obstruct or prevent transportation in interstate commerce can in no circumstances be violations of the Sherman Act. Apart from the Clayton Act it makes no distinction between labor and non-labor cases. We only hold now, as we have previously held both in labor and non-labor cases, that such restraints are not within the Sherman Act unless they are intended to have, or in fact have, the effects on the market on which the Court relied to establish violation in the *Second Coronado* case. Unless the principle of these cases is now to be discarded, an impartial application of the Sherman Act to the activities of industry and labor alike would seem to require that the Act be held inapplicable to the activities of respondents which had an even less substantial effect on the competitive conditions in the industry than the combination of producers upheld in the *Appalachian Coals* case and in others on which it relied.

If, without such effects on the market, we were to hold that a local factory strike, stopping production and shipment of its product interstate, violates the Sherman law, practically every strike in modern industry would be brought within the jurisdiction of the federal courts, under the Sherman Act, to remedy local law violations. The Act was plainly not intended to reach such a result, its language does not require it, and the course of our decisions precludes it. The maintenance in our federal system of a proper distribution between state and national governments of police authority and of remedies private and public for public wrongs is of far-reaching importance. An intention to disturb the balance is not lightly to be imputed to Congress. The Sherman Act is concerned with the character of the prohibited restraints and with their effect on interstate commerce. It draws no distinction between the restraints effected by violence and those achieved by peaceful but oftentimes quite as effective means. Restraints not within the Act, when achieved by peaceful means, are not brought within its sweep merely because, without other differences, they are attended by violence.

Affirmed.[8]

[8] Hughes, C. J., joined by McReynolds, J., and Roberts, J., dissented.

UNITED STATES v. HUTCHESON
312 U.S. 219 (1941)

[As a result of a jurisdictional dispute between the Carpenters Union and the Machinists Union, the Carpenters struck their employer, the Anheuser-Busch brewing company; picketed Anheuser-Busch; and called for a nationwide boycott of Anheuser-Busch beer. Four officers of the Carpenters were charged with a Sherman Act violation pursuant to a policy conceived by the Attorney General of the United States, Thurman Arnold, to prosecute union "bad practices" via the Sherman Act.

The Supreme Court, per Justice Frankfurter (whose book *The Labor Injunction,*[9] written while he was still an academic, was instrumental in causing the Norris-LaGuardia Act to be passed), held the Sherman Act had not been violated. But unlike in *Apex,* where the Court found the union's conduct not within the reach of the antitrust laws' substantive provisions, Justice Frankfurter in the instant case was able to find an exemption for union activity.]

FRANKFURTER, J.

Section 20 of [the Clayton Act] withdrew from the general interdict of the Sherman Law specifically enumerated practices of labor unions by prohibiting injunctions against them — since the use of the injunction had been the major source of dissatisfaction — and also relieved such practices of all illegal taint by the catch-all provision, "nor shall any of the acts specified in this paragraph be considered or held to be violations of any law of the United States." The Clayton Act gave rise to new litigation and to renewed controversy in and out of Congress regarding the status of trade unions. By the generality of its terms the Sherman Law had necessarily compelled the courts to work out its meaning from case to case. It was widely believed that into the Clayton Act courts read the very beliefs which that Act was designed to remove. Specifically the courts restricted the scope of §20 to trade union activities directed against an employer by his own employees. Duplex Co. v. Deering, [254 U.S. 443]. Such a view, it was urged, both by powerful judicial dissents and informed lay opinion, misconceived the area of economic conflict that had best be left to economic forces and the pressure of public opinion and not subjected to the judgment of courts. Agitation again led to legislation and in 1932 Congress wrote the Norris-LaGuardia Act.

The Norris-LaGuardia Act removed the fetters upon trade union activities, which according to judicial construction §20 of the Clayton Act had left untouched, by still further narrowing the circumstances under which the federal courts could grant injunctions in labor disputes. More especially, the Act explicitly formulated the "public policy of the United

[9] F. Frankfurter & N. Greene, The Labor Injunction (1930).

States" in regard to the industrial conflict, and by its light established that the allowable area of union activity was not to be restricted, as it had been in the *Duplex* case, to an immediate employer-employee relation. Therefore, whether trade union conduct constitutes a violation of the Sherman Law is to be determined only by reading the Sherman Law and §20 of the Clayton Act and the Norris-LaGuardia Act as a harmonizing text of outlawry of labor conduct.

Were, then, the acts charged against the defendants prohibited, or permitted, by these three interlacing statutes? If the facts laid in the indictment come within the conduct enumerated in §20 of the Clayton Act they do not constitute a crime within the general terms of the Sherman Law because of the explicit command of that section that such conduct shall not be "considered or held to be violations of any law of the United States." So long as a union acts in its self-interest and does not combine with non-labor groups, the licit and the illicit under §20 are not to be distinguished by any judgment regarding the wisdom or unwisdom, the rightness or wrongness, the selfishness or unselfishness of the end of which the particular union activities are the means. . . .[10]

Note

Hutcheson was both condemned and applauded. The principal criticism was that the legislative history is replete with specific references implying the Norris-LaGuardia Act was intended only to oust federal courts of their injunctive power and not to alter any other judicial remedy (damages and criminal sanctions). Professor Frankfurther had said as much in his book *The Labor Injunction.* But the decision was welcomed by those who believed that judicial antitrust opinions were not proper vehicles for formulating national labor policy. Difficult problems remaining after *Apex*'s pronouncements, such as distinguishing product market from labor market restraints in the many cases at the margin, were put by *Hutcheson* into the hands of Congress. Congress could decide whether to prohibit certain union restraints and, if it did, whether the prohibition should be accomplished by antitrust or other sanctions.

Two questions were largely ignored after *Hutcheson.* First, how does a union act alone? Second, did *Apex* apply when the union was not acting alone?

ALLEN BRADLEY CO. v. INTERNATIONAL BROTHERHOOD OF ELECTRICAL WORKERS, LOCAL 3, 325 U.S. 797 (1945): A New York City local union, having secured closed shop agreements with most of the city's electrical contractors, organized the city's electrical equip-

[10] Stone, J., concurred. Roberts, J., and Hughes, C. J., dissented.

ment manufacturers with promises of a sheltered market. Both manufacturers and contractors agreed to do business only with firms organized by the union. Nonunion firms were excluded by conventional picketing and boycotts, inflated prices, and rigged bids. The scheme was policed by the union and later by employer associations. A Sherman Act suit was brought against Local 3, but not against any of the employers, by non-New York City manufacturers who had been excluded from that market.

Justice Black, writing for the Court, found a violation. Although Local 3 had been "the dynamic force" behind the arrangements,[11] the opinion characterizes the case as presenting a conspiracy of businessmen assisted by Local 3. The Court easily disposed of the question of a substantive violation:

> Quite obviously, this combination of business men has violated both §§1 and 2 of the Sherman Act, unless its conduct is immunized by the participation of the union. For it intended to and did restrain trade in and monopolize the supply of electrical equipment in the New York City area to the exclusion of equipment manufactured in and shipped from other states and did also control its price and discriminate between its would-be customers. Apex Hosiery Co. v. Leader, 310 U.S. 469, 512-513. Our problem in this case is therefore a very narrow one — do labor unions violate the Sherman Act when, in order to further their own interests as wage earners, they aid and abet business men to do the precise things which that Act prohibits?

Thus the case turned on whether the exemption announced in *Hutcheson* applied. It did not:

> We have been pointed to no language in any act of Congress or in its reports or debates, nor have we found any, which indicates that it was ever suggested, considered, or legislatively determined that labor unions should be granted an immunity such as is sought in the present case. It has been argued that this immunity can be inferred from a union's right to make bargaining agreements with its employer. Since union members can without violating the Sherman Act strike to enforce a union boycott of goods, it is said they may settle the strike by getting their employers to agree to refuse to buy the goods. Employers and the union did here make bargaining agreements in which the employers agreed not to buy goods manufactured by companies which did not employ the members of Local No. 3. We may assume that such an agreement standing alone would not have violated the Sherman Act. But it did not stand alone. It was but one element in a far larger program in which contractors and manufacturers united with one another to monopolize all the business in New York City, to bar all other business men from that area, and to charge the public prices above a competitive level. It is true that victory of the union in its

[11] Murphy, J., dissented on this basis.

> disputes, even had the union acted alone, might have added to the cost of goods, or might have resulted in individual refusals of all of their employers to buy electrical equipment not made by Local No. 3. So far as the union might have achieved this result acting alone, it would have been the natural consequence of labor union activities exempted by the Clayton Act from the coverage of the Sherman Act. Apex Hosiery Co. v. Leader. But when the unions participated with a combination of business men who had complete power to eliminate all competition among themselves and to prevent all competition from others, a situation was created not included within the exemptions of the Clayton and Norris-LaGuardia Acts. . . .
>
> The difficulty of drawing legislation primarily aimed at trusts and monopolies so that it could also be applied to labor organizations without impairing the collective bargaining and related rights of those organizations has been emphasized both by congressional and judicial attempts to draw lines between permissible and prohibited union activities. There is, however, one line which we can draw with assurance that we follow the congressional purpose. We know that Congress feared the concentrated power of business organizations to dominate markets and prices. It intended to outlaw business monopolies. A business monopoly is no less such because a union participates, and such participation is a violation of the Act. . . .

Finally, the Court held that an injunction could issue in the case, notwithstanding Norris-LaGuardia, so long as it enjoined "only those prohibited activities in which the union engaged in combination 'with any person, firm or corporation which is a nonlabor group.' "[12]

Notes

1. Which of the following do you think is the best reading of *Allen Bradley:*

a. It applies only to sham arrangements — i.e., employers using unions as an excuse to control the product market.[13]
b. It applies to union-employer combinations that yield market restrictions essentially similar to those devised by businessmen even when they are free from union pressure.[14]
c. The character of management's behavior determines the legality of the union's activity; e.g., did the employers resist the union demand and acquiesce only under pressure?[15]

[12] Roberts, J., concurred.

[13] See Berhardt, The Allen Bradley Doctrine: An Accommodation of Conflicting Policies, 110 U. Pa. L. Rev. 1094, 1099 (1962).

[14] See Meltzer, Labor Unions, Collective Bargaining and the Antitrust Laws, 32 U. Chi. L. Rev. 659, 676 (1965).

[15] See Winter, Collective Bargaining and Competition: The Application of Antitrust Standards to Union Activities, 73 Yale L.J. 14, 49-50 (1963).

2. Given the bid rigging, it seems clear that the New York City manufacturers and contractors in *Allen Bradley* sought to earn supracompetitive profits. Less clear is what the union got out of the scheme.

3. If Local 3 and a single contractor had agreed that only pipe produced by companies employing IBEW members would be installed, would Local 3 have lost its exemption? Would there be a substantive violation? Would the answers be clearer if identical agreements had been entered into between Local 3 and all the other New York City contractors? Suppose a multiemployer bargaining association of contractors had signed such an agreement?

The two cases that follow were decided at the same time and find the Court badly split over the controlling legal principles. In each, the Court divides itself into three groups of three justices each. As you weave your way through the opinions, try to discover the test that each group would apply in deciding whether labor's exemption is lost and, once the exemption is lost, whether a substantive violation is to be found.

UNITED MINE WORKERS v. PENNINGTON
381 U.S. 657 (1965)

[Trustees of the United Mine Workers Welfare and Retirement Fund brought suit against the Phillips Brothers Coal Company for royalty payments allegedly due under a 1950 Wage Agreement. The Company defended and cross-claimed, alleging that the trustees, the UMW, and certain large coal operators had conspired to restrain and to monopolize interstate commerce in violation of §§1 and 2 of the Sherman Act. Actual damages of $100,000 were claimed.]

WHITE, J. . . .

The allegations of the cross claim were essentially as follows: Prior to the 1950 Wage Agreement between the operators and the union, severe controversy had existed in the industry, particularly over wages, the welfare fund and the union's efforts to control the working time of its members. Since 1950, however, relative peace has existed in the industry, all as the result of the 1950 Wage Agreement and its amendments and the additional understandings entered into between UMW and the large operators. Allegedly the parties considered overproduction to be the critical problem of the coal industry. The agreed solution was to be the elimination of the smaller companies, the larger companies thereby controlling the market. More specifically, the union abandoned its efforts to control the working time of the miners, agreed not to oppose the rapid mechanization of the mines which would substantially reduce mine employment, agreed to help finance such mechanization and agreed to impose the terms of the 1950 agreement on all operators without regard to their ability to pay. The benefit to the union was to be increased wages as productivity increased with mechanization, these increases to be demanded of the smaller companies whether mechanized or not. Royalty payments into the welfare fund were to be increased also, and the union was to have effective control over the fund's use. The union and large companies agreed upon other steps to exclude the marketing, production, and sale of nonunion coal. Thus the companies agreed not to lease coal lands to nonunion operators, and in 1958 agreed not to sell or buy coal from such companies. The companies and the union jointly and successfully approached the Secretary of Labor to obtain establishment under the Walsh-Healey Act of a minimum wage for employees of contractors selling coal to the TVA, such minimum wage being much higher than in other industries and making it difficult for small companies to compete in the TVA term contract market. At a later time, at a meeting attended by both union and company representatives, the TVA was urged to curtail its spot market purchases, a substantial portion of which were exempt from the Walsh-Healey order. Thereafter four of the larger companies waged a destructive and collusive price-cutting campaign in the TVA spot market for coal, two of the companies, West Kentucky Coal Co. and its subsidiary Nashville Coal Co., being those in which the union had large investments and over which it was in position to exercise control.

The complaint survived motions to dismiss and after a five-week trial before a jury, a verdict was returned in favor of Phillips and against the trustees and the union, the damages against the union being fixed in the amount of $90,000, to be trebled under 15 U.S.C. §15 (1958 ed.). The trial court set aside the verdict against the trustees but overruled the union's motion for judgment notwithstanding the verdict or in the alternative for a new trial. The Court of Appeals affirmed. 325 F.2d 804. It ruled that the union was not exempt from liability under the Sherman Act on the facts of this case, considered the instructions adequate and found the evidence generally sufficient to support the verdict. We granted certiorari. We reverse and remand the case for proceedings consistent with this opinion.

I

We first consider UMW's contention that the trial court erred in denying its motion for a directed verdict and for judgment notwithstanding the verdict, since a determination in UMW's favor on this issue would finally resolve the controversy. The question presented by this phase of the case is whether in the circumstances of this case the union is exempt from liability under the antitrust laws. We think the answer is clearly in the negative and that the union's motions were correctly denied.

The antitrust laws do not bar the existence and operation of labor unions as such. Moreover, §20 of the Clayton Act and §4 of the Norris-LaGuardia Act permit a union, acting alone, to engage in the conduct therein specified without violating the Sherman Act. United States v. Hutcheson, 312 U.S. 219. . . .

But neither §20 nor §4 expressly deals with arrangements or agreements between unions and employers. Neither section tells us whether any or all such arrangements or agreements are barred or permitted by the antitrust laws. Thus *Hutcheson* itself stated:

> So long as a union acts in its self-interest *and does not combine with nonlabor groups,* the licit and the illicit under §20 are not to be distinguished by any judgment regarding the wisdom or unwisdom, the rightness or wrongness, the selfishness or unselfishness of the end of which the particular union activities are the means. 312 U.S., at 232. (Emphasis added.)

And in Allen Bradley Co. v. Union, 325 U.S. 797, this Court made explicit what had been merely a qualifying expression in *Hutcheson* and held that "when the unions participated with a combination of business men who had complete power to eliminate all competition among themselves and to prevent all competition from others, a situation was created not included within the exemptions of the Clayton and Norris-LaGuardia Acts." Id., at 809. Subsequent cases have applied the *Allen Bradley* doctrine to such combinations without regard to whether they found expression in a collective bargaining agreement, Brotherhood of Carpenters v. United States [330 U.S. 395]; see Teamsters Union v. Oliver, 358 U.S. 283, 296, and even though the mechanism for effectuating the purpose of the combination was an agreement on wages, see Adams Dairy Co. v. St. Louis Dairy Co., 260 F.2d 46 (C.A. 8th Cir. 1958), or on hours of work, Philadelphia Record Co. v. Manufacturing Photo-Engravers Assn., 155 F.2d 799 (C.A. 3d Cir. 1946).

If the UMW in this case, in order to protect its wage scale by maintaining employer income, had presented a set of prices at which the mine operators would be required to sell their coal, the union and the employers who happened to agree could not successfully defend this contract provision if it were challenged under the antitrust laws by the United States or by some party injured by the arrangement. Cf. Allen Bradley Co. v. Union, 325 U.S. 797. In such a case, the restraint on the product market is direct and immediate, is of the type characteristically deemed unreasonable under the Sherman Act and the union gets from the promise nothing more concrete than a hope for better wages to come.

Likewise, if as is alleged in this case, the union became a party to a collusive bidding arrangement designed to drive Phillips and others from the TVA spot market, we think any claim to exemption from antitrust liability would be frivolous at best. For this reason alone the motions of the unions were properly denied.

A major part of Phillips' case, however, was that the union entered into a conspiracy with the large operators to impose the agreed-upon wage and royalty scales upon the smaller, nonunion operators, regardless of their ability to pay and regardless of whether or not the union represented the employees of these companies, all for the purpose of eliminating them from the industry, limiting production and pre-empting the market for the large, unionized operators. The UMW urges that since such an agreement concerned wage standards, it is exempt from the antitrust laws.

It is true that wages lie at the very heart of those subjects about which employers and unions must bargain and the law contemplates agreements on wages not only between individual employers and a union but agreements between the union and employers in a multi-employer bargaining unit. Labor Board v. Truck Drivers Union, 353 U.S. 87, 94-96. The union benefit from the wage scale agreed upon is direct and concrete and the effect on the product market, though clearly present, results from the elimination of competition based on wages among the employers in the bargaining unit, which is not the kind of restraint Congress intended the Sherman Act to proscribe. Apex Hosiery Co. v. Leader, 310 U.S. 469, 503-504. We think it beyond question that a union may conclude a wage agreement with the multi-employer bargaining unit without violating the antitrust laws and that it may as a matter of its own policy, and not by agreement with all or part of the employers of that unit, seek the same wages from those employers.

This is not to say that an agreement resulting from union-employer negotiations is automatically exempt from Sherman Act scrutiny simply because the negotiations involve a compulsory subject of bargaining, regardless of the subject or the form and content of the agreement. Unquestionably the Board's demarcation of the bounds of the duty to bargain has great relevance to any consideration of the sweep of labor's antitrust immunity, for we are concerned here with harmonizing the Sherman Act with the national policy expressed in the National Labor Relations Act of promoting "the peaceful settlement of industrial disputes by subjecting labor-management controversies to the mediatory influence of negotiation," Fibreboard Paper Prods. Corp. v. Labor Board, 379 U.S. 203, 211. But there are limits to what a union or an employer may offer or extract in the name of wages, and because they must bargain does not mean that the agreement reached may disregard other laws.

We have said that a union may make wage agreements with a multi-employer bargaining unit and may in pursuance of its own union interest seek to obtain the same terms from other employers. No case under the antitrust laws could be made out on evidence limited to such union behavior.[2] But we think a union forfeits its exemption from the antitrust laws when it is clearly shown that it has agreed with one set of employers to impose a certain wage scale on other bargaining units. One group of employers may not conspire to eliminate competitors from the industry and the union is liable with the employers if it becomes a party to the conspiracy. This is true even though the union's part in the scheme is an undertaking to secure the same wages, hours or other conditions of employment from the remaining employers in the industry.

We do not find anything in the national labor policy that conflicts with this conclusion. This Court has recognized that a legitimate aim of any national labor organization is to obtain uniformity of labor standards and that a consequence of such union activity may be to eliminate competition based on differences in such standards. Apex Hosiery Co. v. Leader, 310 U.S. 469, 503. But there is nothing in the labor policy indicating that the union and the employers in one bargaining unit are free to bargain about the wages, hours and working conditions of other bargaining units or to attempt to settle these matters for the entire industry. On the contrary, the duty to bargain unit by unit leads to a quite different conclusion. The union's obligation to its members would seem best served if the union retained the ability to respond to each bargaining situation as the individual circumstances might warrant, without being strait-jacketed by some prior agreement with the favored employers.

So far as the employer is concerned it has long been the Board's view that an employer may not condition the signing of a collective bargaining agreement on the union's organization of a majority of the industry.

In such cases the obvious interest of the employer is to ensure that acceptance of the union's wage demands will not adversely affect his competitive position. . . . Permitting insistence on an agreement by the union to attempt to impose a similar contract on other employers would likewise seem to impose a restraining influence on the extent of collective bargaining, for the union could avoid an impasse only by surrendering its freedom to act in its own interest vis-à-vis other employers, something it will be unwilling to do in many instances. Once again, the employer's interest is a competitive interest rather than an interest in

2. Unilaterally, and without agreement with any employer group to do so, a union may adopt a uniform wage policy and seek vigorously to implement it even though it may suspect that some employers cannot effectively compete if they are required to pay the wage scale demanded by the union. The union need not gear its wage demands to wages which the weakest units in the industry can afford to pay. Such union conduct is not alone sufficient evidence to maintain a union-employer conspiracy charge under the Sherman Act. There must be additional direct or indirect evidence of the conspiracy. There was, of course, other evidence in this case, but we indicate no opinion as to its sufficiency.

regulating its own labor relations, and the effect on the union of such an agreement would be to limit the free exercise of the employees' right to engage in concerted activities according to their own views of their self-interest. In sum, we cannot conclude that the national labor policy provides any support for such agreements.

On the other hand, the policy of the antitrust laws is clearly set against employer-union agreements seeking to prescribe labor standards outside the bargaining unit. One could hardly contend, for example, that one group of employers could lawfully demand that the union impose on other employers wages that were significantly higher than those paid by the requesting employers, or a system of computing wages that, because of differences in methods of production, would be more costly to one set of employers than to another. The anticompetitive potential of such a combination is obvious, but is little more severe than what is alleged to have been the purpose and effect of the conspiracy in this case to establish wages at a level that marginal producers could not pay so that they would be driven from the industry. And if the conspiracy presently under attack were declared exempt it would hardly be possible to deny exemption to such avowedly discriminatory schemes.

From the viewpoint of antitrust policy, moreover, all such agreements between a group of employers and a union that the union will seek specified labor standards outside the bargaining unit suffer from a more basic defect, without regard to predatory intention or effect in the particular case. For the salient characteristic of such agreements is that the union surrenders its freedom of action with respect to its bargaining policy. Prior to the agreement the union might seek uniform standards in its own self-interest but would be required to assess in each case the probable costs and gains of a strike or other collective action to that end and thus might conclude that the objective of uniform standards should temporarily give way. After the agreement the union's interest would be bound in each case to that of the favored employer group. It is just such restraints upon the freedom of economic units to act according to their own choice and discretion that run counter to antitrust policy.

Thus the relevant labor and antitrust policies compel us to conclude that the alleged agreement between UMW and the large operators to secure uniform labor standards throughout the industry, if proved, was not exempt from the antitrust laws.

[The Court reversed because the admission of evidence relating to the appeal to the secretary of labor was inconsistent with the holding in Eastern R.R. Presidents Conference v. Noerr Motor Freight, Inc., 365 U.S. 127 (1961), that "joint efforts to influence public officials do not violate the antitrust laws even though intended to eliminate competition."]

DOUGLAS, J., with whom BLACK, J., and CLARK, J., agree, concurring.

As we read the opinion of the Court, it reaffirms the principles of Allen Bradley Co. v. Union, 325 U.S. 797, and tells the trial judge:

First. On the new trial the jury should be instructed that if there were an industry-wide collective bargaining agreement whereby employers and the union agreed on a wage scale that exceeded the financial ability of some operators to pay and that if it was made for the purpose of forcing some employers out of business, the union as well as the employers who participated in the arrangement with the union should be found to have violated the antitrust laws.

Second. An industry-wide agreement containing those features is prima facie evidence of a violation. . . .

GOLDBERG, J., with whom HARLAN, J., and STEWART, J., join, dissenting from the opinion but concurring in the reversal in [*Pennington*] and concurring in the judgment of the Court in [*Jewel Tea*].[16]

[The opinion first reviewed the history of labor antitrust.]

In my view, this history shows a consistent congressional purpose to limit severely judicial intervention in collective bargaining under cover of the wide umbrella of the antitrust laws, and, rather, to deal with what Congress deemed to be specific abuses on the part of labor unions by specific proscriptions in the labor statutes. I believe that the Court should respect this history of congressional purpose and should reaffirm the Court's holdings in *Apex* and *Hutcheson* which, unlike earlier decisions, gave effect to, rather than frustrated, the congressional design. The sound approach of *Hutcheson* is that the labor exemption from the antitrust laws derives from a synthesis of all pertinent congressional legislation — the nature of the Sherman Act itself, §§6 and 20 of the Clayton Act, the Norris-LaGuardia Act, the Fair Labor Standards Act, the Walsh-Healey and Davis-Bacon Acts, and the Wagner Act with its Taft-Hartley and Landrum-Griffin amendments. This last statute, in particular, provides that both employers and unions must bargain over "wages, hours, and other terms and conditions of employment." Following the sound analysis of *Hutcheson,* the Court should hold that, in order to effectuate congressional intent, collective bargaining activity concerning mandatory subjects of bargaining under the Labor Act[17] is not subject to the antitrust laws.[18] This rule flows directly from the *Hutcheson*

[16] Justice Goldberg wrote a single opinion for both *Pennington* and *Jewel Tea.* The portion dealing with *Pennington* is reproduced here.

[17] Was the subject of the alleged agreement, the wage demands the union would make on other employers, a mandatory subject of bargaining?

18. Although I agree with my Brother White in *Jewel Tea* that the doctrine of primary jurisdiction does not apply here, decisions of the Labor Board as to what constitutes a subject of mandatory bargaining are, of course, very significant in determination of the applicability of the labor exemption.

holding that a union acting as a union, in the interests of its members, and not acting to fix prices or allocate markets in aid of an employer conspiracy to accomplish these objects, with only indirect union benefits, is not subject to challenge under the antitrust laws. To hold that mandatory collective bargaining is completely protected would effectuate the congressional policies of encouraging free collective bargaining, subject only to specific restrictions contained in the labor laws, and of limiting judicial intervention in labor matters via the antitrust route — an intervention which necessarily under the Sherman Act places on judges and juries the determination of "what public policy in regard to the industrial struggle demands." Duplex Co. v. Deering, supra, at 485 (dissenting opinion of Mr. Justice Brandeis). See Winter, Collective Bargaining and Competition: The Application of Antitrust Standards to Union Activities, 73 Yale L.J. 14 (1963). . . .

The National Labor Relations Act also declares it to be the policy of the United States to promote the establishment of wages, hours, and other terms and conditions of employment by free collective bargaining between employers and unions. The Act further provides that both employers and unions must bargain about such mandatory subjects of bargaining. This national scheme would be virtually destroyed by the imposition of Sherman Act criminal and civil penalties upon employers and unions engaged in such collective bargaining. To tell the parties that they must bargain about a point but may be subject to antitrust penalties if they reach an agreement is to stultify the congressional scheme. . . .

While purporting to recognize the indisputable fact that the elimination of employer competition based on substandard labor conditions is a proper labor union objective endorsed by our national labor policy and that, therefore, "a union may make wage agreements with a multi-employer bargaining unit and may in pursuance of its own union interests seek to obtain the same terms from other employers," *Pennington,* ante, at 665, the Court holds that "a union forfeits its exemption from the antitrust laws when it is clearly shown that it has agreed with one set of employers to impose a certain wage scale on other bargaining units." Ibid.

This rule seems to me clearly contrary to the congressional purpose manifested by the labor statutes, and it will severely restrict free collective bargaining. Since collective bargaining inevitably involves and requires discussion of the impact of the wage agreement reached with a particular employer or group of employers upon competing employers, the effect of the Court's decision will be to bar a basic element of collective bargaining from the conference room. If a union and employer are prevented from discussing and agreeing upon issues which are, in the great majority of cases, at the central core of bargaining, unilateral force will inevitably be substituted for rational discussion and agreement. Plainly and simply, the Court would subject both unions and employers to antitrust sanctions, criminal as well as civil, if in collective bargaining they concluded a wage agreement and, as part of the agreement, the union has undertaken to use its best efforts to have this wage accepted by other employers in the industry. Indeed, the decision today even goes beyond this. Under settled antitrust principles which are accepted by the Court as appropriate and applicable, which were the basis for jury instructions in *Pennington,* and which will govern it upon remand, there need not be direct evidence of an express agreement. Rather the existence of such an agreement, express or implied, may be inferred from the conduct of the parties. Or, as my Brother Douglas, concurring in *Pennington,* would have it, conduct of the parties could be prima facie evidence of an illegal agreement. Ante, at 673. As the facts of *Pennington* illustrate, the jury is therefore at liberty to infer such an agreement from "clear" evidence that a union's philosophy that high wages and mechanization are desirable has been accepted by a group of employers and that the union has attempted to achieve like acceptance from other employers. For, as I have pointed out, stripped of all adjectives, this is what *Pennington* presents. Yet the Court today holds "the alleged agreement between UMW and the large operators to secure uniform labor standards throughout the industry, if proved, was not exempt from the antitrust laws." Ante, at 669.

The rational thing for an employer to do, when faced with union demands he thinks he cannot meet, is to explain why, in economic terms, he believes that he cannot agree to the union requests. Indeed, the Labor Act's compulsion to bargain in good faith requires that he meaningfully address himself to the union's requests. See Labor Board v. Truitt Mfg. Co., 351 U.S. 149. A recurring and most understandable reason given by employers for their resistance to union demands is that competitive factors prevent them from accepting the union's proposed terms. Under the Court's holding today, however, such a statement by an employer may start both the employer and union on the road to antitrust sanctions, criminal and civil. For a jury may well interpret such discussion and subsequent union action as showing an implicit or secret agreement to impose uniform standards on other employers. Nor does the Court's requirement that there be "direct or indirect evidence of the conspiracy," ante, at 665, n. 2 — whatever those undefined terms in the opinion may mean — provide any substantial safeguard for uninhibited collective bargaining discussions. In *Pennington* itself, the trial court instructed the jury that a union's unilateral actions did not subject it to antitrust sanctions, and yet the jury readily inferred a "conspiracy" from the "direct or indirect evidence" of the union's publicly stated policy in favor of high wages and mechanization, its collective bargaining agreement with a group of employers establishing high wages, and its attempt to obtain similar high wages from other employers.

AMALGAMATED MEAT CUTTERS & BUTCHERS WORKMEN, LOCAL 189 v. JEWEL TEA CO.

381 U.S. 676 (1965)

WHITE, J., announced the judgment[18] of the Court and delivered an opinion, in which WARREN, C.J. and BRENNAN, J., join. . . .

[This case] concerns the lawfulness of the following restriction on the operating hours of food store meat departments contained in a collective bargaining agreement executed after joint multi-employer, multi-union negotiations:

"Market operating hours shall be 9:00 a.m. to 6:00 p.m. Monday through Saturday, inclusive. No customer shall be served who comes into the market before or after the hours set forth above."

This litigation arose out of the 1957 contract negotiations between the representatives of 9,000 Chicago retailers of fresh meat and the seven union petitioners, who are local affiliates of the Amalgamated Meat Cutters and Butcher Workmen of North America, AFL-CIO, representing virtually all butchers in the Chicago area. During the 1957 bargaining sessions the employer group presented several requests for union consent to a relaxation of the existing contract restriction on marketing hours for fresh meat, which forbade the sale of meat before 9 a.m. and after 6 p.m. in both service and self-service markets. The unions rejected all such suggestions, and their own proposal retaining the marketing-hours restriction was ultimately accepted at the final bargaining session by all but two of the employers, National Tea Co. and Jewel Tea Co. (hereinafter "Jewel"). Associated Food Retailers of Greater Chicago, a trade association having about 1,000 individual and independent merchants as members and representing some 300 meat dealers in the negotiations, was among those who accepted. Jewel, however, asked the union negotiators to present to their membership, on behalf of it and National Tea, a counteroffer that included provision for Friday night operations. At the same time Jewel voiced its belief, as it had midway through the negotiations, that any marketing-hours restriction was illegal. On the recommendation of the union negotiators, the Jewel offer was rejected by the union membership, and a strike was authorized. Under the duress of the strike vote, Jewel decided to sign the contract previously approved by the rest of the industry.

In July 1958 Jewel brought suit against the unions, certain of their officers, Associated, and Charles H. Bromann, Secretary-Treasurer of Associated, seeking invalidation under §§1 and 2 of the Sherman Act of the contract provision that prohibited night meat market operations.

[18] Unlike in *Pennington* where Justice White announced the "opinion" of the Court, here he announces the "judgment" of the Court. His analysis in *Jewel Tea* has the agreement of only two other justices.

The gist of the complaint was that the defendants and others had conspired together to prevent the retail sale of fresh meat before 9 a.m. and after 6 p.m. As evidence of the conspiracy Jewel relied in part on the events during the 1957 contract negotiations — the acceptance by Associated of the market-hours restriction and the unions' imposition of the restriction on Jewel through a strike threat. Jewel also alleged that it was a part of the conspiracy that the unions would neither permit their members to work at times other than the hours specified nor allow any grocery firm to sell meat, with or without employment of their members, outside those hours; that the members of Associated, which had joined only one of the 1957 employer proposals for extending marketing hours, had agreed among themselves to insist on the inclusion of the marketing-hours limitation in all collective bargaining agreements between the unions and any food store operator; that Associated, its members and officers had agreed with the other defendants that no firm was to be permitted to operate self-service meat markets between 6 p.m. and 9 p.m.; and that the unions, their officers and members had acted as the enforcing agent of the conspiracy.

The complaint stated that in recent years the prepackaged, self-service system of marketing meat had come into vogue, that 174 of Jewel's 196 stores were equipped to vend meat in this manner, and that a butcher need not be on duty in a self-service market at the time meat purchases were actually made. The prohibition of night meat marketing, it was alleged, unlawfully impeded Jewel in the use of its property and adversely affected the general public in that many persons find it inconvenient to shop during the day. An injunction, treble damages and attorneys' fees were demanded. . . .

After trial, the District Judge ruled the "record was devoid of any evidence to support a finding of conspiracy" between Associated and the unions to force the restrictive provision on Jewel. 215 F. Supp. 839, 845. Testing the unions' action standing alone, the trial court found that even in self-service markets removal of the limitation on marketing hours either would inaugurate longer hours and night work for the butchers or would result in butchers' work being done by others unskilled in the trade. Thus, the court concluded, the unions had imposed the marketing-hours limitation to serve their own interests respecting conditions of employment, and such action was clearly within the labor exemption of the Sherman Act established by Hunt v Crumboch, 325 U.S. 821; United States v. Hutcheson, 312 U.S. 219; United States v. American Federation of Musicians, 318 U.S. 741. Alternatively, the District Court ruled that even if this was not the case, the arrangement did not amount to an unreasonable restraint of trade in violation of the Sherman Act. [The Court of Appeals reversed without disturbing any of the fact findings.] We granted certiorari on the unions' petition, and now reverse the Court of Appeals.

[The Court first holds that this was not within the exclusive jurisdiction of the NLRB.]

II

Here, as in United Mine Workers v. Pennington, the claim is made that the agreement under attack is exempt from the antitrust laws. We agree, but not on the broad grounds urged by the union.

It is well at the outset to emphasize that this case comes to us stripped of any claim of a union-employer conspiracy against Jewel. The trial court found no evidence to sustain Jewel's conspiracy claim and this finding was not disturbed by the Court of Appeals. We therefore have a situation where the unions, having obtained a marketing-hours agreement from one group of employers, have successfully sought the same terms from a single employer, Jewel, not as a result of a bargain between the unions and some employers directed against other employers, but pursuant to what the unions deemed to be in their own labor union interests.

Jewel does not allege that it has been injured by the elimination of competition among the other employers within the unit with respect to marketing hours; Jewel complains only of the unions' action in forcing it to accept the same restriction, the unions acting not at the behest of any employer group but in pursuit of their own policies. It might be argued that absent any union-employer conspiracy against Jewel and absent any agreement between Jewel and any other employer, the union-Jewel contract cannot be a violation of the Sherman Act. But the issue before us is not the broad substantive one of a violation of the antitrust laws — was there a conspiracy or combination which unreasonably restrained trade or an attempt to monopolize and was Jewel damaged in its business? — but whether the agreement is immune from attack by reason of the labor exemption from the antitrust laws. The fact that the parties to the agreement are but a single employer and the unions representing its employees does not compel immunity for the agreement.[19] We must consider the subject matter of the agreement in the light of the national labor policy.

We pointed out in *Pennington* that exemption for union-employer agreements is very much a matter of accommodating the coverage of the Sherman Act to the policy of the labor laws. Employers and unions are required to bargain about wages, hours and working conditions, and this fact weighs heavily in favor of antitrust exemption for agreements on these subjects. But neither party need bargain about other matters and

[19] This is surely startling. Assuming that Justice White is relying on the *Hutcheson-Allen Bradley* "business conspiracy" exception to labor's immunity, he would hold the immunity lost when the union signs an agreement with an unwilling employer who then becomes the plaintiff in the antitrust action.

either party commits an unfair labor practice if it conditions its bargaining upon discussions of a nonmandatory subject. Labor Board v. Borg-Warner Corp., 356 U.S. 342. Jewel, for example, need not have bargained about or agreed to a schedule of prices at which its meat would be sold and the unions could not legally have insisted that it do so. But if the unions had made such a demand, Jewel had agreed and the United States or an injured party had challenged the agreement under the antitrust laws, we seriously doubt that either the unions or Jewel could claim immunity by reason of the labor exemption, whatever substantive questions of violation there might be.[20]

Thus the issue in this case is whether the marketing-hours restriction, like wages, and unlike prices, is so intimately related to wages, hours and working conditions that the unions' successful attempt to obtain that provision through bona fide, arm's-length bargaining in pursuit of their own labor union policies, and not at the behest of or in combination with nonlabor groups, falls within the protection of the national labor policy and is therefore exempt from the Sherman Act.[5] We think that it is.

The Court of Appeals would classify the marketing-hours restriction with the product-pricing provision and place both within the reach of the Sherman Act. In its view, labor has a legitimate interest in the number of hours it must work but no interest in whether the hours fall in the daytime, in the nighttime or on Sundays. . . .

Contrary to the Court of Appeals, we think that the particular hours of the day and the particular days of the week during which employees shall be required to work are subjects well within the realm of "wages, hours, and other terms and conditions of employment" about which employers and unions must bargain. National Labor Relations Act, §8(d); see Timken Roller Bearing Co., 70 N.L.R.B. 500, 504, 515-516, 521 (1946), rev'd on other grounds, 161 F.2d 949 (C.A. 6th Cir. 1947) (employer's unilateral imposition of Sunday work was refusal to bar-

[20] Is this so obvious? Jewel can set its own prices without antitrust implications; the union is acting alone, and in its best interest. If they agree, why a loss of immunity? On the issue of whether there is a substantive violation, Justice White will treat this as tantamount to an agreement among competitors in n. 6, infra.

5. The crucial determinant is not the form of the agreement — e.g., prices or wages — but its relative impact on the product market and the interests of union members. Thus in Teamsters Union v. Oliver, 358 U.S. 283, we held that federal labor policy precluded application of state antitrust laws to an employer-union agreement that when leased trucks were driven by their owners, such owner-drivers should receive, in addition to the union wage, not less than a prescribed minimum rental. Though in form a scheme fixing prices for the supply of leased vehicles, the agreement was designed "to protect the negotiated wage scale against the possible undermining through dimunition of the owner's wages for driving which might result from a rental which did not cover his operating costs." Id., at 293-294. As the agreement did not embody a "'remote and indirect approach to the subject of wages' . . . but a direct frontal attack upon a problem thought to threaten the maintenance of the basic wage structure established by the collective bargaining contract," id., at 294, the paramount federal policy of encouraging collective bargaining proscribed application of the state law.

gain); Massey Gin & Machine Works, Inc., 78 N.L.R.B. 189, 195, 199 (1948) (change in starting and quitting time); Camp & McInnes, Inc., 100 N.L.R.B. 524, 532 (1952) (reduction of lunch hour and advancement of quitting time). And, although the effect on competition is apparent and real, perhaps more so than in the case of the wage agreement, the concern of union members is immediate and direct. Weighing the respective interests involved, we think the national labor policy expressed in the National Labor Relations Act places beyond the reach of the Sherman Act union-employer agreements on when, as well as how long, employees must work. An agreement on these subjects between the union and the employers in a bargaining unit is not illegal under the Sherman Act, nor is the union's unilateral demand for the same contract of other employers in the industry.

Disposing of the case, as it did, on the broad grounds we have indicated, the Court of Appeals did not deal separately with the marketing-hours provision, as distinguished from hours of work, in connection with either service or self-service markets. The dispute here pertains principally to self-service markets.

The unions argue that since night operations would be impossible without night employment of butchers, or an impairment of the butchers' jurisdiction, or a substantial effect on the butchers' workload, the marketing-hours restriction is either little different in effect from the valid working-hours provision that work shall stop at 6 p.m. or is necessary to protect other concerns of the union members. If the unions' factual premises are true, we think the unions could impose a restriction on night operations without violation of the Sherman Act; for then operating hours, like working hours, would constitute a subject of immediate and legitimate concern to union members.[21]

Jewel alleges on the other hand that the night operation of self-service markets requires no butcher to be in attendance and does not infringe any other legitimate union concern. Customers serve themselves; and if owners want to forgo furnishing the services of a butcher to give advice or to make special cuts, this is not the unions' concern since their desire to avoid night work is fully satisfied and no other legitimate interest is being infringed. In short, the connection between working hours and operating hours in the case of the self-service market is said to be so attenuated as to bring the provision within the prohibition of the Sherman Act.

If it were true that self-service markets could actually operate without butchers, at least for a few hours after 6 p.m., that no encroachment on butchers' work would result and that the workload of butchers during

[21] It is so clear as to not require the Justice's comment that the "weighing of the respective interests" come out the same whether the restraint is of the labor market (hours and days employees will work) or of the product market (hours of operation), even assuming a nexus between the two markets?

normal working hours would not be substantially increased, Jewel's position would have considerable merit. For then the obvious restraint on the product market — the exclusion of self-service stores from the evening market for meat — would stand alone, unmitigated and unjustified by the vital interests of the union butchers which are relied upon in this case. In such event the limitation imposed by the unions might well be reduced to nothing but an effort by the unions to protect one group of employers from competition by another, which is conduct that is not exempt from the Sherman Act. Whether there would be a violation of §§1 and 2 would then depend on whether the elements of a conspiracy in restraint of trade or an attempt to monopolize had been proved.[6]

Thus the dispute between Jewel and the unions essentially concerns a narrow factual question: Are night operations without butchers, and without infringement of butchers' interests, feasible? The District Court resolved this factual dispute in favor of the unions. It found that "in stores where meat is sold at night it is impractical to operate without either butchers or other employees. Someone must arrange, replenish and clean the counters and supply customer services." Operating without butchers would mean that "their work would be done by others unskilled in the trade," and "would involve an increase in workload in preparing for the night work and cleaning the next morning." 215 F. Supp., at 846. Those findings were not disturbed by the Court of Appeals, which, as previously noted, proceeded on a broader ground. Our function is limited to reviewing the record to satisfy ourselves that the trial judge's findings are not clearly erroneous. Fed. Rules Civ. Proc. 52 (a). . . .

Reversed.

GOLDBERG, J., with whom HARLAN, J., and STEWART, J., join, dissenting from the opinion but concurring in the . . . judgment of the Court. . . .

The judicial expressions in *Jewel Tea* represent another example of the reluctance of judges to give full effect to congressional purpose in this area and the substitution by judges of their views for those of Congress as to how free collective bargaining should operate. In this case the Court of Appeals would have held the Union subject to the Sherman

6. One issue, for example, would be whether the restraint was unreasonable. Judicial pronouncements regarding the reasonableness of restraints on hours of business are relatively few. Some cases appear to have viewed such restraints as tantamount to limits on hours of work and thus reasonable, even though contained in agreements among competitors. . . .

Other cases have upheld operating-hours restraints in factual circumstances that make it seem likely that the agreement affected hours of operation and hours of work in equal measure but without stressing that fact. . . .

The decided cases thus do not appear to offer any easy answer to the question whether in a particular case an operating-hours restraint is unreasonable.

Act's criminal and civil penalties because in the court's social and economic judgment, the determination of the hours at which meat is to be sold is a "proprietary" matter within the exclusive control of management and thus the Union had no legitimate interest in bargaining over it. My Brother Douglas, joined by Mr. Justice Black and Mr. Justice Clark, would affirm this judgment apparently because the agreement was reached through a multi-employer bargaining unit. But . . . there is nothing even remotely illegal about such bargaining. Even if an independent conspiracy test were applicable to the *Jewel Tea* situation, the simple fact is that multi-employer bargaining conducted at arm's length does not constitute union abetment of a business combination. It is often a self-defensive form of employer bargaining designed to match union strength.

My Brother White, joined by the Chief Justice and Mr. Justice Brennan, while not agreeing with my Brother Douglas, would reverse the Court of Appeals. He also, however, refuses to give full effect to the congressional intent that judges should not, under cover of the Sherman Act umbrella, substitute their economic and social policies for free collective bargaining. My Brother White recognizes that the issue of the hours of sale of meat concerns a mandatory subject of bargaining based on the trial court's findings that it directly affected the hours of work of the butchers in the self-service markets, and therefore, since there was a finding that the Union was not abetting an independent employer conspiracy, he joins in reversing the Court of Appeals. In doing so, however, he apparently draws lines among mandatory subjects of bargaining, presumably based on a judicial determination of their importance to the worker, and states that not all agreements resulting from collective bargaining based on mandatory subjects of bargaining are immune from the antitrust laws, even absent evidence of union abetment of an independent conspiracy of employers. Following this reasoning, my Brother White indicates that he would sustain a judgment here, even absent evidence of union abetment of an independent conspiracy of employers, if the trial court had found "that self-service markets could actually operate without butchers, at least for a few hours after 6 p.m., that no encroachment on butchers' work would result and that the workload of butchers during normal working hours would not be substantially increased. . . ." Ante, at 692. Such a view seems to me to be unsupportable. It represents a narrow, confining view of what labor unions have a legitimate interest in preserving and thus bargaining about. Even if the self-service markets could operate after 6 p.m., without their butchers and without increasing the work of their butchers at other times, the result of such operation can reasonably be expected to be either that the small, independent service markets would have to remain open in order to compete, thus requiring their union butchers to work at night, or that the small, independent service markets would not be able to operate at night and thus would be put at a competitive disadvantage. Since it is clear that the large, automated self-service markets employ fewer butchers per volume of sales than service markets do, the Union certainly has a legitimate interest in keeping service markets competitive so as to preserve jobs. Job security of this kind has been recognized to be a legitimate subject of union interest. . . . The direct interest of the union in not working undesirable hours by curtailing all business at those hours is, of course, a far cry from the indirect "interest" in *Allen Bradley* in fixing prices and allocating markets solely to increase the profits of favored employers.

Indeed, if the Union in *Jewel Tea* were attempting to aid the small service butcher shops and thus save total employment against automation, perhaps at a necessarily reduced wage scale, the case would present the exact opposite union philosophy from that of the Mine Workers in *Pennington.* Putting the opinion of the Court in *Pennington* together with the opinions of my Brothers Douglas and White in *Jewel Tea,* it would seem that unions are damned if their collective bargaining philosophy involves acceptance of automation (*Pennington*) and are equally damned if their collective bargaining philosophy involves resistance to automation (*Jewel Tea*). Again, the wisdom of a union adopting either philosophy is not for judicial determination. . . .

My view that Congress intended that collective bargaining activity on mandatory subjects of bargaining under the Labor Act not be subject to the antitrust laws does not mean that I believe that Congress intended that activity involving all nonmandatory subjects of bargaining be similarly exempt. The direct and overriding interest of unions in such subjects as wages, hours and other working conditions, which Congress has recognized in making them subjects of mandatory bargaining, is clearly lacking where the subject of the agreement is price-fixing and market allocation. Moreover, such activities are at the core of the type of anticompetitive commercial restraint at which the antitrust laws are directed. . . .

DOUGLAS, J., with whom BLACK, J., and CLARK, J., concur, dissenting.

If we followed Allen Bradley Co. v. Union, 325 U.S. 797, we would hold with the Court of Appeals that this multi-employer agreement with the union not to sell meat between 6 p.m. and 9 a.m. was not immunized from the antitrust laws and that respondent's evidence made out a prima facie case that it was in fact a violation of the Sherman Act.

If, in the present case, the employers alone agreed not to sell meat from 6 p.m. to 9 a.m., they would be guilty of an anticompetitive practice, barred by the antitrust laws. . . . That Jewel has been coerced by the unions into respecting this agreement means that Jewel cannot use convenience of shopping hours as a means of competition. . . .

At the conclusion of respondent's case, the District Court dismissed Associated and Bromann from the action, which was tried without a jury, on the ground that there was no evidence of a conspiracy between Associated and the unions. But in the circumstances of this case the collective bargaining agreement itself, of which the District Court said there was clear proof, was evidence of a conspiracy among the employers with the unions to impose the marketing-hours restriction on Jewel via a strike threat by the unions. . . .

My Brother White's conclusion that the concern of the union members over *marketing* hours is "immediate and direct" depends upon there being a necessary connection between marketing hours and working hours. That connection is found in the District Court's finding that "in stores where meat is sold at night it is impractical to operate without either butchers or other employees." 215 F. Supp. 839, 846. It is, however, undisputed that on some nights Jewel does so operate in some of its stores in Indiana, and even in Chicago it sometimes operates without butchers at night in the sale of fresh poultry and sausage, which are exempt from the union ban.

It is said that even if night self-service could be carried on without butchers, still the union interest in store hours would be immediate and direct because competitors would have to stay open too or be put at a disadvantage — and some of these competitors would be non-self-service stores that would have to employ union butchers at night. But *Allen Bradley* forecloses such an expansive view of the labor exemption to the antitrust laws.

Notes

1. What purpose might a union have in agreeing with major coal operators to impose a wage scale on other operators?

2. What is the scope of the *Hutcheson* exemption after *Pennington* and *Jewel Tea?* If the bargaining agreement with the employers in *Pennington* takes the unions' actions out of the exemption, what precisely is the purpose of comparing antitrust policy and national labor policy to the facts of the case? How does the "intimately related" inquiry in *Jewel Tea* fit with an exemption analysis? Suppose the union's exemption had been lost in *Jewel Tea.* Does it follow that the union was liable or does the commercial competition test of *Apex* also have to be met?

3. Employer *A* has been subjected to a stubborn demand for a $2 per hour increase by the union during contract negotiations. He files an antitrust suit against the union and a multiemployer bargaining association in his industry. The union and the association reached a bargaining agreement recently providing for a $2 per hour increase, and employer

A is charging a *Pennington* conspiracy. In discovery, employer *A* learns that the following discussion occurred between the union's business agent and the association's representative at their negotiations:

Business Agent: "We need a $2 per hour increase over the next three years."

Assn. Rep.: "Look, we can't do that. It would drive up our costs too much and we would be undersold by our competitors."

Business Agent: "Don't worry about that, we're going to get the same from them whether they like it or not."

Is this enough evidence for employer *A* to get past a directed verdict motion?

3. In *Jewel Tea,* the union's bargaining agreement with the multiemployer association contained a clause providing that "the unions agree not to enter into a contract with any other employer designating lower wages, or longer hours, or any more favorable conditions of employment." 215 F. Supp. 839, 842 (N.D. Ill. 1963). Should that have been relevant in the Supreme Court?

4. Referring to Justice White's opinion in *Jewel Tea,* Professor Archibald Cox writes:

> [A]lthough there is doubt, Justice White apparently thought it important to appraise whether the benefit of the agreement to the Union outweighed the injury produced by the direct restraint upon the product market. Should this view prevail, the courts will revert to a practice from which they were ousted by the Norris-LaGuardia Act — that of weighing the social desirability or undesirability of the union's objectives. This is contrary to the whole history of labor and antitrust law from 1933 until the 1964 Term's decision.[22]

Do you agree with that description and evaluation of Justice White's balancing test?

AMERICAN FEDERATION OF MUSICIANS v. CARROLL, 391 U.S. 99 (1968): Four orchestra "leaders" brought a Sherman Act action against the Musicians Union. The leaders book one-time engagements to provide music for social events. Their responsibilities include hiring the necessary supporting musicians, called *sidemen,* and attending to bookkeeping details. In addition, the leaders often perform with the orchestras, sometimes only conducting but often playing an instrument. The

[22] Cox, n. [1] supra, at 317, 326 (1966).

leaders belong to the Musicians Union, which regulates labor standards in this market through unilaterally adopted union bylaws and regulations — bargaining agreements with the organizers of these events (weddings, etc.) being impractical. Under these bylaws, the leaders must employ a minimum number of sidemen and must charge purchasers minimum prices prescribed in a "price list." The prices are a total of (1) the minimum wage scales for sidemen, (2) a "leader's fee," which is double the sideman's scale when four or more musicians comprise the orchestra, and (3) an additional 8 percent to cover social security, unemployment insurance, and other expenses. This price floor was challenged under the Sherman Act.

The Court, per Justice Brennan, applied the exemption:

> The Court of Appeals, one judge dissenting, disagreed that the "Price List" was within the labor exemption, stating "the unions' establishment of price floors on orchestra engagements constitutes a per se violation of the Sherman Act." 372 F.2d at 165. The premise of the majority's conclusion was that the "Price List" was disqualified for the exemption because its concern is "prices" and not "wages." But this overlooks the necessity of inquiry beyond the form. Mr. Justice White's opinion in Meat Cutters v. Jewel Tea, 381 U.S. 676, 690, n. 5, emphasized that "[t]he crucial determinant is not the form of the agreement — e.g., prices or wages — but its relative impact on the product market and the interests of union members." It is therefore not dispositive of the question that petitioners' regulation in form establishes price floors. The critical inquiry is whether the price floors in actuality operate to protect the wages of the subleader and sidemen. The District Court found that the price floors were expressly designed to and did function as a protection of sidemen's and subleaders' wage scales against the job and wage competition of the leaders. . . .
>
> [T]he price floors, including the minimums for leaders, are simply a means for coping with the job and wage competition of the leaders to protect the wage scales of musicians who respondents concede are employees on club-dates, namely sidemen and subleaders. As such the provisions of the "Price List" establishing those floors are indistinguishable in their effect from the collective bargaining provisions in Teamsters Union v. Oliver, 358 U.S. 283, which we held governed not prices but the mandatory bargaining subject of wages. [*Oliver* is described in n. 5 of Justice White's opinion in *Jewel Tea.* — Ed.] . . . In other words, the price of the product — here the price for an orchestra for a club-date — presents almost entirely the scale wages of the sidemen and the leader. Unlike most industries, except for the 8% charge, there are no other costs contributing to the price. Therefore, if leaders cut prices, inevitably wages must be cut."[23]

[23] White, J., joined by Black, J., dissented.

CONNELL CONSTRUCTION CO. v. PLUMBERS LOCAL 100[24]

421 U.S. 616 (1975)

POWELL, J. . . .

I

Local 100 is the bargaining representative for workers in the plumbing and mechanical trades in Dallas. When this litigation began, it was party to a multiemployer bargaining agreement with the Mechanical Contractors Association of Dallas, a group of about 75 mechanical contractors. That contract contained a "most favored nation" clause, by which the union agreed that if it granted a more favorable contract to any other employer it would extend the same terms to all members of the Association.

Connell Construction Co. is a general building contractor in Dallas. It obtains jobs by competitive bidding and subcontracts all plumbing and mechanical work. Connell has followed a policy of awarding these subcontracts on the basis of competitive bids, and it has done business with both union and nonunion subcontractors. Connell's employees are represented by various building trade unions. Local 100 has never sought to represent them or to bargain with Connell on their behalf.

In November 1970, Local 100 asked Connell to agree that it would subcontract [jobsite] mechanical work only to firms that had a current contract with the union. . . .

When Connell refused to sign this agreement, Local 100 stationed a single picket at one of Connell's major construction sites. About 150 workers walked off the job, and construction halted. Connell filed suit in state court to enjoin the picketing as a violation of Texas antitrust laws. Local 100 removed the case to federal court. Connell then signed the subcontracting agreement under protest. It amended its complaint to claim that the agreement violated §§1 and 2 of the Sherman Act, and was therefore invalid. Connell sought a declaration to this effect and an injunction against any further efforts to force it to sign such an agreement.

By the time the case went to trial, Local 100 had submitted identical agreements to a number of other general contractors in Dallas. Five others had signed, and the union was waging a selective picketing campaign against those who resisted.

The District Court held that the subcontracting agreement was exempt from federal antitrust laws because it was authorized by the con-

[24] See Leslie, n. [1] supra; St. Antoine, Connell: Antitrust Law at the Expense of Labor Law, 62 Va. L. Rev. 603 (1976).

struction industry proviso to §8(e) of the National Labor Relations Act. The court also held that federal labor legislation pre-empted the State's antitrust laws. The Court of Appeals for the Fifth Circuit affirmed, 483 F.2d 1154 (1973), with one judge dissenting. It held that Local 100's goal of organizing nonunion subcontractors was a legitimate union interest and that its efforts toward that goal were therefore exempt from federal antitrust laws. On the second issue, it held that state law was pre-empted under San Diego Building Trades Council v. Garmon, 359 U.S. 236 (1959). We granted certiorari on Connell's petition. We reverse on the question of federal antitrust immunity and affirm the ruling on state law pre-emption.

II

The basic sources of organized labor's exemption from federal antitrust laws are §§6 and 20 of the Clayton Act, and the Norris-LaGuardia Act. These statutes declare that labor unions are not combinations or conspiracies in restraint of trade, and exempt specific union activities, including secondary picketing and boycotts, from the operation of the antitrust laws. See United States v. Hutcheson, 312 U.S. 219 (1941). They do not exempt concerted action or agreements between unions and nonlabor parties. Mine Workers v. Pennington, 381 U.S. 657, 662 (1965). The Court has recognized, however, that a proper accommodation between the congressional policy favoring collective bargaining under the NLRA and the congressional policy favoring free competition in business markets requires that some union-employer agreements be accorded a limited nonstatutory exemption from antitrust sanctions. Meat Cutters v. Jewel Tea Co., 381 U.S. 676 (1965).

The nonstatutory exemption has its source in the strong labor policy favoring the association of employees to eliminate competition over wages and working conditions. Union success in organizing workers and standardizing wages ultimately will affect price competition among employers, but the goals of federal labor law never could be achieved if this effect on business competition were held a violation of the antitrust laws. The Court therefore has acknowledged that labor policy requires tolerance for the lessening of business competition based on differences in wages and working conditions. See Mine Workers v. Pennington, supra, at 666; *Jewel Tea,* supra, at 692-693 (opinion of White, J.). Labor policy clearly does not require, however, that a union have freedom to impose direct restraints on competition among those who employ its members. Thus, while the statutory exemption allows unions to accomplish some restraints by acting unilaterally, e.g., Federation of Musicians v. Carroll, 391 U.S. 99 (1968), the nonstatutory exemption offers no similar protection when a union and a nonlabor party agree to restrain competition in a business market. See Allen Bradley Co. v. Electrical Workers, 325 U.S.

797, 806-811 (1945); Cox, Labor and the Antitrust Laws — A Preliminary Analysis, 104 U. Pa. L. Rev. 252 (1955); Meltzer, Labor Unions, Collective Bargaining, and the Antitrust Laws, 32 U. Chi. L. Rev. 659 (1965).

In this case Local 100 used direct restraints on the business market to support its organizing campaign. The agreements with Connell and other general contractors indiscriminately excluded nonunion subcontractors from a portion of the market, even if their competitive advantages were not derived from substandard wages and working conditions but rather from more efficient operating methods. Curtailment of competition based on efficiency is neither a goal of federal labor policy nor a necessary effect of the elimination of competition among workers. Moreover, competition based on efficiency is a positive value that the antitrust laws strive to protect.

The multiemployer bargaining agreement between Local 100 and the Association, though not challenged in this suit, is relevant in determining the effect that the agreement between Local 100 and Connell would have on the business market. The "most favored nation" clause in the multiemployer agreement promised to eliminate competition between members of the Association and any other subcontractors that Local 100 might organize. By giving members of the Association a contractual right to insist on terms as favorable as those given any competitor, it guaranteed that the union would make no agreement that would give an unaffiliated contractor a competitive advantage over members of the Association. Subcontractors in the Association thus stood to benefit from any extension of Local 100's organization, but the method Local 100 chose also had the effect of sheltering them from outside competition in that portion of the market covered by subcontracting agreements between general contractors and Local 100. In that portion of the market, the restriction on subcontracting would eliminate competition on all subjects covered by the multiemployer agreement, even on subjects unrelated to wages, hours, and working conditions.

Success in exacting agreements from general contractors would also give Local 100 power to control access to the market for mechanical subcontracting work. The agreements with general contractors did not simply prohibit subcontracting to any nonunion firm; they prohibited subcontracting to any firm that did not have a contract with Local 100. The union thus had complete control over subcontract work offered by general contractors that had signed these agreements. Such control could result in significant adverse effects on the market and on consumers — effects unrelated to the union's legitimate goals of organizing workers and standardizing working conditions. For example, if the union thought the interests of its members would be served by having fewer subcontractors competing for the available work, it could refuse to sign collective-bargaining agreements with marginal firms. Cf. Mine

Workers v. Pennington, supra. Or, since Local 100 has a well-defined geographical jurisdiction, it could exclude "traveling" subcontractors by refusing to deal with them. Local 100 thus might be able to create a geographical enclave for local contractors, similar to the closed market in *Allen Bradley,* supra.

This record contains no evidence that the union's goal was anything other than organizing as many subcontractors as possible.[2] This goal was legal, even though a successful organizing campaign ultimately would reduce the competition that unionized employers face from nonunion firms. But the methods the union chose are not immune from antitrust sanctions simply because the goal is legal. Here Local 100, by agreement with several contractors, made nonunion subcontractors ineligible to compete for a portion of the available work. This kind of direct restraint on the business market has substantial anticompetitive effects, both actual and potential, that would not follow naturally from the elimination of competition over wages and working conditions. It contravenes antitrust policies to a degree not justified by congressional labor policy, and therefore cannot claim a nonstatutory exemption from the antitrust laws.

There can be no argument in this case, whatever its force in other contexts, that a restraint of this magnitude might be entitled to an antitrust exemption if it were included in a lawful collective-bargaining agreement. Cf. Mine Workers v. Pennington, 381 U.S., at 664-665; *Jewel Tea,* 381 U.S., at 689-690 (opinion of White, J.); id., at 709-713, 732-733 (opinion of Goldberg, J.). In this case, Local 100 had no interest in representing Connell's employees. The federal policy favoring collective bargaining therefore can offer no shelter for the union's coercive action against Connell or its campaign to exclude nonunion firms from the subcontracting market.

III

Local 100 nonetheless contends that the kind of agreement it obtained from Connell is explicitly allowed by the construction industry proviso to §8(e) and that antitrust policy therefore must defer to the NLRA. The majority in the Court of Appeals declined to decide this issue, holding that it was subject to the "exclusive jurisdiction" of the NLRB. 483 F.2d, at 1174. This Court has held, however, that the federal courts may decide labor law questions that emerge as collateral issues in

2. There was no evidence that Local 100's organizing campaign was connected with any agreement with members of the multiemployer bargaining unit, and the only evidence of agreement among those subcontractors was the "most favored nation" clause in the collective-bargaining agreement. In fact, Connell has not argued the case on a theory of conspiracy between the union and unionized subcontractors. It has simply relied on the multiemployer agreement as a factor enhancing the restraint of trade implicit in the subcontracting agreement it signed.

suits brought under independent federal remedies including the antitrust laws. We conclude that §8(e) does not allow this type of agreement. [As discussed supra p. 464 of these materials, the Court held the agreement was prohibited by §8(e)].

Finally, Local 100 contends that even if the subcontracting agreement is not sanctioned by the construction-industry proviso and therefore is illegal under §8(e), it cannot be the basis for antitrust liability because the remedies in the NLRA are exclusive. This argument is grounded in the legislative history of the 1947 Taft-Hartley amendments. Congress rejected attempts to regulate secondary activities by repealing the antitrust exemptions in the Clayton and Norris-LaGuardia Acts, and created special remedies under the labor law instead. It made secondary activities unfair labor practices under §8(b)(4), and drafted special provisions for preliminary injunctions at the suit of the NLRB and for recovery of actual damages in the district courts. §10(*l*) of the NLRA and §303 of the Labor-Management Relations Act. But whatever significance this legislative choice has for antitrust suits based on those secondary activities prohibited by §8(b)(4), it has no relevance to the question whether Congress meant to preclude antitrust suits based on the "hot cargo" agreements that it outlawed in 1959. There is no legislative history in the 1959 Congress suggesting that labor-law remedies for §8(e) violations were intended to be exclusive, or that Congress thought allowing antitrust remedies in cases like the present one would be inconsistent with the remedial scheme of the NLRA.[16]

We therefore hold that this agreement, which is outside the context of a collective-bargaining relationship and not restricted to a particular jobsite, but which nonetheless obligates Connell to subcontract work only to firms that have a contract with Local 100, may be the basis of a federal antitrust suit because it has a potential for restraining competition in the business market in ways that would not follow naturally from elimination of competition over wages and working conditions.

16. The dissenting opinion of Mr. Justice Stewart argues that §303 provides the exclusive remedy for violations of §8(e), thereby precluding recourse to antitrust remedies. For that proposition the dissenting opinion relies upon "considerable evidence in the legislative materials." In our view, these materials are unpersuasive. In the first place, Congress did not amend §303 expressly to provide a remedy for violations of §8(e). The House in 1959 did reject proposals by Representatives Hiestand, Alger, and Hoffman to repeal labor's antitrust immunity. Those proposals, however, were much broader than the issue in this case. The Hiestand-Alger proposal would have repealed antitrust immunity for any action in concert by two or more labor organizations. The Hoffman proposal apparently intended to repeal labor's antitrust immunity entirely. That the Congress rejected these extravagant proposals hardly furnished proof that it intended to extend labor's antitrust immunity to include agreements with nonlabor parties, or that it thought antitrust liability under the existing statutes would be inconsistent with the NLRA. The bill introduced by Senator McClellan two years later provides even less support for that proposition. Like most bills introduced in Congress, it never reached a vote.

IV

Although we hold that the union's agreement with Connell is subject to the federal antitrust laws, it does not follow that state antitrust law may apply as well. The Court has held repeatedly that federal law pre-empts state remedies that interfere with federal labor policy or with specific provisions of the NLRA. The use of state antitrust law to regulate union activities in aid of organization must also be pre-empted because it creates a substantial risk of conflict with policies central to federal labor law. . . .

V

Neither the District Court nor the Court of Appeals decided whether the agreement between Local 100 and Connell, if subject to the antitrust laws, would constitute an agreement that restrains trade within the meaning of the Sherman Act. The issue was not briefed and argued fully in this Court. Accordingly, we remand for consideration whether the agreement violated the Sherman Act.[19]

Reversed in part, affirmed in part, and remanded.[25]

STEWART, J., with whom DOUGLAS, J., BRENNAN, J., and MARSHALL, J., join, dissenting. . . .

Contrary to the assertion in the Court's opinion, the deliberate congressional decision to make §303 the exclusive private remedy for unlawful secondary activity is clearly relevant to the question of Local 100's antitrust liability in the case before us. The Court is correct, of course, in noting that §8(e)'s prohibition of "hot cargo" agreements was not added to the Act until 1959, and that §303 was not then amended to cover §8(e) violations standing alone. But as part of the 1959 amendments designed to close "technical loopholes" perceived in the Taft-Hartley Act, Congress amended §8(b)(4) to make it an unfair labor practice for a labor

19. In addition to seeking a declaratory judgment that the agreement with Local 100 violated the antitrust laws, Connell sought a permanent injunction against further picketing to coerce execution of the contract in litigation. Connell obtained a temporary restraining order against the picketing on January 21, 1971, and therefore executed the contract — under protest — with Local 100 on March 28, 1971. So far as the record in this case reveals, there has been no further picketing at Connell's construction sites. Accordingly, there is no occasion for us to consider whether the Norris-LaGuardia Act forbids such an injunction where the specific agreement sought by the union is illegal, or to determine whether, within the meaning of the Norris-LaGuardia Act, there was a "labor dispute" between these parties. If the Norris-LaGuardia Act were applicable to this picketing, injunctive relief would not be available under the antitrust laws. See United States v. Hutcheson, 312 U.S. 219 (1941). If the agreement in question is held on remand to be invalid under federal antitrust laws, we cannot anticipate that Local 100 will resume picketing to obtain or enforce an illegal agreement.

[25] Douglas, J., wrote a separate dissent.

organization to threaten or coerce a neutral employer, either directly or through its employees, where an object of the secondary pressure is to force the employer to enter into an agreement prohibited by §8(e). At the same time, Congress expanded the scope of the §303 damages remedy to allow recovery of the actual damages sustained as a result of a union's engaging in secondary activity to force an employer to sign an agreement in violation of §8(e). In short, Congress has provided an employer like Connell with a fully effective private damages remedy for the allegedly unlawful union conduct involved in this case.

The essence of Connell's complaint is that it was coerced by Local 100's picketing into "conspiring" with the union by signing an agreement that limited its ability to subcontract mechanical work on a competitive basis. If, as the Court today holds, the subcontracting agreement is not within the construction industry proviso to §8(e), then Local 100's picketing to induce Connell to sign the agreement constituted a §8(b)(4) unfair labor practice, and was therefore also unlawful under §303(a).[8] Accordingly, Connell has the right to sue Local 100 for damages sustained as a result of Local 100's unlawful secondary activity pursuant to §303(b), 29 U.S.C. §187(b). Although "limited to actual, compensatory damages," Teamsters v. Morton, 377 U.S., at 260, Connell would be entitled under §303 to recover all damages to its business that resulted from the union's coercive conduct, including any provable damage caused by Connell's inability to subcontract mechanical work to nonunion firms. Similarly, any nonunion mechanical contractor who believes his business has been harmed by Local 100's having coerced Connell into signing the subcontracting agreement is entitled to sue the union for compensatory damages; for §303 broadly grants its damages action to "[w]hoever shall be injured in his business or property" by reason of a labor organization's engaging in §8(b)(4) unfair labor practice.[9]

8. If, contrary to the Court's conclusion, Congress intended what it said in the proviso to §8(e), then the subcontracting agreement is valid and, under the view of the Board and those Courts of Appeals that have considered the question, Local 100's picketing to obtain the agreement would also be lawful. Connell would therefore have neither a remedy under §303 nor one with the Board.

It would seem necessarily to follow that conduct specifically authorized by Congress in the National Labor Relations Act could not by itself be the basis for federal antitrust liability, unless the Court intends to return to the era when the judiciary frustrated congressional design by determining for itself "what public policy in regard to the industrial struggle demands." Duplex Printing Press Co. v. Deering, 254 U.S. 443, 485 (Brandeis, J., dissenting). See United States v. Hutcheson, 312 U.S. 219. In my view, however, even if Local 100's conduct was unlawful, Connell may not seek to invoke the sanctions of the antitrust laws. Accordingly, I find it unnecessary to decide in this case whether the subcontracting agreement entered into by Connell and Local 100 is within the ambit of the construction-industry proviso to §8(e), and if it is, whether it was permissible for Local 100 to utilize peaceful picketing to induce Connell to sign the agreement.

9. If Connell and Local 100 had entered into a purely voluntary "hot cargo" agreement in violation of §8(e), an injured nonunion mechanical subcontractor would have no §303 remedy because the union would not have engaged in any §8(b)(4) unfair labor practice.

Moreover, there is considerable evidence in the legislative materials indicating that in expanding the scope of §303 to include a remedy for secondary pressure designed to force an employer to sign an illegal "hot cargo" clause and in restricting the remedies for violation of §8(e) itself to those available from the Board, Congress in 1959 made the same deliberate choice to exclude antitrust remedies as was made by the 1947 Congress. . . . The judicial imposition of "independent federal remedies" not intended by Congress, no less than the application of state law to union conduct that is either protected or prohibited by federal labor law, threatens "to upset the balance of power between labor and management expressed in our national labor policy." Teamsters v. Morton, 377 U.S., at 260. See Carpenters v. NLRB, 357 U.S., at 98-100; National Woodwork Mfrs. Assn. v. NLRB, 386 U.S., at 619-620. Accordingly, the judgment before us should be affirmed.

Notes

1. Do you agree with the following?

> Justice Powell's opinion is admirably short, but that should not disguise the fact that he is undertaking to lay down general principles of antitrust immunity, left confused after *Pennington* and *Jewel Tea.* The *Hutcheson* immunity has now been all but swallowed up by the "business conspiracy" exception of *Allen Bradley* — the immunity is lost when an unwilling employer signs a bargaining agreement, as was implicit in Justice White's plurality opinion in *Jewel Tea.* The parameters of nonstatutory exemption are determined by accommodating the national labor policy (in *Connell,* a

---

The subcontractor, however, would still be able to seek the full range of Board remedies available for a §8(e) unfair labor practice. Moreover, if Connell had truly agreed to limit its subcontracting without any coercion whatsoever on the part of Local 100, the affected subcontractor might well have a valid antitrust claim on the ground that Local 100 and Connell were engaged in the type of conspiracy aimed at third parties with which this Court dealt in Allen Bradley Co. v. Electrical Workers, 325 U.S. 797. At the very least, an antitrust suit by an injured subcontractor under circumstances in which Congress had failed to provide any form of private remedy for damage resulting from an illegal "hot cargo" agreement would present a very different question from the one before us — a question which it is not now necessary to answer. Cf. Meat Cutters v. Jewel Tea Co., 381 U.S. 676, 708 n. 9 (opinion of Goldberg, J.).

On the other hand, the signatory of a purely voluntary agreement that violates §8(e) is fully protected from any damages that might result from the illegal "hot cargo" agreement by his ability simply to ignore the contract provision that violates §8(e). If the union should attempt to enforce the illicit "hot cargo" clause through any form of coercion, the employer may then bring a §303 damages suit or may file an unfair labor practice charge with the Board. See 29 U.S.C. §158(b)(4)(B). Since §8(e) provides that any prohibited agreement is "unenforceable and void," any union effort to invoke legal processes to compel the neutral employer to comply with his purely voluntary agreement would obviously be unavailing.

policy favoring collective bargaining) and the policy "favoring free competition in business markets."

On the facts of *Connell* the accommodation was not overly difficult. The product market restraint was greater than what was necessary to eliminate competition over wages and working conditions. In other cases the scope of the national labor policy may tolerate a greater (e.g., *Jewel Tea*) or lesser restraint. The important point is that, notwithstanding *Connell's* critics, the test emphatically does not represent a return to the pre-*Apex* days when the federal courts established labor policy in the guise of antitrust regulation. Unlike then, when labor policy turned on the predilection of the individual federal judge, there were now forty years of labor policies set out by Congress and by the agency and courts directed to carry out those policies.

2. How should courts applying *Connell* dispose of antitrust attacks on the union's actions in *National Woodwork*, supra at p. 471, and *Enterprise Association*, supra at p. 479? You should be aware that every "right to control" case has involved a union bargaining agreement with a multiemployer association of specialty subcontractors, and that many of the agreements have provided liquidated damage remedies in case of breach by a subcontractor.

3. Justice Powell argues that the union's tactic in *Connell* "has substantial anticompetitive effects, both actual and potential, that would not follow naturally from the elimination of competition over wages and working conditions." Which of the effects that he cites are actual, and which are potential? Will the union have the opportunity to prove that the "potential" effects are not present in this case? It might begin, for instance, by proving that its collective bargaining agreements in Dallas contained only mandatory subjects of bargaining.

4. What do you think of an argument that many, or even all, secondary boycotts are now also antitrust violations? The argument proceeds as follows. Assume that the union has picketed employer *A* to force it to cease doing business with employer *B*, with whom the union has its dispute. Employer *A*, acting on the advice of its attorney, who has read *Connell*, agrees with the union that the firm will cease business with employer *B*. Now there is an agreement between a union and an employer, so the statutory immunity is lost.

The plaintiff's attorney — either employer *A* or *B* can be the plaintiff — now must exercise some imagination to suggest anticompetitive effects that the union's acts may have. This should not be overly difficult in many cases because the effects need not be real, only "potential." Once anticompetitive effects are identified, national labor policy is consulted. But national labor policy does not help the union because this is a secondary boycott and condemned by the labor statute. Thus the nonstatutory exemption is lost.

Finally, the matter of a substantive violation is easily disposed of in the plaintiff's favor. Because the labor exemption has been lost, ordinary antitrust rules apply. First, the defendant has engaged in a group boycott/refusal to deal. This occasions per se antitrust liability under any number of Supreme Court nonlabor cases. Second, the union fares no better under a rule of reason test because the rule of reason protects only activities that yield net efficiencies. Union acts do not yield net efficiencies.

5. There is no unanimity in the circuit courts on what test of substantive antitrust liability applies to a union defendant that has lost its antitrust exemption after a *Connell* analysis. Several circuits have adopted a rule of reason analysis.[26] The Third Circuit in a secondary boycott context has applied a group boycott per se analysis.[27] The Fifth Circuit has applied the "commercial competition" test of *Apex*.[28]

6. Consider the question left open in *Connell*, the relation between §8(b)(4) liability and antitrust liability. The majority and dissenting opinions agreed that in 1947 Congress chose not to increase the unions' antitrust exposure but to subject them to §8(b)(4). Does this mean that Congress was singling out secondary boycotts as a category of antitrust violations to which antitrust sanctions would not apply? Stated otherwise, if most of the union's activities in *Allen Bradley* would now be prohibited by §8(b)(4), does that mean Congress intended to overrule *Allen Bradley* as a matter of antitrust liability?

One commentator has argued:[29]

> Before the Landrum-Griffin Act of 1959, a union could lawfully negotiate a bargaining agreement clause requiring one employer to cease doing business with another, although the union could not enforce it through concerted action.[139] Concerted action to enforce the clause, such as a strike or a refusal to handle goods, violated §8(b)(4) of the National Labor Relations Act and occasioned several remedies: an injunction in federal district court at the request of the National Labor Relations Board's General Counsel pursuant to §10(l) of the statute, a cease and desist order from the Board, and a damage action in federal district court by an injured private party pursuant to §303 of the Labor-Management Relations Act. The cases suggested, however, that such a clause could be peacefully enforced through grievance arbitration or a breach of contract suit.[144]

[26] See Smith v. Pro Football, 593 F.2d 1173, 1177-1182 (D.C. Cir. 1978); Berman Enterprises v. ILA Local 333, 644 F.2d 930, 936 (2nd Cir. 1981), cert. denied, 454 U.S. 965 (1982); Ackerman-Chillingworth v. Pacific Electrical Contractors Assn., 579 (9th Cir. 1978), cert. denied, 439 U.S. 1089 (1979).

[27] See Larry V. Muko v. Southwestern Pa. Bldg. & Constr. Trades Council, 670 F.2d 421, 426 (3rd Cir.), cert. denied, 103 S. Ct. 229 (1982).

[28] Carpenters Local 1846 v. Pratt-Farnsworth, 690 F.2d 489 (5th Cir. 1982), cert. denied, 104 S. Ct. 335 (1983).

[29] Leslie, supra n. [1] at 1227-1229.

139. Carpenters Local 1976 v. NLRB (Sand Door), 357 U.S. 93 (1958).

144. 357 U.S. at 108.

To prohibit both peaceful enforcement of such a clause and an employer's voluntary compliance with it, the Congress in 1959 added §8(e) to the NLRA. That section makes entering into an agreement with such a clause an unfair labor practice and declares these clauses "unenforceable and void." Persuaded that two industries warranted special treatment, the 1959 Congress added two exceptions, or "provisos," in §8(e). One excepted the apparel and clothing industry, and the one relevant to the *Connell* case declared §8(e) inapplicable to construction industry clauses covering the subcontracting of jobsite work. At the same time, §10(1) of the NLRA was amended to provide for injunctive relief against §8(e) clauses on the General Counsel's petition, and §8(b)(4) was amended to make it an unfair labor practice to use coercion to obtain a clause unlawful under §8(e). Section 303 of the LMRA, however, was not amended to include damage actions for §8(e) violations.

In *Connell,* Local 100 argued that its agreement with Connell was either expressly permitted by the construction industry proviso to §8(e), and thus saved from antitrust liability, or condemned by §8(e). If the clause violated §8(e), the union argued, NLRA remedies were exclusive. A majority of the Court rejected both conclusions. First, Justice Powell held that the clause fell outside the construction industry proviso because Congress had not intended the proviso to give construction industry unions a weapon for "top-down organizing," at least when the union represented none of the signatory firm's employees and when the clause would apply to jobsites where no union members were working. Second, he held that the secondary boycott remedies under the labor statutes did not preclude the application of antitrust remedies. Justice Stewart's dissent focused on the latter holding.

Quoting from the legislative history of the 1947 NLRA amendments, which enacted §§8(b)(4), 10(1), and 303, Justice Stewart demonstrated that Congress had explicitly refused to expand the coverage of the antitrust laws to secondary boycotts and thus to subject them to treble damages, attorneys' fees, and private injunctive actions. Although §8(e) was not added until 1959, Justice Stewart reasoned that the earlier legislative history was relevant because §8(e) was added to these 1947 secondary boycott remedies in order to close "technical loopholes." The labor acts, he concluded, provided a "fully effective" remedy for an employer like Connell. Justice Powell rejected the 1947 legislative history as irrelevant because the enactment critical to *Connell,* §8(e), was passed in 1959[155] when no similar legislative history argued for the exclusiveness of labor law remedies.[156]

155. Justice Powell also noted that §303 was not amended in 1959 to provide a damage remedy for violations of §8(e). See 421 U.S. at 634 n. 16.

156. Id. at 634. In 1947, Congress carefully fashioned cease and desist, injunctive, and damage remedies for secondary boycotts and made sharp distinctions between administrative and private enforcement. In 1959, Congress refined the existing framework. To ask whether Congress intended to supplant antitrust remedies when it passed the secondary boycott provision begs the question, for in both 1947 and 1959 the *Hutcheson* immunity stood largely intact, or to put it more precisely, the narrowness of the *Hutcheson* holding the union could be liable under the antitrust laws for engaging in a secondary boycott or

Neither Justice Powell nor Justice Stewart considered the more fundamental question whether the framework of the labor laws requires that secondary boycott remedies be exclusive even without the direction of express legislative history. If the antitrust laws and the secondary boycott provisions of the labor laws seek the same objectives,[157] the existence of labor laws describing the forbidden conduct with considerable specificity, and providing carefully thought-out remedies, might preclude application of the more generalized antitrust law with its quite different remedies.[158] The secondary boycott prohibitions and the antitrust laws, however, have different objectives. The secondary boycott laws are grounded in the argument that permitting the union to enlist the aid of a secondary employer in a dispute is unfair to the primary employer; that it is unfair to subject a secondary employer to union economic coercion merely because the secondary does business with the primary employer, whose labor policies the secondary does not control; and that secondary boycotts injure the public by needlessly proliferating primary disputes. By contrast, the antitrust laws seek to encourage economic efficiencies through reliance on the competitive process.[159]

These objectives may not conflict, but they are not identical. When a union participates in a business cartel that fixes prices, regulates output, or allocates markets, it has moved beyond the scope of national labor policy, for the labor statutes do not regulate union conduct so as to maintain a free market in the sale of goods and services. National labor policy is not harmed when union conduct is subjected to both labor and antitrust remedies, provided that the conduct violates both statutes.[160] For example, a

---

for exacting a hot cargo clause from an unwilling firm. In short, there were no antitrust remedies to supplant. The Court should have squarely faced these issues in *Connell* rather than relying on the fact that §8(e) was passed in 1959, not 1947.

157. The Third Circuit recently took this view:

> [Sections] 8(b)(4) and 8(e) . . . are, like the Sherman Act, statutes reflecting the basic federal economic policy against restraints upon competition in the marketplace for goods and services as distinct from the labor market. Thus §§8(b)(4) and 8(e) reinforce rather than conflict with the basic policy of the antitrust laws. . . .

Consolidated Express, Inc. v. New York Shipping Assn., 602 F.2d 494, 513 (3d Cir. 1979), vacated and remanded mem., 100 S. Ct. 3040 (1980).

158. One suspects, for instance, that Justice Powell's view on the *Connell* facts would have been different if the 1959 Congress had amended §303's damage provision to say "but not for a violation of §8(e)." In effect, Congress did precisely that when it amended §10(1) to provide for injunctions against §8(e) clauses and amended §303 to cover a strike to secure a §8(e) clause, but not to provide for damages for the clause itself.

159. Other policies may also underlie the antitrust statutes, but it is unnecessary to discuss that issue here. The other policies that have been suggested — for instance, the protection of small businesses — do not affect the point made in the text.

160. If union conduct were found to violate the antitrust laws without a showing of a restraint on commercial competition, the argument for the exclusiveness of labor law remedies would be persuasive. A decision to condemn conduct by subjecting it to specified remedies is not the same as condemning it for any and all purposes; depending on the remedy provided, conduct is more or less prohibited. Supplementing the labor laws' remedies can be as great an interference with the fabric of national labor policy as condemning conduct that labor policy permits. The preemption cases establish that much. See, e.g., Teamsters Local 20 v. Morton, 377 U.S. 252, 259-260 (1963); Garner v. Teamsters Local 776, 346 U.S. 485, 498-499 (1953).

union secondary boycott that enforces a cartel agreement fixing product prices should be found to violate both statutes.[161] It is essential, however, that the union conduct violate the antitrust statutes as well as the labor statutes. The labor laws either prohibit many union actions — for example, recognitional picketing for more than thirty days without filing an election petition — or render them "unprotected" — for example, "quickie strikes." It would be capricious to subject these actions to antitrust scrutiny because they happen to violate one or another of the NLRA sections.[164]

H.A. ARTISTS & ASSOCIATES v. ACTORS' EQUITY ASSOCIATION
451 U.S. 704 (1981)

STEWART, J.

The respondent, Actors' Equity Association (Equity), is a union representing the vast majority of stage actors and actresses in the United States. It enters into collective-bargaining agreements with theatrical producers that specify minimum wages and other terms and conditions of employment for those whom it represents. The petitioners are independent theatrical agents who place actors and actresses in jobs with producers. The Court of Appeals for the Second Circuit held that the respondents' system of regulation of theatrical agents is immune from antitrust liability by reason of the statutory labor exemption from the antitrust laws. We granted certiorari to consider the availability of that exemption in the circumstances presented by this case.

I

A

Equity is a national union that has represented stage actors and actresses since early in this century. Currently representing approximately 23,000 actors and actresses, it has collective-bargaining agreements with virtually all major theatrical producers in New York City, on and off-Broadway, and with most other theatrical producers throughout the United States. The terms negotiated with producers are the minimum

161. Even conduct that the labor statutes expressly authorize should, in a proper case, be subject to antitrust remedies. For example, suppose that a union's agreement with a general contractor falls within the express proviso to §8(e) but the clause is used to enforce a cartel's market allocation plan. The agreement should be unlawful under the antitrust laws notwithstanding its sanctity as a matter of labor policy.

164. Cf. Cox, Labor Law Preemption Revisited, 85 Harv. L. Rev. 1337, 1344 (1972) (improper to permit state law to condemn and remedy union conduct on sole ground that the NLRA also condemns the conduct). It makes even less sense to take the further step and hold that, when conduct violates the NLRA, both the nonstatutory exemption is unavailable and a substantive violation has been committed.

conditions of employment (called "scale"); an actor or actress is free to negotiate wages or terms more favorable than the collectively bargained minima.

Theatrical agents are independent contractors who negotiate contracts and solicit employment for their clients. The agents do not participate in the negotiation of collective-bargaining agreements between Equity and the theatrical producers. If an agent succeeds in obtaining employment for a client, he receives a commission based on a percentage of the client's earnings. Agents who operate in New York City must be licensed as employment agencies and are regulated by the New York City Department of Consumer Affairs pursuant to New York law, which provides that the maximum commission a theatrical agent may charge his client is 10% of the client's compensation.

In 1928, concerned with the high unemployment rates in the legitimate theater and the vulnerability of actors and actresses to abuses by theatrical agents,[3] including the extraction of high commissions that tended to undermine collectively bargaining rates of compensation, Equity unilaterally established a licensing system for the regulation of agents. The regulations permitted Equity members to deal only with those agents who obtained Equity licenses and thereby agreed to meet the conditions of representation prescribed by Equity. Those members who dealt with nonlicensed agents were subject to union discipline.

The system established by the Equity regulations was immediately challenged.[4] In Edelstein v. Gillmore, 35 F.2d 723, the Court of Appeals for the Second Circuit concluded that the regulations were a lawful effort to improve the employment conditions of Equity members. In an opinion written by Judge Swan and joined by Judge Augustus N. Hand, the court said:

> The evils of unregulated employment agencies (using this term broadly to include also the personal representative) are set forth in the defendants' affidavits and are corroborated by common knowledge. . . . Hence the requirement that, as a condition to writing new business with Equity's members, old contracts with its members must be made to conform to the new standards, does not seem to us to justify an inference that the primary purpose of the requirement is infliction of injury upon plaintiff, and other personal representatives in a similar situation, rather than the protection of the supposed interests of Equity's members. *The terms they insist upon are calculated to secure from personal representatives better and more impartial services, at uniform and cheaper rates, and to improve conditions of employment of actors by theater managers.* Undoubtedly the defendants intend to compel

3. Such vulnerability was, and still remains, particularly acute for actors and actresses without established professional reputations, who have always comprised the overwhelming majority of Equity's members.

4. The challenge was grounded on allegations of common law tortious interference with business relationships.

> the plaintiff to give up rights under existing contracts which do not conform to the new standards set up by Equity, but, as already indicated *their motive in so doing is to benefit themselves and their fellow actors in the economic struggle.* The financial loss to plaintiff is incidental to this purpose. 35 F.2d, at 726 (emphasis added).

The essential elements of Equity's regulation of theatrical agents have remained unchanged since 1928. A member of Equity is prohibited, on pain of union discipline, from using an agent who has not, through the mechanism of obtaining an Equity license (called a "franchise") agreed to comply with the regulations. The most important of the regulations requires that a licensed agent must renounce any right to take a commission on an employment contract under which an actor or actress receives scale wages.[8] To the extent a contract includes provisions under which an actor or actress will sometimes receive scale pay — for rehearsals or "chorus" employment, for example — and sometimes more, the regulations deny the agent any commission on the scale portions of the contract. Licensed agents are also precluded from taking commissions on out-of-town expense money paid to their clients. Moreover, commissions are limited on wages within 10% of scale pay,[9] and an agent must allow his client to terminate a representation contract if the agent is not successful in procuring employment within a specified period.[10] Finally, agents are required to pay franchise fees to Equity. The fee is $200 for the initial franchise, $60 a year thereafter for each agent, and $40 for any sub-agent working in the office of another. These fees are deposited by Equity in its general treasury and are not segregated from other union funds.

In 1977, after a dispute between Equity and Theatrical Artists Representatives Associates (TARA) — a trade association representing theatri-

8. The minimum, or "scale" wage varies. In August 1977, for example, the minimum weekly salary was $335 for Broadway performances, and $175 for performances off-Broadway. Scale wages are set by a collective-bargaining agreement between Equity and the producers, to which the agents are not parties. When an agent represents an actor or actress whose professional reputation is not sufficient to demand a salary higher than scale, the agent hopes to develop a relationship that will become continually more remunerative as the performer's professional reputation grows, and with it the power to demand an ever higher salary. No agent is required to represent an actor or actress whom he does not wish to represent.

9. It is Equity's view that commissions in the industry are not necessarily related to efforts by the agents, and that an agent often functions as little more than an "order taker," who is able to collect a percentage of a client's wages for the duration of a show for doing little more than answering a producer's telephone call, Indeed, an agent may collect a commission on the salary of an actor or actress he represents even if the client obtains the job without the agent.

10. Equity argues that this restriction is necessary because there is an incentive for agents to represent as many actors and actresses as possible — and not necessarily to serve them as well — because an agent receives a commission whenever his client is employed at a salary higher than scale, regardless of the extent of his involvement in obtaining employment for the client.

cal agents — a group of agents, including the petitioners, resigned from TARA because of TARA's decision to abide by Equity's regulations. These agents also informed Equity that they would not accept Equity's regulations, or apply for franchises. The petitioners instituted this lawsuit in May 1978, contending that Equity's regulations of theatrical agents violated §§1 and 2 of the Sherman Act.

B

The District Court found, after a bench trial, that Equity's creation and maintenance of the agency franchise system were fully protected by the statutory labor exemptions from the antitrust laws, and accordingly dismissed the petitioners' complaint. Among its factual conclusions, the trial court found that in the theatrical industry, agents play a critical role in securing employment for actors and actresses:

> As a matter of general industry practice, producers seek actors and actresses for their productions through agents. Testimony in this case convincingly established that an actor without an agent does not have the same access to producers or the same opportunity to be seriously considered for a part as does an actor who has an agent. Even principal interviews, in which producers are required to interview all actors who want to be considered for principal roles, do not eliminate the need for an agent, who may have a greater chance of gaining an audition for his client. . . .
>
> Testimony confirmed that agents play an integral role in the industry; without an agent, an actor would have significantly lesser chances of gaining employment. 478 F. Supp., at 497, 502.

The court also found "no evidence to suggest the existence of any conspiracy between Actors' Equity and TARA or between Actors' Equity and Producers," and concluded that "[t]he Actors Equity franchising system was employed by Actors Equity for the purpose of protecting the wages and working conditions of its members." Id., at 499.

The Court of Appeals unanimously affirmed the judgment of the District Court. It determined that the threshold issue was, under United States v. Hutcheson, 312 U.S. 219, 232, whether Equity's franchising system involved any combination between Equity and any "non-labor groups" or persons who are not "parties to a labor dispute." If it did, the court reasoned, the protection of the statutory labor exemption would not apply.

First, the Court of Appeals held that the District Court had not been clearly erroneous in finding no agreement, explicit or tacit, between Equity and the producers to establish or police the franchising system. Next, the court turned to the relationship between the union and those agents who had agreed to become franchised, in order to determine whether those agreements would divest Equity's system of agency regulation of the statutory exemption. Relying on American Federation of Musicians v. Carroll, 391 U.S. 99, the court concluded that the agents were themselves a "labor group," because of their substantial "economic inter-relationship" with Equity, under which "the union could not eliminate wage competition among its members without regulation of the fees of the agents." 622 F.2d, at 650, 651. Accordingly, since the elimination of wage competition is plainly within the area of a union's legitimate self-interest, the court concluded that the exemption was applicable.[11]

After deciding that the central feature of Equity's franchising system — the union's exaction of an agreement by agents not to charge commissions on certain types of work — was immune from antitrust challenge, the Court of Appeals turned to the petitioners' challenge of the franchise fees exacted from agents. Equity had argued that the fees were necessary to meet its expenses in administering the franchise system, but no evidence was presented at trial to show that the costs justified the fees actually levied. The Court of Appeals suggested that if the exactions exceeded the true costs, they could not legally be collected, as such exactions would be unconnected with any of the goals of national labor policy that justify the labor antitrust exemption. Despite the lack of any cost evidence at trial, however, the appellate court reasoned that the fees were sufficiently low that a remand to the District Court on this point "would not serve any useful purpose." 622 F.2d, at 651.

II

A

Labor unions are lawful combinations that serve the collective interests of workers, but they also possess the power to control the character of competition in an industry. Accordingly, there is an inherent tension between national antitrust policy, which seeks to maximize competition, and national labor policy, which encourages cooperation among workers to improve the conditions of employment.[12] In the years immediately following passage of the Sherman Act, courts enjoined strikes as unlawful restraints of trade when a union's conduct or objectives were deemed "socially or economically harmful." Duplex Printing Press Co. v. Deering, 254 U.S. 443, 485 (Brandeis, J., dissenting). In response to these practices, Congress acted, first in the Clayton Act, 38 Stat. 731, and later

11. The Court of Appeals recognized that even if there had been an agreement between Equity and a "non-labor group," the agreement might still have been protected from the antitrust laws under the "non-statutory" exemption. 622 F.2d, at 649, n. 1. See Connell Construction Co. v. Plumbers Local 100, 421 U.S. 616, 622. See n. 19, infra.

12. See generally Meltzer, Labor Unions, Collective Bargaining and the Antitrust Law, 32 U. Chi. L. Rev. 655 (1965); Winter, Collective Bargaining and Competition: The Application of Antitrust Standards to Union Activities, 73 Yale L.J. 14 (1963). See also Leslie, Principles of Labor Antitrust, 66 Va. L. Rev. 1183 (1980).

in the Norris-LaGuardia Act, 47 Stat. 70, to immunize labor unions and labor disputes from challenge under the Sherman Act.

Section 6 of the Clayton Act, 15 U.S.C. §17, declares that human labor "is not a commodity or article of commerce," and immunizes from antitrust liability labor organizations and their members "lawfully carrying out" their "legitimate objectives." Section 20 of the Act prohibits injunctions against specified employee activities, such as strikes and boycotts, that are undertaken in the employees' self-interest and that occur in the course of disputes "concerning terms or conditions of employment" and states that none of the specified acts can be "held to be [a] violation . . . of any law of the United States." 29 U.S.C. §52. This protection is re-emphasized and expanded in the Norris-LaGuardia Act, which prohibits federal court injunctions against single or organized employees engaged in enumerated activities, and specifically forbids such injunctions notwithstanding the claim of an unlawful combination or conspiracy. While the Norris-LaGuardia Act's bar of federal court labor injunctions is not explicitly phrased as an exemption from the antitrust laws, it has been interpreted broadly as a statement of congressional policy that the courts must not use the antitrust laws as a vehicle to interfere in labor disputes.

In United States v. Hutcheson, 312 U.S. 29, the Court held that labor unions acting in their self-interest and not in combination with nonlabor groups enjoy a statutory exemption from Sherman Act liability. After describing the congressional responses to judicial interference in union activity, id., at 229-230, the Court declared that "[s]o long as a union acts in its self-interest and does not combine with non-labor groups, the licit and the illicit under §20 [of the Clayton Act] are not to be distinguished by any judgment regarding the wisdom or unwisdom, the rightness or wrongness, the selfishness or unselfishness of the end of which the particular union activities are the means," Id., at 232 (footnote omitted). The Court explained that this exemption derives not only from the Clayton Act, but also from the Norris-LaGuardia Act, particularly its definition of a "labor dispute," see n. 14, supra, in which Congress "reasserted the original purpose of the Clayton Act by infusing into it the immunized trade union activities as redefined by the later Act." 312 U.S., at 236. Thus under *Hutcheson,* no federal injunction may issue over a "labor dispute," and "§20 [of the Clayton Act] removes all such allowable conduct from the taint of being a 'violation of any law of the United States,' including the Sherman Act." Ibid.[16]

The statutory exemption does not apply when a union combines with

16. See also Apex Hosiery Co. v. Leader, 310 U.S. 469. There, in the Term preceding that in which the *Hutcheson* case was decided, the Court reasoned that the Sherman Act prohibits only restraints on "commercial competition," id., at 497, 499, 510-511 — or those market restraints designed to monopolize supply, control prices, or allocate product distribution — and that unions are not liable where they merely further their own goals in the labor market.

a "non-labor group." Hutcheson, 312 U.S., at 232. Accordingly, antitrust immunity is forfeited when a union combines with one or more employers in an effort to restrain trade. In Allen Bradley v. Electrical Workers, 325 U.S. 797, for example, the Court held that a union had violated the Sherman Act when it combined with manufacturers and contractors to erect a sheltered local business market in order "to bar all other businessmen from [the market], and to charge the public prices above a competitive level." Id., at 809.[17] The Court indicated that the union efforts would, standing alone, be exempt from antitrust liability, ibid., but because the union had not acted unilaterally, the exemption was denied.[18] Congress "intended to outlaw business monopolies. A business monopoly is no less such because a union participates, and such participation is a violation of the Act." Id., at 811.[19]

B

The Court of Appeals properly recognized that the threshold issue was to determine whether or not Equity's franchising of agents involved any combination between Equity and any "non-labor groups," or persons who are not "parties to a labor dispute." 622 F.2d, at 649 (quoting Hutcheson, 312 U.S., at 232).[20] And the court's conclusion that the trial court had not been clearly erroneous in its finding that there was no combination between Equity and the theatrical producers[21] to create or maintain the franchise system is amply supported by the record.

The more difficult problem is whether the combination between Eq-

17. In Hunt v. Crumboch, 325 U.S. 821, decided the same day as *Allen Bradley,* the Court ruled that the labor exemption protected a union's boycott of a truck hauler through successful secondary pressure on purchasers of the hauler's services with whom the union had contracts, because of the absence of union participation in a conspiracy with the hauler's competitors. See 325 U.S., at 824; *Meltzer,* supra n. 12, at 677, and n. 74.

18. United Mine Workers v. Pennington, 381 U.S. 657, also dealt with a union combination with employers, but the grounds of decision were unrelated to the antitrust exemption.

19. Even where there are union agreements with nonlabor groups that may have the effect of sheltering the nonlabor groups from competition in product markets, the Court has recognized a "nonstatutory" exemption to shield such agreements if they are intimately related to the union's vital concerns of wages, hours and working conditions. See, e.g., Meat Cutters v. Jewel Tea, 381 U.S. 676. . . . Neither the District Court nor the Court of Appeals in this case decided whether the nonstatutory exemption would independently shield the respondent from the petitioners' antitrust claims. See n. 11, supra.

20. Of course, a party seeking refuge in the statutory exemption must be a bona fide labor organization, and not an independent contractor or entrepreneur. See Los Angeles Meat Division Local 626 v. United States, 371 U.S. 94; Columbia River Packers Assn. v. Hinton, 315 U.S. 143. See generally 1 Areeda & Turner, Antitrust (1978) §229c, at 195-198. There is no dispute about Equity's status as a bona fide labor organization.

21. As the employers of Equity's members, producers are plainly a "non-labor group." Employers almost always will be a "non-labor group," although an exception has been recognized, for example, when the employer himself is in job competition with his employees. See American Federation of Musicians v. Carroll, 391 U.S. 99 (orchestra leaders who both lead an orchestra and play an instrument).

uity and the agents who agreed to become franchised was a combination with a "non-labor group." The answer to this question is best understood in light of American Federation of Musicians v. Carroll, 391 U.S. 99. There, four orchestra leaders, members of the American Federation of Musicians, brought an action based on the Sherman Act challenging the union's unilateral system of regulating "club dates," or one-time musical engagements. These regulations, inter alia, enforced a closed shop; required orchestra leaders to engage a minimum number of "sidemen," or instrumentalists; prescribed minimum prices for local engagements; prescribed higher minimum prices for traveling orchestras; and permitted leaders to deal only with booking agents licensed by the union.

Without disturbing the finding of the Court of Appeals that the orchestra leaders were employers and independent contractors, the Court concluded that they were nonetheless a "labor group" and parties to a "labor dispute" within the meaning of the Norris-LaGuardia Act, and thus that their involvement in the union regulatory scheme was not an unlawful combination between "labor" and "non-labor" groups. The Court agreed with the trial court that the applicable test was whether there was "job or wage competition or some other economic interrelationship affecting legitimate union interests between the union members and the independent contractors." 391 U.S., at 106.

The Court also upheld the restrictions on booking agents, who were *not* involved in job or wage competition with union members. Accordingly, these restrictions had to meet the "other economic interrelationship" branch of the disjunctive test quoted above. And the test was met because those restrictions were "at least as intimately bound up with the subject of wages '. . . as the price floors.'" Id., at 113. The Court noted that the booking agent restrictions had been adopted, in part, because agents had "charged exorbitant fees, and booked engagements for musicians at wages . . . below union scale."

C

The restrictions challenged by the petitioners in this case are very similar to the agent restrictions upheld in the *Carroll* case.[24] The essential

24. Several cases before *Carroll* also upheld union regulation of the practices of independent entrepreneurs affecting the wages or working conditions of union members. See Milk Wagon Drivers' Union v. Lake Valley Co., 311 U.S. 91; Teamsters Union v. Oliver, 358 U.S. 283 (*Oliver I*); Teamsters Union v. Oliver, 362 U.S. 605 (*Oliver II*). In *Milk Wagon Drivers,* the Court held that the union had engaged in a "labor dispute" within the meaning of the Norris-LaGuardia Act when it attempted to organize independent "vendors" who supplied milk to retail stores. There the union feared that the "vendor system" was designed to escape the payment of union wages and the assumption of union-imposed working conditions. In *Oliver I,* the *Milk Wagon Drivers* decision was invoked to protect from state antitrust challenge a union's successful efforts to prescribe through collective-

features of the regulatory scheme are identical: members are permitted to deal only with agents who have agreed (1) to honor their fiduciary obligations by avoiding conflicts of interest, (2) not to charge excessive commission and (3) not to book members for jobs paying less than the union minimum.[25] And as in *Carroll,* Equity's regulation of agents developed in response to abuses by employment agents who occupy a critical role in the relevant labor market. The agent stands directly between union members and jobs, and is in a powerful position to evade the union's negotiated wage structure.

The peculiar structure of the legitimate theater industry, where work is intermittent, where it is customary if not essential for union members to secure employment through agents, and where agents' fees are calculated as a percentage of a member's wage, makes it impossible for the union to defend even the integrity of the minimum wages it has negotiated without regulation of agency fees.[27] The regulations are "brought within the labor exemption . . . [because they are] necessary to assure that scale wages will be paid. . . ." *Carroll,* 391 U.S., at 112. They "embody a direct frontal attack upon a problem thought to threaten the maintenance of the basic wage structure." Teamsters Union v. Oliver, 358 U.S. 283, at 294. Agents must, therefore, be considered a "labor group," and their controversy with Equity is plainly a "labor dispute" as defined in the Norris-LaGuardia Act: "representation of persons in negotiating, fixing, maintaining, changing, or seeking to arrange terms or conditions of employment, regardless of whether or not the disputants stand in the proximate relation of employer and employee." 29 U.S.C. §113.

Agents perform a function — the representation of union members in the sale of their labor — that in most nonentertainment industries is performed exclusively by unions. In effect, Equity's franchise system

---

bargaining agreements a wage scale for truck drivers, and minimum rental fees for drivers who owned their own trucks. The union feared that driver-owners, whose fees included not only an entrepreneurial component but also a "wage" for the labor of driving, might undercut the union scale by charging a fee that effectively included a sub-scale wage component. The Court stated that "[t]he regulations embod[ied] . . . a direct frontal attack upon a problem thought to threaten the maintenance of the basic wage structure established by the collective bargaining contract." 358 U.S., at 294. See also *Oliver II,* 362 U.S., at 606 (after remand to the state court).

25. . . . The petitioners argue that theatrical agents are indistinguishable from "numerous other groups of persons who merely supply products and services to union members" such as landlords, grocers, accountants and lawyers. But it is clear that agents differ from these groups in two critical respects: the agents control access to jobs and negotiation of the terms of employment. For the actor or actress, therefore, agent commissions are not merely a discretionary expenditure of disposable income, but a virtually inevitable concomitant of obtaining employment.

27. The Court of Appeals found that "the union *cannot* eliminate wage competition among its members without regulation of the fees of the agents." 622 F.2d 647, 651 (emphasis added). Wage competition is prevented not only by the rule precluding commissions on scale jobs. Actors and actresses could also compete over the percentage of their wages they were willing to cede to an agent, subject only to the restrictions imposed by state law.

operates as a substitute for maintaining a hiring hall as the representative of its members seeking employment.

Finally, Equity's regulations are clearly designed to promote the union's legitimate self-interest. Hutcheson, 312 U.S., at 232. In a case such as this, where there is no direct wage or job competition between the union and the group it regulates, the *Carroll* formulation to determine the presence of a nonlabor group — whether there is "some . . . economic interrelationship affecting legitimate union interests . . . ," 391 U.S., at 106 — necessarily resolves this issue.

D

The question remains whether the fees that Equity levies upon the agents who apply for franchises are a permissible component of the exempt regulatory system. We have concluded that Equity's justification for these fees is inadequate. Conceding that *Carroll* did not sanction union extraction of franchise fees from agents, Equity suggests, only in the most general terms, that the fees are somehow related to the basic purposes of its regulations: elimination of wage competition, upholding of the union wage scale, and promotion of fair access to jobs. But even assuming that the fees no more than cover the costs of administering the regulatory system, this is simply another way of saying that without the fees, the union's regulatory efforts would not be subsidized — and that the dues of Equity's members would perhaps have to be increased to offset the loss of a general revenue source. If Equity did not impose these franchise fees upon the agents, there is no reason to believe that any of its legitimate interests would be affected.[31]

III

For the reasons stated, the judgment of the Court of Appeals is affirmed in part and reversed in part, and the case is remanded for proceedings consistent with this opinion.

BRENNAN, J., with whom BURGER, C.J., and MARSHALL, J., join, concurring in part and dissenting in part.

I join all but Part II-D of the Court's opinion. That part holds that respondents' exaction of a franchise fee is not a "permissible component

31. The respondents offer union hiring hall fees as an analogy in support of Equity's collection of franchise fees. In that context, the respondents argue, without citation, a union may impose reasonable fees upon employers to meet the costs of maintaining a union-run hiring hall. But even if the respondents' statement of labor law is correct, the analogy would not be persuasive. Assuming that hiring hall fees are so imposed, the fees are borne by parties who directly benefit from the employment services of the hiring halls and are collected by the entities that provide them. That is not true in the present case.

The view expressed in the separate opinion filed today as to who are the beneficiaries of the franchising system will undoubtedly surprise the agents who brought this lawsuit.

of the exempt regulatory system." Rather, I agree with the Court of Appeals that the approximately $12,000 collected annually in fees is not "incommensurate with Equity's expenses in maintaining a full-time employee to administer the system," 622 F.2d 647, 651 (C.A.2 1980), and thus is not "unconnected with any of the goals of national labor policy which justify the antitrust exemption for labor," ibid.

The Court justifies its conclusion by suggesting that, since the union could increase its dues to offset the revenue lost from invalidation of the fee system, "there is no reason to believe that any of [the union's] legitimate interests would be affected," if the fee system were found to violate the antitrust laws. The union could of course raise its dues, but the issue here is whether the conceded antitrust immunity of the franchising system includes the franchise fee.

I find somewhat incongruous the Court's conclusion that an incident of the overall system constitutes impermissible regulation, but that agents in general may be significantly regulated because they are not a "non-labor group." This incongruity is highlighted by the similarity between union hiring halls and the franchising system, a similarity which the Court itself acknowledges: "Equity's franchise system operates as a substitute for maintaining a hiring hall as the representative of its members seeking employment." The Court disregards this similarity in concluding that the franchising system does not "directly benefit" the agents who are required to pay the fees. It reaches this conclusion by incorrectly assuming that the only parties who directly benefit from the hiring hall and the franchising system are employers and employees and producers and actors, as the case may be. But surely the agents who benefit from the franchising system, which provides an orderly and protective mechanism for pairing actors who seek jobs with producers who seek actors. The system is thus the means by which the agents ultimately receive their commissions; it is as much the source of their livelihood as it is that of the actors.

Because the fee is an incident of a legitimate scheme of regulation and because it is commensurate in amount with the purpose for which it is sought, I would also affirm this holding of the Court of Appeals.

B. FEATHERBEDDING AND UNION SECURITY

1. Featherbedding

NLRB v. GAMBLE ENTERPRISES

345 U.S. 117 (1953)

BURTON, J. . . .

The question here is whether a labor organization engages in an unfair labor practice, within the meaning of §8(b)(6) of the National

Labor Relations Act, when it insists that the management of one of an interstate chain of theaters shall employ a local orchestra to play in connection with certain programs, although that management does not need or want to employ that orchestra. For the reasons hereafter stated, we hold that it does not. . . .

For generations professional musicians have faced a shortage in the local employment needed to yield them a livelihood. They have been confronted with the competition of military bands, traveling bands, foreign musicians on tour, local amateur organizations and, more recently, technological developments in reproduction and broadcasting. To help them conserve local sources of employment, they developed local protective societies. Since 1896, they also have organized and maintained on a national scale the American Federation of Musicians, affiliated with the American Federation of Labor. By 1943, practically all professional instrumental performers and conductors in the United States had joined the Federation, establishing a membership of over 200,000, with 10,000 more in Canada.

The Federation uses its nationwide control of professional talent to help individual members and local unions. It insists that traveling band contracts be subject to its rules, laws and regulations. Article 18, §4, of its By-Laws provides: "Traveling members cannot, without the consent of a Local, play any presentation performances in its jurisdiction unless a local house orchestra is also employed."

From this background we turn to the instant case. For more than 12 years the Palace Theater in Akron, Ohio, has been one of an interstate chain of theaters managed by respondent, Gamble Enterprises, Inc., which is a Washington corporation with its principal office in New York. Before the decline of vaudeville and until about 1940, respondent employed a local orchestra of nine union musicians to play for stage acts at that theater. When a traveling band occupied the stage, the local orchestra played from the pit for the vaudeville acts and, at times, augmented the performance of the traveling band.

Since 1940, respondent has used the Palace for showing motion pictures with occasional appearances of traveling bands. Between 1940 and 1947, the local musicians, no longer employed on a regular basis, held periodic rehearsals at the theater and were available when required. When a traveling band appeared there, respondent paid the members of the local orchestra a sum equal to the minimum union wages for a similar engagement but they played no music.

The Taft-Hartley Act, containing §8(b)(6), was passed, over the President's veto, June 23, 1947, and took effect August 22. Between July 2 and November 12, seven performances of traveling bands were presented on the Palace stage. Local musicians were neither used nor paid on those occasions. They raised no objections and made no demands for "stand-by" payments. However, in October, 1947, the American Federation of Musicians, Local No. 24 of Akron, Ohio, here called the union, opened negotiations with respondent for the latter's employment of a pit orchestra of local musicians whenever a traveling band performed on the stage. The pit orchestra was to play overtures, "intermissions" and "chasers" (the latter while patrons were leaving the theater). The union required acceptance of this proposal as a condition of its consent to local appearances of traveling bands. Respondent declined the offer and a traveling band scheduled to appear November 20 canceled its engagement on learning that the union had withheld its consent.

May 8, 1949, the union made a new proposal. It sought a guaranty that a local orchestra would be employed by respondent on some number of occasions having a relation to the number of traveling band appearances. This and similar proposals were declined on the ground that the local orchestra was neither necessary nor desired. Accordingly, in July, 1949, the union again declined to consent to the appearance of a traveling band desired by respondent and the band did not appear. In December an arrangement was agreed upon locally for the employment of a local orchestra to play in connection with a vaudeville engagement on condition that the union would consent to a later traveling band appearance without a local orchestra. Respondent's New York office disapproved the plan and the record before us discloses no further agreement.

In 1949, respondent filed charges with the National Labor Relations Board asserting that the union was engaging in the unfair labor practice defined in §8(b)(6). . . . After a hearing the trial examiner . . . concluded that the union's conduct "was nothing more or less than a proposal for a stand-by engagement," but he was not convinced that the union's demands were an "attempt to cause" any payment to be made "in the nature of an *exaction*." He, accordingly, recommended dismissal of the complaint. Id., at 1549, 1550, 1551. The Board . . . also ordered dismissal of the complaint, but it did so on grounds differing from those urged by the trial examiner. Id., 1528-1929. It said:

> On the contrary, the instant record shows that in seeking employment of a local orchestra, the . . . [union] insisted that such orchestra be permitted to play at times which would not conflict with the traveling bands' renditions. Thus, the record herein does not justify a finding that, during the period embraced by the charges herein, the . . . [union] was pursuing its old policy and was attempting to cause the charging party to make payments to local musicians for services which were not to be performed. . . .
>
> In our opinion, §8(b)(6) was not intended to reach cases where a labor organization seeks actual employment for its members, even in situations where the employer does not want, does not need, and is not willing to accept such services. Whether it is desirable that such objective should be made the subject of an unfair labor practice is a matter for further congressional action, but we believe that such objective is not proscribed by the limited provisions of §8(b)(6).

> Upon the entire record in the case, we find that the . . . [union] has not been guilty of unfair labor practices within the meaning of §8(b)(6) of the Act. Id., at 1531, 1533-1534.

The Court of Appeals for the Sixth Circuit did not disturb the Board's finding that the union sought actual employment for its members, but it held, nevertheless, that the union was engaging in a labor practice declared unfair by §8(b)(6). It, therefore, set aside the Board's order of dismissal and remanded the cause. . . .

We accept the finding of the Board, made upon the entire record, that the union was seeking actual employment for its members and not mere "stand-by" pay. The Board recognized that, formerly, before §8(b)(6) had taken effect, the union had received "stand-by" payments in connection with traveling band appearances. Since then, the union has requested no such payments and has received none. It has, however, requested and consistently negotiated for actual employment in connection with traveling band and vaudeville appearances. It has suggested various ways in which a local orchestra could earn pay for performing competent work and, upon those terms, it has offered to consent to the appearance of traveling bands which are Federation-controlled. Respondent, with equal consistency, has declined these offers as it had a right to do.

Since we and the Board treat the union's proposals as in good faith contemplating the performance of actual services, we agree that the union has not, on this record, engaged in a practice proscribed by §8(b)(6). It has remained for respondent to accept or reject the union's offers on their merits in the light of all material circumstances. We do not find it necessary to determine also whether such offers were "in the nature of an exaction." We are not dealing here with offers of mere "token" or nominal services. The proposals before us were appropriately treated by the Board as offers in good faith of substantial performances by competent musicians. There is no reason to think that sham can be substituted for substance under §8(b)(6) any more than under any other statute. Payments for "standing-by," or for the substantial equivalent of "standing-by," are not payments for services performed, but when an employer receives a bona fide offer of competent performance of relevant services, it remains for the employer, through free and fair negotiations, to determine whether such offer shall be accepted and what compensation shall be paid for the work done.

The judgment of the Court of Appeals, accordingly, is reversed and the cause is remanded to it.

Reversed and remanded.[30]

[30] Jackson, J., Clark, J., and Vinson, C. J., dissented.

Notes

1. In a companion case, American Newspaper Publishers Assn. v. NLRB, 345 U.S. 100 (1953), the Court dismissed a §8(b)(6) challenge to the Typographers' Union's practice of insisting that its members be paid for setting "bogus" type, type that was destroyed immediately after setting because customers had supplied their own cardboard matrices, obviating the need for typesetting.

2. Could you draft a statute that would reach the unions' demands in *Gamble* and *American Newspaper Publishers Assn.* without prohibiting the union's work preservation efforts in *National Woodwork Mfrs. Assn.*, supra at p. 471?

2. Union Security

NLRB v. GENERAL MOTORS CORP.[31]

373 U.S. 734 (1963)

WHITE, J.

The issue here is whether an employer commits an unfair labor practice, National Labor Relations Act §8(a)(5), when it refuses to bargain with a certified union over the union's proposal for the adoption of the "agency shop." More narrowly, since the employer is not obliged to bargain over a proposal that he commit an unfair labor practice, the question is whether the agency shop is an unfair labor practice under §8(a)(3) of the Act or else is exempted from the prohibitions of that section by the proviso thereto. We have concluded that this type of arrangement does not constitute an unfair labor practice and that it is not prohibited by §8. . . .

In June 1959, the Indiana intermediate appellate court held that an agency shop arrangement would not violate the state right-to-work law. Meade Elec. Co. v. Hagberg, 129 Ind. App. 631, 159 N.E.2d 408. As defined in that opinion, the term "agency shop" applies to an arrangement under which all employees are required as a condition of employment to pay dues to the union and pay the union's initiation fee, but they need not actually become union members. The union [the U.A.W.] thereafter sent respondent a letter proposing the negotiation of a contractual provision covering Indiana plants "generally similar to that set forth" in the *Meade* case. Continued employment in the Indiana plants

[31] See Haggard, A Clarification of the Types of Union Security Agreements Affirmatively Permitted by Federal Statutes, 5 Rut.-Cam. L. Rev. 418 (1974); Grodin & Beeson, State Right-to-Work Laws and Federal Labor Policy, 52 Calif. L. Rev. 95 (1964); Henderson, The Confrontation of Federal Preemption and State Right to Work Laws, 1967 Duke L.J. 1079.

would be conditioned upon the payment of sums equal to the initiation fee and regular monthly dues paid by the union members. The intent of the proposal, the National Labor Relations Board concluded, was not to require membership but to make membership available at the employees' option and on nondiscriminatory terms. Employees choosing not to join would make the required payments and, in accordance with union custom, would share in union expenditures for strike benefits, educational and retired member benefits, and union publications and promotional activities, but they would not be entitled to attend union meetings, vote upon ratification of agreements negotiated by the union, or have a voice in the internal affairs of the union. The respondent made no counterproposal, but replied to the union's letter that the proposed agreement would violate the National Labor Relations Act and that respondent must therefore "respectfully decline to comply with your request for a meeting" to bargain over the proposal.

[The Board found the clause lawful and the employer to have violated §8(a)(5) by refusing to bargain over its inclusion in the agreement.]

The Court of Appeals set the order aside on the grounds that the Act tolerates only "an agreement requiring membership in a labor organization as a condition of employment" when such agreements do not violate state right-to-work laws, and that the Act does not authorize agreements requiring payment of membership dues to a union, in lieu of membership, as a condition of employment. It held that the proposed agency shop agreement would violate §§7, 8(a)(1), and 8(a)(3) of the Act and that the employer was therefore not obliged to bargain over it. We granted certiorari, and now reverse the decision of the Court of Appeals.

Section 8(3) under the Wagner Act was the predecessor to §8(a)(3) of the present law. Like §8(a)(3), §8(3) forbade employers to discriminate against employees to compel them to join a union. Because it was feared that §8(3) and §7, if nothing were added to qualify them, might be held to outlaw union-security arrangements such as the closed shop, the proviso to §8(3) was added expressly declaring:

> *Provided,* That nothing in this Act . . . or in any other statute of the United States, shall preclude an employer from making an agreement with a labor organization . . . to require as a condition of employment membership therein, if such labor organization is the representative of the employees as provided in §9(a). . . ."

The prevailing administrative and judicial view under the Wagner Act was or came to be that the proviso to §8(3) covered both the closed and union shop, as well as less onerous union-security arrangements, if they were otherwise legal. . . .

When Congress enacted the Taft-Hartley Act, it added the following to the language of the original proviso to §8(3):

> on or after the thirtieth day following the beginning of such employment or the effective date of such agreement, whichever is the later . . . *Provided further,* That no employer shall justify any discrimination against an employee for nonmembership in a labor organization (A) if he has reasonable grounds for believing that such membership was not available to the employee on the same terms and conditions generally applicable to other members, or (B) if he has reasonable grounds for believing that membership was denied or terminated for reasons other than the failure of the employee to tender the periodic dues and the initiation fees uniformly required as a condition of acquiring or retaining membership.

These additions were intended to accomplish twin purposes. On the one hand, the most serious abuses of compulsory unionism were eliminated by abolishing the closed shop. On the other hand, Congress recognized that in the absence of a union-security provision "many employees sharing the benefits of what unions are able to accomplish by collective bargaining will refuse to pay their share of the cost." S. Rep. No. 105, 80th Cong., 1st Sess., p. 6, 1 Leg. Hist. L.M.R.A. 412. Consequently, under the new law "employers would still be permitted to enter into agreements requiring all the employees in a given bargaining unit to become members 30 days after being hired," but "expulsion from a union cannot be a ground of compulsory discharge if the worker is not delinquent in paying his initiation fee or dues." S. Rep. No. 105, p. 7, 1 Leg. Hist. L.M.R.A. 413. The amendments were intended only to "remedy the most serious abuses of compulsory union membership and yet give employers and unions who feel that such agreements promoted stability by eliminating 'free riders' the right to continue such arrangements." Ibid. As far as the federal law was concerned, all employees could be required to pay their way. The bill "abolishes the closed shop but permits voluntary agreements for requiring such forms of compulsory membership as the union shop or maintenance of membership. . . ." S. Rep. No. 105, p. 3, 1 Leg. Hist. L.M.R.A. 409.

We find nothing in the legislative history of the Act indicating that Congress intended the amended proviso to §8(a)(3) to validate only the union shop and simultaneously to abolish, in addition to the closed shop, all other union-security arrangements permissible under state law. There is much to be said for the Board's view that, if Congress desired in the Wagner Act to permit a closed or union shop and in the Taft-Hartley Act the union shop, then it also intended to preserve the status of less vigorous, less compulsory contracts which demanded less adherence to the union.

Respondent, however, relies upon the express words of the proviso which allow employment to be conditioned upon "membership": since the union's proposal here does not require actual membership but demands only initiation fees and monthly dues, it is not saved by the proviso. This position, of course, would reject administrative decisions concerning the scope of §8(3) of the Wagner Act, reaffirmed by the Board under the Taft-Hartley amendments. Moreover, the 1947 amendments not only abolished the closed shop but also made significant alterations in the meaning of "membership" for the purposes of union-security contracts. Under the second proviso to §8(a)(3), the burdens of membership upon which employment may be conditioned are expressly limited to the payment of initiation fees and monthly dues. It is permissible to condition employment upon membership, but membership, insofar as it has significance to employment rights, may in turn be conditioned only upon payment of fees and dues. "Membership" as a condition of employment is whittled down to its financial core. . . .

We are therefore confident that the proposal made by the union here conditioned employment upon the practical equivalent of union "membership," as Congress used that term in the proviso to §8(a)(3). The proposal for requiring the payment of dues and fees imposes no burdens not imposed by a permissible union shop contract and compels the performance of only those duties of membership which are enforceable by discharge under a union shop arrangement. If an employee in a union shop unit refuses to respect any union-imposed obligations other than the duty to pay dues and fees, and membership in the union is therefore denied or terminated, the condition of "membership" for §8(a)(3) purposes is nevertheless satisfied and the employee may not be discharged for nonmembership even though he is not a formal member. Of course, if the union chooses to extend membership even though the employee will meet only the minimum financial burden, and refuses to support or "join" the union in any other affirmative way, the employee may have to become a "member" under a union shop contract, in the sense that the union may be able to place him on its rolls. The agency shop arrangement proposed here removes that choice from the union and places the option of membership in the employee while still requiring the same monetary support as does the union shop. Such a difference between the union and agency shop may be of great importance in some contexts, but for present purposes it is more formal than real. To the extent that it has any significance at all it serves, rather than violates, the desire of Congress to reduce the evils of compulsory unionism while allowing financial support for the bargaining agent. . . .

Reversed and remanded.[32]

[32] Goldberg J., took no part in the decision.

Notes

1. Since §8(a)(3) itself bans the union shop (requirement of full membership), it should come as no surprise that §14(b) has been construed to permit states to ban the agency shop (requirement of payment of dues and initiation fees). Otherwise, §14(b) would have no obvious effect. Retail Clerks Local 1625 v. Schermerhorn, 375 U.S. 96 (1963). A state court enforcing state right-to-work laws may enjoin the execution or application of an unlawful union security clause, but it may not enjoin a strike or picketing to secure the clause. The latter remedy is preempted by federal law. Ibid.

The Labor Board has held that right-to-work states may prohibit unions from charging nonunion employees a flat rate for handling their grievances or a graduated fee for handling grievances.[33] It has also held that such states may prohibit a union from charging nonunion employees the actual costs of handling their grievances and arbitrations.[34] See Pipefitters Local 141 v. NLRB, 675 F.2d 1257, 1262 (D.C. Cir. 1982) (Mikva, J., dissenting) (arguing, in dissent, that §14(b) does not authorize states to prohibit unions from charging representation fees and that union proposals to employers for such clauses are mandatory subjects of bargaining).

2. The federal rule that an employee may be required to pay union dues and initiation fees but is free to decline membership[35] does not necessarily create an illusory distinction. Many unions require members to conform to union rules of conduct enforceable by fines. These fines are not deemed union dues and thus a member does not risk discharge from employment by nonpayment,[36] but the fines may be enforceable in state court. An employee refusing membership (while paying dues) would not seem to be subject to these internal union rules and sanctions.

One difficulty is that many (most?) collective bargaining agreements speak in terms of requiring union "membership" after the permitted waiting period and do not spell out that this means only the payment of dues and membership fees. Unions have little interest in disclosing the distinction and employers probably see little reason to incur the union's displeasure by insisting on a candid clause. The Board has not struck down such clauses; indeed, in Keystone Coat, Apron & Towel Supply

[33] Hughes Tool Co., 104 N.L.R.B. 318 (1953).

[34] Machinists Local 697, 223 N.L.R.B. 832 (1976).

[35] See Union Starch & Ref. Co., 87 N.L.R.B. 779 (1949), enforced, 186 F.2d 1008 (7th Cir.), cert. denied, 342 U.S. 815 (1951) (employees may not be discharged for refusing to attend union meetings and to take the membership oath); Marlin Rockwell, 114 N.L.R.B. 553 (1955) (employee cannot be discharged for resigning membership if he or she continues to pay union dues).

[36] Electric Auto-Lite Co., 92 N.L.R.B. 1073 (1950), enforced per curiam, 196 F.2d 500 (6th Cir.) cert. denied, 344 U.S. 823 (1952).

Co., 121 N.L.R.B. 880 (1958), the Board wrote a model union security clause (for contract-bar purposes) requiring "all employees [to] become and remain members in good standing in the Union."

In 1977, a Gallup poll asked the following question: "Do you think a person should or should not be required to join a union if he or she works in a unionized factory or business?" Sixty-three percent of those polled voted no, 31 percent voted yes. Is this good evidence that the public opposes the repeal of §14(b)?

TEAMSTERS, LOCAL 357 v. NLRB
365 U.S. 667 (1961)

DOUGLAS, J.

Petitioner union (along with the International Brotherhood of Teamsters and a number of other affiliated local unions) executed a three-year collective bargaining agreement with California Trucking Associations, which represented a group of motor truck operators in California. The provisions of the contract relating to hiring of casual or temporary employees were as follows:

> Casual employees shall, wherever the Union maintains a dispatching service, be employed only on a seniority basis in the Industry whenever such senior employees are available. An available list with seniority status will be kept by the Unions, and employees requested will be dispatched upon call to any employer who is a party to this Agreement. Seniority rating of such employees shall begin with a minimum of three months service in the Industry, *irrespective of whether such employee is or is not a member of the Union.*
>
> Discharge of any employee by any employer shall be grounds for removal of any employee from seniority status. No casual employee shall be employed by any employer who is a party to this Agreement in violation of seniority status if such employees are available and if the dispatching service for such employees is available. The employer shall first call the Union or the dispatching hall designated by the Union for such help. In the event the employer is notified that such help is not available, or in the event the employees called for do not appear for work at the time designated by the employer, the employer may hire from any other available source. (Emphasis added.)

Accordingly the union maintained a hiring hall for casual employees. One Slater was a member of the union and had customarily used the hiring hall. But in August 1955 he obtained casual employment with an employer who was party to the hiring-hall agreement without being dispatched by the union. He worked until sometime in November of that year, when he was discharged by the employer on complaint of the union that he had not been referred through the hiring-hall arrangement.

Slater made charges against the union and the employer. Though, as plain from the terms of the contract, there was an express provision that employees would not be discriminated against because they were or were not union members, the Board found that the hiring-hall provision was unlawful per se and that the discharge of Slater on the union's request constituted a violation by the employer of §8(a)(1) and §8(a)(3) and a violation by the union of §8(b)(2) and §8(b)(1)(A) of the National Labor Relations Act, as amended by the Taft-Hartley Act.

The Board ordered, inter alia, that the company and the union cease giving any effect to the hiring-hall agreement; that they jointly and severally reimburse Slater for any loss sustained by him as a result of his discharge; and that they jointly and severally reimburse all casual employees for fees and dues paid by them to the union beginning six months prior to the date of the filing of the charge.

The union petitioned the Court of Appeals for review of the Board's action, and the Board made a cross-application for enforcement. That court set aside the portion of the order requiring a general reimbursement of dues and fees. By a divided vote it upheld the Board in ruling that the hiring-hall agreement was illegal per se. . . .

Our decision in Local 60, United Broth. of Carpenters, etc., v. National Labor Relations Board, 365 U.S. 651,[37] is dispositive of the petition of the Board that asks us to direct enforcement of the order of reimbursement. The judgment of the Court of Appeals on that phase of the matter is affirmed.

The other aspect of the case goes back to the Board's ruling in Mountain Pacific Chapter, 119 N.L.R.B. 883. That decision, rendered in 1958, departed from earlier rulings and held, Abe Murdock dissenting, that the hiring-hall agreement, despite the inclusion of a nondiscrimination clause, was illegal per se:

> Here the very grant of work at all depends solely upon union sponsorship, and it is reasonable to infer that the arrangement displays and enhances the Union's power and control over the employment status. Here all that appears is unilateral union determination and subservient employer action with no aboveboard explanation as to the reason for it, and it is reasonable to infer that the Union will be guided in its concession by an eye towards winning compliance with a membership obligation or union fealty in some other respect. The Employers here have surrendered all hiring authority to the Union and have given advance notice via the established hiring hall to the world at large that the Union is arbitrary master and is contractually guaranteed to remain so. From the final authority over hiring vested in the Respondent Union by the three AGC chapters, the inference of the encouragement of union membership is inescapable. Id., 896.

[37] In that case the Court held the Board's general reimbursement order to be punitive, rather than remedial, and disapproved it.

The Board went on to say that a hiring-hall arrangement to be lawful must contain protective provisions. Its views were stated as follows:

> We believe, however, that the inherent and unlawful encouragement of union membership that stems from unfettered union control over the hiring process would be negated, and we would find an agreement to be nondiscriminatory on its face, only if the agreement explicitly provided that:
>
> (1) Selection of applicants for referral to jobs shall be on a nondiscriminatory basis and shall not be based on, or in any way affected by, union membership, bylaws, rules, regulations, constitutional provisions, or any other aspect of obligation of union membership, policies, or requirements.
>
> (2) The employer retains the right to reject any job applicant referred by the union.
>
> (3) The parties to the agreement post in places where notices to employees and applicants for employment are customarily posted, all provisions relating to the functioning of the hiring arrangement, including the safeguards that we deem essential to the legality of an exclusive hiring agreement. Id., 897.

The Board recognizes that the hiring hall came into being "to eliminate wasteful, time-consuming, and repetitive scouting for jobs by individual workmen and haphazard uneconomical searches by employers." Id., 896, n. 8. The hiring hall at times has been a useful adjunct to the closed shop. But Congress may have thought that it need not serve that cause, that in fact it has served well both labor and management — particularly in the maritime field and in the building and construction industry. In the latter the contractor who frequently is a stranger to the area where the work is done requires a "central source" for his employment needs; and a man looking for a job finds in the hiring hall "at least a minimum guarantee of continued employment."

Congress has not outlawed the hiring hall, though it has outlawed the closed shop except within the limits prescribed in the provisos to §8(a)(3). Senator Taft made clear his views that hiring halls are useful, that they are not illegal per se, that unions should be able to operate them so long as they are not used to create a closed shop:

> In order to make clear the real intention of Congress, it should be clearly stated that the hiring hall is not necessarily illegal. The employer should be able to make a contract with the union as an employment agency. The union frequently is the best employment agency. The employer should be able to give notice of vacancies, and in the normal course of events to accept men sent to him by the hiring hall. He should not be able to bind himself, however, to reject nonunion men if they apply to him; nor should he be able to contract to accept men on a rotary-hiring basis. . . .
>
> . . . The National Labor Relations Board and the courts did not find hiring halls as such illegal, but merely certain practices under them. The

> Board and the court found that the manner in which the hiring halls operated created in effect a closed shop in violation of the law. Neither the law nor these decisions forbid hiring halls, even hiring halls operated by the unions as long as they are not so operated as to create a closed shop with all of the abuses possible under such an arrangement, including discrimination against employees, prospective employees, members of union minority groups, and operation of a closed union." S. Rep. No. 1827, 81st Cong., 2d Sess., pp. 13, 14.

There being no express ban of hiring halls in any provisions of the Act, those who add one, whether it be the Board or the courts, engage in a legislative act. The Act deals with discrimination either by the employers or unions that encourages or discourages union membership. As respects §8(a)(3) we said in Radio Officers, etc., v. National Labor Relations Board, 317 U.S. 17:

> The language of §8(a)(3) is not ambiguous. The unfair labor practice is for an employer to encourage or discourage membership by means of discrimination. Thus this section does not outlaw all encouragement or discouragement of membership in labor organizations; only such as is accomplished by discrimination is prohibited. Nor does this section outlaw discrimination in employment as such; only such discrimination as encourages or discourages membership in a labor organization is proscribed.

It is the "true purpose" or "real motive" in hiring or firing that constitutes the test. Id., 347 U.S. 43. Some conduct may by its very nature contain the implications of the required intent; the natural foreseeable consequences of certain action may warrant the inference. Id., 347 U.S. 45. The existence of discrimination may at times be inferred by the Board, for "it is permissible to draw on experience in factual inquiries." Radio Officers', etc., v. National Labor Relations Board, supra, 347 U.S. 49. But surely discrimination cannot be inferred from the face of the instrument when the instrument specifically provides that there will be no discrimination against "casual employees" because of the presence or absence of union membership. The only complaint in the case was by Slater, a union member, who sought to circumvent the hiring-hall agreement. When an employer and the union enforce the agreement against union members, we cannot say without more that either indulges in the kind of discrimination to which the Act is addressed.

It may be that the very existence of the hiring hall encourages union membership. We may assume that it does. The very existence of the union has the same influence. When a union engages in collective bargaining and obtains increased wages and improved working conditions, its prestige doubtless rises and, one may assume, more workers are drawn to it. When a union negotiates collective bargaining agreements that include arbitration clauses and supervises the functioning of those provisions so as to get equitable adjustments of grievances, union membership may also be encouraged. The truth is that the union is a service agency that probably encourages membership whenever it does its job well. But, as we said in Radio Officers, etc., v. National Labor Relations Board, supra, the only encouragement or discouragement of union membership banned by the Act is that which is "accomplished by discrimination," 347 U.S. at page 43.

Nothing is inferable from the present hiring-hall provision except that employer and union alike sought to route "casual employees" through the union hiring hall and required a union member who circumvented it to adhere to it. It may be that hiring halls need more regulation than the Act presently affords. As we have seen, the Act aims at every practice, act, source or institution which in fact is used to encourage and discourage union membership by discrimination in regard to hire or tenure, term or condition of employment. Perhaps the conditions which the Board attaches to hiring-hall arrangements will in time appeal to the Congress. Yet, where Congress has adopted a selective system for dealing with evils, the Board is confined to that system. Where, as here, Congress has aimed its sanctions only at specific discriminatory practices, the Board cannot go farther and establish a broader, more pervasive regulatory scheme.

The present agreement for a union hiring hall has a protective clause in it, as we have said; and there is no evidence that it was in fact used unlawfully. We cannot assume that a union conducts its operations in violation of law or that the parties to this contract did not intend to adhere to its express language. Yet we would have to make those assumptions to agree with the Board that it is reasonable to infer the union will act discriminatorily. Moreover, the hiring hall, under the law as it stands, is a matter of negotiation between the parties. The Board has no power to compel directly or indirectly that the hiring hall be included or excluded in collective agreements. Cf. National Labor Relations Board v. American Nat. Ins. Co., 343 U.S. 395, 404. Its power, so far as here relevant, is restricted to the elimination of discrimination. Since the present agreement contains such a prohibition, the Board is confined to determining whether discrimination has in fact been practiced. If hiring halls are to be subjected to regulation that is less selective and more pervasive, Congress not the Board is the agency to do it.

Affirmed in part and reversed in part.[38]

HARLAN, J., whom STEWART, J., joins, concurring. . . .

The Board's condemnation of these union "hiring hall" procedures as violative of §§8(a)(1), 8(a)(3), 8(b)(1), and 8(b)(2) of the National Labor

[38] Clark, J., and Whittaker, J., dissented. Frankfurter, J., took no part in the decision.

Relations Act ultimately rests on a now well-established line of circuit court cases to the effect that a clause in a collective bargaining agreement may, without more, constitute forbidden discrimination. While seeming to recognize the validity of the proposition that contract terms which are equivocal on their face should ordinarily await an independent evaluation of their actual meaning and effect before being deemed to give rise to an unfair labor practice, such cases have justified short-circuiting that course upon these considerations: The mere existence of a clause that on its face appears to declare preferential rights for union members encourages union membership among employees or job applicants, persons not privy to the undisclosed intent of the parties, yet affected by the apparent meaning of the contract. Hence, the mere possibility that such a clause may actually turn out not to have been administered by the parties so as to favor union members is not enough to save it from condemnation as an unlawful discrimination.

I think this rationale may have validity under certain circumstances, but that it does not carry the day for the Board in these cases. The Board recognizes, as it must, that something more than simply actual encouragement or discouragement of union members must be shown to make out an unfair labor practice, whether the action involved be that of agreeing to a contract term or discharging an employee or anything else. In this regard, it contends that the action of agreeing to the union "hiring" clause should be treated like any other employer or union action and that, on this premise, all that the Board must show in the light of Radio Officers' Union v. National Labor Relations Board, 347 U.S. 17 is that the tendency to encourage or discourage union membership was *foreseeable* to the employer or union. Since one is presumed to intend the foreseeable consequences of his acts, and since acting in order to encourage or discourage union membership is forbidden, the Board's case is said to be made by a simple showing that such encouragement or discouragement is the foreseeable result of employer or union action. The Board then concludes with a showing that encouragement of union membership is a foreseeable consequence of the acts of agreeing to or operating a union-run hiring hall. . . .

While I agree with the opinion of the Court that the Board could not infer from the mere existence of the "hiring hall" clause an intent on the part of employer or union to discriminate in favor of union status, I think it was within the realm of Board expertness to say that the natural and foreseeable effect of this clause is to make employees and job applicants think that union status will be favored. For it is surely scarcely less than a fact of life that a certain number of job applicants will believe that joining the union would increase their chances of hire when the union is exercising the hiring function.

What in my view is wrong with the Board's position in these cases is that a mere showing of foreseeable encouragement of union status is not a sufficient basis for a finding of violation of the statute. It has long been recognized that an employer can make reasonable business decisions, unmotivated by an intent to discourage union membership or protected concerted activities, although the foreseeable effect of these decisions may be to discourage what the act protects. For example, an employer may discharge an employee because he is not performing his work adequately, whether or not the employee happens to be a union organizer. Yet a court could hardly reverse a Board finding that such firing would foreseeably tend to discourage union activity. Again, an employer can properly make the existence or amount of a year-end bonus depend upon the productivity of a unit of the plant, although this will foreseeably tend to discourage the protected activity of striking. A union, too, is privileged to make decisions which are reasonably calculated to further the welfare of all the employees it represents, nonunion as well as union, even though a foreseeable result of the decision may be to encourage union membership.

This Court's interpretation of the relevant statutory provisions has recognized that Congress did not mean to limit the range of either employer or union decision to those possible actions which had *no* foreseeable tendency to encourage or discourage union membership or concerted activities. In general, this Court has assumed that a finding of a violation of §8(a)(3) or §8(b)(2) requires an affirmative showing of a *motivation* of encouraging or discouraging union status or activity. See, e.g., National Labor Relations Board v. Jones & Laughlin Co., 301 U.S. 1, 45-46; Universal Camera Corp. v. National Labor Relations Board, 340 U.S. 474. There have, to be sure, been exceptions to this requirement, but they have been narrow ones, usually analogous to the exceptions made to the requirements for a showing of discrimination in other contexts. For example, in Republic Aviation Corp. v. National Labor Relations Board, 324 U.S. 793, the Court affirmed a Board decision that a company "no solicitation" rule was overbroadly applied to prevent solicitation of union membership on company property during periods when employees were otherwise free to do as they pleased. A finding of a motivation to discourage union membership was there held unnecessary because there was no employer showing of a nondiscriminatory purpose for applying the rule to union solicitation during the employees' free time. . . .

Another field of exceptions to the requirement of a showing of a purpose to encourage or discourage union activity is found in the Court's affirmance of the Second Circuit in Gaynor News Co., Inc., v. National Labor Relations Board, 347 U.S. 17, a companion case to *Radio Officers*: If a union or employer is to be permitted to take action which substantially — though unintentionally — encourages or discourages union activity, the union or employer ends served by the action must not only be of some significance, but they must also be legitimate, or at least not otherwise forbidden by the National Labor Relations Act. In *Gaynor* an employer who, pursuant to a nondiscriminatory business end of paying the least wages possible, agreed with the union which was the statutory representative of the employees to give certain benefits only to union members, was prevented from asserting the justifying business reasons for thus encouraging union membership because of his complicity in the union's breach of its duties as agent for *all* the employees. Indeed, the fact that a nondiscriminatory business purpose forbidden by the Act cannot be used by an employer to justify an action which incidentally encourages union membership, seems to me to be the true basis of the Court's holding in *Radio Officers* that an employer violates §8(a)(3) when a union forces him to take actions in order to encourage union membership. The employer's nondiscriminatory reason for encouraging union membership to avoid the economic pressure the union could impose upon him — was surely no longer intended to be a justification for such employer action after the passage of §8(b)(2), a statutory provision the very wording of which presupposed that union coercion can cause a violation of §§8(a)(3). . . .

There is no reason to decide now whether there are other contexts in which a showing of an actual motivation of encouraging or discouraging union activity might be unnecessary to a finding of a union or employer unfair labor practice. For present purposes, it is sufficient to note that what is involved in the general requirement of finding of forbidden motivation, as well as in the limited scope of the heretofore recognized exceptions to this general requirement, is a realization that the Act was not intended to interfere significantly with those activities of employer and union which are justified by nondiscriminatory business purposes, or by nondiscriminatory attempts to benefit *all* the represented employees. It is against this policy that we should measure the Board's action in finding forbidden the incorporation in collective bargaining contracts of the "hiring hall" clause. We must determine whether the Board's action is consistent with the balance struck by the Wagner and Taft-Hartley Acts between protection of employee freedom with respect to union activity and the privilege of employer and union to make such nondiscriminatory decisions as seem to them to satisfy best the needs of the business and the employees.

Considered in this light, I do not think we can sustain the Board's holding that the "hiring hall" clause is forbidden by the Taft-Hartley Act. The Board has not found that this clause was without substantial justification in terms of legitimate employer or union purposes. Cf. Republic Aviation v. National Labor Relations Board, supra; Gaynor News Co. Inc., v. National Labor Relations Board, supra. Whether or not such a finding would have been supported by the record is not for us now to decide. The Board has not, in my view, made the type of showing of an actual motive of encouraging union membership that is required by

Universal Camera v. National Labor Relations Board, supra. All it has shown is that the clause will tend to encourage union membership, and that without substantial difficulty the parties to the agreement could have taken additional steps to isolate the valid employer or union purposes from the discriminatory effects of the clause. I do not think that these two elements alone can justify a Board holding of an unfair labor practice unless we are to approve a broad expansion of the power of the Board to supervise nondisciminatory decisions made by employer or union. Whether or not such an expansion would be desirable, it does not seem to me consistent with the balance the labor acts have struck between freedom of choice of management and union ends by the parties to a collective bargaining agreement and the freedom of employees from restraint or coercion in their exercise of rights granted by §7 of the Act.

Notes

1. If a union refuses to make a hiring hall referral unless the worker is a union member, or takes out membership, the hiring hall is discriminatory. Some employers have mounted attacks on union hiring halls by sending "ringers" to the halls for referrals. A ringer is an apparently well-qualified, nonunion worker who purports to be seeking a referral and has prearranged with the employer to give Board testimony if the union refuses to refer or demands that a union card be signed. If the Board finds that a hiring hall is being operated in a discriminatory fashion, what remedial order should issue?

2. A nondiscriminatory hiring hall is not subject to state right-to-work laws.[39] Should a state be able to enjoin the operation of a discriminatory hiring hall?

3. Union "stewards" are employees designated by the union to handle union business, e.g., employee grievances, on the job site. How would you analyze for §8(a)(3) purposes a bargaining agreement clause reading, "The steward shall be considered the Senior employee in the craft in which he or she is employed . . ."? The Board held the clause to be unlawful because it accorded super-seniority with respect to all contractual benefits where seniority is a consideration but indicated that such a clause is lawful if limited to layoff and recall seniority.[40] How would you defend the narrower clause before a reviewing court of appeals?

Board members have disagreed about the implications of the rule

[39] Houston Chapter, Associated General Contractors, 143 N.L.R.B. 409 (1963), enforced, 349 F.2d 449 (5th Cir. 1965), cert. denied, 382 U.S. 1026 (1966).

[40] Dairylea Cooperative, 219 N.L.R.B. 656 (1975).

permitting some forms of super-seniority for union stewards, and over the rule's extension to union officers. The nature of the disagreement is summarized in the following passage from American Can Co., 235 N.L.R.B. 704 (1979). The question presented was whether the company and the union violated the Act when they accorded preferential layoff and recall seniority to employees Howard and Schneider. Howard was a trustee for the union. His duties were "to have charge of the hall and all property of the Local Union . . . and perform such other duties as the Local Union may require." The duties of Schneider, a guard, were "to take charge of the door [at union meetings] and see that no one enters who is not entitled to do so." Neither employee performed other official duties for the union. The Board's view was summarized as follows:

> In Dairylea Cooperative Inc., 219 N.L.R.B. 656 (1975), enfd., 531 F.2d 1162 (2nd Cir. 1976), the Board majority held that superseniority clauses which operate to keep a union steward on the job are permissible because the steward's functions benefit all unit employees. The governing considerations were stated in *Dairylea* at 658:
>
> > [I]n view of the inherent tendency of superseniority clauses to discriminate against employees for union-related reasons . . . we do find that superseniority clauses which are not on their face limited to layoff and recall are presumptively unlawful, and that the burden of rebutting that presumption (i.e., establishing justification) rests on the shoulders of the party asserting their legality.
>
> *Dairylea,* however, applied only to superseniority afforded union stewards. In United Electrical, Radio and Machine Workers of America, Local 623 (Limpco Mfg., Inc.), 230 N.L.R.B. 406 (1977), enfd. sub nom., Anna M. D'Amico v. NLRB, 582 F.2d 820, 824 (3d Cir. 1978), the Board majority held that the *Dairylea* presumption that superseniority protection for stewards is lawful because it "furthers the effective administration of the bargaining agreements on the plant level" applies to union officers because they play an important role in contract administration. In Otis Elevator Company, 231 N.L.R.B. 1128 (1977), the Board majority held that union officers may lawfully be given superseniority because they generally contribute, in their official capacities, to the ability of the union to represent the unit effectively and efficiently.
>
> The panel majority issuing the Board's Decision and Order in this proceeding, relying in part on the above-cited cases, found that the superseniority provision involved herein was presumptively lawful because it covered only union officers and committeemen and that the Board would not question a union's decision as to which officers aid the union in effectively representing the unit. Subsequent to that Decision, the Third Circuit issued Anna M. D'Amico v. NLRB, supra. In doing so, the court stated that the respondent "was obligated to produce credible proof that the individual in question was officially assigned duties which helped to implement the collective bargaining agreement in a meaningful way. Any less rigid interpretation of the Board's ruling would leave substantial room to

> dilute the statutory neutrality principle without the requisite collective bargaining justification." (582 F.2d 825)
>
> Upon reflection of the issues involved herein and consideration of the *D'Amico* decision, the Board decided to reconsider sua sponte its earlier Decision and Order herein. As can be seen from the above-cited cases, the Board Members have widely divergent views on *Dairylea* issues, particularly on that involved herein. Thus, this Supplemental Decision and Order is based on an aggregate majority as follows: Chairman Fanning and Member Truesdale do not agree with the restrictions placed on superseniority by *Dairylea* and its progeny (see their dissent herein); Members Jenkins and Penello would not permit union officers to benefit from superseniority except when the officers also serve as stewards or otherwise engage in administration of the contract at the place and during the hours of their employment (see their concurrence herein); and Member Murphy adheres to *Dairylea* and *Limpco,* supra, but finds that the General Counsel has rebutted the presumption that the union officers here involved were lawfully afforded superseniority by showing that Howard and Schneider are not engaged in contract administration (see her separate concurrence herein). Thus, the majority of the Board finds that Respondents violated the Act, as alleged, in their application of the superseniority provision in question to trustee Howard and guard Schneider.

In Gulton Electro-Voice, 266 N.L.R.B. No. 84, 112 L.R.R.M. 1361 (1983), new appointees to the Board reconsidered the super-seniority issue and held that contract super-seniority must be "limited to employees who, as agents of the union, must be on the job to accomplish their duties directly related to administering the collective-bargaining agreement."

6

ENFORCEMENT OF COLLECTIVE BARGAINING AGREEMENTS

A. THE ROLE OF GRIEVANCE ARBITRATION

Most collective bargaining agreements establish a grievance procedure culminating in arbitration. The mechanics of grievance arbitration[1] are varied. Agreements differ in the number of steps in the grievance procedure (perhaps beginning with the foreman, ending with the personnel director), and in the formality of low-level grievance handling (a submission in writing may be required and time limits may be imposed on when a grievance may be filed or carried to the next step). More significant are provisions governing who can file a grievance and what sorts of issues the arbitrator is empowered to decide. Usually the employees and the union are permitted to file grievances; less frequently the agreement permits the employer to grieve as well.

The significance of permitting the employer to grieve will be apparent in some of the following materials. This chapter will also disclose a variety of clauses authorizing an arbitrator to decide disputes. Examples include the following: "any disputes arising between the parties during the term of this agreement may be submitted to arbitration" and "any dispute over the meaning, application or interpretation of this agreement may be submitted to arbitration." Some agreements specifically withdraw certain classes of grievances from the arbitration clause or otherwise limit the arbitrator's authority.

Should a party refuse to submit a grievance to arbitration, the grieving party may file a breach of contract action in court to compel submission to arbitration. An employer's refusal to arbitrate may precipitate a union strike.

[1] Grievance arbitration differs from interest arbitration. The latter refers to the process whereby an employer and union cede to an arbitrator the power to set the terms of a bargaining agreement because the parties cannot agree between themselves. It raises fascinating issues but the rarety of its use means we shall not study it in detail.

Some collective bargaining agreements designate a permanent arbitrator to decide all submitted grievances during the agreement's term. A permanent arbitrator is likely to gain substantial familiarity with the agreement and plant practices. The majority of agreements, however, rely on ad hoc arbitrators. Names of experienced arbitrators may be obtained from either the Federal Mediation and Conciliation Service or the American Arbitration Association. The arbitrators may be engaged in arbitrating grievances full time, or they may be, for example, academics arbitrating on an occasional basis. If the parties have the time, money, and inclination, they may be able to research the past decisions of these arbitrators for "leanings." In any event, the parties typically alternate striking names from the panel until it is reduced to a single arbitrator, who will then hear the case (the process is known in some circles as "knocking brains from the panel").

Arbitration hearings are less formal than court trials. The rules of evidence are relaxed; arbitrators tend to let in evidence "for what it's worth." The parties are not necessarily represented by lawyers. Transcripts are only occasionally made; the usual practice is for the arbitrator to take handwritten notes. The parties rarely file prehearing briefs and sometimes waive posthearing briefs as well. The arbitrator often renders an opinion and award (statement of relief) within a month of the hearing, although considerably longer periods are not unusual. The opinion and award is ordinarily in writing and recites the sum of the important evidence, the arbitrator's reasoning, and a statement of the relief granted. A typical arbitrator's fee is $450 per day (plus expenses), which includes the time necessary to study the evidence and prepare the opinion and award. Costs are most often shared by the parties.

Compliance with the award by the losing party ends the dispute. Otherwise, the winning party must seek judicial enforcement in a breach of contract action. Alternatively, the bargaining agreement may permit a strike if an employer refuses to honor an arbitration award.

It may be that for grievance arbitration to be an effective labor relations device, the cost of arbitrating must not be so high as to prevent its use, nor so low as to make it too attractive an alternative to voluntary settlement. In a recent year, for example, 200,000 grievances were filed under a United Auto Workers-General Motors collective bargaining agreement. Over 1,000 of the grievances were scheduled to be arbitrated but less than 50, having failed to be settled, actually went to arbitration. Ideally, each employer and union would negotiate a grievance and arbitration procedure that would make it neither too difficult nor too easy for those particular parties, in light of their financial capabilities, for example, to carry grievances to arbitration. The greater expense of court enforcement of the bargaining agreement, were that the sole procedure, would presumably encourage intransigence by the nongrieving party, who would realize that a grievant is unlikely to invest more money in taking a grievance to court than would be received if the suit was successful.

This description of the arbitration process should not obscure the difficult and largely unique role assumed by the American labor arbitrator.

> Voluntarism and bargain are also significant ingredients of a collective bargaining agreement. The law leaves the employer and the collectivity of employees free to agree or refrain from agreement subject only to the obligation that they bargain in good faith. The terms of the bargain are not determined by the government; in this respect both management and labor enjoy much greater freedom than a utility or insurance company dealing with the public.
>
> In fact neither the employer nor the employees collectively have the freedom to disagree which characterizes typical contracts between business firms and individuals. Sooner or later the employer and employees must strike some kind of a bargain. For both the costs of delay can be very heavy. The compulsion has two relevant consequences. First, it partially explains the gaps and deliberate ambiguities in collective bargaining agreements which create distinctive problems of interpretation. The pressure to reach an agreement is so great that the parties are willing to contract although each knows that the other places a different meaning on the words and they share only the common intent to postpone the issue and take a gamble upon an arbitrator's ruling if decision is required. Second, the importance of having some agreement means that the arbitrator can hardly say that there was no meeting of the minds upon the question before him, that therefore there was no contract, and that the parties should go back and negotiate a solution.
>
> These consequences of the practical compulsion to sign and preserve collective agreements mean that interpretation must assume a more creative role than in most commercial or property litigations.[2]

TEXTILE WORKERS UNION v. LINCOLN MILLS
353 U.S. 448 (1957)

Douglas, J.

Petitioner-union entered into a collective bargaining agreement in 1953 with respondent-employer, the agreement to run one year and from year to year thereafter, unless terminated on specified notices. The agreement provided that there would be no strikes or work stoppages and that grievances would be handled pursuant to a specified procedure. The last step in the grievance procedure — a step that could be taken by either party — was arbitration.

[2] Cox, The Legal Nature of Collective Bargaining Agreements, 57 Mich. L. Rev. 1, 3-4 (1958).

This controversy involves several grievances that concern work loads and work assignments. The grievances were processed through the various steps in the grievance procedure and were finally denied by the employer. The union requested arbitration, and the employer refused. Thereupon the union brought this suit in the District Court to compel arbitration.

The District Court concluded that it had jurisdiction and ordered the employer to comply with the grievance arbitration provisions of the collective bargaining agreement. The Court of Appeals reversed by a divided vote. It held that, although the District Court had jurisdiction to entertain the suit, the court had no authority founded either in federal or state law to grant the relief. The case is here on a petition for a writ of certiorari which we granted because of the importance of the problem and the contrariety of views in the courts.

The starting point of our inquiry is §301 of the Labor Management Relations Act of 1947. . . . There has been considerable litigation involving §301 and courts have construed it differently. There is one view that §301(a) merely gives federal district courts jurisdiction in controversies that involve labor organizations in industries affecting commerce, without regard to diversity of citizenship or the amount in controversy. Under that view §301(a) would not be the source of substantive law; it would neither supply federal law to resolve these controversies nor turn the federal judges to state law for answers to the questions. Other courts — the overwhelming number of them — hold that §301(a) is more than jurisdictional — that it authorizes federal courts to fashion a body of federal law for the enforcement of these collective bargaining agreements and includes within that federal law specific performance of promises to arbitrate grievances under collective bargaining agreements. . . . That is our construction of §301(a), which means that the agreement to arbitrate grievance disputes, contained in this collective bargaining agreement, should be specifically enforced.

From the face of the Act it is apparent that §301(a) and §301(b) supplement one another. Section 301(b) makes it possible for a labor organization, representing employees in an industry affecting commerce, to sue and be sued as an entity in the federal courts. Section 301(b) in other words provides the procedural remedy lacking at common law. Section 301(a) certainly does something more than that. Plainly, it supplies the basis upon which the federal district courts may take jurisdiction and apply the procedural rules of §301(b). The question is whether §301(a) is more than jurisdictional.

The legislative history of §301 is somewhat cloudy and confusing. But there are a few shafts of light that illuminate our problem.

The bills, as they passed the House and the Senate, contained provisions which would have made the failure to abide by an agreement to arbitrate an unfair labor practice. This feature of the law was dropped in

Conference. As the Conference Report stated, "Once parties have made a collective bargaining contract the enforcement of that contract should be left to the usual processes of the law and not to the National Labor Relations Board." H.R. Conf. Rep. No. 510, 80th Cong., 1st Sess., p. 42.

Both the Senate and the House took pains to provide for "the usual processes of the law" by provisions which were the substantial equivalent of §301(a) in its present form. Both the Senate Report and the House Report indicate a primary concern that unions as well as employees should be bound to collective bargaining contracts. But there was also a broader concern — a concern with a procedure for making such agreements enforceable in the courts by either party. . . .

Congress was also interested in promoting collective bargaining that ended with agreements not to strike.

The Senate Report states:

> If unions can break agreements with relative impunity, then such agreements do not tend to stabilize industrial relations. The execution of an agreement does not by itself promote industrial peace. The chief advantage which an employer can reasonably expect from a collective labor agreement is assurance of uninterrupted operation during the term of the agreement. Without some effective method of assuring freedom from economic warfare for the term of the agreement, there is little reason why an employer would desire to sign such a contract.
>
> Consequently, to encourage the making of agreements and to promote industrial peace through faithful performance by the parties, collective agreements affecting interstate commerce should be enforceable in the Federal courts. Our amendment would provide for suits by unions as legal entities and against unions as legal entities in the Federal courts in disputes affecting commerce.

Thus collective bargaining contracts were made "equally binding and enforceable on both parties." As stated in the House Report, the new provision "makes labor organizations equally responsible with employers for contract violations and provides for suit by either against the other in the United States district courts." To repeat, the Senate Report summed up the philosophy of §301 as follows: "Statutory recognition of the collective agreement as a valid, binding, and enforceable contract is a logical and necessary step. It will promote a higher degree of responsibility upon the parties to such agreements, and will thereby promote industrial peace."

Plainly the agreement to arbitrate grievance disputes is the *quid pro quo* for an agreement not to strike. Viewed in this light, the legislation does more than confer jurisdiction in the federal courts over labor organizations. It expresses a federal policy that federal courts should enforce these agreements on behalf of or against labor organizations and that industrial peace can be best obtained only in that way.

It seems, therefore, clear to us that Congress adopted a policy which placed sanctions behind agreements to arbitrate grievance disputes, by implication rejecting the common-law rule, discussed in Red Cross Line v. Atlantic Fruit Co., 264 U.S. 109, against enforcement of executory agreements to arbitrate. We would undercut the Act and defeat its policy if we read §301 narrowly as only conferring jurisdiction over labor organizations.

The question then is, what is the substantive law to be applied in suits under §301(a)? We conclude that the substantive law to apply in suits under §301(a) is federal law, which the courts must fashion from the policy of our national labor laws. See Mendelsohn, Enforceability of Arbitration Agreements under Taft-Hartley Section 301, 66 Yale L.J. 167. The Labor Management Relations Act expressly furnishes some substantive law. It points out what the parties may or may not do in certain situations. Other problems will lie in the penumbra of express statutory mandates. Some will lack express statutory sanction but will be solved by looking at the policy of the legislation and fashioning a remedy that will effectuate that policy. The range of judicial inventiveness will be determined by the nature of the problem.

Federal interpretation of the federal law will govern, not state law. But state law, if compatible with the purpose of §301, may be resorted to in order to find the rule that will best effectuate the federal policy. Any state law applied, however, will be absorbed as federal law and will not be an independent source of private rights.

It is not uncommon for federal courts to fashion federal law where federal rights are concerned. Congress has indicated by §301(a) the purpose to follow that course here. There is no constitutional difficulty. Article III, §2, extends the judicial power to cases "arising under . . . the Laws of the United States. . . ." The power of Congress to regulate these labor-management controversies under the Commerce Clause is plain. A case or controversy arising under §301(a) is, therefore, one within the purview of judicial power as defined in Article III.

The question remains whether jurisdiction to compel arbitration of grievance disputes is withdrawn by the Norris-LaGuardia Act. Section 7 of that Act prescribes stiff procedural requirements for issuing an injunction in a labor dispute. The kinds of acts which had given rise to abuse of the power to enjoin are listed in §4. The failure to arbitrate was not a part and parcel of the abuses against which the Act was aimed. Section 8 of the Norris-LaGuardia Act does, indeed, indicate a congressional policy toward settlement of labor disputes by arbitration, for it denies injunctive relief to any person who has failed to make "every reasonable effort" to settle the dispute by negotiation, mediation, or "voluntary arbitration." Though a literal reading might bring the dispute within the terms of the Act (see Cox, Grievance Arbitration in the Federal Courts, 67 Harv. L. Rev. 591, 602-604), we see no justification in policy for restricting §301(a) to damage suits, leaving specific performance of a contract to arbitrate grievance disputes to the inapposite procedural requirements of that Act. Moreover, we held in Virginian R. Co. v. System Federation, 300 U.S. 515, and in Graham v. Brotherhood of Firemen, 338 U.S. 232, 237, that the Norris-LaGuardia Act does not deprive federal courts of jurisdiction to compel compliance with the mandates of the Railway Labor Act. The mandates there involved concerned racial discrimination. Yet those decisions were not based on any peculiarities of the Railway Labor Act. We followed the same course in Syres v. Oil Workers International Union, 350 U.S. 892, which was governed by the National Labor Relations Act. There an injunction was sought against racial discrimination in application of a collective bargaining agreement; and we allowed the injunction to issue. The congressional policy in favor of the enforcement of agreements to arbitrate grievance disputes being clear, there is no reason to submit them to the requirements of §7 of the Norris-LaGuardia Act. . . .

The judgment of the Court of Appeals is reversed and the cause is remanded to that court for proceedings in conformity with this opinion.[3]

Notes

1. State courts have concurrent jurisdiction to enforce collective bargaining agreements,[4] but they must apply federal law.[5] Breach of bargaining agreement actions brought in state courts may be removed to federal courts by defendants under the federal question removal jurisdiction.[6]

2. Are the federal courts qualified to establish a common law of collective bargaining agreement enforcement? Shortly after *Lincoln Mills* was decided two academics argued:

> The draftsmen of collective-bargaining contracts are not supermen endowed with total foresight anymore than are the draftsmen of ordinary contracts and the typical case is not likely to involve a stubborn refusal to carry out admitted obligations but rather a dispute concerning what those obligations are. What §301 really demands of the federal courts, therefore, is not the application but the creation in case after case, with the scant

[3] Burton, J., and Harlan, J., concurred in the result, arguing that the federal courts should apply state law and that §301's constitutionality can be upheld on a theory of "protective jurisdiction." In a lengthy dissent, Frankfurter, J., concluded that §301 was intended to be procedural only and was therefore beyond the Constitution's Article III power. Black, J., took no part in the decision.

[4] Dowd Box Co. v. Courtney, 368 U.S. 502 (1962).

[5] Teamsters Local 174 v. Lucas Flour Co., 369 U.S. 95 (1962).

[6] Avco Corp. v. Aero Lodge 735, 390 U.S. 557 (1968).

> assistance of bits and pieces of statutory commands, of a law of labor contracts the chief source of which is to be the common law of commercial contracts. The plain fact is that the courts are enormously unequal to the task and its imposition on them is therefore capable of damaging their usefulness for the essential duties that they are suited to perform.[7]

The three cases that follow comprise the "Steelworkers Trilogy" and represent the major formulation of this federal common law.

UNITED STEELWORKERS v. AMERICAN MANUFACTURING CO.
363 U.S. 564 (1960)

[Employee Sparks left his work because of an injury and settled a workmen's compensation claim against the company on the basis that he was permanently partially disabled. Two weeks later the union filed a grievance charging that Sparks was entitled to return to work by virtue of the seniority provision of the collective bargaining agreement (seniority to control "where ability and efficiency are equal"). The agreement provided that management could discharge "for cause," that the union would not strike unless the company refused to abide by a decision of an arbitrator, and that arbitration could be had of all disputes "as to the meaning, interpretation and application of the provisions of the agreement." The company refused to arbitrate the union's grievance that Sparks be reinstated. The union sued to compel arbitration.]

DOUGLAS, J. . . .

Section 203(d) of the Labor Management Relations Act states, "Final adjustment by a method agreed upon by the parties is hereby declared to be the desirable method for settlement of grievance disputes arising over the application or interpretation of an existing collective-bargaining agreement. . . ." That policy can be effectuated only if the means chosen by the parties for settlement of their differences under a collective bargaining agreement is given full play.

A state decision that held to the contrary announced a principle that could only have a crippling effect on grievance arbitration. The case was International Assn. of Machinists v. Cutler-Hammer, Inc., 271 App. Div. 917, 67 N.Y.S.2d 317, aff'd 297 N.Y. 519, 74 N.E.2d 464. It held that "If the meaning of the provision of the contract sought to be arbitrated is beyond dispute, there cannot be anything to arbitrate and the contract cannot be said to provide for arbitration." 271 App. Div., at 918, 67 N.Y.S.2d, at 318. The lower courts in the instant case had a like preoccupation with ordinary contract law. The collective agreement requires

[7] Bickel & Wellington, Legislative Purpose and the Judicial Process: The *Lincoln Mills* Case, 71 Harv. L. Rev. 1, 22-23 (1957).

arbitration of claims that courts might be unwilling to entertain. In the context of the plant or industry the grievance may assume proportions of which judges are ignorant. Yet, the agreement is to submit all grievances to arbitration, not merely those that a court may deem to be meritorious. There is no exception in the "no strike" clause and none therefore should be read into the grievance clause, since one is the *quid pro quo* for the other. The question is not whether in the mind of the court there is equity in the claim. Arbitration is a stabilizing influence only as it serves as a vehicle for handling any and all disputes that arise under the agreement.

The collective agreement calls for the submission of grievances in the categories which it describes, irrespective of whether a court may deem them to be meritorious. In our role of developing a meaningful body of law to govern the interpretation and enforcement of collective bargaining agreements, we think special heed should be given to the context in which collective bargaining agreements are negotiated and the purpose which they are intended to serve. The function of the court is very limited when the parties have agreed to submit all questions of contract interpretation to the arbitrator. It is confined to ascertaining whether the party seeking arbitration is making a claim which on its face is governed by the contract. Whether the moving party is right or wrong is a question of contract interpretation for the arbitrator. In these circumstances the moving party should not be deprived of the arbitrator's judgment, when it was his judgment and all that it connotes that was bargained for.

The courts, therefore, have no business weighing the merits of the grievance, considering whether there is equity in a particular claim, or determining whether there is particular language in the written instrument which will support the claim. The agreement is to submit all grievances to arbitration, not merely those which the court will deem meritorious. The processing of even frivolous claims may have therapeutic values of which those who are not a part of the plant environment may be quite unaware.

The union claimed in this case that the company had violated a specific provision of the contract. The company took the position that it had not violated that clause. There was, therefore, a dispute between the parties as to "the meaning, interpretation and application" of the collective bargaining agreement. Arbitration should have been ordered. When the judiciary undertakes to determine the merits of a grievance under the guise of interpreting the grievance procedure of collective bargaining agreements, it usurps a function which under that regime is entrusted to the arbitration tribunal.

Reversed.[8]

[8] Brennan, J., Frankfurter, J., Harlan, J., and Whittaker, J., concurred. Black, J., took no part in the decision.

UNITED STEELWORKERS v. WARRIOR & GULF NAVIGATION CO.
363 U.S. 574 (1960)

DOUGLAS, J.

Respondent transports steel and steel products by barge and maintains a terminal at Chickasaw, Alabama, where it performs maintenance and repair work on its barges. The employees at that terminal constitute a bargaining unit covered by a collective bargaining agreement negotiated by petitioner union. Respondent between 1956 and 1958 laid off some employees, reducing the bargaining unit from 42 to 23 men. This reduction was due in part to respondent contracting maintenance work, previously done by its employees, to other companies. The latter used respondent's supervisors to lay out the work and hired some of the laid-off employees of respondent (at reduced wages). Some were in fact assigned to work on respondent's barges. A number of employees signed a grievance which petitioner presented to respondent, the grievance reading:

> We are hereby protesting the Company's actions, of arbitrarily and unreasonably contracting out work to other concerns, that could and previously has been performed by Company employees.
>
> This practice becomes unreasonable, unjust and discriminatory in lieu [sic] of the fact that at present there are a number of employees that have been laid off for about 1 and ½ years or more for allegedly lack of work.
>
> Confronted with these facts we charge that the Company is in violation of the contract by inducing a partial lock-out, of a number of the employees who would otherwise be working were it not for this unfair practice."

The collective agreement had both a "no strike" and a "no lockout" provision. It also had a grievance procedure which provided in relevant part as follows:

> Issues which conflict with any Federal statute in its application as established by Court procedure or matters which are strictly a function of management shall not be subject to arbitration under this section.
>
> Should differences arise between the Company and the Union or its members employed by the Company as to the meaning and application of the provisions of this Agreement, or should any local trouble of any kind arise, there shall be no suspension of work on account of such differences but an earnest effort shall be made to settle such differences immediately in the following manner:
>
> A. For Maintenance Employees:
>
> First, between the aggrieved employees, and the Foreman involved;
>
> Second, between a member or members of the Grievance Committee designated by the Union, and the Foreman and Master Mechanic. . . .

> Fifth, if agreement has not been reached the matter shall be referred to an impartial umpire for decision. . . . The decision of the umpire shall be final.

Settlement of this grievance was not had and respondent refused arbitration. This suit was then commenced by the union to compel it.

The District Court granted respondent's motion to dismiss the complaint. It held after hearing evidence, much of which went to the merits of the grievance, that the agreement did not "confide in an arbitrator the right to review the defendant's business judgment in contracting out work." It further held that "the contracting out of repair and maintenance work, as well as construction work, is strictly a function of management not limited in any respect by the labor agreement involved here." The Court of Appeals affirmed by a divided vote, the majority holding that the collective agreement had withdrawn from the grievance procedure "matters which are strictly a function of management" and that contracting out fell in that exception. The case is here on a writ of certiorari.

We held in Textile Workers v. Lincoln Mills, 353 U.S. 448, that a grievance arbitration provision in a collective agreement could be enforced by reason of §301(a) of the Labor Management Relations Act and that the policy to be applied in enforcing this type of arbitration was that reflected in our national labor laws. Id., at 456-457. The present federal policy is to promote industrial stabilization through the collective bargaining agreement. Id., at 453-454. A major factor in achieving industrial peace is the inclusion of a provision for arbitration of grievances in the collective bargaining agreement.

Thus the run of arbitration cases, illustrated by Wilko v. Swan, 346 U.S. 427, becomes irrelevant to our problem. There the choice is between the adjudication of cases or controversies in courts with established procedures or even special statutory safeguards on the one hand and the settlement of them in the more informal arbitration tribunal on the other. In the commercial case, arbitration is the substitute for litigation. Here arbitration is the substitute for industrial strife. Since arbitration of labor disputes has quite different functions from arbitration under an ordinary commercial agreement, the hostility evinced by courts toward arbitration of commercial agreements has no place here. For arbitration of labor disputes under collective bargaining agreements is part and parcel of the collective bargaining process itself.

The collective bargaining agreement states the rights and duties of the parties. It is more than a contract; it is a generalized code to govern a myriad of cases which the draftsmen cannot wholly anticipate. See Shulman, Reason, Contract, and Law in Labor Relations, 68 Harv. L. Rev. 999, 1004-1005. The collective agreement covers the whole employment relationship. It calls into being a new common law — the common law of a particular industry or of a particular plant. As one observer has put it:[6]

> . . . [I]t is not unqualifiedly true that a collective-bargaining agreement is simply a document by which the union and employees have imposed upon management limited, express restrictions of its otherwise absolute right to manage the enterprise, so that an employee's claim must fail unless he can point to a specific contract provision upon which the claim is founded. There are too many people, too many problems, too many unforeseeable contingencies to make the words of the contract the exclusive source of rights and duties. One cannot reduce all the rules governing a community like an industrial plant to fifteen or even fifty pages. Within the sphere of collective bargaining, the institutional characteristics and the governmental nature of the collective-bargaining process demand a common law of the shop which implements and furnishes the context of the agreement. We must assume that intelligent negotiators acknowledged so plain a need unless they stated a contrary rule in plain words.

A collective bargaining agreement is an effort to erect a system of industrial self-government. When most parties enter into contractual relationship they do so voluntarily, in the sense that there is no real compulsion to deal with one another, as opposed to dealing with other parties. This is not true of the labor agreement. The choice is generally not between entering or refusing to enter into a relationship, for that in all probability preexists the negotiations. Rather it is between having that relationship governed by an agreed-upon rule of law or leaving each and every matter subject to a temporary resolution dependent solely upon the relative strength, at any given moment, of the contending forces. The mature labor agreement may attempt to regulate all aspects of the complicated relationship, from the most crucial to the most minute over an extended period of time. Because of the compulsion to reach agreement and the breadth of the matters covered, as well as the need for a fairly concise and readable instrument, the product of negotiations (the written document) is, in the words of the late Dean Shulman, "a compilation of diverse provisions: some provide objective criteria almost automatically applicable; some provide more or less specific standards which require reason and judgment in their application; and some do little more than leave problems to future consideration with an expression of hope and good faith." Shulman, supra, at 1005. Gaps may be left to be filled in by reference to the practices of the particular industry and of the various shops covered by the agreement. Many of the specific practices which underlie the agreement may be unknown, except in hazy form, even to the negotiators. Courts and arbitration in the context of most commercial contracts are resorted to because there has been a

6. Cox, Reflections upon Labor Arbitration, 72 Harv. L. Rev. 1482, 1498-1499 (1959).

breakdown in the working relationship of the parties; such resort is the unwanted exception. But the grievance machinery under a collective bargaining agreement is at the very heart of the system of industrial self-government. Arbitration is the means of solving the unforeseeable by molding a system of private law for all the problems which may arise and to provide for their solution in a way which will generally accord with the variant needs and desires of the parties. The processing of disputes through the grievance machinery is actually a vehicle by which meaning and content are given to the collective bargaining agreement.

Apart from matters that the parties specifically exclude, all of the questions on which the parties disagree must therefore come within the scope of the grievance and arbitration provisions of the collective agreement. The grievance procedure is, in other words, a part of the continuous collective bargaining process. It, rather than a strike, is the terminal point of a disagreement.

The labor arbitrator performs functions which are not normal to the courts; the considerations which help him fashion judgments may indeed be foreign to the competence of courts.

> A proper conception of the arbitrator's function is basic. He is not a public tribunal imposed upon the parties by superior authority which the parties are obliged to accept. He has no general charter to administer justice for a community which transcends the parties. He is rather part of a system of self-government created by and confined to the parties. . . . Shulman, supra, at 1016.

The labor arbitrator's source of law is not confined to the express provisions of the contract, as the industrial common law — the practices of the industry and the shop — is equally a part of the collective bargaining agreement although not expressed in it. The labor arbitrator is usually chosen because of the parties' confidence in his knowledge of the common law of the shop and their trust in his personal judgment to bring to bear considerations which are not expressed in the contract as criteria for judgment. The parties expect that his judgment of a particular grievance will reflect not only what the contract says but, insofar as the collective bargaining agreement permits, such factors as the effect upon productivity of a particular result, its consequence to the morale of the shop, his judgment whether tensions will be heightened or diminished. For the parties' objective in using the arbitration process is primarily to further their common goal of uninterrupted production under the agreement, to make the agreement serve their specialized needs. The ablest judge cannot be expected to bring the same experience and competence to bear upon the determination of a grievance, because he cannot be similarly informed.

The Congress, however, has by §301 of the Labor Management Relations Act, assigned the courts the duty of determining whether the reluctant party has breached his promise to arbitrate. For arbitration is a matter of contract and a party cannot be required to submit to arbitration any dispute which he has not agreed so to submit. Yet, to be consistent with congressional policy in favor of settlement of disputes by the parties through the machinery of arbitration, the judicial inquiry under §301 must be strictly confined to the question whether the reluctant party did agree to arbitrate the grievance or did agree to give the arbitrator power to make the award he made. An order to arbitrate the particular grievance should not be denied unless it may be said with positive assurance that the arbitration clause is not susceptible of an interpretation that covers the asserted dispute. Doubts should be resolved in favor of coverage.[7]

We do not agree with the lower courts that contracting-out grievances were necessarily excepted from the grievance procedure of this agreement. To be sure, the agreement provides that "matters which are strictly a function of management shall not be subject to arbitration." But it goes on to say that if "differences" arise or if "any local trouble of any kind" arises, the grievance procedure shall be applicable.

Collective bargaining agreements regulate or restrict the exercise of management functions; they do not oust management from the performance of them. Management hires and fires, pays and promotes, supervises and plans. All these are part of its function, and absent a collective bargaining agreement, it may be exercised freely except as limited by public law and by the willingness of employees to work under the particular, unilaterally imposed conditions. A collective bargaining agreement may treat only with certain specific practices, leaving the rest to management but subject to the possibility of work stoppages. When, however, an absolute no-strike clause is included in the agreement, then in a very real sense everything that management does is subject to the agreement, for either management is prohibited or limited in the action it takes, or if not, it is protected from interference by strikes. This comprehensive reach of the collective bargaining agreement does not mean, however, that the language, "strictly a function of management," has no meaning.

"Strictly a function of management" might be thought to refer to any practice of management in which, under particular circumstances prescribed by the agreement, it is permitted to indulge. But if courts, in order to determine arbitrability, were allowed to determine what is permitted and what is not, the arbitration clause would be swallowed up by

7. It is clear that under both the agreement in this case and that involved in *American Manufacturing Co.*, the question of arbitrability is for the courts to decide. Cf. Cox, Reflections upon Labor Arbitration, 72 Harv. L. Rev. 1482, 1508-1509. Where the assertion by the claimant is that the parties excluded from court determination not merely the decision of the merits of the grievance but also the question of its arbitrability, vesting power to make both decisions in the arbitrator, the claimant must bear the burden of a clear demonstration of that purpose.

the exception. Every grievance in a sense involves a claim that management has violated some provision of the agreement.

Accordingly, "strictly a function of management" must be interpreted as referring only to that over which the contract gives management complete control and unfettered discretion. Respondent claims that the contracting out of work falls within this category. Contracting out work is the basis of many grievances; and that type of claim is grist in the mills of the arbitrators.[8] A specific collective bargaining agreement may exclude contracting out from the grievance procedure. Or a written collateral agreement may make clear that contracting out was not a matter for arbitration. In such a case a grievance based solely on contracting out would not be arbitrable. Here, however, there is no such provision. Nor is there any showing that the parties designed the phrase "strictly a function of management" to encompass any and all forms of contracting out. In the absence of any express provision excluding a particular grievance from arbitration, we think only the most forceful evidence of a purpose to exclude the claim from arbitration can prevail, particularly where, as here, the exclusion clause is vague and the arbitration clause quite broad. Since any attempt by a court to infer such a purpose necessarily comprehends the merits, the court should view with suspicion an attempt to persuade it to become entangled in the construction of the substantive provisions of a labor agreement, even through the back door of interpreting the arbitration clause, when the alternative is to utilize the services of an arbitrator.

The grievance alleged that the contracting out was a violation of the collective bargaining agreement. There was, therefore, a dispute "as to the meaning and application of the provisions of this Agreement" which the parties had agreed would be determined by arbitration.

The judiciary sits in these cases to bring into operation an arbitral process which substitutes a regime of peaceful settlement for the older regime of industrial conflict. Whether contracting out in the present case violated the agreement is the question. It is a question for the arbiter, not for the courts.

Reversed.[9]

BRENNAN, J., with whom FRANKFURTER, J., and HARLAN, J., join, concurring. . . .

The issue in the *Warrior* case is essentially no different from that in *American,* that is, it is whether the company agreed to arbitrate a particu-

8. See Celanese Corp. of America, 33 Lab. Arb. Rep. 925, 941 (1959), where the arbiter in a grievance growing out of contracting out work said: "In my research I have located 64 published decisions which have been concerned with this issue covering a wide range of factual situations but all of them with the common characteristic — i.e., the contracting-out of work involved occurred under an Agreement that contained no provision that specifically mentioned contracting-out of work."

[9] Whittaker, J., dissented. Black, J., took no part in the decision.

lar grievance. In contrast to *American,* however, the arbitration promise here excludes a particular area from arbitration — "matters which are strictly a function of management." Because the arbitration promise is different, the scope of the court's inquiry may be broader. Here, a court may be required to examine the substantive provisions of the contract to ascertain whether the parties have provided that contracting out shall be a "function of management." If a court may delve into the merits to the extent of inquiring whether the parties have expressly agreed whether or not contracting out was a "function of management," why was it error for the lower court here to evaluate the evidence of bargaining history for the same purpose? Neat logical distinctions do not provide the answer. The Court rightly concludes that appropriate regard for the national labor policy and the special factors relevant to the labor arbitral process, admonish that judicial inquiry into the merits of this grievance should be limited to the search for an explicit provision which brings the grievance under the cover of the exclusion clause since "the exclusion clause is vague and arbitration clause quite broad." The hazard of going further into the merits is amply demonstrated by what the courts below did. On the basis of inconclusive evidence, those courts found that Warrior was in no way limited by any implied covenants of good faith and fair dealing from contracting out as it pleased — which would necessarily mean that Warrior was free completely to destroy the collective bargaining agreement by contracting out all the work.

The very ambiguity of the *Warrior* exclusion clause suggests that the parties were generally more concerned with having an arbitrator render decisions as to the meaning of the contract than they were in restricting the arbitrator's jurisdiction. The case might of course be otherwise were the arbitration clause very narrow, or the exclusion clause quite specific, for the inference might then be permissible that the parties had manifested a greater interest in confining the arbitrator; the presumption of arbitrability would then not have the same force and the Court would be somewhat freer to examine into the merits.

The Court makes reference to an arbitration clause being the quid pro quo for a no-strike clause. I do not understand the Court to mean that the application of the principles announced today depends upon the presence of a no-strike clause in the agreement.

Notes

1. In Boeing Co. v. UAW, 231 F. Supp. 930 (E.D. Pa. 1964), affd., 349 F.2d 412 (3d Cir. 1965), the company terminated its ten-year practice of giving Christmas turkeys to employees. The union grieved and demanded arbitration, and the company filed a §301 action asking for a declaratory judgment that it was not bound to arbitrate. The union

contended that Christmas turkeys were discussed during negotiations and that although the company's practice was not specifically mentioned in the agreement, it was considered one of the company's obligations under the agreement. The company denied discussing the practice in negotiations. The arbitration clause read:

> The jurisdiction of the arbitrator shall be limited to a determination of the facts and the interpretation and application of the specific provisions of this agreement at issue. The arbitrator shall be bound by the provisions of this agreement and shall have no authority to add to, subtract from, amend or modify any of its provisions, or to rule upon wage scales or management prerogatives.

The court held that the company was not obliged to submit the dispute to arbitration in view of the restrictive language of the arbitration clause and the lack of a specific provision relating to Christmas turkeys.

Was the decision in accord with the guidelines set out in *American Mfg. Co.* and *Warrior & Gulf Navigation Co.*? If so, would a different arbitration clause have sent the dispute to an arbitrator? Does the decision only mean that a court, rather than an arbitrator, should decide whether the company has breached the agreement?

If the arbitration clause had been broader and the grievance submitted to the arbitrator on the merits, how should the arbitrator have ruled? Consider:

> It is more than doubtful that there is any general understanding among employers and unions as to the viability of existing practices during the term of a collective agreement. . . . I venture to guess that in many enterprises the execution of a collective agreement would be blocked if it were insisted that it contain a broad provision that "all existing practices, except as modified by this agreement, shall be continued for the life thereof, unless changed by mutual consent." And I suppose that execution would also be blocked if the converse provision were demanded, namely that "the employer shall be free to change any existing practice except as he is restricted by the terms of this agreement." The reasons for the block would be, of course, the great uncertainty as to the nature and extent of the commitment, and the relentless search for cost-saving changes. . . .[10]

Should the test be whether the practice involves "employee benefits" as opposed to "basic management functions,"[11] or does that merely "encourage the arbitrator to work backward from his [or her] decision"?[12]

[10] Shulman, Reason, Contract and Law in Labor Relations, 68 Harv. L. Rev. 999, 1012 (1955).

[11] F. Elkouri & E. Elkouri, How Arbitration Works 274-275 (1960).

[12] Mittenthal, Past Practice and the Administration of Collective Bargaining Agreements, 59 Mich. L. Rev. 1017, 1038 (1961).

2. Assume the same arbitration clause as in the *Boeing* case, supra. The bargaining agreement says nothing about plant relocation and it was not discussed in negotiations. If the company announces a relocation, should a court send to arbitration a grievance alleging the relocation would violate a clause in the agreement granting recognition of the union as the employees' representative? Wouldn't the union's demand for arbitration be stronger if the agreement had a clause giving management the right to relocate?

3. In *Warrior & Gulf Navigation Co.*, the agreement provided that "matters which are strictly a function of management shall not be subject to arbitration . . ." and Justice Whittaker's dissenting opinion revealed a district court finding that the union had in several negotiations sought to limit management's right to subcontract but with no success. Should parol evidence be considered by a court asked to compel a party to arbitrate? Suppose the company had offered to prove that it had demanded a clause expressly permitting subcontracting and the union negotiator had replied, "Look, that's not necessary. As we read the present agreement you are not prevented from subcontracting and we certainly aren't about to ask you to arbitrate your subcontracting decisions"?

4. Many bargaining agreements impose time limits on raising a grievance or on carrying it to the next step in the grievance-arbitration process. Noncompliance with such a limitation raises a question of "procedural arbitrability." In John Wiley & Sons v. Livingston, 376 U.S. 543 (1964), the Court held that issues of procedural arbitrability are for the arbitrator:

> Doubt whether grievance procedures or some part of them apply to a particular dispute, whether such procedures have been followed or excused, or whether the unexcused failure to follow them avoids the duty to arbitrate cannot ordinarily be answered without consideration of the merits of the dispute which is presented for arbitration. . . . Once it is determined, as we have, that the parties are obligated to submit the subject matter of a dispute to arbitration, "procedural" questions which grow out of the dispute and bear on its final disposition should be left to the arbitrator. . . .
>
> Reservation of "procedural" issues for the courts would not only create the difficult task of separating related issues, but would also produce frequent duplication of effort. In addition, the opportunities for deliberate delay and the possibility of well-intentioned but no less serious delay created by separation of the "procedural" and "substantive" elements of a dispute are clear.

In Operating Engineers Local 150 v. Flair Builders, 406 U.S. 487 (1972), the Court held that a claim of "laches" was for the arbitrator, not a court, to decide even though the claim grew out of matters "extrinsic" to the agreement.

5. Is the arbitrator hearing the *Warrior & Gulf Navigation Co.* dispute free to rule that he or she has no jurisdiction to decide the grievance? If so, and if such a ruling is made, does this mean a court should decide the merits of the grievance?

6. With the Court's attitude toward grievance arbitration, compare the following by a former labor law professor and Second Circuit judge.

> Pending scholarly studies and evaluations, I am forced to the conclusion, based upon observation during twenty-three years of very active practice in the area of arbitration and as an arbitrator, and from suggestions in the more intelligent literature in this field, that labor arbitration has fatal shortcomings as a system for the judicial administration of contract violations. I call labor arbitration "a system for the judicial administration of contract violations," since this is, I believe, all that is basically claimed for it. An arbitrator is a third party called in to determine a controversy over whether one of the parties to the collective bargaining agreement has violated that agreement. He is not a wise counsellor and statesman to whom the management and the union look for advice on how to run their affairs or how to increase production or lessen tensions. He is merely an ad hoc judge to whom is submitted the question of whether the collective bargaining agreement has been violated. The chances are very good that, in all but a tiny percentage of arbitrations, this is the first time he has had anything to do with the plant, and that he knows nothing of the background of the dispute or of the "common law" of the industry. In fact there is a considerable possibility that this is his first arbitration case. He does not in fact have any expertise in these matters and is not actually expected to have any, since it is expected that he will listen to the evidence presented by the two parties and decide on the basis of that evidence whether the charge of contract violation is or is not sustained. For his task he requires exactly the same expertise which judges have and use every day. He must be expert in analyzing issues, in weighing evidence, and in contract interpretation.
>
> There are only a handful of arbitrators who, like Shulman and Cox, have the knowledge, training, skill, and character which would make them good judges and therefore make them good arbitrators. In literally thousands of cases every year decisions are made by arbitrators who are wholly unfitted for their jobs, who do not have the requisite knowledge, training, skill, intelligence and character. In fact, a proportion of arbitration awards, no one knows how large a proportion, is decided not on the basis of the evidence or of the contract or other proper considerations, but in a way calculated to encourage the arbitrator's being hired for other arbitration cases. It makes no difference whether or not a large majority of cases is decided in this way. A system of adjudication in which the judge depends for his livelihood, or for a substantial part of his livelihood or even for substantial supplements to his regular income, on pleasing those who

hire him to judge is per se a thoroughly undesirable system. In no proper system of justice should a judge be submitted to such pressures; on the contrary, a judge should be carefully insulated from any pressure of this type. There are many discussions of arbitration which do not mention this aspect of the process. In my opinion no discussion of arbitration which does not consider the effect of the arbitrator's dependence on the good will of the parties is completely honest.

It is my view that intervention by the courts, even if a broad intervention should be permitted, is not a sufficient answer to the shortcomings of labor arbitration. I believe that the courts should not lend themselves at all to the arbitration process. Labor arbitration is a private system of justice not based on law and not observant of law. There is no reason why it should be able to call upon the legal system to enforce its decrees. On the contrary, there are positive reasons for the courts not exercising their enforcement powers in favor of arbitration. We know that a large proportion of the awards of arbitrators are rendered by incompetents, that another proportion, we do not know how large but are permitted by the circumstances to suspect that it is quite substantial, are rendered not on the basis of any proper concerns, but rather on the basis of what award would be best for the arbitrator's future. We know also that there is another group of cases, though it is true that the courts are not called upon for enforcement in such cases, in which the arbitrator has rendered a rigged award, a practice so vicious as to be unacceptable in any system of justice.

In his lecture [see n.[10] supra] Dean Shulman suggested that "the law stay out" of arbitration. While his reasons for such a conclusion are quite different from mine, I wish to make the same suggestion — that the law get out of labor arbitration and leave the procedure exclusively to the voluntary action of the parties. In this way those who believe that labor arbitration is a praiseworthy system of industrial justice will be able to have such a system working on its highest level, the level Shulman described and advocated. Those who believe, as I do, that labor arbitration is a usually undesirable and frequently intolerable procedure will not be offended by the requirement that our courts rubber stamp the questionable results which the arbitrators have reached.[13]

The Hays view has not gone unchallenged.[14]

7. In Nolde Bros. v. Bakery Workers Local 358, 430 U.S. 243 (1977),[15] the bargaining agreement provided for severance pay on termination of the employment of certain employees. During negotiations for a new agreement, the union gave notice of cancellation and the contract terminated. Negotiations continued but when the union threatened to strike, the company permanently closed its bakery. The com-

[13] Hays, The Future of Labor Arbitration, 74 Yale L.J. 1019, 1034-1035 (1965).

[14] See Meltzer, Ruminations about Ideology, Law, and Labor Arbitration, 34 U. Chi. L. Rev. 545 (1967), and sources there cited.

[15] See Goetz, Arbitration after Termination of a Collective Bargaining Agreement, 63 Va. L. Rev. 693 (1977).

pany paid employees accrued wages and vacation pay under the cancelled contract, but it refused the union's demand for severance pay. It also refused to arbitrate the severance pay claim, contending that its contractual obligation to arbitrate disputes terminated with the collective bargaining agreement. The union brought a §301 suit to compel arbitration.

The Supreme Court, per Chief Justice Burger, held the dispute should be sent to arbitration. The union argued that the employees' right to the severance pay was "accrued" or "vested" under the terminated agreement; the company contended that the substantive right expired with the agreement, as did its obligation to arbitrate. The Court found the substantive dispute to turn on the interpretation of the bargaining agreement, an interpretation that clearly would have been reserved for an arbitrator absent the agreement's termination. Carried to its logical conclusion, in the Court's view, the company's argument would deny arbitration even when a dispute occurred during the term of the agreement but arbitration was not invoked, or its processes not completed, until after the agreement's termination — a result foreclosed by precedent and policy.

The Court relied on John Wiley & Sons v. Livingston, 376 U.S. 543 (1964), where the Court sent similar claims to arbitration when a demand for arbitration was made before the agreement terminated. Absent indications in the expired agreement of a contrary intention, the strong presumption of *Warrior & Gulf Navigation* favoring arbitration applies. For such a dispute to be withheld from arbitration, "the presumptions favoring arbitrability must be negated expressly or by clear implication."

Justices Stewart and Rehnquist dissented on the ground that the assumptions underlying the favored status of arbitration in *Warrior & Gulf Navigation* were absent where

> the closing of the bakery . . . necessarily meant there was no continuing relationship to protect or preserve . . . [a]nd the union's termination of the contract, thereby releasing it from its obligation not to strike, foreclosed any reason for implying a continuing duty on the part of the employer to arbitrate as a quid pro quo for the union's offsetting, enforceable duty to negotiate rather than strike.

Problem. An employee was discharged during the term of a now-expired bargaining agreement. The arbitration clause was broad enough to cover the discharge, and the no-strike clause was broad enough to cover a strike over the discharge. Would a strike to secure reinstatement of the discharged employee be a breach of the expired agreement? Can the employer lawfully refuse to sign a new collective bargaining agreement unless and until the union waives an arbitration award ordering the employee reinstated? See Goya Foods, 238 N.L.R.B. 1465 (1978).

UNITED STEELWORKERS v. ENTERPRISE WHEEL & CAR CORP.
363 U.S. 593 (1960)

Douglas, J.

Petitioner union and respondent during the period relevant here had a collective bargaining agreement which provided that any differences "as to the meaning and application" of the agreement should be submitted to arbitration and that the arbitrator's decision "shall be final and binding on the parties." Special provisions were included concerning the suspension and discharge of employees. The agreement stated:

> Should it be determined by the Company or by an arbitrator in accordance with the grievance procedure that the employee has been suspended unjustly or discharged in violation of the provisions of this Agreement, the Company shall reinstate the employee and pay full compensation at the employee's regular rate of pay for the time lost.

The agreement also provided:

> . . . It is understood and agreed that neither party will institute *civil suits or legal proceedings* against the other for alleged violation of any of the provisions of this labor contract; instead all disputes will be settled in the manner outlined in this Article III — Adjustment of Grievances.

A group of employees left their jobs in protest against the discharge of one employee. A union official advised them at once to return to work. An official of respondent at their request gave them permission and then rescinded it. The next day they were told they did not have a job any more "until this thing was settled one way or the other."

A grievance was filed; and when respondent finally refused to arbitrate, this suit was brought for specific enforcement of the arbitration provisions of the agreement. The District Court ordered arbitration. The arbitrator found that the discharge of the men was not justified, though their conduct, he said, was improper. In his view the facts warranted at most a suspension of the men for 10 days each. After their discharge and before the arbitration award the collective bargaining agreement had expired. The union, however, continued to represent the workers at the plant. The arbitrator rejected the contention that expiration of the agreement barred reinstatement of the employees. He held that the provision of the agreement above quoted imposed an unconditional obligation on the employer. He awarded reinstatement with back pay, minus pay for a 10-day suspension and such sums as these employees received from other employment.

Respondent refused to comply with the award. Petitioner moved the District Court for enforcement. The District Court directed respondent to comply. The Court of Appeals, while agreeing that the District Court had jurisdiction to enforce an arbitration award under a collective bargaining agreement, held that the failure of the award to specify the amounts to be deducted from the back pay rendered the award unenforceable. That defect, it agreed, could be remedied by requiring the parties to complete the arbitration. It went on to hold, however, that an award for back pay subsequent to the date of termination of the collective bargaining agreement could not be enforced. It also held that the requirement for reinstatement of the discharged employees was likewise unenforceable because the collective bargaining agreement had expired. We granted certiorari.

The refusal of courts to review the merits of an arbitration award is the proper approach to arbitration under collective bargaining agreements. The federal policy of settling labor disputes by arbitration would be undermined if courts had the final say on the merits of the awards. As we stated in United Steelworkers of America v. Warrior & Gulf Navigation Co., decided this day, the arbitrators under these collective agreements are indispensable agencies in a continuous collective bargaining process. They sit to settle disputes at the plant level — disputes that require for their solution knowledge of the custom and practices of a particular factory or of a particular industry as reflected in particular agreements.

When an arbitrator is commissioned to interpret and apply the collective bargaining agreement, he is to bring his informed judgment to bear in order to reach a fair solution of a problem. This is especially true when it comes to formulating remedies. There the need is for flexibility in meeting a wide variety of situations. The draftsmen may never have thought of what specific remedy should be awarded to meet a particular contingency. Nevertheless, an arbitrator is confined to interpretation and application of the collective bargaining agreement; he does not sit to dispense his own brand of industrial justice. He may of course look for guidance from many sources, yet his award is legitimate only so long as it draws its essence from the collective bargaining agreement. When the arbitrator's words manifest an infidelity to this obligation, courts have no choice but to refuse enforcement of the award.

The opinion of the arbitrator in this case, as it bears upon the award of back pay beyond the date of the agreement's expiration and reinstatement, is ambiguous. It may be read as based solely upon the arbitrator's view of the requirements of enacted legislation, which would mean that he exceeded the scope of the submission. Or it may be read as embodying a construction of the agreement itself, perhaps with the arbitrator looking to "the law" for help in determining the sense of the agreement. A mere ambiguity in the opinion accompanying an award, which permits the inference that the arbitrator may have exceeded his authority, is not a reason for refusing to enforce the award. Arbitrators have no obligation to the court to give their reasons for an award. To require opinions free of ambiguity may lead arbitrators to play it safe by writing no supporting opinions. This would be undesirable for a well-reasoned opinion tends to engender confidence in the integrity of the process and aids in clarifying the underlying agreement. Moreover, we see no reason to assume that this arbitrator has abused the trust the parties confided in him and has not stayed within the areas marked out for his consideration. It is not apparent that he went beyond the submission. The Court of Appeals' opinion refusing to enforce the reinstatement and partial back pay portions of the award was not based upon any finding that the arbitrator did not premise his award on his construction of the contract. It merely disagreed with the arbitrator's construction of it.

The collective bargaining agreement could have provided that if any of the employees were wrongfully discharged, the remedy would be reinstatement and back pay up to the date they were returned to work. Respondent's major argument seems to be that by applying correct principles of law to the interpretation of the collective bargaining agreement it can be determined that the agreement did not so provide, and that therefore the arbitrator's decision was not based upon the contract. The acceptance of this view would require courts, even under the standard arbitration clause, to review the merits of every construction of the contract. This plenary review by a court of the merits would make meaningless the provisions that the arbitrator's decision is final, for in reality it would almost never be final. This underlies the fundamental error which we have alluded to in United Steelworkers of America v. American Manufacturing Co., decided this day. As we there emphasized, the question of interpretation of the collective bargaining agreement is a question for the arbitrator. It is the arbitrator's construction which was bargained for; and so far as the arbitrator's decision concerns construction of the contract, the courts have no business overruling him because their interpretation of the contract is different from his.

We agree with the Court of Appeals that the judgment of the District Court should be modified so that the amounts due the employees may be definitely determined by arbitration. In all other respects we think the judgment of the District Court should be affirmed. Accordingly, we reverse the judgment of the Court of Appeals, except for that modification, and remand the case to the District Court for proceedings in conformity with this opinion.

It is so ordered.[16]

[16] Brennan, J., Frankfurter, J., and Harlan, J., concurred. Whittaker, J., dissented. Black, J., took no part in the decision.

Notes

1. What is the standard of review of whether the arbitrator had jurisdiction to decide a particular grievance? Should the standard differ depending on whether the party who would challenge the arbitrator's jurisdiction raised the issue before the arbitrator?

2. Do the policies that support sending grievances to arbitration without court inquiry into the merits of the grievances also support judicial deference to arbitration awards at the enforcement stage? Would it substantially interfere with consensual arbitration to require an arbitrator to produce a reasoned opinion supported by some evidence?

In that connection, consider Torrington Co. v. Metal Products Workers, 362 F.2d 677 (2d Cir. 1966). The employer publicly renounced its 20-year practice of giving employees paid time off for voting. The practice was not mentioned in the current bargaining agreement, which then had several months to run before expiration. In negotiations for a new bargaining agreement, the union demanded the practice be reinstated; the company refused. After a strike, during which working employees were not given time off for voting, a new agreement was signed that, like the old, made no mention of paid time off for voting. When the company next refused voting time pay, the union grieved and carried the dispute to arbitration. The arbitrator ruled for the union. In his view, the company had the burden of changing its policy by negotiating the assent of the union, and it had not done so. The company petitioned to vacate the award.

The Second Circuit, Judge Feinberg dissenting, affirmed the district court's vacating of the award. First the court developed its power to review the award:

> Torrington contends that the arbitrator exceeded his authority in this case by "adding" the election day bonus to the terms of the January 1964 agreement. However, the arbitrator held that such a provision was implied by the prior practice of the parties. In some cases, it may be appropriate exercise of an arbitrator's authority to resolve ambiguities in the scope of a collective bargaining agreement on the basis of prior practice, since no agreement can reduce all aspects of the labor-management relationship to writing. However, while courts should be wary of rejecting the arbitrator's interpretation of the implications of the parties' prior practice, the mandate that the arbitrator stay within the confines of the collective bargaining agreement requires a reviewing court to pass upon whether the agreement authorizes the arbitrator to expand its express terms on the basis of the parties' prior practice. Therefore, we hold that the question of an arbitrator's authority is subject to judicial review, and that the arbitrator's decision that he has authority should not be accepted where the reviewing court can clearly perceive that he has derived that authority from sources

> outside the collective bargaining agreement at issue. See Textile Workers Union of America v. American Thread Co., 291 F.2d 894 (4th Cir. 1961).[6]

The court then took the arbitrator to task on the merits of the grievance. The arbitrator had relied upon the fact that the company and union had each initially insisted that their position be incorporated into the agreement and that the company submitted the first written proposal, which did not expressly insist that its election day position be adopted. The arbitrator interpreted the company's action as taking the question "from the table" and used that to bolster his conclusion that the company had failed to carry its burden of negotiating away a past practice. The court rejected the power of an arbitrator to resolve an issue on the basis of past practice when the benefit in question was discussed in negotiations but omitted from the contract. The arbitrator had erroneously ignored the public revocation of the policy and, in the court's view, when that was added to the fact that the agreement prohibited the arbitrator from "adding to" its provisions, the award could not be enforced. The arbitrator had "exceeded his authority by ruling that such a benefit was implied in the terms of the agreement."

Does an arbitrator ever have the authority to construe an agreement erroneously? Professor Theodore St. Antoine writes:

> The difficulty is that any time a court is incensed enough with an arbitrator's reading of the contract and such supplementary data as past practice, bargaining history, and the "common law of the shop," it is simplicity itself to conclude that the arbitrator must have "added to or altered" the collective bargaining agreement. How else can one explain this abomination of a construction? Yet if the courts are to remain faithful to the injunction of *Enterprise Wheel,* they must recognize that most arbitral aberrations are merely the product of fallible minds, not of overreaching power. At bottom, there is an inherent tension (if not inconsistency) between the "final and binding" arbitration clause and the "no additions or modifications" provision. The arbitrator cannot be effective as the parties' surrogate for giving shape to their necessarily amorphous contract unless he is allowed to fill the inevitable lacunae.[17]

6. Of course, it can be argued that our decision authorizes an impermissible review of the "merits" in a case where the principal issue was whether the arbitrator should find an implied substantive obligation in the contract, see Meltzer, The Supreme Court, Arbitrability, and Collective Bargaining, 28 U. Chi. L. Rev. 464, 484-485 (1961), but we think this position is contrary to *Enterprise Wheel.* The question of the arbitrator's authority is really one of his contractual jurisdiction, and the courts cannot be expected to place their stamp of approval upon his action without making some examination of his jurisdiction to act. As stated above, we think more exhaustive judicial review of this question is appropriate after the award has been made than before the award in a suit to compel arbitration; in this way, the court receives the benefit of the arbitrator's interpretive skills as to the matter of his contractual authority.

[17] St. Antoine, Judicial Review of Labor Arbitration Awards: A Second Look at *Enterprise Wheel* and its Progeny, 75 Mich. L. Rev. 1137, 1153 (1977).

3. *Problem.* The collective bargaining agreement provided for paid vacation days based on length of service with the company. Departing from past practice, the company required the employees to take their paid vacation in March, rather than at more attractive times during the summer months. The union grieved and an arbitrator held that the company had breached the agreement. On appeal the company concedes that it breached the agreement, but it challenges the arbitrator's remedy.

The agreement directs that "[t]he arbitrator's decision shall be within the terms of this agreement" and that "the arbitrator shall not add to, subtract from, alter or change the terms." The arbitrator ordered the company to give a second paid vacation to all employees who had been forced to take their vacations in March. He reasoned: "To merely grant an unpaid week off for a summer vacation equates to imposing on the grievants what virtually amounts to a layoff. No recognized principle of equity permits such a penalty on a prevailing party in a contractual dispute."

Should a court enforce the arbitrator's award? See United Electrical Workers, Local 1139 v. Litton Systems, — F.2d — , 115 L.R.R.M. 2633 (8th Cir. 1984).

4. The enforcement of a bargaining agreement may involve overlap and conflict with the NLRA. For example, the conduct claimed to breach the agreement may also be, if proved, an unfair labor practice. Should arbitrators and courts with the responsibility of enforcing bargaining agreements stay their hands while waiting to see how (and whether) the Board will act? The Supreme Court has held that the breach of contract action may go forward, although the maintenance of such an action will not affect the power of the Board to issue a remedy. See Local 174, Teamsters Union v. Lucas Flour Co., 369 U.S. 95, 101 n. 9 (1962); Smith v. Evening News Assn., 371 U.S. 195 (1962). The Court engaged in little discussion of its reasons for so ruling, but you might consider the relative speed of Board and arbitration decisions and the frequency with which such overlap occurs.

Far less settled is what a court or an arbitrator should do when it is contended that a grievance should not be sustained because it would compel the commission of an unfair labor practice or other violation of law. Examples are the enforcement of bargaining agreements with a union security clause that violates §§8(a)(3) and 8(b)(2), with a subcontracting or picket line clause that violates §8(e), or where the validity of the agreement itself is challenged because the union allegedly lacked a majority when it was signed. There are three occasions when such a challenge might be entertained: when a court is petitioned to send a grievance to arbitration, when the arbitrator is deciding the grievance, or when the arbitrator's award is sought to be enforced by the court.

What arguments do you see for and against consideration of the unfair labor practice issues at these points in the proceeding? In that connection consider the following cases.

W. R. GRACE CO. v. RUBBER WORKERS, LOCAL 759, 103 S. Ct. 2177 (1983): The company and the Equal Employment Opportunity Commission were engaged in conciliation discussions over alleged race and sex discrimination in violation of Title VII of the Civil Rights Act of 1964 when the union's collective bargaining agreement with the company expired. A strike settlement was reached and the collective bargaining agreement contained a system of a plantwide seniority. The company then gave female strike replacements shift preferences ahead of returning strikers. These preferences violated the collective bargaining agreement. The union grieved and demanded arbitration. The employer filed suit in federal court for an order prohibiting arbitration and the union counterclaimed to compel arbitration. Before the district court acted, the firm and the EEOC signed a conciliation agreement. The EEOC then joined the lawsuit and claimed the seniority provisions of the bargaining agreement were not bona fide. The district court granted summary judgment for the company and the EEOC. The union appealed to the Fifth Circuit.

While the appeal was pending, the company laid off employees. It followed the conciliation agreement in selecting employees for layoff, thereby breaching the bargaining agreement. The circuit court then reversed the district, held the seniority clauses were valid, and granted the union's request for arbitration.

The employer responded to the court's decision by restoring the laid off employees to the positions to which they were entitled under the bargaining agreement. The union pursued arbitration, seeking backpay for the reinstated workers. Arbitrator Sabella found that the company had violated the bargaining agreement; but he decided it would be unfair to penalize the company, and he refused to award backpay.

Instead of challenging arbitrator Sabella's decision in court, the union decided to challenge his reasoning in seeking backpay for a second worker before another arbitrator, named Barrett. Barrett decided that Sabella had acted outside of the jurisdiction granted to arbitrators by the bargaining agreement, and he declined to give that decision precedential effect. Finding no exception for good faith violations of the seniority clauses, Barrett granted the backpay award. The company challenged the Barrett award in federal court. It argued the award violated public policy. It prevailed in district court but the Fifth Circuit reversed. The case then reached the Supreme Court.

Only the Barrett award was before the Court, which upheld the circuit court and enforced the award. The Court first held that the Barrett award met the *Enterprise Wheel* standard for enforcement. It then stated that federal courts should not enforce arbitration awards that violate "explicit" public policy, but it issued a cautionary note.

> Such a public policy, however, must be well defined and dominant, and is to be ascertained "by reference to the laws and legal precedents and not from general considerations of supposed public interests." Muschany v. United States, 324 U.S. 49, 66 (1945).

The Court then held that no considerations of public policy prevented enforcement of the Barrett award.

> Given the company's desire to reduce its workforce, it is undeniable that the Company was faced with a dilemma; it could follow the conciliation agreement as mandated by the District Court and risk liability under the collective bargaining agreement, or it could follow the bargaining agreement and risk both a contempt citation and Title VII liability. The dilemma, however, was of the Company's own making. The Company committed itself voluntarily to two conflicting contractual obligations. When the Union attempted to enforce its contractual rights, the Company sought a judicial declaration of its respective obligations under the contracts. During the course of this litigation, before the legal rights were finally determined, the Company again laid off employees and dishonored its contract with the Union. For these acts, the Company incurred liability for breach of contract. In effect, Barrett interpreted the collective bargaining agreement to allocate to the Company the losses caused by the Company's decision to follow the District Court order that proved to be erroneous. . . .
>
> Because of the Company's alleged prior discrimination against women, some readjustments and consequent losses were bound to occur. The issue is whether the Company or the Union members should bear the burden of those losses. As interpreted by Barrett, the collective bargaining agreement placed this unavoidable burden on the Company. [T]he Company attempted to shift the loss to its male employees, who shared no responsibility for the sex discrimination. The Company voluntarily assumed its obligations under the collective bargaining agreement and the arbitrators' interpretations of it. No public policy is violated by holding the Company to those obligations, which bar the company's attempted reallocation of the burden.

EVANS PRODUCTS CO. & CARPENTERS LOCAL 550

78-1 A.R.B. ¶8130 (1978)

DAVID E. FELLER, Arbitrator.

Section 9(h) of the 1976-78 master agreement to which both Local 550 and the employer here are parties provides, in relevant part, as follows:

"Neither the Employer nor the Union shall discriminate against any employee or applicant to reemployment on the basis of age, sex, race, creed, color, . . ." Local 550 operates a non-exclusive hiring hall. On July 5, 1977 the union dispatched one [L.] from the hiring hall for the job of "non-production off-bearing tailoff work." On that date Mr. [L.] was 17 years old. The employer refused to hire him on the ground that regulations issued pursuant to the Fair Labor Standards Act, in particular 29 CFR §570.55, prohibited the employment of any person under the age of 18 on this job. The union, disputing the applicability of this regulation to the particular job in question, demanded a grievance hearing. The matter was not resolved in the grievance procedure and was referred to me pursuant to Section 18 of the Agreement between the parties.

The union rested its case upon the showing of the above-stated facts. The employer sought to establish that the hiring of Mr. [L.] would violate the cited provisions of federal law. The union objected, arguing that there was a dispute as to whether the employment of Mr. [L.] would in fact violate the regulations and that I was without authority, under the quoted provision of §18, to resolve that dispute. The employer argued that I was authorized to do so by virtue of the following provisions of §9(i):

> (i) It is expressly agreed by the parties that if any word, phrase, clause, paragraph, subparagraph or section is found to be illegal, the parties intend that the remaining portions of this Agreement shall remain in full force and effect.

In the discussion at the hearing which followed the union made it plain that disagreement between the parties as to the application of the federal regulations involved both a disagreement as to fact and a disagreement as to law. The regulation relied upon by the employer prohibits the employment of any person under the age of 18 in "the occupations of setting up, adjusting, repairing, oiling, or cleaning power-driven wood-working machines." The employer's contention was that the job in question did involve the cleaning of the saw in addition to taking the material away from the saw (the tailoff work). The union disputed the fact that the job required cleaning and also, assuming that the job did require cleaning, was of the view that the cleaning was not of the kind prohibited by the regulation since it did not involve getting into the saw with soap and water but operating a high-powered hose. It asserted, however, that I had no authority to resolve either of these issues under the terms of §18.

With matters in this posture I sought agreement from the parties that I could hear and decide the question of the applicability of the federal regulation, whether or not I would otherwise have jurisdiction to do so. The union refused to so stipulate, but proposed that I hear the factual issues and make findings thereon, leaving to some other tribunal any question as to the ultimate question of whether the federal regulation applied to the facts as found if such question remained. I offered to do so if the parties so stipulated but the employer refused. I then stated my view that §9(i) did not give me authority to interpet and apply the federal regulations and that I was limited by §18(f) to interpretation and application of the specific provisions of the agreement. I indicated that, although this was my view, I would be prepared to hear any testimony which the parties sought to offer and any argument to attempt to persuade me to change my view as to my authority, as well as any other reason than the argued applicability of the federal regulation why the grievance should not be granted.

In response, counsel for the employer asserted that there was another possible defense to the grievance. Specifically, it was said that §9(h) was meant only to include the provisions of the Age Discrimination in Employment Act and that, since that Act applies only between the ages of 40 and 65, there was no violation of the agreement in the refusal to employ Mr. [L.]. Counsel for the employer stated, however, that it was not relying on that defense and that the only defense which it had made to the employment of Mr. [L.] and the only one which it wished me to decide was the claim that his employment would violate the Fair Labor Standards Act regulation.

When I reiterated my view that I did not believe that the agreement gave me authority to resolve a dispute as to the applicability of the federal regulation, the employer requested me to disqualify myself. When I declined to do so and requested the employer to proceed with its case, counsel refused on the ground that I was without authority to hear and decide the matter since I had indicated my view that the agreement did not give me authority to decide the question of federal law.

At this point I inquired of the parties as to their views with respect to remedy if I should find that the refusal to employ Mr. [L.] violated the provisions of the agreement. The union requested that I direct that Mr. [L.] be employed with retroactive salary, benefits and rights to the date of July 5, 1977. The employer declined to present argument with respect to remedy. The hearing then concluded.

No briefs were filed. The union declined the opportunity to present further argument and submitted the matter. The employer declined to participate further in any way.

Transcript of the hearing was received on January 30, 1978.

The principal issue presented by this grievance — the extent of an arbitrator's authority to resolve a grievance on the basis of law external to the collective bargaining agreement — has been the subject of much controversy among arbitrators. See the articles and speeches cited in Feller, The Coming End of Arbitration's Golden Age, in Arbitration — 1976, Proceedings, 29th Annual Meeting, National Academy of Arbitrators (BNA, 1976) at p. 110. I have participated in that controversy and my views are reasonably well known. Indeed, subsequent to my appointment in this case but prior to the hearing, I provided to the parties citations to my published work on this question, and in the case of the employer, reprints of two recent articles: "The Impact of External Law upon Labor Arbitration," in The Future of Labor Arbitration in America (American Arbitration Association, 1976) 83 and "Arbitration: The Days of Its Glory Are Numbered," 2 Industrial Relations Law Journal 97 (1977). The views there expressed parallel recent decisions by both courts and arbitrators. . . . [Consider] the recent decision by the distinguished arbitrator Charles O. Gregory to the following effect:

> After extensive reading and reflection I have concluded that the grievance herein is arbitrable and that I had best fulfill my responsibility as an arbitrator acting under the agreement, in accord with the terms of that agreement, leaving to the courts the interpretation and appropriateness of the various federal antidiscrimination laws, rulings and sanctions. USM Corp., 69 Lab. Arb. Rep. 1050 (1977).

Other arbitrators have a different view. The cases are summarized in The Impact of External Law on Arbitration. For a recent example of a contrary position see International Paper Co., 69 Lab. Arb. Rep. 857 (F. Jay Taylor, 1977).

Whatever one's views may be on this subject in general, however, decision in a particular case must depend upon the authority granted to the arbitrator by the particular agreement which sets forth his jurisdiction. In this case the agreement is particularly clear. It provides that the arbitrator has no "authority to modify or add to any of the terms and provisions of this Agreement, nor to make any decisions on matters not covered by specific provisions of this Agreement." Unless otherwise modified by some other provision of the agreement, this seems to limit me to consideration of whether the employer has violated any specific provision of the agreement, leaving to other tribunals the decision as to whether that violation is justified by a prohibition imposed by law external to the agreement.

The employer argues that the limitation on my authority contained in §18(f) is modified by the provisions of §9(i). Section 9(i) provides that if any provision of the agreement is found to be illegal, the parties intend that the remaining portions of the agreement shall remain in full force and effect. As I indicated at the hearing, the purpose of this provision seems to be to preserve the remainder of the agreement if some portion of it is found to be invalid rather than to vest the arbitrator with authority to find that a portion of the agreement or its application in a particular case is invalid under external law.

I therefore conclude that, whatever the general authority of arbitrators may be, the only authority I have under this agreement is to decide whether the employer's action in refusing to hire Mr. [L.] on July 5, 1977, was a violation of the "specific provisions of this Agreement." Since I find that there is no specific provision which incorporates into the agreement the provisions of the Fair Labor Standards Act or any other federal statute, I am left with the question of whether the employer's action constituted a violation of the provision in §9(h) prohibiting discrimination against an applicant for employment on the basis of age.

The question is somewhat more difficult than might first appear and differs substantially from the cases where an arbitrator is asked to ignore an admitted violation of the agreement because of the anti-discrimination provisions of external law (as in the decision by Arbitrator Gregory cited above). The question is what "discrimination" in this agreement means. It might be possible to argue that this provision, properly construed, refers only to such discrimination as is prohibited by the Age Discrimination in Employment Act and therefore does not reach a refusal to hire an applicant under the age of 40. The employer, at the hearing, however, although raising the question, specifically declined to rest upon any such interpetation of the agreement. The only defense tendered, counsel asserted, was the alleged restriction imposed by the Fair Labor Standards Act.

It might also be possible to argue that the only kind of discrimination intended to be prohibited is invidious or hostile discrimination and that a refusal to hire because of an arguable prohibition under the Fair Labor Standards Act does not constitute discrimination of the kind prohibited by §9(h). Alternatively, it might be possible to contend that it is not discrimination to refuse to hire an individual who because of his age is incapable of performing the job for which he has applied — as would be the case if the applicant were five years old — and that the regulations issued under the Fair Labor Standards Act place such restrictions upon the work which Mr. [L.] could perform that he was thereby rendered unable to fill the requirements of the job. Neither of these latter two arguments, however, was presented to me. The employer rested on the contention that the refusal to hire Mr. [L.] because of his age was justified by the Fair Labor Standards Act and that §9(i) gave me authority to determine the validity of that defense, and declined to proceed further when I indicated my preliminary view that I found no such authority in that section.

Concluding as I do that §9(i) is not such a grant of authority and that I am required, in the absence of agreement to the contrary, to limit myself to the "specific provisions of this Agreement," I am compelled to conclude that the conceded refusal of the employer to hire Mr. [L.] solely because he was 17 years old was discrimination against an applicant for employment on the basis of his age in violation of the provisions of §9(h) of the agreement.

There remains the question of remedy. Any remedy which I might direct is obviously subject to nullification by a court having authority to determine the disputed question of federal law. I need not, therefore, concern myself with any unfairness in providing a remedy if the employer should prove to be correct in the contention with respect to the applicability of federal law to the present case. If, on the other hand, the union should prove to be successful in its view that the federal regulation did not prohibit the employment of Mr. [L.] I must decide what, under this agreement, is the appropriate remedy.

There is no express provision in the agreement as to the remedy to be provided for an applicant who is refused employment in violation of the provisions of the agreement. The union argued, at the hearing, that the appropriate remedy to be implied into the agreement is a direction that Mr. [L.] be currently employed by the employer with retroactive salary, benefits, and rights to the date of July 5, 1977, those rights to be equivalent to those enjoyed by the person or persons hired in lieu of Mr. [L.] from that period to the date when Mr. [L.] is actually employed by the employer. The employer declined to present argument as to the appropriate remedy.

The question of remedy in the case of a refusal to employ is apparently a novel one under this agreement and there has been no experience or practice. In the case of a discharge found to be without just cause, the usual remedy is reinstatement to the position from which the employee was discharged with full back pay minus any compensation from employment earned by the grievant during the period of his discharge and minus any unemployment compensation which the employee might have received during the period of discharge which he is not required to repay. The remedy in case of a refusal to hire should it seems to me be similar, subject only to the uncertainty as to whether the job for which the applicant applied was a permanent job which would have paid full wages for the period in question. Since that cannot be determined on the record made by the parties, the award will simply set forth the principles to be applied in the determination of retroactive pay. Such an award is similar to the remedy provided by the National Labor Relations Board in cases of discriminatory refusal to hire in violation of that Act, see Phelps Dodge Corp. v. NLRB, 313 U.S. 177 (1941), and it seems appropriate to imply agreement upon such a remedy into this agreement.

Award

The employer, having violated §9(h) of the agreement between the parties by refusing to employ [L.] on July 5, 1977, for non-production off-bearing tailoff work because of his age, shall offer employment to him in that position with retroactive salary, benefits and rights equivalent to those person or persons hired in lieu of Mr. [L.], from that date to the date actually employed.

Notes

1. How do you explain the positions taken by the company and the union in *Evans* regarding the arbitrator's authority; especially, why did the company refuse to continue with its presentation after the arbitrator refused to disqualify himself? Is it clear that the arbitrator should have ignored possibly meritorious arguments because the employer declined to present them? How would *W. R. Grace* bear on *Evans*?

2. Should the *Carey* case, supra at p. 498, be reconsidered in light of *W. R. Grace*?

3. *Problems.* a. Employee George Klein filed a grievance alleging that the company had refused to assign him overtime work as required by the bargaining agreement. The agreement had a clause giving union stewards preference for overtime work so long as they were competent to perform it. The company refused to arbitrate on the ground that the preference clause was unlawful. Klein's union filed a §8(a)(5) charge contending that the company had violated §8(a)(5) by refusing to arbitrate. The Regional Director refused to issue a complaint because "[t]he Employer's action in ceasing to honor the superseniority clause is lawful, in view of Dairylea Cooperative, Inc., 219 N.L.R.B. 656." (See p. 690, supra.) The union then filed a §301 suit to compel arbitration of Klein's grievance. What result? See Crescent City Lodge No. 37 v. Boland Marine & Mfg. Co., 591 F.2d 1184 (5th Cir. 1979).

b. The collective bargaining agreement between the union and the employer in the 1950s covered the employer's facilities in both Garland, Texas and nearby Arlington, Texas. A 1961 memorandum of understanding between the union and the employer provided that employees at the Arlington facility were to be covered by the same collective bargaining agreement as the employees at the Garland facility, both facilities being under the "Garland Division" of the company. In 1971 the Arlington plant facilities were shut down, and in 1972 a letter of understanding was entered into which provided that

> all references to the Arlington, Texas, plant would be deleted from the collective bargaining agreement . . . ; [should] the Garland Division resume operations at this facility in the future, references to the Arlington Plant will be returned to the collective bargaining agreement. . . .

In 1978 the employer reopened the Arlington plant under the management of a newly created division of the company called the "Commercial Division." The union asserted that the reopened Arlington facility should be covered by the existing collective bargaining agreement with the Garland Division, but the employer contended that the 1971 memorandum did not apply because the Garland Division was no longer operating the Arlington plant. The union brought suit to compel arbitration under its current collective bargaining agreement. The recognition clause of that agreement stated that the company recognized the union as the bargaining agent of the employer's Garland, Texas Plant and also "those employees designated in . . . the memorandum of understanding dated March 29, 1961."

The employer contended that it should not be required to arbitrate because the issue to be presented to the arbitrator was a jurisdictional one as to whether the contract covers the particular employees. Furthermore, the employer contended that the questions of coverage of the agreement and the union's representation rights at the reopened facility were matters for the National Labor Relations Board. Should the court order arbitration? See United Auto Workers v. E-Systems, 632 F.2d 487 (5th Cir. 1980).

B. ENFORCING THE NO-STRIKE CLAUSE

1. Construction of No-Strike Clauses and Suits for Damages

No-strike clauses usually consist of a promise by a union either not to strike during the term of the agreement or not to strike over any grievance that the employer is bound to arbitrate. Some clauses expressly permit strikes under specified circumstances, such as the refusal of the employer to comply with an arbitrator's award.

The Supreme Court has implied a no-strike promise where the agreement contained none. In Local 174, Teamsters v. Lucas Flour Co., 369 U.S. 95 (1962), the union struck in protest of a worker's discharge. The agreement provided for binding arbitration of disputes and contained a union promise not to suspend work "during such arbitration," but in the instant case no arbitration was pending when the union struck. In a suit by the employer to recover damages caused by the strike, the Court held that

> a strike to settle a dispute which a collective bargaining agreement provides shall be settled exclusively and finally by compulsory arbitration constitutes a violation of the agreement. . . . To hold otherwise would obviously do violence to accepted principles of contract law. Even more in point, a contrary view would be completely at odds with the basic policy of national labor legislation to promote the arbitral process as a substitute for economic warfare. . . . What has been said is not to suggest that a no-strike agreement is to be implied beyond the area which it has been agreed will be exclusively covered by compulsory terminal arbitration.

In Gateway Coal Co. v. UMW, 414 U.S. 368 (1974), the Court again relied on the presence of a broad arbitration clause to imply a no-strike obligation. The implied obligation was sufficient to support an injunction against the strike.

Recall that in Mastro Plastics Corp. v. NLRB, 350 U.S. 270 (1956), supra at p. 344, the Court construed a broad no-strike clause as not covering a strike in protest of serious employer unfair labor practices undermining the union's representative status.

ATKINSON v. SINCLAIR REFINING CO., 370 U.S. 238 (1962): When the company docked three of its employees a total of $2.19, nine hundred ninety-nine employees struck. Count I of the company's district court suit sought damages from the local and international unions for breach of a bargaining agreement promise not to strike over any cause that could be subject to a grievance under the agreement. The Supreme Court concluded that Count I should not be dismissed or stayed while the employer was required to arbitrate his claim against the unions. Whether the company had agreed to arbitrate its breach of contract claims was for judicial determination. Since the contract provided for arbitration of individual and union grievances, but not for employer grievances, the company was not bound to proceed to arbitration and the issue of the union's breach and damage liability was properly before the district court. The union pointed out that individual employees had grieved over their docked pay, and argued that arbitration of those grievances would resolve issues involved in the company's damage claim. The Court concluded that the grievances raised no such common issues.

Count II, based on diversity jurisdiction, charged 24 individual officers and agents of the union with breach of the bargaining agreement and tortious interference with contractual relations. The Court held the count governed by §301, and construed it as charging "the agents for acting on behalf of the principal." The Court found in the final clause of §301(b) a policy requiring "that when a union is liable for damages for violation of the no-strike clause, its officers and members are not liable for these damages."

Notes

1. In Complete Auto Transit v. Reis, 451 U.S. 401 (1981), the Court relied on the legislative history of §301(b) in holding that that section does not create a cause of action against individual union members for a strike in breach of a no-strike clause. The union had not been named a defendant in the suit because it had neither authorized nor approved the strike. The majority opinion suggested that there were other remedies available to employers to prevent wildcat strikes. First, where the union is responsible for the strike, it may be held accountable. Second, an employer may discharge or otherwise discipline a worker who walks

off the job in breach of the no-strike clause. Third, the union may discipline its members. Finally, an injunction may be secured against the union if it is responsible for the stoppage and if the dispute giving rise to the strike is subject to binding arbitration.

Two Justices dissented, arguing that the alternative remedies against wildcat strikers suggested by the majority were inadequate, and that the legislative history did not require the Court's result.

2. In Carbon Fuel Co. v. United Mine Workers, 444 U.S. 212 (1979), the Court addressed the question of whether an international union may be held liable for breach of contract damages if it fails to use all reasonable means available to prevent wildcat strikes by local unions or to bring about their termination. The international union was a party to the collective bargaining agreement between the firm and several of the international's local unions. The locals engaged in 48 unauthorized strikes over a four-year period. The firm made two arguments for why the international should be held liable for not using all reasonable means to prevent the strikes. First, it argued the duty should be implied in law from the bargaining agreement's arbitration clause. Second, it contended that the duty should be implied from a clause in the agreement stating that the parties "agree and affirm that they will maintain the integrity of this contract. . . ." The Court rejected both arguments.

The Court relied on the legislative history of §§301(b) and (e) to reject the company's first argument. "In the face of Congress' clear statement of the limits of an international union's legal responsibility for the acts of one of its local unions, it would be anomalous to hold that an international is nonetheless liable for its failure to take certain steps in response to actions of the local. Such a rule would pierce the shield that Congress took such care to construct."

The Court used bargaining history to reject the company's second argument. In 1950, the company and the union negotiated a promise by the union "to exercise their best efforts through available disciplinary measures to prevent stoppages of work by strike. . . ." This language was deleted in 1952.

Do you think that there are any transaction costs unique to the "best efforts" issue that would prevent unions and firms from bargaining around any Supreme Court decision on the issue?

3. In Drake Bakeries v. Bakery Workers Local 50, 370 U.S. 254 (1962), the Court affirmed a district court's refusal to entertain an action against the union for breach of a no-strike clause since the agreement permitted either party to carry a dispute to arbitration. The employer's remedy lay in arbitration. The employer argued,

> the union's violation of the no-strike clause is sui generis and so basic to what the employer bargained for in the contract and so inherently and fundamentally inconsistent with the grievance and arbitration procedures

> that the faithful observance of the no-strike clause by the union is a condition precedent to the employer's duty to arbitrate . . . , or that the union must be deemed to have waived, or to be estopped from asserting, its right to arbitrate.

The Court rejected the argument, saying

> [a]rbitration provisions, which in themselves have not been repudiated, are meant to survive breaches of contract, in many contexts, even total breach; and in determining whether one party has so repudiated his promise to arbitrate that the other party is excused, the circumstances of the claimed repudiation are critically important. In this case the union denies having repudiated in any respect its promise to arbitrate, denies there was a strike . . . and asserts that it was the company itself which ignored the adjustment and arbitration provisions by [engaging in the conduct which precipitated the dispute].

In Packing House Workers Local 721 v. Needham Packing Co., 376 U.S. 247 (1964), the Court held that a strike in breach of a no-strike clause did not excuse the employer from his or her obligation to send to arbitration the union's grievance over the dispute causing the strike and over the discharge of strikers.

4. Does an employer violate §§8(a)(3) and (1) by singling out union officers for discipline for participating in, fomenting, or failing to take reasonable steps to prevent, a strike in breach of contract? The Board found violations in Precision Casting Co., 233 N.L.R.B. 35 (1977), and Metropolitan Edison Co., 252 N.L.R.B. 1030 (1980). Courts have disagreed. See, e.g., NLRB v. Armour-Dial, 638 F.2d 51 (8th Cir. 1981).

2. Enjoining Strikes in Breach of Contract

BOYS MARKETS v. RETAIL CLERKS, LOCAL 770[18]

398 U.S. 235 (1970)

BRENNAN, J.

In this case we re-examine the holding of Sinclair Refining Co. v. Atkinson, 370 U.S. 195 (1962), that the anti-injunction provisions of the Norris-LaGuardia Act preclude a federal district court from enjoining a strike in breach of a no-strike obligation under a collective-bargaining agreement, even though that agreement contains provisions, enforceable under §301(a) of the Labor Management Relations Act, 1947, for binding arbitration of the grievance dispute concerning which the strike

[18] See Axelrod, The Application of the *Boys Markets* Decision in the Federal Courts, 16 B.C. Ind. & Com. L. Rev. 893 (1975); Cantor, Strikes over Non-Arbitrable Labor Disputes, 23 B.C.L. Rev. 633 (1982); Gould, On Labor Injunctions, Unions and the Judges: The *Boys Markets* Case, 1970 Sup. Ct. Rev. 215.

was called. . . . Having concluded that *Sinclair* was erroneously decided and that subsequent events have undermined its continuing validity, we overrule that decision and reverse the judgment of the Court of Appeals.

I

In February 1969, at the time of the incidents that produced this litigation, petitioner and respondent were parties to a collective-bargaining agreement which provided, inter alia, that all controversies concerning its interpretation or application should be resolved by adjustment and arbitration procedures set forth therein and that, during the life of the contract, there should be "no cessation or stoppage of work, lockout, picketing or boycotts. . . ." The dispute arose when petitioner's frozen foods supervisor and certain members of his crew who were not members of the bargaining unit began to rearrange merchandise in the frozen food cases of one of petitioner's supermarkets. A union representative insisted that the food cases be stripped of all merchandise and be restocked by union personnel. When petitioner did not accede to the union's demand, a strike was called and the union began to picket petitioner's establishment. Thereupon petitioner demanded that the union cease the work stoppage and picketing and sought to invoke the grievance and arbitration procedures specified in the contract.

The following day, since the strike had not been terminated, petitioner filed a complaint in California Superior Court seeking a temporary restraining order, a preliminary and permanent injunction, and specific performance of the contractual arbitration provision. The state court issued a temporary restraining order forbidding continuation of the strike and also an order to show cause why a preliminary injunction should not be granted. Shortly thereafter, the union removed the case to the Federal District Court and there made a motion to quash the state court's temporary restraining order. In opposition, petitioner moved for an order compelling arbitration and enjoining continuation of the strike. Concluding that the dispute was subject to arbitration under the collective-bargaining agreement and that the strike was in violation of the contract, the District Court ordered the parties to arbitrate the underlying dispute and simultaneously enjoined the strike, all picketing in the vicinity of petitioner's supermarket, and any attempts by the union to induce the employees to strike or to refuse to perform their services.

II

At the outset, we are met with respondent's contention that *Sinclair* ought not to be disturbed because the decision turned on a question of statutory construction which Congress can alter at any time. Since Congress has not modified our conclusions in *Sinclair,* even though it has been urged to do so, respondent argues that principles of stare decisis should govern the present case.

We do not agree that the doctrine of stare decisis bars a re-examination of *Sinclair* in the circumstances of this case. We fully recognize that important policy considerations militate in favor of continuity and predictability in the law. Nevertheless, as Mr. Justice Frankfurter wrote for the Court, "[S]tare decisis is a principle of policy and not a mechanical formula of adherence to the latest decision, however recent and questionable, when such adherence involves collision with a prior doctrine more embracing in its scope, intrinsically sounder, and verified by experience." Helvering v. Hallock, 309 U.S. 106, 119 (1940). It is precisely because *Sinclair* stands as a significant departure from our otherwise consistent emphasis upon the congressional policy to promote the peaceful settlement of labor disputes through arbitration and our efforts to accommodate and harmonize this policy with those underlying the anti-injunction provisions of the Norris-LaGuardia Act that we believe *Sinclair* should be reconsidered. Furthermore, in light of developments subsequent to *Sinclair,* in particular our decision in Avco Corp v. Aero Lodge 735, 390 U.S. 557 (1968), it has become clear that the *Sinclair* decision does not further but rather frustrates realization of an important goal of our national labor policy.

Nor can we agree that conclusive weight should be accorded to the failure of Congress to respond to *Sinclair* on the theory that congressional silence should be interpreted as acceptance of the decision. The Court has cautioned that "[i]t is at best treacherous to find in congressional silence alone the adoption of a controlling rule of law." Girouard v. United States, 328 U.S. 61, 69 (1946). Therefore, in the absence of any persuasive circumstances evidencing a clear design that congressional inaction be taken as acceptance of *Sinclair,* the mere silence of Congress is not a sufficient reason for refusing to reconsider the decision.

III

From the time Textile Workers Union v. Lincoln Mills, 353 U.S. 448 (1957), was decided, we have frequently found it necessary to consider various substantive and procedural aspects of federal labor contract law and questions concerning its application in both state and federal courts. *Lincoln Mills* held generally that "the substantive law to apply in suits under §301(a) is federal law, which the courts must fashion from the policy of our national labor laws," 353 U.S., at 456, and more specifically that a union can obtain specific performance of an employer's promise to arbitrate grievances. We rejected the contention that the anti-injunction proscriptions of the Norris-LaGuardia Act prohibited this type of relief, noting that a refusal to arbitrate was not "part and parcel of the abuses against which the Act was aimed," id., at 458, and that the Act itself manifests a policy determination that arbitration should be encouraged. . . .

Subsequent to the decision in *Sinclair,* we held in Avco Corp. v. Aero Lodge 735, supra, that §301(a) suits initially brought in state courts may be removed to the designated federal forum under the federal question removal jurisdiction delineated in 28 U.S.C. §1441. In so holding, however, the Court expressly left open the questions whether state courts are bound by the anti-injunction proscriptions of the Norris-LaGuardia Act and whether federal courts, after removal of a §301(a) action, are required to dissolve any injunctive relief previously granted by the state courts. . . .

The decision in *Avco,* viewed in the context of *Lincoln Mills* and its progeny, has produced an anomalous situation which, in our view, makes urgent the reconsideration of *Sinclair.* The principal practical effect of *Avco* and *Sinclair* taken together is nothing less than to oust state courts of jurisdiction in §301(a) suits where injunctive relief is sought for breach of a no-strike obligation. Union defendants can, as a matter of course, obtain removal to a federal court, and there is obviously a compelling incentive for them to do so in order to gain the advantage of the strictures upon injunctive relief which *Sinclair* imposes on federal courts. The sanctioning of this practice, however, is wholly inconsistent with our conclusion in *Dowd Box* [368 U.S. 502 (1962)] that the congressional purpose embodied in §301(a) was to *supplement,* and not to encroach upon, the pre-existing jurisdiction of the state courts. It is ironic indeed that the very provision that Congress clearly intended to provide additional remedies for breach of collective-bargaining agreements has been employed to displace previously existing state remedies. We are not at liberty thus to depart from the clearly expressed congressional policy to the contrary.

On the other hand, to the extent that widely disparate remedies theoretically remain available in state, as opposed to federal, courts, the federal policy of labor law uniformity elaborated in *Lucas Flour Co.,* [369 U.S. 95 (1982)] is seriously offended. This policy, of course, could hardly require, as a practical matter, that labor law be administered identically in all courts, for undoubtedly a certain diversity exists among the state and federal systems in matters of procedural and remedial detail, a fact that Congress evidently took into account in deciding not to disturb the traditional jurisdiction of the States. The injunction, however, is so important a remedial device, particularly in the arbitration context, that its availability or nonavailability in various courts will not only produce rampant forum shopping and maneuvering from one court to another but will also greatly frustrate any relative uniformity in the enforcement of arbitration agreements.

Furthermore, the existing scheme, with the injunction remedy technically available in the state courts but rendered inefficacious by the removal device, assigns to removal proceedings a totally unintended function. . . . [T]here is no indication that Congress intended by the removal mechanism to effect a wholesale dislocation in the allocation of judicial business between the state and federal courts.

It is undoubtedly true that each of the foregoing objections to *Sinclair-Avco* could be remedied either by overruling *Sinclair* or by extending that decision to the States. While some commentators have suggested that the solution to the present unsatisfactory situation does lie in the extension of the *Sinclair* prohibition to state court proceedings, we agree with Chief Justice Traynor of the California Supreme Court that "whether or not Congress could deprive state courts of the power to give such [injunctive] remedies when enforcing collective bargaining agreements, it has not attempted to do so either in the Norris-LaGuardia Act or section 301." McCarroll v. Los Angeles County Dist. Council of Carpenters, 49 Cal. 2d 45, 63, 315 P.2d 322, 332 (1957), cert. denied, 355 U.S. 932 (1958).

An additional reason for not resolving the existing dilemma by extending *Sinclair* to the States is the devastating implications for the enforceability of arbitration agreements and their accompanying no-strike obligations if equitable remedies were not available. As we have previously indicated, a no-strike obligation, express or implied, is the quid pro quo for an undertaking by the employer to submit grievance disputes to the process of arbitration. See Textile Workers Union v. Lincoln Mills, supra, at 455. Any incentive for employers to enter into such an arrangement is necessarily dissipated if the principal and most expeditious method by which the no-strike obligation can be enforced is eliminated. While it is of course true, as respondent contends, that other avenues of redress, such as an action for damages, would remain open to an aggrieved employer, an award of damages after a dispute has been settled is no substitute for an immediate halt to an illegal strike. Furthermore, an action for damages prosecuted during or after a labor dispute would only tend to aggravate industrial strife and delay an early resolution of the difficulties between employer and union.

Even if management is not encouraged by the unavailability of the injunction remedy to resist arbitration agreements, the fact remains that the effectiveness of such agreements would be greatly reduced if injunctive relief were withheld. Indeed, the very purpose of arbitration procedures is to provide a mechanism for the expeditious settlement of industrial disputes without resort to strikes, lockouts, or other self-help measures. This basic purpose is obviously largely undercut if there is no immediate, effective remedy for those very tactics that arbitration is designed to obviate. Thus, because *Sinclair,* in the aftermath of *Avco,* casts serious doubt upon the effective enforcement of a vital element of stable labor-management relations — arbitration agreements with their attendant no-strike obligations — we conclude that *Sinclair* does not make a viable contribution to federal labor policy.

IV

We have also determined that the dissenting opinion in *Sinclair* states the correct principles concerning the accommodation necessary between the seemingly absolute terms of the Norris-LaGuardia Act and the policy considerations underlying §301(a). 370 U.S., at 215. Although we need not repeat all that was there said, a few points should be emphasized at this time.

The literal terms of §4 of the Norris-LaGuardia Act must be accommodated to the subsequently enacted provisions of §301(a) of the Labor Management Relations Act and the purposes of arbitration. Statutory interpretation requires more than concentration upon isolated words; rather, consideration must be given to the total corpus of pertinent law and the policies that inspired ostensibly inconsistent provisions.

The Norris-LaGuardia Act was responsive to a situation totally different from that which exists today. In the early part of this century, the federal courts generally were regarded as allies of management in its attempt to prevent the organization and strengthening of labor unions; and in this industrial struggle the injunction became a potent weapon that was wielded against the activities of labor groups. The result was a large number of sweeping decrees, often issued ex parte, drawn on an ad hoc basis without regard to any systematic elaboration of national labor policy.

In 1932 Congress attempted to bring some order out of the industrial chaos that had developed and to correct the abuses that had resulted from the interjection of the federal judiciary into union-management disputes on the behalf of management. See declaration of public policy, Norris-LaGuardia Act, §2. Congress, therefore, determined initially to limit severely the power of the federal courts to issue injunctions "in any case involving or growing out of any labor dispute. . . ." §4. Even as initially enacted, however, the prohibition against federal injunctions was by no means absolute. See Norris-LaGuardia Act, §§7, 8, 9. Shortly thereafter Congress passed the Wagner Act, designed to curb various management activities that tended to discourage employee participation in collective action.

As labor organizations grew in strength and developed toward maturity, congressional emphasis shifted from protection of the nascent labor movement to the encouragement of collective bargaining and to administrative techniques for the peaceful resolution of industrial disputes. This shift in emphasis was accomplished, however, without extensive revision of many of the older enactments, including the anti-injunction section of the Norris-LaGuardia Act. Thus, it became the task of the courts to accommodate, to reconcile the older statutes with the more recent ones.

A leading example of this accommodation process is Brotherhood of Railroad Trainmen v. Chicago River & Ind. R. Co., 353 U.S. 30 (1957). There we were confronted with a peaceful strike which violated the statutory duty to arbitrate imposed by the Railway Labor Act. The Court concluded that a strike in violation of a statutory arbitration duty was not the type of situation to which the Norris-LaGuardia Act was responsive, that an important federal policy was involved in the peaceful settlement of disputes through the statutorily mandated arbitration procedure, that this important policy was imperiled if equitable remedies were not available to implement it, and hence that Norris-LaGuardia's policy of nonintervention by the federal courts should yield to the overriding interests in the successful implementation of the arbitration process. The principles elaborated in *Chicago River* are equally applicable to the present case. . . .

The *Sinclair* decision, however, seriously undermined the effectiveness of the arbitration technique as a method peacefully to resolve industrial disputes without resort to strikes, lockouts, and similar devices. Clearly employers will be wary of assuming obligations to arbitrate specifically enforceable against them when no similarly efficacious remedy is available to enforce the concomitant undertaking of the union to refrain from striking. On the other hand, the central purpose of the Norris-LaGuardia Act to foster the growth and viability of labor organizations is hardly retarded — if anything, this goal is advanced — by a remedial device that merely enforces the obligation that the union freely undertook under a specifically enforceable agreement to submit disputes to arbitration. We conclude, therefore, that the unavailability of equitable relief in the arbitration context presents a serious impediment to the congressional policy favoring the voluntary establishment of a mechanism for the peaceful resolution of labor disputes, that the core purpose of the Norris-LaGuardia Act is not sacrificed by the limited use of equitable remedies to further this important policy, and consequently that the Norris-LaGuardia Act does not bar the granting of injunctive relief in the circumstances of the instant case.

V

Our holding in the present case is a narrow one. We do not undermine the vitality of the Norris-LaGuardia Act. We deal only with the situation in which a collective-bargaining contract contains a mandatory grievance adjustment or arbitration procedure. Nor does it follow from what we have said that injunctive relief is appropriate as a matter of course in every case of a strike over an arbitrable grievance. The dissenting opinion in *Sinclair* suggested the following principles for the guidance of the district courts in determining whether to grant injunctive relief — principles that we now adopt:

> A District Court entertaining an action under §301 may not grant injunctive relief against concerted activity unless and until it decides that the case is one in which an injunction would be appropriate despite the Norris-LaGuardia Act. When a strike is sought to be enjoined because it is over a grievance which both parties are contractually bound to arbitrate, the District Court may issue no injunctive order until it first holds that the contract *does* have that effect; and the employer should be ordered to arbitrate, as a condition of his obtaining an injunction against the strike. Beyond this, the District Court must, of course, consider whether issuance of an injunction would be warranted under ordinary principles of equity — whether breaches are occurring and will continue, or have been threatened and will be committed; whether they have caused or will cause irreparable injury to the employer; and whether the employer will suffer more from the denial of an injunction than will the union from its issuance. 370 U.S., at 228. (Emphasis in original.)

In the present case there is no dispute that the grievance in question was subject to adjustment and arbitration under the collective-bargaining agreement and that the petitioner was ready to proceed with arbitration at the time an injunction against the strike was sought and obtained. The District Court also concluded that, by reason of respondent's violations of its no-strike obligation, petitioner "has suffered irreparable injury and will continue to suffer irreparable injury." Since we now overrule *Sinclair,* the holding of the Court of Appeals in reliance on *Sinclair* must be reversed. Accordingly, we reverse the judgment of the Court of Appeals and remand the case with directions to enter a judgment affirming the order of the District Court.

It is so ordered.[19]

Notes

1. From the majority opinion in Sinclair Refining Co. v. Atkinson, 370 U.S. 195, 205-208 (1962):

> When the inquiry is carried beyond the language of §301 into its legislative history, whatever small doubts as to the congressional purpose could have survived consideration of the bare language of the section should be wholly dissipated. For the legislative history of §301 shows that Congress actually considered the advisability of repealing the Norris-LaGuardia Act insofar as suits based upon breach of collective bargaining agreements are

[19] Stewart, J., concurred. Black, J., and White, J., dissented. Marshall, J., took no part in the decision.

> concerned and deliberately choose not to do so. The section as eventually enacted was the product of a conference between Committees of the House and Senate, selected to resolve the differences between conflicting provisions of the respective bills each had passed. Prior to this conference, the House bill had provided for federal jurisdiction of suits for breach of collective bargaining contracts and had expressly declared that the Norris-LaGuardia Act's anti-injunction provisions would not apply to such suits. The bill passed by the Senate, like the House bill, granted federal courts jurisdiction over suits for breach of such agreements but it did not, like the House bill, make the Norris-LaGuardia Act's prohibition against injunctions inapplicable to such suits. Instead it made breach of a collective agreement an unfair labor practice. Under the Senate version, therefore, a breach of a collective bargaining agreement, like any unfair labor practice, could have been enjoined by a suit brought by the National labor Relations Board, but no provision of the Senate version would have permitted the issuance of an injunction in a labor dispute at the suit of a private party. At the conference the provision of the House bill expressly repealing the anti-injunction provisions of the Norris-LaGuardia Act, as well as the provision of the bill passed by the Senate declaring the breach of a collective agreement to be an unfair labor practice, was dropped and never became law. Instead, the conferees, as indicated by the provision which came out of the conference and eventually became §301, agreed that suits for breach of such agreements should remain wholly private and "be left to the usual processes of the law" and that, in view of the fact that these suits would be at the instance of private parties rather than at the instance of the Labor Board, no change in the existing anti-injunction provisions of the Norris-LaGuardia Act should be made. The House Conference Report expressly recognized that the House provision for repeal in contract actions of the anti-injunction prohibitions of the Norris-LaGuardia Act had been eliminated in Conference. . . . And Senator Taft, Chairman of the Conference Committee and one of the authors of this legislation that bore his name, was no less explicit in explaining the results of the conference to the Senate: "The conferees . . . rejected the repeal of the Norris-LaGuardia Act."

Note that Justice Brennan's *Boys Markets* opinion does not speak to the legislative history issue.

2. Where congressional action is paralyzed by powerful opposing public forces, each capable of blocking legislation, is it time for the Court to step in and do justice?[20] Was the Court doing that in *Boys Markets*?

3. Suppose the union has engaged in several recent strikes in breach of contract over arbitrable issues. Should a court issue a prospective injunction prohibiting all such strikes for the duration of the agreement? Would it matter if the recent strikes had been wildcats that the union purported to be unable to control?

[20] See Wellington & Albert, Statutory Interpretation and the Political Process: A Comment upon *Sinclair v. Atkinson,* 72 Yale L.J. 1547 (1963).

4. Suppose the bargaining agreement has a no-strike clause covering "all work stoppages for the duration of the agreement." Another clause reads, "The company has the absolute right to subcontract work and no decision to subcontract shall be subject to the grievance and arbitration procedures of this agreement." The company subcontracts work and the union strikes. Injunction?

In Buffalo Forge Co. v. United Steelworkers, 428 U.S. 397 (1976), the union ordered its members to honor a picket line established by other employees (unionized by another local of the same international union) around the employer's premises. The employer claimed this sympathy strike violated the union's no-strike pledge in its bargaining agreement and sought an injunction. The union denied that a sympathy strike was a contract violation. In a 5-4 decision, the Supreme Court held that an injunction was barred by Norris-LaGuardia.

Acknowledging that the district court had jurisdiction to enforce by injunction an arbitrator's award ordering the sympathy strike to cease, the Court held that a pre-arbitration injunction did not fall within the *Boys Market* exception to Norris-LaGuardia because the strike was not over any dispute between the union and the employer; the dispute causing the sympathy strike was between the employer and another union. The Court refused to extend its limited exception to the Norris-LaGuardia provisions to every strike in breach of a bargaining agreement.

First noting the refusal of Congress as it enacted Taft-Hartley to lift Norris-LaGuardia restraints so as to permit injunctions to enforce bargaining agreements, the Court argued that pre-arbitration relief would enmesh federal courts into "the merits of the factual and legal issues that are subjects for the arbitrator."

The same considerations caused the Court to reject the dissent's suggestion that such strikes be enjoined when the contract violation is clear and the district court is persuaded that the party seeking the injunction will prevail before the arbitrator. The lower courts could not be counted on to hold views of the contract invariably coinciding with those later held by the arbitrator, and some arbitrators were likely to be "heavily influenced or wholly preempted" by the judicial views in the injunction proceedings. Finally, the Court noted that even temporary injunctions against strikes "very often permanently settle the issue. . . ."

In Jacksonville Bulk Terminals v. ILA, 457 U.S. 702 (1982), the Court held that a politically motivated work stoppage protesting the Soviet invasion of Afghanistan by a refusal to load grain destined for the Soviet Union was within the scope of the Norris-LaGuardia Act. The Court relied on *Buffalo Forge* in holding that an injunction against the work stoppage should not issue pending an arbitrator's determination whether the stoppage violated a no-strike clause in the union's collective bargaining agreement.

5. *Problem.* The bargaining agreement in force between the union and the employer bars "all stoppages of work because of any difference of opinion or dispute . . . between the union and the employer." The arbitration clause sends to mandatory arbitration "all disputes over the meaning, application or interpretation of this agreement." Does this agreement bar an employee from honoring a picket line at another employer's place of business? Does it bar an employee from honoring a picket line at this employer's place of business? Does it bar an employee from honoring a picket line at this employer's place of business if the line is established by a sister local union (i.e., one representing another bargaining unit of this employer's employees)?

Are any of these refusals to cross a picket line enjoinable under *Boys Market* and *Buffalo Forge,* if the pickets are picketing over a grievance subject to mandatory arbitration under their own collective bargaining agreement? See Cedar Coal Co. v. United Mine Workers, 560 F.2d 1153 (4th Cir. 1977), cert. denied, 434 U.S. 1047 (1978); Iowa Beef Processors v. Amalgamated Meat Cutters, 597 F.2d 1138 (8th Cir. 1979); Operating Engineers Local 18 (Davis McKee, Inc.), 238 N.L.R.B. 652 (1978).

6. Suppose the union has a bargaining agreement with an employer providing that the employer "will not effectuate any sale of the plant unless the buyer agrees to retain all present employees and continue union recognition." The union has obtained a copy of what is either an agreement to sell the plant, or a proposed draft thereof, which contains no clause respecting employee retention or union recognition. The employer's personnel director has flatly refused to discuss the matter with the union. If the union files a §301 action requesting that the sale be enjoined, is the district court precluded by Norris-LaGuardia from issuing the injunction?[21]

7. The Dow Chemical Company unilaterally announced and implemented a change in the work schedule of its latex department. The change was not sanctioned by Dow's collective bargaining agreement with the Steelworkers' Union. Dow refused to bargain with the Union over the change. The bargaining agreement barred a strike unless and until: (1) all five steps of the grievance procedure had been exhausted; (2) the Union had made a written request for arbitration within 30 days after the receipt of the step-five answer; and (3) arbitration had either been completed or refused.

On the day that Dow implemented the change the Union struck, although it had not invoked step five of the grievance procedure. The Union had made two oral requests for arbitration, which Dow denied, but it had not filed a written request for arbitration. After sustaining the

[21] See Cantor, *Buffalo Forge* and Injunctions Against Employer Breaches of Collective Bargaining Agreements, 1980 Wis. L. Rev. 247; Gould, On Labor Injunctions Pending Arbitration: Recasting *Buffalo Forge,* 30 Stan. L. Rev. 533 (1978).

strike for two months, Dow notified the Union that because of the strike it was rescinding the bargaining agreement. Dow then terminated the strikers.

Subsequently, a majority of Dow's employees then employed signed a petition that they no longer wished to be represented by the Union and Dow withdrew recognition from the Union. Could Dow have enjoined the strike on the authority of *Boys Markets* and *Buffalo Forge*? Would the availability of injunctive relief be relevant to the issue of whether Dow violated §§8(a)(5), (3), and (1) by discharging the strikers and rescinding the bargaining agreements under the rules of Mastro Plastics Corp. v. NLRB, supra at p. 344 and Arlan's Department Stores, supra at p. 346? See Dow Chemical Co., 244 N.L.R.B. 164 (1979), on remand from 530 F.2d 266 (3d Cir. 1976).

C. The Contractual and Bargaining Obligations of Successor Employers[22]

JOHN WILEY & SONS v. LIVINGSTON
376 U.S. 543 (1964)

Harlan, J.

This is an action by a union, pursuant to §301 of the Labor Management Relations Act, to compel arbitration under a collective bargaining agreement. [One of] the major questions presented [is] whether a corporate employer must arbitrate with a union under a bargaining agreement between the union and another corporation which has merged with the employer. . . .

I

District 65, Retail, Wholesale and Department Store Union, AFL-CIO, entered into a collective bargaining agreement with Interscience Publishers, Inc., a publishing firm, for a term expiring on January 31, 1962. The agreement did not contain an express provision making it binding on successors of Interscience. On October 2, 1961, Interscience merged with the petitioner, John Wiley & Sons, Inc., another publishing firm, and ceased to do business as a separate entity. There is no suggestion that the merger was not for genuine business reasons.

At the time of the merger Interscience had about 80 employees, of whom 40 were represented by this Union. It had a single plant in New

[22] See Goldberg, The Labor Obligations of a Successor Employer, 63 Nw. U.L. Rev. 735 (1969); Morris & Gaus, Successorship and the Collective Bargaining Agreement: Accommodating *Wiley* and *Burns*, 59 Va. L. Rev. 1359 (1973); Severson & Wilcoxon, Successorship under *Howard Johnson*: Short Order Justice for Employees, 64 Calif. L. Rev. 795 (1976); Note, 74 Mich. L. Rev. 555 (1976).

York City, and did an annual business of somewhat over $1,000,000. Wiley was a much larger concern, having separate office and warehouse facilities and about 300 employees, and doing an annual business of more than $9,000,000. None of Wiley's employees was represented by a union.

In discussions before and after the merger, the Union and Interscience (later Wiley) were unable to agree on the effect of the merger on the collective bargaining agreement and on the rights under it of those covered employees hired by Wiley. The Union's position was that despite the merger it continued to represent the covered Interscience employees taken over by Wiley, and that Wiley was obligated to recognize certain rights of such employees which had "vested" under the Interscience bargaining agreement. Such rights, more fully described below, concerned matters typically covered by collective bargaining agreements, such as seniority status, severance pay, etc. The Union contended also that Wiley was required to make certain pension fund payments called for under the Interscience bargaining agreement.

Wiley, though recognizing for purposes of its own pension plan the Interscience service of the former Interscience employees, asserted that the merger terminated the bargaining agreement for all purposes. It refused to recognize the Union as bargaining agent or to accede to the Union's claims on behalf of Interscience employees. All such employees, except a few who ended their Wiley employment with severance pay and for whom no rights are asserted here, continued in Wiley's employ.

No satisfactory solution having been reached, the Union, one week before the expiration date of the Interscience bargaining agreement, commenced this action to compel arbitration.

II

The threshold question in this controversy is who shall decide whether the arbitration provisions of the collective bargaining agreement survived the Wiley-Interscience merger, so as to be operative against Wiley. Both parties urge that this question is for the courts. Past cases leave no doubt that this is correct. . . . The duty to arbitrate being of contractual origin, a compulsory submission to arbitration cannot precede judicial determination that the collective bargaining agreement does in fact create such a duty. Thus, just as an employer has no obligation to arbitrate issues which it has not agreed to arbitrate, so a fortiori, it cannot be compelled to arbitrate if an arbitration clause does not bind it at all.

The unanimity of views about who should decide the question of arbitrability does not, however, presage the parties' accord about what is the correct decision. Wiley, objecting to arbitration, argues that it never was a party to the collective bargaining agreement, and that, in any event, the Union lost its status as representative of the former Interscience employees when they were mingled in a larger Wiley unit of employees. The Union argues that Wiley, as successor to Interscience, is bound by the latter's agreement, at least sufficiently to require it to arbitrate. The Union relies on §90 of the N.Y. Stock Corporation Law, which provides, among other things, that no "claim or demand for any cause" against a constituent corporation shall be extinguished by a consolidation. Alternatively, the Union argues that, apart from §90, federal law requires that arbitration go forward, lest the policy favoring arbitration frequently be undermined by changes in corporate organization.

Federal law, fashioned "from the policy of our national labor laws," controls. Textile Workers Union v. Lincoln Mills, 353 U.S. 448, 456. State law may be utilized so far as it is of aid in the development of correct principles or their application in a particular case, id., at 457, but the law which ultimately results is federal. We hold that the disappearance by merger of a corporate employer which has entered into a collective bargaining agreement with a union does not automatically terminate all rights of the employees covered by the agreement, and that, in appropriate circumstances, present here, the successor employer may be required to arbitrate with the union under the agreement.

This Court has in the past recognized the central role of arbitration in effectuating national labor policy. Thus, in *Warrior & Gulf Navigation Co.*, [363 U.S.], at 578, arbitration was described as "the substitute for industrial strife," and as "part and parcel of the collective bargaining process itself." It would derogate from "the federal policy of settling labor disputes by arbitration," United Steelworkers v. Enterprise Wheel & Car Corp., 363 U.S. 593, 596, if a change in the corporate structure or ownership of a business enterprise had the automatic consequence of removing a duty to arbitrate previously established; this is so as much in cases like the present, where the contracting employer disappears into another by merger, as in those in which one owner replaces another but the business entity remains the same.

Employees, and the union which represents them, ordinarily do not take part in negotiations leading to a change in corporate ownership. The negotiations will ordinarily not concern the well-being of the employees, whose advantage or disadvantage, potentially great, will inevitably be incidental to the main considerations. The objectives of national labor policy, reflected in established principles of federal law, require that the rightful prerogative of owners independently to rearrange their businesses and even eliminate themselves as employers be balanced by some protection to the employees from a sudden change in the employment relationship. The transition from one corporate organization to another will in most cases be eased and industrial strife avoided if employees' claims continue to be resolved by arbitration rather than by "the relative strength . . . of the contending forces," *Warrior & Gulf*, supra, at 580.

The preference of national labor policy for arbitration as a substitute for tests of strength between contending forces could be overcome only if other considerations compellingly so demanded. We find none. While the principles of law governing ordinary contracts would not bind to a contract an unconsenting successor to a contracting party,[3] a collective bargaining agreement is not an ordinary contract. ". . . [I]t is a generalized code to govern a myriad of cases which the draftsmen cannot wholly anticipate. . . . The collective agreement covers the whole employment relationship. It calls into being a new common law — the common law of a particular industry or of a particular plant." *Warrior & Gulf*, supra, at 578-579 (footnotes omitted). Central to the peculiar status and function of a collective bargaining agreement is the fact, dictated both by circumstance, see id., at 580, and by the requirements of the National Labor Relations Act, that it is not in any real sense the simple product of a consensual relationship. Therefore, although the duty to arbitrate, as we have said, must be founded on a contract, the impressive policy considerations favoring arbitration are not wholly overborne by the fact that Wiley did not sign the contract being construed.[4] This case cannot readily be assimilated to the category of those in which there is no contract whatever, or none which is reasonably related to the party sought to be obligated. There was a contract, and Interscience, Wiley's predecessor, was party to it. We thus find Wiley's obligation to arbitrate this dispute in the Interscience contract construed in the context of a national labor policy.

We do not hold that in every case in which the ownership or corporate structure of an enterprise is changed the duty to arbitrate survives. As indicated above, there may be cases in which the lack of any substantial continuity of identity in the business enterprise before and after a change would make a duty to arbitrate something imposed from without, not reasonably to be found in the particular bargaining agreement and the acts of the parties involved. So too, we do not rule out the possibility that a union might abandon its right to arbitration by failing to make its claims known. Neither of these situations is before the Court. Although Wiley was substantially larger than Interscience, relevant similarity and continuity of operation across the change in ownership is adequately evidenced by the wholesale transfer of Interscience employ-

3. But cf. the general rule that in the case of a merger the corporation which survives is liable for the debts and contracts of the one which disappears. 15 Fletcher, Private Corporations (1961 rev. ed.), §7121.

4. Compare the principle that when a contract is scrutinized for evidence of an intention to arbitrate a particular kind of dispute, *national labor policy* requires, within reason, that "an interpretation that covers the asserted dispute," *Warrior & Gulf*, supra, pp. 582-583, be favored.

ees to the Wiley plant, apparently without difficulty. The Union made its position known well before the merger and never departed from it. In addition, we do not suggest any view on the questions surrounding a certified union's claim to continued representative status following a change in ownership. This Union does not assert that it has any bargaining rights independent of the Interscience agreement; it seeks to arbitrate claims based on that agreement, now expired, not to negotiate a new agreement.[5]

III

Beyond denying its obligation to arbitrate at all, Wiley urges that the Union's grievances are not within the scope of the arbitration clause. . . .

All of the Union's grievances concern conditions of employment typically covered by collective bargaining agreements and submitted to arbitration if other grievance procedures fail. Specific provision for each of them is made in the Interscience agreement.[7] There is thus no question that had a dispute concerning any of these subjects, such as seniority rights or severance pay, arisen between the Union and Interscience prior to the merger, it would have been arbitrable. Wiley argues, however, that the Union's claims are plainly outside the scope of the arbitration clause: first, because the agreement did not embrace post-merger claims, and, second, because the claims relate to a period beyond the limited term of the agreement.

In all probability, the situation created by the merger was one not expressly contemplated by the Union or Interscience when the agreement was made in 1960. Fairly taken, however, the Union's demands collectively raise the question which underlies the whole litigation: What is the effect of the merger on the rights of covered employees? It would be inconsistent with our holding that the obligation to arbitrate survived the merger were we to hold that the fact of the merger, without more,

5. The fact that the Union does not represent a majority of an appropriate bargaining unit in Wiley does not prevent it from representing those employees who are covered by the agreement which is in dispute and out of which Wiley's duty to arbitrate arises. Retail Clerks Intl. Assn., Local Unions Nos. 128 & 633 v. Lion Dry Goods, Inc., 369 U.S. 17. There is no problem of conflict with another union, since Wiley had no contract with any union covering the unit of employees which received the former Interscience employees.

Problems might be created by an arbitral award which required Wiley to give special treatment to the former Interscience employees because of rights found to have accrued to them under the Interscience contract. But the mere possibility of such problems cannot cut off the Union's right to press the employees' claims in arbitration. While it would be premature at this stage to speculate on how to avoid such hypothetical problems, we have little doubt that within the flexible procedures of arbitration a solution can be reached which would avoid disturbing labor relations in the Wiley plant.

7. See Art. VI: Seniority; Art. XV: Welfare Security Benefits; Art. VII: Discharges and Layoffs; Art. XXIII: Severance Pay; Art. XII: Vacations.

removed claims otherwise plainly arbitrable from the scope of the arbitration clause.

It is true that the Union has framed its issues to claim rights not only "now" — after the merger but during the term of the agreement — but also after the agreement expired by its terms. Claimed rights during the term of the agreement, at least, are unquestionably within the arbitration clause; we do not understand Wiley to urge that the Union's claims to all such rights have become moot by reason of the expiration of the agreement. As to claimed rights "after January 30, 1962," it is reasonable to read the claims as based solely on the Union's construction of the Interscience agreement in such a way that, had there been no merger, Interscience would have been required to discharge certain obligations notwithstanding the expiration of the agreement. We see no reason why parties could not if they so chose agree to the accrual of rights during the term of an agreement and their realization after the agreement had expired. Of course, the Union may not use arbitration to acquire new rights against Wiley any more than it could have used arbitration to negotiate a new contract with Interscience, had the existing contract expired and renewal negotiations broken down.

Whether or not the Union's demands have merit will be determined by the arbitrator in light of the fully developed facts. It is sufficient for present purposes that the demands are not so plainly unreasonable that the subject matter of the dispute must be regarded as nonarbitrable because it can be seen in advance that no award to the Union could receive judicial sanction. See *Warrior & Gulf,* supra, at 582-583. . . .

Affirmed.[23]

NLRB v. BURNS INTERNATIONAL SECURITY SERVICES

406 U.S. 272 (1972)

WHITE, J.

Burns International Security Services, Inc. (Burns), replaced another employer, the Wackenhut Corporation (Wackenhut), which had previously provided plant protection services for the Lockheed Aircraft Service Company (Lockheed) located at the Ontario International Airport in California. When Burns began providing security services, it employed 42 guards; 27 of them had been employed by Wackenhut. Burns refused, however, to bargain with United Plant Guard Workers of America (the union) which had been certified after an NLRB election as the exclusive bargaining representative of Wackenhut's employees less than four months earlier. The issues presented in this case are whether Burns refused to bargain with a union representing a majority of employees in an appropriate unit and whether the National Labor Rela-

[23] Goldberg, J., took no part in the decision.

tions Board could order Burns to observe the terms of a collective-bargaining contract signed by the union and Wackenhut which Burns had not voluntarily assumed. Resolution turns to a great extent on the precise facts involved here.

I

The Wackenhut Corporation provided protection services at the Lockheed plant for five years before Burns took over this task. On February 28, 1967, a few months before the change-over of guard employers, a majority of the Wackenhut guards selected the union as their exclusive bargaining representative in a Board election after Wackenhut and the union had agreed that the Lockheed plant was the appropriate bargaining unit. On March 8, the Regional Director certified the union as the exclusive bargaining representative for these employees, and on April 29, Wackenhut and the union entered into a three-year collective-bargaining contract.

Meanwhile, since Wackenhut's one-year service agreement to provide security protection was due to expire on June 30, Lockheed had called for bids from various companies supplying these services, and both Burns and Wackenhut submitted estimates. At a pre-bid conference attended by Burns on May 15, a representative of Lockheed informed the bidders that Wackenhut's guards were represented by the union, that the union had recently won a Board election and been certified, and that there was in existence a collective-bargaining contract between Wackenhut and the union. Lockheed then accepted Burns' bid, and on May 31, Wackenhut was notified that Burns would assume responsibility for protection services on July 1. Burns chose to retain 27 of the Wackenhut guards, and it brought in 15 of its own guards from other Burns locations.

During June, when Burns hired the 27 Wackenhut guards, it supplied them with membership cards of the American Federation of Guards (AFG), another union with whom Burns had collective bargaining contracts at other locations, and informed them that they must become AFG members to work for Burns, that they would not receive uniforms otherwise, and that Burns "could not live with" the existing contract between Wackenhut and the union. On June 29, Burns recognized the AFG on the theory that it had obtained a card majority. On July 12, however, the UPG demanded that Burns recognize it as the bargaining representative of Burns' employees at Lockheed and that Burns honor the collective-bargaining agreement between it and Wackenhut. When Burns refused, the UPG filed unfair labor practice charges, and Burns responded by challenging the appropriateness of the unit and by denying its obligation to bargain.

The Board . . . found the Lockheed plant an appropriate unit and held that Burns had violated §§8(a)(2) and 8(a)(1) of the Act by unlawfully recognizing and assisting the AFG, a rival of the UPG; that it had violated §§8(a)(5) and 8(a)(1) by failing to recognize the bargain with the UPG and by refusing to honor the collective-bargaining agreement which had been negotiated between Wackenhut and UPG.

Burns did not challenge the §8(a)(2) unlawful assistance finding in the Court of Appeals but sought review of the unit determination and the order to bargain and observe the pre-existing collective-bargaining contract. The Court of Appeals accepted the Board's unit determination and enforced the Board's order insofar as it related to the finding of unlawful assistance of a rival union and the refusal to bargain, but it held that the Board had exceeded its powers in ordering Burns to honor the contract executed by Wackenhut. Both Burns and the Board petitioned for certiorari, Burns challenging the unit determination and the bargaining order and the Board maintaining its position that Burns was bound by the Wackenhut contract, and we granted both petitions, though we declined to review the propriety of the bargaining unit. . . .

II

The trial examiner found, inter alia, that Burns "had in its employ a majority of Wackenhut's former employees," and that these employees had already expressed their choice of a bargaining representative in an election held a short time before. Burns was therefore held to have a duty to bargain, which arose when it selected as its work force the employees of the previous employer to perform the same tasks at the same place they had worked in the past.

The Board, without revision, accepted the trial examiner's findings and conclusions with respect to the duty to bargain, and we see no basis for setting them aside. In an election held but a few months before, the union had been designated bargaining agent for the employees in the unit and a majority of these employees had been hired by Burns for work in an identical unit. It is undisputed that Burns knew all the relevant facts in this regard and was aware of the certification and of the existence of a collective-bargaining contract. In these circumstances, it was not unreasonable for the Board to conclude that the union certified to represent all employees in the unit still represented a majority of the employees and that Burns could not reasonably have entertained a good-faith doubt about that fact. Burns' obligation to bargain with the union over terms and conditions of employment stems from its hiring of Wackenhut's employees and from the recent election and Board certification. It has been consistently held that a mere change of employers or of ownership in the employing industry is not such an "unusual circumstance" as to affect the force of the Board's certification within the normal operative period if a majority of employees after the change of ownership or management were employed by the preceding employer.

It goes without saying, of course, that Burns was not entitled to upset what it should have accepted as an established union majority by soliciting representation cards for another union and thereby committing the unfair labor practice of which it was found guilty by the Board. That holding was not challenged here and makes it imperative that the situation be viewed as it was when Burns hired its employees for the guard unit, a majority of whom were represented by a Board-certified union.

It would be a wholly different case if the Board had determined that because Burns' operational structure and practices differed from those of Wackenhut, the Lockheed bargaining unit was no longer an appropriate one.[4] Likewise, it would be different if Burns had not hired employees already represented by a union certified as a bargaining agent, and the Board recognized as much at oral argument. But where the bargaining unit remains unchanged and a majority of the employees hired by the new employer are represented by a recently certified bargaining agent there is little basis for faulting the Board's implementation of the express mandates of §8(a)(5) and §9(a) by ordering the employer to bargain with the incumbent union. This is the view of several courts of appeal and we agree with those courts.

III

It does not follow, however, from Burns' duty to bargain that it was bound to observe the substantive terms of the collective-bargaining contract the union had negotiated with Wackenhut and to which Burns had in no way agreed. Section 8(d) of the Act expressly provides that the existence of such bargaining obligation "does not compel either party to agree to a proposal or require the making of a concession." Congress has consistently declined to interfere with free collective bargaining and has preferred that device, or voluntary arbitration, to the imposition of compulsory terms as a means of avoiding or terminating labor disputes. . . .

4. The Court of Appeals was unimpressed with the asserted differences between Burns' and Wackenhut's operations: "All of the important factors which the Board has used and the courts have approved are present in the instant case: 'continuation of the same type of product lines, departmental organization, employee identity and job functions.' . . . Both Burns and Wackenhut are nationwide organizations; both performed the identical services at the same facility; although Burns used its own supervisors, their functions and responsibilities were similar to those performed by their predecessors; and finally, and perhaps most significantly, Burns commenced performance of the contract with 27 former Wackenhut employees out of its total complement of 42." R. at 189 (citation omitted). Although the labor policies of the two companies differed somewhat, the Board's determination that the bargaining unit remained appropriate after the changeover meant that Burns would face essentially the same labor relations environment as Wackenhut: it would confront the same union representing most of the same employees in the same unit.

[The] history [of §8(d)] was reviewed in detail and given controlling effect in H. K. Porter Co., Inc. v. NLRB, 397 U.S. 99 (1970). There this Court, while agreeing that the employer violated §8(a)(5) by adamantly refusing to agree to a dues checkoff intending thereby to frustrate the consumation of any bargaining agreement, held that the Board had erred in ordering the employer to agree to such a provision:

> While the Board does have power . . . to require employers and employees to negotiate, it is without power to compel a company or a union to agree to any substantive contractual provision of a collective-bargaining agreement. . . . 397 U.S. at 102 . . . These considerations, evident from the explicit language and legislative history of the labor laws, underlay the Board's prior decisions which until now have consistently held that although successor employers may be bound to recognize and bargain with the union, they are not bound by the substantive provisions of a collective-bargaining contract negotiated by their predecessors but not agreed to or assumed by them. As the Court of Appeals said in this case, "[i]n none of the previous successorship cases has the Board ever reached that result. The successor has always been held merely to have the duty of bargaining with his predecessor's union.

The Board, however, has now departed from this view and argues that the same policies which mandate a continuity of bargaining obligation also require that successor employers be bound to the terms of a predecessor's collective-bargaining contract. It asserts that the stability of labor relations will be jeopardized and that employees will face uncertainty and a gap in the bargained-for terms and conditions of employment, as well as the possible loss of advantages gained by prior negotiations, unless the new employer is held to have assumed, as a matter of federal labor law, the obligations under the contract entered into by the former employer. Recognizing that under normal contract principles a party would not be bound to a contract in the absence of consent, the Board notes that in John Wiley & Sons, Inc. v. Livingston, 376 U.S. 543, 550 (1964), the Court declared that "a collective bargaining agreement is not an ordinary contract" but is rather an outline of the common law of a particular plant or industry. The Court held in *Wiley* that although the predecessor employer who had signed a collective-bargaining contract with the union had disappeared by merger with the successor, the union could compel the successor to arbitrate the extent to which the successor was obligated under the collective-bargaining agreement. The Board contends that the same factors which the Court emphasized in *Wiley*, the peaceful settlement of industrial conflicts and "protection [of] the employees [against] a sudden change in the employment relationship," id., at 549, require that Burns be treated under the collective-bargaining contract exactly as Wackenhut would have been if it had continued protecting the Lockheed plant.

We do not find *Wiley* controlling in the circumstances here. *Wiley* arose in the context of a §301 suit to compel arbitration, not in the context of an unfair labor practice proceeding where the Board is expressly limited by the provisions of §8(d). That decision emphasized "the preference of national labor policy for arbitration as a substitute for tests of strength before contending forces" and held only that the agreement to arbitrate, "construed in the context of national labor policy," survived the merger and left to the arbitrator, subject to judicial review, the ultimate question of the extent to which, if any, the surviving company was bound by other provisions of the contract. Id., at 549, 551.

Wiley's limited accommodation between the legislative endorsement of freedom of contract and the judicial preference for peaceful arbitral settlement of labor disputes does not warrant the Board's holding that the employer commits an unfair labor practice unless he honors the substantive terms of the pre-existing contract. The present case does not involve a §301 suit; nor does it involve the duty to arbitrate. Rather, the claim is that Burns must be held bound by the contract executed by Wackenhut, whether Burns has agreed to it or not and even though Burns made it perfectly clear that it had no intention of assuming that contract. *Wiley* suggests no such open-ended obligation. Its narrower holding dealt with a merger occurring against a background of state law which embodied the general rule that in merger situations the surviving corporation is liable for the obligations of the disappearing corporation. See N.Y. Stock Corporation Law §90; 15 Fletcher, Private Corporations (1961 rev. ed.), §7121. Here there was no merger, no sale of assets, no dealings whatsoever between Wackenhut and Burns. On the contrary, they were competitors for the same work, each bidding for the service contract at Lockheed. Burns purchased nothing from Wackenhut and became liable for none of its financial obligations. Burns merely hired enough of Wackenhut's employees to require it to bargain with the union as commanded by §8(a)(5) and §9(a). But this consideration is a wholly insufficient basis for implying either in fact or in law that Burns had agreed or must be held to have agreed to honor Wackenhut's collective-bargaining contract. . . .

Preventing industrial strife is an important aim of federal labor legislation, but Congress has not chosen to make the bargaining freedom of employers and unions totally subordinate to this goal. When a bargaining impasse is reached, strikes and lockouts may occur. This bargaining freedom means both that parties need not make any concessions as a result of government compulsion and that they are free from having contract provisions imposed upon them against their will. Here, Burns had notice of the existence of the Wackenhut collective-bargaining contract, but it did not consent to be bound by it. The source of its duty to bargain with the union is not the collective-bargaining contract but the fact that it voluntarily took over a bargaining unit that was largely intact and that had been certified within the past year. Nothing in its actions, however, indicated that Burns was assuming the obligations of the contract, and "allowing the Board to compel agreement when the parties themselves are unable to agree would violate the fundamental premise on which the Act is based — private bargaining under governmental supervision of the procedure alone, without any official compulsion over the actual terms of the contract." H. K. Porter Co. v. National Labor Relations Board, supra, 397 U.S., at 108.

We also agree with the Court of Appeals that holding either the union or the new employer bound to the substantive terms of an old collective-bargaining contract may result in serious inequities. A potential employer may be willing to take over a moribund business only if he can make changes in corporate structure, composition of the labor force, work location, task assignment, and nature of supervision. Saddling such an employer with the terms and conditions of employment contained in the old collective-bargaining contract may make these changes impossible and may discourage and inhibit the transfer of capital. On the other hand, a union may have made concessions to a small or failing employer that it would be unwilling to make to a large or economically successful firm. The congressional policy manifest in the Act is to enable the parties to negotiate for any protection either deems appropriate, but to allow the balance of bargaining advantage to be set by economic power realities. Strife is bound to occur if the concessions which must be honored do not correspond to the relative economic strength of the parties.

The Board's position would also raise new problems, for the successor employer would be circumscribed in exactly the same way as the predecessor under the collective-bargaining contract. It would seemingly follow that employees of the predecessor would be deemed employees of the successor, dischargeable only in accordance with provisions of the contract and subject to the grievance and arbitration provisions thereof. Burns would not have been free to replace Wackenhut's guards with its own except as the contract permitted. Given the continuity of employment relationship, the pre-existing contract's provisions with respect to wages, seniority rights, vacation privileges, pension and retirement fund benefits, job security provisions, work assignments and the like would devolve on the successor. Nor would the union commit a §8(b)(3) unfair labor practice if it refused to bargain for a modification of the agreement effective prior to the expiration date of the agreement. A successor employer might also be deemed to have inherited its predecessor's pre-existing contractual obligations to the union which had accrued under past contracts and which had not been discharged when the business was transferred. "[A] successor may well acquire more liabilities as a result of *Burns* than appear on the face of the contract." Finally, a successor will be bound to observe the contract despite good-faith doubts about the union's majority during the time that the contract is a bar to another representation election, Ranch-Way, Inc., 183 N.L.R.B. No. 116 (1970). For the above reasons, the Board itself has expressed doubts as to the general applicability of its *Burns* rule.

In many cases, of course, successor employers will find it advantageous not only to recognize and bargain with the union but also to observe the pre-existing contract rather than to face uncertainty and turmoil. Also, in a variety of circumstances involving a merger, stock acquisition, reorganization, or assets purchase, the Board might properly find as a matter of fact that the successor had assumed the obligations under the old contract. Such a duty does not, however, ensue as a matter of law from the mere fact that an employer is doing the same work in the same place with the same employees as his predecessor, as the Board had recognized until its decision in the instant case. We accordingly set aside the Board's finding of a §8(a)(5) unfair labor practice insofar as it rested on a conclusion that Burns was required to but did not honor the collective-bargaining contract executed by Wackenhut.

IV

It therefore follows that the Board's order requiring Burns to "give retroactive effect to all the clauses of said [Wackenhut] contract and, with interest of 6 percent, make whole its employees for any losses suffered by reason of Respondent's [Burns'] refusal to honor, adopt and enforce said contract" must be set aside. We note that the regional director's charge instituting this case asserted that "on or about July 1, 1967, Respondent unilaterally changed existing wage rates, hours of employment, overtime wage rates, differentials for swing shift and graveyard shift and other terms and conditions of employment of the employees in the appropriate unit . . . ," and that the Board's opinion stated that "[t]he obligation to bargain imposed on a successor-employer includes the negative injunction to refrain from unilaterally changing wages and other benefits established by a prior collective-bargaining agreement even though that agreement had expired. In this respect the successor-employer's obligations are the same as those imposed upon employers generally during the period between collective-bargaining agreements." This statement by the Board is consistent with its prior and subsequent cases which hold that whether or not a successor employer is bound by its predecessor's contract, it must not institute terms and conditions of employment different from those provided in its predecessor's contract, at least without first bargaining with the employees' representative. Thus, if Burns, without bargaining to impasse with the union, had paid its employees on and after July 1 at a rate lower than Wackenhut had paid under its contract or otherwise provided terms and conditions of employment different from those provided in the Wackenhut collective-bargaining agreement, under the Board's view, Burns would have committed a §8(a)(5) unfair labor practice and would be subject to an order to restore to employees what they had lost by this so-called unilateral change.

Although Burns had no obligation to bargain with the union concerning wages and other conditions of employment when the union requested it to do so, this case is not like a §8(a)(5) violation where an employer unilaterally changes a condition of employment without consulting a bargaining representative. It is difficult to understand how Burns could be said to have *changed* unilaterally any pre-existing term or condition of employment without bargaining when it had no previous relationship whatsoever to the bargaining unit and, prior to July 1, no outstanding terms and conditions of employment from which a change could be inferred. The terms on which Burns hired employees for service after July 1 may have differed from the terms extended by Wackenhut and required by the collective-bargaining contract, but it does not follow that Burns changed *its* terms and conditions of employment when it specified the initial basis on which employees were hired on July 1.

Although a successor employer is ordinarily free to set initial terms on which it will hire the employees of a predecessor, there will be instances in which it is perfectly clear that the new employer plans to retain all of the employees in the unit and in which it will be appropriate to have him initially consult with the employees' bargaining representative before he fixes terms. In other situations, however, it may not be clear until the successor employer has hired his full complement of employees that he has a duty to bargain with a union, since it will not be evident until then that the bargaining representative represents a majority of the employees in the unit as required by §9(a) of the Act. Here, for example, Burns' obligation to bargain with the union did not mature until it had selected its force of guards late in June. The Board quite properly found that Burns refused to bargain on July 12 when it rejected the overtures of the union. It is true that the wages it paid when it began protecting the Lockheed plant on July 1 differed from those specified in the Wackenhut collective-bargaining agreement, but there is no evidence that Burns ever unilaterally changed the terms and conditions of employment it had offered to potential employees in June after its obligation to bargain with the union became apparent. If the union had made a request to bargain after Burns had completed its hiring and if Burns had negotiated in good faith and had made offers to the union which the union rejected, Burns could have unilaterally initiated such proposals as the opening terms and conditions of employment on July 1 without committing an unfair labor practice. The Board's order requiring Burns to make whole its employees for any losses suffered by reason of Burns' refusal to honor and enforce the contract, cannot therefore be sustained on the ground that Burns unilaterally changed existing terms and conditions of employment, thereby committing an unfair labor practice which required monetary restitution in these circumstances.

Affirmed.

REHNQUIST, J., with whom BURGER, C.J., BRENNAN, J., and POWELL, J., join, concurring in [part] and dissenting in [part].

Although the Court studiously avoids using the term "successorship" in concluding that Burns did have a statutory obligation to bargain with the union, it affirms the conclusions of the Board and the Court of Appeals to that effect which were based entirely on the successorship doctrine. Because I believe that the Board and the Court of Appeals stretched that concept beyond the limits of its proper application, I would enforce neither the Board's bargaining order nor its order imposing upon Burns the terms of the contract between the union and Wackenhut. . . .

The Court concludes that because the trial examiner and the Board found the Lockheed facility to be an appropriate bargaining unit for Burns' employees, and because Burns hired a majority of Wackenhut's previous employees who had worked at that facility, Burns should have bargained with the union, even though the union never made any showing to Burns of majority representation. There is more than one difficulty with this analysis.

First, it is by no means mathematically demonstrable that the union was the choice of a majority of the 42 employees with which Burns began the performance of its contract with Lockheed. True, 27 of the 42 had been represented by the union when they were employees of Wackenhut, but there is nothing in the record before us to indicate that all 27 of these employees chose the union as their bargaining agent even at the time of negotiations with Wackenhut. There is obviously no evidence whatever that the remaining 15 employees of Burns, who had never been employed by Wackenhut, had ever expressed their views one way or the other about the union as a bargaining representative. It may be that, if asked, all would have designated the union. But they were never asked. Instead, the trial examiner concluded that because Burns was a "successor" employer to Wackenhut, it was obligated by that fact alone to bargain with the union.

The second problem with the Court's reasoning is that it relies on the Board's approval of the Lockheed plant as an appropriate unit to support its conclusion that Burns must bargain with the union. While it is true, as the Court notes, that the trial examiner and the Board found the Lockheed facility to be an appropriate bargaining unit for Burns' employees, it is equally true that the trial examiner's finding to this effect was clearly dependent upon the previous stipulation between Wackenhut and the union. One of the reasons asserted by Burns for declining to recognize the union was its belief that the single Lockheed facility was not an appropriate bargaining unit. This was more than a colorable claim. Unlike Wackenhut, Burns had never bargained with a union consisting of its employees in a single job location. One of the reasons for this difference was that Burns made a practice of transferring employees from one job to another, on a temporary or permanent basis. Both Burns and Wackenhut had numerous security guard job sites in Southern California; for administrative purposes, Wackenhut treated each job site as a separate unit, while Burns treated large numbers of them together. . . .

The rigid imposition of a prior existing labor relations environment on a new employer whose only connection with the old employer is the hiring of some of the latter's employees and the performance of some of the work which was previously performed by the latter, might well tend to produce industrial peace of a sort. But industrial peace in such a case would be produced at a sacrifice of the determination by the Board of the appropriateness of bargaining agents and of the wishes of the majority of the employees which the Act was designed to preserve. These latter principles caution us against extending successorship, under the banner of industrial peace, step by step to a point where the only connection between the two employing entities is a naked transfer of employees. . . .

Burns acquired not a single asset, tangible or intangible, by negotiation or transfer from Wackenhut. It succeeded to the contractual rights and duties of the plant protection service contract with Lockheed not by reason of Wackenhut's assignment or consent, but over Wackenhut's vigorous opposition. I think the only permissible conclusion is that Burns is not a successor to Wackenhut. . . .

This is not to say that Burns would be unilaterally free to mesh into its previously recognized Los Angeles County bargaining unit a group of employees such as were involved here who already have designated a collective-bargaining representative in their previous employment. Burns' action in this regard would be subject to the commands of the Labor Management Relations Act, and to the regulation of the Board under proper application of governing principles. The situation resulting from the addition of a new element of the component work force of an employer has been dealt with by the Board in numerous cases, and various factors are weighed in order to determine whether the new workforce component should be itself a separate bargaining unit, or whether the employees in this component shall be "accreted" to the bargaining unit already in existence. Had the Board made the appropriate factual inquiry and determinations required by the Act, such inquiry might have justified the conclusion that Burns was obligated to recognize and bargain with the union as a representative for its employees at the Lockheed facility. . . .

Notes

1. Isn't it clear that *Wiley* thrusts on labor arbitrators a task fundamentally different from that imposed by the *Steelworkers Trilogy?* What decisional standards would you suggest for an arbitrator asked to decide which substantive provisions of a predecessor's collective bargaining agreement carry over and whether union claims under those provisions have merit?

2. Can *Wiley* survive *Burns*? One possibility is that the union in *Burns* chose the wrong forum. Support for such a reading might be that, unlike the Board, arbitrators are not restricted by §8(d) of the NLRA; also, arbitrators are not limited by the Board's all-or-nothing approach to bargaining agreement carryover. Could it be that *Burns* is not properly deemed a "successorship" case at all and is thus an unfortunate vehicle for doctrinal development?

In Golden State Bottling Co. v. NLRB, 414 U.S. 168 (1973), the Court held that an NLRB order remedying an unfair labor practice could run against the purchaser of the enterprise who took with notice of the outstanding order. The Court approved the Board's reliance on *Wiley* and rejected the view that *Wiley* is applicable only in merger situations. According to the Court, successorship cases have properly shown a "refusal to distinguish among mergers, consolidations, and purchases of assets."

3. If the union's agreement with a predecessor company failed to predict and protect against inflation, or if the successor has a greater ability to pay than the predecessor, wouldn't the successor be well advised to agree with the predecessor to an assumption of the existing collective bargaining agreement? Is the *Burns* Court telling us that the union would have no choice but to be bound to the bargaining agreement if that happens?

HOWARD JOHNSON CO. v. DETROIT LOCAL JOINT EXECUTIVE BOARD, 417 U.S. 249 (1974): The Grissom family operated a motor lodge and restaurant under a Howard Johnson franchise. The Grissoms' collective bargaining agreement with the union provided for the arbitration of disputes and purported to bind all "successors, assigns, purchasers, lessees or transferees." In 1972, the Grissoms sold all the personal property involved in the enterprise, and leased the real property, to the Howard Johnson corporation. Howard Johnson took applications for new employees and hired only a few of the Grissoms' employees and none of its supervisors. The union filed suit to compel Howard Johnson to arbitrate its dismissal of the Grissom employees. The Supreme Court held, 8-1, that Howard Johnson had no duty to arbitrate.

Wiley was distinguished on three grounds. Since that case involved a merger in the context of state law that rendered the surviving corporation liable for the debts of the predecessor, according to the Court the parties in *Wiley* should have anticipated that arbitration might be required. Second, the union could look to the Grissoms for relief (albeit partial) in the instant case, whereas in *Wiley* the merged corporation had gone out of existence. Third, and of greatest significance, in *Wiley* all of the predecessor's employees had been hired, but in *Howard Johnson* the purpose of the arbitration request was to force the corporation to retain the employees. Since only a few of the Grissoms' employees had been hired, the necessary "substantial continuity of identity in the business enterprise was lacking"; and continuity of the work force is a sine qua non of the duty to arbitrate.

The Court took care to point out that Howard Johnson had hired its employees without discriminating against Grissom employees because of their union affiliation. It emphasized that this was "not a case where the successor corporation is the 'alter ego' of the predecessor," and it was "[not] in any sense a paper transaction without meaningful impact on the ownership or operation of the enterprise." The Court also noted that the union had not attempted to secure presale injunctive relief.

Notes

1. Consider Morris and Gaus, supra note [22] at 1395-1396:

> Changes in employment should be significant for the successorship issue only where they are the necessary result of basic entrepreneurial decisions. Thus, if an employer who has purchased a plant intends to discontinue certain products formerly manufactured, and to that end reduces the work force, installs new machinery, and hires new employees to operate the machinery, the resulting discontinuity of the work force would be a forceful reason for finding no successorship. If, however, an employer who has taken over a plant makes no basic changes in operation that require a change in composition or a reduction of the work force, but he nevertheless endeavors to hire predominantly new employees, the resulting discontinuity should have no more significance than if the predecessor had summarily discharged all of his employees and then claimed good faith doubt of majority status. If factors other than the work force indicate that the new employer is enjoying substantial benefits of continuity, he should be regarded as a successor and his mass discharges should be considered arbitrable grievances.

2. *Problems*. a. The Arizona Reclamation Company is a small corporation engaged in recycling aluminum beverage cans. It employs about 75 employees and has a collective bargaining agreement with the Bottlers' Union. Its corporate shares are widely dispersed but not actively

traded. E. N. Trompenur, a client of your law firm, came to you this morning for advice respecting Arizona Reclamation. Trompenur is a business investor interested in securing a controlling interest in the company by purchasing shares on the open market. He predicts Arizona will pass a bottle bill in the next few years requiring a mandatory deposit on all beverage containers and that this will mean increased business for a company like Arizona Reclamation.

The corporate lawyers in your firm have told him he has a lot of flexibility as to how he acquires Arizona Reclamation and he has come to you for labor advice. He wonders if he can get rid of the Bottlers' Union. He feels the union's high wage rate and other benefits are the only drawbacks to a sound investment; that the union is likely to become even more greedy if business booms, as he predicts; and he hates unions. Trompenur has no interest whatever in becoming involved in the active management of the corporation although he would take over as chairman of the board of directors. Advise him.

b. Sam Morton was a grocery store manager and held 18 percent of the shares of stock of the corporation operating the store. The other shareholders decided that the store was financially unsound and prepared to go out of business. Morton obtained two other investors and the three of them purchased the store and its assets from the corporation, each of the owners taking approximately one-third ownership. Morton continued to manage the store, and the location and assets of the store remained the same. The name of the store was changed. When the store reopened under its new ownership, Morton rehired some of the supervisors who had worked in the store, but he did not offer employment to any of the employees who had been members of the union that had had bargaining rights for store employees. Is this a successorship situation? An alter ego situation? See Meatcutters Local 567 v. NLRB, 663 F.2d 223 (D.C. Cir. 1980).

3. The Board has held that a clause barring the sale or transfer of the employer's operations unless the transferee assumes the obligations of the bargaining agreement is a mandatory subject of bargaining. United Mine Workers (Lone Star Steel), 231 N.L.R.B. 573 (1977).

NLRB v. BILDISCO & BILDISCO

104 S. Ct. 1188 (1984)

REHNQUIST, J.

Two important and related questions are presented by these petitions for certiorari: (1) under what conditions can a Bankruptcy Court permit a debtor-in-possession to reject a collective-bargaining agreement; (2) may the National Labor Relations Board find a debtor-in-possession guilty of an unfair labor practice for unilaterally terminating or modifying a collective-bargaining agreement before rejection of that agreement has been approved by the Bankruptcy Court. We decide that the language "executory contract" in 11 U.S.C. §365 of the Bankruptcy Code includes within it collective-bargaining agreements subject to the National Labor Relations Act, and that the Bankruptcy Court may approve rejection of such contracts by the debtor-in-possession upon an appropriate showing. We also decide that a debtor-in-possession does not commit an unfair labor practice when, after the filing of a bankruptcy petition but before court-approved rejection of the collective-bargaining agreement, it unilaterally modifies or terminates one or more provisions of the agreement. We therefore affirm the judgment of the Court of Appeals for the Third Circuit in these cases.

I

A

On April 14, 1980, respondent Bildisco and Bildisco ("Bildisco"), a New Jersey general partnership in the business of distributing building supplies, filed a voluntary petition in bankruptcy for reorganization under Chapter 11 of the Bankruptcy Code. Bildisco was subsequently authorized by the Bankruptcy Court to operate the business as debtor-in-possession under 11 U.S.C. §1107.

At the time of the filing of the petition in bankruptcy, approximately 40 to 45 percent of Bildisco's labor force was represented by Local 408 of the International Brotherhood of Teamsters, Chauffeurs, Warehousemen and Helpers of America ("Union"). Bildisco had negotiated a three-year collective-bargaining agreement with the Union that was to expire on April 30, 1982, and which expressly provided that it was binding on the parties and their successors even though bankruptcy should supervene. Beginning in January, 1980, Bildisco failed to meet some of its obligations under the collective-bargaining agreement, including the payment of health and pension benefits and the remittance to the Union of dues collected under the agreement. In May, 1980, Bildisco refused to pay wage increases called for in the collective-bargaining agreement.

In December, 1980, Bildisco requested permission from the Bankruptcy Court, pursuant to 11 U.S.C. §365(a), to reject the collective-bargaining agreement. At the hearing on Bildisco's request the sole witness was one of Bildisco's general partners, who testified that rejection would save his company approximately $100,000 in 1981. The Union offered no witnesses of its own, but cross-examined the witness for Bildisco. On January 15, 1981, the Bankruptcy Court granted Bildisco permission to reject the collective-bargaining agreement and allowed the Union 30 days in which to file a claim for damages against Bildisco stemming from the rejection of the contract. The District Court upheld the order of the Bankruptcy Court, and the Union appealed to the Court of Appeals for the Third Circuit.

B

During mid-summer 1980, the Union filed unfair labor practice charges with the National Labor Relations Board ("Board"). The General Counsel of the Board issued a complaint alleging that Bildisco had violated §8(a)(5) and §8(a)(1) of the National Labor Relations Act ("NLRA") by unilaterally changing the terms of the collective-bargaining agreement, in failing to pay certain contractually mandated fringe benefits and wage increases and to remit dues to the Union. Ultimately the Board found that Bildisco had violated §8(a)(5) and §8(a)(1) of the NLRA by unilaterally changing the terms of the collective-bargaining agreement and by refusing to negotiate with the Union. Bildisco was ordered to make the pension, health, and welfare contributions and to remit dues to the Union, all as required under the collective-bargaining agreement. The Board petitioned the Court of Appeals for the Third Circuit to enforce its order.

C

The Court of Appeals held that a collective-bargaining agreement is an executory contract subject to rejection by a debtor-in-possession under §365(a) of the Bankruptcy Code. The authority of the debtor-in-possession to seek rejection of the collective-bargaining agreement was not qualified by the restrictions of §8(d) of the NLRA, which established detailed guidelines for mid-term modification of collective-bargaining agreements, because in the court's view, the debtor-in-possession was a "new entity" not bound by the labor agreement. The Court of Appeals concluded, however, that given the favored status Congress has accorded collective-bargaining agreements, a debtor-in-possession had to meet a more stringent test than the usual business judgment rule to obtain rejection. The Court of Appeals . . . required the debtor-in-possession to show not only that the collective-bargaining agreement is burdensome to the estate, but also that the equities balance in favor of rejection. The case was remanded to the Bankruptcy Court for reconsideration in light of the standards enunciated.

The Court of Appeals refused to enforce the Board's order, rejecting the Board's conclusion that Bildisco, as debtor-in-possession, was the alter-ego of the pre-petition employer. Under the Bankruptcy Code, a debtor-in-possession was deemed a "new entity" not bound by the debtor's prior collective-bargaining agreement. Because rejection relates back to the filing of a petition, the Court of Appeals held that if Bildisco were permitted to reject the contract, the Board was precluded from premising an unfair labor practice on Bildisco's rejection of the labor contract. The Court of Appeals implied that if the Bankruptcy Court determined that the collective-bargaining agreement should not be rejected, the Board could find a violation of §8(d) of the NLRA.

II

Section 365(a) of the Bankruptcy Code, 11 U.S.C. §365, provides in full:

> (a) Except as provided in §§765 and 766 of this title and in subsections (b), (c), and (d) of this section, the trustee, subject to the court's approval, may assume or reject any executory contract or unexpired lease of the debtor.

This language by its terms includes all executory contracts except those expressly exempted, and it is not disputed by the parties that an unexpired collective-bargaining agreement is an executory contract. Any inference that collective-bargaining agreements are not included within the general scope of §365(a) because they differ for some purposes from ordinary contracts, see John Wiley & Sons, Inc. v. Livingston, 376 U.S. 543, 550 (1964), is rebutted by the statutory design of §365(a) and by the language of §1167 of the Bankruptcy Code. The text of §365(a) indicates that Congress was concerned about the scope of the debtor-in-possession's power regarding certain types of executory contracts, and purposely drafted §365(a) to limit the debtor-in-possession's power of rejection or assumption in those circumstances. Yet none of the express limitations on the debtor-in-possession's general power under §365(a) apply to collective-bargaining agreements. Section 1167, in turn, expressly exempts collective-bargaining agreements subject to the Railway Labor Act, but grants no similar exemption to agreements subject to the NLRA. Obviously, Congress knew how to draft an exclusion for collective-bargaining agreements when it wanted to; its failure to do so in this instance indicates that Congress intended that §365(a) apply to all collective-bargaining agreements covered by the NLRA.

None of the parties to this case dispute the foregoing proposition. But the Board contends that the standard by which the Bankruptcy Court must judge the request of a debtor-in-possession to reject a collective-bargaining contract must be stricter than the traditional "business judgment" standard applied by the courts to authorize rejection of the ordinary executory contract. The Union also contends that the debtor-in-possession must comply with the procedural requirements of §8(d) of the NLRA, or at a minimum, bargain to impasse before it may request the Bankruptcy Court either to assume or to reject the collective-bargaining agreement.

Although there is no indication in §365 of the Bankruptcy Code that rejection of collective-bargaining agreements should be governed by a standard different from that governing other executory contracts, all of the Courts of Appeals which have considered the matter have concluded that the standard should be a stricter one. We agree with these Courts of Appeals that because of the special nature of a collective-bargaining contract, and the consequent "law of the shop" which it creates, see John Wiley & Sons, supra; United Steelworkers v. Warrior & Gulf Navigation Co., 363 U.S. 574, 578-579 (1960), a somewhat stricter standard should govern the decision of the Bankruptcy Court to allow rejection of a collective-bargaining agreement.

The Union and the Board argue that in light of the special nature of rights created by labor contracts, Bildisco should not be permitted to reject the collective-bargaining agreement unless it can demonstrate that its reorganization will fail unless rejection is permitted. This very strict standard was adopted by the Second Circuit in Brotherhood of Railway and Airline Clerks v. REA Express, Inc., 523 F.2d 164, 167-169 (C.A.2), cert. denied, 423 U.S. 1017 (1975). . . .

The standard adopted by the Court of Appeals for the Second Circuit in *REA Express* is fundamentally at odds with the policies of flexibility and equity built into Chapter 11 of the Bankruptcy Code. The rights of workers under collective-bargaining agreements are important, but the *REA Express* standard subordinates the multiple, competing considerations underlying a Chapter 11 reorganization to one issue: whether rejection of the collective-bargaining agreement is necessary to prevent the debtor from going into liquidation. The evidentiary burden necessary to meet this stringent standard may not be insurmountable, but it will present difficulties to the debtor-in-possession that will interfere with the reorganization process.

We agree with the Court of Appeals below that the Bankruptcy Court should permit rejection of a collective-bargaining agreement under §365(a) of the Bankruptcy Code if the debtor can show that the collective-bargaining agreement burdens the estate, and that after careful scrutiny, the equities balance in favor of rejecting the labor contract. The standard which we think Congress intended is a higher one than that of the "business judgment" rule, but a lesser one than that embodied in the *REA Express* opinion of the Court of Appeals for the Second Circuit.

Before acting on a petition to modify or reject a collective-bargaining agreement, however, the Bankruptcy Court should be persuaded that reasonable efforts to negotiate a voluntary modification have been made and are not likely to produce a prompt and satisfactory solution. The NLRA requires no less. . . . The Bankruptcy Court need step into this process only if the parties' inability to reach an agreement threatens to impede the success of the debtor's reorganization. If the parties are unable to agree, a decision on the rejection of the collective-bargaining agreement may become necessary to the reorganization process. At such a point, action by the Bankruptcy Court is required, while the policies of the Labor Act have been adequately served since reasonable efforts to reach agreement have been made. That court need not determine that the parties have bargained to impasse or make any other determination outside the field of its expertise.

Since the policy of Chapter 11 is to permit successful rehabilitation of debtors, rejection should not be permitted without a finding that that policy would be served by such action. The Bankruptcy Court must make a reasoned finding on the record why it has determined that rejection should be permitted. Determining what would constitute a successful rehabilitation involves balancing the interests of the affected parties — the debtor, creditors, and employees. The Bankruptcy Court must consider the likelihood and consequences of liquidation for the debtor absent rejection, the reduced value of the creditors' claims that would follow from affirmance and the hardship that would impose on them, and the impact of rejection on the employees. In striking the balance, the Bankruptcy Court must consider not only the degree of hardship faced by each party, but also any qualitative differences between the types of hardship each may face.

The Bankruptcy Court is a court of equity, and in making this determination it is in a very real sense balancing the equities, as the Court of Appeals suggested. Nevertheless, the Bankruptcy Court must focus on the ultimate goal of Chapter 11 when considering these equities. The Bankruptcy Code does not authorize free-wheeling consideration of every conceivable equity, but rather only how the equities relate to the success of the reorganization. The Bankruptcy Court's inquiry is of necessity speculative and it must have great latitude to consider any type of evidence relevant to this issue.

III

The second issue raised by this case is whether the NLRB can find a debtor-in-possession guilty of an unfair labor practice for unilaterally rejecting or modifying a collective-bargaining agreement before formal rejection by the Bankruptcy Court. Much effort has been expended by the parties on the question of whether the debtor is more properly characterized as an "alter ego" or a "successor employer" of the pre-bankruptcy debtor, as those terms have been used in our labor decisions. See Howard Johnson Co. v. Detroit Local Joint Executive Board, 417 U.S. 249, 259 n.5 (1974); NLRB v. Burns Security Services, Inc., 406 U.S. 272 (1972); Southport Petroleum Co. v. NLRB, 315 U.S. 100, 106 (1942). We see no profit in an exhaustive effort to identify which, if either, of these terms represents the closest analogy to the debtor-in-possession. Obviously if the latter were a wholly "new entity," it would be unnecessary for the Bankruptcy Code to allow it to reject executory contracts, since it would not be bound by such contracts in the first place. For our purposes, it is sensible to view the debtor-in-possession as the same "entity" which existed before the filing of the bankruptcy petition, but empowered by virtue of the Bankruptcy Code to deal with its contracts and property in a manner it could not have done absent the bankruptcy filing.

The fundamental purpose of reorganization is to prevent a debtor from going into liquidation, with an attendant loss of jobs and possible misuse of economic resources. In some cases reorganization may succeed only if new creditors infuse the ailing firm with additional capital. We recognized the desirability of an analogous infusion of capital in *Burns*; a similarly beneficial recapitalization could be jeopardized if the debtor-in-possession were saddled automatically with the debtor's prior collective-bargaining agreement. Thus, the authority to reject an executory contract is vital to the basic purpose to a Chapter 11 reorganization, because rejection can release the debtor's estate from burdensome obligations that can impede a successful reorganization.

While all parties to this case ultimately concede that the Bankruptcy Court may authorize rejection of a collective-bargaining agreement, the Board and the Union nonetheless insist that a debtor-in-possession violates §8(a)(5) and §8(d) of the NLRA if it unilaterally changes the terms of the collective-bargaining agreement between the date of filing the bankruptcy petition and the date on which the Bankruptcy Court authorizes rejection of the agreement. But acceptance of such a contention would largely, if not completely, undermine whatever benefit the debtor-in-possession otherwise obtains by its authority to request rejection of the agreement. In a Chapter 11 reorganization, a debtor-in-possession has until a reorganization plan is confirmed to decide whether to accept or reject an executory contract, although a creditor may request the Bankruptcy Court to make such a determination within a particular time. In contrast, during a Chapter 7 liquidation the trustee has only 60 days from the order for relief in which to decide whether to accept or reject an executory contract. It seems to us that this difference between the two types of proceedings reflects the considered judgment of Congress that a debtor-in-possession seeking to reorganize should be granted more latitude in deciding whether to reject a contract than should a trustee in liquidation.

Under the Bankruptcy Code proof of claims must be presented to the Bankruptcy Court for administration, or be lost when a plan of reorganization is confirmed. Actions on claims that have been or could have been brought before the filing of a bankruptcy petition are, with limited exceptions not relevant here, stayed through the automatic stay provisions of the Bankruptcy Code. The Bankruptcy Code specifies that the rejection of an executory contract which had not been assumed constitutes a breach of the contract which relates back to the date immediately preceding the filing of a petition in bankruptcy. Consequently, claims arising after filing, such as result from the rejection of an executory contract, must also be presented through the normal administration process by which claims are estimated and classified. Thus suit may not be brought against the debtor-in-possession under the collective-bargaining agreement; recovery may be had only through administration of the claim in bankruptcy.[12]

While the Board insists that §365(g)(1) deals only with priorities of payment, the implications from the decided cases are that the relation back of contract rejection to the filing of the petition in bankruptcy involves more than just priority of claims. Damages on the contract that result from the rejection of an executory contract, as noted, must be administered through bankruptcy and receive the priority provided general unsecured creditors. If the debtor-in-possession elects to continue to receive benefits from the other party to an executory contract pending a decision to reject or assume the contract, the debtor-in-possession is obligated to pay for the reasonable value of those services, which, depending on the circumstances of a particular contract, may be what is specified in the contract. Should the debtor-in-possession elect to assume the executory contract, however, it assumes the contract *cum onere* and the expenses and liabilities incurred may be treated as administrative expenses, which are afforded the highest priority on the debtor's estate.

The necessary result of the foregoing discussion is that the Board is precluded from, in effect, enforcing the contract terms of the collective-bargaining agreement by filing unfair labor practices against the debtor-in-possession for violating §8(d) of the NLRA. Though the Board's action is nominally one to enforce §8(d) of that Act, the practical effect of the enforcement action would be to require adherence to the terms of the collective-bargaining agreement. But the filing of the petition in bankruptcy means that the collective-bargaining agreement is no longer immediately enforceable, and may never be enforceable again. Consequently, Board enforcement of a claimed violation of §8(d) under these circumstances would run directly counter to the express provisions of the Bankruptcy Code and to the Code's overall effort to give a debtor-in-possession some flexibility and breathing space. We conclude that from the filing of a petition in bankruptcy until formal acceptance, the collective-bargaining agreement is not an enforceable contract within the meaning of NLRA §8(d).

12. Section 502(c) provides that any contingent or unliquidated claim shall be estimated for purposes of settling a bankrupt estate. Under this provision losses occasioned by the rejection of a collective-bargaining agreement must be estimated, including unliquidated losses attributable to fringe benefits or security provisions like seniority rights. Section 502(c) is a change from prior law; under §57d of the Bankruptcy Act the court could disallow unliquidated claims if too difficult to estimate. In enacting the Bankruptcy Code Congress also extended the priority for unsecured claims made by workers to cover vacation, severance, sick leave pay, and pension plan obligations and increased the amount of this priority. These provisions indicate Congress's considered judgment regarding the extent to which special provisions should be afforded workers under the Bankruptcy Code for claims arising out of the rejection of the collective-bargaining agreement. In addition, wages paid after the filing of a petition in bankruptcy may be deemed administrative expenses and afforded the highest priority, if necessary to preserve the estate.

The Union, but not the Board, also insists that the debtor-in-possession must comply with the mid-term contract modification procedures set forth in §8(d) of the NLRA. Because the collective-bargaining agreement is not an enforceable contract within the meaning of §8(d), it follows that the debtor-in-possession need not comply with the provisions of §8(d) prior to seeking the Bankruptcy Court's permission to reject the agreement. . . .

The Union maintains, as a fall-back position, that even if §8(d) procedures do not apply fully, the debtor-in-possession should be required to "bargain to impasse" prior to seeking rejection from the Bankruptcy Court. . . . Our rejection of the need for full compliance with §8(d) procedures of necessity means that any corresponding duty to bargain to impasse under §8(a)(5) and §8(d) before seeking rejection must also be subordinated to the exigencies of bankruptcy. Whether impasse has been reached generally is a judgment call for the Board to make; imposing such a requirement as a condition precedent to rejection of the labor contract will simply divert the Bankruptcy Court from its customary area of expertise into a field in which it presumably has little or none.

Our determination that a debtor-in-possession does not commit an unfair labor practice by failing to comply with §8(d) prior to formal rejection of the collective-bargaining agreement does undermine the policy of the NLRA, for that policy, as we have noted, is to protect the process of labor negotiations, not to impose particular results on the parties. Nevertheless, it is important to note that the debtor-in-possession is not relieved of all obligations under the NLRA simply by filing a petition for bankruptcy. A debtor-in-possession is an "employer" within the terms of the NLRA, and is obligated to bargain collectively with the employees' certified representative over the terms of a new contract pending rejection of the existing contract or following formal approval of rejection by the Bankruptcy Court. But while a debtor-in-possession remains obligated to bargain in good faith under NLRA §8(a)(5) over the terms and conditions of a possible new contract, it is not guilty of an unfair labor practice by unilaterally breaching a collective-bargaining agreement before formal Bankruptcy Court action.

Accordingly, the judgment of the Court of Appeals is

Affirmed.[24]

Notes

1. It has been argued that the purpose of the bankruptcy laws is to provide a collective mechanism for the disposition of the assets of the debtor. Absent such a collective mechanism, individual creditors have an

[24] Brennan, J., White, J., Marshall, J., and Blackmun, J., concurred in part and dissented in part.

incentive to spend resources to "grab" an advantage over other creditors, even if the overall asset "pie" would be greater by a distribution mechanism that avoided such grabs.[25]

> In performing that function, however, bankruptcy law should not make determinations in a vacuum. Instead, bankruptcy law best serves its unique collectivizing function simply by attempting to mirror nonbankruptcy assets and liabilities. The proposition follows from the nature and function of bankruptcy law. Successful substitution of a collective regime for a system of individual advantage-taking *attributable to* the substitution process are minimized. This, in turn, requires the rules inside of bankruptcy to mirror, as closely as is consistent with the collectivizing goal, those created by nonbankruptcy law. Only by so replicating the nonbankruptcy universe can the bankruptcy system minimize incentives by an individual claimant to resort to it in order to gain access to a rule change that benefits him but makes the claimants as a group worse off.[26]

How would this reasoning be applied to the facts of *Bildisco*?

2. The summer following *Bildisco,* Congress amended the bankruptcy statute. The statute now requires bankruptcy court approval before a debtor can reject a collective bargaining agreement, and it permits the court to approve rejection only if the union has refused the debtor's proposed contract modifications "without good cause" and if the balance of equities "clearly favors" rejection of the union contract. Only if the bankruptcy court fails to act in a timely fashion on a debtor's application to reject the union contract can the debtor unilaterally implement contract changes. The debtor can make "interim changes" in a union contract with court approval "if essential to the continuation of the debtor's business or in order to avoid irreparable damage to the estate."

D. ENFORCEMENT BY INDIVIDUAL EMPLOYEES AND THE UNION'S DUTY TO FAIRLY REPRESENT

STEELE v. LOUISVILLE & NASHVILLE RAILROAD
323 U.S. 192 (1944)

[A black locomotive fireman brought suit in Alabama state court against his employer, a railroad, and the union which had been designated as the exclusive bargaining representative of the railroad's firemen by the Railway Labor Act. The complaint alleged that the union

[25] See Jackson, Bankruptcy, Non-Bankruptcy Entitlements, and the Creditors' Bargain, 91 Yale L.J. 857 (1982).

[26] Jackson, Translating Assets and Liabilities to the Bankruptcy Forum, 15 J.L. Stud. — (forthcoming, 1985).

had embarked on a course of conduct designed to oust all blacks from positions as firemen on defendant's railroad, and 20 others, and to replace them with white firemen. A collective bargaining agreement was entered into restricting the employment and seniority rights of black firemen. Neither notice nor opportunity to be heard was given to the black firemen before the bargaining agreement provisions went into effect. Pursuant to the agreement, plaintiff lost 16 days of work as a fireman and was then assigned to a harder-working, lower-paying position. The suit asked for an injunction against the enforcement of the current collective bargaining agreement between the union and the railroad, an injunction against the union acting as an exclusive bargaining representative so long as it discriminated against blacks, and for damages from the union for past discrimination. The Alabama Supreme Court held that the Railway Labor Act conferred on the union the right to negotiate and sign such an agreement free from any obligation to treat minorities fairly and without discrimination.]

Stone, C. J. . . .

If, as the state court has held, the Act confers this power on the bargaining representative of a craft or class of employees without any commensurate statutory duty toward its members, constitutional questions arise. For the representative is clothed with power not unlike that of a legislature which is subject to constitutional limitations on its power to deny, restrict, destroy or discriminate against the rights of those for whom it legislates and which is also under an affirmative constitutional duty equally to protect those rights. If the Railway Labor Act purports to impose on petitioner and the other Negro members of the craft the legal duty to comply with the terms of a contract whereby the representative has discriminatorily restricted their employment for the benefit and advantage of the Brotherhood's own members, we must decide the constitutional questions which petitioner raises in his pleading.

But we think that Congress, in enacting the Railway Labor Act and authorizing a labor union, chosen by a majority of a craft, to represent the craft, did not intend to confer plenary power upon the union to sacrifice, for the benefit of its members, rights of the minority of the craft, without imposing on it any duty to protect the minority. Since petitioner and the other Negro members of the craft are not members of the Brotherhood or eligible for membership, the authority to act for them is derived not from their action or consent but wholly from the command of the Act. Section 2, Fourth provides: "Employees shall have the right to organize and bargain collectively through representatives of their own choosing. The majority of any craft or class of employees shall have the right to determine who shall be the representative of the craft or class for the purposes of this Act. . . ." Under §§2, Sixth and Seventh, when the representative bargains for a change of working conditions, the latter section specifies that they are the working conditions of employees "as a class." Section 1, Sixth of the Act defines "representative" as meaning "Any person or . . . labor union . . . designated either by a carrier or group of carriers or by its or their employees, to act for it or them." The use of the word "representative," as thus defined and in all the contexts in which it is found, plainly implies that the representative is to act on behalf of all the employees which, by virtue of the statute, it undertakes to represent. . . .

Section 2, Second, requiring carriers to bargain with the representative so chosen, operates to exclude any other from representing a craft. The minority members of a craft are thus deprived by the statute of the right, which they would otherwise possess, to choose a representative of their own, and its members cannot bargain individually on behalf of themselves as to matters which are properly the subject of collective bargaining.

The labor organization chosen to be the representative of the craft or class of employees is thus chosen to represent all of its members, regardless of their union affiliations or want of them. . . . Unless the labor union representing a craft owes some duty to represent non-union members of the craft, at least to the extent of not discriminating against them as such in the contracts which it makes as their representative, the minority would be left with no means of protecting their interests or, indeed, their right to earn a livelihood by pursuing the occupation in which they are employed. While the majority of the craft chooses the bargaining representative, when chosen it represents, as the Act by its terms makes plain, the craft or class, and not the majority. The fair interpretation of the statutory language is that the organization chosen to represent a craft is to represent all its members, the majority as well as the minority, and it is to act for and not against those whom it represents. It is a principle of general application that the exercise of a granted power to act in behalf of others involves the assumption toward them of a duty to exercise the power in their interest and behalf, and that such a grant of power will not be deemed to dispense with all duty toward those for whom it is exercised unless so expressed.

We think that the Railway Labor Act imposes upon the statutory representative of a craft at least as exacting a duty to protect equally the interests of the members of the craft as the Constitution imposes upon a legislature to give equal protection to the interests of those for whom it legislates. Congress has seen fit to clothe the bargaining representative with powers comparable to those possessed by a legislative body both to create and restrict the rights of those whom it represents, but it has also imposed on the representative a corresponding duty. We hold that the language of the Act to which we have referred, read in the light of the purposes of the Act, expresses the aim of Congress to impose on the bargaining representative of a craft or class of employees the duty to exercise fairly the power conferred upon it in behalf of all those for whom it acts, without hostile discrimination against them.

This does not mean that the statutory representative of a craft is barred from making contracts which may have unfavorable effects on some of the members of the craft represented. Variations in the terms of contract based on differences relevant to the authorized purposes of the contract in conditions to which they are to be applied, such as differences in seniority, the type of work performed, the competence and skill with which it is performed, are within the scope of the bargaining representation of a craft, all of whose members are not identical in their interest or merit. Without attempting to mark the allowable limits of differences in the terms of contracts based on differences of conditions to which they apply, it is enough for present purposes to say that the statutory power to represent a craft and to make contracts as to wages, hours and working conditions does not include the authority to make among members of the craft discriminations not based on such relevant differences. Here the discriminations based on race alone are obviously irrelevant and invidious. Congress plainly did not undertake to authorize the bargaining representative to make such discriminations.

The representative which thus discriminates may be enjoined from so doing, and its members may be enjoined from taking the benefit of such discriminatory action. No more is the Railroad bound by or entitled to take the benefit of a contract which the bargaining representative is prohibited by the statute from making. In both cases the right asserted, which is derived from the duty imposed by the statute on the bargaining representative, is a federal right implied from the statute and the policy which it has adopted. It is the federal statute which condemns as unlawful the Brotherhood's conduct. . . .

So long as a labor union assumes to act as the statutory representative of a craft, it cannot rightly refuse to perform the duty, which is inseparable from the power of representation conferred upon it, to represent the entire membership of the craft. While the statute does not deny to such a bargaining labor organization the right to determine eligibility to its membership, it does require the union, in collective bargaining and in making contracts with the carrier, to represent non-union or minority union members of the craft without hostile discrimination, fairly, impartially, and in good faith. Wherever necessary to that end, the union is required to consider requests of non-union members of the craft and expressions of their views with respect to collective bargaining with the employer and to give to them notice of and opportunity for hearing upon its proposed action. . . .

Section 3, First (i), which provides for reference to the Adjustment Board of "disputes between an employee or group of employees and a carrier or carriers growing out of grievances or out of the interpretation or application of agreements," makes no reference to disputes between employees and their representative. Even though the dispute between the railroad and the petitioner were to be heard by the Adjustment Board, that Board could not give the entire relief here sought. The Adjustment Board has consistently declined in more than 400 cases to entertain grievance complaints by individual members of a craft represented by a labor organization. . . .

In the absence of any available administrative remedy, the right here asserted, to a remedy for breach of the statutory duty of the bargaining representaive to represent and act for the members of a craft, is of judicial cognizance. That right would be sacrified or obliterated if it were without the remedy which courts can give for breach of such a duty or obligation and which it is their duty to give in cases in which they have jurisdiction. . . .

We conclude that the duty which the statute imposes on a union representative of a craft to represent the interests of all its members stands on no different footing and that the statute contemplates resort to the usual judicial remedies of injunction and award of damages when appropriate for breach of that duty.

The judgment is accordingly reversed and remanded for further proceedings not inconsistent with this opinion.[27]

Reversed.

Notes

1. In Syres v. Oil Workers, Local 23, 350 U.S. 892 (1955), the Court made it clear that there is a similar duty to fairly represent under the NLRA.

In Brotherhood of Railroad Trainmen v. Howard, 343 U.S. 768 (1952), the Court applied the doctrine against a union that did not represent the aggrieved employees. The union, representing white brakemen, pressured the carrier into agreeing to discharge black "train porters," not represented by the union, who had been performing brakemen's duties. Implementation of the agreement was enjoined, the Court declaring: "The Federal Act . . . prohibits bargaining agents from using their position and power to destroy colored workers' jobs in order to bestow them on white workers." Three justices dissented on the ground that the train porters were not brakemen and were owed no duty of fair representation by the union.

2. In Miranda Fuel Co., 140 N.L.R.B. 181 (1962), enforcement denied, 326 F.2d 172 (2d Cir. 1963), an employee left three days early for an extended leave of absence. Pressured by some of the employees' fellow workers, the union caused the employer to drop the employee to

[27] Black, J., and Murphy, J., concurred.

the bottom of the seniority list even though the bargaining agreement made no provision for such a seniority loss. A Board majority found a violation of §§8(b)(1)(A) and 8(b)(2), reasoning that the duty to represent employees fairly and impartially flows from §9(a) and is incorporated into employees' §7 rights through their guaranteed freedom "to bargain collectively through representatives of their own choosing." A breach of that duty, whether or not influenced by an employee's union activity, violates §§8(b)(1)(A). A union's instigation of employer action against an employee in such a circumstance violates §8(b)(2) and the employer action itself violates §§8(a)(3) and 8(a)(1).

The Second Circuit reversed, 2-1. Judge Medina was persuaded that §8 of the Act is not violated by "discrimination for reasons wholly unrelated to union membership, loyalty . . . or the performance of union obligations." A concurring judge found insufficient evidence that any fair-representation breach had occurred and therefore found it unnecessary to consider whether such a breach would violate §8(b)(1). Judge Friendly, dissenting, also passed over the fair representation issue. He argued that "discrimination" in §8(a)(3) is broad enough to encompass any distinction made without a proper basis, and that a union's demonstration of sufficient power to bring about such arbitrary employer action would constitute "encouragement" under §8(b)(2).

The Board has persisted in its view despite the Second Circuit setback. Several other circuit courts have sustained the Board.

In Independent Metal Workers, Local 1 (Hughes Tool Co.), 147 N.L.R.B. 573 (1964), the Board held that a union's rejection of an employee grievance on racial grounds violated §§8(b)(1)(A), 8(b)(2), and 8(b)(3) and also ordered the union's certification revoked because it had entered into a racially discriminatory bargaining agreement. Chairman McCulloch and Member Fanning concurred in the finding of a §8(b)(1)(A) violation and in the remedy, but dissented from the majority's reliance on the fair representation doctrine:

> Section 7 was part of the Wagner Act which in its unfair labor practice section was aimed only at employer conduct. The Wagner Act also contained the present §9(a). It hardly seems reasonable to infer, in these circumstances, that §7 contained a protected implied right to fair representation against the bargaining representative, when the entire Wagner Act did not make any conduct by a labor organization unlawful. Section 7 was continued substantially unchanged in the Taft-Hartley Act except for the addition of the 'right to refrain' clause, which is not material to our problem. Although the Taft-Hartley Act added union unfair labor practices to the list of prohibited conduct, neither the Act nor the legislative history contains any mention of the duty of fair representation, despite the fact that the *Steele* and *Wallace* decisions were well known, having been issued 3 years previously. Again, although in the interval between the dates of the Taft-Hartley and Landrum-Griffin Acts, there were addi-

tional court decisions and articles by learned commentators in the law journals dealing with the legal problems of fair representation, Congress made no change in the wording of §7, and ignored the problem completely in adding a "Bill of Rights" section to the existing statute. If Congress had really intended that violation of the duty of fair representation should be an unfair labor practice, it would seem that the 1959 revision afforded it an opportunity to clear up the uncertainty. Instead it remained silent. We do not believe that realistically this silence can be interpreted as in any way favorable to the contention that the right to fair representation is a protected §7 right. There are practical reasons for believing that, if there had been any contemporary understanding that the Act had made it an unfair labor practice for a union to fail in its duty of fair representation, the opposition would have been both strong and loud.

There is another and more important reason why the Board should not undertake to police a union's administration of its duties without a clear mandate from Congress. The purpose of the Act is primarily to protect the organizational rights of employees. But apart from the obligation to bargain in good faith, "Congress intended that the parties would have wide latitude in their negotiations, unrestricted by any governmental power to regulate the substantive solution of their differences." Before *Miranda,* it was assumed that contract or grievance decisions by employers and unions were immune from examination by the Board unless they were influenced by union considerations. But, under the underlying reasoning of the *Miranda* majority and that of the present decision, the Board is now constituted a tribunal to which every employee who feels aggrieved by a bargaining representative's action, whether in contract negotiations or in grievance handling, may appeal, regardless of whether the decision has been influenced in whole or in part by considerations of union membership, loyalty, or activity. The Board must determine on such appeal, without statutory standards, whether the representative's decision was motivated by "unfair or irrelevant or invidious" considerations and therefore to be set aside, or was within the "wide range of reasonableness . . . allowed a statutory representative in serving the unit it represents . . ." and to be sustained. Inevitably, the Board will have to sit in judgment on the substantive matters of collective bargaining, the very thing the Supreme Court has said the Board must not do, and in which it has no special experience or competence. This is not exaggeration. *Miranda* itself did not involve a race issue and since *Miranda,* the Board has had to decide a number of other cases where allegations of violation of the duty of fair representation rested on other than racial grounds, with many more such cases disposed of at the regional level. *Miranda* means that the Board is embarking on a wholly new field of activity for which it has no preparation, and which is likely seriously to interfere with its present activities that are already more than enough to keep it fully occupied. . . .

In Smith v. Evening News Assn., 371 U.S. 195 (1962), the Supreme Court held that §301 grants jurisdiction to federal courts to hear breach of bargaining agreement actions brought by individual employees. But what should the district court do if the employer defends by alleging that the grievance and arbitration provisions of the agreement have not been complied with? Has the individual employee a remedy against the employer in this circumstance, or against the union that failed to exhaust the grievance and arbitration provisions?

VACA v. SIPES[28]

386 U.S. 171 (1967)

White, J. . . .

I

In mid 1959, Owens, [an employee of Swift & Co., a meat packing plant,] a long-time high blood pressure patient, became sick and entered a hospital on sick leave from his employment with Swift. After a long rest during which his weight and blood pressure were reduced, Owens was certified by his family physician as fit to resume his heavy work in the packing plant. However, Swift's company doctor examined Owens upon his return and concluded that his blood pressure was too high to permit reinstatement. After securing a second authorization from another outside doctor, Owens returned to the plant, and a nurse permitted him to resume work on January 6, 1960. However, on January 8, when the doctor discovered Owens' return, he was permanently discharged on the ground of poor health.

Armed with his medical evidence of fitness, Owens then sought the Union's help in securing reinstatement, and a grievance was filed with Swift on his behalf. By mid-November 1960, the grievance had been processed through the third and into the fourth step of the grievance procedure established by the collective bargaining agreement. Swift adhered to its position that Owens' poor health justified his discharge, rejecting numerous medical reports of reduced blood pressure proffered by Owens and by the Union. Swift claimed that these reports were not based upon sufficiently thorough medical tests.

On February 6, 1961, the Union sent Owens to a new doctor at Union expense "to see if we could get some better medical evidence so that we could go to arbitration with his case." This examination did not support Owens' position. When the Union received the report, its executive board voted not to take the Owens grievance to arbitration because of insufficient medical evidence. Union officers suggested to Owens that he

[28] See Clark, The Duty of Fair Representation: A Theoretical Structure, 51 Tex. L. Rev. 1119 (1973); Feller, A General Theory of the Collective Bargaining Agreement, 61 Calif. L. Rev. 663 (1973); Freed, Polsby, & Spitzer, Unions, Fairness and the Conundrums of Collective Choice, 56 S. Cal. L. Rev. 461 (1983); Wellington, Union Democracy and Fair Representation: Federal Responsibility in a Federal System, 67 Yale L.J. 1327 (1958).

accept Swift's offer of referral to a rehabilitation center, and the grievance was suspended for that purpose. Owens rejected this alternative and demanded that the Union take his grievance to arbitration, but the Union refused. With his contractual remedies thus stalled at the fourth step, Owens brought this suit [against petitioners as officers and representatives of the union.] The grievance was finally dismissed by the Union and Swift shortly before trial began in June 1964.

In his charge to the jury, the trial judge instructed that petitioners would be liable if Swift had wrongfully discharged Owens and if the Union had "arbitrarily . . . and without just cause or excuse . . . refused" to press Owens' grievance to arbitration. Punitive damages could also be awarded, the trial judge charged, if the Union's conduct was "willful, wanton and malicious." However, the jury must return a verdict for the defendants, the judge instructed, "if you find and believe from the evidence that the union and its representatives acted reasonably and in good faith in the handling and processing of the grievance of the plaintiff." The jury then returned the general verdict for Owens which eventually was reinstated by the Missouri Supreme Court.[29]

II

Petitioners challenge the jurisdiction of the Missouri courts on the ground that the alleged conduct of the Union was arguably an unfair labor practice and within the exclusive jurisdiction of the NLRB. Petitioners rely on Miranda Fuel Co., 140 N.L.R.B. 181 (1962), enforcement denied, 326 F.2d 172 (C.A. 2d Cir. 1963), where a sharply divided Board held for the first time that a union's breach of its statutory duty of fair representation violates N.L.R.A. §8(b), as amended. [The Court then held that federal and state courts retain their §301 jurisdiction to hear fair representation cases notwithstanding the Board's assertion of jurisdiction.]

III

Petitioners contend, as they did in their motion for judgment notwithstanding the jury's verdict, that Owens failed to prove that the Union breached its duty of fair representation in its handling of Owens' grievance. Petitioners also argue that the Supreme Court of Missouri, in rejecting this contention, applied a standard that is inconsistent with governing principles of federal law with respect to the Union's duty to an individual employee in its processing of grievances under the collective bargaining agreement with Swift. We agree with both contentions. . . .

[29] During the appeal Owens died of a cardiovascular accident and the administrator of his estate was substituted.

Quite obviously, the question which the Missouri Supreme Court thought dispositive of the issue of liability was whether the evidence supported Owens' assertion that he had been wrongfully discharged by Swift, regardless of the Union's good faith in reaching a contrary conclusion. This was also the major concern of the plaintiff at trial: the bulk of Owens' evidence was directed at whether he was medically fit at the time of discharge and whether he had performed heavy work after that discharge.

A breach of the statutory duty of fair representation occurs only when a union's conduct toward a member of the collective bargaining unit is arbitrary, discriminatory, or in bad faith. See Humphrey v. Moore, [375 U.S. 335]; Ford Motor Co. v. Huffman, [345 U.S. 330]. There has been considerable debate over the extent of this duty in the context of a union's enforcement of the grievance and arbitration procedures in a collective bargaining agreement. Some have suggested that every individual employee should have the right to have his grievance taken to arbitration. Others have urged that the union be given substantial discretion (if the collective bargaining agreement so provides) to decide whether a grievance should be taken to arbitration, subject only to the duty to refrain from patently wrongful conduct such as racial discrimination or personal hostility.

Though we accept the proposition that a union may not arbitrarily ignore a meritorious grievance or process it in perfunctory fashion, we do not agree that the individual employee has an absolute right to have his grievance taken to arbitration regardless of the provisions of the applicable collective bargaining agreement. In L.M.R.A. §203(d), Congress declared that "Final adjustment by a method agreed upon by the parties is . . . the desirable method for settlement of grievance disputes arising over the application or interpretation of an existing collective-bargaining agreement." In providing for a grievance and arbitration procedure which gives the union discretion to supervise the grievance machinery and to invoke arbitration, the employer and the union contemplate that each will endeavor in good faith to settle grievances short of arbitration. Through this settlement process, frivolous grievances are ended prior to the most costly and time-consuming step in the grievance procedures. Moreover, both sides are assured that similar complaints will be treated consistently, and major problem areas in the interpretation of the collective bargaining contract can be isolated and perhaps resolved. And finally, the settlement process furthers the interest of the union as statutory agent and as coauthor of the bargaining agreement in representing the employees in the enforcement of that agreement.

If the individual employee could compel arbitration of his grievance regardless of its merit, the settlement machinery provided by the contract would be substantially undermined, thus destroying the employer's confidence in the union's authority and returning the individual grievant to the vagaries of independent and unsystematic negotiation. Moreover, under such a rule, a significantly greater number of grievances would proceed to arbitration. This would greatly increase the cost of the grievance machinery and could so overburden the arbitration process as to prevent it from functioning successfully. It can well be doubted whether the parties to collective bargaining agreements would long continue to provide for detailed grievance and arbitration procedures of the kind encouraged by L.M.R.A. §203(d), supra, if their power to settle the majority of grievances short of the costlier and more time-consuming steps was limited by a rule permitting the grievant unilaterally to invoke arbitration. Nor do we see substantial danger to the interests of the individual employee if his statutory agent is given the contractual power honestly and in good faith to settle grievances short of arbitration. For these reasons, we conclude that a union does not breach its duty of fair representation, and thereby open up a suit by the employee for breach of contract, merely because it settled the grievance short of arbitration.

For these same reasons, the standard applied here by the Missouri Supreme Court cannot be sustained. For if a union's decision that a particular grievance lacks sufficient merit to justify arbitration would constitute a breach of the duty of fair representation because a judge or jury later found the grievance meritorious, the union's incentive to settle such grievances short of arbitration would be seriously reduced. The dampening effect on the entire grievance procedure of this reduction of the union's freedom to settle claims in good faith would surely be substantial. Since the union's statutory duty of fair representation protects the individual employee from arbitrary abuses of the settlement device by providing him with recourse against both employer (in a §301 suit) and union, this severe limitation on the power to settle grievances is neither necessary nor desirable. Therefore, we conclude that the Supreme Court of Missouri erred in upholding the verdict in this case solely on the ground that the evidence supported Owens' claim that he had been wrongfully discharged.

Applying the proper standard of union liability to the facts of this case, we cannot uphold the jury's award, for we conclude that as a matter of federal law the evidence does not support a verdict that the Union breached its duty of fair representation. . . .

In administering the grievance and arbitration machinery as statutory agent of the employees, a union must, in good faith and in a nonarbitrary manner, make decisions as to the merits of particular grievances. In a case such as this, when Owens supplied the Union with medical evidence supporting his position, the Union might well have breached its duty had it ignored Owens' complaint or had it processed the grievance in a perfunctory manner. See Cox, Rights under a Labor Agreement, 69 Harv. L. Rev., at 632-634. But here the Union processed the grievance into the fourth step, attempted to gather sufficient evidence to prove

Owens' case, attempted to secure for Owens less vigorous work at the plant, and joined in the employer's efforts to have Owens rehabilitated. Only when these efforts all proved unsuccessful did the Union conclude both that arbitration would be fruitless and that the grievance should be dismissed. There was no evidence that any Union officer was personally hostile to Owens or that the Union acted at any time other than in good faith. Having concluded that the individual employee has no absolute right to have his grievance arbitrated under the collective bargaining agreement at issue, and that a breach of the duty of fair representation is not established merely by proof that the underlying grievance was meritorious, we must conclude that that duty was not breached here.

IV

In our opinion, there is another important reason why the judgment of the Missouri Supreme Court cannot stand. Owens' suit against the Union was grounded on his claim that Swift had discharged him in violation of the applicable collective bargaining agreement. . . . We hold that such damages are not recoverable from the Union in the circumstances of this case.

The appropriate remedy for a breach of a union's duty of fair representation must vary with the circumstances of the particular breach. In this case, the employee's complaint was that the Union wrongfully failed to afford him the arbitration remedy against his employer established by the collective bargaining agreement. But the damages sought by Owens were primarily those suffered because of the employer's alleged breach of contract. Assuming for the moment that Owens had been wrongfully discharged, Swift's only defense to a direct action for breach of contract would have been the Union's failure to resort to arbitration, and if that failure was itself a violation of the Union's statutory duty to the employee, there is no reason to exempt the employer from contractual damages which he would otherwise have had to pay. The difficulty lies in fashioning an appropriate scheme of remedies.

Petitioners urge that an employee be restricted in such circumstances to a decree compelling the employer and the union to arbitrate the underlying grievance. It is true that the employee's action is based on the employer's alleged breach of contract plus the union's alleged wrongful failure to afford him his contractual remedy of arbitration. For this reason, an order compelling arbitration should be viewed as one of the available remedies when a breach of the union's duty is proved. But we see no reason inflexibly to require arbitration in all cases. In some cases, for example, at least part of the employee's damages may be attributable to the union's breach of duty, and an arbitrator may have no power under the bargaining agreement to award such damages against the union. In other cases, the arbitrable issues may be substantially resolved in the course of trying the fair representation controversy. In such situations, the court should be free to decide the contractual claim and to award the employee appropriate damages or equitable relief.

A more difficult question is, what portion of the employee's damages may be charged to the union: in particular, may an award against a union include, as it did here, damages attributable solely to the employer's breach of contract? We think not. Though the union has violated a statutory duty in failing to press the grievance, it is the employer's unrelated breach of contract which triggered the controversy and which caused this portion of the employee's damages. The employee should have no difficulty recovering these damages from the employer, who cannot, as we have explained, hide behind the union's wrongful failure to act; in fact, the employer may be (and probably should be) joined as a defendant in the fair representation suit, as in Humphrey v. Moore, supra. It could be a real hardship on the union to pay these damages, even if the union were given a right of indemnification against the employer. With the employee assured of direct recovery from the employer, we see no merit in requiring the union to pay the employer's share of the damages.

The governing principle, then, is to apportion liability between the employer and the union according to the damage caused by the fault of each. Thus, damages attributable solely to the employer's breach of contract should not be charged to the union, but increases if any in those damages caused by the union's refusal to process the grievance should not be charged to the employer. In this case, even if the Union had breached its duty, all or almost all of Owens' damages would still be attributable to his allegedly wrongful discharge by Swift. For these reasons, even if the Union here had properly been found liable for a breach of duty, it is clear that the damage award was improper.

Reversed.[30]

BOWEN v. UNITED STATES POSTAL SERVICE

459 U.S. 212 (1983)

POWELL, J.,

[The local union filed a grievance with the employer pursuant to its collective bargaining agreement. The grievance alleged that the discharge of employee Bowen on March 30, 1976, violated the agreement. The union carried the grievance through the grievance process but with-

[30] Fortas, J., joined by Warren, C.J., and Harlan, J., concurred in the result arguing that the breach of duty of fair representation was within the exclusive province of the NLRB and that the Court's discussion of the requisites of an employee action against his or her employer was not revelant. Black, J., dissented, arguing the employee should have an absolute right to have the merits of a grievance heard by a court or arbitrator.

out adequate explanation refused to take the grievance to arbitration. In the lower courts this refusal was held to violate the union's duty to fairly represent Bowen. The district court computed damages to be $52,954 in lost wages and benefits. Finding that had the union carried the grievance to arbitration an arbitrator would have reinstated Bowen by August, 1977, the court apportioned damages between the union and the employer. The employer was liable for Bowen's losses up to the time that he would have been reinstated by the hypothetical arbitrator. The union was liable for the losses accruing thereafter. The Fourth Circuit, citing *Vaca,* held that although the union had breached its duty to fairly represent Bowen, it was not liable for any portion of his lost wages and benefits.]

. . . The interests . . . identified in *Vaca* provide a measure of its principle for apportioning damages. Of paramount importance is the right of the employee, who has been injured by both the employer's and the union's breach, to be made whole. In determining the degree to which the employer or the union should bear the employee's damages, the Court held that the employer should not be shielded from the "natural consequences" of its breach by wrongful union conduct. The Court noted, however, that the employer may have done nothing to prevent exhaustion. Were it not for the union's failure to represent the employee fairly, the employer's breach "could [have been] remedied through the grievance process to the employee-plaintiff's benefit." The fault that justifies dropping the bar to the employee's suit for damages also requires the union to bear some responsibility for increases in the employee's damages resulting from its breach. To hold otherwise would make the employer alone liable for the consequences of the union's breach of duty.

Hines v. Anchor Motor Freight, Inc., 424 U.S. 554 (1976), presented an issue analogous to that in *Vaca*: whether proof of a breach of the duty of fair representation would remove the bar of finality from an arbitral decision. We held that it would, in part because a contrary rule would prevent the employee from recovering

> even in circumstances where it is shown that a union has manufactured the evidence and knows from the start that it is false; or even if, unbeknownst to the employer, the union has corrupted the arbitrator to the detriment of disfavored union members. Id., at 570.

It would indeed be unjust to prevent the employee from recovering in such a situation. It would be equally unjust to require the employer to bear the increase in the damages caused by the union's wrongful conduct.[11] It is true that the employer discharged the employee wrongfully

11. We note that this is not a situation in which either the union or the employer has participated in the other's breach.

and remains liable for the employee's backpay. See *Vaca,* supra, at 197. The union's breach of its duty of fair representation, however, caused the grievance procedure to malfunction resulting in an increase in the employee's damages. Even though both the employer and the union have caused the damage suffered by the employee, the union is responsible for the increase in damages and, as between the two wrongdoers, should bear its portion of the damages.[12]

Vaca's governing principle reflects this allocation of responsibility. As the Court stated, "damages attributable *solely* to the employer's breach of contract should not be charged to the union, but *increases* if any in those damages caused by the union's refusal to process the grievance should not be charged to the employer." 386 U.S., at 197-198 (emphasis added). The Union's position here would require us to read out of the *Vaca* articulation of the relevant principle the words emphasized above. It would also ignore the interests of all the parties to the collective agreement — interests that *Vaca* recognized and *Hines* illustrates . . . .

Fundamental to federal labor policy is the grievance procedure. It promotes the goal of industrial peace by providing a means for labor and management to settle disputes through negotiation rather than industrial strife. Adoption of a grievance procedure provides the parties with a means of giving content to the collective bargaining agreement and determining their rights and obligations under it.

Although each party participates in the grievance procedure, the union plays a pivotal role in the process since it assumes the responsibility of determining whether to press an employee's claims. The employer, for its part, must rely on the union's decision not to pursue an employee's grievance. For the union acts as the employee's exclusive representative in the grievance procedure, as it does in virtually all matters involving the terms and conditions of employment. Just as a nonorganized employer may accept an employee's waiver of any challenge to his discharge as a final resolution of the matter, so should an organized employer be able to rely on a comparable waiver by the employee's exclusive representative.

There is no unfairness to the union in this approach. By seeking and acquiring the exclusive right and power to speak for a group of employees, the union assumes a corresponding duty to discharge that responsibility faithfully — a duty which it owes to the employees whom it represents and on which the employer with whom it bargains may rely. When the union, as the exclusive agent of the employee, waives arbitration or fails to seek review of an adverse decision, the employer should

12. Although the union remains primarily responsible for the portion of the damages resulting from its default, *Vaca* made clear that the union's breach does not absolve the employer of liability. Thus if the petitioner in this case does not collect the damages apportioned against the Union, the Service remains secondarily liable for the full loss of backpay.

be in substantially the same position as if the employee had had the right to act on his own behalf and had done so. Indeed, if the employer could not rely on the union's decision, the grievance procedure would not provide the "uniform and exclusive method for [the] orderly settlement of employee grievances," which the Court has recognized is essential to the national labor policy."[15] See Clayton v. International Union Automobile, Aerospace & Agricultural Implement Workers, 451 U.S. 679, 686-687 (1981).

The principle announced in *Vaca* reflects this allocation of responsibilities in the grievance procedure — a procedure that contemplates that both employer and union will perform their respective obligations. In the absence of damages apportionment where the default of both parties contributes to the employee's injury, incentives to comply with the grievance procedure will be diminished. Indeed, imposing total liability solely on the employer could well affect the willingness of employers to agree to arbitration clauses as they are customarily written.

Nor will requiring the union to pay damages impose a burden on the union inconsistent with national labor policy.[16] It will provide an additional incentive for the union to process its members' claims where warranted. See *Vaca,* supra, at 187. This is wholly consistent with a union's

15. Under the dissent's analysis, the employer may not rely on the union's decision not to pursue a grievance. Rather it can prevent continued liability only by reinstating the discharged employee. This leaves the employer with a dubious option: it must either reinstate the employee promptly or leave itself exposed to open-ended liability. If this were the rule, the very purpose of the grievance procedure would be defeated. It is precisely to provide the exclusive means of resolving this kind of dispute that the parties agree to such a procedure and national labor policy strongly encourages its use.

When the union has breached its duty of fair representation, the dissent justifies its rule by arguing that "only the employer ha(s) the continuing ability to right the wrong by reinstating" the employee, an ability that the union lacks. But an employer has no way of knowing that a failure to carry a grievance to arbitration constitutes a breach of duty. Rather than rehiring, as the dissent suggests, the employer reasonably could assume that the union had concluded the discharge was justified. The union would have the option, if it realized it had committed an arguable breach of duty, to bring its default to the employer's attention. Our holding today would not prevent a jury from taking such action into account.

Moreover, the rule urged by the dissenting opinion would allow the union and the employee, once the case goes to trial, to agree to a settlement pursuant to which the union would acknowledge a breach of its duty of fair representation in exchange for the employee's undertaking to look to his employer for his entire recovery. Although we may assume that this would not occur frequently, the incentive the dissent's rule would provide to agree to such a settlement demonstrates its unsoundness.

16. Requiring the union to pay its share of the damages is consistent with the interests recognized in *International Brotherhood of Electrical Workers* v. *Foust,* 442 U.S. 42 (1979). In *Foust,* we found that a union was not liable for punitive damages. The interest in deterring future breaches by the union was outweighed by the debilitating impact that "unpredictable and potentially substantial" awards of punitive damages would have on the union treasury and the union's exercise of discretion in deciding what claims to pursue. An award of compensatory damages, however, normally will be limited and finite. Moreover, the union's exercise of discretion is shielded by the standard necessary to prove a breach of the duty of fair representation. Thus the threat that was present in *Foust* is absent here.

interest. It is a duty owed to its members as well as consistent with the union's commitment to the employer under the arbitration clause. . . .

IV

In this case, the findings of the District Court, accepted by the Court of Appeals, establish that the damages sustained by petitioner were caused initially by the Service's unlawful discharge and increased by the Union's breach of its duty of fair representation. Accordingly, apportionment of the damages was required by *Vaca*.[19] We reverse the judgment of the Court of Appeals and remand for entry of judgment allocating damages against both the Service and the Union consistent with this opinion.

WHITE, J., with whom MARSHALL, J., BLACKMUN, J., and REHNQUIST, J., (except as to part IV), join, concurring in part in the judgment and dissenting in part.

II

. . . Our precedents notwithstanding, the Court today abandons the *Vaca* rationale and holds that a union's breach of duty does far more than simply remove the exhaustion defense in an employee's §301 suit against his employer. The union's breach, even if totally unrelated to the employer's decision to terminate the employee, now serves to insulate the employer from further backpay liability, as of the hypothetical arbitration date, even though the employer, unlike the union, can stop backpay accretion at any moment it desires, simply by reinstating the discharged employee.

It cannot be denied that, contrary to *Vaca* and its progeny, under the Court's new rule, the "bulk of the award" for backpay in a hybrid §301/breach-of-duty suit will have to be borne by the union, not the employer. In the present case, for example, the jury, which was instructed in accordance with the Court's new test, assessed $30,000 in compensatory damages against the union, and only $17,000 against the employer. The union should well consider itself fortunate that this dispute proceeded to trial less than three years after the cessation of petitioner Bowen's employment. Most of the cases of this nature that have been reviewed by

19. We need not decide whether the District Court's instructions on apportionment of damages were proper. The Union objected to the instructions only on the ground that no back wages at all could be assessed against it. It did not object to the manner of apportionment if such damages were to be assessed. Nor is it necessary in this case to consider whether there were degrees of fault, as both the Service and the Union were found to have acted in "reckless and callous disregard of [Bowen's] rights."

this Court have taken the better part of a decade to run their course.[7] Because the hypothetical arbitration date will usually be less than one year after the discharge, it is readily apparent that, under the Court's rule, in many cases the union will be subject to large liability, far greater than that of the employer, the extent of which will not be in any way related to the union's comparative culpability. Nor will the union have any readily apparent way to limit its constantly increasing liability.[8] . . .

The Court contends that its rule will better enable grievance procedures to provide the uniform and exclusive method for the orderly settlement of employee grievances, because a contrary rule "could well affect the willingness of employers to agree to arbitration clauses as they are customarily written." Why the Court's rule will not "affect the willingness" of *unions* to agree to such clauses is left unexplained. More importantly, since the practical consequence of today's holding is that unions will take many unmeritorious grievances to arbitration simply to avoid exposure to the new breach-of-duty liability, the Court's rule actually impairs the ability of the grievance machinery to provide for orderly dispute resolution. . . .

Notes

1. In Intl. Bd. of Electrical Workers v. Foust, 442 U.S. 42 (1979), the Court held that punitive damages could not be assessed against a union in a fair representation suit. The Court reasoned:

> Just as unlimited access to the grievance process could undermine collective bargaining, so too the threat of punitive damages could disrupt the responsible decision making essential to peaceful labor relations. In order to protect against a future punitive award of unforeseeable magnitude, unions might feel compelled to process frivolous claims or resist fair settlements. Indeed, even those unions confident that most juries would hold in their favor could be deterred by the possibility of punitive damages from taking actions clearly in the interest of union members. Absent clear congressional guidance, we decline to inject such an element of uncertainty into union decisions regarding their representative functions.

7. See, e.g., Clayton v. ITT Gilfillan, 623 F.2d 563, 565 (C.A. 1980), rev'd in part sub nom., Clayton v. Automobile Workers, 451 U.S. 679 (1981) (discharge in February 1975; we remand for trial in May 1981); Electrical Workers v. Foust, 442 U.S. at 43-45 (discharge in February 1971; trial in May 1976; Court of Appeals' judgment in 1978; this Court rules in 1979); Hines v. Anchor Motor Freight, 424 U.S. at 556-559 (discharges in 1967; district court grants summary judgment in 1973; we remand for trial in March 1976); Czosek v. O'Mara, 397 U.S. at 26 (discharge in 1962; we remand for trial in February 1970); Vaca v. Sipes, 386 U.S., at 175-176 (discharge in January 1960; trial begins in June 1964).

8. While remaining disturbingly vague about the point, the Court at least concedes that a union may shift some or all backpay responsibility back to the employer by "bring[ing] its default to the employer's attention." Ante, at 14 n. 15.

Does this reasoning apply with equal force to *Bowen*? See *Bowen,* n. 16.

2. In Clayton v. United Automobile Workers, 451 U.S. 679 (1981), the Court addressed the question of whether an employee who alleges (1) that an employer discharged him or her without just cause, thereby violating the collective bargaining agreement, and (2) that the union involved violated its duty to fairly represent him or her in failing to carry the grievance to arbitration, must attempt to exhaust the internal union grievance procedures established by the union constitution before the employee may maintain a suit under §301. The Court held that lower courts have some discretion in deciding whether to require exhaustion of internal union remedies:

> In exercising this discretion, at least three factors should be relevant: first, whether union officials are so hostile to the employee that he could not hope to obtain a fair hearing on his claim; second, whether the internal union appeals procedures would be inadequate either to reactivate the employee's grievance or to award him the full relief he seeks under §301; and third, whether exhaustion of internal procedures would unreasonably delay the employee's opportunity to obtain a judicial hearing on the merits of his claim.

In this case it was stipulated that the internal union review process had the power to award backpay to the employee from the union treasury; but because the time limit on the union's ability to carry the employee's claim to arbitration under the bargaining agreement had expired, reinstatement of the employee to his job was no longer possible. The Court held that exhaustion was not to be required unless successful exhaustion would provide either the full substantive relief sought by the employee or reactivation of his or her grievance. Having decided that the second factor was not satisfied, the Court declined to consider whether the other factors might also defeat an exhaustion requirement. Four Justices dissented.

3. In DelCostello v. Teamsters, 103 S. Ct. 2281 (1983), the Court held that the six-month statute of limitations period set out in §10(b) of the National Labor Relations Act applies to court suits by individual employees against employers for breach of collective bargaining agreements and against unions for breach of the duty to fairly represent.

NOTE, THE SUBSTANCE OF FAIR REPRESENTATION

At least since the Fourth Circuit's opinion in Griffin v. United Auto Workers, 469 F.2d 181 (4th Cir. 1972), some circuit courts have treated "arbitrary union conduct" as a breach of a union's duty to fairly represent that is distinct from a union's duty to refrain from conduct that is hostile, discriminatory, or in bad faith. The difficulty lies in giving content to the notion of "arbitrary" conduct. The portion of Dean Sandalow's article that follows discusses the content of the term *equal protection of the laws*. Sandalow's insights also provide a framework for understanding the meaning of "arbitrary" in the fair representation context. Following the excerpt are several problems, some of which are taken or adapted from an article by Professor Clyde Summers,[31] which are designed to examine what "arbitrary" means in a variety of contexts.

SANDALOW, RACIAL PREFERENCES IN HIGHER EDUCATION: POLITICAL RESPONSIBILITY AND THE JUDICIAL ROLE[32]

42 U. Chi. L. Rev. 651, 655-657 (1975)

The constitutional guarantee of "the equal protection of the laws," to begin at such a point, does not mean that everyone must be treated equally. The state may tax some individuals at a high rate, some at a low rate, and some not at all. It may maintain a system of publicly supported higher education which admits as students only those who meet established criteria. A prime function of law, indeed, is to mark out the basis for discrimination by government in its relations with the citizenry.

What the equal protection clause does require, stated in the most general terms, is that government treat similarly all those who are similarly situated.[6] But as the literature of moral philosophy articulates more clearly than the literature of the law, the principle of similar treatment for those similarly situated — Aristotle's principle of distributive justice[7] — merely states a formal relationship.[8] Standing alone, it is insufficient to decide any case because it does not indicate how to determine when individuals are similarly situated. All individuals are similar in some respects and different in others. The question that must be answered before it can be determined whether "the equal protection of the laws" requires similar treatment of different individuals is whether the differences among them ought to be taken into account. What is required, in other words, is a material or substantive principle, a standard by which to determine when the differences among individuals justify treating them differently.

[31] Summers, An Individual Employee's Right under the Collective Agreement: What Constitutes Fair Representation, 126 U. Pa. L. Rev. 251 (1977).

[32] Excerpted with permission. Copyright © 1975 by University of Chicago Law Review.

6. Tussman & tenBroek, The Equal Protection of the Laws, 37 Calif. L. Rev. 341, 344 (1949).

7. Nicomachean Ethics, Bk. V.

8. See H. L. A. Hart, The Concept of Law 153-163 (1961); C. Perelman, The Idea of Justice and the Problem of Argument 1-87 (1963).

Now the principle of similar treatment of those similarly situated is merely a prescription for rational behavior and, in that sense, value-free. But the material principles which determine whether individuals are similarly or differently situated necessarily rest upon value choices. A decision whether individuals are similarly or differently situated cannot be made "without positing a certain scale of values, a determination of what is important and what is not. It is our view of the world, the way we distinguish what has value from what has none,"[10] that leads us to conclude whether individuals are similarly or differently situated. Controversy concerning the meaning of the equal protection clause is a product of disagreement not only about those values, but about how and by whom they ought to be determined.

When the issue is whether the administration of law comports with equal protection, the demands imposed by the concept of equal protection are clear. The material principle is provided by the law. Equal protection consists of adherence to its terms. If, for example, the law prescribes a ten percent tax on the income of all individuals, the principle of similar treatment for those similarly situated would be violated by a tax collector who levied a fifteen (or five) percent tax only on blacks. The violation does not depend upon the use of a racial classification (either to the advantage or disadvantage of blacks), but upon the statute's stipulation that income differences alone are relevant to a determination of the taxes that individuals must pay. Thus, the principle of similar treatment for those similarly situated would also be violated if the tax collector were to levy a tax greater (or less) than ten percent upon the income of all individuals who have assets in excess of one million dollars. By stipulating that income differences are the only differences to be taken into account in determining taxes, the lawmaker has ruled out consideration of other differences, however much it might be wished that the tax collector were free to consider them. Wealth and race are equally irrelevant, not because either is in some sense intrinsically irrelevant to taxation, but because they have been made so by a particular material principle — the statute.

The meaning of the equal protection clause is much less clear when the validity of legislation is at issue. A claim that legislation denies the equal protection of the laws is an assertion that the legislation treats differently individuals who are similarly situated. Since the individuals are in fact different and the legislation does distinguish among them, the claim must be that there is a principle extrinsic to the legislation in virtue of which the affected individuals must be deemed similarly situated.[11] But since that extrinsic principle cannot be derived from the formal principle of similar treatment for those similarly situated, the claim must

10. C. Perelman, supra n. 8, at 27.
11. Cf. H. L. A. Hart, supra n. 8, at 157.

be that the equal protection clause embodies one or more material principles from which it can be determined whether persons are similarly situated. Yet nothing in the language of the equal protection clause suggests the values that ought to be given expression by a substantive reading of the clause.

Problems

1. The operation of two plants of a national corporation are consolidated into the newer of the two plants. The national agreement covering both plants explicitly provides that when two plants are consolidated in this fashion, seniority shall be governed by length of service with the company. Application of this rule would result in almost all of the employees from the older, abandoned plant being in the top third of the combined seniority list, and all of the layoffs resulting from the consolidation being suffered by the employees in the newer, continuing plant. To avoid this, officers of the local union, the international union, and management agree to slot the employees according to relative seniority in each plant rather than by straight company seniority. Ordering by relative seniority results in the layoff of some of the employees from the older, abandoned plant. When they file grievances, the local union refuses to process the grievances and the international union refuses to intervene.

Breach of the duty to fairly represent? Is the rule/standard discussion of Ehrlich and Posner, supra at p. 191, relevant in analyzing the case?

2. Company *A*, employing 200 workers, recently bought out Company *B*, who is in the same business and employs 300 workers. Both employee groups are represented by the same local union. Employer *A* announced that only 400 employees will be necessary in a new combined plant.

This has happened twice before in the local union's history, in instances involving far fewer members, and both times the union officers proposed to the surviving employer that seniority lists be dovetailed. The local union membership in this case discussed various bargaining proposals and, by a divided vote, decided to propose the following to Company *A*: "All present employees of Company *A* are to be considered new hires for seniority, layoff, and retention purposes."

Breach of the duty to fairly represent? Choices among collective goods routinely must be made in collective bargaining. Is the good at stake here special? Can you suggest an alternative decision-making procedure for the union? Should it be forced on the union through fair representation suits?

3. Pulaski was discharged for striking a foreman. Pulaski claimed that

the foreman had provoked him with obscene and abusive language containing ethnic slurs. The foreman claimed that Pulaski started the verbal abuse and shoving match. The union refused to carry the case to arbitration because it believed that there was little chance of winning Pulaski's reinstatement and it did not want to condone fighting. In the past, however, the union had carried every discharge case to arbitration, no matter how questionable, including fighting cases. Even in some seemingly hopeless cases, the arbitrator had ordered reinstatement without backpay.

Breach of the duty to fairly represent? Courts seldom announce a new legal rule without also applying the rule to the litigants. Why? Is Pulaski's case distinguishiable?

4. "Bull Whip Pete" had been promoted to supervisor from the ranks, but after several years he became so abusive and overbearing that he could not work with the men under him. When he was demoted back to the bargaining unit, he bid on a job based on seniority accumulated during the years he worked as a supervisor. The company awarded him the job, but when the union protested, the company removed him from the job. The contract language was ambiguous and there were no precedents. The union committee refused to process his grievance, stating, "He should be ridden out of the plant on a rail."

Breach of the duty to fairly represent? What remedy? Does NLRB v. Transportation Management Corp., supra at p. 530, present an analogous situation?

5. Murphy was discharged for theft of company property. He protested his innocence and, following established practice, filled out a grievance form, signed it, and gave it to his shop committeeman. The committeeman lost the form and forgot to do anything about it. By the time that Murphy next inquired, the time for filing a grievance under the contract had expired. The union filed the grievance nonetheless, but an arbitrator dismissed it as untimely.

Breach of the duty to fairly represent? Would it be relevant whether the union had taken cost-effective precautions to safeguard against lost grievances? What will the effect be on future grievants if the union is liable notwithstanding cost-effective precautions?

6. The bargaining agreement states that "when relative skills are equal, the employer shall promote the employee with the greater seniority." Jones was promoted to a better-paying position, although Smith had more seniority. The employer contends that Jones is the better qualified. Smith has filed a grievance. The union would like to arbitrate Smith's grievance. Union officials believe that it is sound practice to arbitrate whenever a less senior employee is promoted and that the union is in a poor position to determine relative work skills among its members.

Breach of the duty to fairly represent Jones if the union presents Smith's grievance? See Smith v. Hussman Refrigeration Co., 619 F.2d 1229 (8th Cir. 1980), cert. denied, 449 U.S. 839 (1981).

7. A union conducts a referendum among its members, but not among nonmembers, to determine whether the union shall present in contract negotiations with the employer a proposal for days off on a fixed rather than a rotating basis.

Does this breach the union's duty to fairly represent nonmember employees in the bargaining unit? Can the situation be distinguished from a union's refusal to permit nonmembers to participate in votes to ratify bargaining agreements? See Branch 6000, Natl. Assn. of Letter Carriers v. NLRB, 595 F.2d 808 (D.C. Cir. 1979).

8. The union business agent revoked the union's prior approval of an employee's temporary work assignment because in the business agent's view such assignments should be allowed to continue no more than 30 days. The business agent did not consult the employee and so he failed to consider the employee's need to find a companion for her blind mother.

Breach of the duty to fairly represent? See U.S. Postal Service, 240 N.L.R.B. 1198 (1979).

7

FEDERAL PREEMPTION OF STATE LEGISLATION

The Supremacy Clause of the Constitution gives Congress the power to preempt state regulation of labor relations by virtue of federal occupancy of the field. The degree to which state regulation is thus preempted is ideally a matter of congressional intent; but Congress, when enacting the various labor statutes, did not speak to the matter of preemption.[1] The Supreme Court, instead, has been left with the task of determining the preclusive effect of federal law in a variety of factual situations.

A test capable of consistent application and fair results is difficult to develop in this area because of the many sorts of state regulations affecting labor-management relations. Consider a few: state tort law may prohibit the intentional interference with business relationships unless justified (secondary and recognitional picketing); state statutes may require the wearing of safety shoes (mandatory subject of bargaining); state statutes may grant (or deny) employment compensation to strikers (economic strikes and lockouts); and state statutes and tort law may prohibit trespass (picketing and handbilling). Certainly the federal statutes were enacted against the backdrop of state law, and it cannot be maintained that all state laws affecting the balance of power in labor-management relations are preempted.

One principle of preemption was established early and has not been seriously challenged. Where conduct is protected by §7, state law is preempted.[2] Although "protected activity" is normally understood to mean protected from employer interference, it would be intolerable to hold that while the employer is precluded from taking direct action against such activity, he or she can be the beneficiary of coercive state pressure. Note that such a rule looks not at the mode of state regulation (statute or judicial decision), but at the activity being regulated. To hold otherwise

[1] An exception is found in Title I of the Labor-Management Reporting and Disclosure Act of 1959, regulating certain aspects of internal union affairs, where state remedies are explicitly left intact.

[2] See Hill v. Florida ex rel. Watson, 325 U.S. 538 (1945); Cox, Labor Law Preemption Revisited, 85 Harv. L. Rev. 1337, 1340 (1972).

would permit state interference with a federally granted substantive right.

The NLRA not only protects some activities, it prohibits others or leaves them apparently unregulated. In a given case, placing conduct into a preempted or nonpreempted category may require a sophisticated choice. Should the states be permitted to supplement federal remedies for prohibited conduct? If conduct is neither expressly protected nor prohibited, may the state act? These inquiries focus on the nature of the conduct potentially subject to state regulation. Alternatively, the inquiry could be focused on the nature of the state regulation, permitting, for example, the operation of state laws of general application while precluding those intended to adjust the labor-management balance of power.

GARNER v. TEAMSTERS LOCAL 776
346 U.S. 485 (1953)

[A Pennsylvania trial court enjoined Teamster picketing of a trucking company that was allegedly for the purpose of coercing the company into compelling or influencing company employees to join the union. The Supreme Court of Pennsylvania ruled that federal law precluded the state court injunction.]

JACKSON, J. . . .

Congress has taken in hand this particular type of controversy where it affects interstate commerce. In language almost identical to parts of the Pennsylvania statute, it has forbidden labor unions to exert certain types of coercion on employees through the medium of the employer [citing §8(b)(2)].[3] It is not necessary or appropriate for us to surmise how the National Labor Relations Board might have decided this controversy had petitioners presented it to that body. The power and duty of primary decision lies with the Board, not with us. But it is clear that the Board was vested with power to entertain petitioners' grievance, to issue its own complaint against respondents and, pending final hearing, to seek from the United States District Court an injunction to prevent irreparable injury to petitioners while their case was being considered. The question then is whether the State, through its courts, may adjudge the same controversy and extend its own form of relief.

Congress did not merely lay down a substantive rule of law to be enforced by any tribunal competent to apply law generally to the parties. It went on to confide primary interpretation and application of its rules to a specific and specially constituted tribunal and prescribed a particular procedure for investigation, complaint and notice, and hearing and

[3] Note that this is prior to the enactment of §8(b)(7).

decision, including judicial relief pending a final administrative order. Congress evidently considered that centralized administration of specially designed procedures was necessary to obtain uniform application of its substantive rules and to avoid these diversities and conflicts likely to result from a variety of local procedures and attitudes toward labor controversies. Indeed, Pennsylvania passed a statute the same year as its labor relations Act reciting abuses of the injunction in labor litigations attributable more to procedure and usage than to substantive rules. A multiplicity of tribunals and a diversity of procedures are quite as apt to produce incompatible or conflicting adjudications as are different rules of substantive law. The same reasoning which prohibits federal courts from intervening in such cases, except by way of review or on application of the federal Board, precludes state courts from doing so. And the reasons for excluding state administrative bodies from assuming control of matters expressly placed within the competence of the federal Board also exclude state courts from like action. . . .

Further, even if we were to assume, with petitioners, that distinctly private rights were enforced by the state authorities, it does not follow that the state and federal authorities may supplement each other in cases of this type. The conflict lies in remedies, not rights. The same picketing may injure both public and private rights. But when two separate remedies are brought to bear on the same activity, a conflict is imminent. It must be remembered that petitioners' remedy was a suit for an injunction prohibiting the picketing. The federal Board, if it should find a violation of the national Labor Management Relations Act, would issue a cease-and-desist order and perhaps obtain a temporary injunction to preserve the status quo. Or if it found no violation, it would dismiss the complaint, thereby sanctioning the picketing. To avoid facing a conflict between the state and federal remedies, we would have to assume either that both authorities will always agree as to whether the picketing should continue, or that the State's temporary injunction will be dissolved as soon as the federal Board acts. But experience gives no assurance of either alternative, and there is no indication that the statute left it open for such conflicts to arise.

The detailed prescription of a procedure for restraint of specified types of picketing would seem to imply that other picketing is to be free of other methods and sources of restraint. For the policy of the national Labor Management Relations Act is not to condemn all picketing but only that ascertained by its prescribed processes to fall within its prohibitions. Otherwise, it is implicit in the Act that the public interest is served by freedom of labor to use the weapon of picketing. For a state to impinge on the area of labor combat designed to be free is quite as much an obstruction of federal policy as if the state were to declare picketing free for purposes or by methods which the federal Act prohibits. . . .

On the basis of the allegations, the petitioners could have presented this grievance to the National Labor Relations Board. The respondents were subject to being summoned before that body to justify their conduct. We think the grievance was not subject to litigation in the tribunals of the State.

Judgment affirmed.

Notes

1. What sorts of "diversities and conflicts" are "likely to result from a variety of local procedures and attitudes toward labor controversies"? Is the Court referring to problems of scheduling hearings and the availability of witnesses, or does this hint at distrust of fact finding in state courts and agencies?

Wouldn't it be too simplistic to say that the federal statute "outlaws" or "prohibits" certain conduct? Conduct is more or less prohibited depending on the remedy provided. If you are of the view that the states should be able to supplement federal labor remedies, then presumably you would approve state damage awards for recognitional picketing and criminal sanctions for secondary boycotts. Would that accord with the congressional purpose in passing the NLRA and its amendments?

2. The normal way of attacking state court or agency action on preemption grounds is to raise the defense throughout state proceedings and hope the Supreme Court will grant a writ of certiorari. A federal statute, 28 U.S.C. §2283, provides that a federal court "may not grant an injunction to stay proceedings in a state court except as expressly authorized by Act of Congress, or where necessary in aid of its jurisdiction, or to protect or effectuate its judgments." This statute prevents a private party from successfully petitioning a federal court to enjoin state court action.[4]

It was early held that the federal courts can enjoin state court action where an unfair labor practice charge has been filed with the NLRB and the NLRB files the injunction request.[5] More recently, the Court held that the federal court may issue such an injunction at the Board's request even though no unfair labor practice charge has been filed; the Board has "implied authority . . . to enjoin state action where its federal power preempts the field."[6]

If a state court enjoins a strike in the face of a preemption argument and the union cannot persuade the NLRB to seek an injunction, even the granting of a writ of certiorari by the Supreme Court (itself unlikely) will come too late to help the union. In In re Green, 369 U.S. 689 (1962), a union lawyer advised his client not to honor an ex parte restraining order issued by a state court against peaceful picketing. The lawyer took

[4] Amalgamated Clothing Workers v. Richman Bros., 348 U.S. 511 (1955).
[5] Capital Service v. NLRB, 347 U.S. 501 (1954).
[6] NLRB v. Nash-Finch Co., 404 U.S. 138, 144 (1971).

the view that the state court injunction was preempted. He was cited for contempt by the state court and was denied the opportunity to prove that the judge issuing the injunction and opposing counsel had agreed to the continuation of the picketing as a method of testing state court jurisdiction. The Supreme Court reversed the contempt citation, declaring "a state court is without power to hold one in contempt for violating an injunction that the state court had no power to enter by reason of federal preemption."

Then in Walker v. City of Birmingham,[7] the Supreme Court upheld contempt convictions for violation of a state court injunction against parading even though the Court agreed that the injunction was constitutionally suspect. Relying on the fact that the state court had had jurisdiction over both the subject matter and the parties, the Court distinguished *Green:*

> In In re Green, 369 U.S. 689, the petitioner was convicted of criminal contempt for violating a labor injunction issued by an Ohio court. Relying on the pre-emptive command of the federal labor law, the Court held that the state courts were required to hear Green's claim that the state court was *without jurisdiction* to issue the injunction. The petitioners in *Green,* unlike the petitioners here, had attempted to challenge the validity of the injunction *before* violating it by promptly applying to the issuing court for an order vacating the injunction. The petitioner in *Green* had further offered to prove that the court issuing the injunction had agreed to its violation as an appropriate means of testing its validity.[8]

SAN DIEGO BUILDING TRADES COUNCIL v. GARMON[9]
359 U.S. 236 (1959)

[The company refused the unions' demand for a collective bargaining agreement establishing a union shop. The unions began to picket peacefully the company's place of business in order to pressure customers and suppliers to stop dealing with the company.[10] A state trial court enjoined the picketing and awarded $1,000 in damages. When the case came to the Supreme Court the first time,[11] the injunction was reversed and the damage award was remanded for further consideration. The California court sustained the damage award and the Supreme Court granted another writ of certiorari.]

[7] 388 U.S. 307 (1967).

[8] Ibid. at 315 n. 6.

[9] See Come, Federal Preemption of Labor-Management Relations: Current Problems in the Application of *Garmon,* 56 Va. L. Rev. 1435 (1970); Cox, Labor Law Preemption Revisited, 85 Harv. L. Rev. 1337 (1972); Lesnick, Preemption Reconsidered: The Apparent Reaffirmation of *Garmon,* 72 Colum. L. Rev. 469 (1972).

[10] At the time of the picketing, the NLRA status of minority picketing was unclear; it might have been protected, prohibited, or neither.

[11] 353 U.S. 26 (1957).

FRANKFURTER, J. . . .

In determining the extent to which state regulation must yield to subordinating federal authority, we have been concerned with delimiting areas of potential conflict; potential conflict of rules of law, of remedy, and of administration. The nature of the judicial process precludes an ad hoc inquiry into the special problems of labor-management relations involved in a particular set of occurrences in order to ascertain the precise nature and degree of federal-state conflict there involved, and more particularly what exact mischief such a conflict would cause. Nor is it our business to attempt this. Such determinations inevitably depend upon judgments on the impact of these particular conflicts on the entire scheme of federal labor policy and administration. Our task is confined to dealing with classes of situations. To the National Labor Relations Board and to Congress must be left those precise and closely limited demarcations that can be adequately fashioned only by legislation and administration. We have necessarily been concerned with the potential conflict of two law-enforcing authorities, with the disharmonies inherent in two systems, one federal the other state, of inconsistent standards of substantive law and differing remedial schemes. But the unifying consideration of our decisions has been regard to the fact that Congress has entrusted administration of the labor policy for the Nation to a centralized administrative agency, armed with its own procedures, and equipped with its specialized knowledge and cumulative experience [quoting *Garner*].

Administration is more than a means of regulation; administration is regulation. We have been concerned with conflict in its broadest sense; conflict with a complex and interrelated federal scheme of law, remedy, and administration. Thus, judicial concern has necessarily focused on the nature of the activities which the States have sought to regulate, rather than on the method of regulation adopted. When the exercise of state power over a particular area of activity threatened interference with the clearly indicated policy of industrial relations, it has been judicially necessary to preclude the States from acting. However, due regard for the presuppositions of our embracing federal system, including the principle of diffusion of power not as a matter of doctrinaire localism but as a promoter of democracy, has required us not to find withdrawal from the States of power to regulate where the activity regulated was a merely peripheral concern of the Labor Management Relations Act. See International Assn. of Machinists v. Gonzales, 356 U.S. 617. Or where the regulated conduct touched interests so deeply rooted in local feeling and responsibility that, in the absence of compelling congressional direction, we could not infer that Congress had deprived the States of the power to act.

When it is clear or may fairly be assumed that the activities which a State purports to regulate are protected by §7 of the National Labor

Relations Act, or constitute an unfair labor practice under §8, due regard for the federal enactment requires that state jurisdiction must yield. To leave the States free to regulate conduct so plainly within the central aim of federal regulation involves too great a danger of conflict between power asserted by Congress and requirements imposed by state law. Nor has it mattered whether the States have acted through laws of broad general application rather than laws specifically directed towards the governance of industrial relations. Regardless of the mode adopted, to allow the States to control conduct which is the subject of national regulation would create potential frustration of national purposes.

At times it has not been clear whether the particular activity regulated by the States was governed by §7 or §8 or was, perhaps, outside both these sections. But courts are not primary tribunals to adjudicate such issues. It is essential to the administration of the Act that these determinations be left in the first instance to the National Labor Relations Board. What is outside the scope of this Court's authority cannot remain within a State's power and state jurisdiction too must yield to the exclusive primary competence of the Board. See, e.g., Garner v. Teamsters Union, 346 U.S. 485.

The case before us is such a case. The adjudication in California has throughout been based on the assumption that the behavior of the petitioning unions constituted an unfair labor practice. This conclusion was derived by the California courts from the facts as well as from their view of the Act. It is not for us to decide whether the National Labor Relations Board would have, or should have, decided these questions in the same manner. When an activity is arguably subject to §7 or §8 of the Act, the States as well as the federal courts must defer to the exclusive competence of the National Labor Relations Board if the danger of state interference with national policy is to be averted.

To require the States to yield to the primary jurisdiction of the National Board does not ensure Board adjudication of the status of a disputed activity. If the Board decides, subject to appropriate federal judicial review, that conduct is protected by §7, or prohibited by §8, then the matter is at an end, and the States are ousted of all jurisdiction. Or, the Board may decide that an activity is neither protected nor prohibited, and thereby raise the question whether such activity may be regulated by the States.[4] However, the Board may also fail to determine the status of the disputed conduct by declining to assert jurisdiction, or by refusal of the General Counsel to file a charge, or by adopting some other disposition which does not define the nature of the activity with unclouded legal significance. This was the basic problem underlying our decision in Guss v. Utah Labor Relations Board, 353 U.S. 1. In that case

4. See Auto Workers v. Wisconsin Board, 366 U.S. 245. The approach taken in that case, in which the Court undertook for itself to determine the status of the disputed activity, has not been followed in later decisions, and is no longer of general application.

we held that the failure of the National Labor Relations Board to assume jurisdiction did not leave the States free to regulate activities they would otherwise be precluded from regulating. It follows that the failure of the Board to define the legal significance under the Act of a particular activity does not give the States the power to act. In the absence of the Board's clear determination that an activity is neither protected nor prohibited or of compelling precedent applied to essentially undisputed facts, it is not for this Court to decide whether such activities are subject to state jurisdiction. The withdrawal of this narrow area from possible state activity follows from our decisions in *Weber* and *Guss.* The governing consideration is that to allow the States to control activities that are potentially subject to federal regulation involves too great a danger of conflict with national labor policy.

In the light of these principles the case before us is clear. Since the National Labor Relations Board has not adjudicated the status of the conduct for which the State of California seeks to give a remedy in damages, and since such activity is arguably within the compass of §7 or §8 of the Act, the State's jurisdiction is displaced.

Nor is it significant that California asserted its power to give damages rather than to enjoin what the Board may restrain though it could not compensate. Our concern is with delimiting areas of conduct which must be free from state regulation if national policy is to be left unhampered. Such regulation can be as effectively exerted through an award of damages as through some form of preventive relief. . . . It may be that an award of damages in a particular situation will not, in fact, conflict with the active assertion of federal authority. The same may be true of the incidence of a particular state injunction. To sanction either involves a conflict with federal policy in that it involves allowing two law-making sources to govern. In fact, since remedies form an ingredient of any integrated scheme of regulation, to allow the State to grant a remedy here which has been withheld from the National Labor Relations Board only accentuates the danger of conflict.

It is true that we have allowed the States to grant compensation for the consequences, as defined by the traditional law of torts, of conduct marked by violence and imminent threats to the public order. United Automobile Workers v. Russell, 356 U.S. 634; United Construction Workers v. Laburnum Corp., 347 U.S. 656. We have also allowed the States to enjoin such conduct. Youngdahl v. Rainfair, 355 U.S. 131; Auto Workers v. Wisconsin Board, 351 U.S. 266. State jurisdiction has prevailed in these situations because the compelling state interest, in the scheme of our federalism, in the maintenance of domestic peace is not overridden in the absence of clearly expressed congressional direction. We recognize that the opinion in United Construction Workers v. Laburnum Corp., 347 U.S. 656, found support in the fact that the state remedy had no federal counterpart. But that decision was determined, as is demonstrated by the question to which review was restricted, by the "type of conduct" involved, i.e., "intimidation and threats of violence." In the present case there is no such compelling state interest.

The judgment below is reversed.

Harlan, J., whom Clark, J., Whittaker, J., and Stewart, J., join, concurring.

I concur in the result upon the narrow ground that the Unions' activities for which the State has awarded damages may fairly be considered protected under the Taft-Hartley Act, and that therefore state action is precluded until the National Labor Relations Board has made a contrary determination respecting such activities. . . .

Note

What, if anything, does the *Garmon* analysis add to *Garner?*

TEAMSTERS LOCAL 24 v. OLIVER, 358 U.S. 283 (1959): Teamster locals signed a multiemployer bargaining agreement with an association of motor carriers doing business in midwestern states, including Ohio. The agreement provided a minimum rental fee (and certain other terms) whenever a motor vehicle was leased to a carrier by an owner-driver working for the carrier. An owner-driver affected by the agreement attacked it in Ohio state court as a form of price fixing violating the state antitrust laws. The Ohio courts enjoined the enforcement of the provision. The United States Supreme Court reversed.

The Supreme Court first found that the objective of the challenged provision was to "protect the negotiated wage scale against the possible undermining through diminution of the owner's wages for driving which might result from a rental which did not cover his operating costs." Deeming this equivalent to a bargaining agreement provision respecting wages, the Court found the subject matter to be a mandatory subject of bargaining. Permitting the state to nullify an agreement on a mandatory subject of bargaining would be inconsistent with the congressional purpose of bringing the parties together to work out their own agreements without government interference in substantive terms. The Court concluded:

> The solution worked out by the parties was not one of a sort which Congress has indicated may be left to prohibition by the several States. Of course, the paramount force of the federal law remains even though it is expressed in the details of a contract federal law empowers the parties to make, rather than in terms in an enactment of Congress. Clearly it is immaterial that the conflict is between federal labor law and the application of what the State characterizes as an antitrust law. . . . Congress has

> sufficiently expressed its purpose to . . . exclude state prohibition, even though that with which the federal law is concerned as a matter of labor relations be related by the State to the more inclusive area of restraint of trade. Weber v. Anheuser-Busch, Inc., 348 U.S. 468, 481. We have not here a case of a collective bargaining agreement in conflict with a local health or safety regulation; the conflict here is between the federally sanctioned agreement and state policy which seeks specifically to adjust relationships in the world of commerce. . . .

Note

Does federal law preempt a state statute that requires employers in a particular industry to provide safety shoes for employees? Is this different, for preemption purposes, from a statute requiring the employees to wear safety shoes while working?

TEAMSTERS LOCAL 20 v. MORTON
377 U.S. 252 (1964)

[Local 20 represented Morton's employees. During an economic strike for a new collective bargaining agreement, Local 20 exerted various forms of secondary pressure violating §8(b)(4). In addition, Local 20 peacefully persuaded management of a Morton customer to cease doing business with Morton during the strike. Although this peaceful persuasion did not even arguably constitute an unfair labor practice, it did violate Ohio law and a federal district court, applying Ohio law, awarded compensatory and punitive damages.]

Stewart, J. . . .

[The] central question to be decided is whether a court, state or federal, is free to apply state law in awarding damages resulting from a union's peaceful strike conduct vis-à-vis a secondary employer, or is confined in the field of damage actions brought for union secondary activities to the specifically limited provisions of §303 of the federal Act. . . .

It is the respondent's contention that since the petitioner union's peaceful conduct was neither arguably protected under §7 nor arguably prohibited under §8 of the National Labor Relations Act, as amended, the trial court was free to award damages on the basis of state law for injuries caused by this conduct. But even though it may be assumed that at least some of the secondary activity here involved was neither protected nor prohibited, it is still necessary to determine whether by enacting §303, "Congress occupied this field and closed it to state regulation."

Automobile Workers v. O'Brien, 339 U.S. 454, 457. The basic question, in other words, is whether "in a case such as this, incompatible doctrines of local law must give way to principles of federal labor law." Teamsters Local 174 v. Lucas Flour Co., 369 U.S. 95, 102. The answer to that question ultimately depends upon whether the application of state law in this kind of case would operate to frustrate the purpose of the federal legislation. Colorado Anti-Discrimination Commn. v. Continental Air Lines, 372 U.S. 714, 722.

Section 303(b) of the Labor Management Relations Act expressly authorizes state and federal courts to award damages to any person injured by certain secondary boycott activities described in §303(a). The type of conduct to be made the subject of a private damage action was considered by Congress, and §303(a) comprehensively and with great particularity "describes and condemns specific union conduct directed to specific objectives." Carpenters Local 1976 v. Labor Board, 357 U.S. 93, 98. In selecting which forms of economic pressure should be prohibited by §303, Congress struck the "balance . . . between the uncontrolled power of management and labor to further their respective interests," id., at 100, by "preserving the right of labor organizations to bring pressure to bear on offending employers in primary labor disputes and [by] shielding unoffending employers and others from pressures in controversies not their own." Labor Board v. Denver Bldg. & Construction Trades Council, 341 U.S. 675, 692.

In this case, the petitioner's request to [the secondary's management to] cease doing business with the respondent was not proscribed by the Act. "[A] union is free to approach an employer to persuade him to engage in a boycott, so long as it refrains from the specifically prohibited means of coercion through inducement of employees." Carpenters Local 1976 v. Labor Board, supra, at 99. This weapon of self-help, permitted by federal law, formed an integral part of the petitioner's effort to achieve its bargaining goals during negotiations with the respondent. Allowing its use is a part of the balance struck by Congress between the conflicting interests of the union, the employees, the employer and the community. Electrical Workers Local 761 v. Labor Board, 366 U.S. 667, 672. If the Ohio law of secondary boycott can be applied to proscribe the same type of conduct which Congress focused upon but did not proscribe when it enacted §303, the inevitable result would be to frustrate the congressional determination to leave this weapon of self-help available, and to upset the balance of power between labor and management expressed in our national labor policy. "For a state to impinge on the area of labor combat designed to be free is quite as much an obstruction of federal policy as if the state were to declare picketing free for purposes or by methods which the federal Act prohibits." Garner v. Teamsters Union, 346 U.S. 485, 500. We hold, therefore, that the damages awarded against the petitioner based upon its peaceful persuasion of [the secondary] not to do business with the respondent during the strike cannot stand.

The same considerations require reversal of the award of punitive damages. Punitive damages for violations of §303 conflict with the congressional judgment, reflected both in the language of the federal statute and in its legislative history, that recovery for an employer's business losses caused by a union's peaceful secondary activities proscribed by §303 should be limited to actual, compensatory damages. And insofar as punitive damages in this case were based on secondary activities which violated only state law, they cannot stand, because, as we have held, substantive state law in this area must yield to federal limitations.[12]

Notes

1. The *Morton* case was easy because evidence of congressional intent and Supreme Court precedent so strongly showed that a peaceful appeal to a secondary employer was a weapon meant to be available to unions under the federal scheme. But in the closer case, who is to decide whether the federal scheme demands the activity be unregulated or permits the states to act — the state court? Applying what standard?

2. The Supreme Court has found imbedded in the NLRA a federal policy to free employers to demand undivided management loyalty from supervisors. Supervisors are excluded from the definition of "employee" under the NLRA (thus support of a union by a supervisor is not protected activity, nor is a discharge because of such support prohibited);[13] and §14(a) provides that "no employer subject to this Act shall be compelled to deem . . . supervisors as employees for the purpose of any law, either national or local, relating to collective bargaining." The Supreme Court held in Hanna Mining Co. v. District 2, Marine Engineers,[14] that a state court was not preempted from enjoining peaceful organizational picketing by a union composed of supervisors, and in Beasley v. Food Fair[15] that the state court was preempted from awarding damages, pursuant to a state right-to-work law, to supervisors discharged for joining a union. In Operating Engineers Local 926,[16] an allegation in a state court action that the union had procured the discharge of a supervisor because he was not a union member was held to be preempted.

[12] Goldberg, J., concurred.

[13] However, the discharge of a supervisor for refusing to engage in conduct itself violative of the Act constitutes an NLRA violation. See, e.g., Russell Stover Candies v. NLRB, 551 F.2d 204 (8th Cir. 1977) (discharging a supervisor for refusing to engage in surveillance that would violate §8(a)(1) itself violates §8(a)(1)).

[14] 382 U.S. 181 (1965).

[15] 416 U.S. 653 (1974).

[16] 460 U.S. 669 (1983).

AMALGAMATED ASSOCIATION OF STREET EMPLOYEES v. LOCKRIDGE

403 U.S. 274 (1971)

[Lockridge, a member of the union, was employed as a bus driver for Western Greyhound Lines. In 1959, Lockridge revoked his dues checkoff authorization and became obligated to pay his union dues directly to the union office. He failed to pay the monthly dues due on October 1, 1959. On November 1, the dues still unpaid, the union suspended Lockridge from membership and requested that Greyhound discharge him. Greyhound promptly complied. On November 10, Lockridge's wife attempted to pay the dues but the union refused to accept them.

The bargaining agreement provided that "[a]ll present employees covered by this contract shall become members of the ASSOCIATION [union] not later than 30 days following its effective date and shall remain members as a condition precedent to continued employment." The union constitution, however, was not precise on when "membership" was lost for dues default. Dues were "due and payable on the first day of each month for that month"; a member in arrears after the fifteenth day was no longer a member "in good standing"; and "where a member allow[ed] his arrearage . . . to run over the last day of the second month without payment, he . . . thereby suspend[ed] himself from membership in [the] Association." Thus Lockridge could reasonably argue that he was a union "member" until November 30 (the "last day of the second month" in arrears) and that only discharge for loss of "membership," not just loss of "good standing," was permitted by the Greyhound bargaining agreement.

There was reason to believe that Lockridge's discharge violated §§8(a)(3) and 8(b)(2). A proviso to §8(a)(3) makes it an unfair labor practice to discharge an employee pursuant to a union security clause "for a reason other than the failure of an employee to tender periodic dues . . . uniformly required as a condition of . . . retaining membership." Lockridge could have made out an unfair labor practice by showing that the union had him fired for a reason other than his dues default (e.g., it was angry at his revocation of dues checkoff) or that he had not lost his "membership" under a proper reading of the union constitution.

Lockridge filed no unfair labor practice charge, probably because the NLRB's regional director had refused to go to complaint upon a charge filed by a similarly situated Greyhound employee. Instead, Lockridge filed a state court action against the union, ultimately amending his complaint to state a willful breach of the union constitution. Lockridge recovered $32,678.56 for wages lost and was restored to union membership.]

HARLAN, J. . . .

II

A

On the surface, this might appear to be a routine and simple case. . . . [I]n San Diego Building Trades Council v. Garmon, 359 U.S., at 245, we held that the National Labor Relations Act pre-empts the jurisdiction of state and federal courts to regulate conduct "arguably subject to §7 or §8 of the Act." On their face, [§§8(a)(3) and 8(b)(2)] at least arguably either permit or forbid the union conduct dealt with by the judgment below. For the evident thrust of this aspect of the federal statutory scheme is to permit the enforcement of union security clauses, by dismissal from employment, only for failure to pay dues. Whatever other sanctions may be employed to exact compliance with those internal union rules unrelated to dues payment, the Act seems generally to exclude dismissal from employment. Indeed, in the course of rejecting petitioner's pre-emption argument, the Idaho Supreme Court stated that, in its opinion, the Union "did most certainly violate 8(b)(1)(A), did most certainly violate 8(b)(2) . . . and probably caused the employer to violate 8(a)(3)." 93 Idaho, at 299, 460 P.2d, at 724. Thus, given the broad pre-emption principle enunciated in *Garmon,* the want of state court power to resolve Lockridge's complaint might well seem to follow as a matter of course.

The Idaho Supreme Court, however, concluded that it nevertheless possessed jurisdiction in these circumstances. That determination, as we understand it, rested upon three separate propositions, all of which are urged here by respondent. The first is that the Union's conduct was not only an unfair labor practice, but a breach of its contract with Lockridge as well. "Pre-emption is not established simply by showing that the same facts will sustain two different legal wrongs." 93 Idaho, at 300, 460 P.2d, at 725. In other words *Garmon,* the state court and respondent assert, states a principle applicable only where the state law invoked is designed specifically to regulate labor relations; it has no force where the State applies its general common law of contracts to resolve disputes between a union and its members. Secondly, it is urged that the facts that might be shown to vindicate Lockridge's claim in the Idaho state courts differ from those relevant to proceedings governed by the National Labor Relations Act. It is said that the conduct regulated by the Act is union and employer discrimination; general contract law takes into account only the correctness of competing interpretations of the language embodied in agreements. 93 Idaho, at 303-304, 460 P.2d, at 728-729. Finally, there recurs throughout the state court opinion, and the arguments of respondent here, the theme that the facts of the instant case render it virtually indistinguishable from Machinists v. Gonzales, 356 U.S. 617 (1958), where this Court upheld the exercise of state court jurisdiction in an opinion written only one Term prior to *Garmon,* by the author of *Garmon* and which was approvingly cited in the *Garmon* opinion itself.

We do not believe that any of these arguments suffice to overcome the plain purport of *Garmon* as applied to the facts of this case. However, we have determined to treat these considerations at some length because of the understandable confusion, perhaps in a measure attributable to the previous opinions of this Court, they reflect over the jurisprudential bases upon which the *Garmon* doctrine rests.

B

. . . The rationale for pre-emption rests in large measure upon our determination that when it set down a federal labor policy Congress plainly meant to do more than simply to alter the then-prevailing substantive law. It sought as well to restructure fundamentally the processes for effectuating that policy, deliberately placing the responsibility for applying and developing this comprehensive legal system in the hands of an expert administrative body rather than the federalized judicial system. Thus, that a local court, while adjudicating a labor dispute also within the jurisdiction of the NLRB, may purport to apply legal rules identical to those prescribed in the federal Act or may eschew the authority to define or apply principles specifically developed to regulate labor relations does not mean that all relevant potential for debilitating conflict is absent.

A second factor that has played an important role in our shaping of the pre-emption doctrine has been the necessity to act without specific congressional direction. The precise extent to which state law must be displaced to achieve those unifying ends sought by the national legislature has never been determined by the Congress. This has, quite frankly, left the Court with few available options. We cannot declare pre-empted all local regulation that touches or concerns in any way the complex interrelationships between employees, employers, and unions; obviously, much of this is left to the States. Nor can we proceed on a case-by-case basis to determine whether each particular final judicial pronouncement does, or might reasonably be thought to, conflict in some relevant manner with federal labor policy. This Court is ill-equipped to play such a role and the federal system dictates that this problem be solved with a rule capable of relatively easy application, so that lower courts may largely police themselves in this regard. Equally important, such a principle would fail to take account of the fact, as discussed above, that simple congruity of legal rules does not, in this area, prove the absence of untenable conflict. Further, it is surely not possible for this Court to treat the National Labor Relations Act section by section, committing enforcement of some of its provisions wholly to the NLRB and others to the concurrent domain of local law. Nothing in the language or underlying purposes of the Act suggests any basis for such distinctions. Finally, treating differently judicial power to deal with conduct protected by the Act from that prohibited by it would likewise be unsatisfactory. Both areas equally involve conduct whose legality is governed by federal law, the application of which Congress committed to the Board, not courts.

This is not to say, however, that these inherent limitations on this Court's ability to state a workable rule that comports reasonably with apparent congressional objectives are necessarily self-evident. In fact, varying approaches were taken by the Court in initially grappling with this pre-emption problem. Thus, for example, some early cases suggested the true distinction lay between judicial application of general common law, which was permissible, as opposed to state rules specifically designed to regulate labor relations, which were pre-empted. See, e.g., Automobile Workers v. Russell, 356 U.S. 634, 645 (1958) [(sustaining a $10,000 state damage judgment against a union in favor of an employee kept away from his job by a mass picket line and threats of violence)]. Others made pre-emption turn on whether the States purported to apply a remedy not provided for by the federal scheme, e.g., Weber v. Anheuser-Busch, Inc., 348 U.S. 468, 479-480 (1955), while in still others the Court undertook a thorough scrutiny of the federal Act to ascertain whether the state courts had, in fact, arrived at conclusions inconsistent with its provisions, e.g., Automobile Workers v. Wisconsin Employment Relations Bd., 336 U.S. 245 (1949). For the reasons outlined above none of these approaches proved satisfactory, however, and each was ultimately abandoned. It was, in short, experience — not pure logic — which initially taught that each of these methods sacrificed important federal interests in a uniform law of labor relations centrally administered by an expert agency without yielding anything in return by way of predictability or ease of judicial application.

The failure of alternative analyses and the interplay of the foregoing policy considerations, then, led this Court to hold in *Garmon,* 359 U.S., at 244:

> When it is clear or may fairly be assumed that the activities which a State purports to regulate are protected by §7 of the National Labor Relations Act, or constitute an unfair labor practice under §8, due regard for the federal enactment requires that state jurisdiction must yield. To leave the States free to regulate conduct so plainly within the central aim of federal regulation involves too great a danger of conflict between power asserted by Congress and requirements imposed by state law.

C

Upon these premises, we think that *Garmon* rather clearly dictates reversal of the judgment below. None of the propositions asserted to support that judgment can withstand an application, in light of those factors that compelled its promulgation, of the *Garmon* rule.

Assuredly the proposition that Lockridge's complaint was not subject to the exclusive jurisdiction of the NLRB because it charged a breach of contract rather than an unfair labor practice is not tenable. Pre-emption, as shown above, is designed to shield the system from conflicting regulation of conduct. It is the conduct being regulated, not the formal description of governing legal standards, that is the proper focus of concerns. Indeed, the notion that a relevant distinction exists for such purposes between particularized and generalized labor law was explicitly rejected in *Garmon* itself.

The second argument, closely related to the first, is that the state courts, in resolving this controversy, did deal with different conduct, i.e., interpretation of contractual terms, than would the NLRB which would be required to decide whether the Union discriminated against Lockridge. At bottom, of course, the Union's action in procuring Lockridge's dismissal from employment is the conduct which Idaho courts have sought to regulate. Thus, this second point demonstrates at best that Idaho defines differently what sorts of such union conduct may permissibly be proscribed. This is to say either that the regulatory schemes, state and federal, conflict (in which case pre-emption is clearly called for) or that Idaho is dealing with conduct to which the federal Act does not speak. If the latter assertion was inherited, it is not accurate. As pointed out supra, the relevant portions of the Act operate to prohibit a union from causing or attempting to cause an employer to discriminate against an employee because his membership in the union has been terminated "on some ground other than" his failure to pay those dues requisite to membership. This has led the Board routinely and frequently to inquire into the proper construction of union regulations in order to ascertain whether the union properly found an employee to have been derelict in his dues-paying responsibilities, where his discharge was procured on the asserted grounds of nonmembership in the union. That a union may in good faith have misconstrued its own rules has not been treated by the Board as a defense to a claimed violation of §8(b)(2). In the Board's view, it is the fact of misapplication by a union of its rules, not the motivation for that discrimination, that constitutes an unfair labor practice.

From the foregoing, then, it would seem that this case indeed represents one of the clearest instances where the *Garmon* principle, properly understood, should operate to oust state court jurisdiction. There being no doubt that the conduct here involved was arguably protected by §7 or prohibited by §8 of the Act, the full range of very substantial interests the pre-emption doctrine seeks to protect is directly implicated here.

However, a final strand of analysis underlies the opinion of the Idaho Supreme Court, and the position of respondent, in this case. Our decision in Machinists v. Gonzales, 356 U.S. 617 (1958), it is argued, fully survived the subsequent reorientation of pre-emption doctrine effected by the *Garmon* decision, providing, in effect, an express exception for the exercise of judicial jurisdiction in cases such as this.

The fact situation in *Gonzales* does resemble in some relevant regards that of the instant case. There the California courts had entertained a complaint by an individual union member claiming he had been expelled from his union in violation of rights conferred upon him by the union's constitution and bylaws, which allegedly constituted a contract between him and his union. Gonzales prevailed on his breach-of-contract theory and was awarded damages for wages lost due to the revocation of membership as well as a decree providing for his reinstatement in the union. This Court confirmed the California courts' power to award the monetary damages, the only aspect of the action below challenged in this Court. The primary rationale for the result reached was that California should be competent to "fill out," 356 U.S., at 620, the reinstatement remedy by utilizing "the comprehensive relief of equity," id., at 621, which the Board did not fully possess. Secondarily, it was said that the lawsuit "did not purport to remedy or regulate union conduct on the ground that it was designed to bring about employer discrimination against an employee, the evil the Board is concerned to strike as an unfair labor practice under §8(b)(2)." Id., at 622.

Although it was decided only one Term subsequent to *Gonzales, Garmon* clearly did not fully embrace the technique of the prior case. It was precisely the realization that disparities in remedies and administration could produce substantial conflict, in the practical sense of the term, between the relevant state and federal regulatory schemes and that this Court could not effectively and responsibly superintend on a case-by-case basis the exertion of state power over matters arguably governed by the National Labor Relations Act that impelled the somewhat broader formulation of the pre-emption doctrine in *Garmon.* It seems evident that the full-blown rationale of *Gonzales* could not survive the rule of *Garmon.* Nevertheless, *Garmon* did not cast doubt upon the result reached in *Gonzales,* but cited it approvingly as an example of the fact that state court jurisdiction is not pre-empted "where the activity regulated was a merely peripheral concern of the . . . Act." 359 U.S., at 243.

Against this background, we attempted to define more precisely the reach of *Gonzales* within the more comprehensive framework *Garmon* provided in the companion cases of Plumbers' Union v. Borden, 373 U.S. 690 (1963), and Iron Workers v. Perko, 373 U.S. 701 (1963).

Borden had sued his union in state courts, alleging that the union had arbitrarily refused to refer him to a particular job which he had lined up. He recovered damages, based on lost wages, on the grounds that this conduct constituted both tortious interference with his right to contract for employment and a breach of promise, implicit in his membership arrangement with the union, not to discriminate unfairly against any member or deny him the right to work. Perko had obtained a large money judgment in the Ohio courts on proof that the union had conspired, without cause, to deprive him of employment as a foreman by demanding his discharge from one such position he had held and representing to others that his foreman's rights had been suspended. We held both Perko's and Borden's judgments inconsistent with the *Garmon* rule essentially for the same reasons we have concluded that Lockridge could not, consistently with the *Garmon* decision, maintain his lawsuit in the state courts. We further held there was no necessity to "consider the present vitality of [the *Gonzales*] rationale in the light of more recent decisions," because in those cases, unlike *Gonzales,* "the crux of the action[s] . . . concerned alleged interference with the plaintiff's existing or prospective employment relations and was not directed to internal union matters." Because no specific claim for restoration of membership rights had been advanced, "there was no permissible state remedy to which the award of consequential damages for loss of earnings might be subordinated." *Perko,* 373 U.S., at 705. See also *Borden,* 373 U.S., at 697.

In sum, what distinguished *Gonzales* from *Borden* and *Perko* was that the former lawsuit "was focused on purely internal union matters," *Borden,* supra, at 697, a subject the National Labor Relations Act leaves principally to other processes of law. The possibility that, in defining the scope of the union's duty to Gonzales, the state courts would directly and consciously implicate principles of federal law was at best tangential and remote. In the instant case, however, this possibility was real and immediate. To assess the legality of his union's conduct toward Gonzales the California courts needed only to focus upon the union's constitution and by-laws. Here, however, Lockridge's entire case turned upon the construction of the applicable union security clause, a matter as to which, as shown above, federal concern is pervasive and its regulation complex. The reasons for Gonzales' deprivation of union membership had nothing to do with matters of employment, while Lockridge's cause of action and claim for damages were based solely upon the procurement of his discharge from employment. It cannot plausibly be argued, in any meaningful sense, that Lockridge's lawsuit "was focused on purely internal union matters." Although nothing said in *Garmon* necessarily suggests that States cannot regulate the general conditions which unions may impose on their membership, it surely makes crystal clear that *Gonzales* does not stand for the proposition that resolution of any union-member conflict is within state competence so long as one of the remedies provided is restoration of union membership. This much was settled by *Borden* and *Perko,* and it is only upon such an unwarrantably broad interpretation of *Gonzales* that the judgment below could be sustained.

III

The pre-emption doctrine we apply today is, like any other purposefully administered legal principle, not without exception. Those same considerations that underlie *Garmon* have led this Court to permit the exercise of judicial power over conduct arguably protected or prohibited by the Act where Congress has affirmatively indicated that such power should exist, Smith v. Evening News Assn., 371 U.S. 195 (1962); Teamsters Union v. Morton, 377 U.S. 252 (1964), where this Court cannot, in spite of the force of the policies *Garmon* seeks to promote, conscientiously presume that Congress meant to intrude so deeply into areas traditionally left to local law, e.g., Linn v. Plant Guard Workers, 383 U.S. 53 (1966); Automobile Workers v. Russell, 356 U.S. 634 (1958),[7] and where the particular rule of law sought to be invoked before another tribunal is so structured and administered that, in virtually all instances, it is safe to presume that judicial supervision will not disserve the interests promoted by the federal labor statutes, Vaca v. Sipes, 386 U.S. 171 (1967).

In his brief before this Court, respondent has argued for the first time since this lawsuit was started that two of these exceptions to the *Garmon* principle independently justify the Idaho courts' exercise of jurisdiction over this controversy. First, Lockridge contends that his action, properly viewed, is one to enforce a collective-bargaining agreement. Alternatively, he asserts the suit, in essence, was one to redress petitioner's breach of its duty of fair representation. As will be seen, these contentions are somewhat intertwined.

In §301 of the Taft-Hartley Act, Congress authorized federal courts to exercise jurisdiction over suits brought to enforce collective-bargaining agreements. We have held that such actions are judicially cognizable, even where the conduct alleged was arguably protected or prohibited by the National Labor Relations Act because the history of the enactment of §301 reveals that "Congress deliberately chose to leave the enforcement of collective agreements 'to the usual processes of the law.'" Charles Dowd Box Co. v. Courtney, 368 U.S. 502, 513 (1962). It is firmly established, further, that state courts retain concurrent jurisdiction to adjudicate such claims, *Charles Dowd Box Co.,* supra, and that individual employees have standing to protect rights conferred upon them by such

7. *Garmon* itself recognized that *Russell* permitted state courts "to grant compensation for the consequences, as defined by the traditional law of torts, of conduct marked by violence and imminent threats to the public order." 359 U.S., at 247. However, whereas the Court in *Russell* had justified that result principally upon the broad grounds that state law not specifically relating to labor relations per se was not pre-empted by the Act, the Court in *Garmon* restated this result as dictated by "the compelling state interest, in the scheme of our federalism, in the maintenance of domestic peace [which] is not overridden in the absence of clearly expressed congressional direction." Ibid. It is, of course, this latter and narrower rationale that survives today.

agreements, Smith v. Evening News, supra; Humphrey v. Moore, 375 U.S. 335 (1964).

Our cases also clearly establish that individual union members may sue their employers under §301 for breach of a promise embedded in the collective-bargaining agreement that was intended to confer a benefit upon the individual. Smith v. Evening News, supra. Plainly, however, this is not such a lawsuit. Lockridge specifically dropped Greyhound as a named party from his initial complaint and has never reasserted a right to redress from his former employer.

This Court has further held in Humphrey v. Moore, supra, that §301 will support, regardless of otherwise applicable pre-emption considerations, a suit in the state courts by a union member against his union that seeks to redress union interference with rights conferred on individual employees by the employer's promises in the collective-bargaining agreement, where it is proved that such interference constituted a breach of the duty of fair representation. Indeed, in Vaca v. Sipes, 386 U.S. 171 (1967), we held that an action seeking damages for injury inflicted by a breach of a union's duty of fair representation was judicially cognizable in any event, that is, even if the conduct complained of was arguably protected or prohibited by the National Labor Relations Act and whether or not the lawsuit was bottomed on a collective agreement. Perhaps Count One of Lockridge's second amended complaint could be construed to assert either or both of these theories of recovery. However, it is unnecessary to pass upon the extent to which *Garmon* would be inapplicable if it were shown that in these circumstances petitioner not only breached its contractual obligations to respondent, but did so in a manner that constituted a breach of the duty of fair representation. For such a claim to be made out, Lockridge must have proved "arbitrary or bad-faith conduct on the part of the Union." Vaca v. Sipes, supra, at 193. There must be "substantial evidence of fraud, deceitful action or dishonest conduct." Humphrey v. Moore, supra, at 348. Whether these requisite elements have been proved is a matter of federal law. Quite obviously, they were not even asserted to be relevant in the proceedings below. As the Idaho Supreme Court stated in affirming the verdict for Lockridge, "[t]his was a misinterpretation of a contract. Whatever the underlying motive for expulsion might have been, this case has been submitted and tried on the interpretation of the contract, not on a theory of discrimination." 93 Idaho, at 303-304, 460 P.2d, at 728-729. Thus, the trial judge's conclusion of law in sustaining Lockridge's claim specifically incorporates the assumption that the Union's "acts . . . were predicted solely upon the ground that [Lockridge] had failed to tender periodic dues in conformance with the requirements of the union Constitution and employment contract as they interpreted [it]. . . ." App. 66. Further, the trial court excluded as irrelevant petitioner's proffer of evidence designed to show that the Union's interpretation of the contract was reasonably based upon its understanding of prior collective-bargaining agreements negotiated with Greyhound. Tr. 259-260. . . .

Reversed.[17]

WHITE, J., with whom BURGER, C.J., joins, dissenting. . . .

I would neither overrule nor eviscerate Machinists v. Gonzales, 356 U.S. 617 (1958). In light of present statutory law and congressional intention gleaned therefrom, state courts should not be foreclosed from extending relief for union deprivation of members' state law rights under the union constitution and bylaws. Even if I agreed that the doctrine of San Diego Building Trades Council v. Garmon, 359 U.S. 236 (1959), properly pre-empts such union member actions based on state law where the challenged conduct is arguably an unfair labor practice, I could not join the opinion of the Court since it unqualifiedly applies the same doctrine where the conduct of the union is only arguably protected under the federal law. . . .

Until today, Machinists v. Gonzales, supra, had been thought to stand for the proposition that *Garmon* did not reach cases "when the possibility of conflict with federal policy is . . . remote." 356 U.S., at 621. But with today's emasculation of *Gonzales,* there is probably little that remains of it. Linn v. Plant Guard Workers, 383 U.S. 53 (1966), was ostensibly based in part on this rationale, but it was equally bottomed on *Laburnum Construction* and other cases upholding state power to regulate matters of "overriding state interest" such as violence or, as in *Linn,* defamation. I see no reason why this exception has not, for all practical purposes, thus expired. In my view, however, *Gonzales* controls this case.[3] . . .

The unmistakable focus of both the NLRA and the LMRA is on labor-management relations, rather than union-member relations, as such. During the 1950's there came to light various patterns of union abuse of power, and in the Labor-Management Reporting and Disclosure Act of 1959 (LMRDA) Congress acted to correct these evils by directly address-

[17] Blackmun, J., and Douglas, J., dissented.

3. With all respect, the majority's attempt to distinguish the instant case from *Gonzales* is unpersuasive. According to the majority, "The reasons for Gonzales' deprivation of union membership had nothing to do with matters of employment, while Lockridge's cause of action and claim for damages were based solely upon the procurement of his discharge from employment." Ante, at 296. In the first place, Lockridge squarely alleged that his damages had been caused by suspension from union membership contrary to the constitution and laws of the union; his cause of action was bottomed upon this breach of duty by the union. More importantly, it is inaccurate to imply, as the foregoing quoted statement does, that *Lockridge* is somehow different from *Gonzales* in that Gonzales' "deprivation of union membership" did not result in his loss of employment. The *Gonzales* Court said, "The evidence adduced at the trial showed that plaintiff, *because* of his loss of membership, was unable to obtain employment and was *thereby* damaged. . . . [T]his damage was not charged nor treated as the result of an unfair labor practice but *as a result* of the breach of contract." 356 U.S., at 622 n. (Quoting the California court's opinion.) (Emphasis added.)

ing itself to some aspects of union-member affairs. . . . Beyond any doubt whatever, although Congress directly imposed some far-reaching *federal* prohibitions on union conduct, it specifically denied any preemption of rights or remedies created by either state law or union constitution and bylaws. Thus, as to union-member relations, any parallel rights created by the States, either directly or indirectly through enforcement of union constitutions or bylaws, were to stand at full strength. . . .

Like many States, Idaho construes the union-member relation to be a contractual one, defined by the constitution and bylaws of the union. As such, the contracts are enforceable through the State's traditional common-law jurisdiction. Here, Lockridge was discharged for alleged nonpayment of dues in accordance with the union constitution and brought suit alleging that he had in fact not been unduly tardy and that the union's action was a breach of the contract. The face of the complaint did not implicate federal law. If the Idaho court were allowed to proceed, it would not have purported to adjudicate an unfair labor practice by reference to federal law but, if it found the conduct unprotected by federal law, would have enforced rights and obligations created by the union constitution. The Court nevertheless holds that because the union conduct alleged in the complaint also constitutes, or arguably so, an unfair labor practice, the controversy must be adjudicated by the National Labor Relations Board. I find little in the Court's opinion to convince me that Congress intended this result. With all respect, I agree with *Gonzales* that this result is at best "abstractly justifiable, as a matter of wooden logic." 356 U.S., at 619. . . .

Note

Is *Gonzales* actually distinguishable from *Lockridge?* If not, which result is your choice? On the one hand, you might argue that the disputes in these cases are between unions and their members and do not bring into play the delicate balance of labor-management power governed by the *Garmon* doctrine. Further, Congress has shown a greater willingness to let state law run its course when union-member matters are at stake (e.g., Title I of the Labor-Management Reporting and Disclosure Act). And the indisputable result in *Lockridge* was to leave Lockridge with no opportunity to prove a meritorious case. A counter argument is that hard cases (i.e., ones involving both arguable unfair labor practices and union-member relationships) must yield to the value of having a rule of general application. And if Lockridge was without remedy, that was the fault of the Board's regional director.

Consider whether the next case settles the matter and, if so, whether the result is grounded in sound policy and lays down a standard capable of consistent application by lower courts.

FARMER v. UNITED BROTHERHOOD OF CARPENTERS

430 U.S. 290 (1977)

POWELL, J.

I

The issue in this case is whether the National Labor Relations Act, as amended, pre-empts a tort action brought in state court by a union member against the union and its officials to recover damages for the intentional infliction of emotional distress.

Petitioner Richard T. Hill[1] was a carpenter and a member of Local 25 of the United Brotherhood of Carpenters and Joiners of America. Local 25 (Union) operates an exclusive hiring hall for employment referral of carpenters in the Los Angeles area. In 1965, Hill was elected to a three-year term as vice president of the Union. Shortly thereafter sharp disagreement developed between Hill and the Union Business Agent, Earl Daley, and other Union officials over various internal Union policies. According to Hill, the Union then began to discriminate against him in referrals to employers, prompting him to complain about the hiring hall operation within the Union and to the District Council and the International Union. Hill claims that as a result of these complaints he was subjected to a campaign of personal abuse and harassment in addition to continued discrimination in referrals from the hiring hall.

In April 1969 petitioner filed in Superior Court for the County of Los Angeles an action for damages against the Union, the District Council and the International with which the Union was affiliated, and certain officials of the Union, including Business Agent Daley. In count two of his amended complaint, Hill alleged that the defendants had intentionally engaged in outrageous conduct, threats, and intimidation, and had thereby caused him to suffer grievous emotional distress resulting in bodily injury. In three other counts, he alleged that the Union had discriminated against him in referrals for employment because of his dissident intra-Union political activities, that the Union had breached the hiring hall provisions of the collective-bargaining agreement between it and a contractors association by failing to refer him on a nondiscriminatory basis, and that the failure to comply with the collective-bargaining agreement also constituted a breach of his membership contract with the Union. He sought $500,000 in actual, and $500,000 in punitive, damages.

The Superior Court sustained a demurrer to the allegations of discrimination and breach of contract on the ground that federal law pre-

1. Hill died after the petition for a writ of certiorari was granted. On June 1, 1976, Joy A. Farmer, special administrator of Hill's estate, was substituted as petitioner. We will refer to Hill as the petitioner.

empted state jurisdiction over them, but allowed the case to go to trial on the allegations in count two. Hill attempted to prove that the Union's campaign against him included "frequent public ridicule," "incessant verbal abuse," and refusals to refer him to jobs in accordance with the rules of the hiring hall. The defendants countered with evidence that the hiring hall was operated in a nondiscriminatory manner. The trial court instructed the jury that in order to recover damages Hill had to prove by a preponderance of the evidence that the defendants intentionally and by outrageous conduct had caused him to suffer severe emotional distress. The court defined severe emotional distress as "any highly unpleasant mental reaction such as fright, grief, shame, humiliation, embarrassment, anger, chagrin, disappointment, or worr[y]." The injury had to be "severe," which in this context meant "substantial or enduring, as distinguished from trivial or transitory. It must be of such substantial quantity or enduring quality that no reasonable man in a civilized society should be expected to endure it. Liability does not extend to mere insults, indignities, annoyances, petty or other trivialities."

The court also instructed that the National Labor Relations Board would not have jurisdiction to compensate petitioner for injuries such as emotional distress, pain and suffering, and medical expenses, nor would it have authority to award punitive damages. The court refused to give a requested instruction to the effect that the jury could not consider any evidence regarding discrimination with respect to employment opportunities or hiring procedures.

The jury returned a verdict of $7,500 actual damages and $175,000 punitive damages against the Union, the District Council, and Business Agent Daley, and the trial court entered a judgment on the verdict.

The California Court of Appeal reversed. Relying on this Court's decisions in Motor Coach Employees v. Lockridge, 403 U.S. 274 (1971); Plumbers v. Borden, 373 U.S. 690 (1963); Iron Workers v. Perko, 373 U.S. 701 (1963); and San Diego Bldg. Trades Council v. Garmon, 359 U.S. 236 (1959), the Court of Appeal held that the state courts had no jurisdiction over the complaint since the "crux" of the action concerned employment relations and involved conduct arguably subject to the jurisdiction of the National Labor Relations Board. . . . The California Supreme Court denied review. We granted certiorari. . . .

[The opinion then reviewed in general terms the *Garmon* rule of preemption and its exceptions.]

The nature of the inquiry is perhaps best illustrated by Linn v. Plant Guard Workers, [383 U.S. 53 (1966)]. Linn, an assistant manager of Pinkerton's National Detective Agency, filed a diversity action in federal court against a union, two of its officers, and a Pinkerton employee, alleging that the defendants had circulated a defamatory statement about him in violation of state law. If unfair labor practice charges had been filed, the Board might have found that the union violated §8 by intentionally circulating false statements during an organizational campaign, or that the issuance of the malicious statements during the campaign had such a significant effect as to require that the election be set aside. Under a formalistic application of *Garmon,* the libel suit could have been pre-empted.

But a number of factors influenced the Court to depart from the *Garmon* rule. First, the Court noted that the underlying conduct — the intentional circulation of defamatory material known to be false — was not protected under the Act, 383 U.S., at 61, and there was thus no risk that permitting the state cause of action to proceed would result in state regulation of conduct that Congress intended to protect. Second, the Court recognized that there was "'an overriding state interest'" in protecting residents from malicious libels, and that this state interest was "'deeply rooted in local feeling and responsibility.'" Id., at 61, 62. Third, the Court reasoned that there was little risk that the state cause of action would interfere with the effective administration of national labor policy. The Board's §8 unfair labor practice proceeding would focus only on whether the statements were misleading or coercive; whether the statements also were defamatory would be of no relevance to the Board's performance of its functions. Id., at 63. Moreover, the Board would lack authority to provide the defamed individual with damages or other relief. Ibid. Conversely, the state law action would be unconcerned with whether the statements were coercive or misleading in the labor context, and in any event the court would have power to award Linn relief only if the statements were defamatory. Taken together, these factors justified an exception to the pre-emption rule.

The Court was careful, however, to limit the scope of that exception. To minimize the possibility that state libel suits would either dampen the free discussion characteristic of labor disputes or become a weapon of economic coercion, the Court adopted by analogy the standards enunciated in New York Times Co. v. Sullivan, 376 U.S. 254 (1964), and held that state damage actions in this context would escape pre-emption only if limited to defamatory statements published with knowledge or reckless disregard of their falsity. The Court also held that a complainant could recover damages only upon proof that the statements had caused him injury, including general injury to reputation, consequent mental suffering, alienation of associates, specific items of pecuniary loss, or any other form of harm recognized by state tort law. The Court stressed the responsibility of the trial judge to assure that damages were not excessive.

Similar reasoning underlies the exception to the pre-emption rule in cases involving violent tortious activity. Nothing in the federal labor statutes protects or immunizes from state action violence or the threat of violence in a labor dispute, Automobile Workers v. Russell, 356 U.S. 634 (1958), and thus there is no risk that state damage actions will fetter the exercise of rights protected by the NLRA. On the other hand, our cases consistently have recognized the historic state interest in "such traditionally local matters as public safety and order and the use of streets and highways." Allen-Bradley Local v. Wisconsin Emp. Rel. Bd., 315 U.S. 740, 749 (1942). And, as with the defamation actions preserved by *Linn,* state court actions to redress injuries caused by violence or threats of violence are consistent with effective administration of the federal scheme: such actions can be adjudicated without regard to the merits of the underlying labor controversy.

Although cases like *Linn* and *Russell* involve state law principles with only incidental application to conduct occurring in the course of a labor dispute, it is well settled that the general applicability of a state cause of action is not sufficient to exempt it from pre-emption. "[I]t [has not] mattered whether the States have acted through laws of broad general application rather than laws specifically directed towards the governance of industrial relations."[9] *Garmon,* 359 U.S., at 244. Instead, the cases reflect a balanced inquiry into such factors as the nature of the federal and state interests in regulation and the potential for interference with federal regulation. As was said in Vaca v. Sipes, 386 U.S., at 180, our cases "demonstrate that the decision to pre-empt federal and state court jurisdiction over a given class of cases must depend upon the nature of the particular interests being asserted and the effect upon the administration of national labor policies of concurrent judicial and administrative remedies."[10]

9. In Plumbers v. Borden, 373 U.S. 690 (1963), for example, an employee sued his union, which operated a hiring hall, claiming that the union had arbitrarily refused to refer him for employment on one particular occasion. He alleged that the union's conduct constituted both tortious interference with his right to contract for employment and breach of a promise, implicit in his membership arrangement with the union, not to discriminate unfairly against any member or deny him the right to work. Under these circumstances, state court jurisdiction would have impaired significantly the functioning of the federal system. If unfair labor practice charges had been filed, the Board might have concluded that the refusal to refer Borden was due to a lawful hiring hall practice, see Teamsters v. NLRB, 365 U.S. 667 (1961). Board approval of various hiring hall practices would be meaningless if state courts could declare those procedures violative of the contractual rights implicit between a member and his union. Accordingly, the state cause of action was pre-empted under *Garmon.* Similar reasoning prompted the Court to apply the *Garmon* rule in the companion case of Iron Workers v. Perko, 373 U.S. 701 (1963).

10. Machinists v. Gonzales, 356 U.S. 617 (1958), established another exception to the general rule of pre-emption for state law actions alleging expulsion from union membership in violation of the applicable union constitution and bylaws and seeking restoration to membership and damages due to the illegal expulsion. *Gonzales* was decided prior to this Court's adoption in *Garmon* of the current pre-emption test, and our decision in *Lockridge* makes it clear that "the full-blown rationale of *Gonzales* could not survive the rule of *Garmon.*" *Lockridge,* 403 U.S., at 295. At the same time, we stated that "*Garmon* did not cast doubt upon the result reached in *Gonzales,*" id., at 295, since *Garmon* cited *Gonzales* as an example of the nonapplicability of the normal pre-emption rule "where the activity regulated was a merely peripheral concern of the . . . Act." 359 U.S. at 243.

Although the *Lockridge* decision has been the subject of extensive criticism, see e.g., Bryson, A Matter of Wooden Logic: Labor Law Pre-emption and Individual Rights, 51

In count two of his amended complaint, Hill alleged that the defendants had intentionally engaged in "outrageous conduct, threats, intimidation, and words" which caused Hill to suffer "grievous mental and emotional distress as well as great physical damage." In the context of Hill's other allegations of discrimination in hiring hall referrals, these allegations of tortious conduct might form the basis for unfair labor practice charges before the Board. On this basis a rigid application of the *Garmon* doctrine might support the conclusion of the California courts that Hill's entire action was pre-empted by federal law. Our cases indicate, however, that inflexible application of the doctrine is to be avoided, especially where the State has a substantial interest in regulation of the conduct at issue and the State's interest is one that does not threaten undue interference with the federal regulatory scheme. With respect to Hill's claims of intentional infliction of emotional distress, we cannot conclude that Congress intended exclusive jurisdiction to lie in the Board.

No provision of the National Labor Relations Act protects the "outrageous conduct" complained of by petitioner Hill in the second count of the complaint. Regardless of whether the operation of the hiring hall was lawful or unlawful under federal statutes, there is no federal protection for conduct on the part of union officers which is so outrageous that "no reasonable man in a civilized society should be expected to endure it." Thus, as in Linn v. Plant Guard Workers, 383 U.S. 53 (1966), and Automobile Workers v. Russell, supra, permitting the exercise of state jurisdiction over such complaints does not result in state regulation of federally protected conduct.

The State, on the other hand, has a substantial interest in protecting its citizens from the kind of abuse of which Hill complained. That interest is no less worthy of recognition because it concerns protection from emotional distress caused by outrageous conduct, rather than protection from physical injury, as in *Russell,* or damage to reputation, as in *Linn.* Although recognition of the tort of intentional infliction of emotional distress is a comparatively recent development in state law, our decisions permitting the exercise of state jurisdiction in tort actions based on violence or defamation have not rested on the history of the tort at issue, but rather on the nature of the State's interest in protecting the health and well-being of its citizens.

Tex. L. Rev. 1037, 1050-1058 (1973); Cox, Labor Law Preemption Revisited, 85 Harv. L. Rev. 1337, 1368-1377 (1972), the instant case presents no occasion for us to reconsider the relationship between *Lockridge* and *Gonzales.* Whatever the scope of *Gonzales* after *Garmon* and *Lockridge,* the analysis used by the Court in those cases is consistent with the framework discussed in the text above. *Lockridge* held that the state court action at issue involved a "real and immediate" potential for conflict with the federal scheme, 403 U.S., at 296, whereas the possibility that the state court in *Gonzales* "would directly and consciously implicate principles of federal law" was considered "at best tangential and remote." Ibid.

There is, to be sure, some risk that the state cause of action for infliction of emotional distress will touch on an area of primary federal concern. Hill's complaint itself highlights this risk. In those counts of the complaint that the trial court dismissed, Hill alleged discrimination against him in hiring hall referrals, which were also alleged to be violations of both the collective-bargaining agreement and the membership contract. These allegations, if sufficiently supported before the National Labor Relations Board, would make out an unfair labor practice[11] and the Superior Court considered them pre-empted by the federal Act.[12] Even in count two of the complaint Hill made allegations of discrimination in "job-dispatching procedures" and "work assignments" which, standing alone, might well be pre-empted as the exclusive concern of the Board. The occurrence of the abusive conduct, with which the state tort action is concerned, in such a context of federally prohibited discrimination suggests a potential for interference with the federal scheme of regulation.

Viewed, however, in light of the discrete concerns of the federal scheme and the state tort law, that potential for interference is insufficient to counterbalance the legitimate and substantial interest of the State in protecting its citizens. If the charges in Hill's complaint were filed with the Board, the focus of any unfair labor practice proceeding would be on whether the statements or conduct on the part of union officials discriminated or threatened discrimination against him in employment referrals for reasons other than failure to pay union dues. See n. 11, supra. Whether the statements or conduct of the respondents also caused Hill severe emotional distress and physical injury would play no role in the Board's disposition of the case, and the Board could not award Hill damages for pain, suffering, or medical expenses. Conversely, the state court tort action can be adjudicated without resolution of the "merits" of the underlying labor dispute. Recovery for the tort of emotional distress under California law requires proof that the defendant intentionally engaged in outrageous conduct causing the plaintiff to

11. . . . Prior to the filing of this suit, Hill filed an unfair labor practice charge with the Board with respect to one specific instance of alleged discrimination. He alleged that the Union violated §§8(b)(1)(A) and 8(b)(2) by refusing to honor an employer's request that he be referred for employment on a particular construction job. The Board awarded Hill $2,517 in backpay.

12. Whether a hiring hall practice is discriminatory and therefore violative of federal law is a determination Congress has entrusted to the Board. See Teamsters v. NLRB, 365 U.S. 667 (1961). Whether there is federal pre-emption with respect to allegations of breach of a *contractual* obligation depends upon the nature of the obligation and the alleged breach. See Motor Coach Employees v. Lockridge, 403 U.S., at 292-297, 298-301. Casting a complaint in terms of breach of a *membership agreement* does not necessarily insulate a state court action from application of the pre-emption doctrine. See n. 9, supra. Allegations of breach of the contract between the union and the employer stand on different ground, since, as noted earlier, §301 of the Labor-Management Relations Act, 29 U.S.C. §185, authorizes suits for breach of a *collective-bargaining agreement* even if the breach is an unfair labor practice within the Board's jurisdiction. See n. 8, supra.

sustain mental distress. The state court need not consider, much less resolve, whether a union discriminated or threatened to discriminate against an employee in terms of employment opportunities. To the contrary, the tort action can be resolved without reference to any accommodation of the special interests of unions and members in the hiring hall context.

On balance, we cannot conclude that Congress intended to oust state court jurisdiction over actions for tortious activity such as that alleged in this case. At the same time, we reiterate that concurrent state court jurisdiction cannot be permitted where there is a realistic threat of interference with the federal regulatory scheme. Union discrimination in employment opportunities cannot itself form the underlying "outrageous" conduct on which the state court tort action is based; to hold otherwise would undermine the pre-emption principle. Nor can threats of such discrimination suffice to sustain state court jurisdiction. It may well be that the threat, or actuality, of employment discrimination will cause a union member considerable emotional distress and anxiety. But something more is required before concurrent state court jurisdiction can be permitted. Simply stated, it is essential that the state tort be either unrelated to employment discrimination or a function of the particularly abusive manner in which the discrimination is accomplished or threatened rather than a function of the actual or threatened discrimination itself.[13]

Two further limitations deserve emphasis. Our decision rests in part on our understanding that California law permits recovery only for emotional distress sustained as a result of "outrageous" conduct. The potential for undue interference with federal regulation would be intolerable if state tort recoveries could be based on the type of robust language and clash of strong personalities that may be commonplace in various labor contexts. We also repeat that state trial courts have the responsibility in cases of this kind to assure that the damages awarded are not excessive.

Although the second count of petitioners' complaint alleged the intentional infliction of emotional distress, it is clear from the record that the trial of that claim was not in accord with the standards discussed above. The evidence supporting the verdict in Hill's favor focuses less on the alleged campaign of harassment, public ridicule, and verbal abuse, than on the discriminatory refusal to dispatch him to any but the briefest and least desirable jobs; and no appropriate instruction distinguishing

13. In view of the potential for interference with the federal scheme of regulation, the trial court should be sensitive to the need to minimize the jury's exposure to evidence of employment discrimination in cases of this sort. Where evidence of discrimination is necessary to establish the context in which the state claim arose, the trial court should instruct the jury that the fact of employment discrimination (as distinguished from attendant tortious conduct under the state law) should not enter into the determination of liability or damages.

the two categories of evidence was given to the jury. The consequent risk that the jury verdict represented damages for employment discrimination rather than for instances of intentional infliction of emotional distress precludes reinstatement of the judgment of the Superior Court.

The judgment of the Court of Appeal is vacated, and the case is remanded to that court for further proceedings not inconsistent with this opinion.

Shortly after the *Lockridge* decision, Professor Archibald Cox penned an article reviewing the Court's labor preemption decisions. Consider the following excerpt.

COX, LABOR LAW PREEMPTION REVISITED

85 Harv. L. Rev. 1337, 1352-1356 (1972)

Two fundamental ideas lie at the core of the national labor policy: (1) freedom of employee self-organization; and (2) the voluntary private adjustment of conflicts of interest over wages, hours, and other conditions of employment through the negotiation and administration of collective bargaining agreements. Both may involve resort to strikes, boycotts, lockouts, and other economic pressures. Providing a legal framework for self-organization and collective bargaining involves determining not only how far the conduct of employers and unions should be regulated but also how far they should be free. In revising the employer unfair labor practice provisions of the Wagner Act in 1947, Congress necessarily decided not only what coercive tactics should be forbidden, but also what methods of persuasion should be permitted employers seeking to induce their employees not to join labor unions. Similarly, the Taft-Hartley restrictions on strikes and secondary boycotts mark a line between the union organizing practices which were outlawed and the freedom allowed. The legal framework also deals with the mutual obligations of employer and bargaining representative in negotiating terms of employment. Since freedom to reject the terms proposed by the other party implies freedom to resort to economic pressures, the framework again necessarily includes a law of lockouts, strikes, and picketing. To restrict either the objectives for which economic pressure can be applied or the forms of pressure which are permissible tips the scale towards management or union. On every point, therefore, formulating the national labor policy required balancing the various interests of management, union, employees, and the public in deciding which tactics should be prohibited and which should be allowed. A priori federal unfair labor practices could conceivably establish minimum standards of conduct for a state to raise if it wished, but the description is inconsistent with the basic conception of labor organization and collective bargaining embodied in the NLRA.

A few examples will illustrate the point. NLRA §8(d) expressly declares that during the term of an unexpired collective bargaining agreement, federal law required an employer to negotiate in good faith about any question arising thereunder, but the employer need not discuss a modification to become effective before the contract expires. For a state to put the latter obligation upon employers subject to the NLRB would reverse a decision reached by Congress. The NLRA is less clear about whether an employer must bargain about some major term or condition of employment not mentioned in the agreement, such as contracting out work that might be done by employees in the bargaining unit. In the first instance a decision on this question turns largely upon a nice judgment as to whether the institutions of collective bargaining will function better under one rule or the other. It can be argued that collective bargaining is a continuous relationship requiring constant conferences and adjustments as circumstances change and new problems arise, and that discussion leads to peaceful settlements whereas refusal to meet and confer on a pressing issue produces industrial strife. The opposing side can argue that collective bargaining works better if each party knows that any contract it may negotiate is the "total package" for its agreed term, that a stable relationship cannot be built upon shifting sands, and that major items can best be negotiated at intervals permitting careful preparation. The current NLRB rule is that there is a continuous duty to negotiate except as to demands discussed during contract negotiations, as to which there is no obligation. A state could not relieve an employer of this federal obligation, because the application of state law would frustrate the national policy. The interference would be no less if the state were to impose an additional obligation to bargain upon demands raised and abandoned during contract talks. In either case there would be state frustration of a national decision as to the best means of implementing the policy of encouraging the negotiated adjustment of differences between labor and management.

The same frustration would occur if states were permitted to impose restrictions upon labor's use of economic weapons going beyond NLRA §8(b) in terms of prohibited objectives or forms of economic pressure. Strikes, boycotts, and picketing are often weapons of union organization. They affect both the progress of unionization and the employees' freedom of choice. The 1947 debates upon secondary boycotts and strikes against NLRB certifications, like the 1959 conflict over organizational picketing, make it plain that Congress was drawing a line between permitted and prohibited times and forms of economic pressure. When the NLRB interprets the complicated secondary boycott provisions of §8(b)(4) it must follow the words of the statute; but where they are ambiguous, the Board inevitably makes policy decisions concerning the effect of expanding or contracting their meanings upon the balance of power between labor and management. To add state restrictions would change the balance Congress struck.

The principle that a state should not upset the balance of freedom and restraint that Congress established as a framework for employee self-organization and collective bargaining explains more than the *Morton* case. It also supplies the ultimate foundation for the rule that state laws may not be used to restrict activities protected by section 7. It may seem obvious today to say that states may not deny a right Congress has granted, but initially the question was whether the rights guaranteed by section 7 were only the correlative of the duties imposed upon employers by section 8 or were also good against the states. The latter question can be answered only by asking how far state curtailment would interfere with the working out of a policy encouraging self-organization and collective bargaining backed by economic weapons.

Similarly, the rule that states may not enforce or remedy violations of the unfair labor practice sections of the federal Act must ultimately rest upon the deeper and broader principle stated above. *Garner* held that divergences in interpretation, procedure, and remedy may be scarcely less upsetting to the balance of interests struck by Congress than differences in rules of substantive law. But if the latter differences were tolerable, the former would be of little concern.

It is obviously too loose to assert that federal law excludes any state law that affects the balance of interests among management, union, employees, and public in union organization and collective bargaining. Jailing strikers for dynamiting a mine tipple or assaulting nonstrikers, indicting a union for a price-fixing conspiracy, regulating insurance funds, and outlawing discrimination in employment may affect the outcome of a labor dispute or influence collective bargaining. Words privileged under NLRA §8(c) may give union leaders a cause of action for defamation. Such incidents ought not to be beyond state control merely because they occur in the course of an organizational campaign or labor dispute, or are covered by a collective bargaining agreement. Consequently, if the underlying rationale for federal preemption is the need for preserving the balance which Congress struck, some formula is required to measure the outer limits of congressional concern.

Here again it seems possible to arrive at an answer by asking what Congress was doing when it enacted the national labor laws. Congress obviously had its own views concerning the special rights and duties to be imposed upon employers, unions, and employees because of their relation to employee self-organization and free collective bargaining. Where further particularization would be appropriate, it delegated the function to a specially constituted administrative agency. But it is equally plain that Congress developed this special framework for self-organization and collective bargaining within a larger context of state law creating rights of property, bodily security, and personality, preserving public order, and promoting public health and welfare. These laws apply to the general public or substantial segments thereof without regard to whether the individual is an employer, union, or employee concerned with unionization or a labor dispute. Neither the laws themselves nor any particular application involves weighing the special interests of employers, unions, employees, or the public in employee self-organization, collective bargaining, or labor disputes. The likelihood that the collateral impact of such laws upon management of labor will upset the national balance is small enough to permit their operation unless interference with a specific federal right can be affirmatively demonstrated. It is only where the state law or rule of decision is based upon an accommodation of the special interests of employers, unions, employees, or the public in employee self-organization, collective bargaining, or labor disputes that the likelihood that its application to persons under NLRB jurisdiction will upset the balance struck by Congress is so great as to require exclusion of state law unless Congress has provided otherwise.

The proposed test has the generality requisite to avoid endless case-by-case adjudication, yet it is also "capable of relatively easy application, so that lower courts may largely police themselves in this regard." Any state statute putting duties upon employers, unions, or employees specifically in connection with union organization, collective bargaining, or labor disputes belongs in the class which could not be applied to industries subject to NLRB jurisdiction. Decisional rules developed as particular applications of general tort principles are likewise preempted because particular application results from weighing the competing interests in a labor dispute. For example, although the general principle is that intentional interference with an advantageous business relation is tortious unless justified, the question of justification in a labor dispute cannot be resolved without appraising the conflicting interests of employer, employees, union, and general public that Congress itself sought to accommodate in NLRA §§7 and 8.

[Professor Cox went on to argue that because the essential controversy in *Lockridge* was between the individual union member and the union, and thus did not implicate the "comprehensive legal framework within which questions of union organization and substantive terms and conditions of employment will be worked out or fought out privately," there should have been no preemption in that case.]

LODGE 76, MACHINISTS v. WISCONSIN EMPLOYMENT RELATIONS COMMISSION

427 U.S. 132 (1976)

[During negotiations for a new collective bargaining agreement, the employer made changes in some of the existing terms and conditions of employment. In support of his demands to raise the work week from 37½ to 40 hours and the work day to eight hours, the employer announced that he was implementing these new hours of work. The union responded with a concerted refusal to work overtime. The employer filed a §8(b)(3) refusal-to-bargain charge against the union, but the regional director refused to go to complaint, relying on NLRB v. Insurance Agents, 361 U.S. 477 (1960) (supra at p. 508). However, the Wisconsin Employment Relations Commission, a state agency, entered a cease and desist order against the union's refusal to work overtime, finding the conduct to be neither arguably prohibited nor arguably protected by the NLRA. The Wisconsin state courts enforced the commission's order.]

BRENNAN, J. . . .

Federal labor policy as reflected in the National Labor Relations Act has been construed not to preclude the States from regulating aspects of labor relations that involve "conduct touch[ing] interests so deeply rooted in local feeling and responsibility that . . . we could not infer that Congress had deprived the States of the power to act." San Diego Unions v. Garmon, 359 U.S. 236, 244 (1959). Policing of actual or threatened violence to persons or destruction of property has been held most clearly a matter for the States. Similarly, the federal law governing labor relations does not withdraw from the States . . . power to regulate where the activity regulated [is] a merely peripheral concern of the Labor Management Relations Act." Id., at 243.

Cases that have held state authority to be pre-empted by federal law tend to fall into one of two categories: (1) those that reflect the concern that "one forum would enjoin, as illegal, conduct which the other forum would find legal" and (2) those that reflect the concern "that the [application of state law by] state courts would restrict the exercise of rights guaranteed by the Federal Acts." Automobile Workers v. Russell, 356 U.S. 634, 644 (1958). "[I]n referring to decisions holding state laws preempted by the NLRA, care must be taken to distinguish pre-emption based on federal protection of the conduct in question . . . from that based predominantly on the primary jurisdiction of the National Labor Relations Board . . . , although the two are often not easily separable." Railroad Trainmen v. Jacksonville Terminal Co., 394 U.S. 369, 383 n. 19 (1969). Each of these distinct aspects of labor law pre-emption has had its own history in our decisions, to which we now turn.

We consider first pre-emption based predominantly on the primary jurisdiction of the Board. This line of preemption analysis was developed in San Diego Unions v. Garmon, supra, and its history was recently summarized in Motor Coach Employees v. Lockridge, 403 U.S. 274, 290-291 (1971). . . .

However, a second line of pre-emption analysis has been developed in cases focusing upon the crucial inquiry whether Congress intended that the conduct involved be unregulated because left "to be controlled by the free play of economic forces." NLRB v. Nash-Finch Co., 404 U.S. 138, 144 (1971). Concededly this inquiry was not made in 1949 in the so-called *Briggs-Stratton* case, Automobile Workers v. Wisconsin Emp. Rel. Board, 336 U.S. 245 (1949), the decision of this Court heavily relied upon by the court below in reaching its decision that state regulation of the conduct at issue is not pre-empted by national labor law. In *Briggs-Stratton,* the union, in order to bring pressure on the employer during negotiations, adopted a plan whereby union meetings were called at irregular times during working hours without advance notice to the employer or any notice as to whether or when the workers would return. In a proceeding under the Wisconsin Employment Peace Act, the Wisconsin Employment Relations Board issued an order forbidding the union and its members from engaging in concerted efforts to interfere with production by those methods. This Court did not inquire whether Congress meant that such methods should be reserved to the union "to be controlled by the free play of economic forces." Rather, because these methods were "neither made a right under federal law nor a violation of it" the Court held that there "was no basis for denying to Wisconsin the power, in governing her internal affairs, to regulate" such conduct. Id., at 265.

However, the *Briggs-Stratton* holding that state power is not pre-empted as to peaceful conduct neither protected by §7 nor prohibited by §8 of the federal Act, a holding premised on the statement that "[t]his conduct is governable by the State or it is entirely ungoverned," 336 U.S., at 254, was undercut by subsequent decisions of this Court. For the Court soon recognized that a particular activity might be "protected" by federal law not only when it fell within §7, but also when it was an activity that Congress intended to be "unrestricted by *any* governmental power to regulate" because it was among the permissible "economic weapons in reserve, . . . actual exercise [of which] on occasion by the parties, is part and parcel of the system that the Wagner and Taft-Hartley Acts have recognized." NLRB v. Insurance Agents, 361 U.S., at 488-489 (emphasis added).

[The Court then reviewed its decision in NLRB v. Insurance Agents, 361 U.S. 477 (1960), p. 508, supra.]

Although many of our past decisions concerning conduct left by Congress to the free play of economic forces address the question in the context of union and employee activities, self-help is of course also the prerogative of the employer because he, too, may properly employ economic weapons Congress meant to be unregulable. . . . "[R]esort to economic weapons should more peaceful measures not avail" is the right of the employer as well as the employee, American Ship Bldg. Co. v. NLRB, 380 U.S., at 317, and the State may not prohibit the use of such weapons or "add to an employer's federal legal obligations in collective bargaining" any more than in the case of employees. Cox, Labor Law Preemption Revisited, 85 Harv. L. Rev. 1337, 1365 (1972). Whether self-help economic activities are employed by employer or union, the crucial inquiry regarding pre-emption is the same: whether "the exercise of plenary state authority to curtail or entirely prohibit self-help would frustrate effective implementation of the Act's processes." Railroad Trainmen v. Jacksonville Terminal Co., 394 U.S., at 380.

There is simply no question that the Act's processes would be frustrated in the instant case were the State's ruling permitted to stand. The employer in this case invoked the Wisconsin law because it was unable to overcome the union tactic with its own economic self-help means. Although it did employ economic weapons putting pressure on the union when it terminated the previous agreement, apparently it lacked sufficient economic strength to secure its bargaining demands under "the balance of power between labor and management expressed in our national labor policy," Teamsters Union v. Morton, 377 U.S., at 260. . . .

Our decisions hold that Congress meant that these activities, whether of employer or employees, were not to be regulable by States any more than by the NLRB, for neither States nor the Board is "afforded flexibility in picking and choosing which economic devices of labor and management shall be branded as unlawful." [*Insurance Agents,* at 498.] Rather, both are without authority to attempt to "introduce some standard of properly 'balanced' bargaining power," id., at 497 (footnote omitted), or to define "what economic sanctions might be permitted negotiating parties in an 'ideal' or 'balanced' state of collective bargaining." Id., at 500. To sanction state regulation of such economic pressure deemed by the federal Act "desirabl[y] . . . left for the free play of contending economic forces, . . . is not merely [to fill] a gap [by] outlaw[ing] what federal law fails to outlaw; it is denying one party to an economic contest a weapon that Congress meant him to have available." Lesnick, Preemption Reconsidered: The Apparent Reaffirmation of *Garmon,* 72 Colum. L. Rev. 469, 478 (1972). Accordingly, such regulation by the State is impermissible because it "'stands as an obstacle to the accomplishment and execution of the full purposes and objectives of Congress.'" Hill v. Florida, 325 U.S. 538, 542 (1945).

There remains the question of the continuing vitality of *Briggs-Stratton.* San Diego Unions v. Garmon, 359 U.S., at 245 n. 4, made clear that the *Briggs-Stratton* approach to pre-emption is "no longer of general application." We hold today that the ruling of *Briggs-Stratton,* permitting state regulation of partial strike activities such as are involved in this case is likewise "no longer of general application." . . .

Our decisions since *Briggs-Stratton* have made it abundantly clear that state attempts to influence the substantive terms of collective-bargaining agreements are as inconsistent with the federal regulatory scheme as are such attempts by the NLRB: "Since the federal law operates here, in an area where its authority is paramount, to leave the parties free, the inconsistent application of state law is necessarily outside the power of the State." Teamsters Union v. Oliver, 385 U.S. 283, 296 (1959). And indubitably regulation, whether federal or State, of "the choice of economic weapons that may be used as part of collective bargaining [exerts] considerable influence upon the substantive terms on which the parties contract." NLRB v. Insurance Agents, 361 U.S., at 490. The availability or not of economic weapons that federal law leaves the parties free to use cannot "depend upon the forum in which the [opponent] presses its claims." Howard Johnson Co. v. Hotel Employees, 417 U.S. 249, 256 (1974). . . .

Reversed.[18]

POWELL, J., with whom BURGER, C. J., joins, concurring.

The Court correctly identifies the critical inquiry with respect to preemption as whether "the exercise of plenary state authority to curtail or entirely prohibit self-help would frustrate effective implementation of the Act's processes." Brotherhood of Railroad Trainmen v. Jacksonville Terminal Co., 394 U.S. 369, 380.

This is equally true whether the self-help activities are those of the employer or the union. I agree with the Court that the Wisconsin law, as applied in this case, is pre-empted since it directly curtails the self-help capability of the union and its members, resulting in a significant shift in the balance of free economic bargaining power struck by Congress. I write to make clear my understanding that the Court's opinion does not, however, preclude the States from enforcing, in the context of a labor dispute, "neutral" state statutes or rules of decision: state laws that are not directed toward altering the bargaining positions of employers or unions but which may have an incidental effect on relative bargaining strength. Except where Congress has specifically provided otherwise, the States generally should remain free to enforce, for example, their law of torts or of contracts, and other laws reflecting neutral public policy.* See Cox, Labor Law Preemption Revisited, 85 Harv. L. Rev. 1337, 1355-1356 (1972).

With this understanding, I join the opinion of the Court.

Note

How do you explain the failure of Justice Brennan's opinion to include the language probably proposed by Justice Powell, and now presented in his separate occurrence? Of what precedential effect is the Powell language?

[18] Stevens, J., Stewart, J., and Rehnquist, J., dissented.

* State laws should not be regarded as neutral if they reflect an accommodation of the special interests of employers, unions, or the public in areas such as employee self-organization, labor disputes, or collective bargaining.

SEARS, ROEBUCK & CO. v. SAN DIEGO DISTRICT COUNCIL OF CARPENTERS

436 U.S. 180 (1978)

STEVENS, J.

The question in this case is whether the National Labor Relations Act, as amended, deprives a state court of the power to entertain an action by an employer to enforce state trespass laws against picketing which is arguably — but not definitely — prohibited or protected by federal law.

I

On October 24, 1973, two business representatives of respondent Union visited the department store operated by petitioner (Sears) in Chula Vista, Cal., and determined that certain carpentry work was being performed by men who had not been dispatched from the Union hiring hall. Later that day, the Union agents met with the store manager and requested that Sears either arrange to have the work performed by a contractor who employed dispatched carpenters or agree in writing to abide by the terms of the Union's master labor agreement with respect to the dispatch and use of carpenters. The Sears manager stated that he would consider the request, but he never accepted or rejected it.

Two days later the Union established picket lines on Sears' property. The store is located in the center of a large rectangular lot. The building is surrounded by walkways and a large parking area. A concrete wall at one end separates the lot from residential property; the other three sides adjoin public sidewalks which are adjacent to the public streets. The pickets patrolled either on the privately owned walkways next to the building or in the parking areas a few feet away. They carried signs indicating that they were sanctioned by the "Carpenters Trade Union." The picketing was peaceful and orderly.

Sears' security manager demanded that the Union remove the pickets from Sears' property. The Union refused, stating that the pickets would not leave unless forced to do so by legal action. On October 29, Sears filed a verified complaint in the Superior Court of California seeking an injunction against the continuing trespass; the court entered a temporary restraining order enjoining the Union from picketing on Sears' property. The Union promptly removed the pickets to the public sidewalks.[2] On November 21, 1973, after hearing argument on the question whether the Union's picketing on Sears' property was protected by state or federal law, the court entered a preliminary injunction. The California Court of Appeals affirmed. While acknowledging the pre-emption

2. Although Sears claimed that some delivery men and repairmen refused to cross the picket lines on the public sidewalks, the Union ultimately concluded that the picketing was then too far removed from the store to be effective. The picketing was discontinued on November 12.

guidelines set forth in San Diego Union v. Garmon, 359 U.S. 236, the court held that the Union's continuing trespass fell within the longstanding exception for conduct which touched interests so deeply rooted in local feeling and responsibility that pre-emption could not be inferred in the absence of clear evidence of congressional intent. [Applying *Garmon,* the Supreme Court of California reversed. Certiorari was granted.]

II

We start from the premise that the Union's picketing on Sears' property after the request to leave was a continuing trespass in violation of state law. We note, however, that the scope of the controversy in the state court was limited. Sears asserted no claim that the picketing itself violated any state or federal law. It sought simply to remove the pickets from its property to the public walkways, and the injunction issued by the state court was strictly confined to the relief sought. Thus, as a matter of state law, the location of the picketing was illegal but the picketing itself was unobjectionable.

As a matter of federal law, the legality of the picketing was unclear. Two separate theories would support an argument by Sears that the picketing was prohibited by §8 of the NLRA and a third theory would support an argument by the Union that the picketing was protected by §7. Under each of these theories the Union's purpose would be of critical importance.

If an object of the picketing was to force Sears into assigning the carpentry work away from its employees to Union members dispatched from the hiring hall, the picketing may have been prohibited by §8(b)(4)(D). Alternatively, if an object of the picketing was to coerce Sears into signing a prehire or members-only type agreement with the Union, the picketing was at least arguably subject to the prohibition on recognitional picketing contained in §8(b)(7)(C). Hence, if Sears had filed an unfair labor practice charge against the Union, the Board's concern would have been limited to the question whether the Union's picketing had an objective proscribed by the Act; the location of the picketing would have been irrelevant.

On the other hand, the Union contends that the sole objective of its action was to secure compliance by Sears with area standards, and therefore the picketing was protected by §7. Longshoremen v. Ariadne Co., 397 U.S. 195. Thus, if the Union had filed an unfair labor practice charge under §8(a)(1) when Sears made a demand that the pickets leave its property, it is at least arguable that the Board would have found Sears guilty of an unfair labor practice.

Our second premise, therefore, is that the picketing was both arguably prohibited and arguably protected by federal law. The case is not, however, one in which "it is clear or may fairly be assumed" that the subject matter which the state court sought to regulate — that is, the location of the picketing — is either prohibited or protected by the Federal Act.

III

In San Diego Building Trades Council v. Garmon, 359 U.S. 236, the Court made two statements which have come to be accepted as the general guidelines for deciphering the unexpressed intent of Congress regarding the permissible scope of state regulation of activity touching upon labor-management relations. The first related to activity which is clearly protected or prohibited by the federal statute. The second articulated a more sweeping prophylactic rule: "When an activity is arguably subject to §7 or §8 of the Act, the States as well as the federal courts must defer to the exclusive competence of the National Labor Relations Board if the danger of state interference with national policy is to be averted." Id., at 245.

While the *Garmon* formulation accurately reflects the basic federal concern with potential state interference with national labor policy, the history of the labor pre-emption doctrine in this Court does not support an approach which sweeps away state-court jurisdiction over conduct traditionally subject to state regulation without careful consideration of the relative impact of such a jurisdictional bar on the various interests affected. As the Court noted last Term: "Our cases indicate . . . that inflexible application of the doctrine is to be avoided, especially where the State has a substantial interest in regulation of the conduct at issue and the State's interest is one that does not threaten undue interference with the federal regulatory scheme." Farmer v. Carpenter, 430 U.S. 290, 302.

Thus the court has refused to apply the *Garmon* guidelines in a literal, mechanical fashion. This refusal demonstrates that "the decision to preempt . . . state court jurisdiction over a given class of cases must depend upon the nature of the particular interests being asserted and the effect upon the administration of national labor policies" of permitting the state court to proceed. Vaca v. Sipes, 386 U.S. 171, 180.

With this limitation in mind, we turn to the question whether preemption is justified in a case of this kind under either the arguably protected or the arguably prohibited branch of the *Garmon* doctrine. While the considerations underlying the two categories overlap, they differ in significant respects and therefore it is useful to review them separately. We therefore first consider whether the arguable illegality of the picketing as a matter of federal law should oust the state court of jurisdiction to enjoin its trespassory aspects. Thereafter, we consider whether the arguably protected character of the picketing should have that effect.

IV

. . . The leading case holding that when an employer grievance against a union may be presented to the National Labor Relations Board it is not subject to litigation in a state tribunal is Garner v. Teamsters Union, 346 U.S. 485. . . . The precise conduct in controversy was arguably prohibited by federal law and therefore state jurisdiction was pre-empted. The reason for pre-emption was clearly articulated:

> Congress evidently considered that centralized administration of specially designed procedures was necessary to obtain uniform application of its substantive rules and to avoid these diversities and conflicts likely to result from a variety of local procedures and attitudes toward labor controversies. Indeed, Pennsylvania passed a statute the same year as its labor relations Act reciting abuses of the injunction in labor litigations attributable more to procedure and usage than to substantive rules. A multiplicity of tribunals and a diversity of procedures are quite as apt to produce incompatible or conflicting adjudications as are different rules of substantive law. The same reasoning which prohibits federal courts from intervening in such cases, except by way of review or on application of the federal Board, precludes state courts from doing so. Cf. Myers v. Bethlehem Shipbuilding Corp., 303 U.S. 41; Amalgamated Utility Workers v. Consolidated Edison Co., 309 U.S. 261. 346 U.S., at 490-491 (footnote omitted).

"The conflict lies in remedies. . . . [W]hen two separate remedies are brought to bear on the same activity, a conflict is imminent." Id., at 498-499.

This reasoning has its greatest force when applied to state laws regulating the relations between employees, their union, and their employer. It may also apply to certain laws of general applicability which are occasionally invoked in connection with a labor dispute. Thus, a State's antitrust law may not be invoked to enjoin collective activity which is also arguably prohibited by the Federal Act. Capital Service, Inc. v. Labor Board, 347 U.S. 501; Weber v. Anheuser Busch, Inc., 348 U.S. 468.[23] In each case, the pertinent inquiry is whether the two potentially conflicting statutes were "brought to bear on precisely the same conduct." Id., at 479.

On the other hand, the Court has allowed a State to enforce certain laws of general applicability even though aspects of the challenged conduct were arguably prohibited by §8 of the Taft-Hartley Act. Thus, for

23. As Professor Cox has noted: "[A]n antitrust statute is not the kind of general law [which should avoid the reach of the pre-emption doctrine.] Such statutes are based upon a view of policy towards combinations and collective action in the market place which is the very subject addressed by Congress in the NLRA. That the state laws primarily apply to business combinations and merely sweep collective action by employees within the same rule does not sufficiently lessen the narrowness of focus." Cox, Labor Law Preemption Revisited, 85 Harv. L. Rev. 1337, 1357 (1972).

example, the Court has upheld state-court jurisdiction over conduct that touches "interests so deeply rooted in local feeling and responsibility that, in the absence of compelling congressional direction, we could not infer that Congress had deprived the States of the power to act." San Diego Building Trades Council v. Garmon, 359 U.S. 236, 244. See United Construction Workers v. Laburnum Construction Corp., 347 U.S. 656 (threats of violence); Youngdahl v. Rainfair, 335 U.S. 131 (violence); Automobile Workers v. Russell, 356 U.S. 634 (violence); Linn v. Plant Guard Workers, 383 U.S. 53 (libel); Farmer v. Carpenters, 430 U.S. 290 (intentional infliction of mental distress). . . .

[In *Farmer,*] the Court identified those factors which warranted a departure from the general pre-emption guidelines in the "local interest" cases. Two are relevant to the arguably *prohibited* branch of the *Garmon* doctrine. First, there existed a significant state interest in protecting the citizen from the challenged conduct. Second, although the challenged conduct occurred in the course of a labor dispute and an unfair labor practice charge could have been filed, the exercise of state jurisdiction over the tort claim entailed little risk of interference with the regulatory jurisdiction of the Labor Board. Although the arguable federal violation and the state tort arose in the same factual setting, the respective controversies presented to the state and federal forums would not have been the same.

The critical inquiry, therefore, is not whether the State is enforcing a law relating specifically to labor relations or one of general application but whether the controversy presented to the state court is identical to (as in *Garner*) or different from (as in *Farmer*) that which could have been, but was not, presented to the Labor Board. For it is only in the former situation that a state court's exercise of jurisdiction necessarily involves a risk of interference with the unfair labor practice jurisdiction of the Board which the arguably prohibited branch of the *Garmon* doctrine was designed to avoid.[27]

In the present case, the controversy which Sears might have presented to the Labor Board is not the same as the controversy presented to the state court. If Sears had filed a charge, the federal issue would have been whether the picketing had a recognitional or work reassignment objective; decision of that issue would have entailed relatively complex factual and legal determinations completely unrelated to the simple question whether a trespass had occurred. Conversely, in the state action, Sears only challenged the location of the picketing; whether the

27. While the distinction between a law of general applicability and a law expressly governing labor relations is, as we have noted, not dispositive for pre-emption purposes, it is of course apparent that the latter is more likely to involve accommodation which Congress reserved to the Board. It is also evident that enforcement of a law of general applicability is less likely to generate rules or remedies which conflict with federal labor policy than the invocation of a special remedy under a state labor relations law.

picketing had an objective proscribed by federal law was irrelevant to the state claim. Accordingly, permitting the state court to adjudicate Sears' trespass claim would create no realistic risk of interference with the Labor Board's primary jurisdiction to enforce the statutory prohibition against unfair labor practices.

The reasons why pre-emption of state jurisdiction is normally appropriate when union activity is arguably prohibited by federal law plainly do not apply to this situation; they therefore are insufficient to preclude a State from exercising jurisdiction limited to the trespassory aspects of that activity.

V

The question whether the arguably protected character of the Union's trespassory picketing provides a sufficient justification for preemption of the state court's jurisdiction over Sears' trespass claim involves somewhat different considerations.

Apart from notions of "primary jurisdiction," there would be no objection to state courts and the NLRB exercising concurrent jurisdiction over conduct prohibited by the Federal Act. But there is a constitutional objection to state court interference with conduct actually protected by the Act.[30] Considerations of federal supremacy, therefore, are implicated to a greater extent when labor-related activity is protected than when it is prohibited. Nevertheless, several considerations persuade us that the mere fact that the Union's trespass was *arguably* protected is insufficient to deprive the state court of jurisdiction in this case.

The first is the relative unimportance in this context of the "primary jurisdiction" rationale articulated in *Garmon.* In theory, of course, that

30. Although it is clear that a state court may not exercise jurisdiction over protected conduct, it is important to note that the word "protected" may refer to two quite different concepts: union conduct which the State may not prohibit and against which the employer may not retaliate because it is covered by §7 or conduct which a State may not prohibit even though it is not covered by §7 of the Act. The Court considered protected conduct in the latter sense in Lodge 76, International Association of Machinists and Aerospace Workers, ALF-CIO v. Wisconsin Employment Relations Commission, 427 U.S. 132. There, the Court relied on a line of pre-emption analysis "focusing upon the crucial inquiry whether Congress intended that the conduct involved be unregulated because left 'to be controlled by the free play of economic forces.' NLRB v. Nash-Finch Co., 404 U.S. 138, 144 (1971)." Id., at 140.

The Union does not claim that trespassory picketing is protected from state interference under this doctrine. We merely identify this line of pre-emption analysis in order to make it perfectly clear that it is unaffected by our consideration of the significance of the status of the picketing as arguably protected under §7 of the Act. We also note, however, that in the cases in which pre-emption exists even though neither §7 nor §8 of the Act is even arguably applicable, there is, by hypothesis, no opportunity for the National Labor Relations Board to make the initial evaluation of the controversy. In these cases, the pre-emption issue is necessarily addressed in the first instance by a state tribunal, and that tribunal must decide whether or not the conduct is actually privileged from governmental regulation.

rationale supports pre-emption regardless of which section of the NLRA is critical to resolving a controversy which may be subject to the regulatory jurisdiction of the NLRB. Indeed, at first blush, the primary jurisdiction rationale provides stronger support for pre-emption in this case when the analysis is focused upon the arguably protected, rather than the arguably prohibited, character of the Union's conduct. For to the extent that the Union's picketing was arguably protected, there existed a potential overlap between the controversy presented to the state court and that which the Union might have brought before the NLRB. Prior to granting any relief from the Union's continuing trespass, the state court was obligated to decide that the trespass was not actually protected by federal law, a determination which might entail an accommodation of Sears' property rights and the Union's §7 rights. In an unfair labor practice proceeding initiated by the Union, the Board might have been required to make the same accommodation.

Although it was theoretically possible for the accommodation issue to be decided either by the state court or by the Labor Board, there was in fact no risk of overlapping jurisdiction in this case. The primary jurisdiction rationale justifies pre-emption only in situations in which an aggrieved party has a reasonable opportunity either to invoke the Board's jurisdiction himself or else to induce his adversary to do so. In this case, Sears could not directly obtain a Board ruling on the question whether the Union's trespass was federally protected. Such a Board determination could have been obtained only if the Union had filed an unfair labor practice charge alleging that Sears had interfered with the Union's §7 right to engage in peaceful picketing on Sears' property. By demanding that the Union remove its pickets from the store's property, Sears in fact pursued a course of action which gave the Union the opportunity to file such a charge. But the Union's response to Sears' demand foreclosed the possibility of having the accommodation of §7 and property rights made by the Labor Board; instead of filing a charge with the Board, the Union advised Sears that the pickets would only depart under compulsion of legal process.

In the face of the Union's intransigence, Sears had only three options: permit the pickets to remain on its property; forcefully evict the pickets; or seek the protection of the State's trespass laws. Since the Union's conduct violated state law, Sears legitimately rejected the first option. Since the second option involved a risk of violence, Sears surely had the right — perhaps even the duty — to reject it. Only by proceeding in state court, therefore, could Sears obtain an orderly resolution of the question whether the Union had a federal right to remain on its property.

The primary jurisdiction rationale unquestionably requires that when the same controversy may be presented to the state court or the NLRB, it must be presented to the Board. But that rationale does not extend to cases in which an employer has no acceptable method of invoking, or inducing the Union to invoke, the jurisdiction of the Board.[33] We are therefore persuaded that the primary jurisdiction rationale does not provide a *sufficient* justification for pre-empting state jurisdiction over arguably protected conduct when the party who could have presented the protection issue to the Board has not done so and the other party to the dispute has no acceptable means of doing so.

This conclusion does not, however, necessarily foreclose the possibility that pre-emption may be appropriate. The danger of state interference with federally protected conduct is the principal concern of the second branch of the *Garmon* doctrine. To allow the exercise of state jurisdiction in certain contexts might create a significant risk of misinterpretation of federal law and the consequent prohibition of protected conduct. In those circumstances, it might be reasonable to infer that Congress preferred the costs inherent in a jurisdictional hiatus to the frustration of national labor policy which might accompany the exercise of state jurisdiction. Thus, the acceptability of "arguable protection" as a justification for pre-emption in a given class of cases is, at least in part, a function of the strength of the argument that §7 does in fact protect the disputed conduct.

The Court has held that state jurisdiction to enforce its laws prohibiting violence, defamation, the intentional infliction of emotional distress, or obstruction of access to property, is not pre-empted by the NLRA. But none of those violations of state law involves protected conduct. In contrast, some violations of state trespass laws may be actually protected by §7 of the Federal Act.

In NLRB v. Babcock & Wilcox, 351 U.S. 105, for example, the Court recognized that in certain circumstances nonemployee union organizers may have a limited right of access to an employer's premises for the purpose of engaging in organization solicitation. And the Court has indicated that *Babcock* extends to §7 rights other than organizational activity, though the "locus" of the "accommodation of §7 rights and the private property rights . . . may fall at differing points along the spectrum depending on the nature and strength of the respective §7 rights and private property rights asserted in any given context." Hudgens v. NLRB, 424 U.S. 507.

For purpose of analysis we must assume that the Union could have

33. Even if Sears had elected the self-help option, it could not have assured that the Union would have invoked the jurisdiction of the Board. The Union may well have decided that the likelihood of success was remote and outweighed by the cost of the effort and the probability that Sears in turn would have charged the Union with violating §8(b)(4)(D) or §8(b)(7)(C) of the Act. Moreover, if Sears had elected this option, and the pickets were evicted with more force than reasonably necessary, it might have exposed itself to tort liability under state law. We are unwilling to presume that Congress intended to require employers to pursue such a risky course in order to ensure that issues involving the scope of §7 rights be decided only by the Labor Board.

proved that its picketing was, at least in the absence of a trespass, protected by §7. The remaining question is whether under *Babcock* the trespassory nature of the picketing caused it to forfeit its protected status. Since it cannot be said with certainty that, if the Union had filed an unfair labor practice charge against Sears, the Board would have fixed the locus of the accommodation at the unprotected end of the spectrum, it is indeed "arguable" that the Union's peaceful picketing, though trespassory, was protected. Nevertheless, permitting state courts to evaluate the merits of an argument that certain trespassory activity is protected does not create an unacceptable risk of interference with conduct which the Board, and a court reviewing the Board's decision, would find protected. For while there are unquestionably examples of trespassory union activity in which the question whether it is protected is fairly debatable, experience under the Act teaches that such situations are rare and that a trespass is far more likely to be unprotected than protected.

Experience with trespassory organizational solicitation by nonemployees is instructive in this regard. While *Babcock* indicates that an employer may not always bar nonemployee union organizers from his property, his right to do so remains the general rule. To gain access, the union has the burden of showing that no other reasonable means of communicating its organizational message to the employees exists or that the employer's access rules discriminate against union solicitation. That the burden imposed on the Union is a heavy one is evidenced by the fact that the balance struck by the Board and the courts under the *Babcock* accommodation principle has rarely been in favor of trespassory organizational activity.

Even on the assumption that picketing to enforce area standards is entitled to the same deference in the *Babcock* accommodation analysis as organizational solicitation,[42] it would be unprotected in most instances. While there does exist some risk that state courts will on occasion enjoin a trespass that the Board would have protected, the significance of this risk is minimized by the fact that in the cases in which the argument in

42. This assumption, however, is subject to serious question. Indeed, several factors make the argument for protection of trespassory area standards picketing as a category of conduct, less compelling than that for trespassory organizational solicitation. First, the right to organize is at the very core of the purpose for which the NLRB was enacted. Area standards picketing in contrast, has only recently been recognized as a §7 right. Hod Carriers Local 41 (Calumet Contractors Assn.), 133 N.L.R.B. 512. Second, *Babcock* makes clear that the interests being protected by according limited access rights to nonemployee, union organizers are not those of the organizers but of the employees located on the employer's property. The Court indicated that "no . . . obligation is owed non-employee organizers"; any right they may have to solicit on an employer's property is a derivative of the right of that employer's employees to exercise their organization rights effectively. Area standards picketing, on the other hand, has no such vital link to the employees located on the employer's property. While such picketing may have a beneficial effect on the compensation of those employees, the rationale for protecting area standards picketing is that a union has a legitimate interest in protecting the wage standards of its members who are employed by competitors of the picketed employer.

favor of protection is the strongest, the union is likely to invoke the Board's jurisdiction and thereby avoid the state forum. Whatever risk of an erroneous state court adjudication does exist is outweighed by the anomalous consequence of a rule which would deny the employer access to any forum in which to litigate either the trespass issue or the protection issue in those cases in which the disputed conduct is least likely to be protected by §7.

If there is a strong argument that the trespass is protected in a particular case, a union can be expected to respond to an employer demand to depart by filing an unfair labor practice charge; the protection question would then be decided by the agency experienced in accommodating the §7 rights of unions and the property rights of employers in the context of a labor dispute. But if the argument for protection is so weak that it has virtually no chance of prevailing, a trespassing union would be well advised to avoid the jurisdiction of the Board and to argue that the protected character of its conduct deprives the state court of jurisdiction.

As long as the union has a fair opportunity to present the protection issue to the Labor Board, it retains meaningful protection against the risk of error in a state tribunal. In this case the Union failed to invoke the jurisdiction of the Labor Board,[43] and Sears had no right to invoke that jurisdiction and could not even precipitate its exercise without resort to self-help. Because the assertion of state jurisdiction in a case of this kind does not create a significant risk of prohibition of protected conduct, we are unwilling to presume that Congress intended the arguably protected character of the Union's conduct to deprive the California courts of jurisdiction to entertain Sears' trespass action.[44]

The judgment of the Supreme Court of California is therefore reversed and the case is remanded to that court for further proceedings not inconsistent with this opinion.[19]

43. Not only could the Union have filed an unfair labor practice charge pursuant to §8(a)(1) of the Act at the time Sears demanded that the pickets leave its property, but the Board's jurisdiction could have been invoked and the protection of its remedial powers obtained even after the litigation in the state court had commenced or the state injunction issued. See Capital Service, Inc. v. NLRB, 347 U.S. 501; NLRB v. Nash-Finch Co., 404 U.S. 138.

44. The fact that Sears demanded that the Union discontinue the trespass before it initiated the trespass action is critical to our holding. While it appears that such a demand was a precondition to commencing a trespass action under California law, see Pet. for Cert. A–4, in order to avoid a valid claim of pre-emption it would have been required as a matter of federal law in any event.

The Board has taken the position that "a resort to court action . . . does not violate §8(a)(1)." NLRB v. Nash-Finch Co., 404 U.S., at 142. If the employer were not required to demand discontinuation of the trespass before proceeding in state court and the Board did not alter its position in cases of this kind, the union would be deprived of an opportunity to present the protection issue to the agency created by Congress to decide such questions. While the union's failure to invoke the Board's jurisdiction should not be a sufficient basis for pre-empting state jurisdiction, the employer should not be permitted to deprive the union of an opportunity to do so.

[19] Brennan, J., Stewart, J., and Marshall, J., dissented.

Blackman, J., concurring. . . .

In this case, as the Court notes, the union failed to file an unfair labor practice charge after being asked to leave. In such a situation pre-emption cannot sensibly obtain because the "risk of an erroneous state court adjudication . . . is outweighed by the anomalous consequence of a rule which would deny the employer access to any forum in which to litigate either the trespass issue or the protection issue." Ante, at 26. It should be made clear, however, that the logical corollary of the Court's reasoning is that if the union *does* file a charge upon being asked by the employer to leave the employer's property and continues to process the charge expeditiously, state court jurisdiction is pre-empted until such time as the General Counsel declines to issue a complaint or the Board, applying the standards of NLRB v. Babcock & Wilcox Co., 351 U.S. 105 (1956), rules against the union and holds the picketing to be unprotected. Similarly, if a union timely files a §8(a)(1) charge, a state court would be bound to stay any pending injunctive or damages suit brought by the employer until the Board has concluded, or the General Counsel by refusal to issue a complaint has indicated, that the picketing is not protected by §7. As the Court also notes, ante, at 21, the primary jurisdiction rationale articulated in *Garmon* "unquestionably requires that when the same controversy may be presented to the state court or the NLRB, it must be presented to the Board." Once the no-man's land has been bridged, as it is once a union files a charge, the importance of deferring to the Labor Board's case-by-case accommodation of employers' property rights and employees' §7 rights mandates pre-emption of state court jurisdiction. . . .*

Powell, J., concurring.

Although I join the Court's opinion, Mr. Justice Blackmun's concurrence prompts me to add a word as to the "no man's land" discussion with respect to trespassory picketing. Mr. Justice Blackmun, relying on the amicus brief of the National Labor Relations Board (Board), observes that "there is a practicable means of getting the issue of trespassory picketing before the Board in a timely fashion without danger of violence," if the union — having been requested to leave the property — files a §8(a)(1) charge.

* . . . The possibility of delay to which my Brother Powell adverts is a double-edged sword. The question really is upon whom the burden of delay should be placed. If it takes the General Counsel "weeks" to decide whether to issue a §8(a)(1) complaint, by the same token there would be no relief available against an erroneous state court injunction interfering with protected picketing for an equal length of time. Section 10(j) permits the Board to seek injunctive relief only after the issuance of a complaint. The Board arguably might seek dissolution of a state court order under NLRB v. Nash-Finch Co., 404 U.S. 138 (1971), but that remedy, too, would encompass some delay. It is worth noting that here by November 12, 1973, the picketing, confined to the public sidewalks by the California Superior Court's temporary restraining order, was abandoned as ineffective. Delay in remedy is desired by neither party in a labor dispute.

With all respect, this optimistic view overlooks the realities of the situation. Trespass upon private property by pickets, to a greater degree than isolated trespass, is usually organized, sustained and sometimes obstructive — without initial violence — of the target business and annoying to members of the public who wish to patronize that business. The "danger of violence" is inherent in many — though certainly not all — situations of sustained trespassory picketing. One cannot predict whether or when it may occur, or its degree. It is because of these factors that, absent the availability of an equivalent remedy under the National Labor Relations Act, a state court should have the authority to protect the public and private interests by granting preliminary relief.

In the context of trespassory picketing not otherwise violative of the Act, the Board has no comparable authority. If a §8(a)(1) charge is filed, nothing is likely to happen "in a timely fashion." The Board cannot issue, or obtain from the federal courts, a restraining order directed at the picketing. And it may take weeks for the General Counsel to decide whether to issue a complaint. Meanwhile, the "no man's land" prevents all recourse to the courts, and is an open invitation to self-help. I am unwilling to believe that Congress intended, by its silence in the Act, to create a situation where there is no forum to which the parties may turn for orderly interim relief in the face of a potentially explosive situation.

I do not minimize the possibility that the Board may find that trespassory activity under certain circumstances is necessary to facilitate the exercise of §7 rights by employees of the target employer. See NLRB v. Babcock & Wilcox Co., 351 U.S. 105 (1956); Central Hardware Co. v. NLRB, 407 U.S. 539 (1972). The union's conduct in this case, however, involved a publicity campaign maintained by nonemployees and directed at the general public. Such "area standards" trespassory picketing is certainly not at the core of the Act's protective ambit. In any event, it is open to the Board upon the issuance of a complaint to seek temporary relief under §10(j) of the Act, 29 U.S.C. §160(j), against the employer's interference with §7 rights. Cf. Capitol Service, Inc. v. NLRB, 347 U.S. 501 (1954). Moreover, it is not an unreasonable assumption that state courts will be mindful of the determination of an expert federal agency that there is probable cause to believe that conduct restrained by state process is protected under the Act. But I find no warrant in the Act to compel the employer to endure the creation, especially by nonemployees, of a temporary easement on his property pending the outcome of the General Counsel's action on a charge.

In sum, I do not agree with Mr. Justice Blackmun that "the logical corollary of the Court's reasoning" in its opinion today is that a state-court jurisdiction is pre-empted forthwith upon the filing of a charge by the union. I would not join the Court's opinion if I thought it fairly could be read to that effect.

Notes

1. The Court does not decide the critical question of what the state court is to do in a case such as this during the months that an unfair labor practice charge works its way through Board processes. Except where the General Counsel refuses to go to complaint against the employer, a Board determination will almost invariably come too late to guide the state court in fashioning interim relief. Therefore the choice respecting arguably protected activity may be between always preempting the state relief and never preempting it.

The seriousness of the problem depends on the rules/standards made by the Board in deciding whether various activities are protected. When the Board sets out a rule involving few factual variables (see *Hudgens* on remand, supra at p. 169), activity is clearly categorized as protected or not and state courts are guided accordingly. But when the Board sets out a test that is to be decided on a "case by case basis" (recall *Babcock* and *Nutone,* supra at pp. 153 and 185), the dilemma of preemption of arguably protected activity must be faced.

2. Professor Cox writes of the *Sears* case:

> It is hard to imagine a narrower decision. One narrowing factor is the weight that Justice Stevens gave to what he deemed the low degree of probability that the union's claim to protection would prevail. Surely, the union's chance of prevailing would have been higher if the picketing had been outside the entrances to a store in a shopping center. Does this mean that state jurisdiction may be preempted in the shopping center case? I suppose not, but the opinion leaves the possibility open.
>
> More important, the opinion skillfully narrows the holding to a situation likely never again to recur. The employer must make a demand upon the pickets before it can maintain an injunctive action in state court. At the same time, *Sears* tells us that the state court has jurisdiction unless and until the picketing union files a charge with the NLRB General Counsel alleging that the employer has violated §8(a)(1). This leaves open several critical questions. Must an existing temporary injunction be vacated when the union files its charge? Suppose that the union files its charge before the state court hearing on the motion for a temporary injunction. Is the charge alone sufficient to oust the jurisdiction of the state court? Finally, since the NLRB will not decide the case for many months — even longer if the union stalls, as unions have often done with charges filed to block an election — does the state court have jurisdiction in the interim, with the duty of ruling on federal question as best it can? Or does the charge protect the union by denying the employer a day in court until aftr the NLRB renders its decision?[20]

[20] Cox, Recent Developments in Federal Labor Law Preemption, 41 Ohio St. L.J. 277, 289 (1980).

NEW YORK TELEPHONE CO. v. NEW YORK STATE DEPARTMENT OF LABOR

440 U.S. 519 (1979)

STEVENS, J., announced the judgment of the Court and an opinion in which WHITE, J., and REHNQUIST, J., joined.

The question presented is whether the National Labor Relations Act, as amended, implicitly prohibits the State of New York from paying unemployment compensation to strikers.

Communication Workers of America, AFL-CIO (CWA), represents about 70% of the nonmanagement employees of companies affiliated with the Bell Telephone Co. In June 1971, when contract negotiations had reached an impasse, CWA recommended a nationwide strike. The strike commenced on July 14, 1971, and, for most workers, lasted only a week. In New York, however, the 38,000 CWA members employed by petitioners remained on strike for seven months.

New York's unemployment insurance law normally authorizes the payment of benefits after approximately one week of unemployment. If a claimant's loss of employment is caused by "a strike, lockout, or other industrial controversy in the establishment in which he was employed," §592(1) of the law suspends the payment of benefits for an additional 7-week period. In 1971, the maximum weekly benefit of $75 was payable to an employee whose base salary was at least $149 per week.

After the 8-week waiting period, petitioners' striking employees began to collect unemployment compensation. During the ensuing five months more than $49 million in benefits were paid to about 33,000 striking employees at an average rate of somewhat less than $75 per week. Because New York's unemployment insurance system is financed primarily by employer contributions based on the benefits paid to former employees of each employer in past years, a substantial part of the cost of these benefits was ultimately imposed on petitioners.

Petitioners brought suit in the United States District Court for the Southern District of New York against the state officials responsible for the administration of the unemployment compensation fund. They sought a declaration that the New York statute authorizing the payment of benefits to strikers conflicts with federal law and is therefore invalid, an injunction against the enforcement of §592(1), and an award recouping the increased taxes paid in consequence of the disbursement of funds to their striking employees. After an 8-day trial, the District Court granted the requested relief. 434 F. Supp. 810. . . .

The Court of Appeals for the Second Circuit reversed. It did not, however, question the District Court's finding that the New York statute "alters the balance in the collective bargaining relationship and therefore conflicts with the federal labor policy favoring the free play of economic forces in the collective bargaining process." 566 F.2d 388,

390. . . . The importance of the question led us to grant certiorari. 435 U.S. 941. We now affirm. . . .

. . . [A]lmost all of the Court's labor law decisions in which state regulatory schemes have been found to be pre-empted have involved state efforts to regulate or to prohibit private conduct that was either protected by §7, prohibited by §8, or at least arguably so protected or prohibited.

In contrast to those decisions, there is no claim in this case that New York has sought to regulate or prohibit any conduct subject to the regulatory jurisdiction of the Labor Board under §8.[15] Nor are the petitioning employers pursuing any claim of interference with employee rights protected by §7. The State simply authorized striking employees to receive unemployment benefits, and assessed a tax against the struck employers to pay for some of those benefits, once the economic warfare between the two groups reached its ninth week. Accordingly, beyond identifying the interest in national uniformity underlying the doctrine, the cases comprising the main body of labor pre-emption law are of little relevance in deciding this case.

There is, however, a pair of decisions in which the Court has held that Congress intended to forbid state regulation of economic warfare between labor and management, even though it was clear that none of the regulated conduct on either side was covered by the federal statute. In Teamsters v. Morton, 377 U.S. 252, the Court held that an Ohio court could not award damages against a union for peaceful secondary picketing even though the union's conduct was neither protected by §7 nor prohibited by §8. Because Congress had focused upon this type of conduct and elected not to proscribe it when §303 of the Labor Management Relations Act was enacted, the Court inferred a deliberate legislative intent to preserve this means of economic warfare for use during the bargaining process.

More recently, in Machinists v. Wisconsin Employment Relations Commn., 427 U.S. 132, the Court held that the state commission could not prohibit a union's concerted refusal to work overtime. Although this type of partial strike activity had not been the subject of special congres-

15. Cf. Nash v. Florida Industrial Commn., 389 U.S. 235, in which the Court held that the NLRA pre-empted a state policy of denying unemployment benefits to persons who filed unfair labor practice charges against their former employer. Relying upon §8(a)(4) of the Act, which makes it an unfair labor practice for an employer to restrain or discriminate against an employee who files charges, the Court concluded that the state statute trenched on the employees' federally protected rights contrary to the Supremacy Clause. 389 U.S., at 238-239.

For similar reasons, we reject petitioners' contention that the NLRA at the least forbids the States from awarding benefits to participants in *illegal* strikes. See Communication Workers of America (New York Telephone Co.), 208 N.L.R.B. 267 (1974) (declaring part of the strike involved in this case illegal). Because such a rule would inevitably involve the States in ruling on the legality of strikes under §8, it would invite precisely the harms that the pre-emption doctrine is designed to avoid.

sional consideration, as had the secondary picketing involved in *Morton,* the Court nevertheless concluded that it was a form of economic self-help that was " 'part and parcel of the process of collective bargaining,' " 427 U.S., at 149 (quoting NLRB v. Insurance Agents, 361 U.S. 477, 495), that Congress implicitly intended to be governed only by the free play of economic forces. The Court identified the crucial inquiry in its pre-emption analysis in *Machinists* as whether the exercise of state authority to curtail or entirely prohibit self-help would frustrate effective implementation of the policies of the National Labor Relations Act.

The economic weapons employed by labor and management in *Morton, Machinists,* and the present case are similar, and petitioners rely heavily on the statutory policy, emphasized in the former two cases, of allowing the free play of economic forces to operate during the bargaining process. Moreover, because of the twofold impact of §592(1), which not only provides financial support to striking employees but also adds to the burdens of the struck employers, we must accept the District Court's finding that New York's law, like the state action involved in *Morton* and *Machinists,* has altered the economic balance between labor and management.

But there is not a complete unity of state regulation in the three cases.[21] Unlike *Morton* and *Machinists,* as well as the main body of labor pre-emption cases, the case before us today does not involve any attempt by the State to regulate or prohibit private conduct in the labor-management field. It involves a state program for the distribution of benefits to certain members of the public. Although the class benefited is primarily made up of employees in the State and the class providing the benefits is primarily made up of employers in the State, and although some of the members of each class are occasionally engaged in labor disputes, the general purport of the program is not to regulate the bargaining relationships between the two classes but instead to provide an efficient means of insuring employment security in the State. It is therefore clear that even though the statutory policy underlying *Morton* and *Machinists* lends support to petitioners' claim, the holdings in those cases are not controlling. The Court is being asked to extend the doctrine of labor law pre-emption into a new area.

II

The differences between state laws regulating private conduct and the unemployment-benefits program at issue here are important from a

21. "[T]he conduct being regulated, not the formal description of governing legal standards, . . . is the proper focus of concern" in pre-emption cases. Motor Coach Employees v. Lockridge, 403 U.S. 274, 292. Nevertheless, in assessing whether there is "conflicting [state and federal] regulation" of the conduct, ibid., the scope, purport, and impact of the state program may not be ignored.

pre-emption perspective. For a variety of reasons, they suggest an affinity between this case and others in which the Court has shown a reluctance to infer a pre-emptive congressional intent.

Section 591(1) is not a "state la[w] regulating the relations between employees, their union, and their employer," as to which the reasons underlying the pre-emption doctrine have their "greatest force." *Sears,* [436 U.S., at 193]. Instead, as discussed below, the statute is a law of general applicability. Although that is not a sufficient reason to exempt it from pre-emption, Farmer v. Carpenters, 430 U.S. 290, 300, our cases have consistently recognized that a congressional intent to deprive the States of their power to enforce such general laws is more difficult to infer than an intent to pre-empt laws directed specifically at concerted activity. See id., at 302; *Sears,* supra, at 194-195; Cox, [Labor Law Preemption Revisited, 85 Harv. L. Rev. 1337,] at 1356-1357.

Because New York's program, like those in other States, is financed in part by taxes assessed against employers, it is not strictly speaking a public welfare program. It nevertheless remains true that the payments to the strikers implement a broad state policy that does not primarily concern labor-management relations, but is implicated whenever members of the labor force become unemployed. Unlike most States,[24] New York has concluded that the community interest in the security of persons directly affected by a strike outweighs the interest in avoiding any impact on a particular labor dispute.

As this Court has held in a related context, such unemployment benefits are not a form of direct compensation paid to strikers by their employer; they are disbursed from public funds to effectuate a public purpose. NLRB v. Gullett Gin Co., 340 U.S. 361, 364-365. This conclusion is no less true because New York has found it most efficient to base employer contributions to the insurance program on "experience ratings." Id., at 365. Although this method makes the struck, rather than all, employers primarily responsible for financing striker benefits, the employer-provided monies are nonetheless funneled through a public agency, mingled with other — and clearly public — funds, and imbued with a public purpose. There are obvious reasons, in addition, why the

24. This may be an overstatement. It is true that only Rhode Island has a statutory provision like New York's that allows strikers to receive benefits after a waiting period of several weeks. See Grinnell Corp. v. Hackett, 475 F.2d 499, 457-459 (C.A.1 1973). But most States provide benefits to striking employees who have been replaced by nonstriking employees, and many States, pursuant to the so-called "American rule" allow strikers to collect benefits so long as their activities have not substantially curtailed the productive operations of their employer. See Hawaiian Telephone Co. v. Hawaii Dept. of Labor & Industrial Relations, 405 F. Supp. 275, 287-288 (Haw. 1976), cert. denied, 435 U.S. 943. For example, in Kimbell, Inc. v. Employment Security Commn., 429 U.S. 804, this Court dismissed for want of a substantial federal question an appeal from the Supreme Court of New Mexico which had held that a retroactive post-strike award of unemployment benefits to strikers under the "American rule" was not pre-empted by federal labor law.

pre-emption doctrine should not "hinge on the myriad provisions of state unemployment compensation laws." Ibid.

New York's program differs from state statutes expressly regulating labor-management relations for another reason. The program is structured to comply with a federal statute, and as a consequence is financed, in part, with federal funds. The federal subsidy mitigates the impact on the employer of any distribution of benefits. More importantly, as the Court has pointed out in the past, the federal statute authorizing the subsidy provides additional evidence of Congress' reluctance to limit the States' authority in this area.

Title IX of the Social Security Act of 1935 established the participatory federal unemployment compensation scheme. The statute authorizes the provision of federal funds to States having programs approved by the Secretary of Labor. In Ohio Bureau of Employment Services v. Hodory, 431 U.S. 471, an employee who was involuntarily deprived of his job because of a strike claimed a federal right under Title IX to collect benefits from the Ohio Bureau. Specifically, he contended that Ohio's statutory disqualification of claims based on certain labor disputes was inconsistent with a federal requirement that all persons involuntarily unemployed must be eligible for benefits.

Our review of both the statute and its legislative history convinced us that Congress had not intended to prescribe the nationwide rule that *Hodory* urged us to adopt. The voluminous history of the Social Security Act made it abundantly clear that Congress intended the several States to have broad freedom in setting up the types of unemployment compensation that they wish. We further noted that when Congress wished to impose or forbid a condition for compensation, it did so explicitly; the absence of such an explicit condition was therefore accepted as a strong indication that Congress did not intend to restrict the States' freedom to legislate in this area.

The analysis in *Hodory* confirmed this Court's earlier interpretation of Title IX of the Social Security Act in Steward Machine Co. v. Davis, 301 U.S. 548, and was itself confirmed by the Court's subsequent interpretation of Title IV of the Act in Batterton v. Francis, 432 U.S. 416. These cases demonstrate that Congress has been sensitive to the importance of the States' interest in fashioning their own unemployment compensation programs and especially their own eligibility criteria. It is therefore appropriate to treat New York's statute with the same deference that we have afforded analogous state laws of general applicability that protect interests "deeply rooted in local feeling and responsibility." With respect to such laws, we have stated "that, in the absence of compelling congressional direction, we could not infer that Congress had deprived the States of the power to act." San Diego Building Trades Council v. Garmon, 359 U.S. 236, 244.

III

. . . Even when there is no express pre-emption, any proper application of the doctrine must give effect to the intent of Congress. Malone v. White Motor Corp., 435 U.S. 497, 504. In this case there is no evidence that the Congress that enacted the National Labor Relations Act in 1935 intended to deny the States the power to provide unemployment benefits for strikers. Cf. *Hodory,* 431 U.S., at 482. Far from the compelling congressional direction on which pre-emption in this case would have to be predicated, the silence of Congress in 1935 actually supports the contrary inference that Congress intended to allow the States to make this policy determination for themselves. [The opinion next reviews certain aspects of the legislative history of the Wagner and the Social Security Acts of 1935.]

Undeniably, Congress was aware of the possible impact of unemployment compensation on the bargaining process. The omission of any direction concerning payment to strikers in either the National Labor Relations Act or the Social Security Act implies that Congress intended that the States be free to authorize, or to prohibit, such payments.

Subsequent events confirm our conclusion that the congressional silence in 1935 was not evidence of an intent to pre-empt the States' power to make this policy choice. On several occasions since the 1930's Congress has expressly addressed the question of paying benefits to strikers, and especially the effect of such payments on federal labor policy. On none of these occasions has it suggested that such payments were already prohibited by an implicit federal rule of law. Nor, on any of these occasions has it been willing to supply the prohibition. The fact that the problem has been discussed so often supports the inference that Congress was well aware of the issue when the Wagner Act was passed in 1935, and that it chose, as it has done since, to leave this aspect of unemployment compensation eligibility to the States.

In all events, a State's power to fashion its own policy concerning the payment of unemployment compensation is not to be denied on the basis of speculation about the unexpressed intent of Congress. New York has not sought to regulate private conduct that is subject to the regulatory jurisdiction of the National Labor Relations Board. Nor, indeed, has it sought to regulate any private conduct of the parties to a labor dispute. Instead, it has sought to administer its unemployment compensation program in a manner that it believes best effectuates the purposes of that scheme. In an area in which Congress has decided to tolerate a substantial measure of diversity, the fact that the implementation of this general state policy affects the relative strength of the antagonists in a bargaining dispute is not a sufficient reason for concluding that Congress intended to pre-empt that exercise of state power.

The judgment of the Court of Appeals is affirmed.

BRENNAN, J., concurring in the result.

I agree that the New York statute challenged in this case does not regulate or prohibit private conduct that is either arguably protected by §7 or arguably prohibited by §8 of the NLRA. Any claim that the New York law is pre-empted must therefore be based on the principles applied in Teamsters v. Morton, 377 U.S. 252 (1964), and Machinists v. Wisconsin Employment Relations Commn., 427 U.S. 132 (1976). Although I agree that the "statutory policy" articulated in those cases has some limits, I am not completely at ease with the distinctions employed by my Brother Stevens in this case to define those limits.* However, since I agree with my Brother Blackmun's conclusion that the legislative histories of the NLRA and the Social Security Act reviewed in my Brother Stevens' opinion provide sufficient evidence of congressional intent to decide this case without relying on those distinctions, I see no reason at this time either to embrace the distinctions or to deny that they may have relevance to pre-emption analysis in other cases.

BLACKMUN, J., with whom MARSHALL, J., joins, concurring in the judgment.

I concur in the result. I agree with that portion of Part III of the plurality's opinion where the conclusion is reached that Congress has made its decision to permit a State to pay unemployment benefits to strikers. (Whether Congress has made that decision wisely is not for this Court to say.) Because I am not at all certain that the plurality's opinion is fully consistent with the principles recently enunciated in Machinists v. Wisconsin Emp. Rel. Commn., 427 U.S. 132 (1976), I refrain from joining the opinion's pre-emption analysis.

The plurality recognizes, that the economic weapons employed in this case are similar to those under consideration in *Machinists;* there, too, the Court concluded that Congress intended to leave the employment of such weapons to the free play of economic forces, and not subject to regulation by either the State or the NLRB. And the opinion also recog-

* My Brother Stevens correctly observes that our past pre-emption cases have dealt with statutes that regulate private conduct, rather than confer public benefits, but does not make clear why these different objectives justify different levels of scrutiny. Furthermore, although the distinction between laws of general applicability and laws directed particularly at labor-management relations perhaps has more significance in the application of the principles of *Machinists* than in the application of pre-emption principles where Congress has arguably protected or prohibited conduct, see Cox, Labor Law Preemption Revisited, 85 Harv. L. Rev. 1337, 1335-1356 (1972), I am not at all sure that the New York statute is a law of general applicability. See id., at 1356; Powell, J., dissenting, post. I find more substance in my Brother Stevens' conclusion that the legislative history of the Social Security Act supports the argument that New York's law should be accorded a deference not unlike that accorded state laws touching interests deeply rooted in local feeling and responsibility. Indeed, he may be correct in suggesting that this case is more a case of conflicting federal statutes than a pre-emption case, ante.

nizes, as the District Court and the Court of Appeals both found, that New York's statutory policy of paying unemployment benefits to strikers does indeed alter the economic balance between labor and management.

But the plurality now appears to hold that the analysis developed in *Machinists* and in its predecessor case, Teamsters v. Morton, 377 U.S. 252 (1964), is inapplicable in the evaluation of the New York statute at issue here. The plurality seems to say that since the state statute does not purport to regulate private conduct in labor-management relations, but rather is intended to serve the State's general purpose of providing benefits to certain members of the public in order to insure employment security, the *Machinists-Morton* analysis is not controlling. Relying on decisions of this Court indicating that Congress has been sensitive to the need to allow the States leeway in fashioning unemployment programs the opinion then finds it appropriate to treat the New York statute with the deference afforded general state laws that protect state interests "deeply rooted in local feeling and responsibility." San Diego Bldg. Trades Council v. Garmon, 359 U.S. 236, 244 (1959). Accordingly, the opinion concludes that " 'in the absence of compelling congressional direction, we could not infer that Congress had deprived the States of the power' " to establish unemployment compensation programs like that of New York, quoting *Garmon,* 359 U.S., at 244.

This requirement that petitioners must demonstrate "compelling congressional direction" in order to establish pre-emption is not, I believe, consistent with the pre-emption principles laid down in *Machinists.* In that case, to repeat, the Court recognized that Congress had committed the use of economic self-help weapons to the free play of economic forces, and held that Wisconsin's attempt to regulate what the federal law had failed to curb denied one party a weapon Congress meant that party to have available to it. 427 U.S., at 150. I believe, however, that *Machinists* indicates that the States are *not* free, entirely and always, directly to enhance the self-help capability of one of the parties to such a dispute so as to result in a significant shift in the balance of bargaining power struck by Congress. Where the exercise of state authority to curtail, prohibit, or enhance self-help " 'would frustrate effective implementation of the Act's processes,' " I believe *Machinists* compels the conclusion that Congress intended to pre-empt such state activity, unless there is evidence of congressional intent to tolerate it.

The difference between *Machinists* and this case, it seems to me, is in the initial premise. In the present case, the plurality appears to be saying that there is no pre-emption unless "compelling congressional direction" indicates otherwise. The premise is therefore one of assumed priority on the state side. In *Machinists,* on the other hand, the Court said, I thought, that there *is* pre-emption unless there is evidence of congressional intent to tolerate the state practice. That premise, therefore, is one of assumed priority on the federal side. The distinction is not semantic.

Despite the distinction, however, either approach leads to the same result in the present case. The evidence recited in Part III of the plurality's opinion establishes that Congress has decided to tolerate any interference caused by an unemployment compensation statute such as New York's. But this fortuity should not obscure a difference in reasoning that could prove important in some other pre-emption case. Where evidence of congressional intent to tolerate a State's significant alteration of the balance of economic power is lacking, *Machinists* might still require a holding of pre-emption notwithstanding the lack of compelling congressional direction that the state statute be pre-empted.

I believe this conclusion to be applicable to a case where a State alters the balance struck by Congress by conferring a benefit on a broadly defined class of citizens rather than by regulating more explicitly the conduct of parties to a labor-management dispute. The crucial inquiry is whether the exercise of state authority "frustrate[s] effective implementation of the Act's processes," not whether the State's purpose was to confer a benefit on a class of citizens. I therefore see no basis for determining the question "whether Congress, explicitly or implicitly, has ruled out such assistance in its calculus of laws regulating labor-management disputes," other than in the very manner set out in *Machinists* in the evaluation of the more direct regulation of labor-management relations at issue in that case.

Nor do I agree that we should depart from the principles of *Machinists* on the ground that "our cases have consistently recognized that a congressional intent to deprive the States of their power to enforce such general laws is more difficult to infer than an intent to pre-empt laws directed specifically at concerted activity." The Court recognized in *Garmon,* 359 U.S., at 244, that it has not "mattered whether the States have acted through laws of broad general application rather than laws specifically directed towards the governance of industrial relations." See Sears, Roebuck & Co. v. Carpenters, 436 U.S. 180, 193-195, and n. 24 (1978); Farmer v. Carpenters, 430 U.S. 290, 296-301 (1977). It is true, of course, that the Court has also recognized an exception to the *Garmon* principle and "allowed a State to enforce certain laws of general applicability even though aspects of the challenged conduct were arguably prohibited" where, for example, "the Court has upheld state-court jurisdiction over conduct that touches 'interests so deeply rooted in local feeling and responsibility that, in the absence of compelling congressional direction, we could not infer that Congress had deprived the States of the power to act.' " *Sears,* 436 U.S., at 194-195, quoting *Garmon,* 359 U.S., at 244. But as the cases make clear, the Court has not extended this exception beyond a limited number of state interests that are at the core of the States' duties and traditional concerns. See, e.g., Youngdahl v. Rainfair, Inc., 355 U.S. 131 (1957) (violence); Linn v. Plant Guard Workers, 383 U.S. 53 (1966) (libel); Farmer v. Carpenters, supra (intentional infliction of mental distress). I do not think the New York statute here at issue fits within the pre-emption exception carved out by those cases, and I therefore would not apply the requirement, found in those cases, that "compelling congressional direction" be established before pre-emption can be found.

In summary, in the adjudication of this case, I would not depart from the path marked out by the Court's decision in *Machinists.* Because, however, I believe the evidence justifies the conclusion that Congress has decided to permit New York's unemployment compensation law, notwithstanding its impact on the balance of bargaining power, I concur in the Court's judgment.

POWELL, J., with whom BURGER, C.J., and STEWART, J., join, dissenting.

The Court's decision substantially alters, in the State of New York, the balance of advantage between management and labor prescribed by the National Labor Relations Act (NLRA). It sustains a New York law that requires the employer, after a specified time, to pay striking employees as much as 50% of their normal wages. In so holding, the Court substantially rewrites the principles of pre-emption that have been developed to protect the free collective bargaining which is the essence of federal labor law.

I. THE POLICY OF FREE COLLECTIVE BARGAINING

Free collective bargaining is the cornerstone of the structure of labor-management relations carefully designed by Congress when it enacted the NLRA. Of the numerous actions that labor or management may take during collective bargaining to bring economic pressure to bear in support of their respective demands, the NLRA protects or prohibits only some. The availability and usefulness of many others depend entirely upon the relative economic strength of the parties.

What Congress left unregulated is as important as the regulations that it imposed. It sought to leave labor and management essentially free to bargain for an agreement to govern their relationship. Congress also intended, by its limited regulation, to establish a fair balance of bargaining power. That balance, once established, obviates the need for substantive regulation of the fairness of collective-bargaining agreements: whatever agreement emerges from bargaining between fairly matched parties is acceptable. Thus, the NLRA's regulations not only are limited in scope but also must be viewed as carefully chosen to create the congressionally desired balance in the bargaining relationship. As the Court observed in Motor Coach Employees v. Lockridge, 403 U.S. 274, 286 (1971), the primary impetus for enactment of "a comprehensive national labor law" was the need to stabilize the labor relations by "equitably and delicately structuring the balance of power among competing forces so as to further the common good."

Because the NLRA's limits represent a clear congressional choice with respect to the freedom and fairness of the bargaining process, the Court has been alert to prevent interference with collective bargaining that is unwarranted by the NLRA. For example, in NLRB v. Insurance Agents, 361 U.S. 477 (1960), the Court rejected the conclusion of the National Labor Relations Board (Board) that certain on-the-job conduct undertaken by employees to support their bargaining demands was inconsistent with the union's duty to bargain in good faith. The Court, noting that the NLRA did not prohibit such actions, id., at 498, concluded that allowing the Board to regulate the availability of such economic weapons would intrude on the area deliberately left unregulated by Congress.

The Court employed the same analysis in reversing the Board's determination that the NLRA was violated by a lockout conducted to bring economic pressure to bear in support of the employer's bargaining position. American Ship Building Co. v. NLRB, 380 U.S. 300, 308 (1965). It rejected the Board's suggestion that in enforcing the employer's duty to bargain in good faith, the Board could deny to the employer the use of certain economic weapons not otherwise proscribed by §8. . . .

The States have no more authority than the Board to upset the balance that Congress has struck between labor and management in the collective-bargaining relationship. . . .

II. Free Collective Bargaining and the New York Statute

. . . The challenged provisions of the New York statute . . . had a "twofold impact" on the bargaining process: they substantially cushioned the economic impact of the lengthy strike on the striking employees, and also made the strike more expensive for the employers.[7]

Nothing in the NLRA or its legislative history indicates that Congress intended unemployment compensation for strikers, let alone employer financing of such compensation, to be part of the legal structure of collective bargaining. The New York law therefore alters significantly the bargaining balance prescribed by Congress in that law. The decision upholding it cannot be squared with *Morton* and *Machinists,* where far less intrusive state statutes were invalidated because they "upset the balance of power between labor and management expressed in our national labor policy." *Morton,* 377 U.S., at 260.

7. The impact of unemployment compensation for strikers on the collective-bargaining process could be reduced significantly if such payments were funded from general tax revenues. The disruptive effect also would be lessened, though not as markedly, if such payments were funded by the unemployment compensation tax but were not taken into account in calculating experience ratings of individual employers. New York has eschewed both of these middle paths, however, in favor of a system in which such payments are financed directly by the struck employer. . . .

The plurality's opinion seeks to avoid this conclusion by ignoring the fact that the petitioners are not challenging the entire New York unemployment compensation law but only that portion of it that provides for benefits for striking employees. Although the plurality characterizes the State's unemployment compensation law as "a law of general applicability" that "implement[s] a broad state policy that does not primarily concern labor-management relations," this description bears no relation to reality when applied to the challenged provisions of the law. Those provisions are "of general applicability" only if that term means — contrary to what the plurality itself says — generally applicable only to labor-management relations. It would be difficult to think of a law more specifically focused on labor-management relations than one that compels an employer to finance a strike against itself.[10]

Even if the challenged portion of the New York statute properly could be viewed as part of a law of "general applicability," this generality of the law would have little or nothing to do with whether it is pre-empted by the NLRA. A state law with purposes and applications beyond the area of industrial relations nonetheless may impinge upon congressional policy when it is applied to the collective-bargaining relationship. The Court has recognized accordingly that pre-emption must turn not on the generality of purpose or applicability of a state law but on the effect of that law when applied in the context of labor-management relations. The "crucial inquiry regarding pre-emption" is whether the application of the state law in question " 'would frustrate effective implementation of the [NLRA's] processes.' " *Machinists,* 427 U.S., at 147-148, quoting Railroad Trainmen v. Jacksonville Terminal Co., 394 U.S. 369, 380 (1969). . . .

The Court has identified several categories of state laws whose application is unlikely to interfere with federal regulatory policy under the NLRA. Mr. Justice Frankfurter described one of these categories in broad terms in San Diego Building Trades Council v. Garmon, 359 U.S. 236, 243-244 (1959): "[States retain authority to regulate] where the regulated conduct touche[s] interests so deeply rooted in local feeling and responsibility that, in the absence of compelling congressional direction, we could not infer that Congress had deprived the States of the power to act." The plurality, attempting to draw support from the foregoing generalization, mistakenly treats New York's requirement that employers pay benefits to striking employees as state action "deeply rooted in local feeling and responsibility." But the broad language from *Garmon* has been applied only to a narrow class of cases. In *Garmon,* Mr. Justice Frankfurter identified, as typical of the kind of state law that

10. This assessment and readjustment of the collective-bargaining relationship by the state legislature is especially obvious in the challenged New York statute, which contains a special eligibility rule requiring strikers to wait seven weeks longer than other unemployed workers before collecting compensation.

would not be pre-empted, "the traditional law of torts." Id., at 247; cf. id., at 244 n. 2. The Court has adhered to this understanding of the "local feeling and responsibility" exception formulated in *Garmon.* See *Machinists,* 427 U.S., at 136, and n. 2 ("Policing of actual or threatened violence to persons or destruction of property has been held most clearly a matter for the States"); id., at 151 n. 13; Farmer v. Carpenters, supra, at 296-300; cf. *Sears,* supra, at 194-197. The provisions of the New York law at issue here have nothing in common with the state laws protecting against personal torts or violence to property that have defined the "local feeling and responsibility" exception to pre-emption.

[Part III of the dissenting opinion, The Lack of Evidence of Congressional Intent to Alter the Policy of the NLRA, explores the legislative history of the Wagner and Social Security Acts and finds no support for an inference of an intent to permit unemployment compensation schemes such as New York's.]

IV

The effect of the New York statute is to require an employer to pay a substantial portion of the wages of employees who are performing no services in return because they have voluntarily gone on strike. This distorts the core policy of the NLRA — the protection of free collective bargaining. Whether that national policy should be subject to such substantial alteration by any state legislature is a decision that the Congress should make after the plenary consideration and public debate that customarily accompany major legislation. The financing of striking employees by employers under unemployment compensation systems such as that of New York has never received any such consideration by Congress. The Court today, finding nothing in any statute, congressional committee report, or debate that indicates any intention to allow States to alter the balance of collective bargaining in this major way, rests its decision on inferences drawn from only the most fragmentary evidence.

I would hold, as it seems to me our prior decisions compel, that the New York statute contravenes federal law. It would then be open to the elected representatives of the people in Congress to address this issue in the way that our system contemplates.

Notes

1. Can you explain the apparent contradiction in these two statements of Justice Powell? First, in *Machinists* in 1976 he writes:

> I write to make clear my understanding that the Court's opinion does not, however, preclude the States from enforcing in the context of a labor

dispute, "neutral" state statutes or rules of decision: state laws that are not directed towards altering the bargaining positions of employers or unions but which may have an incidental effect on relative bargaining strength.

Then, in 1979, in *New York Telephone:*

Even if the challenged portion of the New York statute could be viewed as part of a law of general applicability, this generality of the law would have little or nothing to do with whether it is preempted by the NLRA. A state law with purposes and applications beyond the area of industrial relations may nonetheless impinge upon congressional policy when it is applied to the collective-bargaining relationship.

2. Was the state law in *New York Telephone* one of "general applicability"? Professor Cox on the question:

The disagreement over whether the provision of the New York statute making strikers eligible for unemployment compensation is a "law of general applicability" is a useful reminder that neither formulae nor even precise definitions can take the place of judgment in rendering judicial decisions. The New York unemployment compensation law, taken as a whole, appears to rest on general concerns roughly similar to those supporting the payment of public welfare. Looking to the debates in state legislatures upon whether strikers should be eligible for unemployment compensation, one finds attention focused upon the effect of payment of the benefits on collective bargaining and labor-management disputes. Perhaps the wisest approach is to keep the importance of the distinction between labor-management laws and laws of general application in mind, but to avoid rigid classification in close cases. In a borderline case one would then have only a slight disposition to infer an intent to preempt from the character of the legislation, and one would be quick to accept indications of congressional intent to allow states to decide for themselves.[21]

BELKNAP, INC. v. HALE
103 S. Ct. 3172 (1983)

WHITE, J.

The federal labor relations laws recognize both economic strikes and strikes to protest unfair labor practices. Where employees have engaged in an economic strike, the employer may hire permanent replacements whom it need not discharge even if the strikers offer to return to work unconditionally. If the work stoppage is an unfair labor practice strike, the employer must discharge any replacements in order to accommodate returning strikers. In this case we must decide whether the National

[21] Ibid. at 294.

Labor Relations Act (the NLRA or the Act) preempts a misrepresentation and breach-of-contract action against the employer brought in state court by strike replacements who were displaced by reinstated strikers after having been offered and accepted jobs on a permanent basis and assured they would not be fired to accommodate returning strikers.

I

Petitioner Belknap, Inc., is a corporation engaged in the sale of hardware products and certain building materials. A bargaining unit consisting of all of Belknap's warehouse and maintenance employees selected International Brotherhood of Teamsters Local No. 89 (Union) as their collective bargaining representative. In 1975, the Union and Belknap entered into an agreement which was to expire on January 31, 1978. The two opened negotiations for a new contract shortly before the expiration of the 1975 agreement, but reached an impasse. On February 1, 1978, approximately 400 Belknap employees represented by Local 89 went out on strike. Belknap then granted a wage increase, effective February 1, for union employees who stayed on the job.

Shortly after the strike began, Belknap placed an advertisement in a local newspaper seeking applicants to "permanently replace striking warehouse and maintenance employees." A large number of people responded to the offer and were hired. After each replacement was hired, Belknap presented to the replacement the following statement for his signature:

> "I, the undersigned, acknowledge and agree that I as of this date have been employed by Belknap, Inc. at its Louisville, Kentucky, facility as a regular full time permanent replacement to permanently replace ______________________ in the job classification of ______________________."

On March 7, Local 89 filed unfair labor practice charges against petitioner Belknap. The charge was based on the unilateral wage increase granted by Belknap. Belknap countered with charges of its own. On April 4, the company distributed a letter which said, in relevant part:

> TO ALL PERMANENT REPLACEMENT EMPLOYEES
>
> . . . We recognize that many of you continue to be concerned about your status as an employee. The company's position on this matter has not changed nor do we expect it to change. You will continue to be permanent replacement employees so long as you conduct yourselves in accordance with the policies and practices that are in effect here at Belknap. . . .
>
> We continue to meet and negotiate in good faith with the Union. It is our hope and desire that a mutually acceptable agreement can be reached in the near future. However, we have made it clear to the Union that we

> have no intention of getting rid of the permanent replacement employees just in order to provide jobs for the replaced strikers if and when the Union calls off the strike.

On April 27, the Regional Director issued a complaint against Belknap, asserting that the unilateral increase violated §§8(a)(1), 8(a)(3), and 8(a)(5) of the Act. Three days later, on April 7, the company again addressed the strike replacements:

> We want to make it perfectly clear, once again, that there will be no change in your employment status as a result of the charge by the National Labor Relations Board, which has been reported in this week's newspapers.
>
> We do not believe there is any substance to the charge and we feel confident we can prove in the court's satisfaction that our intent and actions are completely within the law.

A hearing on the unfair labor practice charges was scheduled for July 19. The Regional Director convened a settlement conference shortly before the hearing was to take place. He explained that if a strike settlement could be reached, he would agree to the withdrawal and dismissal of the unfair labor practice charges and complaints against both the Company and the Union. During these discussions the parties made various concessions, leaving one major issue unresolved, the recall of the striking workers. The parties finally agreed that the Company would, at a minimum, reinstate 35 strikers per week. The settlement agreement was then reduced to writing. Petitioner laid off the replacements, including the twelve respondents, in order to make room for the returning strikers.

Respondents sued Belknap in the Jefferson County, Kentucky, Circuit Court for misrepresentation and breach of contract. Belknap, they alleged, had proclaimed that it was hiring permanent employees, knowing both that the assertion was false and that respondents would detrimentally rely on it. The alternative claim was that Belknap was liable for breaching its contracts with respondents by firing them as a result of its agreement with Local 89. Each respondent asked for $250,000 in compensatory damages, and an equal amount in punitive damages.

Belknap, after unsuccessfully seeking to remove the suit to federal court, moved for summary judgment, on the ground that respondents' causes of action were preempted by the NLRA. The trial court agreed and granted summary judgment. The Kentucky Court of Appeals reversed. The court first concluded that preemption was inappropriate because Belknap's alleged activities were not unfair labor practices. Belknap's action was not prohibited by 29 U.S.C. §58(a)(3), which makes unlawful discrimination in personnel decisions for the purpose of encouraging or discouraging membership in a particular union, since plaintiffs did not seek membership in any labor organization. Relying on Linn v. Plant Guard Workers, 383 U.S. 53 (1966), the court also concluded that the suit was not preempted because the contract and misrepresentation claims were of only peripheral concern to the NLRA and were deeply rooted in local law. The Kentucky Supreme Court granted discretionary review, but later vacated its order as having been improvidently entered.

We granted Belknap's petition for certiorari.

We affirm.

II

Our cases have announced two doctrines for determining whether state regulations or causes of action are preempted by the NLRA. Under the first, set out in San Diego Building Trades Council v. Garmon, 359 U.S. 236 (1959), state regulations and causes of action are presumptively preempted if they concern conduct that is actually or arguably either prohibited or protected by the Act. The state regulation or cause of action may, however, be sustained if the behavior to be regulated is behavior that is of only peripheral concern to the federal law or touches interests deeply rooted in local feeling and responsibility. Id., at 243-244; Sears, Roebuck & Co. v. Carpenters, 436 U.S. 180, 200 (1978); Farmer v. Carpenters, 430 U.S. 290, 296-297 (1977). In such cases, the state's interest in controlling or remedying the effects of the conduct is balanced against both the interference with the Board's ability to adjudicate controversies committed to it by the Act, Farmer v. Carpenters, supra, at 297; Sears, Roebuck & Co. v. Carpenters, supra, at 200, and the risk that the state will sanction conduct that the Act protects. Id., at 205. The second preemption doctrine, set out in Machinists v. Wisconsin Employment Relations Commission, 427 U.S. 132 (1976), proscribes state regulation and state-law causes of action concerning conduct that Congress intended to be unregulated, id., at 140, conduct that was to remain a part of the self-help remedies left to the combatants in labor disputes, id., at 147-148.

Petitioner argues that the action was preempted under both *Garmon* and *Machinists.* The Board and the AFL-CIO, in amicus briefs, place major emphasis on *Machinists;* they argue that the Kentucky courts are attempting to impose Kentucky law with respect to areas or subjects that Congress intended to be unregulated. We address first the *Machinists* and then the *Garmon* submissions.

III

It is asserted that Congress intended the respective conduct of the Union and Belknap during the strike beginning on February 1 "'to be controlled by the free play of economic forces'", Machinists v. Wisconsin

Employment Relations Commission, supra, at 140, quoting NLRB v. Nash-Finch, 404 U.S. 138, 144 (1971), and that entertaining the action against Belknap was an impermissible attempt by the Kentucky courts to regulate and burden one of the employer's primary weapons during an economic strike, that is, the right to hire permanent replacements. To permit the suit filed in this case to proceed would upset the delicate balance of forces established by the federal law. Subjecting the employer to costly suits for damages under state law for entering into settlements calling for the return of strikers would also conflict with the federal labor policy favoring the settlement of labor disputes. These arguments, it is urged, are valid whether or not a strike is an economic strike.

We are unpersuaded. It is true that the federal law permits, but does not require, the employer to hire replacements during a strike, replacements that it need not discharge in order to reinstate strikers if it hires the replacements on a "permanent" basis within the meaning of the federal labor law. But when an employer attempts to exercise this very privilege by promising the replacements that they will not be discharged to make room for returning strikers, it surely does not follow that the employer's otherwise valid promises of permanent employment are nullified by federal law and its otherwise actionable misrepresentations may not be pursued. We find unacceptable the notion that the federal law on the one hand insists on promises of permanent employment if the employer anticipates keeping the replacements in preference to returning strikers, but on the other hand forecloses damage suits for the employer's breach of these very promises. Even more mystifying is the suggestion that the federal law shields the employer from damages suits for misrepresentations that are made during the process of securing permanent replacements and are actionable under state law.

Arguments that entertaining suits by innocent third parties for breach of contract or for misrepresentation will "burden" the employer's right to hire permanent replacements are no more than arguments that "this is war," that "anything goes," and that promises of permanent employment that under federal law the employer is free to keep, if it so chooses, are essentially meaningless. It is one thing to hold that the federal law intended to leave the employer and the union free to use their economic weapons against one another, but is quite another to hold that either the employer or the union is also free to injure innocent third parties without regard to the normal rules of law governing those relationships. We cannot agree with the dissent that Congress intended such a lawless regime.

The argument that entertaining suits like this will interfere with the asserted policy of the federal law favoring settlement of labor disputes fares no better. This is just another way of asserting that the employer need not answer for its repeated assurances of permanent employment or for its otherwise actionable misrepresentations to secure permanent replacements. We do not think that the normal contractual rights and other usual legal interests of the replacements can be so easily disposed of by broad-brush assertions that no legal rights may accrue to them during a strike because the federal law has privileged the "permanent" hiring of replacements and encourages settlement.

In defense of this position, Belknap, supported by the Board in an amicus brief, urges that permitting the state suit where employers may, after the beginning of a strike, either be ordered to reinstate strikers or find it advisable to sign agreements providing for reinstatement of strikers, will deter employers from making permanent offers of employment or at the very least force them to condition their offer by stating the circumstances under which replacements must be fired. This would considerably weaken the employer's position during the strike, it is said, because without assuring permanent employment, it would be difficult to secure sufficient replacements to keep the business operating. Indeed, as the Board interprets the law, the employer must reinstate strikers at the conclusion of even a purely economic strike unless it has hired "permanent" replacements, that is, hired in a manner that would "show that the men [and women] who replaced the strikers were regarded by themselves and the [employer] as having received their jobs on a permanent basis." Georgia Highway Express, Inc., 165 N.L.R.B. 514, 516 (1967), affirmed sub. nom, Truck Drivers and Helpers Local No. 728 v. NLRB, 403 F.2d 921 (C.A.D.C.), cert. denied, 393 U.S. 935 (1968).

We remain unconvinced. If serious detriment will result to the employer from conditioning offers so as to avoid a breach of contract if the employer is forced by Board order to reinstate strikers or if the employer settles on terms requiring such reinstatement, much the same result would follow from Belknap's and the Board's construction of the Act. Their view is that, as a matter of federal law, an employer may terminate replacements, without liability to them, in the event of settlement or Board decision that the strike is an unfair labor practice strike. Any offer of permanent employment to replacements is thus necessarily conditional and nonpermanent. This view of the law would inevitably become widely known and would deter honest employers from making promises that they know they are not legally obligated to keep. Also, many putative replacements would know that the proffered job is, in important respects, non-permanent and may not accept employment for that reason. It is doubtful, with respect to the employer's ability to hire, that there would be a substantial difference between the effect of the Board's preferred rule and a rule that would subject the employer to damages liability unless it suitably conditions its offers of employment made to replacements.[7]

7. The dissent's argument that state causes of action such as this must be preempted because they make it more difficult for the employer to hire replacements proves entirely too much. For example, it might be easier for an employer to obtain replacements by mistating the wages or fringe benefits that it would provide. But if the employer did so, surely the employees affected could seek protection in the state courts.

Belknap counters that conditioning offers in such manner will render replacements non-permanent employees subject to discharge to make way for strikers at the conclusion or settlement of a purely economic strike, which would not be the case if replacements had been hired on a "permanent" basis as the Board now understands that term. The balance of power would thus be distorted if the employer is forced to condition its offers for its own protection. Under Belknap's submission, however, which is to some extent supported by the Board, Belknap's promises, although in form assuring permanent employment, would as a matter of law be non-permanent to the same extent as they would be if expressly conditioned on the eventuality of settlement requiring reinstatement of strikers and on its obligation to reinstate unfair labor practice strikers. As we have said, we cannot believe that Congress determined that the employer must be free to deceive by promising permanent employment knowing that it may choose to reinstate strikers or may be forced to do so by the Board.

An employment contract with a replacement promising permanent employment, subject only to settlement with its employees' union and to a Board unfair labor practice order directing reinstatement of strikers, would not in itself render the replacement a temporary employee subject to displacement by a striker over the employer's objection during or at the end of what is proved to be a purely economic strike. The Board suggests that such a conditional offer "might" render the replacements only temporary hires that the employer would be required to discharge at the conclusion of a purely economic strike. Br., at 17. But the permanent-hiring requirement is designed to protect the strikers, who retain their employee status and are entitled to reinstatement unless they have been permanently replaced. That protection is unnecessary if the employer is ordered to reinstate them because of the commission of unfair labor practices. It is also meaningless if the employer settles with the union and agrees to reinstate strikers. But the protection is of great moment if the employer is not found guilty of unfair practices, does not settle with the union, or settles without a promise to reinstate. In that eventuality, the employer, although he has prevailed in the strike, may refuse reinstatement only if he has hired replacements on a permanent basis. If he has promised to keep the replacements on in such a situation, discharging them to make way for selected strikers whom he deems more experienced or more efficient would breach his contract with the replacements. Those contracts, it seems to us, create a sufficiently permanent arrangement to permit the prevailing employer to abide by its promises.[8]

8. The refusal to fire permanent replacements because of commitments made to them in the course of an economic strike satisfies the requirement of NLRB v. Fleetwood Trailer Co., 389 U.S. 375, 380 (1967), that the employer have a "legitimate and substantial justification" for his refusal to reinstate strikers. That the offer and promise of permanent employment are conditional does not render the hiring any less permanent if the conditions do not come to pass. All hirings are to some extent conditional. As the Board recog-

We perceive no substantial impact on the availability of settlement of economic or unfair labor practice strikes if the employer is careful to protect itself against suits like this in the course of contracting with strike replacements.[9] Its risk of liability if it discharges replacements pursuant

---

nizes, Brief of the National Labor Relations Board as Amicus Curiae 16-17 (NLRB Br.), although respondents were hired on a permanent basis, they were subject to discharge in the event of a business slowdown. Had Belknap not settled and no unfair practices been filed, surely it would have been free to retain respondents and obligated to do so by the terms of its promises to them. The result should be the same if Belknap had promised to retain them if it did not settle with the union and if it were not ordered to reinstate strikers.

The dissent and the concurrence make much of conditional offers of employment, asserting that they prevent replacements from being permanent employees. As indicated in the text, however, the Board's position is that even unconditional contracts of permanent employment are as a matter of law defeasible, first, if the strike turns out to be an unfair labor practice strike, and second, if the employer chooses to settle with the union and reinstate the strikers. If these implied conditions, including those dependent on the volitional act of settlement, do not prevent the replacements from being permanent employees, neither should express conditions which do no more than inform replacements what their legal status is in any event.

The dissent and the concurrence suggest that if offers of permanent employment are not necessary to secure the manpower to keep the business operating, returning strikers must be given preference over replacements who have been hired on a permanent basis. That issue is not posed in this case, but we note that the Board has held to the contrary. In Hot Shoppes, Inc., 146 N.L.R.B. 802, 804 (1964), the Board held as follows:

> We however, disagree with the Trial Examiner's premise that an employer may replace economic strikers only if it is shown that he acted to preserve efficient operation of his business. The Supreme Court's decision in Mackay Radio & Telegraph Company, and the cases thereafter, although referring to an employer's right to continue his business during a strike, state that an employer has a legal right to replace economic strikers at will. We construe these cases as holding that the motive for such replacements is immaterial, absent evidence of an independent unlawful purpose. Therefore, we reject the Trial Examiner's conclusion that the plan to replace the economic strikers here was itself improper and that the strike was converted to an unfair labor practice strike on January 4 by Respondent's implementation of such plan.

The Board noted its holding in Hot Shoppes, Inc., at p. 29 of the Twenty-Ninth Annual Report of the National Labor Relations Board, and the holding has not been repudiated by the Board. See, e.g., Pennsylvania Glass Sand Corp., 172 N.L.R.B. 514, n.3, 535 (1968). There are no cases in this Court that require a different conclusion. Indeed, as indicated above, in Hot Shoppes, Inc., supra, the Board read Mackay Radio and Telegraph Company, 314 U.S. 377 (1938), as holding that the motive for hiring permanent replacements is irrelevant. NLRB v. Erie Resistor Corp., 373 U.S. 221 (1963), cited by Justice Blackmun, involved an offer of super-seniority to replacements. The opinion was careful to distinguish cases not involving that element. . . .

9. If, as we hold, an employer may condition his offer to replacements and hence avoid conflicting obligations to strikers and replacements in the event of a settlement providing for reinstatement, the employer will very likely do so. Hence, there will be little occasion for replacements to bring suits for breach of contract or misrepresentation. The employer that nevertheless makes unconditional commitments to replacements and wants to discharge them after settlement with the union will be in much the same position as the employer in W. R. Grace & Co. v. Local 759, 103 S. Ct. 2177 (1983). There the employer signed a conciliation agreement with the EEOC that conflicted with its collective bargaining agreement with the union. We recognized the employer's dilemma, but because it was of the employer's own making we unanimously refused to relieve the employer of either obligation.

to a settlement or to a Board order would then be minimal. We fail to understand why in such circumstances the employer would be any less willing to settle the strike than it would be under the regime proposed by Belknap and the Board, which as a matter of law, would permit it to settle without liability for misrepresentation or for breach of contract.

Belknap and its supporters, the Board and the AFL-CIO, offer no substantial case authority for the proposition that the *Machinists* rationale forecloses this suit. Surely *Machinists* did not deal with solemn promises of permanent employment, made to innocent replacements, that the employer was free to make and keep under federal law. J. I. Case, Co. v. NLRB, 321 U.S. 332 (1944), suggests that individual contracts of employment must give way to otherwise valid provisions of the collective bargaining contract, but it was careful to say that the Board "has no power to adjudicate the validity or effect of such contracts except as to their effect on matters within its jurisdiction," id., at 340. There, the cease-and-desist order, as modified, stated that the discontinuance of the individual contracts was "without prejudice to the assertion of any legal rights the employee may have acquired under such contract or to any defenses thereto by the employer."

There is still another variant or refinement of the argument that the employer and the Union should be privileged to settle their dispute and provide for striker reinstatement free of burdensome law suits such as this. It is said that respondent replacements are employees within the bargaining unit, that the Union is the bargaining representative of petitioner's employees, and the replacements are thus bound by the terms of the settlement negotiated between the employer and "their" representative. The argument is not only that as a matter of federal law the employer cannot be foreclosed from discharging the replacements pursuant to a contract with a bargaining agent, but also that by virtue of the agreement with the Union it is relieved from responding in damages for its knowing breach of contract — that is, that the contracts are not only not specifically enforceable but also may be breached free from liability for damages. We need not address the former issue — the issue of specific performance — since the respondents ask only damages. As to the damages issue, as we have said above, such an argument was rejected in *J. I. Case.*

If federal law forecloses this suit, more specific and persuasive reasons than those based on *Machinists* must be identified to support any such result. Belknap insists that the rationale of the *Garmon* decision, properly construed and applied, furnishes these reasons.

IV

The complaint issued by the Regional Director alleged that on or about February 1, Belknap unilaterally put into effect a 50¢-per-hour wage increase, that such action constituted unfair labor practices under §§8(a)(1), 8(a)(3) and 8(a)(5), and that the strike was prolonged by these violations. If these allegations could have been sustained, the strike would have been an unfair labor practice strike almost from the very start. From that time forward, Belknap's advertised offers of permanent employment to replacements would arguably have been unfair labor practices since they could be viewed as threats to refuse to reinstate unfair labor practice strikers. Furthermore, if the strike had been an unfair labor practice strike, Belknap would have been forced to reinstate the strikers rather than keep replacements on the job. Mastro Plastics Corp. v. NLRB, 350 U.S. 270, 278 (1956). Belknap submits that its offers of permanent employment to respondents were therefore arguably unfair labor practices, the adjudication of which were within the exclusive jurisdiction of the Board, and that discharging respondents to make way for strikers was protected activity since it was no more than the federal law required in the event the unfair labor practices were proved.[12]

Respondents do not dispute that it was the Board's exclusive business to determine, one, whether Belknap's unilateral wage increase was an unfair labor practice, which would have converted the strike into an unfair labor practice strike that required the reinstatement of strikers, and, two, whether Belknap also committed unfair labor practices by offering permanent employment to respondents. They submit, however, that under our cases, properly read, their actions for fraud and breach of contract, are not preempted. We agree with respondents.

Under *Garmon,* a state may regulate conduct that is of only peripheral concern to the Act or which is so deeply rooted in local law that the courts should not assume that Congress intended to preempt the appli-

12. The dissent makes the same ineffective argument, ineffective because it cannot explain in any convincing way why the breach, if required by federal law, should not be subject to a damages remedy. It is not easy to grasp why the employer who settles a purely economic strike (such as one in which no unfair labor practice charge is filed) and fires permanent replacements to make way for returning strikers could be made to respond in damages; yet the employer who violates the labor laws is for that reason insulated from damages liability when it discharges replacements to whom it has promised permanent employment. The dissent asserts that to subject the unfair labor practice employer to damage suits would cause intolerable confusion, but as we see it there would be no interference with the Board's authority to impose its remedy for violating the federal labor law. Performing that function neither requires nor suggests that the replacements must be deprived of their remedy for breach of contract.

Of course, here there was no adjudication of an unfair practice. The employer settled short of that possible outcome. That action was *not* required by federal law. We do not share the dissent's apparent view that federal labor policy favoring settlement privileges the employer to make and break contracts with innocent third parties at will. Nor do we understand why the threat of liability to discharged replacements, in the event the employer loses the unfair labor practice case and discharges them, would deter the employer from settling with the Board where it thinks the unfair labor practice charge will be sustained. Settling would not increase its potential liability to replacements. It may be that the employer would prefer to settle even a case that it is quite confident it could win, but that is surely no reason to deprive the replacements of their contract. Nor in such a case do the equities favor the strikers over the replacements, who would be entitled to stay unless the employer has violated the federal law.

cation of state law. In Linn v. Plant Guard Workers, 383 U.S. 53 (1966), we held that false and malicious statements in the course of a labor dispute were actionable under state law if injurious to reputation, even though such statements were in themselves unfair labor practices adjudicable by the Board. Likewise, in Farmer v. Carpenters, 430 U.S. 290 (1977), we held that the Act did not preempt a state action for intentionally inflicting emotional distress, even though a major part of the cause of action consisted of conduct that was arguably an unfair labor practice. Finally, in Sears, Roebuck & Co. v. Carpenters, 436 U.S. 180 (1978), we held that a state trespass action was permissible and not preempted, since the action concerned only the location of the picketing while the arguable unfair labor practice would focus on the object of the picketing. In that case, we emphasized that a critical inquiry in applying the *Garmon* rules, where the conduct at issue in the state litigation is said to be arguably prohibited by the Act and hence within the exclusive jurisdiction of the NLRB, is whether the controversy presented to the state court is identical with that which could be presented to the Board. There the state court and Board controversies could not fairly be called identical. This is also the case here.

Belknap contends that the misrepresentation suit is preempted because it related to the offers and contracts for permanent employment, conduct that was part and a parcel of an arguable unfair labor practice. It is true that whether the strike was an unfair labor practice strike and whether the offer to replacements was the kind of offer forbidden during such a dispute were matters for the Board. The focus of these determinations, however, would be on whether the rights of strikers were being infringed. Neither controversy would have anything in common with the question whether Belknap made misrepresentations to replacements that were actionable under state law. The Board would be concerned with the impact on strikers not with whether the employer deceived replacements. As in *Linn* v. *Plant Guard Workers,* supra, "the Board [will] not be ignored since its sanctions alone can adjust the equilibrium disturbed by an unfair labor practice." Id., at 66. The strikers cannot secure reinstatement, or indeed any relief, by suing for misrepresentation in state court. The state courts in no way offer them an alternative forum for obtaining relief that the Board can provide. The same was true in *Sears* and *Farmers.* Hence, it appears to us that maintaining the misrepresentation action would not interfere with the Board's determination of matters within its jurisdiction and that such an action is of no more than peripheral concern to the Board and the federal law. At the same time, Kentucky surely has a substantial interest in protecting its citizens from misrepresentations that have caused them grievous harm. It is no less true here than it was in *Linn* v. *Plant Guard Workers,* supra, at 63, that "[t]he injury" remedied by the state law "has no relevance to the Board's function" and that "[t]he Board can award no damages, impose no penalty, or give any other relief" to the plaintiffs in this case. The state interests involved in this case clearly outweigh any possible interference with the Board's function that may result from permitting the action for misrepresentation to proceed.

Neither can we accept the assertion that the breach of contract claim is preempted. The claimed breach is the discharge of respondents to make way for strikers, an action allegedly contrary to promises that were binding under state law. As we have said, respondents do not deny that had the strike been adjudicated an unfair labor practice strike Belknap would have been required to reinstate the strikers, an obligation that the state could not negate.[13] But respondents do assert that such an adjudication has not been made, that Belknap prevented such an adjudication by settling with the Union and voluntarily agreeing to reinstate strikers, and that, in any event, the reinstatement of strikers, even if ordered by the Board, would only prevent the specific performance of Belknap's promises to respondents, not immunize Belknap from responding in damages from its breach of its otherwise enforceable contracts.

For the most part, we agree with respondents. We have already concluded that the federal law does not expressly or impliedly privilege an employer, as part of a settlement with a union, to discharge replacements in breach of its promises of permanent employment. Also, even had there been no settlement and the Board had ordered reinstatement of what it held to be unfair labor practice strikers, the suit for damages for breach of contract could still be maintained without in any way prejudicing the jurisdiction of the Board or the interest of the federal law in insuring the replacement of strikers. The interests of the Board and the NLRA, on the one hand, and the interest of the state in providing a remedy to its citizens for breach of contract, on the other, are "discrete" concerns, cf. *Farmers* v. *Carpenters,* supra, at 304. We see no basis for holding that permitting the contract cause of action will conflict with the rights of either the strikers or the employer or would frustrate any policy of the federal labor laws.

13. Kentucky may not mandate specific performance of the contract between Belknap and respondents nor may it enter an injunction requiring the reinstatement of respondents as a remedy for fraud if either action necessitates the firing of a striker entitled to reinstatement. To do so would be to deprive returning strikers of jobs committed to them by the national labor laws. As the Court said in National Licorice Co. v. NLRB, 309 U.S. 350, 365 (1940):

> The effect of the Board's order, as we construe it, is to preclude the petitioner from taking any benefit of the contracts which were procured through violation of the Act and which are themselves continuing means of violating it, and from carrying out any of the contract provisions, the effect of which would be to infringe the rights guaranteed by the National Labor Relations Act. *It does not forclose the employees from taking any action to secure an adjudication upon the contracts, nor prejudge their rights in the event of such adjudication.* We do not now consider their nature and extent. It is sufficient to say here that it will not be open to any tribunal to compel the employer to perform the acts, which, even though he has bound himself by contract to do them, would violate the Board's order or be inconsistent with any part of it. (Emphasis added.)

V

Because neither the misrepresentation nor the breach-of-contract cause of action is preempted under the *Garmon* or the *Machinists,* the decision of the Kentucky Court of Appeals is

Affirmed.

BLACKMUN, J., concurring in the judgment.

I

Earlier this month, the Court unanimously reaffirmed the principle that the National Labor Relations Board's construction of the National Labor Relations Act (NLRA), if reasonable, is entitled to deference from the courts. NLRB v. Transportation Management, Inc., 103 S. Ct. 2469 (1983). The Court today, it seems to me, ignores this fundamental premise of federal labor law in order to conform the substance of the NLRA to the contract and tort laws of the Commonwealth of Kentucky. Having done so, the Court not surprisingly concludes that those state laws are not pre-empted by the refashioned NLRA. I cannot participate in this extraordinary approach to labor law pre-emption.

The Court recognizes that, "as the Board interprets the law, the employer must reinstate strikers at the conclusion of even a purely economic strike unless it has hired 'permanent' replacements, that is, hired in a manner that would 'show that the men [and women] who replaced the strikers were regarded by themselves and the [employer] as having received their jobs on a permanent basis.'" Ante, quoting Georgia Highway Express, Inc., 165 N.L.R.B. 514, 516 (1967), aff'd. sub nom. Truck Drivers and Helpers Local 728 v. NLRB, 131 U.S. App. D.C. 195, 403 F.2d 921, cert. denied, 393 U.S. 935 (1968). The Court holds today, however, that the employer may refuse to reinstate strikers at the end of an economic strike if the employer has promised its strike replacements "permanent employment, *subject only to settlement with its employees' union* and to a Board unfair labor practice order" (emphasis supplied) — in other words, if the employer has promised that the jobs are permanent unless it later decides they are temporary. Such a promise bears little resemblance to a promise of permanent employment. During settlement negotiations, the union can be counted on to demand reinstatement for returning strikers as a condition for any settlement; the employer can be counted on to acquiesce, at a price the union certainly will be willing to pay.[1]

1. The Court's suggestion that the employer's conditional promise "is of great moment if the employer is not found guilty of unfair practices, does not settle with the union, or settles without a promise to reinstate." ante at 11-12, ignores the significant fact that this is the one situation for which a strike replacement would not need reassurances. An employer that refuses to reinstate strikers as a part of a strike settlement, when it could have

In rejecting the Board's longstanding view of the Act, the Court does not pause to determine whether the Board's view is reasonable, or whether it is contrary to the statutory mandate or frustrates Congress' policy objectives. Rather, it adopts an approach that itself is at wide variance with the NLRA. Under the Act, an employer may eliminate economic strikers' jobs only by showing "'legitimate and substantial business justifications.'" NLRB v. Fleetwood Trailer Co., 389 U.S. 375, 378 (1967), quoting NLRB v. Great Dane Trailers, 388 U.S. 26, 34 (1967). As the Court recognizes, this rule flows from the Act's fundamental premise that economic strikers "retain their employee status and are entitled to reinstatement." The employer may refuse reinstatement if it has promised permanent employment to replacements. But this is true only because such promises are deemed necessary to serve the employer's legitimate and substantial business justification in seeking "to protect and continue his business by supplying places left vacant" by the strikers. NLRB v. Mackay Co., 304 U.S. 333, 345 (1938). See NLRB v. Erie Resistor Corp., 373 U.S. 221, 232 (1963). The Board reasonably has concluded that this purpose is served only by a promise that the job is not subject to cancellation at the employer's option. Covington Furniture Mfg. Corp., 212 N.L.R.B. 214, 220 (1974), enf'd, 514 F.2d 995 (C.A.6 1975).[2] It is patently unreasonable to suppose that the promise the Court substitutes — that the replacements are permanent unless the employer

---

demanded concessions from the union in exchange, is unlikely to fire the replacements and reinstate strikers unilaterally. The Court's conditional promise does not relate to potential replacements' concerns — that in order to end the strike, the employer will agree with the Union to reinstate the strikers at the replacements' expense.

2. As the Court's own quotation from Hot Shoppes, Inc., 146 N.L.R.B. 802 (1964), demonstrates, ante, at 13, n. 8, that case is not the contrary. Hot Shoppes merely holds that, in order to retain strike replacements, the employer need not show in a given case that its offers of permanent employment were motivated by the need to continue the operation of its business. As *Mackay Co.,* makes clear, the Act gives the employer the right to make such promises because it is presumed that they serve this purpose, 304 U.S., at 345; the specific motive for a particular offer is irrelevant. In *Hot Shoppes,* as in this case, permanent offers were made. 146 N.L.R.B., at 804. *Hot Shoppes* obviously does not stand for the proposition that an employer *not* making an offer of permanent employment in the manner set forth in *Covington Furniture* may retain replacement employees in preference to strikers. Yet that is what the Court holds today.

The Court also quotes incompletely from the Board's brief in this Court in an effort to demonstrate that the Board's position is "equivocal at best," and therefore not entitled to deference. Ante, at 13, n.8. The full quote is as follows, and is very clear:

> An employer *could not escape the dilemma* posed by the threat of a state court fraud action simply by informing prospective replacements of all the contingencies that might affect their tenure. In the first place, if an employer were to extend only such a conditional offer, its ability to hire replacement workers quickly would be diminished and its chief weapon for combatting the employees' strike pressure would consequently be weakened. Furthermore, such a conditional offer might well render the replacements only temporary hires *and would mean that the employer would be obligated to reinstate the strikers even if the strike turned out to be an economic one.* . . Brief for NLRB 17 (emphasis supplied).

decides otherwise — would further the employer's legitimate goal at all. It is in order to allay the potential replacements' fear that the employer will replace them as part of a settlement with the Union that the employer must make the promise in the first place.

Indeed, an employer who makes a conditional promise has no legitimate, much less substantial, business justification to refuse to agree with the Union to reinstate the strikers. Under the Court's scenario, the employer has managed to operate its business by hiring replacements on the understanding that they may be fired as part of a settlement of the strike. And whether or not state contract and tort remedies are preempted by the Act, the employer can agree to reinstate the strikers at the replacements' expense without incurring liability. The Court's convoluted attempt to establish that its conditional promise would serve some legitimate business purpose fails to come to grips with these simple facts.

The Court's conditional promise achieves only one thing: it permits an employer, during settlement negotiations with the Union, to threaten to retain replacement employees in preference to returning strikers despite the fact that the employer has not promised to do so. The naked interest in making such a threat, silently endorsed in the Court's opinion, could not be less legitimate under the NLRA. From the employer's point of view, one benefit of offering strike replacements permanent employment is that strikers become fearful that they will lose their jobs. But it is clear that creating this fear, which discourages union membership and concerted activities, is a deleterious side-effect of, rather than a legitimate business justification for, the power to hire permanent strike replacements. See NLRB v. Erie Resistor Corp., 373 U.S., at 232. Promises of permanent employment, and subsequent retention of replacements, are permitted only because it is believed that the harm to protected activities is outweighed by the employer's interest in operating his plant during a strike. Ibid. Thus, an employer who succeeds in operating the plant without promising permanent employment would have no legitimate basis for not reinstating economic strikers. In my view, having made only the Court's conditional promise, an employer who threatened during strike negotiations to retain strike replacements in preference to economic strikers would commit an unfair labor practice. . . .

The Board's construction of the Act is reasonable and entitled to a deference that is wholly lacking in the Court's opinion. By brushing aside the Board's interpretation of the Act, and substituting its own novel construction, the Court side-steps the real question in what is, as the dissent observes, "a difficult case." The question presented is whether respondents' state contract and tort actions are pre-empted by the Act, not whether the Act can be manipulated into a posture consistent with such lawsuits. Taking federal law as it is, however, while the question is close, I conclude that neither of respondents' causes of action is preempted.[3]

II

A

I cannot easily dismiss the basic premises underlying either the Court's opinion or the dissenting opinion. On the one hand, the dissent aptly observes that respondents' state law claims "go to the core of federal labor policy." One would not expect that Congress would have left anything so basic as the respective rights and duties of strike replacements and employers to the nonuniform regulation of the States. On the other hand, there is great strength in the bedrock of the Court's position — it is difficult to believe that Congress could have intended to permit employers and unions "to injure innocent third parties without regard to the normal rules of law governing those relationships."

Any attempt to reconcile these concerns, in my view, must begin with an analysis of the nature of the economic weapon at issue. The heart of the weapon is the power to hire replacements. The promise of permanent employment is simply one means of achieving this end, a means that unquestionably is permitted by the NLRA. The dissent appears to view the self-help weapon as the power to make such promises, and concludes that Congress intended that this power would be largely unregulated. The Court appears to take a different view of the nature of the weapon, implying that the weapon properly is seen as the power to contract with replacement employees, not merely to promise permanent jobs, and that the normal state law accompaniments of contracts were contemplated and accepted by Congress.

I believe that the Court's view is more consistent with the purposes and qualities of this particular economic weapon. One may agree with the dissent that permitting employers to hire replacement workers "is part of the balance struck by the Act between labor and management," without conceding that all means of accomplishing this were meant to be unregulated. As noted above, the very purpose of enabling an employer to offer permanent employment to strike replacements is to permit the employer to keep his business running during a strike. If the promises of permanent employment are unenforceable, "many putative replacements would know that the proffered job is, in important respects, nonpermanent and [might] not accept employment for that reason." The dissent's view that federal law intends those offers to be nonbinding

3. This Court, and not the Board, reviews state court lawsuits said to conflict with federal law. Although it is well established that the Board's construction of the substantive scope of the NLRA is due deference, I am unaware of any case in which this Court has deferred to the Board's views on pre-emption.

would undermine the reason for permitting them. If the promises are enforceable under state law, however, they are credible; this is the only result consistent with the promises' federal purpose.

Moreover, it is difficult to explain the employer's power to prefer permanent strike replacements over returning economic strikers unless, through the promise of permanent employment, the employer has incurred an obligation to those replacements. The employer makes offers of permanent employment to induce replacement workers to take jobs. But what is the legitimate and substantial business justification for later refusing to reinstate returning strikers if, as a matter of federal law, the employer is entitled to discharge the replacements in derogation of his promises to them? This power to override the economic strikers' statutory entitlement to reinstatement must be based on the common-sense notion that, in order to continue to operate the business, the employer was required to obligate himself to third parties in a manner inconsistent with the strikers' right to subsequent reinstatement. Certainly, avoidance of liability for breach of contract is a legitimate business objective. Because federal law apparently does not obligate the employer to fulfill its promises to the replacements, it must be the typical state law obligation to honor one's commitments that justifies the employer's disregard for the returning strikers' otherwise paramount statutory entitlement.

B

Because this case does not fit comfortably within labor preemption doctrine as heretofore developed by this Court and because I share the Court's doubt that Congress could have intended to deprive strike replacements of any remedy for obvious wrongs, the considerations noted above lead me to affirm the judgment below, despite the complex problems identified in the dissent. Cf. New York Tel. Co. v. New York State Labor Dept., 440 U.S., at 549 (concurring opinion) (evidence indicated that Congress decided to tolerate interference with labor law policies caused by unemployment insurance laws). I am not persuaded by the dissent's argument that the *Machinists* doctrine bars respondents' causes of action, for I do not believe that "Congress intended that the conduct involved be unregulated because left 'to be controlled by the free play of economic forces.'" Machinists v. Wisconsin Emp. Rel. Commn., 427 U.S. 132, 140 (1976), quoting NLRB v. Nash-Finch Co., 404 U.S. 138, 144 (1971). Unlike the self-help weapon at issue in *Machinists,* promising permanent employment to strike replacements involves offering to obligate oneself to third parties and inducing their reliance on that offer. In *Machinists,* the union's refusal to work overtime did not involve the rights and duties of anyone but the union and the employer.[4]

4. The right to hire replacements during a strike also differs from the self-help weapon at issue in Teamsters v. Morton, 377 U.S. 252 (1964), where Congress had pro-

The dissent's suggestion that a state action for misrepresentation would frustrate the policies of the Act by making employers more hesitant to promise permanent employment, assumes that under the federal scheme the employer is not meant to hesitate. But I believe that the hesitation engendered by potential contract damages and damages for misrepresentation is as consistent with federal law as it is with common sense and decency. The "free play of economic forces" contemplated by *Machinists* is the clash of weapons used by employer and union against one another. The free play of economic forces does not control one party's pursuit of its goals through imposition of harms on persons external to the dispute, because the economic contest creates no incentive for the other party to impose sanctions for such conduct. In the absence of protection for third parties' rights, the free play of economic forces actually is distorted; the economic cost of a weapon is understated.[5]

Much more troubling is the dissent's argument that the state law action will discourage the settlement of strikes. I agree that, where the employer has chosen to promise permanent employment to strike replacements, its potential liability to them would make the employer reluctant to settle by giving the strikers their old jobs. This problem, it seems to me, is inherent in Congress' choice to permit employers to offer permanent employment in order to obtain replacements. The potential dilemma is one the employer must consider at the time it chooses whether to promise permanent employment. If it makes no promises, settlement will not be impeded.[6]

Finally, I cannot agree that the doctrine of San Diego Building Trades Council v. Garmon, 359 U.S. 236 (1959), pre-empts respondents' contract action. Of course, if the strike is an unfair labor practice strike

---

scribed specific types of secondary boycotts, but not the type of boycott there at issue. Had Congress "focused upon" the power to hire strike replacements and made clear, by omission, that strike replacements were to be left without a remedy for breach of contract or deliberate misrepresentation, these actions would be pre-empted. There is no evidence, however, that Congress focused on this question. Absent congressional attention, the Court must construe the Act and determine its impact on state law in light of the wider contours of federal labor policy. In this case, it appears to me that state enforcement of promises of permanent employment through damages awards for breach of contract and misrepresentation is consistent with the nature of the federal weapon itself.

5. In some circumstances, Congress has permitted parties to a labor dispute to impose harms on third parties with impunity. See e.g., Teamsters v. Morton, 377 U.S. 252 (1964). But when Congress has granted such permission, it has done so with care. See n. 4 supra.

6. It is noteworthy, in light of the argument that permitting these state actions violates the rule in *Machinists*, that neither the Board nor the AFL-CIO can explain in whose favor such actions up the collective bargaining process. See Brief for NLRB 18-19; Brief for AFL-CIO 4-5. "Permanent" strike replacements will have certain rights, but employers will hesitate to make permanent offers; this hesitancy will redound to the benefit of striking unions, but those employers who do make such promises will hesitate to settle with the Union on terms involving return of the strikers. And while the fact that the employer's offers of permanent employment are legally meaningful will make them credible, thereby improving the employer's ability to attract replacement workers during an economic strike, it also will make the offers more costly, and therefore less attractive, for the employer.

and the employer has offered permanent employment to the replacements, federal labor law requires the employer to dismiss the replacements in derogation of his promise. As the dissent implicitly concedes, however, see post, at 8, n. 2, that conduct is "arguably required" does not necessarily mean it is "arguably protected" within the meaning of *Garmon.* Federal law did not require the employer to make the promise or to commit unfair labor practices. Moreover, as discussed above, once the promises are made and relied upon, I believe that federal law presumes they are in some manner enforceable. If federal law recognizes that the employer voluntarily has undertaken an obligation to the replacements, the fact that the employer commits an unfair labor practice making it impossible for him to fulfill that obligation should not shield the employer from compensating the replacement employees.

III

I fully recognize that this view may appear to put the employer between Scylla and Charybdis. Neither the Court's approach, nor the dissent's, however, provides the employer with a safer harbor. The Court's concept of a conditional promise will not help the employer attract replacements, and if the employer wishes to make a meaningful promise, the Court's opinion leaves the employer just where my approach would. And by draining all legal meaning from the promise of permanence, the dissent's approach leaves employers unable to attract any but the most gullible and unfortunate of potential replacement employees.

Although I cannot believe that Congress has reconciled the conflict between the striker's right to reinstatement and the employer's right to operate its business during a strike by requiring lies and broken promises to strike replacements to go unredressed, Congress certainly is free to prove me wrong. Congress also is free to resolve the great tensions inherent in this complex three-way struggle entirely within the framework of federal law. Certainly, some form of federal regulation of promises of permanent employment is the most desirable solution to the perplexing problem before the Court, because it would provide both consistency within federal labor law itself and uniformity throughout the Nation. At this time, however, it appears to me that the logic of the Act permits respondents' damages actions.

Accordingly, I concur in the judgment of the Court.[22]

Notes

1. Was the law in *Belknap* one of "general applicability?" Can you devise an argument that it was not? Is the inquiry relevent?

[22] Brennan, J., Marshall, J., and Powell, J., dissented.

2. As a matter of contract law, would the employer in the state suit have any defenses?

3. Justice White maintains that the legal rule in this case will have few behavior-adaptive effects because under the rule argued for by the Labor Board (state contract liability is preempted), honest employers would not make promises that they are not legally obligated to keep and potential replacements would refuse permanent jobs because they knew the promise of permanency was unenforceable. What are the assumptions underlying this argument? Are they plausible?

The majority opinion suggests that after this decision few, if any, employers will make unconditional offers of permanent jobs to replacements for strikers. One reason why an employer might make an unconditional offer is that a sufficient number of replacements cannot be hired without it. Are there any other reasons?

8

INTERNAL UNION AFFAIRS

A. ADMISSION TO MEMBERSHIP AND POLITICAL EXPENDITURES

Courts have generally refused to order a union to admit an individual into membership, thus affording unions the same freedom that has been accorded to churches and social clubs.[1] The first case that follows is an inroad into the historical practice; the second shows the more dominant view.

DIRECTORS GUILD OF AMERICA v. SUPERIOR COURT OF LOS ANGELES COUNTY

64 Cal. 2d 42, 409 P.2d 934 (1966)

[Plaintiff alleged that he had been promised a position as an assistant director in a television series — a promise that was then withdrawn when he was denied admission to defendant union because of the union's nepotism policy. The union allegedly maintained a closed shop through oral agreements with many employers. The court denied relief, reasoning that employment discrimination, not denial of membership, was at the core of plaintiff's complaint and that the exclusive jurisdiction of the NLRB preempted the state court's power to act. A state remedy would have been available, according to the court, had plaintiff shown that he had actually been employed and then arbitrarily denied union membership (citing California cases barring closed membership by a union controlling a closed shop)].

TOBRINER, J. . . .

The decisions of this court thus recognize that membership in the union means more than mere personal or social accommodation. Such

[1] See Chaffee, The Internal Affairs of Associations Not for Profit, 43 Harv. L. Rev. 993 (1930).

membership affords to the employee not only the opportunity to participate in the negotiation of the contract governing his employment but also the chance to engage in the institutional life of the union. Although in the case which involves interstate commerce the union must legally give fair representation to all the appropriate employees, whether or not they are members of the union, the union official, in the nature of political realities, will in all likelihood more diligently represent union members, who can vote him out of office, than employees whom he must serve only as a matter of abstract law.

Our decisions further recognize that the union functions as the medium for the exercise of industrial franchise. As Summers puts it, "The right to join a union involves the right to an economic ballot." (The Right to Join a Union (1947) 47 Colum. L. Rev. 33.) Participation in the union's affairs by the workman compares to the participation of the citizen in the affairs of his community. The union, as a kind of public service institution, affords to its members the opportunity to record themselves upon all matters affecting their relationships with the employer; it serves likewise as a vehicle for the expression of the membership's position on political and community issues. The shadowy right to "fair representation" by the union, accorded by the Act, is by no means the same as the hard concrete ability to vote and to participate in the affairs of the union.

The above grounds for condemnation of arbitrary rejection from membership apply as forcefully to the situation in which the union does not have a union shop contract as to that in which it does. The need of the worker for union participation is not reduced because the union does not enjoy a union shop; the basis for membership lies in the right and desirability of representation, not in the union's economic control of the job.

Our analysis applies, however, only to union membership for those employed in the appropriate craft or industry. To hold that a union must admit *all* persons who seek membership but are not employed in the craft or industry whose employees are represented by the union would raise serious social and economic questions. Any such sweeping ruling would subject the union to an influx of unemployed persons who could distort its function from representation of those working in the relevant craft or industry to purposes alien to such objectives. It would set up for state courts a test as to the scope of the union's obligation of representation which would conflict with the National Labor Relation Board's counterpart concept of the appropriate bargaining unit. It could gravely affect the basic structure of the union. Although we would hold that the union, even in the absence of the union shop, must admit to membership all qualified employed applicants, the instant complaint, lacking such allegation of employment, must fail. . . .

Notes

1. Professor Blumrosen describes why some unions limit their membership:

> A restrictive admission policy may limit the number of qualified workers, thus insuring jobs for members. It may create a labor shortage which may enhance the value of their services. It insures that the existing members will control the collective bargaining policies of the union which represents them. If the union can control the number of men in the labor market and the order in which employment opportunities are distributed, jobs will be distributed to favor the more entrenched members of the union. Thus, the justification for restricting admission to union membership lies in the economic self-interest of the workers who are already in the unions.[2]

Do §§8(b)(2) and 8(a)(3) provide sufficient protection for the worker whose job opportunities are controlled by the union but who cannot obtain membership? Some experience suggests not.

In parts of the country certain construction industry local unions are known as "closed locals" — membership is virtually impossible to obtain notwithstanding the area's level of employment. If too few union members are available to man a union construction job, the local will permit nonmembers (or travelers from another local of the same international) to be hired and will collect a service fee from them equivalent to union dues.

Union membership is so precious in some of these localities that "book mills" have sprung up from time to time. An unscrupulous local union officer in another part of the country will take a bribe to falsify a union membership (usually at least the applicant's residence requires falsification) and send it to the international union for a membership "book." This book is then deposited at the office of the closed local either in hopes that the closed local will accept a transfer into its membership or that it will permit the new "member" of the international to work by paying a traveler's fee.

These actions are prohibited by federal law. (The book mill practice is a federal crime.) A union employment referral system that discriminates in favor of union members violates §8(b)(2), and a union security agreement cannot be enforced against an employee to whom membership is unavailable. Yet unfair labor practice charges against closed locals are conspicuously rare. A federally guaranteed right to membership may be the only adequate remedy but it presently lacks a statutory basis.

[2] Blumrosen, Legal Protection Against Exclusion from Union Activities, 22 Ohio St. L.J. 21 (1961).

2. Did plaintiff in *Directors Guild* have a fair representation claim against the union on the authority of Brotherhood of Railroad Trainmen v. Howard, 343 U.S. 768 (1952), supra at p. 773?

OLIPHANT v. BROTHERHOOD OF LOCOMOTIVE FIREMEN & ENGINEMEN

156 F. Supp. 89 (N.D. Ohio 1957), affd., 262 F.2d 359 (6th Cir. 1958), cert. denied, 359 U.S. 935 (1959)

JONES, C. J.

This is an action brought by several Negro firemen employed by various southern railroads seeking an order from this court compelling the Brotherhood of Locomotive Firemen and Enginemen to admit them to membership. The Brotherhood has been certified as exclusive bargaining representative for these men, but the constitution of the Brotherhood forbids the admission of Negroes to membership. . . .

The real question is whether Federal action has deprived these Negro citizens of liberty or property without due process of law. It is the considered judgment of this court, without dealing with the question of whether the alleged right to become a member of a labor organization certified as exclusive bargaining representative is concerned with liberty or property, that sufficient Federal action is not shown to enable the courts to declare the Railway Labor Act, or any part thereof, an unconstitutional deprivation of liberty or property. The purpose of the Act was and is to promote industrial peace. Apparently the Act itself would not have been acceptable to the Congress if Negro membership in the agent had been required. In short, the representatives of all the people could not agree that any control over the membership policies of the agents certified was essential to the major purpose of the Act. However, expedience does not remove the taint of unconstitutionality, if such there be.

As is mentioned above, the Federal action taken by an agency of the Congress, was the certification of the Brotherhood of Locomotive Firemen and Enginemen as exclusive bargaining representative for the bargaining unit involved, which included persons who were not acceptable to membership under the Constitution of the Brotherhood. Actions by the Brotherhood can be attributed to the Congress only if the act of certification clothes the Brotherhood with some or all of the attributes of a Federal agency. The court is satisfied that this act is not sufficient to change the character of the organization from that of a private association to that of a governmental agency.

The court can feel that a situation is unjust and may need some remedial action, but unless upon sound equitable principles relief can be granted, the remedy does not lie with the courts. Certainly voluntary action by the defendant or Congressional legislation present the only corrective where a manifest inequality exists. It is pressed upon me that trends and policy with respect to rights not hitherto receiving adequate legislative sanction and security give support and direction to judicial mandate for the accomplishment of the plaintiffs' prayer and purpose here. But I cannot accept such a representation as valid without legislative action. To compel by judicial mandate membership in voluntary organizations where the Congress has knowingly and expressly permitted the bargaining agent to prescribe its own qualifications for membership would be usurping the legislative function. The Congress has entered the field of, and made provision for, labor relations and furnished means of adjusting labor disputes between employers and employees of interstate railways. For injustices due to discrimination or inadequate representation and participation to employees who are not members of the bargaining agent, the employees must look to the legislative, not the judicial branch of constitutional government.

Accordingly, for the reason that there is not sufficient Federal action to render the membership policies of this Brotherhood subject to judicial control, plaintiffs must be denied the relief requested.

Notes

1. Plaintiffs in *Oliphant,* but not the plaintiff in *Directors Guild,* would now have a cause of action under §703(c) of Title VII of the Civil Rights Act of 1964.

2. There are three theories by which union activity might be considered "governmental action" for Fifth and Fourteenth Amendment purposes.[3] The broadest, which might be termed the *totality of regulation theory,* focuses on the extensive federal regulation of unions and on the public functions that unions serve. By virtue of this extensive regulation, the argument goes, the government is so intertwined with the union that all union activity is governmental action. A second theory is that the monopoly of exclusive representation granted to unions by the NLRA, and the corresponding limitation of an individual employee's freedom, clothes the union with governmental action with respect to labor-management matters.

Finally, a theory of governmental action by court enforcement is suggested by NLRB v. Mansion House Center Management Corp., 473 F.2d 471 (8th Cir. 1973). There an employer resisted an order to bargain with a newly certified union on the ground that the union discriminated against blacks by refusing them membership and thus could not "fairly represent" the unit employees. The Eighth Circuit refused to enforce

[3] See Leslie, Governmental Action and Standing: NLRB Certification of Discriminatory Unions, 1974 Ariz. St. L.J. 35.

the Board's bargaining order because to do so, in the court's view, would be unconstitutional:

> When a governmental agency recognizes [a discriminatory] union to be the bargaining representative it significantly becomes a willing participant in the union's discriminatory practices. Although the union itself is not a governmental instrumentality the National Labor Relations Board is. . . . Moreover, here the Board seeks judicial enforcement of its order requiring collective bargaining in a federal court. Obviously, judicial enforcement of private discrimination cannot be sanctioned. Cf. Barrows v. Jackson, 346 U.S. 249 . . . Hurd v. Hodge, 334 U.S. 24 . . . Shelley v. Kraemer, 334 U.S. 1. . . .

The NLRB was initially persuaded by the Eighth Circuit's view[4] but in 1977 reversed itself and held that certification of a union does not involve "governmental action" so as to constitutionally require the Board to examine the union's membership policies.[5] The Board will continue to examine racially discriminatory union practices under its fair representation doctrine but it will not permit employers to raise alleged discriminatory union practices in order to block a union's certification or as a defense against a refusal-to-bargain charge.[6]

It has been suggested that while holding union admission policies to be governmental action would not itself yield unfortunate results, it would be difficult to limit the doctrine's applicability to union membership policies. For example, Professor Harry Wellington has shown that undesirable effects would result if such union activities as lobbying efforts and political campaign expenditures were found to constitute governmental action.[7] He argues that courts considering the constitutionality of union spending would be required to strike a balance among at least four factors: the purpose to which monies are being put, the relative importance of the objectives of spending to the organization, the support the spending has from the union members, and the impact of the spending program on dissenting members. The balance would need to be struck afresh on each challenged expenditure because the union's relationship to particular expenditures will vary from employer to employer, as it will with the passage of time, changed economic conditions, and evolving legal principles.

As Professor Wellington puts it, constitutional scrutiny of union spending "means immersion in collective bargaining, and an understanding of the relationship between economic power and political action." With these comments in mind, consider the next case.

[4] Bekins Moving & Storage Co., 211 N.L.R.B. 138 (1974).

[5] Handy Andy, 228 N.L.R.B. 447 (1977).

[6] Bell & Howell Co., 230 N.L.R.B. 420 (1977) (also suggesting the employer may lack standing to raise the issue).

[7] Wellington, The Constitution, the Labor Union and "Governmental Action," 60 Yale L.J. 345, 364-365, 372 (1961).

ABOOD v. DETROIT BOARD OF EDUCATION
431 U.S. 209 (1977)

STEWART, J.

The State of Michigan has enacted legislation authorizing a system for union representation of local governmental employees. A union and a local government employer are specifically permitted to agree to an "agency shop" arrangement, whereby every employee represented by a union — even though not a union member — must pay to the union, as a condition of employment, a service fee equal in amount to union dues. The issue before us is whether this arrangement violates the constitutional rights of government employees who object to public-sector unions as such or to various union activities financed by the compulsory service fees.

I

[The complaint, filed by a group of teachers, alleged that the dues required to be paid were used for "a number . . . of activities and programs which are economic, political, professional, scientific and religious in nature of which Plaintiffs do not approve . . . and which are not and will not be collective bargaining activities. . . ." It also alleged that the plaintiffs were opposed to public sector unionism itself.]

II

A

Consideration of the question whether an agency-shop provision in a collective-bargaining agreement covering governmental employees is, as such, constitutionally valid must begin with two cases in this Court that on their face go far toward resolving the issue. The cases are Railway Employees' Dept. v. Hanson, [351 U.S. 225], and Machinists v. Street, 367 U.S. 740.

In the *Hanson* case a group of railroad employees brought an action in a Nebraska Court to enjoin enforcement of a union-shop agreement. The challenged clause was authorized, and indeed shielded from any attempt by a State to prohibit it, by the Railway Labor Act. The trial court granted the relief requested. The Nebraska Supreme Court upheld the injunction on the ground that employees who disagreed with the objectives promoted by union expenditures were deprived of the freedom of association protected by the First Amendment. This Court agreed that "justifiable questions under the First and Fifth Amendments were presented," 351 U.S., at 231,[12] but reversed the judgment of the Nebraska Supreme Court on the merits. Acknowledging that "[m]uch might be said pro and con" about the union shop as a policy matter, the Court noted that it is Congress that is charged with identifying "[t]he ingredients of industrial peace and stabilized labor management relations. . . ." Id., at 323-234. Congress determined that it would promote peaceful labor relations to permit a union and an employer to conclude an agreement requiring employees who obtain the benefit of union representation to share its cost, and that legislative judgment was surely an allowable one. Id., at 235.

The record in *Hanson* contained no evidence that union dues were used to force ideological conformity or otherwise to impair the free expression of employees, and the Court noted that "[i]f 'assessments' are in fact imposed for purposes not germane to collective bargaining, a different problem would be presented." Ibid. (footnote omitted). But the Court squarely held that "the requirement for financial support of the collective-bargaining agency by all who receive the benefits of its work . . . does not violate . . . the First . . . Amendmen[t]." Id., at 238.

The Court faced a similar question several years later in the *Street* case, which also involved a challenge to the constitutionality of a union shop authorized by the Railway Labor Act. In *Street,* however, the record contained findings that the union treasury to which all employees were required to contribute had been used "to finance the campaigns of candidates for federal and state offices whom [the plaintiffs] opposed, and to promote the propagation of political and economic doctrines, concepts and ideologies with which [they] disagreed." 387 U.S., at 744.

The Court recognized, id., at 749, that these findings presented constitutional "questions of the utmost gravity" not decided in *Hanson, and* therefore considered whether the Act could fairly be construed to avoid these constitutional issues. 367 U.S., at 749-750. The Court concluded that the Act could be so construed, since only expenditures related to the union's functions in negotiating and administering the collective-bargaining agreement and adjusting grievances and disputes fell within "the reasons . . . accepted by Congress why authority to make union-shop agreements was justified," id., at 768. The Court ruled, therefore, that the use of compulsory union dues for political purposes violated the

12. Unlike §14(b) of the National Relations Act, the Railway Labor Act pre-empts any attempt by a State to prohibit a union-shop agreement. Had it not been for that federal statute, the union-shop provision at issue in *Hanson* would have been invalidated under Nebraska law. The *Hanson* Court accordingly reasoned that government action was present: "[T]he federal statute is the source of the power and authority by which any private rights are lost or sacrificed. . . . The enactment of the federal statute authorizing union shop agreements is the governmental action on which the Constitution operates. . . ." 351 U.S., at 232. See also id., at 232 n. 4 ("Once courts enforce the agreement the sanction of governments is, of course, put behind them. See Shelley v. Kraemer, 334 U.S. 1; Hurd v. Hodge, 334 U.S. 24; Barrows v. Jackson, 346 U.S. 249").

Act itself. Nonetheless, it found that an injunction against enforcement of the union-shop agreement as such as impermissible under *Hanson,* and remanded the case to the Supreme Court of Georgia so that a more limited remedy could be devised.

The holding in *Hanson,* as elaborated in *Street,* reflects familiar doctrines in the federal labor laws. The principle of exclusive union representation, which underlies the National Labor Relations Act as well as the Railway Labor Act, is a central element in the congressional structuring of industrial relations. The designation of a single representative avoids the confusion that would result from attempting to enforce two or more agreements specifying different terms and conditions of employment. It prevents inter-union rivalries from creating dissension within the workforce and eliminating the advantages to the employee of collectivization. It also frees the employer from the possibility of facing conflicting demands from different unions, and permits the employer and a single union to reach agreements and settlements that are not subject to attack from rival labor organizations.

The designation of a union as exclusive representative carries with it great responsibilities. The tasks of negotiating and administering a collective-bargaining agreement and representing the interests of employees in settling disputes and processing grievances are continuing and difficult ones. They often entail expenditure of much time and money. See *Street,* 367 U.S., at 760. The services of lawyers, expert negotiators, economists, and a research staff, as well as general administrative personnel, may be required. Moreover, in carrying out these duties, the union is obliged "fairly and equitably to represent all employees . . . , union and nonunion," within the relevant unit. Id., at 761. A union-shop arrangement has been thought to distribute fairly the cost of these activities among those who benefit; and it counteracts the incentive that employees might otherwise have to become "free riders" — to refuse to contribute to the union while obtaining benefits of union representation that necessarily accrue to all employees. Ibid.

To compel employees financially to support their collective-bargaining representative has an impact upon their First Amendment interests. An employee may very well have ideological objections to a wide variety of activities undertaken by the union in its role as exclusive representative. His moral or religious views about the desirability of abortion may not square with the union's policy in negotiating a medical benefits plan. One individual might disagree with a union policy of negotiating limits on the right to strike, believing that to be the road to serfdom for the working class, while another might have economic or political objections to unionism itself. An employee might object to the union's wage policy because it violates guidelines designed to limit inflation, or might object to the union's seeking a clause in the collective-bargaining agreement proscribing racial discrimination. The examples could be multiplied. To be required to help finance the union as a collective-bargaining agent might well be thought, therefore, to interfere in some way with an employee's freedom to associate for the advancement of ideas, or to refrain from doing so, as he sees fit. But the judgment clearly made in *Hanson* and *Street* is that such interference as exists is constitutionally justified by the legislative assessment of the important contribution of the union shop to the system of labor relations established by Congress. "The furtherance of the common cause leaves some leeway for the leadership of the group. As long as they act to promote the cause which justified bringing the group together, the individual cannot withdraw his financial support merely because he disagrees with the group's strategy. If that were allowed, we would be reversing the *Hanson* case, sub silentio." Machinists v. Street, supra, at 778 (Douglas, J., concurring).

B

The National Labor Relations Act leaves regulation of the labor relations of state and local governments to the States. Michigan has chosen to establish for local government units a regulatory scheme which, although not identical in every respect to the NLRA or the Railway Labor Act, is broadly modeled after federal law. Under Michigan law employees of local government units enjoy rights parallel to those protected under federal legislation: the rights to self-organization and to bargain collectively, and the right to secret-ballot representation elections.

Several aspects of Michigan law that mirror provisions of the Railway Labor Act are of particular importance here. A union that obtains the support of a majority of employees in the appropriate bargaining unit is designated the exclusive representative of those employees. Mich. Comp. Laws §423.211 (1970). A union so designated is under a duty of fair representation to all employees in the unit, whether or not union members. And in carrying out all of its various responsibilities, a recognized union may seek to have an agency-shop clause included in a collective-bargaining agreement. Mich. Comp. Laws §423.210(1)(c) (1970). . . .

The governmental interests advanced by the agency-shop provision in the Michigan statute are much the same as those promoted by similar provisions in federal labor law. The confusion and conflict that could arise if rival teachers' unions, holding quite different views as to the proper class hours, class sizes, holidays, tenure provisions, and grievance procedures, each sought to obtain the employer's agreement, are no different in kind from the evils that the exclusivity rule in the Railway Labor Act was designed to avoid. The desirability of labor peace is no less important in the public sector, nor is the risk of "free riders" any smaller.

Our province is not to judge the wisdom of Michigan's decision to authorize the agency-shop in public employment. Rather, it is to adjudicate the constitutionality of that decision. The same important government interests recognized in the *Hanson* and *Street* cases presumptively support the impingement upon associational freedom created by the agency-shop here at issue. Thus, insofar as the service charge is used to finance expenditures by the Union for the purposes of collective bargaining, contract administration, and grievance adjustment, those two decisions of this Court appear to require validation of the agency-shop agreement before us.

While recognizing the apparent precedential weight of the *Hanson* and *Street* cases, the appellants advance two reasons why those decisions should not control decision of the present case. First, the appellants note that it is *government employment* that is involved here, thus directly implicating constitutional guarantees, in contrast to the private employment that was the subject of the *Hanson* and *Street* decisions. Second, the appellants say that in the public sector collective bargaining itself is inherently "political," and that to require them to give financial support to it is to require the "ideological conformity" that the Court expressly found absent in the *Hanson* case. 351 U.S., at 238. We find neither argument persuasive.

Because it is employment by the State that is here involved, the appellants suggest that this case is governed by a long line of decisions holding that public employment cannot be conditioned upon the surrender of First Amendment rights. But, while the actions of public employers surely constitute "state action," the union shop, as authorized by the Railway Labor Act, also was found to result from governmental action in *Hanson.* The plaintiffs' claims in *Hanson* failed, not because there was no governmental action but because there was no First Amendment violation.[23] The appellants' reliance on the "unconstitutional conditions" doctrine is therefore misplaced.

23. Nothing in our opinion embraces the "premise that public employers are under no greater constitutional constraints than their counterparts in the private sector," post, at 245 (Powell, J., concurring in judgment), or indicates that private collective-bargaining agreements are, without more, subject to constitutional constraints, see post, at 252. We compare the agency-shop agreement in this case to those executed under the Railway Labor Act simply because the existence of governmental action in both contexts requires analysis of the free expression question.

It is somewhat startling, particularly in view of the concession that *Hanson* was premised on a finding that governmental action was present, see post, at 246 (Powell, J., concurring in judgment), to read in Mr. Justice Powell's concurring opinion that *Hanson* and *Street* "provide little or no guidance for the constitutional issues presented in this case," post, at 254. *Hanson* nowhere suggested that the constitutional scrutiny of the agency-shop agreement was watered down because the governmental action operated less directly than is true in a case such as the present one. Indeed, Mr. Justice Douglas, the author of *Hanson,* expressly repudiated that suggestion. . . .

The appellants' second argument is that in any event collective bargaining in the public sector is inherently "political" and thus requires a different result under the First and Fourteenth Amendments. This contention rests upon the important and often-noted differences in the nature of collective bargaining in the public and private sectors. . . .

The distinctive nature of public-sector bargaining has led to widespread discussion about the extent to which the law governing labor relations in the private sector provides an appropriate model. . . . But although Michigan has not adopted the federal model of labor relations in every respect, it has determined that labor stability will be served by a system of exclusive representation and the permissive use of an agency shop in public employment. As already stated, there can be no principled basis for according that decision less weight in the constitutional balance than was given in *Hanson* to the congressional judgment reflected in the Railway Labor Act. The only remaining constitutional inquiry evoked by the appellants' argument, therefore, is whether a public employee has a weightier First Amendment interest than a private employee in not being compelled to contribute to the costs of exclusive union representation. We think he does not.

Public employees are not basically different from private employees; on the whole, they have the same sort of skills, the same needs, and seek the same advantages. "The uniqueness of public employment is *not in the employees* nor in the work performed; the uniqueness is in the special character of the employer." Summers, Public Sector Bargaining: Problems of Governmental Decisionmaking, 44 Cin. L. Rev. 669, 670 (1975) (emphasis added). The very real differences between exclusive-agent collective bargaining in the public and private sectors are not such as to work any greater infringement upon the First Amendment interests of public employees.

We conclude that the Michigan Court of Appeals was correct in viewing this Court's decision in *Hanson* and *Street* as controlling in the present case insofar as the service charges are applied to collective-bargaining, contract administration, and grievance-adjustment purposes.

C

Because the Michigan Court of Appeals rules that state law "sanctions the use of nonunion members' fees for purposes other than collective bargaining," 60 Mich. App., at 99, 230 N.W.2d, at 326, and because the complaints allege that such expenditures were made, this case presents constitutional issues not decided in *Hanson* or *Street*. Indeed, *Street* embraced an interpretation of the Railway Labor Act not without its difficulties, see 367 U.S., at 784-786 (Black, J., dissenting); id., at 799-803

(Frankfurter, J., dissenting), precisely to avoid facing the constitutional issues presented by the use of union-shop dues for political and ideological purposes unrelated to collective bargaining, id., at 749-750. Since the state court's construction of the Michigan statute is authoritative, however, we must confront those issues in this case.

Our decisions establish with unmistakable clarity that the freedom of an individual to associate for the purpose of advancing beliefs and ideas is protected by the First and Fourteenth Amendments. Equally clear is the proposition that a government may not require an individual to relinquish rights guaranteed him by the First Amendment as a condition of public employment. The appellants argue that they fall within the protection of these cases because they have been prohibited, not from actively associating, but rather from refusing to associate. They specifically argue that they may constitutionally prevent the Union's spending a part of their required service fees to contribute to political candidates and to express political views unrelated to its duties as exclusive bargaining representative. We have concluded that this argument is a meritorious one.

One of the principles underlying the Court's decision in Buckley v. Valeo, 424 U.S. 1, was that contributing to an organization for the purpose of spreading a political message is protected by the First Amendment. Because "[m]aking a contribution . . . enables like-minded persons to pool their resources in furtherance of common political goals," id., at 22, the Court reasoned that limitations upon the freedom to contribute "implicate fundamental First Amendment interests," id., at 23.

The fact that the appellants are compelled to make, rather than prohibited from making, contributions for political purposes works no less an infringement of their constitutional rights. For at the heart of the First Amendment is the notion that an individual should be free to believe as he will, and that in a free society one's beliefs should be shaped by his mind and his conscience rather than coerced by the State. . . .

These principles prohibit a State from compelling any individual to affirm his belief in God, or to associate with a political party, as a condition of retaining public employment. They are no less applicable to the case at bar, and they thus prohibit the appellees from requiring any of the appellants to contribute to the support of an ideological cause he may oppose as a condition of holding a job as a public school teacher.

We do not hold that a union cannot constitutionally spend funds for the expression of political views, on behalf of political candidates, or toward the advancement of other ideological causes not germane to its duties as collective-bargaining representative. Rather, the Constitution requires only that such expenditures be financed from charges, dues, or assessments paid by employees who do not object to advancing those ideas and who are not coerced into doing so against their will by the threat of loss of governmental employment.

There will, of course, be difficult problems in drawing lines between collective-bargaining activities, for which contributions may be compelled, and ideological activities unrelated to collective bargaining, for which such compulsion is prohibited. The Court held in *Street,* as a matter of statutory construction, that a similar line must be drawn under the Railway Labor Act, but in the public sector the line may be somewhat hazier. The process of establishing a written collective-bargaining agreement prescribing the terms and conditions of public employment may require not merely concord at the bargaining table, but subsequent approval by other public authorities; related budgetary and appropriations decisions might be seen as an integral part of the bargaining process. We have no occasion in this case, however, to try to define such a dividing line. The case comes to us after a judgment on the pleadings, and there is no evidentiary record of any kind. The allegations in the complaints are general ones, see supra, at 212-213, and the parties have neither briefed nor argued the questions of what specific Union activities in the present context properly fall under the definition of collective bargaining. The lack of factual concreteness and adversary presentation to aid us in approaching the difficult line-drawing questions highlight the importance of avoiding unnecessary decision of constitutional questions. All that we decide is that the general allegations in the complaints, if proved, establish a cause of action under the First and Fourteenth Amendments.

III

In determining what remedy will be appropriate if the appellants prove their allegations, the objective must be to devise a way of preventing compulsory subsidization of ideological activity by employees who object thereto without restricting the Union's ability to require every employee to contribute to the cost of collective-bargaining activities.[35] This task is simplified by the guidance to be had from prior decisions. In *Street,* the plaintiffs had proved at trial that expenditures were being made for political purposes of various kinds, and the Court found those expenditures illegal under the Railway Labor Act. Moreover, in that case each plaintiff had "made known to the union representing his craft or class his dissent from the use of his money for political causes which he opposes." 367 U.S., at 750; see id., at 771. The Court found that "[i]n that circumstance, the respective unions were without power to use pay-

35. It is plainly not an adequate remedy to limit the use of the actual dollars collected from dissenting employees to collective-bargaining purposes. . . .

ments thereafter tendered by them for such political causes." Ibid. Since, however, *Hanson* had established that the union-shop agreement was not unlawful as such, the Court held that to enjoin its enforcement would "[sweep] too broadly." 367 U.S., at 771. The Court also found that an injunction prohibiting the union from expending dues for political purposes would be inappropriate, not only because of the basic policy reflected in the Norris-La Guardia Act against enjoining labor unions, but also because those union members who do wish part of their dues to be used for political purposes have a right to associate to that end "without being silenced by the dissenters." Id., at 772-773.

After noting that "dissent is not to be presumed" and that only employees who have affirmatively made known to the union their opposition to political uses of their funds are entitled to relief, the Court sketched two possible remedies: first, "an injunction against expenditure for political causes opposed by each complaining employee of a sum, from those moneys to be spent by the union for political purposes, which is so much of the moneys exacted from him as is the proportion of the union's total expenditures made for such political activities to the union's total budget"; and second, restitution of a fraction of union dues paid equal to the fraction of total union expenditures that were made for political purposes opposed by the employee. Id., at 774-775.

The Court again considered the remedial question in Railway Clerks v. Allen, 373 U.S. 113. In that case employees who had refused to pay union-shop dues obtained injunctive relief in state court against enforcement of the union-shop agreement. The employees had not notified the union prior to bringing the lawsuit of their opposition to political expenditures, and at trial, their testimony was principally that they opposed such expenditures, as a general matter. The Court held that the employees had adequately established their cause of action by manifesting "opposition to *any* political expenditures by the union," (emphasis in original), and that the requirement in *Street* that dissent be affirmatively indicated was satisfied by the allegations in the complaint that was filed. The Court indicated again the appropriateness of the two remedies sketched in *Street;* reversed the judgment affirming issuance of the injunction; and remanded for determination of which expenditures were properly to be characterized as political and what percentage of total union expenditures they constituted.

The Court in *Allen* described a "practical decree" that could properly be entered, providing for (1) the refund of a portion of the exacted funds in the proportion that union political expenditures bear to total union expenditures, and (2) the reduction of future exactions by the same proportion. Recognizing the difficulties posed by judicial administration of such a remedy, the Court also suggested that it would be highly desirable for unions to adopt a "voluntary plan by which dissenters would be afforded an internal union remedy." This last suggestion is particularly relevant to the case at bar, for the Union has adopted such a plan since the commencement of this litigation.[41]

Although *Street* and *Allen* were concerned with statutory rather than constitutional violations, that difference surely could not justify any lesser relief in this case. Judged by the standards of those cases, the Michigan Court of Appeals' ruling that the appellants were entitled to no relief at this juncture was unduly restrictive. For all the reasons outlined in *Street,* the court was correct in denying the broad injunctive relief requested. But in holding that as a prerequisite to any relief each appellant must indicate to the Union the *specific* expenditures to which he objects, the Court of Appeals ignored the clear holding of *Allen.* As in *Allen,* the employees here indicated in their pleadings that they opposed ideological expenditures of *any* sort that are unrelated to collective bargaining. To require greater specificity would confront an individual employee with the dilemma of relinquishing either his right to withhold his support of ideological causes to which he objects or his freedom to maintain his own beliefs without public disclosure. It would also place on each employee the considerable burden of monitoring all of the numerous and shifting expenditures made by the Union that are unrelated to its duties as exclusive bargaining representative.

The Court of Appeals thus erred in holding that the plaintiffs are entitled to no relief if they can prove the allegations contained in their complaints, and in depriving them of an opportunity to establish their right to appropriate relief, such, for example, as the kind of remedies described in *Street* and *Allen.* In view of the newly adopted Union internal remedy, it may be appropriate under Michigan law, even if not strictly required by any doctrine of exhaustion of remedies, to defer further judicial proceedings pending the voluntary utilization by the parties of that internal remedy as a possible means of settling the dispute.

The judgment is vacated, and the case is remanded for further proceedings not inconsistent with this opinion.[8]

STEVENS, J., concurring.

By joining the opinion of the Court, including its discussion of possible remedies, I do not imply — nor do I understand the Court to imply

41. Under the procedure adopted by the Union, as explained in the appellee's brief, a dissenting employee may protest at the beginning of each school year the expenditure of any part of his agency-shop fee for "'activities or causes of a political nature or involving controversial issues of public importance only incidentally related to wages, hours, and conditions of employment.'" The employee is then entitled to a pro rata refund of his service charge in accordance with the calculation of the portion of total Union expenses for the specified purposes. The calculation is made in the first instance by the Union, but is subject to review by an impartial board.

[8] Rehnquist, J., concurred.

— that the remedies described in Machinists v. Street, 367 U.S. 740, and Railway Clerks v. Allen, 373 U.S. 113, would necessarily be adequate in this case or in any other case. More specifically, the Court's opinion does not foreclose the argument that the Union should not be permitted to exact a service fee from nonmembers without first establishing a procedure which will avoid the risk that their funds will be used, even temporarily, to finance ideological activities unrelated to collective bargaining. Any final decision on the appropriate remedy must await the full development of the facts at trial.

POWELL, J., with whom BURGER, C. J., and BLACKMUN, J., join, concurring in the judgment.

[The opinion first argued that in the *Hanson* and *Street* decisions the Court had not reached the issues presented in the instant case.]

The Court today holds that compelling an employee to finance a union's "ideological activities unrelated to collective bargaining" violates the First Amendment, regardless of any asserted governmental justification. But the Court also decides that compelling an employee to finance any union activity that may be "related" in some way to collective bargaining is permissible under the First Amendment because such compulsion is "relevant or appropriate" to asserted governmental interests. And the Court places the burden of litigation on the individual. In order to vindicate his First Amendment rights in a union shop, the individual employee apparently must declare his opposition to the union and initiate a proceeding to determine what part of the union's budget has been allocated to activities that are both "ideological" and "unrelated to collective bargaining."

I can agree neither with the Court's rigid two-tiered analysis under the First Amendment, nor with the burden it places on the individual. Under First Amendment principles that have become settled since *Hanson* and *Street* were decided, it is now clear, first, that *any* withholding of financial support for a public-sector union is within the protection of the First Amendment; and second, that the State should bear the burden of proving that any union dues or fees that it requires of nonunion employees are needed to serve paramount governmental interests.

The initial question is whether a requirement of a school board that all of its employees contribute to a teachers' union as a condition of employment impinges upon the First Amendment interests of those who refuse to support the union, whether because they disapprove of unionization of public employees or because they object to certain union activities or positions. The Court answers this question in the affirmative: "The fact that [government employees] are compelled to make . . . contributions for political purposes works . . . an infringement of their constitutional rights," and *any* compelled support for a union "has an impact upon" and may be thought to "interfere in some way with" First Amendment interests. I agree with the Court as far as it goes, but I would make it more explicit that compelling a government employee to give financial support to a union in the public sector — regardless of the uses to which the union puts the contribution — impinges seriously upon interests in free speech and association protected by the First Amendment.

In Buckley v. Valeo, 424 U.S. 1 (1976), we considered the constitutional validity of the Federal Election Campaign Act of 1971, as amended in 1974, which in one of its provisions limited the amounts that individuals could contribute to federal election campaigns. We held that these limitations on political contributions "impinge on protected associational freedoms": "Making a contribution, like joining a political party, serves to affiliate a person with a candidate. In addition, it enables like-minded persons to pool their resources in furtherance of common political goals. The Act's contribution ceilings thus limit one important means of associating with a candidate or committee. . . ." Id., at 22.

That *Buckley* dealt with a contribution limitation rather than a contribution requirement does not alter its importance for this case. An individual can no more be required to affiliate with a candidate by making a contribution than he can be prohibited from such affiliation. The only question after *Buckley* is whether a union in the public sector is sufficiently distinguishable from a political candidate or committee to remove the withholding of financial contributions from First Amendment protection. In my view no principled distinction exists.

The ultimate objective of a union in the public sector, like that of a political party, is to influence public decisionmaking in accordance with the views and perceived interests of its membership. Whether a teachers' union is concerned with salaries and fringe benefits, teacher qualifications and in-service training, pupil-teacher ratios, length of the school day, student discipline, or the content of the high school curriculum, its objective is to bring school board policy and decisions into harmony with its own views. Similarly, to the extent that school board expenditures and policy are guided by decisions made by the municipal, State, and Federal Governments, the union's objective is to obtain favorable decisions — and to place persons in positions of power who will be receptive to the union's viewpoint. In these respects, the public-sector union is indistinguishable from the traditional political party in this country.

What distinguishes the public-sector union from the political party — and the distinction is a limited one — is that most of its members are employees who share similar economic interests and who may have a common professional perspective on some issues of public policy. Public school teachers, for example, have a common interest in fair teachers' salaries and reasonable pupil-teacher ratios. This suggests the possibility of a limited range of probable agreement among the class of individuals that a public-sector union is organized to represent. But I am unable to see why the likelihood of an area of consensus in the group should remove the protection of the First Amendment for the disagreements that inevitably will occur. Certainly, if individual teachers are ideologically opposed to public-sector unionism itself, as are the appellants in this case, one would think that compelling them to affiliate with the union by contributing to it infringes their First Amendment rights to the same degree as compelling them to contribute to a political party. Under the First Amendment, the protection of speech does not turn on the likelihood or frequency of its occurrence.

Nor is there any basis here for distinguishing "collective-bargaining activities" from "political activities" so far as the interests protected by the First Amendment are concerned. Collective bargaining in the public sector is "political" in any meaningful sense of the word. This is most obvious when public-sector bargaining extends — as it may in Michigan — to such matters of public policy as the educational philosophy that will inform the high school curriculum. But it is also true when public-sector bargaining focuses on such "bread and butter" issues as wages, hours, vacations, and pensions. Decisions on such issues will have a direct impact on the level of public services, priorities within state and municipal budgets, creation of bonded indebtedness, and tax rates. The cost of public education is normally the largest element of a county or municipal budget. Decisions reached through collective bargaining in the schools will affect not only the teachers and the quality of education, but also the taxpayers and the beneficiaries of other important public services. Under our democratic system of government, decisions on these critical issues of public policy have been entrusted to elected officials who ultimately are responsible to the voters.

Disassociation with a public-sector union and the expression of disagreement with its positions and objectives therefore lie at "the core of those activities protected by the First Amendment." Elrod v. Burns, 427 U.S. 347, 356 (1976) (plurality opinion). . . .

As the public-sector agency shop unquestionably impinges upon the interests protected by the First Amendment, I turn to the justifications offered for it by the Detroit Board of Education.[13]. . .

As the Court points out, the interests advanced for the compulsory agency shop that the Detroit Board of Education has entered into are much the same as those advanced for federal legislation permitting vol-

13. Compelled support of a private association is fundamentally different from compelled support of government. Clearly, a local school board does not need to demonstrate a compelling state interest every time it spends a taxpayer's money in ways the taxpayer finds abhorrent. But the reason for permitting the government to compel the payment of taxes and to spend money on controversial projects is that the government is representative of the people. The same cannot be said of a union, which is representative only of one segment of the population, with certain common interests. The withholding of financial support is fully protected as speech in this context.

untary agency-shop agreements in the private sector. The agency shop is said to be a necessary adjunct to the principle of exclusive union representation; it is said to reduce the risk that nonunion employees will become "free riders" by fairly distributing the costs of exclusive representation; and it is said to promote the cause of labor peace in the public sector. While these interests may well justify encouraging agency-shop arrangements in the private sector, there is far less reason to believe they justify the intrusion upon First Amendment rights that results from compelled support for a union as a condition of government employment.

In Madison School Dist. v. Wisconsin Employment Relations Commn., 429 U.S. 167, 175 (1976), we expressly reserved judgment on the constitutional validity of the exclusivity principle in the public sector. The Court today decides this issue summarily: "The confusion and conflict that could arise if rival teachers' unions, holding quite different views as to the proper class hours, class sizes, holidays, tenure provisions, and grievance procedures, each sought to obtain the employer's agreement, are no different in kind from the evils that the exclusivity in the Railway Labor Act was designed to avoid."

I would have thought that "conflict" in ideas about the way in which government should operate was among the most fundamental values protected by the First Amendment. See New York Times Co. v. Sullivan, 376 U.S. 254, 270 (1964). That the "Constitution does not require all public acts to be done in town meeting or an assembly of the whole," Bi-Metallic Investment Co. v. State Bd. of Equalization, 239 U.S. 441, 445 (1915), does not mean that a State or municipality may agree to set public policy on an unlimited range of issues in closed negotiations with "one category of interested individuals." *Madison School Dist.,* supra, at 175. Such a commitment by a governmental body to exclude minority viewpoints from the councils of government would violate directly the principle that "government must afford all points of view an equal opportunity to be heard." Police Dept. of Chicago v. Mosley, 408 U.S. 92, 96 (1972).

The Court points out that the minority employee is not barred by the exclusivity principle from expressing his viewpoint. In a limited sense this may be true. The minority employee is excluded in theory only from engaging in a meaningful dialogue with his employer on the subjects of collective bargaining, a dialogue that is reserved to the union. It is possible that paramount government interests may be found — at least with respect to certain narrowly defined subjects of bargaining — that would support this restriction on First Amendment interests. But "the burden is on the government to show the existence of such an interest." Elrod v. Burns, 427 U.S., at 362 (plurality opinion). Because this appeal reaches this Court on a motion to dismiss, the record is barren of any demonstration by the State that excluding minority views from the processes by which governmental policy is made is necessary to serve overriding governmental objectives. For the Court to sustain the exclusivity principle in the public sector in the absence of a carefully documented record is to ignore, rather than respect, "the importance of avoiding unnecessary decision of constitutional questions."

The same may be said of the asserted interests in eliminating the "free rider" effect and in preserving labor peace. It may be that the Board of Education is in a position to demonstrate that these interests are of paramount importance and that requiring public employees to pay certain union fees and dues as a condition of employment is necessary to serve those interests under an exclusive bargaining scheme. On the present record there is no assurance whatever that this is the case.[16]

Before today it had been well established that when state law intrudes upon protected speech, the State itself must shoulder the burden of proving that its action is justified by overriding state interests. The Court, for the first time in a First Amendment case, simply reverses this principle. Under today's decision, a nonunion employee who would vindicate his First Amendment rights apparently must initiate a proceeding to prove that the union has allocated some portion of its budget to "ideological activities unrelated to collective bargaining." I would adhere to established First Amendment principles and require the State to come forward and demonstrate, as to each union expenditure for which it would exact support from minority employees, that the compelled contribution is necessary to serve overriding governmental objectives. This placement of the burden of litigation, not the Court's, gives appropriate protection to First Amendment rights without sacrificing ends of government that may be deemed important.

16. Unions in the public sector may be expected to spend money in a broad variety of ways, some of which are more closely related to collective bargaining than others, and some of which are more likely to stimulate "ideological" opposition than others. With respect to many of these expenditures, arriving at the appropriate reconciliation of the employee's First Amendment interests with the asserted governmental interests will be difficult.

I should think that on some narrowly defined economic issues — teachers' salaries and pension benefits, for example — the case for requiring the teachers to speak through a single representative would be quite strong, while the concomitant limitation of First Amendment rights would be relatively insignificant. On such issues the case for requiring all teachers to contribute to the clearly identified costs of collective bargaining also would be strong, while the interest of the minority teacher, who is benefited directly, in withholding support would be comparatively weak. On other issues — including such questions as how best to educate the young — the strong First Amendment interests of dissenting employees might be expected to prevail.

The same may be said of union activities other than bargaining. The processing of individual grievances may be an important union service for which a fee could be exacted with minimal intrusion on First Amendment interests. But other union actions — such as a strike against a public agency — may be so controversial and of such general public concern that compelled financial support by all employees should not be permitted under the Constitution.

ELLIS v. BROTHERHOOD OF RAILWAY CLERKS

104 S. Ct. 1883 (1984)

WHITE, J.

In 1951, Congress amended the Railway Labor Act (the Act or RLA) to permit what it had previously prohibited — the union shop. Section 2, Eleventh of the Act permits a union and an employer to require all employees in the relevant bargaining unit to join the union as a condition of continued employment. 45 U.S.C. §152, Eleventh. In Machinists v. Street, 367 U.S. 740 (1960), the Court held that the Act does not authorize a union to spend an objecting employee's money to support political causes. The use of employee funds for such ends is unrelated to Congress' desire to eliminate "free riders" and the resentment they provoked. The Court did not express a view as to "expenditures for activities in the area between the costs which led directly to the complaint as to 'free riders,' and the expenditures to support union political activities." Petitioners challenge just such expenditures.

I

In 1971, respondent Brotherhood of Railway, Airline and Steamship Clerks (the union or BRAC) and Western Airlines implemented a previously negotiated agreement requiring that all Western's clerical employees join the union within 60 days of commencing employment. As the agreement has been interpreted, employees need not become formal members of the union, but must pay agency fees equal to members' dues. Petitioners are present or former clerical employees of Western who objected to the use of their compelled dues for specified union activities. They do not contest the legality of the union shop as such, nor could they. See Railway Employes' Department v. Hanson, 351 U.S. 225 (1956). They do contend, however, that they can be compelled to contribute no more than their pro rata share of the expenses of negotiating agreements and settling grievances with Western Airlines. Respondents — the national union, its board of adjustment, and three locals — concede that the statutory authorization of the union shop does not permit the use of petitioners' contributions for union political or ideological activities, see Machinists v. Street, supra, and have adopted a rebate program covering such expenditures. The parties disagree about the adequacy of the rebate scheme, and about the legality of burdening objecting employees with six specific union expenses that fall between the extremes identified in *Hanson* and *Street:* the quadrennial Grand Lodge convention, litigation not involving the negotiation of agreements or settlement of grievances, union publications, social activities, death benefits for employees, and general organizing efforts.

The District Court for the Southern District of California granted summary judgment to petitioners on the question of liability. . . .

The Court of Appeals for the Ninth Circuit affirmed in part and reversed in part. . . . We hold that the union's rebate scheme was inadequate and that the Court of Appeals erred in finding that the RLA authorizes a union to spend compelled dues for its general litigation and organizing efforts. . . .

II

B

As the Court of Appeals pointed out, there is language in this Court's cases to support the validity of a rebate program. *Street* suggested "restitution to each individual employee of that portion of his money which the union expended, despite his notification, for the political causes to which he had advised the union he was opposed." 367 U.S., at 775. See also Abood v. Detroit Board of Education, 431 U.S. 209, 238 (1977). On the other hand, we suggested a more precise advance reduction scheme in Railway Clerks v. Allen, 373 U.S. 113, 122 (1963), where we described a "practical decree" comprising a refund of exacted funds in the proportion that union political expenditures bore to total union expenditures and the reduction of future exactions by the same proportion. Those opinions did not, nor did they purport to, pass upon the statutory or constitutional adequacy of the suggested remedies. Doing so now, we hold that the pure rebate approach is inadequate.

By exacting and using full dues, then refunding months later the portion that it was not allowed to exact in the first place, the union effectively charges the employees for activities that are outside the scope of the statutory authorization. The cost to the employee is, of course, much less than if the money was never returned, but this is a difference of degree only. The harm would be reduced were the union to pay interest on the amount refunded, but respondents did not do so. Even then the union obtains an involuntary loan for purposes to which the employee objects.

The only justification for this union borrowing would be administrative convenience. But there are readily available alternatives, such as advance reduction of dues and/or interest-bearing escrow accounts, that place only the slightest additional burden, if any, on the union. Given the existence of acceptable alternatives, the union cannot be allowed to commit dissenters' funds to improper uses even temporarily. A rebate scheme reduces but does not eliminate the statutory violation.

III

Petitioners' primary submission is that the use of their fees to finance the challenged activities violated the First Amendment. This argument assumes that the Act allows these allegedly unconstitutional exactions. When the constitutionality of a statute is challenged, this Court first ascertains whether the statute can be reasonably construed to avoid the constitutional difficulty. As the Court noted when faced with a similar claim in *Street,* "the restraints against unnecessary constitutional decisions counsel against" addressing petitioners' constitutional claims "unless we must conclude that Congress, in authorizing a union shop under §2, Eleventh also meant that the labor organization receiving an employee's money should be free, despite the employee's objection, to spend his money" for these activities. We therefore first inquire whether the statute permits the union to charge petitioners for any of the challenged expenditures.

IV

Section 2, Eleventh contains only one explicit limitation to the scope of the union shop agreement: objecting employees may not be required to tender "fines and penalties" normally required of union members. 45 U.S.C. §152, Eleventh. If there were nothing else, an inference could be drawn from this limited exception that all other payments obtained from voluntary members can also be required of those whose membership is forced upon them. Indeed, several witnesses appearing before the congressional committees objected to the absence of any explicit limitation on the scope or amount of fees and dues that could be compelled. That Congress enacted the provision over these objections arguably indicates that it was willing to tolerate broad exactions from objecting employees.

Furthermore, Congress was well aware of the broad scope of traditional union activities. The hearing witnesses referred in general terms to the costs of "[a]ctivities of labor organizations resulting in the procurement of employee benefits," Hearings on H.R. 7789 before the House Committee on Interstate and Foreign Commerce, 81st Cong., 2d Sess., 10 (1950) (testimony of George Harrison), and the "policies and activities of labor unions," id., at 50 (testimony of George Weaver). Indeed, it was pointed out that not only was the "securing and maintaining of a collective bargaining agreement . . . an expensive undertaking . . . , there are many other programs of a union" that require the financial and moral support of the workers. Id., at 275; Hearings on S. 3295 before a Subcommittee of the Senate Committee on Labor and Public Welfare, 81st Cong., 2d Sess., 236 (1950) (statement of Theodore Brown). In short, Congress was adequately informed about the broad scope of union activities aimed at benefiting union members, and, in light of the absence of express limitations in §2, Eleventh it could be plausibly argued that Congress purported to authorize the collection from involuntary members of the same dues paid by regular members. This view, however, was squarely rejected in *Street,* over the dissents of three Justices, and the cases that followed it.

In *Street,* the Court observed that the purpose of §2, Eleventh was to make it possible to require all members of a bargaining unit to pay their fair share of the costs of performing the function of exclusive bargaining agent. The union shop would eliminate "free riders," employees who obtained the benefit of the union's participation in the machinery of the Act without financially supporting the union. That purpose, the Court held, Congress intended to be achieved without "vesting the unions with unlimited power to spend exacted money." 367 U.S., at 768. Undoubtedly, the union could collect from all employees what it needed to defray the expenses entailed in negotiating and administering a collective agreement and in adjusting grievances and disputes. The Court had so held in Railway Employes Department v. Hanson, 351 U.S. 225 (1936). But the authority to impose dues and fees was restricted at least to the "extent of denying the union the right, over the employee's objection, to use his money to support political causes which he opposes," 367 U.S., at 768, even though Congress was well aware that unions had historically expended funds in the support of political candidates and issues. Employees could be required to become "members" of the union, but those who objected could not be burdened with any part of the union's expenditures in support of political or ideological causes. The Court expressed no view on other union expenses not directly involved in negotiating and administering the contract and in settling grievances.

Railway Clerks v. Allen, 373 U.S. 113 (1963), reaffirmed the approach taken in *Street,* and described the union expenditures that could fairly be charged to all employees as those "germane to collective bargaining." Id., at 121, 122. Still later, in Abood v. Board of Education, 431 U.S. 209 (1977), we found no constitutional barrier to an agency shop agreement between a municipality and a teachers' union insofar as the agreement required every employee in the unit to pay a service fee to defray the cost of collective bargaining, contract administration, and grievance adjustment. The union, however, could not, consistently with the Constitution, collect from dissenting employees any sums for the support of ideological causes not germane to its duties as collective-bargaining agent. In neither *Allen* nor *Abood,* however, did the Court find it necessary further to define the line between union expenditures that all employees must help defray and those that are not sufficiently related to collective bargaining to justify their being imposed on dissenters.

We remain convinced that Congress' essential justification for authorizing the union shop was the desire to eliminate free riders — employees in the bargaining unit on whose behalf the union was obliged to perform its statutory functions, but who refused to contribute to the cost thereof. Only a union that is certified as the exclusive bargaining agent is authorized to negotiate a contract requiring all employees to become members of or to make contributions to the union. Until such a contract is executed, no dues or fees may be collected from objecting employees who are not members of the union; and by the same token, any obligatory payments required by a contract authorized by §2, Eleventh terminate if the union ceases to be the exclusive bargaining agent. Hence, when employees such as petitioners object to being burdened with particular union expenditures, the test must be whether the challenged expenditures are necessarily or reasonably incurred for the purpose of performing the duties of an exclusive representative of the employees in dealing with the employer on labor-management issues. Under this standard, objecting employees may be compelled to pay their fair share of not only the direct costs of negotiating and administering a collective-bargaining contract and of settling grievances and disputes, but also the expenses of activities or undertakings normally or reasonably employed to implement or effectuate the duties of the union as exclusive representative of the employees in the bargaining unit.

With these considerations in mind, we turn to the particular expenditures for which petitioners insist they may not be charged.

V

1. Conventions

Every four years, BRAC holds a national convention at which the members elect officers, establish bargaining goals and priorities, and formulate overall union policy. We have very little trouble in holding that petitioners must help defray the costs of these conventions. Surely if a union is to perform its statutory functions, it must maintain its corporate or associational existence, must elect officers to manage and carry on its affairs, and may consult its members about overall bargaining goals and policy. Conventions such as those at issue here are normal events about which Congress was thoroughly informed and seem to us to be essential to the union's discharge of its duties as bargaining agent. As the Court of Appeals pointed out, convention "activities guide the union's approach to collective bargaining and are directly related to its effectiveness in negotiating labor agreements." In fact, like all national unions, BRAC is required to hold either a referendum or a convention at least every five years for the election of officers. 29 U.S.C. §481(a). We cannot fault it for choosing to elect its officers at a convention rather than by referendum.

2. Social Activities

Approximately .7% of Grand Lodge expenditures go toward purchasing refreshments for union business meetings and occasional social activities. These activities are formally open to nonmember employees. Petitioners insist that these expenditures are entirely unrelated to the union's function as collective-bargaining representative and therefore could not be charged to them. While these affairs are not central to collective bargaining, they are sufficiently related to it to be charged to all employees. As the Court of Appeals noted, "[t]hese small expenditures are important to the union's members because they bring about harmonious working relationships, promote closer ties among employees, and create a more pleasant environment for union meetings."

We cannot say that these de minimus expenses are beyond the scope of the Act. Like conventions, social activities at union meetings are a standard feature of union operations. In a revealing statement, Senator Thomas, Chairman of the Senate Subcommittee, made clear his disinclination to have Congress define precisely what normal, minor union expenses could be charged to objectors; he did not want the bill to say "that the unions . . . must not have any of the . . . kinds of little dues that they take up for giving a party, or something of that nature." Senate Hearings, supra, at 173-174. There is no indication that other Members of Congress were any more inclined to scrutinize the minor incidental expenses incurred by the union in running its operations.

3. Publications

The Grand Lodge puts out a monthly magazine, the *Railway Clerk/interchange,* paid for out of the union treasury. The magazine's contents are varied and include articles about negotiations, contract demands, strikes, unemployment and health benefits, proposed or recently enacted legislation, general news, products the union is boycotting, and recreational and social activities. The Court of Appeals found that the magazine "is the union's primary means of communicating information concerning collective bargaining, contract administration, and employees' rights to employees represented by BRAC." Under the union's rebate policy, objecting employees are not charged for that portion of the magazine devoted to "political causes." App. Exhibits 436. The rebate is figured by calculating the number of lines that are devoted to political issues as a proportion of the total number of lines.

The union must have a channel for communicating with the employees, including the objecting ones, about its activities. Congress can be assumed to have known that union funds go toward union publications; it is an accepted and basic union activity. The costs of "worker education" were specifically mentioned during the hearings. House Hearings, supra, at 275; Senate Hearings, supra, at 236. The magazine is important to the union in carrying out its representational obligations and a reasonable way of reporting to its constituents.

Respondents' limitation on the publication costs charged objecting employees is an important one, however. If the union cannot spend dissenters' funds for a particular activity, it has no justification for spending their funds for writing about that activity. By the same token, the Act surely allows it to charge objecting employees for reporting to them about those activities it can charge them for doing.

4. Organizing

The Court of Appeals found that organizing expenses could be charged to objecting employees because organizing efforts are aimed toward a stronger union, which in turn would be more successful at the bargaining table. Despite this attenuated connection with collective bargaining, we think such expenditures are outside Congress' authorization. Several considerations support this conclusion.

First, the notion that §2, Eleventh would be a tool for the expansion of overall union power appears nowhere in the legislative history. To the contrary, BRAC's president expressly disclaimed that the union shop was sought in order to strengthen the bargaining power of unions.[12] "Nor was any claim seriously advanced that the union shop was necessary to hold or increase union membership." *Street,* 367 U.S., at 763. Thus, organizational efforts were not what Congress aimed to enhance by authorizing the union shop.

Second, where a union shop provision is in place and enforced, all employees in the relevant unit are already organized. By definition, therefore, organizing expenses are spent on employees outside the collective-bargaining unit already represented. Using dues exacted from an objecting employee to recruit members among workers outside the bargaining unit can afford only the most attenuated benefits to collective bargaining on behalf of the dues payer.

Third, the free-rider rationale does not extend this far. The image of the smug, self-satisfied nonmember, stirring up resentment by enjoying benefits earned through other employees' time and money, is completely out of place when it comes to the union's overall organizing efforts. If one accepts that what is good for the union is good for the employees, a proposition petitioners would strenuously deny, then it may be that employees will ultimately ride for free on the union's organizing efforts

12. When asked if the union shop would "strengthen your industry-wide bargaining power as presently exists in the railroad industry," Harrison replied:

> I do not think it would affect the power of bargaining one way or the other. . . . If I get a majority of the employees to vote for my union as the bargaining agent, I have got as much economic power at that stage of development as I will ever have. The man that is going to scab — he will scab whether he is in or out of the union, and it does not make any difference. House Hearings, supra, at 20-21.

outside the bargaining unit. But the free rider Congress had in mind was the employee the union was required to represent and from whom it could not withhold benefits obtained for its members. Non-bargaining unit organizing is not directed at that employee. Organizing money is spent on people who are not union members, and only in the most distant way works to the benefit of those already paying dues. Any free-rider problem here is roughly comparable to that resulting from union contributions to prolabor political candidates. As we observed in *Street,* that is a far cry from the free-rider problem with which Congress was concerned.

5. *Litigation*

The expenses of litigation incident to negotiating and administering the contract or to settling grievances and disputes arising in the bargaining unit are clearly chargeable to petitioners as a normal incident of the duties of the exclusive representative. The same is true of fair representation litigation arising within the unit, of jurisdictional disputes with other unions, and of any other litigation before agencies or in the courts that concerns bargaining unit employees and is normally conducted by the exclusive representative. The expenses of litigation not having such a connection with the bargaining unit are not to be charged to objecting employees. Contrary to the view of the Court of Appeals, therefore, unless the Western Airlines bargaining unit is directly concerned, objecting employees need not share the costs of the union's challenge to the legality of the airline industry mutual aid pact; of litigation seeking to protect the rights of airline employees generally during bankruptcy proceedings; or of defending suits alleging violation of the non-discrimination requirements of Title VII.

6. *Death Benefits*

BRAC pays from its general funds a $300 death benefit to the designated beneficiary of any member or nonmember required to pay dues to the union. In *Street,* the Court did not adjudicate the legality under §2, Eleventh of compelled participation in a death benefit program, citing it as an example of an expenditure in the area between the costs which led directly to the complaint as to "free riders," and the expenditures to support union political activities. In *Allen,* the state trial court, like the District Court in this case, found that compelled payments to support BRAC's death benefit system were not reasonably necessary or related to collective bargaining and could not be charged to objecting employees. We found it unnecessary to reach the correctness of that conclusion.

Here, the Court of Appeals said that death benefits have historically played an important role in labor organizations, that insurance benefits are a mandatory subject of bargaining, and that by providing such benefits itself rather than seeking them from the employer, BRAC is in a better position to negotiate for additional benefits or higher wages. The court added that "the provision of a death benefits plan, which tends to strengthen the employee's ties to the union, is germane to the work of the union within the realm of collective bargaining." This was consistent with the affidavit of one of the union's expert witnesses to the effect that "death benefit funds provide a desirable economic benefit to union members and, therefore, they do serve as an organizational aid and as a means of strengthening the union internally." Affidavit of Lloyd Ulman, 2 App. 210. Petitioners, of course, press the view that death benefits have no connection with collective bargaining at all, let alone one that would warrant forcing them to participate in the system.

We find it unnecessary to rule on this question. Because the union is no longer the exclusive bargaining agent and petitioners are no longer involved in the death benefits system, the only issue is whether petitioners are entitled to a refund of their past contributions. We think that they are not so entitled, even if they had the right to an injunction to prevent future collections from them for death benefits. Although they objected to the use of their funds to support the benefits plan, they remained entitled to the benefits of the plan as long as they paid their dues; they thus enjoyed a form of insurance for which the union collected a premium. We doubt that the equities call for a refund of those payments.

VI

Petitioners' primary argument is that for the union to compel their financial support of these six activities violates the First Amendment. We need only address this contention with regard to the three activities for which, we have held, the RLA allows the union to use their contributions. We perceive no constitutional barrier.

The First Amendment does limit the uses to which the union can put funds obtained from dissenting employees. See generally *Abood,* 431 U.S. 209. But by allowing the union shop at all, we have already countenanced a significant impingement on First Amendment rights. The dissenting employee is forced to support financially an organization with whose principles and demands he may disagree. "To be required to help finance the union as a collective bargaining agent might well be thought . . . to interfere in some way with an employee's freedom to associate for the advancement of ideas, or to refrain from doing so, as he sees fit." Id., at 222. It has long been settled that such interference with First Amendment rights is justified by the governmental interest in industrial peace. Ibid.; *Street,* 367 U.S., at 776, 778 (Douglas, J., concurring); *Hanson,* 351 U.S., at 238. At a minimum, the union may constitutionally "expend uniform exactions under the union-shop agreement in support of activities germane to collective bargaining." Railway Clerks v. Allen,

373 U.S., at 122. The issue is whether these expenses involve additional interference with the First Amendment interests of objecting employees, and, if so, whether they are nonetheless adequately supported by a governmental interest.

Petitioners do not explicitly contend that union social activities implicate serious First Amendment interests. We need not determine whether contributing money to such affairs is an act triggering First Amendment protection. To the extent it is, the communicative content is not inherent in the act, but stems from the union's involvement in it. The objection is that these are *union* social hours. Therefore, the fact that the employee is forced to contribute does not increase the infringement of his First Amendment rights already resulting from the compelled contribution to the union. Petitioners may feel that their money is not being well-spent, but that does not mean they have a First Amendment complaint.

The First Amendment concerns with regard to publications and conventions are more serious; both have direct communicative content and involve the expression of ideas. Nonetheless, we perceive little additional infringement of First Amendment rights beyond that already accepted, and none that is not justified by the governmental interests behind the union shop itself. As the discussion of these expenses indicated, they "relat[e] to the work of the union in the realm of collective bargaining." *Hanson,* 351 U.S., at 235. The very nature of the free-rider problem and the governmental interest in overcoming it require that the union have a certain flexibility in its use of compelled funds. "The furtherance of the common cause leaves some leeway for the leadership of the group." *Abood,* 431 U.S., at 222, quoting *Street,* 367 U.S., at 778 (Douglas, J., concurring). These expenses are well within the acceptable range.

VII

The Court of Appeals erred in holding that respondents were entitled to charge petitioners for their pro rata share of the union's organizing and litigating expenses, and that the former rebate scheme adequately protected the objecting employees from the misuse of their contributions. The decision of the Court of Appeals is affirmed in part and reversed in part and the case remanded for further proceedings consistent with this opinion.[9]

Notes

1. How would you have argued that union organizing creates as much of a "free rider" problem as the other union activities challenged in *Ellis*?

[9] Powell, J., concurred in part and dissented in part.

2. In addition to the restrictions imposed by the line of cases culminating in *Ellis,* unions are prohibited from certain assessments and expenditures with respect to federal election campaigns. 2 U.S.C. §441b makes it unlawful for a labor organization to make a contribution or expenditure in connection with any presidential, vice-presidential, or congressional campaign. Unions are, however, permitted to communicate to the membership and their families with respect to such campaigns on any subject, to conduct nonpartisan get-out-the-vote campaigns directed at members and their families, and to finance "the establishment, administration, and solicitation of contributions to a separate segregated fund to be used for political purposes by a . . . labor organization. . . ."

The Supreme Court held with respect to a forerunner of the present statute that a fund is lawfully constituted even though it is administered and controlled by union officials, so long as the political monies are segregated from other union monies.[10] The government argued unsuccessfully that such a fund was an alter ego of the union and thus did not constitute a "separate" fund.

The statute also prohibits such a fund from utilizing money "secured by physical force, job discrimination, financial reprisals, or the threat [thereof]; or by dues, fees, or other monies required as a condition of membership in labor organization. . . ." A person soliciting an employee on behalf of a fund must inform the employee of the political purposes of the fund and of his or her right to refuse to contribute without any reprisal.

B. UNION CONTROLS ON FREE SPEECH

ATLESON, A UNION MEMBER'S RIGHT OF FREE SPEECH AND ASSEMBLY

51 Minn. L. Rev. 403, 406-409 (1966)

The legislative history of Title I . . . will only be summarized here. Legislative debates, unfortunately, shed little light on the questions and problems raised by the statute. Even the humorous admonition to look at the statute only if legislative history is ambiguous is not helpful since the statute itself is vague and contradictory.

In the late 1950's, the initial bills for internal union reform focused primarily on election and financial controls. The serious disclosures of

[10] Pipefitters Local 562 v. United States, 407 U.S. 385 (1972). See Note, 51 Tex. L. Rev. 936 (1973).

the McClellan special committee hearings dealt with the misuse of union funds for private gain, conflicts of interests, and "sweetheart" arrangements between union officials and employers. The subversion of democratic practices in unions was a "wholly subordinate theme."[13] "[E]vidence pointed to but a handful of irregular or fraudulent union elections, and only scattered instances of arbitrary expulsions, unfair trial procedures, or encroachments on the democratic rights of union members."[14]

After the subcommittee hearings on related bills had terminated, Senator McClellan introduced a comprehensive measure including, as Title I, a bill of rights for union members. Because of McClellan's prestige in the field, the subcommittee reconvened to consider the measure. A bill was reported out of committee, but without the guarantees of individual rights. During the Senate debate on the proposal, Senator McClellan offered as an amendment a "Bill of Rights" embodying the rejected first title of his bill. The combination of McClellan's prestige, the difficulty of voting against a "Bill of Rights," presidential aspirations of various senators, and ignorance of the significance of McClellan's amendment led to its passage by one vote.

Opponents of the bill met during the next two days to prepare a substitute. They feared that lower courts would give the sweeping language of the Bill of Rights its full literal meaning. They were joined by chagrined southern supporters who feared that giving the Secretary of Labor authority to protect private rights would provide an embarrassing precedent in future civil rights debates. Although Kennedy supporters probably had the votes to remove the Bill of Rights provisions, political realities suggested a modified substitute. Thus, one vote had successfully changed the whole thrust of labor reform legislation from regulation of financial practices to protection within unions.

The substitute was introduced by Senator Kuchel. "The draftsmanship left much to be desired, perhaps because of the haste and stress, the number of participants, and the priority of tactical acceptability over nicety of expression." Nevertheless, the amendment in substance was enacted into law as Title I. The substitute specifically enumerated subjects of federal protection and recognized reasonable rulemaking and disciplinary powers of unions.

Senator McClellan's bill had guaranteed equal rights and privileges without detailing the rights included or their scope except that the rights were to include "identical voting rights and equal protection of the union's rules and regulations." In contrast, the Kuchel substitute limited the equal rights provision to four specifically named rights and recog-

13. Summers, American Legislation for Union Democracy, 25 Mod. L. Rev. 273, 274 (1962).

14. Id. at 274.

nized the right of unions to pass reasonable rules and regulations limiting those rights. No explanation was given for narrowing the range of the provision or for limiting the provision to the rights specified. Although a number of Senators stated that enumeration of rights did not exclude other rights, these "other rights" can only refer to rights protected by state law under section 103. The Kuchel substitute removed the broad immunity from penalty, discipline, or interference of any kind, recognized a union's authority to pass reasonable rules for the conduct of meetings, and permitted union discipline for conduct violating obligations owed to the union or interferring with the union's legal or contractual obligations.

"[T]actics also triumphed over sound draftsmanship" in the House.[26] The Landrum-Griffin bill, which eventually passed the House, incorporated the Senate-passed "Bill of Rights."[27] The final House bill was approved on the floor as a substitute to a committee-approved bill, and the report of the house committee contained almost no discussion concerning the basic provisions of its bill. Thus, in neither house was careful committee consideration given to the problems of internal union democracy or the wording of appropriate federal legislation.

Reading the unenlightening debate in both houses supports the analysis of Professor Smith:

> The record of the debate in Congress reveals a deliberate, if not extraordinary, effort to becloud, or clarify, or prejudge, as the case may be. The report filed by the house managers of the conference [House conferees] contains much that is confusing as well as clarifying. Thus, resort to legislative history will at best be difficult, and may serve more to obscure than to illuminate legislative intent.[29]

Turning to the statute for assistance is similarly frustrating. Since Title I was presented from the floor, it contains the purposeful ambiguities and technical compromises thought necessary to insure passage. Moreover, it was hastily drawn to modify what had become an inevitable individual rights section of the act. Consequently, the "courts would be well advised to seek out the underlying rationale without placing great emphasis upon close construction of the words."[30]

The known problems of statutory interpretation take on gargantuan proportions when attempting to find the varying purposes and interests. Common denominators turn out to be those pleasant sounding general principles which cannot decide concrete cases.

26. Cox, Internal Affairs of Labor Unions under the Labor Reform Act of 1959, 58 Mich. L. Rev. 819, 833 (1960).

27. Since the two versions of the Bill of Rights were identical, the conferees had no acknowledged power to alter the language.

29. Smith. The Labor-Management Reporting and Disclosure Act of 1959, 46 Va. L. Rev. 195, 197-198 (1960).

30. Cox, supra note 26, at 852.

SALZHANDLER v. CAPUTO

316 F.2d 445 (2d Cir.), cert. denied, 375 U.S. 946 (1963)

LUMBARD, C. J.

This appeal raises an important question of the rights of union members under the Labor-Management Reporting and Disclosure Act of 1959: whether a union member's allegedly libelous statements regarding the handling of union funds by union officers justify disciplinary action against the member and his exclusion from any participation in the affairs of the union for five years, including speaking and voting at meetings and even attending meetings. We hold that the LMRDA protects the union member in the exercise of his right to make such charges without reprisal by the union; that any provisions of the union constitution which make such criticism, whether libelous or not, subject to union discipline are unenforceable; and that the Act allows redress for such unlawful treatment.

Solomon Salzhandler, a member of Local 442, Brotherhood of Painters, Decorators & Paperhangers of America, brought suit in the district court following the decision of a Trial Board of the union's New York District Council No. 9 that he had untruthfully accused Isadore Webman, the president of the local, of the crime of larceny. The Trial Board found that Salzhandler's "unsupported accusations" violated the union's constitution which prohibited "conduct unbecoming a member . . . ," "acts detrimental to . . . interests of the Brotherhood," "libeling, slandering . . . fellow members [or] officers of local unions" and "acts and conduct . . . inconsistent with the duties, obligations and fealty of a member."

Salzhandler's complaint alleged that his charges against Webman were an exercise of his rights as a member of the union and that the action of the Trial Board was in violation of the provisions of the LMRDA under which he was entitled to relief.

The undisputed facts developed during the trial in the district court amply support Salzhandler's claims for relief.

Salzhandler was elected financial secretary of Local 442 in 1953. He was reelected thereafter and at the times in question he was serving a three-year term which was to end June 30, 1962. His weekly compensation as an officer was $35, of which $25 was salary and $10 was for expenses. The dispute giving rise to this suit was touched off in November 1960 by Salzhandler's distribution to members of Local 442 of a leaflet which accused Webman of mishandling of union funds.

Prior to the audit each July, Salzhandler obtained the checks for the auditor. In going over the union's checks in July 1960 Salzhandler noticed that two checks, one for $800 and one for $375, had been drawn to cover the expenses of Webman and one Max Schneider at two union conventions to which they were elected delegates. The $800 check, drawn on August 21, 1959 to Webman's order, was endorsed by Webman and his wife. The $375 check, drawn on March 4, 1960 to "Cash," was likewise endorsed by Webman and his wife. Schneider's endorsement did not appear on either check. Schneider had died on May 31, 1960.

On July 15, 1960 two checks, each for $6, were drawn as refunds of dues paid by Max Schneider and another deceased member. Such checks were ordinarily mailed to the widows. Webman, however, brought the two checks to Salzhandler and told him to deposit them in a special fund for the benefit of the son of Max Schneider. Salzhandler refused to do this because the checks were not endorsed. Thereafter Sol Feldman and W. Shirpin, who were trustees of the local, each endorsed one of the checks and Salzhandler made the deposit as Webman had requested.

In November 1960 Salzhandler distributed to members of the local a leaflet which accused Webman of improper conduct with regard to union funds and of referring to members of the union by such names as "thieves, scabs, robbers, scabby bosses, bums, pimps, f-bums, [and] jail birds." Attached to the leaflet were photostats of the four checks. With regard to the convention checks, Salzhandler wrote:

> The last convention lasted five days, Monday August 31, to Friday, September 4, 1959. The delegates of 442 presented their credentials Monday, August 31, and on Thursday, September 3, as soon as they got the mileage fare, they disappeared. They were absent at Thursday afternoon session. The most the chairman should have gotten was a weeks pay and allowance — $250.00. The auditor's report shows he got $200 in pay and $300 in expenses — $500, or twice what was coming to him, and also $300 as expenses for the Business Agent. The check was made out to *Cash* for $800 (photostat enclosed). So was the voucher. It does not indicate that Max Schneider got any of it. The same goes for a check made out *only* to I. Webman on March 4, 1960 for another convention, where the chairman was to get $250, but got $375. It does not indicate Schneider got his share. Were the checks legal?

The leaflet also branded Webman as a "petty robber" of the two $6 checks:

> To prove himself most unworthy of any trust, he performed the cheapest petty act ever. Two widows were refunded each $6.00 for overpayment of dues. Two checks were issued to that effect. The petty robber had two of his friends sign their names and the chairman declared these two checks as contributions to the special tax for Michael Schneider — photostats of checks enclosed.

On December 13, 1960, Webman filed charges against Salzhandler with the New York District Council No. 9 of the union, alleging that Salzhandler had violated the union constitution, §267, by libelling and slandering him in implying that he, Webman, had not reimbursed Max Schneider for convention expenses, and that he had been a "petty robber" in causing the two $6 checks to be deposited in the Michael Schneider fund, rather than being paid over to the two widows. The charge went on to state that Salzhandler was guilty of "acts and conduct inconsistent with the duties, obligations and fealty of a member or officer of the Brotherhood" and that the net effect of the leaflet was untruthfully to accuse an officer of the union of the crime of larceny. For over six hours on the evening of Februay 23, 1961, Salzhandler was tried by a five-member Trial Board of the District Council. As the union rules permitted, Salzhandler was represented by a union member who was not a lawyer. At the trial, Webman introduced the leaflet. Salzhandler produced the photostats and was questioned by the Trial Board. Webman's witnesses testified that the convention expenditures were approved by the membership. Salzhandler produced three witnesses who testified that Webman had called members names as alleged in the leaflet.

Not until April 2, 1961 did Salzhandler receive notice of the Trial Board's decision and his removal from office and this was from a printed postal card mailed to all members: "By a decision of the Trial Committee of District Council 9, Sol Saltzhandler [sic] is no longer Financial Secretary of Local Union 442."

Thereafter, on April 4, the District Council mailed to Salzhandler only the final paragraph of its five page "Decision" which read as follows:

> It is our decision that Brother Solomon Salzhandler be prohibited from participating in the affairs of L.U. 442, or of any other Local Union of the Brotherhood, or of District Council 9, for a period of five (5) years. He shall not be permitted during that period to attend meetings of L.U. 442, to vote on any matter, to have the floor at any meeting of any other Local Union affiliated with the District Council, or to be a candidate for any position in any local Union or in the District Council. In all other respects, Brother Salzhandler's rights and obligations as a member of the Brotherhood shall be continued. . . .

On May 15, 1961, Salzhandler attempted to attend a meeting of the local but was prevented from doing so by Webman. The complaint alleges that Webman assaulted Salzhandler and used violence in removing him.

This action was commenced in the federal court under the Labor-Management Reporting and Disclosure Act of 1959, §102, requesting a nullification of the order of the Trial Board, reinstatement in the position as financial secretary, and damages.

Judge Wham dismissed the complaint holding that the Trial Board's conclusion that the leaflet was libelous was sufficiently supported by the evidence. He went further, however, and made an independent finding that the statements were, in fact, libelous. The court held, as a matter of law, that "The rights accorded members of labor unions under Title I of the Labor-Management Reporting and Disclosure Act of 1959 . . . do not include the right of a union member to libel or slander officers of the union." We do not agree.

The LMRDA of 1959 was designed to protect the rights of union members to discuss freely and criticize the management of their unions and the conduct of their officers. The legislative history and the extensive hearings which preceded the enactment of the statute abundantly evidence the intention of the Congress to prevent union officials from using their disciplinary powers to silence criticism and punish those who dare to question and complain. The statute is clear and explicit. . . .

Appellees argue that just as constitutionally protected speech does not include libelous utterances, the speech protected by the statute likewise does not include libel and slander. The analogy to the First Amendment is not convincing. In Beauharnais [v. Illinois, 343 U.S. 250 (1952),] the Supreme Court recognized the possibility that state action might stifle criticism under the guise of punishing libel. However, because it felt that abuses could be prevented by the exercise of judicial authority, 343 U.S. at 263-264, the court sustained a state criminal libel statute. But the union is not a political unit to whose disinterested tribunals an alleged defamer can look for an impartial review of his "crime." It is an economic action group, the success of which depends in large measure on a unity of purpose and sense of solidarity among its members.

The Trial Board in the instant case consisted of union officials, not judges. It was a group to which the delicate problems of truth or falsehood, privilege, and "fair comment" were not familiar. Its procedure is peculiarly unsuited for drawing the fine line between criticism and defamation, yet, were we to adopt the view of the appellees, each charge of libel would be given a trial de novo in the federal court — an impractical result not likely contemplated by Congress, — and such a Trial Board would be the final arbiter of the extent of the union member's protection under §101(a)(2).[7]

In a proviso to §101(a)(2), there are two express exceptions to the broad rule of free expression. One relates to "the responsibility of every member toward the organization as an institution." The other deals with interference with the union's legal and contractual obligations. While the inclusion of only two exceptions, without more, does not mean that

7. See Summers, American Legislation for Union Democracy, 25 Mod. L. Rev. 273, 287:

> The most difficult problem arises when a member is expelled for "slandering a union officer." Union debates are characterized by vitriol and calumny, and campaigns for office are salted with overstated accusations. Defining the scope of fair comment in political contests is never easy, and in this context is nearly impossible. To allow the union to decide this issue in the first instance is to invite retaliation and repression and to frustrate one of the principal reasons for protecting this right — to enable members to oust corrupt leadership through the democratic process.

others were intentionally excluded, we believe that the legislative history supports the conclusion that Congress intended only those exceptions which were expressed. The expression of views by Salzhandler did not come within either exception in the proviso to §101(a)(2). The leaflet did not interfere in any way with the union's legal or contractual obligations and the union has never claimed that it did. Nor could Salzhandler's charges against Webman be construed as a violation of the "responsibility of every member toward the organization as an institution." Quite the contrary; it would seem clearly in the interest of proper and honest management of union affairs to permit members to question the manner in which the union's officials handle the union's funds and how they treat the union's members. It is that interest which motivated the enactment of the statute and which would be immeasurably frustrated were we to interpret it so as to compel each dissatisfied and questioning member to draw, at the peril of union discipline, the thin and tenuous line between what is libelous and what is not. This is especially so when we consider that the Act was designed largely to curtail such vices as the mismanagement of union funds, criticism of which by union members is always likely to be viewed by union officials as defamatory.

The union argues that there is a public interest in promoting the monolithic character of unions in their dealings with employers. But the Congress weighed this factor and decided that the desirability of protecting the democratic process within the unions outweighs any possible weakening of unions in their dealings with employers which may result from the freer expression of opinions within the unions.

The democratic and free expression of opinion in any group necessarily develops disagreements and divergent opinions. Freedom of expression would be stifled if those in power could claim that any charges against them were libelous and then proceed to discipline those responsible on a finding that the charges were false. That is precisely what Webman and the Trial Board did here when they punished Salzhandler with a five-year ban of silence and stripped him of his office. So far as union discipline is concerned Salzhandler had a right to speak his mind and spread his opinions regarding the union's officers, regardless of whether his statements were true or false. It was wholly immaterial to Salzhandler's cause of action under the LMRDA whether he spoke truthfully or not, and accordingly Judge Wham's views on whether Salzhandler's statements were true are beside the point. Here Salzhandler's charges against Webman related to the handling of union funds; they concerned the way the union was managed. The Congress has decided that it is in the public interest that unions be democratically governed and toward that end that discussion should be free and untrammeled and that reprisals within the union for the expression of views should be prohibited. It follows that although libelous statements may be made the basis of civil suit between those concerned, the union may not subject a member to any disciplinary action on a finding by its governing board that such statements are libelous. The district court erred in dismissing the complaint.

Accordingly, we reverse the judgment of the district court and direct entry of judgment for the plaintiff which, among other things, should assess damages and enjoin the defendants from carrying out any punishment imposed by the District Council Trial Board.

FAROWITZ v. MUSICIANS LOCAL 802, 330 F.2d 999 (2d Cir. 1964): Plaintiff Farowitz was expelled by defendant local union for distributing leaflets that urged the membership to refuse to pay taxes assessed by the local. The taxes had been collected through orchestra leaders, but that collection practice was declared unlawful under §302 of the LMRDA by a federal district court. The local then sought to collect the tax directly from the membership and Farowitz contended in his leaflets that the union constitution and bylaws provided no alternative to collection by the leaders. Claiming that his expulsion violated §101(a)(2), Farowitz sought reinstatement to membership and money damages.

The court of appeals, affirming the district court, found Farowitz's actions to be protected by §101(a)(2), relying on *Salzhandler.* The court stated,

> We do not say that there may not be some situations in which a union member would not be protected against disciplinary measures if he were to urge other members to forego paying their dues. Each case of course must turn on its own facts. All we decide is that a member having such good reasons as here to believe that the collection of taxes or dues runs afoul of the law has the right to call this to the attention of the membership and to urge that they refrain from paying such assessments. A member's responsibility to his union as an institution surely cannot include any obligation that he sit idly by while the union follows a course of conduct which he reasonably believes to be illegal because of what a court of law has stated.

AIRLINE MAINTENANCE LODGE 702, IAM v. LOUDERMILK, 444 F.2d 719 (5th Cir. 1971): Plaintiff local union fined union member Loudermilk $500 and sought to enforce the fine in a state small claims court. Loudermilk removed the action to federal district court and there contended that enforcement of the fine would violate his right of free speech under §101(a)(2). Loudermilk was fined because he joined and became president of a rival union, which then tried to oust plaintiff local union as representative of a bargaining unit. The court found the fine violated §101(a)(2):

> The rights of a union member under this statute must be balanced against the right preserved to the union to make rules as to the responsibility of

the member toward the union as an institution, and this balancing process must rest on the facts. Loudermilk was compelled to join plaintiff union under the union shop agreement between Eastern and plaintiff IAM. Some years later he joined and became president of a rival union. He was fined for supporting the rival union, albeit in connection with displacing IAM at another airline. IAM did not choose to expel him or to bar him from meetings and the like, defensive actions which would have protected IAM. Rather, IAM sought to compel his allegiance by the imposition of a fine.

We think this exceeded the authority of the union under the circumstances here which involve compulsory membership under a union shop agreement coupled with the free speech overtones which are inherent in undertaking stemming from dissatisfaction with one union and action seeking to displace that union with another. As the district court said with respect to this factor:

> The Court has the responsibility of balancing the defendant's individual interest against that of the union. If the plaintiff could impose a judicially collectible fine upon a union member who had become [dis]satisfied with the union's representation and sought to replace it with a rival, it could effectively eliminate all criticism of its policies and foreclose any challenge of its right to represent its members. I believe such a result would be inconsistent with the intent of Congress at the time that it passed the Bill of Rights.

Notes

1. With the foregoing decisions promoting the right of free speech, compare this commentary by an attorney representing a major international union:

> The approach exemplified by the *Salzhandler* decision may be deemed proper and wholesome, or strained and dangerous, depending on one's view of the purposes served, or that ought to be served, by labor unions in our industrial society.
>
> As Joel Seidman has pointed out,[8] a labor union has several aspects: (1) economic, since it seeks by collective bargaining to improve the wages and other working conditions of those it represents; (2) political, since it is a membership organization with officers and a governmental apparatus; (3) quasi-military, since it conducts strikes and other kinds of industrial warfare; and (4) social, insofar as it participates in community affairs.
>
> The relative weight and depth of these aspects is affected by the organizational status of the union, that is, whether it is a local, national, or federated union, and by the scope of its bargaining, that is, whether it deals on a single plant, multi-plant, or multi-employer basis.
>
> In considering the problem of democracy in a labor union, it is an oversimplification to give major emphasis to its aspect as a political institution. It is still primarily an economic institution, whose effectiveness de-

8. Democracy in the Labor Movement, Bull, 39 (Cornell University; N.Y. State School of Industrial and Labor Relations, Feb. 1958).

pends on its potential fighting qualities. It is a countervailing force, an opposition group that rose in response to the need of workers to meet and contain the ruthless economic power of employers. Unions must be alert to meet aggressions initiated by the employers; they can never rest secure. Their responsibility to their members depends, in the long run, on their ability to produce — be it higher wages, more fringe benefits, or greater job security — by obtaining these from employers generally reluctant to give more than they must. The enterprises with which they deal are directed by very small groups of men, who can act quickly without the inhibitions of democratic controls. Unions must be able, therefore, to exercise discipline over their members, and to respond quickly and decisively to counter employer tactics if they are to cope successfully with emergency and crisis situations. Internal division in crucial situations may render them impotent. . . .

The American Civil Liberties Union[11] . . . declares that a union has a special responsibility to maintain democratic standards because, first, it speaks for its members in negotiating contracts that determine the basic laws of their working lives. In processing grievances it interprets and enforces those laws. It is, therefore, the workers' economic legislature, policeman, and judge. Second, the power the union has over the worker is derived from the government, particularly through the National Labor Relations Act. Third, the principal moral justification of unions is that they introduce an element of democracy into the government of industry.

A basic flaw in this formulation is that it overlooks the role of the employer. The union is not the workers' economic legislature, policeman, or judge. Under optimum conditions, it is a recognized participant in establishing those laws, a lookout rather than a policeman, and an advocate rather than a judge. Furthermore, the extent to which it introduces an element of democracy into the government of industry is the consequence of its economic power, not its moral posture.

It is generally assumed by commentators that encouragement of increased participation by individual members in the internal affairs of unions is not only essential if the democratic ideal is to be attained, but that increased democracy within unions will strengthen unions and promote the public good. This is a thesis easier to assert than to document. A very plausible argument can be made that democratic procedures do not, as a matter of course, produce more effective or more progressive unions, or promote the public good to a greater degree than autocratic or oligarchic unions, or more fully promote the interests of the members in the areas in which unions are supposed to serve.

Nevertheless, I do not challenge the desirability of the greatest degree of democracy in the internal structure of the unions, which includes freedom for individual members to criticize the leadership and participate in decision making, consistent with maximum effectiveness in dealing with management. The question here is whether the approach of the court in

11. Democracy in Labor Unions, A Report and Statement of Policy, American Civil Liberties Union, 1952, p. 4.

Salzhandler will, in the guise of promoting democracy, seriously prejudice maintenance of union effectiveness.[11]

2. After *Salzhandler, Farowitz,* and *Loudermilk,* what is left of the proviso to §101(a)(2)?

Suppose local union member Baggins is a thorn in the side of the union's officers. At every union meeting Baggins harangues and harasses the presiding officer, accusing the elected leadership of bad faith, personal defaults, and bad decisions on most issues under discussion and many others deemed relevant only by Baggins. He never speaks without being recognized but is prone to filibuster. The leadership would like to shut him off. What do you advise? Can Baggins be barred from the meetings? Can the presiding officer refuse to recognize him?

3. Did the libeled officers in the *Salzhandler* case have a cause of action in tort against Salzhandler? What standard should the state court apply? Isn't the state court required by §103 to apply the same standard that it would in a libel action not involving union affairs?

Would the *Salzhandler* court have upheld a union discipline of Salzhandler for violating a constitutional prohibition of "libeling any officer or fellow member where the libel is made with actual knowledge of its falsity or in reckless disregard of its truth"? Would it help if the union constitution designated three distinguished members of the community to act as a public review board with power to review and set aside union disciplines of this sort?

4. Presumably Farowitz refused to pay the taxes whose collection he challenged. Could he have been disciplined for that? Suppose he urged fellow members to forsake a union strike and picket line (as he himself was doing)?

5. Could the IAM local have expelled Loudermilk for his dual unionism? Consider whether there is a statutory ground for permitting the union to interfere with free speech by expulsion but not by fining. Surely if the IAM local had called a membership meeting to rally support and plan strategy to defeat the takeover bid of the union Loudermilk was heading, it would not have been required to permit Loudermilk to attend.

A line of NLRB decisions is comparable. In Tawas Tube Products, [12] the Board held that the union did not violate §8(b)(1)(A) of the NLRA by expelling members for filing petitions to decertify the union: The members were attacking "the very existence of the union," the union's response was "defensive." But in Molders Local 125 (Blackhawk Tanning Co.),[13] the NLRB found a §8(b)(1)(A) violation where

[11] Sigal, Freedom of Speech and Union Discipline: The "Right" of Defamation and Disloyalty, N.Y.U. Seventeenth Annual Conference on Labor 367, 369-372 (1964).

[12] 151 N.L.R.B. 46 (1965).

[13] 178 N.L.R.B. 208 (1969), enforced, 442 F.2d 92 (7th Cir. 1971).

the union fined a member for filing a decertification petition. Comparing the "union's right to self-defense" with "the public policy against permitting a union to penalize a member because he seeks the aid of the Board," the Board concluded that a fine was punitive rather than defensive.

UNITED STEELWORKERS v. SADLOWSKI

457 U.S. 102 (1982)

MARSHALL, J.

In this case, we confront the question whether §101(a)(2) of the Labor-Management Reporting and Disclosure Act of 1959 (LMRDA) precludes the membership of a union from adopting a rule that prohibits candidates for union office from accepting campaign contributions from nonmembers. . . .

I

A

Petitioner United Steelworkers of America (USWA), a labor organization with 1,300,000 members, conducts elections for union president and other top union officers every four years. The elections for these officers are decided by referendum vote of the membership. In the 1977 election, which was hotly contested, two candidates ran for president: respondent Edward Sadlowski, Jr., the Director of USWA's largest district, and Lloyd McBride, another District Director. Both Sadlowski and McBride headed a slate of candidates for the other top union positions.

McBride was endorsed by the incumbent union leadership, and received substantial financial support from union officers and staff. Sadlowski, on the other hand, received much of his financial support from sources outside the union. During the campaign, the question whether candidates should accept contributions from persons who were not members of the union was vigorously debated. The McBride slate contended that outsider participation in USWA elections was dangerous for the union. McBride ultimately defeated Sadlowski by a fairly wide margin — 57% to 43%. The other candidates on the McBride slate won by similar margins.

After the elections, union members continued to debate the question whether outsider participation in union campaigns was desirable. This debate was finally resolved in 1978, when USWA held its biennial Convention. The Convention, which consists of approximately 5,000 delegates elected by members of USWA's local unions, is USWA's highest governing body. At the 1978 Convention, several local unions submitted resolutions recommending amendment of the USWA Constitution to include an "outsider rule" prohibiting campaign contributions by nonmembers. The union's International Executive Board also recommended a ban on nonmember contributions. Acting on the basis of these recommendations, the Convention's Constitution Committee proposed to the Convention that it adopt an outsider rule. After a debate on the floor of the Convention, the delegates, by a margin of roughly 10 to 1, voted to include such a rule in the Constitution.

The outsider rule, Article V, §27, of the USWA Constitution (1978), provides in pertinent part:

> Sec. 27. No candidate (including a prospective candidate) for any position set forth in Article IV, Section 1, and supporter of a candidate may solicit or accept financial support, or any other direct or indirect support of any kind (except an individual's own volunteered personal time) from any non-member.

Section 27 confers authority upon the International Executive Board to adopt regulations necessary to implement the provision. It also creates a Campaign Contribution Administrative Committee, consisting of three "distinguished, impartial" nonmembers to administer and enforce the provision. The Committee may order a candidate to cease and desist from conduct that breaches §27, and may declare a candidate disqualified. Its decisions are final and binding.

B

In October 1979, Sadlowski and several other individuals filed suit against USWA in the United States District Court for the District of Columbia. They claimed, *inter alia,* that the outsider rule violated the "right to sue" provision of Title I of the LMRDA, §101(a)(4), because it would prohibit a candidate from accepting nonmember contributions to finance campaign-related litigation. Both sides moved for summary judgment. The District Court found that the rule violated §101(a)(4). . . .

The United States Court of Appeals for the District of Columbia Circuit affirmed. . . .

II

A

At the outset, we address respondents' contention that this case can be resolved simply by reference to First Amendment law. Respondents claim that §101(a)(2) confers upon union members rights equivalent to the rights established by the First Amendment. They further argue that in the context of a political election, a rule that placed substantial restrictions on a candidate's freedom to receive campaign contributions would violate the First Amendment. Thus, a rule that substantially restricts contributions in union campaigns must violate §101(a)(2). We are not persuaded by this argument. In light of the legislative history, we do not believe that §101(a)(2) should be read as incorporating the entire body of First Amendment law, so that the scope of protections afforded by the statute coincides with the protections afforded by the Constitution. . . .

This history reveals that Congress modeled Title I after the Bill of Rights, and that the legislators intended §101(a)(2) to restate a principal First Amendment value — the right to speak one's mind without fear of reprisal. However, there is absolutely no indication that Congress intended the scope of §101(a)(2) to be identical to the scope of the First Amendment. Rather, Congress' decision to include a proviso covering "reasonable" rules refutes that proposition. First Amendment freedoms may not be infringed absent a compelling governmental interest. Even then, any government regulation must be carefully tailored, so that rights are not needlessly impaired. Brown v. Hartlage, 456 U.S. 45, 53-54 (1982). Union rules, by contrast, are valid under §101(a)(2) so long as they are reasonable; they need not pass the stringent tests applied in the First Amendment context.

B

To determine whether a union rule is valid under the statute, we first consider whether the rule interferes with an interest protected by the first part of §101(a)(2). If it does, we then determine whether the rule is "reasonable" and thus sheltered by the proviso to §101(a)(2). In conducting these inquiries, we find guidance in the policies that underlie the LMRDA in general and Title I in particular. First Amendment principles may be helpful, although they are not controlling. We must look to the objectives Congress sought to achieve, and avoid "'placing great emphasis upon close construction of the words."' Wirtz v. Glass Bottle Blowers, 389 U.S. 463, 468, and n. 6 (1968) (quoting Cox, Internal Affairs of Labor Unions Under the Labor Reform Act of 1959, 58 Mich. L. Rev. 819, 852 (1960)); Hall v. Cole, 412 U.S. 1, 11, and n. 17 (1973). The critical question is whether a rule that partially interferes with a protected interest is nevertheless reasonably related to the protection of the organization as an institution.

Applying this form of analysis here, we conclude that the outsider rule is valid. Although it may limit somewhat the ability of insurgent union members to wage an effective campaign, an interest deserving some protection under the statute, it is rationally related to the union's legitimate interest in reducing outsider interference with union affairs.

(1)

An examination of the policies underlying the LMRDA indicates that the outsider rule may have some impact on interests that Congress intended to protect under §101(a)(2). Congress adopted the freedom of speech and assembly provision in order to promote union democracy. It recognized that democracy would be assured only if union members are free to discuss union policies and criticize the leadership without fear of reprisal. Congress also recognized that this freedom is particularly critical, and deserves vigorous protection, in the context of election campaigns. For it is in elections that members can wield their power, and directly express their approval or disapproval of the union leadership.

The interest in fostering vigorous debate during election campaigns may be affected by the outsider rule. If candidates are not permitted to accept contributions from persons outside the union, their ability to criticize union policies and to mount effective challenges to union leadership may be weakened. Restrictions that limit access to funds may reduce the number of issues discussed, the attention that is devoted to each issue, and the size of the audience reached. Cf. Buckley v. Valeo, 424 U.S., at 65-66 (per curiam) (First Amendment freedom of expression and association may be "diluted if it does not include the right to pool money through contributions, for funds are often essential if 'advocacy' is to be truly or optimally 'effective' ").[6]

Although the outsider rule does affect rights protected by the statute, as a practical matter the impact may not be substantial. Respondents, as well as the Court of Appeals, suggest that incumbents have a large advantage because they can rely on their union staff during election campaigns. Challengers cannot counter this power simply by seeking funds from union members; the rank and file cannot provide sufficient support. Thus, they must be permitted to seek funds from outsiders. In fact, however, the rank and file probably can provide support. The USWA is a very large union whose members earn sufficient income to make campaign contributions. Requiring candidates to rely solely on contributions from members will not unduly limit their ability to raise campaign funds. Uncontradicted record evidence[7] discloses that challengers have been

6. In several First Amendment cases, we have protected contribution and solicitation of the financial support necessary to further effective advocacy. See, e.g., Citizens Against Rent Control v. Berkeley, 454 U.S. 290 (1981); Village of Schaumburg v. Citizens for Better Environment, 444 U.S. 620 (1980); First National Bank of Boston v. Bellotti, 435 U.S. 765 (1978). These cases are not directly analogous, however. Contribution limitations potentially infringe the First Amendment rights of contributors as well as candidates. Buckley v. Valeo, 424 U.S., at 24-25 (per curiam). Here, the nonmember *contributors* have no right of expression protected by the statute.

7. This case is here on cross-motions for summary judgment. We reach a conclusion opposite to that reached by the Court of Appeals — that the outsider rule is valid. In making this decision, we have assumed that all of the evidence submitted by respondents is

able to defeat incumbents or administration-backed candidates, despite the absence of financial support from nonmembers.[8]

In addition, although there are undoubtedly advantages to incumbency, see Hall v. Cole, 412 U.S., at 13, respondents and the Court of Appeals may overstate those advantages. Staff employees are forbidden by §401(g) of the LMRDA and by internal USWA rules to campaign on union time or to use union funds, facilities, or equipment for campaign purposes. Staff officers have a contractual right to choose whether or not to participate in any USWA campaign without being subjected to discipline or reprisal for their decision. Indeed, USWA elections have frequently involved challenges to incumbents by members of the staff. Many of these challenges have been successful.

The impact of the outsider rule on rights protected under §101(a)(2) is limited in another important respect. The union has stated that the rule would not prohibit union members who are not involved in a campaign from using outside funds to address particular issues. That is, members could solicit funds from outsiders in order to focus the attention of the rank and file on a specific problem. The fact that union members remain free to seek funds for this purpose will serve as a counter to the power of entrenched leadership, and ensures that debate on issues that are important to the membership will never be stifled.

(2)

Although the outsider rule may implicate rights protected by §101(a)(2), it serves a legitimate purpose that is clearly protected under the statute. The union adopted the rule because it wanted to ensure that nonmembers do not unduly influence union affairs. USWA feared that officers who received campaign contributions from nonmembers might be beholden to those individuals and might allow their decisions to be influenced by considerations other than the best interests of the union. The union wanted to ensure that the union leadership remained responsive to the membership.[9] An examination of the policies underlying the

---

true. In addition, we have relied on evidence submitted by the union only when it is uncontradicted.

Here, to support their claim that incumbents have a large advantage in union elections, respondents have submitted numerous affidavits. We do not intend to deny the existence of this advantage. For the purposes of our decision in this case, we think it sufficient to observe that there is uncontradicted evidence demonstrating that effective campaigns have been mounted by nonincumbents — and that interference with interests protected by §101(a)(2) is only partial.

8. USWA has submitted evidence suggesting that the adoption of the outsider rule did not have an adverse effect on the 1981 election campaigns. A nonincumbent candidate for district director in a relatively small district has testified that he had raised in excess of $30,000 from rank-and-file members as early as 15 months before the election. Respondents have not submitted any opposing evidence.

9. Respondents allege that the rule was forced upon the union members by high union officers, who wanted to ensure that they were insulated from effective challenges in future

LMRDA reveals that this is a legitimate purpose that Congress meant to protect.

Evidence that Congress regarded the desire to minimize outsider influence as a legitimate purpose is provided by the history to Title 1. On the Senate floor, Senator McClellan argued that a bill of rights for union members was necessary because some unions had been "invaded" or "infiltrated" by outsiders who had no interest in the members but rather had seized control for their own purposes. He stated that the strongest support for the bill of rights provisions "should come from traditional union leaders. It will protect them from the assaults of those who would capture their unions." And he stated:

> [Infiltration could be ended] by placing the ultimate power in the hands of the members, where it rightfully belongs, so that they may be ruled by their free consent, [and] may bring about a regeneration of union leadership. I believe the unions should be returned to those whom they were designed to serve; they should not be left to the hands of those who act as masters. The union must be returned to their members, to whom they rightfully belong. 105 Cong. Rec. 6472 (1959), 2 Leg. Hist. 1099.

It is true that Senator McClellan was particularly concerned about infiltration of unions by racketeers: he described situations in which "thugs and hoodlums" had taken over unions so that they could exploit the members for pecuniary gain. However, his statements also indicate a more general desire to ensure that union members, and not outsiders, control the affairs of their union.

Additional evidence that Congress regarded the union's desire to maintain control over its own affairs as legitimate is provided by the history of other sections of the LMRDA. In drafting Titles II through VI, Congress was guided by the general principle that unions should be left free to "operate their own affairs, as far as possible." S. Rep. No. 1684, 85th Cong., 2d Sess., 4-5 (1958). It believed that only essential standards should be imposed by legislation, and that in establishing those standards great care should be taken not to undermine union self-government. Given certain minimum standards, "individual members are fully competent to regulate union affairs." Ibid. Thus, for example, in Title IV, which regulates the conduct of union elections, Congress simply set forth certain minimum standards. So long as unions conform with these standards, they are free "to run their own elections." Wirtz v. Glass Bottle Blowers, 389 U.S., at 471. Congress' desire to permit unions to regulate their own affairs and to minimize governmental intervention

---

elections. However, the record does not support respondents' claims. The outsider rule was adopted through democratic processes, and was favored by an overwhelming majority of the delegates to the 1978 Convention. These delegates had been elected by the rank and file.

suggests that it would have endorsed union efforts to reduce outsider influence.

Indeed, specific provisions contained in Title IV provide support for our conclusion that the outsider rule serves a legitimate and protected purpose. Section 401(g), 29 U.S.C. §481(g), prohibits the use of employer as well as union funds in election campaigns. This ban reflects a desire to minimize the danger that employers will influence the outcome of union elections. A union rule that seeks to reduce the influence of outsiders other than employers is clearly consistent with that goal. See also §403 of Title IV of the LMRDA, 29 U.S.C. §483 (authorizing unions to establish their own election rules).

Respondents argue that even if the desire to reduce outside influence is a legitimate purpose, the rule is not rationally related to that purpose. They contend, first, that the union could simply have established contribution ceilings, rather than placing an absolute ban on nonmember contributions. However, USWA feared not only that a few individual nonmembers would make large contributions, but also that outsiders would solicit many like-minded persons for small contributions which, when pooled, would have a substantial impact on the election. This fear appears to have been reasonable. In the 1977 election, Sadlowski received a significant percentage of his campaign funds from individuals who made contributions after receiving mail solicitations signed by prominent nonmembers.

Respondents also contend that even if the union was justified in limiting contributions by true outsiders, it need not have limited contributions by relatives and friends. Again, however, the USWA had a reasonable basis for its decision to impose a broad ban. An exception for family members and friends might have created a loophole that would have made the rule unenforceable: true outsiders could simply funnel their contributions through relatives and friends. See id., at 32. Cf. Buckley v. Valeo, 424 U.S., at 53, n. 59 (Congress could constitutionally subject family members to the same limitations as nonfamily members).

Finally, respondents contend that USWA could simply have required that candidates for union office reveal the sources of their funds. But a disclosure rule, by itself, would not have solved the problem. Candidates who received such funds might still be beholden to outsiders. A disclosure requirement ensures only that union members know about this possibility when they cast their votes. It does not eradicate the threat of outside influence.

III

As an alternative basis for sustaining the result below, respondents ask this Court to hold that the outsider rule impermissibly encroaches upon a union member's right, guaranteed by §101(a)(4) of the LMRDA, to institute legal proceedings, and that the appropriate remedy for this violation is an injunction striking down the rule in toto. However, unlike the District Court and the Court of Appeals, we do not believe that the union's rule violates the right-to-sue provision.

Section 101(a)(4) provides that a union may not "limit the right of any member thereof to institute an action in any court, or in a proceeding before any administrative agency." 29 U.S.C. §411(a)(4). The outsider rule would clearly violate this provision if it prohibited union members from accepting financial or other support from nonmembers for the purpose of conducting campaign-related litigation. In our view, however, the outsider rule simply does not apply where a member uses funds from outsiders to finance litigation. . . .

IV

We hold that USWA's rule prohibiting candidates for union office from accepting campaign contributions from nonmembers does not violate §101(a)(2). Although it may interfere with rights Congress intended to protect, it is rationally related to a legitimate and protected purpose, and this is sheltered by the proviso to §101(a)(2). We reverse the decision below and remand for further proceedings consistent with this opinion.[14]

FINNEGAN v. LEU
456 U.S. 431 (1982)

Burger, C. J.

The question presented in this case is whether the discharge of a union's appointed business agents by the union president, following his election over the candidate supported by the business agents, violated the Labor-Management Reporting and Disclosure Act of 1959. . . .

I

In December 1977, respondent Harold Leu defeated Omar Brown in an election for the presidency of Local 20 of the International Brotherhood of Teamsters, Chauffeurs, Warehousemen and Helpers of America, a labor organization representing workers in a 14-county area of northwestern Ohio. During the vigorously contested campaign, petitioners, then business agents of Local 20, openly supported the incumbent president, Brown. Upon assuming office in January 1978, Leu discharged petitioners and the Local's other business agents, all of whom

[14] White, J., Burger, C. J., Brennan, J., and Blackmun, J., dissented.

had been appointed by Brown following his election in 1975. Leu explained that he felt the agents were loyal to Brown, not to him, and therefore would be unable to follow and implement his policies and programs.

Local 20's bylaws — which were adopted by, and may be amended by, a vote of the union membership — provide that the president shall have authority to appoint, direct, and discharge the Union's business agents. The duties of the business agents include participation in the negotiating of collective-bargaining agreements, organizing of union members, and processing of grievances. In addition, the business agents, along with the president, other elected officers, and shop stewards, sit as members of the Stewards Council, the legislative assembly of the Union. Petitioners had come up through the union ranks, and as business agents they were also members of Local 20. Discharge from their positions as business agents did not render petitioners ineligible to continue their union membership.

Petitioners filed suit in the United States District Court, alleging that they had been terminated from their appointed positions in violation of the Labor-Management Reporting and Disclosure Act, 29 U.S.C. §§411(a)(1), 411(a)(2), 412, and 529. The District Court granted summary judgment for respondents Leu and Local 20, holding that the Act does not protect a union employee from discharge by the president of the union if the employee's rights as a union member are not affected. The United States Court of Appeals for the Sixth Circuit affirmed. . . .

II

The Labor-Management Reporting and Disclosure Act of 1959 was the product of congressional concern with widespread abuses of power by union leadership. The relevant provisions of the Act had a history tracing back more than two decades in the evolution of the statutes relating to labor unions. Tensions between union leaders and the rank-and-file members and allegations of union wrongdoing led to extended congressional inquiry. As originally introduced, the legislation focused on disclosure requirements and the regulation of union trusteeships and elections. However, various amendments were adopted, all aimed at enlarged protection for members of unions paralleling certain rights guaranteed by the Federal Constitution; not surprisingly, these amendments — ultimately enacted as Title I of the Act — were introduced under the title of "Bill of Rights of Members of Labor Organizations." The amendments placed emphasis on the rights of union members to freedom of expression without fear of sanctions by the union, which in many instances could mean loss of union membership and in turn loss of livelihood. Such protection was necessary to further the Act's primary objective of ensuring that unions would be democratically governed and responsive to the will of their memberships.

Sections 101(a)(1) and (2) of the Act, on which petitioners rely, guarantee equal voting rights, and rights of speech and assembly, to "[e]very *member* of a labor organization" (emphasis added). In addition, §609 of the Act renders it unlawful for a union or its representatives "to fine, suspend, expel, or otherwise discipline any of its *members* for exercising any right to which he is entitled under the provisions of this Act." (Emphasis added.) It is readily apparent, both from the language of these provisions and from the legislative history of Title I, that it was rank-and-file union members — not union officers or employees, as such — whom Congress sought to protect.

Petitioners held a dual status as both employees and members of the Union. As *members* of Local 20, petitioners undoubtedly had a protected right to campaign for Brown and support his candidacy. At issue here is whether they were thereby immunized from discharge at the pleasure of the president from their positions as appointed union *employees.*

III

Petitioners contend that discharge from a position as a union employee constitutes "discipline" within the meaning of §609; and that termination of union employment is therefore unlawful when predicated upon an employee's exercise of rights guaranteed to members under the Act. However, we conclude that the term "discipline," as used in §609, refers only to retaliatory actions that affect a union member's rights or status *as a member* of the union. Section 609 speaks in terms of disciplining "members"; and the three disciplinary sanctions specifically enumerated — fine, suspension, and expulsion — are all punitive actions taken against union members as members. In contrast, discharge from union employment does not impinge upon the incidents of union membership, and affects union members only to the extent that they happen also to be union employees. See Sheridan v. Carpenters Local No. 626, 306 F.2d 152, 156 (C.A.3 1962). We discern nothing in §609, or its legislative history, to support petitioners' claim that Congress intended to establish a system of job security or tenure for appointed union employees.

Congress used essentially the same language elsewhere in the Act with the specific intent not to protect a member's status as a union employee or officer. Section 101(a)(5) states that "[n]o member of any labor organization may be fined, suspended, expelled, or otherwise disciplined" without enumerated procedural protections. The Conference Report accompanying S. 1555 as finally enacted, H.R. Conf. Rep. No. 1147, 86th Cong., 1st Sess., 31 (1959), 1 Leg. Hist. 935, explains that this "prohibition on suspension without observing certain safeguards applies only to suspension of membership in the union; *it does not refer to suspension of a member's status as an officer of the union*" (emphasis added). This too is a persuasive indication that the virtually identical language in §609 was likewise meant to refer only to punitive actions diminishing membership rights, and not to termination of a member's status as an appointed union employee.[9]

We hold, therefore, that removal from appointive union employment is not within the scope of those union sanctions explicitly prohibited by §609.

IV

Our analysis is complicated, however, by the fact that §102 provides independent authority for a suit against a union based on an alleged violation of Title I of the Act. Section 102 states that

> [a]ny person whose rights secured by the provisions of this title have been infringed by any violation of this title may bring a civil action in a district court of the United States for such relief (including injunctions) as may be appropriate.

Although the intended relationship between §§102 and 609 is not entirely clear, it seems evident that a litigant may maintain an action under §102 — to redress an "infringement" of "rights secured" under Title I — without necessarily stating a violation of §609.[10]

9. In Grand Lodge of International Assn. of Machinists v. King, 335 F.2d, at 344, the court held that Congress had used the "identical words . . . with quite different meanings" in the two sections. The court found that the "legislative gloss" on the words "otherwise disciplined" in §101(a)(5) stemmed primarily from congressional concern that "wrongdoing union officials" — and particularly those guilty of misappropriating union funds — might be permitted "to remain in control while the time-consuming 'due process' requirements of the section were met." See 105 Cong. Rec. 17899 (1959) (remarks of Sen. Kennedy). However, viewing this concern as inapplicable with regard to §609, the court concluded that "although Congress did not intend the words 'otherwise discipline' to include removal from union office in section 101(a)(5), it did intend the words to include such action in section 609."

We agree that the purposes of the two sections are different, and that the distinction drawn in *King* is one Congress plausibly could have chosen to make. However, we are hard pressed to discern any such distinction from either the language or legislative history of the Act. Certainly one would expect that if Congress had intended identical language to have substantially different meanings in different sections of the same enactment it would have manifested its intention in some concrete fashion.

10. Section 609, of course, applies to disciplinary action taken in retaliation for the exercise of *any* right secured under the Act, whereas §102 protects only rights secured by Title I. Although the two sections may be somewhat duplicative as regards union discipline imposed in retaliation for the exercise of Title I rights, this seems due in large part to the fact that the provisions derived from different sources and were originally intended to serve quite different purposes. Section 102 was first included as part of the so-called Kuchel Amendment, and was designed to enforce the provisions of Title I by creating an individual right of action for union members. 105 Cong. Rec. 6719 (1959), 2 Leg. Hist.

The question still remains, however, whether petitioners' "rights secured" under Title I were "infringed" by the termination of their union employment. Petitioners, as union members, had a right under §§101(a)(1) and (2) to campaign for Brown and to vote in the union election, but they were not prevented from exercising those rights. Rather, petitioners allege only an *indirect* interference with their membership rights, maintaining that they were forced to "choos[e] between their rights of free expression . . . and their jobs." See Retail Clerks Union Local 648 v. Retail Clerks International Assn., 299 F. Supp. 1012, 1021 (DC 1969).

We need not decide whether the retaliatory discharge of a union member from union office — even though not "discipline" prohibited under §609 — might ever give rise to a cause of action under §102. For whatever limits Title I places on a union's authority to utilize dismissal from union office as "part of a purposeful and deliberate attempt . . . to suppress dissent within the union," cf. Schonfeld v. Penza, 477 F.2d 899, 904 (C.A.2 1973), it does not restrict the freedom of an elected union leader to choose a staff whose views are compatible with his own.[11] Indeed, neither the language nor the legislative history of the Act suggests that it was intended even to address the issue of union patronage.[12] To the contrary, the Act's overriding objective was to ensure that unions would be democratically governed, and responsive to the will of the union membership as expressed in open, periodic elections. See Wirtz v. Hotel Employees, 391 U.S. 492, 497 (1968). Far from being inconsistent with this purpose, the ability of an elected union president to select his

---

1232. In contrast, the precursor of §609 created *criminal* penalties for retaliatory discipline, and was included in the Senate bill prior to the addition of the bill of rights, see S. 1555, 86th Cong., 1st Sess., §506 (1959) (as reported), 2 Leg. Hist. 390; it apparently was thought to be primarily applicable to violations of the election provisions. See 105 Cong. Rec. 6534 (1959), 2 Leg. Hist. 1140; Rothman, Legislative History of the "Bill of Rights" for Union Members, 45 Minn. L. Rev. 199, 218 (1960). The Landrum-Griffin bill retained this provision, but "temper[ed] the remedy," 105 Cong. Rec. 15531 (1959), 2 Leg. Hist. 1567 (remarks of Rep. Griffin), providing for civil enforcement by the Secretary of Labor instead of criminal sanctions. H.R. 8400, 86th Cong., 1st Sess., §609 (1959), 1 Leg. Hist. 676. Finally, one day before passage of the Landrum-Griffin bill, §609 was amended to authorize private suits, by making "[t]he provisions of section 102 . . . applicable in the enforcement of this section." The amendment was promoted by Congressmen who thought that enforcement by the Secretary would lead to "unnecessary injection of the executive branch on the Federal level into law enforcement matters," 105 Cong. Rec. 15830 (1959), 2 Leg. Hist. 1662 (remarks of Rep. Cramer). See Rothman, supra, at 219.

11. We leave open the question whether a different result might obtain in a case involving nonpolicymaking and nonconfidential employees.

12. We think it virtually inconceivable that Congress would have prohibited the longstanding practice of union patronage without any discussion in the legislative history of the Act. See Wood v. Dennis, 489 F.2d, at 858 (Stevens, J., concurring in result). Had such a result been contemplated, it undoubtedly would have encountered substantial resistance. Moreover, Congress likely would have made some express accommodation to the needs of union employers to appoint and remove policymaking officials. See ibid.

own administrators is an integral part of ensuring a union administration's responsiveness to the mandate of the union election.

Here, the presidential election was a vigorous exercise of the democratic processes Congress sought to protect. Petitioners — appointed by the defeated candidate — campaigned openly against respondent Leu, who was elected by a substantial margin. The Union's bylaws, adopted, and subject to amendment, by a vote of the union membership, grant the president plenary authority to appoint, suspend, discharge, and direct the Union's business agents, who have significant responsibility for the day-to-day conduct of union affairs. Nothing in the Act evinces a congressional intent to alter the traditional pattern which would permit a union president under these circumstances to appoint agents of his choice to carry out his policies.

No doubt this poses a dilemma for some union employees; if they refuse to campaign for the incumbent they risk his displeasure, and by supporting him risk the displeasure of his successor. However, in enacting Title I of the Act, Congress simply was not concerned with perpetuating appointed union employees in office at the expense of an elected president's freedom to choose his own staff. Rather, its concerns were with promoting union democracy, and protecting the rights of union *members* from arbitrary action by the union or its officers.

We therefore conclude that petitioners have failed to establish a violation of the Act. Accordingly, the decision of the Court of Appeals is Affirmed.

BLACKMUN, J., with whom BRENNAN, J. joins, concurring.

I am not prepared to hold that a newly elected president of a local union may discipline, without violating the Labor-Management Reporting and Disclosure Act of 1959, and as a matter of retaliation, *all* union member-employees who opposed his candidacy. As the Court notes, a union member possesses, under the Act, rights to freedom of expression and of speech and assembly, and a right to support the candidate of his choice.

I must assume that what the Court holds today is that the newly elected president may discharge the union's appointed business agents and other appointed union member-employees who will be instrumental in evolving the president's administrative policies. See Elrod v. Burns, 427 U.S. 347 (1976); Branti v. Finkel, 445 U.S. 507 (1980). Indeed, the Court uses the terms "staff," and "his own administrators." In addition, this particular union's bylaws expressly give the president plenary authority over the business agents. With that much, I have no difficulty.

On the understanding, but only on the understanding, that the Court by its opinion is not reaching out further to decide the same issue with respect to nonpolicymaking employees, that is, rank-and-file member-employees (a matter which, for me, presents another case for another day), I join the Court's opinion.

Note

The *Sadlowski* and *Finnegan* decisions raise the same policy issues. To what extent can and should legal rules facilitate monitoring of union officers by the memberships? In *Sadlowski* it appeared that the union had taken special steps to promote open elections and that incumbents had mounted successful campaigns in the past. Does the holding apply to unions without a similar history? If it does not, then the statutory language must be thought to be quite flexible; but if it does, is not reliance on the special circumstances of the Steelworkers Union misplaced?

C. UNION DISCIPLINE

12. NLRA Limitations[15]

NLRB v. ALLIS-CHALMERS MANUFACTURING CO.
388 U.S. 175 (1967)

BRENNAN, J.

The question here is whether a union which threatened and imposed fines [from $20 to $100] and brought suit [in state court] for their collection against members who crossed the union's picket line and went to work during an authorized strike against their employer, committed the unfair labor practice under §8(b)(1)(A) of the National Labor Relations Act of engaging in conduct "to restrain or coerce" employees in the exercise of their right guaranteed by §7 to "refrain from" concerted activities. . . .

It is highly unrealistic to regard §8(b)(1), and particularly its words "restrain or coerce," as precisely and unambiguously covering the union conduct involved in this case. On its face court enforcement of fines imposed on members for violation of membership obligations is no more conduct to "restrain or coerce" satisfaction of such obligations than court

[15] See Atleson, Union Fines and Picket Lines: The NLRA and Union Disciplinary Power, 17 U.C.L.A.L. Rev. 681 (1970); Gould, Some Limitations upon Union Discipline under the National Labor Relations Act: The Radiations of *Allis-Chalmers,* 1970 Duke L.J. 1967; Silard, Labor Board Regulations of Union Discipline after *Allis-Chalmers, Marine Workers* and *Scofield,* 38 Geo. Wash. L. Rev. 187 (1969); Wellington, Union Fines and Workers' Rights, 85 Yale L.J. 1022 (1976).

enforcement of penalties imposed on citizens for violation of their obligations as citizens to pay income taxes, or court awards of damages against a contracting party for nonperformance of a contractual obligation voluntarily undertaken. But even if the inherent imprecision of the words "restrain or coerce" may be overlooked, recourse to legislative history to determine the sense in which Congress used the words is not foreclosed. . . .

To say that Congress meant in 1947 by the §7 amendments and §8(b)(1)(A) to strip unions of the power to fine members for strikebreaking, however lawful the strike vote, and however fair the disciplinary procedures and penalty, is to say that Congress preceded the Landrum-Griffin amendments with an even more pervasive regulation of the internal affairs of unions. It is also to attribute to Congress an intent at war with the understanding of the union-membership relation which has been at the heart of its effort "to fashion a coherent labor policy" and which has been a predicate underlying action by this Court and the state courts. More importantly, it is to say that Congress limited unions in the powers necessary to the discharge of their role as exclusive statutory bargaining agents by impairing the usefulness of labor's cherished strike weapon. It is no answer that the proviso to §8(b)(1)(A) preserves to the union the power to expel the offending member. Where the union is strong and membership therefore valuable, to require expulsion of the member visits a far more severe penalty upon the member than a reasonable fine. Where the union is weak, and membership therefore of little value, the union faced with further depletion of its ranks may have no real choice except to condone the member's disobedience. Yet it is just such weak unions for which the power to execute union decisions taken for the benefit of all employees is most critical to effective discharge of its statutory function.

Congressional meaning is of course ordinarily to be discerned in the words Congress uses. But when the literal application of the imprecise words "restrain or coerce" Congress employed in §8(b)(1)(A) produces the extraordinary results we have mentioned we should determine whether this meaning is confirmed in the legislative history of the section. . . .

What legislative materials there are dealing with §8(b)(1)(A) contain not a single word referring to the application of its prohibitions to traditional internal union discipline in general, or disciplinary fines in particular. On the contrary there are a number of assurances by its sponsors that the section was not meant to regulate the internal affairs of unions. . . .

It is true that there are references in the Senate debate on §8(b)(1)(A) to an intent to impose the same prohibitions on unions that applied to employers as regards restraint and coercion of employees in their exercise of §7 rights. However apposite this parallel might be when applied to organizational tactics, it clearly is inapplicable to the relationship of a union member to his own union. Union membership allows the member a part in choosing the very course of action to which he refuses to adhere, but he has of course no role in employer conduct, and nonunion employees have no voice in the affairs of the union.

Cogent support for an interpretation of the body of §8(b)(1) as not reaching the imposition of fines and attempts at court enforcement is the proviso to §8(b)(1). It states that nothing in the section shall "impair the right of a labor organization to prescribe its own rules with respect to the acquisition or retention of membership therein. . . ." Senator Holland offered the proviso during debate and Senator Ball immediately accepted it, stating that it was not the intent of the sponsors in any way to regulate the internal affairs of unions. At the very least it can be said that the proviso preserves the rights of unions to impose fines, as a lesser penalty than expulsion, and to impose fines which carry the explicit or implicit threat of expulsion for nonpayment. Therefore, under the proviso the rule in the UAW constitution governing fines is valid and the fines themselves and expulsion for nonpayment would not be an unfair labor practice. Assuming that the proviso cannot also be read to authorize court enforcement of fines, a question we need not reach, the fact remains that to interpret the body of §8(b)(1) to apply to the imposition and collection of fines would be to impute to Congress a concern with the permissible *means* of enforcement of union fines and to attribute to Congress a narrow and discrete interest in banning court enforcement of such fines. Yet there is not one word in the legislative history evidencing any such congressional concern. And, as we have pointed out, a distinction between court enforcement and expulsion would have been anomalous for several reasons, First, Congress was operating within the context of the "contract theory" of the union-member relationship which widely prevailed at that time. The efficacy of a contract is precisely its legal enforceability. A lawsuit is and has been the ordinary way by which performance of private money obligations is compelled. Second, as we have noted, such a distinction would visit upon the member of a strong union a potentially more severe punishment than court enforcement of fines, while impairing the bargaining facility of the weak union by requiring it either to condone misconduct or deplete its ranks.

There may be concern that court enforcement may permit the collection of unreasonably large fines. However, even were there evidence that Congress shared this concern, this would not justify reading the Act also to bar court enforcement of reasonable fines.

The 1959 Landrum-Griffin amendments, thought to be the first comprehensive regulation by Congress of the conduct of internal union affairs, also negate the reach given §8(b)(1)(A) by the majority en banc below. . . . In 1959 Congress did seek to protect union members in their relationship to the union by adopting measures to insure the provision of democratic processes in the conduct of union affairs and procedural due process to members subjected to discipline. Even then, some Senators emphasized that, "in establishing and enforcing statutory standards great care should be taken not to undermine union self-government or weaken unions in their role as collective-bargaining agents." S. Rep. No. 187, 86th Cong., 1st Sess., 7. The Eighty-sixth Congress was thus plainly of the view that union self-government was not regulated in 1947. Indeed, that Congress expressly recognized that a union member may be "fined, suspended, expelled, or otherwise disciplined," and enacted only procedural requirements to be observed. 29 U.S.C. §411(a)(5). Moreover, Congress added a proviso to the guarantee of freedom of speech and assembly disclaiming any intent "to impair the right of a labor organization to adopt and enforce reasonable rules as to the responsibility of every member toward the organization as an institution. . . ." 29 U.S.C. §411(a)(2).

The 1959 provisions are significant for still another reason. . . . [T]he only indication in the debates over §8(b)(1)(A) of a reach beyond organizational tactics which restrain or coerce nonmembers was Senator Taft's concern with arbitrary and undemocratic union leadership. The 1959 amendments are addressed to that concern. The kind of regulation of internal union affairs which Senator Taft said protected stockholders of a corporation, and made necessary a "right of protest against arbitrary powers which have been exercised by some of the labor union leaders," is embodied in the 1959 Act. The requirements of adherence to democratic principles, fair procedures and freedom of speech apply to the election of union officials and extend into all aspects of union affairs. In the present case the procedures followed for calling the strikes and disciplining the recalcitrant members fully comported with these requirements, and were in every way fair and democratic. Whether §8(b)(1)(A) proscribes arbitrary imposition of fines, or punishment for disobedience of a fiat of a union leader, are matters not presented by this case, and upon which we express no view.

Thus this history of congressional action does not support a conclusion that the Taft-Hartley prohibitions against restraint or coercion of an employee to refrain from concerted activities included a prohibition against the imposition of fines on members who decline to honor an authorized strike and attempts to collect such fines. Rather, the contrary inference is more justified in light of the repeated refrain throughout the debates on §8(b)(1)(A) and other sections that Congress did not propose any limitations with respect to the internal affairs of unions, aside from barring enforcement of a union's internal regulations to affect a member's employment status.

The collective bargaining agreements with the locals incorporate union security clauses. Full union membership is not compelled by the clauses: an employee is required only to become and remain "a member of the Union . . . to the extent of paying his monthly dues. . . ." The majority en banc below nevertheless regarded full membership to be "the result not of individual voluntary choice but of the insertion of [this] union security provision in the contract under which a substantial minority of the employees may have been forced into membership." 358 F.2d, at 660. But the relevant inquiry here is not what motivated a member's full membership but whether the Taft-Hartley amendments prohibited disciplinary measures against a full member who crossed his union's picket line. It is clear that the fined employees involved herein enjoy full union membership. Each executed the pledge of allegiance to the UAW constitution and took the oath of full membership. Moreover, . . . two disciplined employees testified that they had fully participated in the proceedings leading to the strike. They attended the meetings at which the secret strike vote and the renewed strike vote were taken. It was upon this and similar evidence that the [state court] found that [a disciplined employee] "had by his actions become a member of the union for all purposes. . . ." Allis-Chalmers offered no evidence in this proceeding that any of the fined employees enjoyed other than full union membership. We will not presume the contrary. Indeed, it is and has been Allis-Chalmers' position that the Taft-Hartley prohibitions apply whatever the nature of the membership. Whether those prohibitions would apply if the locals had imposed fines on members whose membership was in fact limited to the obligation of paying monthly dues is a question not before us and upon which we intimate no view.

The judgment of the Court of Appeals is reversed.

White, J., concurring.

It is true that §8(b)(1)(A) makes it an unfair labor practice for a union to restrain or coerce any employees in the exercise of §7 rights, but the proviso permits the union to make its own rules with respect to acquisition and retention of membership. Hence, a union may expel to enforce its own internal rules, even though a particular rule limits the §7 rights of its members and even though expulsion to enforce it would be a clear and serious brand of "coercion" imposed in derogation of those §7 rights. Such restraint and coercion Congress permitted by adding the proviso to §8(b)(1)(A). Thus, neither the majority nor the dissent in this case questions the validity of the union rule against its members crossing picket lines during a properly called strike, or the propriety of expulsion to enforce the rule. Section 8(b)(1)(A), therefore, does not bar *all* restraint and coercion by a union to prevent the exercise by its members of their §7 rights. "Coercive" union rules are enforceable at least by expulsion.

The dissenting opinion in this case, although not questioning the enforceability of coercive rules by expulsion from membership, questions whether fines for violating such rules are enforceable at all, by expulsion or otherwise. The dissent would at least hold court collection of fines to be an unfair labor practice, apparently for the reason that fines collectible in court may be more coercive than fines enforceable by expulsion. My Brother Brennan, for the Court, takes a different view, reasoning that since expulsion would in many cases — certainly in this one involving a strong union — be a far more coercive technique for enforcing a union rule and for collecting a reasonable fine than the threat of court enforcement, there is no basis for thinking that Congress, having accepted expulsion as a permissible technique to enforce a rule in derogation of §7 rights, nevertheless intended to bar enforcement by another method which may be far less coercive.

I do not mean to indicate, and I do not read the majority opinion otherwise, that every conceivable internal union rule which impinges upon the §7 rights of union members is valid and enforceable by expulsion and court action. There may well be some internal union rules which on their face are wholly invalid and unenforceable. But the Court seems unanimous in upholding the rule against crossing picket lines during a strike and its enforceability by expulsion from membership. On this premise I think the opinion written for the Court is the more persuasive and sensible construction of the statute and I therefore join it, although I am doubtful about the implications of some of its generalized statements.

BLACK, J., whom DOUGLAS, J., HARLAN, J., and STEWART, J., join, dissenting. . . .

In determining what the Court here holds, it is helpful to note what it does not hold. Since the union resorted to the courts to enforce its fines instead of relying on its own internal sanctions such as expulsion from membership, the Court correctly assumes that the proviso to §8(b)(1)(A) cannot be read to authorize its holding. Neither does the Court attempt to sustain its holding by reference to §7 which gives employees the right to refrain from engaging in concerted activities. To be sure, the Court in characterizing the union-member relationship as "contractual" and in emphasizing that its holding is limited to situations where the employee is a "full member" of the union, implies that by joining a union an employee gives up or waives some of his §7 rights. But the Court does not say that a union member is without the §7 right to refrain from participating in such concerted activity as an economic strike called by his union. Such a holding would be clearly unwarranted even by resort to the legislative history of the 1947 addition to §7 of "the right to refrain from any or all of such activities." According to Senator Taft, that phrase was added by the Conference Committee to "make the prohibition contained in section 8(b)(1) apply to coercive acts of unions against employees who did not wish to join or *did not care to participate in a strike or a picket line.*" 93 Cong. Rec. 6859, II Leg. Hist. 1623. (Emphasis added.)

With no reliance on the proviso to §8(b)(1)(A) or on the meaning of §7, the Court's holding boils down to this: a court-enforced reasonable fine for nonparticipation in a strike does not "restrain or coerce" an employee in the exercise of his right not to participate in the strike. In holding as it does, the Court interprets the words "restrain or coerce" in a way directly opposed to their literal meaning, for the Court admits that fines are as coercive as penalties imposed on citizens for the nonpayment of taxes. Though Senator Taft, in answer to charges that these words were ambiguous, said their meaning "is perfectly clear," 93 Cong. Rec. 4021, II Leg. Hist. 1025, and though any union official with sufficient intelligence and learning to be chosen as such could hardly fail to comprehend the meaning of these plain, simple English words, the Court insists on finding an "inherent imprecision" in these words. And that characterization then allows the Court to resort to "[w]hat legislative materials there are." . . .

The real reason for the Court's decision is its policy judgment that unions, especially weak ones, need the power to impose fines on strikebreakers and to enforce those fines in court. It is not enough, says the Court, that the unions have the power to expel those members who refuse to participate in a strike or who fail to pay fines imposed on them for such failure to participate; it is essential that weak unions have the choice between expulsion and court-enforced fines, simply because the latter are more effective in the sense of being more punitive. Though the entire mood of Congress in 1947 was to curtail the power of unions, as it had previously curtailed the power of employers, in order to equalize the power of the two, the Court is unwilling to believe that Congress intended to impair "the usefulness of labor's cherished strike weapon." I cannot agree with this conclusion or subscribe to the Court's unarticulated premise that the Court has power to add a new weapon to the union's economic arsenal whenever the Court believes that the union needs that weapon. That is a job for Congress, not this Court. . . .

Contrary to the Court, I am not at all certain that a union's right under the proviso to prescribe rules for the retention of membership includes the right to restrain a member from working by trying him on the vague charge of "conduct unbecoming a union member" and fining him for exercising his §7 right of refusing to participate in a strike, even though the fine is only enforceable by expulsion from membership. It is one thing to say that Congress did not wish to interfere with the union's power, similar to that of any other kind of voluntary association, to prescribe specific conditions of membership. It is quite another thing to say that Congress intended to leave unions free to exercise a court-like power to try and punish members with a direct economic sanction for exercising their right to work. Just because a union might be free, under the proviso, to expel a member for crossing a picket line does not mean that Congress left unions free to threaten their members with fines. Even though a member may later discover that the threatened fine is only enforceable by expulsion, and in that sense a "lesser penalty," the direct threat of a fine, to a member normally unaware of the method the union might resort to for compelling its payment, would often be more coercive than a threat of expulsion.

Even on the assumption that §8(b)(1)(A) permits a union to fine a member as long as the fine is only enforceable by expulsion, the fundamental error of the Court's opinion is its failure to recognize the practical and theoretical difference between a court-enforced fine, as here, and a fine enforced by expulsion or less drastic intra-union means. As the Court recognizes, expulsion for nonpayment of a fine may, especially in the case of a strong union, be more severe than judicial collection of the fine. But, if the union membership has little value and if the fine is great, then court-enforcement of the fine may be more effective punishment, and that is precisely why the Court desires to provide weak unions with this alternative to expulsion, an alternative which is similar to a criminal court's power to imprison defendants who fail to pay fines. . . .

The Court disposes of this tremendous practical difference between court-enforced and union-enforced fines by suggesting that Congress was not concerned with "the permissible *means* of enforcement of union fines" and that court-enforcement of fines is a necessary consequence of the "contract theory" of the union-member relationship. And then the Court cautions that its holding may only apply to court enforcement of "reasonable fines." Apparently the Court believes that these considerations somehow bring reasonable court-enforced fines within the ambit of "internal union affairs." There is no basis either historically or logically for this conclusion or the considerations upon which it is based. First, the Court says that disciplinary fines were commonplace at the time the Taft-Hartley Act was passed, and thus Congress could not have meant to prohibit these "traditional internal union discipline" measures without saying so. Yet there is not one word in the authorities cited by the Court that indicates that court enforcement of fines was commonplace or traditional in 1947, and, to the contrary, until recently unions rarely resorted to court enforcement of union fines. Second, Congress' unfamiliarity in 1947 with this recent innovation and consequent failure to make any distinction between union-enforced and court-enforced fines cannot support the conclusion that Congress was unconcerned with the "means" a union uses to enforce its fines. Congress was expressly concerned with enacting "rules of the game" for unions to abide by. . . .

The union here had a union security clause in its contract with Allis-Chalmers. That clause made it necessary for all employees, including the ones involved here, to pay dues and fees to the union. But §8(a)(3) and §8(b)(2) make it clear that "Congress intended to prevent utilization of union security agreements for any purpose other than to compel payment of union dues and fees." Radio Officers' Union v. Labor Board, 347 U.S. 17, 41. If the union uses the union security clause to compel employees to pay dues, characterizes such employees as members, and then uses such membership as a basis for imposing court-enforced fines upon those employees unwilling to participate in a union strike, then the union security clause is being used for a purpose other than "to compel payment of union dues and fees." It is being used to coerce employees to join in union activity in violation of §8(b)(2).

The Court suggests that this problem is not present here, because the fined employees failed to prove they enjoyed other than full union membership, that their role in the union was not in fact limited to the obligation of paying dues. For several reasons, I am unable to agree with the Court's approach. Few employees forced to become "members" of the union by virtue of the union security clause will be aware of the fact that they must somehow "limit" their membership to avoid the union's court-enforced fines. Even those who are brash enough to attempt to do so may be unfamiliar with how to do it. Must they refrain from doing anything but paying dues, or will signing the routine union pledge still leave them with less than full membership? And finally, it is clear that what restrains the employee from going to work during a union strike is the union's threat that it will fine him and collect the fine from him in court. How many employees in a union shop whose names appear on the union's membership rolls will be willing to ignore that threat in the hope that they will later be able to convince the Labor Board or the state court that they were not full members of the union? By refusing to decide whether 8§(b)(1)(A) prohibits the union from fining an employee who does nothing more than pay union dues as a condition to retaining his job in a union shop, the Court adds coercive impetus to the union's threat of fines. Today's decision makes it highly dangerous for an employee in a union shop to exercise his §7 right to refrain from participating in a strike called by a union in which he is a member in name only. . . .

NLRB v. MARINE WORKERS, 391 U.S. 418 (1968): Union member Holder filed charges with his local union alleging that its president had violated the union constitution. The local ruled that the president had committed no violation. Holder then filed §§8(b)(1)(A) and 8(b)(2) charges against the union alleging the same facts. The local union charged Holder with violating a union constitutional provision requiring members to exhaust all remedies and appeals within the union before resorting to an outside court or tribunal. Holder was found guilty and expelled. He then filed a §8(b)(1)(A) charge challenging his expulsion. The Supreme Court, per Justice Douglas, held the union had violated §8(b)(1)(A):

> We held in NLRB v. Allis-Chalmers Mfg. Co that §8(b)(1)(A) does not prevent a union from imposing fines on members who cross a picket line created to implement an authorized strike. The strike, we said, "is the ultimate weapon in labor's arsenal for achieving agreement upon its terms," and the power to fine or expel as strikebreaker "is essential if the union is to be an effective bargaining agent." Thus §8(b)(1)(A) assures a union freedom of self-regulation where its legitimate internal affairs are concerned. But where a union rule penalizes a member for filing an unfair labor practice charge with the Board, other considerations of public policy come into play. . . .
>
> A healthy interplay of the forces governed and protected by the Act means that there should be as great a freedom to ask the Board for relief as there is to petition any other department of government for a redress of grievances. Any coercion used to discourage, retard, or defeat that access is beyond the legitimate interest of a labor organization. . . . [T]he overriding public interest makes unimpeded access to the Board the only healthy alternative, except and unless plainly internal affairs of the union are involved. . . .

SCOFIELD v. NLRB, 394 U.S. 423 (1969): The union represented production employees, about half of whom were paid on a piecework or incentive basis. The union had established a ceiling on production — employees could produce more than the ceiling rate, but were forbidden to demand immediate payment for production above the ceiling rate; they could only "bank" the excess production with the company against the day when the ceiling rate was not reached because of machine breakdown or other cause. Violation of these union-imposed rules resulted in fines, and a refusal to pay a fine could result in expulsion. When the union imposed such fines ($50 to $100) on several union members and sought to enforce the fines in state court, the members filed §8(b)(1)(A) charges[16] against the union. The Supreme Court, affirming the Board and the court of appeals, found no violation. The Court described the approach of *Allis-Chalmers* and *Marine Workers* as

> [leaving] a union free to enforce a properly adopted rule which reflects a legitimate union interest, impairs no policy Congress has imbedded in the labor laws, and is reasonably enforced against union members who are

[16] Since the union had bargained with the company over the existence and content of the union rules, there was no §8(b)(3) refusal to bargain. The Board has ruled that union enforcement, through its disciplinary procedures, of a unilaterally imposed production ceiling violates §8(b)(3). Painters District Council (Westgate Painting & Decorating Corp.), 136 N.L.R.B. 964 (1970), enforced, 453 F.2d 783 (2d Cir. 1971), cert. denied, 408 U.S. 930 (1972).

> free to leave the union and escape the rule. This view of the statute must be applied here.
>
> In the case at hand, there is no showing in the record that the fines were unreasonable or the mere fiat of a union leader, or that the membership of petitioners in the union was involuntary. Moreover, the enforcement of the rule was not carried out through means unacceptable in themselves, such as violence or employer discrimination. It was enforced solely through the internal technique of union fines, collected by threat of expulsion or judicial action. The inquiry must therefore focus on the legitimacy of the union interest vindicated by the union-imposed production ceiling.

The Court then noted the historic union concern that piecework pay systems drive up productivity and create pressure to lower piecework rates, thus forcing employees to exert intolerable efforts at no greater pay. The Court admitted that the rule was "intended to have an impact beyond the confines of the union organization," but refused to find the required "impairment of a statutory labor policy" since the rule had been the subject of collective bargaining and did not violate the bargaining agreement.

CARPENTERS LOCAL 22 (GRAZIANO CONSTRUCTION CO.)

195 N.L.R.B. 1 (1972)

[Respondent union contended that it fined union member Shanley for violating legitimate union rules but the Board found that the union was retaliating against Shanley for his opposition of certain activities by the union's officers. No labor-management activities were involved in the case.]

It is by now well settled that although Section 8(b)(1)(A) "leaves a union free to enforce a properly adopted rule which reflects a legitimate union interest" and "impairs no policy Congress has imbedded in the labor laws,"[1] it does not permit enforcement, by fine or expulsion, of a rule which "invades or frustrates an overriding policy of the labor laws. . . ."[2] Cases decided to date, holding that union enforcement of a rule by fining a member violates Section 8(b)(1)(A) of the Act, have involved the protection of important policies embodied in the Act itself, such as the right of employees to gain access to the processes of the Board to seek to remedy union conduct violative of the Act, or the right of employees who sought to observe contractual responsibilities to protection against union efforts to punish them for refusing to breach such

1. Scofield v. NLRB, 394 U.S. 423, 430.
2. Id. at 429.

responsibilities. The policies which the Union's conduct here seeks to frustrate are embodied in the Labor-Management Reporting and Disclosure Act of 1959, rather than specifically in the National Labor Relations Act. This difference does not, however, impel a different conclusion.

As the above-quoted language from the Supreme Court's decision in *Scofield* implies, the Board is charged with considering the full panoply of congressional labor policies in determining the legality of a union fine. Here the Union, in the guise of enforcing internal discipline, has sought to deprive its members of the right, as guaranteed by the Labor-Management Reporting and Disclosure Act, to participate fully and freely in the internal affairs of his own union. A fine for that purpose not only in our opinion fails to reflect a legitimate union interest but rather in fact impairs a policy that Congress has imbedded in the labor laws. For these reasons, we conclude that the Respondent Union's conduct in fining Shanley because of his intraunion activity violated Section 8(b)(1)(A) of the Act.

Having found that the Respondent unlawfully cited and fined Bernard Shanley the sum of $75 because of his intraunion activity, we shall order that said fine be rescinded, that all references and other evidence in Respondent's records and files relating to the proceeding against Shanley be expunged, and that Shanley be reimbursed for any sums paid toward said fine with interest thereon at the rate of 6 percent per annum from the time said sums were paid. . . .

Member Fanning, dissenting:

The Trial Examiner found that Shanley was in fact disciplined because of his violations of the union rules, and that such violations were not utilized as a pretext to discipline him for other reasons. I would not reverse the Trial Examiner on this pretext finding and would, therefore, dismiss the complaint in its entirety without reaching the further legal issue decided by my colleagues.

Notes

1. Recall that most collective bargaining agreement union security clauses do not make it clear that an employee is obligated only to pay dues and fees and is not obligated to assume the duties required by full membership. Should that be relevant to §8(b)(1)(A) scrutiny of union discipline?

2. Is the Court saying in *Allis-Chalmers* that the fining of a nonmember violates §8(b)(1)(A)? If so, doesn't that concede that fines constitute "coercion"? What precisely is the Court's rationale? Do *Allis-Chalmers, Marine Workers,* and *Scofield* yield a consistent line of analysis or did the Court redirect its test?

Recall that in *Mackay,* supra at p. 373, the Court permitted permanent replacement of strikers by employers despite an obvious interference with §7 rights. In *Republic Aviation,* supra at p. 170, the balance came down the other way. Could those cases have been used by analogy in *Allis-Chalmers*? How would they cut?

3. Would a union violate §8(b)(1)(A) by fining a member for refusing to participate in a strike later found to be a secondary boycott[17] or in breach of a collective bargaining agreement? If so, what result if the strike were not in breach of the bargaining agreement but the member had a good faith belief that it was?

4. *Graziano* may be an isolated case but its implications for Board enforcement of the LMRDA are staggering. How would you have argued the case for the union opposing a Board enforcement petition in a court of appeals?

5. *Problem.* The Elevator Constructors Union has a rule that no member may install a factory pre-assembled escalator. When the Otis Elevator Company raised an objection to this rule in bargaining negotiations, the union discussed but refused to abolish it. Yesterday, Otis brought a pre-assembled escalator on the jobsite and ordered two employees (both union members) to install it. They complied. Today the union summarily fined each of them $500 and also expelled one of the two. The bargaining agreement with Otis has broad no-strike and grievance/arbitration clauses. Any §8(b)(1)(A) violation?

NLRB v. BOEING CO.[18]

412 U.S. 67 (1973)

[The union fined 143 members $540 each for working behind an economic picket line called by the union. The union filed suit in state court against nine employees to collect the fines and the employer filed a §8(b)(1)(A) charge contending the fines were unreasonable in amount. The Board held it had no authority to scrutinize the size of union fines.]

REHNQUIST, J. . . .

We have previously held that §8(b)(1)(A) was not intended to give the Board power to regulate internal union affairs, including the imposition of disciplinary fines, with their consequent court enforcement, against members who violate the unions' constitutions and bylaws. NLRB v. Allis-Chalmers Mfg. Co., 388 U.S. 175 (1967); Scofield v. NLRB (394 U.S. 423 (1969). . . .

[17] In Longshoremens Local 30, 223 N.L.R.B. 1257, enforced, 549 F.2d 698 (9th Cir. 1977), the Board found it a §8(b)(1)(A) violation to fine a union member for refusing to honor a secondary picket line; but see NLRB v. Local 18, IUOE, 503 F.2d 780 (6th Cir. 1974) (finding no violation where union expels members for refusing to honor illegal secondary picket lines.)

[18] See Craver, The *Boeing* Decision: A Blow to Federalism, Individual Rights and Stare Decisis, 122 U. Pa. L. Rev. 556 (1974).

In deciding these cases, the Court several times referred to the unions' imposition of "reasonable" fines. In particular, the *Scofield* Court concluded "that the union rule is valid and that its enforcement by *reasonable* fines does not constitute the restraint or coercion proscribed by §8(b)(1)(A)." 394 U.S., at 436 (emphasis added). The Company contends, not illogically, that the Court's use of the adjective "reasonable" was intended to suggest to the Board that an unreasonable fine would amount to an unfair labor practice.

This interpretation, however, permissible as it may be, is only dicta, since in both *Allis-Chalmers* and in *Scofield* the reasonableness of the fines was assumed. Being squarely presented with the issue in this case, we recede from the implications of the dicta in these earlier cases. While "unreasonable" fines may be more coercive than "reasonable" fines, all fines are coercive to a greater or lesser degree. The underlying basis for the holdings of *Allis-Chalmers* and *Scofield* was not that reasonable fines were noncoercive under the language of §8(b)(1)(A) of the Act, but was instead that those provisions were not intended by Congress to apply to the imposition by the union of fines not affecting the employer-employee relationship and not otherwise prohibited by the Act. The reason for this determination, in turn, was that Congress had not intended by enacting this section to regulate the internal affairs of unions to the extent that would be required in order to base unfair labor practice charges on the levying of such fines. . . .

Inquiry by the Board into the multiplicity of factors that the parties and the Court of Appeals correctly thought to have a bearing on the issue of reasonableness would necessarily lead the Board to a substantial involvement in strictly internal union affairs. While the line may not always be clear between those matters that are internal and those that are external, to the extent that the Board was required to examine into such questions as a union's motivation for imposing a fine it would be delving into internal union affairs in a manner which we have previously held Congress did not intend. Given the rationale of *Allis-Chalmers* and *Scofield*, the Board's conclusion that §8(b)(1)(A) of the Act has nothing to say about union fines of this nature, whatever their size, is correct. Issues as to the reasonableness or unreasonableness of such fines must be decided upon the basis of the law of contracts, voluntary associations, or such other principles of law as may be applied in a forum competent to adjudicate the issue. Under our holding, state courts will be wholly free to apply state law to such issues at the suit of either the union or the member fined. . . .

The Court of Appeals and the Company have suggested several policy reasons why the Board should not leave the determinations of reasonableness entirely to the state courts. Their basic reasons are, first, that more uniformity in the determination of what is reasonable will result if the Board suggests standards and, second, that more expertise in labor matters will be brought to bear if the issue is decided by the Board rather than solely by the Courts. Even if we were to concede the relevance of policy factors in determining congressional intent, we are not persuaded that the Board is necessarily the better forum for determining the reasonableness of a fine.

As we noted in *Allis-Chalmers,* court enforcement of union fines is not a recent innovation but has been known at least since 1867. The relationship between a member and his union is generally viewed as contractual in nature, and the local law of contracts or voluntary associations usually governs the enforcement of this relationship.

We alluded to state court enforcement of unusually harsh union discipline in *Allis-Chalmers* when we stated that "state courts, in reviewing the imposition of union discipline, find ways to strike down 'discipline [which] involves a severe hardship.'" 388 U.S., at 193 n. 32, quoting Summers, Legal Limitations on Union Discipline, 64 Harv. L. Rev. 1049, 1078 (1951). The Board assumed that in view of this statement, our reference to "reasonable" fines, when reasonableness was not in issue, in *Allis-Chalmers* and in *Scofield,* was merely adverting to the usual standard applied by state courts in deciding whether to enforce union-imposed fines. The Board reads these cases, therefore, as encouraging state courts to use a reasonableness standard, not as a directive to the Board.

Our review of state court cases decided both before and after our decisions in *Allis-Chalmers* and *Scofield* reveals that state courts applying state law are quite willing to determine whether disciplinary fines are reasonable in amount. Indeed, the expertise required for a determination of reasonableness may well be more evident in a judicial forum that is called upon to assess reasonableness in varying factual contexts than it is in a specialized agency. In assessing the reasonableness of disciplinary fines, for example, state courts are often able to draw on their experience in areas of the law apart from labor relations.

Nor is it clear, as contended by the Court of Appeals, that the Board's setting of standards of reasonableness will necessarily result in greater uniformity in this area even if uniformity is thought to be a desirable goal. Since state courts will have jurisdiction to determine reasonableness in the enforcement context in an event, the Board's independent determination of reasonableness in an unfair labor practice context might well yield a conflict when the two forums are called upon to review the same fine.

For all of the foregoing reasons, we conclude that the Board was warranted in determining that when the union discipline does not interfere with the employee-employer relationship or otherwise violate a policy of the National Labor Relations Act, the Congress did not authorize it "to evaluate the fairness of union discipline meted out to protect a legitimate union interest." The judgment of the Court of Appeals is, therefore, reversed.[19]

[19] Burger, C.J., Douglas, J., and Blackmun, J., dissented.

Note

In NLRB v. Granite State Joint Board, Textile Workers Local 1029, 409 U.S. 213 (1972), the Court ruled that a union violates §8(b)(1)(A) when it fines strike-breaking members who have effectively resigned from the union. In Booster Lodge 405, IAM v. NLRB, 412 U.S. 84 (1973), the Court refused to imply a commitment into a union constitution prohibiting members from strike breaking after an effective resignation from union membership. The court left open the question of whether a union could avoid violating §8(b)(1)(A) by relying on a provision in the constitution or bylaws expressly limiting a member's power to resign and avoid union discipline.[20] Is there any policy argument for voiding such a limitation in a union's constitution, especially if you assume that members were aware of the limitation when they joined?

Presumably a state court would not enforce the fine imposed in *Granite State* because a contractual basis would be lacking. How is it, then, that an enforceable fine does not violate §8(b)(1)(A) but an unenforceable fine does? The Board has stated, "A man who is held up at gunpoint is coerced whether or not the gun is loaded."[21]

AMERICAN BROADCASTING CO. v. WRITERS GUILD OF AMERICA WEST

437 U.S. 411 (1978)

[The respondent union represents writers in the television and motion picture industries. The petitioners are the three major television networks, ABC, NBC, and CBS, and the Association of Motion Picture and Television Producers.

Among the union's members are a substantial number of persons hired by the employers to perform executive and supervisory functions including the selection and direction of writers and limited writing duties not covered by the union's contract. These persons are called "hyphenates."

During a union strike, many hyphenates reported to work. They performed supervisory functions and no writing work covered by past union contracts. The union charged 30 hyphenates who worked during the strike with violating union rules. After hearings, these hyphenates were subjected to various penalties, including expulsions, suspensions, and fines from $100 to $50,000.

[20] The Board has held that a union cannot restrict the right of members to resign during a strike. Machinists Local Lodge 1414 (Neufeld Porsche-Audi), 270 N.L.R.B. No. 209, 116 L.R.R.M. 1257 (1984). Accord, Pattern Makers' League v. NLRB, 115 L.R.R.M. 2264 (7th Cir. 1983); but see, Machinists Local Lodge 1327 v. NLRB, 725 F.2d 1212 (9th Cir. 1984).

[21] Booster Lodge No. 405, IAM, 185 N.L.R.B. 380, 381 (1970), modified, 459 F.2d 1143 (D.C. Cir. 1972), aff'd in part and rev'd in part, 412 U.S. 67, 84 (1973).

Petitioners filed §8(b)(1)(B) unfair labor practice charges. An administrative law judge found that the hyphenates were supervisors, that one of their functions was the adjustment of grievances, and that during the strike they had done their normal work, which included grievance adjustment, but they had performed no rank-and-file work. The ALJ found that by disciplining the hyphenates the union had restrained and coerced the employers in the selection of their representatives for grievance adjustment. Finally, he held that the Supreme Court's decision in Florida Power & Light Co. v. International Bhd. of Elec. Workers Local 641, 417 U.S. 790 (1974) (FP&L) was not controlling.

The Board adopted the findings and conclusions of the ALJ. It reasoned that *FP&L* was distinguishable because there the union had disciplined supervisors who had performed bargaining unit work during a strike, and in the instant case the disciplined union members had performed only their ordinary supervisory work during the strike. A court of appeals denied enforcement.]

WHITE, J. . . .

II

As the Court has set out in greater detail in its comprehensive review of §8(b)(1)(B) in *FP&L,* the prohibition against restraining or coercing an employer in the selection of his bargaining representative was, until 1968, applied primarily to pressures exerted by the union directly upon the employer to force him into a multiemployer bargaining unit or otherwise to dictate or control the choice of his representative for the purpose of collective bargaining or adjusting grievances in the course of administering an existing contract. In San Francisco-Oakland Mailers' Union No. 18, International Typographical Union (Northwest Publications, Inc.), 172 N.L.R.B. 2173 (1968), however, the Board applied the section to prohibit union discipline of one of its member-supervisors for the manner in which he had performed his supervisory task of grievance adjustment. Although the union "sought the substitution of attitudes rather than persons, and may have exerted its pressures upon the [employer] by indirect rather than direct means," the ultimate fact was that the pressure interfered with the employer's control over his representative. "Realistically, the Employer would have to replace its foremen or face *de facto* nonrepresentation by them." *Oakland Mailers,* supra, at 2173.

The application of the section to indirect coercion of employers through pressure applied to supervisory personnel continued to evolve until the *FP&L* and *Illinois Bell*[18] cases reached the Court of Appeals for

18. IBEW, Local 134 v. NLRB, 159 U.S. App. D.C. 242, 487 F.2d 1113, rev'd on rehearing en banc, 159 U.S. App. D.C. 272, 487 F.2d 1143 (1973), refusing to enforce IBEW, Local 134, 192 N.L.R.B. 85 (1971) (Illinois Bell), and IBEW Systems Council U-4, 193 N.L.R.B. 30 (1971) (FP&L).

the District of Columbia Circuit and then this Court. In each of those cases, the union disciplined supervisor-members who had performed rank-and-file work behind a union picket line during a strike. In a companion case to *Illinois Bell,* upon which *Illinois Bell* explicitly relied, the Board found an infraction of §8(b)(1)(B), broadly construing its purpose "to assure to the employer that its selected collective-bargaining representatives will be completely faithful to its desires" and holding that this could not be achieved "if the union has an effective method, union disciplinary action, by which it can pressure such representatives to deviate from the interests of the employer." In like fashion, in *FP&L,* the Board held that fining supervisors for doing rank-and-file work during a work stoppage "struck at the loyalty an employer should be able to expect from its representatives for the adjustment of grievances and therefore restrained and coerced employers in their selection of such representatives."

The Court of Appeals overturned both decisions of the Board, holding that although the section could be properly applied to union efforts to discipline supervisors for their performance as collective-bargaining or grievance-adjustment representatives, it could not reasonably be applied to prohibit union discipline of supervisors crossing picket lines to perform bargaining-unit work: "When a supervisor forsakes his supervisory role to do rank-and-file work ordinarily the domain of nonsupervisory employees, he is no longer acting as a management representative and no longer merits any immunity from discipline." 159 U.S. App. D.C., at 286, 487 F.2d, at 1157.

This Court affirmed the judgment of the Court of Appeals:

> The conclusion is thus inescapable that a union's discipline of one of its members who is a supervisory employee can constitute a violation of §8(b)(1)(B) only when that discipline may adversely affect the supervisor's conduct in performing the duties of, and acting in his capacity as, grievance adjuster or collective bargainer on behalf of the employer. 417 U.S., at 804-805.

The Court thus rejected the claim that "even if the effect of [union] discipline did not carry over to the performance of the supervisor's grievance adjustment or collective bargaining functions," it was enough to show that the result would be "to deprive the employer of the full allegiance of, and control over, a representative he has selected for grievance adjustment or collective bargaining purposes." Id., at 807. Assuming without deciding that the Board's decision in *Oakland Mailers* fell within the outer reaches of §8(b)(1)(B), the Court concluded that the *Illinois Bell* and *FP&L* decisions did not, because it was "certain that these supervisors were not engaged in collective bargaining or grievance adjustment, or in any activities related thereto, when they crossed union picket lines during an economic strike to engage in rank-and-file struck work." 417 U.S., at 805.

Subsequent to *FP&L,* in applying §8(b)(1)(B) to cases involving union discipline of supervisor-members, the Board directed its attention, as it understood *FP&L* to require, to the question whether the discipline may adversely affect the supervisor's conduct in performing his grievance-adjustment or collective-bargaining duties on behalf of the employer. In *Hammond Publishers,* supra, and *Triangle Publishers,* supra, the Board held that it was an unfair practice under §8(b)(1)(B) for a union to discipline a supervisor-member whose regular duties included the adjustment of grievances for crossing a picket line to perform his regular functions during a strike. These cases rested on the Board's conclusion that such discipline imposed on the supervisor would have a "carryover" effect and would influence the supervisor in the performance of his adjustment functions after the strike and hence interfere with and coerce the employer in the choice of his grievance representative. The *Triangle* decision was not challenged in the courts, but *Hammond* was enforced. 176 U.S. App. D.C. 240, 539 F.2d 242 (1976), as was *Skippy Enterprises,* 532 F.2d 47 (C.A.7 1976).[23] . . .

IV

We cannot agree with what appears to be the fundamental position of the Court of Appeals and the union that under §8(b)(1)(B), as the section was construed in *FP&L,* it is never an unfair practice for a union to discipline a supervisor-member for working during a strike, regardless of the work that he may perform behind the picket line. The opinion in *FP&L* expressly refrained from questioning *Oakland Mailers* or the proposition that an employer could be coerced or restrained within the meaning of §8(b)(1)(B) not only by picketing or other direct actions aimed at him but also by debilitating discipline imposed on his collective-bargaining or grievance-adjustment representative. Indeed, after focusing on the purposes of the section, the Court in *FP&L* delineated the boundaries of when that "carryover" effect would violate §8(b)(1)(B): whenever such discipline may adversely affect the supervisor's conduct in his capacity as a grievance adjustor or collective bargainer. In these situations — that is, when such impact might be felt — the employer would be deprived of the full services of his representatives and hence would be restrained and coerced in his selection of those representatives.

23. In *Hammond* and *Skippy,* the supervisor also performed some rank-and-file work during the strike. The Board in *Hammond* characterized the amount of rank-and-file work as minimal, and only incidental to the supervisory functions, but in *Skippy,* the supervisor performed rank-and-file work for about 30% of his time. In light of the finding that the supervisors performed no rank-and-file writing in this case, we are not presented with that element of the Board's reasoning in *Hammond* and *Skippy.*

Furthermore, because this was the test prescribed and employed by the Court to adjudicate the very situation where union discipline was imposed for crossing picket line, it is unlikely that the Court anticipated that the test could *never* be satisfied in such disciplinary cases, that it could *never* be true that the sanction could or would affect the supervisor's collective-bargaining or grievance-adjustment functions, or that the employer in such circumstances could *never* be restrained or coerced in the selection of his representatives.

This is not to say that *every* effort by a union to discipline a supervisor for crossing a picket line to do supervisory rather than rank-and-file work would satisfy the standards specified by *FP&L,* or that on facts present here there is necessarily a violation of §8(b)(1)(B). But we are of the view that the Board correctly understood *FP&L* to mean that in ruling upon a §8(b)(1)(B) charge growing out of union discipline of a supervisory member who elects to work during a strike, it may — indeed, it must — inquire whether the sanction may adversely affect the supervisor's performance of his collective-bargaining or grievance-adjustment tasks and thereby coerce or restrain the employer contrary to §8(b)(1)(B). The Board addressed those issues here, and if its ultimate factual conclusions in this regard are capable of withstanding judicial review, it seems to us that its construction of the section fairly recognizes and respects the outer boundaries established by *FP&L,* and represents an "acceptable reading of the statutory language and a reasonable implementation of the purposes of the relevant statutory sections." NLRB v. Iron Workers, 434 U.S. 335, 341 (1978).

Respondent objects that this construction of the Act impermissibly intrudes on the union's right to resort to economic sanctions during a strike. However, an employer also has economic rights during a strike, and the statute declares that, in the unrestrained freedom to select a grievance-adjustment and collective-bargaining representative, the employer's rights dominate. Ample leeway is already accorded to a union in permitting it to discipline any member, even a supervisor, for performing struck work — to carry that power over to the case of purely supervisory work is an inappropriate extension and interference with the employer's prerogative. The Board has so ruled, and as the Court has often observed, "'[t]he function of striking [the] balance to effectuate national labor policy is often a difficult and delicate responsibility, which the Congress committed primarily to the National Labor Relations Board, subject to limited judicial review,'" NLRB v. Iron Workers, supra, at 350, quoting NLRB v. Truck Drivers, 353 U.S. 87, 96 (1957); NLRB v. Insurance Agents, 361 U.S. 477, 499 (1960). Here, in adjudicating as it did the intertwining interests of union, employer, and supervisor-member during an economic strike, we cannot say that the Board has moved into a new area of regulation not committed to it by Congress, ibid., or conclude that the role assumed by the Board is "fundamentally inconsistent with the structure of the Act and the function of the sections relied upon." American Ship Building Co. v. NLRB, 380 U.S. 300, 318 (1965); NLRB v. Iron Workers, supra.

V

. . . We are also unpersuaded that the Board's findings and conclusions are infirm on any of the grounds submitted.

[A]s to those hyphenates who reported for work, it is strenuously urged that there is no basis for concluding that the discipline imposed upon them would adversely affect the performance of their grievance-adjustment duties either during or after the strike. . . .

[I]t does not strike us as groundless or lacking substantial evidence for the Board to conclude on this record that the discipline imposed would have the necessary adverse effect. Strike rules were distributed in February; the strikes against the Association began on March 4 and terminated June 24; the strikes against the networks began on March 29 and ended on July 12. Between April 6 and November 8 — both during and after the strikes — some 31 hyphenates who had worked during the strikes were charged with violating union rules, 15 hearings had been held prior to the closing of evidence in November 1973, and from June 25 to September 28, very substantial penalties were imposed in 10 cases although 9 have already been reduced on appeal. These penalties were widely publicized at the time of their imposition. Other charges were pending and remained to be tried when the record was closed in this case.

These penalties were meted out at least in part because the accused hyphenates had complied with the orders of their employers by reporting for work and performing only their normal supervisory functions, including the adjustment of grievances, during the strike. Hyphenates who worked were thus faced not only with threats but also with the *actuality* of charges, trial, and severe discipline simply because they were working at their normal jobs. And if this were not enough, they were threatened with a union blacklist that might drive them from the industry. How long such hyphenates would remain on the job under such pressure was a matter no one, particularly the employer, could predict.

Moreover, after the strike, with the writers back at work, the hyphenates who had worked during the strike still faced charges and trials or were appealing large fines and long suspensions. At the same time, they were expected to perform their regular supervisory duties and to adjust grievances whenever the occasion demanded, functions requiring them to deal with the same union which was considering the appeal of their personal sanctions. As to these supervisors, who had felt the union's wrath, not for doing rank-and-file work contrary to union rules, but for performing only their primary supervisory duties during the strike and who were in a continuing controversy with the union, it was not untenable for the Board to conclude that these disciplined hyphenates had a diminished capacity to carry out their grievance-adjustment duties effectively and that the employer was deprived of the full range of services from his supervisors. Such a hyphenate might be tempted to give the union side of a grievance a more favorable slant while the threat of discipline remained, or while his own appeal of a union sanction was pending. At the very least, the employer could not be certain that a fined hyphenate would willingly answer the employer's call to duty during a subsequent work stoppage, particularly if it occurred in the near future. For an employer in these circumstances to insure having satisfactory collective-bargaining and grievance-adjustment services would require a change in his representative.

As the Board has construed the Act from *Oakland Mailers* to *Triangle, Hammond,* and the cases now before us, such a likely impact on the employer constitutes sufficient restraint and coercion in connection with the selection of collective-bargaining and grievance-adjustment representatives to violate §8(b)(1)(B). In *FP&L* the Court declined the invitation to overrule *Oakland Mailers,* and we do so again. Union pressure on supervisors can affect either their willingness to serve as grievance adjustors or collective bargainers, or the manner in which they fulfill these functions; and either effect impermissibly coerces the employer in his choice of representative.

Third, it is further urged that union discipline could not adversely affect a supervisor's later performance of his §8(b)(1)(B) duties because the employer could require him to leave the union and thus free himself from further threats of union discipline. This submission has little force in this case, since, as the Administrative Law Judge found, the union's known policy was not to permit a member to resign during a strike and for a period of six months thereafter. For the entire period to which the Board's findings were addressed, hyphenates could not terminate their membership, and the employer's only recourse would have been to replace them as his grievance representatives.

Carried to its logical end, this submission is simply another argument that union sanctions applied to supervisor-members who work during a strike can never violate §8(b)(1)(B), because the employer could always insist that his supervisors either terminate union affiliation or face discharge. Yet, as we have noted, the test posited by this Court in *FP&L* plainly recognizes the possibility of a §8(b)(1)(B) violation arising from union fines imposed during a strike. Moreover, if the argument were to be accepted, indirect pressures on the employer by sanctioning supervisor-members for the manner in which they perform their grievance-adjusting function (as in *Oakland Mailers*) would never be a violation because the supervisor could, at the employer's request, escape from union threats and sanctions. The Board's construction of the Act is to the contrary, however, and as we have said, we are not prepared at this juncture to override it.

Because we have concluded that the Board's construction of §8(b)(1)(B) is not an unreasonable reading of its language or inconsistent with its purposes, and because we cannot say that the Board's findings lacked substantial evidence, we must reverse the judgment of the Court of Appeals.[22]

Notes

1. If an employee has been a member of a unionized bargaining unit for several years, he or she may have accumulated valuable union benefits, such as an entitlement to a death benefit payable to the family upon the member's death, a share in a union strike fund, medical insurance coverage, and the like. These union benefits may persuade the employee not to accept a position as a low-level supervisor if acceptance requires resignation from union membership — and this is especially true for a senior rank-and-file employee who may earn only slightly more as a supervisor and who is old enough to have little expectation of advancing further in management ranks.

2. Recall the Elevator Constructors hypothetical, supra at p. 945. If the rank-and-file employees had refused to install the escalator and so two supervisors performed the installation, could the union lawfully fine the supervisors (assuming they were union members)?

3. Would it violate §8(a)(5) for an employer to insist to impasse on a bargaining agreement clause limiting the union's power to discipline either rank-and-file strikebreakers or supervisors who perform rank-and-file work during a strike?

2. LMRDA Limitations[23]

DETROY v. AMERICAN GUILD OF VARIETY ARTISTS
286 F.2d 75 (2d Cir. 1961)

Lumbard, C.J.

The appellant, manager and trainer of a troupe of chimpanzees with which he performs professionally under the name of the "Marquis Family" in theaters, night clubs, circuses, on television, and in motion pictures, instituted this proceeding under §102 of the Labor-Management Reporting and Disclosure Act of 1959 demanding injunctive relief and

[22] Stewart, J., Brennan, J., Marshall, J., and Stevens, J., dissented.

[23] See Etelson & Smith, Union Discipline under the Landrum-Griffin Act, 82 Harv. L. Rev. 727 (1969); Beaird & Player, Union Discipline of its Membership under Section 101(a)(5) of the Landrum-Griffin, 9 Ga. L. Rev. 383 (1975).

damages for an alleged violation of the procedural rights granted union members by §101(a)(5) of the Act. Upon a motion for summary judgment, the district court dismissed the complaint on the ground that under §101(a)(4) the plaintiff could bring no court action against a labor union without first exhausting the internal remedies provided by the union, and that in this case the defendant union had established reasonable procedures by its constitution whereby claims against it by members could be heard within the four-month period permitted by the law.

The controversy between the appellant and the American Guild of Variety Artists, a labor union representing variety entertainers in the United States and Canada, arose out of a breach-of-contract claim made against the appellant by a resort hotel in Las Vegas, Nevada. After failing to settle the dispute by negotiation, the AGVA requested the parties to submit it to arbitration, which they did. A panel of three, one selected by each of the parties to the dispute and the third chosen by the two so designated, met in Los Angeles County, California, on January 12, 1960, and decided in favor of the hotel. The union then advised the appellant that if he did not abide by the award, it would place him on the "National Unfair List" appearing in its monthly periodical "AGVA News." The appellant replies that he intended to move to vacate the arbitration award in the California courts, but never began any such proceedings. When the three months provided by California law for vacating arbitration awards had elapsed, the union proceeded to publish the appellant's name in the August 1960 issue of the periodical under a heading which read as follows:

> Notice to Members
>
> The rules require that you may not work for any employer, agent, booker or third party who is marked "Unfair" by AGVA. Violation of these rules subjects you to disciplinary action.
>
> Notice to Agents
>
> . . . You are not authorized to book AGVA members in unfair establishments or book performers not in good standing in AGVA. Violation of rules subjects you to revocation of your franchise.

The appellant then began this proceeding in the Southern District of New York, claiming that the listing amounted to disciplinary action within the meaning of §101(a)(5) of the Labor-Management Reporting and Disclosure Act of 1959 and that he was, therefore, entitled to specific written charges, a reasonable time to defend, and a full and fair hearing before having his name placed on the list.

The appellant did not, however, seek to utilize the procedure made available by Article XX of the Constitution of the AGVA. This article, entitled "Claims of Members," establishes procedures whereby claims asserted against the union are heard and determined by its Board or

Executive Committee. Thus, the first issue before us now is whether the proviso in §101(a)(4), which protects the right of a union member to sue his union, "Provided, That any such member may be required to exhaust reasonable hearing procedures (but not to exceed a four-month lapse of time) within such organization, before instituting legal or administrative proceedings against such organizations or any officer thereof," required of the appellant in this case that he first have recourse to the internal procedures established by the union's constitution. The exhaustion proviso of §101(a)(4) does not appear in §102, which grants members who claim that their rights under §101 have been infringed a federal forum in which to litigate their disputes with the union. . . . However, the broad language of the proviso in §101(a)(4) includes suits instituted against labor unions in any court on any claim. Absent a clear directive by Congress, the policy formulated over a course of time by courts reluctant to interfere in the internal affairs of private organizations should not be superseded. We hold, therefore, that the provision in §101(a)(4) applies, as well, to suits brought in the federal courts for violations of the rights secured by §101.

Judge Dimock in this case read §101(a)(4) as imposing upon the union member an absolute duty to exhaust union remedies before applying to the federal courts. The legislative history of the section indicates, however, that Congress had no intention of establishing such a rule. The statute provides that any member of a labor organization "may be required" to exhaust the internal union remedies, not that he "must" or "is required to" exhaust them. When read in light of the statements made on the floor of Congress by the authors of the statute, it appears clear that the proviso was incorporated in order to preserve the exhaustion doctrine as it had developed and would continue to develop in the courts, lest it otherwise appear to be Congress' intention to have the right to sue secured by §101 abrogate the requirement of prior resort to internal procedures. In addition, the proviso dictated an outside limit beyond which the judiciary cannot extend the requirements of exhaustion — no remedy which would require proceedings exceeding four months in duration may be demanded. We therefore construe the statute to mean that a member of a labor union who attempts to institute proceedings before a court or an administrative agency may be required *by that court or agency* to exhaust internal remedies of less than four months' duration before invoking outside assistance. . . .

If we look to the substantial body of state law on the subject, we find that the general rule requiring exhaustion before resort to a court has been almost entirely swallowed up by exceptions phrased in broad terms. Rather than decide whether exhaustion is proper by determining whether the union's action can be characterized as "void" or as "affecting property rights," we believe it preferable to consider each case on its own facts.

The Congressionally approved policy of first permitting unions to correct their own wrongs is rooted in the desire to stimulate labor organizations to take the initiative and independently to establish honest and democratic procedures. Other policies, as well, underlie the exhaustion rule. The possibility that corrective action within the union will render a member's complaint moot suggests that, in the interest of conserving judicial resources, no court step in before the union is given its opportunity. Moreover, courts may find valuable the assistance provided by prior consideration of the issues by appellate union tribunals. Congress has provided a safeguard against abuse by a union of the freedom thus granted it by not requiring exhaustion of union remedies if the procedures will exceed four months in duration. But in any case, if the state of facts is such that immediate judicial relief is warranted, Congress' acceptance of the exhaustion doctrine as applied to the generality of cases should not bar an appropriate remedy in proper circumstances.

The affidavits and exhibits submitted in the district court on the motion for summary judgment establish that the only hearing given the appellant before his name was placed on the National Unfair List was that of the arbitration proceeding. The union was not a party to the arbitration, and the issue decided by the arbitrators was not whether the appellant should be disciplined by the union but whether he owed an obligation to an employer with whom he had contracted. It is undisputed that no hearing was held in which the appellant could respond to the union's intention of taking disciplinary action. Quite clearly, a hearing in which some liability between a union member and a third party is determined is not the type of hearing demanded by §101(a)(5). At no time was the appellant given the opportunity of arguing before the union's hearing board that placing him on the Unfair List exceeded the powers granted to the union by its constitution, nor could he raise other mitigating circumstances in response to an expressed intention to place his name on such a list. The facts on their face, therefore, reveal a violation of the rights guaranteed union members by §101(a)(5). If the question before us were whether the union's constitution authorized the listing of the appellant's name on an unfair list after a hearing with due procedural safeguards, a union tribunal might provide some insight to aid our decision. But no prior consideration by such a tribunal is necessary or helpful on the question whether the treatment of the appellant violated §101(a)(5).

In addition, the particular form of the disciplinary action makes it difficult for the union to provide an adequate remedy. The appellant, from the date his name appeared on the list, was virtually barred from employment by those dealing regularly with the AGVA. Since he is an independent contractor whose weekly pay varies according to the terms of the contracts he signs with his employers, the precise extent of damages suffered by the appellant as a result of the listing can never be determined. Even were the union to permit him to present his case before a review board, the board could merely order his name removed from the list and, in order to provide a more satisfactory remedy, award as damages for the period during which he was barred from employment a sum which, at best, could only be an approximation. It appears unlikely that Congress intended that its expressed desire to provide minimum safeguards against arbitrary union discipline be avoided by the union's imposition of a sanction which has its most severe effect within a four-month period, if the consequences of such action cannot be precisely measured in order to assess damages. Early judicial intervention providing an adequate remedy by means of the court's power to enjoin further violations is therefore proper. . . .

Moreover, it is by no means clear that the union's own rules afforded the appellant a remedy within the organization. The section of the union's constitution which relates to disciplinary proceedings (Article XVII) authorizes fines, censure, suspension, or expulsion pursuant to a hearing and determination made by the Board or Executive Committee of the union. An appeal may be taken from such a decision to the next following annual or special convention of the union. No provision is made anywhere for any proceeding either before or after the printing of a member's name on the National Unfair List. . . .

Taking due account of the declared policy favoring self-regulation by unions, we nonetheless hold that where the internal union remedy is uncertain and has not been specifically brought to the attention of the disciplined party, the violation of federal law clear and undisputed, and the injury to the union member immediate and difficult to compensate by means of a subsequent money award, exhaustion of union remedies ought not to be required. The absence of any of these elements might, in light of Congressional approval of the exhaustion doctrine, call for a different result. The facts of this case, however, warrant immediate judicial intervention.

Nor can we agree with the union's claim that the listing of the appellant's name did not constitute discipline within the meaning of §101(a)(5). If a union such as the AGVA undertakes to enforce the contracts made by its members with employers, it does so because such enforcement is to the ultimate benefit of all the members, in that it promotes stability within the industry. A breach of contract or a refusal to abide by an arbitration award, therefore, is not damaging merely to the employer but to the union as well, and the union's listing of those of its members who do violate their contracts is an act of self-protection. In thus furthering its own ends the union must abide by the rules set down for it by Congress in §101(a)(5), and any member against whom steps are taken by the union in the interest of promoting the welfare of the group is entitled to these guarantees. . . .

FIGUEROA v. NATIONAL MARITIME UNION
342 F.2d 400 (2d Cir. 1965)

MEDINA, J. . . .

Many years ago each of the appellees [three seamen union members] was convicted of unlawfully possessing narcotics, but they had been employed for some time as seamen and were members of the appellant Union until March 6, 1958. On that date Government Customs Agents became aware of these old convictions and arrested the three seamen on board the SS "Independence," charging that they had left the country without registering as violators of the narcotics laws. These charges were not pressed, but the result was that the Union thereafter refused to register these men at the hiring hall or to refer them to shipowners for employment as seamen.

As stated previously, the policy of the shipowners bargaining with the National Maritime Union had for some time been not to employ on their vessels any persons known to have participated in any crime involving narcotics. In 1957 the collective bargaining agreement negotiated by the Union with the shipowners provided in terms that the Union shall not be required to register a seaman "whom it does not consider to be suitable for employment," and it was agreed that "in passing upon the suitability of applicants for registration" the Union shall give consideration to such matters as habitual drunkenness, illegal possession of lethal weapons, immoral or indecent conduct, and "illegal possession or use of narcotics." Admittedly, union and nonunion applicants for employment received the same treatment.

After discovery of the narcotics convictions events moved swiftly. The Union not only refused to register and refer the three seamen, but it also applied automatic suspension of membership under Article 22, Section 3 of the Union constitution, although the convictions of two of the seamen were long prior to the period of their membership in the Union, and the conviction of the third preceded the adoption by the Union of this section of the constitution. . . .

We turn to the merits of the case. Here again we eschew the attempt to distinguish between "employment" rights and "membership" rights. We affirm *Detroy* and hold that under certain circumstances union interference with the employment opportunities of its members may constitute "discipline" within §101(a)(5).

But in this case, unlike *Detroy* where the union acted unilaterally in blacklisting the plaintiff member, the refusal to register and refer was pursuant to the terms of a collective bargaining agreement and in compliance with the declared policy of the shipowners that they will hire no seamen known to have a narcotics conviction. This was no more "discipline," once appellees admitted their convictions and the applicability to them of the terms of the collective bargaining agreement, than it would have been to turn down an applicant who admitted that he lacked a physical requirement for the job or who admitted that he fell outside the age limits specified by the employer.

Had appellees disputed the fact of their convictions, the determination by the Union or its agent that they had been convicted would, of course, have constituted "discipline" entitling the members to the procedural safeguards of §101(a)(5). Having admitted their convictions and consequent disqualification from employment under the collective bargaining agreement, appellees' claim to a hearing must fail.

Whether or not the refusal by the Union to refer appellees constituted a breach of the Union's duty of fair representation, a matter not presented to us and which we do not decide, it is clear that, under the circumstances of this case, the Union's conduct did not amount to "discipline." Nothing in §101(a)(5) compels a union to grant a hearing concerning whether it ought to negotiate with an employer regarding a change in hiring policies expressed in a collective agreement. Such matters of collective bargaining strategy are not to be confused with the union discipline at which §101(a)(5) is aimed. . . .

Notes

1. In Ryan v. International Brotherhood of Electrical Workers, 361 F.2d 942 (7th Cir.), cert. denied, 385 U.S. 935 (1966), union members were expelled for filing a lawsuit prior to exhausting their internal union remedies. Acknowledging that a court might have dismissed the members' suit for failure to exhaust, the Seventh Circuit nonetheless held that union discipline for a failure to exhaust was barred by §101(a)(4). The Supreme Court approved this reading of §101(a)(4) in NLRB v. Marine Workers, 391 U.S. 418 (1968), supra at p. 941, where the issue was argued by analogy in a §8(b)(1)(A) case.

2. According to the court in *Figueroa,* if the seamen "had disputed the fact of their convictions," they would have been entitled by §101(a)(5) to a hearing. Is the only purpose of a union disciplinary hearing with procedural safeguards to determine the guilt or innocence of the accused? Certainly the seamen would have wanted to argue for clemency, or that their conduct fell outside of the spirit, if not the language, of the rule.

3. On the question of what constitutes §101(a)(5) "discipline," are *Detroy* and *Figueroa* compatible? Would *Detroy* have been decided the other way if the AGVA's right to place a member on the unfair list in these circumstances was embodied in a collective bargaining agreement with an employer?

4. *Problem.* An employer operating a lunch counter suspected the theft of money or food by employees but was unable to apprehend the

culprit. The employer and the union agreed that rather than a discharge of the entire crew of 11, five employees would be temporarily laid off and replaced by new people. If the thefts stopped, the layoffs would become permanent; if the thefts continued, the laid-off employees would be reinstated. The thefts did stop and the five employees were discharged. Plaintiff was one of those discharged and the union refused to file a grievance in her behalf. She filed a fair representation action in federal court and lost.[24] Would she have fared better charging a violation of §101(a)(5)? If not, would her chances be substantially improved under either that or the fair representation doctrine if she alleged and proved that the union business agent disliked her personally?

5. *Problem.* A local carpenters union has engaged in several wildcat strikes in recent years, causing much of the local carpentry work to go nonunion. If the parent international union revokes the local's charter and establishes a new local in the area, has there been a violation of §101(a)(5)? Would it matter whether some, or all, of the members of the old local were granted membership in the new local? How would you advise the international to proceed?

INTERNATIONAL BROTHERHOOD OF BOILERMAKERS v. HARDEMAN

401 U.S. 233 (1971)

BRENNAN, J. . . .

Respondent was expelled from membership in petitioner union and brought this action under §102 in the District Court for the Southern District of Alabama. He alleged that in expelling him the petitioner violated §101(a)(5) of the Act. . . . A jury awarded respondent damages of $152,150. The Court of Appeals for the Fifth Circuit affirmed. 420 F.2d 485 (1969). We granted certiorari limited to the questions whether the subject matter of the suit was pre-empted because exclusively within the competence of the National Labor Relations Board and, if not pre-empted, whether the courts below had applied the proper standard of review to the union proceedings. We reverse.

The case arises out of events in the early part of October 1960. Respondent, George Hardeman, is a boilermaker. He was then a member of petitioner's Local Lodge 112. On October 3, he went to the union hiring hall to see Herman Wise, business manager of the Local Lodge and the official responsible for referring workmen for jobs. Hardeman had talked to a friend of his, an employer who had promised to ask for him by name for a job in the vicinity. He sought assurance from Wise that he would be referred for the job. When Wise refused to make a

[24] Union News Co. v. Hildreth, 295 F.2d 658 (6th Cir. 1961).

definite commitment, Hardeman threatened violence if no work was forthcoming in the next few days.

On October 4, Hardeman returned to the hiring hall and waited for a referral. None was forthcoming. The next day, in his words, he "went to the hall . . . and waited from the time the hall opened until we had the trouble. I tried to make up my mind what to do, whether to sue the Local or Wise or beat hell out of Wise, and then I made up my mind." When Wise came out of his office to go to a local jobsite, as required by his duties as business manager, Hardeman handed him a copy of a telegram asking for Hardeman by name. As Wise was reading the telegram, Hardeman began punching him in the face.

Hardeman was tried for this conduct on charges of creating dissension and working against the interest and harmony of the Local Lodge, and of threatening and using force to restrain an officer of the Local Lodge from properly discharging the duties of his office. The trial committee found him "guilty as charged," and the Local Lodge sustained the finding and voted his expulsion for an indefinite period. Internal union review of this action, instituted by Hardeman, modified neither the verdict nor the penalty. Five years later, Hardeman brought this suit alleging that petitioner violated §101(a)(5) by denying him a full and fair hearing in the union disciplinary proceedings.

I

We consider first the union's claim that the subject matter of this lawsuit is, in the first instance, within the exclusive competence of the National Labor Relations Board. The union argues that the gravamen of Hardeman's complaint — which did not seek reinstatement, but only damages for wrongful expulsion, consisting of loss of income, loss of pension and insurance rights, mental anguish and punitive damages — is discrimination against him in job referrals; that any such conduct on the part of the union is at the very least arguably an unfair labor practice under §§8(b)(1)(A) and 8(b)(2) of the National Labor Relations Act, and that in such circumstances, "the federal courts must defer to the exclusive competence of the National Labor Relations Board if the danger of . . . interference with national policy is to be averted." San Diego Building Trades Council v. Garmon, 359 U.S. 236, 245 (1959); see Local 100, Journeymen v. Borden, 373 U.S. 690 (1963).

We think the union's argument is misdirected. Hardeman's complaint alleged that his expulsion was unlawful under §101(a)(5), and sought compensation for the consequences of the claimed wrongful expulsion. The critical issue presented by Hardeman's complaint was whether the union disciplinary proceedings had denied him a full and fair hearing within the meaning of §101(a)(5)(C). Unless he could establish this claim, Hardeman would be out of court. We hold that this claim was not within the exclusive competence of the National Labor Relations Board. . . . Those factors suggesting that resort must be had to the administrative process are absent from the present case. The fairness of an internal union disciplinary proceeding is hardly a question beyond "the conventional experience of judges," nor can it be said to raise issues "within the special competence" of the NLRB. See NLRB v. Allis-Chalmers Mfg. Co., 388 U.S. 175, 181, 193-194 (1967). As we noted in that case, the 86th Congress which enacted §101(a)(5) was "plainly of the view" that the protections embodied therein were new material in the body of federal labor law.

And that same Congress explicitly referred claims under §101(a)(5), not to the NLRB, but to the federal district courts. This is made explicit in the opening sentence of §102: "Any person whose rights secured by the provisions of this title have been infringed by any violation of this title may bring a civil action in a district court of the United States for such relief (including injunctions) as may be appropriate." Of course, "[t]he purpose of Congress is the ultimate touchstone." Retail Clerks Local 1625 v. Schermerhorn, 375 U.S. 96, 103 (1963). And in §102 Congress has clearly indicated a purpose to refer claims regarding violation of §101(a)(5) to the district courts.

The union argues that Hardeman's suit should nevertheless have been dismissed because he did not seek an injunction restoring him to membership, and because he did seek damages for loss of employment said to be the consequence of his expulsion from the union. Taken together, these factors are said to shift the primary focus of the action from a review of Hardeman's expulsion to a review of alleged union discrimination against him in job referrals. Since this is a matter normally within the exclusive competence of the NLRB, see Local 100, Journeymen v. Borden, 373 U.S., at 695-696, the union argues that Hardeman's suit was beyond the competence of the district court.

The argument has no merit. To begin with, the language of §102 does not appear to make the availability of damages turn upon whether an injunction is requested as well. If anything, §102 contemplates that damages will be the usual, and injunctions the extraordinary form of relief. Requiring that injunctive relief be sought as a precondition to damages would have little effect other than to force plaintiffs, as a matter of course, to add a few words to their complaints seeking an undesired injunction. We see no reason to import into §102 so trivial a requirement.

Nor are our prior cases authority for such a result. We have repeatedly held, of course, that state law may not regulate conduct either protected or prohibited by the National Labor Relations Act. Where it has not been clear whether particular conduct is protected, prohibited, or left to state regulation by that Act, we have likewise required courts to stay their hand, for "courts are not primary tribunals to adjudicate such issues. It is essential to the administration of the Act that these determinations be left in the first instance to the National Labor Relations Board." Building Trades Council v. Garmon, supra, at 244-245. . . .

The present case, however, implicates none of the principles discussed above. There is no attempt, in this lawsuit, to apply state law to matters pre-empted by federal authority. Nor is there an attempt to apply federal law of general application, which is limited in the particular circumstances by the National Labor Relations Act. Nor is there an attempt to have the District Court enforce the provisions of the National Labor Relations Act itself, without guidance from the NLRB. As we have said, the critical question in this action is whether Hardeman was afforded the rights guaranteed him by §101(a)(5) of the LMRDA. If he was denied them, Congress has said that he is entitled to damages for the consequences of that denial. Since these questions are irrelevant to the legality of conduct under the National Labor Relations Act, there is no danger of conflicting interpretation of its provisions. And since the law applied is federal law explicitly made applicable to such circumstances by Congress, there is no danger that state law may come in through the back door to regulate conduct that has been removed by Congress from state control. Accordingly, this action was within the competence of the District Court.

II

Two charges were brought against Hardeman in the union disciplinary proceedings. He was charged with violation of Art. XIII, §1, of the Subordinate Lodge Constitution, which forbids attempting to create dissension or working against the interest and harmony of the union, and carries a penalty of expulsion. He was also charged with violation of Art. XII, §1, of the Subordinate Lodge By-Laws, which forbids the threat or use of force against any officer of the union in order to prevent him from properly discharging the duties of his office; violation may be punished "as warranted by the offense." Hardeman's conviction on both charges was upheld in internal union procedures for review.

The trial judge instructed the jury that "whether or not he [respondent] was rightfully or wrongfully discharged or expelled is a pure question of law for me to determine." He assumed, but did not decide, that the transcript of the union disciplinary hearing contained evidence adequate to support conviction of violating Art. XII. He held, however, that there was no evidence at all in the transcript of the union disciplinary proceedings to support the charge of violating Art. XIII. This holding appears to have been based on the Fifth Circuit's decision in Boilermakers v. Braswell, 388 F.2d 193 (C.A.5 1968). There the Court of Appeals for the Fifth Circuit had reasoned that "penal provisions in union constitutions must be strictly construed," and that as so construed Art. XIII was directed only to "threats to the union as an organization and to the effective carrying out of the union's aims," not to merely personal altercations. 388 F.2d, at 199. Since the union tribunal had returned only a general verdict, and since one of the charges was thought to be supported by no evidence whatsoever, the trial judge held that Hardeman had been deprived of the full and fair hearing guaranteed by §101(a)(5). The Court of Appeals affirmed, simply citing *Braswell.*

We find nothing in either the language or the legislative history of §101(a)(5) that could justify such a substitution of judicial for union authority to interpret the union's regulations in order to determine the scope of offenses warranting discipline of union members. Section 101(a)(5) began life as a floor amendment to S. 1555, the Kennedy-Ervin Bill, in the 86th Congress. As proposed by Senator McClellan, and as adopted by the Senate on April 22, 1959, the amendment would have forbidden discipline of union members "except for breach of a published written rule of [the union]." 105 Cong. Rec. 6476, 6492-6493. But this language did not long survive. Two days later, a substitute amendment was offered by Senator Kuchel, who explained that further study of the McClellan amendment had raised "some rather vexing questions." The Kuchel substitute, adopted the following day, deleted the requirement that charges be based upon a previously published, written union rule; it transformed Senator McClellan's amendment, in relevant part, into the present language of §101(a)(5). As so amended, S. 1555 passed the Senate on April 25. Identical language was adopted by the House and appears in the statute as finally enacted.

The Congress understood that Senator Kuchel's amendment was intended to make substantive changes in Senator McClellan's proposal. Senator Kennedy had specifically objected to the McClellan amendment because "[i]n the case of . . . the . . . official who bribed a judge, unless there were a specific prohibition against bribery of judicial officers written into the constitution of the union, then no union could take disciplinary action against [an] officer or member guilty of bribery. . . . It seems to me that we can trust union officers to run their affairs better than that." Id., at 6491.

Senator Kuchel described his substitute as merely providing "the usual reasonable constitutional basis" for union disciplinary proceedings: union members were to have "constitutionally reasonable notice and a reasonable hearing." Id., at 6720. After the Kuchel amendment passed the Senate, Senator Goldwater explained it to the House Committee on Labor and Education as follows:

> [T]he bill of rights in the Senate bill requires that the union member be served with written specific charges prior to any disciplinary proceedings but it does not require that these charges, to be valid, must be based on activity that the union had proscribed prior to the union member having

> engaged in such activity. Labor-Management Reform Legislation, Hearings before a Joint Subcommittee of the House Committee on Education and Labor, 86th Cong., 1st Sess., pt. 4, p. 1595 (1959).

And Senator McClellan's testimony was to the same effect.

We think that this is sufficient to indicate that §101(a)(5) was not intended to authorize courts to determine the scope of offenses for which a union may discipline its members.[11] And if a union may discipline its members for offenses not proscribed by written rules at all, it is surely a futile exercise for a court to construe the written rules in order to determine whether particular conduct falls within or without their scope.

Of course, §101(a)(5)(A) requires that a member subject to discipline be "served with written specific charges." These charges must be, in Senator McClellan's words, "specific enough to inform the accused member of the offense that he has allegedly committed." Where, as here, the union's charges make reference to specific written provisions, §101(a)(5)(A) obviously empowers the federal courts to examine those provisions and determine whether the union member had been misled or otherwise prejudiced in the presentation of his defense. But it gives courts no warrant to scrutinize the union regulations in order to determine whether particular conduct may be punished at all.

Respondent does not suggest, and we cannot discern, any possibility of prejudice in the present case. Although the notice of charges with which he was served does not appear as such in the record, the transcript of the union hearing indicates that the notice did not confine itself to a mere statement or citation of the written regulations that Hardeman was said to have violated: the notice appears to have contained a detailed statement of the facts relating to the fight that formed the basis for the disciplinary action. Section 101(a)(5) requires no more.

III

There remains only the question whether evidence in the union disciplinary proceeding was sufficient to support the finding of guilt. Section 101(a)(5)(C) of the LMRDA guarantees union members a "full and fair" disciplinary hearing, and the parties and the lower federal courts are in full agreement that this guarantee requires the charging party to provide some evidence at the disciplinary hearing to support the charges made. This is the proper standard of judicial review. We have repeatedly

11. State law, in many circumstances, may go further. See Summers, The Law of Union Discipline: What the Courts Do in Fact, 70 Yale L.J. 175 (1960). But Congress, which preserved state law remedies by §103 of the LMRDA, was well aware that even the broad language of Senator McClellan's original proposal was more limited in scope than much state law. See 105 Cong. Rec. 6481-6489.

held that conviction on charges unsupported by any evidence is a denial of due process, and we feel that §101(a)(5)(C) may fairly be said to import a similar requirement into union disciplinary proceedings. Senator Kuchel, who first introduced the provision, characterized it on the Senate floor as requiring the "usual reasonable constitutional basis" for disciplinary action, 105 Cong. Rec. 6720, and any lesser standard would make useless §101(a)(5)(A)'s requirement of written, specific charges. A stricter standard, on the other hand, would be inconsistent with the apparent congressional intent to allow unions to govern their own affairs, and would require courts to judge the credibility of witnesses on the basis of what would be at best a cold record.[15]

Applying this standard to the present case, we think there is no question that the charges were adequately supported. Respondent was charged with having attacked Wise without warning, and with continuing to beat him for some time. Wise so testified at the disciplinary hearing, and his testimony was fully corroborated by one other witness to the altercation. Even Hardeman, although he claimed he was thereafter held and beaten, admitted having struck the first blow. On such a record there is no question but that the charges were supported by "some evidence."

Reversed.[25]

DOUGLAS, J., dissenting. . . .

I agree that a court does not sit in review of a union as it does of an administrative agency. But by reason of §101(a)(5) judicial oversight is much more than procedural; it provides in subsection (C) for "a full and fair hearing." Even if every conceivable procedural guarantee is provided, a hearing is not "fair" when all substantive rights are stripped away to reach a preordained result. If there is to be a "fair hearing" there must, I submit, be some evidence directed to the charges to support the conclusion.

Membership in a union may be the key to livelihood itself. Without membership, the member may be cast into the outer darkness, so far as employment is concerned. Just as this Court concluded Congress did not authorize exclusive bargaining agents to make invidious discriminations, Steele v. Louisville & Nashville R. Co., 323 U.S. 192, it is unthinkable to me that Congress in designing §101(a)(5) gave unions the authority to expel members for such reasons as they chose. For courts to lend their hand to such oppressive practices is to put the judicial imprimatur on the union's utter disregard of due process to reach its own ends.

In Boilermakers v. Braswell, arising out of the same incident, the Court of Appeals followed that reasoning. 388 F.2d 193, 199. It said:

15. Although a transcript was made of the union proceedings in the present case, we have no reason to believe that this is a universal practice.

[25] White, J., concurred.

> [T]he act charged to Braswell was a blow struck in anger, and nothing more. However reprehensible this act may be, it did not constitute a violation of the provisions in the charges. Article XIII, Section 1 of the constitution on its face is directed at threats to the union as an organization and to the effective carrying out of the union's aims. Braswell's fist was not such a threat.

As stated by a student in this area: "[H]ow can there be a 'full and fair hearing' when it results in a verdict which mocks the evidence?"[8] Of course, the reviewing court does not give a hearing de novo; nor does it review the merits of the dispute. But it does sit to check intemperate use of union power; and if it is to discharge its duties, it must conclude that there is some evidence to sustain the charge. This is the view of the Second, Third, and Fifth Circuits, Vars v. Boilermakers, 320 F.2d 576; Kelsey v. Philadelphia Local No. 8, 419 F.2d 491; Boilermakers v. Braswell, 388 F.2d 193, and I would adopt it as the controlling legal principle. . . .

Notes

1. Wouldn't the union's refusal to refer Hardeman violate §8(b)(1)(A) whether he made out his Landrum-Griffin §101(a)(5) claim or not? What issues would be litigated in the Board proceedings? Presumably the extent of the damages suffered by Hardeman would be a principal point of contention. Is the Board deemed to have expertise in determining these damages? If only damages for lost referrals are sought, why no primary jurisdiction in the Board? Isn't the six-month limitation on Board charges (§10(b) of the NLRA) intended to preclude damages for stale claims of union refusals to refer?

2. Which of the following procedural rights of an accused would you deem guaranteed by §101(a)(5): to be present during the taking of evidence, to cross-examine witnesses, to be represented by a lawyer, to be represented by a fellow member, to be provided a transcript of the hearing, to take an appeal to the union membership and then to the international union?

3. *Problem.* Suppose union member Frodo is charged with assaulting the union business agent at a tavern. Frodo and the business agent disagree over who started the fight. The notice of hearing to Frodo reads, in part: "Member Gandalf is appointed hearing officer in this case to determine the truth or falsity of the charge. Member Gandalf was present at the tavern the night when the fight occurred and is thus best able to evaluate the conflicting accounts of what happened." If Gandalf

8. Christensen, Union Discipline under Federal Law: Institutional Dilemmas in an Industrial Democracy, 43 N.Y.U.L. Rev. 227, 251.

is the hearing officer, has the union violated §101(a)(5)? If so, and if Frodo is found guilty, what remedy: acquittal or new trial?

4. In Hall v. Cole, 412 U.S. 1 (1972), the Court held that an award of attorney fees is permissible in a suit under §102 of the LMRDA that establishes a violation of §101(a)(2).

> [B]y vindicating his own right of free speech guaranteed by §101(a)(2) respondent necessarily rendered a substantial service to his union as an institution and to all of its members. When a union member is disciplined for the exercise of any of the rights protected by Title I, the rights of all members of the union are threatened. And, by vindicating his own right, the successful litigant dispels the "chill" cast upon the rights of others. Indeed, to the extent that such lawsuits contribute to the preservation of union democracy, they frequently prove beneficial "not only in the immediate impact of the results achieved but in their implications for the future conduct of the union's affairs." Yablonski v. United Mine Workers of America, 150 U.S. App. D.C. 253, 260, 466 F.2d 424, 431 (1972). Thus, . . . reimbursement of respondent's attorneys' fees out of union treasury simply shifts the costs of litigation to "the class that has benefited from them and that would have had to pay them had it brought the suit."

The Court rejected the argument that since §§201(c) and 501(b) of the LMRDA expressly authorize the recovery of attorney fees, the failure of §102 to so provide demonstrates a congressional purpose to preclude them. Presumably, then, attorney fees also are recoverable if the suit charges a violation of §101(a)(5).

D. ELECTION OF UNION OFFICERS[26]

NOTE, ELECTION REMEDIES UNDER THE LABOR-MANAGEMENT REPORTING AND DISCLOSURE ACT

78 Harv. L. Rev. 1617, 1617-1618 (1965)

Historically, control of internal union affairs was left to the state courts without any legislative guidance. The common law provided few if any principles applicable to union elections, primarily because of the general reluctance of the courts to interfere in affairs of voluntary associations. The union member who brought suit for violation of his election rights was unable to recover damages, since he had sustained no

[26] See Topol, Union Elections under the LMRDA, 74 Yale L.J. 1282 (1965); Comment, 81 Yale L.J. 407 (1972).

calculable loss. The alternative of seeking relief in equity was often barred by the practice of protecting only property rights. Although some courts found a property right in a candidate's holding office or in a member's voting for officials, and others simply disregarded the property requirement altogether, when the courts did intervene, it was generally on the theory that the union constitution and bylaws created a contract between union and members. These documents became, at least ostensibly, the standard for judicial resolution of internal union disputes. They proved to be an unsuccessful standard because they were frequently too general, ambiguous, and incomplete, and the courts were therefore forced to adjudicate disputes without clear guiding principles.

State courts granted union members both preelection and postelection relief. The willingness of the courts to intervene, the form of the remedy they provided, and the effectiveness of judicial action depended largely on when suit was brought. The great majority of suits appear to have been brought for temporary injunctions, prior to the holding of an election. If there was no time for a hearing, the judge might grant an order to show cause and issue an ex parte restraining order effective until the hearing. If an interlocutory order issued, the union could either correct the defect and proceed with the election, or postpone the election pending determination of whether a permanent injunction should be granted. On the other hand, state courts were very reluctant to void an election already held and would deny relief if the plaintiff failed to show that the alleged defect had been responsible for the election result, or if the complaint charged preelection defects that could have been raised earlier.

STEELWORKERS LOCAL 3489 v. USERY
429 U.S. 305 (1977)

BRENNAN, J.

The Secretary of Labor brought this action in the District Court for the Southern District of Indiana under §402(b) of the Labor-Management Reporting and Disclosure Act of 1959 (LMRDA) to invalidate the 1970 election of officers of Local 3489, United Steelworkers of America. The Secretary alleged that a provision of the Steelworkers' International Constitution, binding on the Local, that limits eligibility for local union office to members who have attended at least one-half of the regular meetings of the local for three years previous to the election (unless prevented by union activities or working hours), violated §401(e) of the LMRDA. The District Court dismissed the complaint, finding no violation of the Act. The Court of Appeals for the Seventh Circuit reversed. . . . We affirm.

I

At the time of the challenged election, there were approximately 660 members in good standing of Local 3489. The Court of Appeals found that 96.5% of these members were ineligible to hold office, because of failure to satisfy the meeting attendance rule. Of the 23 eligible members, nine were incumbent union officers. The Secretary argues, and the Court of Appeals held, that the failure of 96.5% of the local members to satisfy the meeting attendance requirement, and the rule's effect of requiring potential insurgent candidates to plan their candidacies as early as 18 months in advance of the election when the reasons for their opposition might not have yet emerged, established that the requirement has a substantial antidemocratic effect on local union elections. Petitioners argue that the rule is reasonable because it serves valid union purposes, imposes no very burdensome obligation on the members, and has not proved to be a device that entrenched a particular clique of incumbent officers in the local.

II

The opinions in three cases decided in 1968 have identified the considerations pertinent to the determination whether the attendance rule violates §401(e). Wirtz v. Hotel, etc. Employees Union Local 6, 391 U.S. 492; Wirtz v. Bottle Glass Blowers Assn., 389 U.S. 463 (1968); Wirtz v. Local Union No. 125, Laborers Intl. Union, 389 U.S. 477 (1968).

LMRDA does not render unions powerless to restrict candidacies for union office. The injunction in §401(e) that "every member in good standing shall be eligible to be a candidate and to hold office" is made expressly "subject to . . . reasonable qualifications uniformly imposed." But "Congress plainly did not intend that the authorization . . . of 'reasonable qualifications . . .' should be given a broad reach. The contrary is implicit in the legislative history of the section and its wording. . . ." Wirtz v. Hotel Employees, supra, 391 U.S., at 499.

The basic objective of Title IV of LMRDA is to guarantee "free and democratic" union elections modeled on "political elections in this country" where "the assumption is that voters will exercise common sense and judgment in casting their ballots." Id., at 504. Thus, Title IV is not designed merely to protect the right of a union member to run for a particular office in a particular election. ". . . Congress emphatically asserted a vital public interest in assuring free and democratic union elections that transcends the narrower interest of the complaining union member." Wirtz v. Bottle Blowers Assn., supra, 389 U.S., at 475; Wirtz v. Local 125, Laborers Intl. Union, 389 U.S., at 483.

The goal was to "protect the rights of rank-and-file members to participate fully in the operation of their union through processes of democratic self-government, and, through the election process, to keep the union leadership responsive to the membership." Wirtz v. Hotel Employees, supra, 391 U.S., at 497.

Whether a particular qualification is "reasonable" within the meaning of §401(e) must therefore "be measured in terms of its consistency with the Act's command to unions to conduct 'free and democratic' union elections." Wirtz v. Hotel Employees, supra, 391 U.S., at 499. Congress was not concerned only with corrupt union leadership. Congress chose the goal of "free and democratic" union elections as a preventive measure "to curb the possibility of abuse by benevolent as well as malevolent entrenched leadership." Id., at 503. *Hotel Employees* expressly held that that check was seriously impaired by candidacy qualifications which substantially deplete the ranges of those who might run in opposition to incumbents, and therefore held invalid the candidacy limitation there involved that restricted candidacies for certain positions to members who had previously held union office. "Plainly, given the objective of Title IV, a candidacy limitation which renders 93% of union members ineligible for office can hardly be a 'reasonable qualification.'" Id., at 502.

III

Applying these principles to this case, we conclude that here too the antidemocratic effects of the meeting attendance rule outweigh the interests urged in its support. Like the by-law in Hotel Employees, an attendance requirement that results in the exclusion of 96.5% of the members from candidacy for union office hardly seems to be a "reasonable qualification" consistent with the goal of free and democratic elections. A requirement having that result obviously severely restricts the free choice of the membership in selecting their leaders.

Petitioners argue however that the by-law held violative of §401(e) in *Hotel Employees* differs significantly from the attendance rule here. Under the *Hotel Employees* by-law no member could assure by his own efforts that he would be eligible for union office, since others controlled the criterion for eligibility. Here, on the other hand, a member can assure himself of eligibility for candidacy by attending some 18 brief meetings over a three-year period. In other words, the union would have its rule treated not as excluding a category of member from eligibility, but simply as mandating a procedure to be followed by any member who wishes to be a candidate.

Even examined from this perspective, however, the rule has a restrictive effect on union democracy.[6] In the absence of a permanent "opposi-

6. Petitioners argue that attendance at 18 relatively short meetings over three years is no very onerous burden on a union member. But this argument misconceives the evil at which the statute aims. We must judge the eligibility rule not by the burden it imposes on the individual candidate, but by its effect on free and democratic processes of union government. Wirtz v. Hotel Employees, supra, 391 U.S., at 499.

tion party" within the union, opposition to the incumbent leadership is likely to emerge in response to particular issues at different times, and member interest in changing union leadership is therefore likely to be at its highest only shortly before elections. Thus it is probable that to require that a member decide upon a potential candidacy at least 18 months in advance of an election when no issues exist to prompt that decision may not foster but discourage candidacies and to that extent impair the general membership's freedom to oust incumbents in favor of new leadership.

Nor are we persuaded by the Union's argument that the Secretary has failed to show an antidemocratic effect because he has not shown that the incumbent leaders of the Union became "entrenched" in their offices as a consequence of the operation of the attendance rule. The reasons why leaderships become entrenched are difficult to isolate. The election of the same officers year after year may be a signal that antidemocratic election rules have prevented an effective challenge to the regime, or might well signal only that the members are satisfied with their stewardship; if elections are uncontested, opposition factions may have been denied access to the ballot, or competing interests may have compromised differences before the election to maintain a front of unity. Conversely, significant turnover in offices may result from an open political process, or from a competition so limited as to offer no real opposition to an entrenched establishment. But Congress did not saddle the courts with the duty to search out and remove improperly entrenched union leaderships. Rather, Congress chose to guarantee union democracy by regulating not the results of a union's electoral procedure, but the procedure itself. Congress decided that if the elections are "free and democratic," the members themselves are able to correct abuse of power by entrenched leadership. Procedures that unduly restrict free choice among candidates are forbidden without regard to their success or failure in maintaining corrupt leadership.

Petitioners next argue that the rule is reasonable within §401(e) because it encourages attendance at union meetings, and assures more qualified officers by limiting election to those who have demonstrated an interest in union affairs, and are familiar with union problems. But the rule has plainly not served these goals. It has obviously done little to encourage attendance at meetings, which continue to attract only a handful of members.[8] Even as to the more limited goal of encouraging the attendance of potential dissident candidates, very few members, as we have said, are likely to see themselves as such sufficiently far in advance of the election to be spurred to attendance by the rule.

As for assuring the election of knowledgeable and dedicated leaders,

8. Attendance at Local 3489's meetings averages 47 out of approximately 660 members. There is no indication in the record that this total represents a significant increase over attendance before the institution of the challenged rule.

the election provisions of LMRDA express a congressional determination that the best means to this end is to leave the choice of leaders to the membership in open democratic elections, unfettered by arbitrary exclusions. Pursuing this goal by excluding the bulk of the membership from eligibility for office, and thus limiting the possibility of dissident candidacies, run directly counter to the basic premise of the statute. We therefore conclude that Congress, in guaranteeing every union member the opportunity to hold office, subject only to "reasonable qualifications," disabled unions from establishing eligibility qualifications as sharply restrictive of the openness of the union political process as is petitioners' attendance rule.

IV

Finally, petitioners argue that the absence of a precise statement of what the Secretary of Labor and the courts will regard as reasonable prevents the drafting of a meeting-attendance rule with any assurance that it will be valid under §401(e). The Secretary, to whom Congress has assigned a special role in the administration of the Act, has announced the view that:

> Experience has demonstrated that it is not feasible to establish arbitrary guidelines for judging the reasonableness of [a meeting-attendance eligibility requirement]. Its reasonableness must be gauged in the light of all the circumstances of the particular case, including not only the frequency of meetings, the number of meetings which must be attended and the period of time over which the requirement extends, but also such factors as the nature, availability and extent of excuse provisions, whether all or most members have the opportunity to attend meeting, and the impact of the rule, i.e., the number or percentage of members who would be rendered ineligible by its application. 29 C.F.R. §452-38(a).

Obviously, this standard leads to more uncertainty than would a less flexible rule. But in using the word "reasonable," Congress clearly contemplated exactly such a flexible result. Moreover, on the facts of this case and in light of *Hotel Employees,* petitioners' contention that they had no way of knowing that a rule disqualifying over 90% of a local's members from office would be regarded as unreasonable in the absence of substantial justification is unpersuasive.[9]

Affirmed.

9. Also unpersuasive is the argument that a union cannot know in advance how many of its members will be disqualified by a meeting attendance rule. While the precise number may not be predictable, petitioners must have had some awareness of the general attendance rate at union meetings, and if Local 3489's attendance rate is at all typical (and there is no contention that it is not), it should have been fairly obvious that a rule disqualifying all who had not maintained 50% attendance for three years, admittedly one of the most stringent such rules among labor unions, would have a significant antidemocratic impact.

POWELL, J., with whom STEWART, J., and REHNQUIST, J., join, dissenting. . . .

As this holding seems to me to be an unwarranted interference with the right of the union to manage its own internal affairs, I dissent.

Stated broadly, the purpose of Title IV of the Act is to insure "free and democratic" elections. But, "[t]he legislative history [of the Act] shows that Congress weighed how best to legislate against revealed abuses in union elections without departing needlessly from its long-standing policy against unnecessary governmental intrusion into internal union affairs." Wirtz v. Local 153, Glass Bottle Blowers Association, 389 U.S. 463, 470-471; Wirtz v. Hotel Employees, 391 U.S. 492, 496.

Section 401(e) reflects a congressional intent to accommodate both of these purposes. It provides that a labor organization may set "reasonable qualifications uniformly imposed" for members in good standing who wish to be candidates and to hold office. There is no contention that the attendance rule in question was not "uniformly imposed." Nor does the rule render ineligible for office any member who displays enough interest to attend half of his local's meetings.

The Court nevertheless, relying heavily on *Hotel Employees,* holds that this rule imposes an unreasonable qualification, violative of §401(e). *Hotel Employees* involved a "prior office" rule that limited candidates for local union office to members who previously had held elective union office. The Court's opinion in that case emphasized that the effect of the prior office rule was to disqualify 93.1% of the union's membership. In this case, the Government argues that *Hotel Employees* enunciated a per se "effects" rule, requiring invalidation of union elections whenever an eligibility rule disqualifies all but a small percentage of the union's membership. Although the Court today does not in terms adopt a per se "effects" analysis, it comes close to doing so. The fact that 96.5% of Local 3489's members chose not to comply with its rule was given controlling weight.

In my view, the Court has extended the reach of *Hotel Employees* far beyond the holding and basic rationale of that case. Indeed, the rule there involved was acknowledged to be a sport — "virtually unique in trade union practice." Id., at 505. It was a rule deliberately designed, as intimated by the Court's opinion, to entrench union leadership.

Moreover, the general effect of the rule in *Hotel Employees* was predictable at the time the rule was adopted. By limiting eligibility to members who held or previously had held elective office, the disqualification of a large proportion of the membership was a purposeful and inevitable effect of the structure of the rule itself. The attendance rule before the Court today has no comparable feature. No member is precluded from establishing eligibility. Nor can the effect of the rule be predicted, as any member who demonstrates the requisite interest in union affairs is eligible to seek office. In short, the only common factor between the prior office rule in *Hotel Employees* and that before the Court today is the similarity in the percentage of ineligible members. But in one case the effect was predetermined for the purpose of perpetuating control of a few insiders, whereas here the effect resulted from the free choice — perhaps the indifference — of the rank and file membership. . . .

Although the opinion of Court today discounts the weight to be given these purposes, . . . at least facially they serve legitimate and meritorious union purposes: (i) encouraging attendance at meetings; (ii) requiring candidates for office to demonstrate a meaningful interest in the union and its affairs; and (iii) assuring that members who seek office have had an opportunity to become informed as to union affairs. One may argue that requiring attendance at 18 of the 36 meetings prior to the election goes beyond what may be necessary to serve these purposes. But this is a "judgment call" best left to the unions themselves absent a stronger showing of potential for abuse than has been made in this case.

The record in this case is instructive. Twenty-three members were eligible to run for office in the 1970 election. These were members who were nominated and who also had complied with the attendance requirement. The record does not show, and indeed no one knows, how many members were eligible under the rule but who were not nominated. Three candidates competed for the office of president, four for the three trustee offices, and six ran unopposed for the remaining offices. Of the 10 officers elected, six were incumbents. Nonincumbents were elected to the offices of vice president, treasurer, recording secretary, and the minor office of guide. There was no history of entrenched leadership and no evidence of restrictive union practices precluding free and democratic elections. Indeed, the record is to the contrary. Five different presidents had been elected during the preceding 10 years, and an estimated 40 changes in officers had occurred in the course of four separate elections. Bernard Frye, who initiated this case by complaint to the Secretary, won the presidency in an election subsequent to 1970 and thereafter lost it.

In the final analysis, respondent, which bears the burden of proving that the rule is "unreasonable," rests its entire case on a facial attack upon the attendance rule itself, an attack supported by a statistical "effects test" that at best is ambiguous and one that could invalidate almost any attendance requirement that served legitimate union purposes. In my view, the respondent has failed to prove that the rule is unreasonable. For these reasons, I would reverse the judgment of the Court of Appeals.

Notes

1. Once an election is held, the Secretary of Labor is the only party who may sue to set it aside, and the Secretary can act only upon the

complaint of a member who has satisfied the exhaustion requirements of §402(a). In Hodgson v. Steelworkers Local 6799, 403 U.S. 333 (1971), a member exhausted his internal remedies with respect to several grounds but when filing with the Secretary added a new challenge to the Steelworkers' meeting attendance rule. The Supreme Court held the Secretary was precluded from challenging the attendance rule since the member had not exhausted.

In Dunlop v. Bachowski, 421 U.S. 560 (1975), the Court held that a complainant was entitled to a statement of reasons from the Secretary of Labor supporting a decision of the Secretary not to bring suit. A district court then has jurisdiction to determine whether "the Secretary's decision is so irrational as to constitute the decision arbitrary and capricious." Where the statement is inadequate, according to the Court, the Secretary should be given leave to supplement the statement. The Court expressly left open the question of whether a district court would have the power to order the Secretary to bring suit.

If the Secretary sues to set aside the election, affected union members may intervene, under §24(a) of the Federal Rules of Civil Procedure, for the limited purpose of presenting evidence and argument in support of the Secretary's proffered grounds for setting aside the election.[27] No additional grounds may be raised. In Trbovich v. United Mine Workers, 401 U.S. 528 (1972), the Court reasoned that such limited intervention was not inconsistent with the policies underlying the grant of exclusivity to the Secretary of Labor to bring suit: "to protect unions from frivolous litigation and unnecessary judicial interference with their elections, and . . . to centralize in a single proceeding such litigation as might be warranted with respect to a single election."

If the Secretary proves a violation of §401, this will be considered a prima facie case that the violation "may have affected" the outcome of the election (§402(c)(1)) and the burden shifts to the respondent union to prove the violation did not affect the result.[28] The wrongful disqualification of a candidate, while not, in the Supreme Court's words, "automatically" proving a violation that affected the result, establishes a prima facie case. It is not apparent what evidence could constitute a sufficient rebuttal.

2. *Problem.* In June of 1976, a Sheet Metal Workers local union conducted an election of union officers. All of the union's members classi-

[27] In Brennan v. Steelworkers District 15, 554 F.2d 586 (3d Cir. 1977), cert. denied, 435 U.S. 977 (1978), the court held that such intervenors might be entitled to attorney fees from the union on a "common benefit" theory. The court stated, "although union members should not be required to pay for unnecessary duplication of legal services, it should not be presumed that mere duplication of effort by either counsel for [intervenor] or counsel for the Department of Labor was unnecessary or nonbeneficial."

[28] Wirtz v. Hotel, Motel & Club Employees Union, Local 6, 391 U.S. 492 (1968).

fied as journeymen received proper notice of the election but, through carelessness, notice to some of the union's members classed as production members was defective. The union admitted that a prima facie case of a §401 violation had been made out but argued that the violation had not affected the outcome of the 1976 election. The union relied on evidence supporting the following factual conclusions:

a. No production workers were shown to have wanted to run for office or nominate anyone else in 1976.
b. The winners of the 1976 election prevailed by such a large margin that the outcome could not have been affected by greater participation of production workers.
c. In the 1979 election, when notice in full compliance with Title IV was given, there were even fewer participants than there were in the 1976 election, and in particular there was less participation by production workers.

Has the union carried its burden of showing that the violation did not affect the outcome of the election? If not, does an intervening, valid 1979 election moot the necessity of a court-ordered 1981 election? See Usery v. Sheet Metal Workers Local 20, 105 L.R.R.M. 3203 (D.N.J. 1980).

CALHOON v. HARVEY
379 U.S. 134 (1964)

BLACK, J., . . .

The respondents, three members of District No. 1, National Marine Engineers' Beneficial Association, filed a complaint in Federal District Court against the union, its president, and its secretary-treasurer, alleging that certain provisions of the union's bylaws and national constitution violated the Act in that they infringed "the right of members of defendant District No. 1, NMEBA, to nominate candidates in elections of defendant, which right is guaranteed to each member of defendant, and to each plaintiff, by Section 101(a)(1) of the LMRDA. . . ." It was alleged that §102 of Title I of the Act gave the District Court jurisdiction to adjudicate the controversy. The union bylaws complained of deprived a member of the right to nominate anyone for office but himself. The national constitution in turn provided that no member could be eligible for nomination or election to a full-time elective office unless he had been a member of the national union for five years and had served 180 days or more of seatime in each of two of the preceding three years on vessels covered by collective bargaining agreements with the national or its subsidiary bodies. On the basis of these allegations respondents asked that the union be enjoined from preparing for or conducting any election until it revised its system of elections so as to afford each of its members a fair opportunity to nominate any persons "meeting fair and reasonable eligibility requirements for any or all offices to be filled by such election."

The union moved to dismiss the complaint on the grounds that (1) the court lacked jurisdiction over the subject matter, and (2) the complaint failed to state a claim upon which relief could be granted. The District Court dismissed for want of "jurisdiction," holding that the alleged conduct of the union, even if true, failed to show a denial of the equal rights of all members of the union to vote for or nominate candidates guaranteed by §101(a)(1) of Title I of the Act, so as to give the District Court jurisdiction of the controversy under §102. The allegations, said the court, showed at most imposition of qualifications of eligibility for nomination and election so restrictive that they might violate §401(e) of Title IV by denying members a reasonable opportunity to nominate and vote for candidates. The District Court further held that it could not exercise jurisdiction to protect §401(e) rights because §402(a) of Title IV provides a remedy, declared by §403 to be "exclusive," authorizing members to vindicate such rights by challenging elections after they have been held, and then only by (1) first exhausting all remedies available with the union, (2) filing a complaint with the Secretary of Labor, who (3) may, after investigating the violation alleged in the complaint, bring suit in a United States district court to attack the validity of the election. The Court of Appeals reversed, holding that "the complaint alleged a violation of §101(a)(1) and the federal jurisdiction existed under §102." 324 F.2d 486, 487. . . .

I

Jurisdiction of the District Court under §102 of Title I depends entirely upon whether this complaint showed a violation of rights guaranteed by §101(a)(1), for we disagree with the Court of Appeals' holding that jurisdiction under §102 can be upheld by reliance in whole or in part on allegations which in substance charge a breach of Title IV rights. An analysis and understanding of the meaning of §101(a)(1) and of the charges of the complaint are therefore essential to a determination of this issue. Respondents charge that the bylaws and constitutional provisions referred to above infringed their right guaranteed by §101(a)(1) to nominate candidates. The result of their allegations here, however, is an attempt to sweep into the ambit of their right to sue in federal court if they are denied an equal opportunity to nominate candidates under §101(a)(1), a right to sue if they are not allowed to nominate anyone they choose regardless of his eligibility and qualifications under union restrictions. But Title IV, not Title I, sets standards for eligibility and qualifications of candidates and officials and provides its own separate and different administrative and judicial procedure for challenging those standards. And the equal-rights language of §101(a)(l) would have to be stretched far beyond its normal meaning to hold that it guarantees members not just a right to "nominate candidates," but a right to nominate anyone, without regard to valid union rules. . . .

Plainly, [§101(a)(1)] is no more than a command that members and classes of members shall not be discriminated against in their right to nominate and vote. And Congress carefully prescribed that even this right against discrimination is "subject to reasonable rules and regulations" by the union. The complaining union members here have not been discriminated against in any way and have been denied no privilege or right to vote or nominate which the union has granted to others. They have indeed taken full advantage of the uniform rule limiting nominations by nominating themselves for office. It is true that they were denied their request to be candidates, but that denial was not a discrimination against their right to nominate, since the same qualifications were required equally of all members. Whether the eligibility requirements set by the union's constitution and bylaws were reasonable and valid is a question separate and distinct from whether the right to nominate on an equal basis given by §101(a)(1) was violated. The District Court therefore was without jurisdiction to grant the relief requested here unless, as the Court of Appeals held, the "*combined* effect of the eligibility requirements and the restriction to self-nomination" is to be considered in determining whether §101(a)(1) has been violated.

II

We hold that possible violations of Title IV of the Act regarding eligibility are not relevant in determining whether or not a district court has jurisdiction under §102 of Title I of the Act. Title IV sets up a statutory scheme governing the election of union officers, fixing the terms during which they hold office, requiring that elections be by secret ballot, regulating the handling of campaign literature, requiring a reasonable opportunity for the nomination of candidates, authorizing unions to fix "reasonable qualifications uniformly imposed" for candidates, and attempting to guarantee fair union elections in which all the members are allowed to participate. Section 402 of Title IV, as has been pointed out, sets up an exclusive method for protecting Title IV rights, by permitting an individual member to file a complaint with the Secretary of Labor challenging the validity of any election because of violations of Title IV. Upon complaint the Secretary investigates and if he finds probable cause to believe that Title IV has been violated, he may file suit in the appropriate district court. It is apparent that Congress decided to utilize the special knowledge and discretion of the Secretary of Labor in order best to serve the public interest. Cf. San Diego Building Trades Council v. Garmon, 359 U.S. 236, 242. In so doing Congress, with one exception not here relevant,[13] decided not to permit individuals to block or delay union elections by filing federal-court suits for violations of Title IV. Reliance on the discretion of the Secretary is in harmony with the general congressional policy to allow unions great latitude in resolving their own internal controversies, and, where that fails, to utilize the agencies of Government most familiar with union problems to aid in bringing about a settlement through discussion before resort to the courts. Without setting out the lengthy legislative history which preceded the passage of this measure, it is sufficient to say that we are satisfied that the Act itself shows clearly by its structure and language that the disputes here, basically relating as they do to eligibility of candidates for office, fall squarely within Title IV of the Act and are to be resolved by the administrative and judicial procedures set out in that Title.

Accordingly, the judgment of the Court of Appeals is reversed and that of the District Court is affirmed.[29]

STEWART, J., whom HARLAN, J., joins concurring.

This case marks the first interpretation by this Court of the significant changes wrought by the Labor-Management Reporting and Disclosure Act of 1959 increasing federal supervision of internal union affairs. At issue are subtle questions concerning the interplay between Title I and Title IV of that Act. In part, both seem to deal with the same subject matter: Title I guarantees "equal rights and privileges . . . to nominate candidates"; Title IV provides that "a reasonable opportunity shall be given for the nomination of candidates." Where the two Titles of the legislation differ most substantially is in the remedies they provide. If a Title I right is at issue, the allegedly aggrieved union member has direct, virtually immediate recourse to a federal court to obtain an adjudication of his claim and an injunction if his complaint has merit. Vindication of claims under Title IV may be much more onerous. Federal-court suits can be brought only by the Secretary of Labor, and then, only after the election has been held. An additional barrier is thus placed between the union member and the federal court. Remedies shape the significance of rights, and I think the Court too casually forecloses the direct access to a federal court which the Court of Appeals held was given these respondents by Congress. . . .

13. Section 401(c) of the Act permits suits prior to election in the United States District Courts by any bona fide candidate for union office to enforce the rights guaranteed by that section, to equal treatment in the distribution of campaign literature and access to membership lists.

[29] Douglas, J., concurred.

[T]he Court forecloses early adjudication of claims concerning participation in the election process. But there are occasions when eligibility provisions can infringe upon the right to nominate. Had the NMSBA issued a regulation that only Jesse Calhoon was eligible for office, no one could place great store on the right to self-nomination left to the rest of the membership. This Court long ago recognized the subtle ways by which election rights can be removed through discrimination at a less visible stage of the political process. The decisions in the *Texas Primary Cases* were founded on the belief that the equal right to vote was impaired where discrimination existed in the method of nomination. Smith v. Allwright, 321 U.S. 649; Nixon v. Herndon, 273 U.S. 536. See United States v. Classic, 313 U.S. 299. No less is the equal right to nominate infringed where onerous burdens drastically limit the candidates available for nomination. In scrutinizing devices designed to erode the franchise, the Court has shown impatience with arguments founded in the form of the device. If Congress has told the courts to protect a union member from infringement of his equal right to nominate, the courts should do so whether such discrimination is sophisticated or simple-minded.

After today, simply by framing its discriminatory rules in terms of eligibility, a union can immunize itself from pre-election attack in a federal court even though it makes deep incursions on the equal right of its members to nominate, to vote, and to participate in the union's internal affairs. . . .

[T]he Court finds a "general congressional policy" to avoid judicial resolution of internal union disputes. That policy, the Court says, was designed to limit the power of individuals to block and delay elections by seeking injunctive relief. Such an appraisal might have been accurate before the addition of Title I, but it does not explain the emphasis on prompt judicial remedies there provided. In addition to the injunctive relief authorized by §102 and the saving provisions of §103, §101(a)(4) modifies the traditional requirement of exhausting internal remedies before resort to litigation. Even §403 is not conclusive on the elimination of pre-election remedies. At the least, state-court actions may be brought in advance of an election to "enforce the constitution and bylaws." And as to federal courts, it is certainly arguable that recourse through the Secretary of Labor is the exclusive remedy only after the election has been held. By reading Title I rights so narrowly, and by construing Title IV to foreclose absolutely pre-election litigation in the federal courts, the Court sharply reduces meaningful protection for many of the rights which Congress was so assiduous to create. By so simplifying the tangled provisions of the Act, the Court renders it virtually impossible for the aggrieved union member to gain a hearing when it is most necessary — when there is still an opportunity to make the union's rules comport with the requirements of the Act.

My difference with the Court does not reach to the disposition of this particular case. Whether in terms of restrictions on the right to nominate, or in terms of limitations on eligibility for union office, I think the rules of a labor organization would operate illegally to curtail the members' equal right to nominate within the meaning of Title I only if those rules effectively distorted the basic democratic process. The line might be a shadowy one in some cases. But I think that in this case the respondents did not allege in their complaint nor demonstrate in their affidavits that this line was crossed. I would therefore remand the case to the District Court with directions to dismiss the complaint for failure to state a claim for relief.

Notes

1. Suppose the union's constitution provides that "no apprentice member shall be eligible to run for office." Would such a rule be challengeable in federal court before the election under §101(a)(1)? After the election (with a request to set aside the election)? In state court? Consult §403.

2. Does the Secretary of Labor have the power to engage in a preballoting investigation of union conduct later challengeable in a Title IV suit?[30] See §601. The purpose of the investigation might be to gather facts not obtainable later and to prevent the destruction of potential evidence, or it might be to deter civil and criminal violations. Would such an investigation provide the challenger with too potent a propaganda opportunity against the incumbent officers?

In Local 82, Furniture and Piano Movers v. Crowley, 104. S. Ct. 2557 (1984), members of a local union brought a suit under Title I alleging that they had been denied their rights to nominate candidates for union office. The suit was filed after election ballots had been distributed to the membership. The district court enjoined the election. After several months of litigation on the matter, the court declared the interrupted election to be invalid, and it ordered a new election to be held in accordance with procedures mandated by the court. The Supreme Court reversed. The appropriateness of maintaining a Title I suit during the course of a union election depends on the remedies sought in the Title I case. Court supervision of union election is not an appropriate Title I remedy. If the remedy sought is the invalidation of an election already conducted, the exclusive course is to request action by the Secretary of Labor persuant to Title IV.

[30] For a spirited debate on this issue, see Rauh, LMRDA — Enforce It or Repeal It, 5 Ga. L. Rev. 643 (1971); Silberman & Driesen, the Secretary and the Law: Preballoting Investigations under the Landrum-Griffin Act, 7 Ga. L. Rev. 1 (1972).

3. In Driscoll v. Operating Engineers, Local 139, 484 F.2d 682 (7th Cir. 1973), Driscoll, a union member, exhausted his internal union remedies and then filed a complaint with the Secretary of Labor challenging the union's requirement that all candidates for union office must execute a noncommunist affidavit. The Secretary declined to litigate under Title IV. Driscoll then brought suit against the union under §102 alleging violations of §§101(a)(1), 101(a)(2), and 101(a)(5). The Seventh Circuit held there was no jurisdiction because "Driscoll's allegations 'basically relate' to eligibility and charge 'in substance' that he has been denied the right to run for office. . . ." The court found that Driscoll's complaint did not fall into the exception to *Calhoon* that the court was prepared to recognize:

> The complaint does not allege that the candidacy requirement is part of a purposeful program of suppressing any expression of dissent by plaintiff. Nor does it appear that the eligibility requirement is a discriminatory ad hoc device calculated to perpetuating certain individuals in office.

BLISS v. HOLMES
721 F.2d 156 (6th Cir. 1983)

Per curiam. Plaintiff Bliss is a candidate for office of president of defendant Local 337, International Brotherhood of Teamsters, Chauffeurs, Warehousemen and Helpers of America. Plaintiff Savage is a candidate for vice president. They allege that the excessive publicity given to Robert F. Holmes and Lawrence Brennan, incumbent president and vice president of Local 337, in the union newsletter, "TEAM 337," is an impermissible use of the membership lists and union funds by defendants in violation of 29 U.S.C. §481(c) and §481(g).

Plaintiffs sought an injunction against use of the newsletter as campaign literature for the incumbents while denying them reasonable mention.

The District Court found nothing unusual in the union newsletter devoting the bulk of its attention to incumbent officers. It also held that plaintiffs could obtain adequate relief in the post-election remedy of having the election set aside. Concerned with avoiding entanglement in union affairs and interfering with the local union's first amendment rights, it denied injunctive relief.

We share the District Court's first amendment concerns as well as its concern that the courts refrain from involving themselves in internal union controversies when possible. However, Congress adopted §§481(c) and (g) of the Labor-Management Reporting and Disclosure Act of 1959 to maintain democratic and fair conduct in election of union officials and expressly gave the right to enforce LMRDA guarantees in the federal courts.

Once a member's candidacy is announced, if the union uses the union mailing lists to mail a newsletter the newsletter must refrain from discrimination in favor of or against any candidate. A "[n]ewsletter laudatory of the incumbent President and derogatory of his opponent paid for by the Union and distributed from its mailing list was prohibited campaign literature in violation of Section 481(g). See Hodgson v. Liquor Salesmen's Union Local No. 2, 334 F. Supp. 1369, 1377 aff'd, 44 F.2d 1344 (2d Cir. 1971); Wirtz v. Independent Workers Union of Florida, 272 F. Supp. 31 (M.D. Fla. 1967)." Usery v. International Organization of Masters, etc., 538 F.2d 946, 949 (2d Cir. 1976).

After plaintiff Bliss announced his candidacy for president of Local 337 in May 1983 and incumbent president, Holmes, announced his intention to run for re-election in the May, 1983 issue of "TEAM 337," the union was required to refrain from discrimination in favor of or against any candidate. The publication is paid for by the union and uses the union's membership lists for distribution. Our review of the May, June, July, and September issues of "TEAM 337" discloses numerous pages devoted to laudatory articles about the incumbent president and numerous columns by both the incumbent president and vice president, the effect of which is to advance their candidacies. No mention is made of plaintiffs Bliss or Savage, except their inclusion in the masthead as secretary-treasurer and trustee. The September issue, which was not available to the District Court, devotes 3 out of a total of 7 pages to President Holmes and Vice President Brennan. We conclude that this excessive publicity, not balanced by any publicity for other candidates, or even an announcement of their candidacies, constitutes the distribution of campaign literature for defendants Holmes and Brennan distributed at the expense of the defendant union.

Plaintiffs are entitled, therefore, to have a piece of their campaign literature distributed in a similar manner, i.e., at union expense. We, therefore, order that defendant union pay for the mailing of a piece of campaign literature prepared by plaintiffs to be mailed at the same time the September, 1983 newsletter is mailed. The preparation of the literature itself, including folding, if that is necessary for using the union's mailing process, shall be paid for by plaintiffs. Defendant union is required only to pay for the mailing which shall be mailed in the same manner as is the newsletter.

Defendants are further ordered to refrain from discrimination in any further newsletters distributed before the November 1983 election which are prepared and mailed at union expense and use union membership lists.

KEITH, J., dissenting.

I respectfully dissent. I am convinced after hearing oral arguments in this case that the Teamsters' newsletter, "337," for the months in question, does not contain excessive publicity for President Robert F. Holmes, Vice-President Lawrence Brennan and Richard Leebove. I therefore would vacate the preliminary injunction for the stay heretofore entered on October 6, 1983, and allow defendant-appellees to proceed with the distribution of all election materials. Our Court's decision to grant the stay in this case will have a chilling effect on the First Amendment rights of the officers of Local 337. I feel very strongly that courts should not interfere with the internal operations and politics of unions.

Notes

1. Suppose that an examination of the newsletter during a period when there was no election campaign going on showed a similar attention to the union officers. Would that call for a different result in *Bliss*?

2. *Problem.* The national Rural Letter Carriers' Association has negotiated a new collective bargaining agreement with the employer, the United States Postal Service. The union constitution requires that the agreement be ratified by the membership before it is effective. The Knox County (Tennessee) Local opposes ratification. The Local has submitted a full-page advertisement opposing ratification to the national association for inclusion in the union's official weekly magazine, which is circulated nationwide to the union's dues-paying members. The Local has offered to pay the standard rate for advertising in the magazine. If the officers refuse to run the advertisement, have they violated the LMRDA? Why might they want to refuse? See Knox County Rural Carrier's Assn., 720 F.2d 936 (6th Cir. 1983).

E. THE FIDUCIARY DUTY OF UNION OFFICERS[31]

MORRISSEY v. CURRAN

423 F.2d 393 (2d Cir.), cert. denied, 399 U.S. 928, 400 U.S. 826 (1970)

ANDERSON, J.

This case arises under §501 of the Labor-Management Reporting and Disclosure Act of 1959 and concerns the propriety of certain payments made into the Officers' Pension Fund of the National Maritime Union

[31] See Leslie, Federal Courts and Union Fiduciaries, 76 Colum. L. Rev. 1205 (1976); Clark, the Fiduciary Duties of Union Officials under Section 501 of the LMRDA, 52 Minn. L. Rev. 437 (1967); Note, 75 Colum. L. Rev. 1189 (1975).

(NMU). The plaintiffs, James M. Morrissey,[32] Joseph Padilla, and Ralph Ibrahim, have been members in good standing of the NMU since approximately 1950. The defendant Joseph Curran is the national president and the defendant Shannon Wall is the national secretary-treasurer of the NMU, both elective positions. The defendant William Perry is the recently retired assistant to the president of the Union, a non-elective position. . . .

The structure of the NMU and the powers and duties of its officers and various internal governing bodies are set out in the Union's constitution. It makes provision for three governing units which have nationwide jurisdiction. The ultimate authority is vested in the National Convention, which meets triennially and is composed of the elected delegates from various ships and ports. When the National Convention is not in session, the Union is governed by the National Council, which holds regular annual meetings and consists of the elected national officials and certain other delegated representatives. When the National Council is not in session, governing authority rests in the National Office, made up of the national president, secretary-treasurer, three vice presidents, and three national representatives. This body is primarily responsible for the day to day, internal administration of NMU affairs.

In 1951 the NMU constitution was amended to permit the National Council, subject to membership approval, to provide pension benefits for all NMU officers and employees. On December 29, 1952, pursuant to this authority, the National Council entered into an Agreement and Declaration of Trust with three trustees which gave them the authority to establish a pension plan. On February 16, 1953, the trustees adopted a plan whereby pension rights accrued to the various elected officials of the Union, including the president, secretary, treasurer, vice-president, national port committee member, branch agent, field patrolman, and patrolman. No non-elected employee of the Union was included under its coverage. The majority of the administrative employees of the NMU were represented by this or other unions in their employment relationship with the NMU and had been granted pension rights, as permitted by the 1961 NMU constitution, as a part of their respective collective bargaining agreements.

On October 28, 1961, the National Office (as opposed to the National Council) authorized an amendment to the Agreement and Declaration of Trust, the effect of which was to extend its coverage to certain executive and supervisory employees of the Union who held appointive rather than elective positions, such as the assistant to the president, organizer, executive secretary, publicity director, editor of the Pilot (the union

[32] Plaintiff Morrissey was an unsuccessful candidate for Secretary-Treasurer of the NMU in 1966. Another plaintiff was an unsuccessful candidate for vice-president in the same election.

house organ), and supervisors over maintenance, bookkeeping, records and supplies.

Prior to the adoption of the amended Declaration of Trust, however, the NMU constitution had been subjected to an extensive revision whereby, along with other changes, the authority vested in the National Council to fix the salaries of certain employees was shifted to the National Office and the requirement for membership approval thereof was deleted. This revision became effective on December 2, 1960.

The plaintiffs contend that the 1961 amendments to Declaration of Trust, by the National Office, permitting benefits to be paid to non-elected employees under the Officers' Pension Plan were not authorized by and were in contravention of the NMU constitution, as amended in 1960. After Union officials refused to take any action, as requested, to obtain the return of funds paid into the Trust fund for the benefit of non-elected employees under the revised Plan, the plaintiffs filed a complaint in the district court seeking an accounting, a money judgment for any damages suffered by the Union or the Trust fund, and an injunction against further payments to non-elected employees. . . .

The [district] court held that the defendants should account for and repay pension funds accrued and paid to non-elected Union employees, that the defendant trustees should be enjoined from paying out of the Officers' Pension Plan fund further benefits to non-officers and the plaintiffs should recover costs and attorneys' fees. Immediately following the district court decision, the National Council of the Union convened and proposed amendments to the constitution which gave the National Office of the NMU the authority, which the trial court had found it did not have under the 1960 amended constitution, to designate certain non-elected employees to be eligible for benefits under the Officers' Pension Plan as well as the authority "to validate retroactively all pensions heretofore paid under the plan." The approval of these amendments was voted on June 24, 1969. The plaintiffs promptly moved to have the June 24th amendments declared invalid as exculpatory, and therefore void, under §501(a) and to enjoin any implementation of them. The relief sought was denied without prejudice on July 3, 1969. The defendants moved that the entire action be dismissed as moot on the ground that the new amendments removed any question of the power of the defendants to act as they did. . . .

The defendants have appealed from the district court decision granting summary judgment to the plaintiffs, denying their own similar motion and their motions for reargument. The plaintiffs have filed an interlocutory appeal from the trial court's denial of their motion to declare invalid and enjoin the use of the June 24 amendments to the NMU constitution. The major dispute on these appeals concerns the proper interpretation of the provisions for establishing employee pension funds under the 1951 NMU constitution, as amended in 1960.

Defendants argue that the 1960 amendments were designed to shift the responsibility for the establishment of employee salaries from the National Council to the National Office and did not limit in any way the power of the National Office to establish employee pension funds. They assert that the term "salaries," as used in Article 8, §11, must be construed to include pensions, from which they claim it follows that the National Office was acting within its authority when it amended the Officers' Pension Plan in 1961. In support of this position they rely upon cases which hold that pensions are compensation for past services as opposed to gratuities, and in that sense, are included within the term "salary." But as the district court pointed out in its opinion, the framers of the NMU constitution, when drafting the 1960 revision, clearly had in mind a distinction between salaries and pensions, as evidenced by the use of the term "compensation" in Article 14 to include both types of remuneration. The NMU constitution, as amended in 1960, was clear and explicit with regard to the persons covered by the pension provisions, and in the light of the history, context and wording of those provisions, the district court's rejection of the defendants' claim is correct. There was no genuine issue of material fact concerning the charge of a breach of duty on the part of the defendants, and summary judgment in favor of the plaintiffs should be affirmed.

In support of their claim that the 1969 amendments to the NMU constitution, made immediately following the district court decision, are exculpatory and that their application should be enjoined, the plaintiffs rely on Highway Truck Drivers and Helpers Local 107 v. Cohen, 182 F. Supp. 608 (E.D. Pa.), aff'd, 284 F.2d 162 (3d Cir. 1960), cert. denied, 365 U.S. 833 (1961), and Highway Truck Drivers and Helpers Local 107 v. Cohen, 215 F. Supp. 938 (E.D. Pa. 1963), aff'd, 334 F.2d 378 (3d Cir.), cert. denied, 379 U.S. 921 (1964). In the first of these two cases the district court found that it was improper for the local union to pay the attorney fees of union officers who were under criminal indictment. These fees were to be paid pursuant to a resolution of the local which permitted such payment, and that resolution was declared invalid because it authorized "action beyond the powers of the union as derived from its constitution and was inconsistent with the aims and purposes of the Labor-Management Reporting and Disclosure Act." 284 F.2d at 164. The international union then amended its constitution to permit such authorizations. Thereafter in the second *Cohen* case the union officers claimed that the payments were valid as the amendment purported to be retroactive. In rejecting this claim the Third Circuit said:

> That abortive attempt to validate the illegal 1959 resolution, could not of course in 1961 legitimatize the 1959 payments which have been held to have been wrongful. And the action of the International was just as incon-

> sistent with Section 501 of the Labor Management Act as was the Local's ill conceived resolution. 334 F.2d at 381.

The defendants in the present case, however, assert that the cases cited actually support the defense. It is their contention that the trial court held in the 1960 *Cohen* case that a resolution authorizing an expenditure of union funds was not an exculpatory provision in violation of §501(a) and, in the 1963 *Cohen* case, that a constitutional amendment authorizing expenditures already incurred was not exculpatory unless the expenditures themselves were in violation of §501 of the Act. Turning to the present case they argue that the court below did not find that the payments into the Officers' Pension Plan for the benefit of employees were per se violative of §501(a), and therefore any subsequent constitutional provision purporting to validate the past payments cannot be exculpatory within the meaning of §501(a). In making this assertion, the defendants conveniently overlook the fact that the trial court did find that they had breached their duties because the expenditures in question were not authorized by the NMU constitution and that they were in violation of §501 of the Act. In the *Cohen* cases the trial court was affirmed because the local union authorized actions beyond its powers as derived from the constitution and because its effort to pay attorneys' fees for officers was "inconsistent with the aims and purposes of the Labor-Management Reporting and Disclosure Act." We agree with the position taken by the Third Circuit. Otherwise the provisions of §501 would be completely emasculated if, every time a court, at the behest of complaining members of a union, found that the officers had breached their duties, the officers could find sanctuary by putting through a constitutional amendment or by-law retroactively to legitimatize their former derelictions of duty.

The defendants also argue that the district court "has not imposed any personal liability upon the defendants from which they needed to be 'exculpated,'" but we do not agree with this argument. The district court ordered the defendants to account for all moneys paid into the Officers' Pension Plan and return to the NMU all moneys received by the trustees for the benefit of non-officers with interest. It follows that if they are unable to recoup that money, they may be held personally liable.

The trial court's decision, however, on the plaintiffs' motion for an injunction, that the purpose of the 1969 amendments to the NMU constitution was to include non-officer employees in the NMU officers' pension plan and that the amendments were, therefore, not exculpatory provisions prohibited by §501, is at odds with its holding that there was an obvious breach of duty on the part of the defendants in causing union funds to be paid out to persons who were not entitled to them. His conclusions might have been correct if the provisions were prospective only in their application but the amendment to Article 14, §7 provides in part: "the National Office shall have the authority to validate retroactively all pensions heretofore paid under the plan." This is clearly exculpatory in intent and language. The NMU exercised its authority under the 1969 amendments to attempt to validate retroactively all the pensions previously paid. The determination that the 1969 amendments were not exculpatory is reversed and will be reconsidered on remand. . . .

We affirm denial of the defendants' motion for summary judgment and the entry of summary judgment in favor of the plaintiffs. As the June 24, 1969, amendments to the NMU constitution are clearly exculpatory as prohibited by §501(a), we reverse the denial of plaintiffs' motion to have these amendments declared void, and remand to the district court for appropriate action declaring the amendments to be without effect and enjoining defendants from acting in reliance upon them. As the district court apparently did not pass on so much of plaintiffs' motion as requested that defendants be enjoined from retaining counsel paid or to be paid with Union funds, this question should also be determined on remand. The controlling cases on this point are Tucker v. Shaw, supra, and Holdeman v. Sheldon, 311 F.2d 2 (2d Cir. 1962), in which we held that all that is necessary for enjoining of the defendants in a §501 action is that the plaintiff make "a reasonable showing that he is likely to succeed." We also note that the district court maintains continuing jurisdiction to insure that the accounting and return of funds to the Union treasury proceed as ordered, and, of course, it retains the power to issue the necessary orders to assure full compliance.

Affirmed in part, reversed in part, and remanded for further proceedings in compliance with this opinion.

Danaher, J. (dissenting). . . .

The National Maritime Union of America (hereinafter NMU) was founded in 1937. Some fourteen years later, the still-young Union adopted a Constitution which, so far as is here pertinent, provided that "considering the financial state of the Union," the Union's National Council was empowered to make adequate and appropriate provisions for pensions, welfare and similar benefits for officers and employees of the Union. That power was never rescinded, I suggest, but was later transferred to the National Office.

Agreeably to such authorization, effective as of February, 1953, the NMU Officers' Pension Plan was adopted, then covering all elected offices of NMU. There has been no challenge here to the validity of that Plan.

NMU in the management of its properties, in the administration of its far-flung business and in furtherance of its purposes, utilized the services of a staff of lawyers, economists, pension administrators, staff experts in Washington, doctors, and supervisory staffs of Union-owned real estate. For their protection as well as to further its own interest in their retention in its service NMU negotiated with various unions of which its employees were members for the establishment of pension and welfare plans. As an employer, NMU was bound to bargain respecting hours, wages and conditions of employment. Although clearly authorized to do so, NMU had not until the events here at issue, set up a separate plan for a few of its supervisory personnel, not elected officers and not represented by some union.

Some sixteen years after the original Plan had become effective, the plaintiffs here alleged that without authorization a lump-sum benefit[3] had been accorded to the defendant Perry following his resignation as Executive Assistant to the National President. Purporting to base the action upon §501, the plaintiffs had sought an accounting, a money judgment against the defendants, and an injunction to restrain the Trustees from paying benefits to Perry or any other non-elected employees of NMU. The Union was not made a party. Under date of May 23, 1969, the District Judge filed an Opinion holding, compendiously, that there was no authority[4] for covering non-employees into the Plan, and so he granted summary judgment for the plaintiffs. . . .

[T]he 1951 Constitution was revised at an NMU Convention held in October, 1960, with ratification by the membership after a referendum vote concluded in December of 1960.

I deem it unthinkable that the NMU membership supposed for a moment that the amended Constitution was intended to wipe out whatever rights to coverage had been acquired since 1952. There was no repealer clause in the 1960 revision. To me, it is inconceivable that the eligibility established in 1952, followed by good faith reliance under the express terms of the earlier Constitution, was to be deemed obliterated. I reject the suggestion that the Constitution, as revised, had narrowed the authority of this Union to provide pensions for any of its 47,000 members, whether they be elected officers or employees or whatever their status.

On the contrary the 1960 Constitution even broadened benefits to be accorded to members whose rights had previously accrued, as for example where Article 15, Section 8(f), specified that members "receiving a monthly pension under the NMU Welfare and Pension Plan or the NMU Officers' Pension Plan shall not be required to pay dues and shall be regarded as honorary members. . . ."

Against such background, lacking representation by any employee

3. The original Plan had specifically provided that the Trustees in their discretion might make a lump-sum payment in lieu of benefits otherwise provided. Indeed, the authorization was amended and extended in 1958.

4. There was no evidence that the officer defendants or the Trustees personally benefitted in any way or otherwise acted unlawfully, or that they had exercised bad faith.

union and not possessing the status of elected officers, a few non-elected employees were brought into the Plan. Perry as Assistant to the President was included, certain others being identified as Organizer, Maintenance Supervisor, Bookkeeper Supervisor, Records and Supply Supervisors, Executive Secretary, Publicity Director and the Editor of the NMU official News Organ, The Pilot.

In sum, my reading of the record and my construction of the NMU Constitution convince me, first, that it had always been the plain intendment of this Union that pensions for both officers and employees be authorized; and next, that the power to establish any plans had been created in 1951, with continuing authorization to amend whatever plan might thereafter be established. . . .

Nothing to be discerned from the revised Constitution, ratified December 2, 1960, detracted one whit from that authority. Rather, I suggest, the later revision must be read with the former. The only difference in giving effect to the continuing intent of the Union membership was that after the 1960 revision, the authority to act was transferred from the National Council to the National Office. I conclude that even without more than my analysis suggests, the District Judge erred in concluding that at the time the challenged action was taken, there had been a lack of authority to provide pensions for all past and present employees of the Union.

But there was more. After the release of Judge Bonsal's May 23, 1969 Opinion, the Union promptly took steps to reiterate the NMU intention. If the judge could be heard to say that NMU had failed to make clear its intention, two amendments to the Constitution were immediately proposed. The amendments [were passed] by the membership by an overwhelming vote. Accordingly, the revised 1960 Constitution was further amended by the addition to Article 8, Section 11, of the following:

> (d) — The National Office shall have the authority to provide pensions for all past and present employees of the Union and to protect the pension rights of all past and present employees of the Union.

The membership further amended Article 14, Section 7, to read as follows:

> Pensions: All officers and such employees as the National Office may designate shall be eligible for benefits under the NMU Officers' Pension Plan, subject to such rules and regulations as the Trustees of that Plan may establish. The National Office shall have the authority to validate retroactively all pensions heretofore paid under the Plan.

These plaintiffs then attacked the amendments as "exculpatory" within the meaning of §501, and they sought an injunction. The District

Judge flatly — and correctly — rejected that contention and ruled that the amendments "were not exculpatory provisions prohibited by §501. *Their purpose is obviously to include non-officer employees in the NMU Officers' Plan.*" (Emphasis added.)

Granting that the constitution had validly been amended, the District Judge's July 3, 1969 Memorandum observed, "It does not appear that the National Office has exercised this authority."

I read him to be saying, "I do not perceive that the necessary authority existed to include non-officers at the time they were covered into the Plan. But now NMU has conferred that authority. Even so as of this moment, the National Office has not so far exercised its power." And accordingly he concluded *only* that since the inclusion of non-officers "was beyond the power of the defendants, plaintiffs are entitled to appropriate relief."

Thereupon after such prompting, as the record shows, the National Office acted to implement the authority so recently reaffirmed. It adopted a resolution based upon the desire of the National Office "to confirm the pension rights of all employees of the Union, both retroactively and prospectively." . . .

Right then and there, having been advised in the premises, the assumed omission having been cured by NMU, the District Judge should have entered summary judgment in behalf of the *defendants,* thus rendering moot whatever claims had previously been urged upon the Court by these plaintiffs. To take any other view, as it seems to me, is not only to deny NMU its right to manage its own affairs, but in view of the rectification of whatever oversight the Judge thought he had detected, the membership clearly restated its approval of the authority of the National Office and the Trustees to provide pensions for all officers and all employees.

The purpose and the intent of the Union emerged conclusively, I respectfully submit, and the conferred authority was exercised. . . .

Notes

1. Plaintiffs in *Morrissey* would receive their attorney fees out of the monetary recovery and they would have the satisfaction of seeing the union treasury restored (of which a very small portion might loosely be deemed theirs). Had they lost, they would have had to bear their own attorney fees and expenses (and undoubtedly the wrath of the defendants, for whatever that is worth). Why do you suppose they brought the case? Is Title V likely to generate sufficient litigation to force others to adhere to a fiduciary standard?

2. Isn't there a difference between misinterpreting one's authority

under the union constitution[33] and committing a fiduciary breach? Should there be? Should the presence or absence of personal gain be a factor? The potential personal liability in *Morrissey* was over $100,000. Would you pause before accepting the office of president of a large union in light of the risk of this sort of loss if you erroneously interpreted your authority to act? Maximum protection against liability would be provided by a union constitution giving an officer unfettered power to act in broad areas. If this is an outgrowth of cases like *Morrissey*, §501 will have had an unintended effect.

3. Was the action of the membership an attempt at exculpation or ratification? Is there a difference? Was there any way for the membership to announce that it was Curran's interpretation, not the court's, that they deemed the more accurate?

The courts in *Morrissey* and in the *Cohen* case, cited in *Morrissey*, may be worried about the possibility that some union memberships will vote in support of any proposition put forward by their officers. Is §501 an appropriate vehicle for curtailing the effects of this domination?

4. Section 501(b) permits the reasonable part of a recovery to be used to pay plaintiff's attorney. Even where a finding of a §501 violation produces no monetary recovery, the ferreting out of the violation has been held to confer a "benefit" on all the members of the union, rendering the union liable for plaintiff's attorney fees.[34] The fees are to be measured in light of the value of the benefit conferred.

Once a §501 suit is filed against union officers, the courts routinely disqualify regular union counsel from representing the officers. However, if the officers prevail, the union is permitted to reimburse the officers their attorney fees from the union treasury. Union counsel are occasionally permitted to represent the union's "institutional interest" in §501 cases, but the courts carefully scrutinize such representation to ensure it is not a sham for representing the officers.

JOHNSON v. NELSON
325 F.2d 646 (8th Cir. 1963)

[Political opponents of incumbent local union officers had earlier brought suit under Title I of the LMRDA to enjoin disciplinary action taken against them by the local. The suit was settled by the withdrawal of the discipline and, following settlement, the plaintiffs secured a membership vote directing that their attorney fees be paid from local union

[33] Splits between a local union and its parent international over a breach of the international constitution may be brought in federal court under §301 of the LMRA. See United Association v. Local 334, 452 U.S. 615 (1981).

[34] See Bakery & Confectionary Workers v. Ratner, 335 F.2d 691 (D.C. Cir. 1964); Dawson, Lawyers and Involuntary Clients in Public Interest Litigation, 88 Harv. L. Rev. 849 (1975). See also Hall v. Cole, page 970, supra.

funds. The incumbent officers had this vote rescinded by the membership at the next meeting. The parent international union then intervened. An international representative persuaded the quarrelling groups to rescind all charges and countercharges, and recommended that the membership pay the attorney fees of both plaintiffs and defendants in the settled Title I suit. The membership so voted, but the incumbent officers refused to pay plaintiffs' attorney and instead appealed the vote to the international union.

Eventually the international union, relying on broad constitutional authority,[35] declared a union policy against paying plaintiffs' attorney fees in such a situation and directed that the local's officers should not pay unless directed to do so by a secret mail ballot of the entire membership. The local union officers were bound by the international constitution to follow the policy directive of the international's executive council. The disappointed plaintiffs then filed a §501 suit alleging that the officers were violating their fiduciary duty in withholding payment.]

MATTHES, J. . . .

There are two basic questions presented for our consideration and determination: (1) the scope of Title V; (2) whether the conduct of appellants constitutes a violation of their fiduciary responsibilities and duties under Title V.

In summary, appellants' position as to question (1) is that Title V of the Landrum-Griffin Act was designed to apply to situations where the action or nonaction of union officials results in some *pecuniary* loss or disallowance to the membership as a group, and that the trust relationship imposed by Title V relates to financial or money-related responsibilities rather than to a broad "trustee" responsibility in regard to all activities and relationships between the officers of a union and the membership.

Careful analysis of Title V refutes the notion that the statute is narrow in its terms and scope and that it is limited solely to pecuniary responsibilities or the proper or improper use of union funds.

In explicit language, §501(a) provides that officers and other repre-

[35] The district court cited the following provisions from the International's constitution:

> Sec. 60(b) [T]he General Executive Board is authorized and empowered to conduct and manage the affairs of this organization between conventions, and to manage, invest, expend, contribute, use, lend and acquire union funds and property in the pursuit and accomplishment of the objectives set forth in the Constitution of the Brotherhood.
>
> Sec. 63(a) The General Executive Board shall decide all points of law arising under the jurisdiction of the Brotherhood and also all grievances and appeals, unless otherwise provided in this constitution; their decisions shall be in force and effect unless reversed in accordance with the procedure set forth in this constitution. 212 F. Supp. at 245 n. 9.

sentatives of a labor organization "occupy positions of trust in relation to such organization and its members as a group." It is the duty of each such person, "taking into account the special problems and functions of a labor organization," not only to hold its money and property solely for the benefit of the organization and its members, but to "refrain from dealing with such organization as an adverse party . . . in any matter connected with his duties and from holding or acquiring any pecuniary or personal interest which conflicts with the interests of such organization."

Thus it plainly appears that the statute is broad in its reach. Officers and other union representatives may not act adversely to their organization or to the members as a group, or acquire a personal interest which is contrary to the interests of the organization. Being trustees the officers must subvert their own personal interests to the lawful mandates and orders of the organization.

The legislative history of the Act demonstrates that Congress intended that it should not be interpreted by the courts narrowly or strictly, but, to the contrary, that its confines are broad. . . . [W]e note that H. Rep. No. 741 on H.R. 8342 — known as the Elliot Bill — contained fiduciary provisions *identical* with those which became §501(a) of the Landrum-Griffin Act.

The report in pertinent part provides:

> Union officials occupy positions of trust. They hold property of the union and manage its affairs on behalf of the members. It is the duty of union officers just as it is the duty of all similar trustees to put their obligations to the union and its members ahead of any personal interest. . . .
>
> We affirm that the committee bill is broader and stronger than the provisions of S. 1555 which relate to fiduciary responsibilities. S. 1555 applied the fiduciary principle to union officials only in their handling of 'money or other property' (see S. 1555, sec. 610), apparently leaving other questions to the common law of the several States. Although the common law covers the matter, we considered it important to write the fiduciary principle explicitly into Federal labor legislation. *Accordingly the committee bill extends the fiduciary principle to all the activities of union officials and other union agents or representatives.* (Emphasis supplied.)

The courts have with consistency refused to accede to the contention that §501 is designed for the single purpose of establishing responsibility on the part of officers and other representatives in relation to the handling and managing of fiscal matters of the labor organization. Quite to the contrary, indication is clearly present in the reported cases that §501 should receive a broad and liberal interpretation and application. . . . In summary, we hold that §501 imposes fiduciary responsibility in its broadest application and is not confined in its scope to union officials in their handling of money and property affairs.

Appellants' second contention — that even if Title V imposes a fiduciary responsibility in the broadest sense, the action complained of would not constitute a violation of such responsibility — has given rise to certain misapprehensions that are in need of clarification. Appellants have seemingly misconstrued the true nature of this action, have diverted attention away from themselves as *local* officers, have attempted to focus upon the directive of the *International* General Executive Board reinforcing appellants' action, and have stated the issues in terms of a mere ministerial policy determination controversy between the International and the Local union members. Appellants assert that:

> [T]he policy directive of the General Executive Board — found by the court below to be the basis for its ultimate determination against appellants — goes only to a requirement that any use of local union funds for the payment of legal expenses incurred in private litigation in which it was sought to protect the rights of such individual members must be submitted to a vote of the membership *as a whole* before such payments could be permitted as a matter of general policy. There was no attempt to discipline members who had brought such litigation merely because of their resort to the courts; all that was required was that repayment of expenses be agreed to by a majority of *all* whose funds were to be used for that purpose. . . . While it may be true that Landrum-Griffin protects the rights of individuals to seek relief for vindication of their rights, it cannot be said that any portion of Landrum-Griffin requires that individual members be given reimbursement by their local union for any costs that they might have incurred in defense of their rights. . . .
>
> [T]he policy determination which the General Executive Board was authorized to make was consistent with and guided by the provisions of . . . the International Constitution which prohibit loaning or donating money from the local union treasury to members. . . .
>
> In union affairs, personality clashes are the order of the day; it takes no imagination to conclude that the courts will be flooded with litigation if Title V has a scope and application, as found below, sufficient to permit the courts to question every policy determination made by the governing body of a parent international union. (Emphasis supplied.)

But the International is not a party to this action and its directive was considered below only for the purpose of determining whether it afforded appellants a valid reason for violating their fiduciary duty under Title V in not paying the bills as ordered by the duly authorized majority vote of the Local members. The trial court struck down the International directive, finding that it conflicted with Congressional policy as established in Title I of the Landrum-Griffin Act by discouraging the Local members from resorting "to the federal courts when internal redress for patent federal wrongs has proven futile in the past."

"This case nominally involves the alleged breach of a fiduciary duty and the non-payment of attorneys' fees, but what is really at stake here are the rights which were jeopardized by the union trials of July, 1960." 212 F. Supp. at 256.

In essence, this controversy narrows down to the following factual features: (1) Appellees — as revealed in the findings of fact below — were denied Title I rights in internal union trials, which culminated after much local internal union strife in which appellees had dared to express opposition to the incumbent local officers (appellants). In their brief, appellants "take no exception to the formal findings of fact made by Judge Larson and as otherwise set forth in his opinion," thereby conceding such treatment of appellees during the union trials as their presumption of guilt — in violation of the procedures set forth in the union constitution; (2) Despite the obvious violations by the Local Trial Board of the trial procedures and rights of appellees as set forth in the union constitution, the International Union affirmed the unlawful action of the Local Trial Board in suspending and fining appellees; (3) Charging violation of Title I — §101(a)(2) and (5) of the LMRDA, appellees sought to set aside the improper disciplinary awards in federal court. By stipulation approved and adjudged binding by the court, the decisions of guilt made by the Local Trial Board and the penalties imposed thereby were set aside and withdrawn; (4) After further local internal strife over payment of attorneys' fees incurred by appellees in their Title I action, and after further charges were levied against appellees, a Special Trial Board, constituted pursuant to stipulation entered into in the first federal court action, dismissed the charges against appellee Nelson, reprimanded both groups, and recommended that the attorneys' fees and expenses for *both* sides in the union conflict be paid by Local; (5) Although payment of appellees' attorneys' fees and related expenses was duly approved by a constitutional vote of the membership of Local, appellants refused to pay these bills. On the contrary, appellants followed a course against the wishes of the majority vote by soliciting support for their refusal from International; (6) Despite efforts by appellees, pursuant to Title V — §501(b) of LMRDA, to have the union officers take remedial action, appellants still refused to pay the duly approved bills; (7) Appellees brought this action in the federal court below under Title V to force appellants to comply with the desires of the majority of Local — as expressed in their authorized vote — and pay appellees' attorneys' fees and related expenses; (8) One month after this litigation began, the General Executive Board of the International Union, on its own motion sent a directive to Local stating that the majority vote approval was null and void because it was "the subject of an unauthorized recommendation and because [it was] not properly voted upon." No union constitutional provision was cited in support of its conclusion or its further suggestion that a vote of the *entire* Local membership be taken.

Under these pertinent facts and stripped of the details discussed in the opinion below, we are of the view that appellants' refusal to pay appellees' attorneys' fees and related expenses as duly authorized by a majority vote of the local members constituted a violation of appellants' fiduciary responsibility within the meaning of Title V of the Landrum-Griffin Act — *independent of any action by the International Union.* According to Title V — §501(a), appellants "occupy positions of trust," yet they have breached that trust relationship, and contrary to the statutory provision, have failed "to refrain from dealing with such organization [Local] as an adverse party or in behalf of an adverse party in any matter connected with his [their] duties. . . ." Appellants — opponents of appellees in previous proceedings — have allowed their personal feelings towards appellees to interfere with their duties as officers; have refused to pay the bills even though approved by the membership; have employed various tactics in an unsuccessful attempt to attain local approval for their conduct; have solicited support for their wrongful behavior from the International; and have thus assumed positions adverse to the interests of the local union as expressed in a majority vote, duly authorized by the union constitution. And contrary to appellants' assertion, the authorized payments do not constitute "donations," for the local union itself received substantial benefit from the first federal action brought by appellees. Fair and orderly procedures were restored to union trials; integrity was restored to the internal democratic processes of Local. Additionally, we agree with the trial court's conclusion that the eleventh-hour directive of International furnished no excuse for the action taken by appellants.

Implicit in our determinations is the recognition that, under the circumstances of this case, denial of relief to appellees under Title V would discourage resort to the courts by union members to establish their Title I rights. Likewise, to allow the directive of the International to stand as a defense to appellants' conduct would seriously undermine and frustrate appellees' rights under Title I. No *alleged* policy determination, no directive by any union official will be allowed to impair freedom of speech within the union. As stated by the court below, "it seems obvious . . . that there is no point in these Petitioners [appellees] or any other union members going to their union meetings if they are going to be met with letters such as the one in this case sent by the GEB on November 15, 1961." 212 F. Supp. at 269. The directive from International — though seemingly a mere policy determination on its face — not only attempts to contramand the majority vote taken by Local and to deprive appellees of "reimbursement for their legal expenses for the first Federal trials; it suggested that if more kangaroo courts were forthcoming, there would be no help from GEB. This would in turn cause the Petitioners [appellees], men of modest means, to have to again seek the aid of the Federal courts. This is the way that freedom of speech in the union hall is snuffed out; this is the way that tyranny begins." 212 F. Supp. at 270.

Of course, it is of prime significance here that a duly authorized constitutional majority of Local's members voted to pay appellees' expenses; that these expenses were incurred pursuing rights which are of substantial benefit to Local as a whole; that a personal animosity toward appellees motivated appellants' refusal to pay the expenses; and that Internationals' eleventh-hour "policy" directive was not based upon union constitutional authority, and was not, in fact, the real cause for appellants' conduct. We are by no means announcing a rule requiring payment of attorneys' fees to successful union member litigants in every Title I court proceeding — regardless of the circumstances. . . .

Accordingly, we affirm.

Notes

1. Was the breach the refusal to pay in accordance with the membership vote, or the appeal to the international union?

2. In Pignotti v. Local 3, Sheet Metal Workers, 477 F.2d 825 (8th Cir.), cert. denied, 414 U.S. 1067 (1973), a group of employers agreed with a local union to make pension contributions to a pension plan to be subsequently designated by the local. Alternatives were the national plan established by the local's parent international for the benefit of its locals, or one of several possible local plans. Several membership meetings were held on the issue of which plan to designate, but the results were inconclusive.

Finally, the international president ordered a special membership meeting to decide the pension plan issue. The national plan was adopted at that meeting and contributions were begun. Shortly thereafter, opponents of the national plan petitioned for another special meeting and at that meeting the members voted out the national plan. The international then imposed a formal trusteeship over the local and the appointed trustee indicated the local would participate in the national plan. Members of the local union brought a §501 suit alleging that the international president, among others, had violated his fiduciary duty to the local. The district court found that the international president breached his fiduciary duty because he allowed his "personal feelings" (?) to interfere with his duty as an officer. The Eighth Circuit affirmed. There was no suggestion in either opinion that the international president ever exceeded his constitutional authority or that he sought or received any personal gain.

Should a personally motivated, authorized act be a §501 violation? Suppose a union president, acting pursuant to constitutional authority, discharges an appointed union subordinate for incompetence, and as a result is charged with violation of §501. Evidence at trial convinces the judge that the subordinate was, in fact, incompetent but that the union president was substantially motivated by a desire to rid himself of a political rival. What result?

3. The first use of the technique of striking down an officer's authorization as "inconsistent with the policies of the LMRDA" and then finding a fiduciary breach was Highway Truck Drivers & Helpers, Local 107 v. Cohen, 182 F. Supp. 608 (E.D. Pa.), affd., 284 F.2d 163 (3d Cir. 1960), cert. denied, 365 U.S. 833 (1961); 215 F. Supp. 938 (E.D. Pa. 1963), affd., 334 F.2d 378 (3d Cir.), cert. denied, 379 U.S. 921 (1964) (discussed in *Morrissey,* supra). There, union officers were charged with a fiduciary duty of using union funds to defend themselves against state charges of corruption. Payment of the officers' fees was authorized by a vote of the union membership. The court found the approval of the payment to be inconsistent with the policies of the LMRDA and, therefore, that the disbursing officers had committed a fiduciary breach.

If the membership wants to spend its money for such a purpose, is that properly the business of the federal courts? Again, domination may be a central, but unarticulated concern. Can union officers conform their conduct to the standard set out in *Cohen* and *Johnson*?

F. TRUSTEESHIPS[36]

There are a variety of methods by which international unions control their subordinate local unions. Most common is control of the collective bargaining process. Where the employer is national in scope (e.g., automotive industry), the international union is likely to bargain for a contract binding nationally with only local issues of relatively minor importance left to local unions. When local unions do their own bargaining, they may be assisted by a representative of the international who exerts substantial de facto control. Some local unions are required by their international's constitution to send their bargaining agreements to the national office for approval. Other methods of control range from the use of national strike funds doled out at the discretion of international officers, to the ability of some international unions to control jobs by reassigning the geographical work jurisdictions of local unions.

Disciplinary control over local unions may take the form of expulsion from the international union, merger into another (usually larger) local, or a trusteeship. The trusteeship is the most common of these devices. A trusteeship is accomplished by sending in a representative of the international union to direct the affairs of the local union: the union treasury

[36] See Anderson, Landrum-Griffin and the Trusteeship Imbroglio, 71 Yale L.J. 1460 (1962); Beaird, Union Trusteeship Provisions of the Labor-Management Reporting and Disclosure Act of 1959, 2 Ga. L. Rev. 469 (1968).

is often put solely at the trustee's direction and democratic procedures are suspended; officers may be ousted, or are likely to serve only at the pleasure of the trustee. The trustee may also take over the process of collective bargaining and sign bargaining agreements binding the local.

While a trusteeship is arguably a necessary tool for the orderly functioning of international unions, its potential for abuse is high. It has been used to loot local treasuries, cement personal political power, and establish an autocracy by the international. The following two cases are an introduction to the LMRDA regulation of the use of trusteeship.

UNITED BROTHERHOOD OF CARPENTERS v. BROWN

343 F.2d 872 (10th Cir. 1965)

[The general president of the carpenters international union ordered Carpenters Local 201 to affiliate with a union district council and raise membership dues from $5.80 to $8 per month as required by the district council's bylaws. Local 201 initially complied, but some members became disenchanted with the dues increase and membership voted to withdraw from the council and rescind the dues increase. The international union imposed a trusteeship and individual members of Local 201 sued to set the trusteeship aside. The district court held the trusteeship invalid.]

HILL, J. . . .

The primary reason for the organization of [the] district council was to attempt to fully utilize the work force on various missile sites in the area and to supply contractors on those sites with an adequate force of carpenters. One of the benefits accruing to members of the local unions by organizing the district council was that the members of a local union could go anywhere in the territory of the council, even into that of another local union, and work without being required to pay the usual "journeymen's permit" or "service permit" fee that would be charged without a district council. Thus, the members of Local 201 would gain substantial benefits from the formation of a district council since Local 201 was the largest local in the area and only three of the missile sites were in its territory.

[The court first held that Title III did not require plaintiffs to file a complaint with the Secretary of Labor and exhaust that remedy before filing this lawsuit.]

Appellants also contend that the judgment must be reversed and the action dismissed for the reason that the plaintiffs have failed to exhaust the internal remedies afforded by United Brotherhood's Constitution and Laws as required by §101(a)(4) of the Act. We do not agree. Section

101(a)(4) is applicable only where individual violations of the so-called Bill of Rights provisions are alleged and does not apply where, as here, the validity of a trusteeship is being challenged. . . .

The basic issue in this case is, of course, the validity of the trusteeship imposed upon Local 201 by United Brotherhood. That issue must be determined by reference to §302 of the Act which provides that a trusteeship may be established and administered by a labor organization over its subordinate body ". . . only in accordance with the constitution and bylaws of the organization which has assumed trusteeship. . . ." The statute is mandatory in its terms and has nullified or removed whatever inherent power an international union had prior to its enactment to impose such a trusteeship. Unless the constitution and bylaws of the parent organization make provision therefor, such organization has no power to establish a trusteeship over a subordinate body. An examination of the constitution and bylaws of United Brotherhood discloses that there is no specific provision authorizing it to impose a trusteeship on any of its subordinate local unions.

It is suggested, however, that United Brotherhood's power to impose the trusteeship in question may be derived from the general authority granted to it in §§6B and 6D of its Constitution and Laws, as implemented by the provision in §10K, which empowers the General Executive Board ". . . to take such action as is necessary and proper for the welfare . . ." of the national union. Appellant's argument is that while its constitution and laws do not specifically grant it the authority to impose trusteeships, such authority may be implied from §§6B, 6D and 10K and that implied authority is sufficient. We do not agree. . . . Obviously, a trusteeship cannot conform to the constitution and bylaws of a labor organization where, as here, the constitution and bylaws make no provision for trusteeships. We think the statute not only contemplates, but requires, more than some vague general reference to the effect that the parent organization shall have power to take such action as is necessary and proper for its welfare. It requires at the very least that the organization's constitution and bylaws set forth the circumstances under which a trusteeship may be established over its local unions and the manner or procedure in which it is to be imposed. It goes without saying, of course, that the constitution and bylaws in that respect must not conflict with applicable provisions of the Act.

A second limitation upon the imposition of trusteeships is that under section 302 it must be for one of the following purposes: (1) To correct corruption or financial malpractice; (2) to assure the performance of collective bargaining agreements or other duties of a bargaining representative; or (3) to restore democratic procedures, or otherwise carry out the legitimate objects of the labor organization. Congress recognized that the use of trusteeships by an international union is a particularly effective device for the maintenance of order within the organization and that ". . . they have been widely used to prevent corruption, mismanagement of union funds, violation of collective bargaining agreements, infiltration of Communists; in short, to preserve the integrity and stability of the organization itself. . . ." But, Congress also recognized that ". . . in some instances trusteeships have been used as a means of consolidating the power of corrupt union officers, plundering and dissipating the resources of local unions, and preventing the growth of competing political elements within the organization." 2 U.S. Code Cong. & Adm. News, 86th Cong., 1st Sess., 1959, p. 2333. To preserve the legitimate use of trusteeships, Congress in enacting §302 enumerated the purposes for which a trusteeship could be imposed in language of a broad and general nature. However, in order to prevent their misuse, Congress obviously intended those purposes to have limitations as well and therefore in determining whether a particular case meets the test, the statute must be construed in the light of the various other provisions of the Act.

The purpose of the Act as a whole is not only to stop and prevent outrageous conduct by thugs and gangsters but also to stop lesser forms of objectionable conduct by those in positions of trust and to protect democratic processes within union organizations. To accomplish that purpose, a "Bill of Rights of Members of Labor Organizations" was incorporated into the Act. . . . Thus, the rights of individual members of a labor union are protected by federal statute with a view to allowing those members to conduct local matters with a minimum of outside interference. In short, local affairs are to be governed by local members under democratic processes.

With this background in mind we turn to a consideration of the purposes for which the instant trusteeship was imposed. The trial court found, and the evidence confirms, that United Brotherhood established the trusteeship over Local 201 because it would not affiliate with the District Council and would not raise its dues. The court also found, and the evidence shows, that it was not imposed because of "dissension" within the local union. The result is that the trusteeship was established for the purposes of affiliating Local 201 with the District Council and raising the dues of its membership. In determining whether these are proper purposes under §302, we must remember that a majority of the local membership consistently voted against having anything to do with the District Council and on at least two occasions, by secret ballot, voted against the proposal to raise the monthly dues. We must also remember that the provisions of §411 were designed to afford them protection in that respect. Under these circumstances, we have no hesitancy in holding that the purposes for which this trusteeship was imposed do not fall within any of the categories set forth in §302. Beyond question, they do not come under the category of correcting corruption or financial malpractice and have nothing whatever to do with collective bargaining. It is also clear to us that the specified purposes are not within the category of restoring democratic processes or otherwise carrying out the legitimate objects of United Brotherhood. To the contrary, the imposition of the trusteeship in question could have no other effect than to stifle democratic processes by, in effect, voiding the results of the properly conducted elections on the issues involved. If we were to hold that the asserted purposes were proper, this court would be placed in the position of allowing a national union to establish a trusteeship over a local union because the members of the local union insisted upon exercising a right granted them by statute. This would in effect nullify and frustrate not only the plain purpose but the express terms of the Act.

It is true that there is a presumption as to the validity of a trusteeship for a period of eighteen months from the date of its establishment. But, it is quite clear from the statute itself and from the legislative history that Congress intended for the presumption of validity to be available only where the trusteeship has been established ". . . in conformity with the procedural requirements of its [the labor organization's] constitution and bylaws and authorized or ratified after a fair hearing either before the executive board or before such other body as may be provided in accordance with its constitution or bylaws. . . ." 29 U.S.C.A. §464(c); 2 U.S. Code Cong. & Adm. News, 86th Cong., 1st Sess., 1959, p. 2334. Since the trusteeship in this case was not established in conformity with the constitution and bylaws, the presumption is not available to appellants.

CARPENTERS LOCAL 1302 v. UNITED BROTHERHOOD OF CARPENTERS

447 F.2d 612 (2d Cir. 1973)

[The Metal Trades Department of the AFL-CIO was established to enable local craft unions, acting jointly, to establish bargaining rights with employers when a single craft union would find it difficult or impossible to secure representative status for an employerwide bargaining unit. In the instant case, a Metal Trades Council comprised of 11 constituent local unions had had exclusive recognition for 8,000 shipyard employees for over 25 years. The local carpenters union, comprised of about 400 of the shipyard's employees, pursuant to a vote of its membership sought to sever its relationship with the council and filed a petition with the NLRB for separate certification for a unit of shipyard carpenters. The carpenters international union, complying with the procedures of the international constitution, put the local in trusteeship for refusing an order to refrain from filing the NLRB petition. The trustee thereupon withdrew the petition and the council signed a new collective bargaining agreement with the shipyard. The international indicated that a trusteeship would again be imposed if the local sought separate bargaining rights. The local sued under Title III of the LMRDA for an injunction against the international's interference. The court of appeals held, 2-1, that the trusteeship was for a proper purpose.]

HAYS, J. . . .

In connection with imposing the trusteeship on the Local, the committee of the International which heard the charges found that collective bargaining by the Metal Trades Council on behalf of Local 1302 and the ten other affiliated local unions had resulted over many years in stable bargaining relationships under which the members of the affiliated locals had received substantial benefits. The committee also found that the filing by the Local of the petition for disaffiliation had resulted in delaying the then current collective negotiations. The committee concluded that the Local's disaffiliation would have a detrimental effect on the process of collective bargaining and would constitute a failure to carry out its duties to its members in a responsible manner.

It appears to us that the Committee's conclusions were clearly justified. Not only would separate bargaining negotiations delay the execution of a collective agreement, but disaffiliation by the Local might well lead to attempts at disaffiliation by other locals of the eleven unions representing the 8000 employees of the Electric Boat Division, and the undermining of the Council's position as bargaining representative. Such a development would almost inevitably result in instability of the whole bargaining relationship with the eleven locals vying to outdo one another and resorting to strikes to accomplish their aim. It was to avoid just such results that the Metal Trades Department was organized.

Thus the trusteeship was imposed to prevent the destruction of the existing bargaining unit and to preserve the status of the certified bargaining representative. The International action was designed, in our opinion, to carry out "the legitimate objects" of the organization within the meaning of Section 302.

It should be noted that our decision does not mean that the members of the local are being locked in to the union. If the members of Local 1302 wish to repudiate the United Brotherhood of Carpenters and Joiners and start a new union through which to bargain, they are free to do so. However, this is not what they have attempted to do. Instead they have attempted to stay within the International while at the same time withdrawing from the Metal Trades Section and from the established bargaining system. . . .[37]

[37] Oakes, J., dissented.

Notes

1. Are *Brown* and *Carpenters Local 1302* compatible?

2. Suppose a local carpenters union has engaged in several wildcat strikes in recent years, causing much of the local carpentry to go non-union. If the parent international union revokes the local's charter and establishes a new local in the area, is Title III applicable? Would it matter whether some, or all, of the members of the old local were granted membership in the new local? Would you reach a different result if the charter were revoked because the local's president had announced his candidacy for the office of international president?

3. Section 301 jurisdiction has been held to extend to suits between local and international unions to enforce the international constitution (deemed a contract "between . . . labor organizations").[38] Thus, §301 suits have been filed to strike down trusteeships allegedly established contrary to the union constitution,[39] and to enforce a trusteeship by an injunction.[40]

[38] United Association v. Local 334, 452 U.S. 615 (1981).

[39] Parks v. IBEW, 314 F.2d 886 (4th Cir. 1963), cert. denied, 372 U.S. 976 (1963).

[40] Brotherhood of Painters v. Local 127, 264 F. Supp. 301 (N.D. Cal. 1966).

9

PUBLIC EMPLOYEE UNIONISM

Regulated by the individual states, public employee unionism raises most of the issues that we have examined with respect to unionism in the private sector and its federal regulation. The reaction of state legislatures to these issues, and to the legitimacy of bargaining by state and local government employees, has been varied:[1]

> Public employees are the largest bloc of workers in the national work force and one of the largest blocs of union members. About three million federal, state, and local employees are members of thirty-two AFL-CIO unions. The full organizing potential is about thirteen million and growing.
>
> While collective bargaining is authorized in the federal sector as a result of presidential executive orders, it has no statutory base. . . . In the states the situation is in chaos.
>
> Six states have authorized the limited right to strike. They are Alaska, Hawaii, Montana, Oregon, Pennsylvania, and Vermont (local employees only).
>
> Fifteen states have authorized union shop and/or agency shop. This provision is required by law in three states — Hawaii, Minnesota, and Rhode Island (for state employees). The remaining eleven states make this provision negotiable. They are Alaska, California (just teachers), Kentucky (just fire fighters), Maine (university employees only), Massachusetts, Michigan, Montana, Oregon, Vermont (local employees only), Washington, and Wisconsin. One state, Pennsylvania, provides for maintenance of membership.
>
> Twenty-four states have mandatory comprehensive bargaining laws for all public employees, both state and local. They are Alaska, California, Connecticut, Delaware, Florida, Hawaii, Iowa, Kansas, Maine, Massachusetts, Minnesota, Montana, Nebraska, New Hampshire, New Jersey, New York, North Dakota, Oregon, Pennsylvania, Rhode Island, South Dakota, Vermont, Washington, and Wisconsin. Two states, Indiana and Missouri, exclude police and fire fighters only. Michigan excludes certain categories of civil service workers.
>
> Two states have mandatory comprehensive bargaining laws for state employees only. These are Illinois and New Mexico.

[1] Meany, Union Leaders and Public Sector Unions, in Institute for Contemporary Studies, Public Employee Unions 167-168 (A. Chickering, ed. 1976)

One state, Nevada, has a comprehensive bargaining law only for local employees.

Details of public employee unionism must be left to a separate course. What follows is in the nature of a debate over the critical question of the extent to which the values and teachings of private sector labor relations are applicable in the public sector.

WELLINGTON AND WINTER, THE LIMITS OF COLLECTIVE BARGAINING IN PUBLIC EMPLOYMENT

78 Yale L.J. (1969) 1107, 1111-1127

I. The Claims for Collective Bargaining in the Private Sector

Those who deny the validity of the claims for collective bargaining in the private sector will surely not find those claims to have merit in the public. We do not intend to debate the merits of these claims. We must, however, if we are fully to test our thesis that a full transplant of collective bargaining to the public sector is inappropriate, assume a minimal validity of the claims that are made for it in the private.

Four claims then, are made for private-sector collective bargaining. First, it is a way to achieve industrial peace. The point was put as early as 1902 by the Industrial Commission:

> The chief advantage which comes from the practice of periodically determining the conditions of labor by collective bargaining directly between employers and employees is that thereby each side obtains a better understanding of the actual state of the industry, of the conditions which confront the other side, and of the motives which influence it. Most strikes and lockouts would not occur if each party understood exactly the position of the other.[17]

Second, collective bargaining is a way of achieving industrial democracy — that is, participation by workers in their own governance. It is the industrial counterpart of the contemporary demand for community participation.

Third, unions that bargain collectively with employers represent workers in the political arena as well. And political representation through interest groups is one of the most important types of political representation that the individual can have. Government at all levels acts in large part in response to the demands made upon it by the groups to which its citizens belong.

Fourth, and most important, as a result of a belief in the unequal

17. Final Report of the Industrial Commission 844 (1902).

bargaining power of employers and employees, collective bargaining is claimed to be a needed substitute for individual bargaining. Monopsony — a buyer's monopoly,[21] in this case a buyer of labor — is alleged to exist in many situations and to create unfair contracts of labor as a result of individual bargaining. While this, in turn, may not mean that workers as a class and over time get significantly less than they should — because monopsony is surely not a general condition but is alleged to exist only in a number of particular circumstances[22] — it may mean that the terms and conditions of employment for an individual or group of workers at a given period of time and in given circumstances may be unfair. What tends to insure fairness in the aggregate and over the long run is the discipline of the market.[23] But monopsony, if it exists, can work substantial injustice to individuals. Governmental support of collective bargaining represents the nation's response to a belief that such injustice occurs. Fairness between employee and employer in wages, hours, and terms and conditions of employment is thought more likely to be ensured where private ordering takes the collective form.

There are, however, generally recognized social costs resulting from this resort to collectivism. In the private sector these costs are primarily economic, and the question is, given the benefits of collective bargaining as an institution, what is the nature of the economic costs? Economists who have turned their attention to this question are legion, and disagreement among them monumental. The principal concerns are of two intertwined sorts. One is summarized by Professor Albert Rees of Princeton:

> If the union is viewed solely in terms of its effect on the economy, it must in my opinion be considered an obstacle to the optimum performance of our economic system. It alters the wage structure in a way that impedes the growth of employment in sectors of the economy where productivity and income are naturally high and that leaves too much labor in low-income sectors of the economy like southern agriculture and the least skilled trades. It benefits most those workers who would in any case be relatively well off, and while some of this gain may be at the expense of the owners

21. Our use of the term monopsony is not intended to suggest a labor market with a single employer. Rather we mean any market condition in which the terms and conditions of employment are generally below that which would have existed if the employers behaved competitively.

22. There is by no means agreement that monopsony is a significant factor. For a theoretical discussion, see F. Machlup, The Political Economy of Monopoly 333-79 (1952); for an empirical study, see R. Bunting, Employer Concentration in Local Labor Markets (1962).

23. See, e.g., L. Reynolds, Labor Economic and Labor Relations 18-19 (3d ed. 1961).

To the extent that monopsonistic conditions exist at any particular time one would expect them to be transitory. For even if we assume a high degree of labor immobility, a low wage level in a labor market will attract outside employers. Over time, therefore, the benefits of monopsony seem to carry with them the seeds of its destruction. But the time may seem a very long time in the life of any individual worker.

of capital, most of it must be at the expense of consumers and the lower-paid workers. Unions interfere blatantly with the use of the most productive techniques in some industries, and this effect is probably not offset by the stimulus to higher productivity furnished by some other unions.[27]

The other concern is stated in the 1967 Report of the Council of Economic Advisors:

> Vigorous competition is essential to price stability in a high employment economy. But competitive forces do not and cannot operate with equal strength in every sector of the economy. In industries where the number of competitors is limited, business firms have a substantial measure of discretion in setting prices. In many sectors of the labor market, unions and managements together have a substantial measure of discretion in setting wages. The responsible exercise of discretionary power over wages and prices can help to maintain general price stability. Its irresponsible use can make full employment and price stability incompatible.[28]

And the claim is that this "discretionary power" too often is exercised "irresponsibly."

Disagreement among economists extends to the quantity as well as to the fact of economic malfunctioning that properly is attributable to collective bargaining. But there is no disagreement that at some point the market disciplines or delimits union power. As we shall see in more detail below, union power is frequently constrained by the fact that consumers react to a relative increase in the price of a product by purchasing less of it. As a result any significant real financial benefit, beyond that justified by an increase in productivity, which accrues to workers through collective bargaining, may well cause significant unemployment among union members. Because of this employment-benefit relationship, the economic costs imposed by collective bargaining as it presently exists in the private sector seem inherently limited.

II. The Claims for Collective Bargaining in the Public Sector

In the area of public employment the claims upon public policy made by the need for industrial peace, industrial democracy and effective political representation point toward collective bargaining. This is to say that three of the four arguments that support bargaining in the private sector — to some extent, at least — press for similar arrangements in the public sector.

Government is a growth industry, particularly state and municipal government. While federal employment between 1963 and 1968 has increased from 2.36 million to 2.73 million, state and local employment

27. A. Rees, The Economics of Trade Unions 194-95 (1962).
28. Council of Econ. Advisors, 1967 Annual Report 119 (1967).

has risen from 6.87 to 9.42 million, and the increase continues apace. With size comes bureaucracy, and with bureaucracy comes the isolation and alienation of the individual worker. His manhood, like that of his industrial counterpart, is threatened. Lengthening chains of command necessarily depersonalize the employment relationship and contribute to a sense of powerlessness on the part of the worker. If he is to share in the governance of his employment relationship as he does in the private sector, it must be through the device of representation, which means unionization. Accordingly, just as the increase in the size of economic units in private industry fostered unionism, so the enlarging of governmental bureaucracy has encouraged public employees to look to collective action for a sense of control over their employment destiny. The number of government employees, moreover, makes it plain that those employees are members of an interest group which can organize for political representation as well as for job participation.

The pressures thus generated by size and bureaucracy lead inescapably to disruption — to labor unrest — unless these pressures are recognized and unless existing decision-making procedures are accommodated to them. Peace in government employment too, the argument runs, can best be established by making union recognition and collective bargaining accepted public policy.

Much less clearly analogous to the private model, however, is the unequal bargaining power argument. In the private sector that argument really has two aspects. The first, which we have just adumbrated, is affirmative in nature. Monopsony is believed sometimes to result in unfair individual contracts of employment. The unfairness may be reflected in wages, which are less than they would be if the market were more nearly perfect, or in working arrangements which may lodge arbitrary power in a foreman, i.e., power to hire, fire, promote, assign or discipline without respect to substantive or procedural rules. A persistent assertion, generating much heat, relates to the arbitrary exercise of managerial power in individual cases. This assertion goes far to explain the insistence of unions on the establishment in the labor contract of rules, with an accompanying adjudicatory procedure, to govern industrial life.

Judgments about the fairness of the financial terms of the public employee's individual contract of employment are even harder to make than for private sector workers. The case for the existence of private employer monopsony, disputed as it is, asserts only that some private sector employers in some circumstances have too much bargaining power. In the public sector, the case to be proven is that the governmental employer ever has such power. But even if this case could be proven, market norms are at best attenuated guides to questions of fairness. In employment as in all other areas, governmental decisions are properly political decisions, and economic considerations are but one criterion among many. Questions of fairness do not centrally relate to how much imperfection one sees in the market, but more to how much imperfection one sees in the political process. "Low" pay for teachers may be merely a decision — right or wrong, resulting from the pressure of special interests or from a desire to promote the general welfare — to exchange a reduction in the quality or quantity of teachers for higher welfare payments, a domed stadium, etc. And we are limited in our ability to make informed judgments about such political decisions because of the understandable but unfortunate fact that the science of politics has failed to supply us with either as elegant or as reliable a theoretical model as has its sister disciplines.

Nevertheless, employment benefits in the public sector may have improved relatively more slowly than in the private sector during the last three decades. An economy with a persistent inflationary bias probably works to the disadvantage of those who must rely on legislation for wage adjustments. Moreover, while public employment was once attractive for the greater job security and retirement benefits it provided, quite similar protection is now available in many areas of the private sector. On the other hand, to the extent that civil service, or merit, systems exist in public employment and these laws are obeyed, the arbitrary exercise of managerial power is substantially reduced. Where it is reduced, a labor policy that relies on the individual employment contract must seem less unacceptable.

The second, or negative aspect of the unequal bargaining power argument, relates to the social costs of collective bargaining. As we have seen, the social costs of collective bargaining in the private sector are principally economic, and seem inherently limited by market forces. In the public sector, however, the costs seem to us economic only in a very narrow sense and are on the whole political. It further seems to us that, to the extent union power is delimited by market or other forces in the public sector, these constraints do not come into play nearly as quickly as in the private. An understanding of why this is so requires further comparison between collective bargaining in the two sectors.

III. The Private Sector Model

While the private sector is, of course, extraordinarily diverse, the paradigm case is an industry which produces a product that is not particularly essential to those who buy it and for which dissimilar products can be substituted. Within the market or markets for this product, most — but not all — of the producers must bargain with a union representing their employees, and this union is generally the same through the industry. A price rise of this product relative to others will result in a decrease in the number of units of the product sold. This in turn will result in a cutback in employment. And an increase in price would be dictated by an increase in labor cost relative to output, at least in most situations. Thus, the union is faced with some sort of rough trade-off between, on the one hand, larger benefits for some employees and unemployment for others, and on the other hand, smaller benefits and more employment. Because unions are political organizations, with a legal duty to represent *all* employees fairly, and with a treasury that comes from per capita dues, there is pressure on the union to avoid the road that leads to unemployment.

This picture of the restraints that the market imposes on collective bargaining settlements undergoes change as the variables change. On the one hand, to the extent that there are non-union firms within a product market, the impact of union pressure will be diminished by the ability of consumers to purchase identical products from non-union and, presumably, less expensive sources. On the other hand, to the extent that union organization of competitors within the product market is complete, there will be no such restraint and the principal barriers to union bargaining goals will be the ability of a number of consumers to react to a price change by turning to dissimilar but nevertheless substitutable products.

Two additional variables must be noted. First, where the demand for an industry's product is rather insensitive to prove — i.e., relatively inelastic — and where all the firms in a product market are organized, the union need fear less the employment-benefit trade-off, for the employer is less concerned about raising prices in response to increased costs. By hypothesis, a price rise affects unit sales of such an employer only minimally. Second, in an expanding industry, wage settlements which exceed increases in productivity may not reduce union employment. They will reduce expansion, hence the employment effect will be experienced only by workers who do not belong to the union. This means that in the short run the politics of the employment-benefit trade-off do not restrain the union in its bargaining demands.

In both of these cases, however, there are at least two restraints on the union. One is the employer's increased incentive to substitute machines for labor, a factor present in the paradigm case and all other cases as well. The other restraint stems from the fact that large sections of the nation are unorganized and highly resistant to unionization. Accordingly, capital will seek non-union labor, and in this way the market will discipline the organized sector.

The employer, in the paradigm case and in all variations of it, is motivated primarily by the necessity to maximize profits (and this is so no matter how political a corporation may seem to be). He therefore is not inclined (absent an increase in demand for his product) to raise prices and thereby suffer a loss in profits, and he is organized to transmit and represent the market pressures described above. Generally he will resist, and resist hard, union demands that exceed increases in productivity, for if he accepts such demands he may be forced to raise prices. Should he be unsuccessful in his resistance too often, and should it cost him too much, he can be expected to put his money and energy elsewhere.

What all this means is that the social costs imposed by collective bargaining are economic costs; that usually they are limited by powerful market restraints; and that these restraints are visible to anyone who is able to see the forest for the trees.

IV. The Public Sector Model

The paradigm case in the public sector is a municipality with an elected board of aldermen, and an elected mayor who bargains (through others) with unions representing the employees of the city. He bargains also, of course, with other permanent and ad hoc interest groups making claims upon government (business groups, save-the-park committees, neighborhood groups, etc.). Indeed, the decisions that are made may be thought of roughly as a result of interactions and accommodations among those interest groups, as influenced by perceptions about the attitudes of the electorate, and by the goals and programs of the mayor and his aldermanic board.

Decisions that cost the city money are generally paid for from taxes and, less often, by borrowing. Not only are there many types of taxes, but also there are several layers of government which may make tax revenue available to the city; federal and state as well as local funds may be employed for some purposes. Formal allocation of money for particular uses is made through the city's budget, which may have within it considerable room for adjustments. Thus, a union will bargain hard for as large a share of the budget as it thinks it possibly can obtain, and beyond this to force a tax increase if it deems that possible.

In the public sector too, the market operates. In the long run, the supply of labor is a function of the price paid for labor by the public employer relative to what workers earn elsewhere. This is some assurance that public employees in the aggregate — with or without collective bargaining — are not paid too little. The case for employer monopsony, moreover, may be much weaker in the public sector than it is in the private. First, to the extent that most public employees work in urban areas, as they probably do, there may often be a number of substitutable and competing private and public employers in the labor market. When that is the case, there can be little monopsony power.[49] Second, even if

49. This is based on the reasonable but not unchallengeable assumption that the number of significant employers in a labor market is related to the existence of monopsony. See R. Bunting, Employer Concentration in Local Labor Markets 3-14 (1962). The greater the number of such employers in a labor market, the greater the departure from the classic case of the monopsony of the single employer. The number of employers would clearly seem to affect their ability to make and enforce a collusive wage agreement.

public employers occasionally have monopsony power, governmental policy is determined only in part by economic criteria, and there is no assurance, as there is in the private sector where the profit motive prevails, that the power will be exploited.

As we have seen, market-imposed unemployment is an important restraint on unions in the private sector. In the public sector, the trade-off between benefits and employment seems much less important. Government does not generally sell a product the demand for which is closely related to price. There usually are not close substitutes for the products and services provided by government and the demand for them is inelastic. Such market conditions are, as we have seen, favorable to unions in the private sector because they permit the acquisition of benefits without the penalty of unemployment, subject to the restraint of non-union competitors, actual or potential. But no such restraint limits the demands of public employee unions. Because much government activity is, and must be, a monopoly, product competition, non-union or otherwise, does not exert a downward pressure on prices and wages. Nor will the existence of a pool of labor ready to work for a wage below union scale attract new capital and create a new, and competitively less expensive, governmental enterprise. The fear of unemployment, however, can serve as something of a restraining force in two situations. First, if the cost of labor increases, the city may reduce the quality of the service it furnishes by reducing employment. For example, if teachers' salaries are increased, it may decrease the number of teachers and increase class size. However, the ability of city government to accomplish such a change is limited not only by union pressure, but also by the pressure of other affected interest groups in the community. Political considerations, therefore, may cause either no reduction in employment or services, or a reduction in an area other than that in which the union members work. Both the political power exerted by the beneficiaries of the services, who are also voters, and the power of the public employee union as a labor organization, then, combine to create great pressure on political leaders either to seek new funds or to reduce municipal services of another kind. Second, if labor costs increase, the city may, even as a private employer would, seek to replace labor with machines. The absence of a profit motive, and a political concern for unemployment, however, may be a deterrent in addition to the deterrent of union resistance. The public employer which decides it must limit employment because of unit labor costs will likely find that the politically easiest decision is to restrict new hires, rather than to lay off current employees.

Even if we are right that a close relationship between increased economic benefits and unemployment does not exist as a significant deterrent to unions in the public sector, might not the argument be made that in some sense the taxpayer is the public sector's functional equivalent of the consumer? If taxes become too high, the taxpayer can move to another community. While it is generally much easier for a consumer to substitute products than for a taxpayer to substitute communities, is it not fair to say that, at the point at which a tax increase will cause so many taxpayers to move that it will produce less total revenue, the market disciplines or restrains union and public employer in the same way and for the same reasons that the market disciplines parties in the private sector? Moreover, does not the analogy to the private sector suggest that it is legitimate in an economic sense for unions to push government to the point of substitutability?

Several factors suggest that the answer to this latter question is at best intermediate, and that question of legitimacy must be judged not by economic, but by political criteria.

In the first place, there is no theoretical reason — economic or political — to suppose that it is desirable for a governmental entity to liquidate its taxing power, to tax up to the point where another tax increase will produce less revenue because of the number of people it drives to different communities. In the private area, profit maximization is a complex concept, but its approximation generally is both a legal requirement and socially useful as a means of allocating resources. The liquidation of taxing power seems neither imperative nor useful.

Second, consider the complexity of the tax structure and the way in which different kinds of taxes (property, sales, income) fall differently upon a given population. Consider, moreover, that the taxing authority of a particular governmental entity may be limited (a municipality may not have the power to impose an income tax). What is necessarily involved, then, is principally the redistribution of income by government rather than resource allocation, and questions of income redistribution surely are essentially political questions.

For his part, the mayor in our paradigm case will be disciplined not by a desire to maximize profits, but by a desire — in some cases at least — to do a good job (to effectuate his programs), and in virtually all cases either to be reelected or to move to a better elective office. What he gives to the union must be taken from some other interest group or from taxpayers. His is the job of coordinating these competing claims while remaining politically viable. And that coordination will be governed by the relative power of the competing interest groups. Our inquiry, therefore, must turn to the question of how much power public employee unions will exercise if the full private model of collective bargaining is adopted in the public sector.

V. Public Employee Strikes and the Political Process

Although the market does not discipline the union in the public sector to the extent that it does in the private, the paradigm case, nevertheless, would seem to be consistent with what Robert A. Dahl has called the "'normal' American political process," which is "one in which there is a high probability that an active and legitimate group in the population can make itself heard effectively at some crucial stage in the process of decision,"[54] for the union may be seen as little more than an "active and legitimate group in the population." With elections in the background to perform, as Mr. Dahl tells us, "the critical role . . . in maximizing political equality and popular sovereignty,"[55] all seems well, at least theoretically, with collective bargaining and public employment.

But there is trouble even in the house of theory if collective bargaining in the public sector means what it does in the private. The trouble is that if unions are able to withhold labor — to strike — as well as to employ the usual methods of political pressure, they may possess a disproportionate share of effective power in the process of decision. Collective bargaining would then be so effective a pressure as to skew the results of the "'normal' American political process."

One should straightaway make plain that the strike issue is not *simply* the essentiality of public services as contrasted with services or products produced in the private sector. This is only half of the issue, and in the past the half truth has beclouded analysis. The services performed by a private transit authority are neither less nor more essential to the public than those that would be performed if the transit authority were owned by a municipality. A railroad or a dock strike may be much more damaging to a community than "job action" by teachers. This is not to say that governmental services are not essential. They are, both because the demand for them is inelastic and because their disruption may seriously injure a city's economy and occasionally the physical welfare of its citizens. Nevertheless, essentiality of governmental services is only a necessary part of, rather than a complete answer to, the question: What is wrong with strikes in public employment?

What is wrong with strikes in public employment is that because they disrupt essential services, a large part of a mayor's political constituency will press for a quick end to the strike with little concern for the cost of settlement. The problem is that because market restraints are attenuated and because public employee strikes cause inconvenience to voters, such strikes too often succeed. Since other interest groups with conflicting claims on municipal government do not, as a general proposition, have anything approaching the effectiveness of this union technique — or at least cannot maintain this relative degree of power over the long run — they are put at a significant competitive disadvantage in the political process. Where this is the case, it must be said that the political process has been radically altered. And because of the deceptive simplicity of the analogy to collective bargaining in the private sector, the alteration may take place without anyone realizing what has happened.

54. R. Dahl, A Preface to Democratic Theory 145 (1956).
55. Id.

Therefore, while the purpose and effect of strikes by public employees may seem in the beginning merely designed to establish collective bargaining or to "catch up" with wages and fringe benefits in the private sector, in the long run strikes must be seen as a means to redistribute income, or, put another way, to gain a subsidy for union members, not through the employment of the usual types of political pressure, but through the employment of what might appropriately be called political force.

As is often the case when one generalizes, this picture may be thought to be overdrawn. In order to refine analysis, it will be helpful to distinguish between strikes that occur over monetary issues and strikes involving non-monetary issues. The generalized picture sketched above is essentially valid as to the former. Because there is usually no substitute for governmental service, the citizen-consumer faced with a strike of teachers, or garbage men, or social workers is likely to be seriously inconvenienced. This in turn places enormous pressure on the mayor, who is apt to find it difficult to look to the long-run balance sheet of the municipality. Most citizens are directly affected by a strike of sanitation workers. Few, however, can decipher a municipal budget or trace the relationship between today's labor settlement and next year's increase in the mill rate. Thus, in the typical case the impact of a settlement is less visible — or can more often be concealed — than the impact of a disruption of services. Moreover, the cost of settlement may be borne by a constituency much larger — the whole state or nation — than that represented by the mayor. It follows that the mayor usually will look to the electorate which is clamoring for a settlement, and in these circumstances, the union's fear of a long strike, a major check on its power in the private sector, is not a consideration.[58] In the face of all of these factors other interest groups with priorities different from the union's are apt to be much less successful in their pursuit of scarce tax dollars than is the union with power to withhold services.

With respect to strikes over some non-monetary issues — decentralization of the governance of schools might be an example — the intensity of concern on the part of well-organized interest groups opposed to the union's position would support the mayor in his resistance to union demands. But even here, if union rank-and-file back their leadership, the pressures for settlement from the general public, which may be

58. Contrast the situation in the private sector: "[M]anagement cannot normally win the short strike. Management can only win the long strike. Also management frequently tends in fact to win the long strike. As a strike lengthens, it commonly bears more heavily on the union and the employees than on management. Strike relief is no substitute for a job. Even regular strike benefits, which few unions can afford, and which usually exhaust the union treasury quite rapidly (with some exceptions), are no substitute for a job." Livernash, The Relation of Power to the Structure and Process of Collective Bargaining, 6 J. Law & Econ. 10, 15 (1963).

largely indifferent as to the underlying issue, would in time become irresistible.

VI. Sovereignty and Delegation Revisited

As applied to public employment, there is a concept of sovereignty entitled to count as a reason for making strikes by public employees illegal. For what sovereignty should mean in this field is not the location of ultimate authority — on that the critics are dead right — but the right of government, through its laws, to ensure the survival of the "'normal' American political process." As hard as it may be for some to accept, strikes by public employees may, as a long run proposition, threaten that process.[61]

Moreover, it is our view — although this would seem to be much less clear — that the public stake in some issues makes it appropriate for government either not to have to bargain with its employees on these issues at all or to follow bargaining procedures radically different from those of the private sector. It is in this respect that the judicial doctrine of illegal delegation of power should have relevance.

Consider, for example, the question of a public review board for police; or, for that matter, the question of school decentralization. These issues, viewed by the unions involved primarily as questions of job security, engage the interest of so many disparate groups in a relevant population, that it may be thought unfair to allow one group — the police, the teachers — to exert pressure through collective bargaining (quite apart from the strike) in which competing groups do not directly participate as well as through the channels (e.g., lobbying) open to other interest groups.

Our hesitation in this area is caused by two factors. First, models of the political process have trouble with fine-grained distinctions about too much power. Given the vulnerability of most municipal employers, one can say with some confidence that the strike imparts too much power to an interest group only because the distinction addressed there is not fine-grained at all. Second, it is difficult indeed for any governmental institution to make judgments about the issues that should be included in the non-bargainable class. The courts are badly suited to this task; and the legislature is not well constituted to come in after the fact and effect a change. Nevertheless, limits will have to be set or bargaining procedures radically changed, and this will in a sense be giving content to the doctrine of delegation as it bears upon the subject of public employment.

While there is increasing advocacy for expanding the scope of bar-

61. It should be understood that this claim is with respect to the employment of the strike once collective bargaining is established. In our opinion the opportunity for public employees to organize and bargain through a union is compelled by the private sector analogy and is consistent with the survival of the "normal American political process."

gaining in public employment and in favor of giving public employees the right to strike — advocacy not just by unionists but by disinterested experts as well — the law generally limits the scope of bargaining and forbids strikes. This is often done with little attention to supporting reasons. Ours has been an attempt to supply these reasons and thereby to give some legitimate content to sovereignty and delegation.

We do not, however, mean to suggest that legislatures should abdicate to the courts the task of constructing a new system of collective bargaining for the public sector through the elaboration of sovereignty and delegation. Legislation is needed, for the problems we have explored require solutions beyond the power of the courts to fashion. In the future, if strikes are to be barred, sophisticated impasse procedures must be established. If, on the other hand, some strikes are to be tolerated, changes in the political structure which will make the municipal employer less vulnerable to work stoppages must be developed. And, in any event, legislative action will be necessary either to separate out those non-monetary issues which might not be decided solely through collective bargaining, or to change bargaining procedures so that all interested groups may participate in the resolution of such issues. These legislative choices and legal procedures will be the subject of a forthcoming article.

BURTON AND KRIDER, THE ROLE AND CONSEQUENCES OF PUBLIC EMPLOYEE STRIKES

79 Yale L.J. 418, 418-440 (1970)

> Reason is the life of the law.
>
> SIR EDWARD COKE

> The life of the law has not been logic: it has been experience.
>
> OLIVER WENDELL HOLMES

The vexing problem of strikes by public employees has generated a number of assertions based largely on logical analysis. One common theme is that strikes fulfill a useful function in the private sector, but are inappropriate in the public sector, because they distort the political decision-making process. Another is that strikes in nonessential government services should not be permitted because it is administratively infeasible to distinguish among the various government services on the basis of their essentiality. The present article attempts to evaluate these assertions in terms of labor relations experience at the local level of government.

The assertions concerning strikes by public employees which we shall discuss have been drawn mainly from The Taylor Report, a report on public employee labor relations submitted to the Governor of New York State,[1] and "The Limits of Collective Bargaining in Public Employment," a recent article by Harry Wellington and Ralph Winter.[2] Most of the evidence used to evaluate these assertions has been gathered in connection with the Brookings Institution Study of Unionism and Collective Bargaining in the Public Sector. Statistical information on all local public employee strikes which have occurred between 1965 and 1968 has been provided by the Bureau of Labor Statistics. Because education is outside the scope of our portion of the Brookings study, the data used in this article primarily relate to strikes by groups other than teachers.

I. The Role of Strikes in the Private Sector

Wellington and Winter have catalogued four claims which are made to justify collective bargaining in the private sector. First, collective bargaining is a way to achieve industrial peace. Second, it is a way of achieving industrial democracy. Third, unions that bargain collectively with employers also represent workers in the political arena. Fourth, and in their view the most important reason, collective bargaining compensates for the unequal bargaining power which is believed to result from individual bargaining. Wellington and Winter recognize that the gains to employees from collective bargaining, such as protection from monopsony power, are to be balanced against the social costs resulting from the resort to collectivism, such as distortion of the wage structure. While noting that considerable disagreement exists among economists concerning the extent of the benefits and costs, they stress the fact that costs are limited by economic constraints. Unions can displace their members from jobs by ignoring the discipline of the market. These four justifications for private sector collective bargaining are presumably relevant to some degree whether or not strikes are permitted. Nonetheless, one can conceptualize two models of collective bargaining — the Strike Model, which would normally treat strikes as legal, and the No-Strike Model, which would make all strikes illegal — and evaluate whether, in terms of the above justifications, society benefits from permitting strikes.

Most scholars of industrial relations accept the view that the right to strike is desirable in the private sector. Chamberlain and Kuhn assert, "[T]he possibility or ultimate threat of strikes is a necessary condition for collective bargaining." The distinguished scholars who comprised the Taylor Committee asserted similarly, "[T]he right to strike remains an integral part of the collective bargaining process in the private enter-

1. Governor's Committee on Public Employee Relations. Final Report (State of New York, 1966) [hereinafter cited as Taylor Committee Report]. The committee chairman was George W. Taylor.

2. Wellington & Winter, The Limits of Collective Bargaining in Public Employment, 78 Yale L.J. 1107 (1969).

prise sector and this will unquestionably continue to be the case." One reason for this endorsement of the strike is that its availability is often essential to the union in its bid for recognition by the employer. In addition, once the bargaining relationship is established, the possibility that work may be interrupted forces the parties to bargain seriously. The possibility of a strike thus increases the likelihood that the parties will reach an agreement without third-party intervention. More important, the ability to strike increases the bargaining power of employees and their union so that unlike the No-Strike Model, the employer cannot dominate the employer-employee relationship.

Use of the Strike Model instead of the No-Strike Model appears to enhance all but the third of the four claims for private sector collective bargaining offered by Wellington and Winter.[10] While they do not provide a claim by claim analysis of the consequences of permitting strikes, their endorsement of strikes in the private sector must indicate that they believe the Strike Model preferable to the No-Strike Model.

II. The Role of Strikes in the Public Sector

What are the virtues of collective bargaining in the public sector, and what are the consequences of permitting strikes by public employees?

The advocates of one view presumably assume that the four reasons offered by Wellington and Winter to justify collective bargaining in the private sector have equal relevance in the public sector. They also assert that strikes play the same role in the public and private sectors, and that our private sector strike policy should be replicated in the public sector. Strikes would not be banned ab initio in any function, but could be dealt with ex post facto by injunction if an emergency occurred.

This approach has been argued by Theodore W. Kheel, a noted labor arbitrator. He asserts that it is now "evident that collective bargaining is the best way of composing differences between workers and their employers in a democratic society. . . ." The only alternatives to collective bargaining are two: "either the employer makes the final determination or it is made by a third party, an arbitrator." While collective bargaining is the superior type of industrial relations, "collective bargaining cannot

10. The first reason offered — it is a way to achieve industrial peace — appears to be inconsistent with the notion of permitting strikes as a method of increasing the employees' bargaining power. One possible resolution of this apparent contradiction is that the enhanced bargaining power of the employees will enable them to work out mutually satisfactory terms with their employer without having to resort to the strike, while workers with limited bargaining power will often engage in strikes as an expression of their futility. This explanation is not totally compelling, however, and one may therefore have to justify collective bargaining among parties with equal power on grounds other than the diminution of strikes. The favorable consequences of the last three claims offered by Wellington and Winter for private sector collective bargaining presumably offset any possible increase in strikes.

exist if employees may not withdraw their services or employers discontinue them."

> [However, this does not mean] that the right to strike is sacrosanct. On the contrary, it is a right like all other rights that must be weighed against the larger public interest, and it must be subordinated where necessary to the superior right of the public to protection against injury to health or safety. . . .
>
> These principles, in my judgment, apply to the private sector as well as to the public sector. Moreover, their application cannot be determined in advance.[11]

Instead, Kheel believes, a procedure should be developed which would halt a strike only after it could be demonstrated that the public health and safety were endangered.

Proponents of the opposing view of public sector strikes argue that such strikes are invariably inappropriate. The Taylor Committee concluded that in the public services, "the strike cannot be a part of the negotiating process." And Wellington and Winter clearly believe that overall the four claims for collective bargaining are valid in the public sector only if strikes are illegal. Their primary concern is the fourth reason offered for collective bargaining — collective activity is needed as a substitute for individual activity because individuals are weak. This reason is always troublesome because increased bargaining power involves costs as well as benefits. They do not endorse the Strike Model in the public sector because the costs which result from increasing employee bargaining power by permitting strikes are higher and the benefits are less in the public sector than in the private sector.

The benefits of collective action are less in the public sector for several reasons. The problem of employer monopsony is not as consequential, not only because employer monopsony is less likely to occur, but also because existing monopsony power is less likely to be utilized. In addition, the low pay given to certain groups in the public sector, such as teachers, may reflect society's view about the best uses of its resources, while low pay in the private sector for a particular occupation presumably reflects a misallocation of resources.

The costs of substituting collective for individual bargaining are also likely to be higher in the public sector. According to Wellington and Winter, the market restraints on trade union activity are weak, reflecting the inelastic demand for public services, a lack of substitutes for these services, and the fact that many public services are essential. Second, strikes in the public sector lead to public pressure on officials which compels quick settlements. Further, there are no other pressure groups

11. All quotations are from Kheel, Resolving Deadlocks Without Banning Strikes, 92 Monthly Lab. Rev. 62-63 (July 1969).

competing for public resources which have weapons comparable to the strike, and, thus, unions have a more advantageous arsenal of weapons. The net result of the lack of market restraints, the pressure on public officials to settle strikes quickly, and the absence of comparable weaponry by other pressure groups is that strikes in the public sector impose high costs by distorting the normal political process.

Because the cost-benefit ratio which results from the substitution of collective action, including strikes, for individual action is so high in the public sector, Wellington and Winter argue that public employee strikes should be illegal. Their argument is based on their notion of sovereignty. This is not the traditional doctrine of sovereignty, which they specifically reject, but a new version of sovereignty which asserts that the government has the right, through its laws, "to ensure the survival of the 'normal' American political process." This rationale for sovereignty, fully articulated in Wellington and Winter and implicit in the Taylor Report analysis, deserves a careful scrutiny in terms of empirical evidence.

III. Consequences of Strikes in the Public Sector

The best procedure for evaluating public sector strikes would be to investigate the respective impacts of the Strike Model and the No-Strike Model on each of the claims made for collective bargaining. Such an analysis should consider the economic, political, and social effects produced. An inquiry into these effects is particularly important since several authors who have implicitly endorsed the Strike Model in the private sector have done so more on the basis of noneconomic reasons than economic reasons. Nonetheless, the attack on the Strike Model in the *public* sector has been based largely on the evaluation of the fourth claim for collective bargaining, that relating to unequal bargaining power. We will attempt to meet this attack by confining our discussion to the economic consequences of collective bargaining with and without strikes.

Even an examination confined to economic consequences is difficult. The most desirable economic data, which would measure the impact of unions on wages and other benefits, is unavailable. A major examination of the relative wage impact of public sector unions is now being conducted by Paul Hartman, but pending the outcome of his study we have to base our evaluation on less direct evidence. Our approach will be to review carefully the various steps in the analytical model developed by Wellington and Winter by which they arrive at the notion of sovereignty. If we find that the evidence available on public sector strikes contradicts this model, we shall conclude that the differential assessment they provide for public and private strikes is unwarranted.

A. BENEFITS OF COLLECTIVE BARGAINING

Wellington and Winter believe the benefits of collective action, including strikes, are less in the public sector than in the private sector since (1) the problem of employer monopsony is less serious, and (2) any use of monopsony power in the public sector which results in certain groups, such as teachers, receiving low pay may reflect, not a misallocation of resources, but rather a political determination of the desired use of resources.

Wellington and Winter assert that employer monopsony is less likely to exist or be used in the public than in the private sector. But as they concede, referring to Bunting, monopsony is not widespread in the private sector and, except in a few instances, cannot be used as a rationale for trade unions. They provide no evidence that monopsony is less prevalent in the public than in the private sector. Moreover, other labor market inefficiencies, common to the public and private sectors, are probably more important than monopsony in providing an economic justification for unions. For example, the deficiencies of labor market information are to some extent overcome by union activities, and there is no reason to assume that this benefit differs between the public and private sectors.

Assuming there is monopsony power, Wellington and Winter believe that collective bargaining in the private sector can eliminate unfair wages "which are less than they would be if the market were more nearly perfect." They assert, however, that low pay for an occupation in the public sector may reflect a political judgement which ought not to be countered by pressures resulting from a strike. To say, however, that the pay for an occupation would be higher if the employees had the right to strike than if they did not is not independent proof that strikes are inappropriate. The same criticism could be made of any activity by a public employee group which affects its pay. An independent rationale must be provided to explain why some means which are effective in raising wages (strikes) are inappropriate while other means which are also effective (lobbying) are appropriate. Whether the Wellington and Winter discussion of the politically based decision-making model for the public sector provides this rationale will be discussed in more detail subsequently.

B. COSTS OF COLLECTIVE BARGAINING

Wellington and Winter's discussion of the cost of substituting collective for individual bargaining in the public sector includes a chain of causation which runs from (1) an allegation that market restraints are weak in the public sector, largely because the services are essential; to (2) an assertion that the public puts pressure on civic officials to arrive at a quick settlement; to (3) a statement that other pressure groups have no weapons comparable to a strike; to (4) a conclusion that the strike thus imposes a high cost since the political process is distorted.

Let us discuss these steps in order:

(1) Market Restraints

A key argument in the case for the inappropriateness of public sector strikes is that economic constraints are not present to any meaningful degree in the public sector. This argument is not entirely convincing. First, wages lost due to strikes are as important to public employees as they are to employees in the private sector. Second, the public's concern over increasing tax rates may prevent the decision-making process from being dominated by political instead of economic considerations. The development of multilateral bargaining in the public sector is an example of how the concern over taxes may result in a close substitute for market constraints. In San Francisco, for example, the Chamber of Commerce has participated in negotiations between the city and public employee unions and has had some success in limiting the economic gains of the unions. A third and related economic constraint arises for such services as water, sewage and, in some instances, sanitation, where explicit prices are charged. Even if representatives of groups other than employees and the employer do not enter the bargaining process, both union and local government are aware of the economic implications of bargaining which leads to higher prices which are clearly visible to the public. A fourth economic constraint on employees exists in those services where subcontracting to the private sector is a realistic alternative.[24] Warren, Michigan, resolved a bargaining impasse with an American Federation of State, County and Municipal Employees (AFSCME) local by subcontracting its entire sanitation service; Santa Monica, California, ended a strike of city employees by threatening to subcontract its sanitation operations. If the subcontracting option is preserved, wages in the public sector need not exceed the rate at which subcontracting becomes a realistic alternative.

An aspect of the lack-of-market-restraints argument is that public services are essential. Even at the analytical level, Wellington and Winter's case for essentiality is not convincing. They argue:

> The Services performed by a private transit authority are neither less nor more essential to the public than those that would be performed if the

24. The subcontracting option is realistic in functions such as sanitation and street or highway repairs, and some white collar occupations. Several other functions, including hospitals and education, may be transferred entirely to the private sector. The ultimate response by government is to terminate the service, at least temporarily. In late 1968, Youngstown, Ohio, closed its schools for five weeks due to a taxpayer's revolt. 281 Gov. Emp. Rel. Rep. B-6 (1969). In late 1969, 10 Ohio school districts ran out of money and were closed down. Wall Street Journal, Dec. 19, 1969, at 1, col. 1.

> transit authority were owned by a municipality. A railroad or a dock strike may be much more damaging to a community than "job action" by teachers. This is not to say that government services are not essential. They are both because they may seriously injure a city's economy and occasionally the physical welfare of its citizens.

This is a troublesome passage. It ends with the implicit conclusion that all government services are essential. This conclusion is important in Wellington and Winter's analysis because it is a step in their demonstration that strikes are inappropriate in all governmental services. But the beginning of the passage, with its example of "job action" by teachers, suggests that essentiality is not an *inherent* characteristic of government services but depends on the specific service being evaluated. Furthermore the transit authority example suggests that many services are interchangeable between the public and private sectors. The view that various government services are not of equal essentiality and that there is considerable overlap between the kinds of services provided in the public and private sectors is reinforced by our field work and strike data from the Bureau of Labor Statistics. Examples include:

1. Where sanitation services are provided by a municipality, such as Cleveland, sanitationmen are prohibited from striking. Yet, sanitationmen in Philadelphia, Portland, and San Francisco are presumably free to strike since they are employed by private contractors rather than by the cities.

2. There were 25 local government strikes by the Teamsters in 1965-68, most involving truck drivers and all presumably illegal. Yet the Teamsters' strike involving fuel oil truck drivers in New York City last winter was legal even though the interruption of fuel oil service was believed to have caused the death of several people.

(2) Public Pressure

The second argument in the Wellington and Winter analysis is that public pressure on city officials forces them to make quick settlements. The validity of this argument depends on whether the service is essential. Using as a criterion whether the service is essential in the short run, we believe a priori that services can be divided into three categories: (1) essential services — police and fire — where strikes immediately endanger public health and safety; (2) intermediate services — sanitation, hospitals, transit, water, and sewage — where strikes of a few days might be tolerated; (3) nonessential services — streets, parks, education, housing, welfare and general administration — where strikes of indefinite duration could be tolerated.[27] These categories are not exact since essentiality

27. We consider education a nonessential service. However, because our portion of the Brookings Institution study excludes education, our analysis in this article will also largely exclude education.

depends on the size of the city. Sanitation strikes will be critical in large cities such as New York but will not cause much inconvenience in smaller cities where there are meaningful alternatives to governmental operation of sanitation services.

Statistics on the duration of strikes which occurred in the public sector between 1965 and 1968 provide evidence not only that public services are of unequal essentiality, but also that the a priori categories which we have used have some validity. As can be seen from Table 1, strikes in the essential services (police and fire) had an average duration of 4.7 days, while both the intermediate and the nonessential services had an average duration of approximately 10.5 days. It is true that the duration of strikes in the intermediate and nonessential services is only half the average duration of strikes in the private sector during these years. However, this comparison is somewhat misleading since all of the public sector strikes were illegal, and many were ended by injunction, while presumably a vast majority of the private sector strikes did not suffer from these constraints. It would appear that with the exception of police and fire protection, public officials are, to some degree, able to accept long strikes. The ability of governments to so choose indicates that political pressures generated by strikes are not so strong as to undesirably distort the entire decision-making process of government. City officials in Kalamazoo, Michigan, were able to accept a forty-eight day strike by sanitationmen and laborers; Sacramento County, California, survived an eighty-seven day strike by welfare workers. A three month strike of hospital workers has occurred in Cuyahoga County (Cleveland), Ohio.

(3) *The Strike as a Unique Weapon*

The third objection to the strike is that it provides workers with a weapon unavailable to the employing agency or to other pressure groups. Thus, unions have a superior arsenal. The Taylor Committee Report opposes strikes for this reason, among others, arguing that "there can scarcely be a countervailing lockout." Conceptually, we see no reason why lockouts are less feasible in the public than in the private sector. Legally, public sector lockouts are now forbidden, but so are strikes; presumably both could be legalized. Actually, public sector lockouts have occurred. The Social Service Employees Union (SSEU) of New York City sponsored a "work-in" in 1967 during which all of the caseworkers went to their office but refused to work. Instead, union-sponsored lectures were given by representatives of organizations such as CORE, and symposia were held on the problems of welfare workers and clients. The work-in lasted for one week, after which the City locked out the caseworkers.

A similar assertion is made by Wellington and Winter, who claim that no pressure group other than unions has a weapon comparable to the strike. But this argument raises a number of questions. Is the distinctive characteristic of an inappropriate method of influencing decisions by public officials that it is economic as opposed to political? If this is so, then presumably the threat of the New York Stock Exchange to move to New Jersey unless New York City taxes on stock transfers were lowered and similar devices should be outlawed along with the strike.

(4) Distortion of the Political Process

The ultimate concern of both the Taylor Committee and Wellington and Winter is that "a strike of government employees . . . introduces an alien force in the legislative process." It is "alien" because, in the words of the Taylor Committee Report:

> Careful thought about the matter shows conclusively, we believe, that while the right to strike normally performs a useful function in the private enterprise sector (where relative economic power is the final determinant in the making of private agreements), it is not compatible with the orderly functioning of our democratic form of representative government (in which relative political power is the final determinant).

The essence of this analysis appears to be that certain means used to influence the decision-making process in the public sector — those which are political — are legitimate, while others — those which are economic — are not. For several reasons, we believe that such distinctions among means are tenuous.

First, any scheme which differentiates economic power from political power faces a perplexing definitional task. The *International Encyclopedia of the Social Sciences* defines the political process as "the activities of people in various groups as they struggle for — and use — power to achieve personal and group purposes." And what is power?

> Power in use invariably involves a mixture of many different forms — sometimes mutually reinforcing — of persuasion and pressure. . . .
>
> Persuasion takes place when A influences B to adopt a course of action without A's promising or threatening any reward or punishment. It may take the form of example, expectation, proposals, information, education, or propaganda. . . .
>
> Pressure is applied by A upon B whenever A tries to make a course of action more desirable by promising or threatening contingent rewards or punishments. It may take the form of force, commands, manipulation, or bargaining. . . .
>
> Physical force is a blunt instrument. . . . Besides, more flexible and reliable modes of pressure are available. Rewards, in the form of monetary payments, new positions, higher status, support, favorable votes, cooperation, approval, or the withdrawal of any anticipated punishment, may be bestowed or promised. Punishment, in the form of fines, firing, reduction in status, unfavorable votes, noncooperation, rejection, disapproval, or withdrawal of any anticipated reward, may be given or threatened. . . .

> Bargaining is a still more fluid — and far more persuasive — form of using pressure. In bargaining, all sides exercise power upon each other through reciprocal promises or threats. . . . Indeed, force, command, and manipulation tend to become enveloped in the broader and more subtle processes of bargaining.

We have quoted at length from this discussion of the political process because we believe it illustrates the futility of attempting to distinguish between economic and political power. The former concept would seem to be encompassed by the latter. The degree of overlap is problematical since there can be economic aspects to many forms of persuasion and pressure. It may be possible to provide an operational distinction between economic power and political power, but we do not believe that those who would rely on this distinction have fulfilled their task.

Second, even assuming it is possible to operationally distinguish economic power and political power, a rationale for utilizing the distinction must be provided. Such a rationale would have to distinguish between the categories either on the basis of characteristics inherent in them as a means of action or on the basis of the ends to which the means are directed. Surely an analysis of ends does not provide a meaningful distinction. The objectives of groups using economic pressure are of the same character as those of groups using political pressure — both seek to influence executive and legislative determinations such as the allocation of funds and the tax rate. If it is impossible effectively to distinguish economic from political pressure groups in terms of their ends, and it is desirable to free the political process from the influence of all pressure groups, then effective lobbying and petitioning should be as illegal as strikes.

If the normative distinction between economic and political power is based, not on the ends desired, but on the nature of the means, our skepticism remains undiminished. Are all forms of political pressure legitimate? Then consider the range of political activity observed in the public sector. Is lobbying by public sector unions to be approved? Presumably it is. What then of participation in partisan political activity? On city time? Should we question the use of campaign contributions or kickbacks from public employees to public officials as a means of influencing public sector decisions? These questions suggest that political pressures, as opposed to economic pressures, cannot *as a class* be considered more desirable.

Our antagonism toward a distinction based on means does not rest solely on a condemnation of political pressures which violate statutory provisions. We believe that perfectly legal forms of political pressure have no automatic superiority over economic pressure. In this regard, the evidence from our field work is particularly enlightening. First, we have found that the availability of political power varies among groups of employees within a given city. Most public administrators have respect for groups which can deliver votes at strategic times. Because of their links to private sector unions, craft unions are invariably in a better position to play this political role than a union confined to the public sector, such as AFSCME. In Chicago, Cleveland and San Francisco, the public sector craft unions are closely allied with the building trades council and play a key role in labor relations with the city. Prior to the passage of state collective bargaining laws such unions also played the key role in Detroit and New York City. In the No-Strike Model, craft unions clearly have the comparative advantage because of their superior political power.

Second, the range of issues pursued by unions relying on political power tends to be narrow. The unions which prosper by eschewing economic power and exercising political power are often found in cities, such as Chicago, with a flourishing patronage system. These unions gain much of their political power by cooperating with the political administration. This source of political power would vanish if the unions were assiduously to pursue a goal providing job security for their members since this goal would undermine the patronage system. In Rochester, for example, a union made no effort to protect one of its members who was fired for political reasons. For the union to have opposed the city administration at that time on an issue of job security would substantially have reduced the union's influence on other issues. In Chicago, where public sector strikes are rare (except for education) but political considerations are not, the unions have made little effort to establish a grievance procedure to protect their members from arbitrary treatment.

Third, a labor relations system built on political power tends to be unstable since some groups of employees, often a substantial number, are invariably left out of the system. They receive no representation either through patronage or through the union. In Memphis, the craft unions had for many years enjoyed a "working relationship" with the city which assured the payment of the rates that prevailed in the private sector and some control over jobs. The sanitation laborers, however, were not part of the system and were able to obtain effective representation only after a violent confrontation with the city in 1968. Having been denied representation through the political process, they had no choice but to accept a subordinate position in the city or to initiate a strike to change the system. Racial barriers were an important factor in the isolation of the Memphis sanitation laborers. Similar distinctions in racial balance among functions and occupations appear in most of the cities we visited.

C. CONCLUSIONS IN REGARD TO STRIKES AND THE POLITICAL PROCESS

Wellington and Winter and the Taylor Committee reject the use of the Strike Model in the public sector. They have endorsed the No-Strike Model in order "to ensure the survival of the 'normal' American political process." Our field work suggests that unions which have actually helped their members either have made the strike threat a viable weapon despite its illegality or have intertwined themselves closely with their nominal employer through patronage-political support arrangements. If this assessment is correct, choice of the No-Strike Model is likely to lead to patterns of decision making which will subvert, if not the "normal" American political process, at least the political process which the Taylor Committee and Wellington and Winter meant to embrace. We would not argue that the misuse of political power will be eliminated by legalizing the strike; on balance, however, we believe that, in regard to most governmental functions, the Strike Model has more virtues than the No-Strike Model. Whether strikes are an appropriate weapon for all groups of public employees is our next topic.

IV. Differentiation among Public Sector Functions

The most important union for local government employees, The American Federation of State, County, and Municipal Employees (AFSCME), issued a policy statement in 1966 claiming the right of public employees to strike:

> AFSCME insists upon the right of public employees . . . to strike. To forestall this right is to handicap free collective bargaining process [sic]. Wherever legal barriers to the exercise of this right exist, it shall be our policy to seek the removal of such barriers. Where one party at the bargaining table possesses all the power and authority, the bargaining becomes no more than formalized petitioning.

Significantly, AFSCME specifically excluded police and other law enforcement officers from this right. Any local or police officers that engages in a strike or other concerted refusal to perform duties will have its charter revoked.

Can a distinction among functions, such as is envisioned by AFSCME, be justified? In view of the high costs associated with the suppression of strikes, could each stoppage be dealt with, as Theodore Kheel suggests, only when and if it becomes an emergency?

Despite arguments to the contrary, we feel that strikes in some essential services, such as fire and police, would immediately endanger the public health and safety and should be presumed illegal. We have no evidence from our field work to support our fears that any disruption of essential services will quickly result in an emergency. But the events which occurred on September 9, 1919, during a strike by Boston policemen provide strong proof; those which occurred on October 7, 1969, following a strike by Montreal policemen would appear to make the argument conclusive. Contemporary accounts amply describe the holocausts:

> Boston, 1919
>
> About me milled a crowd of aimless men and women, just seeing what they could see. . . . There was an air of expectancy without knowing what was expected.
>
> Then came the sound of two hard substances in sharp impact, followed a second later by a louder one and the thrilling crash of falling splintering glass. A plate show-window had been shattered. Instantly the window and its immediate vicinity were filled with struggling men, a mass of action, from which emerged from time to time bearers of shirts, neckties, collars, hats. In a few seconds the window was bare. Some with loot vanished; others lingered.
>
> Lootless ones were attacking the next window. Nothing happened. That is, the fear of arrest abated after the first shock of the lawless acts. I saw men exchanging new shirts each with the other, to get their sizes . . . good-looking men, mature in years, bearing all the earmarks of a lifetime of sane observance of property rights.
>
> Montreal, 1969
>
> "You've never seen the city like this," said the owner of a big women's clothing store surveying his premises, strewn with dummies from which the clothing had been torn. "It's like the war."
>
> A taxi driver carrying a passenger up Sherbrooke Street in Montreal today blamed the police for "not knowing the effect their absence would have on people." He continued: "I don't mean hoodlums and habitual lawbreakers, I mean just plain people committed offenses they would not dream of trying if there was a policeman standing on the corner. I saw cars driven through red lights. Drivers shot up the wrong side of the street because they realized no one would catch them."

In the case of strikes by essential employees, such as policemen, the deterioration of public order occurs almost immediately. During the first few hours of the police walkout in Montreal, robberies occurred at eight banks, one finance company, two groceries, a jewelry store and a private bank. In the case of the Boston police strike of 1919, outbreaks began within four hours after the strike had commenced. Such consequences require that strikes by police and other essential services be outlawed in advance. There is simply no time to seek an injunction.

Even if a distinction in the right to strike can be made among government functions on the basis of essentiality, is such a distinction possible to implement? The Taylor Committee based their argument against prohibiting strikes in essential functions but allowing them elsewhere on this difficulty:

> We come to this conclusion [to prohibit all strikes] after a full consideration of the views . . . that public employees in non-essential government services, at least, should have the same right to strike as has been accorded to employees in private industry. We realize, moreover, that the work performed in both sectors is sometimes comparable or identical. Why,

> then, should an interruption of non-essential governmental services be prohibited?
>
> To begin with, a differentiation between essential and non-essential governmental services would be the subject of such intense and never ending controversy as to be administratively impossible.

Despite the conclusion of the Taylor Committee it appears that in practice a distinction is emerging between strikes in essential services and strikes in other services. Employee organizations and public officials do in fact treat some strikes as critical, while other strikes cause no undue concern.

Our analysis of the Bureau of Labor Statistics strike data pertaining to the last four years suggests that it is possible to devise an operational definition of essential service. First, as we have indicated above, strike duration was considerably shorter in the essential services than in the intermediate or nonessential services [see Table 1]. These data suggest that, except in police and fire services, public officials have some discretion in choosing to accept long strikes. Second, the statistics reveal that managers have been able to distinguish between essential and nonessential services in their use of counter sanctions. In strikes involving essential services, injunctions were sought more frequently and employees, because of their short run indispensability, were fired less frequently. Injunctions were granted in 35% of the essential strikes, and in 25% of the intermediate, but only in 19% of the nonessential strikes. Third, partial operation was attempted more frequently in essential services [see Table 2]. By using nonstrikers, supervisors, replacements or volunteers, local governments were able to continue partial operation during 92% of the essential strikes, but in only 80% of the intermediate, and 77% of the nonessential strikes. Such data suggest that it may be administratively feasible to differentiate among public services so as to permit some, but not all, public employees to strike. Indeed, public administrators already seem to be making such distinctions.

The idea that distinctions among functions are appropriate is also beginning to emerge among legislators. The first state to move in this

TABLE 1*
Duration of Strikes by Essentiality of Function

	Average duration in days	*Standard deviation** in days*
Essential	4.7	7.9
Intermediate	10.3	18.5
Nonessential	10.6	20.1
Education	7.2	8.9

* Based on data collected by the Bureau of Labor Statistics on strikes during 1965-68 involving employees of local government.

** Standard deviation is a measure of dispersion around the average or the mean.

TABLE 2*
Partial Operation by Essentiality of Function (Noneducation)

	Essential		*Intermediate*		*Nonessential*		*Total***	
	Number	*Percentage*	*Number*	*Percentage*	*Number*	*Percentage*	*Number*	*Percentage*
Total Number of Strikes	37	100.0	221	100.0	43	100.0	301	100.0
Partial Operation***	34	91.9	175	79.2	33	76.7	242	80.4
Supervisors	(28)	(75.5)	(154)	(69.7)	(29)	(67.4)	(211)	(70.1)
Nonstrikers	(27)	(73.0)	(137)	(62.0)	(28)	(65.1)	(192)	(63.8)
Replacements	(3)	(9.1)	(34)	(15.4)	(4)	(9.3)	(41)	(13.6)
Volunteers	(5)	(13.5)	(16)	(7.2)	—	—	(21)	(7.0)
No Partial Operation	3	8.1	46	2.08	10	23.3	59	(19.6)

* Based on data collected by the Bureau of Labor Statistics on strikes during 1965-68 involving employees of local governments.

** Twenty-eight strikes in such miscellaneous functions as libraries, museums, and electric or gas utilities were not classified. There was partial operation in 18 (64.3%) of these strikes.

*** The sub-totals for partial operation do not add to 100% because more than one method may have been used in each strike.

direction has been Vermont, which apparently restricts municipal employee strikes only if they endanger the health, safety, or welfare of the public. Unfortunately — at least from the viewpoint of researchers — there has been no experience under the statute. Montana prohibits strikes in private or public hospitals only if there is another strike in effect in a hospital within a radius of 150 miles. Study commissions in other states have accepted the distinction between essential and nonessential services. In 1968, the Governor's Commission in Pennsylvania recommended a limited right to strike for all public employees except police and firemen. In 1969, the Labor Law Committee of the Ohio State Bar Association recommended repeal of the Ferguson Act, which prohibits strikes by public employees. They proposed a Public Employment Relations Act which would permit strikes by recognized employee organizations in nonessential occupations following mandatory use of fact-finding procedures. The proposed statute states:

> [I]n the event a public employer and a certified labor organization are unable to reach an agreement within forty-five days following the date of the receipt of the recommendation of the fact-finding board, the public employees in the bargaining unit . . . and/or the labor organization shall not thereafter be prohibited from engaging in any strike until such time as the labor organization and the public employer reach agreement on a collective bargaining agreement.

V. Implications for Public Policy

We have expressed our views on the market restraints that exist in the public sector, the extent of the public pressure on public officials to reach quick settlements, the likely methods by which decisions would be made in the No-Strike Model, and the desirability and feasibility of differentiating among government services on the basis of essentiality. In this light, what public policy seems appropriate for strikes at the local government level?

In general, we believe that strikes in the public sector should be legalized for the same reasons they are legal in the private sector. For some public sector services, however — namely, police and fire protection — the probability that a strike will result in immediate danger to public health and safety is so substantial that strikes are almost invariably inappropriate. In these essential functions, the strike should be presumed illegal; the state should not be burdened with the requirement of seeking an injunction. We would, however, permit employees in a service considered essential to strike if they could demonstrate to a court that a disruption of service would not endanger the public. Likewise, we would permit the government to obtain an injunction against a strike in a service presumed nonessential if a nontrivial danger to the public could be shown.

The decision to permit some, but not all, public employee strikes cannot, of course, take place in vaccus publicum jus. Mediation, fact finding, or advisory arbitration may be appropriate for those functions where strikes are permitted. Where strikes are illegal because of the essential nature of the service, it may be necessary to institute compulsory arbitration. The choice of a proper role for third parties in the public sector is difficult, and we do not wish to leave the impression that we are unaware of the problem. In our portion of the Brookings Institution study, we will examine the experience which many cities have had in the use of neutral third parties. Our initial reaction is that such experience does not undermine the feasibility of a public policy which would permit some, but not all, public employees the right to strike, and include that decision in a comprehensive public policy for collective bargaining.

While we have indicated our support for the right of public employees to strike, we do not mean to suggest that all strikes are desirable. In particular, strikes which are necessary solely because the employer refuses to establish a bargaining relationship seem anachronous. The right of employees to deal with their employer through a representative of their choosing should be reflected in our public policy. The obligation on employers to recognize and to bargain with properly certified unions has eliminated many strikes in the private sector. The evidence in Table 3 suggests that, in the public sector, strikes on such issues can be sharply reduced. In those states in which local governments are required to recognize and to bargain with unions representing a majority of their employees, strikes to establish the bargaining relationship have been virtually eliminated. States with permissive laws, which require minimal

TABLE 3
Local Government Strikes by Public Policy and Issue*

	Noneducation strikes		*Education strikes*	
	Number	*Duration in days*	*Number*	*Duration in days*
Mandatory Law				
Strikes to establish bargaining relationship*	1	10.0	5	3.4
Other strikes	56	6.7	104	8.7
Permissive Law				
Strikes to establish bargaining relationship	20	19.6	2	7.0
Other strikes	34	10.4	16	6.5
No Law				
Strikes to establish bargaining relationship	68	21.6	29	5.9
Other strikes	150	5.8	93	6.2

* Based on data collected by the Bureau of Labor Statistics on strikes during 1965-68 involving employees of local governments.

** Includes strikes where union was demanding recognition as well as strikes where union was demanding bona fide collective bargaining.

recognition of unions and which require only that employers "meet and confer," as opposed to "bargain," with these unions, have perhaps aggravated the strike problem.

Similarly, our general endorsement of public sector strikes does not mean that we are unconcerned about the circumstances under which such strikes take place. Public policy has an important role to play in shaping the structure and, hence, influencing the outcome of collective bargaining. An example is the inclusion or exclusion of supervisors in the bargaining unit. As indicated in Table 2, supervisors are often used during strikes to provide partial operation. Presumably, this enhances the ability of local governments to resist union demands. Some states, such as Wisconsin, have wisely stipulated that supervisors are to be excluded from bargaining units, while other states, such as New York, have not. A supervisor who belongs to a striking union is likely to be of limited usefulness to management in attempting to counteract the strike. Another way in which a state's public policy could enhance local government's ability to resist strikes would be to enact a statute prohibiting public employers from signing away their right to subcontract. The absolute right to subcontract operations would thereby be preserved. While it is unlikely that some services, such as police and fire protection, will ever be placed under private management, other services can be subcontracted if union demands raise the cost of a public service to a level at which private service becomes competitive. Excluding the education sector, subcontracting was threatened by management in 16 local government strikes and implemented in five between 1965 and 1968.

VI. Conclusions

This article has offered a policy to deal with public sector strikes. It has also examined several propositions concerning public sector strikes which have been based largely on logical analysis. The assertions that strikes by public employees inevitably distort the decision-making process in the public sector and that differential treatment of public employees in their right to strike would be infeasible have been found to be wanting when evaluated in the light of our actual experience with public sector strikes. This evaluation suggests that logic alone is an inadequate basis for public policy in this area. Yet we would not want to suggest that a literal interpretation of Holmes' view on the relative merits of logic and experience is appropriate. If we were forced to choose a mentor in any debate concerning the proper bases for law, we endorse Cardozo:

"My analysis of the judicial process comes then to this, and little more: logic, and history, and custom, and utility, and the accepted standards of right conduct, are the forces which singly or in combination shape the progress of the law."

WELLINGTON AND WINTER, MORE ON STRIKES BY PUBLIC EMPLOYEES

79 Yale L.J. 441, 441-443 (1970)

We have two brief observations on the paper by Messrs. Burton and Krider. First, we suggest that society is not limited to a choice between their strike and no-strike alternatives. Our earlier article argued that the typical municipal political structure is vulnerable to strikes by well entrenched public employee unions, and that, given this existing political structure, the no-strike model is preferable to the strike model. We stated, however, that changes in the political structure which reduce the vulnerability of municipal employers to strikes by public employees can be made and that we intended (and we still do intend) to explore these possibilities in a future article. There is, therefore, a third model — one which permits some strikes in conjunction with various changes in municipal political structures.

Second, we wish to define what seems to be the principal area of our disagreement with Messrs. Burton and Krider. All agree that the services performed by some public employees are in one way or another "essential" and that this "essentiality" is in some sense related to society's ability to tolerate strikes. However, which employees under the Burton-Krider strike model are to have union activities limited depends very much on one's view of essentiality. It is now clear that our vision is different from theirs.

For them, the essentiality of the service depends on the extent to which disruption of the service by a strike would "immediately endanger public health and safety." They limit the concept to situations creating an immediate danger to the public health and safety and, therefore, advocate a prohibition on strikes affecting municipal police and fire functions. They would permit strikes in other areas, such as education. We agree that strikes which create an immediate danger to public health and welfare cannot be tolerated, and that any concept of essentiality must, at a minimum, embrace such situations.

We claim more for the concept, however.[5] Many government services are essential in two additional senses, senses which are of critical importance to the issues before us. First, the demand for numerous governmental services is relatively inelastic; that is, relatively insensitive to changes in price. Indeed, the lack of close substitutes is typical of many governmental endeavors.[6] And, since at least the time of Marshall's Principles of Economics, the elasticity of demand for the final service or product has been considered a major determinant of union power. Because the demand for labor is derived from the demand for the product, inelasticity on the product side tends to reduce the employment-benefit trade-off unions face. As our earlier article noted, this is as much the case in the private as in the public sector. But, in the private sector product inelasticity is not typical. Moreover, there is the future restraint on union power created by the real possibility of non-union entrants into the product market. In the public sector, inelasticity of demand seems to us more the rule than the exception, and non-union rivals are not generally a serious problem.

Consider education. A strike by teachers may never create an immediate danger to public health and welfare. Nevertheless, teachers rarely need fear unemployment as a result of union-induced wage increases, and the threat of an important non-union rival (competitive private schools) is not to be taken seriously so long as potential consumers of private education must pay taxes to support the public school system.

The third sense in which the concept of essentiality has significance is the extent to which the disruption of a government service inconve-

5. If one were using "essentiality" in merely a descriptive sense, the Burton-Krider definition might well be satisfactory. They employ this concept, however, as the touchstone for resolving the strike question. When so used, their definition is totally inadequate.

6. Sometimes this is so because of the nature of the endeavor, national defense, for example, and sometimes because the existence of the governmental operation necessarily inhibits entry by private entities, as in the case of elementary education.

niences municipal voters. A teachers' strike may not endanger public health or welfare. It may, however, seriously inconvenience parents and other citizens who, as voters, have the power to punish one of the parties — and always the same party, the political leadership — to the dispute. How can anyone any longer doubt the vulnerability of a municipal employer to this sort of pressure? Was it simply a matter of indifference to Mayor Lindsay in September, 1969, whether another teachers' strike occurred on the eve of a municipal election? Did the size and the speed of the settlement with the U.F.T. suggest nothing about one first-rate politician's estimate of his vulnerability?

Messrs. Burton and Krider's disagreement with us on this point seems based principally on their conviction that anticipation of increased taxes as the result of a large labor settlement will countervail the felt inconvenience of a strike, and that municipalities are not, therefore, overly vulnerable to strikes by public employees. We remain convinced, however, that governmental budgets are so complex that the effect of any particular labor settlement on the typical municipal budget is a matter of very low visibility. It will not, therefore, significantly deter voters, inconvenienced by a strike, from compelling political leaders to settle quickly. Moreover, as we noted in our earlier article, municipalities are often subsidized by other political entities — the nation or state — and the cost of a strike settlement may not be borne by those demanding an end to the strike. Surely Mayor Lindsay's pleas for federal and state aid because of the increased cost of municipal services are not totally unrelated to his labor problems.

The sum of our position then is — given today's typical municipal structure — that once public employee unions become well established, they will, if they are allowed to strike, have too much power. For the effect of the strike weapon[8] is to put competing claimants in the political process (at all levels of government) at a disadvantage substantial enough for us to insist that it constitutes, what in our earlier article we called, a "distortion" of the "'normal' American political process." This distortion, moreover, may make everyone from large taxpayers to welfare recipients poorer than they are, and the cities less livable, but more volatile, than they have become.

8. Our convictions remain unshaken in the face of Messrs. Burton and Krider's argument that the threat of the New York Stock Exchange to move to New Jersey is analogous to a public employee strike. When teachers strike, education ceases. If the Stock Exchange moved, citizens of New York would continue to buy and sell stock. New York City might get less tax revenue, to be sure, but it also might get more, depending on what kind of business takes the Exchange's place.

Table of Cases

Italics indicate principal cases

Index